Choice Modelling: Foundational Contributions

Classics in Transport and Environmental Valuation

Series Editor: David A. Hensher
Professor of Management
Founding Director, Institute of Transport and Logistic Studies (ITLS)
University of Sydney, Australia

1. Choice Modelling: Foundational Contributions
   David A. Hensher and John M. Rose

Future titles will include:

Urban Form and Transport Accessibility
Corinne Mulley

Transport, the Environment and Public Health: Classic Papers on Non-motorised Travel
Stephen Greaves and Jan Garrard

Wherever possible, the articles in these volumes have been reproduced as originally published using facsimile reproduction, inclusive of footnotes and pagination to facilitate ease of reference.

For a list of all Edward Elgar published titles visit our website at
www.e-elgar.com

Choice Modelling: Foundational Contributions

Edited by

David A. Hensher

Professor of Management and Founding Director, Institute of Transport and Logistic Studies University of Sydney, Australia

and

John M. Rose

Professor, Institute of Transport and Logistic Studies University of Sydney, Australia

CLASSICS IN TRANSPORT AND ENVIRONMENTAL VALUATION

An Elgar Research Collection
Cheltenham, UK • Northampton, MA, USA

Published by
Edward Elgar Publishing Limited
The Lypiatts
15 Lansdown Road
Cheltenham
Glos GL50 2JA
UK

Edward Elgar Publishing, Inc.
William Pratt House
9 Dewey Court
Northampton
Massachusetts 01060
USA

A catalogue record for this book is available from the British Library

Library of Congress Control Number: 2011927324

MIX
Paper from responsible sources
FSC® C018575
FSC www.fsc.org

ISBN 978 0 85793 727 8

Printed and bound by MPG Books Group, UK

Contents

Acknowledgements

The editors and publishers wish to thank the authors and the following publishers who have kindly given permission for the use of copyright material.

American Economic Association for article: André de Palma, Gordon M. Myers and Yorgos Y. Papageorgiou (1994), 'Rational Choice Under an Imperfect Ability to Choose', *American Economic Review*, **84** (3), June, 419–40.

American Marketing Association via the Copyright Clearance Center for articles: Jordan J. Louviere and George Woodworth (1983), 'Design and Analysis of Simulated Consumer Choice or Allocation Experiments: An Approach Based on Aggregate Data', *Journal of Marketing Research,* **XX**, November, 350–67; Peter E. Rossi and Greg M. Allenby (1993), 'A Bayesian Approach to Estimating Household Parameters', *Journal of Marketing Research,* **XXX**, May, 171–82; Joffre Swait and Jordan Louviere (1993), 'The Role of the Scale Parameter in the Estimation and Comparison of Multinomial Logit Models', *Journal of Marketing Research,* **XXX**, August, 305–14.

Blackwell Publishing Ltd for article: Daniel McFadden and Kenneth Train (2000), 'Mixed MNL Models for Discrete Response', *Journal of Applied Econometrics*, **15** (5), 447–70; David A. Hensher (2006), 'How do Respondents Process Stated Choice Experiments? Attribute Consideration Under Varying Information Load', *Journal of Applied Econometrics*, **21**, 861–78.

Econometric Society for articles: Charles F. Manski and Steven R. Lerman (1977), 'The Estimation of Choice Probabilities from Choice Based Samples', *Econometrica*, **45** (8), November, 1977–88; Kenneth A. Small and Harvey S. Rosen (1981), 'Applied Welfare Economics with Discrete Choice Models', *Econometrica*, **49** (1), January, 105–30; Jeffrey A. Dubin and Daniel L. McFadden (1984), 'An Econometric Analysis of Residential Electric Appliance Holdings and Consumption', *Econometrica,* **52** (2), March, 345–62; W. Michael Hanemann (1984), 'Discrete/Continuous Models of Consumer Demand', *Econometrica*, **52** (3), May, 541–61; Daniel McFadden (1989), 'A Method of Simulated Moments for Estimation of Discrete Response Models Without Numerical Integration', *Econometrica,* **57** (5), September, 995–1026.

Elsevier Ltd for articles and excerpts: Daniel McFadden (1974), 'Conditional Logit Analysis of Qualitative Choice Behavior', in Paul Zarembka (ed.), *Frontiers in Econometrics*, Chapter 4, 105–42; John I. Yellott, Jr. (1977), 'The Relationship between Luce's Choice Axiom, Thurstone's Theory of Comparative Judgment, and the Double Exponential Distribution', *Journal of Mathematical Psychology*, **15** (2), April, 109–44; R. Duncan Luce (1977), 'The

Choice Axiom after Twenty Years', *Journal of Mathematical Psychology*, **15** (3), 215–33; J. Hayden Boyd and Robert E. Mellman (1980), 'The Effect of Fuel Economy Standards on the U.S. Automotive Market: An Hedonic Demand Analysis', *Transportation Research Part A*, **14A**, 367–78; N. Scott Cardell and Frederick C. Dunbar (1980), 'Measuring the Societal Impacts of Automobile Downsizing', *Transportation Research Part A*, **14A**, 423–34; Andrew Daly (1987), 'Estimating 'Tree' Logit Models', *Transportation Research Part B*, **21B** (4), August, 251–67; Axel Börsch-Supan (1990), 'On the Compatibility of Nested Logit Models with Utility Maximization', *Journal of Econometrics*, **43** (3), March, 373–88; Moshe Ben-Akiva and Takayuki Morikawa (1990), 'Estimation of Travel Demand Models from Multiple Data Sources', in M. Koshi (ed.), *Transportation and Traffic Theory*, Proceedings of the 11th ISTTT, 461–76; David S. Bunch (1991), 'Estimability in the Multinomial Probit Model', *Transportation Research Part B*, **25B** (1), February, 1–12; M.A. Bradley and A.J. Daly (1997), 'Estimation of Logit Choice Models using Mixed Stated-Preference and Revealed-Preference Information', in Peter Stopher and Martin Lee-Gosselin (eds), *Understanding Travel Behaviour in an Era of Change*, Chapter 9, 209–31; Frank S. Koppelman and Chieh-Hua Wen (1998), 'Alternative Nested Logit Models: Structure, Properties and Estimation', *Transportation Research Part B*, **32B** (5), June, 289–98; David Brownstone and Kenneth Train (1999), 'Forecasting New Product Penetration with Flexible Substitution Patterns', *Journal of Econometrics*, **89**, 109–29; David Hensher, Jordan Louviere and Joffre Swait (1999), 'Combining Sources of Preference Data', *Journal of Econometrics*, **89**, 197–221; Paula Armstrong, Rodrigo Garrido and Juan de Dios Ortúzar (2001), 'Confidence Intervals to Bound the Value of Time', *Transportation Research Part E*, **37** (2–3), April–July, 143–61; Chandra R. Bhat (2001), 'Quasi-Random Maximum Simulated Likelihood Estimation of the Mixed Multinomial Logit Model', *Transportation Research Part B*, **35** (7), August, 677–93; David A. Hensher and William H. Greene (2002), 'Specification and Estimation of the Nested Logit Model: Alternative Normalisations', *Transportation Research Part B*, **36** (1), January, 1–17; William H. Greene and David A. Hensher (2003), 'A Latent Class Model for Discrete Choice Analysis: Contrasts with Mixed Logit', *Transportation Research Part B*, **37** (8), September, 681–98; Chandra R. Bhat (2005), 'A Multiple Discrete–Continuous Extreme Value Model: Formulation and Application to Discretionary Time-Use Decisions', *Transportation Research Part B*, **39** (8), September, 679–707; Lesley Chiou and Joan L. Walker (2007), 'Masking Identification of Discrete Choice Models Under Simulation Methods', *Journal of Econometrics*, **141** (2), December, 683–703.

Institute for Operations Research and Management Science (INFORMS) for articles: Carlos F. Daganzo, Fernando Bouthelier and Yosef Sheffi (1977), 'Multinomial Probit and Qualitative Choice: A Computationally Efficient Algorithm', *Transportation Science,* **11** (4), November, 338–58; Joel L. Horowitz (1983), 'Statistical Comparison of Non-Nested Probabilistic Discrete Choice Models', *Transportation Science*, **17** (3), August, 319–50.

MIT Press Journals and the President and Fellows of Harvard College for article: David Revelt and Kenneth Train (1998), 'Mixed Logit with Repeated Choices: Households' Choices of Appliance Efficiency Level', *Review of Economics and Statistics*, **LXXX** (4), 647–57.

Pion Ltd for article: H.C.W.L. Williams (1977), 'On the Formation of Travel Demand Models and Economic Evaluation Measures of User Benefit', *Environment and Planning A*, **9**, 285–344.

Springer Science and Business Media for excerpt and articles: Charles F. Manski (1977), 'The Structure of Random Utility Models', *Theory and Decision*, **8**, 229–54; Michael P. Keane (1997), 'Current Issues in Discrete Choice Modeling', *Marketing Letters,* **8** (3), July, 307–22; David A. Hensher and William H. Greene (2003), 'The Mixed Logit Model: The State of Practice', *Transportation*, **30** (2), May, 133–76; Kenneth Train and Melvyn Weeks (2005), 'Discrete Choice Models in Preference Space and Willing-to-Pay Space', in Riccardo Scarpa and Anna Alberini (eds), *Applications of Simulation Methods in Environmental and Resource Economics*, Chapter 1, 1–16, references.

Stanford University Press for excerpt: Jacob Marschak (1960), 'Binary-Choice Constraints and Random Utility Indicators', in Kenneth J. Arrow, Samuel Karlin and Patrick Suppes (eds), *Mathematical Methods in Social Sciences, 1959*, Chapter 21, 312–29.

Taylor and Francis Ltd (http://www.informaworld.com) for excerpts: Daniel McFadden (1979), 'Quantitative Methods for Analysing Travel Behaviour of Individuals: Some Recent Developments', in David A. Hensher and Peter R. Stopher (eds), *Behavioural Travel Modelling*, Chapter 13, 279–318; Moshe Ben-Akiva and Steven R. Lerman (1979), 'Disaggregate Travel and Mobility-Choice Models and Measures of Accessibility', in David A. Hensher and Peter R. Stopher (eds), *Behavioural Travel Modelling*, Chapter 30, 654–79.

Transportation Research Board via the Copyright Clearance Center for article: Joel L. Horowitz (1984), 'Testing Disaggregate Travel Demand Models by Comparing Predicted and Observed Market Shares', *Transportation Research Record,* **976**, 1–7.

University of Chicago Press for article: Kelvin J. Lancaster (1966), 'A New Approach to Consumer Theory', *Journal of Political Economy*, **74** (2), April, 132–57.

Every effort has been made to trace all the copyright holders but if any have been inadvertently overlooked the publishers will be pleased to make the necessary arrangement at the first opportunity.

Introduction

David A. Hensher and John M. Rose

The study of choice is well recognised as a significant research area as well as being important in real world applications associated with fields as diverse as marketing, finance, transportation, logistics, health, environmental sciences, agriculture, tourism and economics. Fundamentally every decision that an individual, a household and an organisation makes involves a choice, including the choice to not choose, and thus having a set of methods to identify the drivers of choice making (referred to as attributes of alternatives on offer, conditioned on the characteristics of the decision making unit) provides a powerful framework within which to undertake predictions of demand for alternative goods and services, as well as a way of establishing how much decision makers are willing to pay for a specific level of an attribute. The application of choice modelling is now widespread in many disciplines and accommodates both active and passive use. Examples include the choice of mode and time of day to travel, the choice of tourism destination, the choice of health insurance or a medical treatment for an illness, choice of investment portfolio, choice of wine to drink, choice of automobile type, and choice of support for alternative heritage protection regulations. The list of applications is growing at a fast pace.

This book brings together a number of papers that have made foundational contributions to the methods that are increasingly being used to develop choice models that are now extensively used by academics, consultants and researchers in government and industry. This introduction provides a brief historical overview of the journey from the very beginning in 1927 to today in the development of theory and statistical methods that might be described as the state of practice tools now readily available in software packages. It is important to note that many of the early contributions were published in psychology, economics, transportation, and marketing sources but are very much portable in relevance to all disciplinary areas of research.

It is 84 years since Thurstone's classic paper on the law of comparative judgment (Chapter 1), in which he assumes the response of an individual to a pair of alternatives, i, j, is determined by the discriminal processes $v_i = f(\alpha_i) + \varepsilon_i$ and $v_j = f(\alpha_j) + \varepsilon_j$. The terms $f(\alpha_i)$ and $f(\alpha_j)$ represent a single-valued function of unknown parameters α_i and α_j characteristics of the 'objects participating in the i, j pair'. These parameters are referred to by Thurstone as 'affective values' of the corresponding objects (or alternatives); ε_i and ε_j are elements of the discriminal processes specific to the randomly selected individual and are assumed by Thurstone to obey a normal bivariate distribution function. The difference process $(v_i - v_j)$ is distributed normally with mean $f(\alpha_i) - f(\alpha_j)$ and variance $\sigma^2_{ij} = \sigma^2_i + \sigma^2_j + 2\rho_{ij}\sigma_i\sigma_j$ where ρ_{ij} is the correlation between the alternatives. The individual is assumed to judge $X_i > X_j$ when $(v_j - v_i) > 0$. Thus the probability that a randomly sampled individual will be observed to judge $X_i > X_j$ is $\text{Prob}_{ij} = \Phi\{f(\alpha_i) - f(\alpha_j)/\sigma_{ij}\}$. This response function is referred to as a statement of the law of comparative judgment. McFadden (2001) described the Thurstone contribution as a model of imperfect discrimination in which alternative i with true stimulus level V_i is perceived with a normal error as $V_i + \varepsilon_i$ and

Thurstone showed that the probability $P_{\{i,j\}}(i)$ that alternative i is chosen over alternative j has a form that we now call binomial probit. The emphasis on probabilistic choice theory can be credited to both Thurstone (1945) and Hull (1943).

An alternative to the normal response function proposed by Bradley and Terry (1952) and Luce (1959) is of special interest because of its psychological interpretation (Restle 1961, Bock and Jones 1968). The authors proposed a model for the probability that X_i is ranked above X_j in the pair X_i, X_j, as $\text{Prob}_{ij} = \{\pi_i/(\pi_i + \pi_j)\}$, $I = 1,2,\ldots,n$; $j = 1,2,\ldots,n$. π_i and π_j are positive parameters characteristic of alternatives X_i and X_j. Bradley and Terry (1952) introduce $\pi_i + \pi_j$ in the denominator to normalise π_i so that $\text{Prob}_{ij} + \text{Prob}_{ji} = 1$. Luce (1959) developed the theoretical foundations in a precise form, in which π_i can be interpreted as the probability that X_i will be ranked first among all n alternatives. The probability that X_i will be ranked first in any subset of alternatives, and in particular in the subset $\{X_i, X_j\}$ in any subset of alternatives follows from Luce's principle of independence from irrelevant alternatives, which states that the ratio π_i/π_j is constant regardless of what other alternatives are in the subset. This became known as the IIA rule or constant shares assumption. Importantly, this model was transformed into the logistics response function by setting $\pi_i/\pi_j = \exp(\alpha_i - \alpha_j)$. Bradley and Terry (1952) were the first (in the psychological literature) to estimate the logit response function by using a maximum likelihood estimator, although the logistic form goes back many years in Bioassay (see Ashton 1972 for a review and summary of the contribution of Berkson 1944). Estimates of the natural log of π_i/π_j were obtained by employing logistic deviates $y_{ij} = \ln\{\text{prob}_{ij}/(1 - \text{prob}_{ij})\}$. After exponential transformation of parameters (what later became the representative or observed component of utility), the Bradley–Terry–Luce (BTL) model becomes equivalent to Thurstone's Case V model, except that the logistic's density replaces the Gaussian density of Thurstone's response function. The principle of IIA has the exact same effect as constant correlation of discriminal processes for all pairs of alternatives (stimuli). This implies that the conditional probability of an individual's choice between any two alternatives, given his choice between any other two alternatives, is equal to the unconditional probability. The famous *red bus/blue bus* example, introduced by Mayberry in Quandt (1970) and due to Debreu (1960), has been used extensively to highlight the risk of empirical validity of IIA, which became the springboard for many of the developments in discrete choice models to circumvent the rigidity of IIA.

Marschak (1959, Chapter 2) generalised the BTL model to stochastic utility maximisation over multiple alternatives, and introduced it to economics, referring for the first time to Random Utility Maximisation (RUM) (also see Georgescu-Roegen 1954). Marschak explored the testable implications of maximisation of random preferences, and proved for a finite set of alternatives that choice probabilities satisfying Luce's IIA axiom were consistent with RUM. An extension of this result established that a necessary and sufficient condition for RUM with independent errors to satisfy the IIA axiom was that the ε_i be identically distributed with a Type I Extreme Value distribution, $\text{Prob}(\varepsilon_i \leq c) = \exp(-e^{-c/\sigma})$, where σ is a scale factor. The sufficiency was proved by Anthony Marley and reported by Luce and Suppes (1965).

In the 1960s a number of researchers had realised that the study of choices amongst mutually exclusive (discrete) alternatives was not appropriate through the application of ordinary least squares (OLS) regression. Given that the dependent variable of interest was discrete, typically binary (1, 0), the use of OLS would result in predicted outcomes violating the boundary limits of probability. Although under a binary choice setting, probabilities in the range 0.3 to 0.7

tended to satisfy a common range of a linear OLS (or linear probability model form), any probabilities at the extremities were likely to be greater than 1.0 and less than 0. To avoid this, a transformation is required, the most popular being the logistic (log of the odds) transformation. Software to estimate a binary logit (or probit) model started to appear in the 1960s, replacing the popular discriminant analysis method. The early programs included PROLO (PRObit-LOgit) written by Cragg at the University of British Columbia and which was used in many Ph.D. theses in the late 1960s (including Charles Lave (1970a), Thomas Lisco (1967), and David Hensher(1972)). Peter Stopher in the late 1960s had written a program to allow for more than two alternatives, but as far as we are aware, it was rarely used. During the period of the late 1960s and early 1970s there were a number of researchers developing logit software for multinomial logit, including McFadden's code that became the basis of QUAIL, Charles Manski's program (XLogit) used by MIT students such as Ben-Akiva, Andrew Daly's ALogit, Hensher and Johnson's BLogit, and Daganzo and Sheffi's TROMP. Bill Greene had a version of Limdep in the 1970s that began with Tobit and then Logit.

Despite the developments in software (mainly binary choice and some limited multiple choice capability), it was not until the link was made between McFadden's contribution at Berkeley (McFadden 1968) and a project undertaken by Charles River Associates to develop a joint mode and destination choice model (Domencich and McFadden 1975), that we saw a significant growth in research designed to deliver practical tools for modelling interdependent discrete choices involving more than two alternatives. By the late 1960s, Dan McFadden had developed an empirical model from Luce's choice axiom (centred on IIA as described above). Letting $P_C(i)$ denote the probability that a subject confronted with a set of mutually exclusive and exhaustive alternatives C will choose alternative i, given the IIA property, Luce showed that if his axiom holds, then one can associate with each alternative a positive 'strict utility' w_i such that $P_C(i) = w_i / \Sigma_{k \in C} w_k$. Taking the strict utility for alternative i to be a parametric exponential function of its attributes x_i, $w_i = \exp(x_i\beta)$, gave a practical statistical model for individual choice data. McFadden called this the 'conditional logit model' because it reduced to a logistic in the two-alternatives case, and had a ratio form analogous to the form for conditional probabilities (McFadden 1968, 1974, Chapter 8). McFadden (1968, 1974) proved necessity (given sufficiency had already been shown), starting from the implication of the Luce axiom that multinomial choice between an object with strict utility w_1 and m objects with strict utilities w_2 matched binomial choice between an object with strict utility w_1 and an object with strict utility mw_2.

In McFadden (2001), Dan McFadden explains that he '…initially interpreted the conditional logit model as a model of a decision-making bureaucracy, with random elements coming from heterogeneity of tastes of various bureaucrats. It was then transparent that in an empirical model with data across decision-makers, the randomness in utility could come from both inter-personal and intra-personal variation in preferences, and from variations in the attributes of alternatives known to the decision-maker but not to the observer.' This led in his 1974 paper (Chapter 8) on the conditional logit model to introduce '…the idea of an *extensive* margin for discrete decisions in contrast to the *intensive* margin that operates for a representative consumer making continuous decisions.' This was a defining distinction between the economist's and the psychologist's interpretation of randomness.

The 1970s saw much activity in finessing the multinomial logit model based on the form developed by Dan McFadden. In addition to the Charles River Associates project (published as the book by Domencich and McFadden 1975), which introduced inclusive value to connect levels calculated as probability weighted averages of systematic utility components at the next level down in the tree (with Ben Akiva separately developing the log sum formula for exact calculation of inclusive values; see Ben Akiva and Lerman (1979)), McFadden directed the Travel Demand Forecasting Project (TDFP), which set out to develop a comprehensive framework for transportation policy analysis using disaggregate behavioural tools. TDFP used the introduction of BART to test the ability of disaggregate travel demand models to forecast a new transportation mode. On the methodological front, TDFP developed methods for choice-based sampling and for simulation, and statistical methods for estimating and testing nested logit models, that laid the foundation for later results. Some of the ideas that led to the eventual discovery of the nested logit had been laid down by Manheim (1973), and Alan Wilson barely missed it when proposing the combined distribution-mode split function for the famous SELNEC transport model (Wilson *et al.* 1969), although he referred to logsum in Wilson (1969, page 47).

The concern with the limitation of the IIA condition led to the development of the nested logit model (referred to as tree logit by Daly) in which the idea of dissimilarity noted over 45 years before in psychology finally was treated explicitly in the RUM framework through the recognition that the variance associated with the unobserved influences in the random component is likely to be different across the finite set of alternatives in a choice set, but possibly similar for subsets of alternatives. This had appeal to those interested in decision trees although it must be pointed out that the nesting structure is a mechanism to accommodate differential variance in the unobserved effects which may not align with intuition in the construction of decision trees. With the knowledge that the distribution of the variance associated with the unobserved effects can be defined by a location and a scale parameter, the nested logit model had found a way of explicitly identifying and parameterising this scale, which became known alternatively as composite cost, inclusive value, log sum and expected maximum utility. The contributions to this literature, in particular the theoretical justification under RUM, are attributable to Williams (1977, Chapter 9) and Daly and Zachary (1978), with a later generalisation by McFadden (2001). In particular, the Williams–Daly–Zachary analysis provides the foundation for derivation of RUM-consistent choice models from social surplus functions, and connects RUM-based models to Willingness-To-Pay (WTP) for projects.

The period from the mid 1970s to 2010 saw an explosion of contributions to theory, computation and empirical applications of closed-form discrete choice models of the multinomial logit (MNL) and nested logit (NL) variety. The most notable development of closed form models occurred when it was recognised that the nested logit model reveals crucial information to accommodate the pooling of multiple data sets, especially revealed and stated preference data. Although Louviere and Hensher (1982, 1983) and Louviere and Woodworth (1983, Chapter 35) had recognised the role of stated choice data in the study of discrete choices in situations where new alternatives and/or existing alternatives with stretched attribute levels outside of these observed in real markets exist, it was the contribution of Morikawa (see Ben Akiva and Morikawa 1990, Chapter 37) that developed a way to combine data sets while accounting for differences in scale (or variance) that was the essential feature of the choice model that had to be satisfied if the resulting model was able to satisfy the theoretical properties of RUM. Bradley and Daly (1997, but written in 1991, Chapter 38) and Hensher and Bradley (1993) had shown how the nested logit method can be used as a 'nested logit trick', to identify the scale parameter(s) associated with pooled data sets and to adjust the parameter estimates so that all absolute parameters can be compared across data sets.

Despite great progress in linking multiple choices and multiple data sets, some critical challenges remained. These centred initially on open-form models such as multinomial probit, which was difficult to estimate beyond a few alternatives, given the need to accommodate multiple integrals through analytical solutions. The need for numerical integration was required, but it was not until a number of breakthroughs associated with the notion of simulated moments (McFadden 1989, Chapter 16) that the door opened to ways of accommodating more complex choice models, including models that could account for the fuller range of sources of unobserved heterogeneity in preferences. The era of open-form models such as random parameter logit (also referred to as mixed logit) and error components logit, enabled researchers to account for random and systematic sources of taste (or preference) heterogeneity, to allow for the correlated structure of data common to each sampled individual (especially the case for stated choice data), and to obtain richer insights into preference and scale heterogeneity (and heteroscedasticity) associated with structural and latent influences on choices.

This volume brings together a selection of papers that we describe as *Foundational Contributions*. Within the limits of space, we believe that we have a relevant suite of articles that trace the contributions from the 1920s through to the beginning of the 21st century. We will be criticised for omissions (and even possibly for inclusions); however we expect that readers will find that this volume captures what we believe are important contributions at least up to the beginning of the 1990s, with some articles after 2000 that synthesise major developments from the era of open-form discrete choice models. The growing interest in the field will assure a follow up volume in the future to capture the literature of recent times. But first, such contributions must be out there and pass the test of time.

References

Ashton, W.D. (1972), *The Logit Transformation*, Griffin, London.

Ben Akiva, M.E. and Lerman, S.R. (1979), 'Disaggregate travel and mobility choice models and measures of accessibility', in D.A. Hensher and P.R. Stopher (eds), *Behavioural Travel Modelling*, Croom Helm, London.

Ben-Akiva, M.E., and Morikawa, T. (1991), Estimation of travel demand models from multiple data sources, in Koshi, M. (ed.) *Transportation and Traffic Theory*, Proceedings of the 11th ISTTT, Elsevier, Amsterdam, 461–476.

Berkson, J. (1944), 'Application of the logistics function to bioassay', *Journal of the American Statistical Association*, **39**, 357–65.

Bock, R.D. and Jones, L.V. (1968), *The Measurement and Prediction of Judgment and Choice*, Holden-Day, San Francisco.

Bradley, R.A. and Terry, M.E. (1952), 'Rank analysis of incomplete block designs. I The method of paired comparison, *Biometrika*, **39**, 324–45.

Daly, A.J. and Zachary, S. (1978), 'Improved multiple choice models', in D.A. Hensher and M.Q. Dalvi (eds), *Determinants of Travel Choice*, Saxon House, Farnborough.

Debreu, G. (1960), 'Review of R.D. Luce *Individual Choice Behavior*', *American Economic Review*, **50**, 186–8.

Domencich, T. and McFadden, D. (1975), *Urban Travel Demand*, North Holland, Amsterdam.

Georgescu-Roegen, N. (1954), 'Choice, expectations, and measurability', *Quarterly Journal of Economics*, **LXVIII**, 503–34.

Hensher, D.A. (1972), *The Consumer's Choice Function: A Study of Traveller Behaviour and Values*, Department of Economics, University of New South Wales.

Hensher, D.A. (1974), 'A probabilistic disaggregate model of binary mode choice', in D.A. Hensher (ed.), *Urban Travel Choice and Demand Modelling*, Special Report No. 12, Melbourne, *Australian Road Research Board*, August, 61–99.

Hensher, D.A. and Bradley, M. (1993), 'Using stated response data to enrich revealed preference discrete choice models', *Marketing Letters*, **4** (2), 139–52.

Hull, C.L. (1943), *Principles of Behavior*, Appleton-Century, New York.

Lave, C.A. (1970a), *Value of Time*, Department of Economics, Stanford University.

Lave, C. (1970b), 'The demand for urban mass transit', *Review of Economics and Statistics*, **52**, 320–23.

Lisco, T. (1967), *The Value of Commuters' Travel Time: A Study in Urban Transportation*, University of Chicago, Ph.D. dissertation.

Louviere, J.J. and Hensher, D.A. (1982), 'On the design and analysis of simulated choice or allocation experiments in travel choice modelling', *Transportation Research Record No. 890*, 11–17.

Louviere, J.J. and Hensher, D.A. (1983), 'Using discrete choice models with experimental design data to forecast consumer demand for a unique cultural event', *Journal of Consumer Research*, **10** (3), 348–61.

Louviere, J. and Woodworth, G. (1983), 'Design and analysis of simulated consumer choice or allocation experiments: an approach based on aggregate data', *Journal of Marketing Research*, **20**: 350–367.

Luce, R.D. (1959), *Individual Choice Behavior*, Wiley, New York.

Luce, R.D. and Suppes, P. (1965), 'Preference, utility and subjective probability, in R.D. Luce, R.R. Bush and E. Galanter (eds), *Handbook of Mathematical Psychology, Volume III*, Wiley, New York.

Manheim, C.F. (1973), 'Practical implications of some fundamental properties of travel demand models', *Highway Research Record*, **244**, 21–38.

McFadden, D. (1968), *The Revealed Preferences of a Public Bureaucracy*, Department of Economics, University of California, Berkeley.

McFadden, D. (2001), 'Disaggregate behavioural travel demand RUM side – a 30 years retrospective', in D.A. Hensher (ed.), *Travel Behaviour Research: The Leading Edge*, Pergamon, Oxford, 17–64.

Quandt, R.E. (1970), *The Demand for Travel: Theory and Measurement*, Heath, Lexington.

Restle, F. (1961), *Psychology of Judgment and Choice*, Wiley, New York.

Rumelhart, D.L. and Greeno, J.G. (1968), 'Choice between similar and dissimilar objects: an experimental test of the Luce and Restle choice models', presented at the *Midwestern Psychological Association* meeting, May.

Stopher, P.R. and Lisco, T. (1970), 'Modeling travel demand: a disaggregate behavioral approach, issues and applications', *Transportation Research Forum Proceedings*, 195–214.

Thurstone, L.L. (1945), 'The prediction of choice', *Psychometrika*, **10**, 237–53.

Wilson, A.G. (1969), The use of entropy maximising models in the theory of trip distribution, mode split and route split, *Journal of Transport Economics and Policy*, **3**, 108-126.

Williams, H.C.W.L. (1977), 'On the formation of travel demand models and economic evaluation measures of user benefit', *Environment and Planning* A, 9 (3), 285–344.

Wilson, A.G., Hawkins, A.F., Hill, G.J. and Wagon, D.J. (1969), 'Calibrating and testing of the SELNEC transport model', *Regional Studies*, **3** (3), 340–345.

[1]

A LAW OF COMPARATIVE JUDGMENT[1]

BY L. L. THURSTONE

The University of Chicago

The object of this paper is to describe a new psychophysical law which may be called the *law of comparative judgment* and to show some of its special applications in the measurement of psychological values. The law of comparative judgment is implied in Weber's law and in Fechner's law. The law of comparative judgment is applicable not only to the comparison of physical stimulus intensities but also to qualitative comparative judgments such as those of excellence of specimens in an educational scale and it has been applied in the measurement of such psychological values as a series of opinions on disputed public issues. The latter application of the law will be illustrated in a forthcoming study. It should be possible also to verify it on comparative judgments which involve simultaneous and successive contrast.

The law has been derived in a previous article and the present study is mainly a description of some of its applications. Since several new concepts are involved in the formulation of the law it has been necessary to invent several terms to describe them, and these will be repeated here.

Let us suppose that we are confronted with a series of stimuli or specimens such as a series of gray values, cylindrical weights, handwriting specimens, children's drawings, or any other series of stimuli that are subject to comparison. The first requirement is of course a specification as to what it is that we are to judge or compare. It may be gray values, or weights, or excellence, or any other quantitative or qualitative attribute about which we can think 'more' or 'less' for each specimen. This attribute which may be assigned, as it were, in differing amounts to each specimen defines what we shall call the *psychological continuum* for that particular project in measurement.

[1] This is one of a series of articles by members of the Behavior Research Staff of the Illinois Institute for Juvenile Research, Chicago, Herman M. Adler, Director. Series B, No. 107.

As we inspect two or more specimens for the task of comparison there must be some kind of process in us by which we react differently to the several specimens, by which we identify the several degrees of excellence or weight or gray value in the specimens. You may suit your own predilections in calling this process psychical, neural, chemical, or electrical but it will be called here in a non-committal way *the discriminal process* because its ultimate nature does not concern the formulation of the law of comparative judgment. If then, one handwriting specimen *seems* to be more excellent than a second specimen, then the two discriminal processes of the observer are different, at least on this occasion.

The so-called 'just noticeable difference' is contingent on the fact that an observer is not consistent in his comparative judgments from one occasion to the next. He gives different comparative judgments on successive occasions about the same pair of stimuli. Hence we conclude that the discriminal process corresponding to a given stimulus is not fixed. It fluctuates. For any handwriting specimen, for example, there is one discriminal process that is experienced more often with that specimen than other processes which correspond to higher or lower degrees of excellence. This most common process is called here *the modal discriminal process for the given stimulus.*

The psychological continuum or scale is so constructed or defined that the frequencies of the respective discriminal processes for any given stimulus form a normal distribution on the psychological scale. This involves no assumption of a normal distribution or of anything else. The psychological scale is at best an artificial construct. If it has any physical reality we certainly have not the remotest idea what it may be like. We do not assume, therefore, that the distribution of discriminal processes is normal on the scale because that would imply that the scale is there already. We *define* the scale in terms of the frequencies of the discriminal processes for any stimulus. This artificial construct, the psychological scale, is so spaced off that the frequencies of the discriminal processes for any given stimulus form a normal distribution on the scale. The separation on the scale between the discriminal process for a given stimulus on any particular occasion and the modal discriminal process for that stimulus we shall call *the discriminal deviation* on that occasion. If on a particular occasion, the observer perceives more than the usual degree of excellence or weight in the specimen in question, the discriminal deviation is at that instant positive. In a similar manner the discriminal deviation at another moment will be negative.

The standard deviation of the distribution of discriminal processes on the scale for a particular specimen will be called its *discriminal dispersion.*

This is the central concept in the present analysis. An ambiguous stimulus which is observed at widely different degrees of excellence or weight or gray value on different occasions will have of course a large discriminal dispersion. Some other stimulus or specimen which is provocative of relatively slight fluctuations in discriminal processes will have, similarly, a small discriminal dispersion.

The scale difference between the discriminal processes of two specimens which are involved in the same judgment will be called *the discriminal difference* on that occasion. If the two stimuli be denoted A and B and if the discriminal processes corresponding to them be denoted a and b on any one occasion, then the discriminal difference will be the scale distance $(a - b)$ which varies of course on different occasions. If, in one of the comparative judgments, A seems to be better than B, then, on that occasion, the discriminal difference $(a - b)$ is positive. If, on another occasion, the stimulus B seems to be the better, then on that occasion the discriminal difference $(a - b)$ is negative.

Finally, the scale distance between the modal discriminal processes for any two specimens is the separation which is assigned to the two specimens on the psychological scale. The two specimens are so allocated on the scale that their separation is equal to the separation between their respective modal discriminal processes.

We can now state the law of comparative judgment as follows:

$$S_1 - S_2 = x_{12} \cdot \sqrt{\sigma_1^2 + \sigma_2^2 - 2r\sigma_1\sigma_2}, \qquad (1)$$

in which

S_1 and S_2 are the psychological scale values of the two compared stimuli.

x_{12} = the sigma value corresponding to the proportion of judgments $p_{1>2}$. When $p_{1>2}$ is greater than .50 the numerical value of x_{12} is positive. When $p_{1>2}$ is less than .50 the numerical value of x_{12} is negative.

σ_1 = discriminal dispersion of stimulus R_1.

σ_2 = discriminal dispersion of stimulus R_2.

r = correlation between the discriminal deviations of R_1 and R_2 in the same judgment.

This law of comparative judgment is basic for all experimental work on Weber's law, Fechner's law, and for all educational and psychological scales in which comparative judgments are involved. Its derivation will not be repeated here because it has been described in a previous article.[2] It applies fundamentally to the judgments of *a single observer* who compares a series of stimuli by the method of paired comparison when no 'equal' judgments are allowed. It is a rational equation for the method of constant stimuli. It is assumed that the single observer compares each pair of stimuli a sufficient number of times so that a proportion, $p_{a>b}$, may be determined for each pair of stimuli.

For the practical application of the law of comparative judgment we shall consider five cases which differ in assumptions, approximations, and degree of simplification. The more assumptions we care to make, the simpler will be the observation equations. These five cases are as follows:

Case I.—The equation can be used in its complete form for paired comparison data obtained from a single subject when only two judgments are allowed for each observation such as 'heavier' or 'lighter,' 'better' or 'worse,' etc. There will be one observation equation for every observed proportion of judgments. It would be written, in its complete form, thus:

$$S_1 - S_2 - x_{12} \cdot \sqrt{\sigma_1^2 + \sigma_2^2 - 2r\sigma_1\sigma_2} = 0. \qquad (1)$$

[2] Thurstone, L. L., 'Psychophysical Analysis,' *Amer. J. Psychol.*, July, 1927.

According to this equation every pair of stimuli presents the possibility of a different correlation between the discriminal deviations. If this degree of freedom is allowed, the problem of psychological scaling would be insoluble because every observation equation would introduce a new unknown and the number of unknowns would then always be greater than the number of observation equations. In order to make the problem soluble, it is necessary to make at least one assumption, namely that the correlation between discriminal deviations is practically constant throughout the stimulus series and for the single observer. Then, if we have n stimuli or specimens in the scale, we shall have $\frac{1}{2} \cdot n(n - 1)$ observation equations when each specimen is compared with every other specimen. Each specimen has a scale value, S_1, and a discriminal dispersion, σ_1, to be determined. There are therefore $2n$ unknowns. The scale value of one of the specimens is chosen as an origin and its discriminal dispersion as a unit of measurement, while r is an unknown which is assumed to be constant for the whole series. Hence, for a scale of n specimens there will be $(2n - 1)$ unknowns. The smallest number of specimens for which the problem is soluble is five. For such a scale there will be nine unknowns, four scale values, four discriminal dispersions, and r. For a scale of five specimens there will be ten observation equations.

The statement of the law of comparative judgment in the form of equation 1 involves one theoretical assumption which is probably of minor importance. It assumes that all positive discriminal differences $(a - b)$ are judged $A > B$, and that all negative discriminal differences $(a - b)$ are judged $A < B$. This is probably not absolutely correct when the discriminal differences of either sign are very small. The assumption would not affect the experimentally observed proportion $p_{A>B}$ if the small positive discriminal differences occurred as often as the small negative ones. As a matter of fact, when $p_{A>B}$ is greater than .50 the small positive discriminal differences $(a - b)$ are slightly more frequent than the negative perceived differences $(a - b)$. It is probable that rather refined experimental procedures are necessary to isolate this effect. The effect is ignored in our present analysis.

Case II.—The law of comparative judgment as described under Case I refers fundamentally to a series of judgments *of a single observer.* It does not constitute an assumption to say that the discriminal processes for a single observer give a normal frequency distribution on the psychological continuum. That is a part of the definition of the psychological scale. But it does constitute an assumption to take for granted that the various degrees of an attribute of a specimen perceived in it by *a group* of subjects is a normal distribution. For example, if a weight-cylinder is lifted by an observer several hundred times in comparison with other cylinders, it is possible to define or construct the psychological scale so that the distribution of the apparent weights of the cylinder for the single observer is normal. It is probably safe to assume that the distribution of apparent weights for *a group* of subjects, each subject perceiving the weight only once, is also normal on the same scale. To transfer the reasoning in the same way from a single observer to a group of observers for specimens such as handwriting or English Composition is not so certain. For practical purposes it may be assumed that when *a group* of observers perceives a specimen of handwriting, the distribution of excellence that they read into the specimen is normal on the psychological continuum of perceived excellence. At least this is a safe assumption if the group is not split in some curious way with prejudices for or against particular elements of the specimen.

With the assumption just described, the law of comparative judgment, derived for the method of constant stimuli with two responses, can be extended to data collected from a group of judges in which each judge compares each stimulus with every other stimulus only once. The other assumptions of Case I apply also to Case II.

Case III.—Equation 1 is awkward to handle as an observation equation for a scale with a large number of specimens. In fact the arithmetical labor of constructing an educational or psychological scale with it is almost prohibitive. The equation can be simplified if the correlation r can be assumed to be either zero or unity. It is a safe assumption that when the stimulus series is very homogeneous with no distracting attributes, the correlation between discriminal deviations is low and possibly even zero unless we encounter the effect of simultaneous or successive contrast. If we accept the correlation as zero, we are really assuming that the degree of excellence which an observer perceives in one of the specimens has no influence on the degree of excellence that he perceives in the comparison specimen. There are two effects that may be operative here and which are antagonistic to each other.

(1) If you look at two handwriting specimens in a mood slightly more generous and tolerant than ordinarily, you may perceive a degree of excellence in specimen A a little higher than its mean excellence. But at the same moment specimen B is also judged a little higher than its average or mean excellence for the same reason. To the extent that such a factor is at work the discriminal deviations will tend to vary together and the correlation r will be high and positive.

(2) The opposite effect is seen in *simultaneous contrast.* When the correlation between the discriminal deviations is negative the law of comparative judgment gives an exaggerated psychological difference $(S_1 - S_2)$ which we know as simultaneous or successive contrast. In this type of comparative judgment the discriminal deviations are negatively associated. It is probable that this effect tends to be a minimum when the specimens have other perceivable attributes, and that it is a maximum when other distracting stimulus differences are removed. If this statement should be experimentally verified, it would constitute an interesting generalization in perception.

If our last generalization is correct, it should be a safe assumption to write $r = 0$ for those scales in which the specimens are rather complex such as handwriting specimens and childrens drawings. If we look at two handwriting specimens and perceive one of them as unusually fine, it probably tends to depress somewhat the degree of excellence we would ordinarily perceive in the comparison specimen, but this effect is slight compared with the simultaneous contrast perceived in lifted weights and in gray values. Furthermore, the simultaneous contrast is slight with small stimulus differences and it must be recalled that psychological scales are based on comparisons in the subliminal or barely supraliminal range.

The correlation between discriminal deviations is probably high when the two stimuli give simultaneous contrast and are quite far apart on the scale. When the range for the correlation is reduced to a scale distance comparable with the difference limen, the correlation probably is reduced nearly to zero. At any rate, in order to simplify equation 1 we shall assume that it is zero. This represents the comparative judgment in which the evaluation of one of the specimens has no influence on the evaluation of the other specimen in the paired judgment. The law then takes the following form.

$$S_1 - S_2 = x_{12} \cdot \sqrt{\sigma_1^2 + \sigma_2^2}. \tag{2}$$

Case IV.—If we can make the additional assumption that the discriminal dispersions are not subject to gross variation, we can considerably simplify the equation so that it becomes linear and therefore much easier to handle. In equation (2) we let

$$\sigma_2 = \sigma_1 + d,$$

in which d is assumed to be at least smaller than σ_1 and preferably a fraction of σ_1 such as .1 to .5. Then equation (2) becomes

$$\begin{aligned} S_1 - S_2 &= x_{12} \cdot \sqrt{\sigma_1^2 + \sigma_2^2} \\ &= x_{12} \cdot \sqrt{\sigma_1^2 + (\sigma_1 + d)^2} \\ &= x_{12} \cdot \sqrt{\sigma_1^2 + \sigma_1^2 + 2\sigma_1 d + d^2}. \end{aligned}$$

If d is small, the term d^2 may be dropped. Hence

$$\begin{aligned} S_1 - S_2 &= x_{12} \cdot \sqrt{2\sigma_1^2 + 2\sigma_1 d} \\ &= x_{12} \cdot \sqrt{2\sigma_1}(\sigma_1 + d)^{\frac{1}{2}}. \end{aligned}$$

Expanding $(\sigma_1 + d)^{1/2}$ we have

$$(\sigma_1 + d)^{1/2} = \sigma_1^{1/2} + \tfrac{1}{2}\sigma_1^{-(1/2)}d - \tfrac{1}{4}\sigma_1^{-(3/2)}d^2$$

$$= \sqrt{\sigma_1} + \frac{d}{2\sqrt{\sigma_1}} - \frac{d^2}{4\sqrt{\sigma_1^3}}.$$

The third term may be dropped when d^2 is small. Hence

$$(\sigma_1 + d)^{1/2} = \sqrt{\sigma_1} + \frac{d}{2\sqrt{\sigma_1}}.$$

Substituting,

$$S_1 - S_2 = x_{12} \cdot \sqrt{2\sigma_1}\left[\sqrt{\sigma_1} + \frac{d}{2\sqrt{\sigma_1}}\right]$$

$$= x_{12}\left[\sigma_1\sqrt{2} + \frac{d}{\sqrt{2}}\right].$$

But $d = \sigma_2 - \sigma_1$;

$$\therefore\ S_1 - S_2 = x_{12}\frac{\sigma_2}{\sqrt{2}} + x_{12}\frac{\sigma_1}{\sqrt{2}}$$

or

$$S_1 - S_2 = .707x_{12}\sigma_2 + .707x_{12}\sigma_1. \tag{3}$$

Equation (3) is linear and very easily handled. If $\sigma_2 - \sigma_1$ is small compared with σ_1, equation (3) gives a close approximation to the true values of S and σ for each specimen.

If there are n stimuli in the scale there will be $(2n - 2)$ unknowns, namely a scale value S and a discriminal dispersion σ for each specimen. The scale value for one of the specimens may be chosen as the origin or zero since the origin of the psychological scale is arbitrary. The discriminal dispersion of the same specimen may be chosen as a unit of measurement for the scale. With n specimens in the series there will be $\tfrac{1}{2}n(n - 1)$ observation equations. The minimum number of specimens for which the scaling problem can be solved is then four, at which number we have six observation equations and six unknowns.

Case V.—The simplest case involves the assumption that all the discriminal dispersions are equal. This may be legitimate for rough measurement such as Thorndike's handwriting scale or the Hillegas scale of English Composition. Equation (2) then becomes

$$S_1 - S_2 = x_{12} \cdot \sqrt{2\sigma^2}$$
$$= x_{12}\sigma \cdot \sqrt{2}.$$

But since the assumed constant discriminal dispersion is the unit of measurement we have

$$S_1 - S_2 = 1.4142 x_{12}. \tag{4}$$

This is a simple observation equation which may be used for rather coarse scaling. It measures the scale distance between two specimens as directly proportional to the sigma value of the observed proportion of judgments $p_{1>2}$. This is the equation that is basic for Thorndike's procedure in scaling handwriting and children's drawings although he has not shown the theory underlying his scaling procedure. His unit of measurement was the standard deviation of the discriminal differences which is $.707\sigma$ when the discriminal dispersions are constant. In future scaling problems equation (3) will probably be found to be the most useful.

Weighting the Observation Equations

The observation equations obtained under any of the five cases are not of the same reliability and hence they should not all be equally weighted. Two observed proportions of judgments such as $p_{1>2} = .99$ and $p_{1>3} = .55$ are not equally reliable. The proportion of judgments $p_{1>2}$ is one of the observations that determine the scale separation between S_1 and S_2. It measures the scale distance $(S_1 - S_2)$ in terms of the standard deviation, σ_{1-2}, of the distribution of discriminal differences for the two stimuli R_1 and R_2. This distribution is necessarily normal by the definition of the psychological scale.

The standard error of a proportion of a normal frequency distribution is

$$\sigma_p = \frac{\sigma}{Z} \cdot \sqrt{\frac{pq}{N}}.[3]$$

[3] See Kelley, T. L., 'Statistical Method,' p. 90, equation 43.

in which σ is the standard deviation of the distribution, Z is the ordinate corresponding to p, and $q = 1 - p$ while N is the number of cases on which the proportion is ascertained. The term σ in the present case is the standard deviation σ_{1-2} of the distribution of discriminal differences. Hence the standard error of $p_{1>2}$ is

$$\sigma_{p1>2} = \frac{\sigma_{1-2}}{Z} \cdot \sqrt{\frac{pq}{N}}. \tag{5}$$

But since, by equation (2)

$$\sigma_{1-2} = \sqrt{\sigma_1^2 + \sigma_2^2} \tag{6}$$

and since this may be written approximately, by equation (3), as

$$\sigma_{1-2} = .707(\sigma_1 + \sigma_2) \tag{7}$$

we have

$$\sigma_{p1>2} = \frac{.707(\sigma_1 + \sigma_2)}{Z} \cdot \sqrt{\frac{pq}{N}}. \tag{8}$$

The weight, w_{1-2}, that should be assigned to observation equation (2) is the reciprocal of the square of its standard error. Hence

$$w_{1-2} = \frac{1}{\sigma_{p1>2}^2} = \frac{Z^2 N}{.5(\sigma_1 + \sigma_2)^2 p \cdot q}. \tag{9}$$

It will not repay the trouble to attempt to carry the factor $(\sigma_1 + \sigma_2)^2$ in the formula because this factor contains two of the unknowns, and because it destroys the linearity of the observation equation (3), while the only advantage gained would be a refinement in the weighting of the observation equations. Since only the weighting is here at stake, it may be approximated by eliminating this factor. The factor .5 is a constant. It has no effect, and the weighting then becomes

$$w_{1-2} = \frac{Z^2 N}{pq}. \tag{10}$$

By arranging the experiments in such a way that all the observed proportions are based on the same number of judgments the factor N becomes a constant and therefore has no effect on the weighting. Hence

$$w_{1-2} = \frac{Z^2}{pq}. \tag{11}$$

This weighting factor is entirely determined by the proportion, $p_{1>2}$ of judgments '1 is better than 2' and it can therefore be readily ascertained by the Kelley-Wood tables. The weighted form of observation equation (3) therefore becomes

$$wS_1 - wS_2 - .707wx_{12}\sigma_2 - .707wx_{12}\sigma_1 = 0. \tag{12}$$

This equation is linear and can therefore be easily handled. The coefficient $.707wx_{12}$ is entirely determined by the observed value of p for each equation and therefore a facilitating table can be prepared to reduce the labor of setting up the normal equations. The same weighting would be used for any of the observation equations in the five cases since the weight is solely a function of p when the factor σ_{1-2} is ignored for the weighting formula.

Summary

A law of comparative judgment has been formulated which is expressed in its complete form as equation (1). This law defines the psychological scale or continuum. It allocates the compared stimuli on the continuum. It expresses the experimentally observed proportion, $p_{1>2}$ of judgments '1 is stronger (better, lighter, more excellent) than 2' as a function of the scale values of the stimuli, their respective discriminal dispersions, and the correlation between the paired discriminal deviations.

The formulation of the law of comparative judgment involves the use of a new psychophysical concept, namely, the *discriminal dispersion.* Closely related to this concept are those of the *discriminal process*, the *modal discriminal process*, the *discriminal deviation*, the *discriminal difference.* All of these psychophysical concepts concern the ambiguity or qualitative variation with which one stimulus is perceived by the same observer on different occasions.

The psychological scale has been defined as the particular linear spacing of the confused stimuli which yields a normal distribution of the discriminal processes for any one of the stimuli. The validity of this definition of the psychological continuum can be experimentally and objectively tested. If the stimuli are so spaced out on the scale that the distribution of discriminal processes for one of the stimuli is normal, then these scale allocations should remain the same when they are defined by the distribution of discriminal processes of any other stimulus within the confusing range. It is physically impossible for this condition to obtain for several psychological scales defined by different types of distribution of the discriminal processes. Consistency can be found only for one form of distribution of discriminal processes as a basis for defining the scale. If, for example, the scale is defined on the basis of a rectangular distribution of the discriminal processes, it is easily shown by experimental data that there will be gross discrepancies between experimental and theoretical proportions, $p_{1>2}$. The residuals should be investigated to ascertain whether they are a minimum when the normal or Gaussian distribution of discriminal processes is used as a basis for defining the psychological scale. Triangular and other forms of distribution might be tried. Such an experimental demonstration would constitute perhaps the most fundamental discovery that has been made in the field of psychological measurement. Lacking such proof and since the Gaussian distribution of discriminal processes yields scale values that agree very closely with the experimental data, I have defined the psychological continuum that is implied in Weber's Law, in Fechner's Law, and in educational quality scales as that particular linear spacing of the stimuli which gives a Gaussian distribution of discriminal processes.

The law of comparative judgment has been considered in this paper under five cases which involve different assumptions and degrees of simplification for practical use. These may be summarized as follows.

Case I.—The law is stated in complete form by equation (1). It is a rational equation for the method of paired comparison. It is applicable to all problems involving the method of constant stimuli for the measurement of both quantitative and qualitative stimulus differences. It concerns the repeated judgments of a single observer.

Case II.—The same equation (1) is here used for *a group* of observers, each observer making only one judgment for each pair of stimuli, or one serial ranking of all the stimuli. It assumes that the distribution of the perceived relative values of each stimulus is normal for the group of observers.

Case III.—The assumptions of Cases I. and II. are involved here also and in addition it is assumed that the correlation between the discriminal deviations of the same judgment are uncorrelated. This leads to the simpler form of the law in equation (2).

Case IV.—Besides the preceding assumptions the still simpler form of the law in equation (3) assumes that the discriminal deviations are not grossly different so that in general one may write

$$\sigma_2 - \sigma_1 < \sigma_1$$

and that preferably

$$\sigma_2 - \sigma_1 = d$$

in which d is a small fraction of σ_1.

Case V.—This is the simplest formulation of the law and it involves, in addition to previous assumptions, the assumption that all the discriminal dispersions are equal. This assumption should not be made without experimental test. Case V. is identical with Thorndike's method of constructing quality scales for handwriting and for children's drawings. His unit of measurement is the standard deviation of the distribution of discriminal differences when the discriminal dispersions are assumed to be equal.

Since the standard error of the observed proportion of judgments, $p_{1>2}$, is not uniform, it is advisable to weight each of the observation equations by a factor shown in equation (11) which is applicable to the observation equations in any of the five cases considered. Its application to equation (3) leads to the weighted observation equation (12).

[2]

Binary-Choice Constraints and Random Utility Indicators

JACOB MARSCHAK
Yale University

1. The Problem

This paper contains suggestions for combining various available types of information on economic choice. There are in the main three types.

(i) Controlled experiments on choices from small sets (usually pairs) of alternatives.

(ii) Surveys of consumers' choices from large sets of alternatives, each set being determined by the market prices and by each consumer's monetary resources; similar surveys (*mutatis mutandis*) of producers' choices are also available, especially in the case of farmers.

(iii) Time series of total consumption (or production) of individual commodities, total incomes, and market prices, over a given geographical area.

Various researchers (Marschak [16], and more recently Tobin [19], Wold [22], and Farrell [9]) have tried to combine information on (ii) and (iii). The present paper deals with combining the materials in (i) and (ii), albeit only to the extent of outlining the general problem and of concluding with an example.

Suppose that, given a set of consumers' budgets at varying prices, we want to estimate a function on the commodity space that might be used as a utility indicator (defining a system of "indifference surfaces") to describe the tastes of the sampled group of people. The desired statistical estimation will usually be preceded by the "specification" of a class of eligible functions on the commodity space. The continuity and convexity ("diminishing marginal satisfaction") properties postulated in economic theory, partly in connection with its requirement of "consumer's equilibrium," permit such specification only within very broad limits.

Dedicated to Ragnar Frisch, an old and esteemed friend, on the occasion of his sixty-fifth birthday.

The paper was completed during a year's visit at the Carnegie Institute of Technology. The research was carried out partly under a contract of the Office of Naval Research with the Cowles Foundation for Research in Economics at Yale University, Task NR047-006. Previous collaboration with H. D. Block and discussions with Herman Chernoff, Gerard Debreu, Morris DeGroot, Tjalling Koopmans, and R. Duncan Luce were most helpful.

Suppose, however, that, in addition to the consumers' survey data, laboratory data are available that imply that the choices being made by people of a given socio-economic group obey certain constraints. The knowledge of these constraints might provide help in further restricting the set of eligible utility indicators.

It will be realistic to assume that a man's choice from a given set of alternatives is not unique but obeys some probability distribution. This agrees with the approach usual in psychometrics and psychophysics, and may also explain a part of the statistical variations in economic survey data. Accordingly, our approach will be "stochastic" throughout. We shall study the logical connections between different behavior assumptions made in stochastic theories of decision.

2. Binary-Choice Probabilities

Unless specified to the contrary, all concepts in this paper are associated with a single given person, the "subject" of experiments. The only experiments considered in this paper—except for cursory remarks on other kinds of experiments, especially in Sections 4, 5, and 11—are *binary choices*: the subject is forced to choose one of the pair (x, y) of alternatives. On the other hand, the data resulting from a consumer survey are, of course, *multiple choices* since a consumer's monetary resources permit him, given the prices of goods, to choose from among more than a pair of alternative budgets.

The following notation will be used:

$\boldsymbol{X}$, the set of *alternatives*, with generic elements $x, y, \cdots$.

$\boldsymbol{n}$, the number of elements of X when X is finite; in this case the elements will be identified by integers: $X = (1, \cdots, n)$.

$\boldsymbol{p}$, the class of functions p on $X \times X$ (or, with X finite, the set of matrices $p = [p_{xy}]$) such that

(1) $$p_{xy} = 1 - p_{yx} \geqq 0 .$$

Hence $p_{xx} = \frac{1}{2}$. When $x \neq y$, the function p_{xy} is called the *probability of a binary choice, viz.*, of the choice of x out of the subset (x, y) of X. A region $\boldsymbol{p}_C \subseteqq \boldsymbol{p}$ defines a condition (C) on all p_{xy} and is called a *binary-choice constraint*. It will be convenient to identify such constraints, and other conditions, by symbols in parentheses, thus: (C).

Binary-choice constraints involving no other quantities but the p_{xy} are called *directly testable*: it will be assumed that they can be accepted or rejected, in the sense of statistical inference, on the basis of binary-choice experiments. (However, except in the case of finite X and very large samples permitting the approximation of each p_{xy} by the corresponding observed frequency, difficult statistical problems that cannot be treated here present themselves, but see [1, Section 10].) Constraints on the p_{xy} that are not "directly testable" involve in particular the existence of the variously defined "utilities," a theoretical construct. It will be important to find which of the "directly testable" constraints imply or are implied by the existence of "utilities" in the various senses of this term.

EXAMPLE. Let $X = (1, 2, 3)$. A function p is completely described by any six numbers p_{xy} obeying (1). The relation $1 \leqq p_{12} + p_{23} + p_{31} \leqq 2$ exemplifies a binary-choice constraint. It is "directly testable" and is implied by certain "utility" statements, as will be seen in Section 6.

3. Random Utility Indicator

A probability measure on the set of real-valued functions on X defines a real-valued random function on X (a random vector if X is finite); its values are random numbers.

DEFINITION. *$U^{(2)}$, a real-valued random function on X, is called a* random utility indicator "in the binary sense" *if, for every $x \neq y$,*

$$\Pr(U_x^{(2)} \geqq U_y^{(2)}) = p_{xy} \,. \tag{2}$$

(The idea goes back to Thurstone's "law of comparative judgment" [18].)

It follows that if F is a random utility indicator in the binary sense, and G is a strictly increasing transform of F (that is, $F_x \geqq F_y$ if and only if $G_x \geqq G_y$, for all x, y), then G is also a random utility indicator in the binary sense.

The following theorem was suggested by M. DeGroot:

THEOREM 1. *If $U^{(2)}$ is a random utility indicator in the binary sense, then $\Pr(U_x^{(2)} = U_y^{(2)}) = 0$ for every $x \neq y$.*

PROOF. Let $x \neq y$ and suppose $\Pr(U_x^{(2)} = U_y^{(2)}) > 0$. Then

$$\begin{aligned} p_{xy} + p_{yx} &= \Pr(U_x^{(2)} \geqq U_y^{(2)}) + \Pr(U_y^{(2)} \geqq U_x^{(2)}) \\ &= \Pr(U_x^{(2)} > U_y^{(2)}) + \Pr(U_y^{(2)} > U_x^{(2)}) + 2\Pr(U_x^{(2)} = U_y^{(2)}) \\ &= \{\Pr(U_x^{(2)} > U_y^{(2)}) + \Pr(U_y^{(2)} > U_x^{(2)}) + \Pr(U_x^{(2)} = U_y^{(2)})\} \\ &\qquad\qquad + \Pr(U_x^{(2)} = U_y^{(2)}) \\ &= 1 + \Pr(U_x^{(2)} = U_y^{(2)}) > 1 \,, \end{aligned}$$

contradicting (1).

EXAMPLES. (i) Let $X = (1, 2, 3)$; then $U^{(2)}$ is a random utility indicator if the six numbers $\Pr(U_x^{(2)} > U_y^{(2)})$ are respectively equal to the six numbers p_{xy} which (or some constraints on which) are obtained from observations.

(ii) Let X denote the real m-space with generic point $x = (x_1, \cdots, x_m)$; let $T = (T_1, \cdots, T_m)$ be a random vector such that $0 < T_i < 1$ $(i = 1, \cdots, m)$ and $\sum T_i = 1$. Let

$$U_x^{(2)} = \prod_{i=1}^{m} x_i^{T_i} \tag{3}$$

(the "Cobb-Douglas function" frequently used in economics, with X being the commodity space). If $\Pr(U_x^{(2)} \geqq U_y^{(2)}) = p_{xy}$, then $U^{(2)}$ is a random utility indicator "in the binary sense." This example will be used again in Section 12.

CONDITION ($U^{(2)}$). The function p is such that $U^{(2)}$ exists.

4. A Remark on Multiple-Choice Probabilities

The concepts and the condition just defined can be easily generalized to multiple-choice probabilities. For every $x \in X^*$ and $X^* \subseteq X$, one defines $p_x(X^*)$, obeying

$$(4) \qquad p_x(X^*) \geqq 0 , \qquad \sum_{x \in X^*} p_x(X^*) = 1 .$$

The number $p_x(X^*)$ is interpreted as the probability that the subject, forced to choose from the subset X^*, will choose x. Clearly, p_{xy} is a special case, with $X^* = (x, y)$. The following condition exemplifies an important and plausible constraint that would be directly testable if multiple choices from subsets of various sizes were observable:

$$(5) \qquad \text{if} \quad x \in X^{**} \subseteq X^* \subseteq X, \quad \text{then} \quad p_x(X^*) \leqq p_x(X^{**}) .$$

In [1], Block and Marschak dealt with multiple-choice probabilities, and had accordingly used the following definition of the random utility indicator, stronger than the one given in Section 3:

DEFINITION. *U, a random function on X, is a* random utility indicator *if, for all $X^* \subseteq X$,*

$$(6) \qquad \Pr(U_x \geqq U_y , \quad y \in X^*) = p_x(X^*) .$$

Correspondingly, Condition ($U^{(2)}$) is replaced by the stronger

CONDITION (U). The set of probabilities $p_x(X^*)$, where $x \in X^*$ and $X^* \subseteq X$, is such that U, in the sense of (6), exists.

Clearly, Condition (U) implies ($U^{(2)}$) and also implies (5).

Some other properties of U will be used later, in Section 11. However, because of experimental difficulties with large subsets of alternatives, it seems worthwhile to devote a special and intensive study to binary-choice probabilities. They cover much of the existing materials on human responses, and many practical situations ("pairwise comparisons"). Moreover, the following needs no proof:

THEOREM 2. *If the p_{xy} admit the existence of a function $U^{(2)}$ satisfying Condition ($U^{(2)}$), then, for every $x \in X^*$* and *$X^* \subseteq X$, there exists a number $q_x(X^*) \geqq 0$ such that, putting $p_x(X^*) = q_x(X^*)$ and $U = U^{(2)}$, condition* (6) *is satisfied.*

That is, Condition ($U^{(2)}$) guarantees the existence of numbers which, if they were the observed multiple-choice probabilities, would satisfy Condition (U).

Except in Section 11, it will not be assumed in this paper that constraints on non-binary-choice probabilities—such as (5)—can be inferred from observations.

5. Probability of Ranking

Similarly, and possibly on still stronger grounds, no reference will be made in this paper to experiments in which the subject is requested, not to make an actual choice but to rank three or more alternatives according to his preferences (with two alternatives, choosing and ranking may be regarded as identical). It will not be assumed that responses obtained in such experiments are in any sense consistent with choices of single alternatives from subsets. To be sure, we shall use the term "probability of ranking," but not to denote a number that is estimated (or, more generally, whose properties are inferred) from experiments on ranking. Rather, we give the following definition:

DEFINITION. *If $U^{(2)}$ is a random utility indicator, then, for any $x_1, x_2, \cdots, x_m$ in X, the number*

$$P(x_1x_2 \cdots x_m) = \Pr(U^{(2)}_{x_1} > U^{(2)}_{x_2} > \cdots > U^{(2)}_{x_m}) \tag{7}$$

is called the probability of the ranking *(permutation)* $x_1x_2 \cdots x_m$. *It follows that* $P(xy) = p_{xy}$.

THEOREM 3. *If* $(U^{(2)})$ *is satisfied and* $X^* = M = (1, \cdots, m)$ *is a finite subset of* X, *then for any* $i, j \in M$,

$$p_{ij} = \sum_{r \in R_{ij}} P(r) \, , \tag{8}$$

where R_{ij} *is the set of all rankings* r *on* M *in which* i *precedes* j.

PROOF. By (2), (7).

THEOREM 4. $(U^{(2)})$ *is satisfied for* X *finite,* $X = N = (1, \cdots, n)$, *if there is a non-negative function* P *on the set of rankings* r *on* N *such that equation* (8) *holds, provided* R_{ij} *is redefined as the set of all rankings on* N *in which* i *precedes* j.

PROOF. Denote by $r = 1_r2_r \cdots n_r$ the ranking in which the ith place is occupied by i_r. Then, by (7)

$$P(r) = P(1_r2_r \cdots n_r) = \Pr(U^{(2)}_{1_r} > U^{(2)}_{2_r} > \cdots > U^{(2)}_{n_r}) \, ,$$

and by (8) the condition (2) is satisfied.

6. A Condition for the Existence of a Random Utility Indicator

CONDITION (Δ) ["triangular"]. For all x, y, z in X,

$$p_{xy} + p_{yz} \geqq p_{xz} \, . \tag{9}$$

By virtue of (1), this can be rewritten more symmetrically as

$$1 \leqq p_{xy} + p_{yz} + p_{zx} \leqq 2 \, . \tag{9a}$$

Define

$$\Delta_{xyz} = p_{xy} + p_{yz} + p_{zx} - 1 \, ; \tag{10}$$

then by (1), $\Delta_{xyz} + \Delta_{zyx} = 1$; and (9a) can be rewritten as

$$0 \leqq \Delta_{xyz} \leqq 1 . \tag{9b}$$

Condition (Δ) was probably first noticed by Guilbaud [13].

THEOREM 5. *($U^{(2)}$) implies (Δ). [And therefore, clearly, (U) also implies (Δ).]*

PROOF. Denote by x, y, z the generic elements of the subset (1, 2, 3) of X. Then, by the definition (7), the six $P(xyz)$ add up to 1, and each is greater than or equal to 0. If ($U^{(2)}$) is true, then, by Theorem 3,

$$\begin{aligned} p_{13} &= P(132) + P(123) + P(312) , \\ p_{23} &= P(123) + P(213) + P(231) , \\ p_{31} &= P(312) + P(231) + P(321) . \end{aligned} \tag{11}$$

In (11) the sum of the left sides is $\Delta_{123} + 1$; on the right side, the three off-diagonal terms of the symmetric matrix add up to s, say, where $0 \leqq s \leqq 1$; and all nine terms add up to $1 + s$. Hence

$$0 \leqq \Delta_{123} = s = P(123) + P(231) + P(312) \leqq 1 ,$$

and (9b) is satisfied.

THEOREM 6. *If $X = (1, 2, 3)$, then (Δ) implies ($U^{(2)}$).*[1]

PROOF. Denote by x, y, z the generic elements of X. We shall show that, for any six numbers p_{xy} satisfying (1) and such that $0 \leqq \Delta_{123} = p_{12}+p_{21}+p_{31}-1$, one can find six numbers $P(xyz)$, non-negative, adding up to 1, and satisfying (11). We have just seen that if $\sum_{xyz} P(xyz) = 1$, then (11) implies

$$\Delta_{123} = P(123) + P(231) + P(312) . \tag{12}$$

Subtracting (12) from each of the equations (11), we obtain

$$\begin{aligned} p_{12} - \Delta_{123} &= P(132) - P(231) , \\ p_{23} - \Delta_{123} &= P(213) - P(312) , \\ p_{31} - \Delta_{123} &= P(321) - P(123) . \end{aligned} \tag{13}$$

Put $0 = P(231)$ or $P(132)$ according as $p_{12} \geqq$ or $\leqq \Delta_{123}$; put $0 = P(312)$ or $P(213)$ according as $p_{23} \geqq$ or $\leqq \Delta_{123}$. Substituting into (13) and (12), one obtains the remaining four $P(xyz)$, non-negative and adding up to 1. Hence, by Theorem 4, ($U^{(2)}$) is satisfied.

AN ALTERNATIVE PROOF OF THEOREM 5. A probability distribution on the set of rankings on $X = (1, \cdots, n)$ is a vector P whose components $P(r^k)$, where $k = 1, \cdots, n!$, are non-negative and add up to 1. The set $\boldsymbol{P}$ of all such vectors is convex and has $n! - 1$ dimensions and $n!$ vertices. The vertex P_k shall represent the distribution in which $P(r^k) = 1$. Suppose ($U^{(2)}$) holds and let $[p_{xy}(P)]$ be the $n \times n$ matrix of binary probabilities generated by P in $\boldsymbol{P}$. Consider the vertex P_k of $\boldsymbol{P}$ and denote by r^k_x the rank assigned to x when the ranking is r^k. Then, for $x \neq y$,

[1] See also [1], Theorems 5.7, 5.1.

$$p_{xy}(P_k) = \begin{cases} 1 & \text{if} \quad r_x^k < r_y^k , \\ 0 & \text{if} \quad r_x^k > r_y^k . \end{cases}$$

Let x, y, z be all distinct. Since $r_x^k < r_y^k$ and $r_y^k < r_z^k$ imply $r_z^k > r_x^k$, the triple

$$\{p_{xy}(P_k), p_{yz}(P_k), p_{zx}(P_k)\}$$

cannot consist of 1's only or of 0's only. Hence the sum of these three probabilities, for every ranking r^k, is either 1 or 2. Now, every vector P is a convex combination of the unit vectors P_k:

$$P = \sum P_k \cdot P(r^k) \qquad (\sum P(r^k) = 1;\ P(r^k) \geqq 0;\ k = 1, \cdots, n!)$$

and

$$p_{xy}(P) = \sum p_{xy}(P_k) \cdot P(r^k) .$$

Hence every sum $p_{xy}(P) + p_{yz}(P) + p_{zx}(P)$ is a weighted average of the numbers 1 and 2, so that (Δ) is satisfied.

This proof was obtained after a conversation with Herman Chernoff, who had suggested the following way to prove (or disprove) the converse of Theorem 5.

CONVERSE OF THEOREM 5. Denote by $\boldsymbol{S_P}$ the set of all matrices $[p_{xy}]$ generated by the distributions P in $\boldsymbol{P}$; denote by $\boldsymbol{S_\Delta}$ the set of all matrices $[p_{xy}]$ satisfying (Δ). Each of these sets has $n(n-1)/2$ dimensions and is convex. $\boldsymbol{S_P}$ has $n!$ vertices, each corresponding to precisely one vertex of $\boldsymbol{P}$, and such that for x, y, z distinct, $p_{xy} = 1$ or 0, and $p_{xy} + p_{yz} + p_{zx} = 1$ or 2. Hence all vertices of $\boldsymbol{S_P}$ are elements and are, in fact vertices, of $\boldsymbol{S_\Delta}$, and (another way to state Theorem 5) $\boldsymbol{S_\Delta}$ contains $\boldsymbol{S_P}$. If it were possible to prove that *all* vertices of $\boldsymbol{S_\Delta}$ are vertices of $\boldsymbol{S_P}$, the converse of Theorem 5 would be proved for any n, thus extending Theorem 6. We therefore register (but do not assert to be true!) the following

CONJECTURE 1. *For any finite* $\boldsymbol{X}$, (Δ) *implies* $(U^{(2)})$.[2]

While (Δ) is necessary for $(U^{(2)})$ and therefore for (U), and even if it were true that (Δ) is sufficient for $(U^{(2)})$, it is certainly not sufficient for (U) since (Δ) does not put any constraints on non-binary choices while (U) does [we have seen that (U) implies (5)]. Some sufficient conditions for $(U^{(2)})$ and (U), respectively, will be given in Sections 10 and 11.

7. Transitivity of Stochastic Preferences

DEFINITION. *Alternative x is* stochastically preferred (stochastically indifferent) *to y if* $p_{xy} > \frac{1}{2}$ $(p_{xy} = \frac{1}{2})$.

In what follows, the words "transitivity of stochastic preferences" will be abbreviated to "transitivity."

CONDITIONS (t_w) [weak transitivity], (t_m) [mild transitivity], and (t_s) [strong

[2] I am told by Professor T. Motzkin that he has proved the conjecture for $n \leqq 5$. Because of applications to the commodity space or to the space of wagers, the continuous case (as in Theorems 19 and 14) would deserve study.

transitivity].[3] If $\min(p_{xy}, p_{yz}) \geqq \frac{1}{2}$, then

$$p_{xz} \geqq \begin{cases} \frac{1}{2} & \text{Condition } (t_w)\,, \\ \min(p_{xy}, p_{yz}) & \text{Condition } (t_m)\,, \\ \max(p_{xy}, p_{yz}) & \text{Condition } (t_s)\,. \end{cases}$$

Equivalently, by (1): if $\max(p_{xy}, p_{yz}) \leqq \frac{1}{2}$, then

$$p_{xz} \leqq \begin{cases} \frac{1}{2} & \text{Condition } (t_w)\,, \\ \max(p_{xy}, p_{yz}) & \text{Condition } (t_m)\,, \\ \min(p_{xy}, p_{yz}) & \text{Condition } (t_s)\,. \end{cases}$$

A more symmetric equivalent form for (t_w) is, by (1),

$$\min(p_{xy}, p_{yz}, p_{zx}) \leqq \tfrac{1}{2} \leqq \max(p_{xy}, p_{yz}, p_{zx})\,.$$

Theorem 7. *Condition (t_s) is equivalent to the following conditions: if $p_{xy} \geqq \frac{1}{2}$, then $p_{xz} \geqq p_{yz}$, for all $z \in X$; and if $z \in X$ and $p_{xz} \geqq p_{yz}$, then $p_{xy} \geqq \frac{1}{2}$.*

Proof. See [1], Theorem 4. 1.

Theorem 8. *Condition (t_s) is strictly stronger than (t_m), and (t_m) is strictly stronger than (t_w).*

Proof. Obvious.

Theorem 9. *Condition (t_w) is neither sufficient nor necessary for $(\varDelta)$.*

Proof. Let $n = 3$, and $p_{13} = .6$. If $p_{12} = p_{23} = .9$, then (t_w) is satisfied but $(\varDelta)$ is not. If $p_{12} = p_{23} = .4$, then $(\varDelta)$ is satisfied but (t_w) is not.

Theorem 10. *Condition (t_m) is strictly stronger than $(\varDelta)$.*

Proof. (i) Sufficiency. Consider $(1, 2, 3) \subseteqq X$. Using the notation of Section 6, we have to prove that (t_m) implies $0 \leqq \varDelta_{xyz} \leqq 1$. By (1) we can let $p_{12} \geqq p_{23} \geqq \frac{1}{2} \geqq p_{32} \geqq p_{21}$ without loss of generality; then

$$p_{12} + p_{23} \geqq 1 \geqq p_{32} + p_{21}\,, \qquad p_{12} + p_{23} + p_{31} - 1 = \varDelta_{123} \geqq 0\,,$$
$$1 - \varDelta_{123} = p_{21} + p_{32} + p_{13} - 1 = \varDelta_{321} \leqq 1\,.$$

Now assume (t_m). Then

$$p_{31} \leqq \max(p_{32}, p_{21}) = p_{32}\,, \qquad \varDelta_{123} \leqq p_{12} + p_{23} + p_{32} - 1 = p_{12} \leqq 1$$

and

$$p_{13} \geqq \min(p_{12}, p_{23}) = p_{12}\,, \qquad \varDelta_{321} \geqq p_{21} + p_{32} + p_{12} - 1 = p_{32} \geqq 0\,.$$

(ii) No necessity. By Theorems 8, 9.

Theorem 11. *Condition (t_m) is strictly stronger than the conjunction of (t_w) and $(\varDelta)$.*

---

[3] Conditions (t_w) and (t_s) were formulated by S. Valavanis-Vail [21] and originated in his work with C. Coombs. Condition (t_m) was formulated by N. Georgescu-Roegen [12] and by John Chipman [4]. Experimental tests of stochastic transitivity conditions were undertaken by Papandreou *et al.* [17] and by Davidson and Marschak [5].

PROOF. (i) Sufficiency. By Theorems 8, 10. (ii) No necessity. Let $X = (1, 2, 3)$, $p_{12} = .8$, $p_{23} = .7$, and $p_{31} = .4$. Then (t_w) and (Δ) are satisfied. But since $p_{12} > p_{23} > .5$ while $p_{13} = .6 < p_{23}$, Condition (t_m) is violated.

Write $\rightarrow$ for "implies", $\leftrightarrow$ for "implies and is implied by", $\mapsto$ for "implies but is not implied by", $\vdash\!\dashv$ for "does not imply nor is implied by". Then our results can be summarized in

THEOREM 12.

$$\begin{array}{ccccccc} (t_s) & \longmapsto & (t_m) & \longmapsto & (t_w, \Delta) & & \\ & & & & \downarrow & & \\ (\Delta; n = 3) & \longmapsto & (U^{(2)}) & \longrightarrow & (\Delta) & \vdash\!\!\!\longrightarrow\!\!\!\dashv & (t_w)\,. \\ & & \uparrow & & & & \\ & & (U) & & & & \end{array}$$

In political science the fact that Condition $(U^{(2)})$ does not imply Condition (t_w) is interpreted as "intransitivity of the majority rule." It was pointed out by Kenneth Arrow. We have shown in [1, Theorem 3.2] that even the stronger Condition (U) does not imply (t_w).

8. Weak Utility Function

DEFINITION. *A real-valued function w on X is called a* weak utility function *if* $w_x \geqq w_y$ when and only when $p_{xy} \geqq \frac{1}{2}$.

CONDITION (w). The function p is such that w exists. It follows that w is unique up to an increasing monotone transformation.

THEOREM 13. $(w) \longmapsto (t_w)$.

PROOF. (i) Sufficiency. Let $p_{ab} \geqq \frac{1}{2}$, $p_{bc} \geqq \frac{1}{2}$, $a, b, c \in X$. If (w) is true, then $w_a \geqq w_b \geqq w_c$ and $p_{ac} \geqq \frac{1}{2}$. (ii) No necessity. Let X be a real 2-space with generic points $x = (x_1, x_2)$ and assume that $p_{xy} > \frac{1}{2}$ when either $x_1 > y_1$ or $x_1 = y_1$ and $x_2 > y_1$ (lexicographical ordering) Compare Debreu [6].

CONDITION (D). X is perfectly separable (i.e., contains a countable and dense subset); and for every a in X, the sets $(x \mid p_{xa} \geqq \frac{1}{2})$ and $(x \mid p_{xa} \leqq \frac{1}{2})$ are closed. This is adapted from Debreu's paper just cited, which also contains, *mutatis mutandis*, the proof of

THEOREM 14. *If (D) is satisfied, then (w) and (t_w) are equivalent.*

REMARK. Condition (D) is trivially satisfied on X finite. Moreover, every subset of a finite-dimensional real space is perfectly separable; and it is reasonable to assume that Condition (D) is satisfied on a commodity space.

We summarize some of the previous results in

THEOREM 15.

$$\begin{array}{ccccccccccc} (t_w; n \text{ finite}) & \longmapsto & (t_w, D) & \longmapsto & (w) & \longmapsto & (t_w) & & & & \\ & & & & & & \uparrow & & & & \\ (\Delta; n = 3) & \longmapsto & U^{(2)} & \longrightarrow & (\Delta) & \longleftarrow\!\!\dashv & (t_w, \Delta) & \longleftarrow\!\!\dashv & (t_m) & \longleftarrow\!\!\dashv & (t_s) \end{array}$$

9. Strong Utility Function

DEFINITION. *A real-valued function* v *on* X *is called a* strong utility function *if there exists a monotone increasing function* ϕ_v *such that*

$$(14) \qquad \phi_v(v_x - v_y) = p_{xy};\ \phi_v(0) = \tfrac{1}{2}\ .$$

CONDITION (v). The function p is such that v exists.

THEOREM 16. *If* X *is continuous and* ϕ_v *is strictly monotone, then* (i) v *is unique up to an increasing linear transformation, and* (ii) *for any real number* λ,

$$(15) \qquad \phi_v(\lambda) + \phi_v(-\lambda) = 1\ .$$

PROOF. For (i), see [1, Section 2]; (ii) is obvious.

Equation (15) implies that ϕ_v is anti-symmetrical about $(0, \frac{1}{2})$; the median and the mean (if it exists) are 0.

The strong utility v_x of alternative x corresponds to the "sensation" produced by a stimulus x, as defined by Fechner [10] in 1859. It also corresponds to the relative position of a gene in the chromosome when inferred from the probability of a "crossover": this generation of a real line from a set of probabilities was noticed by D. Hilbert.[4]

CONDITION (q) [quadruple condition]. For any x, y, z, t in X,

$$(16) \qquad \text{if} \quad p_{xy} \geqq p_{zt}, \quad \text{then} \quad p_{xz} \geqq p_{yt}\ .$$

THEOREM 17. *Condition* (v) *implies Condition* (q) [PROOF. By monotonicity of ϕ_v]; *Condition* (q) *implies Condition* (t_s) [PROOF. In (16) put $z = t$ and use Theorem 7]; *Condition* (v) *implies Condition* (w) [PROOF. In (14), put $v = w$].

THEOREM 18. *If* X *is finite,* $X = (1, \cdots, n)$, *then* (q) *implies* (v) *only for* $n \leqq 4$.

PROOF. See [1], Proof of Theorem 4. 1.

For X continuous it is useful to consider the following

CONDITION ($s{\cdot}c$) ["stochastic continuity"]. If $p_{xy} < q < p_{xz}$, then there is a t in X such that $p_{xt} = q$. In [7] Debreu has proved

THEOREM 19. *If Condition* ($s{\cdot}c$) *is satisfied, then* (q) *implies* (v).

If both ($U^{(2)}$) and (v) are satisfied, we can define a random function V_x by

$$(17) \qquad U_x^{(2)} = v_x + V_x\ , \qquad EV_x = 0\ ,$$

and set up the following three conditions, each stronger than the preceding one:

There exist two functions on X, a real-valued v and a random-valued V, and a distribution function ϕ_v such that

$$p_{xy} = \phi_v(v_x - v_y)\ , \qquad \Pr(V_y - V_x \leqq \lambda) = \phi_v(\lambda)\ ,$$

[4] In a paper [14] pointed out to me by Hans Rademacher.

where

CONDITION (V): $\lambda = v_x - v_y$;

CONDITION (V'): $\lambda =$ any real number;

CONDITION (V''): $\Pr(V_x \leqq \alpha,\ V_y \leqq \beta) = \Pr(V_x \leqq \beta,\ V_y \leqq \alpha)$, $\lambda, \alpha, \beta =$ any real numbers.

In Condition (V) the distribution of the differences $V_x - V_y$ is defined only for each pair of alternatives (possibly finite in number); in (V') this distribution is defined for any real argument; in (V''), in addition, the (multivariate) distribution function of V is symmetrical in its arguments. From (17) and Theorem 16 one obtains

THEOREM 20. $(V'') \longmapsto (V') \longmapsto (V) \longleftrightarrow (U^{(2)}, v)$ *if X is finite;*
$(V'') \longmapsto (V') \longleftrightarrow (V) \longleftrightarrow (U^{(2)}, v)$ *if X is continuous.*

In the work of Thurstone and his school a condition even stronger than (V'') is used: the distribution function of V is assumed to be normal and symmetric (zero means, equal variances, equal covariances). Actually, a normal distribution of differences ϕ_v (as assumed by Fechner) is consistent also with a normal distribution of V non-symmetrical in its arguments.

For possible application to the commodity space some of our results can be summarized in

THEOREM 21. *If X is continuous and the conditions (D) and (s·c) are satisfied, then*

$$\begin{array}{ccccccccccccc}
(V'') & \longmapsto & (V') & \longleftrightarrow & (U^{(2)}, v) & \longmapsto & (v) & \longleftrightarrow & (q) & \longmapsto & (t_s) & \longmapsto & (t_w) \\
 & & & & \downarrow & & & & & & \downarrow & & \updownarrow \\
 & & & & (U^{(2)}) & & \longrightarrow & & & & (\Delta) & \longmapsto & (w)\ .
\end{array}$$

10. Strict Utility Function (in the "binary" sense)

DEFINITION. *A* positive-valued function $u^{(2)}$ on X *is called a* strict utility function (in the "binary" sense) *if*

$$p_{xy} = \frac{u_x^{(2)}}{u_x^{(2)} + u_y^{(2)}}\ . \tag{18}$$

Clearly, every positive multiple of a strict utility function is also a strict utility function.

CONDITION $(u^{(2)})$. The function p is such that $u^{(2)}$ exists. Applying (18) one obtains

THEOREM 22. *Condition* $(u^{(2)})$ *is true only if* (i) $0 < p_{xy} < 1$ *for every x, y in X, and* (ii) *for any subset* $(1, \cdots, m) \subseteqq X$ $(m > 1)$, *the following equation holds:*

$$p_{12} \cdot p_{23} \cdots p_{m-1,m} \cdot p_{m1} = p_{21} \cdot p_{32} \cdots p_{m,m-1} \cdot p_{1m}\ . \tag{19}$$

Note that (19) is "directly testable." Condition $(u^{(2)})$ was formulated by

Törnqvist [20], Bradley and Terry [3], and L. R. Ford [11]. It is a weak form of a postulate that has been proposed by Luce [15] and that involves multiple-choice probabilities: see Section 11 below.

THEOREM 23. $(u^{(2)}) \longmapsto (v)$.

PROOF. (i) Necessity. Put $u_y^{(2)} = e^{v_y}$; then by (18) $p_{xy} = \phi_v(v_x - v_y)$, where

$$\phi_v(\lambda) = \frac{1}{1 + e^{-\lambda}}, \tag{20}$$

the "logistic curve." (ii) No sufficiency. For X continuous, by the above proof of necessity (due to Luce) and by Theorem 16, we see that Condition $(u^{(2)})$ is not implied by (v), since $(u^{(2)})$ restricts the function ϕ_v to the form (20). For X finite, let

$$X = (1, 2, 3); \quad p_{12} = .6, \quad p_{23} = .7, \quad p_{13} = .8 . \tag{21}$$

Then (v) is satisfied[5] by $v_1 = .3$, $v_2 = .2$, $v_3 = .0$, and $\phi_v(\lambda) = .5 + \lambda$. But (19), and therefore $(u^{(2)})$, is not.

THEOREM 24. *If X is finite, then $(u^{(2)})$ implies $(U^{(2)})$.*

PROOF. We shall use an arithmetical identity proved in [1, Theorem 3.6] and [8]:

LEMMA. *Let $N = (1, \cdots, n)$ and denote by $r = (1_r 2_r \cdots n_r)$ the permutation on N in which the kth place is occupied by the element k_r; denote by R_{iM} the set of permutations on N in which i precedes all other elements of $M \subseteq N$. Then, for any positive $u_1, \cdots, u_n$,*

$$\frac{u_i}{\sum_{h \in M} u_h} \equiv \sum_{r \in R_{iM}} \prod_{j=1}^{n-1} \frac{u_{j_r}}{\sum_{k=j}^{n} u_{k_r}} . \tag{22}$$

To prove Theorem 24 from this Lemma, let $X = N$, $M = (i, j)$, $u_x = u_x^{(2)}$; then by (18) the left side of (22) becomes p_{ij}, and the set $R_{iM} = R_{ij}$, as defined in Theorem 3. Since each of the products on the right side is positive and they add up to p_{ij}, we can equate each of them to a probability of ranking in the sense of (7), so that, for any ranking r on N,

$$P(r) = P(1_r 2_r \cdots n_r) = \frac{u_{1_r}}{u_{1_r} + \cdots + u_{n_r}} \cdot \frac{u_{2_r}}{u_{2_r} + \cdots + u_{n_r}} \cdots \frac{u_{(n-1)_r}}{u_{(n-1)_r} + u_{n_r}} . \tag{23}$$

Since we interpret each u_i as $u_i^{(2)}$, then by Theorem 4 $(U^{(2)})$ is satisfied.

If X is continuous, the reasoning just used can be applied to any finite subset of X. Hence the following

CONJECTURE 2. *Theorem 24 applies to any X.*

[5] It is noteworthy that for $n = 3$, Condition (t_s) is not only necessary but also sufficient for (v). This follows from Theorems 17 and 18.

Remark. The proof of Theorem 24 could be much simplified if Conjecture 1 (Section 6) were proved to to be true. For it would then suffice to prove that $(u^{(2)})$ implies (Δ). This is indeed the case: for, writing $u_y^{(2)}/u_x^{(2)} = a$, $u_z^{(2)}/u_y^{(2)} = b$, and $u_x^{(2)}/u_z^{(2)} = c$, we have $abc = 1$, and by (10), (18), we obtain

$$(24) \qquad 0 < \Delta_{xyz} = \frac{1}{1+a} + \frac{1}{1+b} + \frac{1}{1+c} - 1 = \frac{1}{1+k} < 1\,,$$

where $k = (1 + ab + bc + ca)/(1 + a + b + c) > 0$, since $a, b, c, > 0$.

Theorem 25. *$(U^{(2)})$ does not imply $(u^{(2)})$.*

Proof: Consider again example (21). Since $p_{31} = .2$, it follows that $\Delta_{123} = .5$; hence Condition (Δ) and, by Theorem 6, Condition $(U^{(2)})$ are satisfied But (19) is not.

Since example (21) was seen to satisfy (v), Theorem 25 can be replaced by the even stronger

Theorem 26. *The conjunction of $(U^{(2)})$ and (v) does not imply $(u^{(2)})$.*

Some of the results of this and the preceding section can be summarized in

Theorem 27. *For X finite,*

$$\begin{array}{ccccccccccccc}
(u^{(2)}) & \longmapsto & [(U^{(2)}),(v)] & \longmapsto & (v) & \longmapsto & (q) & \longmapsto & (t_s) & \longmapsto & (t_w) & \longleftrightarrow & (w) \\
 & & \downarrow & & & & & & \downarrow & & & & \\
 & & (U^{(2)}) & & \longrightarrow & & \longrightarrow & & (\Delta)\,. & & & &
\end{array}$$

Remark on the commodity space. If Condition (D) is satisfied on the continuous commodity space and if Conjecture 2 is correct, Theorem 27 applies also to the commodity space; if, in addition, $(s \cdot c)$ is satisfied, then $(v) \leftrightarrow (q)$.

11. Some Results on Multiple-Choice Probabilities

In Section 4, the Condition (U) was stated. Clearly, (U) implies $(U^{(2)})$. Similarly, $(u^{(2)})$ can be replaced by the following stronger

Condition (u). There exists a positive-valued function u on X such that for any finite subset $M = (x_1, \cdots, x_m) \subseteq X$, the multiple-choice probability

$$(25) \qquad p_{x_i}(M) = \frac{u_i}{\sum\limits_{j \in M} u_j}\,.$$

The function u may be called a *strict utility function in the multiple-choice sense.*

As was proved in [1], (u) implies that the probability of each ranking in the multiple-choice sense, defined as

$$P(r) = \Pr(U_{1_r} > U_{2_r} > \cdots > U_{n_r}), \quad \text{with} \quad \sum_{R_{iM}} P(r) = p_i(M)\,,$$

exists and is precisely the expression on the right side of (23). For example, if $\boldsymbol{X} = (1, 2, 3)$, then

$$P(xyz) = \frac{u_x}{u_x + u_y + u_z} \cdot \frac{u_y}{u_y + u_z} = p_x(\boldsymbol{X}) \cdot p_y(y, z) \, , \tag{26}$$

by (25). Thus (u) implies (and, as shown in [1], is equivalent to) the proposition that the probability of a given ranking of a finite set of alternatives is the product of probabilities of multiple choices made successively, from the set itself, then from the subset remaining after eliminating the first choice, then from the subset remaining after eliminating the second choice, etc. Applying the Lemma of Section 10 we obtain, using (25),

THEOREM 28. $(u) \longrightarrow (U)$ *when* $\boldsymbol{X}$ *is finite.*

This result is discussed in more detail in [1]. We can prove the even stronger

THEOREM 29. $(u) \longmapsto [(U), (v)]$ *when* $\boldsymbol{X}$ *is finite.*

PROOF. (i) Necessity. By Theorems 28 and 23, remembering that (u) of course implies $(u^{(2)})$. (ii) No sufficiency. Note that for $\boldsymbol{X} = (1, 2, 3)$, condition (u) implies, by (19) and (26) respectively,

$$p_{12} \cdot p_{23} \cdot p_{31} = p_{13} \cdot p_{32} \cdot p_{21} \, , \tag{27}$$

and

$$P(123) \cdot P(231) \cdot P(312) = P(213) \cdot P(132) \cdot P(321) \, . \tag{28}$$

Moreover, (U) implies $p_{xy} = P(xyz) + P(xzy) + P(zxy)$ and $p_x(\boldsymbol{X}) = P(xyz) + P(xzy)$. It is easy to construct examples satisfying (v) and (U) but not (27) or (28). For example, use (21), which we have seen satisfies (v) and which contradicts (27); and put, in addition, the following values: for the probabilities of rankings, $P(123) = P(132) = .3$, $P(231) = P(213) = .2$, $P(312) = P(321) = 0$; for the ternary probabilities, $p_1(\boldsymbol{X}) = .6$, $p_2(\boldsymbol{X}) = .4$, and $p_3(\boldsymbol{X}) = 0$. The foregoing results, together with some obtained in the previous section, can be summarized in

THEOREM 30.

$$\begin{array}{ccccc}
(u) & \longmapsto & [(U), (v)] & \longmapsto & (U) \\
\downarrow & & \downarrow & & \downarrow \\
(u^{(2)}) & \longmapsto & [(U^{(2)}), (v)] & \longmapsto & (U^{(2)}) \\
 & & \downarrow & & \downarrow \\
 & & (v) & \longmapsto & (\Delta)
\end{array}$$

Luce [15] proposed a condition still stronger than (u), being a conjunction of (u) and the following

CONDITION (u'). Denote by $p'_x(\boldsymbol{X}^*)$ the probability that x is the *last* choice out of the subset $\boldsymbol{X}^* \subseteq \boldsymbol{X}$. There exists a real-valued function u' on $\boldsymbol{X}$ such that for any finite subset $\boldsymbol{M} = (x_1, \cdots, x_m) \subseteq \boldsymbol{X}$, the probability

$$p'_{x_i}(M) = \frac{u'_i}{\sum_{j \in M} u'_j} .$$

The function u' may be called a *strict disutility function*. However, apart from trivial cases, the functions u and u' cannot both exist:

THEOREM 31. *Conditions* (u) *and* (u') *can both hold only if all first choices are equally probable and all last choices are equally probable, or if* X *has only two elements.*

PROOF. If $n \geqq 3$, let $M \subseteq X$ consist of three elements, to be denoted generically by x, y, z. Assume both Conditions (u) and (u'). Without loss of generality, let $u_x + u_y + u_z = 1 = u'_x + u'_y + u'_z$, so that $p_x(M) = u_x$, $p'_x(M) = u'_x$, for all x in M. Then

$$u_x \cdot \frac{u'_z}{1 - u'_x} = u'_z \cdot \frac{u_x}{1 - u_z}, \qquad \text{all } x, z \text{ in } M,$$

since both the left and the right side express the probability of the same event, viz., of x being the first, and z the last choice. Hence $u'_x = u_z$, $p'_x(M) = p_z(M)$ for any pair x, z of the arbitrary three-elements subset M. Interchanging variables x, y, z, and applying (u), (u'),

$$p'_x(X) = p_y(X) = p'_y(X) = p_x(X), \qquad \text{all } x, y \text{ in } X.$$

This proves the Theorem for $n \geqq 3$. When $n = 2$, the same reasoning yields trivially the identity $p_x(x, y) = p'_y(x, y)$. For a more detailed proof see [1, Theorem 3.8].

It has been pointed out by Luce (in private correspondence) that while in experiments on choices the probabilities of last choices may or may not be accessible to observations, they definitely are in experiments on perceptions: the subject's decision as to which is the loudest of three sounds is as observable as his decision as to which sound is the softest. If one accepts (u), symmetry requires one to accept (u') also. But, as we have shown, these two conditions are mutually inconsistent.

Therefore, we must limit ourselves to the weaker Condition $(u^{(2)})$. It involves binary choices only, so that, when identifying the loudest sound, the subject identifies also the softest. That is, if the subset X^* consists of two elements, then Conditions $(u^{(2)})$, (u), and (u') are identical. A strict utility function in this limited sense—$u^{(2)}$ rather than u—is compatible with the existence of the corresponding strict disutility function and of a random utility indicator $U^{(2)}$ involving binary choices only.

12. Binary-Choice Constraints and the Form of the Random Utility Indicator

Consider Example (ii) of Section 3, and let $m = 2$, $0 < T_1 = A < 1$, and $T_2 = 1 - A$. Then

$$U_x^{(2)} = x_1^A x_2^{1-A} ; \tag{29}$$

the function $U^{(2)}$ is monotone increasing in x in the sense that if $x = (x_1, x_2)$, $y = (y_1, y_2)$, $x_1 \geqq y_1$, and $x_2 > y_2$, then $U_x^{(2)} > U_y^{(2)}$. $U^{(2)}$ is a random function depending on the random parameter A.[6] If $U^{(2)}$ is a utility indicator in the "binary" sense of (2), then $p_{xy} = \Pr(U_x^{(2)} \geqq U_y^{(2)}) = \Pr(y_1^A y_2^{1-A} \leqq x_1^A x_2^{1-A})$. Let $y_1 > x_1$ and $y_2 < x_2$ (so that x does not dominate y, and conversely). Then $\log(y_1/x_1) > 0$, $\log(x_2/y_2) > 0$, and

$$p_{xy} = \Pr\left(\frac{A}{1-A} \leqq \frac{\log(x_2/y_2)}{\log(y_1/x_1)}\right) = F(\mu_{xy}),$$

where $\mu_{xy} = \log(x_2/y_2)/\log(y_1/x_1)$ and F is a monotone non-decreasing function depending on the distribution of A. We shall now show that the form (29) of the random utility indicator is not consistent with some binary-choice constraints:

Theorem 32. *If the random utility indicator has the form* (29), *then the strong transitivity condition* (t_s) *is, in general, not satisfied.*

Proof. Consider three points x, y, z with $z_1 > y_1 > x_1$ and $z_2 < y_2 < x_2$. Then

$$p_{xy} = F(\mu_{xy}), \quad \mu_{xy} = (\log x_2 - \log y_2)/(\log y_1 - \log x_1),$$
$$p_{yz} = F(\mu_{yz}), \quad \mu_{yz} = (\log y_2 - \log z_2)/(\log z_1 - \log y_1),$$
$$p_{xz} = F(\mu_{xz}), \quad \mu_{xz} = (\log x_2 - \log z_2)/(\log z_1 - \log x_1),$$
$$\mu_{xz} = \frac{\mu_{xy}(\log y_1 - \log x_1) + \mu_{yz}(\log z_1 - \log y_1)}{(\log y_1 - \log x_1) + (\log z_1 - \log y_1)},$$

a convex combination of μ_{xy} and μ_{yz}. Hence $\min(\mu_{xy}, \mu_{yz}) \leqq \mu_{xz} \leqq \max(\mu_{xy}, \mu_{yz})$; and since F is non-decreasing, $\min(p_{xy}, p_{yz}) \leqq p_{xz} \leqq \max(p_{xy}, p_{yz})$. This is consistent with the Weak and the Mild Transitivity Conditions, (t_w) and (t_m) of Section 7, but not with the Strong Transitivity Condition (t_s). All three conditions are directly testable.

Thus (29) is in general inconsistent with the existence of strict or strong utility functions, since those imply strong transitivity (Theorems 17 and 27).

Consider now another random form of the "Cobb-Douglas function":

$$U_x^{(2)} = x_1^\alpha x_2^{1-\alpha} + V_x, \tag{30}$$

where α is a constant, $0 < \alpha < 1$, and V is a random function on $\boldsymbol{X}$. If $U^{(2)}$ is a random utility indicator, then

$$p_{xy} = \Pr(U_x^{(2)} \geqq U_y^{(2)}) = \Pr(V_y - V_x \leqq x_1^\alpha x_2^{1-\alpha} - y_1^\alpha y_2^{1-\alpha}).$$

Suppose we have found V such that $\Pr(V_y - V_x \leqq \lambda) = \phi(\lambda)$ for any real λ, with ϕ being a distribution function independent of x, y. Then Condition (V') of Section 9 is satisfied, and

$$U_x^{(2)} - V_x = v_x = x_1^\alpha x_2^{1-\alpha} \tag{31}$$

[6] Maximizing $U_x^{(2)}$ with respect to x, subject to the constancy of income $x_1 + x_2$, we see that A is the (random) proportion spent on the 1th commodity. Hence the observed frequency distribution of this proportion should help to estimate the distribution of A—assuming that members of the sampled population were characterized by the same random function $U^{(2)}$. (But we shall not pursue this matter here.)

is a strong utility function consistent with the assumed random utility indicator.[7]

If we could accept the still stronger condition (V''), i.e., let the (infinite-dimensional) distribution of V be symmetrical in its arguments $(x, y, \cdots)$, we would have to search for such distributions. However, the symmetry assumption is hardly realistic: for example, in the case of normality it implies that deviations from the average budget composition have not only the same variances everywhere but also the same correlations for any two points of the X-plane, however close or remote in relation to each other.

The examples used in this section have the purpose merely of illustrating the problem: to find a class of random utility indicators consistent with a given set of binary-choice constraints.

REFERENCES

[1] BLOCK, H. D. and J. MARSCHAK. "Random Orderings and Stochastic Theories of Responses," in Olkin *et al.*, *Contributions to Probability and Statistics*, Stanford, Calif.: Stanford University Press, 1960, pp. 97–132.

[2] BLOCK, H. D. and J. MARSCHAK. "An Identity in Arithmetic," *Bulletin of the American Mathematical Society*, **65** (1959), 123–24.

[3] BRADLEY, R. A., and M. E. TERRY. "Rank Analysis of Incomplete Block Designs. I. The Method of Paired Comparisons," *Biometrika*, **39** (1952), 324-44.

[4] CHIPMAN, J. S. "Stochastic Choice and Subjective Probability" (abstract), *Econometrica*, **26** (1958), 613.

[5] DAVIDSON, D., and J. MARSCHAK. "Experimental Tests of Stochastic Decision Theories." Ch. 13 of C. W. Churchman, and Ph. Ratoosh, eds., *Measurement: Definition and Theories*, New York: John Wiley and Sons, 1959, pp. 233–69.

[6] DEBREU, G. "Representation of a Preference Ordering by a Numerical Function," in R. M. Thrall, C. Coombs, and R. L. Davis, eds., *Decision Processes*, New York: John Wiley and Sons, 1954, pp. 159-66.

[7] DEBREU, G. "Stochastic Choice and Cardinal Utility." *Econometrica*, **26** (1958), 440–44.

[8] DEBREU, G. "On An Identity in Arithmetic," *Proceedings of the American Mathematical Society*, **11** (1960) (in press).

[9] FARRELL, M. J. "The Demand for Motor-Cars in the United States." *Journal of the Royal Statistical Society, A*, **117** (1954), 171-93.

[10] FECHNER, G. TH. *Elemente der Psychophysik*, 1859 (see especially pp. 70-103 of the 1889 edition).

[11] FORD, L. R. "Solution of a Ranking Problem from Binary Comparisons," *American Mathematical Monthly*, **64** (1957), No. 8 (supplement), 28-33.

[7] One may want to use indifference lines to picture some relevant aspect of a given random utility indicator, and in particular, its mean. In the case just discussed, described by (30) and (31), we may choose V to have 0 expectation; then $EU_x^{(2)} = v_x$. Accordingly, an indifference line through x consists of all points y, with $v_y = v_x$ and $p_{yx} = \phi_v(0) = \frac{1}{2}$ as in (14); it is then the common boundary of the two sets used in Condition (D), Section 8. On the other hand, if the random utility indicator is described by (29), equation $EU_y^{(2)} = EU_x^{(2)}$, or possibly $E \log U_y^{(2)} = E \log U_x^{(2)}$, gives quite a different representation.

[12] GEORGESCU-ROEGEN, N. "Threshold in Choice and the Theory of Demand," *Econometrica*, **26** (1958), 157–68.

[13] GUILBAUD, G. "Sur une difficulté de la théorie du risque," *Colloques Internationaux du Centre National de la Recherche Scientifique* (*Econométrie*), **40** (1953), 19–25.

[14] HILBERT, D. "Naturerkenntis und Logik," *Gesammelte Abhandlungen*, **3** (1935), esp. pp. 379–80.

[15] LUCE, R. D. *Individual Choice Behavior*, New York: John Wiley and Sons, 1959.

[16] MARSCHAK, J. "Money Illusion and Demand Analysis," *Review of Economic Statistics* **25** (1943), 40–48.

[17] PAPANDREOU, A. G. (with the collaboration of O. H. Sauerlender, O. H. Brownlee, L. Hurwicz, W. Franklin). "A Test of a Stochastic Theory of Choice," *University of California Publications in Economics*, **16** (1957), 1–18.

[18] THURSTONE, L. L. "A Law of Comparative Judgment," *Psychological Review*, **34** (1927), 273–86.

[19] TOBIN, J. "A Statistical Demand Function for Food in the U. S. A.," *Journal of the Royal Statistical Society A*, **113** (1951), 113–49.

[20] TÖRNQVIST, L. "A Model for Stochastic Decision Making," *Cowles Commission Discussion Paper*, Economics 2100, 1954 (duplicated).

[21] VALAVANIS-VAIL, S. "A Stochastic Model for Utilities," seminar on the application of mathematics to social sciences, University of Michigan, 1957 (duplicated).

[22] WOLD, H. (with L. Jureen). *Demand Analysis*, New York: John Wiley and Sons, 1953.

[3]

JOURNAL OF MATHEMATICAL PSYCHOLOGY 15, 215–233 (1977)

The Choice Axiom after Twenty Years*

R. DUNCAN LUCE

Department of Psychology and Social Relations, Harvard University, Cambridge, Massachusetts 02138

This survey is divided into three major sections. The first concerns mathematical results about the choice axiom and the choice models that devolve from it. For example, its relationship to Thurstonian theory is satisfyingly understood; much is known about how choice and ranking probabilities may relate, although little of this knowledge seems empirically useful; and there are certain interesting statistical facts. The second section describes attempts that have been made to test and apply these models. The testing has been done mostly, though not exclusively, by psychologists; the applications have been mostly in economics and sociology. Although it is clear from many experiments that the conditions under which the choice axiom holds are surely delicate, the need for simple, rational underpinnings in complex theories, as in economics and sociology, leads one to accept assumptions that are at best approximate. And the third section concerns alternative, more general theories which, in spirit, are much like the choice axiom.

Perhaps I had best admit at the outset that, as a commentator on this scene, I am qualified no better than many others and rather less well than some who have been working in this area recently, which I have not been. My pursuits have led me along other, somewhat related routes. On the one hand, I have contributed to some of the recent, purely algebraic aspects of fundamental measurement (for a survey of some of this material, see Krantz, Luce, Suppes, & Tversky, 1971). And on the other hand, I have worked in the highly probabilistic area of psychophysical theory; but the empirical materials have led me away from axiomatic structures, such as the choice axiom, to more structural, neural models which are not readily axiomatized at the present time. After some attempts to apply choice models to psychophysical phenomena (discussed below in its proper place), I was led to conclude that it is not a very promising approach to these data, and so I have not been actively studying any aspect of the choice axiom in over 12 years. With that understood, let us begin.

MATHEMATICAL AND STATISTICAL RESULTS

The Choice Axiom

Anyone reading this article is probably already familiar with the choice axiom (axiom 1 of Luce, 1959), so I confine myself to a brief reminder. One part says that if a choice set S

* A slightly abridged version of this article will appear in a memorial volume for P. F. Lazarsfeld edited by J. S. Coleman, R. K. Merton, and P. Rossi. Drs. D. M. Green, T. Indow, A. A. J. Marley, P. Suppes, A. Tversky, and J. I. Yellott, Jr. commented on an earlier draft of this paper. In several cases, errors of fact or interpretation were pointed out as well as various omissions and obscurities; my thanks to each for his thoughtful remarks.

ISSN 0022–2496

contains two elements, *a* and *b*, such that *a* is never chosen over *b* when the choice is restricted to just *a* and *b*; then *a* can be deleted from *S* without affecting any of the choice probabilities. The other, more substantive part, concerns choice situations where all the deletions of the first part have been carried out. Suppose *R* is a subset of *S*; then the choice probabilities for the choice set *R* are assumed to be identical to the choice probabilities for the choice set *S* conditional on *R* having been chosen, i.e., for *a* in *R*

$$P_R(a) = P_S(a \mid R).$$

Several easy consequences of this are that the ratio $P_R(a)/P_R(b)$ is independent of *R* (the constant-ratio rule), that the pairwise probabilities satisfy

$$P(a, b)\, P(b, c)\, P(c, a) = P(a, c)\, P(c, b)\, P(b, a)$$

(the product rule), and that there exists a numerical ratio scale v over T such that for all *a* in *R*,

$$P_R(a) = v(a) \Big/ \sum_{b \text{ in } R} v(b).$$

We say $v(a)$ is a response strength associated with response *a*, and the axiom implies response probability is proportional to response strength. This representation is closely related to the logit analysis used in statistics. For two-element choice sets, it was proposed earlier by Bradley and Terry (1952), and so some authors (e.g., Suppes & Zinnes, 1963) refer to these as BTL models. Others, especially economists, refer to it as the strict utility model. As Fantino and Navarick (1974) note, it recurs repeatedly in people's thinking about choice probabilities.

The Relation to Thurstone's Theory

It was apparent from the outset that in many situations the numbers predicted by the choice axiom differ but little from those predicted by the special case of Thurstone's discriminable dispersion model (called the random utility model by economists and probit analysis by statisticians) in which the random variables are independent, are normally distributed, and have the same variance. Indeed, the paired comparison situation leads to the logistic distribution for the choice model and the normal ogive for Thurstone's, and these are well known to be very similar except in the tails. One study (Burke & Zinnes, 1965), aimed at empirical tests, concerned ways to try to maximize the difference between the two models. Large differences in the prediction of $P(a, c)$ in terms of $P(a, b)$ and $P(b, c)$ arise only when one of these probabilities is very near 0 and the other is very near 1, but it is not practical to estimate such extreme values with sufficient accuracy to make the test workable.

The first major step in understanding the exact relationship between these two models, due to Block and Marschak (1960), is the theorem that for any system of probabilities satisfying the choice axiom, there is an independent Thurstone model defined on the whole real line that yields these probabilities. Their proof was very indirect and later

E. Holman and A. A. J. Marley (reported in Luce & Suppes, 1965) gave a direct proof. In particular, an independent Thurstone model with random variables of the form

$$P(X \leqslant t) = f(t)^{v(x)}, \qquad f(-\infty) = 0, f(\infty) = 1, \; -\infty < t < \infty,$$

yields the choice model. If one restricts this to random variables that differ only in their means—a shift family—then one obtains the double exponential[1] of the form

$$P(X \leqslant t) = e^{-e^{-\alpha t+\beta}}.$$

A question not then answered, and only recently resolved by McFadden (1974) and independently and under appreciably less restrictive conditions[2] by Yellott (1977), is whether this distribution is unique or not. That is to say, while we can reproduce any set of probabilities satisfying the choice axiom by using appropriate double exponential distributions, can we do the same thing with some different distribution? The answer is "No" provided the Thurstone model is restricted to a shift family and the choice set has at least three elements. This is by no means obvious, nor is it easy to prove. The case of just binary choices is more complex; Bradley (1965) discussed it.

In the course of investigating this problem, Yellott has brought to our attention two related facts. The first, which was also pointed out earlier in the context of paired comparison models by Thompson and Singh (1967) (see also Beaver & Rao, 1972), is that the double exponential distribution arose very many years ago in statistics (Fisher & Tippett, 1928; Gumbel, 1958) as an answer to the question: given n independent, identically distributed random variables, what is the asymptotic ($n \to \infty$) distribution of the maximum? This is similar to the question answered in the central limit theorem, but with "maximum" substituted for "average" (or "sum"). There are various possibilities, one of which is the double exponential which arises when the underlying distribution has an upper exponential tail.

The second fact is a new and very pretty result which, had Thurstone known it, might have led him to postulate the double exponential rather than the normal distribution. Yellott asked and answered the following question. Suppose choices are determined by a Thurstone model involving random variables that are independent and a shift family and that the choice probabilities exhibit the following plausible invariance property: let each element of a choice set be replicated k times—think of choices among books or phonograph records with several identical copies of each—the probability of choosing any particular element is independent of the value of k. Yellott has shown that under this invariance assumption the distributions in the Thurstone model must be double

[1] There is a good deal of terminological confusion. Sometimes the LaPlace distribution is called the double exponential, whereas $e^{-e^{-x}}$ is often called the log–Weibull distribution because the distribution e^{-x^k}, $x \geqslant 0$, is known as the Weibull distribution. Both Holman and Marley and McFadden stated the result in Weibull form, but in order to have the variables run from $-\infty$ to ∞, Yellott uses the double exponential form.

[2] McFadden's proof is more restrictive in two respects. He assumed that the distribution of the random variable is translation complete and that there are infinitely many objects of choice; neither is required in Yellott's proof.

exponentials, and hence the choice axiom must hold. In many contexts, Yellott's condition is so compelling that his theorem means Thurstone's model with a shift family of independent random variables and the choice axiom stand or fall together.

It should be noted that Yellott's invariance condition is closely related to Debreu's (1960) counterexample to the choice axiom: Suppose a person is indifferent between a and b and a' and b, $P(a, b) = P(a', b) = \frac{1}{2}$ and that a and a' are very similar so $P(a, a') = \frac{1}{2}$. Because of the similarity of a and a', Debreu contends $P_A(a) = P(a, b) = \frac{1}{2}$, where $A = \{a, a', b\}$. However, according to the choice axiom

$$P(a', b) = P(a, b) \quad \text{iff} \quad P_A(a) = P_A(a'),$$
$$P(a', a) = P(a', b) \quad \text{iff} \quad P_A(b) = P_A(a),$$

whence $P_A = \frac{1}{3} < P(a, b)$. The key difference between Yellott and Debreu is that the former uses equal numbers of replications whereas the latter does not.

Limit Properties

Let L_n denote a probability distribution on the first n integers, $n \geqslant 2$. Steele (1974) called a sequence of such distributions, $n = 2, 3, \ldots$, a *Luce process* provided they exhibit the constant-ratio rule, i.e., for each $m < n$ and for $i, j \leqslant m$,

$$P_n(i)/P_n(j) = P_m(i)/P_m(j).$$

Next, let us define for each L_n a measure P_n on the unit interval by placing atoms at the points k/n, $1 \leqslant k \leqslant n$, with mass $P_n(k)$. Using the results of Karamata (1933) on regularly varying functions, Steele showed that if the sequence L_n is a Luce process and if the associate measures P_n converge in distribution to P, then for some α, $0 \leqslant \alpha \leqslant \infty$, $P[0, x] = x^\alpha$. So far as I know, this result has yet to be put to use.

Discard and Acceptance Mechanisms

Luce (1960) suggested that choices may be effected by systematically discarding elements from a choice set. If so and if we denote the probability of discarding b from A by $Q_A{}^*(b)$, then a natural inductive hypothesis is

$$P_A(a) = \sum_{b \text{ in } A-\{a\}} Q_A{}^*(b)\, P_{A-\{b\}}(a).$$

There it was shown that if the choice axiom also holds, then

$$Q_A{}^*(b) = [1 - P_A(b)]/[|A| - 1],$$

where $|A|$ is the number of elements in A. So in this very special case the choice probabilities can arise from a discard mechanism.

Marley (1965) studied the problem more generally. We say the choice probabilities satisfy *regularity* if, for a in $A \subseteq B$, $P_A(a) \geqslant P_B(a)$. This is a very weak property which almost everyone believes to be true of choice probabilities. However, as Corbin and Marley (1974) have pointed out, even it may not always be true. For example, a guest in deference to his host selects the second most expensive item on a menu; this choice of course is altered by adding an entree more expensive than any on the current menu. Marley showed that regularity is sufficient, but not necessary, for the discard equation to hold, that the discard probabilities are unique when the inequality in regularity is strict, and he gave an expression for them.

Following Marley (1968), let P^* denote aversion probabilities, i.e., $P_A{}^*(a)$ is the probability that a is selected from A as the least desired element. One can define an acceptance condition that parallels the discard one by

$$P_A{}^*(a) = \sum_{b \text{ in } A-\{a\}} Q_A(b)\, P^*_{A-\{b\}}(a).$$

These two conditions, discard and acceptance, are called strong if $Q^* = P^*$ and $Q = P$.

Another plausible relation between the two kinds of probabilities is Marley's *concordant condition*

$$P_A(a)\, P^*_{A-\{a\}}(b) = P_A{}^*(b)\, P_{A-\{b\}}(a).$$

He showed that the concordant condition implies that both the strong discard and the strong acceptance conditions hold, but that neither set of choice probabilities can satisfy the choice axiom.

Rankings

Georgescu-Roegen (1958, 1969) and Luce (1959) independently discussed how choice and ranking probabilities might interrelate, and Block and Marschak (1960) and Marschak (1960) extended some of these results considerably.

Let us denote the choice probabilities by $P_A(a)$ and the probability of the rank order $a_1 > a_2 > \cdots > a_n$ by $p(a_1, \ldots, a_n)$. Let U be the universal, finite set under consideration. A major difference among assumptions is whether the rankings are just of U or of all of its subsets.

Georgescu-Roegen (1958) discussed the following two interrelations.

A. Suppose ranking probabilities exist for all subsets of U, then for any set $\{a_1, \ldots, a_n\} \subseteq U$,

$$p(a_2, a_3, \ldots, a_n) = p(a_1, a_2, a_3, \ldots, a_n) + p(a_2, a_1, a_3, \ldots, a_n) + \cdots + p(a_2, a_3, \ldots, a_n, a_1).$$

B. Suppose the ranking probabilities exist for all subsets of U, then for $A_n = \{a_1, \ldots, a_n\} \subseteq U$,

$$P_{A_n}(a_1) = \sum_{\rho} p(a_1, a_{\rho(2)}, \ldots, a_{\rho(n)}),$$

where the sum extends over all permutations of $a_2, \ldots, a_n$.

Note that for $A_2 = \{a_1, a_2\}$, B yields

$$P(a_1, a_2) = p(a_1, a_2),$$

which together with A applied inductively yields that $P(a_1, a_2)$ can be expressed as the sum of the probabilities of all rankings of U for which a_1 is ahead of a_2. This property was suggested by Luce (1959) and generalized by Block and Marschak (1960) to the following. Let $R(a, A)$ denote all of the rank orderings of U in which a in A ranks ahead of all elements in $A - \{a\}$.

B′. $$P_A(a) = \sum_{\rho \text{ in } R(a,A)} p(\rho).$$

Luce (1959) proposed that the ranking probabilities might arise by repeated selections of the best element. This can be formulated in either of two ways depending on which ranking probabilities are assumed to exist.

R. If the ranking probabilities exist for all subsets of U,
$$p(a_1, a_2, \ldots, a_n) = P_{A_n}(a_1)\, p(a_2, a_3, \ldots, a_n).$$

R′. If the ranking probabilities exist on U,
$$p(a_1, a_2, \ldots, a_n) = P_U(a_1)\, P_{U-\{a_1\}}(a_2) \cdots P(a_{n-1}, a_n).$$

The major results appear to be these:

(1) (Block & Marschak, 1960) A system of choice probabilities on the subsets of U form a random utility (Thurstone) model iff there exist ranking probabilities on U such that B′ holds.

(2) (Block & Marschak, 1960; Luce, 1959 for $n = 3$) A system of choice probabilities on the subsets of U satisfy the choice axiom iff there exists ranking probabilities on U such that B′ and R′ hold.

(3) (Georgescu-Roegen, 1969) Suppose a system of choice probabilities and ranking probabilities on the subsets of U satisfy R. Then the choice axiom is equivalent to A.

Georgescu-Roegen (1958) asserted that if there are systems of rankings and choice probabilities satisfying A and B, then it is not possible for the choice probabilities to be a function just of the binary ones. In particular, then, the choice axiom may not hold. This has been questioned by Chakrabarti (1969) and by me in correspondence and replied to by Georgescu-Roegen (1969). It is clear that some misunderstanding exists. By (3) above and by the simple fact, pointed out by Georgescu-Roegen (1969), that B follows from R, we see that R and the choice axiom imply A and B. But if he is correct, these imply that the choice axiom cannot hold. The difficulty lies in the proof in the 1958 paper.

A complication arises when we admit that rankings can be generated by choice mechanisms in at least two ways—either by repeatedly selecting the best alternative or by repeatedly selecting the worst. Luce and Suppes (1965) summarize the impossibility theorem that arises if one demands both that the probability of the ranking not depend on which process is sused and that the choice axiom holds. More insight is provided by Marley (1968) who showed that this ranking hypothesis is equivalent to assuming the concordant condition which, as we noted above, implies that the choice axiom does not hold.

Applications

As we see in the next section, psychologists have been at pains to test the adequacy of the choice axiom as a descriptive model, but there has been relatively little application of it as the foundation of some other theory. I made some attempts in Luce (1959, 1963) and Luce and Galanter (1963) to build a psychophysical theory on it, and Nakatani (1972) and Shipley (1965) extended those ideas, but realistically I do not think it has been a particularly successful program.

In sociology, there are two large texts on mathematical sociology. There is a brief mention of the choice axiom in the introduction to Coleman (1964), but he does not appear to employ it later; whereas Fararo (1973) devotes much of one of 25 chapters to expositing the idea. However, so far as I can see, nothing is really built on it.

In economics, there appear to be two sorts of applications. One is typified by the work of McFadden and his colleagues (for a survey, see McFadden, 1976) in which different possible models of choice are used to fit empirical data which arise in economic contexts of some complexity. This work is more in the spirit of data handling and reduction of statistics than economic theory. The other, which is more deeply theoretical, attempts to reconstruct the foundations of rational economic theory, basing it on probabilistic rather than algebraic assumptions. Work of this sort was initiated by Georgescu-Roegen (1936, 1958). The latter paper raised the key questions: "I. What axioms are logically necessary and experimentally justified, to relate the multiple choice probability to that of the binary choice? II. Granted these axioms, what is the reflection of the 'average' demand into the binary choice map?" Halldin (1974) undertook the investigation of the second question on the assumption that the choice axiom is a reasonable answer to the first question. As he pointed out, the choice axiom is a possible probabilistic formulation of "... a leading ... and powerful ... principle in the traditional economic theory of consumer behavior: by the definition of rationality, the choice made from any given budget set B depends exclusively on the ordering of the alternatives in B." He proceeds to develop on this foundation a generalization of the classical theory of demand. He summarizes his results as follows. "On the basis of Luce's theory then, we conclude that whereas the mode or most probable demand of the uncertain consumer will always coincide with his classical and optimal demand, his mean or expected demand will not, that is, his expected demand will not reveal preferences as demand reveals preferences in the classical case, nor can it be identified with the demand he would have if, as in classical theory, his preferences were perfectly certain."

Experimental Tests

By now, quite a variety of experiments have either been performed to test or been interpreted in terms of the choice axiom, and so it is helpful to group them into related categories. Even so, only the briefest mention of individual studies is possible. I have elected to group most of the animal studies together at the end.

Binary Data

Because the choice axiom implies the binary constraint

$$\frac{P(a, b)\, P(b, c)\, P(c, a)}{P(b, a)\, P(c, b)\, P(a, c)} = 1,$$

known as the product rule, binary (paired comparison) data provide an indirect test of the axiom. This property is equivalent to the binary choice model of Bradley and Terry (1952),

$$P(a, b) = \frac{v(a)}{v(a) + v(b)}.$$

In an early paper on taste preferences, Hopkins (1954) used Bradley's (1953) estimation scheme and a χ^2 evaluation and found the Bradley–Terry model satisfactory. Burke and Zinnes (1965) fitted both the binary Thurstone and the Bradley–Terry model to three published sets of data—Gulliksen and Tukey (1958) in which 200 subjects evaluated pairs of handwriting specimens, Guilford (1954) in which a single subject judged each pair of weights 200 times, and Thurstone (1959) in which 266 subjects judged the seriousness of crimes. They estimated two of the three probabilities, predicted the third, and used χ^2 as a measure of goodness of fit. Thurstone's data were indecisive and the other two favored the Thurstone model. As they pointed out, assigning all of the variability to just one of the three probabilities is not really very satisfactory. Hohle (1966) carried out another analysis of existing data: lifted weights (Guilford, 1931), preferences among vegetables (Guilford, 1954), samples of handwriting (Hevner, 1930), and numerousness (Hohle). His more sophisticated analysis involved maximum likelihood estimates for the scale values of both the Bradley–Terry and Thurstone models and evaluated the fit in terms of $-2 \ln \lambda$, where λ is the likelihood ratio, which is asymptotically distributed as χ^2. By this test, the Bradley–Terry model was favored, although in over half of the comparisons the discrepancies were significant. In the worst case, the average absolute deviation was 0.032. Skvoretz, Windell, and Fararo (1974) used as stimuli two sets of five occupations each, with one occupation in common. A group of 79 subjects were presented with all 36 pairs and asked to "choose that occupation which, *in general*, you accord a higher social standing." Using Bradley's procedures, these were fitted to the binary model and the appropriate χ^2 test yielded $p > .25$. So, for the average subject, the binary model fit very well. Later, under rankings, I discuss other data from this study.

Several authors, probably motivated by Debreu's (1960) counter example to the choice axiom (actually, to simple scalability; see below), have emphasized the need to take into account similarity relations among the stimuli. Restle (1961) proposed a binary choice theory which has recently been generalized by Tversky (1972a, b) to arbitrary sets of alternatives. Rumelhart and Greeno (1971) designed a study in which certain subgroups of stimuli were similar, but different groups were not. Their data clearly disconfirmed the Bradley–Terry model and were consistent with the Restle model. Their procedure of estimation was criticized by Edgell, Geisler, and Zinnes (1973), but their conclusion was not altered by correcting the estimates.

Nonbinary Data: The Constant Ratio Rule

The constant ratio rule (CRR) (Clarke, 1957) version of the choice model has attracted considerable attention, especially as a way of dealing with confusion matrices. Early studies include Anderson (1959), Clarke (1957, 1959), Clarke and Anderson (1957), and Egan (1957a, b). These authors all concluded that the CRR is reasonably satisfactory. Later studies along much the same lines, including Atkinson, Bower, and Crothers (1965, pp. 146–150, analyzing data of W. K. Estes), Hodge (1967), Hodge and Pollack (1962), Pollack and Decker (1960), and Waganaar (1968), continued to interpret the data as reasonably favorable, although not always. Hodge (1967, p. 435) put it this way: "Taken as a whole, the predictions are good enough to make the CRR a useful tool in designing practical stimulus displays and response systems (cf., Engstrand & Moeller, 1962). As a model of choice behavior, however, the rule as presently formulated is somewhat unsatisfactory. The results of the present experiment and those of Hodge and Pollack demonstrate that the CRR has difficulty predicting the response proportions of single dimensional ensembles, especially when the 2 by 2 matrices involve variations in the spacing-range conditions and practice on the task."

But even the apparently favorable cases are cast into doubt by Morgan (1974) who worked out a likelihood ratio test for the CRR and reexamined some of the published data, which he found departs significantly from predicted values. His discussion of the difficulties in running a suitable experiment to test the CRR is illuminating.

Yellott and Curnow (1967) ran a study in which one of three possible target letters was flashed briefly at random in a 4×4 matrix along with 15 other nontarget letters. On some trials the subject had all three responses available and on the remainder one of the two incorrect responses was eliminated by the experimenter after the presentation and before the response. Assuming that choices were a mixture of guesses and observations, it was found that the choice axiom accounted well for the data of the four subjects. When an error was made, on trials for which all three responses were available, they required a second choice. These were not well predicted, but they argued that this is not a satisfactory test of the choice axiom because of sequential effects introduced by the selection of trials.

Tversky (1972b) conducted a psychophysical and two preference studies of the CRR. The psychophysical data exhibited no significant departure, but in the preference data the observed binary proportions were larger than those predicted from trinary data. This is plausible in the light of his model, which generalizes both Restle and the CRR (see below), in which stimulus similarity plays a role.

Nonbinary Data: Response Biases

In Luce (1959) and more fully in Luce (1963) a class of models was developed in which the scale values associated with responses are decomposed multiplicatively into two factors, a response bias b_j associated solely with the response and a stimulus factor, η_{ij} being the impact of stimulus i on response j. The choice axiom then yields the form

$$P(r_j \mid s_i) = \eta_{ij} b_j \Big/ \sum_k \eta_{ik} b_k .$$

In the latter paper I attempted, with some degree of success, to use this to account for various psychophysical data, but certain phenomena proved recalcitrant to this approach. Perhaps the most striking of these occurs in absolute identification, where the information transmitted for stimuli spread over a large range grows almost linearly with $\log n$ until about $n = 7$ at which point it becomes constant (Miller, 1956) or for 10 or more stimuli it grows linearly with a range up to a point (15–20 dB in auditory intensity) after which its rate is greatly reduced (Braida & Durlach, 1972). Indeed, until very recently no model has successfully accounted for these phenomena (Luce, Green, & Weber, 1976).

Shipley and Luce (1964) collected considerable data (weights) and attempted to fit them with this model with, at best, modest success. Shipley (1965) collected additional auditory data and found that the simple model would not do and she developed a number of elaborate modifications of it which, however, have not been pursued. Townsend (1971) fit the model to an alphabet confusion matrix with rather better results. Broadbent (1967) argued that it is a suitable model to explain the word-frequency effect in the perception of words, but his interpretation was sharply questioned by Catlin (1969) and Nakatani (1970) and defended by Treisman (1971).

Nakatani (1968, 1972) proposed a generalization of the response bias model which he calls confusion-choice recognition theory. He has had success in fitting it to word recognition data. For a summary, see Luce and Green (1974, p. 307).

β-Learning Model

The form of biased choices just described suggested (Luce, 1959) a possible mechanism for learning, not unrelated to the linear operator models then in vogue. The idea was that on trial n there is a set of response strengths $v_n(a)$, a in A, and if alternative a is selected on trial n then depending on the outcome it is changed to $\beta v_n(a) = v_{n+1}(a)$ on trial $n + 1$. A positive reinforcement corresponds to $\beta > 1$ and a negative one to $0 < \beta < 1$. In terms of the probabilities, these operators are nonlinear, but they exhibit instead of linearity the very powerful property of commutativity. This captures a learning process in which there is no forgetting or attenuation of the past.

Mathematical properties of these operators were investigated by Bush (1960), Kanal (1960, 1962a, b), Lamperti & Suppes (1960), and Luce (1959). In Luce (1964) whole families of commutative operators were investigated and, in general, were shown to behave much like the β model. Bush, Galanter, & Luce (1959) conducted some experimental tests of the model, using animals, but their conclusions were sharply questioned by Sternberg (1963, p. 96–97) who pointed out that optimal estimates of the parameters were considerably different from their nonoptimal ones.

Rankings

Although some nice theoretical results relate rankings to choices, few relevant data have been reported. Part of the reason for this is that once one goes beyond three alternatives, the number of observations required to get reasonably accurate estimates of ranking probabilities is nearly prohibitive. For example, with $n = 5$ there are 120 possible rankings, and so 100 observations per rank yields a total of 12,000 judgments.

I am aware of only two sets of data. One, collected by W.K. Estes, was analyzed by

Atkinson *et al.* (1965, pp. 150–155). The averages from 17 subjects seem to provide support for the ranking hypothesis R (see above).

The other study is in Skvoretz, Windell, and Fararo (1974) who had 155 subjects rank order the two sets of occupations that had been used in the paired comparisons study with another group of subjects. They then employed assumption B to estimate the pairwise choice probabilities, fit the binary choice model to get scale values, used these to generate choice probabilities, and from these and the ranking postulate R predicted the ranking probabilities. A χ^2 test strongly rejected this model. They concluded that the ranking postulate is in error; however, it is really the combination of B, the choice axiom, and R that are rejected. In particular, they do not report for these data how well the binary choice model works.

Simple Scalability

Although the evidence so far reviewed makes one suspicious that the choice axiom is not terribly accurate empirically, to me the most compelling data against it are the several studies that were explicitly designed to undermine the whole broad class of models satisfying simple scalability. Luce and Suppes (1965) defined the ***constant utility models*** to be those for which there is a real-valued function u over the alternatives and real function F_n on n real arguments such that

$$P_A(a_1) = F_n[u(a_1); u(a_2),..., u(a_n)],$$

where $A = \{a_1, a_2, ..., a_n\}$. If, in addition, we assume that F_n is strictly increasing in the first argument and strictly decreasing in the remaining $n - 1$, then we say *simple scalability* holds. Tversky (1972a) showed this to be equivalent to the following simple observable property called *order independence*: for a, b in $A - B$ and c in B,

$$P_A(a) \geqslant P_A(b) \quad \text{iff} \quad P_{B\cup\{b\}}(c) \geqslant P_{B\cup\{a\}}(c),$$

provided none of the probabilities is 0. This generalizes earlier results on binary simple scalability (Krantz, 1967; Tversky & Russo, 1969) which had been shown to be equivalent to each of the following well-known properties:

Strict Stochastic Transitivity. $P(a, b) \geqslant \frac{1}{2}$ and $P(b, c) \geqslant \frac{1}{2}$ imply $P(a, c) \geqslant \max[P(a, b), P(b, c)]$, and $>$ in either hypothesis implies $>$ in the conclusion.

Substitutability. $P(a, c) \geqslant P(b, c)$ iff $P(a, b) \geqslant \frac{1}{2}$.

Independence. $P(a, c) \geqslant P(b, c)$ iff $P(a, d) \geqslant P(b, d)$.

To begin with, against simple scalability is Debreu's (1960) example. It was raised against the choice axiom, but the argument actually only uses order independence (see p. 7). Almost everyone, including me, agrees that Debreu is empirically correct, and so simple scalability must be wrong.

Empirically, we also have several unambiguous studies. Coombs (1958) showed that preferences among shades of gray include triples of alternatives, which he could identify on the basis of his unfolding ideas, that violate strict stochastic transitivity and hence simple scalability (the full impact of his result was not fully realized by most of us at the time). Chipman (1960) found in a study of subjective probability that he could reject strict stochastic transitivity for 6 of 10 subjects. Krantz (1967) showed that substitutability, and hence simple scalability, failed for judgments about monochromatic colors. Whether or not one alternative can be substituted for another was found to be context dependent. And Tversky and Russo (1969) exhibited failures of independence, and hence simple scalability, in judgments of the relative size of simple geometric figures that varied in two dimensions. "It was found that the similarity between stimuli facilitate the discrimination between them. But since the similarity between two stimuli can be varied without changing their scale values, simple scalability, and hence independence, must be violated" (p. 11).

These results are deeply disturbing because their variety of domains make it difficult to see in what domain simple scalability, let alone the choice axiom, may hold. And at the same time, all of the data reported are in large part consistent with simple scalability, and so it is difficult to abandon the idea completely. As we see, Tversky was led from these problems to his choice-by-elimination model, but even that may not be without problems.

Expected Random Utility (Thurstone) Model

Becker, DeGroot, and Marschak (1963b), drawing upon a theoretical analysis in Becker, DeGroot, and Marschak (1963a), designed a study of choices among gambles which had the following property. No expected random utility model predicts that one of the alternatives (which was an average of the other two) in each choice set would ever be chosen. There were 25 such sets and 60 of the 62 subjects selected the forbidden alternative at least once in 25 times. This study casts doubt upon just about any way of generalizing the expected utility property in a probabilistic context.

Animal Data

In his text, Greeno (1968) analyzed several sets of data. Food preferences of rats (Young, 1947) gave good agreement with the product rule. However, the proportions of time spent in alternative activities (Allison, 1964) did not satisfy the product rule very well. And finally, monkey data on times devoted to activities allowed good predictions.

By far the most systematic program of animal research that bears on these matters is that of R. J. Herrnstein and his collaborators. He has concerned himself with choice situations defined in an operant framework in terms of different keys associated with different reinforcement schedules. The behavior observed is key presses and reinforcements received. The major generalization from these data is that strength of responding is proportional to its relative rate of reinforcement. Put more formally, if there are n alternative responses, r_i denotes the number of reinforcements delivered per ith response, r_0 is a constant, and R_i is the number of occurrences of response i, then

$$R_i = kr_i \Big/ \sum_{j=0}^{n} r_j .$$

If P_i denotes the proportion of i responses, then

$$P_i = R_i \Big/ \sum_{j=1}^{n} R_j$$

$$= \left(kr_i \Big/ \sum_{j=0}^{n} r_j\right) \Big/ \left(\sum_{j=1}^{n} kr_j \Big/ \sum_{h=0}^{n} r_h\right)$$

$$= r_i \Big/ \sum_{j=1}^{n} r_j$$

which, of course, is the choice axiom representation, but with the scale value having an explicit empirical interpretation.

For a general discussion of these ideas, summaries of the data, and more detailed references, see Fantino and Navarick (1974), Herrnstein (1970, 1974), and de Villiers and Herrnstein (1976). Herrnstein and Loveland (1976) have studied the product rule during extinction trials and found that the choice axiom prediction is not nearly as extreme as the data.

Generalizations

As we have seen, there is much evidence that choices are not generally governed by axioms as simple as the choice axiom. Indeed, the difficulty pervades the whole broad class of models exhibiting simple scalability. That being so, various other approaches have been taken.

There is of course the general class of Thurstone models, which economists call random utility models. These are the ones with a random variable U_a associated with each response alternative and the assumption that

$$P_A(a) = \Pr(U_a \geqslant U_b \text{ for all } b \text{ in } A).$$

Mostly, only independent random utility models have been used; these are ones in which the random variables are assumed to be independent of each other. As Tversky (1972b) pointed out, a familiar example (Luce & Raiffa, 1957, p. 375) makes clear that this model will not suffice. Consider nearly equivalent trips to Paris and to Rome, and let the added symbol $+$ denote some minor added benefit, such as a slight reduction in price. It is evident that for $a =$ either Paris or Rome, $P(a+, a) = 1$, but that it is quite possible for both $P(\text{Paris}+, \text{Rome}) < 1$ and $P(\text{Rome}+, \text{Paris}) < 1$. Assuming an independent Thurstone model, the first two equalities imply no overlap between the distributions of a and $a+$ for $a =$ Paris and $a =$ Rome, whereas the last two inequalities imply an overlap between Paris $+$ and Rome and between Rome $+$ and Paris. These statements are mutually inconsistent for independent random variables.

So the only remaining real possibility that retains the intuitive idea of a utility indicator is some form of a nonindependent Thurstone model. Although Restle (1961) and Eisler

(1964) have suggested binary generalizations, it was not until Tversky (1972a, b) (see also Corbin & Marley, 1974) that a full generalization was proposed. Tversky took as his point of departure an equation which in spirit is much like the discard condition stated above but which admits that more than one alternative may be discarded at a time. If $B \subseteq A$, let $Q_A(B)$ denote the probability that the alternatives A–B are discarded, then he proposed the Markovian condition

$$P_A(a) = \sum_{\substack{B \\ B \subseteq A}} Q_A(B)\, P_B(a)$$

as describing the elimination process. By itself, this imposes no restrictions on the choice probabilities. However, he suggested that the transition probabilities A may satisfy the following condition: Suppose $B, C \subseteq A \subseteq T$, then

$$Q_A(B)/Q_A(C) = \sum_{\substack{D \\ D \cap A = B}} Q_T(D) \Big/ \sum_{\substack{D \\ D \cap A = C}} Q_T(D),$$

provided that both denominators are positive. No rationalization was offered for this condition. From it and the Markovian condition on the elimination process, he showed that there is a function U over the subsets of T such that

$$P_A(a) = \sum_{\substack{B \\ B \cap A \neq A}} U(B)\, P_{A \cap B}(a) \Big/ \sum_{\substack{B \\ B \cap A \neq \phi}} U(B).$$

An alternative argument for this recursive form is given in Tversky (1972b), where he identified each alternative by the set of aspects (or components) that characterizes it. He suggested that people proceed by selecting an aspect in proportion to its measure and then eliminate all alternatives not possessing it. This process is continued until exactly one alternative remains, which is their choice. Such a process can be translated into an equation of the above form.

This model reduces to the choice model in the special circumstance where the pairs of alternatives are aspect disjoint. Furthermore, for binary alternatives it is equivalent to Restle's (1961) model. But perhaps its nicest feature is the number of desirable consequences that can be derived from it. Tversky (1972a) showed that it implies regularity (see the section on Discard and Acceptance Mechanisms), moderate stochastic transitivity: if $P(a, b) \geqslant \frac{1}{2}$ and $P(b, c) \geqslant \frac{1}{2}$, then $P(a, c) \geqslant \min[P(a, b), P(b, c)]$; and $P_{\{a,b,c\}}(a) \geqslant P(a, b)\, P(a, c)$. The latter multiplicative inequality was generalized in Sattath and Tversky (1976) to: $P_{A \cup B}(a) \geqslant P_A(a)\, P_B(a)$. Thus, it and regularity provide lower and upper bounds on $P_{A \cup B}(a)$ in terms of $P_A(a)$ and $P_B(a)$. It is recalled that regularity is a condition that nearly everyone believes to be true of most choices. And whereas strong stochastic transitivity (max for min above), which is equivalent to binary simple scalability, has been rejected in data, moderate stochastic transitivity has not been.

Tversky also showed how to construct ranking probabilities so that property B of the section on ranking holds. Since by Block and Marschak's theorem, this is equivalent to the choice probabilities satisfying a random utility model, this means Tversky's model has this property (of course, it does not involve independent random variables).

To the best of my knowledge, the only data so far reported that conceivably might reject this elimination-by-aspects model are the gambling ones of Becker, DeGroot, and Marschak (1963b) that reject every expected random utility model; however, the trouble may well be with the expected utility property. Corbin and Marley's (1974) example against regularity raises doubts about any random utility model and so EBA, but it has not yet been explored empirically. Indow (1975) in a survey article on the choice axiom and Tversky's model questions whether it or any mathematical model can capture all that is involved. "... It may not be quite realistic as a [substantive] model for actual choice behavior of human beings. Choice is in essence *conflict* and will not proceed in such a straightforward way defined in the eliminating process. Such cases occur rather frequently in which no alternative is easily eliminated from a certain stage of decision making on and they create conflict or attractiveness of aspects changes their balance from moment to moment, which also leads to conflict. Certainly, to take all these features into consideration will make mathematical formulation untractable. Then, computer simulation will be a possible way of approach." Others, however, are unwilling yet to give up the quest for a general structural model or at least for several classes of such models to cover different domains.

Conclusion

After somewhat less than 20 years, where does the choice axiom stand? As a descriptive tool, it is surely imperfect; sometimes it works well, other times not very well. As Debreu and Restle made clear and as has been repeatedly demonstrated experimentally, it fails to describe choice behavior when the stimulus set is structured in such a way that several alternatives are treated as substantially the same. It probably also fails whenever the experimental subjects have the belief—which I fear may often be the case—that they should employ the response alternatives about equally often. This tends to introduce some form of response bias which can well differ from one experimental run to another. Keep in mind that once we enter the path of strict rejection of models on the basis of statistically significant differences, little remains. To the best of my knowledge, the only property of general choice probabilities that has never been empirically disconfirmed is regularity—a decrease in the choice set does not decrease the probability of choosing any of the remaining alternatives—but even that looks suspect in a Gedanken experiment. Despite these empirical difficulties, there remains a tendency to invoke the choice axiom in many behavioral models—often implicitly. This is partly because it is so simple and the resulting computations are so easy.

Perhaps the greatest strength of the choice axiom, and one reason it continues to be used, is as a canon of probabilistic rationality. It is a natural probabilistic formulation of K. J. Arrow's famed principle of the independence of irrelevant alternatives, and as such it is a possible underpinning for rational, probabilistic theories of social behavior. Thus, in the development of economic theory based on the assumption of probabilistic individual choice behavior, it can play a role analogous to the algebraic rationality postulates of the traditional theory.

However long the choice axiom may prove useful, at least during the 1960s and 1970s it contributed to the interplay of ideas about choices that arose in economics, psychology, and statistics.

References

Allison, J. Strength of preference for food, magnitude of food reward, and performance in instrumental conditioning. *Journal of Comparative and Physiological Psychology*, 1964, **57**, 217–223.

Anderson, C. D. The constant-ratio rule as a predictor of confusions among various stimuli of brief exposure duration. Technical Note, AFCRC-TN-58-60, Hearing and Communication Laboratory, Indiana University, 1959.

Atkinson, R. C., Bower, G. H., & Crothers, E. J. *An introduction to mathematical learning theory*. New York: Wiley, 1965.

Beaver, R. J., & Rao, P. V. The use of limit theorems in paired and triple comparison model building. *Journal of Mathematical Psychology*, 1972, **9**, 92–103.

Becker, G. M., DeGroot, M. H., & Marschak, J. Stochastic models of choice behavior. *Behavioral Science*, 1963, **8**, 41–55. (a)

Becker, G. M., DeGroot, M. H., & Marschak, J. An experimental study of some stochastic models for wagers. *Behavioral Science*, 1963, **8**, 199–202. (b)

Block, H. D., & Marschak, J. Random orderings and stochastic theories of responses. In I. Olkin, S. Ghurye, W. Hoeffding, W. Madow, & H. Mann (Eds.), *Contributions to probability and statistics*. Stanford, Calif.: Stanford University Press, 1960. Pp. 97–132.

Bradley, R. A. Some statistical methods in taste testing and evaluation. *Biometrics*, 1953, **9**, 22–38.

Bradley, R. A. Another interpretation of a model for paired comparisons. *Psychometrika*, 1965, **30**, 315–318.

Bradley, R. A., & Terry, M. E. Rank analysis of incomplete block designs. I. The method of paired comparisons. *Biometrika*, 1952, **39**, 324–345.

Braida, L. D., & Durlach, N. I. Intensity perception II. Resolution in one-interval paradigms. *Journal of the Acoustical Society of America*, 1972, **51**, 483–502.

Broadbent, D. E. Word-frequency effect and response bias. *Psychological Review*, 1967, **74**, 1–15.

Burke, C. J., & Zinnes, J. L. A paired comparison of pair comparisons. *Journal of Mathematical Psychology*, 1965, **2**, 53–76.

Bush, R. R. Some properties of Luce's beta model for learning. In K. J. Arrow, S. Karlin, & P. Suppes (Eds.), *Mathematical methods in the social sciences*, 1959. Stanford, Calif.: Stanford University Press, 1960. Pp. 254–264.

Bush, R. R., Galanter, E., & Luce, R. D. Tests of the "beta model." In R. R. Bush & W. K. Estes (Eds.), *Studies in mathematical learning theory*. Stanford, Calif.: Stanford University Press, 1959. Pp. 382–399.

Catlin, J. On the word-frequency effect. *Psychological Review*, 1969, **76**, 504–506.

Chakrabarti, S. K. A note on the relation between binary and multiple choice probabilities. *Econometrica*, 1969, **37**, 726–727.

Chipman, J. S. Stochastic choice and subjective probability. In D. Willner (Ed.), *Decisions, values and groups*, Vol. 1. New York: Pergamon, 1960. Pp. 70–95.

Clarke, F. R. Constant-ratio rule for confusion matrices in speech communication. *Journal of the Acoustical Society of America*, 1957, **29**, 715–720.

Clarke, F. R. Proportion of correct responses as a function of the number of stimulus-response alternatives. *Journal of the Acoustical Society of America*, 1959, **31**, 835.

Clarke, F. R., & Anderson, C. D. Further test of the constant-ratio rule in speech communication. *Journal of the Acoustical Society of America*, 1957, **29**, 1318–1320.

Coleman, J. S. *Introduction to mathematical sociology.* Glencoe, Ill.: Free Press, 1964.

Coombs, C. H. On the use of inconsistency of preferences in psychological measurement. *Journal of Experimental Psychology*, 1958, **55**, 1–7.

Corbin, R., & Marley, A. A. J. Random utility models with equality: An apparent, but not actual, generalization of random utility models. *Journal of Mathematical Psychology*, 1974, **11**, 274–293.

Debreu, G. Review of R. D. Luce, Individual choice behavior: A theoretical analysis. *American Economic Review*, 1960, **50**, 186–188.

de Villiers, P. A., & Herrnstein, R. J. Toward a law of response strength. *Psychological Bulletin*, 1976, **83**, 1131–1153.

Edgell, S. E., Geisler, W. S. III, & Zinnes, J. L. A note on a paper by Rumelhart and Greeno. *Journal of Mathematical Psychology*, 1973, **10**, 86–90.

Egan, J. P. Message repetition, operating characteristics, and confusion matrices in speech communication. Technical Report 57-50, Hearing and Communication Laboratory, Indiana University, 1957. (a)

Egan, J. P. Monitoring task in speech communication. *Journal of the Acoustical Society of America*, 1957, **29**, 482–489. (b)

Eisler, H. A choice model for paired comparison data based on imperfectly nested sets. *Psychometrika*, 1964, **29**, 363–370.

Engstrand, R. D., & Moeller, G. The relative legibility of ten simple geometric figures. *American Psychologist*, 1962, **17**, 386.

Fantino, E., & Navarick, D. Recent developments in choice. In G. H. Bower (Ed.), *The psychology of learning and motivation*, Vol. 8. New York: Academic Press, 1974. Pp. 147–185.

Fararo, T. J. *Mathematical sociology.* New York: Wiley, 1973.

Fisher, R. A., & Tippett, L. H. C. Limiting forms of the frequency distribution of the largest or the smallest of a sample. *Proceedings of the Cambridge Philosophical Society*, 1928, **24**, 180–190.

Georgescu-Roegen, N. The pure theory of consumer's behavior. *Quarterly Journal of Economics*, 1936, **50**, 545–593.

Georgescu-Roegen, N. Threshold in choice and the theory of demand. *Econometrica*, 1958, **26**, 157–168.

Georgescu-Roegen, N. The relation between binary and multiple choices: some comments and further results. *Econometrica*, 1969, **37**, 728–730.

Greeno, J. G. *Elementary theoretical psychology.* Reading, Mass.: Addison–Wesley, 1968.

Guilford, J. P. Some empirical tests of the method of paired comparisons. *Journal of Genetic Psychology*, 1931, **5**, 64–77.

Guilford, J. P. *Psychometric methods* (2nd ed.). New York: McGraw–Hill, 1954.

Gulliksen, H., & Tukey, J. W. Reliability for the law of comparative judgment. *Psychometrika*, 1958, **23**, 95–110.

Gumbel, E. J. *Statistics of extremes.* New York: Columbia Press, 1958.

Halldin, C. The choice axiom, revealed preferences, and the theory of demand. *Theory and Decision*, 1974, **5**, 139–160.

Herrnstein, R. J. On the law of effect. *Journal of the Experimental Analysis of Behavior*, 1970, **13**, 243–266.

Herrnstein, R. J. Formal properties of the matching law. *Journal of the Experimental Analysis of Behavior*, 1974, **21**, 159–164.

Herrnstein, R. J., & Loveland, D. H. Matching in a network. *Journal of the Experimental Analysis of Behavior*, 1976, **26**, 143–153.

Hevner, K. An empirical study of three psychophysical methods. *Journal of Genetic Psychology*, 1930, **4**, 191–212.

Hodge, M. H. Some further tests of the constant-ratio rule. *Perception & Psychophysics*, 1967, **2**, 429–437.

Hodge, M. H., & Pollack, I. Confusion matrix analysis of single and multidimensional auditory displays. *Journal of Experimental Psychology*, 1962, **63**, 129–142.

HOHLE, R. H. An empirical evaluation and comparison of two models for discriminability scales. *Journal of Mathematical Psychology*, 1966, **3**, 174–183.

HOPKINS, J. W. Incomplete block rank analysis: Some taste test results. *Biometrics*, 1954, **10**, 397–399.

INDOW, T. On choice probability. *Behaviometrika*, 1975, **2**, 13–31.

KANAL, L. Analysis of some stochastic processes arising from a learning model. Ph.D. dissertation, University of Pennsylvania, 1960.

KANAL, L. A functional equation analysis of two learning models. *Psychometrika*, 1962, **27**, 89–104.(a)

KANAL, L. The asymptotic distribution for the two-absorbing-barrier beta model. *Psychometrika*, 1962, **27**, 105–109. (b)

KARAMATA, J. Sur un mode de croissance régulière: Théorèmes fondamentaux. *Bulletin de la Société Mathématique de France*, 1933, **61**, 55–62.

KRANTZ, D. H. Rational distance functions for multidimensional scaling. *Journal of Mathematical Psychology*, 1967, **4**, 226–245.

KRANTZ, D. H., LUCE, R. D., SUPPES, P., & TVERSKY, A. *Foundations of measurement*, Vol. 1. New York: Academic Press, 1971.

LAMPERTI, J., & SUPPES, P. Some asymptotic properties of Luce's beta learning model. *Psychometrika*, 1960, **25**, 233–241.

LUCE, R. D. *Individual choice behavior*. New York: Wiley, 1959.

LUCE, R. D. Response latencies and probabilities. In K. J. Arrow, S. Karlin, & P. Suppes (Eds.), *Mathematical methods in the social sciences*, 1959. Stanford: Stanford University Press, 1960. Pp. 298–311.

LUCE, R. D. Detection and recognition. In R. D. Luce, R. R. Bush, & E. Galanter (Eds.), *Handbook of mathematical psychology*, Vol. 1. New York: Wiley, 1963. Pp. 103–189.

LUCE, R. D. Some one-parameter families of commutative learning operators. In R. C. Atkinson (Ed.), *Studies in mathematical psychology*. Stanford, Calif.: Stanford University Press, 1964. Pp. 380–398.

LUCE, R. D., & GALANTER, E. Discrimination. In R. D. Luce, R. R. Bush, & E. Galanter (Eds.), *Handbook of mathematical psychology*, Vol. 1. New York: Wiley, 1963. Pp. 193–243.

LUCE, R. D., & GREEN, D. M. Detection, discrimination, and recognition. In E. C. Carterette & M. P. Friedman (Eds.), *Handbook of perception*, Vol. II. New York: Academic Press, 1974. Pp. 299–342.

LUCE, R. D., GREEN, D. M., & WEBER, D. L. Attention bands in absolute identification. *Perception & Psychophysics*, 1976, **20**, 49–54.

LUCE, R. D., & RAIFFA, H. *Games and decisions*. New York: Wiley, 1957.

LUCE, R. D., & SUPPES, P. Preference, utility, and subjective probability. In R. D. Luce, R. R. Bush, & E. Galanter (Eds.), *Handbook of mathematical psychology*, Vol. 3. New York: Wiley, 1965. Pp. 249–410.

MARLEY, A. A. J. The relation between the discard and regularity conditions for choice probabilities. *Journal of Mathematical Psychology*, 1965, **2**, 242–253.

MARLEY, A. A. J. Some probabilistic models of simple choice and ranking. *Journal of Mathematical Psychology*, 1968, **5**, 333–357.

MARSCHAK, J. Binary-choice constraints and random utility indicators. In K. J. Arrow, S. Karlin, & P. Suppes (Eds.), *Mathematical methods in the social sciences*, 1959. Stanford: Stanford University Press, 1960. Pp. 312–329.

MCFADDEN, D. Conditional logit analysis of quantitative choice behavior. In P. Zarembka (Ed.), *Frontiers in econometrics*. New York: Academic Press, 1974. Pp. 105–142.

MCFADDEN, D. Quantal choice analysis: a survey. *Annals of Economic and Social Measurement*, 1976, **5**, 363–390.

MILLER, G. A. The magical number seven, plus or minus two: Some limits on our capacity for processing information. *Psychological Review*, 1956, **63**, 81–97.

MORGAN, B. J. T. On Luce's choice axiom. *Journal of Mathematical Psychology*, 1974, **11**, 107–123.

NAKATANI, L. H. *A confusion-choice stimulus recognition model applied to word recognition*. Ph.D. dissertation, University of California at Los Angeles, 1968.

NAKATANI, L. H. Comments on Broadbent's response bias model for stimulus recognition. *Psychological Review*, 1970, **77**, 574–576.

NAKATANI, L. H. Confusion-choice model for multidimensional psychophysics. *Journal of Mathematical Psychology*, 1972, **9**, 104–127.

POLLACK, I., & DECKER, L. Consonant confusions and the constant-ratio rule. *Language and Speech*, 1960, **3**, 1–6.

RESTLE, F. *Psychology of judgment and choice.* New York: Wiley, 1961.

RUMELHART, D. L., & GREENO, J. G. Similarity between stimuli: an experimental test of the Luce and Restle choice models. *Journal of Mathematical Psychology*, 1971, **8**, 370–381.

SATTATH, S., & TVERSKY, A. Unite and conquer: A multiplicative inequality for choice probabilities. *Econometrica*, 1976, **44**, 79–89.

SHIPLEY, E. F. Detection and recognition: experiments and choice models. *Journal of Mathematical Psychology*, 1965, **2**, 277–311.

SHIPLEY, E. F., & LUCE, R. D. Discrimination among two- and three-element sets of weights. In R. C. Atkinson (Ed.), *Studies in Mathematical Psychology*. Stanford, Calif.: Stanford University Press, 1964. Pp. 218–232.

SKVORETZ, J., WINDELL, P., & FARARO, T. J. Luce's axiom and occupational prestige: test of a measurement model. *Journal of Mathematical Sociology*, 1974, **3**, 147–162.

STEELE, J. M. Limit properties of Luce's choice theory. *Journal of Mathematical Psychology*, 1974, **11**, 124–131.

STERNBERG, S. Stochastic learning theory. In R. D. Luce, R. R. Bush, & E. Galanter (Eds.), *Handbook of mathematical psychology*, Vol. 2. New York: Wiley, 1963. Pp. 1–120.

SUPPES, P., & ZINNES, J. L. Basic measurement theory. In R. D. Luce, R. R. Bush, & E. Galanter (Eds.), *Handbook of mathematical psychology*, Vol. 1. New York: Wiley, 1963. Pp. 1–76.

THOMPSON, W. A., JR., & SINGH, J. The use of limit theorems in paired comparison model building. *Psychometrika*, 1967, **32**, 255–264.

THURSTONE, L. L. *The measurement of values*. Chicago: University of Chicago Press, 1959.

TOWNSEND, J. J. Theoretical analysis of an alphabetic confusion matrix. *Perception & Psychophysics*, 1971, **9**, 40–50.

TREISMAN, M. On the word frequency effect: Comments on papers by J. Catlin and L. H. Nakatani. *Psychological Review*, 1971, **78**, 420–425.

TVERSKY, A. Choice by elimination. *Journal of Mathematical Psychology*, 1972, **9**, 341–367. (a)

TVERSKY, A. Elimination by aspects: a theory of choice. *Psychological Review*, 1972, **79**, 281–299. (b)

TVERSKY, A., & RUSSO, J. E. Substitutability and similarity in binary choices. *Journal of Mathematical Psychology*, 1969, **6**, 1–12.

WAGENAAR, W. A. Application of Luce's choice axiom to form-discrimination. *Nederlands Tijdschrift voor de Psychologie*, 1968, **23**, 96–108.

YELLOTT, J. I., JR. The relationship between Luce's choice axiom, Thurstone's theory of comparative judgment, and the double exponential distribution. *Journal of Mathematical Psychology*, 1977, **15**, 109–144.

YELLOTT, J. I., JR., & CURNOW, P. F. Second choices in a visual span of apprehension task. *Perception & Psychophysics*, 1967, **2**, 307–311.

YOUNG, P. T. Studies of food preference, appetite, and dietary habit: VII. Palatability in relation to learning and performance. *Journal of Comparative and Physiological Psychology*, 1947, **40**, 37–72.

RECEIVED: September 8, 1976

[4]

JOURNAL OF MATHEMATICAL PSYCHOLOGY 15, 109–144 (1977)

The Relationship between Luce's Choice Axiom, Thurstone's Theory of Comparative Judgment, and the Double Exponential Distribution[1]

JOHN I. YELLOTT, JR.

School of Social Sciences, University of California, Irvine 92717

Holman and Marley have shown that Thurstone's Case V model becomes equivalent to the Choice Axiom if its discriminal processes are assumed to be independent double exponential random variables instead of normal ones. It is shown here that for pair comparisons, this representation is not unique; other discriminal process distributions (specifiable only in terms of their characteristic functions) also yield a model equivalent to the Choice Axiom. However, none of these models is equivalent to the Choice Axiom for triple comparisons: There the double exponential representation is unique. It is also shown that within the framework of Thurstone's theory, the double exponential distribution, and hence the Choice Axiom, is implied by a weaker assumption, called "invariance under uniform expansions of the choice set."

1. INTRODUCTION

1.1. *Historical Background*

As premises for a model of choice behavior, Luce's (1959) Choice Axiom and Thurstone's (1927) Theory of Comparative Judgment seem at first glance to be not only different, but quite unrelated. The Axiom simply imposes an intuitively plausible constraint on observable choice probabilities, while the theory postulates an imaginary psychological process, underlying observable behavior, wherein choice objects are represented by random variables ("discriminal processes") which the subject compares in order to arrive at a decision. However, it has been recognized since the earliest days of the Choice Axiom that this apparent dissimilarity is only superficial, and that the two ideas are in fact surprisingly closely related. In his 1959 monograph, Luce included a table showing that for pair-comparison experiments, the predictions of the Choice Axiom are virtually identical to those of Case V of Thurstone's theory. (Recall that in Case V the discriminal processes corresponding to a set of objects $o_1, o_2, \ldots$ take the form $u_1 + \mathbf{X}_1$, $u_2 + \mathbf{X}_2, \ldots$, where $u_1, u_2, \ldots$ are constants (scale values) and $\mathbf{X}_1, \mathbf{X}_2, \ldots$ are independent identically distributed normal random variables.) He then

[1] I thank J. Aczel, D. A. Darling, I. I. Kotlarski, R. D. Luce, A. A. J. Marley, J. E. K. Smith, B. Wandell, and J. L. Zinnes for helpful advice; M. Vernoy for assistance in preparing Fig. 1, and the Institute for Advanced Study, Princeton, for support in the form of a visiting membership during 1970–1971, when this research was begun.

ISSN 0022-2496

pointed out that this near identity is not simply coincidental; instead, it reflects the mathematical fact that for pair-comparison experiments the Choice Axiom is equivalent to a version of Thurstone's theory in which the differences between the discriminal processes (that is, the random variables $(u_i + \mathbf{X}_i) - (u_j + \mathbf{X}_j)$) have a logistic distribution instead of the normal distribution implied by Case V. This fact had already been noted by Adams and Messick (1957), who had also shown that the logistic is unique in this respect: A Thurstone model with independent discriminal processes is equivalent to the Choice Axiom for pair comparisons if and only if the differences between discriminal processes are logistic random variables. (This result is proved here in Section 2.6.)

Luce then raised two questions: (1) What must be the distribution of the discriminal processes themselves, in order for their differences to be logistic (so that the resulting model is equivalent to the Choice Axiom for pair comparisons)? (2) Are there any discriminal process distributions for which the resulting model is equivalent to the Choice Axiom for experiments with larger sets of alternatives? (see Luce, 1959, open problem B-2, p. 144.).

A partial answer to both questions was subsequently supplied by Holman and Marley (cited in Luce & Suppes, 1965), who showed that if Thurstone's discriminal processes are assumed to have the *double exponential distribution*:

$$P[u_i + \mathbf{X}_i \leqslant x] = \exp\{-e^{-[a(x-u_i)+b]}\} \qquad (-\infty < x < \infty)$$

(where a and b are arbitrary constants, $a > 0$; see Fig. 1B), then $\mathbf{X}_i - \mathbf{X}_j$ will be logistic, and the resulting model is equivalent to the Choice Axiom for any choice experiment, not simply for pair comparisons. (This result is proved here in Section 2.6.) However, Holman and Marley did not show that the double exponential is the *only* distribution with this property. In presenting their result, Luce and Suppes (1965) remarked that "it is conjectured that [the double exponential distribution is] the only reasonably well behaved example, but no proof has yet been devised" (p. 339).

The present paper carries this line of development two steps further. First, it provides a solution to the uniqueness problem: For pair-comparison experiments the double exponential is *not* the only distribution that yields a Thurstone model equivalent to the Choice Axiom (Section 3.2), but for experiments involving both pair and triple comparisons, it *is* (Theorem 5, Section 3.4). Second, it provides a kind of explanation for the special status of the double exponential distribution: This distribution (and consequently, the Choice Axiom) can be derived in a straightforward way, starting from Thurstone's original discriminal process notion, by applying Luce's idea that observable choice probabilities ought to satisfy some intuitively plausible constraint. It turns out that there is a constraint ("invariance under uniform expansions of the choice set") which is a good deal weaker than the Choice Axiom itself, but which implies that Axiom when combined with Thurstone's discriminal process assumption.

In order to solve the original uniqueness problem, it was natural to generalize it, and consequently a good deal of the paper is devoted to the uniqueness properties of arbitrary discriminal process distributions.

1.2. *Overview and Summary of Results*

1.2.1. *Uniqueness*

We start with Thurstone's basic idea that choice objects $o_1, \ldots, o_n$ are represented by discriminal processes $u_1 + \mathbf{X}_1, \ldots, u_n + \mathbf{X}_n$, where $\mathbf{X}_1, \ldots, \mathbf{X}_n$ are independent identically distributed random variables with a common distribution function F, and, for any given set of objects, $u_1, \ldots, u_n$ are real constants—the scale values of those objects. When the subject is presented with a set of objects and required to choose one, he picks the object with the largest discriminal process. Now we can imagine a class of *Thurstone models* of this type, each one corresponding to a different probability distribution F: Thurstone's original Case V model corresponds to the assumption that F is a normal distribution, and Holman and Marley's result shows that if F is a double exponential distribution, the resulting model is *equivalent* to the Choice Axiom, in the sense that any set of choice probabilities generated by assigning arbitrary values to the $\{u_i\}$ will satisfy the Choice Axiom, and any set of choice probabilities that satisfy the Choice Axiom can be duplicated by a suitable choice of values for the $\{u_i\}$. Then our specific uniqueness problem is to determine whether any other type of distribution also yields a model equivalent to the Choice Axiom.

One might suppose that this problem could be solved by appealing to Adams and Messick's result, since a model with F arbitrary could be equivalent to the Choice Axiom for pair comparison experiments only if F is a distribution for which the differences $\mathbf{X}_i - \mathbf{X}_j$ are logistic. However, it turns out that F need not be double exponential in order for $\mathbf{X}_i - \mathbf{X}_j$ to be logistic: There are other distributions, technically acceptable as bases for Thurstone models, though not at all appealing, that have the same property. (This is shown in Section 3.2.) Consequently, if we restrict our attention to pair-comparison experiments, the double exponential discriminal process distribution is *not* the only one that yields a Thurstone model equivalent to the Choice Axiom.

Generalizing the problem, let $\mathscr{T}_F$ denote the Thurstone model corresponding to distribution function F, and consider the set $\{\mathscr{T}_F\}$ consisting of all such models, one for every distribution function that satisfies certain minimal constraints designed to preserve the spirit of Thurstone's original idea. (See Definition 3, Section 2.6.) Then the general uniqueness question is whether two models $\mathscr{T}_F$ and $\mathscr{T}_G$ can be equivalent if F and G are different distributions. We know already, from the case of the double exponential distribution, that this can happen if we consider only pair-comparison experiments, and this turns out to be true for other distributions as well; the model with F exponential is another example (Section 3.2. This has a bearing on the "Threshold" model proposed by Dawkins, 1969.) In fact the only important exception seems to be the normal (i.e., Case V) model, whose pair-comparison predictions cannot be entirely duplicated by any other Thurstone model (Section 3.2).

Since pair-comparison predictions alone do not uniquely identify the discriminal process distribution of a Thurstone model, it is natural to wonder whether this is also true of experiments in which the subject is confronted with more than two objects at a time. We define a *complete choice experiment* to be one in which choice probabilities are determined for every subset of objects, the simplest nontrivial case being a complete experiment with three objects. It is not difficult to show that two models $\mathcal{T}_F$ and $\mathcal{T}_G$ cannot be equivalent for complete experiments involving choice sets that are arbitrarily large unless F and G are both distributions of the same type (e.g., both double exponential, but perhaps with different means and variances). This is proved in Section 3.3 (Theorem 3). However, this still leaves open the possibility that models with different types of discriminal process distributions might be equivalent for all practical purposes. For an important subclass of Thurstone models—all those in which the distribution F has a nonvanishing characteristic function—this possibility can be ruled out, because it can be shown that if F has a nonvanishing characteristic function, and G is an arbitrary distribution, the models $\mathcal{T}_F$ and $\mathcal{T}_G$ can be equivalent for complete experiments with three (or more) objects if and only if F and G are distributions of the same type (Theorem 4, Section 3.4). Since double exponential distributions have nonvanishing characteristic functions, and we know that $\mathcal{T}_F$ is equivalent to the Choice Axiom if F is double exponential, it follows that another model $\mathcal{T}_G$ can also be equivalent to the Choice Axiom (and consequently to $\mathcal{T}_F$) for complete experiments with three objects only if G is also double exponential (Theorem 5, Section 3.4).

This result provides the sharpest possible solution to our original uniqueness problem. However, the general version of that problem cannot be disposed of quite so neatly, because F can have a characteristic function with zeros and still yield a perfectly acceptable Thurstone model $\mathcal{T}_F$. Thus the general question, whether $\mathcal{T}_F$ and $\mathcal{T}_G$ can be equivalent for complete experiments with three objects if F and G are distributions of different types, remains open. Arguments given in Section 3.4 show that if there are distributions with this property, they must be fairly exotic, and my conjecture is that they do not exist at all. However, I have not been able to prove this. Technically, the answer turns out to depend on whether a certain functional equation involving characteristic functions (Eq. (23)) has only solutions of a certain form (Eq. (24)). I have not been able to answer this question, but I suspect that a specialist in characteristic functions would find it fairly straightforward. In any event, it is left here as an open problem.

1.2.2. *Deriving the Choice Axiom*

When Thurstone decided to assign normal distributions to his discriminal processes, his choice was tentative, and he clearly envisioned the possibility that some other distribution might do a better job:

> The residuals [discrepancies between observed and predicted results] should be investigated to ascertain whether they are a minimum when the normal or Gaussian distribution of discriminal processes is used as a basis for defining the psychological scale. Triangular and other forms of distribution might be tried. Such an experimental demonstration would constitute perhaps the most fundamental discovery that has yet been made in the field of psychological measurement. Lacking such proof and since the Gaussian distribution of discriminal processes yields scale values that agree very closely with the experimental data, I have defined the psychological continuum that is implied in Weber's Law, in Fechner's Law, and in educational quality scales, as that particular linear spacing of the stimuli which gives a Gaussian distribution of discriminal processes (1927, p. 285).

Now if Thurstone had, for some reason, decided on the double exponential distribution instead of the normal, he would in effect have discovered the Choice Axiom. Since this distribution was in those days quite unknown (it only began to become prominent in statistics in 1928, when Fisher and Tippet showed that it is one of three possibilities for the limit distribution of the maximum of a sequence of random variables. See Section 2.6) Thurstone would not have been likely to think of it offhand. But it is interesting to speculate on how he might have been led to it in a logical way, starting from some intuitively plausible premise about choice behavior. Section 4 describes one such premise: that choice probabilities should be "invariant under uniform expansions of the choice set." This notion is motivated by examples of the following kind: Imagine a subject confronted either with a choice set containing a cup of coffee, a cup of tea, and a glass of milk, or with a set containing k cups of coffee, all indistinguishable from the first one, and similarly k identical cups of tea and k identical glasses of milk. In both cases the subject only gets to choose one object. Under these circumstances it seems fairly reasonable to suppose that the probability of choosing coffee (that is, the sum of the probabilities for each individual cup) should be the same in both cases, no matter what the value of k. Invariance of this sort is implied by the Choice Axiom, but taken alone it is clearly a weaker assumption than the Choice Axiom, and does not imply it. However, Section 4 shows that a Thurstone model $\mathscr{T}_F$ guarantees this sort of invariance only when F is a double exponential distribution (Theorem 6). Thus within the framework of Thurstone's basic discriminal process idea, invariance under uniform expansions of the choice set is an axiomatic filter that singles out the double exponential distribution, which in turn implies the Choice Axiom. It is natural to wonder whether, if Thurstone had thought along these lines, he would still have settled on the normal distribution, or whether the prominent role played by that distribution in the history of psychometrics might not have fallen instead to the double exponential.

Outline of the Balance of the Paper

Section 2 deals with preliminary matters: Sections 2.1 and 2.2 introduce the notation for choice probabilities and systems of such probabilities; Section 2.3 explicates the notion of equivalence between choice models (that is, theories); Sections 2.4 and 2.5 review Luce's Choice Axiom and Thurstone's Theory of Comparative Judgment; Section 2.6 defines the general class of Thurstone models and discusses three cases of special interest: the normal (Case V) model, the double exponential model (earlier work on the relationship between this model and the Choice Axiom is reviewed here), and the exponential model (which turns out to be equivalent to Dawkin's (1969) Threshold Model, but only for pair comparisons). Then Section 3 deals with the uniqueness problem: Section 3.1 provides an overview of the results; Section 3.2 considers the special case of pair comparisons, with particular emphasis on the three specific models just mentioned; Section 3.3 considers the case of complete experiments with choice sets of arbitrary size, and Section 3.4 deals with triple comparisons—this section contains the final solution for the special problem of the Choice Axiom. Section 4 defines the idea of "invariance under uniform expansions of the choice set" and, by appealing back to an earlier result, shows how this principle implies the double exponential distribution. Finally, Section 5 comments briefly on an "irreversibility" theorem proved by Luce in his 1959 monograph, and also outlines the relationship between Thurstone models and the more general class of "independent random utility models" defined by Luce and Suppes (1965). New results of central interest are called theorems; old results and those that are only preparatory are called lemmas. To make the paper self-contained, explicit proofs are given for every important step in the mathematical development, even though in a few places this has meant re-proving results already available in the literature.

2. Notation, Definitions, Conventions

2.1. *Basic Notation*

Suppose $o_1, o_2, \ldots, o_n$ is a set of n *choice objects* (e.g., n tones, to be compared for loudness), and that on each trial of an experiment the subject is presented with a subset of these objects and required to choose one (e.g., "which tone seems loudest?"). In a *pair-comparison experiment* only subsets containing exactly two objects are presented, and here p_{ij} *denotes the probability that* o_i *is chosen when* $\{o_i, o_j\}$ *is presented.* In the general case, when the subsets are not always pairs, we identify each subset of objects with the set of integers that are the indices of these objects, and then $p_S(i)$ *denotes the probability that* o_i *is chosen when* $\{o_j \mid j \in S\}$ *is presented.* C_n denotes the total set of indices of the n choice objects, i.e., $C_n = \{1, 2, \ldots, n\}$. Thus, p_{ij} is shorthand for $p_{\{i,j\}}(i)$; $p_{C_n}(i) = p_{\{1,2,\ldots,n\}}(i)$; the probability of choosing o_i from the set $\{o_i, o_j, o_k\}$ is $p_{\{i,j,k\}}(i)$, etc.

An experiment that determines the probability $p_S(i)$ for every i in every subset S ($S \subseteq C_n$, $|S| \geqslant 2$) will be called a *complete choice experiment with n objects.*

2.2. *Systems of Choice Probabilities*

A pair-comparison experiment with n objects results in $\binom{n}{2}$ binary probability distributions, each of the form $\{p_{ij}, p_{ji}\}$. The entire set $\{\{p_{ij}, p_{ji}\} \mid i, j \in C_n, i < j\}$ will be called a *system of pair-comparison probabilities for n objects,* and be denoted by $\{p_{ij}/C_n\}$.

The result of a *complete* choice experiment with n objects is a set of the form

$$\{\{p_S(i) \mid i \in S\} \mid S \subseteq C_n, |S| \geqslant 2\},$$

containing $2^n - (n + 1)$ discrete probability distributions; one for each subset of two or more objects. A set of this form will be called a *complete system of choice probabilities for n objects,* and be denoted by $\{p_S/C_n\}$.

Convention: *Choice probabilities can never be zero or one.* The Thurstone models considered below all imply that no choice probability can ever be zero or one. To save repetition, we stipulate at the outset that every system $\{p_S\}$ or $\{p_{ij}\}$ mentioned later contains only probabilities in the open interval (0, 1).

Convention on terminology: *"Model" used in the sense of "theory."* Some writers use "model" to mean a numerical structure that satisfies a "theory" (e.g., Luce & Suppes, 1965): They would say, for example, that a system $\{p_S/C_n\}$ which satisfies the Choice Axiom is a "model of the Choice Axiom." Here model has the same logical status as theory, as in "the Case V model is a special case of Thurstone's Theory of Comparative Judgment."

2.3. *Equivalence between Choice Theories*

Intuitively, two choice theories are *equivalent* (that is, indistinguishable) for a certain kind of experiment if no potential result of such an experiment could allow us to reject one theory in favor of the other. To formalize this idea in the standard way (Burke & Zinnes, 1965; Luce & Suppes, 1965), let R_n denote the set of all possible complete systems of choice probabilities $\{p_S/C_n\}$, and $R^* = \bigcup_2^\infty R_n$. Then R_n is the set of all possible results of a complete choice experiment with n objects, and R is the set of all possible results of complete experiments of any size. A *theory of complete choice experiments* (e.g., Luce's Choice Axiom; any of the Thurstone models defined in Section 2.6) can be thought of as partitioning every R_n into two disjoint subsets: A set of *admissible* systems (those that satisfy the theory) and a set of *inadmissible* systems (those that do not). (In line with this way of thinking, theories will be defined here by specifying the systems they admit.) If two theories partition R_n in exactly the same way, then no complete choice experiment with n objects can distinguish between them. In this case, the two theories will be called *completely equivalent for (choice experiments with) n objects.* If two theories are equivalent for n objects for every n (i.e., partition R^* in exactly the same way), then no complete choice experiment can distinguish between them. In this case the theories will simply be called *completely equivalent.*

It is also useful to define a restricted type of equivalence that reflects only the pair-comparison predictions of two theories. Let B_n denote the set of all possible pair-comparison systems $\{p_{ij}/C_n\}$. Two theories will be called *equivalent for pair-comparison experiments with n objects* if they admit exactly the same systems in B_n. If this is true for every n, the two theories are *equivalent for pair comparisons.*

Relationships between different types of equivalence. Every complete system $\{p_S/C_n\}$ contains a pair comparison system $\{p_{ij}/C_n\}$, and for the theories considered here, a given pair-comparison system is admissible iff it is contained in some admissible complete system. Thus by definition *complete equivalence for n objects implies pair-comparison equivalence for n objects, and complete equivalence implies pair-comparison equivalence.* By the same token, *complete equivalence for n objects implies complete equivalence for* $n - 1$.

The converses of these statements, however, are not logically implied. In particular, pair-comparison equivalence does not imply complete equivalence: The Choice Axiom, for example, is equivalent to several different Thurstone models for pair comparisons (Section 3.2), but it turns out to be completely equivalent to only one—the model with double exponential discriminal processes (Section 3.3 and 3.4). In general, for the class of Thurstone models defined in Section 2.6, pair-comparison equivalence does not imply complete equivalence, except in one special case (Section 3.2). Nor does complete equivalence for $n-1$ objects imply complete equivalence for n. However, it will be shown that for an important subset of Thurstone models, complete equivalence for three objects implies that both models have the same type of discriminal process distribution, and consequently are completely equivalent (Section 3.4).

The next two sections review the Choice Axiom and Thurstone's Theory of Comparative Judgment. Then Section 2.6 defines a general class of "Thurstone models"—models like Thurstone's original Case V except that their discriminal processes need not be normal.

2.4. *Luce's Choice Axiom*

DEFINITION 1. A complete system of choice probabilities $\{p_S/C_n\}$ satisfies the *Choice Axiom* (Axiom 1 in Luce, 1959) iff, for every i and S, $i \in S \subseteq C_n$:

$$p_S(i) = p_{C_n}(i) \Big/ \sum_{j \in S} p_{C_n}(j). \tag{1}$$

The following fundamental result is proved in Luce, 1959:

LEMMA 1. *A complete system $\{p_S/C_n\}$ satisfies the Choice Axiom iff there exists a set of numbers $v_1, v_2, \ldots, v_n$ ("v scale values") such that*

$$p_S(i) = v_i \Big/ \sum_{j \in S} v_j \tag{2}$$

for every i, S; $i \in S \subseteq C_n$. The scale values $v_1, \ldots, v_n$ are uniquely determined by the system $\{p_S/C_n\}$ up to multiplication by a constant.

Equation (2) implies that the pair-comparison probabilities of any complete system satisfy the following relationship:

LEMMA 2. *For every $i, j, k \in C_n$*

$$p_{ik} = p_{ij}p_{jk}/(p_{ij}p_{jk} + p_{ji}p_{kj}). \tag{3}$$

Proof. Equation (3) follows directly from the fact that

$$p_{ik}/p_{ki} = (p_{ij}/p_{ji})(p_{jk}/p_{kj}),$$

which follows in turn from the relationship $v_i/v_k = (v_i/v_j)(v_j/v_k)$. ∎

2.5. *Thurstone's Theory of Comparative Judgment*

This theory (Thurstone, 1927) is based on the idea that choice objects $o_1, o_2, \ldots, o_n$ are represented in an underlying psychological space by real valued random variables $\mathbf{D}_1, \mathbf{D}_2, \ldots, \mathbf{D}_n$ called *discriminal processes*. When o_i and o_j are presented the subject picks o_i iff $\mathbf{D}_i > \mathbf{D}_j$, so that $p_{ij} = P[\mathbf{D}_i > \mathbf{D}_j] = P[\mathbf{D}_j - \mathbf{D}_i < 0]$. To generate testable predictions, Thurstone arbitrarily (but not thoughtlessly) assumed that the discriminal processes were normal random variables, and considered five special cases corresponding to increasingly severe constraints on their variances and covariances. Of these, only Case V is directly comparable to the Choice Axiom—the others have too many free parameters. In Case V, the discriminal processes are assumed to have identical variances ($\operatorname{Var} \mathbf{D}_i \equiv \sigma^2$) and a common covariance ($\operatorname{Cov}(\mathbf{D}_i, \mathbf{D}_j) \equiv r\sigma^2$), so that their marginal distributions differ only in their locations along the axis. Then $\mathbf{D}_i - \mathbf{D}_j$ has a normal distribution with mean $E(\mathbf{D}_i) - E(\mathbf{D}_j)$ and variance $2\sigma^2(1 - r)$. To capture the idea that the discriminal process $\mathbf{D}_i$ of an object o_i represents a "true" scale value that is perturbed by random noise, it is natural to express $\mathbf{D}_i$ in the form $u_i + \mathbf{X}_i$, where u_i is a real number (the Thurstone scale value of o_i) and $\mathbf{X}_i$ is a normal random variable, with $E(\mathbf{X}_i) \equiv \mu$, $\operatorname{Var}(\mathbf{X}_i) \equiv \sigma^2$, $\operatorname{Cov}(\mathbf{X}_i, \mathbf{X}_j) \equiv r\sigma^2$. Then the pair comparison probability p_{ij} is the probability that $u_i + \mathbf{X}_i$ is greater than $u_j + \mathbf{X}_j$, and consequently it can be expressed as

$$p_{ij} = N[(u_i - u_j)/\sigma(2 - 2r)^{1/2}], \tag{4}$$

where N is the normal distribution function

$$N(x) = \int_{-\infty}^{x} (1/(2\pi)^{1/2})\, e^{-(1/2)t^2}\, dt.$$

Equation (4) is Case V of Thurstone's *Law of Comparative Judgment* for pair comparisons. Its testable consequences are entirely captured by the following well-known relationship:

LEMMA 3. *If a system of pair-comparison probabilities* $\{p_{ij}/C_n\}$ *satisfies* (4), *then for every* $i, j, k \in C_n$

$$p_{ik} = N[N^{-1}(p_{ij}) + N^{-1}(p_{jk})]. \tag{5}$$

Proof. (5) follows directly from (4). ∎

Equation (5) is analogous to Eq. (3). Thus for both the Choice Axiom and Case V of Thurstone's law, there is a *triples function* $t(p, p')$ from $(0, 1) \otimes (0, 1) \to (0, 1)$ such that for any p_{ij}, p_{jk}, p_{ik}, $p_{ik} = t(p_{ij}, p_{jk})$. It turns out (Section 3.2) that all of the generalized Thurstone models defined in Section 2.6 also imply triples functions—of the same form as (5), but with N not necessarily a normal distribution function. These functions play a central role in determining whether two models are equivalent for pair comparisons, because the triples function of a model completely determines the pair-comparison systems admitted by that model, and consequently two models can be equivalent for pair comparisons iff they imply the same triples function. (This is shown explicitly in the proof of Theorem 2, Section 3.2.)

Thurstone developed his Case V model explicitly only for the case of pair-comparison experiments, but the following generalization to complete experiments is straightforward:

DEFINITION 2. A complete system of choice probabilities $\{p_S/C_n\}$ satisfies the *Case V* model $T(\mu, \sigma^2, r)$ iff there exist numbers (*scale values*) $u_1, u_2, \ldots, u_n$ such that for every i and S, $i \in S \subseteq C_n$,

$$p_S(i) = P[u_i + \mathbf{X}_i = \text{Max}\{u_j + \mathbf{X}_j \mid j \in S\}], \tag{6}$$

where $\mathbf{X}_1, \mathbf{X}_2, \ldots, \mathbf{X}_n$ are normally distributed random variables with common mean μ, common variance σ^2, and $\text{Cov}(\mathbf{X}_i, \mathbf{X}_j) \equiv r\sigma^2$ for all i and j, $i \neq j$. The random variable $u_i + \mathbf{X}_i$ is the *discriminal process* associated with object o_i.

Definition 2 is stated in such a way that to every triple (μ, σ^2, r) there corresponds a distinct Case V model. However, it is well known that in the case of pair comparisons, the parameters μ, σ^2, and r cannot be identified. That is, if a pair-comparison system satisfies any $T(\mu, \sigma^2, r)$, then it satisfies all of them, and in particular it satisfies the model $T(0, 1, 0)$ in which the $\mathbf{X}_i$ have mean zero, variance 1, and are independent. The same is true of the generalization to complete experiments represented by Definition 2, as the following Lemma shows.

LEMMA 4. *Every Case* V *model* $T(\mu, \sigma^2, r)$ *is completely equivalent to the model* $T(0, 1, 0)$.

Proof. Suppose $\{p_S/C_n\}$ is a complete system of choice probabilities admitted by $T(\mu, \sigma^2, r)$, with scale values $u_1, u_2, \ldots, u_n$. To show that this system is also admitted by $T(0, 1, 0)$, observe that if $\{u_i + \mathbf{X}_i \mid i = 1, \ldots, n\}$ are the discriminal processes of $T(\mu, \sigma^2, r)$, their joint moment generating function $m(\theta_1, \ldots, \theta_n) = E[\exp(\sum \theta_i(u_i + \mathbf{X}_i))]$ is

$$\exp\left[\sum_{i=1}^{n} \theta_i(u_i + \mu) + \tfrac{1}{2}\sigma^2 \sum_{i=1}^{n} \theta_i^2 + r\sigma^2 \sum_{i \neq j} \theta_i\theta_j\right].$$

However, a straightforward calculation shows that this is also the joint m.g.f. of a set of n normal random variables of the form $\mathbf{X}_i' = u_i + \mu + \mathbf{X}_i^* + \mathbf{Y}$, where X_1^*, $X_2^*, \ldots, \mathbf{X}_n^*$ are n independent identically distributed (i.i.d.) normal R.V.'s with mean zero, variance $\sigma^2(1 - r)$, and $\mathbf{Y}$ is another normal random variable, independent of all the others, with mean zero, and variance $r\sigma^2$. Consequently for any $p_S(i)$ in $\{p_S/C_n\}$

$$\begin{aligned} p_S(i) &= P[u_i + \mathbf{X}_i = \text{Max}\{u_j + \mathbf{X}_j \mid j \in S\}] \\ &= P[u_i + \mu + \mathbf{X}_i^* + \mathbf{Y} = \text{Max}\{u_j + \mu + \mathbf{X}_j^* + \mathbf{Y} \mid j \in S\}] \\ &= P[u_i + \mathbf{X}^* = \text{Max}\{u_j + \mathbf{X}_j^* \mid j \in S\}] \\ &= P[(u_i/c) + (\mathbf{X}_i^*/c) = \text{Max}\{(u_j/c) + (\mathbf{X}_j^*/c) \mid j \in S\}]. \end{aligned}$$

where $c = (\sigma^2(1 - r))^{1/2}$. The random variables $\mathbf{X}_1^*/c, \mathbf{X}_2^*/c, \ldots, \mathbf{X}_n^*/c$ are normal, i.i.d., and have mean zero and variance one. Consequently if $\{p_S/C_n\}$ is admitted by $T(\mu, \sigma^2, r)$ with scale values $u_1, u_2, \ldots, u_n$, it is also admitted by $T(0, 1, 0)$ with scale values $u_1/(\sigma^2(1-r))^{1/2},\ldots, u_n/(\sigma^2(1-r))^{1/2}$. The converse is proved by working backward along the same route. ∎

Remark on nonidentifiable correlations. The proof of the last lemma shows explicitly why correlated and independent discriminal processes in a Case V model yield the same results: If $\{u_i + \mathbf{X}_i \mid i = 1,\ldots, n\}$ is a set of jointly distributed normal discriminal processes with common variances and a common nonzero covariance, then there is another set $\{u_i + \mathbf{X}_i^* + \mathbf{Y} \mid i = 1,\ldots, n\}$, with $\{\mathbf{X}_i^*\}$ i.i.d., and $\mathbf{Y}$ independent of the $\{\mathbf{X}_i^*\}$, which have the same joint distribution and consequently yield the same predictions. In this equivalent set of processes the correlation between the original $\mathbf{X}_i$ is represented entirely by the extra random variable $\mathbf{Y}$. Because this random variable has no effect on the probability of an inequality of the form $u_i + \mathbf{X}_i^* + \mathbf{Y} > u_j + \mathbf{X}_j^* + \mathbf{Y}$, its distribution has no effect on choice probabilities based on such inequalities, and in particular we can assume that $\mathbf{Y}$ is a degenerate R.V. equal to zero. In fact, we could assume that $\mathbf{Y}$ has a nonnormal distribution and the resulting model (in which the discriminal processes would no longer be normal or independent) would yield the same results, since

$$p_S(i) = P[u_i + \mathbf{X}_i^* + \mathbf{Y} = \operatorname{Max}\{u_j + \mathbf{X}_j^* + \mathbf{Y} \mid j \in S\}]$$

is independent of the distribution of $\mathbf{Y}$. This shows that if we start with a Case V model with independent normal discriminal processes, we can then construct an infinite number of distinct models with correlated nonnormal discriminal processes, all of which will yield the same predictions as the original.

The same argument applies also in the general case developed in the next section, and so it can be seen that in general, if the discriminal processes are not assumed to be independent, there is no hope of identifying their distribution from their predictions for choice experiments.

2.6. *Generalization: Thurstone Models with Independent Discriminal Processes*

The essential features of Case V of Thurstone's Theory of Comparative Judgment are (1) the idea that choice objects $o_1, o_2,\ldots, o_n$ are represented on an underlying psychological continuum by random variables $u_1 + \mathbf{X}_1,\ldots, u_n + \mathbf{X}_n$, with

$$p_S(i) = P[u_i + \mathbf{X}_i = \operatorname{Max}\{u_j + \mathbf{X}_j \mid j \in S\}];$$

(2) the $\mathbf{X}_i$ are independent and identically distributed, so that the discriminal processes $\{u_i + \mathbf{X}_i\}$ are themselves independent and identically distributed except for shifts along the axis; (3) the (cumulative) distribution function of the difference $\mathbf{X}_j - \mathbf{X}_i$ is continuous and strictly increasing, so that $p_{ij} = P[\mathbf{X}_j - \mathbf{X}_i \leqslant u_i - u_j]$ is a continuous and strictly increasing function of the scale value difference $u_i - u_j$.

A general class of models that share these properties without presupposing normal distributions can be defined as follows.

Notation. If F is a distribution function, its *difference distribution* D_F is the distribution function

$$D_F(x) = \int_{-\infty}^{\infty} F(x + y)\, dF(y).$$

(Thus if $\mathbf{X}_1$, $\mathbf{X}_2$ are i.i.d. with common distribution function F, D_F is the distribution function of $\mathbf{X}_1 - \mathbf{X}_2$.)

DEFINITION 3. Suppose F is a distribution for which D_F is continuous and strictly increasing over $(-\infty, \infty)$. A complete system of choice probabilities $\{p_S/C_n\}$ satisfies the ***Thurstone model*** $\mathcal{T}_F$ if and only if there exist numbers $u_1, u_2, \ldots, u_n$ (*scale values*) such that for every $i \in S \subseteq C_n$

$$p_S(i) = P[u_i + \mathbf{X}_i = \mathrm{Max}\{u_j + \mathbf{X}_j \mid j \in S\}]$$

where $\mathbf{X}_1, \mathbf{X}_2, \ldots, \mathbf{X}_n$ are n independent random variables with F as their common distribution function (i.e., $P(\mathbf{X}_i \leqslant x) = F(x)$).[2]

In other words: A given Thurstone model $\mathcal{T}_F$ can be thought of as a specific collection of complete systems of choice probabilities, all those that can be generated by the distribution function F together with every possible set of scale values $u_1, u_2, \ldots$. F here is regarded as completely specified: It has no free parameters of its own. Thus, the model corresponding to the normal distribution with mean zero and variance 1 is conceptually distinct from the model corresponding to the normal distribution with mean 1 and variance 2. Lemma 4 showed that in the case of normal distributions this distinction is artificial, and as might be expected the same is true for any other type of distribution. Theorem 1 in Section 3.1 makes this explicit: Models with distributions of the same type are completely equivalent. Consequently there is usually no harm in talking about, e.g., "the normal model," without specifying precisely which normal distribution we have in mind. Still, it is necessary to have some convention in this regard to keep things logically straight, and the one adopted here has at least the advantage of not taking anything for granted.

For pair-comparison experiments the difference distribution D_F plays a central role, because

$$p_{ij} = P[u_i + \mathbf{X}_i > u_j + \mathbf{X}_j] = D_F(u_i - u_j).$$

The assumption that D_F is continuous and strictly increasing over the whole line guarantees the third essential Thurstone condition, i.e., that p_{ij} be a continuous strictly increasing function of $u_i - u_j$. Note that the scale values of a Thurstone model are uniquely determined by a system $\{p_S/C_n\}$ up to addition of a constant (i.e., if $\mathcal{T}_F$ generates

[2] It should perhaps be emphasized that the class of "Thurstone models" defined here represents a generalization only of Thurstone's Case V, and consequently the theorems proved below for this class need not apply to generalized version of his other cases.

$\{p_S/C_n\}$ with scale values $\{u_i\}$, scale values of the form $\{a + u_i\}$ will work also—but no others, since $u_i - u_j = D_F^{-1}(p_{ij})$).

Definition 3 excludes discriminal process distributions concentrated on finite intervals. Models of that sort are intriguing, because they admit the possibility that choice probabilities can be zero and one, but they are awkward to deal with for the same reason. We can afford to exclude them here without loss of generality, because—for reasons spelled out in Section 4—none of them can be equivalent to the Choice Axiom.

Of the following three examples, only (c) requires special motivation. It is included partly because of its uniqueness properties, which are similar to those of (b), the case of central interest, but easier to demonstrate explicitly. Example (c) also shows that the Choice Axiom is not the only theory of choice behavior that inadvertently turns out to be equivalent to a Thurstone model. However, in (c), this equivalence only extends to pair comparisons.

Examples of Thurstone Models (*Fig.* 1)

(a) *The Normal Model* (Thurstone's Case V). If F is the normal distribution with mean u, and variance σ^2, $\mathscr{T}_F$ is the Case V model $T(\mu, \sigma^2, 0)$ of Definition 2. Here D_F is again normal, with mean zero and variance $2\sigma^2$.

(b) *The Double Exponential Model* (*Luce's Choice Axiom*). If $\mathbf{Y}$ is an exponential random variable with density e^{-y}, the random variable $\mathbf{X} = -\log \mathbf{Y}$ has distribution function

$$P(\mathbf{X} \leqslant x) = F(x) = e^{-e^{-x}} \qquad (-\infty < x < \infty). \tag{6}$$

Equation (6) is the ***double exponential*** distribution function, with mean γ (where γ is Euler's constant 0.5772,...) and variance $\pi^2/6$. (The mean can be derived from formulas found in most handbooks of integrals. The variance takes more work, but it can be obtained using a formula for the derivatives of the γ function given by Whittaker and Watson (1963, p. 241).) This distribution is famous in statistics, because it is one of three possible distributions for the limit (as $n \to \infty$) of the maximum $\mathbf{Z}_n{}^*$ of n i.i.d. random variables $\mathbf{Z}_1, \ldots, \mathbf{Z}_n$. Of course if the $\mathbf{Z}_i$ are not bounded from above, $\mathbf{Z}_n{}^* \to \infty$ with probability 1, but in many cases sequences of normalizing constants $\{a_n\}$, $\{b_n\}$, can be found such that the distribution of $a_n\mathbf{Z}_n{}^* - b_n$ converges to a nondegenerate limit. If this is true when $a_n \equiv 1$ (i.e., if $\mathbf{Z}_n{}^* - b_n$ has a limit distribution), then that distribution must be of the double exponential type. (Gumbel (1958) discusses all this very throughly.) This fact is used in Section 4 to derive the Choice Axiom from a weaker assumption about choice probabilities in experiments with "redundant" objects.

The difference distribution corresponding to (6) is quickly found to be the logistic distribution

$$D_F(x) = (1 + e^{-x})^{-1}. \tag{7}$$

Relationship to the Choice Axiom. Adams and Messick (1957) showed that a Thurstone

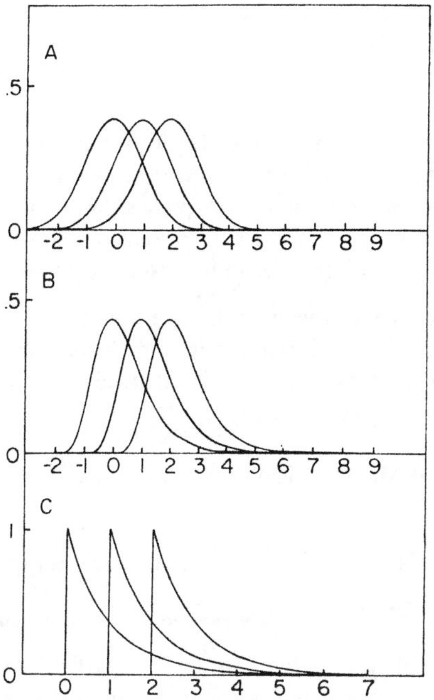

FIG. 1. Discriminal process distributions (shown as probability density functions) for three different Thurstone models. Each panel depicts the density functions $f(x)$ for three discriminal process random variables of the form $u_i + \mathbf{X}_i$, with $u_1 = 0$, $u_2 = 1$, $u_3 = 2$ in each case. Every distribution has variance 1. (A) The Normal (Case V) Model: $f(x) = (2\pi)^{-1/2} \exp[-\frac{1}{2}(x - u_i)^2]$. (B) The Double Exponential (Choice Axiom) Model: $f(x) = a \exp[-a(x - u_i)] \exp[-\exp[-a(x - u_i)]]$, $a = \pi/6^{1/2}$. (The means are $u_i + \gamma a^{-1}$, $\gamma =$ Euler's constant.) (C) The exponential model: $f(x) = \exp[-(x - u_i)]$. (The means are 1, 2, 3.)

model is equivalent to the Choice Axiom for pair comparisons if and only if its difference distribution is logistic (any logistic with mean zero, not just (7)):

LEMMA 5 (Adams and Messick's theorem). *A Thurstone model $\mathcal{T}_F$ is equivalent to the Choice Axiom for pair-comparison experiments iff $D_F(x) = (1 + e^{-ax})^{-1}$, with $a > 0$.*

Proof. One method (the original) is to show by a functional equation argument that only the logistic implies the triples function (3). Here we can take a shorter route. Suppose $D_G(x)$ is $(1 + e^{-x})^{-1}$, and $\mathcal{T}_G$ admits $\{p_{ij}/C_n\}$. Then

$$\begin{aligned} p_{ij} &= P[u_i + \mathbf{X}_i > u_j + \mathbf{X}_j] \\ &= D_G(u_i - u_j) \\ &= (1 + e^{-(u_i - u_j)})^{-1}. \end{aligned}$$

Setting $u_i = \log v_i$, the last line becomes

$$p_{ij} = v_i/(v_i + v_j).$$

Consequently (via Lemma 1), the system $\{p_{ij}/C_n\}$ satisfies the Choice Axiom. Conversely, if $\{p_{ij}/C_n\}$ satisfies the Choice Axiom, with scale values $v_1, ..., v_n$, then it satisfies $\mathcal{T}_G$ with $u_i = \log v_i$. Then to establish uniqueness, we appeal to Theorem 2 below, which shows that in general, two Thurstone models $\mathcal{T}_F$ and $\mathcal{T}_G$ can be equivalent for pair comparisons iff $D_F(x) = D_G(ax)$ for some positive constant a. ∎

In view of (7) and Lemma 5, it is clear that the double exponential Thurstone model (6) is equivalent to the Choice Axiom for pair comparisons. Holman and Marley (cited in Luce and Suppes, 1965) showed that this is also true for complete choice experiments for any model of the double exponential type:

LEMMA 6 (Holman and Marley's theorem). *If F is a distribution function of the double exponential type*

$$F(x) = e^{-e^{-(ax+b)}} \qquad (a > 0,\ b \text{ arbitrary})$$

then the Thurstone model $\mathcal{T}_F$ is completely equivalent to the Choice Axiom.

Proof. It is sufficient to prove this only for the particular case $a = 1$, $b = 0$, and then appeal to Theorem 1 below, which shows that two models $\mathcal{T}_F$ and $\mathcal{T}_G$ with distributions of the same type (i.e., $F(x) = G(ax + b)$) are always completely equivalent. Suppose then that a complete system $\{p_S/C_n\}$ is admitted by $\mathcal{T}_G$ $(G(x) = e^{-e^{-x}})$ with scale values $u_1, ..., u_n$. Set $u_i = \log v_i$, and $\mathbf{X}_i = -\log \mathbf{Y}_i$. Then $\mathbf{Y}_i$ has the exponential distribution function $1 - e^{-y}$, and

$$\begin{aligned}
p_S(i) &= P[u_i + \mathbf{X}_i = \text{Max}\{u_j + \mathbf{X}_j \mid j \in S\}] \\
&= P[v_i/\mathbf{Y}_i = \text{Max}\{v_j/\mathbf{Y}_j \mid j \in S\}] \\
&= P[\mathbf{Y}_i/v_i = \text{Min}\{\mathbf{Y}_j/v_j \mid j \in S\}] \\
&= \int_0^\infty v_i e^{-v_i y} \Big(\prod_{j \in S-i} e^{-v_j y} \Big)\, dy \\
&= v_i \Big/ \sum_{j \in S} v_j .
\end{aligned}$$

Consequently $\{p_S/C_n\}$ also satisfies the Choice Axiom, with v scale values $v_i = e^{u_i}$. The converse is immediate. ∎

Notice that Lemma 6 does not say that the double exponential is the *only* Thurstone model that is completely equivalent to the Choice Axiom. In citing Holman and Marley's result, Luce and Suppes (1965, p. 339) mentioned that the uniqueness question was open. At that time all that was known by way of uniqueness was Adams and Messick's theorem, which shows that any other model that is completely equivalent to the Choice

Axiom must, like the double exponential, have the logistic as its difference distribution. That property, however, does not uniquely characterize the double exponential distribution, for reasons elaborated in Section 3.2. Subsequently, both the author (1971) and McFadden (1974) have independently given proofs (along quite similar lines) that a Thurstone model $\mathscr{T}_F$ can be completely equivalent to the Choice Axiom only if F is a double exponential distribution. Both proofs depend on extra assumptions about F: Mine assumed that F has a density f, with $\lim_{x \to \infty} xf(\log x) \neq 0$;[3] McFadden's assumed that F is translation complete (e.g., has a nonvanishing characteristic function). Theorem 3 below has as a consequence the somewhat better result that without any additional assumptions (beyond those of Definition 3) $\mathscr{T}_F$ is equivalent to the Choice Axiom if and only if F is double exponential. This result, however, is still weak; the strongest one possible is proved in Section 3.4 (Theorem 5).

(c) *The Exponential Model (Dawkins' Threshold Model).* If $F(x)$ is the exponential distribution $1 - e^{-x}$, then D_F is the Laplace distribution

$$D_F(x) = \int_{-\infty}^{x} \tfrac{1}{2} e^{-|y|}\, dy.$$

This model turns out to be equivalent, for pair comparisons, to the *Threshold Model* proposed by Dawkins (1969). That model assumes the existence of a set of "thresholds" $t_1, t_2, \ldots, t_n$, corresponding to the choice objects $o_1, o_2, \ldots, o_n$: The more preferred the object, the lower its threshold—if $t_1 < t_2 < \cdots < t_n$, then o_1 is most preferred, o_n least. $\mathbf{V}$ denotes an "excitation" random variable, with $P(\mathbf{V} \leqslant v) = H(v)$. (We assume $0 < H(v) < 1$ and strictly increasing for all v. H turns out to be unidentifiable.) When a pair o_i, o_j is presented, with $t_i \leqslant t_j$, the subjects' choice depends on where $\mathbf{V}$ is relative to these thresholds: If $\mathbf{V} < t_i \leqslant t_j$, the subject makes no choice, and instead draws another sample of $\mathbf{V}$. If $t_i < \mathbf{V} \leqslant t_j$, he chooses o_i. If $t_i \leqslant t_j < \mathbf{V}$, he picks either o_i or o_j, each with probability .5. Dawkins (1969) showed that the triples function for this model (analogous to (3) and (5)) is given by

$$p_{ik} = 1 - 2p_{kj}p_{ji} \tag{8}$$

in the case $p_{ij} \geqslant 0.5$, $p_{jk} \geqslant 0.5$. The remaining cases can be derived from this expression. (Since the subject might not choose either object—if $\mathbf{V}$ falls below both thresholds—it is necessary to redefine p_{ij} here to mean the probability that i is chosen when $\{o_i, o_j\}$ is presented and the subject actually chooses an object.)

Any Thurstone model with the Laplace distribution as its difference distribution will also imply this same triples function, and consequently be equivalent to Dawkins' model for pair-comparison experiments. The following lemma also shows that this representation is unique: The Laplace stands in the same relationship to Dawkins' model that the logistic does to the Choice Axiom.

[3] This condition makes somewhat more sense in the context $F(x) = P(\mathbf{X} \leqslant x)$; $\mathbf{Y} = e^{-\mathbf{X}}$: Then it implies that the density of $\mathbf{Y}$ is positive at the origin.

LEMMA 7. *A Thurstone model $\mathcal{T}_F$ is equivalent to Dawkins' Threshold model for pair comparisons if and only if its difference distribution D_F is a Laplace distribution:*

$$D_F(x) = \tfrac{1}{2}e^{ax}, \qquad x \leqslant 0, \\ = 1 - \tfrac{1}{2}e^{-ax}, \qquad x > 0. \tag{9}$$

Proof. Here again we need only show that (9) implies the triples function (8), and then Theorem 2 below establishes uniqueness. Assuming p_{ij} and p_{jk} both $\geqslant 0.5$, $u_i - u_j$ and $u_j - u_k$ are both nonnegative, and

$$\begin{aligned} p_{ik} &= D_F(u_i - u_j + u_j - u_k) \\ &= 1 - \tfrac{1}{2}e^{-a(u_i-u_j)}e^{-a(u_j-u_k)} \\ &= 1 - 2(\tfrac{1}{2}e^{a(u_j-u_i})(\tfrac{1}{2}e^{a(u_k-u_j)}) \\ &= 1 - 2p_{ji}p_{kj}. \quad \blacksquare \end{aligned}$$

Surprisingly, this equivalence breaks down as soon as we consider complete experiments. In fact, for complete experiments with three objects, Dawkins' Threshold model is not equivalent to any Thurstone model. To see why, suppose o_1 is preferred to o_2 is preferred to o_3, so that in the Threshold model $t_1 < t_2 < t_3$, and in any corresponding Thurstone model $u_1 > u_2 > u_3$. In this case the Threshold model implies that the following relationship holds regardless of where t_2 is located in the interval (t_1, t_3):

$$p_{\{1,2,3\}}(3) = \tfrac{1}{3}(1 - H(t_3))/(1 - H(t_1)) = \tfrac{2}{3}p_{31}. \tag{10}$$

No Thurstone model can duplicate this prediction, because to do so would mean that the probability of the event

$$u_3 + \mathbf{X}_3 = \text{Max}\{u_i + \mathbf{X}_i \mid i = 1, 2, 3\}$$

depended only on the difference between u_1 and u_3, and not on the location of u_2 within the interval (u_3, u_1). For any Thurstone model, however, this probability clearly must always be a strictly decreasing function of u_2.

In his 1969 paper, Dawkins reports a great deal of pair comparison data which is all very well fit by either his model or the Choice Axiom or Thurstone's Case V (the predictions of all three models are nearly identical–not surprisingly, in view of the similarity of their difference distributions). Equation (10), however, seems much too strong to be generally true, and so it seems fair to attribute the success of Dawkins' model for pair-comparison experiments to the fact that in that special case it happens to be a Thurstone model.

3. Uniqueness Properties of Thurstone Models

3.1. *Preliminaries*

The general question here is whether two Thurstone models $\mathcal{T}_F$ and $\mathcal{T}_G$ can be equivalent even though F and G are different distributions. An overview of the results was given earlier in Section 1.2.1, and Fig. 2 shows a graphical summary. Theorem 1 disposes of the trivial case in which F and G are distributions of the same type (e.g., F and G are both double exponential distributions, differing only in their means and variances).

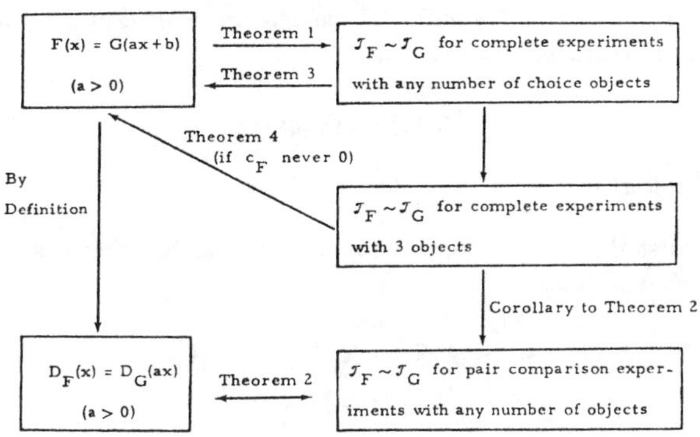

FIG. 2. Logical structure of the relationship between two discriminal process distributions F and G and various types of equivalence ($\sim$) between their corresponding Thurstone models $\mathcal{T}_F$ and $\mathcal{T}_G$. Arrows signify the direction of implication.

THEOREM 1. *If $\mathcal{T}_F$ and $\mathcal{T}_G$ are Thurstone models, and F and G are distributions of the same type (i.e., $F(x) = G(ax + b)$ for all x and some pair of constants a, b, with $a > 0$), then $\mathcal{T}_F$ is completely equivalent to $\mathcal{T}_G$.*

Proof. Suppose $\mathcal{T}_F$ admits the system $\{p_S/C_n\}$ with scale values $u_1, u_2, \ldots, u_n$, and that $p_S(i)$ is an arbitrary probability in that system. Then

$$\begin{aligned} p_S(i) &= P[u_i + \mathbf{X}_i = \text{Max}\{u_j + \mathbf{X}_j \mid j \in S\}] \\ &= P[au_i + a\mathbf{X}_i + b = \text{Max}\{au_j + a\mathbf{X}_j + b \mid j \in S\}] \\ &= P[au_i + \mathbf{X}_i{}^* = \text{Max}\{au_j + \mathbf{X}_j{}^* \mid j \in S\}] \end{aligned}$$

where

$$\begin{aligned} P[\mathbf{X}_j{}^* \leqslant x] &= P[a\mathbf{X}_j + b \leqslant x] \\ &= F[(x - b)/a] \\ &= G(x). \end{aligned}$$

Consequently $\{p_S/C_n\}$ is also admitted by $\mathcal{T}_G$, with scale values $au_1, au_2, \ldots, au_n$. ∎

In view of Theorem 1 it is unnecessary to maintain a strict distinction between Thurstone models whose discriminal process distributions belong to the same type: There is no ambiguity in talking about, e.g., "the double exponential model" without specifying exactly which double exponential distribution we mean, because all such models are completely equivalent.

3.2. *Implications of Pair-Comparison Equivalence*

The starting point is the following result:

THEOREM 2. *Two Thurstone models $\mathscr{T}_F$ and $\mathscr{T}_G$ are equivalent for pair comparisons if and only if their difference distributions satisfy*

$$D_F(x) = D_G(ax)$$

for some $a > 0$ and all x.

Proof. Note first that any model $\mathscr{T}_F$ implies a triples function analogous to Eq. 5 for the Case V Model. Since

$$\begin{aligned} p_{ij} &= P[\mathbf{X}_j - \mathbf{X}_i \leqslant u_i - u_j] \\ &= D_F(u_i - u_j), \end{aligned}$$

it follows that for any three pairwise probabilities p_{ij}, p_{jk}, p_{ik} in a pair-comparison system admitted by $\mathscr{T}_F$:

$$p_{ik} = D_F(D_F^{-1}(p_{ij}) + D_F^{-1}(p_{jk})). \tag{11}$$

Equation (11) is the *triples function* for $\mathscr{T}_F$.

Next, observe that the triples function (11) completely determines the set of pair-comparison systems admitted by $\mathscr{T}_F$: That set consists exactly of those systems in which (a) $p_{12}, p_{23}, \ldots, p_{n-1,n}$ are arbitrary probabilities; (b) p_{1i} is the probability obtained by applying the triples function t of $\mathscr{T}_F$ to this chain, i.e.,

$$\begin{aligned} p_{13} &= t(p_{12}, p_{23}), \\ p_{1i} &= t(p_{1,i-1}, p_{i-1,i}), \end{aligned}$$

and (c)

$$p_{ij} = t(p_{i1}, p_{1j}).$$

Consequently two models $\mathscr{T}_F$ and $\mathscr{T}_G$ are equivalent for pair comparisons iff they have the same triples function, i.e., iff for every p, p' in (0, 1)

$$D_F(D_F^{-1}(p) + D_F^{-1}(p')) = D_G(D_G^{-1}(p) + D_G^{-1}(p')). \tag{12}$$

To solve this functional equation, let $x = D_F^{-1}(p)$, $x' = D_F^{-1}(p')$. Then

$$D_G^{-1}D_F(x + x') = D_G^{-1}D_F(x) + D_G^{-1}D_F(x'),$$

so $D_G^{-1}D_F$ satisfies the Cauchy equation $f(x + x') = f(x) + f(x')$ for every x and x'. Since $D_G^{-1}D_F$ is continuous, the only solution is $D_G^{-1}D_F(x) = ax$, and so $D_F(x) = D_G(ax)$. The constant a must be positive because $a = D_G^{-1}D_F(1)$ and $D_F(1) > 0.5$ (since $D_F(0) = 0.5$, and D_F is strictly increasing by assumption), so that $D_G^{-1}D_F(1) > 0$. ▮

The following is included here for use later in Sections 3.3 and 3.4.

COROLLARY 1 (to Theorem 2). *If $\mathscr{T}_F$ and $\mathscr{T}_G$ are equivalent for complete experiments with three (or more) objects, then: (1) They are equivalent for pair-comparison experiments with any number of objects; and (2) if $\{p_S/C_n\}$ is a system admitted by both models, and the scale values for this system are $u_1, \ldots, u_n$ according to $\mathscr{T}_F$, and $u_1', \ldots, u_n'$ according to $\mathscr{T}_G$, then*

$$u_i' - u_j' = a(u_i - u_j) \tag{13}$$

where a is the positive constant for which $D_F(x) = D_G(ax)$.

Proof. (1) Complete equivalence for three objects implies pair-comparison equivalence for three objects, which implies that $\mathscr{T}_F$ and $\mathscr{T}_G$ have the same triples function. The proof of Theorem 2 shows that this implies pair-comparison equivalence for any number of objects. (2) Pair-comparison equivalence implies $D_F(x) = D_G(ax)$. If p_{ij} is in $\{p_S/C_n\}$, $p_{ij} = D_F(u_i - u_j) = D_G(u_i' - u_j')$. Then

$$\begin{aligned} D_G^{-1}(p_{ij}) &= u_i' - u_j' \\ &= D_G^{-1}D_F(u_i - u_j) \\ &= a(u_i - u_j). \end{aligned}$$ ▮

Now suppose that two models $\mathscr{T}_F$ and $\mathscr{T}_G$ are equivalent for pair comparisons, and that one of them has a known distribution—say, F is the double exponential distribution (6). What can we infer about G? From Theorem 2 we know that pair-comparison equivalence implies only that $D_F(x) = D_G(ax)$. Clearly one solution is $F(x) = G(ax + b)$, with $a > 0$: That corresponds to the case in which F is the distribution function of $\mathbf{X}$ and G is the distribution function of $a\mathbf{X} + b$ ($a > 0$), so that F and G are distributions of the same type. The other obvious solution is $F(x) = 1 - G(-ax + b)$ (again, $a > 0$): This corresponds to G being the distribution of $-a\mathbf{X} + b$. In this case G is a distribution of the same type as ${}^-F$, where

$${}^-F(x) = 1 - F(-x),$$

i.e., ${}^-F$ is the distribution function of $-\mathbf{X}$. (If F is not a symmetrical distribution, ${}^-F$ and F are not of the same type. For example, if F is a double exponential, hence not symmetrical, as can be seen from Fig. 1B, ${}^-F$ is not.)

If the only solutions to $D_F(x) = D_G(ax)$ were $F(x) = G(ax + b)$ and $F(x) =$

$1 - G(-ax + b)$, Adams and Messick's theorem (Lemma 5) would permit a simple solution to the uniqueness problem for the Choice Axiom, because we would know that $\mathscr{T}_G$ could be equivalent to the Choice Axiom only if G were either a double exponential distribution, or a distribution function of the same type as $1 - e^{-e^x}$. Then a quick calculation would show that the latter possibility does not yield the Choice Axiom for complete experiments, and so the problem would be solved.

However, things are not that simple, because in addition to the obvious solutions, which correspond to linear transformations of random variables, $D_F(x) = D_G(ax)$ also has other solutions, in which F and G are not related to one another in any readily interpretable way. These hidden possibilities emerge when things are considered from the standpoint of characteristic functions. Recall that if $\mathbf{X}$ has distribution function F, its characteristic function (c.f.) $c_F(t)$ is the complex valued function of a real variable t defined by $c_F(t) = E(e^{it\mathbf{X}})$: This function always exists; two distributions F and G are identical iff c_F and c_G are identical; the c.f. of $\alpha X + \beta$ is $e^{i\beta t}c_F(\alpha t)$; and the c.f. of a sum of independent random variables is the product of their individual c.f.'s (e.g., Feller, 1966, Chap. XV). Thus if X_1, X_2 are i.i.d. with distribution function F, their difference $X_1 - X_2$ has the c.f. $c_{D_F}(t) = c_F(t)\, c_F(-t)$.

In terms of characteristic functions, our original equation $D_F(x) = D_G(x)$ (where to simplify appearances we set $a = 1$, without loss of generality) takes the form

$$c_F(t)\, c_F(-t) = c_G(t)\, c_G(-t),$$

and the two obvious solutions are represented by

$$c_G(t) = e^{ibt}c_F(t) \qquad (F(x) = G(x + b)),$$

and

$$c_G(t) = e^{ibt}c_F(-t) \qquad (F(x) = 1 - G(-x + b)).$$

However, in general, these are not the only possible solutions: In the theory of characteristic functions there are many examples in which $c_F(t)\, c_F(-t) = c_G(t)\, c_G(-t)$ even though c_G is not either of the obvious solutions. (Lukacs, 1960, discusses the problem in detail.) In these cases the extra solutions G are not related to F in any probabilistically obvious way,[4] but they can nevertheless often be shown to be well-behaved distributions, with continuous densities and finite moments—distributions, in other words, that would yield plausible Thurstone models in their own right.

The Exponential Case

Suppose, for example, that F is the exponential distribution function $1 - e^{-x}$. Then $c_F(t) = (1 - it)^{-1}$, and $D_F(x)$ is the Laplace distribution, with c.f. $(1 + t^2)^{-1}$. But Lukacs (1960, p. 94) notes that the function

$$c_G(t) = \frac{(1 + it/v)(1 + it/\bar{v})}{(1 - it)(1 - it/v)(1 - it/\bar{v})}$$

[4] In fact these extra solutions are distributions whose Fourier components have the same amplitudes as those of F, but differ in phase.

(where $v = 1 + ir$, $\bar{v} = 1 - ir$, $r \geqslant 2(2^{1/2})$) is also a c.f. (of a continuous density) and it is easy to see that $c_G(t)\, c_G(-t) = (1 + t^2)^{-1} = c_F(t)\, c_F(-t)$ even though $c_G(t)$ is not of the form $e^{ibt}c_F(t)$ or $e^{ibt}c_F(-t)$. Thus $D_G(x) = D_F(x)$, even though G is not an exponential distribution, or the distribution of the negative of an exponential random variable.

This counterexample shows there is a Thurstone model $\mathcal{T}_G$ that is equivalent to the exponential model for pair comparisons even though neither G or ^{-}G is an exponential distribution. Consequently Dawkin's Threshold model is equivalent to both exponential and nonexponential Thurstone models for pair comparisons, and (as noted earlier) not equivalent to any Thurstone model for complete experiments with three or more objects.

The Double Exponential Case

If F is the double exponential distribution $F(x) = e^{-e^{-x}}$, $c_F(t) = \Gamma(1 - it)$ (where Γ is the gamma function), and so the difference distribution $D_F(x) = (1 + e^{-x})^{-1}$ has c.f. $\Gamma(1 - it)\, \Gamma(1 + it)$. However, an example due to Laha (1964) shows that this c.f. can also be factored into $c_G(t)\, c_G(-t)$, where neither factor is the c.f. of a double exponential distribution. Laha studied the general question: If $\mathbf{Y}_1$ and $\mathbf{Y}_2$ are i.i.d. and positive, and $\mathbf{Y}_1/(\mathbf{Y}_1 + \mathbf{Y}_2)$ has the β distribution, must $\mathbf{Y}_1$ and $\mathbf{Y}_2$ be γ distributed? The special case where $\mathbf{Y}_1$ and $\mathbf{Y}_2$ are exponential is relevant here. In this case $\mathbf{Y}_1/(\mathbf{Y}_1 + \mathbf{Y}_2)$ has the uniform distribution on (0, 1) (a special case of the β) which implies that $\log \mathbf{Y}_1 - \log \mathbf{Y}_2$ has the logistic distribution function (7). Thus if there exist positive nonexponential i.i.d. random variables $\mathbf{Y}_1$, $\mathbf{Y}_2$ such that $\mathbf{Y}_1/(\mathbf{Y}_1 + \mathbf{Y}_2)$ is uniform, then $\mathbf{X}_1 = -\log \mathbf{Y}_1$ and $\mathbf{X}_2 = -\log \mathbf{Y}_2$ (and also—but less interestingly, $-\mathbf{X}_1$, $-\mathbf{X}_2$) will be a pair of i.i.d. random variables that are not double exponential, but nevertheless have the logistic as their difference distribution.

Adapted to the problem at hand, Laha's results can be summarized as follows. If $\mathbf{X}_1$ and $\mathbf{X}_2$ are i.i.d., each having distribution function F, and $\mathbf{X}_1 - \mathbf{X}_2$ is logistic, then: (i) F is absolutely continuous and strictly increasing over the whole line; (ii) if F has finite absolute moments of all orders and is infinitely divisible, then ^{-}F or F must be double exponential; (iii) there exist solutions F that have finite absolute moments of all orders, but neither F or ^{-}F is double exponential. The last result is proved by constructing the characteristic function of such a distribution. The expression for this c.f. is very complicated, noninformative to the naked eye, and fills at least an entire page (Laha, 1964, pp. 296–297). So it will not be reproduced here—suffice it to say that no one would ever be tempted to use the corresponding distribution as the basis for a theory of choice behavior, even though from a technical standpoint it makes a perfectly acceptable Thurstone model.

Laha's results show that there exists a Thurstone model in which the discriminal process distribution is not related in any obvious way to the double exponential, but which is equivalent to the double exponential model (hence, to the Choice Axiom) for pair comparisons. This model cannot be excluded unless one is willing to require that "reasonable" Thurstone Models must have infinitely divisible distributions, which does not seem to be a justifiable restriction. (Recall that a distribution is infinitely divisible if, for every n, it is the distribution of the sum of n i.i.d. random variables. Put another way, F is infinitely divisible if $(c_F)^{1/n}$ is a characteristic function for every n.) It is true that the three examples of Thurstone models given in Section 2 all involve discriminal process distributions that are infinitely divisible. (For the normal, infinite divisibility is obvious: this is the prototype of the concept. Feller (1966, Chap. XVII) shows that the exponential distribution is infinitely divisible, and Laha (1966) shows that the double exponential is also.) But Laha's example shows that this is not an essential property, and it is easy to find less exotic distributions that are not infinitely divisible and still lead to perfectly acceptable Thurstone models. For example, if $\mathbf{Y}$ is normal and another, independent, random variable $\mathbf{U}$ is uniform on $(-1, 1)$, the sum $\mathbf{X} = \mathbf{U} + \mathbf{Y}$ has a positive density, and consequently its distribution F satisfies Definition 3. This distribution is not infinitely divisible, because its c.f. vanishes infinitely often (since the c.f. of the uniform term is $\sin t/t$), whereas the c.f. of an infinitely divisible distribution can never be zero (Feller, 1966, p. 532).

The Normal Case

The two examples just considered illustrate the general rule that a difference distribution D_F does not imply the type of the discriminal process distribution F, because F and G can be distributions of nontrivially different types (i.e., $G \neq$ either F or ^-F) and still yield $D_F = D_G$. However, there is one important exception. A famous theorem due to Cramér (Feller, 1966, p. 408) shows that if $\mathbf{X}_1$ and $\mathbf{X}_2$ are independent and $\mathbf{X}_1 + \mathbf{X}_2$ is normal, then $\mathbf{X}_1$ and $\mathbf{X}_2$ must both be normal also. It follows that if D_F is normal, then F itself must be normal:

COROLLARY 2 (to Theorem 2). *A Thurstone model $\mathcal{T}_F$ is equivalent to the normal (i.e., Case* V) *model for pair comparisons iff F is a normal distribution.*

In other words, the pair-comparison predictions of the normal model, taken altogether, uniquely characterize that model; they cannot be entirely duplicated by any other model.

As a historical note, it is interesting that in his original 1927 paper, Thurstone seems to have taken for granted that experimental confirmation of the Law of Comparative Judgment (i.e., confirmation of the triples function (5)) would imply that the discriminal processes must be normal. Cramér's theorem, however, was not proved until 1936. In the interim, no one could have known whether confirmation of the normal model for pair comparisons actually implied normal discriminal processes, or whether there might not also be nonnormal discriminal process distributions that could yield the same set of pair-comparison predictions. As things turned out, of course, Thurstone was right to ignore the problem for his Case V model. But if he had started with virtually any other distribution, he would have either been wrong, or else the answer would still be unknown, because Cramér's theorem seems to be the only one of its kind (except for an analogous result for Poisson distributions, Raikov's theorem (Lukacs, 1960), which is not helpful here).

3.3. *Uniqueness Implications of Complete Equivalence*

The last section showed that two models $\mathscr{T}_F$ and $\mathscr{T}_G$ can be equivalent for pair comparisons even though F and G are distributions of completely different types—distributions for which the corresponding random variables are not related by any linear transformation. A natural question is whether $\mathscr{T}_F$ and $\mathscr{T}_G$ can be equivalent for all complete experiments when F and G are not the same type of distribution. The next theorem shows that this cannot happen: The set of all complete systems admitted by $\mathscr{T}_F$ determines F, up to its type.

THEOREM 3. *Two Thurstone models $\mathscr{T}_F$ and $\mathscr{T}_G$ are completely equivalent if, and only if, $F(x) = G(ax + b)$, with $a > 0$.*

Proof. The proof of this theorem depends on the characteristic function analysis developed in Section 3.4, and so is deferred to the end of that section.

As a solution to our uniqueness problem, Theorem 3 is incomplete, because it leaves open the question of whether two models $\mathscr{T}_F$ and $\mathscr{T}_G$ can be equivalent for complete experiments with a *finite* number of objects when F and G are distributions of different types. If this were true for a sufficiently large number of objects, then $\mathscr{T}_F$ and $\mathscr{T}_G$ could be equivalent for all practical purposes even though they corresponded to different discriminal process distributions. The next section shows that for an important subset of cases, this possibility can be ruled out.

3.4. *Uniqueness Implications of Complete Equivalence for Experiments with Three Objects*

The sharpest possible result would be to show that $\mathscr{T}_F$ and $\mathscr{T}_G$ can be equivalent for complete experiments with three objects iff F and G are distributions of the same type. The following lemma provides the basis for obtaining such a result by way of a functional equation involving the characteristic functions of F and G:

LEMMA 8. *If $\mathscr{T}_F$ and $\mathscr{T}_G$ are equivalent for complete experiments with n objects ($n \geqslant 3$), the characteristic functions of F and G satisfy the equation*

$$c_G(t_1)\, c_G(t_2) \cdots c_G(t_{n-1})\, c_G\left(-\sum_{i=1}^{n-1} t_i\right)$$
$$= c_F(at_1)\, c_F(at_2) \cdots c_F(at_{n-1})\, c_F\left(-\sum_{i=1}^{n-1} at_i\right), \tag{16}$$

where a is the constant for which $D_F(x) = D_G(ax)$.

Proof. To avoid cumbersome expressions we prove the special case $n = 3$; the reasoning in the general case is exactly the same. Suppose $\mathscr{T}_F$ and $\mathscr{T}_G$ are equivalent for complete experiments with three objects, that both admit an arbitrary system $\{p_S/C_3\}$, and that the scale values for this system according to $\mathscr{T}_F$ are u_1, u_2, u_3. Then from Corollary 2 to Theorem 2 we know that the corresponding scale values for $\mathscr{T}_G$,

u_1', u_2', u_3', satisfy the relationship $u_i' - u_j' = a(u_i - u_j)$ where a is the positive constant that makes $D_F(x) = D_G(ax)$. Let $\{u_i + \mathbf{X}_i \mid i = 1, 2, 3\}$ denote the discriminal processes of $\mathcal{T}_F$, and $\{au_i + \mathbf{X}_i' \mid i = 1, 2, 3\}$ the discriminal processes of $\mathcal{T}_G$. Then

$$\begin{aligned} p_{C_3}(1) &= P[\mathbf{X}_2 - \mathbf{X}_1 \leqslant u_1 - u_2, \mathbf{X}_3 - \mathbf{X}_1 \leqslant u_1 - u_3], \\ &= P[\mathbf{X}_2' - \mathbf{X}_1' \leqslant a(u_1 - u_2), \mathbf{X}_3' - \mathbf{X}_1' \leqslant a(u_1 - u_3)]. \end{aligned} \tag{17}$$

Let

$$J_F(x, y) = P(\mathbf{X}_2 - \mathbf{X}_1 \leqslant x, \mathbf{X}_3 - \mathbf{X}_1 \leqslant y),$$

and

$$J_G(x, y) = P(\mathbf{X}_2' - \mathbf{X}_1' \leqslant x, \mathbf{X}_3' - \mathbf{X}_1' \leqslant y).$$

Then (17) implies

$$J_F(x, y) = J_G(ax, ay). \tag{18}$$

Now consider the joint characteristic function of $(\mathbf{X}_2' - \mathbf{X}_1', \mathbf{X}_3' - \mathbf{X}_1')$:

$$\begin{aligned} E[\exp(it_1(\mathbf{X}_2' - \mathbf{X}_1') + it_2(\mathbf{X}_3' - \mathbf{X}_1')] &= E[e^{it_1\mathbf{X}_2'} e^{it_2\mathbf{X}_3'} e^{-i(t_1+t_2)\mathbf{X}_1'}] \\ &= c_G(t_1)\, c_G(t_2)\, c_G(-t_1 - t_2) \end{aligned} \tag{19}$$

since the $\mathbf{X}_i$ are i.i.d. The same c.f. can also be expressed as the integral

$$\int_{-\infty}^{\infty} \int_{-\infty}^{\infty} e^{it_1x + it_2y}\, dJ_G(x, y). \tag{20}$$

Making the change of variable $x = ax'$, $y = ay'$, and using (18), (20) becomes

$$\int_{-\infty}^{\infty} \int_{-\infty}^{\infty} e^{it_1ax' + it_2ay'}\, dJ_F(x', y'). \tag{21}$$

However, this last integral is also the joint c.f. of $(\mathbf{X}_2 - \mathbf{X}_1, \mathbf{X}_3 - \mathbf{X}_1)$ evaluated at (at_1, at_2), so (21) equals

$$E[\exp[iat_1(\mathbf{X}_2 - \mathbf{X}_1) + iat_2(\mathbf{X}_3 - \mathbf{X}_1)]] = c_F(at_1)\, c_F(at_2)\, c_F(-at_1 - at_2). \tag{22}$$

Consequently (19) and (22) are equal, as claimed.[5] ∎

Specializing to the case $n = 3$, Lemma 8 says that if $\mathcal{T}_F$ and $\mathcal{T}_G$ are completely equivalent for experiments with three objects, the characteristic functions of F and G satisfy the functional equation

$$c_G(t_1)\, c_G(t_2)\, c_G(-t_1 - t_2) = c_F(at_1)\, c_F(at_2)\, c_F(-at_1 - at_2). \tag{23}$$

[5] It can be seen from this proof that the uniqueness problem for Thurstone models boils down to the question of whether the distribution of a set of independent R.V.'s. $\mathbf{X}_1, \mathbf{X}_2, \ldots, \mathbf{X}_n$ is determined by the joint distribution of the differences $\mathbf{X}_2 - \mathbf{X}_1, \mathbf{X}_3 - \mathbf{X}_1, \ldots, \mathbf{X}_n - \mathbf{X}_1$. I. I. Kotlarski has pointed out to me that there is a rather extensive literature on this question, beginning with his 1966 paper which shows that if the joint c.f. of the differences is nonvanishing, the answer is yes. Although arrived at independently, Theorem 4 is essentially a corollary of Kotlarski's result.

One acceptable solution to (23) is

$$c_G(t) = e^{ibt}c_F(at), \tag{24}$$

which implies $F(x) = G(ax + b)$. (The solution $c_G(t) = e^{wt}e^{ibt}c_F(at)$ (w, b real) is not acceptable because it cannot be a characteristic function. This follows from the fact that if $c(t) = c_1(t) + ic_2(t)$ is a c.f., c_1 must be even and c_2 must be odd (Feller, 1966, p. 474). Consequently, $e^{wt}c(t)$ (w real) can never be a c.f., because $e^{wt}c_1(t)$ will not be even, and $e^{wt}c_2(t)$ will not be odd. Since we know that $e^{ibt}c_F(at)$ is a c.f., $e^{wt}e^{ibt}c_F(at)$ is not). If (24) is the only solution to (23), then complete equivalence for experiments with three objects implies that F and G are distributions of the same type. The next theorem shows that this is always true if F (or G) has a nonvanishing characteristic function.

THEOREM 4. *If $\mathscr{T}_F$ and $\mathscr{T}_G$ are equivalent for complete choice experiments with three objects and the characteristic function of F (or G) is never zero, then $F(x) = G(ax + b)$.*

Proof. To simplify the notation, let $f(t) = c_F(t)$, $g(t) = c_G(t)$. Then (23) becomes

$$g(s)\,g(t)\,g(-s - t) = f(as)\,f(at)\,f(-as - at), \tag{25}$$

which holds for all real s and t. The problem is to show that the only acceptable solutions to (25) are of the form

$$g(t) = e^{ibt}f(at), \tag{26}$$

where b is an arbitrary constant. Observe first that when $s = 0$, (25) becomes

$$g(t)\,g(-t) = |\,g(t)|^2 = f(at)\,f(-at) = |\,f(at)|^2 \tag{27}$$

(since $g(0) = f(0) = 1$). Clearly if f never vanishes, neither does g, and vice versa, so the factors in (25) can be divided freely. Using (27) to rewrite $f(-as - at)/g(-s - t)$, (25) becomes

$$\frac{g(s)}{f(as)}\frac{g(t)}{f(at)} = \frac{g(s + t)}{f(as + at)}\,. \tag{28}$$

Now let $h(t) = g(t)/f(at)$. Then (28) becomes

$$h(s)\,h(t) = h(s + t). \tag{29}$$

Functional equation (29) is a complex version of the well-known Cauchy equation—if h were a real valued function, the only continuous nonzero solution would be $h(t) = e^{bt}$ (Aczél, 1966, p. 38). Since h is a complex function of a real variable, the solution here takes a bit more work, but in the end the result (when h is a ratio of c.f.'s) is a complex analog of the real solution: $h(t) = e^{ibt}$. To show this, let h_1 and h_2 denote the real and imaginary parts of h, i.e., $h(t) = h_1(t) + ih_2(t)$, and similarly, $f(t) = f_1(t) + if_2(t)$ and $g(t) = g_1(t) + ig_2(t)$. Then using the fact that f_1 and g_1 are even, and f_2 and g_2 are odd, it is straightforward to show that h_1 is even and h_2 is odd. Writing (29) in terms of h_1 and h_2, expanding, and equating the real and imaginary parts on both sides, we obtain a pair of real functional equations:

$$h_1(s)\,h_1(t) - h_2(s)\,h_2(t) = h_1(s + t), \tag{30}$$

$$h_1(s)\,h_2(t) + h_2(s)\,h_1(t) = h_2(s + t). \tag{31}$$

Putting $-s$ in place of s in (30), and using the fact that h_1 is even, and h_2 odd, (30) becomes

$$h_1(s)\,h_1(t) + h_2(s)\,h_2(t) = h_1(t - s). \tag{32}$$

Aczél (1966, pp. 176–180) shows that the only continuous nonconstant solution to (32) is $h_1(t) = \cos bt$, $h_2(t) = \sin bt$. Since h is the ratio of two continuous functions (every c.f. is continuous) h_1 and h_2 are continuous, and h cannot be any constant except one (i.e., $b = 0$) because $h(0) = 1$. Consequently the only acceptable solution to (29) is

$$h(t) = \cos bt + i \sin bt = e^{ibt}.$$

Thus (26) is the only solution to (25) under the assumption that f and g are c.f.'s, one of which is known to be nonvanishing. ▮

Applying Theorem 4 to the special case of the double exponential distribution, we obtain finally a complete solution to the uniqueness problem for the Choice Axiom:

THEOREM 5. *A Thurstone model $\mathscr{T}_F$ is equivalent to the Choice Axiom for complete experiments with three (or more) objects if, and only if, F is a double exponential distribution, i.e., iff $F(x) = e^{-e^{-(ax+b)}}$, with $a > 0$.*

Proof. Holman and Marley's theorem (Lemma 6) shows that any double exponential model implies the Choice Axiom, in particular, the model $\mathscr{T}_G$, with $G(x) = e^{-e^{-x}}$. This distribution has the nonvanishing characteristic function $\Gamma(1 - it)$, and consequently any model $\mathscr{T}_F$ that is equivalent to $\mathscr{T}_G$ (hence, to the Choice Axiom) for complete experiments with three objects must have $F(x) = G(ax + b)$. (To show explicitly that $\Gamma(1 - it)$ is never zero we can use the fact that for any complex z, $\Gamma(z)\,\Gamma(1 - z) = \pi/(\sin \pi z)$ (e.g., Ahlfors, 1966, p. 198). Recall also that $\Gamma(1 + z) = z\Gamma(z)$, and that by definition $\sin z = (e^{iz} - e^{-iz})/zi$. Then if $g(t) = \Gamma(1 - it)$:

$$\begin{aligned} |\,g(t)|^2 &= \Gamma(1 - it)\,\Gamma(1 + it) \\ &= it\pi/\sin it\pi \\ &= 2\pi t/(e^{\pi t} - e^{-\pi t}). \end{aligned}$$

Clearly this last expression could only vanish at $t = 0$, and applying L'Hospital's rule shows that $|\,g(0)|^2 = 1$. ▮

(Notice that Theorem 5 does not simply state that the double exponential is the only distribution with a nonvanishing c.f. that is equivalent to the Choice Axiom; that would be a weaker result than the one actually proved, which is completely general.)

From a general standpoint, there remains the open question of whether Theorem 4 can be strengthened to cover all Thurstone models, rather than just those that are equivalent to models with nonvanishing characteristic functions. The answer hinges on whether the functional equation (23) can have solutions other than (24) if we drop the requirement that c_F never vanishes. Ignoring for the moment the fact that such solutions are relevant here only if they actually represent characteristic functions, it is not difficult to construct alternative solutions to (23) when c_F is allowed to vanish over entire intervals. For example, suppose

$$\begin{aligned} c_F(t) &= 1 - |t|, && t \in [-1, 1], \\ &= 1 - ||t| - 5|, && |t| \in [4, 6], \\ &= 0, && \text{elsewhere} \end{aligned}$$

(so that the graph of c_F consists of three triangles, centered at -5, 0, and $+5$, each two units wide), and (for some real r)

$$\begin{aligned} c_G(t) &= c_F(t), && |t| \notin [4, 6], \\ &= e^{ir} c_F(t), && t \in [4, 6], \\ &= e^{-ir} c_F(t), && t \in [-4, -6]. \end{aligned}$$

Then clearly $c_G(t)$ does not have the form $e^{ibt} c_F(t)$, but by considering the various possible values of s and t, one can see that

$$c_G(s)\, c_G(t)\, c_G(-s - t) = c_F(s)\, c_F(t)\, c_F(-s - t),$$

so c_G and c_F satisfy (23), but not (24). (That is, if s and t both lie in $[-1, 1]$, then either $-s - t$ does also, in which case $c_G = c_F$, so the equation is satisfied, or else $c_F(-s - t) = c_G(-s - t) = 0$, in which case the same is true. And so on.) However, I have not been able to determine whether examples constructed along these lines can also be the characteristic functions of distributions satisfying Definition 3. This is left as an open problem, for someone with a better understanding of characteristic functions.

One incomplete, but still useful, way to broaden the scope of Theorem 4 is to notice that even if c_F has zeros, there will always be a neighborhood of the origin in which $|c_F(t)|^2$ is strictly positive (since $c_F(0) = 1$ and c_F is continuous), and consequently if $\mathcal{T}_F$ and $\mathcal{T}_G$ are equivalent for three objects, the ratio $h = c_F/c_G$ will always satisfy (29) for all s and t in some neighborhood of zero. It follows (applying Theorem 1 in Aczél, 1966, p. 46, to the real and imaginary parts of $\log h$) that the solution (24) is always valid for $|t|$ sufficiently close to zero, and consequently the c.f. of $F(x)$ always agrees with that of $G(ax + b)$ in some neighborhood of the origin. This means that all the moments of F agree with the moments of $G(ax + b)$. Consequently *if F is a distribu-*

tion that is determined by its moments, $\mathscr{T}_G$ can be equivalent to $\mathscr{T}_F$ for complete experiments with three or more objects iff *G is another distribution of the same type.* This argument applies to many special cases that are not covered by Theorem 4. But F need not have finite moments or a nonvanishing c.f. in order to make an acceptable discriminal process distribution: The convolution of a Cauchy distribution with any symmetric distribution having one of the periodic c.f.'s described by Feller (1966 Example "a," p. 594) will have a positive density (so that Definition 3 is satisfied), but its c.f. will vanish over intervals, and its moment sequence will be uninformative (since only the odd moments will exist, and these will all be zero because of symmetry).

To prove Theorem 3 using c.f.'s, notice that (16) implies

$$c_G{}^n(t)\, c_G(-nt) = c_F{}^n(at)\, c_F(-ant). \tag{33}$$

As noted in the last paragraph, (24) holds in some neighborhood N of the origin. If $\mathscr{T}_F$ and $\mathscr{T}_G$ are completely equivalent, (16) holds for every n, and for any s, there will be a t in N such that $s = -nt$ for some n. Then $c_G{}^n(-t) = e^{-ibs}c_F{}^n(-at)$ and substituting in (33), we get $c_G(s) = e^{ibs}c_F(as)$ for all s.

4. Invariance under Uniform Expansions of the Choice Set: An Assumption That Implies the Choice Axiom

It is evident from his 1927 paper that Thurstone's grounds for assigning normal distributions to his discriminal processes were entirely heuristic, and had nothing to do with considerations specific to choice behavior: The normal distribution was chosen because of its ubiquitous role in statistics, and the suitability of this choice was left as an open problem, to be decided empirically. Another strategy, more in keeping with modern trends in choice theory, would have been to start with some intuitively plausible assumption about choice behavior, and then derive from this the type of the discriminal process distribution. For example, Thurstone might have begun (anachronistically) by postulating the Choice Axiom, which (in the general case, as shown in the previous section) would have led him to the double exponential distribution instead of the normal. Of course in that case the discriminal process mechanism would have been redundant excess baggage, because the Choice Axiom alone leads to the same predictions as the double exponential Thurstone model, and does so in a much more direct fashion.

There is, however, another assumption, weaker than the Choice Axiom itself (and therefore perhaps intuitively more attractive), which also implies that the discriminal process distribution must be double exponential, and which consequently implies the Choice Axiom—under the assumption that some Thurstone model is true.

To motivate this assumption, suppose that $T_{n,1} = \{o_{11}, o_{21}, \ldots, o_{n1}\}$ is a set of n choice objects (the reason for the double subscript will become clear in a moment), and let $p_{C_{n,1}}(i)$ denote the probability of choosing object o_{i1} from $T_{n,1}$. Then suppose we expand this choice set by adding $k-1$ objects that are identical to o_{11} (call these $o_{12}, o_{13}, \ldots, o_{1k}$), and $k-1$ objects identical to o_{21} ($o_{22}, o_{23}, \ldots, o_{2k}$), and so on for each of the original objects, so that the new choice set is $T_{n,k} = \{o_{11}, ..., o_{1k}; o_{21}, ..., o_{2k}; ...; o_{n1}, ..., o_{nk}\}$. This new set $T_{n,k}$ will be called the (kth-order) ***uniform expansion*** of the original set $T_{n,1}$.

Now let $p^*_{C_{n,k}}(i)$ denote the probability that in choosing from the expanded set $T_{n,k}$ (where again the subject chooses only one object), the object chosen is one of the type i objects, i.e., one of the objects $o_{i1}, o_{i2}, ..., o_{ik}$. In some contexts it seems intuitively plausible that $p^*_{C_{n,k}}(i)$ should be constant for all values of k, i.e., the probability of choosing a type i object should not be affected by a uniform expansion of the choice set.

For example, suppose the original set consists of three objects: a cup of coffee, a cup of tea, and a glass of milk. Then the kth-order uniform expansion of this set consists of k identical cups of coffee, k cups of tea, and k glasses of milk. Assuming that the desirability of the choice objects themselves is the only consideration, it seems natural to suppose that the probability of choosing a cup of coffee from the expanded set (as opposed to tea or milk) will be the same as it was originally, regardless of k.

Clearly this is what the Choice Axiom predicts, since the redundant objects in the expanded choice set will have the same v scale values as those in the original set: If o_{i1} has scale value v_i, then $o_{i2}, o_{i3}, ..., o_{ik}$ must also have scale value v_i, since they are all identical to o_{i1}, and consequently

$$p^*_{C_{n,k}}(i) = kv_i/k \sum_{j=1}^{n} v_j = p_{C_{n,1}}(i).$$

To state our assumption concisely, we will say that *the predictions of a choice model are invariant under uniform expansions of the choice set iff* $p^*_{C_{n,k}}(i) \equiv p_{C_{n,1}}(i)$ *for all* k.

Now consider what it would mean for a Thurstone model $\mathscr{T}_F$ to imply this sort of invariance. Suppose the original objects $o_{11}, o_{21}, ..., o_{n1}$ have discriminal processes $u_1 + \mathbf{X}_{11}, u_2 + \mathbf{X}_{21}, ..., u_n + \mathbf{X}_{n1}$ (where the $\mathbf{X}_{i1}$ are all i.i.d.), so that

$$\begin{aligned} p_{C_{n,1}}(i) &= P[u_i + \mathbf{X}_{i1} = \text{Max}\{u_j + \mathbf{X}_{j1} \mid j = 1, ..., n\}] \\ &= \int_{-\infty}^{\infty} \left[\prod_{\substack{j=1 \\ j \neq i}}^{n} F(x + u_i - u_j)\right] dF(x). \end{aligned} \tag{34}$$

In the kth-order uniform expansion of this set the discriminal processes of the type i objects will be $u_i + \mathbf{X}_{i1}, u_i + \mathbf{X}_{i2}, ..., u_i + \mathbf{X}_{ik}$, and the probability of choosing a type i object (as opposed to a type j object, $j \neq i$) will be the probability that one of these random variables is the maximum of the entire set of discriminal processes

$$\{u_j + \mathbf{X}_{jm} \mid j = 1, ..., n; m = 1, ..., k\}.$$

Clearly it does not matter whether the subject ranks all of these discriminal processes without regard for object type, and then selects the object corresponding to the largest, or first ranks the discriminal processes within each type (i.e., determines $\text{Max}\{u_j + \mathbf{X}_{jm} \mid m = 1, ..., k\}$ for each j) and then rank orders these maximums. Consequently the probability of selecting a type i object is the probability that the largest of the type i

discriminal processes is greater than the largest discriminal process for every other object type:

$$
\begin{aligned}
p^*_{C_{n,k}}(i) = P[\text{Max}\{u_i + \mathbf{X}_{im} \mid m = 1,..., k\} &= \text{Max}\{\text{Max}\{u_1 + \mathbf{X}_{1m} \mid m = 1,..., k\}, \\
&\quad \text{Max}\{u_2 + \mathbf{X}_{2m} \mid m = 1,..., k\},..., \text{Max}\{u_n + \mathbf{X}_{nm} \mid m = 1,..., k\}\}] \\
= P[u_i + \text{Max}\{\mathbf{X}_{im} \mid m = 1,..., k\} & \qquad (35) \\
&= \text{Max}\{u_1 + \text{Max}\{\mathbf{X}_{1m} \mid m = 1,..., k\},..., u_n + \text{Max}\{\mathbf{X}_{nm} \mid m = 1,..., k\}\}].
\end{aligned}
$$

Since the random variable $\text{Max}\{\mathbf{X}_{jm} \mid m = 1,..., k\}$ has distribution function $F^k(x)$, (35) can be written as

$$p^*_{C_{n,k}}(i) = \int_{-\infty}^{\infty} \left[\prod_{\substack{j=1 \\ j \neq i}}^{n} F^k(x + u_i - u_j) \right] dF^k(x). \tag{36}$$

Now the model $\mathcal{T}_F$ is invariant under uniform expansions iff the integrals in (34) and (36) are equal for every choice of scale values $\{u_j\}$ and every integer k. However this is the same as saying that the Thurstone model $\mathcal{T}_{F^k}$ is completely equivalent to the model $\mathcal{T}_F$, since a given set of scale values $u_1, u_2,..., u_n$ will yield exactly the same choice probabilities in either model (that is, when inserted into either (36) or (34).) Consequently it follows from Theorem 3 that

$$F^k(x) = F(a_k x + b_k). \tag{37}$$

Moreover the constant a_k here must always be one, since if $u_1 = 0$, $u_2 = -u$, we have $p_{C_{2,1}}(1) = D_F(u) = p^*_{C_{2,k}}(1) = D_{F^k}(u)$, and (37) implies $D_{F^k}(u) = D_F(a_k u)$. Thus, the Thurstone model $\mathcal{T}_F$ can be invariant under uniform expansions of the choice set if and only if, for every k,

$$F^k(x) = F(x + b_k), \tag{38}$$

where b_k is a constant that depends on k.

Now functional Eq. (38) is precisely the one that Fisher and Tippet used in 1928 to prove that the limit distribution of the (normalized) maximum Z_k^* of k i.i.d. random variables $Z_1,..., Z_k$ (that is, the limit distribution of $Z_k^* - b_k$ as $k \to \infty$) is the double exponential. Their original argument is explained by Gumbel (1958). However, to obtain a proof that is sufficiently general for the present context we use here a different argument, based on Feller's version of a theorem due to Gnedenko:

LEMMA 9. *F is a distribution function that satisfies functional Eq. (38) (i.e., for every k there exists a b_k such that $F^k(x) = F(x + b_k)$ for all x) iff F is a distribution of the double exponential type, i.e.,*

$$F(x) = e^{-e^{-(ax+b)}}.$$

Proof. If F is double exponential, then

$$\begin{aligned} F^k(x) &= e^{-ke^{-(ax+b)}} \\ &= \exp\{-e^{-[a(x-(1/a)\log k)+b]}\} \\ &= F(x + b_k) \end{aligned}$$

where $b_k = -(1/a) \log k$.

To show the converse, suppose $\mathbf{X}_1, \mathbf{X}_2, ..., \mathbf{X}_k, ...,$ are i.i.d., with F as their common distribution function. Let $\mathbf{X}_k^* = \text{Max}\{\mathbf{X}_1, ..., \mathbf{X}_k\}$, and $\mathbf{Y}_k = e^{\mathbf{X}_k}$. Then $\mathbf{Y}_k^* = e^{\mathbf{X}^*}$. Feller (1966, pp. 270–271) shows that if a sequence of constants $\{a_k\}$ exists such that $G(y) = \lim_{k\to\infty} P[\mathbf{Y}_k^*/a_k \leqslant y]$ exists and is not concentrated at the origin, then

$$G(y) = e^{-cy^{-a}} \qquad (c > 0, a > 0, y > 0).$$

Now

$$\begin{aligned} P[\mathbf{Y}_k^*/a_k \leqslant y] &= P[e^{\mathbf{X}_k^*} \leqslant a_k y] \\ &= P[\mathbf{X}_k^* \leqslant \log y + \log a_k] \\ &= F^k[\log y + \log a_k] \\ &= F(\log y + \log a_k + b_k). \end{aligned}$$

So if F satisfies (38) for some sequence b_k (in fact we can readily show that $b_k = D_F^{-1}(1/(k+1))$), then $G(y)$ exists (for the sequence $a_k = e^{-b_k}$) and equals $F(\log y)$, which clearly is not concentrated at the origin. Thus

$$F(\log y) = e^{-cy^{-a}}$$

i.e.,

$$F(x) = e^{-ce^{-ax}} = e^{-e^{-(ax+b)}},$$

as claimed. ∎

Combining Lemma 9 with the argument that preceded it, we obtain the following result:

THEOREM 6. *The predictions of a Thurstone model $\mathcal{T}_F$ are invariant under uniform expansions of the choice set if and only if F is a double exponential distribution, i.e., iff* $F(x) = e^{-e^{-(cx+d)}}$, *where* $c > 0$.

In other words, within the class of Thurstone models, invariance under uniform expansions implies the Choice Axiom.[6]

Theorem 6 could stand to be sharpened a bit, so that it requires only invariance under uniform expansions of choice sets with three objects, instead of an arbitrary number as in the present version. This would be straightforward if Theorem 4 could

[6] For a different approach to motivating the double exponential distribution, also based on the statistics of extremes, see Thompson and Singh, 1967.

be strengthened to cover arbitrary discriminal process distributions instead of just those with nonvanishing characteristic functions. (If the invariance condition is stated only for initial choice sets with three objects, it implies the functional equation $c_{F^k}(x)\, c_{F^k}(y)\, c_{F^k}(-x-y) = c_F(x)\, c_F(y)\, c_F(-x-y)$, by the same argument used to prove Lemma 8 in Section 3.4. Then if Theorem 4 held generally, it would follow that $F^k(x) = F(x + b_k)$, and applying Lemma 9 would complete the proof.)

Thurstone Models with Discriminal Processes Concentrated on Finite Intervals

It was noted earlier (in Section 2.6) that no Thurstone model $\mathscr{T}_F$ with F concentrated on a finite interval (say (α, β)) can be equivalent to the Choice Axiom. This is readily seen by considering the predictions of such a model under uniform expansions of the choice set. Suppose the discriminal processes of the original objects $o_{11}, o_{21}, \ldots, o_{n1}$ are $u_1 + \mathbf{X}_{11}, \ldots, u_n + \mathbf{X}_{n1}$, where the $\mathbf{X}_{i1}$ are bounded between α and β. Then for the kth-order uniform expansion of this set, the probability $p^*_{C_{n,k}}(i)$ of choosing a type i object is the probability that

$$u_i + \mathbf{X}^*_{i,k} = \mathrm{Max}\{u_j + \mathbf{X}^*_{j,k} \mid j = 1, \ldots, n\},$$

where

$$\mathbf{X}^*_{j,k} = \mathrm{Max}\{\mathbf{X}_{j1}, X_{j2}, \ldots, \mathbf{X}_{jk}\}.$$

Now as $k \to \infty$, the random variables $\mathbf{X}^*_{j,k}$ will all converge to β, and consequently $u_j + \mathbf{X}^*_{j,k}$ will converge to $u_j + \beta$, so that the probabilities $p^*_{C_{n,k}}(i)$ will all converge to zero, except for the one corresponding to the largest scale value. In other words, if the discriminal processes are concentrated on a finite interval, then under uniform expansions the subject will always wind up deterministically choosing one of the type i objects, where u_i is the largest scale value.

5. Remarks on Irreversibility and on Independent Random Utility Models

5.1. *The Irreversibility Paradox*

In his 1959 monograph Luce proved a very surprising and counterintuitive result: No Thurstone model can simultaneously satisfy the Choice Axiom both for choices based on the principle "pick the object with the *largest* discriminal process" and for choices based on the principle "pick the object with the *smallest* discriminal process." To motivate this result, consider two complete choice experiments, with the same set of three objects o_1, o_2, o_3: In Experiment B (for best) the subject is instructed to always choose the object he prefers most, and in Experiment W (for worst) he is instructed to always choose the object he prefers least. Let $\{b_S(i)/C_3\}$ denote the system of choice probabilities resulting from Experiment B, and $\{w_S(i)/C_3\}$ the system resulting from Experiment W. It seems almost inescapable that these systems should satisfy the condition

$$b_{\{i,j\}}(i) = w_{\{i,j\}}(j). \tag{39}$$

It is easily shown that (39) will hold and both $\{b_S/C_3\}$ and $\{w_S/C_3\}$ will satisfy the Choice Axiom if there exist v scale values v_1, v_2, v_3 such that

$$b_S(i) = v_i \Big/ \sum_{j \in S} v_j, \tag{40}$$

and

$$w_S(i) = (1/v_i) \Big/ \sum_{j \in S} (1/v_j). \tag{41}$$

Now suppose we apply a Thurstone model $\mathscr{T}_F$ to the same situation. It seems natural to assume that the discriminal processes of the objects will be the same in both experiments, i.e., o_i corresponds to $u_i + \mathbf{X}_i$ in both cases, and then to suppose that in Experiment B, the subject picks the object with the largest discriminal process, while in Experiment W he picks the object with the smallest. These assumptions seem quite innocuous, but Luce (1959, p. 57) showed that if they hold there is no distribution F for which the resulting systems $\{b_S/C_3\}$ and $\{w_S/C_3\}$ will both satisfy the Choice Axiom and also condition (39), except in the trivial special case in which all objects are chosen with equal probability.

This impossibility theorem was proved without reference to the double exponential representation of the Choice Axiom. In light of the results described here in Section 3 we can now see why it is true: In order for a Thurstone model to satisfy the Choice Axiom for Experiment B, the $\mathbf{X}_i$ must be double exponential, but when the subject in Experiment W picks the object with the smallest discriminal process (i.e., "pick o_i from S iff $u_i + \mathbf{X}_i = \text{Min}\{u_j + \mathbf{X}_j \mid j \in S\}$") he is actually following the rule "pick o_i iff $-u_i - \mathbf{X}_i = \text{Max}\{-u_j - \mathbf{X}_j \mid j \in S\}$". Consequently in Experiment W the subject is behaving according to a Thurstone model in which the discriminal processes are not double exponential (since that distribution is not symmetrical, $u_i + \mathbf{X}_i$ and $-u_i - \mathbf{X}_i$ cannot both be double exponential), and which therefore is not equivalent to the Choice Axiom.

There is, however, a simple way around this difficulty. Suppose that in Experiment W the subject reverses only the scale values of each object (instead of the entire discriminal process) so that his decision rule is "pick o_i from subset S iff $-u_i + \mathbf{X}_i = \text{Max}\{-u_j + \mathbf{X}_j \mid j \in S\}$". Then if the random variables $\mathbf{X}_i$ are double exponential in both Experiments B and W, the resulting choice probabilities will satisfy the Choice Axiom in both directions, i.e., Eqs. 39, 40, and 41 will all hold simultaneously. (To see this explicitly, set $\mathbf{X}_j = -\log \mathbf{Y}_j$, where $\mathbf{Y}_j$ is exponential with density e^{-y}, and $u_j = \log v_j$. Then all three equations fall out immediately.)

5.2. *Relationship between Thurstone Models and Independent Random Utility* (IRU) *Models*

Luce and Suppes (1965) have defined a class of IRU models which represent the ultimate generalization of Thurstone's Case V notion: A system of choice probabilities $\{p_S/C_n\}$ satisfies an IRU model iff there exist independent random variables $\mathbf{U}_1, \ldots, \mathbf{U}_n$ such that for every $i \in S \subseteq C_n$

$$p_S(i) = P[\mathbf{U}_i = \text{Max}\{\mathbf{U}_j \mid j \in S\}].$$

The $\{\mathbf{U}_i\}$ here need not have any systematic relationship between their distributions, and in particular, these distributions need not be identical except for shifts along the axis—the Thurstone models of Section 2.6 represent that special case, where $\mathbf{U}_i = u_i + \mathbf{X}_i$, with the $\mathbf{X}_i$ all i.i.d. Clearly if the discriminal processes of any Thurstone model $\mathscr{T}_F$ are transformed monotonically (i.e., from $\mathbf{U}_i = u_i + \mathbf{X}_i$ to $\mathbf{U}_i' = m(\mathbf{U}_i)$, where m is strictly increasing), the result will be a non-Thurstonian IRU model that is completely equivalent to $\mathscr{T}_F$. It is natural to define equivalence classes of IRU models of the form M_F, where M_F represents the set of all IRU models obtained by applying monotonic transformations to the Thurstone model $\mathscr{T}_F$: Then the application of the basic uniqueness theorems of Section 3 to these classes of IRU models is straightforward.

Starting from the other direction, Levine (1970) has considered the question, When can an arbitrary family of independent random variables be transformed by a common monotonic transformation in such a way that the resulting distribution functions are identical except for shifts along the axis? The essential condition turns out to be that none of the original distribution functions can intersect (i.e., if $F \neq G$, then either $F(x) < G(x)$ for all x, or vice versa). If Levine's conditions hold for an arbitrary set of random variables that constitute an IRU model, then that model is equivalent to some Thurstone model, and its uniqueness status can be determined accordingly, using the results of Section 3.

References

Aczél, J. *Lectures on functional equations.* New York: Academic Press, 1966.

Adams, E., & Messick, S. An axiomatization of Thurstone's successive intervals and paired comparisons scaling models. Technical Report 12, Applied Mathematics and Statistics Laboratory, Stanford University, 1957.

Ahlfors, L. V. *Complex analysis*, 2nd ed. New York: McGraw–Hill, 1966.

Burke, C. J., & Zinnes, J. L. A paired comparison of pair comparisons. *Journal of Mathematical Psychology*, 1965, **2**, 53–76.

Dawkins, R. A threshold model of choice behavior. *Animal Behavior*, 1969, **17**, 120–133.

Feller, W. *An introduction to probability theory and its applications, Vol. II.* New York: Wiley, 1966.

Gumbel, E. G. *Statistics of extremes.* New York: Columbia University Press, 1958.

Kotlarski, I. I. On some characterizations of probability distributions in Hilbert spaces. *Annali di Mathematica pura ed applicata*, 1966, **74**, 129–134.

Laha, R. G. On a problem connected with beta and gamma distributions. *Transactions of the American Mathematical Society*, 1964, **113**, 287–298.

Levine, M. V. Transformations that render curves parallel. *Journal of Mathematical Psychology*, 1970, **7**, 410–443.

Luce, R. D. *Individual choice behavior.* New York: Wiley, 1959.

Luce, R. D., & Suppes, P. Preference, utility, and subjective probability. In R. D. Luce, R. R. Bush, & E. Galanter (Eds.) *Handbook of Mathematical Psychology, Vol. III.* New York: Wiley, 1965.

Lukacs, E. *Characteristic functions.* London: Griffen, 1960.

McFadden, D. Conditional logit analyses of qualitative choice behavior. In P. Zarembka (Ed.), *Frontiers in econometrics.* New York: Academic Press, 1974.

Thompson, W. A., & Singh, J. The use of limit theorems in paired comparison model building. *Psychometrika*, 1967, **32**, 255–264.

THURSTONE, L. L. A law of comparative judgment. *Psychological Review*, 1927, **34**, 273–286.
TVERSKY, A. Choice by elimination. *Journal of Mathematical Psychology*, 1972, **9**, 340–367.
WHITTAKER, E. T., & WATSON, G. N. *A course of modern analysis*, 4th ed. Cambridge: Cambridge University Press, 1963.
YELLOTT, J. Generalized Thurstone representations for three choice theories: uniqueness theorems. Paper given at annual Mathematical Psychology Meeting, Princeton, September 1971.

RECEIVED: November 14, 1975

[5]

A NEW APPROACH TO CONSUMER THEORY*

KELVIN J. LANCASTER
Johns Hopkins University

I. THE CURRENT STATUS OF CONSUMER THEORY

The theory of consumer behavior in deterministic situations as set out by, say, Debreu (1959, 1960) or Uzawa (1960) is a thing of great aesthetic beauty, a jewel set in a glass case. The product of a long process of refinement from the nineteenth-century utility theorists through Slutsky and Hicks-Allen to the economists of the last twenty-five years,[1] it has been shorn of all irrelevant postulates so that it now stands as an example of how to extract the minimum of results from the minimum of assumptions.

To the process of slicing away with Occam's razor, the author made a small contribution (1957). This brought forth a reply by Johnson (1958) which suggested, somewhat tongue-in-cheek, that the determinateness of the sign of the substitution effect (the only substantive result of the theory of consumer behavior) could be derived from the proposition that goods are goods.

Johnson's comment, on reflection, would seem to be almost the best summary that can be given of the current state of the theory of consumer behavior. All *intrinsic* properties of particular goods, those properties that make a diamond quite obviously something different from a loaf of bread, have been omitted from the theory, so that a consumer who consumes diamonds alone is as rational as a consumer who consumes bread alone, but one who sometimes consumes bread, sometimes diamonds (*ceteris paribus*, of course), is irrational. Thus, the only property which the theory can build on is the property shared by all goods, which is simply that they are goods.

Indeed, we can continue the argument further, since goods are simply what consumers would like more of; and we must be neutral with respect to differences in consumer tastes (some consumers might like more of something that other consumers do not want), that the ultimate proposition is that *goods are what are thought of as goods.*

In spite of the denial of the relevance of intrinsic properties to the pure theory, there has always been a subversive undercurrent suggesting that economists continue to take account of these properties. Elementary textbooks bristle with substitution examples about butter and margarine, rather than about shoes and ships, as though the authors believed that there was something intrinsic to butter and margarine that made them good substitutes and about automobiles and gasoline that made them somehow intrinsically complementary. Market re-

* The author wishes to acknowledge helpful comments from various sources, including Gary Becker, Harry Johnson, and colleagues and students at Johns Hopkins University, especially Carl Christ, F. T. Sparrow, William Poole, C. Blackorby, T. Amemiya, and T. Tsushima.

[1] The American Economic Association *Index of Economic Journals* lists 151 entries under category 2.111 (utility, demand, theory of the household) over the period 1940–63.

searchers, advertisers, and manufacturers also act as though they believe that knowledge of (or belief in) the intrinsic properties of goods is relevant to the way consumers will react toward them.

The clearest case of conflict between a belief that goods do have intrinsic properties relevant to consumer theory but that they are not taken into account has been the long search for a definition of "intrinsic complementarity." The search was successful only where Morishima (1959) turned from traditional theory to an approach somewhat similar to that of the present paper.

Perhaps the most important aspects of consumer behavior relevant to an economy as complex as that of the United States are those of consumer reactions to new commodities and to quality variations. Traditional theory has nothing to say on these. In the case of new commodities, the theory is particularly helpless. We have to expand from a commodity space of dimension n to one of dimension $n + 1$, replacing the old utility function by a completely new one, and even a complete map of the consumer's preferences among the n goods provides absolutely no information about the new preference map. A theory which can make no use of so much information is a remarkably empty one. Even the technique of supposing the existence of a utility function for all possible goods, including those not yet invented, and regarding the prices of nonexistent goods as infinite—an incredible stretching of the consumers' powers of imagination—has no predictive value.

Finally we can note the unsuitability of traditional theory for dealing with many of the manifestly important aspects of actual relationships between goods and consumers in I. F. Pearce's (1964) recent heroic but rather unsuccessful attempts to deal with complementarity, substitution, independence, and neutral want associations within the conventional framework.

II. A NEW APPROACH

Like many new approaches, the one set out in this paper draws upon several elements that have been utilized elsewhere. The chief technical novelty lies in breaking away from the traditional approach that goods are the direct objects of utility and, instead, supposing that it is the properties or characteristics of the goods from which utility is derived.

We assume that consumption is an activity in which goods, singly or in combination, are inputs and in which the output is a collection of characteristics. Utility or preference orderings are assumed to rank collections of characteristics and only to rank collections of goods indirectly through the characteristics that they possess. A meal (treated as a single good) possesses nutritional characteristics but it also possesses aesthetic characteristics, and different meals will possess these characteristics in different relative proportions. Furthermore, a dinner party, a combination of two goods, a meal and a social setting, may possess nutritional, aesthetic, and perhaps intellectual characteristics different from the combination obtainable from a meal and a social gathering consumed separately.

In general—and the richness of the approach springs more from this than from anything else—even a single good will possess more than one characteristic, so that the simplest consumption activity will be characterized by joint outputs. Furthermore, the same characteristic (for example, aesthetic properties) may be included among the joint outputs of many consumption activities so that goods which are apparently unrelated in certain of their characteristics may be related in others.

We shall assume that the structure we have interposed between the goods themselves and the consumer's preferences is, in principle, at least, of an objective kind. That is, the characteristics possessed by a good or a combination of goods are the same for all consumers and, given units of measurement, are in the same quantities,[2] so that the personal element in consumer choice arises in the choice between collections of characteristics only, not in the allocation of characteristics to the goods. The objective nature of the goods-characteristics relationship plays a crucial role in the analysis and enables us to distinguish between objective and private reactions to such things as changes in relative prices.

The essence of the new approach can be summarized as follows, each assumption representing a break with tradition:

1. The good, per se, does not give utility to the consumer; it possesses characteristics, and these characteristics give rise to utility.

2. In general, a good will possess more than one characteristic, and many characteristics will be shared by more than one good.

3. Goods in combination may possess characteristics different from those pertaining to the goods separately.

A move in the direction of the first assumption has already been made by various workers including Strotz (1957, 1959) and Gorman (1959), with the "utility tree" and other ideas associating a particular good with a particular type of utility. The theory set out here goes much further than these ideas. Multiple characteristics, structurally similar to those of the present paper but confined to a particular problem and a point utility function, are implicit in the classical "diet problem" of Stigler (1945), and multidimensioned utilities have been used by workers in other fields, for example, Thrall (1954). The third assumption, of activities involving complementary collections of goods, has been made by Morishima (1959) but in the context of single-dimensioned utility.

A variety of other approaches with similarities to that of the present paper occur scattered through the literature, for example, in Quandt (1956), or in Becker (1965), or in various discussions of investment-portfolio problems. These are typically set out as *ad hoc* approaches to particular problems. Perhaps the most important aspect of this paper is that the model is set out as a general replacement of the traditional analysis (which remains as a special case), rather than as a special solution to a special problem.

It is clear that only by moving to multiple characteristics can we incorporate many of the intrinsic qualities of individual goods. Consider the choice between a gray Chevrolet and a red Chevrolet. On ordinary theory these are either the same commodity (ignoring what may be a relevant aspect of the choice situation) or different commodities (in which case there is no a priori presumption that they are close substitutes). Here we regard them as goods associated with satisfaction vectors which differ in only one component, and we can proceed to look at the situation in much the same way as the consumer—or even the economist, in private life—would look at it.

Traditional theory is forever being forced to interpret quite common real-life

[2] Since the units in which the characteristics are measured are arbitrary, the objectivity criterion relating goods and characteristics reduces to the requirement that the *relative* quantities of a particular characteristic between unit quantities of any pair of goods should be the same for all consumers.

happenings, such as the effects of advertising in terms of "change of taste," an entirely non-operational concept since there is no way of predicting the relationship between preference before and after the change. The theory outlined here, although extremely rich in useful ways of thinking about consumer behavior, may also be thought to run the danger of adding to the economist's extensive collection of non-operational concepts. If this were true, it need not, of course, inhibit the heuristic application of the theory. Even better, however, the theory implies predictions that differ from those of traditional theory, and the predictions of the new approach seem to fit better the realities of consumer behavior.

III. A MODEL OF CONSUMER BEHAVIOR

To obtain a working model from the ideas outlined above, we shall make some assumptions which are, on balance, neither more nor less heroic than those made elsewhere in our present economic theorizing and which are intended to be no more and no less permanent parts of the theory.

1. We shall regard an individual good or a collection of goods as a consumption activity and associate a scalar (the level of the activity) with it. We shall assume that the relationship between the level of activity k, y_k, and the goods consumed in that activity to be both linear and objective, so that, if x_j is the jth commodity we have

$$x_j = \sum_k a_{jk} y_k , \qquad (1)$$

and the vector of total goods required for a given activity vector is given by

$$x = Ay . \qquad (2)$$

Since the relationships are assumed objective, the equations are assumed to hold for all individuals, the coefficients a_{jk} being determined by the intrinsic properties of the goods themselves and possibly the context of technological knowledge in the society.

2. More heroically, we shall assume that each consumption activity produces a fixed vector of characteristics[3] and that the relationship is again linear, so that, if z_i is the amount of the ith characteristic

$$z_i = \sum_k b_{ik} y_k , \qquad (3)$$

or

$$z = By . \qquad (4)$$

Again, we shall assume that the coefficients b_{ik} are objectively determined—in principle, at least—for some arbitrary choice of the units of z_i.

3. We shall assume that the individual possesses an ordinal utility function on characteristics $U(z)$ and that he will choose a situation which maximizes $U(z)$. $U(z)$ is provisionally assumed to possess the ordinary convexity properties of a standard utility function.

The chief purpose of making the assumption of linearity is to simplify the problem. A viable model could certainly be produced under the more general set of relationships

$$F_k(z, x) = 0 , \quad k = 1 \ldots m . \qquad (5)$$

The model could be analyzed in a similar way to that used by Samuelson (1953*b*) and others in analyzing production, although the existence of much jointness among outputs in the present model presents difficulties.

[3] The assumption that the consumption technology A, B is fixed is a convenience for discussing those aspects of the model (primarily static) that are the chief concern of this paper. The consequences of relaxing this particular assumption is only one of many possible extensions and expansions of the ideas presented and are discussed by the author elsewhere (Lancaster, 1966).

In this model, the relationship between the collections of characteristics available to the consumer—the vectors z—which are the direct ingredients of his preferences and his welfare, and the collections of goods available to him—the vectors x—which represent his relationship with the rest of the economy, is not direct and one-to-one, as in the traditional model, but indirect, through the activity vector y.

Consider the relationships which link z and x. These are the equation systems: $x = Ay$ (2) and $z = By$ (4). Suppose that there are r characteristics, m activities, and n goods. Only if $r = m = n$ will there be a one-to-one relationship between z and x. In this case both the B and A matrixes are square (the number of variables equals the number of equations in both sets of equations) and we can solve for y in terms of x, $y = A^{-1}x$, giving $z = BA^{-1}x$. $U(z)$ can be written directly and unambiguously as a function $u(x)$. Otherwise the relations are between vectors in spaces of different dimensions. Consider some x^* in the case in which $m > n$: equation (2) places only n restrictions on the m-vector y, so that y can still be chosen with $m - n$ degrees of freedom. If $r < m$, then there are $m - r$ degrees of freedom in choosing y, given some z, but whether the ultimate relationship gives several choices of z for a given x, or several x for a given z, and whether all vectors z are attainable, depends on the relationships between r, m, and n and the structures of the matrixes A, B. In general, we will expect that the consumer may face a choice among many paths linking goods collections with characteristics collections. The simple question asked (in principle) in the traditional analysis—does a particular consumer prefer collection x_1 or collection x_2—no longer has a direct answer, although the question, does he prefer characteristics collection z_1 or z_2, does have such an answer.

If we take the standard choice situation facing the consumer in a free market, with a linear budget constraint, this situation, in our model, becomes:

$$\begin{aligned} &\text{Maximize } U(z) \\ &\text{subject to } px \leqq k \\ &\text{with} \quad z = By \\ &\qquad\quad\ x = Ay \\ &\qquad\quad\ x, y, z \geqq 0\,. \end{aligned}$$

This is a non-linear program of an intractable kind. The problem of solution need not worry us here, since we are interested only in the properties of the solution.

IV. THE SIMPLIFIED MODEL

We shall simplify the model in the initial stages by supposing that there is a one-to-one correspondence between goods and activities so that we can write the consumer-choice program in the simpler form

$$\begin{aligned} &\text{Maximize } U(z) \\ &\text{subject to } px \leqq k \\ &\text{with} \quad z = Bx \\ &\qquad\quad\ z, x \geqq 0\,. \end{aligned}$$

This is still, of course, a non-linear program, but we now have a single step between goods and characteristics.

The model consists of four parts. There is a maximand $U(z)$ operating on characteristics, that is, U is defined on characteristics-space (C-space). The budget constraint $px \leqq k$ is defined on goods-space (G-space). The equation system $z = Bx$ represents a transformation between G-space and C-space. Finally, there are non-negativity constraints z,

$x \geqq 0$ which we shall assume to hold initially, although in some applications and with some sign conventions they may not always form part of the model.

In traditional consumer analysis, both the budget constraint and the utility function are defined on G-space, and we can immediately relate the two as in the ordinary textbook indifference-curve diagram. Here we can only relate the utility function to the budget constraint after both have been defined on the same space. We have two choices: (1) We can transform the utility function into G-space and relate it directly to the budget constraint; (2) we can transform the budget constraint into C-space and relate it directly to the utility function $U(z)$.

Each of these techniques is useful in different circumstances. In the case of the first, we can immediately write $U(z) = U(Bx) = u(x)$, so we have a new utility function directly in terms of goods, but the properties of the function $u(x)$ depend crucially on the structure of the matrix B and this, together with the constraints $x \geqq 0$ and $z = Bx \geqq 0$ give a situation much more complex than that of conventional utility maximization. The second technique again depends crucially on the structure of B and again will generally lead to a constraint of a more complex kind than in conventional analysis.

The central role in the model is, of course, played by the transformation equation $z = Bx$ and the structure and qualitative[4] properties of the matrix B. Most of the remainder of the paper will be concerned with the relationship between the properties of B, which we can call the *consumption technology*[5] of the economy, and the behavior of consumers.

Certain properties of the transformations between G- and C-space follow immediately from the fact that B is a matrix of constants, and the transformation $z = Bx$ is linear. These can be stated as follows, proof being obvious.

a) A convex set in G-space will transform into a convex set in C-space, so that the budget constraint $px \leqq k$, $x \geqq 0$ will become a convex constraint on the z's.

b) An inverse transformation will not necessarily exist, so that an arbitrary vector z in C-space may have no vector x in G-space corresponding to it.

c) Where an inverse transformation does exist from C-space into G-space, it will transform convex sets into convex sets so that, for any set of z's which do have images in G-space, the convexity of the U function on the z's will be preserved in relation to the x's.

The properties are sufficient to imply that utility maximization subject to constraint will lead to determinate solutions for consumer behavior.

V. THE STRUCTURE OF CONSUMPTION TECHNOLOGY

The consumption technology, which is as important a determinant of consumer behavior as the particular shape of the utility function, is described fully only by the A and B matrixes together, but certain types of behavior can be related to more generalized descriptions of the technology. We shall distinguish broadly between structural properties of the technology, such as the relationship between the number of rows and columns of B and/or A and whether A, B are decomposable, and qualitative properties, such as the signs of the elements of A and B.

The leading structural property of the

[4] "Qualitative" is used here in a somewhat more general sense than in the author's work on the properties of qualitatively defined systems for which see Lancaster (1962, 1965).

[5] If the relationship between goods and activities is not one-to-one, the consumption technology consists of the two matrixes B, A, as in the technology of the Von Neumann growth model.

consumption technology is the relationship between the number of characteristics (r) and the number of activities (m), that is, between the number of rows and columns of B. It will be assumed that B contains no linear dependence, so that its rank is the number of rows or columns, whichever is less. We shall assume, unless otherwise stated, a one-to-one relationship between goods and activities.

1. The number of characteristics is equal to the number of goods. In this case, there is a one-to-one relationship between activities vectors and characteristics vectors. We have $z = Bx$, $x = B^{-1}z$. If B is a permutation of a diagonal matrix then there is a one-to-one relationship between each component of z and each component of y, and the model becomes, by suitable choice of units, exactly the same as the traditional model. If B is not a diagonal permutation, the objects of utility are composite goods rather than individual goods, and the model has some important differences from the conventional analysis. Note how specialized is the traditional case in relation to our general model.

If B is a diagonal permutation but there is not a one-to-one relationship between activities and goods so that A is not a diagonal permutation, we have a model similar to that of Morishima (1959).

2. The number of characteristics is greater than the number of goods. In this case, the relationships $Bx = z$ contain more equations than variables x_i so that we cannot, in general, find a goods vector x which gives rise to an arbitrarily specified characteristics vector z. We can take a basis of any arbitrarily chosen n characteristics and consider the reduced $n \times n$ system $\bar{B} = \bar{z}$, which gives a one-to-one relationship between n characteristics and the n goods, with the remaining $r-n$ characteristics being determined from the remaining $r-n$ equations and the goods vector x corresponding to $\bar{z}$. In this case, it is generally most useful to analyze consumer behavior by transforming the utility function into G-space, rather than the budget constraint into C-space. What does the transformed utility function look like?

As shown in the Appendix, the utility function transformed into G-space retains its essential convexity. An intuitive way of looking at the situation is to note that all characteristics collections which are actually available are contained in an n-dimensional slice through the r-dimensional utility function, and that all slices through a convex function are themselves convex. The transformation of this n-dimensional slice into G-space preserves this convexity.

For investigation of most aspects of consumer behavior, the case in which the number of characteristics exceeds the number of goods—a case we may often wish to associate with simple societies—can be treated along with the very special case (of which conventional analysis is a special subcase) in which the number of characteristics and goods is equal. In other words, given the consumption technology, we concern ourselves only with the particular n-dimensional slice of the r-dimensional utility function implied by that technology[6] and, since the slice of the utility function has the same general properties as any n-dimensional utility function, we can proceed as if the utility function was defined on only n characteristics.

[6] Assuming no decomposability or singularities in the consumption technology matrix B, then, if z_n is the vector of any n components of z and B_n, the corresponding square submatrix of B, the subspace of C-space to which the consumer is confined, is that defined by $z_{r-n} = B_{r-n}B_n^{-1} z_n$, where z_{r-n}, B_{r-n} are the vector and corresponding submatrix of B consisting of the components not included in z_n, B_n.

3. In the third case, in which the number of goods exceeds the number of characteristics, a situation probably descriptive of a complex economy such as that of the United States, there are properties of the situation that are different from those of the two previous cases and from the conventional analysis.

Here, the consumption technology, $z = Bx$, has fewer equations than variables so that, for every characteristics vector there is more than one goods vector. For every point in his characteristics-space, the consumer has a choice between different goods vectors. Given a price vector, this choice is a pure efficiency choice, so that for every characteristics vector the consumer will choose the most efficient combination of goods to achieve that collection of characteristics, and the efficiency criterion will be minimum cost.

The efficiency choice for a characteristics vector z^* will be the solution of the canonical linear program

$$\begin{aligned} &\text{Minimize} \quad px \\ &\text{subject to } Bx = z^* \\ &\qquad\qquad x \geqq 0 . \end{aligned}$$

Since this is a linear program, once we have the solution x^* for some z^*, with value k^*, we can apply a scalar multiple to fit the solution to any budget value k and characteristics vector $(k/k^*)z^*$. By varying z^*, the consumer, given a budget constraint $px = k$, can determine a characteristics frontier consisting of all z such that the value of the above program is just equal to k. There will be a determinate goods vector associated with each point of the characteristics frontier.

As in the previous case, it is easy to show that the set of characteristics vectors in C-space that are preferred or indifferent to z transforms into a convex set in G-space if it is a convex set in C-space; it is also easy to show that the set of z's that can be obtained from the set of x's satisfying the convex constraint $px \leqq k$ is also a convex set. The characteristics frontier is, therefore, concave to the origin, like a transformation curve. For a consumption technology with four goods and two characteristics, the frontier could have any of the three shapes shown in Figure 1. Note that, in general, if B is a positive matrix, the positive orthant in G-space transforms into a cone which lies in the interior of the positive orthant in C-space, a point illustrated in the diagrams.

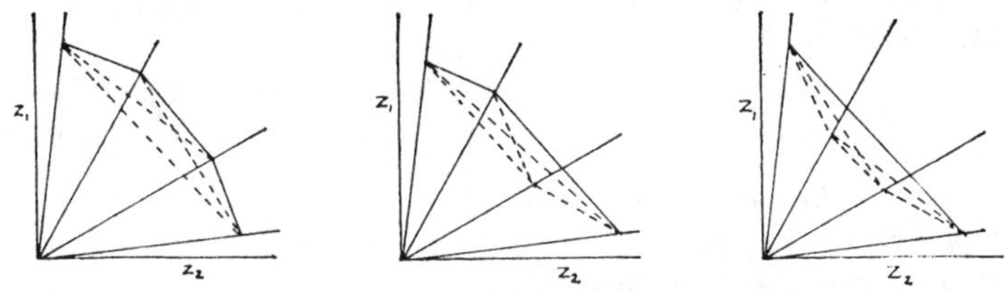

FIG. 1

A consumer's complete choice subject to a budget constraint $px \leqq k$ can be considered as consisting of two parts:

a) An efficiency choice, determining the characteristics frontier and the associated efficient goods collections.

b) A private choice, determining which point on the characteristics frontier is preferred by him.

The efficiency choice is an objective not a subjective choice. On the assumption that the consumption technology is objective, the characteristics frontier is also objective, and it is the same for all consumers facing the same budget constraint. Furthermore the characteristics frontier is expanded or contracted linearly and proportionally to an increase or decrease in income, so that the frontier has the same *shape* for all consumers facing the same prices, income differences simply being reflected in homogeneous expansion or contraction.

We should note that, if the consumption technology matrix has certain special structural properties, we may obtain a mixture of the above cases. For example, a matrix with the structure

$$B \equiv \begin{bmatrix} B_1 0 \\ 0 B_2 \end{bmatrix},$$

where B_1 is an $(s \times k)$ matrix and B_2 is an $(r-s) \times (n-k)$ matrix, partitions the technology into two disconnected parts, one relating s of the characteristics to k of the goods, the other separately relating $r-s$ of the characteristics to $n-k$ of the goods. We can have $s \geqq k$ and $r-s < n-k$ giving a mixed case.

Dropping the assumption of a one-to-one relationship between goods and activities does not add greatly to the difficulties of the analysis. We have, as part of the technology, $x = Ay$, so that the budget constraint $px \leqq k$ can be written immediately as $pAy \leqq k$. The goods prices transform directly into implicit activity prices $q = pA$. Interesting cases arise, of course. If the number of goods is less than the number of activities, then not all q's are attainable from the set of p's; and if the number of goods exceeds the number of activities, different p vectors will correspond to the same q vector. This implies that certain changes in relative goods prices may leave activity prices, and the consumer's choice situation, unchanged.

In most of the succeeding analysis, we will be concerned with the B matrix and the relationship between activities and characteristics, since this represents the most distinctive part of the theory.

VI. THE EFFICIENCY SUBSTITUTION EFFECT AND REVEALED PREFERENCE

At this stage, it is desirable to examine the nature of the efficiency choice so that we can appreciate the role it plays in the consumer behavior implied by our model. Consider a case in which there are two characteristics, a case that can be illustrated diagrammatically, and, say, four activities.

The activities-characteristics portion of the consumption technology is defined by the two equations

$$\begin{aligned} z_1 &= b_{11}y_1 + b_{12}y_2 + b_{13}y_3 + b_{14}y_4 ; \\ z_2 &= b_{21}y_1 + b_{22}y_2 + b_{23}y_3 + b_{24}y_4 . \end{aligned} \tag{6.1}$$

With activity 1 only, the characteristics will be obtained in proportion, b_{11}/b_{21} (the ray labeled 1 in Fig. 2). Similarly with activities 2, 3, 4, one at a time, characteristics will be obtained in proportions b_{12}/b_{22}, b_{13}/b_{23}, b_{14}/b_{24}, respectively, corresponding to the rays 2, 3, 4 in the diagram.

We are given a budget constraint in goods space of the form $\Sigma_i p_i x_i \leqq k$. If there is a one-to-one correspondence between goods and activities, the prices of the activities are given by p_i. If there is not a one-to-one relationship, but a goods-activities portion of the consumption technology

$$x_i = a_{i1}y_1 + a_{i2}y_2 + a_{i3}y_3 + a_{i4}y_4 \qquad i = 1 \ldots n, \tag{6.2}$$

then the budget constraint can be transformed immediately into characteristics space

$$\left(\sum_i p_i a_{i1}\right) y_1 + \left(\sum_i p_i a_{i2}\right) y_2 + \left(\sum_i p_i a_{i3}\right) y_3 + \left(\sum_i p_i a_{i4}\right) y_4 \leqq k \tag{6.3}$$

where the composite prices $q_j = \Sigma_i p_i a_{ij}$, $j = 1 \ldots 4$ represent the prices of each activity. The number of goods in relation to the number of activities is irrelevant at this stage, since each activity has a unique and completely determined price q_j, given the prices of the goods.

Given q_1, q_2, q_3, q_4, and k, the maximum attainable level of each activity in isolation can be written down (corresponding to the points E_1, E_2, E_3, E_4 in Fig. 2,) and the lines joining these points represent combinations attainable subject to the budget constraint. In the diagram it has been assumed that prices are such that combinations of 1 and 2, 2 and 3, 3 and 4 are efficient, giving the characteristics frontier, while combinations 1 and 3, 2 and 4, or 1 and 4 are inefficient.

Suppose that the consumer chooses characteristics in the combination represented by the ray z^*, giving a point E^* on the frontier. Now suppose that relative prices change: in particular, that the price of activity 2 rises so that, with income still at k, the point E_2 moves inward on ray 2. If the movement is small enough, the characteristics frontier continues to have a corner at E_2, and the consumer will continue to obtain characteristics in proportion z^* by a combination of activities 1 and 2. If income is adjusted so that the new frontier goes through E^*, the consumer will use the same activities in the same proportions as before.

If the price of activity 2 rises sufficiently, however, the point E_2 will move inward past the line joining E_1 and E_3 to E_2'. Combinations of 1 and 2 and of 2 and 3 are now inefficient combinations

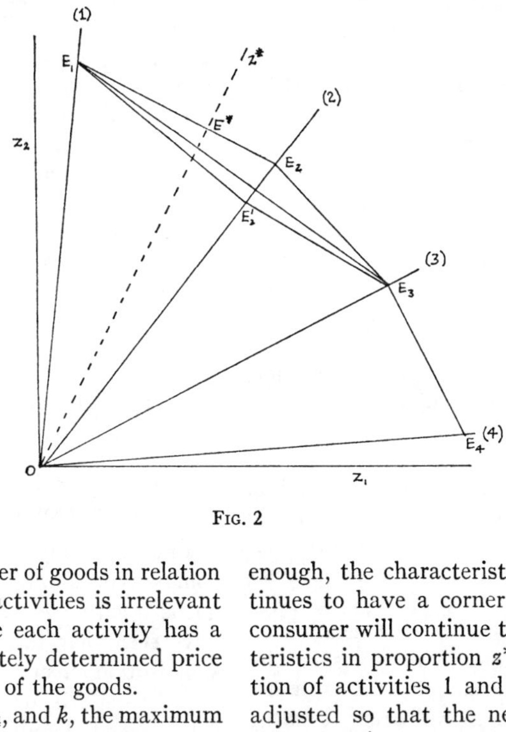

FIG. 2

of activities, their place on the efficiency frontier being taken by a combination of 1 and 3. The consumer will switch from a combination of activities 1 and 2 to a combination of 1 and 3.

Thus there is an efficiency substitution effect which is essentially a switching effect. If price changes are too small to cause a switch, there is no efficiency substitution effect: If they are large enough, the effect comes from a complete switch from one activity to another.

The manifestation of the efficiency substitution effect in goods space depends on the structure of the A (goods-activities) matrix. There are two polar cases:

a) If there is a one-to-one relationship between goods and activities, the efficiency substitution effect will result in a complete switch from consumption of one good to consumption of another. This might be regarded as typical of situations involving similar but differentiated products, where a sufficiently large price change in one of the products will result in widespread switching to, or away from, the product.

b) If there is not a one-to-one relationship between goods and activities and, in particular, if all goods are used in all activities, the efficiency substitution effect will simply result in less consumption of a good whose price rises, not a complete disappearance of that good from consumption. If all cakes require eggs but in different proportions, a rise in the price of eggs will cause a switch from egg-intensive cakes to others, with a decline in the consumption of eggs, but not to zero.

The existence of an efficiency substitution effect depends, of course, on the number of activities exceeding the number of characteristics (otherwise switching of activities will not, in general, occur[7]) but does not require that the number of goods exceed the number of characteristics. In fact, with two goods, two characteristics, and three activities, the effect may occur. With two goods, two characteristics and one hundred activities (well spread over the spectrum), an almost smooth efficiency substitution effect would occur.

Since the efficiency substitution effect implies that consumers may change goods collections as a result of compensated relative price changes, simply in order to obtain the same characteristics collection in the most efficient manner, it is obvious that the existence of substitution does not of itself either require or imply convexity of the preference function on characteristics. In other words, the axiom of revealed preference may be satisfied even if the consumer always consumes characteristics in fixed proportions (and possibly even if the consumers had *concave* preferences), so that the "revelation" may be simply of efficient choice rather than convexity. A formal proof is given in the Appendix.

VII. OBJECTIVE AND SUBJECTIVE CHOICE AND DEMAND THEORY

In an economy or subeconomy with a complex consumption technology (many goods relative to characteristics), we have seen that there are two types of substitution effect:

1. Changes in relative prices may result in goods bundle I becoming an *in-*

[7] This is a somewhat imprecise statement in that, if the B matrix is partitionable into disconnected subtechnologies, for some of which the number of activities exceeds the number of characteristics and for others the reverse, an efficiency-substitution effect may exist over certain groups of activities, although the number of activities is less than the number of characteristics over-all.

efficient method of attaining a given bundle of characteristics and being replaced by goods bundle II even when the characteristics bundle is unchanged.

2. Changes in relative prices, with or without causing efficiency substitutions as in type 1, may alter the slope of the characteristics frontier in a segment relevant to a consumer's characteristics choice. The change in the slope of the frontier is analogous to the change in the budget line slope in the traditional case and, with a convex preference function, will result in a substitution of one characteristics bundle for another and, hence, of one goods bundle for another. Note that, even with smoothly convex preferences, this effect may not occur, since the consumer may be on a corner of the polyhedral characteristics frontier, and thus his characteristics choice could be insensitive to a certain range of slope changes on the facets.

The first effect, the efficiency substitution effect, is universal and objective. Subject to consumer ignorance or inefficiency,[8] this substitution effect is independent of the shapes of individual consumers' preference functions and hence of the effects of income distribution.

The second effect, the private substitution effect, has the same properties, in general, as the substitution effect in traditional theory. In particular, an aggregately compensated relative price change combined with a redistribution of income may result in no substitution effect in the aggregate, or a perverse one.

These two substitution effects are independent—either may occur without the other in certain circumstances—but in general we will expect them both to take place and hence that their effects will be reinforcing, if we are concerned with a complex economy. Thus, the consumer model presented here, in the context of an advanced economy, has, in a sense, more substitution than the traditional model. Furthermore, since part of the total substitution effect arises from objective, predictable, and income-distribution-free efficiency considerations, our confidence in the downward slope of demand curves is increased even when income redistribution takes place.

Since it is well known that satisfaction of the revealed preference axioms *in the aggregate* (never guaranteed by traditional theory) leads to global stability in multimarket models (see, for example, Karlin, 1959), the efficiency substitution effect increases confidence in this stability.

In a simple economy, with few goods or activities relative to characteristics, the efficiency substitution effect will be generally absent. Without this reinforcement of the private substitution effect, we would have some presumption that perverse consumer effects ("Giffen goods," backward-bending supply curves) and lower elasticities of demand would characterize simple economies as compared with complex economies. This seems to be in accord with at least the mythology of the subject, but it is certainly empirically verifiable. On this model, consumption technology as well as income levels differentiate consumers in different societies, and we would not necessarily expect a poor urban American to behave in his consumption like a person at the same real-income level in a simple economy.

[8] One of the properties of this model is that it gives scope for the consumer to be more or less efficient in achieving his desired characteristics bundle, although we will usually assume he is completely efficient. This adds a realistic dimension to consumer behavior (traditional theory never permits him to be out of equilibrium) and gives a rationale for the Consumers' Union and similar institutions.

VIII. COMMODITY GROUPS, SUBSTITUTES, COMPLEMENTS

In a complex economy, with a large number of activities and goods as well as characteristics, and with a two-matrix (A, B) consumption technology, it is obvious that taxonomy could be carried out almost without limit, an expression of the richness of the present approach. Although an elaborate taxonomy is not very useful, discussion of a few selected types of relationships between goods can be of use. One of the important features of this model is that we can discuss relationships between goods, as revealed in the structure of the technology. In the conventional approach, there are, of course, no relationships between goods as such, only properties of individual's preferences.

The simplest taxonomy is that based on the zero entries in the technology matrixes. It may be that both matrixes A, B are almost "solid," in which case there is little to be gained from a taxonomic approach. If, however, the B matrix contains sufficient zeros to be decomposable as follows,

$$B \equiv \begin{bmatrix} B_1 0 \\ 0 B_2 \end{bmatrix}, \qquad (7.1)$$

so that there is some set of characteristics and some set of activities such that these characteristics are derived only from these activities and these activities give rise to no other characteristics, then we can separate that set of characteristics and activities from the remainder of the technology. If, further, the activities in question require a particular set of goods which are used in no other activities (implying a decomposition of the A matrix), then we can regard the goods as forming an *intrinsic commodity group.* Goods within the group have the property that efficiency substitution effects will occur only for relative price changes within the group and will be unaffected by changes in the prices of other goods. If the utility function on characteristics has the conventional properties, there may, of course, be *private* substitution effects for goods within the group when the prices of other goods changes. For an intrinsic commodity group, the whole of the objective analysis can be carried out without reference to goods outside the group.

Goods from different intrinsic commodity groups can be regarded as *intrinsically unrelated*, goods from the same group as *intrinsically related.*

If, within a group, there are two activities, each in a one-to-one relationship with a different good, and if the bundles of characteristics derived from the two goods differ only in a scalar (that is, have identical proportions), we can regard the two goods in question as *intrinsic perfect substitutes*. If the associated characteristics bundles are similar, the goods are *close substitutes*. We can give formal respectability to that traditional butter-margarine example of our texts by considering them as two goods giving very similar combinations of characteristics.

On the other hand, if a certain activity requires more than one good and if these goods are used in no other activity we can consider them as *intrinsic total complements* and they will always be consumed in fixed proportions, if at all.

Many goods within a commodity group will have relationships to each other which are partly complementary and partly substitution. This will be true if two goods, for example, are used in different combinations in each of several activities, each activity giving rise to a similar combination of characteristics. The goods are complements within each activity, but the activities are substitutes.

IX. LABOR, LEISURE, AND OCCUPATIONAL CHOICE

Within the structure of the present theory, we can regard labor as a reversed activity, using characteristics as inputs and producing commodities or a commodity as output. This is similar to the standard approach of generalized conventional theory, as in Debreu (1959).

We can add to this approach in an important way within the context of the present model by noting that a work activity may produce characteristics, as well as the commodity labor, as outputs. This is structurally equivalent to permitting some of the columns of the B matrix to have both negative and positive elements, corresponding to activities that "use up" some characteristics (or produce them in negative quantities) and produce others. In a work activity, the corresponding column of the A matrix will contain a single negative coefficient for the commodity labor, or, more differentiated, for one or more types of labor. If a work activity corresponds to a column of mixed signs in the B matrix, it is a recognition of the obvious truth that some work activities give rise to valued characteristics directly from the work itself.

Consider a very simple model of two characteristics with two commodities, labor and consumption goods. Both labor and consumption goods correspond to separate activities giving rise to the two characteristics in different proportions—perhaps negative in the case of labor. With no income other than labor, and only one good available to exchange for labor, we can collapse work and consumption into a single work-consumption activity. Given the wage rate in terms of the consumption good, the characteristics resulting from the work-consumption activity are given by a linear combination of the characteristics from work and consumption separately, the weights in the combination being given by the wage rate.

Add another activity, leisure, which gives rise to the two characteristics, and the constraint that the weighted sum of the levels of activity labor and activity leisure is a constant.

The model is illustrated in Figure 3. W represents a work-consumption activity giving positive levels of both characteristics, l represents a leisure activity, also giving positive levels of both characteristics. The constraint on total time (so that a linear combination of w and l is a constant) is represented by some line joining w, l.

If the constraint line has, like AB in the diagram, a negative slope, then individual consumers' utility functions will be tangent to the constraint at different points (like m, m') and we will have a neoclassical type of labor-leisure choice in which the proportions depend on individual preferences. Some consumers' preferences may be such that they will choose A (maximum work) or B (maximum leisure), but it is a private choice.

In this model, however, for a certain level of the wage, given the coefficients of the technology, the constraint may have a positive slope as in $A'B$, or AB'. If the constraint is $A'B$ (corresponding, *ceteris paribus*, to a sufficiently low real wage), *all* individuals will choose B, the only efficient point on the constraint set $OA'B$. At a sufficiently high wage, giving constraint set OAB', A, the maximum labor choice, is the only efficient choice and will be chosen by *all* individuals.

The above effect, in which for some wage range there is a private labor-leisure choice between efficient points while outside the range all individuals will take maximum work or maximum leisure, can only occur if both the work-consumption and leisure activities give both characteristics in positive amounts. If the using up of characteristic 2 in labor exceeded the amount of that characteristic gained by consumption, then the work-consumption activity might lie outside the positive quadrant, like w'. In this case, a constraint like $A'B$ can exist, but not one like AB'. Furthermore, if the consumer will choose only positive characteristics vectors, no consumer will choose maximum work.

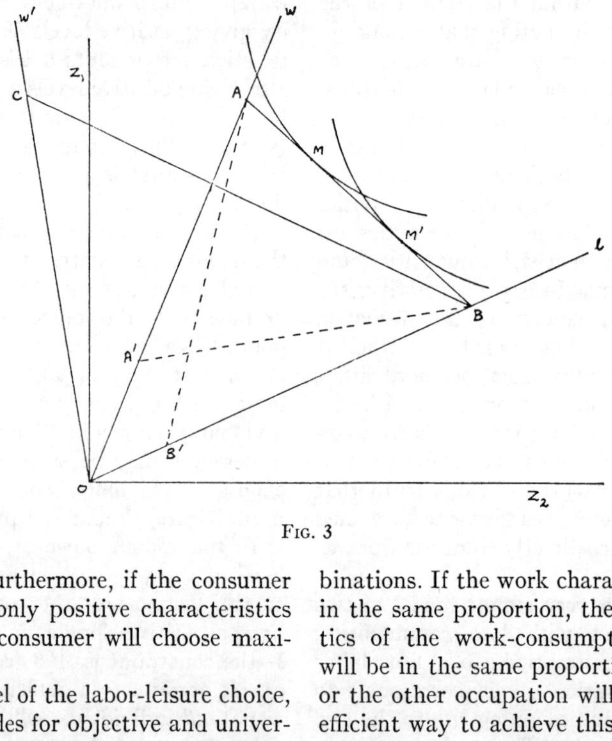

FIG. 3

This model of the labor-leisure choice, which provides for objective and universal efficiency choices as well as private choices, may be the basis for a useful working model for an underdeveloped area. If the "leisure" be defined as "working one's own field," the work-consumption activity as entering the market economy, we see that there will be wages below which no peasant will offer himself as paid labor and that this is an *efficiency* choice and not a private choice.

We can use the same type of model also to analyze occupational choice. Suppose that we have two types of work (occupations) but otherwise the conditions are as above. If and only if the characteristics arising from the work itself are different in the two occupations, the two work-consumption activities will give rise to activities in different combinations. If the work characteristics are in the same proportion, the characteristics of the work-consumption activity will be in the same proportions and one or the other occupation will be the only efficient way to achieve this characteristics bundle.

Figure 4 illustrates one possible set of relationships for such a model. In the diagram, w_1, w_2 represent the characteristics combinations from work-consumption activities in occupations 1 and 2, l the characteristics combinations from leisure. The frontier consists of the lines AC (combinations of w_1 and leisure) and AB (combinations of w_2 and leisure). We shall impose the realistic restriction that an individual can have only a single occupation so that AB is not a possible combination of activities.

The choice of occupation, given the relationships in the figure, depends on personal preferences, being M_1 (combination of w_2 and leisure) for an individual with preferences skewed towards z_2 and M_2 for an individual with preferences skewed towards z_1. But note a special effect. For some individuals whose indifference curves cannot touch BC but can touch AC, the efficient choice will be the corner solution M_3 (= B). There is, in fact, a segment of AC to the left of w_2 (the part of AC to the right of w_2 is dominated by BC), lying below the horizontal through B which is inefficient relative to B and will never be chosen.

In a configuration like the above we have the very interesting effect, where those who choose occupation 1 will work very hard at it; leisure-lovers will choose private combinations of occupation 2 and leisure—surely a good description of effects actually observed.

The loss to certain individuals from confinement to a single occupation is obvious. Could he choose a combination of occupations 1 and 2, the individual at M_2 would do so and be better off than with a combination of occupation 1 and leisure. In a two-characteristic, three-activity model, of course, two activities will be chosen at most, so that leisure plus both occupations will not appear.

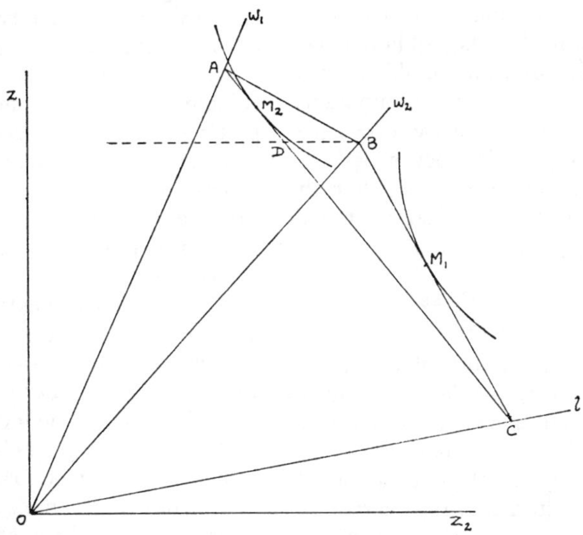

FIG. 4

The configuration in the diagram (Fig. 4) represents the situation for some set of technical coefficients and specific wages in the two occupations. A large number of other configurations is possible. In particular, if the wage rate in occupation 2 fell sufficiently, BC would lie inside AC and occupation 2 would cease to be chosen by any individual. All individuals, in this case, would choose their various personal combinations of occupation 1 and leisure.

Confinement to a single occupation need not result in a welfare loss, even when neither occupation dominates the other in an efficiency sense. If the technical coefficients were different, so that the characteristics vectors representing occupation 2 and leisure changed places, then the work-leisure combinations would be given by AB and BC, both efficient relative to any combination of occupations 1 and 2. In this case, all individuals would optimize by some combination of leisure and any one of the occupations.

Approaches similar to those outlined above seem to provide a better basis for analysis of occupational choice than the traditional, non-operational, catch-all "non-monetary advantages."

X. CONSUMER DURABLES, ASSETS, AND MONEY

Within the framework of the model, we have a scheme for dealing with durable goods and assets. A durable good can be regarded simply as giving rise to an activity in which the output consists of dated characteristics, the characteristics of different dates being regarded as different characteristics.

Given characteristics as joint outputs and two types of dimension in characteristics space—cross-section and time—any asset or durable good can be regarded as producing a combination of several characteristics at any one time, and that combination need not be regarded as continuing unchanged through time. In the decision to buy a new automobile, for example, the characteristic related to "fashion" or "style" may be present in relative strength in the first season, relatively less in later seasons, although the characteristics related to "transportation" may remain with constant coefficients over several seasons.

Elementary textbooks stress the multidimensional characteristics of money and other assets. The present model enables this multidimensionality to be appropriately incorporated. "Safety," "liquidity," and so forth become workable concepts that can be related to characteristics. We can use analysis similar to that of the preceding sections to show why efficiency effects will cause the universal disappearance of some assets (as in Gresham's Law) while other assets will be held in combinations determined by personal preferences. It would seem that development along these lines, coupled with development of some of the recent approaches to consumer preferences over time as in Koopmans (1960), Lancaster (1963), or Koopmans, Diamond, and Williamson (1964) might eventually lead to a full-blooded theory of consumer behavior with respect to assets—saving and money—which we do not have at present.

In situations involving risk, we can use multiple characteristics better to analyze individual behavior. For example, we might consider a gamble to be an activity giving rise to three characteristics—a mathematical expectation, a maximum gain, and a maximum loss. One consumer's utility function may be such that he gives more weight to the maximum gain than to the maximum loss or the expected value, another's utility function may be biased in the opposite direction. All kinds of models can be developed along these lines, and they are surely more realistic than the models (Von Neumann and Morgenstern, 1944; Friedman and Savage, 1952) in which the expected value, alone, appears in the utility-maximizing decisions.

XI. NEW COMMODITIES, DIFFERENTIATED GOODS, AND ADVERTISING

Perhaps the most difficult thing to do with traditional consumer theory is to introduce a new commodity—an event that occurs thousands of times in the U.S. economy, even over a generation, without any real consumers being unduly disturbed. In the theory of production, where activity-analysis methods have become widely used, a new process or product can be fitted in well enough; but in consumer theory we have traditionally had to throw away our n-dimensional preference functions and replace them by totally new $(n + 1)$ dimensional functions, with no predictable consequences.

In this model, the whole process is extraordinarily simple. A new product simply means addition of one or more activities to the consumption technology. Given the technology (or the relevant portion of it) and given the intrinsic characteristic of the activity associated with the new good, we simply insert it in the appropriate place in the technology, ***and we can predict the consequences.***

If a new good possesses characteristics in the same proportions as some existing good, it will simply fail to sell to anyone if its price is too high, or will completely replace the old good if its price is sufficiently low.

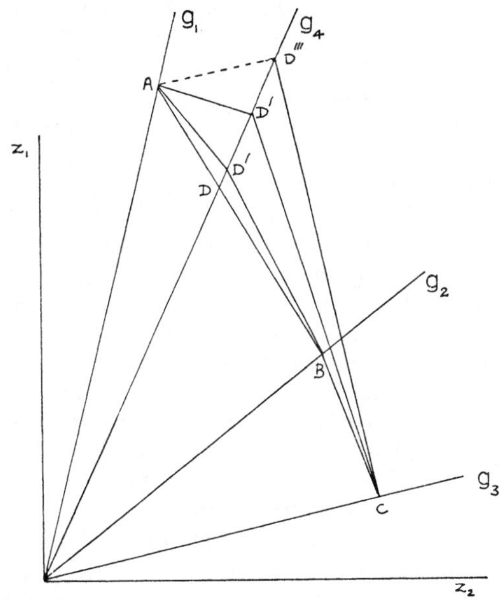

FIG. 5

More usually, we can expect a new good to possess characteristics in somewhat different proportions to an existing good. If its price is too high, it may be dominated by some ***combination*** of existing goods and will fail to sell. If its price is sufficiently low, it will result in adding a new point to the efficiency frontier. In Figure 5, ABC represents the old efficiency frontier, on which some individuals will consume combinations of goods g_1 and g_2 in various proportions, some combinations of g_2 and g_3. If the price of the new good, g_4, is such that it represents a point, D, on the old efficiency frontier, some persons (those using combinations of g_1 and g_2) will be indifferent between their old combinations and combinations of either g_1 and g_4 or g_2 and g_4. If the price of g_4 is a little lower, it will push the efficiency frontier out to D'. Individuals will now replace combinations of g_1 and g_2 with combinations of g_1 and g_4 or g_2 and g_4, depending on their preferences. The new good will have taken away some of the sales from both g_1 and g_2, but completely replaced neither.

If the price of g_4 were lower, giving point D'', then combinations of g_4 and g_3 would dominate g_2, and g_2 would be replaced. At an even lower price, like D''', combinations of g_4 and g_3 would dominate g_2, and the corner solution g_4 only would dominate all combinations of g_1 and g_4 (since AD''' has a positive slope), so that g_4 would now replace both g_1 and g_2.

Differentiation of goods has presented almost as much of a problem to traditional theory as new commodities. In the present analysis, the difference is really one of degree only. We can regard a differentiated good typically as a new good within an existing intrinsic commodity group, and within that group analyze it as a new commodity. Sometimes there appear new commodities of a more fundamental kind whose characteristics cut across those of existing groups.

We may note that differentiation of goods, if successful (that is, if the differentiated goods are actually sold) represents a welfare improvement since it pushes the efficiency frontier outward an enables the consumer more efficiently to reach his preferred combination of characteristics.

Many economists take a puritanical view of commodity differentiation since their theory has induced them to believe that it is some single characteristic of a commodity that is relevant to consumer decisions (that is, automobiles are only for transportation), so that commodity variants are regarded as wicked tricks to trap the uninitiated into buying unwanted trimmings. This is not, of course, a correct deduction even from the conventional analysis, properly used, but is manifestly incorrect when account is taken of multiple characteristics.

A rather similar puritanism has also been apparent in the economist's approach to advertising. In the neoclassical analysis, advertising, if it does not represent simple information (and little information is called for in an analysis in which a good is simply a good), is an attempt to "change tastes" in the consumer. Since "tastes" are the ultimate datum in welfare judgments, the idea of changing them makes economists uncomfortable.

On the analysis presented here, there is much wider scope for informational advertising, especially as new goods appear constantly. Since the consumption technology of a modern economy is clearly very complex, consumers require a great deal of information concerning that technology. When a new version of a dishwashing detergent is produced which contains hand lotion, we have a product with characteristics different from those of the old. The consumption technology is changed, and consumers are willing to pay to be told of the change. Whether the new product pushes out the efficiency frontier (compared, say, with a combination of dishwasher and hand lotion consumed separately) is, of course, another matter.

In any case, advertising, product design, and marketing specialists, who have a heavy commitment to understanding how consumers actually do behave, themselves act as though consumers regard a commodity as having multiple characteristics and as though consumers weigh the various combinations of characteristics contained in different commodities in reaching their decisions. At this preliminary stage of presenting the model set out here, this is strong evidence in its favor.

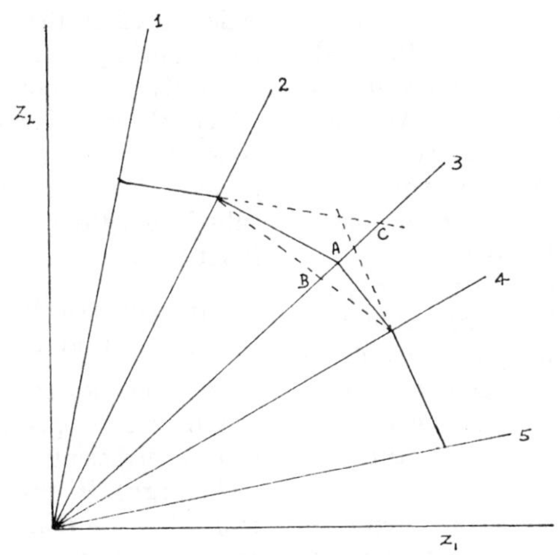

FIG. 6

XII. GENERAL EQUILIBRIUM, WELFARE, AND OTHER MATTERS

Since the demand for goods depends on objective and universal efficiency effects as well as on private choices, we can draw some inferences relative to equilibrium in the economy.

A commodity, especially a commodity within an intrinsic commodity group, must have a price low enough relative to the prices of other commodities to be represented on the efficiency frontier, otherwise it will be purchased by no one and will not appear in the economy. This implies that if there are n viable commodities in a group, each in a one-to-one relation to an activity, the equilibrium prices will be such that the efficiency frontier has $n-1$ facets in the two-characteristic case. In Figure 6, for example, where the price of commodity 3 brings it to point A on the efficiency frontier, that price could not be allowed to rise to a level bringing it inside point B, or it would disappear from the market; and if its price fell below a level corresponding to C, commodities 2 and 4 would disappear from the market. Thus the limits on prices necessary for the existence of all commodities within a group can be established (in principle) from objective data. Only the demand within that price range depends on consumer preferences.

With a large number of activities relative to characteristics, equilibrium prices would give a many-faceted efficiency frontier that would be approximated by a smooth curve having the general shape of a production possibility curve. For many purposes it may be mathematically simple to analyze the situation in terms of a smooth efficiency frontier. We can then draw on some of the analysis that exists, relating factor inputs to outputs of goods, as in Samuelson (1953*b*). Goods in our model correspond to factors in the production model, and characteristics in our model to commodities in the production model.

The welfare implications of the model set out here are quite complex and deserve a separate treatment. We might note several important aspects of the welfare problem, however, which arise directly from a many-faceted, many-cornered efficiency frontier:

1. Consumers whose choices represent a corner on the efficiency frontier are not, in general, *equating* marginal rates of substitution between characteristics to the ratio of any parameters of the situation or to marginal rates of substitution of other consumers.

2. Consumers whose choices represent points on different facets of the efficiency frontier are equating their marginal rates of substitution between characteristics to different implicit price ratios between characteristics. If there is a one-to-one relationship between goods and activities, the consumers are reacting to relative prices between different sets of goods. The traditional marginal conditions for Paretian exchange optimum do not hold because the price ratio relevant to one consumer's decisions differs from the price ratio relevant to another's. In common-sense terms, the price ratio between a Cadillac and a Continental is irrelevant to my decisions, but the price ratio between two compact cars is relevant, while there are other individuals for whom the Cadillac/Continental ratio is the relevant datum. If the A matrix is strongly connected, however, the implicit price ratios between different activities can correspond to price ratios between the same sets of goods, and the Paretian conditions may be relevant.

Finally, we may note that the shape of the equilibrium efficiency frontier and the existence of the efficiency substitution effect can result in demand conditions with the traditionally assumed properties, even if the traditional, smooth, convex utility function does not exist. In particular, a simple utility function in which characteristics are consumed in constant proportions—the proportions perhaps changing with income—can be substituted for the conventional utility function.

XIII. OPERATIONAL AND PREDICTIVE CHARACTERISTICS OF THE MODEL

In principle, the model set out here can be made operational (that is, empirical coefficients can be assigned to the technology). In practice, the task will be more difficult than the equivalent task of determining the actual production technology of an economy.

To emphasize that the model is not simply heuristic, we can examine a simple scheme for sketching out the efficiency frontier for some commodity group. We shall assume that there is a one-to-one relationship between activities and goods, that at least one characteristic shared by the commodities is capable of independent determination, and that a great quantity of suitable market data is available.

In practice, we will attempt to operate with the minimum number of characteristics that give sufficient explanatory power. These may be combinations of fundamental characteristics (a factor-analysis situation) or fundamental characteristics themselves.

Consider some commodity group such as household detergents. We have a primary objective characteristic, cleaning power, measured in some chosen way. We wish to test whether one or more other characteristics are necessary to describe the consumer-choice situation.

We take a two-dimensional diagram with characteristic "cleaning power" along one axis. Along the axis we mark the cleaning power per dollar outlay of all detergents observed to be sold at the same time. If this is the same for all detergents, this single characteristic describes the situation, and we do not seek further. However, we shall assume this is not so. From our observed market data, we obtain cross-price elasticities between all detergents, taken two at a time. From the model, we know that cross-price elasticities will be highest between detergents with adjacent characteristics vectors, so that the order of the characteristics vectors as we rotate from one axis to the other in the positive quadrant can be established.

The ordering of "cleaning power per dollar" along one axis can be compared with the ordering of the characteristics vectors. If the orderings are the same, an equilibrium efficiency frontier can be built up with two characteristics as in Figure 7a. The slopes of the facets can be determined within limits by the limiting prices at which the various detergents go off the market. If the ordering in terms of cleaning power does not agree with the ordering in terms of cross-elasticity, as in Figure 7b, two characteristics do not describe the market appropriately, since detergent with cleaning power 3 in the figure cannot be on the efficiency frontier. But with a third characteristic, detergent 3 could be adjacent to detergents 2 and 1 in an extra dimension, and we could build up an efficiency frontier in three characteristics.

Other evidence could, of course, be used to determine the efficiency frontier for a given market situation. Among this evidence is that arising from ordinary activity-analysis theory, that, with r characteristics we would expect to find some consumers who used r commodities at the same time, unless all consumers were on corners or edges of the efficiency frontier.

Last, but possibly not least, simply asking consumers about the characteristics associated with various commodities may be much more productive than attempts to extract information concerning preferences within the context of conventional theory.

In general, if consumer preferences are well dispersed (so that all facets of the efficiency frontier are represented in some consumer's choice pattern), a combination of information concerning interpersonal variances in the collections of goods chosen and of the effects of price changes on both aggregate and individual choices can, in principle, be used to ferret out the nature of the consumption technology. Some of the problems that arise are similar to those met by psychologists in measuring intelligence, personality, and other multidimensional traits, so that techniques similar to those used in psychology, such as factor analysis, might prove useful.

Even without specification of the consumption technology, the present theory makes many predictions of a structural kind which may be contrasted with the predictions of conventional theory. Some of these are set out in Chart 1.

XIV. CONCLUSION

In this model we have extended into consumption theory activity analysis, which has proved so penetrating in its application to production theory. The crucial assumption in making this application has been the assumption that goods possess, or give rise to, multiple characteristics in fixed proportions and that it is these characteristics, not goods themselves, on which the consumer's preferences are exercised.

The result, as this brief survey of the possibilities has shown, is a model very many times richer in heuristic explanatory and predictive power than the con-

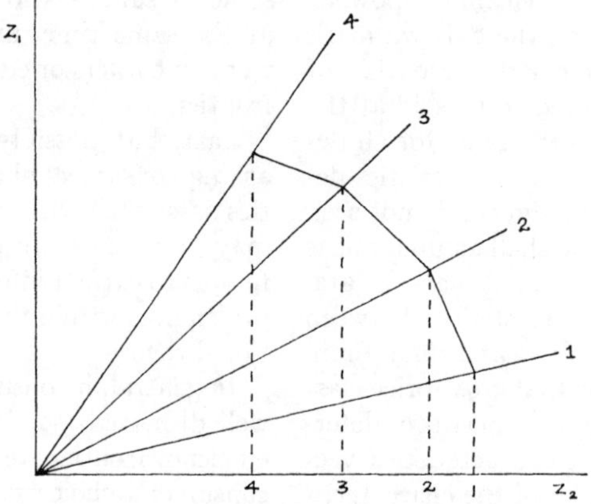

FIG. 7a

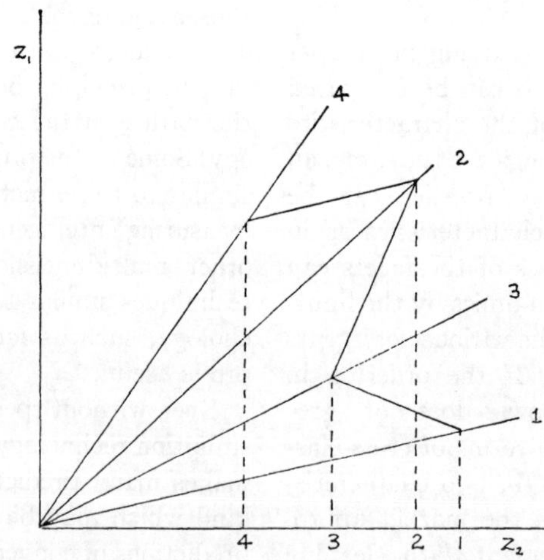

FIG. 7b

ventional model of consumer behavior and one that deals easily with those many common-sense characteristics of actual behavior that have found no place in traditional exposition.

This paper is nothing more than a condensed presentation of some of the great number of possible ways in which the model can be used. It is hoped that a door has been opened to a new, rich treasure house of ideas for the future development of the most refined and least powerful branch of economic theory, the theory of the consumer himself.

CHART 1

This Theory	Conventional Theory
Wood will not be a close substitute for bread, since characteristics are dissimilar	No reason except "tastes" why they should not be close substitutes
A red Buick will be a close substitute for a gray Buick	No reason why they should be any closer substitutes than wood and bread
Substitution (for example, butter and margarine) is frequently intrinsic and objective, will be observed in many societies under many market conditions	No reason why close substitutes in one context should be close substitutes in another
A good may be displaced from the market by new goods or by price changes	No presumption that goods will be completely displaced
The labor-leisure choice may have a marked occupational pattern	Labor-leisure choice determined solely by individual preferences; no pattern, other than between individuals, would be predicted
(Gresham's Law) A monetary asset may cease to be on the efficiency frontier, and will disappear from the economy	No ex ante presumption that any good or asset will disappear from the economy
An individual is completely unaffected by price changes that leave unchanged the portion of the efficiency frontier on which his choice rests	An individual is affected by changes in all prices
Some commodity groups may be intrinsic, and universally so	No presumption that commodities forming a group (defined by a break in spectrum of cross-elasticities) in one context will form a group in another context

APPENDIX

I. TRANSFORMATION OF THE UTILITY FUNCTION INTO G-SPACE

Consider some characteristics vector z^* which does have an image x^* in G-space, and consider the set P of all vectors z preferred or indifferent to z^*. If U has the traditional properties, the set P is convex with an inner boundary which is the indifference surface through z^*. Now $z \geqq z^*$ implies z is in P so that every x such that $Bx \geqq z^*$, a set S, is preferred or indifferent to x^*. If we take some other z' in P, every x in S' such that $Bx \geqq z'$ is also preferred or indifferent to x'^*. Similarly for z'' in P and S'' such that that $Bx \geqq z''$, and so on. From the theory of inequalities, the sets S, S', S'' . . . are all convex, and since P is convex, a linear combination of z', z'' is in P, so that a linear combination of x's in S', S'' is also preferred or indifferent to x^*. Hence the set $\bar{P}$ of all x preferred or indifferent to x^* is the linear combination of all the sets $S, S', S'', \ldots$ and so is convex.

Thus the utility function transformed into G-space retains its essential convexity. A more intuitive way of looking at the situation is to note that all characteristics collections which are actually available are contained in an n-dimensional slice through the r-dimensional utility function and that all slices through a convex function are themselves convex. The transformation of this n-dimensional slice into G-space preserves this convexity.

II. "REVEALED PREFERENCE" IN A COMPLEX ECONOMY

We shall use the structural properties of the consumption technology A, B (dropping the assumption of a one-to-one relationship between goods and activities) to show that in a complex economy with more activities than characteristics the efficiency choice always satisfies the weak axiom of revealed preference and will satisfy the strong axiom for sufficiently large price changes, so that satisfaction of even the strong axiom does not "reveal" convexity of the preference function itself.

Consider an economy with a consumption technology defined by

$$z = By\,,$$
$$x = Ay\,,$$

and a consumer subject to a budget constraint of the form $p^*x \leqq k$ who has chosen goods x^* for activities y^*, giving characteristics z^*.

We know that if the consumer has made an efficient choice, y^* is the solution of the program (the value of which is k).

$$\text{Minimize } p^*Ay\ (= p^*x): \quad By = z^*\,, y \geqq 0\,, \tag{8.1a}$$

which has a dual (solution v^*).

$$\text{Maximize } vz^*: vB \leqq p^*A\,. \tag{8.1b}$$

The dual variables v can be interpreted as the implicit prices of the characteristics themselves. From the Kuh-Tucker Theorem, we can associate the vector v with the slope of the separating hyperplane between the set of attainable z's and the set of z's preferred or indifferent to z^*.

For the same satisfactions vector Z^* and a new price vector p^{**} the efficiency choice will be the solution y^{**} (giving x^{**}), v^{**}, of

$$\begin{aligned} &\text{Min } p^{**}Ay: By = z^*\,, y \geqq 0\,, \\ &\text{Max } vz^*: vb \leqq p^{**}A\,. \end{aligned} \tag{8.2}$$

Since z^* is the same in (8.1) and (8.2), y^{**} is a feasible solution of (8.1) and y^* of (8.2). From the fundamental theorem of linear programing we have

$$p^{**}Ay^* \geqq v^{**}z^* = p^{**}Ay^{**}\,, \tag{8.3}$$

$$p^*Ay^{**} \geqq v^*z^* = p^*Ay^*\,. \tag{8.4}$$

A program identical with (8.2) except that z^* is replaced by hz^* will have a solution hy^{**}, v^{**}. Choose h so that $hp^{**}Ay^{**} = p^{**}Ay^*$. From (8.3) $h \geqq 1$. From (8.4),

$$hp^*Ay^{**} \geqq p^*Ay^{**} \geqq p^*Ay^*\,. \tag{8.5}$$

If we now write p for p^*, p' for p^{**}; $x = Ay^*$, $x' = hAy^{**}$, we have

$$p'x' = p'x \text{ implies } px' \geqq px\,, \tag{8.6}$$

satisfying the *weak axiom of revealed preference.*

The equality will occur on the right in (8.6) only if equalities hold in *both* (8.3) and (8.4), and these will hold only if y^{**} is optimal as well as feasible in (8.1), and y^* is optimal as well as feasible in (8.2). In general, if the number of activities exceeds the number of characteristics, we can always find two prices p^*, p^{**} so related that neither of the solutions y^{**}, y^* is optimal in the other's program.

Hence, if the number of activities exceeds the number of characteristics (representing the number of primary constraints in the program), we can find prices so related that the strong axiom of revealed preference is satisfied, even though the consumer has obtained characteristics in unchanged proportions (z^*, hz^*) and has revealed nothing of his preference map.

The above effect represents an *efficiency substitution effect* which would occur even if characteristics were consumed in absolutely fixed proportions. If the consumer substitutes between different satisfactions bundles when his budget constraint changes, this private substitution effect is additional to the efficiency substitution effect.

Just as the conceptual experiment implicit in revealed preference implies "overcompensation" in the conventional analysis (see Samuelson 1948, 1953*a*), so the efficiency effect leads to "external overcompensation" additional to private overcompensation.

REFERENCES

Becker, Gary S. "A Theory of the Allocation of Time," *Econ. J.*, September, 1965.

Debreu, Gerald. *Theory of Value*. Cowles Foundation Monograph 17, 1959.

———. "Topological Methods in Cardinal Utility Theory," in K. J. Arrow, S. Karlin, and P. Suppes (eds.). *Mathematical Methods in the Social Sciences, 1959*. Stanford, Calif.: Stanford Univ. Press, 1960.

Friedman, Milton, and Savage, L. J. "The Expected-Utility Hypothesis and the Measurability of Utility," *J.P.E.*, Vol. LX (December, 1952).

Gorman, W. M. "Separable Utility and Aggregation," *Econometrica*, Vol. XXVII (July, 1959).

Johnson, Harry G. "Demand Theory Further Revised or Goods Are Goods," *Economica*, N.S. 25 (May, 1958).

Karlin, S. *Mathematical Methods and Theory in Games, Programming and Economics*. New York: Pergamon Press, 1959.

Koopmans, T. C. "Stationary Ordinal Utility and Impatience," *Econometrica*, Vol. XXIII (April, 1960).

Koopmans, T. C., Diamond, P. A., and Williamson, R. E. "Stationary Utility and Time Perspective," *ibid.*, Vol. XXXII (January–April, 1964).

Lancaster, Kelvin J. "Revising Demand Theory," *Economica*, N.S. 24 (November, 1957).

———. "The Scope of Qualitative Economics," *Rev. Econ. Studies*, Vol. XXIX (1962).

———. "An Axiomatic Theory of Consumer Time Preference," *Internat. Econ. Rev.*, Vol. IV (May, 1963).

———. "The Theory of Qualitative Linear Systems," *Econometrica*, Vol. XXXIII (April, 1965).

———. "Change and Innovation in the Technology of Consumption," *A.E.R.*, Papers and Proceedings, May, 1966 (to be published).

Morishima, M. "The Problem of Intrinsic Complementarity and Separability of Goods," *Metroeconomica*, Vol. XI (December, 1959).

Pearce, I. F. *A Contribution to Demand Analysis*. New York: Oxford Univ. Press, 1964.

Quandt, R. E. "A Probabilistic Theory of Consumer Behaviour," *Q.J.E.*, Vol. LXX (November, 1956).

Samuelson, P. A. "Consumption Theory in Terms of Revealed Preference," *Economica*, N.S. 15 (November, 1948).

———. "Consumption Theorems in Terms of Over-Compensation Rather than Indifference Comparisons," *ibid.*, N.S. 20 (February, 1953). (*a*)

———. "Prices of Factors and Goods in General Equilibrium," *Rev. Econ. Studies*, Vol. XXI (1953). (*b*)

Stigler, G. J. "The Cost of Subsistence," *J. Farm Econ.*, Vol. XXVII (1945).

Strotz, Robert, "The Empirical Implications of a Utility Tree," *Econometrica*, Vol. XXV (April, 1957).

———. "The Utility Tree: A Correction and Further Appraisal," *ibid.*, Vol. XXVII (July, 1959).

Thrall, Robert M., Coombs, C., and Davis, R. L. *Decision Processes*. New York: Wiley & Sons, 1954.

Uzawa, H. "Preference and Rational Choice in the Theory of Consumption," in K. J. Arrow, S. Karlin, and P. Suppes (eds.). *Mathematical Methods in the Social Sciences, 1959*. Stanford, Calif.: Stanford Univ. Press, 1960.

Von Neumann, J., and Morgenstern, O. *Theory of Games and Economic Behaviour*. Princeton, N.J.: Princeton Univ. Press, 1944.

[6]

Rational Choice Under an Imperfect Ability To Choose

By ANDRÉ DE PALMA, GORDON M. MYERS, AND YORGOS Y. PAPAGEORGIOU*

We consider an individual who lacks the information-processing capacity required for a direct comparison of all feasible allocations. Instead of finding at once a best allocation, the individual myopically adjusts his current allocation toward higher utility. The individual makes adjustment errors inversely proportional to his ability to choose. We compare the stationary state of this process with the standard model. We see how an imperfect ability to choose modifies both positive and normative predictions of the standard model and how the standard model can be obtained from our more general one as the special case corresponding to perfect ability. (*JEL* D11)

The standard model of consumer behavior asserts that individuals have unlimited information-processing capacity, which allows them to solve their choice problem in a strictly optimal manner irrespective of the difficulty of the problem. However, existing evidence indicates that individuals have only limited information-processing capacity.[1] In consequence, when deciding among alternative courses of action, individuals use simple, local and myopic choice procedures which adapt choice behavior to their capacity limitations (see e.g., Allen Newell and Herbert A. Simon, 1972). The quality of choice procedures used reflects the *ability to choose*. Since such procedures are imperfect, they cause random errors when the choice problem is of sufficient complexity. Thus, within our framework, individual choice behavior can only be determined up to a probability distribution which serves as a "black box" to summarize complex behavioral aspects of the individual. Such ambiguity in choice predictions is deeply rooted in the real world. It arises because individuals may not know their preferences perfectly well, and it differs from that generated by an uncertain future in the context of rational choice (von Neumann and Morgenstern, 1944). Of course, variance may well arise through uncertainty about the future. But it may also arise as an inherent property of choice behavior even when the future can be known (James G. March, 1978 pp. 598–99).

We consider the choice problem of an individual who does not have the information-processing capacity required for a direct comparison of all feasible allocations. Instead of finding at once a best allocation

*De Palma: Département COMIN, Université Genève, 102 Boulevard Carl Vogt, CH-1211 Genève 4, Switzerland; Myers: Department of Economics, University of Waterloo, 200 University Ave. West, Waterloo, ON N2L 3G1, Canada; Papageorgiou: BSB 329, McMaster University, 1280 Main Street West, Hamilton, ON L8S 4K1, Canada. We thank Richard Arnott, Tom Muller, the participants of a McMaster economics workshop, and three anonymous referees for their comments. G.M.M. and Y.Y.P. acknowledge SSHRCC grants 410-91-1851 and 410-91-0906, respectively.

[1]This observation has given rise to information-processing theories of choice, which are dominant in the behavioral sciences (see e.g., James R. Bettman, 1979; Daniel Kahneman et al., 1982). In those theories, individuals acquire information from various sources in their environment, which they perceive, interpret, and evaluate drawing upon past experience and upon the context in which they obtained it. Thus information-processing theories are not just about what individuals know, but also about how individuals use what they know. In economics, such processing-capacity limitations have been expressed as a "competence–difficulty" gap (Ronald A. Heiner, 1983), whereby the competence of individuals to solve a choice problem does not match the difficulty of that problem.

as in the standard model of consumer behavior, the individual adjusts myopically his current consumption in order to improve utility. Beginning with some initial commodity stock, the individual spends at a constant rate which defines periods corresponding to one unit of expenditure. The individual's commodity stock changes between periods following the rates at which he consumes the various commodities on the one hand, and his purchasing decisions on the other. At the beginning of each period, the individual spends the unit of money currently available on a single commodity. The problem now is to find a commodity which gives the highest marginal utility. Thus the individual reduces the unmanageable problem of comparing all feasible consumption bundles to a manageable problem of comparing the utility increments derived by adding in turn an amount of unit value to each current commodity stock. In principle, all that is necessary to solve this problem is knowledge about marginal abilities at a point, rather than about the utility function itself.

Following the information-processing approach to choice, we allow for the possibility that the individual makes errors in comparing marginal utilities. This creates a difference between perceived and true marginal utilities, which decreases as the ability to choose increases. For a particular degree of ability, the above choice procedure corresponds to a particular stationary state in consumption. As the ability to choose increases, the stationary level of utility also increases. At the limit, where the ability to choose becomes perfect, the stationary state coincides with the solution of the standard consumer choice problem. Thus, for different degrees of ability to choose, our model predicts a dispersion of choice decisions even in cases where rational individuals have identical preferences, endowments, and access to information—a phenomenon which has been observed experimentally (R. J. Herrnstein, 1991). In the context of the standard consumer choice model, such dispersion must signify irrational behavior.

When the individual can choose to improve his ability, he faces a trade-off between the level of ability and the income left for consumption. Under these conditions, a maximum feasible level of utility can be reached, provided the individual does not make errors in improving his ability. In the presence of such errors, our framework leads to a failure of both fundamental welfare theorems which does not arise from externalities or a lack of information, but rather because the individual does not have the information-processing capacity necessary to equate the marginal cost of improving ability with the corresponding marginal benefit. In such cases, paternalism may be justified.

We next examine the possibility that random errors are biased. A natural interpretation for such errors can be found in the context of image advertisement. In most economic models, such advertisement has been treated as a good that yields either information or utility. We, on the other hand, focus on the manipulative characteristics of image advertisement which can be either good (if error bias encourages consumption that increases utility) or bad (if it encourages consumption that decreases utility). The impact of such advertisement becomes smaller for higher ability to choose until, when the ability to choose is perfect, manipulative advertisement is rendered completely ineffective. It follows that, when individuals are perfect instruments of choice and have fixed preferences, as in standard economic theory, there is no conceptual basis for manipulative advertisement: individuals either benefit from it or eventually discard it. In contrast, an imperfect ability to choose does not negate existing economic approaches to advertisement. For example, image advertisement can enter the utility function as a complement to the good advertised (Gary Becker and Kevin M. Murphy, 1993) and, at the same time, bias the perception of true utility when the individual has an imperfect ability to choose. Our approach provides a rationale for laws against false advertisement, for the regulation of advertisement of commodities for which errors may become dangerous, and for advertisement aimed specifically at low-ability groups such as young children.

Throughout the paper, we provide examples about how an imperfect ability to choose modifies both the positive and normative implications of the standard consumer model.[2] In the final section we provide a model of socially optimal product differentiation with fixed prices in which normative implications vary systematically with the degree of ability to choose. When the ability to choose is perfect, we derive the standard solution. The optimal products become increasingly similar for lower ability until, below a certain level, there remains only one optimal product. Besides providing a formalization of the familiar idea that there can be too much product variety, this example provides another case in which the implications of variable ability to choose cannot be dismissed as insignificant.

I. Myopic Adjustments

If an individual can evaluate and rank all feasible consumption bundles, the description of the choice procedure adopted becomes trivial: the individual simply ranks all feasible consumption bundles according to his preferences and chooses a most preferred one. Under these circumstances, the choice problem can be expressed in the familiar, compact form:

$$(1) \qquad \max_{Q_1,\ldots,Q_n} U(Q_1,\ldots,Q_n)$$

subject to

$$\sum_{i=1}^{n} p_i Q_i = Y$$

where $U(\cdot)$ is the ordinal utility function, p_i and Q_i are the price and the consumption of the ith commodity, and Y is income. If, however, the individual does not have the ability for making the global comparisons required to solve a problem (1), then he is bound to adjust his choice behavior accordingly. For example, if we confronted you with a complete display of all the consumption choices you made last month, together with a reasonable (for you) alternative display of consumption choices, we doubt that you would be prepared to undertake the global comparisons required for expressing preference between those two consumption bundles. You would be prepared, however, to discuss the advantages of choosing this brand of cereal over that brand, or the excessive amounts you spent last month on entertainment. More generally, excepting some well-defined cases in which the problem of choosing among a small number of alternatives is independent of everything else, consumption choices rarely, if at all, concern entire consumption bundles. Typically *consumption choices are about elements of the consumption bundle and about consumption-bundle change*. In this sense, consumption choices are typically *local* rather than global.[3]

One main goal of our paper is to model a sequence of consumption choices that describes local consumption-bundle adjustments. We imagine that this sequence occurs during a time interval of length T. At the beginning of the time interval, the individual receives a fixed income Y, which it spends on the n commodities. To fix ideas, let T represent a month and let Y represent the salary received at the beginning of the month. There is no borrowing or saving across months. We assume that spending occurs at a uniform rate $y = Y/T$ which determines the partitioning of the month into periods of length Δt corresponding to one unit of expenditure:

$$(2) \qquad y\Delta t = 1.$$

[2] See also George A. Akerlof and Janet L. Yellen (1985) for a discussion about how even small errors in consumption decisions can have large effects on equilibria.

[3] This is closer to a Marshallian point of view (Alfred Marshall, 1920 [Vol. 3, Chapter III]). It is interesting to note that John R. Hicks, a protagonist in the establishment of ordinal utility theory, later recognised the descriptive accuracy of the old consumer theory (Hicks, 1976 pp. 137–38).

At the beginning of each period $[t, t+\Delta t]$ $(t = 0, \Delta t, 2\Delta t, \ldots, (Y-1)\Delta t)$ the individual spends the available unit on a single commodity. We thus replace the global choice of one among an infinite number of commodity combinations in the feasible consumption set with a sequence of simpler, local decisions about spending one unit of money on one out of n discrete alternatives.

Let $Q_{i,t}$ represent the stock of commodity i at the beginning of the period $[t, t+\Delta t]$. During that period, this stock is consumed at a uniform rate $q_{i,t}$ determined at the beginning of the period. The continuous decrease of the stock during that period is given by

$$Q_{i,t}(\tau) = Q_{i,t}(1 - c_i\tau) \tag{3}$$

where $0 \leq \tau \leq \Delta t$, $c_i\tau \leq 1$, and c_i is a constant that determines how fast one unit of commodity i is depleted. It follows that the uniform consumption rate for commodity i during the period $[t, t+\Delta t]$ is given by

$$q_{i,t} = c_i Q_{i,t}. \tag{4}$$

If, at the beginning of the next period, the individual spends the newly accumulated unit of money on commodity i, the corresponding stock increases by $1/p_i$, and the consumption rate increases by c_i/p_i. Thus, although consumption rates remain fixed within periods, they can vary between periods according to the size of stock owned at the beginning of each period, where a larger stock implies a higher rate of consumption.

The problem of the individual at the beginning of each period is to spend the unit of money on a commodity i that generates the largest utility increment. Utility in our model is determined by the rate of consumption, rather than by the stock itself: if you do not use what you have, you do not derive utility from it. Let $u(q_{1,t}, \ldots, q_{n,t})$ represent the individual's perception of the utility derived from the n consumption rates. We can now replace the global choice problem (1) with the following sequence of local choice problems:

at the beginning t of each period in $[0, T]$ spend $y\Delta t$ on a commodity i such that

$$\Delta_{i,t}u > \max\{\Delta_{j,t}u;\ j \neq i\} \tag{5}$$

where $\Delta_{i,t}u$ is the utility increment derived from buying commodity i at t. If we assume that $u(\cdot)$ represents the utility derived from the n consumption rates during the period $[t, t+\Delta t]$, then (5) is akin to *melioration*, "(the) process of comparing the rates of return and shifting toward the alternative that is currently yielding the better return..." (Herrnstein, 1991 p. 361). This is a widely observed type of choice behavior in various species, including humans. For example, in series of experiments designed to determine whether individuals maximize utility in the global sense or meliorate, Herrnstein found strong evidence in support of the second alternative.[4] Individual behavior, at least in the environment provided by those experiments, was consistently myopic as implied by (5). Herrnstein uses his findings as evidence that individuals do not maximize utility. In contrast, we shall argue that the Herrnstein experiments are consistent with utility maximization subject to error.

II. Errors of Perception

We have proposed the sequence of local choice problems as a more accurate description of individual consumption behavior because we believe that individuals do not have the ability to make the global comparisons required for solving problem (1). In

[4]There were three types of experiment, involving a sequence of binary choices where current return depended on previous choices in a systematic way which could be understood given the information available. Maximizing utility would require taking into account the consequences of the current choice on future returns. In the first type of experiment, utility maximization predicted indifference between alternatives, while melioration predicted a unique outcome. In the second type, the predictions were reversed. Finally, in the third type, both choice procedures predicted diammetrically opposed, unique outcomes. In every type of experiment, individuals tended to meliorate quite strongly.

the Herrnstein experiments, such behavior led to suboptimal choice outcomes because the alternative yielding the better strictly current return is not necessarily the alternative yielding the better current return after taking into account the consequences of current choice on future returns. This is just one out of many ways people make errors along a choice procedure such as (5).[5] In general, those errors can be defined as

$$\Delta_{i,t}u - \Delta_{i,t}v = \varepsilon_{i,t} \tag{6}$$

where $\Delta_{i,t}u$ denotes *perceived* utility increments and $\Delta_{i,t}v$ denotes *true* utility increments. This distinction is fundamental for our paper. Since the ways people can make errors are many and unpredictable, we assume that $\varepsilon_{i,t}$ is random. Its variance reflects the ability of the individual to choose, where smaller variance implies higher ability. At the limit, where perceived and true utility increments coincide, we say that the ability to choose is perfect.

Our objective is to study the outcomes of (5) for consumer choice by recognizing explicitly that individuals make errors. Substituting (6) in (5), we have the following:

at the beginning t of each period in $[0,T]$ *spend* $y\Delta t$ *on a commodity i such that*

$$\Delta_{i,t}v + \varepsilon_{i,t} > \max\{\Delta_{j,t}v + \varepsilon_{j,t};\ j \neq i\}. \tag{7}$$

In the context of problem (1), this choice procedure portrays an individual who applies a gradient process to climb myopically toward the peak of the intersection between his utility surface and the hyperplane that describes the fixed amount of resources available. If the individual does not make errors, since his true utility surface has a single peak, the outcome of this procedure will also maximize utility on average.

Since errors are random, individual choices in (7) can be determined only up to a probability distribution. Accordingly,

$$\mathbb{P}_{i,t} \equiv \Pr\{\Delta_{i,t}v + \varepsilon_{i,t} > \max\{\Delta_{j,t}v + \varepsilon_{j,t};\ j \neq i\}\} \tag{8}$$

denotes the probability that the individual will spend the unit of money on commodity i at t. We shall first examine the simple case in which error variance remains the same over time. If those errors are independently and identically distributed[6] and if the preference ordering of the individual is invariant under uniform expansions of the choice set then, according to theorem 6 in John I. Yellott (1977), the random errors are double-exponential.[7] Under these circumstances, we can write the random errors as

$$\varepsilon_{i,t} = \frac{1}{\mu}\varepsilon \qquad \mu > 0 \tag{9}$$

where $1/\mu$ is the dispersion parameter of $\varepsilon_{i,t}$, and where ε is double-exponential with a zero location parameter and unit

[5] Following information-processing theories, we can imagine that the individual uses information from the environment as an input to an individual-specific processing technology and produces decisions. The processing technology will reflect the individual's investment for improving his processing capacity through, for example, education. However, it will also reflect inherent characteristics of the individual, such as perceptiveness, intelligence, quality of memory, and so forth, which make some individuals better instruments of choice than others. In this framework, errors can arise from incomplete information, the distortion of information during processing, or wrong deductions. The last possibility has been called a "lack of logical omniscience" by Barton L. Lipman (1992). Better processing technology implies smaller errors on average.

[6] A justification for stochastic independence can be made if a commodity is understood to represent a distinct class of differentiated products sold at the same price by a large number of competing firms. There is no restriction on the entry or exit of firms, or on the introduction of new products and discontinuation of old ones. We imagine that the individual draws a random combination of products of unit value belonging to the same commodity. Since the choice environment is in continuous flux, the individual can make errors in predicting the consumption effect of the particular draw on utility; and since every draw consists of a random combination, those errors can be independent.

[7] A uniform expansion of a set can be obtained by replicating every element in the set the same number of times.

dispersion parameter. Then, following Daniel McFadden (1974), the marginal allocation probabilities (8) are given by the multinomial logit model:

$$\mathbb{P}_{i,t} = \frac{\exp(\mu \Delta_{i,t} v)}{\sum_{j=1}^{n} \exp(\mu \Delta_{j,t} v)}. \tag{10}$$

Since errors become smaller for larger μ, this parameter can be interpreted as the ability of the individual to choose, where a larger μ signifies higher ability. We also have

$$\lim_{\mu \to 0} \mathbb{P}_{i,t} = \frac{1}{n} \tag{11}$$

$$\lim_{\mu \to \infty} \mathbb{P}_{i,t} = \begin{cases} 1 & \text{if } \Delta_{i,t} v > \max\{\Delta_{j,t} v, j \neq i\} \\ 0 & \text{otherwise.} \end{cases}$$

When there is no ability to choose, discrete choices are equiprobable, irrespective of differences in the true marginal value of alternatives; and when the ability to choose is perfect, the best choice is made with certainty. More generally, the individual's ability to choose is reflected by the distribution of marginal allocation probabilities around alternatives of higher marginal utility. As the ability to choose increases, the distribution of marginal allocation probabilities tightens around better alternatives until, at the limit, the individual adjusts only toward the best alternative.

III. Stationary Choice Behavior

Changes in the value of the commodity stock between periods are driven by the flows of expenditure and consumption. We have already argued that choice, and hence expenditure, can be determined only up to a probability distribution. Using (2), the expected expenditure on commodity i during the period equals $y \Delta t \mathbb{P}_{i,t}$, while the corresponding consumption equals $p_i q_{i,t} \Delta t$. Therefore expected changes in the value of the commodity stock between intervals obey

$$\Delta p_i Q_{i,t} = (y \mathbb{P}_{i,t} - p_i q_{i,t}) \Delta t. \tag{12}$$

Since the individual aims to improve his utility level, $y\mathbb{P}_{i,t}$ in (12) can be interpreted as the value of the currently desired consumption rate on commodity i. Thus (12) implies that expected changes in the value of the commodity stock are driven by the difference between the values of currently desired and experienced consumption rates.

Through $\mathbb{P}_{i,t}$, (12) depends on the entire distribution of commodity stocks. Thus the dynamics of (12) may be complicated, and they may or may not lead the individual to stationary choice behavior, such that no further changes in the value of the commodity stock are observed between intervals.[8] We do not study these dynamics here. Instead, we confine our analysis to stationary choice behavior which corresponds to the time-invariant system

$$y \mathbb{P}_i \Delta t = p_i q_i \Delta t. \tag{13}$$

Summing over one interval, (13) implies

$$Y \mathbb{P}_i = T p_i q_i. \tag{14}$$

Summing (14) over the n commodities, we obtain the stationary budget constraint

$$y = \sum_{i=1}^{n} p_i q_i \tag{15}$$

since $\Sigma_i \mathbb{P}_i = 1$. Furthermore, substituting (10) into (13), we have

$$\Delta_i v - \Delta_1 v = \frac{1}{\mu} \ln \frac{p_i q_i}{p_1 q_1} \qquad i > 1 \tag{16}$$

[8]A stationary solution exists (see e.g., proposition 4 in Victor Ginsburgh et al. [1985]). Sufficient conditions for the stability of stationary states for systems more general than ours are given in proposition 5 of Ginsburgh et al. (1985).

IV. Relationship with Maximizing Behavior

Let us begin by defining a simple expression for true utility increments at the stationary state. We consider the decision of spending the unit of money on commodity i at the beginning of a period and its consequences for future periods along the stationary path. Denote the initial change in the stock of commodity i by $\Delta Q_i^{(0)}$, and denote the portion of $\Delta Q_i^{(0)}$ remaining after m periods by $\Delta Q_i^{(m)}$. Taking into account $\Delta Q_i^{(0)} = 1/p_i$ and (3), we have

$$(17)\quad \Delta Q_i^{(m)} = \frac{1}{p_i}(1-c_i\Delta t)^m \qquad m = 0,1,2,\ldots.$$

Using (4), the correspondence change in the consumption flow is

$$(18)\quad \Delta q_i^{(m)} = \frac{c_i}{p_i}(1-c_i\Delta t)^m \qquad m = 0,1,2,\ldots.$$

We require that the true utility increment takes fully into account the future consequences on utility of the initial spending decision:

$$(19)\qquad \Delta_i v = \sum_{m=0}^{\infty} \Delta_i v^{(m)}.$$

We also assume that the function $v(q_1,\ldots,q_n)$, which determines the true current utility generated by the n consumption rates, is differentiable, strictly increasing, and strictly quasi-concave. If we expand $v(\cdot)$ in Taylor series around q_i and retain only linear terms, we can express true utility increments as

$$(20)\quad \Delta_i v \cong \sum_{m=0}^{\infty} \Delta q_i^{(m)} v_i = \frac{c_i v_i}{p_i}\sum_{m=0}^{\infty}(1-c_i\Delta t)^m = \frac{v_i}{p_i \Delta t}$$

where $v_i \equiv \partial v/\partial q_i$ and where the intermediate step follows from (18). From now on, we shall assume that (20) holds as an equality.

Introducing (20) in (16), we obtain

$$(21)\quad \frac{v_i}{p_i} - \frac{v_1}{p_1} = \frac{\Delta t}{\mu}\ln\frac{p_i q_i}{p_1 q_1} \qquad i>1$$

where v_i/p_i is the marginal utility per unit of expenditure. Equations (15) and (21) can be used to determine the stationary consumption rates $(\bar{q}_1,\ldots,\bar{q}_n)$ where, from now on, an overbar will denote variables at stationary state. According to our interpretation of (12), stationary consumption rates also represent desired consumption rates: since, in this case, the aspirations of the individual match its experiences, there is no need for further change in the commodity stock. Solving (15) and (21), we have

$$(22)\qquad \bar{q}_i = \bar{q}_i(y,\mathbf{p};\mu)$$

where $\mathbf{p}$ is the vector of prices. Using (13) and (22), the corresponding stationary utility level can be written as

$$(23)\quad v(\bar{q}_1,\ldots,\bar{q}_n) = v\left(\frac{y\bar{\mathbb{P}}_1}{p_1},\ldots,\frac{y\bar{\mathbb{P}}_n}{p_n}\right) \equiv \bar{v}(y,\mathbf{p};\mu).$$

When there is no ability to choose, (21) implies $p_i\bar{q}_i = p_j\bar{q}_j$ for all i and j, which is consistent with (11). That is, under complete inability to determine what constitutes a good choice, the individual allocates an equal amount of money per unit of time to all commodities. On the other hand, when the ability to choose is perfect, (21) implies that, for all i and j, at least one of the following conditions must hold: (a) $\bar{v}_i/p_i = \bar{v}_j/p_j$; (b) $\bar{q}_i = 0$; (c) $\bar{q}_j = 0$; (d) both $\bar{q}_i = 0$ and $\bar{q}_j = 0$. It follows immediately that the stationary consumption rates corresponding to a perfect ability to choose satisfy the necessary conditions of maximizing $v(\cdot)$ subject to $\Sigma_i p_i q_i \le y$, which is consistent with (11). Furthermore, it can be shown that the stationary consumption rates tend to the solution of the constrained maximization problem as $\mu \to \infty$, which implies the continuity of the stationary solutions for $\mu > 0$.

V. Satisficing Behavior

We now turn to a main result of our paper, namely, that the behavior of the individual under an imperfect ability to choose is *satisficing* in the sense that its stationary choice behavior corresponds to a level of utility that is below the maximum possible (Simon, 1955; Leibenstein, 1976 Ch. 5). In particular, we shall prove that $d\bar{v}/d\mu > 0$ for $0 < \mu < \infty$. Notice that, since utility is differentiable, strictly increasing, and strictly quasi-concave, any $(\bar{q}_1, \ldots, \bar{q}_n) \equiv \bar{\mathbf{q}}$ is equivalent to the solution of a standard utility maximization problem with adjusted income and prices. This happens because a single indifference surface passes through $\bar{\mathbf{q}}$ and, in turn, a single hyperplane is tangent to this surface at $\bar{\mathbf{q}}$. We call this an equivalent maximization problem (EMP). As $\bar{\mathbf{q}}$ changes smoothly, so do the income and prices of the EMP, given a particular good as the numeraire. Also notice that

$$(24)\quad \sigma^2 \equiv \sum_{i=1}^{n} \mathbb{P}_i \left(\frac{v_i}{p_i}\right)^2 - \left(\sum_{i=1}^{n} \mathbb{P}_i \frac{v_i}{p_i}\right)^2$$

can be interpreted as the variance of a discrete random variable having realizations v_i/p_i which occur with probability $\mathbb{P}_i$. Now since $\bar{v}(\cdot)$ can also be treated as the solution of an EMP, we may use the envelope theorem on the definition in (23) to obtain

$$(25)\quad \frac{d\bar{v}}{d\mu} = y\bar{\sigma}^2$$

which is positive provided that $\bar{\sigma}^2 \to 0$ only if $\mu \to \infty$. The qualification placed on this result is not restrictive: the only exception occurs when the conditions $v_i/p_i = v_j/p_j$ for all i and j are satisfied for any value of μ, in which case system (21) admits a solution independent of μ and defined by $p_i q_i = p_j q_j$ for all i and j. Then $\bar{\sigma}^2 = 0$ for all μ. In any other case, $\bar{\sigma}^2 \to 0$ only if $\mu \to \infty$.[9]

It is interesting to note the dependence of $d\bar{v}/d\mu$ in (25) on the distribution of marginal utilities. For a given ability to choose, larger variance of this distribution implies larger gains in stationary utility caused by an ability improvement. This agrees with intuition. Since an improvement in the ability to choose tightens the distribution of marginal allocation probabilities around better alternatives, the expected benefit of such an improvement will increase with a larger variance of the distribution. To fix ideas, imagine first a choice among commodities with very similar characteristics. Since, in this case, the choice is not particularly important, the benefit from an ability improvement is not large. Now imagine that the consumption of some commodities has health or safety implications: some could save your life, others could kill you. In this high-variance environment, one would expect that an ability improvement may be crucially important for the individual's well-being.

The analysis of demand functions and comparative statics for an exogenous ability to choose appears in Appendix A-1. Not surprisingly, this is a straightforward generalization of the standard analysis.

VI. The Case of Two Commodities

In this section we present two graphs of stationary choice behavior when there are only two commodities. The line AB in Figure 1 represents the stationary budget constraint. Point C, the point of tangency between the budget constraint and the highest possible difference curve I^{∞}, represents stationary consumption rates under a perfect ability to choose. Point D, where $p_1 q_1 =$

[9]Directly computing the sign of $d^2\bar{v}/d\mu^2$ shows $\bar{v}(\cdot)$ to be convex for small μ and concave for large μ. In consequence, the marginal return to improving the ability to choose first increases and then decreases. In particular, the concavity of the curve when μ is sufficiently large guarantees that $d\bar{v}/d\mu$ in (25) remains finite as $\mu \to \infty$.

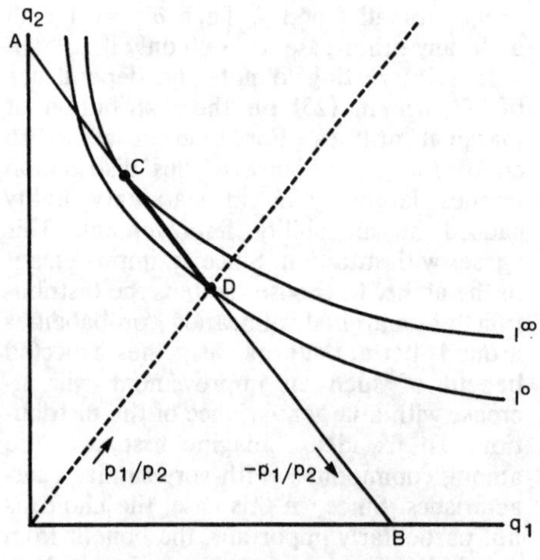

FIGURE 1. STATIONARY CONSUMPTION RATES

p_2q_2, represents stationary consumption rates under no ability to choose on a lower indifference curve I^0. In between these two indifference curves lies the range of stationary utility indifference curves as μ changes. Every particular indifference curve within that range intersects only once with the line segment CD to define an associated set of stationary consumption rates. Clearly, CD is the set of all possible stationary consumption rates. A dispersion of stationary consumption rates over CD implies different abilities to choose, where higher ability is located closer to C. Such dispersion can be observed in the third experiment of Herrnstein (1991). In that experiment, subjects had the same preferences, endowments, and access to information. Consequently, the dispersion of stationary states in that experiment implies different abilities to solve the same economic problem, that is, different abilities to choose.

An alternative, more detailed point of view stems from a direct study of (21) in the case of two commodities, namely,

$$\frac{v_2}{p_2} - \frac{v_1}{p_1} = \frac{\Delta t}{\mu} \ln \frac{y - p_1q_1}{p_1q_1}. \tag{26}$$

Figure 2A shows the right-hand side (RHS) of this equation for different values of μ. When μ approaches 0, the function tends to a vertical line crossing the axis q_1 at $y/2p_1$. On the other hand, when μ approaches infinity, the function tends to zero for every possible value of q_1 except for $q_1 = 0$ and $q_1 = y/p_1$. Intermediate values of μ will generate graphs between these two extremes.

We now proceed on the assumption that the left-hand side (LHS) of (20) satisfies[10]

$$\frac{d}{dq_1}\left(\frac{v_2}{p_2} - \frac{v_1}{p_1}\right) > 0. \tag{27}$$

Figure 2B displays four possible graphs of the LHS of (26) superimposed on the graphs of the associated RHS of Figure 2A. Points A and B represent corner solutions at $\lim \mu \to \infty$, while points C and D represent corresponding interior solutions. The solution D is independent of μ, a case which was identified as the only exception to $d\bar{v}/d\mu > 0$ in Section V. Notice that if $\mu < \infty$ then there can be no corner solution. Furthermore, with the exception of D, stationary consumption rates change monotonically as the ability to choose improves or deteriorates. It is evident from (21) that the absence of corner solutions for $\mu < \infty$ is generally true. Monotonicity, however, which must hold in both Figures 1 and 2A, does not apply in general.[11]

[10] When this assumption does not hold, the LHS of (26) cannot cross the horizontal axis of Figure 2B. Otherwise, the uniqueness of the stationary consumption rates for $\lim \mu \to \infty$ is violated. It follows that (27) rules out only some cases with corner solutions at $\lim \mu \to \infty$. Everything else, which represents the vast majority of cases, is consistent with (27).

[11] An example will suffice. Let $v(\mathbf{q}) \equiv q_1^\alpha q_2^\beta q_3^\gamma$, with q_1 the numeraire. Also let $y = 1$, $\alpha = 1/3$, and $\beta + \gamma = 2/3$. It follows that $\bar{q}_1 = 1/3$ for $\mu = 0$. Since we know that $\bar{q}_1$ attains the same value for $\mu = \infty$, it is enough to show that there exists $\mu^* > 0$ such that $\bar{q}_1 \neq 1/3$ for $\mu = \mu^*$. Applying (21), we conclude that $\bar{q}_1 = 1/3$ for $\mu = \mu^*$ is violated at $\mu^* = \bar{v}(\cdot)$ because it requires solving two independent equations for a single unknown. It is always possible to select such μ^* since $\bar{v}(\cdot)$ is continuous and bounded, and since $\mu > 0$.

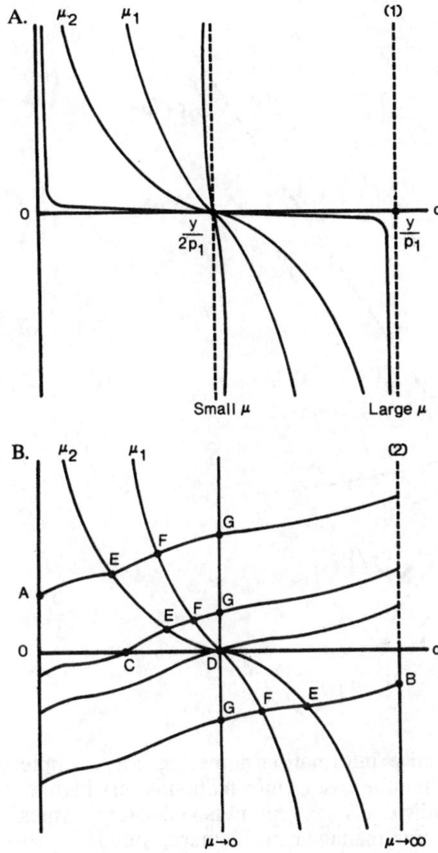

FIGURE 2. A) THE RIGHT-HAND SIDE OF EQUATION (26); B) SOLUTIONS TO EQUATION (26)

VII. Improving the Ability to Choose

When the individual can spend money on information processing, he faces a trade-off between his ability to choose and disposable income. Let $\mu(c)$ represent the ability to choose achieved at the expenditure rate c, where $\mu'(c) > 0$. Also let $\psi \equiv y + c$; that is, ψ is the total expenditure rate. The stationary level of utility $\bar{v}(\cdot)$ can now be written as $\bar{v}(\psi - c, \mathbf{p}; \mu(c))$ and, therefore,

$$\text{(28)} \qquad \frac{d\bar{v}}{dc} = \frac{\partial \bar{v}}{\partial c}\bigg|_{\mu} + \frac{\partial \bar{v}}{\partial \mu}\frac{d\mu}{dc}\bigg|_{\psi - c}.$$

The individual can aim toward the best level of ability as follows. At the beginning of each interval $[(k-1)T, kT]$, $k = 1, 2, \ldots$, the individual decides to spend at a rate c_k on information acquisition and processing, thus determining both the ability to choose $\mu_k \equiv \mu(c_k)$ and a corresponding stationary utility level $\bar{v}_k \equiv \bar{v}(\psi - c_k, \mathbf{p}; \mu(c_k))$ for the interval. We assume that all adjustments are fast, so that the individual enjoys $\bar{v}_k$ over the entire interval. For every interval, the decision of the individual about c_k is based on past performance: if his efforts to improve ability have reduced the stationary utility level, the individual will relapse to a lower level of effort; and if it pays to improve ability, the individual will intensify effort.

We begin with a stationary utility level $\bar{v}_0$, which corresponds to $c_0 = 0$. In the first interval the individual allocates $c_1 = h\bar{v}_0$ toward improving ability, where h is a constant. For $k \geq 2$, changes in c_k are determined by

$$\text{(29)} \qquad \Delta c_k = \begin{cases} h\Delta\bar{v}_{k-1} & \text{if sign } \Delta\bar{v}_{k-1} = \text{sign } \Delta c_{k-1} \\ -h\Delta\bar{v}_{k-1} & \text{otherwise.} \end{cases}$$

For h small enough, the simple adjustment process in (29) can lead the individual to an optimum. This is illustrated in Figure 3, which is a detailed version of Figure 1, where the discrete stationary path just described belongs to the continuous line DFE. This line represents the locus of stationary consumption rates as a function of the expenditure rate. A movement toward the left of the line corresponds to a higher expenditure rate and, therefore, to a lower budget constraint. It has been drawn so that, near zero ability to choose, improving ability also improves the stationary utility level. We also know that DFE passes through the origin (if you spend everything on improving your ability to choose, you can buy nothing else). Thus there must be at least one level of ability to choose that maximizes the stationary utility level. When DFE is strictly concave, as in Figure 3, the single optimum will be found at F, where DFE is tangent to the

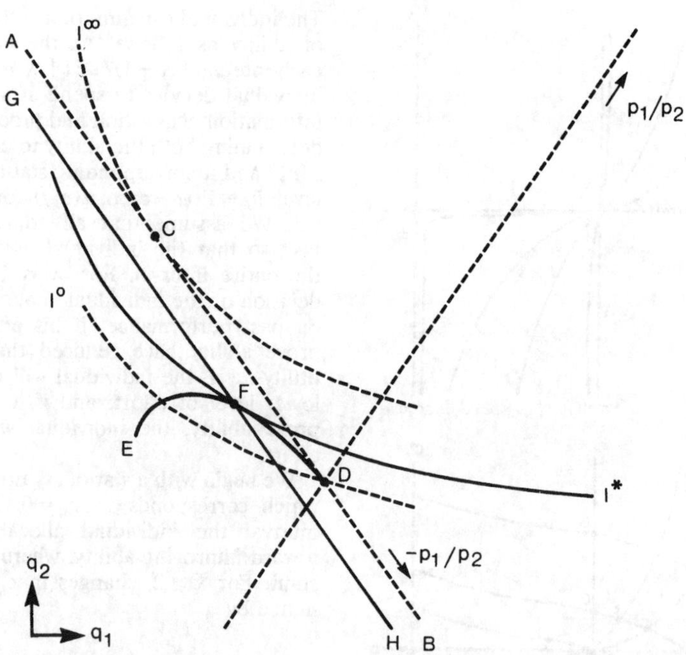

FIGURE 3. OPTIMAL ABILITY TO CHOOSE

indifference curve I*, and intersects with the budget constraint GH which is lower than the original AB. At the limit $h \to 0$, c^*, μ^*, and $\bar{v}^*$ will become independent of the interval, and a stationary state analogous to that of Section III will obtain. When DFE is not that well-behaved, the individual may attain only a local optimum.

Following our remarks in Section V, one should expect a higher marginal return from investment in the ability to choose for a larger variance in the distribution of marginal utilities. That is, individuals will benefit more by investing in ability improvements if decisions to be taken are more important. Once a stationary equilibrium has been achieved in which individuals have appropriately taken into account the trade-off between their ability to choose and disposable income, there is no way left to improve on stationary consumption rates. Further improvements can be made only if there are advantages to be explored in collective information gathering, for example, when the cost of information is very high for individuals as in personal-safety issues. Home-management courses, public warnings about cigarette use or about alcohol abuse, fire drills, and the like serve as examples of methods aiming at further improvements of the ability to choose. If the cost of such methods is equally borne by the individuals, $\mu(c)$ reflects returns to scale in collective information gathering. More generally, efforts to improve ability at the individual and the public levels seem complementary, and the optimal mix of these efforts largely remains an empirical question.

When individuals optimize their ability to choose, differences in ability will arise because of inherent differences in their information-processing capacity (intelligence, quality of memory, judgment, etc.). This happens because processing capacity represents an indivisible resource for individuals. Since some individuals are better instruments of choice than others, the utility-possibility frontier becomes asymmetric, and unless the Rawlsian principle applies, individuals should be treated unequally even if their preferences are identical.[12]

The analysis of demand functions for an endogenous ability to choose appears in Appendix A-2.

VIII. Paternalism

The adjustment process in (29) assumes no error in the decision to spend for improving the ability to choose. If, however, we admit the existence of errors in consumption choices, why preclude analogous errors in the context of (29)? For example, if spending c_k now increases μ only at the beginning of the next interval, someone following (29) will decide against investment to improve ability. A typical case is provided by a child who underestimates the future benefit of the current effort required for education. Since taxing the individual and then subsidizing ability improvements would improve welfare, we conclude that the first welfare theorem can fail under an imperfect ability to choose, even in the absence of externalities. With more than one individual and under the same myopic conditions, the second welfare theorem also fails because no redistribution can induce individuals to choose their optimal ability improvements. Such failures need not arise from a lack of information, but rather because individuals may not have the information-processing capacity necessary to equate the marginal cost of improving ability with the corresponding marginal benefit. For example, a child may have complete and accurate information provided by his parents, yet lack the judgment necessary to use the information appropriately to make the utility-maximizing decision.

There is a case for paternalism in our framework. Parents insisting that their child must go to school may well improve the child's welfare. Similarly, governments insisting that all children must be provided with medical care may well improve the welfare of children whose parents have a religious objection to medicine. Notice, however, that paternalism does not only require an "inferior" ability to choose from the subject and a "superior" ability to choose from the decision-maker, but also an ability for imposing coercive decisions. Thus, although paternalism in our framework cannot be rejected on the basis of consumer sovereignty as under a perfect ability to choose, it could still be rejected on the basis of an aversion to the coercive power it entails.

IX. Systematic Distortions in Perception

Advertisement in economics is modeled either as providing direct information about the product (Lester G. Telser, 1964; Gene M. Grossman and Carl Shapiro, 1984) or as creating an "image" for the product which can either serve as a signal of product quality (Paul Milgrom and John Roberts, 1986) or enter the utility function as a complement to the product advertised (Becker and Murphy, 1993).[13] Such models imply that advertisement can be good since it provides either useful information or utility, and they offer powerful ways of thinking about some advertisement-related phenomena. There are, however, those who believe that image advertisement can be bad since it is meant to manipulate consumers (John K. Galbraith, 1967). A standard example is provided by a number of competing firms which produce highly similar products and which use image advertisement to create artificial differentiation for their product. A

[12] This result is well known in urban economics (J. A. Mirrlees, 1972), where unequal treatment at the optimum arises because location quality is also indivisible. For a diagrammatic exposition, in which differences in location advantage can be reinterpreted as differences in processing capacity, see David Levhari et al. (1978).

[13] An exception is provided by Avinash Dixit and Victor Norman (1978), who modeled advertisement as changing preferences.

$$(32)\qquad \frac{v_2}{p_2}-\frac{v_1}{p_1}=\frac{\Delta t}{\mu}\ln\left(\left[\frac{y}{2}-p_1q_1+\sqrt{\left(\frac{y}{2}-p_1q_1\right)^2+e^{-(b_1+b_2)}p_1q_1(y-p_1q_1)}\,\right]\Big/p_1q_1e^{-b_1}\right)$$

firm in this context aims to bias consumers in favor of its product even though there is no intrinsic reason for preference. More generally, bias from manipulative advertisement can arise only in the context of errors made because of an imperfect ability to choose.[14] As the ability to choose improves, manipulative advertisement should become less effective, and hence bias should become smaller. At the limit, where the ability to choose is perfect, the individual should not rely any longer on biased information, but only on the intrinsic character of products. We express this possibility by assuming that manipulative advertisement in favor of commodity i can lead to errors having a positive expectation $E(\varepsilon_{i,t})=b_i$, where b_i is the bias associated with that commodity. Our previous remarks suggest that (9) can be generalized as

$$(30)\qquad \varepsilon_{i,t}=\frac{1}{\mu}(\varepsilon+b_i)$$

which implies that the marginal allocation probabilities are now given by

$$(31)\qquad \mathbb{P}_{i,t}=\frac{\exp(\mu\Delta_{i,t}v+b_i)}{\sum_{j=1}^{n}\exp(\mu\Delta_{j,t}v+b_j)}.$$

We consider only the case of two commodities. Introducing (31) in (13), and taking into account (20), we have equation (32) above at steady-state, which reduces to (21) for $b_1=b_2=0$. Figure 4A shows the RHS of this equation for different values of μ.

Relative to Figure 2A, it is seen that systematic distortions in perception shift the point common to all curves along the abscissa. If $b_2<(>)\ b_1$, the common point shifts to the right (left) of $y/2p_1$. In the first case, shown in Figure 2A, the bias encouraging adjustments toward the first commodity is stronger than that encouraging adjustments away from it. Furthermore, the length of the shift depends on the difference between b_1 and b_2. Thus the amount of effort spent on advertisement is not important—only the differential effort: when $b_1=b_2$, biases cancel each other and Figure 4A reduces to Figure 2A. As b_1-b_2 increases, the RHS of (32) changes as in Figure 4B. Two possible graphs of the LHS are also shown in that figure. Applying the logic of Figure 2B, the stationary consumption rate of a better-advertised commodity increases. In combination, parts A and B of Figure 4 suggest how, as the ability to choose improves, systematic distortions become less important until, under perfect ability to choose, they cannot any longer affect marginal allocation adjustments for any degree of differential effort.

There is a scope for control of manipulative advertisement in our framework. In a world of perfect ability to choose, as that of the standard model, there is no rationale for the regulation of the effects of advertisement on the individual since advertisement is either good or it is discarded. However, in a world of imperfect ability to choose, laws against false advertisement and regulation of some advertisement may be accounted for on the basis of removing bias that decreases utility. This seems particularly true for commodities such as tobacco and alcohol, where errors may become dangerous, as well as for advertisement aimed specifically at low-ability groups such as young children. There is also a scope for the public manipulation of bias. For example, in the

[14] In models of rational expectations, errors are unbiased because, even though individuals lack information, they are otherwise perfect instruments of choice; hence they do not make systematic errors.

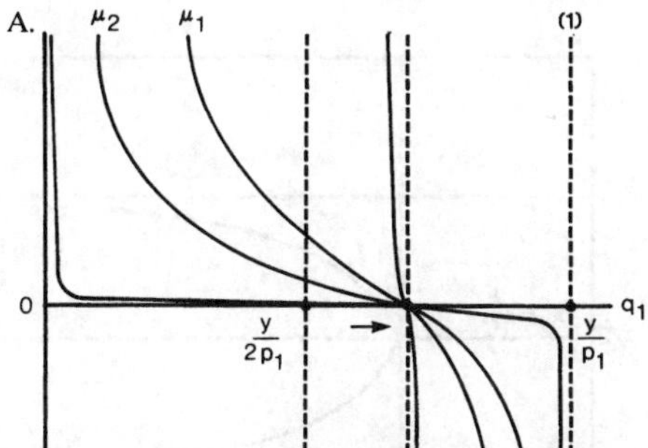

FIGURE 4. A) THE RIGHT-HAND SIDE OF EQUATION (32); B) SOLUTIONS TO EQUATION (32)

presence of externalities, correction could involve public advertisement instead of Pigouvian taxes and subsidies. Furthermore, given a particular ability to choose, Figure 4B indicates that bias may either decrease (line AB) or increase (line CD) the stationary level of utility. In particular, there is $b_1 - b_2$ which will generate the optimal allocation at stationary state. It follows that the quantities b_i can be used as controls. Unlike firms, which waste resources by trying to overcome the advertising effects of their competitors, government in our model can simply determine $b_1 > 0$ and $b_2 < 0$ for which the stationary consumption rates in the case of line CD are found at G. In any case, if no other advertisement is allowed, the planner can determine a combination of biases such that $b_1^* - b_2^*$ will accomplish G at minimum cost. Only when the ability to choose is perfect will it be unnecessary to influence the individual. Since both the ability to choose and the pattern of systematic distortions to perception can be affected, the problem is to find a best combination of ability-improvement programs and systematic distortion strategies. One cannot depend exclusively upon ability-improvement programs, since it becomes more costly to raise already higher ability while, at the same time, the corresponding savings on systematic manipulation strategies decline. Finally, public manipulation of bias can become bad, as suggested by propaganda.

X. Optimal Product Differentiation

We have already provided some examples indicating how standard welfare results can change under an imperfect ability to choose. In this section we reinforce this implication by developing a model in which we specify precisely how a welfare result changes with the degree of ability. We examine optimal product differentiation using the simplest model consistent with our framework. There is a population of individuals identical with respect to income and ability to choose. Following the tradition of Harold Hotelling (1929), we assume that this population is continuously distributed at a unit density over a line interval $[0,1]$ representing the space of the single characteristic over which products are defined. Location on that space determines the preferences of those located there because the ideal product for an individual located at $x \in [0,1]$ has a characteristic of size x. There are only two products which are produced at the same, fixed marginal cost and sold at the same price. We consider a single interval $[0,T]$, at the beginning of which every individual spends a disposable income of one unit on a single product, which it consumes at a uniform rate $1/T$. In terms of Section I, $T = \Delta t = c^{-1}$. For an individual located at x, the utility of spending the unit of money on product i is simply

$$(33)\qquad v_i(x) = -\theta|x - x_i|$$

where $\theta > 0$ measures the intensity of preference for the ideal product and $x_i \in [0,1]$ is the address of product i. Using (10), the probability that an individual located at x will choose product i is

$$(34)\quad \mathbb{P}_i(x) = \frac{\exp(-\mu\theta|x - x_i|)}{\sum_{j=1}^{2}\exp(-\mu\theta|x - x_j|)}.$$

The expected utility of that individual can be written as

$$(35)\quad V(x, x_1, x_2) \equiv -[\theta|x - x_1|\mathbb{P}_1(x) + \theta|x - x_2|\mathbb{P}_2(x)]$$

and the total expected utility in the system is given by

$$(36)\quad W(x_1, x_2) \equiv \int_0^1 V(x, x_1, x_2)\,dx.$$

Since firms produce under the same linear technology and sell at the same price, and since total demand is fixed, we may disregard profits in constructing a socially optimal rule. Therefore our problem is to determine the optimal products (x_1^*, x_2^*), so that $W(\cdot)$ is maximized for a given ability to choose. In Appendix B-1 we prove that the optimal products are symmetrically located on $[0,1]$ and behave as in Figure 5. When the ability to choose is perfect, we obtain the standard solution on the first and third quarters of the characteristic space (see e.g., Melvin L. Greenhut et al., 1987). As the ability to choose declines, optimal products become increasingly similar, and Hotelling's principle of minimum differentiation is eventually restored when the ability to choose becomes sufficiently low (also see de Palma et al., 1985). This could be interpreted as a justification of the familiar belief that less product variety can be better.

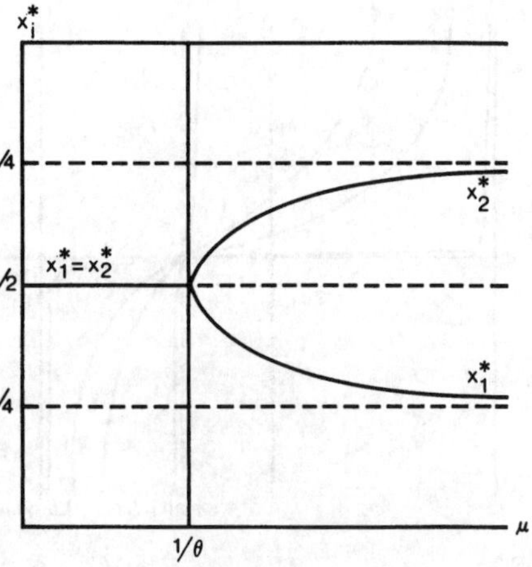

FIGURE 5. OPTIMAL PRODUCTS

For stronger intensity of preference, the range over which the principle is restored becomes smaller. Thus intensity of preference, as ability to choose, requires more differentiation. These conclusions are similar to the optimal location policies developed by Simon P. Anderson and de Palma (1988). We compare the two approaches in Appendix B-2.

XI. Concluding Remarks

The power and the success of perfectly rational behavior as a model of choice is to be found in the observation that many real events can be explained by assuming that individuals behave *as if* they have a perfect ability to choose. Yet there are phenomena for which explanations alternative to those provided within the context of perfectly rational behavior might appear closer to experience in some respects; and there are cases in which the "as if" principle itself breaks down. A positive example of "as if" failure is provided by the Herrnstein (1991) experiments in Section I, and a normative example is provided by the optimal product differentiation of Section X. Our basic premise, which provided the foundation for our model, is that those difficulties arise because the ability to choose often affects behavior in ways that cannot be dismissed as insignificant. With this in mind, we have strived to attain some meaningful balance between descriptive accuracy and analytical tractability. On the one hand, our model comes closer to observation than the model of perfectly rational behavior. On the other, modeling such behavior seems fruitful: the limited experience presented here indicates that our model can offer some analytical results which provide new insights.

Appendix A: Demand Functions

1. *Exogenous Ability To Choose*

At stationary consumption,

$$\text{(A1)} \qquad y\bar{\mathbb{P}}_i = p_i\bar{q}_i,$$

Total differentiation yields

$$\text{(A2)} \quad (\mathbf{A}-\mathbf{I}\cdot\mathbf{p})\,d\bar{\mathbf{q}} = -y\frac{\partial\bar{\mathbb{P}}}{\partial\mu}d\mu - (\mathbf{B}-\mathbf{I}\cdot\bar{\mathbf{q}})\,d\mathbf{p} - \bar{\mathbb{P}}\,dy$$

where $\mathbf{A}$ and $\mathbf{B}$ are $n\times n$ matrices with elements

$$\text{(A3)} \qquad a_{ij} \equiv y\sum_{k=1}^{n}\frac{\partial\bar{\mathbb{P}}_i}{\partial\bar{v}_k}\frac{\partial\bar{v}_k}{\partial\bar{q}_j}$$

$$b_{ij} \equiv y\frac{\partial\bar{\mathbb{P}}_i}{\partial\bar{q}_j}$$

respectively, $\bar{\mathbb{P}}$ is the vector of stationary probabilities, and $\partial\bar{\mathbb{P}}/\partial\mu$ is the vector with components $\partial\bar{\mathbb{P}}_i/\partial\mu$. Equation (A2) describes the local changes in the stationary demand caused by any combination of local changes in the ability to choose, prices, and the expenditure rate. The effect on the equilibrium allocation of a change in the ability to choose when prices and the expenditure rate remain fixed is given by

$$\text{(A4)} \quad d\bar{\mathbf{q}} = -(\mathbf{A}-\mathbf{I}\cdot\mathbf{p})^{-1}y\frac{\partial\bar{\mathbb{P}}}{\partial\mu}d\mu$$

provided that the matrix $\mathbf{A}-\mathbf{I}\cdot\mathbf{p}$ is nonsingular.

Consider now the associated EMP. For any $(y,\mathbf{p};\mu)$ there is $(\bar{y},\bar{\mathbf{p}})$ such that $\bar{\mathbf{q}}(y,\mathbf{p};\mu)$ is the solution to the problem of maximizing $v(\cdot)$ subject to $\Sigma_i\bar{p}_iq_i \le \bar{y}$. Thus at $\bar{\mathbf{q}}+d\bar{\mathbf{q}}$ there is another $(\bar{y}+d\bar{y},\bar{\mathbf{p}}+d\bar{\mathbf{p}})$ such that

$$\text{(A5)} \quad y\frac{\partial\bar{\mathbb{P}}}{\partial\mu}d\mu = (\mathbf{B}-\mathbf{I}\cdot\bar{\mathbf{q}})/d\bar{\mathbf{p}} - \bar{\mathbb{P}}\,d\bar{y}.$$

Equations (A4) and (A5) imply

$$\text{(A6)} \quad d\bar{\mathbf{q}} = -(\mathbf{A}-\mathbf{I}\cdot\bar{\mathbf{p}})^{-1}\Big[(\mathbf{B}+\bar{\mathbb{P}}\cdot\bar{\mathbf{q}}'-\mathbf{I}\cdot\bar{\mathbf{q}})\,d\bar{\mathbf{p}} + \bar{\mathbb{P}}(d\bar{y}-\bar{\mathbf{q}}'\cdot d\bar{\mathbf{p}})\Big]$$

$$\equiv \frac{\partial\bar{\mathbf{q}}}{\partial\bar{\mathbf{p}}}\bigg|_{\bar{v}}\cdot d\bar{\mathbf{p}} + \frac{\partial\bar{\mathbf{q}}}{\partial\bar{y}}(d\bar{y}-\bar{\mathbf{q}}'\cdot d\bar{\mathbf{p}})$$

where $\partial\bar{\mathbf{q}}/\partial\bar{\mathbf{p}}$ is the $n\times n$ matrix with elements $\partial\bar{q}_i/\partial\bar{p}_j$, $\partial\bar{\mathbf{q}}/\partial\bar{y}$ is the vector with components $\partial\bar{q}_i/\partial\bar{y}$, and $\bar{\mathbf{q}}'$ is the transpose of $\bar{\mathbf{q}}$. The RHS of (A6) represents the decomposition of a change in the ability to choose into substitution and income effects of the EMP. How $\bar{y}$ and $\bar{\mathbf{p}}$ vary with μ can be determined through (A5), keeping a particular commodity as the numeraire.

Figure A1 illustrates those points in the case of two commodities. AB corresponds to the stationary budget constraint determined by the fixed y and $\mathbf{p}$. As in Figure 1, CD is the set of all possible stationary consumptions, where C corresponds to perfect ability and D to zero ability. Let E represent $\bar{\mathbf{q}}(y,\mathbf{p};\mu+d\mu)$ and let F represent $\bar{\mathbf{q}}(y,\mathbf{p};\mu)$. Both can be thought of as solutions to an EMP, the former with budget constraint GH and the latter with budget constraint JK. Both these new constraints involve changes in prices and the expenditure rate described by $d\bar{\mathbf{p}}$ and $d\bar{y}$ in (A5). As the ability to choose deteriorates, the stationary consumption moves from point E to point F on a lower indifference curve.

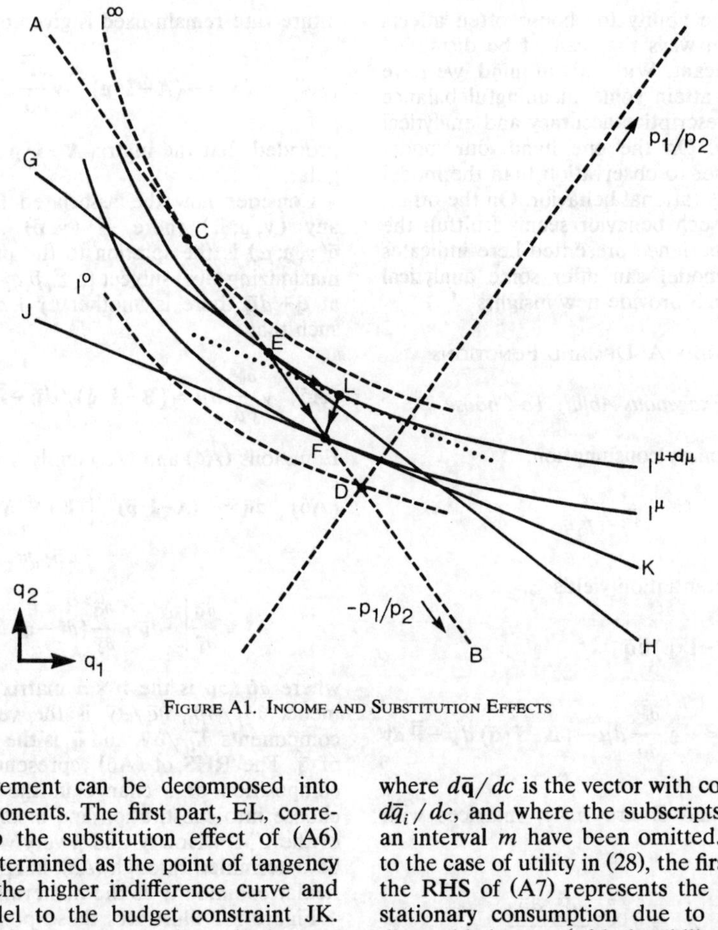

FIGURE A1. INCOME AND SUBSTITUTION EFFECTS

This movement can be decomposed into two components. The first part, EL, corresponds to the substitution effect of (A6) with L determined as the point of tangency between the higher indifference curve and the parallel to the budget constraint JK. The second, LF, corresponds to the income effect of (A6).

2. *Endogenous Ability To Choose*

The impact of improving ability on stationary consumption can be determined through a modification of (A2) Holding only prices fixed,

$$\text{(A7)} \quad \frac{d\bar{\mathbf{q}}}{dc} = (\mathbf{A} - \mathbf{I}\cdot\mathbf{p})^{-1}\cdot\bar{\mathbb{P}} - (\mathbf{A} - \mathbf{I}\cdot\mathbf{p})^{-1}(y-c)\frac{\partial\bar{\mathbb{P}}}{\partial\mu}\frac{d\mu}{dc}$$

where $d\bar{\mathbf{q}}/dc$ is the vector with components $d\bar{q}_i/dc$, and where the subscripts denoting an interval m have been omitted. Similarly to the case of utility in (28), the first term on the RHS of (A7) represents the change in stationary consumption due to a smaller disposable income (with the ability to choose held constant), while the second term represents the corresponding change due to an improved ability (with the disposable income held constant).

Figure A2 illustrates (28) and (A7) in the case of two commodities. Its structure and notation resemble those of Figure A1. Let AB represent the stationary budget constraint when $c = 0$. Suppose now that the initial position is at E, where the individual spends a positive amount c to maintain a particular ability to choose and, consequently, has a stationary budget constraint GH lower than AB. In contrast, the stationary utility level lies on an indifference curve

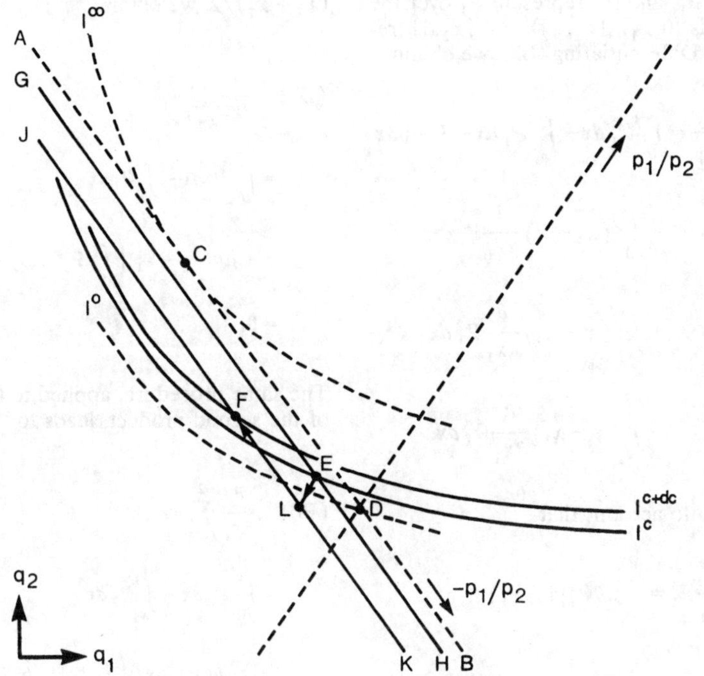

FIGURE A2. INCOME AND ABILITY EFFECTS

I^c which is higher than I^0 because, here, the improvement in ability dominates the corresponding loss of disposable income. The same continues to be true for further ability improvements in our example. Increasing c by dc results in the stationary consumption F, which lies at the intersection between a lower budget constraint JK and a higher difference curve I^{c+dc}. The movement from E to F can be partitioned into two components. The first, EL, corresponds to the first term on the RHS of (A7) and the second, LF, corresponds to the second term.

APPENDIX B: DETAILS ON OPTIMAL PRODUCT DIFFERENTIATION

Some calculations, which have not been included in this appendix, are available from the authors upon request.

1. *Optimal Products*

We first prove that the optimal products are symmetric in [0,1]. Let

$$\text{(B1)} \qquad w_i \equiv \int_0^1 |x - x_i| \mathbb{P}_i \, dx.$$

Since $W(\cdot) = -\theta \Sigma_i w_i$, maximizing $W(\cdot)$ is equivalent to minimizing $\Sigma_i w_i$ with first-order conditions given by $\partial(\Sigma_i w_i)/\partial x_j = 0$ for $j = 1,2$. Now using

$$\text{(B2)} \qquad w_1 = \int_0^{x_1} (x_1 - x) \mathbb{P}_1^1 \, dx + \int_{x_1}^{x_2} (x - x_1) \mathbb{P}_1^2 \, dx + \int_{x_2}^1 (x - x_1) \mathbb{P}_1^3 \, dx$$

where $\mathbb{P}_1^1$, $\mathbb{P}_1^2$, and $\mathbb{P}_1^3$ represent $\mathbb{P}_1$ over the subintervals $[0, x_1)$, $[x_1, x_2)$ and $[x_2, 1]$, respectively. Differentiating (B2), we obtain

$$\text{(B3)} \quad \frac{\partial w_1}{\partial x_1} = \int_0^{x_1} \mathbb{P}_1^1\,dx - \int_{x_1}^{x_2} \mathbb{P}_1^2\,dx - \int_{x_2}^{1} \mathbb{P}_1^3\,dx + \int_0^{x_1} (x_1 - x)\frac{\partial}{\partial x_1}\mathbb{P}_1^1\,dx + \int_{x_1}^{x_2} (x - x_1)\frac{\partial}{\partial x_1}\mathbb{P}_1^2\,dx + \int_{x_2}^{1} (x - x_1)\frac{\partial}{\partial x_1}\mathbb{P}_1^3\,dx.$$

Taking into account that

$$\text{(B4)} \quad \frac{\partial}{\partial x_1}\mathbb{P}_1^1 = -\mu\theta\mathbb{P}_1^1(1 - \mathbb{P}_1^1)$$

$$\frac{\partial}{\partial x_1}\mathbb{P}_1^k = \mu\theta\mathbb{P}_1^k(1 - \mathbb{P}_1^k) \qquad k = 2,3$$

equation (B3) reduces to

$$\text{(B5)} \quad \frac{\partial w_1}{\partial x_1} = \int_0^{x_1} \mathbb{P}_1\,dx - \int_{x_2}^{1} \mathbb{P}_1\,dx + \mu\theta\int_0^1 (x - x_1)\mathbb{P}_1\mathbb{P}_2\,dx.$$

Similarly,

$$\text{(B6)} \quad \frac{\partial w_2}{\partial x_1} = -\mu\theta + \mu\theta\int_{x_1}^{x_2} (x - x_2)\mathbb{P}_1\mathbb{P}_2\,dx - \mu\theta\int_{x_2}^{1} (x - x_2)\mathbb{P}_1\mathbb{P}_2\,dx.$$

Adding (B5) and (B6), and taking into account that $\mathbb{P}_i$ is symmetric with respect to $(x_1 + x_2)/2$, we obtain

$$\text{(B7)} \quad \frac{\partial}{\partial x_1}\sum_{i=1}^{2} w_i = \int_0^{x_1} \mathbb{P}_1\,dx - \int_{x_1}^{1} \mathbb{P}_1\,dx + \mu\theta(x_2 - x_1)\left(\int_0^{x_1} \mathbb{P}_1\mathbb{P}_2\,dx + \int_{x_2}^{1} \mathbb{P}_1\mathbb{P}_2\,dx\right) = 0.$$

The same procedure, applied to the address of the second product, leads to

$$\text{(B8)} \quad \frac{\partial}{\partial x_2}\sum_{i=1}^{2} w_i = \int_0^{x_2} \mathbb{P}_2\,dx - \int_{x_2}^{1} \mathbb{P}_2\,dx - \mu\theta(x_2 - x_1)\left(\int_0^{x_1} \mathbb{P}_1\mathbb{P}_2\,dx + \int_{x_2}^{1} \mathbb{P}_1\mathbb{P}_2\,dx\right) = 0.$$

Finally, adding (B7) and (B8), we conclude that

$$\text{(B9)} \qquad x_2^* = 1 - x_1^*$$

as required for symmetry.

We next examine the behavior of optimal products in relation to θ and μ. Upon substitution of (B9) into (B7) and taking into account the symmetry of $\mathbb{P}_i$ when the two product addresses are symmetric, the first-order condition (FOC) of the optimization problem can be written as

$$\text{(B10)} \quad \text{FOC} \equiv 4\mu\theta\mathbb{P}_1^1(1 - \mathbb{P}_1^1)\left(\frac{1}{2} - x_1\right)x_1 + \left(2\mathbb{P}_1^2 x_1 - \frac{1}{2}\right) = 0$$

where

$$\text{(B11)}\quad \mathbb{P}_1^1 = \{1+\exp[\mu\theta(2x_1-1)]\}^{-1}.$$

The corresponding second-order condition (SOC) is

$$\text{(B12)}\quad \text{SOC} \equiv 2\mathbb{P}_1^1\left\{1-2\mu\theta(1-\mathbb{P}_1^1)\right.$$
$$\left.\times\left[3x_1-\frac{1}{2}+2\mu\theta\left(\frac{1}{2}-x_1\right)(1-2\mathbb{P}_1^1)\right]\right\}\geq 0.$$

At $x_1 = 1/2$ we have $\mathbb{P}_1^1 = 1/2$. Hence, for the same location, FOC = 0, and SOC = 1 − $\mu\theta$. It follows that $x_1 = 1/2$ corresponds to a local maximum of $W(\cdot)$ for $\mu \leq 1/\theta$ and to a local minimum for $\mu > 1/\theta$. We prove below that the maximum is global. Therefore $x_1^* = 1/2$ if and only if $\mu \leq 1/\theta$. For $\mu > 1/\theta$, x_1^* also corresponds to a global maximum of $W(\cdot)$. Total differentiation of (B10) further yields that x_1^* is strictly decreasing and convex in μ for $\mu > 1/\theta$. Hence the minimum occurs at $\mu = \infty$. In order to evaluate this minimum notice that $\lim \mathbb{P}_1^1 = 1$ and $\lim \mu\mathbb{P}_1^1 = 0$ for $\mu \to \infty$. These, in conjunction with the FOC, imply $\lim_{\mu\to\infty} x_1^* = 1/4$.

It remains to prove that the result is global. Using $x_1 \equiv 1/2 - z$, after some calculations, we can write (B10) as

$$\text{(B13)}\quad z[(\mu\theta-1)-2\mu\theta z]$$
$$=\left(z-\frac{1}{4}\right)\exp(2\mu\theta z)+\frac{1}{4}\exp(-2\mu\theta z).$$

When $\mu \leq 1/\theta$, the LHS of (B13) is null for $z = 0$ and negative for $z > 0$, while the RHS of (B13) is null for $z = 0$ and positive for $z > 0$. In consequence (B13) admits a unique solution $z = 0$. This implies that $x_1^* = x_2^* = 1/2$ corresponds to the global maximum of $W(\cdot)$. We now examine the case $\mu > 1/\theta$. The LHS of (B13) is a concave parabola as shown in Figure B1, where LHS(1/2) < 0. After some calculations, we also establish that the RHS of (B13) is a convex function as shown in Figure B1 where RHS(1/2) > 0. Since, in Figure B1, $z = 0$ is a solution to

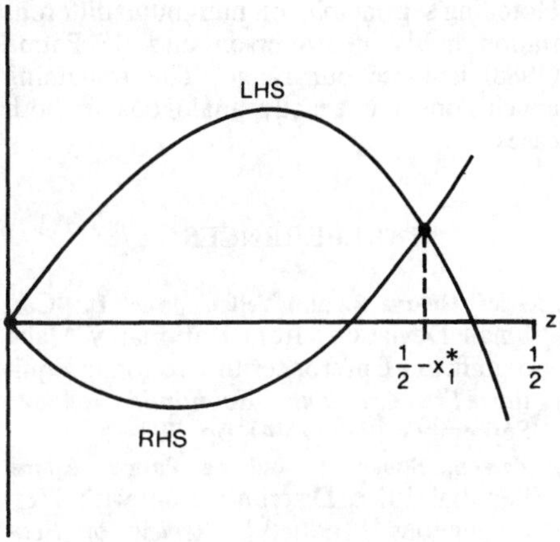

FIGURE B1. SOLUTIONS TO EQUATION (B13)

(B13) that corresponds to a local minimum of $W(\cdot)$, the only other solution must correspond to a global maximum.

2. *Anderson and de Palma (1988)*

In order to determine optimal location policies analogous to our optimal design policies, Anderson and de Palma (1988) employed the consumer-surplus function

$$\text{(B14)}\quad \text{CS}(x_1,x_2)$$
$$\equiv \frac{1}{\mu}\int_0^1 \ln\left(\sum_{i=1}^{2}\exp[\mu\theta|x-x_i|]\right)$$

which was derived for the logit model by Kenneth A. Small and Harvey S. Rosen (1981). Taking into account symmetry, the first- and second-order conditions are

$$\text{(B15)}\quad \text{FOC} \equiv 2\mu\theta\left(\frac{1}{2}-x_1\right)+\ln(4x_1-1)=0$$

$$\text{(B16)}\quad \text{SOC} \equiv 4-2\mu\theta(4x_1-1)\geq 0.$$

At $x_1 = 1/2$ we have FOC = 0 and SOC = $2-\mu\theta$. It follows that $x_1 = 1/2$ corresponds to a local maximum of CS($\cdot$) for $\mu \leq 2/\theta$, and to a local minimum for $\mu > 2/\theta$. As in our case, the maximum is also global. Thus the range over which

Hotelling's principle of minimum differentiation holds in Anderson and de Palma (1988) is twice our range. The remaining conclusions are exactly analogous in both cases.

REFERENCES

Akerlof, George A. and Yellen, Janet L. "Can Small Deviations from Rationality Make Significant Differences to Economic Equilibria?" *American Economic Review*, September 1986, *75*(4), pp. 708–20.

Anderson, Simon P. and de Palma, André. "Spatial Price Discrimination with Heterogeneous Products." *Review of Economic Studies*, October 1988, *55*(4), pp. 573–92.

Becker, Gary and Murphy, Kevin M. "A Simple Theory of Advertisement as a Good or Bad." *Quarterly Journal of Economics*, November 1993, *108*(4), pp. 941–64.

Bettman, James R. *An information processing theory of consumer choice*. Reading MA: Addison-Wesley, 1979.

de Palma, A.; Ginsburgh, V.; Papageorgiou, Y. Y. and Thisse, J.-F. "The Principle of Minimum Differentiation Holds Under Sufficient Heterogeneity." *Econometrica*, July 1985, *53*(4), pp. 767–81.

Dixit, Avinash and Norman, Victor. "Advertising and Welfare." *Bell Journal of Economics*, Spring 1978, *9*(1), pp. 1–17.

Galbraith, John K. *The new industrial state*. Boston: Houghton Mifflin, 1967.

Ginsburgh, Victor; Papageorgiou, Yorgos and Thisse, Jacques-François. "On Existence and Stability of Spatial Equilibria and Steady-States." *Regional Science and Urban Economics*, June 1985, *15*(2), pp. 149–58.

Greenhut, Melvin L.; Norman, George and Hung, Chao-Shun. *The economics of imperfect competition*. Cambridge: Cambridge University Press, 1987.

Grossman, Gene M. and Shapiro, Carl. "Informative Advertising with Differentiated Products." *Review of Economic Studies*, January 1984, *51*(1), pp. 63–82.

Heiner, Ronald A. "The Origin of Predictable Behavior." *American Economic Review*, September 1983, *73*(4), pp. 560–95.

Herrnstein, R. J. "Experiments on Stable Suboptimality in Individual Behavior." *American Economic Review*, May 1991 (*Papers and Proceedings*), *81*(2), pp. 360–64.

Hicks, John R. "Some Questions of Time in Economics," in Anthony M. Tang, Fred M. Westfield, and James S. Worley, eds., *Evolution, welfare, and time in economics*. Lexington MA: Lexington Books, 1976, pp. 135–51.

Hotelling, Harold. "Stability in Competition." *Economic Journal*, March 1929, *39*(1), pp. 41–57.

Kahneman, Daniel; Slovic, Paul and Tversky, Amos. *Judgment under uncertainty: Heuristics and biases*, Cambridge: Cambridge University Press, 1982.

Leibenstein, Harvey. *Beyond economic man: A new foundation for microeconomics*. Cambridge MA: Harvard University Press, 1976.

Levhari, David; Oron, Yitzhak and Pines, David. "A Note on Unequal Treatment of Equals in an Urban Setting." *Journal of Urban Economics*, January 1978, *5*(2), pp. 278–84.

Lipman, Barton L. "Decision Theory with Impossible Possible Worlds." Mimeo, Queen's University, 1992.

March, James G. "Bounded Rationality, Ambiguity, and the Engineering of Choice." *Bell Journal of Economics*, Autumn 1978, *9*(2), pp. 587–608.

Marshall, Alfred. *Principles of economics*, 8th Ed. London: Macmillan, 1920.

McFadden, Daniel. "Conditional Logit Analysis of Qualitative Choice Behavior," in P. Zarembka, ed., *Frontiers in econometrics*. New York: Academic Press, 1974, pp. 105–42.

Milgrom, Paul and Roberts, John. "Price and Advertising Signals of Product Quality." *Journal of Political Economy*, August 1986, *94*(4), pp. 796–821.

Mirrlees, J. A. "The Optimum Town." *Swedish Journal of Economics*, Winter 1972, *74*(1), pp. 114–35.

Newell, Allen and Simon, Herbert A. *Human problem solving*. Englewood Cliffs, NJ: Prentice-Hall, 1972.

Simon, Herbert A. "A Behavioral Model of Rational Choice." *Quarterly Journal of Economics*, February 1955, *69*(1), pp. 99–118.

Small, Kenneth A. and Rosen, Harvey S. "Applied Welfare Economics with Discrete Choice Models." *Econometrica*, January 1981, *49*(1), pp. 105–30.

Telser, Lester G. "Advertising and Competition." *Journal of Political Economy*, December 1964, *72*(6), pp. 537–62.

von Neumann, John and Morgenstern, Oskar. *Theory of games and economic behavior*. New York: Wiley, 1944.

Yellott, John I. "The Relationship Between Luce's Choice Axiom, Thurstone's Theory of Comparative Judgement, and the Double Exponential Distribution." *Journal of Mathematical Psychology*, April 1977, *15*(2), pp. 109–44.

[7]

CHARLES F. MANSKI*

THE STRUCTURE OF RANDOM UTILITY MODELS

INTRODUCTION

This paper presents a formal analysis of the distributional structure of random utility models. Its essential conceptual contribution lies in its explicit treatment of the processes making perfect predictions of choice behavior unattainable. The paper's technical contribution is its demonstration of the manner in which these processes induce the distributional properties of a model. In contrast to the approach adopted here, the existing literature on random utility models generally imposes distributional assumptions directly. Because it leaves so much implicit, this practice has often caused researchers to remain unaware of the restrictiveness of their models. Only a few authors, working with specific simple models, have chosen to lay the foundations of their research more deeply. Their efforts will be described shortly.

Historically, random utility models, a subset of the class of probabilistic choice models, were first developed by psychologists in the attempt to characterize observed inconsistencies in patterns of individual behavior.[1] A definition offered by Block and Marschak (1960) can be paraphrased for our purposes as follows:

> Let $\mathfrak{a}$ be a finite set of alternatives, T be a finite population of decision makers and let $\in^c$ mean 'is chosen from'. Then choice is consistent with a random utility model if there exist real valued random variables U_{at}, all $a \in \mathfrak{a}$, $t \in T$ such that $\Pr_t(a \in^c C) = \Pr(U_{at} \geqslant U_{a't}$, all $a' \in C)$ for all alternatives $a \in C$, all non-null choice sets $C \subset \mathfrak{a}$ and all decision makers $t \in T$.

Later, economists, beginning with McFadden (1968) embraced such models as an econometric representation of maximizing behavior. In this formulation, utilities are treated as random variables not to reflect a lack of rationality in the decision maker but to reflect a lack of information regarding the characteristics of alternatives and/or decision makers on the part of the observer.[2]

Theory and Decision 8 (1977) 229–254. *All Rights Reserved*

Differing substantive interpretations not withstanding, both the econometric and psychometric literatures focussed early on one simple specification for the random utility function, the form $U_{at} = V_{at} + \epsilon_{at}$ where $(V_{at}, a \in \mathfrak{a}, t \in T)$ are a set of constants and $(\epsilon_{at}, a \in \mathfrak{a}, t \in T)$ are a set of independent and identically distributed random variables. Among such 'independent and identically distributed random utilities' (IIDRU) models, the Luce (1959, 1965) and McFadden (1968, 1973) model undoubtedly has the best analytical and computational properties. Domenchic and McFadden (1975) offer other examples of IIDRU models.

Although empirical practice still confines itself to the exclusive use of IIDRU models, the special nature of such models has long been recognized. Beginning in Debreu's (1960) review of Luce's pioneering work (Luce, 1959), examples of situations in which IIDRU models yield counter-intuitive behavioral forecasts have become numerous.[3] Concern with the development of tractable but less restrictive models has, to a degree, increased as well. Two such models, Tversky's elimination-by-aspects model (Tversky, 1972a, 1972b) and a model constructed by Quandt and Young (1969) and generalized by Domenchic and McFadden (1975) are now available. Both models derive their distributional properties from more basic assumptions, both behave more intuitively than do IIDRU models yet both contain an IIDRU model as a special case.

While the above developments have contributed in important ways to our grasp of the structure of random utility models, our understanding of such models remains fragmentary and in many ways superficial. Our continuing inability to delineate the appropriate domain for IIDRU models typefies the situation. Instead of turning to formal analysis of the problem, discussion has become mired in the search for ad hoc corrections to be applied to existing models so as to make them behave more plausibly. An ill-defined dichotomy between 'similar' alternatives, for which IIDRU models are supposed to be inappropriate and 'distinct' alternatives, which such models are said to suitably handle, has also arisen.[4]

Repeated frustration in my own attempts to operationalize the similar-distinct dichotomy gradually convinced me that further progress requires not new technique but rather a reformulation of the random utility model at a position logically prior to that hitherto adopted. That reformulation, in terms of the processes making perfect choice predictions unattainable, is contained in Part I of the present paper. Part II then examines the distributional properties of random utility models.

In order not to raise unjustified hopes to applied researchers, I must point out that this paper's scope is limited to theoretical issues. Questions of operationalizing the models presented in terms of tractable estimation and forecasting procedures are, by and large, not considered.[5]

I. THE GENERAL MODEL

This development of the random utility model begins with a statement of primitive concepts and definitions. Next, the decision rule governing the behavior of a given decision maker faced with a specified choice set is specified. Then the process associating decision makers with choice sets is introduced.

At this point, attention shifts to the observer. I detail the limited information regarding the choice problem generating process, the decision rule governing choice, and the characteristics of decision makers and alternatives – he possesses. Finally, I show how lack of complete information induces the random utility model and its associated choice probabilities.

Mathematically, this paper uses only the concepts of elementary set and probability theory. Nevertheless, the proper interpretation of certain assumptions and results can be quite subtle. Throughout the model's development, I attempt to point our where steps are restrictive and to interpret their import.[6]

A. *Primitive Concepts and Definitions*

Let *choice* be an operation mapping a set into one of its non-null elements and a *decision maker* be an agent performing choice operations according to a fixed rule. A finite population of decision makers, designated T, is assumed to exist. Assume the existence of a finite set $\mathfrak{a}$, termed the *alternative space*, such that the choice operation is defined over each of $\mathfrak{a}$'s non-null subsets. The elements of $\mathfrak{a}$ are then termed *alternatives*, the ordered non-null subsets of $\mathfrak{a}$ are termed *choice sets* and the set of all ordered non-null subsets of $\mathfrak{a}$ is termed the *choice set space*, designated Γ.

DISCUSSION: In the above, choice sets are defined as ordered sets for analytical reasons. To the utility maximizing decision maker, the ordering of the elements of such a set is irrelevant.

B. *The Decision Rule*

Let U_t be a real valued function defined over $\mathfrak{a}$ and termed a ***utility function***. Faced with any choice set $C \in \Gamma$, decision maker t is assumed to select an $a \in C$ such that $U_{at} \geqslant U_{a't}$, all $a' \in C$.[7]

Let X and S be finite subsets of real spaces and $\mathfrak{a} \rightarrow X$, $T \rightarrow S$ be mappings associating every $a \in \mathscr{A}$ with an $x_a \in X$, every $t \in T$ with an $s_t \in S$. X and S are ***attribute*** representations of the alternative space $\mathfrak{a}$ and decision maker space T while x_a and s_t are attribute vectors for a and t respectively. The attribute representations X and S are said to be ***utility relevant*** if there exists a real valued function w, defined over $X \times S$ such that

$$U_{at} = w(x_a, s_t) \quad \text{all} \quad a \in \mathfrak{a}, \quad t \in T.$$

DISCUSSION: (1) If X is an attribute representation for $\mathfrak{a}$, then the choice set space Γ has a corresponding representation, namely the class of ordered sets $R = (r_c, C \in \Gamma)$ where $r_c = [(x_a, \text{all } a \in C)]$. If the mapping $\mathfrak{a} \rightarrow X$ is one-to-one, then R is the set of all non-null subsets of X.[8]

(2) We shall, in this paper, be interested only in utility relevant representations for $\mathfrak{a}$ and T.

In general, each $\mathfrak{a}$ and T admit infinitely many such representations and the observer must select among them. While often this choice is merely one of normalization, sometimes it is less trivial. For example, the utility of a transportation mode might be specified to be a function of its physical characteristics or of its 'qualities', comfort, convenience, privacy etc., appropriately scaled. Both types of specification are found in the literature. The observer's selection of a representation will depend on the nature of his attribute data and on his ability to specify the w function associated with alternative representations.

Our concern will be with the derivation of a random utility model from a given representation, not with the choice among representations.

(3) In establishing real valued attribute representations for the primitive sets $\mathfrak{a}$ and T, it is natural to inquire what properties of real spaces are being exploited. At this stage, these representations are merely formalisms. Even later, the only property used is the expressibility of a real space as a Cartesian product set.[9]

Nowhere are X and S viewed as generating linear spaces. In fact, linear combinations of elements in X need correspond not only to no element of $\mathfrak{a}$ but to no logically possible alternative. For example, in mode choice models travel time must be positive and the number of occupants in a vehicle is confined to the positive integers.[10]

C. *The Generation of Choice Problems*

The framework of classical choice theory, within which the present effort lies, explains individual behavior as the outcome of a two step recursive process. First, exogeneous forces pose a choice problem, that is an individual and an associated choice set. Then, with the choice set well-defined, the individual selects among the available alternatives.

In general, research on choice theory has focused on the second stage process, the characterization of classes of decision rules, formalization of choice set structure and study of the properties of the outcome when decision rules of a given class are applied to choice sets of a specified structure.[11] In the present development of the random utility model, the description of the first stage, the mechanism generating choice problems, occupies an equally central position. Having already assumed a decision rule, utility maximization, and a choice set structure, finite point sets, we now describe the generation of choice problems, first formally and then through an interpretive discussion.

Let a *choice problem* be a pair (C, t) drawn from the product space $\Gamma \times T$ according to a probability measure $M_{\Gamma T}$, defined over $\Gamma \times T$. $M_{\Gamma T}$ is the *choice problem generating process*.

From $M_{\Gamma T}$, a variety of useful probability measures may be derived. These include the following:

M_T, a distribution with domain T and defined by $M_T(t) = \Sigma_{C \in \Gamma} M_{\Gamma T}(C, t)$ is the *decision maker generating process.*

$M_\Gamma(C/t)$, $t \in T$, a set of distributions each with domain Γ and defined by $M_\Gamma(C/t) = M_{\Gamma T}(C, t)/M_T(t)$ are the *choice set generating processes.*

Because the ordering of elements within a choice set is arbitrary, we shall adopt the convention that $M_{\Gamma T}(C, t) = M_{\Gamma T}(\tilde{C}, t)$ whenever C and $\tilde{C}$ are identical except for order.

DISCUSSION: Specification of a distribution $M_{\Gamma T}$ and a set of utility values U_{at}, $a \in \mathfrak{a}$, $t \in T$ fully characterizes a classical choice process. The conciseness of this formalization is both pleasing and powerful. At the same time, however, it is implicitly restrictive and undeniably unintuitive. The discussion below attempts to provide the intuition for and make explicit the restrictions in this model of choice problem generation.

(1) Noting that $M_{\Gamma T}(C, t) = M_{\Gamma}(C \mid t)\, M_T(t)$, consider first the generation of choice sets, as embodied in $M_{\Gamma}(C \mid t)$. This process is most easily interpreted when there exist a set of decision makers TT who control the alternatives $\mathfrak{a}$. The generation of choice sets for T is then the outcome of a set of prior decisions made by the members of TT. These are the (not necessarily independent) binary decisions specifying whether each $a \in \mathfrak{a}$ will or will not be made available to each $t \in T$.

For example, if T is a set of students and $\mathfrak{a}$ is a set of colleges, then college choice sets are generated for T through the admissions decisions of the intitutional administrators TT controlling $\mathfrak{a}$. Similarly, T might be a set of workers, $\mathfrak{a}$ a set of jobs and TT a set of firms making job offers. Or T might be the set of draft eligible males, $\mathfrak{a}$, a set of military and civilian alternatives and TT 'nature' operating through the draft lottery to restrict the availability of civilian alternatives.

Turn now to the process generating decision makers, M_T. In the context of random utility function estimation, where the observer draws a sample from T and then notes their choices, interpretation of M_T as describing the sampling process is straightforward. A different interpretation of M_T derives from the psychological model of random utilities. There T specifies a set of decision rules from which the individual draws, according to the distribution M_T, when faced with a choice situation.[12]

(2) The classical assumption of a recursive choice process often restricts its empirical utility. In particular, when TT is a set of conscious decision makers (as opposed to 'nature'), symmetric treatment of T and TT seems more appropriate. A recursive structure gains attractiveness if it allows recontracting. While the present development of the random utility model is static in the sense that it describes only one move by each actor, a sequence of such models could conceivably be linked so as to describe a recontracting process. Such a sequence might capture the essence of game theoretic models while retaining the analytically useful concept of a choice set.[13]

(3) While we have presented $M_{\Gamma T}$ as a distribution characterizing a single choice problem drawn from $\Gamma \times T$, greater interest lies in describing a sequence of such draws. For this purpose, $M_{\Gamma T}$ continues to suffice only if choice problems are generated independently. More generally, if $(C, t)_n$, $n = 1, \dots N$ were a sequence of choice problems, a probability measure over $(\Gamma \times T)^N$ would be required.[14]

D. *The Observer's Information Base*

We now postulate an *observer*, external to the choice process described by $M_{\Gamma T}$ and U, and endowed with limited information regarding that process. The present task, the final step in developing the random utility model, is to specify the observer's information base.

We assume the following:

(1) The observer has no direct knowledge of the utility values U_{at}, $a \in \mathfrak{a}$, $t \in T$.

(2) There exist utility relevant attribute representations X and S with an associated utility function w such that for every specified $x \in X$, $s \in S$, $w(x, s)$ is known.

(3) The attribute values x_a, $a \in \mathfrak{a}$ and s_t, $t \in T$ are only partially known to the observer. In particular, there exists a partitioning of X, defined by $X = [X_o{:}X_u]$ and one of S, $S = [S_o{:}S_u]$ such that the subvectors $X_o = (x_{ao}, a \in \mathfrak{a})$ and $S_o = (s_{to}, t \in T)$ are observed without error but $X_u = (x_{au}, a \in \mathfrak{a})$ and $S_u = (s_{tu}, t \in T)$ are unobserved.

(4) For every choice problem (C, t), the probability, conditioned on knowledge of the observed attributes $r_{co} = (x_{ao}, a \in C)$ and s_{to}, that the unobserved attributes $r_{cu} = (x_{au}, a \in C)$ and s_{tu} take on any values $\bar{r}_{cu}$ and $\bar{s}_{tu}$ is known. This probability is given by

$$\Pr(\bar{r}_{cu}, \bar{s}_{tu} \mid r_{co}, s_{to}) = \Pr(\bar{r}_c, \bar{s}_t) \,/\, \Pr(r_{co}, s_{to}) =$$

$$= \sum_{\substack{(\tilde{C}, \tilde{t}):\, r_{\tilde{c}} = \bar{r}_c \\ s_{\tilde{t}} = \bar{s}_t}} M_{\Gamma T}(\tilde{C}, \tilde{t}) \Bigg/ \sum_{\substack{(\tilde{C}, \tilde{t}):\, r_{\tilde{c}o} = r_{co} \\ s_{\tilde{t}o} = s_{to}}} M_{\Gamma T}(\tilde{C}, \tilde{t}).$$ [15]

DISCUSSION: (1) Our informational assumptions place the locus of observer ignorance totally in his inability to observe certain attributes of alternatives and of decision makers. The resulting random utility model is consistent with the classical notion of probability. An informationally weaker model would permit incomplete knowledge of the structure of w and/or of the probabilities $\Pr(\bar{r}_{cu}, \bar{s}_{tu} \mid r_{co}, s_{to})$.[16] In such a model, these probabilities would be subjective and w a subjectively random function. Explicit Bayesian analysis of random utility models is beyond the scope of the present paper.[17]

(2) It will become apparent in the next section that the present develop-

ment of the random utility model does not formally require that the choice problem generating process $M_{\Gamma T}$ be known, only the derived probabilities $\Pr(\bar{r}_{cu}, \bar{s}_{tu} \mid r_{co}, s_{to})$. Unfortunately, the latter probabilities are very difficult to substantively interpret. Hence, we choose to work with the former ones. Calculation of 'outcome probabilities' in Section F does require knowledge of $M_{\Gamma T}$.

(3) In writing $X = [X_o : X_u]$ and $S = [S_o : S_u]$ we assume that X and S partition 'conformably' into observed and unobserved parts. That is, there exist no attributes which are observed for some alternatives (decision makers) but unobserved for others. This assumption, which is in no way crucial, simplifies the presentation.

(4) In the random utility literature, the function w is often written in the additive form $w(x, s) \equiv V(x_o, s_o) + \epsilon(x, s)$, where V captures that part of w additively separable in observed attributes and ϵ the residual. Note that V is a well-defined function only if X and S each partitions conformably into observed and unobserved parts.

E. *The Random Utility Model*

We now show that the decision rule, the choice problem generating process and the observational information assumed in Sections B, C, and D induce a random utility model describing behavior.

In every choice problem (C, t), the vector of utilities $W_{ct} = w((x_{ao}, x_{au}), (s_{to}, s_{tu}))$, $a \in C$ are functions of the unobserved attributes x_{au}, $a \in C$ and s_{tu}. Hence, the utilities are *observationally random* with the following distribution:

$$\Pr(\bar{W}_{ct} \mid r_{co}, s_{to}) = \Sigma_{(\bar{r}_c, \bar{s}_t): W = \bar{W}_{ct}} \Pr(\bar{r}_c, \bar{s}_t) / \Pr(r_{co}, s_{to})$$

$$= \frac{\displaystyle\sum_{\substack{(\bar{C}, \bar{t}):\, r_{\bar{c}o} = r_{co} \\ s_{\bar{t}o} = s_{to} \\ W_{\bar{c}\bar{t}} = \bar{W}_{ct}}} M_{\Gamma T}(\bar{C}, \bar{t})}{\displaystyle\sum_{\substack{(\bar{C}, \bar{t}):\, r_{\bar{c}o} = r_{co} \\ s_{\bar{t}o} = s_{to}}} M_{\Gamma T}(\bar{C}, \bar{t})}$$

Recall that for each choice problem $(C, t) \in \Gamma \times T$ and any $a \in C$, t chooses a from C if and only if $w((x_{ao}, x_{au}), (s_{to}, s_{tu})) \geqslant w((x_{\bar{a}o}, x_{\bar{a}u}), (s_{to}, s_{tu}))$, all

$\bar{a} \in C$. Letting $w_{at} = w(x_a, s_t)$, it follows that observationally

$$\Pr_t(a \in^c C) = \Sigma_{\bar{W}_{ct}: \bar{w}_{at} \geq \bar{w}_{a't}, a \in C} \Pr(\bar{W}_{ct} \mid r_{co}, s_{to}).$$

That is, choice is consistent with the random utility model.[18]

DISCUSSION: An example may help to summarize the model. Let

$$\mathfrak{a} = (\alpha, \beta, \gamma) \qquad T = (\sigma, \tau)$$

$$x = \begin{array}{c|ccc} & \alpha & \beta & \gamma \\ \hline x_1 & 1 & 1 & 2 \\ x_2 & \frac{1}{2} & \frac{1}{2} & -1 \end{array} \qquad S = s \begin{array}{|cc} \sigma & \tau \\ \hline 1 & 0 \end{array}$$

That is, there are three alternatives, α, β, and γ each characterized by the two real valued attributes x_1 and x_2 and there are two decision makers σ and τ each characterized by the one real attribute s.

Assume that the utility function governing behavior is $w(x, s) = x_1 + x_2\, s$.

Furthermore, let the choice problem generating process be defined by the following probabilities:

$M_{\Gamma T}\,[(\alpha, \beta, \gamma), \sigma] = \frac{2}{36}$	for each of the six ordered choice sets whose elements are α, β, and γ.
$M_{\Gamma T}\,[(\alpha, \beta), \sigma] = \frac{1}{12}$	for each of the two ordered choice sets whose elements are α and β.
$M_{\Gamma T}\,[(\alpha, \beta, \gamma), \tau] = \frac{1}{36}$	for each of the six ordered choice sets whose elements are α, β and γ.
$M_{\Gamma T}\,[(\alpha, \beta), \tau] = \frac{2}{12}$	for each of the two ordered choice sets whose elements are α and β.

If x_1 and s are observed but x_2 is not, then it can be deduced that for any ordered choice set composed of α, β and γ,

$$\Pr_\sigma(\alpha \in^c (\alpha, \beta, \gamma)) = \tfrac{1}{2} \qquad \Pr_\tau(\alpha \in^c (\alpha, \beta, \gamma)) = 0$$

$$\Pr_\sigma(\beta \in^c (\alpha, \beta, \gamma)) = \tfrac{1}{2} \qquad \Pr_\tau(\beta \in^c (\alpha, \beta, \gamma)) = 0$$

$$\Pr_\sigma(\gamma \in^c (\alpha, \beta, \gamma)) = 0 \qquad \Pr_\tau(\gamma \in^c (\alpha, \beta, \gamma)) = 1.$$

However, if s as well as x_2 are unobserved, then

$$\Pr_\sigma(\alpha \in^c (\alpha, \beta, \gamma)) = \Pr_\tau(\alpha \in^c (\alpha, \beta, \gamma)) = \tfrac{1}{3}$$

$$\Pr_\sigma(\beta \in^c (\alpha, \beta, \gamma)) = \Pr_\tau(\beta \in^c (\alpha, \beta, \gamma)) = \tfrac{1}{3}$$

$$\Pr_\sigma(\gamma \in^c (\alpha, \beta, \gamma)) = \Pr_\tau(\gamma \in^c (\alpha, \beta, \gamma)) = \tfrac{1}{3}.$$

F. *The Outcome of the Choice Process*

The descriptive power of a random utility model is contained in the set of *choice probabilities* $[\Pr_t(a \in^c C)$, all $a \in C \in \Gamma$, all $t \in T]$ it induces. Although the preceding derivation of these probabilities required specification of both steps in the classical choice process, the probabilities themselves describe only the outcome of the second step. That is, they characterize choice from a well-defined choice set by a given decision maker.

Often, ultimate interest rests in obtaining a description of the outcome of the entire choice process. The following *outcome probabilities* provide this description:

Let $\Pr(a)$ designate the probability that a is the outcome of the choice process. Then, for every $a \in \mathfrak{a}$,

$$\Pr(a) = \Sigma_{C \in \Gamma} \Sigma_{t \in T} \Pr_t(a \in^c C) M_{\Gamma T}(C, t).$$

DISCUSSION: (1) Where the concern is to forecast aggregate market shares, for example transportation modal splits and relative sales volumes of competing manufacturers, the outcome probabilities are sufficient statistics. Sometimes, it is desired to forecast the composition as well as the aggregate levels of outcomes. For example, we may wish to forecast the racial composition of college enrollments or the socio-economic patterns in residential location. To provide these forecasts, we need simply partition $\mathfrak{a}$ and T into the categories of interest and construct the relevant probabilities. Formally,

Let

$$\mathscr{A} = \bigcup_{n=1}^{N} \mathfrak{a}_n, T = \bigcup_{m=1}^{M} T_m,$$

where

$$\mathfrak{a}_n \cap \mathfrak{a}_{n'} = \phi \text{ if } n \neq n' \text{ and } T_m \cap T_{m'} = \phi \text{ if } m \neq m'.$$

Then

$$\Pr(a \in \mathfrak{a}_n, t \in T_m) = \Sigma_{a \in \mathfrak{a}_n} \Sigma_{t \in T_m} \Sigma_{C \in \Gamma} \Pr_t (a \in^c C) M_{\Gamma T}(C, t).$$

(2) Current methods for estimating the parameters of random utility functions require ex post observation of a sequence of choice problems for each of which the decision maker, choice set and chosen alternative are known. Often, however, the survey instrument used in estimation supplies the identities of the decision makers and his chosen alternative but not those of his feasible inferior alternatives. In such situations, the probability of the observation is

$$\Pr_t(\mathrm{a}) = \Sigma_{C \in \Gamma} \Pr_t(a \in^c C) M_\Gamma (C \mid t, a \in C),$$

where $M_\Gamma (C \mid t, a \in C)$ is the probability that C is drawn given that a must be an element of the realized choice set.

(3) Empirical application of outcome probabilities often presents a serious computational problem. That is, the summation $\Sigma_{C \in \Gamma}$ contains $2^{|\Gamma|} - 1$ terms, where $|\Gamma|$ is the order of Γ. As a result, it has become common practice in estimation studies to 'impute' the identities of unobserved inferior alternatives and view choices as if they had been made from the imputed choice sets. That is, if $\tilde{C}$ is the imputed set, the probability of the observation is taken to be $\Pr_t(a \in^c \tilde{C})$ rather than $\Pr_t(a)$ as defined above.

In the literature, two different imputation procedures have been used. Ben-Akiva and Lerman (1974), and other analysts of modal choice impute an 'expected choice set'.[19] Kohn *et al.* (1974) draw a choice set randomly from Γ according to the distribution $M_\Gamma (C \mid t, a \in C)$. Their choice probability $\Pr_t (a \in^c \tilde{C})$ is then an unbiased estimate of $\Pr_t(a)$. As yet, no general analysis of the consequences of alternative imputation rules has been attempted. McFadden and Reid (1974) and Westin (1974) do, however, show in a binary choice context that expected choice set imputation generates biased parameter estimates and biased forecasts.

II. SPECIAL MODELS

The work of Part I has demonstrated that if decision makers are utility maximizers and if the process associating decision makers with choice sets can be specified, then, to an observer possessing incomplete knowledge of the characteristics of decision makers and alternatives, a random utility model describes behavior. We now probe beneath this basic result to explain the formation of random utility models with special distributional properties.

Assume that the behavioral and informational conditions described earlier are met so that the statement

$$\Pr(\bar{W}_{ct} \mid r_{co}, s_{to}) = \Sigma_{\substack{(\bar{C},\bar{t}):\, r_{\bar{c}o} = r_{co} \\ s_{\bar{t}o} = s_{to} \\ W_{\bar{c}\bar{t}} = W_{ct}}} M_{\Gamma T}(\bar{C}, \bar{t}) \Big/ \Sigma_{\substack{(\bar{C},\bar{t}):\, r_{\bar{c}o} = r_{co} \\ s_{\bar{t}o} = s_{to}}} M_{\Gamma T}(\bar{C}, \bar{t})$$

characterizes observed choice behavior. Within the context of this general random utility model, the probability distribution of the random vector W_{ct} is determined by three factors, the form of the utility function $w(x, s)$, the nature of the choice problem generating process $M_{\Gamma T}$ and the extent of the observer's information which partitions the attributes $(x_a, a \in \alpha)$ and $(s_t, t \in T)$ into observed and unobserved parts.

We should like to demonstrate exactly how conditions placed on $w(x, s)$, $M_{\Gamma T}$, x_{ao} and s_{to} induce the distributional structure of random utility models. Equally strong is a desire to shed light on the substantive restrictions implied by the various particular models developed in the literature. To meet these dual objectives, the following analysis will focus on three familiar classes of random utility models, the independent random utilities, the independent and identically distributed random utilities and the random coefficients models. In what follows, each class of models is defined, theorems giving structural conditions inducing the class are presented and each theorem is discussed.

A. *The Independent Random Utility Models*

Consider a choice problem (C, t) drawn from $\Gamma \times T$. The associated random utility vector W_{ct} is said to have the *independent random utilities* (IRU) property if

$$\Pr(\bar{W}_{ct} \mid r_{co}, s_{to}) = \prod_{a \in C} \Pr(\bar{w}_{at} \mid x_{ao}, s_{to})$$

for all values of $\bar{W}_{ct}$.[20]

The theorem below gives conditions sufficient to ensure that a utility vector W_{ct} has the IRU property.

THEOREM: *Assume the following*:

(i) *for every*

$$(C, t) \in \Gamma \times T, M_\Gamma(C \mid t) = (\Pi_{a \in C} P(a \mid t)) (\Pi_{\beta \notin C} (1-P(\beta \mid t)))$$

where

$$P(a \mid t) = \Sigma_{\bar{C}:\, a \in \bar{C}} M_{\Gamma T}(\bar{C}, t) \Big/ \Sigma_{\bar{C} \in \Gamma} M_{\Gamma T}(\bar{C}, t)$$

is the probability that alternative a is an element of the choice set faced by decision maker t. Furthermore, for every t, $P(a \mid t) = 1$ *for at least one* $a \in \alpha$.[21]

(ii) For every $(a, t) \in \alpha \times T$, $P(a \mid t) = P(a \mid s_t)$. *That is, decision makers whose utility relevant attributes are equal face equal probabilities* $P(a \mid t)$.

(iii) *For every* $t \in T$, $s_{to} = s_t$. *That is, all utility relevant decision maker attributes are observed.*

Let (C, t) *be a choice problem such that the observed attributes* $(x_{ao}, a \in C)$ *are distinct. Then, for all values of*

$$\bar{W}_{ct}, \Pr(\bar{W}_{ct} \mid r_{co}, s_{to}) = \prod_{a \in C} \Pr(\bar{w}_{at} \mid x_{ao}, s_{to}).$$

Proof: Under the assumptions of the theorem,

$$\Sigma_{\substack{(\bar{C}, \bar{t}):\, r_{\bar{c}o} = r_{co} \\ s_{\bar{t}o} = s_{to} \\ W_{\bar{c}\bar{t}} = \bar{W}_{ct}}} M_{\Gamma T}(\bar{C}, \bar{t})$$

$$= \Sigma_{\substack{\bar{C}:\, r_{\bar{c}o} = r_{co} \\ W_{\bar{c}t} = \bar{W}_{ct}}} \Sigma_{\bar{t}:\, s_{\bar{t}o} = s_{to}} M_\Gamma(\bar{C} \mid \bar{t}) M_T(\bar{t})$$

$$= \left[\Sigma_{\substack{\bar{C}:\, r_{\bar{c}o} = r_{co} \\ W_{\bar{c}t} = \bar{W}_{ct}}} \left(\Pi_{\alpha \in \bar{C}} P(\alpha \mid s_{to}) \right) \left(\Pi_{\substack{\beta:\, \beta \notin \bar{C} \\ x_{\beta o} \in r_{co}}} (1-P(\beta \mid s_{to})) \right) \right.$$

$$\left. \times \left(\Pi_{\substack{\gamma:\, \gamma \notin \bar{C} \\ x_{\gamma o} \notin r_{co}}} (1-P(\gamma \mid s_{to})) \right) \right] \cdot \left(\Sigma_{\bar{t}:\, s_{\bar{t}o} = s_{to}} M_T(\bar{t}) \right)$$

$$= \left[\Sigma_{\substack{\bar{C}:\ r_{\bar{c}o} = r_{co} \\ W_{\bar{c}t} = \bar{W}_{ct}}} \left(\Pi_{\alpha\in\bar{C}} P(\alpha \mid s_{to})\right)\left(\Pi_{\substack{\beta:\beta\notin\bar{C} \\ x_{\beta o}\in r_{co}}} (1-P(\beta \mid s_{to}))\right)\right]$$

$$\times \left(\Pi_{\gamma:x_{\gamma o}\notin r_{co}} (1-P(\gamma \mid s_{to}))\right)\left(\Sigma_{\bar{t}:\ s_{\bar{t}o}=s_{to}} M_T(\bar{t})\right)$$

In the above, assumption (iii) guarantees the first equality while assumptions (i) and (ii) guarantee the second. The third equality rearranges the resulting expression.

By analogous transformations, it can be shown that

$$\Sigma_{\substack{(\bar{C},\bar{t})\, r_{\bar{c}o} = r_{co} \\ s_{\bar{t}o} = s_{to}}} M_{\Gamma T}(\bar{C},\bar{t}) = \left[\Sigma_{\bar{C}:r_{\bar{c}o}=r_{co}} \left(\Pi_{\alpha\in c} P(\alpha \mid s_{to})\right)\right.$$

$$\left.\left(\Pi_{\substack{\beta:\ \beta\notin\bar{C} \\ x_{\beta o}\in r_{co}}} (1-P(\beta \mid s_{to}))\right)\right]\left(\Pi_{\gamma:x_{\gamma o}\notin r_{co}} (1-P(\gamma \mid s_{to}))\right)$$

$$\times \left(\Sigma_{\bar{t}:s_{\bar{t}o}=s_{to}} M_T(\bar{t}).\right)$$

Hence

$$\Pr(\bar{W}_{ct} \mid r_{co}, s_{to}) =$$

$$\frac{\Sigma_{\substack{\bar{C}:r_{\bar{c}o}=r_{co} \\ W_{\bar{c}t}=\bar{W}_{ct}}} \left(\Pi_{\alpha\in\bar{C}} P(\alpha \mid s_{to})\right)\left(\Pi_{\substack{\beta:\beta\notin\bar{C} \\ x_{\beta o}\in r_{co}}} (1-P(\beta \mid s_{to}))\right)}{\Sigma_{\bar{C}:r_{\bar{c}o}=r_{co}} \left(\Pi_{\alpha\in\bar{C}} P(\alpha \mid s_{to})\right)\left(\Pi_{\substack{\beta\notin\bar{C} \\ x_{\beta o}\in r_{co}}} (1-P(\beta \mid s_{to}))\right)}$$

Observe that the class of choice sets

$$\begin{pmatrix}\bar{C}:\ r_{\bar{c}o} = r_{co} \\ W_{\bar{c}t} = \bar{W}_{ct}\end{pmatrix} = \bigtimes_{a\in C} \begin{pmatrix}\alpha:\ x_{\alpha o} = x_{ao} \\ w_{\alpha t} = w_{at}\end{pmatrix}$$

and that the class

$$(\bar{C}:\ r_{\bar{c}o} = r_{co}) = \bigtimes_{a\in C} (\alpha:\ x_{\alpha o} = x_{ao})$$

where $\times_{a \in C}$ denotes the Cartesian product operator.

Additionally, observe that if $(x_{ao}, a \in C)$ are distinct attribute vectors, then for any $\bar{C}$: $r_{\bar{c}o} = r_{co}$,

$$\left(\Pi_{\alpha \in \bar{C}} P(\alpha \mid s_{to})\right)\left(\Pi_{\substack{\beta: \beta \notin \bar{C} \\ x_{\beta o} \in r_{co}}} (1 - P(\beta \mid s_{to}))\right)$$

$$= \Pi_{a \in C}\left(P(\alpha_a \mid s_{to})\, \Pi_{\substack{\beta: \beta \neq \alpha_a \\ x_{\beta o} = x_{ao}}} (1 - P(\beta \mid s_{to}))\right),$$

where α_a is the unique element of $\bar{C}$ such that $x_{\alpha_a o} = x_{ao}$. It follows from the above that

$\Pr(W_{ct} \mid r_{co}, s_{to})$

$$= \Pi_{a \in C}\left(\frac{\Sigma_{\substack{\alpha: x_{\alpha o} = x_{ao} \\ w_{\alpha t} = \bar{w}_{at}}} \left(P(\alpha \mid s_{to})\, \Pi_{\substack{\beta: \beta \neq \alpha \\ x_{\beta o} = x_{ao}}} (1 - P(\beta \mid s_{to}))\right)}{\Sigma_{\alpha: x_{\alpha o} = x_{ao}} \left((P(\alpha \mid s_{to})\, \Pi_{\substack{\beta: \beta \neq \alpha \\ x_{\beta o} = x_{ao}}} (1 - P(\beta \mid s_{to}))\right)}\right) =$$

$$\Pi_{a \in C} \Pr(\bar{w}_{at} \mid x_{ao}, s_{to}).$$

DISCUSSION: Four points focus our discussion of the theorem. These include first an interpretation of the theorem's assumptions; second an explanation of the condition that $(x_{ao}, a \in C)$ be distinct; third a look at alternative assumptions yielding the IRU property; and fourth a comment on the IRU property.

(1) Of the three assumptions, (i) and (ii) place restrictions on the process generating choice problems while (iii) places an informational requirement on the observer. The form of the utility function is left arbitrary.

Statistically, assumption (i) asserts that each decision maker's choice set is the realization of a set of independent draws of alternatives across α. Substantively, the assumption is most easily interpreted if the existence of a conscious set of decision makers TT controlling α is assumed. In this context, the assumption requires 'offers' of alternatives to be mutually independent.

For example, if $\mathfrak{a}$ is a set of jobs, assumption (i) prohibits any interdependence among job offers. In particular, both bandwagon effects and collusion among firms to segment the labor market would violate the assumption.[22]

Assumption (ii) limits the diversity of choice set generating processes across T. The assumption does not, however, require that all $t \in T$ face identical processes.

Assumption (iii) is straightforward in interpretation. As a practical matter, this assumption can be difficult to fulfill.

(2) The theorem demonstrates the IRU property only for choice sets whose observed attribute vectors are distinct. To analyze the more general case where $(x_{ao}, a \in C)$ need not be distinct, let D be an ordered subset of C such that $(x_{ao}, a \in D)$ includes, without duplication, all the distinct elements of $(x_{ao}, a \in C)$. For each $a \in D$, let $n(a)$ be the number of alternatives in C whose observed attribute vector is x_{ao} and designate those alternatives by a_i, $i = 1, \dots n(a)$. It can be shown that

$$\Pr(\bar{W}_{ct} \mid r_{co}, s_{to}) = \Pi_{a \in D}$$

$$\left(\frac{\displaystyle\sum_{\substack{\left(\alpha_i : x_{\alpha_i} = x_{ao} \atop w_{\alpha_i t} = w_{a_i t}\right) \\ i=1,\dots,n(a)}} \Sigma \left(\Pi_{i=1}^{n(a)} P(\alpha_i \mid s_t) \right) \left(\Pi_{\substack{\beta : \beta \neq \alpha_i,\, i=1,\dots,n(a) \\ x_{\beta o} = x_{ao}}} (1 - P(\beta \mid s_t)) \right)}{\displaystyle\sum_{\substack{(\alpha_i : x_{\alpha_i o} = x_{ao}) \\ i=1,\dots,n(a)}} \Sigma \left(\Pi_{i=1}^{n(a)} P(\alpha_i \mid s_t) \right) \left(\Pi_{\substack{\beta : \beta \neq \alpha_i,\, i=1,\dots,n(a) \\ x_{\beta o} = x_{ao}}} (1 - P(\beta \mid s_t)) \right)} \right) =$$

$$= \Pi_{a \in D} \Pr(\bar{w}_{a_i t}, i = 1,..,n(a) \mid x_{ao}, n(a), s_{to})$$

That is, alternatives with distinct observed attribute vectors have independently distributed utilities. Alternatives whose observed attributes are identical have interdependent utilities.[23]

(3) The assumptions of the theorem are sufficient to induce the IRU property but are not necessary. For example, the reader may verify that the following assumptions can substitute for assumptions (ii) and (iii).

(ii′) For every $(a, t) \in \mathfrak{a} \times T$, $P(a \mid t) = P(a \mid s_{to})$.

(iii′) The mappings $a \to x_a$, $t \to s_t$ and $(x, s) \to w(x, s)$ are all one-to-one.

Moreover, we shall later, within the discussion of random coefficients models, describe an IRU model sharing none of the structural assumptions presented thus far.

As a general matter, sets of minimal structural conditions, whether for the basic random utility model developed in Part I or for the special models examined here, have remained beyond my reach. Efforts seeking to better define the range of validity of these models are to be encouraged.

(4) The independent random utilities property, while helpful, has not by itself proved sufficient to render random utility models analytically or computationally tractable. At this date, only the more restrictive independent and identically distributed random utilities models have found practical application. An examination of this class of models follows.

B. *The Independent and Identically Distributed Random Utilities Models*

Write the utility function $w(x, s)$ as $w(x, s) = V(x_o, s_o) + \epsilon(x, s)$ where $V(x_o, s_o)$ is that part of $w(x, s)$ additively separable in the observed x_o and s_o attributes. Note that for every $a \in \alpha, t \in T$, $V_{at} = V(x_{ao}, s_{to})$ is known to the observer but $\epsilon_{at} = \epsilon(x_a, s_t)$ is unobserved. A random utility vector W_{ct} is said to have the *independent and identically distributed random utilities* (IIDRU) property if

$$\Pr(\bar{W}_{ct} \mid r_{co}, s_{to}) = \Pi_{a\in C} \Pr(V_{at} + \bar{\epsilon}_{at})$$

where $\bar{\epsilon}_{at}$, $a \in C$ are realizations of a set of independent and identically distributed random variables. The theorem below gives conditions sufficient to ensure that W_{ct} has the IIDRU property.

THEOREM: *Assume that conditions* (i), (ii) *or* (ii′), *and* (iii) *or* (iii′) *stated previously are met. Also assume the following*:

(iv) *There exists a real function* $\delta(x_u)$ *such that* $w(x_a, s_t) = V(x_{ao}, s_{to}) + \delta(x_{au})$, all $a \in \alpha$, $t \in T$.

(v) *For all values of* x_o, $\bar{x}_u$, *and* s_o, $\Pr(\bar{x}_u \mid x_o, s_o) = \Pr(\bar{x}_u)$.[24]

Let (C, t) be a choice problem such that the observed attributes (x_{ao}, $a \in C$) *are distinct. Then, for all values of*

$$\bar{W}_{ct}, \Pr(\bar{W}_{ct} \mid r_{co}, s_{to}) = \Pi_{a\in C} \Pr(V_{at} + \bar{\epsilon}_{at})$$

where ϵ_{at}, $a \in C$ *are independent and identically distributed.*

Proof: The theorem's assumptions guarantee that W_{ct} has the IRU property. That is,

$$\Pr(\bar{W}_{ct} \mid r_{co}, s_{to}) = \Pi_{a\in C} \Pr(\bar{w}_{at} \mid x_{ao}, s_{to}) =$$

$$\Pi_{a\in C} \Pr(V_{at} + \bar{\epsilon}_{at} \mid x_{ao}, s_{to}),$$

where ϵ_{at}, $a \in C$ are independent random variables.

Assumptions (iv) and (v) guarantee that for given a and t, ϵ_{at} is neither functionally nor distributionally dependent on x_{ao} or s_{to}.
Hence, ϵ_{at}, $a \in C$ have observationally identical distributions and

$$\Pr(\bar{W}_{ct} \mid r_{co}, s_{to}) = \Pi_{a\in C} \Pr(V_{at} + \bar{\epsilon}_{at}),$$

where ϵ_{at}, $a \in C$ are i.i.d.

DISCUSSION: Our discussion first interprets the two new assumptions introduced by the theorem. We then examine an interesting weakened form of the IIDRU property.

(1) Both assumptions (iv) and (v) place conditions on the 'fine structure' of the choice process.

Assumption (iv) concerns both the form of the utility function and the extent of the observer's information. What seems most restrictive about this separability assumption is its requirement that the sub-utility function $\delta(x_u)$ not be dependent on t.[25] That is, preferences with respect to the x_u attributes are assumed homogeneous among the decision makers T.

Assumption (v) relates to the choice problem generating process and to the observer's information. In its requirement that x_u be distributed independently of s_o, (v) enforces a certain limited uniformity among the choice set generating processes faced by the members of T. In its requirement that x_u be distributed independently of x_o, the assumption is analogous, although stronger than, the usual linear model condition that excluded variables be uncorrelated with included ones.

Because fulfillment of (v) depends in detailed ways on the structure of the mapping from the alternative space to its attribute space and on the nature of the processes generating choice sets, it is difficult to interpret the assumption substantively. Consequently, it is difficult to provide the empirical researcher with guidance as to when he might reasonably conclude that the assumption is satisfied. Lack of any meaningful interpretation of assumption (v) constitutes an important gap in our understanding of the structure of random utility models.[26]

(2) Consider a choice process satisfying the following assumptions:

(i) For every

$$(C, t) \in \Gamma \times T, M_\Gamma(C \mid t) = (\Pi_{a \in C} P(a \mid t))\,(\Pi_{\beta \notin C}(1 - P(\beta \mid t))).$$

(iv′) There exists a real function $\delta(x_u, s_o)$ such that $w(x_a, s_t) = V(x_{ao}, s_{to}) + \delta(x_{au}, s_t)$, all $a \in \mathfrak{a}$, $t \in T$.

(v′) For all values of x_o and $\bar{x}_u$, $\Pr(\bar{x}_u \mid x_o, t) = \Pr(\bar{x}_u \mid t)$.

Let C be a choice set such that $(x_{ao}, a \in C)$ are distinct. It is straightforward to show that W_{ct} then satisfies the *conditionally independent and identically distributed random utilities* (CIIDRU) property:

$$\Pr(\bar{W}_{ct} \mid r_{co}, t) = \Pi_{a \in C} \Pr(V_{at} + \bar{\epsilon}_{at} \mid t),$$

where ϵ_{at}, $a \in C$ are, conditional on t, i.i.d.r.v.'s.

The CIIDRU property, avoiding as it does any restriction of the distributional relation between W_{ct} and t, is a significantly weakened form of the IIDRU property.[27] Nevertheless, models possessing this property are amenable to estimation by existing methods. See Manski (1975) where it is proved that under suitable regularity conditions, 'maximum score' estimates of CIIDRU models are consistent.

C. *The Random Coefficients Models*

Consider a choice problem $(C, t) \in \Gamma \times T$. Let $\hat{W}(C, t, \bar{s}_u) = (w(x_a, s_{to}, \bar{s}_u), a \in C)$, all $\bar{s}_u \in S_u$. The random utility vector W_{ct} has the *random coefficients* (RC) property if, for all values of $\bar{W}_{ct}$,

$$\Pr(\bar{W}_{ct} \mid r_{co}, s_{to}) = \Sigma_{\bar{s}_u:\, \hat{W}(C, t, \bar{s}_u) = \bar{W}_{ct}} \Pr(\bar{s}_u \mid s_{to}),$$

where

$$\Pr(\bar{s}_u \mid s_{to}) = \Sigma_{\bar{t}:\, s_{\bar{t}o} = s_{to},\ s_{\bar{t}u} = \bar{s}_u} M_T(\bar{t}) \Big/ \Sigma_{\bar{t}:\, s_{\bar{t}o} = s_{to}} M_T(\bar{t}).$$

The theorem below gives conditions sufficient to ensure that a utility vector W_{ct} has the random coefficients property.

THEOREM: *Assume that*

(vi) *For all* $(C, t) \in \Gamma \times T, M_\Gamma(C \mid t) = M_\Gamma(C \mid s_{to})$.

(vii) *For all* $a \in \mathfrak{a}, x_{ao} = x_a$.

Then, for all values of $\bar{W}_{ct}$,

$$\Pr(\bar{W}_{ct} \mid r_{co}, s_{to}) = \Sigma_{\bar{s}_u:\ \hat{W}(C,t,\bar{s}_u) = \bar{W}_{ct}} \Pr(\bar{s}_u \mid s_{to}).$$

Proof: By the assumptions of the theorem,

$$\Pr(\bar{W}_{ct} \mid r_{co}, s_{to}) =$$

$$\Sigma_{\substack{(\bar{C},\bar{t}):\ r_{\bar{c}o} = r_{co} \\ s_{\bar{t}o} = s_{to} \\ W_{\bar{c}\bar{t}} = \bar{W}_{ct}}} M_{\Gamma T}(\bar{C}, \bar{t}) \Bigg/ \Sigma_{\substack{(\bar{C},\bar{t}):\ r_{\bar{c}o} = r_{co} \\ s_{\bar{t}o} = s_{to}}} M_{\Gamma T}(\bar{C}, \bar{t}) =$$

$$\frac{\Sigma_{\bar{C}:\ r_{\bar{c}o} = r_{co}} \Sigma_{\substack{\bar{t}:\ s_{\bar{t}o} = s_{to} \\ \hat{W}(C,t,s_{\bar{t}u}) = \bar{W}_{ct}}} M_\Gamma(C \mid s_{to}) M_T(t)}{\Sigma_{\bar{C}:\ r_{\bar{c}o} = r_{co}} \Sigma_{\bar{t}:\ s_{\bar{t}o} = s_{to}} M_\Gamma(C \mid s_{to}) M_T(\bar{t})}$$

$$= \Sigma_{\substack{\bar{t}:\ s_{\bar{t}o} = s_{to} \\ \hat{W}(C,\bar{t},s_{\bar{t}u}) = \bar{W}_{ct}}} M_T(\bar{t}) \Bigg/ \Sigma_{\bar{t}:\ s_{\bar{t}o} = s_{to}} M_T(\bar{t}) =$$

$$= \Sigma_{\bar{s}_u:\ \hat{W}(C,t,\bar{s}_u) = \bar{W}_{ct}} \Pr(\bar{s}_u \mid s_{to}).$$

DISCUSSION: (1) In random coefficients models, the existence of unobserved decision maker attributes s_u forms the sole source of observational randomness in W_{ct}. Furthermore, knowledge of the choice set faced by t yields no information as to the value of s_{tu}. In the above theorem, assumption (vi) guarantees the latter property while (vii) guarantees the former. Both assumptions have straightforward interpretations.

(2) The random utility models developed by psychometricians generally fall within the random coefficients class. For example, in Tversky's elimination by aspects model, alernatives have 0–1 'aspects', all of which are observed, and the decision maker draws a lexicographic decision rule from a set of such

rules. The rule drawn in any choice situation is unobserved and is drawn independently of the choice set faced.[28]

(3) Interestingly, there exist random coefficients models which also have the IIDRU property. Assume that $w(x, s) = x_o \cdot s_o + x_o \cdot s_u$ where x_o, s_o and s_u are each K element vectors and s_u is distributed independently of C. Thus, the model has the RC property. Also assume that for every $a \in \mathfrak{a}$, x_{ao} is a permutation of the vector (1, 0, ..., 0) and that the K components of s_u are mutually independent and identically distributed and distributed independently of s_o as well. Letting $V_{at} = x_{ao} \cdot s_{to}$ and $\epsilon_{at} = x_{ao} \cdot s_{tu}$, it follows that if $(x_{ao}, a \in C)$ are distinct, $\epsilon_{at}, a \in C$ are i.i.d.[29]

SOME OBSERVATIONS

My work on this paper was motivated by an uneasiness about the econometric literature's assymetric handling of the 'systematic' and 'disturbance' components of a random utility model. There is an essential symmetry between V and ϵ in the equation $U = V + \epsilon$. Nevertheless, attention in empirical analyses has focussed almost exclusively on the functional form of V to the neglect of the probability distribution of ϵ. Furthermore, theoretical discussion of distributional specification has been very limited. These trends, I felt, needed correction.

At its completion, I have mixed feelings about the success of my endeavor. On the positive side, Part I presents an internally consistent and structurally meaningful derivation of the random utility model. Moreover, as the theorems of Part II indicate, that derivation can be a powerful tool for interpreting the special models found in the literature.

My misgivings, ironically enough, arise out of a perceived assymetry in my work. The classical choice process, Section IC emphasizes, is a recursive one. First, a choice problem is generated and then the specified decision maker selects from his realized choice set. In this paper, a specific rule for the decision maker, namely utility maximization, is assumed but the choice problem generating process is described only as a probability distribution over $\Gamma \times T$. An interpretation of $M_{\Gamma T}$ in terms of the behavior of TT is offered and is helpful but, like the similar-distinct dichotomy, it is not fully satisfying. Thus, this paper may have resolved some questions about the distributional specification of random utility models only to replace them with questions about the distribution governing the generation of choice problems.

Looking beyond the present paper, I see a number of directions for future research, corresponding to the four sets of assumptions laid out in Section IA through ID.

One direction obviously is the structural investigation of choice problem generation. Processes assuming conscious decision makers *TT* seem particularly ripe for analysis but 'natural' processes should not be ignored.

A second focus would be the study of alternative information bases for the observer. As alluded to earlier, a weakening of our informational assumptions would seem to lead to Bayesian random utility models. On the other side, information not considered in the present analysis is sometimes available to the observer. For example, knowledge of non-utility relevant attributes can be valuable.

Third, the utility maximizing decision rule we assume might be dispensed with or strengthened. For example, Tversky has shown that a conceptually different rule, elimination-by-aspects, is consistent with a random utility model. Lancaster has demonstrated the analytical power that linear attribute spaces yield in the presence of utility maximization.

A final set of questions concerns the structure of the spaces $\mathfrak{a}$ and T. In particular, it is not clear whether the extension of our work to infinite alternative and decision maker spaces involves merely matters of mathematical interest or more.

Carnegie – Mellon University

NOTES

*Assistant Professor of Economics, School of Urban and Public Affairs, Carnegie-Mellon University.

I am grateful to Joseph B. Kadane for numerous constructive suggestions offered during discussions of this research. The financial sponsorship of the U.S. Department of Transportation through grant DOT-OS-4006 is also acknowledged. The opinions and conclusions expressed herein are solely those of the author.

[1] Luce and Suppes (1965) and Tversky (1972b) provide good overviews of this literature.

[2] McFadden (1974) provides a comprehensive survey of this literature.

[3] Debreu's observation was made with respect to Luce's 'strict utility' model before a random utility interpretation of that model had been obtained. Although the problem with the Luce model was first attributed to its peculiar 'independence of irrelevant alternatives' property, it was later recognized by Luce and Suppes (1965) that the strict utility model can be restated as a particular IIDRU model and that all IIDRU models share the Luce Model's deficiency.

[4] The 'similar-distinct' dichotomy arose through interpretation of the examples in which IIDRU models make implausible choice forecasts. In all of those examples, the problem appears when a new alternative, identical to an existing one in all utility-relevant respects, is added to the choice set. The failure of IIDRU models in such a situation is easily shown. If alternatives i and j form the original choice set so that

$$\Pr(i \in^c (i, j)) = \Pr(U_i \geqslant U_j),$$

addition of a third alternative k, identical to j yields

$$\Pr(i \in^c (i, j, k)) = \Pr(U_i \geqslant U_j, U_k) < \Pr(U_i > U_j) = \Pr(i \in^c (i, j)),$$

certainly a counter-intuitive result. The interpretation of the problem to extend to 'similar' as well as identical alternatives seemed straightforward. Nevertheless, a definition of similarity has remained elusive. See Ginsberg (1972), Luce and Suppes (1965), McFadden (1974), (1975), Kohn *et al.* (1974), McLynn and Goodman (1973) and Varian (1974) for discussions of the problem and examples of the ad hoc corrections proposed to resolve it.

[5] Papers dealings with estimation and forecasting methodology include McFadden (1973), McFadden and Reid (1974), Manski (1975), Manski and Lerman (1975), and Westin (1974).

[6] Some aspects of the development are only seemingly restrictive. In particular, although the presentation assigns the source of randomness to incomplete observer information, it does not rule out inconsistent individual behavior. In order to interpret the model in this way, one need only view T as defining not a population of individually rational decision makers but a population of decision rules from which an individual makes random draws.

[7] The utility maximizing model does not specify how the choice among alternatives bearing equal utilities is resolved. For our purposes, it is perhaps easiest to assume simply that each decision maker orders the finite set $\mathfrak{a}$ completely. That is, indifference among alternatives does not exist.

[8] In this case X may itself be defined as the alternative space.

[9] This becomes relevant when we seek to distinguish between observed and unobserved attributes in Section IID.

[10] Lancaster (1971) assumes linear space properties in his attribute model of consumer demand. His quite restrictive specification does yield analytical results which our weak assumptions cannot.

[11] Formal treatments within the classical framework include Arrow (1958, 1959), Fishburn (1970), Gorman (1968), Luce (1959), and Weddepohl (1970).

[12] For psychological models, it seems more natural to decompose $M_{\Gamma T}$ as follows: $M_{\Gamma T}(\mathcal{C}, t) = M_T(t \mid C) M_\Gamma(C)$. In this formulation, $M_T(t \mid C)$ is the probability that the decision maker draws decision rule t given that he is faced with choice set C and $M_\Gamma(C)$ is the probability that he is faced with this choice set. We note that the psychological models developed thus far usually do not allow the distribution governing the drawing of choice rules to be influenced by the choice set faced. That is, they assume $M_T(t \mid C) = M_T(t)$.

[13] Because most game theoretic models assume simultaneous decisions on the part of all players, no well-defined concept of a choice set exists for such models. Only equilibrium solutions are well-defined.

[14] An example distinguishing independent from non-independent processes may be

useful. If TT is a set of colleges and every $tt \in TT$ evaluates each of its applicants in isolation from its other applicants, college choice sets will be independently generated. However, if because of capacity constraints, colleges make comparative decisions about applicants and if T contains more than one applicant to a given college, independence is violated.

[15] In these expressions and hereafter, a bar (–) over a variable symbol indicates that it is a realization of an observationally random variable. Thus, $\bar{s}_t$ is some realization of the observationally random decision maker attribute vector while s_t is the unknown true value of this vector.

[16] It might be thought that our model actually allows incomplete knowledge of w, since an unknown parameter of w and an unobserved constant element in x_u or s_u are indistinguishable. However, the assumption that the probabilities $\Pr(\bar{r}_{cu}, \bar{s}_{tu} \mid r_{co}, s_{to})$ are known implies that the value of any constant attribute, even if directly unobserved, can be determined. We therefore must keep unknown function parameters and unobserved constant attributes conceptually distinct.

[17] We do not rule out the potential of Bayes procedures. The random utility model literature has been totally confined to classical point estimation of the unknown parameters of w and application of the estimated function $\hat{w}$ in forecasting as if it were w. It would seem more appropriate, although considerably more complicated, to go to the empirical Bayes route; that is, use the output of the parametric estimation process to obtain a distribution for w and treat w as a random function with this distribution in forecasting.

[18] We adopt the convention that if $a \notin C$, then $\Pr_t(a \in^c C) = 0$.

[19] Expected choice set imputation is well-defined only if $\mathfrak{A}$ partitions into N categories (such as auto, bus, taxi), each choice set with positive probability contains one alternative from each category and convex combinations of alternatives are themselves alternatives. Treating choice sets as ordered sets of alternatives, the expected choice set is then $C = \Sigma_{C \in \Gamma} C M_\Gamma \, (C \mid t, a \in C)$. It should be pointed out that practitioners have not attempted to define the expected choice set procedure formally. I believe however that the above definition does describe the essence of their practice.

[20] Note that the definition of the IRU property is phrased directly in terms of our development of the random utility model and not more abstractly. More general definitions of the property tend to be ambiguous. For example, Luce and Suppes simply state that an IRU model is one in which the utilities U_{at}, $a \in C$ are independently distributed. Such a definition leaves unclear the information conditioning the utility vector's distribution. See Luce and Suppes (1965) p. 338.

[21] This last assumption ensures that the realized choice set is non-empty.

[22] As a second example, let $\mathfrak{A}$ be a set of transportation mode-route alternatives and TT be a metropolitan transportation planning agency whose 'master plan' is reflected in the existing network. The agency might well view the construction of a new highway in an area of good transit service (or vice versa) as redundant. If so, the probability that a community with given characteristics has both good auto and transit links will be smaller than the product of the probabilities of good auto and good transit. Hence, the independence assumption would be violated.

[23] The interdependence among the utilities of alternatives with identical observed attributes arises because for any x_o, the population of alternatives α: $x_{\alpha o} = x_o$ is finite and the process of drawing alternatives with attributes x_o into the choice set is one of sampling without replacement from that population.

[24] In words, let x_o be the observed attributes of an alternative within the choice set faced by a decision maker with observed attributes s_o. The probability that this alternative has unobserved attributes $\bar{x}_u$ is independent of both x_o and s_o.
[25] Note that in the degenerate case where all alternative attributes are observed, this restriction is not effective.
[26] As an example of the problems in interpreting (v), let $\mathfrak{a}$ be a set of differentiated jobs. Then fulfillment of (v) depends on the structure of the distribution of job offers. Clearly, this distribution itself is determined by the operation of the labor market. It would therefore seem that meaningful interpretation of (v) requires a detailed model of a labor market with heterogeneous jobs and workers.
[27] Note that a CIIDRU model need not even have the IRU property. Such a model is, however, a 'conditionally independent random utilities' (CIRU) model.
[28] See Tversky (1972). Note that Tversky's model is a random utility model in spite of the fact that his decision rules are lexicographic. This follows because his alternative space is assumed finite, implying that a utility function can explain any ordering of alternatives. It seems likely that Tversky's model in the presence of an uncountable alternative space would no longer be a random utility model.
[29] A similar derivation of the IIDRU property is given by Tversky for his elimination-by-aspects model.

BIBLIOGRAPHY

Arrow, K., 'Utilities, Attitudes, Choices: A Review Note', *Econometrica* **26** (1958), 1–23.

Arrow, K., 'Rational Choice Functions and Orderings', *Economica* **26** (1959), 121–127.

Ben-Akiva, M. and Lerman, S., 'A Disaggregate Behavioral Model of Automobile Ownership', presented at the Annual Meeting of the Transportation Research Board, January 1975.

Block, H. and Marschak, J., 'Random Orderings and Stochastic Theories of Response', in Olkin (ed.), *Contributions to Probability and Statistics*, Stanford University Press, 1960.

Debreu, G., 'Review of R. Luce, Individual Choice Behavior', *American Economic Review* (1960), 186–188.

Domenchic, T. and McFadden, D., *Urban Travel Demand: A Behavioral Analysis*, North Holland, 1975.

Fishburn, P., *Utility Theory for Decision Making*, Wiley and Son, 1970.

Ginsberg, R., 'Incorporating Causal Structure and Exogenous Information With Probabilistic Models: With Special Reference to Choice, Gravity, Migration, and Markov Chains', *Journal of Mathematical Sociology* **2** (1972), 83–103.

Gorman, T., 'The Structure of Utility Functions', *Review of Economic Studies* **35** (1968), 367–390.

Kelley, J., *General Topology*, Van Nostrand, 1955.

Kohn, M., Manski, C., and Mundel, D., 'An Empirical Investigation of Factors Which Influence College Going Behavior', Rand Corporation Report R-1470-NSF, September, 1974.

Lancaster, K., *Consumer Demand: A New Approach*, Columbia University Press, 1971.

Luce, R., *Individual Choice Behavior*, Wiley, 1959.

Luce, R. and Suppes, P., 'Preference, Utility and Subjective Probability', in Luce, Bush and Galanter (eds.), *Handbook of Mathematical Psychology III*, Wiley, pp. 249–410.

McFadden, D., 'The Revealed Preferences of a Government Bureaucracy', forthcoming, *Bell Journal of Economics and Management Science* (1968).

McFadden, D., 'Conditional Logit Analysis of Qualitative Choice Behaviour', in Zarembka (ed.), *Frontiers in Econometrics*, Academic Press, 1973.

McFadden, D., 'Quantal Choice Analysis', 1974, unpublished.

McFadden, D. and Reid, F., 'Aggregate Travel Demand Forecasting from Disaggregated Behavioral Models', presented at the Annual Meeting of the Transportation Research Board, January, 1975.

McFadden, D., 'On Independence, Structure and Simultaneity in Transportation Demand Analysis', May, 1975, unpublished.

McLynn, J. and Goodman, K., 'Mode Choice and the Shirley Highway Experiment', Urban Mass Transportation Administration Report UMTA-IT-06-0024-73-1, November, 1973.

Manski, C., 'Maximum Score Estimation of the Stochastic Utility Model of Choice', *Journal of Econometrics* 3 (1975), 205–228.

Manski, C. and Lerman, S., 'The Estimation of Choice Probabilities from Choice Based Samples', October, 1975, unpublished.

Quandt, R. and Young, K., 'Cross Sectional Travel Demand Models: Estimation and Tests', *Journal of Regional Science* 9 (1969), 201–214.

Tversky, A., 'Elimination by Aspects: A Theory of Choice', *Psychological Review* 79 (1972), 281–299.

Tversky, A., 'Choice by Elimination', *Journal of Mathematical Psychology* 9 (1972), 341–367.

Varian, H., 'A Note on Conditional Logit Models and the Independence of Irrelevant Alternatives', 1974, unpublished.

Weddepohl, H., *Axiomatic Choice Models*, Rotterdam University Press, 1970.

Westin, R., 'Predictions From Binary Choice Models', *Journal of Econometrics* 2 (1974) 1–16.

[8]

Conditional logit analysis of qualitative choice behavior

DANIEL McFADDEN[1]
UNIVERSITY OF CALIFORNIA AT BERKELEY
BERKELEY, CALIFORNIA

A fundamental concern of economics is understanding human choice behavior. Models or hypotheses are formed on the nature of decision processes, and are evaluated in the light of observed behavior. This task is complicated

[1] The research for this paper was done with the support of National Science Foundation Grant GS-27226, the Ford Foundation, the University of Chicago, and the U.S. Department of Transportation. I am indebted to P. Cottingham, J. Craig, G. Debreu, T. Domencich, R. Hall, M. Richter, and B. Saffran for useful comments at various stages of this research, but retain sole responsibility for errors.

because the econometrician cannot observe or control all the factors influencing behavior, and because the process of observation itself influences acts of the decision-maker through the vehicle of experience. It becomes necessary to make statistical inferences on a model of *individual* choice behavior from data obtained by sampling from a *population* of individuals (or sampling from a population of "experience levels" for a single individual). When the model of choice behavior under examination depends on unobserved characteristics in the population, the testable implications of the individual choice model are obscured. However, it is possible to deduce from the individual choice model properties of population choice behavior which can be subjected to empirical test.

The link between models of individual behavior and data on population choices is most critical when the decision-maker's alternatives are qualitative, or "lumpy." In conventional consumer analysis with a continuum of alternatives, one can often plausibly assume that all individuals in a population have a *common* behavior rule, except for purely random "optimization" errors, and that systematic variations in aggregate choice reflect common variations in individual choice at the *intensive* margin. By contrast, systematic variations in aggregate choice among lumpy alternatives must reflect shifts in individual choice at the *extensive* margin, resulting from a *distribution* of decision rules in the population.

This paper outlines a general procedure for formulating econometric models of population choice behavior from distributions of individual decision rules. A concrete case with useful empirical properties, conditional logit analysis, is developed in detail. The relevance of these methods to economic analysis can be indicated by a list of the consumer choice problems to which conditional logit analysis has been applied: choice of college attended, choice of occupation, labor force participation, choice of geographical location and migration, choice of number of children, housing choice, choice of number and brand of automobiles owned, choice of shopping travel mode and destination.

Section I of this paper derives the relation between individual behavioral models and the distribution of population choices, and discusses the behavioral axiom which leads to the conditional logit model. Section II discusses estimation of the conditional logit model, and Section III discusses its statistical properties. Section IV summarizes an application of the method to the problem of shopping travel mode and destination choice.

I. Preferences and Selection Probabilities

A study of choice behavior is described by (1) the objects of choice and sets of alternatives available to decision-makers, (2) the observed attributes of decision-makers, and (3) the model of individual choice and behavior and distribution of behavior patterns in the population. Observed data are assumed to be generated by the *trial* of drawing an individual randomly from the population and recording his attributes, the set of alternatives available to him, and his actual choice. A sample is obtained by a sequence of independent trials, with or without *replications* in which a sequence of choices are observed for individuals with the same measured attributes and alternative sets.

We let X denote the universe of objects of choice, S the universe of vectors of measured attributes of decision-makers. An individual drawn at random from the population will have some attribute vector $s \in S$ and will face some set of available alternatives, which we now assume to be finite and denote by $B \subseteq X$. Let $P(x \mid s, B)$ denote the conditional probability that an individual drawn at random from the population will choose alternative x, given that he has measured attributes s and faces the alternative set B. The observed choice in a trial with attributes s and alternatives B can then be viewed as a drawing from a multinomial distribution with selection probabilities $P(x \mid s, B)$ for $x \in B$.

An individual behavior rule is a function h which maps each vector of measured attributes s and possible alternative set B into a chosen member of B. A *model* of individual behavior is a set of behavior rules H. For example, h may be a demand function resulting from maximization of a specific utility function, and H may be the set of demand functions which result from maximization of *some* utility function. With unmeasured attributes varying across the population, a model H can contain many behavior rules.

If a model H truly describes a population, then there exists a probability π defined on the (measurable) subsets of H specifying the distribution of behavior rules in the population.[2] The selection probability that an individual drawn at random from the population will choose x, given measured attributes s and alternative set B, equals the probability of occurrence of a decision rule yielding this choice, or

$$(1) \qquad P(x \mid s, B) = \pi[\{h \in H \mid h(s, B) = x\}].$$

An econometric model of qualitative choice behavior can be constructed for a specified model of individual behavior by assuming π to be a member of a

[2] To be precise, each trial represents a drawing of a triple (s, B, ω) from an underlying universe, where s is a vector of measured attributes, B is an alternative set, and ω determines a unique decision rule h_ω, with $h_\omega(s', B') \in B'$ for all possible arguments (s', B'). A probability defined on the underlying universe induces a probability π on the set of h_ω, conditioned on values of (s, B). When the pair (s, B) and ω are statistically independent [e.g., the underlying probability is a product of a probability defined on the universe of (s, B) and a probability defined on the universe of ω], the probability π is independent of the conditioning values (s, B). We confine our attention to this case, noting that satisfaction of this condition is one of the criteria for a carefully designed laboratory experiment or sample survey.

parametric family of probability distributions and using the fact that the observed choices are multinomially distributed with the probabilities (1) to obtain estimators of the underlying parameters. The following paragraphs carry through this program for the classical model of the utility-maximizing economic consumer.

Suppose an individual in the population has a vector of measured attributes s, and faces J alternatives, indexed $j = 1, \ldots, J$ and described by vectors of attributes x_j. The individual has a utility function that can be written in the form

$$U = V(s, x) + \varepsilon(s, x),$$

where V is nonstochastic and reflects the "representative" tastes of the population, and ε is stochastic and reflects the idiosyncracies of this individual in tastes for the alternative with attributes x. The individual chooses the alternative which maximizes utility; let h_ε denote his behavior rule, and $B = \{x_1, \ldots, x_J\}$. The probability that an individual drawn randomly from the population, with attributes s and alternative set B, will choose x_i equals

$$\begin{aligned} P_i \equiv P(x_i \mid s, B) &= \pi[\{h_\varepsilon \in H \mid h_\varepsilon(s, B) = x_i\}] \\ &= P[\varepsilon(s, x_j) - \varepsilon(s, x_i) < V(s, x_i) - V(s, x_j) \quad \text{for all} \quad j \neq i]. \end{aligned} \tag{2}$$

The probability π induces a joint cumulative distribution function $F(\varepsilon_1, \ldots, \varepsilon_J)$ over the values $\varepsilon_j = \varepsilon(s, x_j)$ for $j = 1, \ldots, J$; i.e.,

$$F(\varepsilon_1, \ldots, \varepsilon_J) = \pi[\{h_\varepsilon \in H \mid \varepsilon(s, x_j) \leqslant \varepsilon_j \quad \text{for} \quad j = 1, \ldots, J\}].$$

Let F_i denote the partial derivative of F with respect to its ith argument, and let $V_i = V(s, x_i)$. Then Equation (2) can be written

$$P_i = \int_{\varepsilon = -\infty}^{+\infty} F_i(\varepsilon + V_i - V_1, \ldots, \varepsilon + V_i - V_J)\, d\varepsilon. \tag{3}$$

We may proceed by specifying a joint distribution, such as joint normal, which will yield a family of probabilities depending on the unknown parameters of the distribution. It will generally be necessary to impose rather stringent maintained hypotheses on the unknown parameters to make them identifiable in a choice experiment, particularly in the absence of repetitions.

In practice, it is difficult to define joint distributions F which allow the computation of econometrically useful formulas for the P_i in Equation (3). An alternative approach is to specify formulas for the selection probabilities and then examine the question of whether these formulas could be obtained via Equation (3) from *some* distribution of utility-maximizing consumers. This problem is the population analog of the conventional theory of revealed preference for individual consumers. The author and Professor Marcel K.

Richter have elsewhere (1971) characterized the necessary and sufficient condition on selection probabilities for satisfaction of Equation (3). We shall follow this method, using a particular specification of the selection probabilities that allows direct verification of condition (3).

We consider a powerful axiom on selection probabilities introduced by Luce (1959) which states that the relative odds of one alternative being chosen over a second should be independent of the presence or absence of unchosen third alternatives. Formally, we make the following assumption.

AXIOM 1. (Independence of Irrelevant Alternatives). For all possible alternative sets B, measured attributes s, and members x and y of B,

$$P(x \mid s, \{x, y\})\, P(y \mid s, B) = P(y \mid s, \{x, y\})\, P(x \mid s, B). \tag{4}$$

We show below that this axiom is consistent with condition (3) and leads to a simple econometric specification of the selection probabilities. Luce has presented evidence that the axiom is consistent with behavior in some choice experiments; we shall point out later some of its limitations.

When $P(x \mid s, B)$ is positive, Equation (4) implies $P(x \mid s, \{x, y\})$ positive, and

$$\frac{P(y \mid s, \{x, y\})}{P(x \mid s, \{x, y\})} = \frac{P(y \mid s, B)}{P(x \mid s, B)}. \tag{5}$$

This condition states that the odds of y being chosen over x in a multiple choice situation B, where both are available, equals the odds of a binary choice of y over x.

Since empirically a zero probability is indistinguishable from one that is extremely small, there is little loss of generality in assuming that the selection probabilities are all positive for the possible alternative sets in an experiment.

AXIOM 2 (Positivity). $P(x \mid s, B) > 0$ for all possible alternative sets B, vectors of measured attributes s, and $x \in B$.

Consider a choice set B containing alternatives x, y, z, and let $p_{xy} = P(x \mid s, \{x, y\})$. Define $p_{xx} = \frac{1}{2}$. From Equation (4),

$$P(y \mid s, B) = \frac{p_{yx}}{p_{xy}} P(x \mid s, B) \tag{6}$$

and

$$1 = \sum_{y \in B} P(y \mid s, B) = \left(\sum_{y \in B} \frac{p_{yx}}{p_{xy}} \right) P(x \mid s, B). \tag{7}$$

Hence, the multiple choice selection probabilities can be written in terms of binary odds,

$$P(x \mid s, B) = \frac{1}{\sum_{y \in B}(p_{yx}/p_{xy})}. \tag{8}$$

Permuting the indices x, y, z in Equation (6) and multiplying yields the condition

$$\frac{p_{yx}}{p_{xy}} = \frac{p_{yz}/p_{zy}}{p_{xz}/p_{zx}}. \tag{9}$$

Taking z to be a "benchmark" member of the alternative set B and defining $V(s, x, z) = \log(p_{xz}/p_{zx})$, Equation (8) can be written

$$P(x \mid s, B) = \frac{e^{V(s,x,z)}}{\sum_{y \in B} e^{V(s,y,z)}}. \tag{10}$$

In the function $V(s, x, z)$, one may think of the argument s as giving a "measured taste effect," the argument x as giving a "choice alternative effect," and the argument z as giving an "alternative set effect." In an experiment with sufficient variation in measured attributes s and the alternative set B, and replications for each (s, B) pair, one can normally identify each of these effects. In the absence of replications, it is impossible to identify the "alternative set effect," and an identifying restriction is necessary to isolate the "choice alternative effect"; we shall assume the following.[3]

Axiom 3 (Irrelevance of Alternative Set Effect). The function $V(s, x, z)$ determining the selection probabilities in Equation (10) has the additively separable form

$$V(s, x, z) = v(s, x) - v(s, z). \tag{11}$$

Then, Equation (10) becomes

$$P(x \mid s, B) = e^{v(s,x)} \Big/ \sum_{y \in B} e^{v(s,y)}, \tag{12}$$

and the function v can be interpreted as a "utility indicator" of "representative" tastes. The following result justifies this terminology in terms of the behavior of a population of consumers.

[3] Axiom 3 follows from Axioms 1 and 2 if there exists some "universal benchmark" alternative z such that if B is a possible alternative set, then $B \cup \{z\}$ is also. This follows by noting that Equation (9) holds for $z \notin B$, provided Axioms 1 and 2 holds for $B \cup \{z\}$. Then, taking z to be the universal benchmark in Equation (10) and defining $v(s, x) = V(s, x, z)$ for all alternative sets yields the result.

LEMMA 1. Suppose each member of a population of utility-maximizing consumers has a utility function $U(s,x) = v(s,x) + \varepsilon(s,x)$, where v is a non-stochastic function reflecting "representative" tastes and $\varepsilon(s,x)$ is a function that varies randomly in the population with the property that in each possible alternative set $B = \{x_1, \ldots, x_J\}$, the values $\varepsilon(s,x_j)$ are independently identically distributed with the Weibull (Gnedenko, extreme value) distribution[4]

$$P(\varepsilon(s,x_j) \leqslant \varepsilon) = e^{-e^{-\varepsilon}}. \tag{13}$$

Then the selection probabilities given by Equation (3) satisfy Equation (12).

Proof: From Equation (13), letting $V_i = v(s,x_i)$,

$$\begin{aligned} &F_i(\varepsilon + V_i - V_1, \ldots, \varepsilon + V_i - V_J) \\ &\quad = \exp(-\varepsilon) \prod_{j=1}^{J} \exp(-\exp(-\varepsilon - V_i + V_j)) \\ &\quad = \exp(-\varepsilon) \exp\left\langle -[\exp(-\varepsilon)] \left[\sum_{j=1}^{J} \exp(V_j - V_i) \right] \right\rangle . \end{aligned}$$

Substituting this expression in Equation (3) yields the result.

A nonconstructive proof of this result was first given by Marschak (1959); the argument above appears in Luce and Suppes (1965), and is attributed to E. Holman and A. Marley. The next lemma establishes that under mild conditions the distribution (13) characterizes the population choice models whose selection probabilities satisfy Equation (12). A random variable ε is said to be *translation complete* if for a function h of bounded absolute variation with $h(\pm\infty) = 0$, the condition $Eh(\varepsilon + a) = 0$ for all real a implies $h \equiv 0$ (except possibly on a set of measure zero). Most common distributions have this property; in particular, the Weibull distribution above is translation complete.[5]

[4] Monotone increasing transformations of the utility function $U(s,x)$ do not affect utility maximization or the selection probabilities, but transform the distribution of the random component. In particular, $e^{U(s,x)} = e^{V(s,x)}\eta(s,x)$ has η distributed with the reciprocal exponential distribution $P(\eta \leqslant y) = e^{-1/y}$ $(y \geqslant 0)$; $-e^{-U(s,x)} = e^{-V(s,x)}\eta(s,x)$ has η distributed with the negative exponential distribution $P(\eta \leqslant y) = e^{y}$ $(y \leqslant 0)$; and $e^{-\beta \exp[-U(s,x)]} = \eta(s,x)^{\exp[-V(s,x)]}$ has η distributed with the power distribution $P(\eta \leqslant y) = y^{1/\beta} (0 \leqslant y \leqslant 1)$. These examples demonstrate that the moments of the distribution of utility in the population (or their existence) do not provide a useful guide to the degree of dispersion of tastes. We note for later reference that the Weibull distribution (13) has the characteristic function $\Gamma(1 + it)$, which is nonzero for real t, and has all positive moments finite.

[5] A distribution whose characteristic function is nonzero for real arguments is translation complete [apply Feller (1966), p. 479]; the Weibull distribution satisfies this condition.

LEMMA 2. Suppose selection probabilities are given by Equation (12) for all finite alternative sets B in a universe X, and suppose that for each vector of measured attributes s, the values of $v(s,x)$ range over the real line; i.e., $v(s,X) = (-\infty, +\infty)$. Suppose the selection probabilities satisfy Equation (3) with independently identically distributed $\varepsilon(s,x_i)$ having a translation complete cumulative distribution function G. Then, $G(\varepsilon) = e^{-\alpha \exp(-\varepsilon)}$, where α is an arbitrary positive parameter. Fixing the parameter α by specifying $G(0) = e^{-1}$ yields the distribution (13).

Proof: Consider the choice between an alternative yielding "utility" $v_x = v(s,x)$ and K alternatives, each yielding v_y. Equations (3) and (12) imply that the probability P_x of choosing x is

$$(14) \qquad P_x = \frac{e^{v_x}}{e^{v_x} + Ke^{v_y}} = \int_{\varepsilon=-\infty}^{+\infty} G(\varepsilon + v_x - v_y)^K \, dG(\varepsilon).$$

On the other hand, consider a binary choice between x and an alternative z yielding $v_z = v(s,z) = v_y + \log K$, implying

$$(15) \qquad P_{xz} = \frac{e^{v_x}}{e^{v_x} + e^{v_z}} = \int_{\varepsilon=-\infty}^{+\infty} G(\varepsilon + v_x - v_z) \, dG(\varepsilon).$$

The construction of v_z makes Equations (14) and (15) equal, implying

$$\int_{\varepsilon=-\infty}^{+\infty} [G(\varepsilon + v_x - v_y - \log K) - G(\varepsilon + v_x - v_y)^K] \, dG(\varepsilon) = 0.$$

But this can be true for all values of $v_x \in (-\infty, +\infty)$ only if the term in brackets is zero, since G is translation complete, implying

$$G(v_x - \log K) = G(v_x)^K.$$

Taking $v_x = 0$ implies $G(-\log K) = e^{-\alpha K}$, where $\alpha = -\log G(0) > 0$, and taking $v_x = \log K - \log L$ implies $G(-\log L) = G(\log K/L)^K$. Hence, $G(\log K/L) = e^{-\alpha L/K}$ for all positive integers K, L. Since G is monotone, it follows in the limit that $G(\log k) = e^{-\alpha/k}$ for all positive real k. Then $G(\varepsilon) = e^{-\alpha \exp(-\varepsilon)}$.

We summarize the advantages, and then the limitations, of the axioms leading to the formula (12) for the selection probabilities. First, this formula allows a ready interpretation of the selection probabilities in terms of the relative representative utilities of alternatives, and is relatively amenable to computation. Second, the formula makes it simple to ascertain the effect of introducing a new alternative to an alternative set; the proportional decrease in the selection probability of each old alternative equals the selection probability of the new alternative. This also points out a weakness of the model in that one cannot postulate a pattern of differential substitutability and complementarity between alternatives. Third, the axioms provide the identifying restrictions necessary to estimate choice alternative effects without replications, and to predict choice behavior resulting from extrapolation of observed alternative sets. Any set of identifying restrictions meeting these conditions will require powerful axioms on behavior, and care must be exercised in avoiding application of these models in situations where the axioms are implausible. The model above is subject to this general caveat.

The primary limitation of the model is that the independence of irrelevant alternatives axiom is implausible for alternative sets containing choices that are close substitutes. An example illustrates this point. Suppose a population faces the alternatives of travel by auto and by bus, and two-thirds choose to use auto. Suppose now a second "brand" of bus travel is introduced that is in all essential respects the same as the first. Intuitively, two-thirds of the population will still choose auto, and the remainder will split between the bus alternatives. However, if the selection probabilities satisfy Axiom 1, only half the population will use auto when the second bus is introduced. The reason this is counter-intuitive is that we expect individuals to lump the two bus alternatives together in making the auto-bus choice. This example suggests that application of the model should be limited to situations where the alternatives can plausibly be assumed to be distinct and weighed independently in the eyes of each decision-maker.

II. Conditional Logit Estimation

Formula (12) for the selection probabilities, obtained from Axioms 1–3, can be adapted for empirical analysis by specifying the functional form of "representative" utility $v(s, x)$. A particularly convenient assumption is that v is linear in unknown parameters.

AXIOM 4. The function $v(s, x)$ has the form

$$v(s, x) = \theta_1 v^1(s, x) + \cdots + \theta_K v^K(s, x),$$

where the $v^k(s, x)$ are specified numerical functions and the θ_k are unknown parameters.

A choice experiment yields observations on N distinct trials (s_n, B_n), where s_n is a vector of measured attributes of an individual and B_n is an alternative set. Let B_n contain J_n alternatives, indexed $j = 1, \ldots, J_n$, with vectors of attributes x_{jn}. Define $z_{jn}^k = v^k(s_n, x_{jn})$ and $z_{jn} = (z_{jn}^1, \ldots, z_{jn}^K)$. From Equation (12), the selection probabilities then satisfy

$$(16) \qquad P_{in} = P(x_{in} \mid s_n, B_n) = \frac{e^{z_{in}\theta}}{\sum_{j=1}^{J_n} e^{z_{jn}\theta}},$$

where $\theta' = (\theta_1, \ldots, \theta_K)$.[6] The experiment provides R_n repetitions of trial n, and the ith alternative is observed to be chosen S_{in} times. Of particular interest is the case without repetition,

$$R_n = \sum_{j=1}^{J_n} S_{jn} = 1.$$

We term this the *conditional logit model.* Note that it is an immediate generalization to the case of unequal, possibly unranked, alternatives of the multinomial logit model appearing in the literature.[7] The derivation of this model from a theory of population choice behavior appears to be new.

[6] The generality and limits of this form deserve emphasis. A variable $z^k = v^k(s, x)$ may be a component of x, a function specifying a nonlinear transformation or interaction between components of x, or a function specifying an interaction between x and s variables. It cannot be a component of s (or x) that is invariant over each alternative set, as this shifts the origin of the "representative" utility function leaving all the selection probabilities unchanged, and the associated θ_k is nonidentified. In general, the alternatives x_j have no natural ranking, and the indexing j is arbitrary. We would then say the attributes of the alternatives are generic, or "hedonic." However, in some application the alternatives are ranked, and the rank j is a component of the vector of attributes of alternative x_j summarizing the "unique" characteristics of this position. Then z^k may be a variable such that $z_j^k = 1$ and $z_l^k = 0$ for $l \neq j$, yielding a "specific jth alternative" effect θ_k. Further, the interaction of such a variable with other components of x can give variable alternative-specific interaction effects. An extreme case is that in which the specific alternative effect is the only attribute varying across the alternative set, and all variables are as an example of the form $z_j^j = s^1$ and $z_l^j = 0$ for $l \neq j$, implying $v(s, x_j) = \sum_{j=1}^{J} s^1 \theta_j$, where only the parameters θ_j vary in j. Since translation of all θ_j leaves the selection probabilities unchanged, identification requires a normalization, say $\theta_1 = 0$.

[7] Binomial logit analysis was popularized by Berkson (1951, 1955) and has been analyzed extensively in the statistical literature: Antle (1970), Cox (1958, 1966, 1970), Gart (1967), Gilbert (1968), Grizzle (1962, 1971), Gupta (1967), Harter and Moore (1967), and Walker and Duncan (1967). Multinomial logit was developed for a special case by Gurland (1960), and more generally by Bloch (1967), Bock (1969), Rassam (1971), McFadden (1968), Stopher (1969), and Theil (1969, 1970). An analogous development has occurred for probit analysis, in which the cumulative normal rather than logistic distribution is used to determine the selection probabilities (Aitchison and Silvey, 1957; Aitchison and Bennett, 1970; Amemiya, 1972).

The notion of a distribution of tastes in a population of consumers as a source of stochastic components of demand has been implicit in much of the literature on consumer demand theory, particularly in random coefficients models of demand. The use of this concept in analyzing qualitative choice has been made explicit in the work of Quandt (1968, 1970; Quandt and Young, 1969; Quandt and Baumol, 1966), where selection probabilities are assumed to result from maximization of a log-linear utility function with random parameters. The relationship of logit models to distributions of utility functions was worked out in the context of models of stochastic choice behavior by Marschak (1960) and Block (1960), and explored further by Luce and Suppes (1965); the econometric implications of this work were apparently first noted by the author (1968). The foundations of the theory of testing hypotheses on individual behavior from population data were developed in a later paper by the author and Richter (1971).

The vector $(S_{1n}, \ldots, S_{J_n n})$ can be viewed as the result of R_n independent drawings from a multinomial distribution with probabilities given by Equation (16) for $i = 1, \ldots, J_n$. Hence, the likelihood of the given sample is a function $L = L(\theta) = L((S_{jn}, z_{jn}); \theta)$ satisfying

$$e^L = \prod_{n=1}^{N} \frac{R_n!}{S_{1n}! \cdots S_{J_n n}!} \prod_{i=1}^{J_n} P_{in}^{S_{in}}. \tag{17}$$

Substitution of Equation (16) yields the log-likelihood function

$$\begin{aligned} L &= C - \sum_{n=1}^{N} \sum_{i=1}^{J_n} S_{in} \log \sum_{j=1}^{J_n} e^{(z_{jn} - z_{in})\theta} \\ &= C + \sum_{n=1}^{N} \left[\left(\sum_{j=1}^{J_n} S_{jn} z_{jn} \right) \theta - R_n \log \sum_{j=1}^{J_n} e^{z_{jn}\theta} \right], \end{aligned} \tag{18}$$

where

$$C = \sum_{n=1}^{N} \left[\log R_n! - \sum_{j=1}^{J_n} \log S_{jn}! \right].$$

An estimator for θ with good large sample properties under very general conditions is obtained by a vector $\hat{\theta}$, depending on the observations, which maximizes the likelihood (18) of the given sample. We discuss the computation and statistical properties of the maximum likelihood estimator. Several alternative estimation methods are discussed at the end of this section.

Differentiation of Equation (18) with respect to θ yields the formulas

$$\frac{\partial L}{\partial \theta} = \sum_{n=1}^{N} \left[\sum_{j=1}^{J_n} (S_{jn} - R_n P_{jn}) z_{jn} \right], \tag{19}$$

$$\frac{\partial^2 L}{\partial \theta \, \partial \theta'} = -\sum_{n=1}^{N} R_n \sum_{j=1}^{J_n} (z_{jn} - \bar{z}_n)' P_{jn} (z_{jn} - \bar{z}_n), \tag{20}$$

where

$$\bar{z}_n = \sum_{i=1}^{J_n} z_{in} P_{in}.$$

Since Equation (20) is the negative of a weighted moment matrix of the independent variables, it is negative semidefinite and the log-likelihood function is concave in θ. Then L is maximized at any critical point θ where $\partial L / \partial \theta = 0$.

Binomial logit and probit analyses have been used in a number of economic applications: Allouche (1972), Amemiya and Boskin (1972), Fisher (1962), Korbel (1966), Lave (1968), Lee (1963), Lisco (1967), McGillivray (1970), Moses *et al.* (1967), Reichman and Stopher (1971), Stopher (1969), Stopher and Lisco (1970), Talvitie (1972), Thomas and Thompson (1971), Uhler (1968), Walker (1968), Warner (1967), and Zellner and Lee (1965).

If, further, the matrix $\partial^2 L/\partial\theta\,\partial\theta'$ is nonsingular, L has a unique maximum in θ (provided one exists). A necessary and sufficient condition for $\partial^2 L/\partial\theta\,\partial\theta'$ to be negative definite is the following.

AXIOM 5 (Full Rank). The $\sum_{n=1}^{N} J_n \times K$ matrix whose rows are $(z_{in}-\bar{z}_n)$ for $i = 1, \ldots, J_n$ and $n = 1, \ldots, N$ is of rank K.

Since N linear dependency conditions are present in this matrix due to the subtraction of weighted means, a necessary order condition is $\sum_{n=1}^{N} J_n \geqslant K+N$. This will hold in particular if $N \geqslant K$ since $J_n \geqslant 2$, but may also hold for $N < K$ if the J_n are large. Analogously to the hypothesis of full rank in the linear statistical model, we can expect Axiom 5 to hold when the order condition is satisfied provided the data vary across alternative sets and are not collinear.

We next introduce an inequalities condition that guarantees the existence of a vector θ maximizing L.

AXIOM 6. There exists no nonzero K-vector γ satisfying $S_{in}(z_{jn}-z_{in})\gamma \leqslant 0$ for $i,j = 1, \ldots, J_n$ and $n = 1, \ldots, N$.

Note that there is a positive probability that Axiom 6 may fail in a finite sample since the S_{in} are random. We show later that this probability is negligible in samples of reasonable size and approaches zero asymptotically. The following result establishes the existence of a θ maximizing L.

LEMMA 3. Suppose Axioms 1–5 hold. Then Axiom 6 is necessary and sufficient for the existence of a vector θ maximizing L.

Proof: We first show Axiom 6 to be necessary. Suppose L has a maximum at $\hat{\theta}$, but Axiom 6 fails for some $\gamma \neq 0$. Recall that

$$\log P_{in}(\theta) = -\log\left(\sum_{j=1}^{J_n} e^{(z_{jn}-z_{in})\theta}\right).$$

If $S_{in} > 0$, then $(z_{jn}-z_{in})(\hat{\theta}+\gamma) \leqslant (z_{jn}-z_{in})\hat{\theta}$ and $\log P_{in}(\hat{\theta}+\gamma) \geqslant \log P_{in}(\hat{\theta}_n)$. Then $L(\hat{\theta}+\gamma) \geqslant L(\hat{\theta})$. Since L is strictly concave, $L(\hat{\theta}+\gamma/2) > L(\hat{\theta})$, contradicting the definition of $\hat{\theta}$. Hence, Axiom 6 is necessary.

Next suppose that Axiom 6 holds. Define $A = \{\gamma \mid \gamma'\gamma = 1\}$. For each $\gamma \in A$, there exists j, i, n such that $S_{in}(z_{jn}-z_{in})\gamma > 0$. Define

$$b(\gamma) = \max_{n=1,\ldots,N}\ \max_{i,j=1,\ldots,J_n} S_{in}(z_{jn}-z_{in})\gamma. \tag{21}$$

Then b is a positive continuous function on the compact set A, and has a positive lower bound b^* on this set. Let $|\theta| = (\theta'\theta)^{1/2}$ and define

$$D = \{\theta \mid |\theta| \leqslant [-L(0)+C]/b^*\}.$$

Consider any $\theta \neq 0$, and let $\gamma = \theta/|\theta|$. Then $\gamma \in A$, and there exist indices i, j, n such that $b(\gamma) = S_{in}(z_{jn} - z_{in})\gamma$. From Equation (18),

$$\begin{aligned} L(\theta) - C \leqslant S_{in} \log P_{in} &= -S_{in} \log \sum_{k=1}^{J_n} e^{(z_{kn} - z_{in})\gamma|\theta|} \\ &\leqslant -S_{in}(z_{jn} - z_{in})\gamma|\theta| = -b(\gamma)|\theta| \\ &\leqslant -b^*|\theta|. \end{aligned}$$

For $\theta \notin D$, $L(\theta) - C \leqslant -b^*|\theta| < L(0) - C$. Hence, L can be maximized on the compact set D, and an optimal θ exists.

The following lemma establishes that Axiom 6 can be tested by solving a quadratic programming problem. This can be done by using a finite computational algorithm such as Lemke's method. In practice it is unnecessary to carry out this computation for sample sizes N exceeding the number of parameters K, as the probability of nonexistence rapidly becomes negligible.

LEMMA 4. Suppose Axioms 1–5 hold. Then Axiom 6 holds if and only if the minimum in the following quadratic programming problem is zero:

$$\operatorname*{Min}_{y,\alpha} y'y$$

subject to

$$y' = \sum_{n=1}^{N} \sum_{i,j=1}^{J_n} \alpha_{ijn} S_{in}(z_{jn} - z_{in}) \quad \text{and} \quad \alpha_{ijn} \geqslant 1. \tag{22}$$

Proof: Suppose the program has a zero minimum, achieved at some $y' = 0$, but that Axiom 6 fails. Then there exists $\gamma \neq 0$ such that $S_{in}(z_{jn} - z_{in})\gamma \leqslant 0$, with at least one inequality strict by Axiom 5. Then

$$0 = y'\gamma = \sum_{n=1}^{N} \sum_{i,j=1}^{J_n} \alpha_{ijn} S_{in}(z_{jn} - z_{in})\gamma < 0,$$

a contradiction. Thus, if the program has a zero minimum, Axiom 6 holds.

Let K denote the convex cone generated by the vectors $S_{in}(z_{jn} - z_{in})$ for $n = 1, \ldots, N$ and $i, j = 1, \ldots, J_n$. If the origin is in the interior of K, then there exist positive scalars α_{ijn} such that $y' = \sum_{n=1}^{N} \alpha_{ijn} S_{in}(z_{jn} - z_{in}) = 0$, and the quadratic program achieves a minimum of zero. If the origin is not in the interior of K, then there exists a separating hyperplane with normal $\gamma \neq 0$ such that $S_{in}(z_{jn} - z_{in})\gamma \leqslant 0$ for all $n = 1, \ldots, N$ and $i, j = 1, \ldots, J_n$. Hence, Axiom 6 fails. This proves the lemma.

Computation of the maximum likelihood estimator can be carried out using a variety of standard programs for unconstrained nonlinear optimization.

Since the likelihood function is strictly concave, any algorithm which converges will attain the maximum. Experience has shown that a standard Newton–Raphson algorithm may converge slowly for this problem; we have found that one efficient procedure is to use Davidon's variable metric method to determine direction of search and a one-dimensional procedure employing a cubic approximation to determine the optimal step size.[8]

The maximum likelihood procedure has proved practical for problems of up to 20 variables and 2000 observations, but is relatively costly for large samples. A quick procedure which can be used for screening models is to make a linear expansion of the gradient of the likelihood function (19) in θ about some initial vector $\bar{\theta}$, and then solve for the value of θ equating this approximate gradient to zero, or

$$(23)\qquad \tilde{\theta} = \bar{\theta} + \left[\sum_{n=1}^{N} R^n \sum_{j=1}^{J_n} (z_{jn}-\bar{z}_n)'\bar{P}_{jn}(z_{jn}-\bar{z}_n)\right]^{-1} \times \left[\sum_{n=1}^{N}\sum_{j=1}^{J_n} (z_{jn}-\bar{z}_n)'(S_{jn}-R_n\bar{P}_{jn})\right],$$

where $\bar{P}_{jn} = P_{jn}(\bar{\theta})$ and $\bar{z}_n = \sum_{j=1}^{J_n} z_{jn}\bar{P}_{jn}$. Note that $\tilde{\theta}$ is the result of one iteration of a Newton–Raphson procedure for maximizing the likelihood function, and can also be interpreted as the ordinary least squares estimator in the linear model (with R_n observations for each n)

$$(24)\qquad (\bar{P}_{jn})^{-1/2}[(S_{jn}/R_n)-\bar{P}_{jn}] = (\bar{P}_{jn})^{1/2}(z_{jn}-\bar{z}_n)(\theta-\bar{\theta}) + \varepsilon_{jn}.$$

Equation (24) is termed the *linear probability model*, and is sometimes taken as a specification of selection probabilities $P_{jn} = E(S_{jn}/R_n)$. The estimator $\tilde{\theta}$ is not a consistent estimate of the true parameter vector θ when the specification of Axioms 1–6 is valid; however, as a practical matter it usually agrees in magnitude and sign with the maximum likelihood estimator provided the terms $|(z_{jn}-\bar{z}_n)(\theta-\bar{\theta})|$ are less than unity. Equation (24) is inappropriate for use in forecasting selection probabilities because the requirement that the forecasts lie in the unit interval is not met.

When the number of repetitions for each trial is large, a method of estimation developed by Berkson (1951) and generalized to the multinomial case by Theil (1969) can be employed. When S_{in}, S_{ln} are large,[9] $\log(S_{in}/S_{ln})$ is a close approximation to the left-hand side of

$$(25)\qquad \log(P_{in}/P_{ln}) = (z_{in}-z_{ln})\theta,$$

and an estimate of θ can be obtained by applying ordinary or weighted least

[8] The author is indebted to H. Wills and H. Varian for work on the numerical methods and programming of this problem.

[9] A rule-of-thumb is $S_{in} \geqslant 5$.

squares to the model

$$\log(S_{in}/S_{ln}) = (z_{in} - z_{ln})\theta + \varepsilon_{in}, \tag{26}$$

taking into account linear restrictions across equations.[10] This procedure is asymptotically equivalent to maximum likelihood estimation as the S_{in} approach infinity (for appropriate weights in the regression), and is to be preferred to the maximum likelihood procedure on computational grounds. It should be noted, however, that grouping observations that are not exact replications in order to achieve the cell frequencies required for application of the Berkson–Theil method introduces an "errors in variables" component that makes the estimator inconsistent and may make it seriously biased. In such cases the maximum likelihood procedure should be more reliable.

III. Statistical Properties

Maximum likelihood estimation of the conditional logit model can be shown under very general conditions to provide estimators that are asymptotically efficient and normally distributed. Examples suggest that the approximation is reasonably good even in quite small samples. These results can be used to construct approximate large-sample confidence bounds and tests of hypotheses for the parameters.

We have noted that for finite sample sizes, there will be a positive probability that a maximum of the likelihood function cannot be attained. This corresponds to the case where the system of inequalities in Axiom 6 has a nontrivial solution and the sample is "explained" by maximization of this linear combination of the independent variables. We first show that when the sample is in fact generated by probabilities satisfying Axioms 1–5, then the probability that the likelihood function has a maximum approaches one as the sample size increases. We impose the following condition on the data.

AXIOM 7. The numbers of alternatives J_n are uniformly bounded by an integer J_*. The independent variables z_{in} are uniformly bounded by a scalar

[10] Some improvement in the statistical properties of the unweighted Berkson–Theil estimator can be obtained by replacing Equation (26) with the regression equation

$$\log\left(\frac{S_{in}+\frac{1}{2}}{S_{ln}+\frac{1}{2}}\right) = (z_{in} - z_{ln})\theta + \varepsilon_{in}. \tag{26a}$$

This modification, suggested by Haldane (1955) for the binomial logit model, makes $E\log[(S_{in}+\frac{1}{2})/(S_{ln}+\frac{1}{2})]$ equal to $\log(P_{in}/P_{ln})$ up to a term of order $1/R_n^2$, rather than of order $1/R_n$, as R_n approaches infinity. This improves the speed of convergence of the estimators to their large-sample values. Minor modifications of the Haldane argument establish its validity in the multinomial case.

M.[11] The limit of the weighted moment matrix, as $\sum_{n=1}^{N} R_n \to +\infty$,

$$\lim\left(\sum_{n=1}^{N} R_n\right)^{-1} \sum_{n=1}^{N} R_n \sum_{i=1}^{J_n} (z_{in} - \bar{z}_n)' P_{in} (z_{in} - \bar{z}_{in}) = \Omega, \tag{27}$$

exists and is positive-definite.

The last part of this axiom strengthens the full-rank condition assumed earlier, implying that an infinite number of blocks of K trials can be found satisfying Axiom 5.[12] One can expect Axiom 7 to hold provided the data are not multicollinear and do not tend to become explosive or degenerate as the sample size increases. The following results are proved in the Appendix.

LEMMA 5. Suppose Axioms 1–4 and 7 hold. Then the probability that Axiom 6 holds and the maximum likelihood estimator exists approaches unity as $\sum_{n=1}^{N} R_n$ approaches infinity.

LEMMA 6. Suppose Axioms 1–4 and 7 hold, θ^0 is the true parameter vector, and $\hat{\theta}^M$ is the maximum likelihood estimator for a sample of size $M = \sum_{n=1}^{N} R_n$. Then $\hat{\theta}^M$ is consistent and asymptotically normal, with

$$\left(\sum_{n=1}^{N} R_n\right)^{1/2} \Omega^{1/2} (\hat{\theta}^M - \theta^0), \tag{28}$$

tending to a multivariate normal distribution with mean zero and a covariance matrix equal to the identity matrix.

This lemma implies that $\hat{\theta}^M$ tends to be distributed normally with mean θ^0 and covariance matrix $(\sum_{n=1}^{N} R_n)^{-1}\Omega^{-1}$, and that the quadratic form

$$Q(\hat{\theta}^M) \equiv \left(\sum_{n=1}^{N} R_n\right)(\hat{\theta}^M - \theta^0)'\Omega(\hat{\theta}^M - \theta^0)$$

tends to be chi-square distributed with K degrees of freedom. These statistics can be used to carry out large sample tests of hypotheses on θ^0. In particular, diagonal elements of the inverse of the information matrix $(\sum_{n=1}^{N} R_n)^{-1}\Omega^{-1}$ provide estimates of the variances of the estimators.[13] To test a hypothesis

[11] I.e., $|z_{in}| \leqslant M$, where the norm $|A|$ of any array A is the sum of the absolute values of its elements.

[12] Otherwise, all but a finite number of vectors $z_{in} - \bar{z}_n$ can be written as linear combinations of less than K linearly independent vectors. Then, Ω must also have this property, contradicting the hypothesis that it is nonsingular.

[13] Some improvement in the speed of convergence can be attained by multiplying these estimates by a correction factor for degrees of freedom,

$$\frac{\sum_{n=1}^{N} R_n(J_n - 1)}{\sum_{n=1}^{N} R_n(J_n - 1) - K}.$$

that the true parameter vector θ^0 lies in a $(K-K_1)$ dimensional manifold, calculate the maximum likelihood estimator $\hat{\theta}^H$ under the null hypothesis and the unconstrained maximum likelihood estimator $\hat{\theta}$. Then the statistic

$$(29) \quad -2[L(\hat{\theta}^H)-L(\hat{\theta})] = (\hat{\theta}^H-\hat{\theta})' \sum_{n=1}^{N} R_n \sum_{i=1}^{J_n} (z_{in}-\bar{z}_n)' P_{in}(z_{in}-\bar{z}_n)(\hat{\theta}^H-\hat{\theta}),$$

with P_{in} evaluated at $\hat{\theta}$, is distributed approximately chi-square with K_1 degrees of freedom. If the null hypothesis is that θ^0 is zero, or that it is zero except for pure alternative effects, then this statistic provides a test of the significance of an estimation equation, indicating respectively the "mean square error" explained or the "variance" explained. Noting that the extreme case is $L(\hat{\theta}) \approx 0$, we can define a coefficient of determination that is analogous to the multiple-correlation coefficient in the linear statistical model,

$$(30) \qquad \rho^2 = 1 - \frac{L(\hat{\theta})}{L(\hat{\theta}^H)} .$$

If $\hat{\theta}^H$ is zero, or if $\hat{\theta}^H$ is zero except for pure alternative effects and the model contains such effects, then ρ^2 lies in the unit interval. If, in the latter case, the model has no pure alternative effects, it is possible for ρ^2 to be negative.

A second measure of goodness of fit is based on deviations of observed from fitted relative frequencies. Define the weighted residuals

$$(31) \qquad D_{in} = \frac{S_{in} - R_n P_{in}}{(R_n P_{in})^{1/2}} ,$$

for $i = 1, \ldots, J_n$ and $n = 1, \ldots, N$, where P_{in} is evaluated at the maximum likelihood estimate. These residuals satisfy the first-order conditions for maximization of the likelihood function,

$$(32) \qquad \sum_{n=1}^{N} (r_n)^{1/2} \sum_{i=1}^{J_n} D_{in}(P_{in})^{1/2}(z_{in}-\bar{z}_n) = 0,$$

where

$$(33) \qquad r_n = \frac{R_n}{\sum_{m=1}^{N} R_m} ,$$

and the conditions

$$(34) \qquad \sum_{i=1}^{J_n} (P_{in})^{1/2} D_{in} = 0,$$

for $n = 1, \ldots, N$, a total of $N+K$ restrictions. Now suppose $\sum_{n=1}^{N} R_n$ approaches infinity, with each r_n approaching a limit. We show in the Appendix that the

D_{in} are distributed asymptotically with mean zero and covariances

$$\Lambda_{in,jm} \equiv ED_{in}D_{jm} = \delta_{nm}[\delta_{ij} - (P^0_{in}P^0_{jn})^{1/2}] \tag{35}$$
$$- (r_m r_n P^0_{in} P^0_{jm})^{1/2}(z_{in} - \bar{z}_n)\Omega^{-1}(z_{jm} - \bar{z}_m).$$

Consider the case in which N remains finite and the R_n approach infinity. Then Λ is an idempotent matrix of rank $N^* = \sum_{n=1}^{N} J_n - N - K$, and the asymptotic distribution of the D_{in} is multivariate normal. Hence,

$$G = \sum_{n=1}^{N} \sum_{i=1}^{J_n} D_{in}^2 \tag{36}$$

has an asymptotic chi-square distribution with N^* degrees of freedom.[14] The statistics D_{in} and G can be used to carry out large-sample tests of the model specification. For example, regression of the D_{in} on potential independent variables provides evidence on the validity of their exclusion from the model. A test of the significance of G provides evidence on the validity of the logit specification of the selection probabilities and the absence of "alternative set" effects. Further, one can define an analog of the multiple-correlation coefficient,

$$R^2 = 1 - G/G^H, \tag{37}$$

where G is given by Equation (36) and G^H is given by the same equation when the numerators of the residuals are evaluated under the hypothesis that the parameter vector is zero, or is zero except for pure alternative choice effects.

In evaluating the results of regressions of the D_{in} on potential independent variables, one should adjust for the nonindependence and heteroskedasticity of the D_{in}. This can be achieved in part by using the linearly transformed residuals

$$Y_{in} = D_{in} - \frac{D_{1n}(P_{in})^{1/2}[1-(P_{1n})^{1/2}]}{1-P_{1n}}, \tag{38}$$

defined for $i = 2, \ldots, J_n$ and $n = 1, \ldots, N$. The Y_{in} are asymptotically multivariate normal with mean zero and covariances

$$\Gamma_{in,jm} \equiv EY_{in}Y_{jm} = \delta_{nm}\delta_{ij} - q'_{in}q_{jm}, \tag{39}$$

[14] Treating G as a function of θ and minimizing it at a value $\hat{\theta}$ provides a *minimum chi-square* estimator of the parameter vector. The first-order conditions for this minimization coincide with Equation (32) except for a term, reflecting the effect of changing θ on the weights in the denominator of Equation (31), which has probability limit zero when the $R_n \to +\infty$. Thus, the maximum likelihood and minimum chi-square estimators are asymptotically equivalent under these limiting conditions. On the other hand, the minimum chi-square procedure is not consistent under the limiting conditions that $N \to +\infty$ and R_n remain finite.

where

$$q'_{in} = (r_n P^0_{in})^{1/2}\left((z_{in} - \bar{z}_n) + \frac{P^0_{1n} - (P^0_{1n})^{1/2}}{1 - P^0_{1n}}(z_{1n} - \bar{z}_n)\right)\Omega^{-1/2}. \tag{40}$$

The matrix Γ is idempotent of rank N^*. When the r_n are small, the matrix Γ is nearly diagonal, and the regression of any subset of N^* of the Y_{in} on potential independent variables can, as a good approximation, be treated as independent and homoskedastic with unit variance.

We next consider the case in which N approaches infinity and the limiting values of the r_n are zero. Then, the residuals D_{in} have an asymptotic multinomial distribution with mean zero and covariances given by Equation (35), with the second term in this expression vanishing. The D_{in} and the transformed residuals Y_{in} defined in Equation (38) are independent across n, and the Y_{in} have zero mean, unit variance, and zero covariances. Suppose integers N_m satisfy $\sum_{m=1}^{M} N_m = N$ and $N_m \to +\infty$. Then the statistics

$$Y^m = \frac{\sum_{n=N_{m'}+1}^{N_{m'}+1} \sum_{j=2}^{J_n} Y_{jn}}{(\sum_{n=N_{m'}+1}^{N_{m'}+1} J_n - N_m)^{1/2}}, \tag{41}$$

where $N_m' = N_1 + \cdots + N_{m-1}$, are asymptotically independent standard normal, and can be used to test the specification of the absence of alternative set effects. When the R_n remain small, the distributions of the D_{in} and Y_{in} depart substantially from asymptotic normality. The statistics G and R^2 defined in Equations (36) and (37) remain useful summary measures, although the robustness of the asymptotic distributions obtained in the previous case has not been investigated. Since the Y_{in} satisfy the Gauss–Markov assumptions when the model is specified correctly, the usual asymptotic theory for the linear statistical model can be applied to test the validity of excluding potential independent variables.

The small sample properties of the maximum likelihood estimator of the conditional logit model are unknown except for a few special cases. Monte Carlo studies of related models suggest that maximum likelihood, minimum chi-square, and Berkson–Theil estimators are all reasonably well behaved in small samples, even when the number of repetitions is small.[15] We next consider several simple examples in which the maximum likelihood estimator can be calculated analytically. These examples suggest that the maximum likelihood estimator is well behaved in samples of sizes likely to be encountered in applications, 50 and greater, but may be inferior to the linear probability model estimator in very small samples provided the range of the data is not too large.

[15] Berkson (1955), Gart and Zweifel (1967), Gilbert (1968), and Talvitie (1972).

TABLE 1

SAMPLING PROPERTIES OF THE MAXIMUM LIKELIHOOD ESTIMATOR: EXAMPLE 1

Parameter value (θ_1)	Sample size	Probability of existence of maximum likelihood estimator	Conditional expectation of maximum likelihood estimator	Percent bias	Conditonal variance of maximum likelihood estimator	Calculated variance of maximum likelihood estimator	Percent bias	Linear probability model estimator	Percent bias
0.01	5	0.93748	0.00828	−17.2	0.75018	1.21529	62.0	0.01000	a
	10	0.99814	0.01103	10.3	0.49988	0.50943	1.9	0.01000	a
	20	1.0	0.01057	5.7	0.22422	0.22314	−0.5	0.01000	a
	30	1.0	0.01036	3.6	0.14334	0.14308	a	0.01000	a
	50	1.0	0.01021	2.1	0.08343	0.08338	a	0.01000	a
	75	1.0	0.01014	1.4	0.05482	0.05481	a	0.01000	a
	100	1.0	0.01010	1.0	0.04083	0.04082	a	0.01000	a
0.1	5	0.93594	0.08272	−17.3	0.74726	1.21643	67.0	0.09992	−0.1
	10	0.99782	0.11023	10.2	0.50044	0.51128	2.2	0.09992	−0.1
	20	1.0	0.10575	5.8	0.22503	0.22387	−0.5	0.09992	−0.1
	30	1.0	0.10364	3.6	0.14379	0.14349	a	0.09992	−0.1
	50	1.0	0.10211	2.1	0.08366	0.08360	a	0.09992	−0.1
	75	1.0	0.10138	1.4	0.05497	0.05497	a	0.09992	−0.1
	100	1.0	0.10103	1.0	0.04093	0.04093	a	0.09992	−0.1
0.5	5	0.89888	0.40054	−20.0	0.68164	1.24250	83.0	0.48984	−2.0
	10	0.99121	0.54433	8.9	0.50916	0.55472	8.9	0.48984	−2.0
	20	0.99992	0.53020	6.0	0.24536	0.24215	−1.3	0.48984	−2.0
	30	1.0	0.51912	3.8	0.15515	0.15391	−0.8	0.48984	−2.0
	50	1.0	0.51101	2.2	0.08955	0.08922	a	0.48984	−2.0
	75	1.0	0.50720	1.4	0.05865	0.05852	a	0.48984	−2.0
	100	1.0	0.50535	1.1	0.04361	0.04354	a	0.48984	−2.0

1.0	5	0.78978	0.73234	−26.8	0.52531	1.30757	148.0	0.92423	−7.6
	10	0.95639	1.04040	4.0	0.49435	0.67376	36.5	0.92423	−7.6
	20	0.99810	1.06643	6.6	0.30950	0.30826	−0.4	0.92423	−7.6
	30	0.99992	1.04437	4.4	0.19662	0.19146	−2.6	0.92423	−7.6
	50	1.0	1.02525	2.5	0.11041	0.10881	−1.5	0.92423	−7.6
	75	1.0	1.01641	1.6	0.07145	0.07083	−0.8	0.92423	−7.6
	100	1.0	1.01216	1.2	0.05285	0.05252	−0.6	0.92423	−7.6
2.0	5	0.46885	1.12824	−44.5	0.23655	1.44030	510.0	1.5232	−23.8
	10	0.71897	1.71841	−14.1	0.30827	0.95333	209.0	1.5232	−23.8
	20	0.92102	2.04023	2.0	0.37726	0.60123	59.4	1.5232	−23.8
	30	0.97780	2.09760	4.9	0.35233	0.41411	17.6	1.5232	−23.8
	50	0.99825	2.08151	4.0	0.23948	0.23167	−3.3	1.5232	−23.8
	75	0.99993	2.05384	2.2	0.15052	0.14352	−4.7	1.5232	−23.8
	100	1.0	2.03925	2.0	0.10754	0.10383	−3.5	1.5232	−23.8
3.0	5	0.21568	1.28953	−57.1	0.09262	1.51321	1655.0	1.8103	−39.7
	10	0.38484	2.01670	−32.8	0.13505	1.11987	830.0	1.8103	−39.7
	20	0.62158	2.59216	−13.6	0.21698	0.88161	307.0	1.8103	−39.7
	30	0.76721	2.84486	−5.2	0.27726	0.74378	162.0	1.8103	−39.7
	50	0.91191	3.04643	1.5	0.33452	0.54907	64.4	1.8103	−39.7
	75	0.97385	3.10492	3.5	0.32443	0.38745	19.4	1.8103	−39.7
	100	0.99224	3.10337	3.4	0.27741	0.28459	2.5	1.8103	−39.7

[a] Negligible.

Example 1. Suppose N observations are taken of a binary choice with a selection probability $P_1 = 1/(1+e^{-\theta_1})$ for the first alternative, and suppose this alternative is chosen S times. The maximum likelihood estimator exists if $0 < S < N$, and equals $\hat{\theta}_1 = \log[S/(N-S)]$. Table 1 gives the actual expectation and variance of $\hat{\theta}_1$, conditioned on existence, and the large sample variance calculated from the information matrix. The last columns give the linear probability model approximation (23) to the logit model from starting value zero. For sample sizes exceeding 20, the maximum likelihood estimator and its calculated variance have expectations that are within 10% of true values except for extreme selection probabilities (e.g., $\theta_1 = 2.0$ yields $P_1 = 0.88$). The linear probability model approximation is quite accurate for small parameter values, even for small sample sizes. The bias is severe however for extreme selection probabilities, and is independent of sample size. The probability of existence of the maximum likelihood estimator rises rapidly with sample size, even for extreme selection probabilities.

Example 2. Suppose $N = 2R$ observations are taken of a binary choice with selection probabilities $P_{1n} = 1/(1+e^{-\theta_1-\theta_2 x_n})$, where $x_n = 0$ for $n = 1, \ldots, R$ and $x_n = 1$ for $n = R+1, \ldots, N$. Suppose the first alternative is chosen S_1 times in the first R observations and S_2 times in the second R observations. The maximum likelihood estimator exists if $0 < S_1 < R$ and $0 < S_2 < R$, and equals $\hat{\theta}_1 = \log[S_1/(R-S_1)]$ and $\hat{\theta}_2 = \log[S_2/(R-S_2)] - \log[S_1/(R-S_1)]$. Table 2 gives the conditional expectations of these estimators and the expectations of the variances calculated from the information matrix for selected parameter values. The pattern of the biases generally conforms to that of the previous example. For a sample size of 10, the estimator and its calculated variance are substantially biased, the former downward and the latter upward. As sample size increases, the bias in the estimator swings positive, but never more than 10% and then approaches zero. The calculated variances show similar behavior with reversed sign, their bias going from positive to negative as sample size increases and then approaching zero. As the parameter values and selection probabilities become more extreme, there is an increase in the sample size at which the maximum positive bias in the estimator occurs. The linear probability model approximation provides an accurate estimator for small sample sizes and parameter values, and indicates correctly signs and orders of magnitude of parameters even for extreme values, but with substantial biases. In samples of size 100 or 200 the biases and probabilities of nonexistence of the maximum likelihood estimator are acceptably small even for extreme selection probabilities.

One must be cautious in generalizing too far the conclusions drawn from these examples. In particular, we have not explored the behavior of the estimators in samples in which the observations are generated by mixtures of

TABLE 2

SAMPLING PROPERTIES OF THE MAXIMUM LIKELIHOOD ESTIMATOR: EXAMPLE 2

	Sample size					
	10	20	40	80	140	200
First parameter (all cases)						
True value	0.10000	0.10000	0.10000	0.10000	0.10000	0.10000
Expect. of M.L. estimate	0.08272	0.11023	0.10575	0.10267	0.10148	0.10103
Per cent bias of est.	−17.28364	10.22808	5.74896	2.66732	1.48170	1.02609
True variance of M.L. est.	0.74726	0.50044	0.22503	0.10576	0.05902	0.04094
Calc. variance of M.L. est.	0.80200	0.40100	0.20050	0.10025	0.05729	0.04010
Per cent bias of var. est.	7.32580	−19.87098	−10.90107	−5.21060	−2.93154	−2.04035
Linear prob. model est.	0.09992	0.09992	0.09992	0.09992	0.09992	0.09992
Per cent bias of linear est.	−0.08325	−0.08325	−0.08325	−0.08325	−0.08325	−0.08325
Second parameter						
True value	−0.50000	−0.50000	−0.50000	−0.50000	−0.50000	−0.50000
Expect. of M.L. estimate	−0.40695	−0.54780	−0.52948	−0.51365	−0.50757	−0.50524
Per cent bias of est.	−18.60931	9.56094	5.89654	2.72972	1.51402	1.04790
True variance of M.L. est.	1.45241	1.00740	0.46265	0.21631	0.12049	0.08353
Calc. variance of M.L. ext.	1.63443	0.81722	0.40861	0.20430	0.11675	0.08172
Per cent bias of var. est.	12.53225	−18.87888	−11.68067	−5.54934	−3.11136	−2.16302
Linear prob. model est.	−0.49467	−0.49467	−0.49467	−0.49467	−0.49467	−0.49467
Per cent bias of linear est.	−1.06652	−1.06652	−1.06652	−1.06652	−1.06652	−1.06652
Prob. of existence of M.L. est.	0.85421	0.99181	0.99996	1.00000	1.00000	1.00000
True value	0.10000	0.10000	0.10000	0.10000	0.10000	0.10000
Expect. of M.L. estimate	0.08204	0.10990	0.10582	0.10270	0.10150	0.10104
Per cent bias of est.	−17.96158	9.90456	5.82398	2.69820	1.49773	1.03691
True variance of M.L. est.	1.48579	1.00250	0.45254	0.21246	0.11852	0.08220
Calc. variance of M.L. ext.	1.61003	0.80501	0.40251	0.20125	0.11500	0.08050
Per cent bias of var. est.	8.36201	−19.69933	−11.05610	−5.27618	−2.96650	−2.06423
Linear prob. model est.	0.09942	0.09942	0.09942	0.09942	0.09942	0.09942
Per cent bias of linear est.	−0.58076	−0.58076	−0.58076	−0.58076	−0.58076	−0.58076
Prob. of existence of M.L. est.	0.87160	0.99496	0.99999	1.00000	1.00000	1.00000

TABLE 2—continued

	Sample size					
	10	20	40	80	140	200
True value	1.00000	1.00000	1.00000	1.00000	1.00000	1.00000
Expect. of M.L. estimate	0.70474	1.01873	1.06783	1.03421	1.01864	1.01282
Per cent bias of est.	−29.52618	1.87276	6.78330	3.42109	1.86412	1.28241
True variance of M.L. est.	1.23857	0.98412	0.55049	0.25613	0.14019	0.09663
Calc. variance of M.L. ext.	1.86941	0.93470	0.46735	0.23368	0.13353	0.09347
Per cent bias of var. est.	50.93327	−5.02084	−15.10210	−8.76667	−4.75197	−3.26642
Linear prob. model est.	0.90112	0.90112	0.90112	0.90112	0.90112	0.90112
Per cent bias of linear est.	−9.88763	−9.88763	−9.88763	−9.88763	−9.88763	−9.88763
Prob. of existence of M.L. est.	0.71254	0.94144	0.99680	0.99999	1.00000	1.00000
First parameter (all cases)						
True value	1.00000	1.00000	1.00000	1.00000	1.00000	1.00000
Expect. of M.L. estimate	0.73234	1.04040	1.06643	1.03222	1.01764	1.01216
Per cent bias of est.	−26.76589	4.04022	6.64324	3.22242	1.76425	1.21578
True variance of M.L. est.	0.52531	0.49435	0.30950	0.14142	0.07686	0.05285
Calc. variance of M.L. est.	1.01723	0.50862	0.25431	0.12715	0.07266	0.05086
Per cent bias of var. est.	93.64346	2.88570	−17.83370	−10.08782	−5.46810	−3.76027
Linear prob. model est.	0.92423	0.92423	0.92423	0.92423	0.92423	0.92423
Per cent bias of linear est.	−7.57657	−7.57657	−7.57657	−7.57657	−7.57657	−7.57657
Second parameter						
True value	−0.50000	−0.50000	−0.50000	−0.50000	−0.50000	−0.50000
Expect. of M.L. estimate	−0.33180	−0.49607	−0.53624	−0.51826	−0.50991	−0.50681
Per cent bias of est.	−33.64020	−0.78652	7.24721	3.65173	1.98177	1.36160
True variance of M.L. est.	1.20695	1.00351	0.55487	0.25493	0.13986	0.09646
Calc. variance of M.L. ext.	1.86828	0.93414	0.46707	0.23354	0.13345	0.09341
Per cent bias of var. est.	54.79349	−6.91277	−15.82285	−8.39383	−4.58190	−3.15818
Linear prob. model est.	−0.43440	−0.43440	−0.43440	−0.43440	−0.43440	−0.43440
Per cent bias of linear est.	−13.12060	−13.12060	−13.12060	−13.13060	−13.12060	−13.12060
Prob. of existence of M.L. est.	0.70992	0.94799	0.99802	1.00000	1.00000	1.00000

True value	0.10000	0.10000	0.10000	0.10000	0.10000	0.10000
Expect. of M.L. estimate	0.05511	0.08855	0.10715	0.10465	0.10248	0.10169
Per cent bias of est.	−44.88654	−11.44656	7.14974	4.65396	2.48035	1.69241
True variance of M.L. est.	1.01662	0.97802	0.63496	0.29179	0.15804	0.10854
Calc. variance of M.L. ext.	2.08464	1.04232	0.52116	0.26058	0.14890	0.10423
Per cent. bias of var. est.	105.05601	6.57426	−17.92244	−10.69591	−5.78006	−3.96928
Linear prob. model est.	0.07681	0.07681	0.07681	0.07681	0.07681	0.07681
Per cent bias of linear est.	−23.19389	−23.19389	−23.19389	−23.19389	−23.19389	−23.19389
Prob. of existence of M.L. est.	0.60127	0.90235	0.99491	0.99999	1.00000	1.00000
True value	1.00000	1.00000	1.00000	1.00000	1.00000	1.00000
Expect. of M.L. estimate	0.39590	0.67801	0.97380	1.06299	1.04043	1.02706
Per cent bias of est.	−60.40966	−12.19939	−2.62020	6.29931	4.04250	2.70572
True variance of M.L. est.	0.76186	0.80262	0.68676	0.43638	0.24022	0.16047
Calc. variance of M.L. ext.	2.92211	1.46106	0.73053	0.36526	0.20872	0.14611
Per cent bias of var. est.	283.54796	82.03495	6.37315	−16.29632	−13.11233	−8.94926
Linear prob. model est.	0.59895	0.59895	0.59895	0.59895	0.59895	0.59895
Per cent bias of linear est.	−40.10460	−40.10460	−40.10460	−40.10460	−40.10460	−40.10460
Prob. of existence of M.L. est.	0.37108	0.68762	0.91927	0.99376	0.99986	1.00000

extreme and nonextreme selection probabilities. On the other hand, we anticipate that the qualitative structure of biases will be unchanged by the addition of independent variables or of multiple-choice alternatives, as the estimator is analogous to a linear statistical estimator except for the nonlinear dependence of the selection probabilities on the parameters.

IV. An Empirical Application

The theory of qualitative choice behavior outlined above has been applied to several areas of consumer choice. The author (1968) has investigated the criteria employed by a state highway department in selecting urban freeway routes. The determinants of college choice have been studied by Professor Miller and Professor Radner (1970), and the results have been used to forecast the effects of changing educational policy on college enrollment. Professor Boskin (1972) has applied the model to the problem of occupational choice. Studies in progress are investigating urban trip generation, distribution, and modal choice; labor force participation and job search decisions; housing location and type; recidivism; child-bearing decisions and the implications of population control policy; choice of consumer durables; and rural-urban migration decisions. To illustrate the method, we reproduce here selected results on shopping trip mode and destination decisions obtained in a study of travel demand models by T. Domencich and D. McFadden (1972).[16]

The objective of this study is to develop disaggregated, policy-oriented, behavioral models of urban trip generation, distribution, and mode. The behavioral unit studied is the individual trip-maker, faced with decisions on whether to take a trip, mode, and destination. The empirical analysis is based on a household survey in Pittsburgh conducted by the Southwestern Pennsylvania Regional Planning Commission in 1967, supplemented with time and cost data collected by the study authors. A detailed description of the sample frame and variables collected is given in the study.

The analysis of shopping travel behavior is separated into three decisions: (1) choice of mode for trips actually made at the observed time and to the observed destination; (2) choice of destination for trips made at an observed time by preferred mode; and (3) choice of whether or not to make a trip, given a preferred time, mode, and destination.[17] The results of each analysis are summarized in turn.

[16] The results below are reproduced with the permission of Charles River Associates, Inc.

[17] The separation of these decisions is justified in the study by postulating a "tree" utility structure; we shall not repeat the argument here.

Shopping choice of mode

Choice between public transit and auto mode is examined for a sample of 140 individual shopping trips. For each observation, walk access to transit is available. The sample is drawn from a southern suburban corridor of Pittsburgh and a central city corridor running from downtown to the east. A number of alternative models were fitted; those giving the most satisfactory results in terms of fitting the base data are described in Table 3. All coefficients in these models are of the expected sign. The coefficients of transit walk time, auto in-vehicle less transit station-to-station time, and auto operating costs less transit fares imply a value of walk time of \$5.46 per hour and a value of in-vehicle time of \$0.95 per hour in Model 1. These values are in close accord

TABLE 3

CONDITIONAL LOGIT MODEL OF SHOPPING MODE CHOICE; DEPENDENT VARIABLE EQUALS THE LOG ODDS OF CHOICE OF AUTO MODE; BINARY LOGIT MAXIMUM LIKELIHOOD ESTIMATES; STANDARD ERRORS IN PARENTHESES

Independent variable	Model 1	Model 2	Model 3	Model 4
Pure auto mode preference effect (constant)[a]	−6.77 (1.66)	−6.20 (2.10)	−6.65 (1.54)	−6.37 (1.82)
Transit walk time (minutes)	0.374 (0.328)	0.398 (0.410)	0.30 (0.351)	0.274 (0.612)
Transit wait plus transfer time (minutes)	—	—	0.0647 (0.0403)	—
Transit station-to-station time (minutes)	—	—	—	0.0532 (0.0455)
Auto in-vehicle time (minutes)	—	—	—	−0.0486 (0.0956)
Auto in-vehicle time less transit station-to-station time (minutes)	−0.0654 (0.0320)	−0.0636 (0.0398)	—	—
Auto in-vehicle time less transit line-haul time (minutes)	—	—	−0.0287 (0.0715)	—
Auto operating cost less transit fares (dollars)	−4.11 (1.67)	−4.66 (2.06)	−4.10 (2.13)	−4.06 (1.74)
Ratio of number of autos to number of workers in the household	2.24 (1.11)	2.26 (1.14)	2.01 (1.04)	1.89 (0.76)
Race of respondent (0 if white, 1 if non-white)	—	−2.18 (1.26)	—	—
Occupation of head of household (0 if blue-collar, 1 if white collar)	—	−1.53 (1.10)	—	—

[a] Because of the sample selection procedure and the presence of the last three variables giving socioeconomic-auto mode interaction effects, this constant cannot be interpreted as a "transit" bias that would be replicated in a random sample of the population.

with shopping trip value of time studies. Thus, the estimates seem quite stable despite the relatively large standard errors. The models provide excellent fits of the base-line data; in Model 1, the probability of selecting the actual mode is greater than one-half for 133 of the 140 observations, and greater than 0.9 for 116 of the 140 observations.

Shopping choice of destination

The choice of shopping destination is analyzed for 63 auto-mode trips starting from the southern suburban corridor. The possible alternative destinations for each observation are selected by dividing the city into zones and choosing all destination zones to which there is a trip in the sample from the origin zone. The number of alternatives varies from three to five in this sample.

This model is estimated using only three explanatory variables, an inclusive index of the "price" of a trip in terms of time and cost, an index of the "attractiveness" of each shopping destination, and an interaction of the inclusive price index and a socioeconomic variable, the number of preschool children. The inclusive price is defined from the shopping mode choice Model 1 to be

$$[\text{Inclusive price}] = 0.0654[\text{Auto in-vehicle time}] + 4.11[\text{Auto operating cost}].$$

The measure of destination attractiveness is taken to be the retail employment in the zone as a percentage of total retail employment in the region. Because the alternative destinations are unranked and vary from one observation to the next, the explanatory variables enter generically. In particular, it is assumed that there are no "specific destination" effects. The results of the estimation are given in Table 4. The two independent variables above are both found to be

TABLE 4

CONDITIONAL LOGIT MODEL OF SHOPPING DESTINATION CHOICE; DEPENDENT VARIABLE EQUALS THE LOG ODDS THAT ONE DESTINATION ZONE IS CHOSEN OVER A SECOND; MULTINOMIAL LOGIT MAXIMUM LIKELIHOOD ESTIMATES; STANDARD ERRORS IN PARENTHESES

Independent variable	Model 5	Model 6
Inclusive price of trip (weighted time and cost using Model 1 weights)	−1.06 (0.28)	−0.602 (0.159)
Index of attractiveness of destination	0.844 (0.227)	0.832 (0.224)
Interaction effect equals the inclusive price of trip times the number of preschool children	—	−0.521 (0.343)

highly significant. Model 6 yields calculated selection probabilities which are maximum for the actual destination in 29 cases, as opposed to a match for 16 cases which would be expected by chance.

Shopping trip frequency

The decision of whether to take a shopping trip on a given day is analyzed for a sample of 80 households in the southern suburban corridor, of whom 59 recorded a shopping trip on the survey day. An inclusive price of a trip for nontrip takers is calculated by assuming that the distribution of destination preferences is that determined in Model 6, and that utility has a separable form implying this distribution is independent of the distribution of tastes for taking auto trips. The independent variables in the model are the preference-distribution-weighted inclusive price, the measure of attractiveness of shopping zone used above, similarly weighted, and a household-income shopping trip

TABLE 5

CONDITIONAL LOGIT MODEL OF SHOPPING TRIP FREQUENCY; DEPENDENT VARIABLE EQUALS THE LOG ODDS OF MAKING A SHOPPING TRIP ON SAMPLED DAY; BINOMIAL LOGIT MAXIMUM LIKELIHOOD ESTIMATES; STANDARD ERRORS IN PARENTHESES

Independent variable	Model 7	Model 8
Inclusive price of trip (weighted time and cost using Model 6 weights)	−1.72 (0.54)	−2.25 (0.68)
Index of attractiveness of destination	3.90 (1.08)	2.85 (1.19)
Family income	—	−0.199 (0.195)

interaction variable. The estimates are given in Table 5. Model 7 predicts the actual decision with probability 0.5 or better for 60 of the 80 observations.

The models above of shopping mode, destination, and frequency decisions can be combined with distributions of the independent variables in an urban area to produce trip generation and distribution tables by mode.[18] These

[18] Such tables could also be generated by aggregating over individuals for a random sample of the population, a procedure that requires a smaller sample than that necessary to obtain accurate cell frequencies for a detailed classification of multiple-independent variables. In particular, the sample used to calibrate the models may be utilized to produce trip tables. On the other hand, when samples of sufficient size are available to obtain cell frequencies, it may be possible to calibrate the model using the Berkson–Theil estimation procedure.

tables are functions of policy variables such as transit fares and wait times, and can be recalculated to forecast the effects of policy changes on the transportation system. Because the parameters are estimated from data at the level of the individual decision, they do not suffer from the "fallacy of composition" that could occur in attempting to infer response elasticities from data on behavior of heterogeneous groups. Thus, this modeling approach has the potential of providing accurate forecasts of the response of shopping travel demand to policy variables, in a framework that exploits the common thread of utility maximization and taste distribution in a variety of choice situations.

The empirical study summarized above represents a typical application of the theory of qualitative choice behavior of populations of consumers, with the conditional logit specification of the distribution of tastes. For applications in which the independence of irrelevant alternatives is plausible, this statistical procedure provides an analog for qualitative dependent variables of the conventional linear statistical model.

Appendix: Proofs of Statistical Properties

This section outlines proofs of Lemmas 5 and 6, and the properties of statistics based on weighted residuals.

LEMMA 5. Suppose Axioms 1–4 and 7 hold. Then the probability that the maximum likelihood estimator exists approaches unity as $\sum_{n=1}^{N} R_n$ approaches infinity.

Proof: As noted in the text, Axiom 7 implies that Axiom 5 holds when $\sum_{n=1}^{N} R_n$ is large. We next show that Axiom 7 implies a second linear independence condition. Let m be a serial index of trials and repetition; e.g., m identifies the r_mth repetition of trial n_m. We shall show that there exists an infinite subset M of the indices m, and integers i_m, j_m satisfying $1 \leqslant i_m$, $j_m \leqslant J_{n_m}$ such that each sequence of K successive vectors $z_{i_m n_m} - z_{j_m n_m}$ for $m \in M$ are linearly independent. We proceed by induction. Axiom 7 implies there is some m, i, j such that $z_{in_m} - z_{jn_m} \neq 0$; set $M_1 = \{m\}$, $i_1 = i$, and $j_1 = j$. Suppose that we have constructed a set M_{l-1} containing $l-1$ indices that satisfy the required property. Suppose there does not exist an index m_l such that $M_l = M_{l-1} \cup \{m_l\}$ has the desired property. Then, for all $m > m_{l-1}$ and $1 \leqslant i, j \leqslant J_{n_m}$, the vector $z_{in_m} - z_{jn_m}$ can be written as a linear combination of vectors $z_{i_p n_p} - z_{j_p n_p}$ for the last $K-1$ or fewer elements p of M_{l-1}. But then $z_{in_m} - \bar{z}_{n_m} = \sum_{j=1}^{J_{n_m}} P_{jn_m}(z_{in_m} - z_{jn_m})$ also has this property, implying that the limiting matrix Ω in Axiom 7 is singular, for a contradiction. Hence, by induction, the set $M = \bigcup_{l=1}^{\infty} M_l$ has the desired property.

Partition the set M into successive subsets $M^1, M^2, \ldots$, each containing K

elements. Let W^q denote the matrix with rows $z_{i_m n_m} - z_{j_m n_m}$ for $m \in M^q$. Then, W^q is nonsingular and the linear transformation $(W^{q-1})(W^q)^{-1}$ is continuous. Hence, for even q one can define a strictly positive vector a^{q-1} and a vector a^q with no zero elements such that $a^q W^q = a^{q-1} W^{q-1}$.

For q even, consider the event in which alternative i_m is chosen for $m \in M^{q-1}$; alternative i_m is chosen for $m \in M^q$ if $a_m{}^q$ is negative; and alternative j_m is chosen for $m \in M^q$ if $a_m{}^q$ is positive. Suppose this event occurs, but Axiom 6 fails, and let $\gamma \neq 0$ be such that $S_{in}(z_{jn} - z_{in})\gamma \leqslant 0$ for all i, j, n. Then, $W^{q-1}\gamma$ is a nonnegative vector. Since W^{q-1} is nonsingular, it has at least one component positive. Hence, $a^q W^q \gamma = a^{q-1} W^{q-1} \gamma > 0$. But z^q and $W^q\gamma$ have opposite signs in each component, contradicting the last inequality. Therefore, when this event occurs, Axiom 6 holds and the maximum likelihood estimator exists.

The selection probabilities are bounded below by

$$P_{in} \geqslant 1/J_* e^{2M|\theta|} \equiv P_* > 0, \tag{42}$$

where J_* and M are the bounds given by Axiom 7. Hence, the probability that the event above occurs for an even q is at least P_*^{2K}, and the probability that this event occurs for some even $q \leqslant 2q'$ is at least $1 - (1 - P_*^{2K})^{q'}$. This last probability approaches unity as $q' \to +\infty$, proving the lemma.

LEMMA 6. Suppose Axioms 1–4 and 7 hold, θ^0 is the true parameter vector and $\hat{\theta}^m$ is the maximum likelihood estimator for a sample of size $m = \sum_{n=1}^{N} R_n$. Then $\hat{\theta}^m$ is consistent and asymptotically normal as $m \to +\infty$, with

$$\sqrt{m}\,\Omega^{1/2}(\hat{\theta}^m - \theta^0),$$

tending to a multivariate normal distribution with mean zero and identity covariance matrix.

Proof: We shall first establish that $\hat{\theta}^m$ is a consistent estimator of θ^0. From Axiom 7, $|z_{in}| \leqslant M$ for a positive scalar M. Differentiation of Equation (16) yields the bounds

$$\left|\frac{\partial \log P_{in}}{\partial \theta}\right| \leqslant 2M,$$

$$\left|\frac{\partial^2 \log P_{in}}{\partial \theta\, \partial \theta'}\right| \leqslant 4M^2, \tag{43}$$

$$\left|\frac{\partial^3 \log P_{in}}{\partial \theta\, \partial \theta'\, \partial \theta_k}\right| \leqslant 8M^3,$$

uniform in θ.

Let m be a serial index of trials and repetitions, and let S_{im} equal unity if alternative i is chosen at this observation and zero otherwise, for $1 \leqslant i \leqslant J_{n_m}$. Define a sequence of independent random variables

(44) $$\lambda^m(\theta) = \sum_{i=1}^{J_{nm}} S_{im} \log P_{in}(\theta).$$

Then

(45) $$L^q(\theta) = C_q + \sum_{m=1}^{q} \lambda^m(\theta),$$

with C_q a constant independent of θ, is the log likelihood function. From Equation (43), the derivatives of λ^m, denoted $\partial\lambda^m/\partial\theta = \lambda_\theta{}^m$, etc., satisfy the uniform bounds $|\lambda_\theta{}^m| \leqslant 2M$, $|\lambda^m_{\theta\theta'}| \leqslant 4M^2$, and $|\lambda^m_{\theta\theta'\theta_k}| \leqslant 8M^3$. Further,

(46) $$E\lambda_\theta{}^m(\theta^0) = \left[\sum_{i=1}^{J_{nm}} \frac{\partial P_{in_m}}{\partial\theta}\right]_{\theta^0} = 0.$$

Define

(47) $$\begin{aligned}\Omega_m &= -E\lambda^m_{\theta\theta'}(\theta^0)\\ &= \sum_{i=1}^{J_{nm}} (z_{in_m} - \bar{z}_{n_m})' P_{in_m}(z_{in_m} - \bar{z}_{n_m}).\end{aligned}$$

Then by Axiom 7,

(48) $$\lim_{q\to\infty} \frac{1}{q} \sum_{m=1}^{q} \Omega_m = \Omega.$$

Let β denote the smallest characteristic value of Ω. Then there exists q_0 such that for $q \geqslant q_0$, the smallest characteristic value of $(1/q)\sum_{m=1}^{q} \Omega_m$ is at least $\beta/2$.

Given a small positive scalar ε, choose $\delta = \min\{\varepsilon, \beta/4(1+4KM^3)\}$. The strong law of large numbers (Feller, 1966, Vol. II, p. 233) implies that there exists $q_1 \geqslant q_0$ such that for $q \geqslant q_1$, $L_\theta{}^q(\theta^0) = \sum_{m=1}^{q} \lambda_\theta{}^m(\theta^0)$ satisfies

(49) $$\left|\frac{1}{q} L_\theta{}^q(\theta^0)\right| < \delta^2,$$

with probability at least $1-\varepsilon$.

A second-order Taylor's expansion of $L^q_{\theta_k}$ about θ^0 yields

(50) $$\frac{1}{q} L^q_{\theta_k}(\theta) - \frac{1}{q} L^q_{\theta_k\theta}(\theta^0)(\theta-\theta^0) = \frac{1}{q} L^q_{\theta_k}(\theta^0) + \frac{1}{2}\frac{1}{q}(\theta-\theta^0)' L^q_{\theta_k\theta\theta'}(\bar{\theta})(\theta-\theta^0),$$

where $\tilde{\theta}$ lies between θ and θ^0. Consider $q \geqslant q_1$ and θ satisfying

$$(\theta-\theta^0)'(\theta-\theta^0) = \delta^2,$$

and suppose Equation (49) holds. Then

$$(51)\qquad \left|\frac{1}{q}L^q_{\theta_k}(\theta) - \frac{1}{q}L^q_{\theta_k\theta}(\theta^0)(\theta-\theta^0)\right| \leqslant \delta^2(1+4K^2M^3) \leqslant \delta\beta/4.$$

Hence,

$$(52)\qquad \frac{1}{q}|(\theta-\theta^0)'L_\theta{}^q(\theta) - (\theta-\theta^0)'L_{\theta\theta'}(\theta^0)(\theta-\theta^0)| \leqslant \delta^2\beta/4.$$

But $(1/q)(\theta-\theta^0)'L_{\theta\theta'}(\theta^0)(\theta-\theta^0) \leqslant -\delta^2\beta/2$, implying

$$(53)\qquad \frac{1}{q}(\theta-\theta^0)'L_\theta{}^q(\theta) \leqslant -\delta^2\beta/4.$$

Hence, at each point on the sphere $(\theta-\theta^0)'(\theta-\theta^0) = \delta^2$, the gradient $L_\theta{}^q(\theta)$ is directed inward. Since L^q is concave in θ, this implies that a maximum $\hat{\theta}^q$ of L^q is achieved inside this sphere. Since this event occurs with probability at least $1-\varepsilon$, we have proved the estimator to be consistent.

We next show that $\sqrt{q}\,\Omega^{1/2}(\hat{\theta}^q-\theta^0)$ is asymptotically standard multivariate normal. Evaluating the Taylor's expansion (50) at the maximum likelihood estimator yields

$$(54)\qquad 0 = \frac{1}{q}L^q_{\theta_k}(\theta^0) + \frac{1}{q}L^q_{\theta_k\theta}(\theta^0)(\theta-\theta^0) + 4M^3|\hat{\theta}^q-\theta^0|\,a_k(\theta-\theta^0),$$

where a_k is a $1\times K$ vector depending on $\hat{\theta}^q$, which satisfies $|a_k| \leqslant 1$. Letting A denote the matrix with rows a_k and defining

$$(55)\qquad D_q = \Omega^{-1/2}\left(\frac{1}{q}\sum_{m=1}^{q}\Omega_m - 4M^3|\hat{\theta}^q-\theta^0|A\right)\Omega^{-1/2},$$

Equation (54) can be written

$$(56)\qquad \frac{1}{\sqrt{q}}\Omega^{1/2}D_q[\sqrt{q}\,\Omega^{1/2}(\hat{\theta}^q-\theta^0)] = \frac{1}{q}L_\theta{}^q(\theta^0).$$

Then,

$$(57)\qquad \operatorname*{plim}_{q\to\infty} D_q = I - 4M^3\Omega^{-1/2}A\Omega^{-1/2}\operatorname*{plim}_{q\to\infty}|\hat{\theta}^q-\theta^0| = I.$$

Hence, $\sqrt{q}\,\Omega^{1/2}(\hat{\theta}^q-\theta^0)$ has the same asymptotic distribution as

$$(58)\qquad \frac{1}{q}\Omega^{-1/2}L_\theta{}^q(\theta^0) = \frac{1}{q}\sum_{m=1}^{q}\Omega^{-1/2}\lambda_\theta{}^m(\theta^0).$$

But the independent random variables $\Omega^{-1/2}\lambda_\theta{}^m(\theta^0)$ satisfy the Lindeberg–Levy theorem (Feller, 1966, Vol. II, pp. 256–258), implying that Equation (58) is asymptotic standard normal. This proves the lemma.

Since $\sqrt{q}\,\Omega^{1/2}(\hat{\theta}^q-\theta^0)$ is asymptotically standard multivariate normal, it follows that $q(\hat{\theta}^q-\theta^0)'\Omega(\hat{\theta}^q-\theta^0)$ is asymptotically chi-square with K degrees of freedom. Further, a second-order Taylor's expansion of the log-likelihood function about $\hat{\theta}^q$ can be used to establish that $q(\hat{\theta}^q-\theta^0)'\Omega(\hat{\theta}^q-\theta^0)$ and $2[L(\theta^0)-L(\hat{\theta})]$ converge in probability, and hence have the same asymptotic distribution. This argument justifies use of the statistic (29). Details of the proof can be found in Theil (1971, p. 396), Rao (1968, pp. 347–351), and Kendall and Stuart (1967, Vol. II, pp. 230–236). Rao gives several asymptotically equivalent forms for the test.

Consider the weighted residuals D_{in} in Equation (31). Define

$$D_{in}^0 = \frac{S_{in}-R_n P_{in}^0}{(R_n P_{in}^0)^{1/2}}, \tag{59}$$

$$D_{in}^1 = \sum_{m=1}^{N}\sum_{j=1}^{J_m}(r_n r_m P_{in}^0 P_{jm}^0)^{1/2}(z_{in}-\bar{z}_n)\Omega^{-1}(z_{jm}-\bar{z}_m)'D_{jm}^0, \tag{60}$$

where $P_{in}^0 = P_{in}(\theta^0)$. Then D_{in}^0 has a multivariate distribution with $ED_{in}^0=0$ and $ED_{in}^0 D_{jm}^0 = \delta_{nm}[\delta_{ij}-(P_{in}^0 P_{jn}^0)^{1/2}]$, implying $ED_{in}^1 = 0$,

$$ED_{in}^0 D_{jm}^1 = (r_n r_m P_{in}^0 P_{jm}^0)^{1/2}(z_{in}-\bar{z}_n)\Omega^{-1}(z_{jm}-\bar{z}_m), \tag{61}$$

and asymptotically

$$ED_{in}^1 D_{jm}^1 = (r_n r_m P_{in}^0 P_{jm}^0)^{1/2}(z_{in}-\bar{z}_n)\Omega^{-1}(z_{jm}-\bar{z}_m). \tag{62}$$

Making Taylor's expansions, one can show that the random variables

$$\frac{(R_n)^{1/2}(P_{in}^0-P_{in})}{(P_{in}^0)^{1/2}} \quad \text{and} \quad (r_n P_{in}^0)^{1/2}(z_{in}-\bar{z}_n)\left(\sum_{n=1}^{N} R_n\right)^{1/2}(\theta^0-\hat{\theta})$$

differ from $-D_{in}^1$ by terms with probability limits zero. It then follows, since $(\sum_{n=1}^{N} R_n)^{1/2}(\theta^0-\hat{\theta})$ is asymptotic normal with mean zero and covariance matrix Ω, that these three random variables have a common asymptotic normal distribution. Hence, $D_{in}^0 - D_{in}^1$ has an asymptotic distribution with mean zero and covariance

$$\begin{aligned}\Lambda_{in,jm} &= \delta_{nm}[\delta_{ij}-(P_{in}^0 P_{jm}^0)^{1/2}] \\ &\quad -(r_n r_m P_{in}^0 P_{jm}^0)^{1/2}(z_{in}-\bar{z}_n)\Omega^{-1}(z_{jm}-\bar{z}_m).\end{aligned} \tag{63}$$

Write

$$D_{in} = \frac{S_{in}-R_n P_{in}^0}{(R_n P_{in})^{1/2}} + \frac{(R_n)^{1/2}(P_{in}^0-P_{in}^0)}{(P_{in})^{1/2}}. \tag{64}$$

The first term differs from D_{in}^0, and the second from $-D_{in}^1$, by factors with probability limits zero. Hence, D_{in} has the same asymptotic distribution as $D_{in}^0 - D_{in}^1$. When the R_n approach infinity, D_{in}^0 is asymptotically normal, implying D_{in} asymptotically normal. The covariance matrix can be written

$$(65) \qquad \Lambda = I - \sum_{m=0}^{N} q_m q_m',$$

where

$$(q_0)_{in} = (r_n P_{in}^0)^{1/2}(z_{in} - \bar{z}_n)\Omega^{-1/2},$$
$$(q_m)_{in} = \delta_{mn}(P_{in}^0)^{1/2}, \qquad m = 1, \ldots, N.$$

The vectors q_m are orthonormal, implying Λ idempotent of rank $N^* = \sum_{n=1}^N J_n - N - K$. Then $G = \sum_{n=1}^N \sum_{j=1}^{J_n} D_{in}^2$ has an asymptotic chi-square distribution with N^* degrees of freedom (Rao, 1968, p. 149).

Next consider the linear transformations

$$(66) \qquad Y_{in} = D_{in} - D_{1n}(P_{in})^{1/2}\alpha_n, \qquad i = 2, \ldots, J_n,$$

where $\alpha_n = [1 - (P_{1n})^{1/2}](1 - P_{1n})$. Then, Y_{in} has the same asymptotic distribution as the random variable Y_{in}^0 formed by replacing P_{in} with P_{in}^0 in Equation (66), and the latter random variable has asymptotic moments $EY_{in}^0 = 0$ and

$$\begin{aligned} \Gamma_{in,jm} = EY_{in}^0 Y_{jm}^0 &= ED_{in}D_{jm} - (P_{jm}^0)^{1/2}\alpha_m ED_{in}D_{1m} \\ &\quad - (P_{in}^0)^{1/2}\alpha_n ED_{1n}D_{jm} + (P_{in}^0 P_{jm}^0)^{1/2}\alpha_n\alpha_m ED_{1n}D_{1m} \\ &= \delta_{nm}\delta_{ij} - q_{in}' q_{jm}, \end{aligned}$$

with

$$q_{in}' = (r_n P_{in}^0)^{1/2}\left((z_{in} - \bar{z}_n) + \frac{P_{1n}^0 - (P_{1n}^0)^{1/2}}{1 - P_{1n}^0}(z_{1n} - \bar{z}_n)\right)\Omega^{-1/2}.$$

Then, $\sum_{n=1}^N \sum_{i=2}^{J_n} q_{in} q_{in}' = I_K$ and Γ is idempotent of rank N^*. Hence,

$$\sum_{n=1}^{N}\sum_{i=2}^{J_n} Y_{in}^2 = \sum_{n=1}^{N}\sum_{i=1}^{J_n} D_{in}^2$$

has an asymptotic chi-square distribution with N^* degrees of freedom.

REFERENCES

Aitchison, J. and J. Bennett (1970). "Polychotomous quantal response by maximum indicant," *Biometrika* **57**, 253–262.

Aitchison, J. and S. Silvey (1957). "The Generalization of Probit Analysis to the Case of Multiple Responses," *Biometrika* **44**, 131–140.

Allouche, J. (1972). "Approach to Probability Distribution of Value of Walking Time and Pedestrian Circulation Models," *Highway Res. Rec.* **392**, 121–133.

Amemiya, T. (1972). "Bivariate Probit Analysis: Minimum Chi-Square Methods," Dept. of Econ., Stanford Univ., Stanford, California, unpublished.

Amemiya, T. and M. Boskin (1972). "Regression Analysis when the Dependent Variable is Truncated Lugnormal, with An Application to the Determinants of the Duration of Welfare Dependency," Inst. for Math. Stud. in the Soc. Sci., Stanford Univ., Stanford, California, Tech. Rep. No. 75.

Antle, C., L. Klimko and W. Harkness (1970). "Confidence intervals for the parameters of the logistic distribution," *Biometrika* **57**, 397–402.

Atkinson, A. (1972). "A Test of the Linear Logistic and Bradley-Terry Models," *Biometrika* **59**, 37–42.

Berkson, J. (1951). "Why I prefer Logits to Probits," *Biometrics* **7**, 327–339.

Berkson, J. (1955). "Maximum Likelihood and Minimum Chi-Square Estimates of the Logistic Function," *J. Amer. Statist. Ass.* **50**, 130–162.

Bloch, D. and G. Watson (1967). "A Bayesian Study of the Multinomial Distribution," *Ann. Math. Statist.* **38**, 1423–1435.

Block, H. and J. Marschak (1960). "Random Orderings and Stochastic Theories of Response," *In Contributions to Probability and Statistics* (I. Olkin, ed.). Stanford Univ. Press, Stanford, California.

Bock, R. (1969). "Estimating Multinomial Response Relations," *In Contributions to Statistics and Probability: Essays in Memory of S. N. Roy* (R. Bose, ed.). Univ. of North Carolina Press.

Boskin, M. (1972). "A Conditional Logit Model of Occupational Choice," Dept. of Econ., Stanford Univ., Stanford, California, unpublished.

Cox, D. (1958). "The Regression Analysis of Binary Sequences," *J. Roy. Statist. Soc. Ser. B*, **20**, 215–242.

Cox, D. (1966). "Some Procedures Connected with the Logistic Qualitative Response Curve," *Research Papers in Statistics* (F. David, ed.), pp. 55–71. Wiley, New York.

Cox, D. (1970). *Analysis of Binary Data.* Methuen, London.

Cox, D. and E. Snell (1968). "A General Definition of Residuals," *J. Roy. Statist. Soc. Ser B* **30**, 248–265.

Cox, D. and E. Snell (1971). "On Test Statistics Calculated from Residuals," *Biometrika* **58**, 589–594.

Domencich, T. and D. McFadden (1972). *A Disaggregated Behavioral Model of Urban Travel Demand,* Report No. CRA-156-2, Charles River Associates, Inc., Cambridge, Massachusetts.

Ergun, G. (1971). "Development of a Downtown Parking Mode," *Highway Res. Rec.* **369**, 118–134.

Feller, W. (1966). *An Introduction to Probability Theory and Its Applications*, Vol. 2, Wiley, New York.

Finney, D. (1952). *Probit Analysis.* Cambridge Univ. Press, London and New York.

Fisher, J. (1962). "An Analysis of Consumer Goods Expenditures in 1957," *Rev. Econ. Statist.* **44**, 64–71.

Gart, J. and J. Zweifel (1967). "On the Bias of Various Estimators of the Logit and its Variance," *Biometrika* **54**, 181–187.

Gilbert, E. (1968). "On Discrimination Using Qualitative Variables," *J. Amer. Statist. Ass.* **63**, 1399–1412.

Goodman, L. (1970). "The Multivariate Analysis of Qualitative Data: Interactions Among Multiple Classifications," *J. Amer. Statist. Ass.* **65**, 226–256.

Goodman, L. (1972). "A Modified Multiple Regression Approach to the Analysis of Dichotomous Variables," *Amer. Sociolog. Rev.* **37**, 28–46.

Grizzle, J. (1962). "Asymptotic Power of Tests of Linear Hypotheses Using the Probit and Logit Transformation," *J. Amer. Statist. Ass.* **57**, 877–894.

Grizzle, J. (1971). "Multivariate Logit Analysis," *Biometrics* **27**, 1057–1062.

Gupta, S., A. Qureishi and B. Shah (1967). "Best Linear Unbiased Estimators of the Parameters of the Logistic Distribution Using Order Statistics," *Technometrics* **9**, 43–56.

Gurland, J., I. Lee and P. Dolan (1960). "Polychotomous quantal response in biological assay," *Biometrics* **16**, 382–398.

Harter, J. and A. Moore (1967). "Maximum likelihood estimation, from censored samples, of the parameters of a logistic distribution," *J. Amer. Statist. Ass.* **62**, 675–683.

Kendall, M. and A. Stuart (1967). *The Advanced Theory of Statistics*. Vol. 2. Hafner, New York.

Korbel, J. (1966). "Labor Force Entry and Attachment of Young People," *J. Amer. Statist. Ass.* **61**, 117–127.

Lave, C. (1968). Modal Choice in Urban Transportation: A Behavioral Approach. Dept. of Econ., Stanford Univ., Stanford, California, Ph.D. dissertation.

Lee, T. (1963). "Demand for Housing: A Cross-Section Analysis," *Rev. Econ. Statist.* **45**, 190–196.

Leonard, T. (1972). "Bayesian Methods for Multinomial Data," *American College Testing Program*, Tech. Bull. No. 4.

Lisco, T. (1967). The Value of Commuters' Travel Time: A Study in Urban Transportation. Dept. of Econ., Univ. of Chicago, Chicago, Illinois, Ph.D. dissertation.

Luce, R. (1959). *Individual Choice Behavior*. Wiley, New York.

Luce, R. and P. Suppes (1965). "Preference, Utility, and Subjective Probability," *In Handbook of Mathematical Psychology* (R. Luce, R. Bush, and E. Galanter, eds.), Vol. 3. Wiley, New York.

Marschak, J. (1960). "Binary Choice Constraints on Random Utility Indicators," *In Stanford Symp. Math. Methods Soc. Sci.* (K. Arrow, ed.). Stanford Univ. Press, Stanford, California.

McFadden, D. (1968). "The Revealed Preferences of a Government Bureaucracy," Dept. of Econ., Univ. of California, Berkeley, California, unpublished.

McFadden, D. and M. Richter (1971). "On the extension of a set function to a probability on the Boolean algebra generated by a family of events, with applications," Working Paper 14, MSSB Workshop on the Theory of Markets under Uncertainty, Dept. of Econ., Univ. of California, Berkeley, California.

McGillivray, R. (1969). Binary Choice of Transport Mode in the San Francisco Bay Area, Dept. of Econ., Univ. of California, Berkeley, California, Ph.D. dissertation.

McGillivray, R. (1970). "Demand and Choice Models of Modal Split," *J. Transport Econ. Policy* **4**, 192–207.

Miller, L. and R. Radner (1970). "Demand and Supply in U.S. Higher Education," *Amer. Econ. Rev. Papers & Proceedings*, **60**, 326–340.

Miller, L. and R. Radner (forthcoming). *Demand and Supply in U.S. Higher Education*, Carnegie Commission on the Future of U.S. Higher Education.

Moses, L., R. Beals and M. Levy (1967). "Rationality and Migration in Ghana," *Rev. Econ. Statist.* **49**, 480–486.

Quandt, R. (1968). "Estimation of Modal Splits," *Transportat. Res.* **2**, 41–50.

Quandt, R. (1970). *The Demand for Travel*. Heath.

Quandt, R. and W. Baumol (1966). "The Demand for Abstract Transport Modes: Theory and Measurement," *J. Regional Sci.* **6**, 13–26.

Quandt, R. and K. Young (1969). "Cross Sectional Travel Demand Models: Estimation and Tests," *J. Regional Sci.* **9**, 201–214.

Quarmby, D. (1967). "Choice of Travel Mode for the Journey to Work: Some Findings," *J. Transport Econ. Policy*.

Rao, C. (1965). *Linear Statistical Inference and its Applications*. Wiley, New York.

Rassam, P., R. Ellis and J. Bennett (1971). "The n-Dimensional Logit Model: Development and Application," *Highway Res. Rec.* **369**, 135–147.

Reichman, S. and P. Stopher (1971). "Disaggregate Stochastic Models of Travel-Mode Choice," *Highway Res. Rec.* **369**, 91–103.

Stopher, P. (1969). "A Multinomial Extension of the Binary Logit Model for Choice of Mode of Travel," Northwestern Univ., unpublished.

Stopher, P. and T. Lisco (1970). "Modelling Travel Demand: A Disaggregate Behavioral Approach—Issues and Applications," *Transportat. Res. Forum Proc.* pp. 195–214.

Stopher, P. (1969). "A Probability Model of Travel Mode Choice for the Work Journey," *Highway Res. Rec.* **283**, 57–65.

Talvitie, A. (1972). "Comparison of Probabilistic Modal-Choice Models: Estimation Methods and System Inputs," *Highway Res. Rec.* **392**, 111–120.

Theil, H. (1969). "A Multinomial Extension of the Linear Logit Model," *Int. Econ. Rev.* **10**, 251–259.

Theil, H. (1970). "On the Estimation of Relationships involving Qualitative Variables," *Amer. J. Sociol.* **76**, 103–154.

Theil, H. (1971). *Principles of Econometrics*, Wiley, New York.

Thomas, T. and G. Thompson (1971). "Value of Time Saved by Trip Purpose," *Highway Res. Rec.* **369**, 104–113.

Thurstone, L. (1927). "A Law of Comparative Judgment," *Psycholog. Rev.* **34**, 273–286.

Tobin, J. (1958). "Estimation of Relationships for Limited Dependent Variables," *Econometrica* **26**.

Tversky, A. and J. Russo (1969). "Substitutability and Similarity in Binary Choice ," *J. Math. Psychol.* **6**, 1–12.

Uhler, R. (1968). "The Demand for Housing: An Inverse Probability Approach," *Rev. Econ. Statist.* 50, 129–134.

Walker, F. (1968). "Determinants of auto scrappage," *Rev. Econ. Statist.* **50**, 503–506.

Walker, S. and D. Duncan (1967). "Estimation of the Probability of an Event as a Function of Several Independent Variables," *Biometrika* **54**, 167–179.

Warner, S. (1962). *Stochastic Choice of Mode in Urban Travel: A Study in Binary Choice*. Northwestern Univ. Press, Evanston, Illinois.

Zellner, A. and T. Lee (1965). "Joint Estimation of Relationships Involving Discrete Random Variables," *Econometrica* **33**, 382–394.

Zinnes, J. (1969). "Scaling," *Ann. Rev. Psychol.* **20**, 447–478.

[9]

Environment and Planning A, 1977, volume 9, pages 285-344

On the formation of travel demand models and economic evaluation measures of user benefit†

H C W L Williams¶
Institute for Transport Studies, University of Leeds, Leeds, LS2 9JT, England
Received 16 August 1976, in revised form 26 October 1976

Abstract. This paper examines a variety of issues within the context of two main themes: the formation of travel demand models and economic evaluation measures which are mutually consistent within a theory of rational choice; and a consideration of the structure of models which are representations of the trip decision process over several dimensions: location, mode, and route. Random utility theory is invoked to explore both the role and properties of composite costs or index prices in the 'recursive' approach to the structuring of travel choice models, and their significance in the economic evaluation problem. It is shown that the specification of these costs must be made very precisely, with respect to the demand model form chosen, in order to retain the underlying assumption that the traveller is an optimal decisionmaker. It is argued that the structure of 'simultaneous' models *currently in use* is inconsistent with the form of utility function assumed to generate those models. Furthermore, it is shown that the 'simultaneous' and 'recursive' forms are special cases of a more general choice model structure which takes specific account of correlation or 'commonality' of trip attributes.

A number of applications are discussed in which consistent demand models and perceived user benefit measures are constructed. These include the formation of strategic transport planning models and of models for mixed-mode, multimode, and multiroute systems. The formalism allows definitive answers to be given to a number of problems of current interest in transportation planning, which have been incorrectly or incompletely treated.

1 Introduction and summary

Over the past twenty years, work in universities, government agencies, and transportation studies has spawned a vast literature relating to the theoretical, methodological, and computational aspects of travel demand forecasting and its role in the transport planning process. Excellent reviews of passenger-demand forecasting models developed both within a research and planning context have been provided by Charles River Associates (CRA, 1972), Ruiter (1973), Brand (1973), and Wilson (1973a).

In recent years the Urban Transport Planning process, which evolved during the 1950s and through the 1960s, has received a battery of criticism, and not least the mathematical models which lie at its heart. The fundamental limitations of traditional demand models and the framework within which they are applied are both being subjected to considerable reappraisal. Four aspects which have attracted particular attention are: the descriptive rather than causal nature of travel demand relationships; the nonpolicy orientation of the models; the development of models at an aggregate level rather than the level of the decisionmaking unit; and the internal inconsistencies of the representation of the trip decision process itself.

This paper will be concerned directly with these four issues and with the naturally related but sadly neglected problem of developing an economic evaluation methodology, based on generalised consumer surplus, which is fully consistent with the demand models used to predict the effect of transport system changes. This consistency is indeed required by the theory of revealed preference.

† An initial version of this paper was presented by the author at the conference on Urban Transport Planning, University of Leeds, Leeds, England, 29 March-1 April 1976.

¶ Present address: School of Geography, University of Leeds, Leeds, LS2 9JT, England.

The main conclusions of the paper, which I have attempted to justify theoretically, are threefold. *First,* the models used in transportation studies, which purport to represent the collective choice of rational decisionmakers, are, without exception, inconsistent with the theory of choice, and are thus subject to misspecification errors. A consistent analytic representation of the trip decision process and compatible measures of user benefit may be found within the framework of random utility theory. The assumption of optimality, which characterises the decision process, imposes restrictions on the resultant choice models, the analytic structure of which is governed by the form and properties of utility (or, alternatively, suitably defined disutility or cost) functions which are used to record preferences.

Second, much recent research which has been devoted to the formation of behavioural models within the framework of probabilistic choice theory may be shown to be theoretically incorrect for failing to relate the analytic structure of models to the utility functions which are assumed to generate them, and, in particular, for the failure to recognise the role of attribute correlation in the choice process.

Third, the 'trapezoidal' or 'rule-of-a-half' measure which is used to determine user benefit is not only computationally inefficient, but also its marginal basis renders it inappropriate for assessing the economic value of a large number of transport systems which involve the introduction of new facilities (or movements). In contrast to the common method of extracting user benefits *after* the forecasting process, the condition of optimality which underpins the behavioural models allows the economic evaluation measures to be extracted directly from the calculations performed *during* model implementation. For urban transport planning models this distinction is between the assessment of benefits at the trip generation stage rather than *after* the assignment submodel. The resultant measures lay emphasis on quantities commonly interpreted as accessibility indices or rents rather than on movement costs in the conventional measure.

The paper itself is divided into three segments: the first, comprising sections 2 and 3, is concerned essentially with the statement and characteristics of problems to be tackled, some of which are rather well-known but have, in the author's opinion, been unsatisfactorily treated; the second, containing sections 4 and 5, sets out a theoretical framework within which the problems may be interpreted, analysed, and solved; and a final segment, consisting of section 6, deals with a considerable number of applications of the theory, which involve models of multidimensional choice, and the representation of travel demand in mixed-mode, multimode, and multiroute systems. Finally, urban travel demand models are analysed. Throughout, the emphasis is on generating an operational methodology.

2 Demand models, composite costs, and benefit analysis—some preliminaries

2.1 *Some characteristics of strategic transport planning models*

The general approach to forecasting travel demand in urban transport studies has traditionally been through the well-known sequence of generation, distribution, modal-split, and assignment submodels. Undoubtedly the greatest variation in the structures employed both by British and American studies has been associated with the modal-split stage—whether it has preceded, followed, or indeed combined with the distribution submodel.

The most common structures which have been imposed on the general urban travel demand model may be written in the product share forms (Manheim, 1973)

$$T_{ij}^{nkr} = G_i^n M_i^{nk} M_{ij}^{nk} M_{ij}^{nkr} , \quad (1)$$

$$T_{ij}^{nkr} = G_i^n M_{ij}^n M_{ij}^{nk} M_{ij}^{nkr} , \quad (2)$$

$$T_{ij}^{nkr} = G_i^n M_{ij}^{nk} M_{ij}^{nkr} . \quad (3)$$

These correspond respectively to predistribution, postdistribution, and joint-distribution modal-split models. Here T_{ij}^{nkr} represents the total demand for trips by mode k and route r between zones i and j by persons from households with socioeconomic characteristics n, while G_i^n denotes the number of trips generated in zone i by persons of type n. The definition of the shares M follows immediately. Thus, for example, M_i^{nk} represents the proportion of the G_i^n trips which selects mode k, while M_{ij}^{nk} in equation (1) is the proportion of the modal demand $G_i^n M_i^{nk}$ which is attracted to zone j. The shares may be given a probabilistic interpretation in terms of the probability of a person, drawn randomly from a suitably defined population, selecting a particular movement. For example, M_i^{nk}, which is subject to the normalisation condition

$$\sum_{k \in H(n)} M_i^{nk} = 1 , \tag{4}$$

represents the probability of a person, drawn randomly from the population G_i^n, selecting mode k. The notation $\sum_{k \in H(n)}$ denotes summation over all modes available to persons of type n. The share M_{ij}^{nkr} is the proportion of interzonal trips by mode k which selects route r from the set R of all routes between zones i and j available to mode k. M_{ij}^{nkr} usually has a very simple structure in transportation studies. If the allocation of demand to routes is taken to be consistent with Wardrop's (1952) first principle then

$$\sum_{r \in R^*(i, j)} M_{ij}^{nkr} = 1 , \tag{5}$$

$$M_{ij}^{nkr} = 0 , \quad \text{for} \quad r \notin R^*(i, j) , \tag{6}$$

with $R^*(i, j)$ denoting the set of routes between zones i and j, determined within the assignment procedure, which have perceived costs or disutilities equal to the minimum value

$$c_{ij}^k = \min_{r \in R(i, j)} c_{ij}^{kr} , \tag{7}$$

where c_{ij}^{kr} is the measure of disutility on route r. When $R^*(i, j)$ consists of a single route, an all-or-nothing assignment results. The quantities c_{ij}^k and c_{ij}^{kr}, which are usually taken as a combination of time and out-of-pocket costs, are frequently referred to as generalised costs and may be expressed in money or time units. The route index r will be dropped when the Wardrop conditions (5) to (7) are satisfied.

The problems of analytic structure, with which this paper is concerned, relate to the mathematical representation of the trip decision process and, in particular, the form of the demand function and the relationship between the socioeconomic, land-use, and transportation-system variables which enter it. Conventional urban transport planning models are calibrated with data pertaining to groups of people. Here I shall be concerned with aggregate models of this type, but mainly with disaggregate probabilistic models expressed and calibrated at the level of individual decisionmakers.

The first problem presents itself. What determines the analytic structure of the demand model, and which of the above forms (1) to (3), if any, is most appropriate for any given trip purpose? In section 5 below I shall compare my own discussion on this issue with the recent contributions of Manheim (1973), CRA (1972), Ben-Akiva (1973), and others.

2.2 *Composite costs*

In both the (pre' and postdistribution modal-split) structures (1) and (2) it has proved necessary, in order to implement the models, to define so-called composite costs, which have been the subject of much debate over the years. A penetrating discussion

Table 1. A selection of transportation models from British Studies. (For notation see appendix A.)

Study	Distribution model (work)	Composite cost function	Modal-split model
London Transport Study (Phase III), 1968	$T_{ij}^{n} = g_i^n a_j^n G_i^n A_j^n F_j^n(t_{ij}^n)\,, \quad n = 1$ $T_{ij}^{k} = g_i^k a_j^k G_i^k A_j^k F_j^k(t_{ij}^k)\,, \quad k = 2$	$t_{ij}^{n=1} = t_{ij}^{k=1}$	diversion curves
MALTS, 1969 (Merseyside Area)	$T_{ij}^{n} = g_i^n a_j^n G_i^n A_j^n F^n(t_{ij}^n)$	$F^n(t_{ij}^n) = \sum_{k \in H(n)} F^{nk}(t_{ij}^k)$	diversion curves
SELNEC Transportation Study, 1971 (South East Lancashire, North East Cheshire)	$T_{ij}^{n} = g_i^n a_j G_i^n A_j \exp(-\beta^n c_{ij}^n)$	$\exp(-\beta^n c_{ij}^n) = \sum_{k \in H(n)} \exp(-\beta^n c_{ij}^k)$	$M_{ij}^{nk} = \dfrac{\exp(-\lambda^n c_{ij}^k)}{\sum_{k \in H(n)} \exp(-\lambda^n c_{ij}^k)}$
Coventry Transportation Study, 1973	$T_{ij}^{n} = g_i^n a_j G_i^n A_j F^n(c_{ij}^n)$	$F^n(c_{ij}^n) = \sum_{k \in H(n)} F^k(c_{ij}^k)$	$M_{ij}^{nk} = \dfrac{F^k(c_{ij}^k)}{\sum_{k \in H(n)} F^k(c_{ij}^k)}$
Nottingham and Environs Transportation Study, 1974	$T_{ij}^{n} = g_i^n a_j G_i^n A_j \exp(-\beta^n c_{ij}^n)$	$\exp(-\beta^n c_{ij}^n) = \dfrac{1}{M} \sum_{k \in H(n)} \exp(-\beta^n c_{ij}^k)$ $M = 2 \text{ if } n = 1\,, \quad M = 1 \text{ if } n = 2$	$M_{ij}^{nk} = \dfrac{\exp(-\lambda^n c_{ij}^k)}{\sum_{k \in H(n)} \exp(-\lambda^n c_{ij}^k)}$
Sheffield-Rotherham Land-Use-Transportation Study, 1974	$T_{ij}^{n} = g_i^n a_j^n G_i^n A_j^n K_{ij}^n \exp(-\beta^n c_{ij}^n)$	$c_{ij}^n = \sum_{k \in H(n)} M_{ij}^{nk} c_{ij}^k$	$M_{ij}^{nk} = \dfrac{\exp(-\lambda^n c_{ij}^k)}{\sum_{k \in H(n)} \exp(-\lambda^n c_{ij}^k)}$

of this topic has been given by Wilson (1969). In the model form (2), for example, costs c_{ij}^{n}, which represent for persons of type n a perceived disutility of spatial separation, are defined in terms of the modal disutilities c_{ij}^{k}, $k \in H(n)$, through the relation

$$c_{ij}^{n} = c_{ij}^{n}(c_{ij}^{k_1}, c_{ij}^{k_2}, ...) , \tag{8}$$

which transfers modal cost information from the modal-split to the distribution process. A very popular form of composite cost is the weighted average

$$c_{ij}^{n} = \sum_{k \in H(n)} M_{ij}^{nk} c_{ij}^{k} , \tag{9}$$

in which M_{ij}^{nk} is the share of interzonal trips associated with mode k. A variety of other forms and their accompanying distribution and modal-split models, taken from British Transport Studies, are given in table 1. A similar specification problem occurs for the structure (1), in this case in the form

$$c_{i}^{nk} = c_{i}^{nk}(c_{ij_1}^{k}, c_{ij_2}^{k}, ...) , \tag{10}$$

which expresses the location dependent costs c_{i}^{nk} in terms of the interaction costs $c_{ij_1}^{k}, c_{ij_2}^{k}, ...$.

Further questions must be answered. Out of the rich variety of composite costs shown in table 1, which, if any, is appropriate? Does the choice of composite cost represent an extra degree of freedom in the model-building procedure—is the modeller at liberty to inject an arbitrary functional form? What is the role of composite cost in the representation of the trip decision process?

2.3 *User benefit analysis and composite costs*

Since its introduction in the London Transportation Study (Phase III, Tressider et al, 1968) the 'rule-of-a-half' (ROH) has been used widely for the purpose of determining user benefits arising from specific transport policies. If D_{ξ} and c_{ξ} represent the demand for, and cost associated with, movement ξ, such that

$$D_{\xi} = D_{\xi}(c_1, ..., c_{\xi}, ..., c_N) , \qquad \xi = 1, ..., N , \tag{11}$$

the 'rule-of-a-half' benefit measure may be written

$$\Delta S = \tfrac{1}{2}\sum_{\xi} (D_{\xi}^{\star} + D_{\xi}^{\bigstar})(c_{\xi}^{\star} - c_{\xi}^{\bigstar}) , \tag{12}$$

in which the superscripts ☆, ★ denote evaluation of the variable in the initial ('do nothing' or 'do minimum') and final (design) transportation systems, characterised by vectors of *perceived* costs $\boldsymbol{c}^{\star}$ and $\boldsymbol{c}^{\bigstar}$ respectively. [A discussion of the 'resource correction' has been given by McIntosh and Quarmby (1970).] The vectors $\boldsymbol{c}^{\star}$ and $\boldsymbol{c}^{\bigstar}$ have the following components:

$$\boldsymbol{c}^{\star} = (c_1^{\star}, ..., c_{\xi}^{\star}, ..., c_N^{\star}) , \qquad \boldsymbol{c}^{\bigstar} = (c_1^{\bigstar}, ..., c_{\xi}^{\bigstar}, ..., c_N^{\bigstar}) .$$

In terms of $\boldsymbol{c}$, the demand function D_{ξ} may be written

$$D_{\xi} = D_{\xi}(\boldsymbol{c}) , \qquad \xi = 1, ..., N . \tag{13}$$

In transportation studies the function D_{ξ} in equation (12) is taken as T_{ij}^{k} which corresponds to the total modal demand between zone pairs. ΔS becomes

$$\Delta S = \tfrac{1}{2}\sum_{ijk} (T_{ij}^{k\star} + T_{ij}^{k\bigstar})(c_{ij}^{k\star} - c_{ij}^{k\bigstar}) , \tag{14}$$

with T_{ij}^{k} given by

$$T_{ij}^{k} = \sum_{n \in K(k)} T_{ij}^{nk} . \tag{15}$$

Summation here is over all socioeconomic classes (usually taken as classes of car-ownership) which have the choice of mode k available to them.

A more fundamental measure of user benefit is given by the generalised surplus form proposed by Hotelling (1938)

$$\Delta S = -\sum_{\xi} \int_{c_\xi^*}^{c_\xi^\star} \mathrm{d}c_\xi D_\xi(c) \,, \tag{16}$$

in which the line integration is defined along a path P in cost-space parameterised by $\hat{\sigma}$

$$P : \boldsymbol{c} = \boldsymbol{c}(\hat{\sigma}) \,, \tag{17}$$

between the initial and final cost states $\boldsymbol{c}^*$ and $\boldsymbol{c}^\star$. The Hotelling measure (16) is a natural extension of the Marshallian measure,

$$\Delta S = -\sum_{\xi} \int_{c_\xi^*}^{c_\xi^\star} \mathrm{d}c_\xi D_\xi(c_\xi) \,, \tag{18}$$

to a general equilibrium setting in which the demand functions depend on all movement costs $c_1, ..., c_\xi, ..., c_N$.

As there are an infinity of ways of specifying the function (17), and therefore the paths between the initial and final cost states, it would appear that ΔS, as defined by equation (16), is completely arbitrary. If, however, the following integrability conditions

$$\frac{\partial D_\xi}{\partial c_{\xi'}} = \frac{\partial D_{\xi'}}{\partial c_\xi} \,, \qquad \xi, \xi' = 1, ..., N \,, \tag{19}$$

are satisfied by the demand function, the generalised surplus change ΔS is independent of path and defined uniquely.

It has been shown (Williams, 1976a) that the ROH benefit measure (12) may be generated from equation (16) by adopting a linear path of integration

$$\boldsymbol{c}(\hat{\sigma}) = [c_1^* + \hat{\sigma}(c_1^\star - c_1^*), ..., c_\xi^* + \hat{\sigma}(c_\xi^\star - c_\xi^*), ..., c_N^* + \hat{\sigma}(c_N^\star - c_N^*)] \,, \quad 0 \leqslant \hat{\sigma} \leqslant 1 \,, \tag{20}$$

such that

$$\Delta S = \sum_{\xi} (c_\xi^* - c_\xi^\star) \int_0^1 \mathrm{d}\hat{\sigma} D_\xi(\hat{\sigma}) \,, \tag{21}$$

and retaining terms up to first order in $\hat{\sigma}$ in a Taylor expansion of the demand function about the initial cost state $\boldsymbol{c}^* = \boldsymbol{c}$ $(\sigma = 0)$. Although the demand function may violate the integrability conditions, the linear path measure (12), a marginal approximation by virtue of the rejected terms in the expansion, may be regarded as an 'average' value of user benefit—a pragmatic rather than mathematical interpretation!

Consider now postdistribution models of the form

$$T_{ij}^k = T_{ij}(\boldsymbol{c}) M_{ij}^k(\boldsymbol{c}_{ij}) \,, \tag{22}$$

in which M_{ij}^k, the modal share, is a function of all modal costs associated with the zone pair $\{i, j\}$, which are the components of a vector $\boldsymbol{c}_{ij}$, and T_{ij} is a function of all interzonal composite costs c_{ij}, contained in $\boldsymbol{c}$. By straightforward differentiation we have

$$\frac{\partial T_{ij}^k}{\partial c_{i'j'}^k} = M_{ij}^k \frac{\partial T_{ij}}{\partial c_{i'j'}} \frac{\partial c_{i'j'}}{\partial c_{i'j'}^k} + T_{ij} \frac{\partial M_{ij}^k}{\partial c_{i'j'}^k} \,. \tag{23}$$

It can be seen from equation (23) that the integrability of the demand function is clearly dependent on the analytic forms of T_{ij}, M_{ij}^k, and, in particular, of the composite cost function c_{ij}.

The questions raised in this section are the following: what forms of demand function and composite cost are consistent with a unique definition of the generalised surplus economic evaluation measure, and what is the significance of a violation of the integrability conditions (19)?

2.4 *General issues*

Discussion has so far centred on some of the problems embedded in the conventional urban travel demand methodology. There are of course many other related issues in transport analysis which involve the construction of a consistent representation of trip decision processes and corresponding evaluation measures. In addition to general urban travel forecasting models, I shall discuss in section 6 the formation of demand models for multimode, mixed-mode, and multiroute transportation systems.

Traditionally, movement through a transportation system has been represented in terms of travel demand over modal networks, defined for *public* and *private* trips, in which movements are coded in terms of 'principal' mode. A submode split between public transport modes, such as bus and rail, is frequently made by an 'all-or-nothing' assignment to a public transport network defined over all public transport services. The adequacy of this approach has been questioned on a number of occasions. What is the definition of a 'mode' in this case? Are we to treat the multimode demand problem in a 'hierarchical' structure involving 'principal' and 'submode' split models, or is it more appropriate to treat the modes on an equal footing in a joint model? In the above example this modelling distinction is between a nested form with a public transport subsplit, and a three-way modal-split function. These alternative model forms are sometimes called 'sequential' and 'simultaneous' structures.

A related problem concerns the modelling of mixed modes when substantial portions of a journey are taken by different modes, and a significant number of such trips occur. Currently, mixed-mode trips tend to be classified in terms of principal mode. The emergence of policies which are designed to encourage mixed-mode travel necessitates a close look at the formation of appropriate travel demand models and user-benefit measures, particularly because the introduction of interchange facilities gives rise to the possibility of selecting a new movement, which in turn may be regarded as a 'nonmarginal' change to the transportation choice environment. This raises the issue of movement aggregation itself.

An important assumption underpinning the evaluation measure (14) is the satisfaction at the assignment stage of Wardrop's principle, embodied in equations (5) to (7), which essentially states that the cost on any route used between a pair of zone centroids is less than or equal to those on all unused routes. In recent years several attempts have been made to relax the assumption that individuals in the route selecting population T_{ij}^k have an identical perception of route costs, and so introduce dispersion over routes other than that implicit in capacity diversion. The evaluation implications of such probabilistic assignment issues will be briefly considered in section 6.

Finally, a class of problems may be generated by combining various aspects of those discussed above. A well-known issue, for example, concerns the forecasting of demand for modes each of which has a (possibly large) number of associated routes or services. Is a 'sequential' or 'simultaneous' approach more appropriate?

Before proceeding to examine the theoretical aspects of demand models and their analytic structure, the concept and properties of composite costs, which pervade the above discussion, are considered further.

3 The structure and properties of composite costs

3.1 *The different cost forms*

In order to consider in more detail the properties of composite costs I shall analyse a simple multiple choice situation in which a person is confronted by a choice dimension X with N alternatives $\{X_1, ..., X_\rho, ..., X_N\}$ and a choice dimension Y with M alternatives $\{Y_1, ..., Y_\mu, ..., Y_M\}$. There are thus $N \times M$ combinations of which one must be selected. A typical alternative will be denoted $\{\rho, \mu\}$, the demand for which is given by $D_{\rho\mu}$.

Suppose there is good reason to believe (this supposition will be considered further in section 5 below) that a suitable demand model is given by

$$D_{\rho\mu} = TM_\rho M_{\mu|\rho} , \tag{24}$$

in which T is the total number of trips. M_ρ, the probability of selecting alternative X_ρ, is given by

$$M_\rho = \frac{\exp(-\beta\tilde{c}_{\rho\bullet})}{\sum\limits_\rho \exp(-\beta\tilde{c}_{\rho\bullet})} , \qquad \rho = 1, ..., N , \tag{25}$$

while $M_{\mu|\rho}$, the probability of selecting Y_μ given that X_ρ has been chosen, is

$$M_{\mu|\rho} = \frac{\exp(-\lambda c_{\rho\mu})}{\sum\limits_\mu \exp(-\lambda c_{\rho\mu})} , \qquad \mu = 1, ..., M . \tag{26}$$

Here $c_{\rho\mu}$ is the disutility, or perceived cost, associated with the choice combination $\{\rho, \mu\}$, while $\tilde{c}_{\rho\bullet}$, a composite cost, is written in the form

$$\tilde{c}_{\rho\bullet} = \tilde{c}_{\rho\bullet}(c_{\rho 1}, ..., c_{\rho\mu}, ..., c_{\rho M}) , \qquad \rho = 1, ..., N . \tag{27}$$

λ and β are dispersion parameters which determine the sensitivity of the shares $M_{\mu|\rho}$ and M_ρ to changes in the perceived costs. The structure of the model (24) and the corresponding choice alternatives may be represented as in figure 1.

The more popular contenders for the composite cost function are contained in the following forms:

$$\exp(-\beta\tilde{c}_{\rho\bullet}) = \sum_\mu M_{\mu|\rho} \exp(-\beta c_{\rho\mu}) , \tag{28}$$

$$\exp(-\beta\tilde{c}_{\rho\bullet}) = \sum_\mu \exp(-\beta c_{\rho\mu}) , \tag{29}$$

$$\exp(-\beta\tilde{c}_{\rho\bullet}) = \frac{1}{M}\sum_\mu \exp(-\beta c_{\rho\mu}) , \tag{30}$$

$$\tilde{c}_{\rho\bullet} = \min_\mu c_{\rho\mu} , \tag{31}$$

$$\tilde{c}_{\rho\bullet} = \sum_\mu M_{\mu|\rho} c_{\rho\mu} , \qquad \rho = 1, ..., N . \tag{32}$$

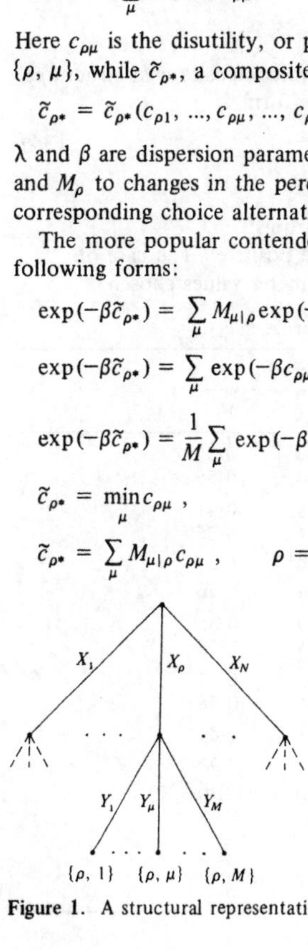

Figure 1. A structural representation of the model form $D_{\rho\mu} = TM_\rho M_{\mu|\rho}$.

In the postdistribution modal-split model (2), the index pairings $\{\rho\} \leftrightarrow \{ij\}$ and $\{\mu\} \leftrightarrow \{k\}$ and the composite cost forms (29) to (32) correspond to those used in the SELNEC, Nottingham, London, and Sheffield–Rotherham Transport Studies appearing in table 1.

3.2 *An example*

The salient properties of these forms (28) to (32) become apparent in a simple numerical example which involves two alternatives, X_1 and X_2, in the X choice dimension and two, Y_1 and Y_2, in the Y dimension. The four resultant choices $\{X_1Y_1, X_1Y_2, X_2Y_1, X_2Y_2\}$ might correspond, for example, to two modes to each of two shopping centres. The changes in the shares M_ρ and composite costs $\tilde{c}_{\rho\bullet}$ have been determined when one of the movement costs c_{22} is reduced from fifty units to seven units while maintaining the costs on the other movements as follows: $c_{11} = 10{\cdot}0$, $c_{12} = 8{\cdot}0$, $c_{21} = 6{\cdot}0$. The results are shown in table 2. Note that for the composite costs (29) and (30), and for the form [see equation (34) below] which contains the parameter λ instead of β in equation (29), the share $M_{\rho=1}$ is *larger* than $M_{\rho=2}$ before the cost reduction of c_{22}. The behaviour is in contrast to that for the forms (28), (31), and (32). Perhaps the most significant feature of this example is the behaviour of the composite cost $\tilde{c}_{2\bullet}$ as a function of c_{22} for a constant value of c_{21}, that is

$$\tilde{c}_{2\bullet}(x) = \tilde{c}_{2\bullet}(c_{21} = 6{\cdot}0, x)\,, \tag{33}$$

where x is any value of c_{22}.

The form of this function is given in figure 2 for the five composite cost structures (28) to (32) over the range $4 < x < 30$, together with the form

$$\exp(-\lambda\tilde{c}_{\rho\bullet}) = \sum_{\mu} \exp(-\lambda c_{\rho\mu})\,, \tag{34}$$

the significance of which will become apparent below.

Examination of the results reveals several interesting features:

(a) The composite cost $\tilde{c}_{2\bullet}$ is not in all cases assured to be positive. The case of function (29) is most dramatic in this respect for the parameter values chosen

Table 2. Composite costs $\tilde{c}_{\rho\bullet}$ and shares M_ρ before and after the change in c_{22}.

Composite cost function [a] $\tilde{c}_{\rho\bullet} = c^j_{\rho\bullet}(c_{\rho 1}, ..., c_{\rho\mu}, ..., c_{\rho M})$		Composite costs $\tilde{c}_{\rho\bullet}$		Shares M_ρ	
		$\tilde{c}_{1\bullet}$	$\tilde{c}_{2\bullet}$	M_1	M_2
$j = 1$ [equation (28)]	before [b]	8·76	6·00	0·43	0·57
	after [c]	8·76	6·44	0·44	0·56
$j = 2$ [equation (29)]	before	2·02	5·88	0·59	0·41
	after	2·02	−0·44	0·44	0·56
$j = 3$ [equation (30)]	before	8·95	12·81	0·59	0·41
	after	8·95	6·49	0·44	0·56
$j = 4$ [equation (31)]	before	8·00	6·00	0·45	0·55
	after	8·00	6·00	0·45	0·55
$j = 5$ [equation (32)]	before	8·80	6·01	0·43	0·57
	after	8·80	6·45	0·44	0·56
$j = 6$ [equation (34)]	before	5·43	6·00	0·51	0·49
	after	5·43	3·01	0·44	0·56

[a] The composite cost functions $c^j_{\rho\bullet}$, $j = 1, ..., 6$, correspond to equations (28) to (32) and (34), respectively.

[b] $c^*_{11} = 10{\cdot}0$ $c^*_{12} = 8{\cdot}0$ $c^*_{21} = 6{\cdot}0$ $c^*_{22} = 50{\cdot}0$

[c] $c^*_{11} = 10{\cdot}0$ $c^*_{12} = 8{\cdot}0$ $c^*_{21} = 6{\cdot}0$ $c^*_{22} = 7{\cdot}0$

($\beta = 0{\cdot}1$, $\lambda = 0{\cdot}2$). It was indeed precisely for this reason that Wilson (1969) suggested modification of form (29) to form (30).

(b) For the forms (29) to (31), and (34) the derivative $\partial\tilde{c}_{2*}/\partial c_{22} \geqslant 0$ over the whole range of costs c_{22}, whereas over particular ranges for the forms (28) and (32) $\partial\tilde{c}_{2*}/\partial c_{22} < 0$.

(c) For the cost functions (29), (31), and (34), $\tilde{c}_{2*}$ is less than or equal to the minimum of c_{21} and c_{22}, whereas $\tilde{c}_{2*}$ is greater than this value for the forms (28), (30), and (32).

(d) The demand for the various movements is the same for cost forms (29) and (30) by virtue of the fact that the same number of choices is associated with X_1 and X_2 (namely Y_1 and Y_2 in this case).

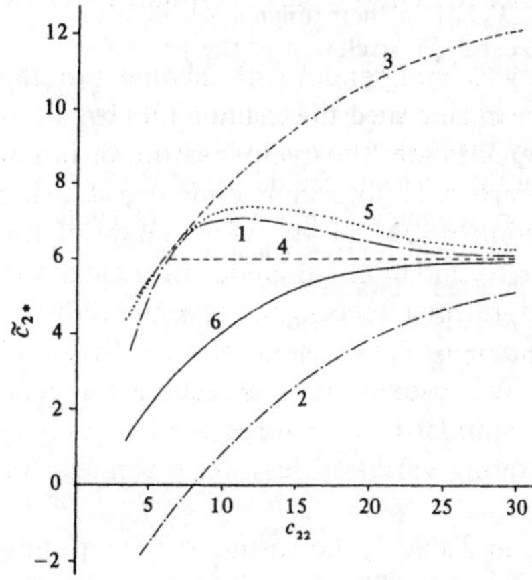

$$1\quad \exp(-\beta\tilde{c}_{\rho*}) = \sum_{\mu} M_{\mu|\rho} \exp(-\beta c_{\rho\mu})$$

$$2\quad \exp(-\beta\tilde{c}_{\rho*}) = \sum_{\mu} \exp(-\beta c_{\rho\mu})$$

$$3\quad \exp(-\beta\tilde{c}_{\rho*}) = \frac{1}{M}\sum_{\mu} \exp(-\beta c_{\rho\mu})$$

$$4\quad \tilde{c}_{\rho*} = \min_{\mu} c_{\rho\mu}$$

$$5\quad \tilde{c}_{\rho*} = \sum_{\mu} M_{\mu|\rho} c_{\rho\mu}$$

$$6\quad \exp(-\lambda\tilde{c}_{\rho*}) = \sum_{\mu} \exp(-\lambda c_{\rho\mu})$$

$$M_\rho = \frac{\exp(-\beta c_{\rho*})}{\sum_{\rho} \exp(-\beta c_{\rho*})}$$

$$M_{\mu|\rho} = \frac{\exp(-\lambda c_{\rho\mu})}{\sum_{\mu} \exp(-\lambda c_{\rho\mu})}$$

$$\beta = 0{\cdot}1, \qquad \lambda = 0{\cdot}2$$

Figure 2. The form of six composite cost structures $\tilde{c}_{2*} = \tilde{c}_{2*}(c_{21}, c_{22})$, $c_{21} = 6{\cdot}0$. [The composite cost functions $j = 1, ..., 6$ correspond to equations (28) to (32) and (34) respectively.]

3.3 *Properties of composite costs*

I shall show below, within the context of probabilistic choice theory, that the following four conditions should be satisfied by a composite cost $\tilde{c}_{\rho*}$

$$\tilde{c}_{\rho*} \geqslant 0\,, \qquad \rho = 1, ..., N\,, \tag{35}$$

$$\frac{\partial\tilde{c}_{\rho*}}{\partial c_{\rho\mu}} \geqslant 0\,, \qquad \rho = 1, ..., N\,, \quad \mu = 1, ..., M\,, \tag{36}$$

$$\tilde{c}_{\rho*} < \min_{\mu} c_{\rho\mu}\,, \qquad \rho = 1, ..., N\,, \tag{37}$$

$$\lim_{\lambda\to\infty} \tilde{c}_{\rho*}(\lambda) = \min_{\mu} c_{\rho\mu}\,, \qquad \rho = 1, ..., N\,. \tag{38}$$

Indeed it will be shown that under certain general conditions a far more restrictive condition replaces equation (36), which may be used to determine $\tilde{c}_{\rho*}$ if the choice model is known. The properties of five composite cost forms are given in table 3, and it can be seen that all violate at least one of the conditions (35) to (38). I shall argue below that, while it is undesirable to have a negative composite cost, it is not a pathological condition, and may in certain circumstances be tolerated. The issue here relates to the definition of the costs $c_{\rho\mu}$.

Consider now a violation of the conditions (36) and (37) which is associated with some of the cost forms chosen. In the former case a negative value for the derivative would imply that a marginal increase in $c_{\rho\mu}$ would result in a decrease in $\tilde{c}_{\rho *}$ (other costs being held constant). For demand shares which satisfy the usual elasticity properties,

$$\frac{\partial M_\rho}{\partial \tilde{c}_{\rho *}} < 0 , \qquad \frac{\partial M_\rho}{\partial \tilde{c}_{\rho' *}} > 0 , \qquad \rho' \neq \rho , \tag{39}$$

$$\frac{\partial M_{\mu|\rho}}{\partial c_{\rho\mu}} < 0 , \qquad \frac{\partial M_{\mu|\rho}}{\partial c_{\rho\mu'}} > 0 , \qquad \mu' \neq \mu , \tag{40}$$

this behaviour would do much violence to the notion of rational choice underpinning the demand model (24), because an increase in the share M_ρ must arise from those who have already rejected $\{X_\rho Y_1, ..., X_\rho Y_\mu, ..., X_\rho Y_M\}$ in their original selection of movements and for whom an *increase* in the cost $c_{\rho\mu}$ is irrelevant in the process of reselection among the alternatives.

If the condition (37) [which may be shown to be related to condition (36) by path integration] were violated, it would imply that a new alternative, Y^ρ_{M+1}, associated with X_ρ, would in fact *decrease* the total demand for the set of choices $\{X_\rho Y_1, ..., X_\rho Y_\mu, ..., X_\rho Y_M, X_\rho Y^\rho_{M+1}\}$. In the corresponding shopping centre (X) and mode (Y) example, the violation of condition (37) which arises when a new mode is added to the centre X_ρ would manifest itself in a reduction of trips to X_ρ!

Finally consider condition (38). The share $M_{\mu|\rho}$ is here considered to be parameterised by λ, as in the multinomial logit model (26), such that

$$M_{\mu|\rho}(\lambda \to \infty) = 1 , \qquad \text{for} \quad c_{\rho\mu} = \min_\pi c_{\rho\pi} , \tag{41}$$

and

$$M_{\alpha|\rho}(\lambda \to \infty) = 0 , \qquad \text{if} \quad \alpha \neq \mu . \tag{42}$$

Table 3. The properties of several common composite cost functions.

Composite cost	Property 1	Property 2	Property 3	Property 4
$\tilde{c}_{\rho *} = \tilde{c}_{\rho *}(c_{\rho 1}, ..., c_{\rho\mu}, ..., c_{\rho M})$ $c_{\rho\mu} > 0$	$\tilde{c}_{\rho *} \geqslant 0$	$\frac{\partial \tilde{c}_{\rho *}}{\partial c_{\rho\mu}} \geqslant 0$	$\tilde{c}_{\rho *} < \min_\mu c_{\rho\mu}$	$\lim_{\lambda \to \infty} \tilde{c}_{\rho *}(\lambda) = \min_\mu c_{\rho\mu}$
$\exp(-\beta\tilde{c}_{\rho *}) = \sum_\mu M_{\mu\mid\rho} \exp(-\beta c_{\rho\mu})$	+	$\frac{\partial \tilde{c}_{\rho *}}{\partial c_{\rho\mu}} < 0$ [b]	−	+
$\exp(-\beta\tilde{c}_{\rho *}) = \sum_\mu \exp(-\beta c_{\rho\mu})$	$\tilde{c}_{\rho *} < 0$ [a]	+	+	−
$\exp(-\beta\tilde{c}_{\rho *}) = \frac{1}{M} \sum_\mu \exp(-\beta c_{\rho\mu})$	+	+	−	−
$\tilde{c}_{\rho *} = \min_\mu c_{\rho\mu}$	+	+	−	+
$\tilde{c}_{\rho *} = \sum_\mu M_{\mu\mid\rho} c_{\rho\mu}$	+	$\frac{\partial \tilde{c}_{\rho *}}{\partial c_{\rho\mu}} < 0$ [b]	−	+

[a] If $\sum_\mu \exp(-\beta c_{\rho\mu}) > 0$.
[b] Over limited range.

+ indicates that the composite cost form satisfies the condition.
− indicates that the composite cost form violates the condition.

When λ becomes very large the total share is associated with the least cost alternative Y_μ. In the limit $\lambda \to \infty$ either one choice $X_\rho Y_\mu$ from the set $\{X_\rho Y_1, ..., X_\rho Y_\mu, ..., X_\rho Y_M\}$ is selected, which is characterised by perceived cost $c_{\rho\mu}$ or several choices are selected by the population as a whole, each of which has the cost $c_{\rho\mu}$. The composite cost $\tilde{c}_{\rho\bullet}$, which is representative of the costs on the selected alternatives associated with X_ρ, must therefore equal $c_{\rho\mu}$. The property (38) follows immediately.

In this section the properties of composite costs have been introduced. I have argued on the basis of the conditions (35) to (38), which have been justified by a general and qualitative reference to rational choice behaviour, that none of the forms (28) to (32) are suitable for use in travel demand models. In order to derive equations (35) to (38) rigorously, the role played by composite costs in analytic structure must be explored, and further, to answer the questions posed in section 2, one must appeal to a general theory of tripmaking based on rational choice. This is the subject of the following two sections.

4 The formation of travel demand models and user benefit measures

4.1 *Introduction*

It is widely accepted that, with the possible exception of leisure trips, travel itself does not improve the human condition. It is a means to an end, and demand for transport is thus regarded as a derived demand. In the choice problem with which I shall be concerned, it will be assumed that demand for a good, service, or activity may be satisfied at any one of N locations $L_1, ..., L_\rho, ..., L_N$, while there exist several possible means of transportation $T_{\rho 1}, ..., T_{\rho\mu}, ..., T_{\rho M}$ to each (for example the combination of mode and route etc). In the general case, the number of options M may depend on the particular location choice L_ρ. Each combination $\{L_\rho, T_{\rho\mu}\}$ may be characterised by a set of attributes, some of which are observable, say $\{Z_\rho, Z_\mu, Z_{\rho\mu}\}$, and some of which are not. The decisionmaker, characterised by a set of socio-economic variables E, is assumed to select a single alternative $\{\rho, \mu\}$ from the product set $L \otimes T$.

It is well to consider at this point various possible explanations an observer may invoke to account for trip dispersion—the variation in choice behaviour in a population characterised by trip destination, mode, route, and the same origin. Among the several possibilities are (a) an irrational or probabilistic decisionmaking process at the level of the individual; (b) imperfect information on trip or location opportunities; (c) misspecification of the attributes characterising trip or location alternatives; (d) the precise location of the trip ends, and therefore choice attributes, varies over the population; (e) traveller behaviour varies with the socioeconomic characteristics of the tripmaker; (f) the perception of costs or prices of the alternatives varies over the population for a given socioeconomic category; (g) individuals rank alternatives differently—utility functions vary over the population; (h) individuals have identical preferences but make several nonsynchronised trips; (i) constraints exist on traveller behaviour.

These sources of variability have considerable influence on, and implications for, the formation of travel demand models and their forecasting ability. The proposed theory will thus vary according to whether a person makes one or several trips, whether market information is regarded as perfect, whether decisionmaking is considered to be rational, etc.

In the early development stages (1950–1960) of the transportation planning process it was recognised that trip behaviour, when aggregated to the level of the zone or other spatial unit, showed discernable patterns which bore statistically significant *correlative* relations with land-use, socioeconomic, and transport system level-of-service variables. It therefore seemed not unreasonable to base forecasts on trip group patterns rather than to deal directly with the large amount of variability associated with the behaviour of individuals or households. The zone was thus adopted as the fundamental 'behavioural' unit in the trip prediction process, and the models, such as those in table 1, were expressed in terms of variables which were average values determined over trip groups.

It took several years after Warner's (1962) pioneering study of modal choice for the merits of a disaggregate approach to be recognised. As Fleet and Robertson (1968), Wootton and Pick (1967), and others so forcefully pointed out in the context of trip generation modelling, it is precisely the variability between the fundamental decisionmaking units in the system which must be explained if causal relations upon which confident forecasts may be based are to be established. The aggregate approach, while generating deceptively good results in terms of conventional goodness-of-fit statistics when applied to zonal data, frequently resulted, through loss of information arising from grouping, in models with poor explanatory power and forecasting ability.

In principle, forecasts of demand at the macrolevel may be established by constructing a model at the microlevel and performing an aggregation process. The nature of this process and its inherent difficulties have been discussed by Wilson (1973b), Domencich and McFadden (1975), Cesario and Smith (1975), and others. Here I shall confine attention to the formation of choice models in which the variables pertain to an individual or household. The four model-building methods discussed, each of which makes different assumptions about the nature of the trip decision process, are: the constant utility and random utility approaches of probabilistic choice theory; the entropy maximising methodology; and a procedure based on the maximisation of group consumer surplus.

In this section the one-dimensional choice problem—the selection of a single alternative from a set $X \equiv \{X_1, ..., X_\rho, ..., X_N\}$—will be considered in order to compare the underlying assumptions of the model building approaches, and their suitability for extension to the treatment of the more general multidimensional choice problem outlined at the start of the section. The models constructed express the choice probability $P_\rho(Z_1^t, ..., Z_\rho^t, ..., Z_N^t)$ of an individual t selecting a single alternative, say X_ρ, in terms of the observable attribute vectors $Z_1^t, ..., Z_\rho^t, ..., Z_N^t$. Each vector, Z_ρ say, will contain a set of attributes associated with the corresponding alternative.

4.2 *Probabilistic choice theory—the constant utility approach*

Choice among the set of alternatives $X \equiv \{X_1, ..., X_\rho, ..., X_N\}$ is assumed to be governed by the net utility or surplus value s, attributed to each alternative, which is defined by

$$s_\rho(Z_\rho) = u_\rho(Z'_\rho) - c_\rho(Z''_\rho)\,, \qquad \rho = 1, ..., N\,. \tag{43}$$

Here u_ρ, the benefit associated with X_ρ, is expressed in the same units as the incurred (transport) cost or disutility c_ρ. In the *constant utility* approach (or more appropriately named, in this context, the *constant surplus* approach) it is assumed that the values $s_1, ..., s_\rho, ..., s_N$ are discrete (not subject to variation), but that the decisionmaking process is of a probabilistic nature. (The *random utility* approach on the other hand is characterised by a deterministic selection mechanism but the utility and/or cost of each alternative are regarded as random variables.)

An important theoretical construct in the constant utility approach, derived from mathematical psychology, is *Luce's choice axiom* (Luce, 1959; Luce and Suppes, 1965), which has been described as a probabilistic version of the axioms of *transitivity* and *independence from irrelevant alternatives* from deterministic choice theory. If $P(X_\rho \in X)$ is the probability of selection X_ρ from a set X, the choice axiom would assert that the relative probability of choice among any two remaining alternatives would be unaffected by the removal of a subset of alternatives. Thus

$$\frac{P(X_\rho \in X)}{P(X_{\rho'} \in X)} = \frac{P(X_\rho \in X')}{P(X_{\rho'} \in X')} , \qquad \forall X_\rho, X_{\rho'} \in X, X' , \tag{44}$$

where X_ρ and $X_{\rho'}$ refer to two alternatives in sets X and X', with X' a subset of X.

Luce has proved that if the choice axiom holds, then, given a utility measure V_ρ proportional to the choice probability $P(X_\rho \in X)$, there exists a ratio scale such that

$$P(X_\rho \in X) = \frac{V_\rho}{\sum_{X_\rho \in X} V_\rho} , \qquad \forall X_\rho \in X . \tag{45}$$

If V_ρ is proportional to the exponential transform of the surplus s_ρ then the multinomial logit model

$$P_\rho = \frac{\exp(\lambda s_\rho)}{\sum_\rho \exp(\lambda s_\rho)} \tag{46}$$

results[(1)]. If the utility values $u_1, ..., u_\rho, ..., u_N$ are equal across all alternatives the familiar perceived cost model is obtained

$$P_\rho = \frac{\exp(-\lambda c_\rho)}{\sum_\rho \exp(-\lambda c_\rho)} , \qquad \rho = 1, ..., N , \tag{47}$$

in which

$$c_\rho = c_\rho(Z''_\rho, \boldsymbol{\alpha}) . \tag{48}$$

The perceived generalised cost c_ρ is here considered to be a function of the attributes Z''_ρ and a set of parameters $\boldsymbol{\alpha}$.

The benefit ΔS arising from a change in the vector of costs $\boldsymbol{c}^* \rightarrow \boldsymbol{c}^\star$ may be expressed in terms of a change in the expectation value of the surplus over the discrete probability distribution $\{P_1, ..., P_\rho, ..., P_N\}$. That is

$$\Delta S = \sum_\rho (P^\star_\rho s^\star_\rho - P^*_\rho s^*_\rho) . \tag{49}$$

A well-known example, which illustrates the caution needed in applying the choice axiom, concerns the choice between several modes. Consider a traveller who is initially indifferent between car and bus. Clearly $P_{\text{car}} = P_{\text{bus}} = \frac{1}{2}$, and this is what would result from applying the choice axiom. If now half the buses were painted red and the other half blue, then, by regarding the individual as having three alternatives available to him, equation (44) would predict $P_{\text{car}} = P_{\text{red bus}} = P_{\text{blue bus}} = \frac{1}{3}$. The increase of the total public transport share caused simply by modification of a superficial aspect of the service is clearly unrealistic. The red bus–blue bus conundrum, as it is known, may readily be resolved by applying Luce's axiom in the sequence involving car and public transport, and then between two public transport 'modes'. This must be done in order to isolate 'identifiable' choices. This simple example has important characteristics to which I shall return in the next section.

4.3 *Probabilistic choice theory—the random utility approach*

In constant utility theory the probability measure P_ρ may be interpreted as the proportion of a population Π, whose choice is characterised by the same vector of observable attributes $\boldsymbol{Z}$, selecting the alternative X_ρ, or alternatively, as a frequency of

(1) If the quantities s_ρ, or net benefits, are expressed in money units, then λ has dimension $(\text{money})^{-1}$. On the other hand, if the net utility is expressed in utils, then λ is dimensionless.

choice from repeated trials by a single person. The essential feature is that decision-making varies probabilistically over the population or for each trial. In random utility theory each individual in the hypothetical population Π is assumed to select that alternative which offers him maximum net utility or surplus. If each choice were endowed with the same surplus value then the same alternative would be chosen by all members of Π. However, in general, the benefit and cost of available choices will be perceived differently. Because some of the attributes of any individual are unobserved, and because the *valuation* of observable attributes may be nonuniform, it is not certain which alternative will be selected by that individual. The uncertainty here is associated with the observer who attributes random components to the utility and cost functions—the traveller himself is, in the theory of rational choice, considered to choose optimally and consistently within his own utility frame of reference.

4.3.1 *The formalism of random utility theory*

The probability of an individual selecting a given option may be computed if a functional form is assigned to the random components of the surplus attached to each alternative. The essence of the approach is embodied in the formal expression

$$P_\rho = \int_{R_\rho} \mathrm{d}s H(s_1, ..., s_\rho, ..., s_N) \equiv \int_{R_\rho} \mathrm{d}s H(s) \,, \tag{50}$$

where $H(s_1, ..., s_\rho, ..., s_N)$ is the joint density function of the surplus variables $s_1, ..., s_\rho, ..., s_N$, $\mathrm{d}s$ is the volume element $\prod_\rho \mathrm{d}s_\rho$, and R_ρ is the region of integration defined by

$$s_\rho = \max_{\rho'} s_{\rho'} \,, \qquad \text{and} \quad s_\rho \geqslant 0 \,. \tag{51}$$

Over the region R_ρ, X_ρ is therefore the preferred option. If no alternative may be found which gives positive surplus, then no trip will be made. It should be noted that the choice process is not subject directly to a budget constraint, because only those alternatives which are feasible are considered.

Two methods of generating random utility models have been widely used. In the random coefficient approach the net utilities are expressed as functions of a vector of random parameters $\boldsymbol{\alpha}$, with mean value $\bar{\boldsymbol{\alpha}}$, such that

$$s_\rho = s_\rho(\boldsymbol{\alpha}, Z) \,, \qquad \rho = 1, ..., N \,. \tag{52}$$

Equation (50) is then transformed into ($\boldsymbol{\alpha}$ – space) to give

$$P_\rho(\bar{\boldsymbol{\alpha}}, Z) = \int_{R_\rho} \mathrm{d}\boldsymbol{\alpha} H^\alpha(\boldsymbol{\alpha}) \,, \tag{53}$$

and integration is over the portion of that space equivalent to R_ρ defined by equations (51) and (52). Such an approach has been adopted by Quant (1968), Blackburn (1970), Golob and Beckmann (1971), Harris and Tanner (1974), and others.

The alternative approach is to specify a functional form for each random variable s_ρ directly. The net utility is written

$$s_\rho = \bar{s}_\rho(\bar{\boldsymbol{\alpha}}, Z) + \epsilon_\rho \,, \qquad \rho = 1, ..., N \,, \tag{54}$$

in terms of a 'representative' component $\bar{s}_\rho(\bar{\boldsymbol{\alpha}}, Z)$ which is assumed to be equal for all members of Π, and a stochastic component ϵ_ρ *for which a distribution is assumed*. All the variation in tastes represented by the random coefficients $\boldsymbol{\alpha}$ in equation (52), together with the variation arising from unobserved factors, is condensed into the random variable ϵ_ρ. Such an approach has been adopted by CRA (1972), McFadden (1974), Domencich and McFadden (1975), and Cochrane (1975) and will be used in this paper.

An important class of problems is that for which the distributions of the random variables ϵ_ρ ($\rho = 1, ..., N$) (and therefore s_ρ) are independent. If $\Gamma_\rho(s, \bar{s}_\rho)$ is the probability that the perceived surplus for alternative X_ρ lies in the range $[s_\rho, s_\rho + \mathrm{d}s_\rho]$, while $\Theta_\rho(s)$ is the probability that all other alternatives have surplus less than s, then we may write

$$P_\rho = \mathrm{prob}(s_\rho > s_{\rho'}, \ \forall X_{\rho'} \in X; \ s_\rho \geqslant 0) \tag{55}$$

$$= \int_0^\infty \mathrm{d}s \Gamma_\rho(s, \bar{s}_\rho) \Theta_\rho(s) \tag{56}$$

$$= \int_0^\infty \mathrm{d}s \Gamma_\rho(s, \bar{s}_\rho) \prod_{\rho' \neq \rho} \int_{-\infty}^{s} \mathrm{d}s' \Gamma_{\rho'}(s', \bar{s}_{\rho'}) \, . \tag{57}$$

The probability of making no trip is

$$P_0 = 1 - \sum_\rho P_\rho \, . \tag{58}$$

If now the benefit associated with all alternatives is considerably greater than all transport costs, the lower limit of integration may be extended from zero to minus infinity, with negligible approximation for 'bell-shaped' distributions, to give

$$P_\rho = \int_{-\infty}^\infty \mathrm{d}s \Gamma_\rho(s, \bar{s}_\rho) \prod_{\rho' \neq \rho} \int_{-\infty}^{s} \mathrm{d}s' \Gamma_{\rho'}(s', \bar{s}_{\rho'}) \, . \tag{59}$$

In this case a trip is definitely made.

It may be shown (CRA, 1972) that the multinomial logit model (46) is generated if the stochastic component ϵ_ρ varies according to a Weibull distribution

$$\Gamma(\epsilon_\rho, \lambda) = \Gamma(s - \bar{s}_\rho, \lambda) \, , \tag{60}$$

$$= \lambda \exp(-\lambda \epsilon_\rho) \exp[-\exp(-\lambda \epsilon_\rho)] \, , \tag{61}$$

which has standard deviation σ, given by[(2)]

$$\sigma = \pi(\lambda \sqrt{6})^{-1} \, , \tag{62}$$

as noted, for example, by Cochrane (1975). The relation (62) confirms, as would be expected, that the dispersion parameter λ is inversely related to the standard deviation of the underlying distributions of net utility.

The linear model

$$P_\rho = \frac{\exp\left(\lambda \sum_\eta \alpha_\eta Z_\rho^\eta\right)}{\sum_\rho \exp\left(\lambda \sum_\eta \alpha_\eta Z_\rho^\eta\right)} \, , \tag{63}$$

is much favoured by demand analysts due to its ease of calibration and manipulation. A very full discussion of its application to modelling choice behaviour has been given by McFadden (1974). Alternative models may be generated by taking different functional forms for the values $\bar{s}_\rho$ in terms of the attributes Z_ρ or of the form for the residual ϵ_ρ. It should be noted that ϵ_ρ is distributed according to the difference between the random components of the utility and cost functions

$$\epsilon_\rho = \epsilon_\rho^u - \epsilon_\rho^c \, . \tag{64}$$

The generation of models from given distributions ϵ_ρ^u and ϵ_ρ^c is considered in section 5. Here I have assumed that ϵ_ρ has a Weibull form.

(2) The mean value of the distribution (61) is not in fact $\bar{s}_\rho$ but $\bar{s}_\rho + \gamma/\lambda$ where γ, Euler's constant, is approximately 0·577. Since the distributions $\Gamma_1, ..., \Gamma_\rho, ..., \Gamma_N$ and the resultant demand model are (translationally) invariant with respect to addition or subtraction of constants to the quantities $\bar{s}_1, ..., \bar{s}_\rho, ..., \bar{s}_N$, the distinction between $\bar{s}_\rho$ and the mean value may effectively be ignored.

The computation of a consumer surplus measure of benefit which is fully consistent with the model generated within the random utility approach, may now be expressed in terms of the change in the expectation value of surplus $\langle s\rangle$. For given values of the attribute vectors Z, $\langle s\rangle$ is defined by

$$\langle s\rangle = \sum_{\rho} \int_{R_\rho} \mathrm{d}s\, s_\rho H(s, Z)\ . \tag{65}$$

The formalism of benefit calculations, to which I shall return, has been explored for one dimensional models by Cochrane (1975), and by Harris and Tanner (1974) who have investigated the conditions under which random utility models are compatible with a unique definition of the expectation value of surplus $\langle s\rangle$.

In order to extend the random utility approach to problems of multidimensional choice, the characteristics and properties of certain cost and utility distributions must be explored. The full significance of the benefit expression (65) and of the occurrence of different cost, utility, and surplus measures in the theory will then become apparent.

4.3.2 *Utility distributions and their properties*

Consider choice over the set of alternatives X for which the utility is constant[3] and considerably greater than the perceived values of disutility c_ρ ($\rho = 1, ..., N$), which are distributed according to Γ_ρ ($\rho = 1, ..., N$) respectively. (This problem is of considerable importance in the multidimensional choice models discussed later.) For each individual, the problem of selecting the option with maximum surplus is clearly equivalent to that of determining the minimum perceived cost alternative. It is important now to distinguish between three cost or disutility measures $\bar{c}_\rho$, $\bar{\bar{c}}_\rho$, and $\tilde{c}_*$ which are defined as follows:

$\bar{c}_\rho$ is the mean value of the distribution of disutility Γ_ρ for alternative X_ρ, as perceived by the choicemaking population Π.

$\bar{\bar{c}}_\rho$ is the mean value of the distribution of disutility $\tilde{\Gamma}_\rho$ for alternative X_ρ, as perceived by that portion Π_ρ of the population Π which selects X_ρ.

$\tilde{c}_*$ is the mean value of the distribution of disutility Λ_* over the selected choices. Λ_* will be described as the distribution of minimum perceived costs. The asterisk is used to denote an operation, defined below, over the set of distributions associated with the dimension X.

The distributions $\tilde{\Gamma}_\rho$ and Λ_*, and their respective mean values $\bar{\bar{c}}_\rho$, $\tilde{c}_*$ are defined (for independent normalised distributions Γ_ρ) as follows:

$$\tilde{\Gamma}_\rho(c) = \Gamma_\rho(c) \prod_{\rho' \neq \rho} \int_c^\infty \mathrm{d}c' \Gamma_{\rho'}(c')\ , \tag{66}$$

$$\Lambda_*(c) = \sum_\rho \tilde{\Gamma}_\rho(c) \tag{67}$$

$$= \sum_\rho \left[\Gamma_\rho(c) \prod_{\rho' \neq \rho} \int_c^\infty \mathrm{d}c' \Gamma_{\rho'}(c') \right]\ , \tag{68}$$

with

$$\bar{\bar{c}}_\rho = \left[\int_{-\infty}^{\infty} \mathrm{d}c\, c \tilde{\Gamma}_\rho(c) \right] \Big/ \left[\int_{-\infty}^{\infty} \mathrm{d}c \tilde{\Gamma}_\rho(c) \right]\ , \tag{69}$$

and

$$\tilde{c}_* = \int_{-\infty}^{\infty} \mathrm{d}c\, c \Lambda_*(c)\ . \tag{70}$$

The distribution Λ_* is normalised if the distributions Γ are themselves normalised.

(3) This condition should not be taken to indicate a constant utility model of the type discussed in section 4.2. The distribution of the disutility or perceived cost measure gives rise to the random surplus model.

We may write immediately from equations (67) and (70)

$$\tilde{c}_* = \sum_p \left[\int_{-\infty}^{\infty} \mathrm{d}c\, c\, \tilde{\Gamma}_p(c)\right]\left[\int_{-\infty}^{\infty} \mathrm{d}c \tilde{\Gamma}_p(c)\right] \Big/ \int_{-\infty}^{\infty} \mathrm{d}c \tilde{\Gamma}_p(c) \,, \tag{71}$$

$$= \sum_p P_p \tilde{\bar{c}}_p \,, \tag{72}$$

on using the relation

$$P_p = \int_{-\infty}^{\infty} \mathrm{d}c\, \tilde{\Gamma}_p(c) \,. \tag{73}$$

$\tilde{c}_*$ is thus the weighted mean of N values $\tilde{\bar{c}}_p$. The quantity $\tilde{c}_p$ will be less than $\bar{c}_p$ because the population Π_p which selects X_p does so precisely because that option is perceived as the least-cost alternative, while those in the population Π who are involved in the calculation of $\bar{c}_p$ do not all select that option.

For later reference, the distribution of minimum costs Λ_*, defined by equation (68) will be written in terms of the operator relation

$$\Lambda_*(c, \bar{c}_1, ..., \bar{c}_p, ..., \bar{c}_N) = \mathrm{O}_{\min}[\Gamma_p(c, \bar{c}_p), \ p = 1, ..., N] \,. \tag{74}$$

$\tilde{c}_*$, the mean value of Λ_*, is a function of the costs $\bar{c}_1, ..., \bar{c}_p, ..., \bar{c}_N$, which I shall write

$$\tilde{c}_* = \tilde{c}_*(\bar{c}_1, ..., \bar{c}_p, ..., \bar{c}_N) = \tilde{c}_*(\bar{c}) \,. \tag{75}$$

In appendix 2 it is shown that the function $\tilde{c}_*$ has the following interesting properties

(a) $\tilde{c}_* > 0$ if the distributions $\Gamma_p(c)$ vanish for $c < 0$, (76)

(b) $$\frac{\partial \tilde{c}_*}{\partial \bar{c}_p} = P_p(\bar{c}_1, ..., \bar{c}_p, ..., \bar{c}_N) \,, \tag{77}$$

(c) $$\tilde{c}_* < \min_p(\bar{c}_1, ..., \bar{c}_p, ..., \bar{c}_N) \,, \tag{78}$$

(d) $$\lim_{\lambda \to \infty} \tilde{c}_*(\lambda) = \min_p(\bar{c}_1, ..., \bar{c}_p, ..., \bar{c}_N) \,, \tag{79}$$

where the distributions $\boldsymbol{\Gamma}$ are parameterised by λ. The general conditions under which these relations hold are discussed along with their derivation. By comparing equations (76) to (79) with equations (35) to (38) it will be of no surprise if $\tilde{c}_*$, the mean of a suitably defined distribution of minimum costs, assumes the status of a composite cost[(4)] function in the more complex choice models discussed in section 5.

It is clear that for any model we may similarly define the distributions of surplus $\Gamma_p(s)$, $\tilde{\Gamma}_p(s)$ ($p = 1, ..., N$) and $\Lambda_*(s)$ together with their mean values $\bar{s}_p$, $\tilde{\bar{s}}_p$, and $\tilde{s}_*$. In this case

$$\Lambda_*(s, \bar{s}_1, ..., \bar{s}_p, ..., \bar{s}_N) = \mathrm{O}_{\max}[\Gamma_p(s, \bar{s}_p), \ p = 1, ..., N] \,. \tag{80}$$

For a model in which $\boldsymbol{\Gamma}$ are independent, the benefit ΔS, defined by equation (65), reduces to

$$\Delta S = \langle \tilde{s}^{\star} \rangle - \langle \tilde{s}^{*} \rangle = \int_{-\infty}^{\infty} \mathrm{d}s s[\Lambda_*(s, \boldsymbol{Z}^{\star}) - \Lambda_*(s, \boldsymbol{Z}^{*})] \,, \tag{81}$$

where $\tilde{s}_*^{\star}$ and $\tilde{s}_*^{*}$ are computed with the two sets of vectors $\boldsymbol{Z}^{\star}$ and $\boldsymbol{Z}^{*}$ respectively.

(4) Cochrane (1975) has noted the possibility of using the mean of the distribution of minimum costs for integrating mode-split and distribution models, and has quoted a result for $\tilde{c}_*$ for a random parameter binary choice model.

If the utility is constant over all choices, then ΔS is given by

$$\Delta S = (u-\tilde{c}_*^{\star})-(u-\tilde{c}_*^{\star}) = \tilde{c}_*^{\star}-\tilde{c}_*^{\star} . \tag{82}$$

The computation of benefit now directly involves the mean value of the distribution $\Lambda_*(c)$.

4.3.3 *Examples*

A distinction between the distributions $\Gamma_\rho(c)$, $\tilde{\Gamma}_\rho(c)$, and $\Lambda_*(c)$, and between their mean values $\bar{c}_\rho$, $\bar{\bar{c}}_\rho$, and $\tilde{c}_*$ is illustrated in figure 3 for binary selection. The functions $\Gamma_\rho(c, \bar{c}_\rho)$ are taken as independent normal distributions

$$\Gamma(c, \bar{c}_\rho) = \frac{1}{(2\pi)^{1/2}\sigma} \exp\left[-\frac{(c-\bar{c}_\rho)^2}{2\sigma^2}\right], \qquad \rho = 1, 2 . \tag{83}$$

Figure 3(a) corresponds to the condition $\bar{c}_1 = \bar{c}_2$, in which the underlying normal distributions completely overlap, which results in equal choice between the movements, $P_1 = P_2 = 0{\cdot}5$, while figure 3(b) illustrates the case in which $(\bar{c}_2 - \bar{c}_1)$ equals σ, the common standard deviation, and corresponds to the share probability $P_1 = 0{\cdot}76$. The form of the probit (cumulative normal) model

$$P_1(\chi) = \frac{1}{(2\pi)^{1/2}} \int_{-\infty}^{\chi} dx \exp(-\tfrac{1}{2}x^2) , \tag{84}$$

with

$$\chi = \frac{\bar{c}_2 - \bar{c}_1}{\sigma} ,$$

which results from the normal distributions (83), and the accompanying cost statistics $\bar{c}_\rho$, $\bar{\bar{c}}_\rho$, and $\tilde{c}_*$, appear in figures 4 and 5, respectively[(5)]. The sigmoid curves are illustrated for a number of σ values. The binary probit model presented here is virtually indistinguishable from the binary logit model

$$P_\rho(\bar{c}_1, \bar{c}_2) = \frac{\exp(-\Delta\bar{c}_\rho)}{\sum_\rho \exp(-\Delta\bar{c}_\rho)} , \tag{85}$$

when

$$\Delta = \frac{\pi}{\sigma_{\text{Weibull}}\sqrt{6}} \cong \frac{4}{\sigma_{\text{Normal}}\sqrt{2\pi}} , \tag{86}$$

a relation which may be derived by examining cross-elasticities at $\bar{c}_1 = \bar{c}_2$.

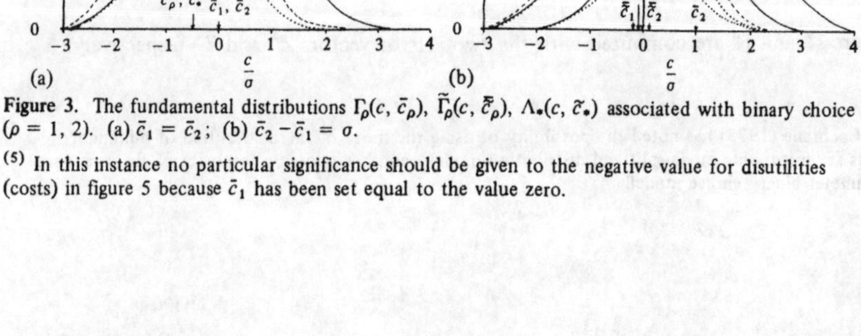

Figure 3. The fundamental distributions $\Gamma_\rho(c, \bar{c}_\rho)$, $\tilde{\Gamma}_\rho(c, \bar{\bar{c}}_\rho)$, $\Lambda_*(c, \tilde{c}_*)$ associated with binary choice ($\rho = 1, 2$). (a) $\bar{c}_1 = \bar{c}_2$; (b) $\bar{c}_2 - \bar{c}_1 = \sigma$.

(5) In this instance no particular significance should be given to the negative value for disutilities (costs) in figure 5 because $\bar{c}_1$ has been set equal to the value zero.

The property (77) may be exploited directly for the estimation of benefit in cases for which the utility values u_ρ are equal. For a differential change $(\mathrm{d}\bar{c}_1, ..., \mathrm{d}\bar{c}_\rho, ..., \mathrm{d}\bar{c}_N)$ the change in the quantity $\tilde{c}_*$, which from equation (82) gives the benefit $\mathrm{d}S$, is given immediately by

$$\mathrm{d}\tilde{c}_* = \sum_\rho \frac{\partial \tilde{c}_*}{\partial \bar{c}_\rho} \mathrm{d}\bar{c}_\rho \tag{87}$$

$$= \sum_\rho P_\rho \mathrm{d}\bar{c}_\rho \, . \tag{88}$$

For the finite change $\bar{c}_X^* \rightarrow \bar{c}_X^*$ the change in $\tilde{c}_*$ may be computed by line integration as

$$\Delta\tilde{c}_* = \sum_\rho \int_0^1 \mathrm{d}\hat{\sigma} \frac{\mathrm{d}\bar{c}_\rho(\hat{\sigma})}{\mathrm{d}\hat{\sigma}} P_\rho(\hat{\sigma}) \, , \tag{89}$$

where the evaluation is along a path parameterised by $\hat{\sigma}$, between the initial and final cost states $\bar{c}_X^*$ and $\bar{c}_X^*$. The integral (89) may readily be shown to be unique and $\Delta\tilde{c}_*$ may be defined unambiguously because the necessary integrability conditions,

$$\frac{\partial P_\rho}{\partial \bar{c}_{\rho'}} = \frac{\partial P_{\rho'}}{\partial \bar{c}_\rho} \, , \quad \forall \, X_\rho, X_{\rho'} \in X \, , \tag{90}$$

follow directly from equation (77) when the symmetry of the second derivative $\partial^2\tilde{c}_*/\partial\bar{c}_\rho\partial\bar{c}_{\rho'}$ is exploited. Thus $\Delta\tilde{c}_*$ may be computed directly from a knowledge of the distributions Γ_ρ through equation (70) or, if it is known that the demand function P_ρ is derivable from translationally invariant distributions, directly from equation (89), which is formally equivalent to the generalised surplus integral of Hotelling (1938). For the multinomial logit model (47) the path integral (89), which is equal to ΔS, is given by

$$\Delta S = -\Delta\tilde{c}_* = \frac{1}{\Delta} \ln \frac{\sum_\rho \exp(-\Delta\bar{c}_\rho^*)}{\sum_\rho \exp(-\Delta\bar{c}_\rho^*)} \, , \tag{91}$$

a result which has been derived by Wilson and Kirwan (1969), and by Neuberger (1971).

The absolute value for $\tilde{c}_*$ (given $\bar{c}_\rho$) may be obtained by direct integration from its definition or, by exploiting the property shown in equation (77), through path integration by defining initial and final cost states c_X^* and c_X^* as follows

$$c^* = (\infty \, ... \, \infty, \bar{c}_\rho, \infty \, ... \, \infty) \, , \qquad c^* = (\bar{c}_1, ..., \bar{c}_\rho, ..., \bar{c}_N) \, . \tag{92}$$

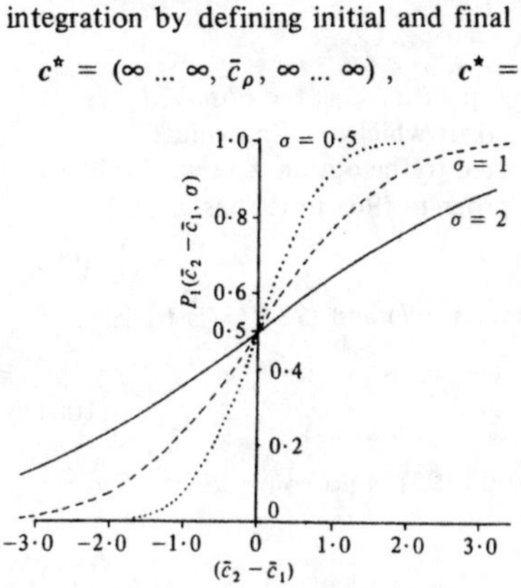

Figure 4. The cumulative normal (probit) model.

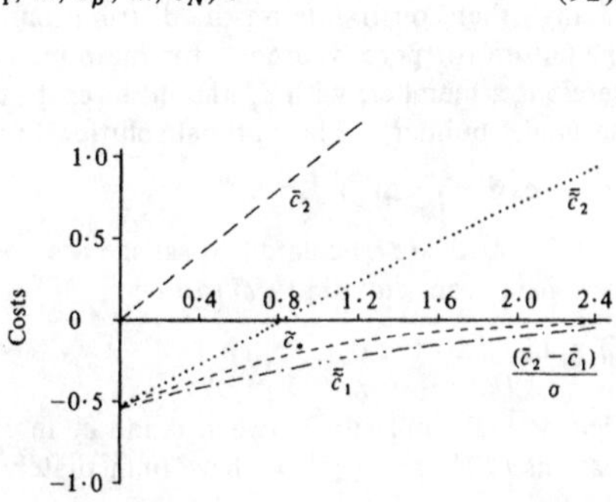

Figure 5. Costs $\bar{c}_\rho$, $\bar{\bar{c}}_\rho$, and $\tilde{c}_*$ as functions of (reduced) separation $(\bar{c}_2 - \bar{c}_1)/\sigma$ for the binary probit model ($\bar{c}_1 = 0{\cdot}0$).

For the Weibull distribution we have

$$\tilde{c}_*^* - \tilde{c}_*^\star = -\sum_\rho \int_0^1 \mathrm{d}\hat{\sigma}\, \frac{\mathrm{d}\bar{c}_\rho}{\mathrm{d}\hat{\sigma}} P_\rho(\hat{\sigma}) = \frac{1}{\Delta} \ln \left[\frac{\sum_\rho \exp(-\Delta \bar{c}_\rho^\star)}{\sum_\rho \exp(-\Delta \bar{c}_\rho^*)} \right] \tag{93}$$

$$= \frac{1}{\Delta} \ln \left[\sum_\rho \exp(-\Delta \bar{c}_\rho) \right] + \bar{c}_\rho \,. \tag{94}$$

Now, $\tilde{c}_*^*$ is the mean value of the Weibull distribution $\Gamma_\rho(c)$ so finally

$$\tilde{c}_* = \tilde{c}_*^\star = -\frac{1}{\Delta} \ln \sum_\rho \exp(-\Delta \bar{c}_\rho) + \frac{\gamma}{\Delta} \,. \tag{95}$$

This result will be used extensively in the multidimensional choice models of section 5.

4.4 *The entropy maximising and group surplus maximising approaches*

The random utility models described above are underpinned by a rational assessment of choice alternatives in which the probabilistic component of the theory arises because of the different perception of utility associated with any choice alternative. The approach is essentially *behavioural* in nature. An alternative, and widely used, method of generating travel demand and activity location models is that proposed by Wilson (1967; 1970) based on the concept of entropy, in which the most probable distribution of trips is determined subject to any known constraints.

To date, all *applications* of the entropy maximising methodology have been at the aggregate level, and it is at this level that the constraints on demand have been expressed. It is important to note, however, as Wilson has stressed, that the procedure may equally be applied at the microlevel. The entropy of the discrete probability distribution $\{P_1, ..., P_\rho, ..., P_N\}$, defined as

$$W = -\sum_\rho P_\rho \ln P_\rho \,, \tag{96}$$

is maximised subject to the normalisation condition

$$\sum_\rho P_\rho = 1 \,, \tag{97}$$

the cost constraint

$$\sum_\rho P_\rho \bar{c}_\rho = C \,, \tag{98}$$

and any other constraints on the distribution. The quantity C is the *observed* expenditure (or perceived cost) for the population Π of which the 'individual' of interest is a member, with $\bar{c}_\rho$ the mean cost attributed to the option X_ρ by an observer (the model builder). The optimal solution of the program (96) to (98) is given by

$$P_\rho = \exp(-\tilde{\eta} - \Delta \bar{c}_\rho) \,, \tag{99}$$

where $\tilde{\eta}$ and Δ are calculated to satisfy the constraints (97) and (98). $\tilde{\eta}$ is trivially determined from equation (97) to be

$$\tilde{\eta} = \ln \sum_\rho \exp(-\Delta \bar{c}_\rho) \,. \tag{100}$$

The formal similarity between $\tilde{\eta}$ and $\tilde{c}_*$ in equation (95) is no coincidence. From equations (100) and (95) we have immediately

$$\tilde{\eta} = -\Delta \tilde{c}_* + \gamma \,. \tag{101}$$

It can also be seen from equations (89), (91), (96), and (100) that, for fixed value of Δ, the generalised surplus may be written

$$\Delta S = -\sum_{\rho} \int_{0}^{1} \mathrm{d}\hat{\sigma} \frac{\mathrm{d}\bar{c}_{\rho}(\hat{\sigma})}{\mathrm{d}\hat{\sigma}} P_{\rho}(\hat{\sigma}) = \tilde{c}_{\star}^{\star} - \tilde{c}_{\star}^{\star} = \frac{1}{\Delta}(\tilde{\eta}^{\star} - \tilde{\eta}^{\star}) \tag{102}$$

$$= C^{\star} - C^{\star} + \frac{1}{\Delta}(W^{\star} - W^{\star}) \, , \tag{103}$$

where the ☆ and ★ notation again denotes evaluation of a variable in the initial and final cost states corresponding to $\boldsymbol{c}^{\star}$ and $\boldsymbol{c}^{\star}$ respectively.

Several comments about the entropy maximising method and its application are appropriate at this point. The methodology, which may be applied with equal validity at the macrolevel and microlevels, is characterised by the *lack* of assumptions made concerning the decisionmaking process at the level of the individual. The probability distribution (99) obtained by maximising entropy is, as Wilson (1970) has pointed out, that which makes the weakest assumptions consistent with what is known and reflected in the constraints. The method can be viewed as a statistical aggregation procedure, and trip variability may be considered to arise from any of the sources outlined in section 4.1. It is not, however, generally within the spirit of the approach to pin down the variation to any particular source as this would, in effect, present additional assumptions or hypotheses which could be exploited in model formation. In the above calculation, which gives the result (103), for example, the population must in fact be endowed with economic rationality in order to be able to interpret ΔS as the appropriate measure of benefit. In this case W/Δ in equation (103) becomes formally equivalent to a utility function for the group, measured in money units.

Derivation of the relation (103) by path integration of the demand function is not restricted to the form of the entropy function (96) and may be obtained for *any* program with the following structure

$$\max_{\{\boldsymbol{P}\}} \frac{1}{\Delta}\hat{W}(\boldsymbol{P}) - \sum_{\rho} P_{\rho}\bar{c}_{\rho} \, , \tag{104}$$

subject to

$$\sum_{\rho} P_{\rho} = 1 \, , \tag{105}$$

plus any other constraints on the probability distribution. Here the objective function may be interpreted as the net utility or surplus function for the group Π *in the sense that maximisation of this quantity reproduces the variability existing at the individual level.* Where one seeks to explain trip variability in terms of *economic rationality* it is more appropriate to start from a utility-based approach rather than an information-theory approach, as noted by Beckmann and Golob (1971) and Neuberger (1971). If the economic implications of a change in the vector of perceived costs are to be determined and interpreted it is indeed essential that the basis upon which decisions are considered to be made is fully recognised. It can be seen from equations (49) and (82) that the results are indeed sensitive to the decision process imputed by an observer to the choicemaking population.

If, however, the observer is not prepared to attribute the variability at the microlevel or macrolevel to any particular source, or is confronted by several sources of variability, which would overtax theoretical or data capability at the level of resolution considered, the entropy maximising method would seem to be the appropriate model building device, and in fact possibly the only approach. The methodology, by its very nature, generates descriptive rather than causal models because the fundamental sources of variability are not subject to a causal interpretation.

For the remainder of the paper I shall assume that the choice models are underpinned by a *rational decision process* for which *random utility theory* is appropriate. All other approaches considered in this paper will be used on occasion for comparative purposes.

4.5 *Notation*

In later discussion on theoretical issues it proves very convenient to relax the *notational* distinction between utility or benefit u, disutility c, and surplus s. In the following section, a single variable u will be used to denote all components, which will be termed utility components. Perceived generalised cost will thus be included implicitly as a negative utility measured in money units. The net utility or surplus will, as before, be calculated consistently. In section 6, I shall, where it proves convenient, reintroduce the generalised cost notation c.

It will also prove convenient on occasion to absorb the dispersion parameter, say θ, into the utility function u in an expression such as $\exp(\theta u)$ which will be written $\exp(\hat{u})$. If u is in money units then θ will be the coefficient of the attribute money (out-of-pocket cost) in the linear expression

$$\hat{u}_p = \sum_{\eta} \bar{\alpha}_\eta Z_p^\eta \, .$$

5 The analytic structure of travel demand models

In this section I shall extend, within the framework of random utility theory, the work of Neuberger (1971), Harris and Tanner (1974), Cochrane (1975), and Domencich and McFadden (1975), and build on the work of section 4, in the development of consistent demand models and evaluation measures for multidimensional choice situations. A derivation is given of Manheim's partial share models, for which choice is governed by specific, additive, separable utility functions, and the full significance and role of composite costs, discussed earlier, will be established. Finally, the class of demand functions treated will be extended to a general choice model which allows the 'recursive' and 'simultaneous' approaches to multiple-choice modelling to be placed within a broader perspective. Throughout, emphasis is given to the role of *attribute correlation* in the structuring of behavioural models.

5.1 *Approaches to equilibrium modelling*

5.1.1 *Demand models as representations of the trip decision process*

The traditional urban-transport planning process involved a decomposition in which a set of submodels was used to correspond to the address sequence shown in table 4. The form of demand model was based on a dynamic scenario of the trip decision process in which a person decided whether to make a trip, then whether to take public or private transport, where to perform a given activity, and then finally which route to take. The trip decision was thus conceived within a time framework in which successive choices were conditional on the predecessor.

The ambivalence of the position of the modal-split model in the sequence with respect to the distribution submodel was recognised at an early stage. In order to accommodate modal competition in a more satisfactory way, trip interchange models of modal split were developed by the Traffic Research Corporation in the early 1960s within the model structure (2), and have dominated applications to date, with analytic forms recently replacing the diversion curve approach (see table 1). A person was now considered to choose mode *after* the location decisions had been settled.

Four basic approaches to forecasting travel demand in equilibrium are now usually identified: aggregate sequential; disaggregate sequential; aggregate simultaneous; and disaggregate simultaneous. The first descriptor refers, as explained earlier, to whether the model addresses data pertaining to groups or to individuals (or households), whereas the latter characterises the representation of the trip decision process itself. A full range of examples of these distinct approaches is given by CRA (1972) and by Ruiter (1973). A small number of recent British studies have employed hybrid forms. In the model developed by Bonsall et al (1974) and the models in the Coventry Transportation Study (1973)(6) and Greater London Study (Havers et al, 1974), for example, the trip generation stage has been developed at the household level with other submodels addressing aggregate data, and the distribution and modal-split models have been combined in a joint structure similar to that proposed by Wilson (1969).

It has been argued that the 'simultaneous' (or 'joint') and 'recursive' (or 'sequential') model structures are based on different hypotheses about the underlying travel decisionmaking process. Thus Ben-Akiva (1974) remarks "The simultaneous structure is very general and does not require any specific assumptions. The recursive structure represents a specific conditional decision structure, ie the traveller is assumed to decompose his trip decision into several stages. Thus, simultaneous and recursive structures represent simultaneous and sequential decision making processes". The existence of a semantic difficulty in relation to the descriptors 'simultaneous' and 'sequential' and time ordering of the trip decision process has been noted on several occasions (see for example Kraft, 1974). However, the important point is that both representations of the trip decision process are underpinned by a utility function which, in the theory of rational choice, governs an optimal selection over the set of alternatives. Once this function has been specified the generation of the demand model becomes a mathematical exercise within a specific theoretical framework. Thus, in the random utility framework, the model may in principle be developed through multiple integration as in equation (50). Any classification of the analytic structure of the demand function, insofar as it pertains to the *behavioural* context of the model, is thus determined by the properties and structure of the utility function itself. How, in fact, a traveller identifies his optimal choice in a maze of possibilities and disregards suboptimal alternatives is not particularly relevant in an equilibrium (cross-sectional) approach, although a mental picture of how this *may* occur can be useful in interpreting certain characteristics of the resultant model.

Table 4. Address sequence for conventional transport model system.

Submodel	Address
Urban-regional growth model	What will be the magnitude of urban-regional growth?
Activity location land use allocation model	Where will the activities be located?
Generation	How many trips will the activities generate?
Modal split	Which mode of travel will be used?
Distribution	Where will these trips go?
Assignment	Which route will these trips take?
Evaluation	What is the 'best' transportation system?

5.1.2 *The 'recursive' and 'simultaneous' approaches*

I shall now discuss the 'recursive' and 'simultaneous' approaches insofar as they relate to behavioural issues. In particular, the recent work of Ben-Akiva (1973), who was the first to perform a structural sensitivity analysis in a multiple-choice context, will be discussed briefly to provide a basis for model development. I shall argue later that the models examined by Ben-Akiva, and indeed any 'joint-choice' model structure based on the multinomial logit function [equation (106)], with a trivial exception, are theoretically unsound.

(6) The Coventry Transport model in table 1 is an indirect representation of a 'simultaneous' structure.

Recursive structures such as those listed in table 1, involve the assumptions of '*separability*' and of '*sequence*'. The first concept relates to the properties of the underlying utility function, which allows the various choices to be modelled separately. Thus the conditional probability $P_{\mu|\rho}$, say, is dependent only on a subset of the variables, namely those appropriate to the choices $X_\rho Y_1, ..., X_\rho Y_\mu, ..., X_\rho Y_\eta$ associated with X_ρ, and is independent of those associated with $X_{\rho' \neq \rho}$. The basic assumption of separability is that the marginal rate of substitution between two variables which determine a particular choice is functionally independent of other choices. The separability-of-choices assumption is also usually made with respect to 'simultaneous' structures.

The sequence assumption relates to the nature of the 'hierarchical' structure of the utility function and indicates the nature of the interdependence between the choices in different dimensions, which is frequently interpreted in terms of the conditional dependence of the decision process. The sequence is expressed in a recursive model both in the way alternatives are partitioned, or choice dimensions are ordered, and in the formation of composite costs. Recently much work has been done in improving consistency in recursive models by incorporating generalised costs (Wilson, 1969; Manheim, 1973; CRA, 1972), which maintain the same marginal rate of substitution between variables entering more than one dimension in the choice hierarchy, and by appropriately defining composite costs or index prices (Strotz, 1957).

The separability assumption is introduced to simplify the modelling process. CRA (1972), who were the first to apply the disaggregate modelling framework to an entire set of choices, exploited the separability properties of the independence axiom in the calibration of a shopping trip model. By assuming a utility function in which the components associated with a shopping trip itself, destination, time of day, and mode, were additive, the properties of the multinomial logit model allowed the complex choice process over these 'dimensions' to be decoupled into a series of simple steps. Composite costs, equivalent to the function (32), were formed in order to preserve the 'utility' computed in one dimension, in other dimensions.

In order to illustrate, and later develop, the implications of these concepts I shall refer now to the work of Ben-Akiva (1973), who has calibrated a multinomial logit model, for choice over frequency, destination, and mode of shopping trips, both directly and indirectly (see Manheim, 1973), and compared the results with those of recursive models based on two possible sequencies, each with different composite cost functions. These processes may be illustrated most simply for choice in two dimensions $X = \{X_1, ..., X_\rho, ..., X_N\}$ and $Y = \{Y_1, ..., Y_\mu, ..., Y_M\}$. The simultaneous model structure was of the form

$$P_{\rho\mu} = \frac{\exp[\bar{u}(\rho, \mu)]}{\sum_{\rho\mu}\exp[\bar{u}(\rho, \mu)]}, \tag{106}$$

with

$$\bar{u}(\rho, \mu) = \bar{u}_\rho + \bar{u}_\mu + \bar{u}_{\rho\mu} ; \tag{107}$$

$$\bar{u}_\rho = \sum_\eta \bar{\alpha}_\eta^X Z_\rho^\eta , \tag{108}$$

$$\bar{u}_\mu = \sum_{\eta'} \bar{\alpha}_{\eta'}^Y Z_\mu^{\eta'} , \tag{109}$$

$$\bar{u}_{\rho\mu} = \sum_{\eta''} \bar{\alpha}_{\eta''}^{XY} Z_{\rho\mu}^{\eta''} . \tag{110}$$

The multinomial logit model is of linear form in the attribute vector $\boldsymbol{Z}$, with $\bar{u}_\rho$ and $\bar{u}_\mu$ denoting the components which are constant over the choice dimensions Y and X respectively, and $\bar{u}_{\rho\mu}$ is that component which varies across both dimensions.

Now equation (106) may be written in the following form

$$P_{\rho\mu} = \frac{\exp(\bar{u}_\rho+\bar{u}_{\rho\mu})}{\sum\limits_\rho \exp(\bar{u}_\rho+\bar{u}_{\rho\mu})}\,\frac{\exp(\bar{u}_\mu+\hat{\tilde{u}}_{\mu *})}{\sum\limits_\mu \exp(\bar{u}_\mu+\hat{\tilde{u}}_{\mu *})}\,, \tag{111}$$

where

$$\hat{\tilde{u}}_{\mu *} = \ln \sum_\rho \exp(\bar{u}_\rho+\bar{u}_{\rho\mu})\,. \tag{112}$$

The conditional probability $P_{\rho|\mu}$ and marginal probability P_μ can thus be identified as

$$P_{\rho|\mu} = \frac{\exp(\bar{u}_\rho+\bar{u}_{\rho\mu})}{\sum\limits_\rho \exp(\bar{u}_\rho+\bar{u}_{\rho\mu})}\,, \tag{113}$$

and

$$P_\mu = \frac{\exp(\bar{u}_\mu+\hat{\tilde{u}}_{\mu *})}{\sum\limits_\mu \exp(\bar{u}_\mu+\hat{\tilde{u}}_{\mu *})}\,. \tag{114}$$

Equally, we can write

$$P_{\rho\mu} = P_{\mu|\rho}P_\rho\,, \tag{115}$$

with

$$P_{\mu|\rho} = \frac{\exp(\bar{u}_\mu+\bar{u}_{\rho\mu})}{\sum\limits_\mu \exp(\bar{u}_\mu+\bar{u}_{\rho\mu})}\,, \tag{116}$$

and

$$P_\rho = \frac{\exp(\bar{u}_\rho+\tilde{u}_{\rho *})}{\sum\limits_\rho \exp(\bar{u}_\rho+\hat{\tilde{u}}_{\rho *})}\,, \tag{117}$$

with

$$\tilde{u}_{\rho *} = \ln \sum_\mu \exp(\bar{u}_\mu+\bar{u}_{\rho\mu})\,. \tag{118}$$

The expressions (106), (111), and (115) are mathematically equivalent. The parameters $\bar{\boldsymbol{\alpha}}^X$, $\bar{\boldsymbol{\alpha}}^Y$, and $\bar{\boldsymbol{\alpha}}^{XY}$ in the 'simultaneous' model may therefore be estimated directly from the multinomial logit model (106) or indirectly from either of the forms (111) and (115). Ben-Akiva has compared this model with two recursive forms, which may be written as follows:

$$P_{\rho\mu} = P_\mu P_{\rho|\mu} = \frac{\exp(\bar{u}_\mu+\hat{\tilde{u}}_{\mu *}\delta)}{\sum\limits_\mu \exp(\bar{u}_\mu+\hat{\tilde{u}}_{\mu *}\delta)}\,\frac{\exp(\bar{u}_\rho+\bar{u}_{\rho\mu})}{\sum\limits_\rho \exp(\bar{u}_\rho+\bar{u}_{\rho\mu})}\,, \tag{119}$$

and

$$P_{\rho\mu} = P_\rho P_{\mu|\rho} = \frac{\exp(\bar{u}_\rho+\hat{\tilde{u}}_{\rho *}\delta')}{\sum\limits_\rho \exp(\bar{u}_\rho+\hat{\tilde{u}}_{\rho *}\delta')}\,\frac{\exp(\bar{u}_\mu+\bar{u}_{\mu\rho})}{\sum\limits_\mu \exp(\bar{u}_\mu+\bar{u}_{\rho\mu})}\,, \tag{120}$$

where δ and δ' are coefficients of the composite variables. The possible forms of the composite functions (for $\tilde{u}_{\mu *}$) considered were

'weighted prices' $\hat{\tilde{u}}_{\mu *}(\eta) = \sum\limits_\rho P_{\rho|\mu} Z_\rho^\eta\,,$ (121)

'weighted generalised costs' $\hat{\tilde{u}}_{\mu *} = \sum\limits_\rho P_{\rho|\mu}\bar{u}_{\rho\mu}\,,$ (122)

'weighted utilities' $\hat{\tilde{u}}_{\mu *} = \sum\limits_\rho P_{\rho|\mu}(\bar{u}_\rho+\bar{u}_{\rho\mu})\,,$ (123)

and 'log of the denominator' $\hat{\tilde{u}}_{\mu *} = \ln \sum\limits_\rho \exp(\bar{u}_\rho+\bar{u}_{\rho\mu})\,.$ [equation (112)]

The functional form (122) was used by CRA (1972) in their disaggregate shopping model[(7)]. Similar forms exist for $\hat{u}_{\rho *}$.

It can be seen that if the unity constraint on the coefficient in equation (114) is relaxed, a model similar to the recursive structure (119) is obtained with the composite cost form (112), and corresponds to one of Manheim's Special Product (MSP) models. As Ben-Akiva notes "Writing the indirect structure of the simultaneous model without the unity constraint corresponds to an alternative formulation of a recursive model ... An empirical 'test of simultaneity' can be made by estimating the unconstrained model (MSP *model*) and performing a statistical test to determine *whether the δ parameter* is significantly different from one". (The italics have been inserted by the author.)

Much has been written about the advantages and disadvantages of the recursive and simultaneous approaches (see Brand, 1973). It is usually argued that separability is a more reasonable assumption than sequence, for there is often no *a priori* way to distinguish between several possible sequences, and that in fact travellers do not make choices 'sequentially' anyway. The latter aspect, I have argued, can be misleading in the conceptualisation and formation of *equilibrium* models.

It is clear from the above discussion on the two approaches that the parameter δ plays an important role in the distinction between the structures, although its significance is not elucidated in the work of Ben-Akiva (1973) or in Manheim's (1973) characterisation of demand models. Why does the assumption of sequence destroy the property of independence from irrelevant alternatives of the choice axiom when the recursive structure involves the composite cost (112)? Is the argument concerning the maintenance of utility in recursive models through the composite cost form (122) justified? Are, in fact, the models (106) and (119) consistent with the utility functions assumed to have generated them? These issues centre directly on the phenomenon of *attribute correlation* to which I shall now turn.

5.2 *The existence and implications of attribute correlation*

5.2.1 *Attribute correlation and Luce's choice axiom*

Consider again the red bus–blue bus conundrum. The problem of apportioning trips was seen as one of mode definition, or how to prespecify alternatives which in some sense had equal 'weight' in the choice process. In this example the attribute colour has (presumably) negligible effect on bus patronage, which suggests that the notion of 'weight' has something to do with 'independent' contributions to the cost or utility functions. Here the red and blue buses are endowed with attributes which are perfectly correlated. That is, the times, costs, comfort factors, etc of the two public transport alternatives are adjudged to be identical by each individual although there will in general be an interpersonal variation in the perception of these attributes.

The phenomenon of attribute correlation and the violence rendered to Luce's axiomatic approach, when choice between 'similar' alternatives has been considered, has long been recognised in mathematical psychology. Luce's model would suggest that the relative probability of complex choice alternatives could be computed by summing the values of the component attributes to produce a total utility value V_ρ as in equation (94). [This is, in effect, assumed in equation (106).] That this could yield absurd results when common elements were present in the choices was pointed out by Restle (1961), who argued that the choice between two complex and 'overlapping' alternatives depends not at all on the elements common to the two alternatives, but only on differential elements. Restle developed a set-theoretical

(7) A full discussion of the implications of these forms for the marginal rate of substitution between pairs of variables throughout the model is given by Ben-Akiva (1973).

approach to accommodate the effect while maintaining the flavour of the axiomatic formulation. The red bus–blue bus anomaly here is simply a manifestation of the problems arising from applying Luce's axiom in a condition of substantial 'overlapping' or 'correlation' of attributes.

The effect of correlation in the random utility interpretation of probabilistic choice theory can be simply demonstrated in the case of binary choice between alternatives X_1 and X_2 with normally distributed utility values (see, for example, Restle, 1971). The probability that X_1 is chosen is clearly the probability that the utility difference $u_1 - u_2$ is positive. The distribution of $u_1 - u_2$, which is central to the calculation, has standard deviation $\sigma_{1,2}$ given by

$$\sigma_{1,2} = (\sigma_1^2 + \sigma_2^2 - 2r_{1,2}\sigma_1\sigma_2)^{1/2} , \tag{124}$$

where σ_1 and σ_2 are the standard deviations of the distributions of u_1 and u_2, respectively, while $r_{1,2}$ is the product moment correlation between them. If σ_1 and σ_2 are equal and $r_{1,2}$ is approximately equal to unity, the quantity $\sigma_{1,2}$ will be very small and the probability of choosing X_1, which depends on the difference between the means $\bar{u}_1$ and $\bar{u}_2$ divided by the standard deviation of the difference, $\sigma_{1,2}$, can be near unity even though the means are not far apart. Langdon (1976) has exploited this argument in a multimode selection problem (see section 6.3). I shall now show how correlation manifests itself in random utility models of multidimensional choice.

5.2.2 *The generation of share models from additive separable utility functions*
Consider choice in the two dimensions X and Y to be governed by a utility function of the form

$$U(X, Y) = U^X + U^{XY} , \tag{125}$$

such that

$$u(\rho, \mu) = u_\rho + u_{\rho\mu} , \qquad \rho = 1, ..., N , \quad \mu = 1, ..., M . \tag{126}$$

In the function (126) the existence of correlation between the utility distributions for the choices $\{X_\rho Y_1, ..., X_\rho Y_\mu, ..., X_\rho Y_M\}$ is explicitly recognised through the commonality of the component u_ρ which is a function of attributes that are perceived, by any individual, to be identical for all choices in the Y dimension. (The subscripts ρ and μ will denote, as before, components in X and Y dimensions respectively.) Now if u_ρ and $u_{\rho\mu}$ are random variables drawn from distributions $\Gamma_\rho(u, \bar{u}_\rho)$ and $\Gamma_{\rho\mu}(u, \bar{u}_{\rho\mu})$, respectively, then $u(\rho, \mu)$ can be expressed as follows:

$$u(\rho, \mu) = \bar{u}_\rho + \bar{u}_{\rho\mu} + \epsilon_\rho + \epsilon_{\rho\mu} , \tag{127}$$

where ϵ_ρ and $\epsilon_{\rho\mu}$ are stochastic residuals with means equal to zero and standard deviations σ_ρ and $\sigma_{\rho\mu}$ respectively. [The consequence of neglecting attribute correlation would be to generate the multinomial logit model as Domencich and McFadden (1975) have done.]

$P_{\rho\mu}$, the probability that alternative $\{\rho, \mu\}$ will be selected, can be written

$$P_{\rho\mu} = \text{prob}(u(\rho, \mu) > u(\rho', \mu') \ \forall \rho' \in X, \mu' \in Y) , \tag{128}$$

and will be characterised as follows:

$$P_{\rho\mu} = F_{\rho\mu}(\bar{\boldsymbol{u}}_X, \bar{\boldsymbol{u}}_{XY}; \boldsymbol{\sigma}_X, \boldsymbol{\sigma}_{XY}) , \tag{129}$$

where the vectors $\bar{\boldsymbol{u}}_X$, $\bar{\boldsymbol{u}}_{XY}$ contain all mean values of the utility components in the $\{X, Y\}$ choice complex, with $\boldsymbol{\sigma}_X$ and $\boldsymbol{\sigma}_{XY}$ the corresponding vectors of standard deviations. That is $\bar{\boldsymbol{u}}_X = (\bar{u}_1, ..., \bar{u}_\rho, ..., \bar{u}_N)$, $\bar{\boldsymbol{u}}_{XY} = (\bar{u}_{11}, ..., \bar{u}_{\rho\mu}, ..., \bar{u}_{NM})$ and $\boldsymbol{\sigma}_X = (\sigma_1, ..., \sigma_\rho, ..., \sigma_N)$, $\boldsymbol{\sigma}_{XY} = (\sigma_{11}, ..., \sigma_{\rho\mu}, ..., \sigma_{NM})$.

I shall assume that each of the sets of random variables ϵ_ρ ($\rho = 1, ..., N$) and $\epsilon_{\rho\mu}$ ($\rho = 1, ..., N$; $\mu = 1, ..., M$) are independent. It is clear in this case that the function $F_{\rho\mu}$ must satisfy the boundary condition

$$\lim_{\sigma_X \to 0} \lim_{\bar{u}_X \to 0} F_{\rho\mu}(\bar{u}_X, \bar{u}_{XY}; \sigma_X, \sigma_{XY}) = f_{\rho\mu}(\bar{u}_{XY}, \sigma_{XY}), \quad \forall \rho \in X, \quad \mu \in Y, \tag{130}$$

where $f_{\rho\mu}(\bar{u}_{XY}, \sigma_{XY})$ is the independent random utility model generated by the function

$$u(\rho, \mu) = \bar{u}_{\rho\mu} + \epsilon_{\rho\mu}. \tag{131}$$

Similarly the generalised surplus function, or mean value of the distribution of maximum surplus $\tilde{U}_{\bullet\bullet}$, must satisfy

$$\lim_{\sigma_X \to 0} \lim_{\bar{u}_X \to 0} \tilde{U}_{\bullet\bullet}(\bar{u}_X, \bar{u}_{XY}; \sigma_X, \sigma_{XY}) = \tilde{u}_{\bullet\bullet}(\bar{u}_{XY}; \sigma_{XY}), \tag{132}$$

where $\tilde{u}_{\bullet\bullet}$ is the composite utility derived from equation (131). Thus if $\epsilon_{\rho\mu}$ ($\rho = 1, ..., N$, $\mu = 1, ..., M$) are drawn from independent Weibull distributions with common standard deviation, $\sigma_{\rho\mu} = \sigma_{XY}$, the limiting conditions become

$$\lim_{\sigma_X \to 0} \lim_{\bar{u}_X \to 0} F_{\rho\mu}(\bar{u}_X, \bar{u}_{XY}; \sigma_X, \sigma_{XY}) = \frac{\exp(\Delta\bar{u}_{\rho\mu})}{\sum_{\rho\mu} \exp(\Delta\bar{u}_{\rho\mu})}, \tag{133}$$

and

$$\lim_{\sigma_X \to 0} \lim_{\bar{u}_X \to 0} \tilde{U}_{\bullet\bullet}(\bar{u}_X, \bar{u}_{XY}; \sigma_X, \sigma_{XY}) = \frac{1}{\Delta} \ln \sum_{\rho\mu} \exp(\Delta\bar{u}_{\rho\mu}), \tag{134}$$

where

$$\Delta = \frac{\pi}{\sigma_{XY}\sqrt{6}}. \tag{135}$$

Now the choice process *may* be conceptualised in terms of the way an individual acquires full information in order to act optimally. The additive separable utility function lends itself naturally to a partitioning of the alternatives in the hierarchy shown in figure 1. This is essentially a representation of *Strotz's utility tree* (Strotz, 1957). For each alternative, X_ρ, an individual t will determine the maximum value

$$u^t_{\rho\bullet} = \max_\mu u^t_{\rho\mu}, \tag{136}$$

and then select alternative X_ρ if

$$u^t_\rho + u^t_{\rho\bullet} = \max_{\rho'} (u^t_{\rho'} + u^t_{\rho'\bullet}). \tag{137}$$

Over the whole population

$$P_{\rho\mu} = \text{prob}(u_\rho + u_{\rho\bullet} > u_{\rho'} + u_{\rho'\bullet}, \ \forall \rho' \in X; \ \text{and} \ u_{\rho\mu} > u_{\rho\mu'}, \ \forall \mu' \in Y), \tag{138}$$

where $u_{\rho\bullet}$ is a random variable drawn from the distribution of maximum utility

$$\Lambda_{\rho\bullet} = \text{O}_{\max}[\Gamma_{\rho\mu}, \ \mu = 1, ..., M]. \tag{139}$$

Because of the independence of the distributions in the separate choice dimensions, we may write

$$P_{\rho\mu} = \text{prob}(u^\dagger_{\rho\bullet} > u^\dagger_{\rho'\bullet}, \ \forall \rho' \in X)\,\text{prob}(u_{\rho\mu} > u_{\rho\mu'}, \ \forall \mu' \in Y), \tag{140}$$

where $u^\dagger_{\rho\bullet}$ is distributed according to the sum of the independent random variables u_ρ and $u_{\rho\bullet}$. This distribution $\Lambda^\dagger_{\rho\bullet}$ has mean $\bar{u}^\dagger_{\rho\bullet}$ and standard deviation $\sigma^\dagger_{\rho\bullet}$ given by

$$\bar{u}^\dagger_{\rho\bullet} = \bar{u}_\rho + \bar{u}_{\rho\bullet}, \tag{141}$$

$$\sigma^\dagger_{\rho\bullet} = (\sigma^2_\rho + \sigma^2_{\rho\bullet})^{1/2}. \tag{142}$$

$P_{\rho\mu}$ may thus be expressed in the product form

$$P_{\rho\mu} = P_\rho(\bar{u}^\dagger_{1*}, ..., \bar{u}^\dagger_{\rho*}, ..., \bar{u}^\dagger_{N*})P_{\mu|\rho}(\bar{u}_{\rho 1}, ..., \bar{u}_{\rho\mu}, ..., \bar{u}_{\rho M}) ,$$

$$\equiv P_\rho(\bar{u}^\dagger_{X*})P_{\mu|\rho}(\bar{u}_{\rho Y}) , \tag{143}$$

in an obvious vector notation, while the difference in generalised consumer surplus ΔS arising from the change $(\bar{u}^*_{11}, ..., \bar{u}^*_{\rho\mu}, ..., \bar{u}^*_{NM}) \rightarrow (\bar{u}^\star_{11}, ..., \bar{u}^\star_{\rho\mu}, ..., \bar{u}^\star_{NM})$ becomes

$$\Delta S = \sum_{\rho\mu} \int_0^1 \mathrm{d}\hat{o} \frac{\mathrm{d}\bar{u}_{\rho\mu}}{\mathrm{d}\hat{o}} P_\rho(\bar{u}^\dagger_{X*})P_{\mu|\rho}(\bar{u}_{\rho Y}) \tag{144}$$

$$= \sum_\rho \int_0^1 \mathrm{d}\hat{o} P_\rho(\bar{u}^\dagger_{X*}) \sum_\mu P_{\mu|\rho}(\bar{u}_{\rho Y}) \frac{\mathrm{d}\bar{u}_{\rho\mu}}{\mathrm{d}\hat{o}} . \tag{145}$$

For translationally invariant distributions

$$\frac{\mathrm{d}\tilde{u}_{\rho*}}{\mathrm{d}\hat{o}} = \sum_\mu P_{\mu|\rho} \frac{\mathrm{d}\bar{u}_{\rho\mu}}{\mathrm{d}\hat{o}} , \tag{146}$$

which reduces equation (145) to

$$\Delta S = \sum_\rho \int_0^1 \mathrm{d}\hat{o} \frac{\mathrm{d}\bar{u}^\dagger_{\rho*}}{\mathrm{d}\hat{o}} P_\rho(\bar{u}^\dagger_{X*}) , \tag{147}$$

on using the independence of $\bar{u}_\rho$ from the path parameter $\hat{o}$. This result has important implications which I shall now explore.

5.2.3 *The properties of utility trees in random utility theory*

In essence, equations (144) and (147) indicate to us that the surplus change evaluated at the level $(X_1Y_1, ..., X_\rho Y_\mu, ..., X_N Y_M)$ is equal to that computed at the level $(X_1, ..., X_\rho, ..., X_N)$. That is, the benefit corresponding to the change $(\bar{u}^*_{11}, ..., \bar{u}^*_{\rho\mu}, ..., \bar{u}^*_{NM}) \rightarrow (\bar{u}^\star_{11}, ..., \bar{u}^\star_{\rho\mu}, ..., \bar{u}^\star_{NM})$ computed with the choice probabilities $P_{\rho\mu}$ is identical to that for the change $(\bar{u}^{\dagger *}_{1*}, ..., \bar{u}^{\dagger *}_{\rho*}, ..., \bar{u}^{\dagger *}_{N*}) \rightarrow (\bar{u}^{\dagger\star}_{1*}, ..., \bar{u}^{\dagger\star}_{\rho*}, ..., \bar{u}^{\dagger\star}_{N*})$ computed with the probabilities P_ρ. This property of vertical aggregation in the utility tree is not surprising, and arises because of the optimality condition underpinning the choice process. All relevant information for optimal choices to be made is passed 'up the tree', as was illustrated in the possible conceptualisation of the decision process for the individual.

This argument may be immediately generalised to an arbitrary number of dimensions over which choice is governed by an additive, separable utility function of the form

$$u(\rho, \mu, ..., \zeta) = u_\rho + u_{\rho\mu} + ... + u_{\rho\mu ... \zeta} ,$$

$$\rho = 1, ..., N ; \quad \mu = 1, ..., M ; \quad \zeta = 1, ..., W . \tag{148}$$

The resultant probability distribution $P_{\rho\mu ... \zeta}$ can be written

$$P_{\rho\mu ... \zeta} = P_\rho P_{\mu|\rho} ... P_{\zeta| ... \mu\rho} , \tag{149}$$

where

$$P_\rho = P_\rho(\bar{u}_X ; \tilde{u}_{X* ... *}) ,$$

$$P_{\mu|\rho} = P_{\mu|\rho}(\bar{u}_{\rho Y} ; \tilde{u}_{\rho Y* ... *}) , \tag{150}$$

and

$$P_{\zeta| ... \mu\rho} = P_{\zeta| ... \mu\rho}(\bar{u}_{\rho\mu ... 1}, ..., \bar{u}_{\rho\mu ... \zeta}, ..., \bar{u}_{\rho\mu ... W}) .$$

The surplus change, ΔS satisfies the relations

$$\Delta S = \sum_{\rho\mu \dots \zeta} \int_0^1 d\hat{o} \frac{d\bar{u}_{\rho\mu \dots \zeta}}{d\hat{o}} P_{\rho\mu \dots \zeta} , \tag{151}$$

$\vdots$

$$= \sum_{\rho} \int_0^1 d\hat{o} \frac{d\bar{u}^{\dagger}_{\rho * \dots *}}{d\hat{o}} P_{\rho} , \tag{152}$$

$$= \tilde{U}^{\star}_{* \dots *} - \tilde{U}^{\star}_{* \dots *} , \tag{153}$$

where the quantities $\bar{u}^{\dagger}_{\rho * \dots *}$ and $\tilde{U}_{* \dots *}$ denote the mean values of the corresponding distributions $\Lambda^{\dagger}_{\rho * \dots *}$ and $\Lambda_{* \dots *}$, with

$$\bar{u}^{\dagger}_{\rho * \dots *} = \bar{u}_{\rho} + \tilde{u}_{\rho * \dots *} .$$

The quantity $\tilde{u}_{\rho * \dots *}$, which appears in equation (152) associated with $\bar{u}^{\dagger}_{\rho * \dots *}$, is the mean of the distribution defined by

$$\Lambda_{\rho * \dots *} = \mathrm{O}_{\max}[\Lambda^{\dagger}_{\rho\mu * \dots *}(u, \bar{u}_{\rho\mu} + \tilde{u}_{\rho\mu * \dots *}), \ \mu = 1, \dots, M] , \tag{154}$$

and $\Lambda^{\dagger}_{\rho\mu * \dots *}$ is, in turn, the distribution of the sum of the independent random variables $u_{\rho\mu}$ and $u_{\rho\mu * \dots *}$. In equation (153), $\tilde{U}^{\star}_{* \dots *}$ and $\tilde{U}^{\star}_{* \dots *}$ are the values of $\tilde{U}_{* \dots *}$ evaluated in the final and initial states respectively.

Thus the computation of choice probabilities and consumer-surplus change may be performed by identifying with each node in the tree a *composite utility*, which is the mean value of the distribution of maximum utility corresponding to that node, and by identifying with each branch a common component of utility. This information accompanies the general tree structure shown in figure 6. The benefit accruing from a system change involving the utilities $\bar{u}_{\rho\mu \dots \zeta}$ is determined from the change in the composite function $\tilde{U}_{** \dots *}$ at the highest vertex in the tree. Another implication of the property (146) concerns the aggregation of alternatives in the tree. A set of

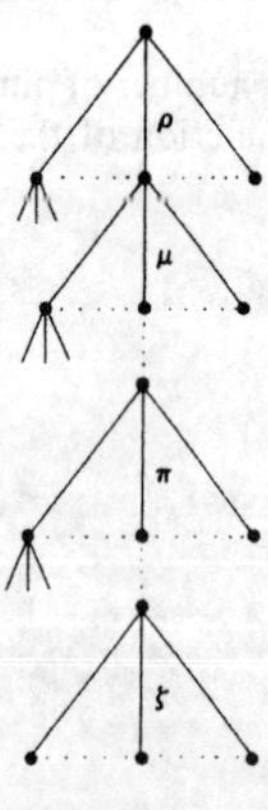

Feature of the structure	Distribution of utility	Mean value	Parameter
Node	$\Lambda_{** \dots * \dots *}$	$\tilde{U}_{** \dots * \dots *}$	β
Branches	Γ_{ρ}	$\bar{u}_{\rho}$	σ_{ρ}
Nodes	$\Lambda_{\rho * \dots * \dots *}$	$\tilde{u}_{\rho * \dots * \dots *}$	λ
Branches	$\Gamma_{\rho\mu}$	$\bar{u}_{\rho\mu}$	$\sigma_{\rho\mu}$
Nodes	$\Lambda_{\rho\mu * \dots * \dots *}$	$\tilde{u}_{\rho\mu \dots * \dots *}$	ϕ
Nodes	$\Lambda_{\rho\mu \dots \gamma * \dots *}$	$\tilde{u}_{\rho\mu \dots \gamma * \dots *}$	ψ
Branches	$\Gamma_{\rho\mu \dots \gamma\pi}$	$\bar{u}_{\rho\mu \dots \gamma\pi}$	$\sigma_{\rho\mu \dots \pi}$
Nodes	$\Lambda_{\rho\mu \dots \gamma\pi * \dots *}$	$\tilde{u}_{\rho\mu \dots \gamma\pi * \dots *}$	ω
Nodes	$\Lambda_{\rho\mu \dots \pi \dots *}$	$\tilde{u}_{\rho\mu \dots \pi \dots *}$	Δ
Branches	$\Gamma_{\rho\mu \dots \pi \dots \zeta}$	$\bar{u}_{\rho\mu \dots \pi \dots \zeta}$	$\sigma_{\rho\mu \dots \zeta}$
Nodes	–	–	–

Figure 6. The generation of partial share models within random utility theory. The distribution of utility, their mean values, and associated parameters are shown for the model $P_{\rho\mu \dots \pi \dots \zeta} = P_{\rho} P_{\mu|\rho} \dots P_{\zeta| \dots \mu\rho}$ generated by a utility function of the form $u(\rho, \mu, \dots, \pi, \dots, \zeta) = u_{\rho} + u_{\rho\mu} + \dots + u_{\rho\mu \dots \pi} + \dots + u_{\rho\mu \dots \pi \dots \zeta}$.

submovements (or dimensions) in the hierarchy, that correspond to a node at *any* level, may be completely replaced by an aggregate movement with the appropriate composite utility index.

5.2.4 *The logit function approximation*

The distributions $\Lambda^{\dagger}$ at any node in the tree will not, in general, result in analytically tractable calculations. Although the relations (148) to (154) hold in general, and require only the translational invariance of the underlying distributions of utility, an approximation must be made in order to derive workable demand functions, while retaining the properties of the utility tree.

The Weibull distribution, as Domencich and McFadden (1975) note, is the only distribution which retains its functional form under the maximisation process (80), whereas the Gaussian retains its form under the addition process—that is, the sum of normal variates is itself normally distributed. As the random variables u_ρ and $u_{\rho *}$ ($\rho = 1, ..., N$) will be drawn from bell-shaped distributions, I shall adopt an approximation in which the stochastic residual $\epsilon^{\dagger}_{\rho *}$, defined in the two-dimensional problem by

$$u_\rho + u_{\rho *} = \bar{u}_\rho + \tilde{u}_{\rho *} + \epsilon^{\dagger}_{\rho *}\,, \qquad \rho = 1, ..., N\,, \tag{155}$$

is distributed according to a Weibull function with zero mean and standard deviation $\sigma^{\dagger}_{\rho *}$ given by

$$\sigma^{\dagger}_{\rho *} = (\sigma_X^2 + \sigma_{X *}^2)^{\frac{1}{2}} \tag{156}$$

$$= \left(\sigma_X^2 + \frac{\pi^2}{6\Delta^2}\right)^{\frac{1}{2}}\,, \tag{157}$$

where σ_X and $\sigma_{X *}$ are the standard deviations of the distributions Γ_ρ and $\Lambda_{\rho *}$ ($\rho = 1, ..., N$) respectively. Equation (157) follows from equation (156) since $\Lambda_{\rho *}$ are Weibull distributions with parameter Δ. The resultant probabilistic choice model then becomes

$$P_{\rho\mu} = \frac{\exp[\beta(\bar{u}_\rho + \tilde{u}_{\rho *})]}{\sum\limits_\rho \exp[\beta(\bar{u}_\rho + \tilde{u}_{\rho *})]} \, \frac{\exp(\Delta \bar{u}_{\rho\mu})}{\sum\limits_\mu \exp(\Delta \bar{u}_{\rho\mu})}\,, \tag{158}$$

with

$$\beta = \frac{\pi}{\sqrt{6}}\left(\sigma_X^2 + \frac{\pi^2}{6\Delta^2}\right)^{-\frac{1}{2}}\,, \tag{159}$$

and

$$\tilde{u}_{\rho *} = \frac{1}{\Delta} \ln \sum_\mu \exp(\Delta \bar{u}_{\rho\mu})\,. \tag{160}$$

The virtual indistinguishability of the probit and logit models, both generated from bell-shaped utility distributions, suggests that the logit approximation will be an extremely good one.

The surplus change ΔS can be written in the following forms

$$\Delta S = \sum_{\rho\mu} \int_0^1 \mathrm{d}\hat{\sigma} \, \frac{\mathrm{d}\bar{u}_{\rho\mu}}{\mathrm{d}\hat{\sigma}} P_{\rho\mu} \tag{161}$$

$$= \sum_\rho \int_0^1 \mathrm{d}\hat{\sigma} \, \frac{\exp[\beta(\bar{u}_\rho + \tilde{u}_{\rho *})]}{\sum\limits_{\rho'} \exp[\beta(\bar{u}_{\rho'} + \tilde{u}_{\rho' *})]} \, \frac{\mathrm{d}\tilde{u}_{\rho *}(\hat{\sigma})}{\mathrm{d}\hat{\sigma}} \tag{162}$$

$$= \frac{1}{\beta} \ln \left\{ \frac{\sum\limits_\rho \exp[\beta(\bar{u}_\rho + \tilde{u}^{\star}_{\rho *})]}{\sum\limits_\rho \exp[\beta(\bar{u}_\rho + \tilde{u}^{\star}_{\rho *})]} \right\}. \tag{163}$$

The composite function $\tilde{U}_{\bullet\bullet}$ is thus given by

$$\tilde{U}_{\bullet\bullet} = \frac{1}{\beta} \ln \sum_{\rho} \exp[\beta(\bar{u}_{\rho} + \tilde{u}_{\rho\bullet})] \tag{164}$$

$$= \frac{1}{\beta} \ln \left\{ \sum_{\rho} \exp(\beta \bar{u}_{\rho}) \left[\sum_{\mu} \exp(\Delta \bar{u}_{\rho\mu}) \right]^{\beta/\Delta} \right\} \tag{165}$$

$$= \frac{1}{\beta} \ln \left\langle \sum_{\rho} \left\{ \sum_{\mu} \exp[\Delta(\bar{u}_{\rho} + \bar{u}_{\rho\mu})] \right\}^{\beta/\Delta} \right\rangle \tag{166}$$

$$= \frac{1}{\beta} \ln \left\langle \sum_{\rho} \left\{ \sum_{\mu} \exp[\Delta \bar{u}(\rho, \mu)] \right\}^{\beta/\Delta} \right\rangle \tag{167}$$

It is straightforward to show that $P_{\rho\mu}$ and $\tilde{U}_{\bullet\bullet}$ satisfy the boundary conditions (133) and (134), because

$$\lim_{\sigma_X \to 0} \beta(\sigma_X, \Delta) = \Delta . \tag{168}$$

The difference in the parameters β and Δ is attributable to the dispersion associated with the distribution of u_X. From equation (159) we note that $\beta \leqslant \Delta$. The relations (158) and (167) may readily be generalised to several dimensions for utility functions of the form

$$u(\rho, \mu, \ldots, \omega, \zeta) = u_{\rho} + u_{\rho\mu} + \ldots + u_{\rho\mu \ldots \omega} + u_{\rho\mu \ldots \omega\zeta} , \tag{169}$$

giving

$$P_{\rho\mu \ldots \omega\zeta} = P_{\rho}(\beta) P_{\mu|\rho}(\lambda) \ldots P_{\omega|\ldots \mu\rho}(\chi) P_{\zeta|\omega \ldots \mu\rho}(\Delta) , \tag{170}$$

where

$$P_{\rho}(\beta) = \frac{\exp[\beta(\bar{u}_{\rho} + \tilde{u}_{\rho\bullet \ldots \bullet})]}{\sum_{\rho} \exp[\beta(\bar{u}_{\rho} + \tilde{u}_{\rho\bullet \ldots \bullet})]} , \tag{171}$$

$\vdots$

$$P_{\zeta|\omega \ldots \rho}(\Delta) = \frac{\exp(\Delta \bar{u}_{\rho \ldots \zeta})}{\sum_{\zeta} \exp(\Delta \bar{u}_{\rho \ldots \zeta})} , \tag{172}$$

with

$$\tilde{u}_{\rho\mu \ldots \omega\bullet} = \frac{1}{\Delta} \ln \sum_{\zeta} \exp(\Delta \bar{u}_{\rho \ldots \zeta}) , \tag{173}$$

$\vdots$

$$\tilde{u}_{\rho\bullet \ldots \bullet} = \frac{1}{\lambda} \ln \sum_{\mu} \exp[\lambda(\bar{u}_{\rho\mu} + \tilde{u}_{\rho\mu\bullet \ldots \bullet})] . \tag{174}$$

If $\bar{u}(\rho, \mu, \ldots, \omega, \zeta)$ is the mean value of $u(\rho, \mu, \ldots, \omega, \zeta)$ in equation (169), then by writing

$$R_{\rho\mu \ldots \omega\zeta} = \exp[\Delta \bar{u}(\rho, \mu, \ldots, \omega, \zeta)] , \tag{175}$$

and

$$R_{\rho\mu \ldots \omega\bullet} = \sum_{\zeta} R_{\rho\mu \ldots \omega\zeta} , \tag{176}$$

it may readily be shown from equations (170) to (176) that

$$P_{\rho\mu \ldots \omega\zeta} = \frac{\left\{ \sum_{\mu} [\ldots (R_{\rho\mu \ldots \omega\bullet})^{\chi/\Delta} \ldots]^{\lambda/\psi} \right\}^{\beta/\lambda}}{\sum_{\rho} \left\{ \sum_{\mu} [\ldots (R_{\rho\mu \ldots \omega\bullet})^{\chi/\Delta} \ldots]^{\lambda/\psi} \right\}^{\beta/\lambda}} \cdots \frac{(R_{\rho\mu \ldots \omega\bullet})^{\chi/\Delta}}{\sum_{\omega} (R_{\rho\mu \ldots \omega\bullet})^{\chi/\Delta}} \frac{R_{\rho\mu \ldots \omega\zeta}}{R_{\rho\mu \ldots \omega\bullet}} , \tag{177}$$

with

$$\Delta \geqslant \chi \geqslant \dots \geqslant \lambda \geqslant \beta \,. \tag{178}$$

Equation (177) is of the form of Manheim's special product model

$$P_{\rho\mu \dots \omega\zeta} = \frac{[\dots (R_{\rho\mu \dots \omega *})^{\delta_1} \dots]^{\delta_n}}{\sum\limits_{\rho} [\dots (R_{\rho\mu \dots \omega *})^{\delta_1} \dots]^{\delta_n}} \cdots \frac{(R_{\rho\mu \dots \omega *})^{\delta_1}}{\sum\limits_{\omega} (R_{\rho\mu \dots \omega *})^{\delta_1}} \frac{R_{\rho\mu \dots \omega\zeta}}{R_{\rho\mu \dots \omega *}} \,. \tag{179}$$

The origin and relative size of the parameters δ_i ($i = 1, \dots, n$), and the relationship between them, is now clear from equations (159) and (177).

The composite utility $\tilde{U}_{* \dots *}$ corresponding to the model (177), which appears in the benefit calculation, takes the form

$$\tilde{U}_{* \dots *} = \frac{1}{\beta} \ln \sum_{\rho} \exp [\beta(\bar{u}_{\rho} + \tilde{u}_{\rho * \dots *})] \tag{180}$$

$$\vdots$$

$$= \frac{1}{\beta} \ln \left\langle \sum_{\rho} \left\{ \sum_{\mu} [\dots (R_{\rho\mu \dots \omega *})^{\chi/\Delta} \dots]^{\lambda/\psi} \right\}^{\beta/\lambda} \right\rangle \,. \tag{181}$$

That the models (158) and (170) violate the 'independence from irrelevant alternatives' axiom (as indeed they should do) may readily be shown. The ratio $P_{\rho\mu}/P_{\rho'\mu'}$ for the model (158) is, for example, given by

$$\frac{P_{\rho\mu}}{P_{\rho'\mu'}} = \frac{\exp(\beta\bar{u}_{\rho} + \Delta\bar{u}_{\rho\mu})}{\exp(\beta\bar{u}_{\rho'} + \Delta\bar{u}_{\rho'\mu'})} \left[\frac{\sum\limits_{\nu} \exp(\Delta\bar{u}_{\rho\nu})}{\sum\limits_{\nu'} \exp(\Delta\bar{u}_{\rho'\nu'})} \right]^{(\beta-\Delta)/\Delta} , \tag{182}$$

which is seen to depend on the utility values of alternatives other than $\{\rho, \mu\}$ and $\{\rho', \mu'\}$. Only if the parameter relation $\beta = \Delta$ holds will the independence axiom be satisfied and, from equation (159), it is apparent that this will only be the case if the variance associated with the utility component $\boldsymbol{u}_X$ is zero. The corresponding properties hold for the model (170).

The analysis here has involved selection of alternatives in many dimensions in which distinct alternatives are components of a complete decision. Although it was assumed that the stochastic components of the utility function within any given dimension were independent, it is most important to note that this assumption may readily be relaxed to accommodate commonality effects among the attributes of alternatives in any dimension. Thus, for example, if the dimension X corresponds to a set of modes it may well be that certain characteristics of the public transport modes correlate strongly. The stochastic components of the utility function will no longer be independent, and it may be necessary to form a utility function with an appropriate substructure. This example will be treated below in section 6.3.

5.2.5 *The entropy maximising method applied to multidimensional choice*

It is well-known that the product shares in equation (170) may be generated by the entropy maximising method. For example $P_{\mu|\rho}$ may be generated from the program

$$\max_{\{P_{\mu|\rho}\}} \left(-\sum_{\mu} P_{\mu|\rho} \ln P_{\mu|\rho} \right) , \tag{183}$$

subject to

$$\sum_{\mu} P_{\mu|\rho} = 1 \,, \tag{184}$$

and

$$\sum_{\mu} P_{\mu|\rho} (\bar{u}_{\rho\mu} + \tilde{u}_{\rho\mu * \dots *}) = U_{\rho} \,. \tag{185}$$

The composite function $\tilde{u}_{\rho\mu * \ldots *}$ must, however, be injected into the program—the methodology is not based on any behavioural theory which would indicate what these values should be. As was shown in section 4.4 the functions which correspond to equation (174) are in fact related to the Lagrange multipliers associated with the constraint

$$\sum_{\eta} P_{\eta|\mu\rho} = 1 , \tag{186}$$

in the corresponding program for the partial share $P_{\eta|\mu\rho}$. Thus the entropy maximising method will generate a correct 'behavioural' model of rational choice if the necessary behavioural parameters are injected into the program, in which case the objective function can be treated like a utility function. Similarly, a constant utility model appropriate to a *probabilistic decision mechanism* can be generated if $\tilde{u}_{\rho\mu * \ldots *}$ is taken as

$$\tilde{u}_{\rho\mu * \ldots *} = \sum_{\eta} P_{\eta|\rho\mu}(\bar{u}_{\rho\mu\eta} + \tilde{u}_{\rho\mu\eta * \ldots *}) , \tag{187}$$

in which case the total 'observed' utility is conserved in the choice process

5.3 *Towards a general model structure*

5.3.1 *The general nature of the choice process*

A fundamental problem must now be confronted. It has been argued strongly (see for example Ben-Akiva, 1973; Brand, 1973) that there are many instances where the specification of a decision sequence is *a priori* unjustified and inappropriate. If this statement is interpreted in terms of the form of the utility function, it is not clear which, if any, of the forms

$$u(\rho, \mu, \ldots, \zeta) = u_{\rho} + u_{\rho\mu} + \ldots + u_{\rho\mu \ldots \zeta} , \tag{188}$$

$$u(\mu, \rho, \ldots, \zeta) = u_{\mu} + u_{\mu\rho} + \ldots + u_{\mu\rho \ldots \zeta} , \tag{189}$$

$$\vdots$$

$$u(\zeta, \omega, \ldots, \rho) = u_{\zeta} + u_{\zeta\omega} + \ldots + u_{\zeta\omega \ldots \rho} , \tag{190}$$

is appropriate to a choice decision over several dimensions. This is precisely the nature of the dilemma over selecting a model structure from equations (1) to (3). It is increasingly argued that where choices in several dimensions are 'interdependent' it is appropriate to use the 'simultaneous' approach and exploit the separability properties of the multinomial logit model

$$P_{\rho\mu \ldots \zeta} = \frac{\exp[\Delta(\bar{u}_{\rho} + \bar{u}_{\mu} + \ldots + \bar{u}_{\rho\mu} + \ldots + \bar{u}_{\rho\mu \ldots \zeta})]}{\sum\limits_{\rho, \ldots, \zeta} \exp[\Delta(\bar{u}_{\rho} + \bar{u}_{\mu} + \ldots + \bar{u}_{\rho\mu} + \ldots + \bar{u}_{\rho\mu \ldots \rho})]} . \tag{191}$$

From the above discussion it is clear that the model (191), which is 'derived' from a utility function of the form

$$u(\rho; \mu; \ldots; \zeta) = u_{\rho} + u_{\mu} + \ldots + u_{\zeta} + \ldots + u_{\rho\mu} + \ldots + u_{\omega\zeta} + \ldots + u_{\rho\mu \ldots \omega\zeta} , \tag{192}$$

is, in general, fundamentally inconsistent with the structure of the stochastic component of equation (192). While the multinomial logit form (191) assumes independence between the distributions of $\epsilon(\rho; \mu; \ldots; \omega; \zeta)$, it is clear that extensive commonality effects will be present in the form

$$\epsilon(\rho; \mu; \ldots; \omega; \zeta) = \epsilon_{\rho} + \epsilon_{\mu} + \ldots + \epsilon_{\rho\mu} + \ldots + \epsilon_{\rho\mu \ldots \omega\zeta} , \tag{193}$$

which is appropriate to the utility function (192). Clearly all the 'tree structures' (188) to (190) are simply special cases of equation (192). It is thus necessary to determine the more general form of demand function which is appropriate to the correlative structure of $\epsilon(\rho; \mu; ...; \omega; \zeta)$ given by equation (193) and which reduces to the partial share models corresponding to structures (188) to (190) when the appropriate components in expression (193) vanish.

It is unfortunately of no use appealing to the multiple integral expressions (50) and (53) to generate the model. These are interactable for a general form of the residual (193). Progress may be made, however, if the conditions which the probability function $P_{\rho\mu ... \zeta}$ and composite function $\tilde{U}_{\bullet ... \bullet}$ must satisfy under certain limiting conditions are identified. Take the case of two-dimensional choice (dimensions X and Y) governed by a utility function of the form

$$u(\rho, \mu) = u_\rho + u_\mu + u_{\rho\mu} \, . \tag{194}$$

In a notation which corresponds to that of section 5.2, $P_{\rho\mu}$, which is characterised by the functional form

$$P_{\rho\mu} = F_{\rho\mu}(\bar{u}_X, \bar{u}_Y, \bar{u}_{XY}; \sigma_X, \sigma_Y, \sigma_{XY}) \, , \tag{195}$$

must satisfy the following conditions:

$$\sum_{\rho\mu} P_{\rho\mu} = 1 \, , \tag{196}$$

and

$$F_{\rho\mu}(0, \bar{u}_Y, \bar{u}_{XY}; 0, \sigma_Y, \sigma_{XY}) = F_{\rho\mu}(\bar{u}_Y, \bar{u}_{XY}; \sigma_Y, \sigma_{XY}) \, , \tag{197}$$

$$F_{\rho\mu}(\bar{u}_X, 0, \bar{u}_{XY}; \sigma_X, 0, \sigma_{XY}) = F_{\rho\mu}(\bar{u}_X, \bar{u}_{XY}; \sigma_X, \sigma_{XY}) \, , \tag{198}$$

$$F_{\rho\mu}(0, 0, \bar{u}_{XY}; 0, 0, \sigma_{XY}) = F_{\rho\mu}(0, \bar{u}_{XY}; 0, \sigma_{XY}) \, , \tag{199}$$

$$F_{\rho\mu}(\bar{u}_X, \bar{u}_Y, \bar{u}_{XY}; 0, \sigma_Y, \sigma_{XY}) = F_{\rho\mu}(\bar{u}_Y, \bar{u}_X + \bar{u}_{XY}; \sigma_Y, \sigma_{XY}) \, , \tag{200}$$

$$F_{\rho\mu}(\bar{u}_X, \bar{u}_Y, \bar{u}_{XY}; \sigma_X, 0, \sigma_{XY}) = F_{\rho\mu}(\bar{u}_X, \bar{u}_Y + \bar{u}_{XY}; \sigma_X, \sigma_{XY}) \, , \tag{201}$$

$$F_{\rho\mu}(\bar{u}_X, \bar{u}_Y, 0; \sigma_X, \sigma_Y, 0) = F_\rho(0, \bar{u}_X; 0, \sigma_X) F_\mu(0, \bar{u}_Y; 0, \sigma_Y) \, , \tag{202}$$

where the function F is given by equation (129). These are the expressions which must be satisfied when the general utility function (192) collapses to the 'hierarchical' forms corresponding to equations (188) to (190).

Similar conditions must be satisfied by the composite utility function $\tilde{U}_{\bullet\bullet}$ given by

$$\tilde{U}_{\bullet\bullet} = \tilde{U}_{\bullet\bullet}(\bar{u}_X, \bar{u}_Y, \bar{u}_{XY}; \sigma_X, \sigma_Y, \sigma_{XY}) \, . \tag{203}$$

For example

$$\tilde{U}_{\bullet\bullet}(\bar{u}_X, 0, \bar{u}_{XY}; \sigma_X, 0, \sigma_{XY}) = \tilde{U}_{\bullet\bullet}(\bar{u}_X, \bar{u}_{XY}; \sigma_X, \sigma_{XY}) \, . \tag{204}$$

In addition to which, $\tilde{U}_{\bullet\bullet}$ and F should be related by

$$F_{\rho\mu} = \frac{\partial \tilde{U}_{\bullet\bullet}}{\partial \bar{u}_{\rho\mu}} \, , \qquad \forall \, \rho \in X \, , \quad \mu \in Y \, , \tag{205}$$

if the Hotelling conditions are to be satisfied.

We have seen that it was necessary to invoke a logit approximation to obtain a manageable demand function (170). Similarly, a search must be made here for a closed form which is computationally manageable and, at the same time, captures the essence of the correlative structure of the utility function and obeys the appropriate limiting conditions.

5.3.2 *A general choice model*

Equations (158) and (167) give an insight into the appropriate structure for a general choice model. Consider the following expressions:

$$P_{\rho\mu} = \frac{\exp(\beta u_\rho^\# + \lambda u_\mu^\# + \Delta \bar{u}_{\rho\mu})}{\sum\limits_{\rho\mu} \exp(\beta u_\rho^\# + \lambda u_\mu^\# + \Delta \bar{u}_{\rho\mu})} , \tag{206}$$

and

$$\tilde{u}_{**} = \frac{1}{\beta + \lambda - \Delta} \ln \sum_{\rho\mu} \exp(\beta u_\rho^\# + \lambda u_\mu^\# + \Delta \bar{u}_{\rho\mu}) , \tag{207}$$

in which the utility functions $u_\rho^\#$ and $u_\mu^\#$ are defined by

$$u_\rho^\# = \bar{u}_\rho + \left(\frac{\beta - \Delta}{\beta}\right) \tilde{u}_{\rho *} , \tag{208}$$

$$u_\mu^\# = \bar{u}_\mu + \left(\frac{\lambda - \Delta}{\lambda}\right) \tilde{u}_{\mu *} , \tag{209}$$

and the composite utilities by

$$\tilde{u}_{\rho *} = \frac{1}{\Delta} \ln \sum_\mu \exp(\Delta \bar{u}_{\rho\mu} + \lambda \bar{u}_\mu) , \tag{210}$$

$$\tilde{u}_{\mu *} = \frac{1}{\Delta} \ln \sum_\rho \exp(\Delta \bar{u}_{\rho\mu} + \beta \bar{u}_\rho) , \tag{211}$$

with

$$\beta = \frac{\pi}{\sqrt{6}} \left(\sigma_X^2 + \frac{\pi^2}{6\Delta^2}\right)^{-\frac{1}{2}} , \tag{212}$$

and

$$\lambda = \frac{\pi}{\sqrt{6}} \left(\sigma_Y^2 + \frac{\pi^2}{6\Delta^2}\right)^{-\frac{1}{2}} . \tag{213}$$

Just as the structure of the model (170) and of the composite costs may be illustrated with reference to the utility tree in figure 6, so too may the structure of the model (206) be illustrated by figure 7. Thus the composite index at node X_ρ is 'related' through each of the interactions $u_{\rho\mu}$ ($\mu = 1, ..., M$) to nodes Y_μ ($\mu = 1, ..., M$) endowed with the parameter λ and with branch specific utility components $\bar{u}_\mu$.

Now, it is the case that boundary conditions alone do not determine a function uniquely (I have in fact sacrificed rather more general forms for the quantities β, λ, $\tilde{u}_{\rho *}$, and $\tilde{u}_{\mu *}$ to Occam's razor), and it must be said that the condition (205) is not

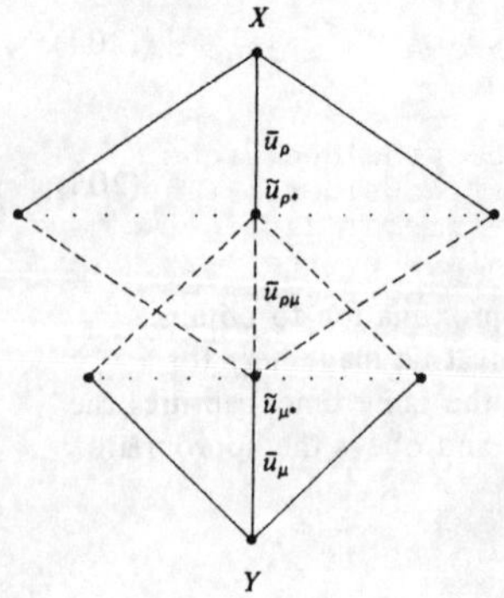

Figure 7. A representation of the interrelated structure of the general choice model [equation (206)].

satisfied exactly, which indicates that equations (206) and (207) are not fully compatible in the Hotelling sense. This is not entirely surprising because it is known that no exact analytic expression may be obtained from equation (194). It may readily be shown, however, by examining the limiting forms of the parameters β and λ in the various cases, that the limiting forms (197) to (202) are satisfied exactly. Extension of the two-dimensional model to several dimensions is given in appendix 3.

5.3.3 *Calibration of the general choice model*

Because the presence of attribute correlation gives rise to complex interdependencies between alternative choices in different dimensions, it is not surprising to find that the calibration process is somewhat more involved than that for the multinomial logit model (191). The quantities $u_\rho^\#$, $u_\mu^\#$, and $\bar{u}_{\rho\mu}$, it should be noted, have the following dependencies

$$u_\rho^\# = \bar{u}_\rho(\bar{\alpha}^X, Z_\rho) + \frac{\beta-\Delta}{\beta}\tilde{u}_{\rho\bullet}(\bar{\alpha}^Y, \bar{\alpha}^{XY};\ Z_1, ..., Z_\mu, ..., Z_M;\ Z_{\rho 1}, ..., Z_{\rho\mu}, ..., Z_{\rho M}) , \tag{214}$$

$$u_\mu^\# = \bar{u}_\mu(\bar{\alpha}^Y, Z_\mu) + \frac{\lambda-\Delta}{\lambda}\tilde{u}_{\mu\bullet}(\bar{\alpha}^X, \bar{\alpha}^{XY};\ Z_1, ..., Z_\rho, ..., Z_N;\ Z_{1\mu}, ..., Z_{\rho\mu}, ..., Z_{N\mu}) , \tag{215}$$

$$\bar{u}_{\rho\mu} = \bar{u}_{\rho\mu}(\bar{\alpha}^{XY};\ Z_{\rho\mu}) . \tag{216}$$

The parameters to be estimated are therefore β, λ, Δ, $\bar{\alpha}^X$, $\bar{\alpha}^Y$, and $\bar{\alpha}^{XY}$. (β, λ, and Δ may be multiplied directly into the linear functions $\bar{\boldsymbol{u}}_X$, $\bar{\boldsymbol{u}}_Y$, and $\bar{\boldsymbol{u}}_{XY}$ and extracted after calibration as the coefficients of those factors which are expressed in money units.) The quantities $u_\rho^\#$ and $u_\mu^\#$ are, through the composite functions $\tilde{u}_{\rho\bullet}$ and $\tilde{u}_{\mu\bullet}$, nonlinear functions of the attributes in the dimensions Y and X respectively.

Unless the parameters may be estimated by maximum likelihood from the model expressed in direct form (206), which would be infeasible for a large number of choices, it would be necessary to resort to an indirect method. Just as the multinomial logit model may be written in the form (115), so too may the model (206) be written indirectly as

$$P_{\rho\mu} = P_\rho P_{\mu|\rho} , \tag{217}$$

with

$$P_\rho = \frac{\exp(\beta u_\rho^\# + \Delta\tilde{u}_{\rho\bullet}^\#)}{\sum\limits_\rho \exp(\beta u_\rho^\# + \Delta\tilde{u}_{\rho\bullet}^\#)} , \tag{218}$$

$$P_{\mu|\rho} = \frac{\exp(\lambda u_\mu^\# + \Delta\bar{u}_{\rho\mu})}{\sum\limits_\mu \exp(\lambda u_\mu^\# + \Delta\bar{u}_{\rho\mu})} , \tag{219}$$

and

$$\tilde{u}_{\rho\bullet}^\# = \frac{1}{\Delta}\ln\sum_\mu \exp(\lambda u_\mu^\# + \Delta\bar{u}_{\rho\mu}) . \tag{220}$$

For the multinomial logit model it was argued that the parameters $\bar{\alpha}^Y$ and $\bar{\alpha}^{XY}$ could be estimated in the conditional probability model $P_{\mu|\rho}$ and transferred directly to the marginal probability model P_ρ, through a composite index. However, in the model (206) $u_\mu^\#$ in $P_{\mu|\rho}$ is, through its dependence on the composite term $\tilde{u}_{\mu\bullet}$, a function of the components $\bar{u}_\rho$ and $\bar{u}_{\rho\mu}$ ($\rho = 1, ..., N$), and similarly $u_\rho^\#$ in P_ρ is a function of the parameters in the Y dimension. This interdependency characterises the very nature of attribute correction in several dimensions. [Note the distinction between $\tilde{u}_{\rho\bullet}^\#$ defined by equation (220) and $u_\rho^\#$ defined by equation (208).]

It is possible to calibrate the model by iteration through either of the processes shown in figures 8(a) and 8(b) which correspond to the two indirect, and mathematically equivalent, formulations of the expression (206), the first of which is appropriate to the form (217). It remains to test the feasibility and convergence properties of these processes and the consistency of the parameter estimates between them. Presumably the most efficient method will depend on the relative sizes of σ_X and σ_Y.

The alternatives to such approaches are either to accept the current joint approach based on the multinomial logit model (191) which, I have argued, is an incorrect representation of the choice process governed by the function (192), or otherwise to attempt to justify *a priori* a particular structure of utility tree [one of the forms (188) to (190)] and perform a structural sensitivity test on alternatives. I shall return to this issue in the context of developing strategic transport planning models in the following section.

(a)

1 Set $\lambda = \Delta$

2 $u_\mu^\# = \bar{u}_\mu + \left(\dfrac{\lambda-\Delta}{\lambda\Delta}\right) \ln \sum_\rho \exp(\beta\bar{u}_\rho + \Delta\bar{u}_{\rho\mu})$

3 Determine λ, Δ, $\bar{\boldsymbol{\alpha}}^Y$, and $\bar{\boldsymbol{\alpha}}^{XY}$ from $P_{\mu|\rho}$

4 $\tilde{u}_{\rho*}^\# = \dfrac{1}{\Delta} \ln \sum_\mu \exp(\lambda u_\mu^\# + \Delta\bar{u}_{\rho\mu})$

5 Determine β and $\bar{\boldsymbol{\alpha}}^X$ from P_ρ

6 Return to *step 2* if $\bar{\boldsymbol{\alpha}}^X, \bar{\boldsymbol{\alpha}}^Y, \bar{\boldsymbol{\alpha}}^{XY}$, and β, λ, Δ are outside convergence limits

(b)

1 Set $\beta = \Delta$

2 $u_\rho^\# = \bar{u}_\rho + \left(\dfrac{\beta-\Delta}{\beta\Delta}\right) \ln \sum_\mu \exp(\lambda\bar{u}_\mu + \Delta\bar{u}_{\rho\mu})$

3 Determine β, Δ, $\bar{\boldsymbol{\alpha}}^X$, and $\bar{\boldsymbol{\alpha}}^{XY}$ from $P_{\rho|\mu}$

4 $\tilde{u}_{\mu*}^\# = \dfrac{1}{\Delta} \ln \sum_\rho \exp(\beta u_\rho^\# + \Delta\bar{u}_{\rho\mu})$

5 Determine λ and $\bar{\boldsymbol{\alpha}}^Y$ from P_μ

6 Return to *step 2* if $\bar{\boldsymbol{\alpha}}^X, \bar{\boldsymbol{\alpha}}^Y, \bar{\boldsymbol{\alpha}}^{XY}$, and β, λ, Δ are outside convergence limits

Figure 8. Stages in the indirect estimation of the general choice model. (a) $P_{\rho\mu} = P_\rho P_{\mu|\rho}$; (b) $P_{\rho\mu} = P_\mu P_{\rho|\mu}$.

6 The formation of travel demand models and economic evaluation measures—some examples

6.1 *Introduction*

A number of applications that involve the construction of consistent demand models and evaluation measures will now be discussed. These deal successively with: models for multiroute, multimode, mode-route, and mixed-mode transport systems, and with 'strategic' transport planning models. The examples will involve the structuring of demand functions appropriate to additive, separable utility functions for which the theory developed in section 5.2 may be appealed to directly. The fundamental problem is one of devising a suitable structure for the underlying utility function in any particular example, which does not exclude from the resultant model a possible source of attribute correlation.

Since the model represented by the fan structure in figure 9(b) is a special case of that appropriate to figure 9(a), in which all correlation effects represented by the 'intermediate' branches in figure 9(a) are zero, it is usually desirable to adopt the model corresponding to figure 9(a) and be guided by the results of the calibration process on the extent of the correlation. Of course, the appropriate common attributes or factors must be provided in the specification of the model. If the multinomial logit model is adopted, there should be good reason to believe that the movements involved will be perceived as distinct with no appreciable commonality effects. In all the examples to follow it is important to recognise the fundamental inconsistency of assuming the existence of factors which give rise to dispersion, while neglecting the influence of these factors in the benefit calculation.

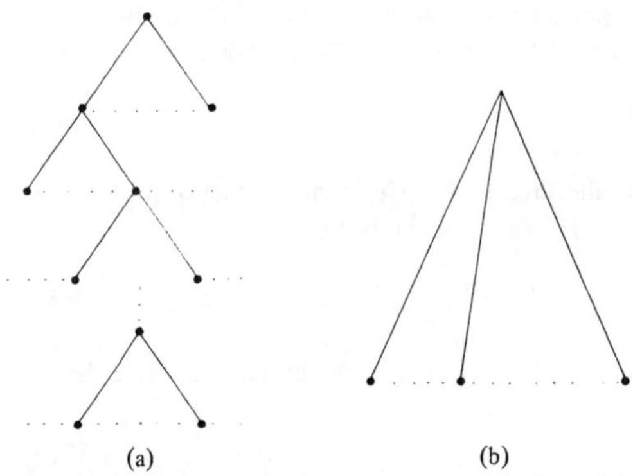

Figure 9. A representation of alternative structures for multiple choice models. (a) 'Recursive' structure; (b) 'Simultaneous' structure.

6.2 *Route choice analysis*

The road traffic assignment stage of the transport planning process concerns the computation of a network equilibrium in which the level-of-service (times and costs) on each link is consistent with the demand assumed to be generated by these costs, and that the demand is also consistent with a behavioural principle of route choice. It is usually assumed that drivers are sufficiently familiar with the network for a single optimal decision to be made on choice of route. This is very reasonable for such trip purposes as shopping and work.

Dispersion of traffic over several routes between a zone pair, other than that arising from capacity diversion (and neglecting zonal aggregation effects), is brought about by the distribution in utility values associated with links and therefore routes. There are two principal sources: the perceived variation of network variables (for example link times); and the stochastic variation over the population of the parameters in a utility or cost function defined in terms of a precise set of network variables. The former arises through lack of perfect information, while the latter results from a dispersion of preferences—a source discussed at some length in sections 4 and 5. The mathematics of the demand estimation problem are similar in the two cases.

A variety of probabilistic assignment procedures have been suggested over the past fifteen years, their forerunner being the diversion curve methods used in the USA through the 1950s. The challenge has been to produce a computationally efficient device for allocating trips to routes in a way consistent with a realistic route choice criterion. The most widely implemented approaches nowadays are those introduced by Burrell (1968) and Dial (1971)—the former has been adopted in over twenty British transport studies, while the latter has been incorporated in the UMTA Transport Planning System.

As Beilner and Jacobs (1972), Le Clercq (1975), and others have pointed out, random utility theory offers a unifying context for these various approaches. Here I wish to comment briefly on the two suggestions of Dial (1971)—the single-pass (SP) and double-pass (DP) algorithms—in order to point out some interesting connections with the notions of composite cost and separability developed earlier.

Any network between two nodes N_1 and N_2 may be decomposed into a tree structure involving possible routes from N_1 to N_2. There is a natural mapping of an additive separable utility function onto this tree if the route costs are linear additions of the link costs, as in the usual case for private transport. The tree corresponding to the link network of figure 10(a) is illustrated in figure 10(b).

It may be shown (the details are provided by Williams, 1976b) that the division of trips between N_1 and N_2 to routes $r \in R(i, j)$ in Dial's methods may be written in the partial share representation

$$P_r = \prod_{L(l,\,l') \in r} P_{ll'} \,, \tag{221}$$

in which P_r, the proportion of trips allocated to route r, is the product of probabilities $P_{ll'}$ for those links $L(l, l')$ along that route. $P_{ll'}$ is of the form

$$P_{ll'} = \frac{\exp[-\theta(c_{ll'} + \tilde{c}_{l'*})]}{\sum_{l'} \exp[-\theta(c_{ll'} + \tilde{c}_{l'*})]} \,, \tag{222}$$

in which $c_{ll'}$ is the link disutility, and $\tilde{c}_{l*}$, the composite cost at node l, is given in the single-pass algorithm by

$$\tilde{c}_{l*} = \min_{l'} \, (c_{ll'} + \tilde{c}_{l'*}) \,, \tag{223}$$

and in the double-pass method by

$$\tilde{c}_{l*} = -\frac{1}{\theta} \ln \sum_{l'} \exp[-\theta(c_{ll'} + \tilde{c}_{l'*})] \,. \tag{224}$$

Note that at each node the dispersion parameter θ has the same value. It can also be shown for the double-pass method that the benefit accruing from network changes is of the form

$$\Delta S = \frac{1}{\theta} \sum_{ij} T_{ij} \ln \left[\frac{\sum_{r \in R(i,j)} \exp(-\theta c_r^{*})}{\sum_{r \in R(i,j)} \exp(-\theta c_r^{\star})} \right] \tag{225}$$

$$= \sum_{ij} T_{ij} (\tilde{c}_{ij}^{*} - \tilde{c}_{ij}^{\star}) \,, \tag{226}$$

where $\tilde{c}_{ij}$ is the average of the distribution of minimum perceived disutility between zones i and j. An intimate relationship exists between these composite cost measures, the nodal weights employed by Dial in the implementation of the algorithm, and a dual variable in an entropy maximising derivation of the probabilistic assignment model (Williams, 1976b). No analytic form exists for the benefit which corresponds to the SP algorithm because the route demand functions violate the integrability conditions.

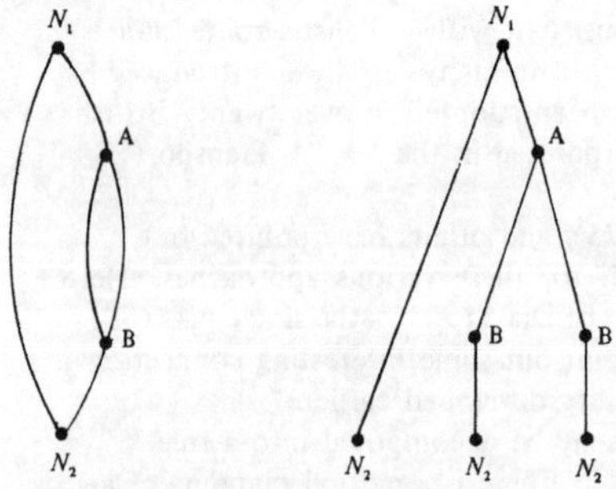

Figure 10. A representation of a network in the form of a (dis)utility tree (a simple example). (a) A network; (b) a tree representation.

In the particular case of Dial's double-pass algorithm the tree structure in fact collapses to the fan form because the equations (221) and (222) are simply an indirect representation of the simultaneous structure

$$P_r = \frac{\exp\left(-\theta \sum_{L(l,\,l') \in r} c_{ll'}\right)}{\sum_{r \in R(i,\,j)} \exp\left(-\theta \sum_{L(l,\,l') \in r} c_{ll'}\right)} \,. \tag{227}$$

This is a direct result of assuming an identical θ at each node and is an indictment of the double-pass method, which, if applied in urban areas, directs too many trips into the areas where the network is most dense (Van Vliet, 1976). The reason is clear—the correlation between different routes which arises from common links is completely ignored. On the other hand, the single-pass method, through its composite cost structure, results in inconsistent route demand functions and can produce unrealistic routings in areas where a network is sparse.

The task of incorporating the effects of correlation which will allow a consistent formulation of route allocation and a benefit analysis measure is a formidable one. Clearly the parameter θ at each node must be related to the standard deviations of the independent distributions associated with that node. The efficient automation of this process in a non-path-enumeration method of the Dial type is a challenging problem. An added theoretical difficulty presents itself when congestion is present and relates to the very existence of supply–demand equilibria in probabilistic assignments for which the set of efficient routes (a concept adopted in the Dial algorithm) is itself dependent on the level of network service (Murchland, 1975, private communication).

6.3 *Multimode and multimode/multiroute choice problems*

It is easily forgotten that the private and public modes in binary choice modal-split models are each composites or aggregates of several possible means of transportation. For example, in the Greater London Transportation Study (Havers et al, 1974) surveyed movements were initially grouped into eleven classes by stage: (1) car, van, or motorcycle driver; (2) goods vehicle driver; (3) car, van, or motorcycle passenger; (4) underground rail; (5) British rail (surface train); (6) taxi or minicab; (7) scheduled bus; (8) coach; (9) walk or pedal cycle; (10) goods passenger; (11) other passenger.

For the distribution and assignment stages of the strategic passenger-demand model, two *distribution* modes are defined: (a) travel by private transport, including trips by car, van, or motorcycle; and (b) travel by public transport, incorporating trips by underground, British rail, and scheduled bus. (The treatment of mixed-mode trips involving combined 'distribution' modes will be considered below.) The initial two-fold classification recognises the existence of common attributes, which, in this case, concern the degree of personalisation of the movement and the influence of comfort, convenience, and mode flexibility.

Traditionally the 'submodal'-split calculation between public transport modes, for example bus and train, has involved a 'primary' split between the two composites in which the public transport disutility is taken as the minimum disutility of the available submodes. Such a model in fact assumes an additive, separable utility function $u(k)$ defined over modal attributes in which 'public' modes contain a common attribute $u_{\tilde{k}}$. Thus

$$u(k) = u_{\tilde{k}} + u_{k(\tilde{k})} \,, \tag{228}$$

where $u_{k(\tilde{k})}$ is that component of the utility function which varies over modes k in the 'public' movement composite $\tilde{k}$. Now it is clear that, for any individual, the perception of specifically 'public transport' elements of the utility function would not be identical for bus and rail. What has been assumed in the formation of equation (228), and hence in the resultant demand model, is that the grouping criterion is satisfied for which the rank correlation associated with these elements, attributed to any 'individual' or group, is considerably higher for the public/private choice dichotomy than for any pair of public transport modes. In other words, if other factors such as journey times, money costs, etc, were considered equal, a group tendency to prefer car to bus and train or vice versa would be exhibited. The appropriate utility tree is shown in figure 11(a). The rejected structure is that of figure 11(b).

In the notation of appendix 1 a suitable multimodal demand model would be of the form

$$T_{ij}^{nk(\bar{k})} = T_{ij}^{n}(u^n - \tilde{c}^n)\frac{\exp[-\lambda^n(\delta^{\bar{k}} + \tilde{c}_{ij}^{n\bar{k}})]}{\sum\limits_{\bar{k} \in H(n)} \exp[-\lambda^n(\delta^{\bar{k}} + \tilde{c}_{ij}^{n\bar{k}})]}\,\frac{\exp[-\Delta^n c_{ij}^{k(\bar{k})}]}{\sum\limits_{k \in Y(\bar{k})} \exp[-\Delta^n c_{ij}^{k(\bar{k})}]}\,, \tag{229}$$

where

$$c_{ij}^{k} = \sum_{\eta} \alpha_\eta Z_{ijk}^{\eta}\,, \tag{230}$$

and

$$\tilde{c}_{ij}^{nk} = -\frac{1}{\Delta^n}\ln \sum_{k \in Y(\bar{k})} \exp[-\Delta^n c_{ij}^{k(\bar{k})}]\,, \tag{231}$$

$$\tilde{c}_{ij}^{n} = -\frac{1}{\lambda^n}\ln \sum_{\bar{k} \in H(n)} \exp[-\lambda^n(\delta^{\bar{k}} + \tilde{c}_{ij}^{n\bar{k}})]\,. \tag{232}$$

Here Z_{ijk} denotes a set of variables, such as time, distance, and cost, which varies over modes and destination. $\delta^{\bar{k}}$ is the source of correlation between the submodes in the composite set $\bar{k}$ and $\sum_{k \in Y(\bar{k})}$ denotes summation over all modes in that composite set. The evaluation procedure is now straightforward, and consumer surplus measures may be extracted from the balancing factors of the distribution model as described in section 6.5 below.

The quantities $\delta^{\bar{k}}$ may be regarded as calibration parameters—their maximum likelihood values would ensure that the predicted and observed modal-shares at the composite level are equal over the whole system. Progress in modelling these 'modal-penalty' parameters explicitly in terms of causal variables has been reported recently by Stopher (1975).

It is interesting to note that the solution to the multimode problem discussed here is similar to that envisaged by Domencich and McFadden (1975), who recognise that in a car-multiple transit mode system the stochastic components of disutility of the transit modes will be 'interdependent' and that the "logit framework can be adapted to describe a tree decision structure in which the independence of irrelevant alternatives does not hold". The problem of attribute correlation in a mode selection context has

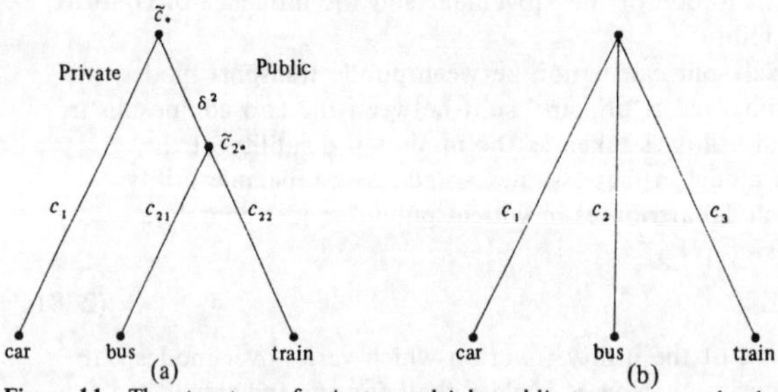

Figure 11. The structure of private-multiple public transport mode choice models. (a) 'Recursive' structure; (b) 'Simultaneous' structure.

also been treated by Langdon (1976), who recently formulated and solved numerically a three-mode model, within the random utility approach, which explicitly contains correlation between modal disutility values through bivariate normal distributions. Langdon has also investigated the resultant benefit implications within a consumer surplus framework.

As δ^k tends to zero, the model (229) collapses to one appropriate to a fan structure in which all modes are given equal 'weight'. Perhaps the best-known example of such a 'simultaneous' structure is that of Rassam et al (1971), who developed and applied a multidimensional logit model for four access modes—private car, rental car, taxi, and limousine—to airports in the Baltimore-Washington, DC region. More recently Richards (1975) and Lawson and Mullen (1976) have documented applications of the multinomial logit model to choice selection over several modes.

In any conurbation transport system the car thus competes with possibly several public transport modes, each of which consists of many services operating over different routes through a network. The problem of demand forecasting in a situation that entails mode- and route-choice was first considered in detail by Wilson (1969), who addressed the issues of mode definition itself. Two share models were developed through the entropy maximising approach, the first corresponding to a joint mode-route multinomial logit model, and the second to a recursive structure in which route share is determined conditional on the choice of mode. Wilson explored the consequences of adopting a variety of composite costs in the recursive form. In the language of random utility theory these two forms correspond respectively to the utility functions $u(k, r)$ defined over mode (k)-route (r) combinations as follows

$$u(k, r) = \bar{u}_{kr} + \epsilon_{kr} \qquad \text{('simultaneous' model),} \tag{233}$$

$$u(k, r) = \bar{u}_k + \bar{u}_{kr} + \epsilon_k + \epsilon_{kr} \qquad \text{('recursive' model).} \tag{234}$$

The correct model specification and evaluation measures may now be obtained in the usual way.

A multinomial logit model, similar to Wilson's 'route dominant' form, was incorporated in the TRANSEPT package developed by LGORU (Last, 1974). The alternative movement options for car owners included car, walk, and the two cheapest bus paths, and for nonowners of cars the three latter. The structure of the model corresponds to figure 12(a). The package has recently been modified (Daly and Zachary, 1976) to include a more appropriate 'three-level' logit model corresponding to the utility tree shown in figure 12(b). The correct forms of composite cost have been identified and correlation between the public transport modes, and between the walk and public transport modes have been suitably catered for. In the Huddersfield bus study four public transport service options were included.

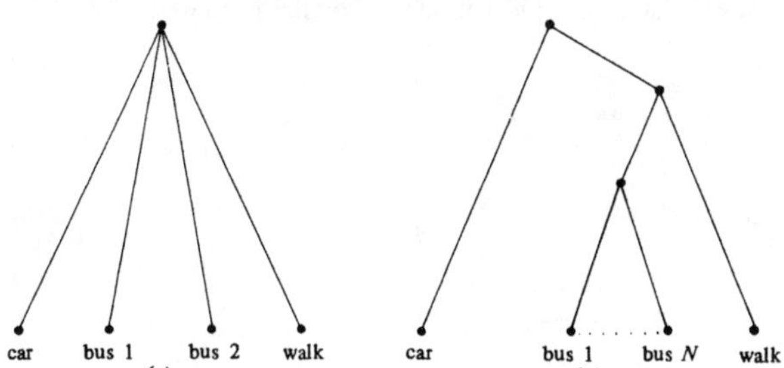

Figure 12. The structure of multimode-multiroute choice models. (a) TRANSEPT 1; (b) TRANSEPT 2.

Given an existing set of mode–route alternatives, it is sometimes required to model the impact of an additional transportation alternative. The class of *abstract-mode* models developed in the United States in the mid-sixties was developed to address precisely this type of problem. The issue frequently reduces to one of labelling the new option a 'route' or a 'mode', and the classification must depend on the extent and nature of the common attributes thought to characterise that movement with respect to the current set. It is usually the case, however, that in 'one-off' situations there will be specific factors which distinguish the new option, for which *existing* information can shed little or no light. The forecasting of the demand for new transportation options will, because of this, always be a somewhat hazardous exercise.

6.4 *Mixed-mode demand models*

In a British context, the Merseyside Study (MALTS, 1969) was one of the first to give serious consideration to the problem of modelling mixed-mode (in this case car-to-rail) trips. Usually mixed-mode trips are classified along with their majority stage. The fundamental hypothesis underlying the procedure for estimating car-to-rail travel was that a tripmaker from a car-owner household first chooses between driving the car and taking one of the available public transport services, and then, if the choice is car, whether to park-and-ride or to take private transport to the city centre (Liverpool). Primary and secondary modal-split models were constructed based on diversion curves, for which the composite private transport mode level-of-service variables were taken to be those of the car.

In common with most other transport studies MALTS found that, although mixed-mode trips may be significant in certain corridors for long trips to the city-centre (Liverpool), a small proportion of internal journey-to-work trips involve park-and-ride or feeder-bus travel. Under present conditions of restraint, there is indeed little incentive, nor are the facilities available, in the majority of British cities for car-owners, who may use their car, to switch mode. However, by time or price penalty measures, or through the operation of exclusion schemes for central areas, private-transport restraint policies coupled with public-transport priority schemes could induce extensive use of mixed modes. The Nottingham Collar Scheme is the first example in Britain of a policy that encourages mode change on a 'strategic' scale for the journey-to-work.

The problem of building a demand model for a car–public transport interchange scheme has been considered within the general framework presented below (Williams et al, 1975). The structure of the model currently being implemented for the Leeds area is shown in figure 13. It has been assumed that if the car journey to the interchange forms a large proportion of the overall trip time or cost to the destination, the mixed mode will be perceived as an addition to the private transport (composite) alternative, whereas if the park is close to the origin the park–ride option would be regarded as part of the composite public transport mode. (For the purpose of

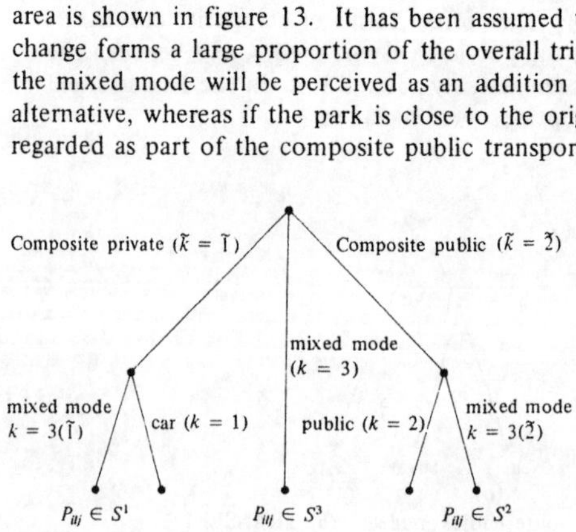

Figure 13. A representation of a mixed-mode choice model.

exposition of the main features of the model structure the 'kiss-and-ride' option is ignored here.) In these two cases the characteristics (attributes) of the majority journey leg dominate the characteristics of the mixed mode, and are the source of correlation between the respective alternatives. In an intermediate 'range' the three alternatives, car, public transport, and park-and-ride, correlate rather less strongly and may well be considered with equal 'weight'. The classification of the mixed mode is therefore a function of the spatial configuration of origin, interchange, and destination, and is specified in the following way: movements P_{ilj} through an interchange at l, with generalised cost c_{ilj}^{3}, which correspond to a composite private mode, composite public mode, and the 'distinct' third mode are identified in terms of the sets S^1, S^2, and S^3 respectively, such that

$$P_{ilj} \in S^1\,, \qquad \text{for } \frac{c_{il}^{k=1}}{c_{ilj}^{k=3}} \geqslant \varphi_1\,, \tag{235}$$

$$P_{ilj} \in S^2\,, \qquad \text{for } \frac{c_{lj}^{k=2}}{c_{ilj}^{k=3}} \geqslant \varphi_2\,, \tag{236}$$

$$P_{ilj} \in S^3\,, \qquad \text{for } (1-\varphi_2) \leqslant \frac{c_{il}^{k=1}}{c_{ilj}^{k=3}} \leqslant \varphi_1\,, \tag{237}$$

The thresholds φ_1, φ_2 must be specified, and subjected to a sensitivity analysis.

The functional form of the model corresponding to the structure in figure 13 is

$$T_{ij}^{1k(k)} = T_{ij}^{1}M_{ij}^{k}M_{ij}^{k(k)}\,, \qquad k = 1, 2\,, \tag{238}$$

$$T_{ilj}^{13(k)} = T_{ij}^{1}M_{ij}^{k}M_{ilj}^{3(k)}\,, \qquad P_{ilj} \in S^k\,, \qquad \tilde{k} = 1, 2\,, \tag{239}$$

$$T_{ilj}^{13} = T_{ij}^{1}M_{ilj}^{3}\,, \qquad P_{ilj} \in S^3\,, \tag{240}$$

where the shares M are taken of logit form. The possibility for apportioning mixed-mode trips between two or more interchanges in a given set for a given origin–destination pair may easily be incorporated (Williams et al, 1975).

The perceived user-benefits arising from the introduction of the interchange system may now be written

$$\Delta S = -\sum_{ij}\sum_{n}\sum_{k \in H(n)} \int_{c_{ij}^{k*}}^{c_{ij}^{k*}} \mathrm{d}c_{ij}^{k} T_{ij}^{nk} - \sum_{\nu=1}^{3}\sum_{ij}\sum_{\substack{l \\ \{P_{ilj} \in S^{\nu}\}}} \int_{\infty}^{c_{ilj}^{*}} \mathrm{d}c_{ilj}^{3}\, T_{ilj}^{13(\tilde{\nu})}\,. \tag{241}$$

The absence of an interchange corresponds to an infinite cost for the mixed-mode movements. The consumer surplus change reduces to the following form

$$\Delta S = \sum_{ij} T_{ij}^{n=2,\,k=2}(c_{ij}^{2*} - c_{ij}^{2*}) + \frac{1}{\lambda}\sum_{ij} T_{ij}^{k=1} \ln\left[\frac{\exp(-\lambda c_{ij}^{\bar{1}*}) + \exp(-\lambda c_{ij}^{\bar{2}*}) + \exp(-\lambda c_{ij}^{\bar{3}*})}{\exp(-\lambda c_{ij}^{\bar{1}*}) + \exp(-\lambda c_{ij}^{\bar{2}*})}\right] \tag{242}$$

where the first term is the perceived cost change accruing to the captive public-transport users. [A fixed trip matrix $\mathbf{T}_{ij}$ has been assumed in equation (242).] $c^{\bar{1}}$ and $c^{\bar{2}}$ are the disutilities associated with the composite private and public modes. The example considered here is clearly one for which the rule-of-a-half is inapplicable because of its marginal domain of validity.

6.5 *Strategic transport planning models*

Strategic transport planning models, such as those represented by equations (1) to (3), involve the dimensions of route choice (r), mode choice (k), location choice (d), and frequency (f). I am now in a position to offer a consistent formulation of those models and the associated benefit measures. Each model will be considered to be underpinned by an additive, separable, utility function. The following structures

$$u(f, k, d, r) = u(f)+u(k\,|\,f)+u(d\,|\,kf)+u(r\,|\,dkf) \,, \tag{243}$$

$$u(f, d, k, r) = u(f)+u(d\,|\,f)+u(k\,|\,df)+u(r\,|\,kdf) \,, \tag{244}$$

$$u(f, d, k, r) = u(f)+u(dk\,|\,f)+u(r\,|\,dkf) \,, \tag{245}$$

correspond to the forms (1) to (3) respectively.

It will be assumed now, for the purpose of discussing operational forms, that a sufficiently fine zoning system exists in the study area to render small the aggregation bias when the partial share models are interpreted with aggregate data. The full specification of the common postdistribution form (2), if the Wardrop conditions are assumed to hold and the logit function approximation adopted, becomes

$$T_{ij}^{nk} = G_i^n M_{ij}^n M_{ij}^{nk} \,, \tag{246}$$

with

$$G_i^n = G_i^n(E_i^n, \tilde{u}_{i\bullet}^n) \,, \tag{247}$$

$$M_{ij}^n = \frac{A_j \exp[-\beta^n(-u_{ij}^n + \tilde{c}_{ij}^n + b_j)]}{\sum_j A_j \exp[-\beta^n(-u_{ij}^n + \tilde{c}_{ij}^n + b_j)]} \,, \tag{248}$$

$$M_{ij}^{nk} = \frac{\exp(-\lambda^n c_{ij}^k)}{\sum_{k \in H(n)} \exp(-\lambda^n c_{ij}^k)} \,, \tag{249}$$

and the appropriate composite functions are given by

$$\tilde{c}_{ij}^n = -\frac{1}{\lambda^n} \ln \sum_{k \in H(n)} \exp(-\lambda^n c_{ij}^k) \,, \tag{250}$$

$$\tilde{u}_{i\bullet}^n = \frac{1}{\beta^n} \ln \sum_j A_j \exp[-\beta^n(-u_{ij}^n + \tilde{c}_{ij}^n + b_j)] \,, \tag{251}$$

$$= a_i^n \,, \tag{252}$$

where a_i^n is the dual variable associated with the origin trip-end constraints in the programming derivation of the spatial interaction model[8]. $\boldsymbol{b}$ is a vector of shadow prices or dual variables accompanying any constraints on trip attractions into any zone. $\boldsymbol{a}$ and $\boldsymbol{b}$ depend on modal travel costs through the composite costs $\tilde{c}_{ij}^n$. The spatial interaction model featuring in equation (248) is *not* equivalent to an entropy maximising model, which would be expressed as

$$M_{ij}^{nk} = \frac{A_j \exp[-\hat{b}_j - \beta^n(-u_{ij}^n + \tilde{c}_{ij}^n)]}{\sum_j A_j \exp[-\hat{b}_j - \beta^n(-u_{ij}^n + \tilde{c}_{ij}^n)]} \,. \tag{253}$$

It is noted that the dual variable $\boldsymbol{b}$ in equation (248) is incorporated into the cost function, and thus has dimensions of cost, rather than being dimensionless, as in the corresponding entropy model. In cases where different market segments (for example car owners and noncar owners) interact through competition for an activity in any zone, this difference has important implications for the resultant demand predictions and user-benefit calculations. The model (253) is developed from the perspective of *information theory* whereas model (248) corresponds to the approach of *maximising group surplus* (see section 4.4). The distinction creates interesting calibration and benefit measurement issues which have been discussed in detail by Champernowne, et al (1976).

(8) The weight $A_j / \sum_j A_j$ which appears in the composite utility function $\tilde{u}_{i\bullet}^n$ is proportional to the *a priori* probability that the destination will fall in zone i.

An exact expression for the change in total perceived benefit which accompanies a network modification may now be written

$$\Delta S = -\sum_{ij}\sum_{n}\sum_{k\in H(n)}\int_0^1 \mathrm{d}\hat{\sigma}\,\frac{\mathrm{d}c_{ij}^k(\hat{\sigma})}{\mathrm{d}\hat{\sigma}}\,T_{ij}^{nk}(\hat{\sigma}) \tag{254}$$

$$= -\sum_{ij}\sum_{n}\int_0^1 \mathrm{d}\hat{\sigma}\,G_i^n(\tilde{u}_{i*}^n(\hat{\sigma}))M_{ij}^n(\hat{\sigma})\sum_{k\in H(n)} M_{ij}^{nk}\,\frac{\mathrm{d}c_{ij}^k}{\mathrm{d}\hat{\sigma}} \tag{255}$$

$$= -\sum_{ij}\sum_{n}\int_0^1 \mathrm{d}\hat{\sigma}\,G_i^n(\hat{\sigma})M_{ij}^n(\tilde{\kappa}_{ij}^n(\hat{\sigma}))\,\frac{\mathrm{d}\tilde{\kappa}_{ij}^n}{\mathrm{d}\hat{\sigma}} + \sum_j A_j(b_j^\star - b_j^\star)\ , \tag{256}$$

where $\tilde{\kappa}_{ij}^n(\hat{\sigma})$ denotes the variable

$$\tilde{\kappa}_{ij}^n(\hat{\sigma}) = -u_{ij}^n + \tilde{c}_{ij}^n(\hat{\sigma}) + b_j(\hat{\sigma})\ . \tag{257}$$

Finally

$$\Delta S = -\sum_{n}\sum_{i}\int_0^1 \mathrm{d}\hat{\sigma}\,G_i^n(\tilde{u}_{i*}^n(\hat{\sigma}))\,\frac{\mathrm{d}\tilde{u}_{i*}^n(\hat{\sigma})}{\mathrm{d}\hat{\sigma}} + \sum_j A_j(b_j^\star - b_j^\star)\ , \tag{258}$$

which, for inelastic trip ends, may be written

$$\Delta S = \sum_{n}\sum_{i} G_i^n(a_i^{n\star} - a_i^{n\star}) + \sum_j A_j(b_j^\star - b_j^\star)\ . \tag{259}$$

This is a generalisation of Neuberger's (1971) result for the singly constrained model, and its full interpretation, which in turn depends on the interpretation of the doubly-constrained spatial interaction form as a location choice model, has been given by Champernowne et al (1976). Because of a redundancy of one of the constraints in the doubly-constrained gravity model it is necessary to set one dual variable (in a given plan) to zero in order to give the terms in equation (259) an 'independent' interpretation in terms of user benefit and changes in location rent respectively. This procedure is fully discussed by Senior and Williams (1977). The ROH measure is an approximation to the exact result (259), the latter being valid for arbitrary changes in the transport cost matrix.

Several comments are appropriate at this point. The result (259) indicates that the correct form of composite cost allows extraction of the benefit measure from the 'top' of the model—in this case from the 'accessibility' or 'balancing' factors of the distribution model—rather than after the assignment stage as at present. This is not an indication that the assignment stage is superfluous to the evaluation process. What is assumed is that the dual variables $\boldsymbol{a}$ and $\boldsymbol{b}$ are computed with level-of-service variables appropriate to a state in which demand and supply are in equilibrium. Note also that here the calibration, and implementation of the model in the forecasting phase, proceed from the route choice model to the generation stage rather than the reverse. (This process is explicit in Manheim's special product models.) For example, the parameters of the modal-split model must be estimated and transferred through the composite cost function to the distribution submodel. This is in contrast to the calibration processes involved in the SELNEC and Nottingham models in table 1, in which the (incorrect) specification of composite costs for the distribution model does not involve the parameters of the modal share function. The relative computational efficiency of benefit calculations based on the dual variable measure and the ROH measure has been discussed by Williams (1976a).

Experience with the model form (246) and with the composite cost form (250) (Senior and Williams, 1977) has shown that, for certain modal share parameters, the composite cost may become negative for some trip interchanges. This is indeed not unexpected (see figure 2). This feature may readily be averted, in practical cases involving two modes, by computing the absolute value of c_{ij}^n, as in equation (95), through addition of the quantity γ/λ^n (see footnote 2). It does not remove completely the possibility of the composite cost becoming negative, and indeed in aggregation over several movements this behaviour becomes more likely. If this facet is considered too unsavory then a different form for the functions $\mathbf{\Gamma}(c)$ must be chosen which is consistent with a positive mean value for $\Lambda(c)$. Unfortunately there are no such convenient forms which generate simple and realistic closed form models. It should be reemphasised, however, that the negative cost phenomenon in no way influences the demand or benefit calculations because the demand functions are invariant with respect to addition of *arbitrary* constants to all costs, whereas for the computation of benefit we are interested in consumer surplus *changes* between transport plans (and therefore cost matrices).

The location-specific component of utility $u(d)$ generates a term which I shall label $u^n_{i,j}$. If the distribution model is interpreted as a residential location model for fixed workplace, $u^n_{i,j}$ will denote a location specific component u^n_i, whereas a workplace-location model for fixed residence will involve a component u^n_j. $u^n_{i,j}$ will thus in general involve both location and activity variable characteristics. The presence of this quantity is vital to the interpretation of equation (246) as a recursive model, which, in an obvious notation, I shall label G/D/MS/A. If $u^n_{i,j}$ vanishes, the value of the parameter β^n, which depends on the variance of the distribution $\Gamma_{ij}(u, u^n_{ij})$, tends to λ^n and the model collapses to

$$T^{nk}_{ij} = G^n_i \frac{A_j \exp[-\lambda^n(c^k_{ij}+b_j)]}{\sum\limits_j \sum\limits_{k \in H(n)} A_j \exp[-\lambda^n(c^k_{ij}+b_j]}\,, \tag{260}$$

which is the joint distribution modal-split form G/D–MS/A. The implication of this result is clear. The joint model is only appropriate in circumstances for which there is good reason to believe that the location specific component of the utility function is small compared with the transportation component (or more specifically its *variance* is small—money costs, such as parking charges and rents, are perceived at their face value and have zero variance). The relatively greater substitutability between mode and destination pairs for shopping trips is, indeed, precisely because the corresponding component $u(d)$ is presumably small compared with that associated with work trips. For the latter (in the workplace selection interpretation of the distribution model), the component $u(d)$ will tend to be a proxy for the characteristics of employment, which will indirectly depend on location. In this context it is not surprising that relatively large K-factors are introduced in some studies to obtain a reasonable fit with distribution data. The scope for disaggregation of activity variables in a journey-to-work context is indeed considerable. It is clear that the insertion of the location specific utility components emphasises the location choice model characteristics of the conventional transport demand forms[9].

So far it has been assumed that the number of trips generated is invariant with respect to the level of transport service—trip ends are inelastic. The formalism for incorporating a 'no-trip' option has already been set out in equations (247) and (251). The crucial feature is the incorporation of the nonnegativity constraint (51) on the level of trip surplus. Recently a logit model of frequency choice, constructed within the framework of probabilistic choice theory, has been developed and applied by CRA (1972) at the microlevel, and includes a composite cost of travel of the type (32).

[9] It should be noted that the term $\exp(\beta u_j)$ may be regarded as an attraction weight A_j. The nature of this quantity must be carefully distinguished from the weight A_j, which can arise in macromodels from the *aggregation* of trip ends in the zone. In the work-trip model, for example, the proportion of total trips to any given zone will, *ceteris paribus*, be proportional to the total number of opportunities in that zone.

It is clear from the above discussion that if a model of trip production is developed to correspond to the underlying utility structure (244), then the appropriate measure of net utility, which involves level-of-service variables in the logit approximation, is of the form (251), which is seen to be proportional to the log transform of a modified Hansen measure of accessibility (Hansen, 1959) and is of similar structure to the index proposed by Koenig (1975). Recently much effort has gone into developing regression- and category-analysis models of trip production which incorporate accessibility indices (see, for example, Daor, 1975; Dalvi and Martin, 1976). It is apparent that the appropriate index $\tilde{u}_{i\bullet}^{n}$ depends directly on the model for location choice through an expression of the form (146). If an elastic trip-end model is developed the consumer surplus in equation (258) must be integrated to form an overall composite utility of travel $\tilde{U}_{\bullet\bullet}$, which is then used in benefit calculations.

The recursive model (246) corresponds to the structure of the utility function (244). The alternative models, which will be distinguished by G/MS/D/A and G/D–MS/A, can now be written down immediately and are included in table 5. The calibration and a full comparison of these alternative structures, together with a sensitivity analysis of demand and benefit measures to alternative forms of composite cost, have recently been carried out by Senior and Williams (1977).

I have argued in section 5 that the choice (or demand) models, which are expressed in sequences such as those in equations (1) to (3), are merely special cases of a general choice model in which correlation effects between different dimensions are incorporated. The choice model G/D*MS/A, which includes such correlating components in the location and mode choice dimensions, is included in the table for completeness. A decision must be made either to develop the more general form of model, or, as has always been the case, to provide justification for one particular sequence. In terms of the models specified in table 5 a rule-of-thumb would be to compute the *microparameters* $\beta^{*} = |(\beta' - \lambda')/\lambda'|$ in equation (2) and $\lambda^{*} = |(\lambda' - \beta')/\beta'|$ in model (1), for any journey purpose, and adopt the following criteria:

(a) If $\beta^{*} \gg \lambda^{*}$ develop G/D/MS/A,
(b) If $\lambda^{*} \gg \beta^{*}$ develop G/MS/D/A,
(c) If $\lambda^{*} \approx \beta^{*} \approx 0$ develop G/D–MS/A,
(d) If $\lambda^{*} \approx \beta^{*} \gg 0$ develop G/D*MS/A.

These conditions aim at establishing the relative sizes of the standard deviation of the utility components in the utility structures (243) to (245), which contain no 'cross-correlating components' as in equation (192).

A more accurate set of criteria may be developed by examining the limiting properties of the general choice micromodel G/D*MS/A embodied in equations (197) to (202). When $\sigma_d \gg \sigma_k$, for example, the model G/D*MS/A may be approximated by the 'postdistribution modal-split' form G/D/MS/A with M_{ij}^{n} given by equation (248), and M_{ij}^{nk} by

$$M_{ij}^{nk} = \frac{\exp[-\lambda^{n}(c_{ij}^{k} + \delta^{k})]}{\sum\limits_{k \in H(n)} \exp[-\lambda^{n}(c_{ij}^{k} + \delta^{k})]}\,, \tag{261}$$

where δ^{k} is a 'mode specific penalty'. By comparing the value of λ^{n} with that obtained with $\delta^{k} = 0$, an estimate of the standard deviation of the correlating component δ^{k} in the mode dimension may, in principle, be established. Similarly the standard deviation of the location specific component of the utility function may be estimated from the relative sizes of the λ^{n} and β^{n} parameters, and the initial assumption that $\sigma_d \gg \sigma_k$ may be checked. The converse assumption, which involves the model G/MS/D/A, may be checked if it is found that $\sigma_d \ll \sigma_k$. If $\sigma_d \approx \sigma_k \ll \sigma_{dk}$ the multinomial logit function (191) is an appropriate approximation, whereas if

Table 5. A specification of alternative transport planning models.

Model descriptor	Model structure	Composite functions	Benefit measures $\Delta S = B^* - B^*$
Predistribution modal split G/MS/D/A [equation (1)]	$T_{ij}^{nk} = G_i^n \dfrac{\exp[-\lambda^n(\delta_i^{nk} + \tilde{c}_{i*}^{nk})]}{\sum_{k \in H(n)} \exp[-\lambda^n(\delta_i^{nk} + \tilde{c}_{i*}^{nk})]} \dfrac{A_j \exp[-\beta^n(c_{ij}^k + b_j)]}{\sum_j A_j \exp[-\beta^n(c_{ij}^k + b_j)]}$	$\tilde{c}_{i*}^{nk} = -\dfrac{1}{\beta^n} \ln \sum_j A_j \exp[-\beta^n(c_{ij}^k + b_j)]$ $\tilde{c}_{i*}^{n} = -\dfrac{1}{\lambda^n} \ln \sum_{k \in H(n)} \exp[-\lambda^n(\delta_i^{nk} + \tilde{c}_{i*}^{nk})]$	$B = -\sum_{in} G_i^n \tilde{c}_{i*}^n + \sum_j A_j b_j$
Postdistribution modal split G/D/MS/A [equation (2)]	$T_{ij}^{nk} = G_i^n \dfrac{A_j \exp[\beta^n(u_{i,j}^n - \tilde{c}_{ij}^n - b_j)]}{\sum_j A_j \exp[\beta^n(u_{i,j}^n - \tilde{c}_{ij}^n - b_j)]} \dfrac{\exp(-\lambda^n c_{ij}^k)}{\sum_{k \in H(n)} \exp(-\lambda^n c_{ij}^k)}$	$\tilde{c}_{ij}^{n} = -\dfrac{1}{\lambda^n} \ln \sum_{k \in H(n)} \exp(-\lambda^n c_{ij}^k)$ $\tilde{u}_{i*}^{n} = \dfrac{1}{\beta^n} \ln \sum_j A_j \exp[\beta^n(u_j^n - \tilde{c}_{ij}^n - b_j)]$	$B = \sum_{in} G_i^n \tilde{u}_{i*}^n + \sum_j A_j b_j$ $= \sum_{in} G_i^n a_i^n + \sum_j A_j b_j$
Joint-distribution modal split G/D-MS/A [equation (3)]	$T_{ij}^{nk} = G_i^n \dfrac{A_j \exp[-\beta^n(c_{ij}^k + b_j)]}{\sum_j \sum_{k \in H(n)} A_j \exp[-\beta^n(c_{ij}^k + b_j)]}$	$\tilde{u}_{i*}^{n} = \dfrac{1}{\beta^n} \ln \sum_j \sum_{k \in H(n)} A_j \exp[-\beta^n(c_{ij}^k + b_j)]$ $= a_i^n$	$B = \sum_{in} G_i^n \tilde{u}_{i*}^n + \sum_j A_j b_j$ $= \sum_{in} G_i^n a_i^n + \sum_j A_j b_j$
Joint-distribution modal split (general choice) G/D*MS/A	$T_{ij}^{nk} = G_i^n \dfrac{A_j \exp[\beta^n u_j^{\#} + \lambda^n u_k^{\#} - \Delta(c_{ij}^k + b_j)]}{\sum_j \sum_{k \in H(n)} A_j \exp[\beta^n u_j^{\#} + \lambda^n u_k^{\#} - \Delta(c_{ij}^k + b_j)]}$	See text [equations (206) to (211)]	$B = \sum_{in} G_i^n (\beta^n + \lambda^n - \Delta)^{-1} \ln Z + \sum_j A_j b_j$ where Z is given by $Z = \sum_j \sum_{k \in H(n)} A_j \exp[\beta^n u_j^{\#} + \lambda^n u_k^{\#} - \Delta(c_{ij}^k + b_j)]$

$\sigma_d \approx \sigma_k \approx \sigma_{dk}$ the model G/D*MS/A *must* be developed. This investigation must, of course, be made in a research context rather than 'on-line' in a transportation study.

It should be noted in conclusion that the model forms above have been developed for a fixed land-use pattern. Much work has recently been devoted to the integration of activity location and transport models to incorporate the mutual interaction of these systems, and Ben-Akiva et al (1976) note the attractive possibilities of developing a hierarchical framework in which nonwork travel decisions are conditional on a 'mobility' decision process involving location choices. The formalism presented above may also be extended to embrace the processes of design, analysis, and evaluation of land-use–transport plans, which involve alternative networks and distributions of activities (see Williams, 1976a; Coelho and Williams, 1977).

7 Conclusion

It is important at this point to reconsider briefly the issues raised in section 2, and the general perspective of the paper. At the outset we should recall the static equilibrium nature of the models, and the assumption of optimal choice behaviour in random utility theory. I have argued that the analytic structure and functional form of travel demand models are uniquely determined by the underlying utility functions, and the presence of common (correlating) components of that function governs the structuring process.

Manheim's (1973) partial share model and the special product model have been derived from additive, separable utility functions, and the significance of *index prices* or *composite costs* in the formation of those models and the corresponding benefit measures has been established. Once a component of the utility function (or resultant partial share) has been specified, the form of composite cost is determined *uniquely* within any given theoretical framework. Thus in *random utility theory* the form of function is specified by equation (70).

One of the arguments sometimes used in support of the composite cost structure (32),

$$\tilde{c}_{p*} = \sum_{\mu} M_{\mu|p} \bar{c}_{p\mu} ,$$

is that the same modal transportation (generalised) cost is involved in different partial shares. Although this is consistent with a *probabilistic* decision process (see section 4.2), it is totally inappropriate in a theory underpinned by consistent rational choice behaviour. In random utility theory the *actual* disutilities perceived by the decision-makers are involved, as in the form

$$\tilde{c}_{p*} = \sum_{\mu} M_{\mu|p} \bar{\bar{c}}_{p\mu} ,$$

rather than the costs attributed by the analyst to the choicemaking population Π as a whole.

Within the theory of rational choice there is thus *no* flexibility in the selection of the composite cost function. Indeed the penalties for not including the correct form are considerable. Not only may counterintuitive behaviour be generated in the choice process (see section 3) but also, by foregoing the conditions of optimality in which the composite costs play an essential role, the aggregation properties of the utility tree, which are indispensable in developing exact benefit measures, are no longer attainable. The opportunity for developing consistent demand models and evaluation measures is then immediately sacrificed.

It is becoming increasingly popular to invoke the multinomial logit model (191) in 'joint-choice' calculations. This popularity rests on the separability properties of that model, the ease of its calibration, and the feeling that it somehow genuinely represents a simultaneous decision process. I have argued that, in general, the latter contention is without foundation. The severe limitations of Luce's choice axiom are too well-known for one to take any comfort in the optimism of those who propose such a form as representing the choice process over several dimensions. Although there is a fine balance to be made between what is theoretically preferable and the practical necessities of implementation, I feel that, in this case, the Gordian knot has been cut too readily. A more suitable general choice model has been suggested, which takes full account of the effects of commonality of the attributes in the utility function. It remains to explore the characteristics and calibration of this new model, as set out in section 5.

In considering the theoretical aspects of forecasting here, I do not wish to discount the problems of data availability and of general calibration issues. It is, however, essential that a sound framework, based on preference theory, is developed in order that consistent demand forecasts and economic evaluation measures can be established.

Acknowledgements. I should like to acknowledge a number of useful discussions with Professor A G Wilson and Dr M Q Dalvi.

References

Beckmann M J, Golob T, 1971 "On the metaphysical foundation of traffic theory; entropy revisited" in *Proceedings of the Fifth International Symposium on the Theory of Traffic Flow and Transportation* Ed. G F Newell (Elsevier, New York)

Beilner H, Jacobs F, 1972 "Probabilistic aspects of traffic assignment" in *Proceedings of the Fifth International Symposium on the Theory of Traffic Flow and Transportation* Ed. G F Newell (Elsevier, New York) pp 183-194

Ben-Akiva M E, 1973 "Structure of passenger travel demand models" PhD dissertation, Department of Civil Engineering, MIT, Cambridge, Mass

Ben-Akiva M E, 1974 "Structure of passenger travel demand models" *Transportation Research Record* number 526, 26-42

Ben-Akiva M E, Lerman S R, Manheim M L, 1976 "Disaggregate models: an overview of some recent research results and practical applications" paper presented at PTRC Summer Meeting, University of Warwick, Coventry, England, 12-16 July

Blackburn A J, 1970 "A non-linear model of the demand for travel" and "An alternative approach to aggregation and estimation in the non-linear model" in *The Demand for Travel: Theory and Measurement* Ed. R E Quant (Lexington Books, D C Heath, Lexington, Mass) pp 163-196

Bonsall P W, and others, 1974 "A transport model for West Yorkshire" WP 46, Institute for Transport Studies, University of Leeds, Leeds, England

Brand D, 1973 "Travel demand forecasting, some foundations and a review" in *Urban Travel Demand Forecasting* special report 143, Highway Research Board, Washington, DC

Burrell J E, 1968 "Multiple route assignment and its application to capacity restraint" paper presented at Fourth International Symposium on the Theory of Traffic Flow, Karlsruhe, West Germany

Cesario F J, Smith T E, 1975 "Direction for future research in spatial interaction modelling" *Papers of the Regional Science Association* **35** 57-72

Champernowne A F, Williams H C W L, Coelho J D, 1976 "Some comments on urban travel demand analysis, model calibration, and the economic evaluation of transport plans" *Journal of Transport Economics and Policy* **10** (3) 267-285

CRA, 1972 "A disaggregate behavioural model of urban travel demand" Charles River Associates, Federal Highway Administration, US Department of Transportation, Washington, DC

Le Clercq F, 1975 "Some remarks on probabilistic route choice models" in *Urban Traffic Models* PTRC Summer Meeting, University of Warwick, Coventry, England, pp 89-98

Cochrane R A, 1975 "A possible economic basis for the gravity model" *Journal of Transport Economics and Policy* **9** (1) 34-49

Coelho J D, Williams H C W L, 1977 "On the analysis, evaluation and design of land use-transportation plans" Institute for Transport Studies, University of Leeds, Leeds, England (forthcoming)

Coventry Transportation Study, 1973 *Report on Phase Two: Technical Report, Parts I and II* Coventry City Council, Coventry, England

Dalvi M Q, Martin K M, 1976 "Estimation of non-work trip demand" paper presented to Conference on Urban Transport Planning, University of Leeds, Leeds, England, 29 March-1 April

Daly A J, Zachary S, 1976 "Improved multiple choice models" in *Urban Traffic Models* PTRC Summer Meeting, University of Warwick, Coventry, England, 12-16 July

Daor E, 1975 "The GLTS trip generation model" GLTS note 183, Greater London Council, London, England (unpublished)
Dial R B, 1971 "A probabilistic multipath assignment model which obviates path enumeration" *Transportation Research* **5** (2) 83-111
Domencich T, McFadden D, 1975 *Urban Travel Demand: A Behavioural Analysis* (North-Holland, Amsterdam)
Fleet C R, Robertson S R, 1968 "Trip generation in the transport planning process" *Highway Research Record* number 240, Highway Research Board, Washington, DC
Golob T F, Beckmann M J, 1971 "A utility model for travel forecasting" *Transportation Science* **5** (1) 79-90
Hansen W G, 1959 "How accessibility shapes land use" *Journal of the American Institute of Planners* **25** 73-76
Harris A J, Tanner J C, 1974 "Transport demand models based on personal characteristics" paper presented at Sixth International Symposium on Transportation and Traffic Theory, Sydney, Australia
Havers G, Van Vliet D, and others, 1974 "GLTS models: the state of the art" Greater London Transportation Study, note number 71, Greater London Council, London, England
Hotelling H, 1938 "The general welfare in relation to taxation and of railway and utility rates" *Econometrica* **6** 242-269
Koenig J G, 1975 "A theory of urban accessibility: a new working tool for the urban planner" in *Urban Traffic Models* PTRC Summer Meeting, University of Warwick, Coventry, England, pp 99-147
Kraft G, 1974 "Alternative travel behaviour structures: comments" *Transportation Research Record* number 526, Highway Research Board, Washington, DC, pp 52-55
Langdon M, 1976 "Modal split models for more than two modes" in *Urban Traffic Models* PTRC Summer Meeting, University of Warwick, Coventry, England, 12-16 July
Last A, 1974 "How TRANSEPT works: (1) predicting bus patronage" Local Government Operational Research Unit, Reading, Berks, England
Lawson G P, Mullen P, 1976 "The use of disaggregate modelling techniques in the Telford transportation study" PTRC Summer Meeting, University of Warwick, Coventry, England, 12-16 July
London Transport Study (Phase III), 1968, Part I, Chapters 19 and 20, Freeman, Fox, Wilbur Smith, and Associates, London, England
Luce R D, 1959 *Individual Choice Behavior* (John Wiley, New York)
Luce R D, Suppes P, 1965 "Preference, utility and subjective probability" in *Handbook of Mathematical Psychology Volume 3* Eds R D Luce, R Bush, E Galanter (John Wiley, New York)
Manheim M L, 1973 "Practical implications of some fundamental properties of travel demand models" *Highway Research Record* number 422, Highway Research Board, Washington, DC, pp 21-38
McFadden D, 1974 "Conditional logit analysis of qualitative choice behavior" in *Frontiers in Econometrics* Ed. P Zarembka (Academic Press, New York)
McIntosh P T, Quarmby D A, 1970 "Generalised cost, and the estimation of movement costs and benefit in transport planning" MAU note 179, Department of the Environment, London, England
MALTS, 1969 "The development of a person trip forecasting procedure" Merseyside Area Land Use Transportation Study, Traffic Research Corporation, Liverpool, England
Neuberger H L I, 1971 "User benefit in the evaluation of transport and land use plans" *Journal of Transport Economics and Policy* **5** 52-75
Nottingham and Environs Transportation Study, 1974 "Calibration of the transportation model" Freeman, Fox, and Associates, London, England
Quant R E, 1968 "Estimation of modal splits" *Transportation Research* **2** 41-50
Rassam P R, Ellis R H, Bennet J C, 1971 "The n-dimensional logit model: development and application" *Highway Research Record* number 369, Highway Research Board, Washington, DC, pp 135-147
Restle F, 1961 *Psychology of Judgement and Choice* (John Wiley, Chichester, Sussex)
Restle F, 1971 *Mathematical Models in Psychology: An Introduction* (Penguin Books, Harmondsworth, Middx)
Richards M G, 1975 "An application of disaggregate modelling techniques to transportation planning studies" in *Urban Traffic Models* PTRC Summer Meeting, University of Warwick, Coventry, England, pp 246-262
Ruiter E, 1973 "Analytic structures" in *Urban Travel Demand Forecasting* special report 143, Highway Research Board, Washington, DC

SELNEC Transportation Study, 1971 "The mathematical model" technical working paper 5, Town Hall, Manchester, England
Senior M L, Williams H C W L, 1977 "The structure of urban travel demand models and user benefit measures: a comparative study and sensitivity analysis" Institute for Transport Studies, University of Leeds, Leeds, England (forthcoming)
Sheffield-Rotherham Land-Use-Transportation Study, 1974 "Transportation model calibration" technical memorandum 10, A M Voorhees, Sheffield, England
Stopher P R, 1975 "Comfort and convenience in travel demand models: some recent advances" in *Urban Traffic Models* PTRC Summer Meeting, University of Warwick, Coventry, England, pp 263-272
Strotz R H, 1957 "The empirical implications of a utility tree" *Econometrica* **25** 269-280
Tressider J O, Meyers D A, Burrell J E, Powell T J, 1968 "The London Transportation Study: methods and techniques" *Proceedings of the Institute of Civil Engineers* **39** 433-464
Van Vliet D, 1976 "Road assignment III: comparative tests of stochastic methods" *Transportation Research* **10** 151-157
Wardrop J G, 1952 "Some theoretical aspects of road traffic research" *Proceedings of the Institute of Civil Engineers, Part II* **1** 325-378
Warner S L, 1962 *Stochastic Choice of Mode in Urban Travel: A Study in Binary Choice* (Northwestern University Press, Evanston, Ill.)
Williams H C W L, 1976a "Travel demand models, duality relations and user benefit analysis" *Journal of Regional Science* **16** (2) 147-166
Williams H C W L, 1976b "The formation of travel demand models and user benefit measures" paper presented to the Conference on Urban Transport Planning, University of Leeds, Leeds, England, 29 March-1 April
Williams H C W L, Sanderson I R, Senior M L, 1975 "The design and evaluation of an urban park-and-ride system: some methodological issues" *Environment and Planning A* **7** 689-702
Wilson A G, 1967 "A statistical theory of spatial distribution models" *Transportation Research* **1** 253-269
Wilson A G, 1969 "Entropy maximising models in the theory of trip distribution, mode split and route split" *Journal of Transport Economics and Policy* **3** 108-126
Wilson A G, 1970 *Entropy in Urban and Regional Modelling* (Pion, London)
Wilson A G, 1973a "Travel demand forecasting: achievements and problems" in *Urban Travel Demand Forecasting* special report 143, Highway Research Board, Washington, DC
Wilson A G, 1973b "Further developments of entropy maximising transport models" *Transportation Planning and Technology* **1** 183-193
Wilson A G, Kirwan R M, 1969 "Measures of benefit in the evaluation of urban transport improvements" WP 43, Centre for Environmental Studies, London, England
Wootton H J, Pick G W, 1967 "A model for trips generated by households" *Journal of Transport Economics and Policy* **1** 137-153

APPENDIX 1

Principal notation

D_ξ is the demand for a movement characterised by the index ξ.
D_ξ^*, $D_\xi^\star$ are demand functions evaluated in the initial and final cost states c^* and $c^\star$.
M_ξ is a share function for movement ξ.
c_ξ is the perceived generalised cost or disutility associated with ξ.
ΔS is the change in consumer surplus associated with the change $c^* \rightarrow c^\star$.
$\hat{\sigma}$ is a path parameter in cost or utility space.
σ is the standard deviation of utility, cost, or surplus distributions.
T_{ij}^{nkr} is the number of trips between zones i and j by persons of type n by mode k and route r. $n = 1, 2$ frequently refer to car-owner and noncar-owner households in distribution models. In modal-split shares, M_{ij}^{nk}, n is frequently disaggregated to refer to 0, 1, 2+ car-owner households.
$T_{ij}^{nk(\tilde{k})}$ is the modal trip matrix for composite mode $\tilde{k}$. $\tilde{k} = 1, 2$ denotes private and public modes respectively. $k(\tilde{k})$ refers to a submode within the composite movement $\tilde{k}$.
δ^k is a modal penalty.

---

c_{ij}^k is the generalised cost between zones i and j by mode k.
G_i^n is the number of trips generated in zone i from households with characteristic n.
A_j is a destination weight in aggregate models. In aggregate work trip models, A_j is the number of trips attracted to zone j.
W is an entropy function.
$\boldsymbol{a}, \boldsymbol{b}$ are vectors of dual variables (or Lagrange multipliers).
P_ρ is the probability that an individual will select alternative X_ρ from a set X.
Z_ρ is a vector of attributes associated with X_ρ.
$\beta, \lambda, ..., \Delta$ are dispersion parameters in a logit function.
$\bar{\alpha}$ is a vector of parameters in a utility function.

APPENDIX 2

The properties of $\tilde{c}_{\bullet}$, the mean value of the distribution of minimum costs $\Lambda_{\bullet}(c)$
In this appendix the properties of the cost $\tilde{c}_{\bullet}$, defined by

$$\tilde{c}_{\bullet} = \int_{-\infty}^{+\infty} \mathrm{d}c\, c\, \Lambda_{\bullet}(c) \tag{A1}$$

with

$$\Lambda_{\bullet}(c) = \sum_\rho \Gamma_\rho(c, \bar{c}_\rho) \prod_{\rho' \neq \rho} \int_c^{\infty} \mathrm{d}c' \Gamma_{\rho'}(c', \bar{c}_{\rho'}) , \tag{A2}$$

will be formally examined. The N distributions $\Gamma_\rho(c, \bar{c}_\rho)$, $(\rho = 1, ..., N)$, which are characterised by mean values $\bar{c}_\rho$ $(\rho = 1, ..., N)$ and standard deviations σ_ρ, are considered to be normalised

$$\int_{-\infty}^{\infty} \mathrm{d}c\, \Gamma_\rho(c, \bar{c}_\rho) = 1 , \qquad \rho = 1, ..., N . \tag{A3}$$

Property 1: The sign of $\tilde{c}_{\bullet}$
The perceived generalised costs associated with transport alternatives are regarded (by definition) as positive measures of disutility. If the function $\Gamma_\rho(c, \bar{c}_\rho)$ is a realistic distribution of disutility it must therefore be normalised over the positive c axis. That is

$$\int_0^{\infty} \mathrm{d}c\, \Gamma_\rho(c, \bar{c}_\rho) = 1 , \qquad \rho = 1, ..., N , \tag{A4}$$

whence

$$\tilde{c}_{\bullet} = \int_0^{\infty} \mathrm{d}c\, c\, \Lambda_{\bullet}(c) . \tag{A5}$$

Because $\Lambda(c)$ is positive for $c > 0$, the nonnegativity of $\tilde{c}_{\bullet}$ follows immediately.

Tailed distributions, such as the Gaussian or Weibull, which are not normalised over the positive axis may, in certain circumstances, give rise to negative values of $\tilde{c}_{\bullet}$. It is interesting to note in this context, as Domencich and McFadden (1975) have shown, that the Weibull is the only distribution which maintains its functional form under the operation [see equation (74)]

$$\Lambda_{\bullet}(c) = \mathrm{O}_{\min}[\Gamma_\rho(c, \bar{c}_\rho),\ \rho = 1, ..., N] .$$

Thus for

$$\Gamma_\rho(c, \bar{c}_\rho) = \Delta \exp[-\Delta(\bar{c}_\rho - c)] \exp\{-\exp[-\Delta(\bar{c}_\rho - c)]\} , \tag{A6}$$

the distribution of minimum costs, $\Lambda(c)$, is given by

$$\Lambda_{\bullet}(c, \tilde{c}_{\bullet}) = \Gamma\left[c, -\frac{1}{\Delta} \ln \sum_\rho \exp(-\Delta\bar{c}_\rho)\right] , \tag{A7}$$

and the value

$$\tilde{c}_{*} = -\frac{1}{\Delta}\ln\sum_{\rho}\exp(-\Delta\bar{c}_{\rho})+\frac{\gamma}{\Delta} \tag{A8}$$

becomes negative for the values of $\{\Delta; \bar{c}_{\rho}\}$ $(\rho = 1, ..., N)$ satisfying

$$\sum_{\rho}\exp(-\Delta\bar{c}_{\rho}) > e^{\gamma} = 1\cdot 78 . \tag{A9}$$

Properties of the derivative $\partial\tilde{c}_{*}/\partial\bar{c}_{\rho}$

By direct differentiation of equation (A1) we have

$$\frac{\partial\tilde{c}_{*}}{\partial\bar{c}_{\rho}} = \int_{-\infty}^{\infty} dc\, c\, \frac{\partial\Gamma_{\rho}}{\partial\bar{c}_{\rho}} \prod_{\rho'\neq\rho}\int_{c}^{\infty} dc'\,\Gamma_{\rho'}(c', \bar{c}_{\rho'})$$

$$+\sum_{\rho''\neq\rho}\int_{-\infty}^{\infty} dc\, c\,\Gamma_{\rho''}(c, \bar{c}_{\rho''})\int_{c}^{\infty} dc'\,\frac{\partial\Gamma_{\rho}}{\partial\bar{c}_{\rho}}\prod_{\substack{\rho'\neq\rho''\\ \neq\rho}}\int_{c}^{\infty} dc''\,\Gamma_{\rho'}(c'', \bar{c}_{\rho'}) . \tag{A10}$$

If the distributions $\Gamma_{\rho}(c)$ may be written in the form

$$\Gamma_{\rho}(c, \bar{c}_{\rho}) = \Gamma_{\rho}(\tau_{\rho}, \sigma_{\rho}) \equiv \Gamma_{\rho}(c-\bar{c}_{\rho}, \sigma_{\rho}(\bar{c}_{\rho})) , \tag{A11}$$

where σ_{ρ} is the standard deviation, then

$$\frac{\partial\Gamma_{\rho}(c, \bar{c}_{\rho})}{\partial\bar{c}_{\rho}} = \frac{\partial\Gamma_{\rho}}{\partial\tau_{\rho}}\frac{d\tau_{\rho}}{d\bar{c}_{\rho}}+\frac{\partial\Gamma_{\rho}}{\partial\sigma_{\rho}}\frac{d\sigma_{\rho}}{d\bar{c}_{\rho}} \tag{A12}$$

$$= -\frac{\partial\Gamma_{\rho}}{\partial\tau_{\rho}}+\frac{\partial\Gamma_{\rho}}{\partial\sigma_{\rho}}\frac{d\sigma_{\rho}}{d\bar{c}_{\rho}} \tag{A13}$$

$$= -\frac{\partial\Gamma_{\rho}}{\partial c}+\frac{\partial\Gamma_{\rho}}{\partial\sigma_{\rho}}\frac{d\sigma_{\rho}}{d\bar{c}_{\rho}} . \tag{A14}$$

Thus

$$\frac{\partial\tilde{c}_{*}}{\partial\bar{c}_{\rho}} = \Phi_{\rho}+\Psi_{\rho} , \tag{A15}$$

with

$$\Phi_{\rho} = -\int_{-\infty}^{\infty} dc\, c\,\frac{\partial\Gamma_{\rho}}{\partial c}\prod_{\rho'\neq\rho}\int_{c}^{\infty} dc'\,\Gamma_{\rho'}(c', \bar{c}_{\rho'})$$

$$-\sum_{\rho''\neq\rho}\int_{-\infty}^{\infty} dc\, c\,\Gamma_{\rho''}(c, \bar{c}_{\rho''})\int_{c}^{\infty} dc'\,\frac{\partial\Gamma_{\rho}}{\partial c'}\prod_{\substack{\rho'\neq\rho''\\ \neq\rho}}\int_{c}^{\infty} dc''\,\Gamma_{\rho'}(c'', \bar{c}_{\rho'}) , \tag{A16}$$

and

$$\Psi_{\rho} = \frac{\partial\tilde{c}_{*}}{\partial\sigma_{\rho}}\frac{d\sigma_{\rho}}{d\bar{c}_{\rho}} . \tag{A17}$$

The first term in the expression for Φ_{ρ}, which will be denoted Φ'_{ρ}, may be integrated by parts to give

$$\Phi'_{\rho} = \left[-c\,\Gamma_{\rho}(c, \bar{c}_{\rho})\prod_{\rho'\neq\rho}\int_{c}^{\infty} dc'\,\Gamma_{\rho'}(c', \bar{c}_{\rho'})\right]_{-\infty}^{\infty}$$

$$-\sum_{\rho''\neq\rho}\int_{-\infty}^{\infty} dc\, c\,\Gamma_{\rho}(c, \bar{c}_{\rho})\Gamma_{\rho''}(c, \bar{c}_{\rho''})\prod_{\substack{\rho'\neq\rho''\\ \neq\rho}}\int_{c}^{\infty} dc''\,\Gamma(c'', \bar{c}_{\rho'})$$

$$+\int_{-\infty}^{\infty} dc\,\Gamma_{\rho}(c, \bar{c}_{\rho})\prod_{\rho'\neq\rho}\int_{c}^{\infty} dc'\,\Gamma_{\rho'}(c', \bar{c}_{\rho'}) . \tag{A18}$$

The first term of equation (A18) vanishes at both limits, while the second cancels the second term on the right-hand side of equation (A16). It then follows that

$$\Phi_\rho = \int_{-\infty}^{\infty} \mathrm{d}c\, \Gamma_\rho(c, \bar{c}_\rho) \prod_{\rho' \neq \rho} \int_{c}^{\infty} \mathrm{d}c' \Gamma_{\rho'}(c', \bar{c}_{\rho'})$$

$$= P_\rho \,, \qquad \text{(A19)}$$

and

$$\frac{\partial \tilde{c}_*}{\partial \bar{c}_\rho} = P_\rho + \Psi_\rho \qquad \text{(A20)}$$

$$= P_\rho + \frac{\partial \tilde{c}_*}{\partial \sigma_\rho} \frac{\mathrm{d}\sigma_\rho}{\mathrm{d}\bar{c}_\rho} \,. \qquad \text{(A21)}$$

Therefore

$$\frac{\partial P_\rho}{\partial \bar{c}_{\rho'}} + \frac{\mathrm{d}\sigma_\rho}{\mathrm{d}\bar{c}_\rho} \frac{\partial^2 \tilde{c}_*}{\partial \bar{c}_{\rho'} \partial \sigma_\rho} = \frac{\partial P_{\rho'}}{\partial \bar{c}_\rho} + \frac{\mathrm{d}\sigma_{\rho'}}{\mathrm{d}\bar{c}_{\rho'}} \frac{\partial^2 \tilde{c}_*}{\partial \bar{c}_\rho \partial \sigma_{\rho'}} \,. \qquad \text{(A22)}$$

No further progress may be made in reducing Ψ_ρ until the specific dependence of the standard deviation σ_ρ on the mean $\bar{c}_\rho$ is established. I shall not pursue this general problem further. When the underlying distributions are *translationally invariant*, with σ_ρ independent of $\bar{c}_\rho$, then from equation (A21) we have

$$\frac{\partial \tilde{c}_*}{\partial \bar{c}_\rho} = P_\rho \geqslant 0 \,. \qquad \text{(A23)}$$

An alternative demonstration of the validity of this special case is given by Harris and Tanner (1974). It can be seen from equation (A22) that Hotelling's integrability condition (19) is immediately implied by translational invariance. The presence of correlation between alternative movements does not destroy this basic result which relies fundamentally on the relation

$$\frac{\partial H(c, \bar{c}_\rho)}{\partial \bar{c}_\rho} = -\frac{\partial H(c, \bar{c}_\rho)}{\partial c} \qquad \text{(A24)}$$

for any function H.

The property $\tilde{c}_* < \min_\rho \bar{c}_\rho$

The normalised distribution Λ_*^N characterises the *selected* choices of a hypothetical population with equal observable attributes. Consider the introduction of an additional choice X_{N+1}. A person now compares the disutility of the new option with his preferred alternative. Switching will only occur if the alternative is perceived as the optimal choice in the modified set.

The new distribution of minimum costs will have a mean value $\tilde{c}_*^{N+1}$ given by

$$\tilde{c}_*^{N+1} = \int_{-\infty}^{\infty} \mathrm{d}c\, c\, \Gamma_{N+1}(c, \bar{c}_{N+1}) \int_{c}^{\infty} \mathrm{d}c' \Lambda_*^N(c') + \int_{-\infty}^{\infty} \mathrm{d}c\, c\, \Lambda_*^N(c) \int_{c}^{\infty} \mathrm{d}c' \Gamma_{N+1}(c', \bar{c}_{N+1}) \,. \qquad \text{(A25)}$$

Now, by inverting the order of integration in the first term of the right-hand side of equation (A25), in the (c, c') plane, $\tilde{c}_*^{N+1}$ may be written

$$\tilde{c}_*^{N+1} = \int_{-\infty}^{\infty} \mathrm{d}c\, \Lambda_*^N(c) \int_{-\infty}^{c} \mathrm{d}c' c' \Gamma_{N+1}(c') + \int_{-\infty}^{\infty} \mathrm{d}c\, c\, \Lambda_*^N(c) \int_{c}^{\infty} \mathrm{d}c' \Gamma_{N+1}(c') \qquad \text{(A26)}$$

$$= \int_{-\infty}^{\infty} \mathrm{d}c\, c\, \Lambda_*^N(c) + \int_{-\infty}^{\infty} \mathrm{d}c\, \Lambda_*^N(c) \int_{-\infty}^{c} \mathrm{d}c' \Gamma_{N+1}(c')(c' - c) \qquad \text{(A27)}$$

$$\leqslant \tilde{c}_*^N \,. \qquad \text{(A28)}$$

The inequality holds because the second integral in equation (A27) is always negative and will be zero only when the distributions $\Lambda(c)$ and $\Gamma_{N+1}(c)$ do not overlap. Similarly it may be shown that

$$\tilde{c}_{\bullet}^{N+1} \leqslant \bar{c}_{N+1} , \tag{A29}$$

giving

$$\tilde{c}_{\bullet}^{N+1} \leqslant \min(\tilde{c}_{\bullet}^{N}, \bar{c}_{N+1}) . \tag{A30}$$

By recursion we have

$$\tilde{c}_{\bullet}^{N+1} \leqslant \min[\min(\tilde{c}_{\bullet}^{N-1}, \bar{c}_{N}), \bar{c}_{N+1}] \tag{A31}$$

$$\overset{\cdots}{\leqslant} \min(\bar{c}_{N+1}, ..., \bar{c}_1) . \tag{A32}$$

It should be emphasised that the equality holds in the independent random utility model when the distributions $\{\Gamma_1, ..., \Gamma_\rho, ..., \Gamma_N\}$ do not overlap.

The property $\lim_{\lambda \to \infty} \tilde{c}_{\bullet}(\lambda) = \min_{\rho} c_\rho$

The parameter λ is taken to characterise the standard deviation of the distributions Γ_ρ $(\rho = 1, ..., N)$ such that

$$\sigma_\rho \approx \frac{1}{\lambda} . \tag{A33}$$

The function $\tilde{c}_{\bullet}$ may be written [equation (72)]

$$\tilde{c}_{\bullet} = \sum_{\rho} P_\rho \bar{\bar{c}}_\rho ,$$

with

$$P_\rho = \int_{-\infty}^{\infty} \mathrm{d}c\, \Gamma_\rho(c, \bar{c}_\rho) \prod_{\rho' \neq \rho} \int_{c}^{\infty} \mathrm{d}c' \Gamma_{\rho'}(c', \bar{c}_{\rho'}) .$$

It is clear that in the limit $\lambda \to \infty$ the normalised distributions Γ_ρ will have the characteristics of the Dirac delta function, $\delta(c - \bar{c}_\rho)$, and the probability distribution and costs will then satisfy

$$P_\rho = 1 , \quad \text{if} \quad \bar{c}_\rho = \min_{\rho'} \bar{c}_{\rho'} ,$$
$$= 0 , \quad \text{otherwise,} \tag{A34}$$

and

$$\bar{\bar{c}}_\rho = \bar{c}_\rho . \tag{A35}$$

The property $\lim_{\lambda \to \infty} \tilde{c}_{\bullet}(\lambda) = \min_{\rho} \bar{c}_\rho$ follows immediately.

APPENDIX 3

The general choice model in N' dimensions

The multiple choice problem in the N'*-dimensions* $X^{(1)}, ..., X^{(N')}$ involves specification of the probability function $P_{\rho\mu ... \zeta}$, for selection of $\{X_\rho^{(1)}, X_\mu^{(2)}, ..., X_\zeta^{(N')}\}$, appropriate to a utility function with the following form

$$U[X^{(1)}, ..., X^{(N')}] = U^{(X^1)} + ... + U^{(X^{N'})} + U^{(X^1X^2)} + ... + U^{(X^1X^2 ... X^{N'})} , \tag{A36}$$

which has the following elements

$$u(\rho\mu, ..., \zeta) = u_\rho + ... + u_\zeta + u_{\rho\mu} + ... + u_{\rho\mu ... \zeta} ,$$
$$X_\rho \in X^{(1)}, X_\mu \in X^{(2)}, ..., X_\zeta \in X^{(N')} . \tag{A37}$$

The component $U^{(X^1)}$ contains attributes $Z^{(X^1)}$, which vary across the dimension $X^{(1)}$ alone, $U^{(X^1X^2)}$ contains attributes $Z^{(X^1X^2)}$, which vary across the $X^{(1)}$ and $X^{(2)}$ dimensions, whereas $U^{(X^1 \dots X^{N'})}$ varies across all dimensions.

The extension of equation (206) to N dimensions $X^{(1)}, \dots, X^{(N')}$ may now be written

$$P_{\rho\mu \dots \zeta} = \frac{\exp(\beta_1 u_\rho^{\#} + \beta_2 u_\mu^{\#} + \dots + \beta_{12} u_{\rho\mu}^{\#} + \dots + \beta_{12 \dots N'} u_{\rho\mu \dots \zeta}^{\#})}{\sum\limits_{\rho \dots \zeta} \exp(\beta_1 u_\rho^{\#} + \beta_2 u_\mu^{\#} + \dots + \beta_{12} u_{\rho\mu}^{\#} + \dots + \beta_{12 \dots N'} u_{\rho\mu \dots \zeta}^{\#})}, \tag{A38}$$

where

$$u_\rho^{\#} = \bar{u}_\rho + \left(\frac{\beta_1 - \beta_{12 \dots N'}}{\beta_{12 \dots N'}}\right) \tilde{u}_{\rho * \dots *}, \tag{A39}$$

$$u_\mu^{\#} = \bar{u}_\mu + \left(\frac{\beta_2 - \beta_{12 \dots N'}}{\beta_{12 \dots N'}}\right) \tilde{u}_{*\mu * \dots *}, \tag{A40}$$

$$u_{\rho\mu}^{\#} = \bar{u}_{\rho\mu} + \left(\frac{\beta_{12} - \beta_{12 \dots N'}}{\beta_{12 \dots N'}}\right) \tilde{u}_{\rho\mu * \dots *}, \tag{A41}$$

$$u_{\rho\mu \dots \zeta}^{\#} = \bar{u}_{\rho\mu \dots \zeta}. \tag{A42}$$

The notation $\bar{u}_{\rho\mu}$, for example, denotes the mean value of the distribution of utility $\Gamma_{\rho\mu}(u, \bar{u}_{\rho\mu})$. The composite functions are in turn defined by

$$\tilde{u}_{\rho * \dots *} = \frac{1}{\beta_{12 \dots N'}} \times \ln \sum_{X_\mu \in X^{(2)}} \dots \sum_{X_\zeta \in X^{(N')}} \exp(\beta_2 \bar{u}_\mu + \dots + \beta_{N'} \bar{u}_\zeta + \beta_{12} \bar{u}_{\rho\mu} + \dots + \beta_{12 \dots N'} \bar{u}_{\rho\mu \dots \zeta}) \tag{A43}$$

$\vdots$

$$\tilde{u}_{\rho\mu * \dots *} = \frac{1}{\beta_{12 \dots N'}} \ln \sum_{X_\tau \in X^{(3)}} \dots \sum_{X_\zeta \in X^{(N')}} \exp(\beta_3 \bar{u}_\tau + \dots + \beta_{13} \bar{u}_{\rho\tau} + \dots + \beta_{12 \dots N'} \bar{u}_{\rho\mu \dots \zeta}) \tag{A44}$$

$\vdots$

$$\tilde{u}_{\rho\mu \dots \omega *} = \frac{1}{\beta_{12 \dots N'}} \ln \sum_{X_\zeta \in X^{(N')}} \exp(\beta_{N'} \bar{u}_\zeta + \beta_{1N'} \bar{u}_{\zeta\rho} + \dots + \beta_{12 \dots N'} \bar{u}_{\rho\mu \dots \zeta}). \tag{A45}$$

A measure of consumer surplus may be obtained from the logarithm of the denominator in equation (A38) as before.

[10]

Econometrica, Vol. 49, No. 1 (January, 1981)

APPLIED WELFARE ECONOMICS WITH DISCRETE CHOICE MODELS[1]

BY KENNETH A. SMALL AND HARVEY S. ROSEN

Economists have been paying increasing attention to the study of situations in which consumers face a discrete rather than a continuous set of choices. Such models are potentially very important in evaluating the impact of government programs upon consumer welfare. But little has been said in general regarding the tools of applied welfare economics in discrete choice situations.

This paper shows how the conventional methods of applied welfare economics can be modified to handle such cases. It focuses on the computation of the excess burden of taxation, and the evaluation of quality change. The results are applied to stochastic utility models, including the popular cases of probit and logit analysis. Throughout, the emphasis is on providing rigorous guidelines for carrying out applied work.

1. INTRODUCTION

ECONOMISTS ARE PAYING increasing attention to the study of situations in which consumers face a discrete rather than a continuous set of choices. A considerable literature has grown covering econometric methodology and applications to a wide variety of situations.[2] In a few specific cases, estimates of discrete choice models have been employed for welfare analysis.[3] Travel demand researchers have developed "composite cost" and "accessibility" measures to evaluate the desirability of various states (Williams [**34**], Ben-Akiva and Lerman [**4**]), but the relationship of these to conventional welfare criteria has not been thoroughly explored. Indeed, very little has been said in general regarding the validity of the tools of applied welfare economics in discrete choice situations.

Nevertheless, in at least two areas in which discrete choice models are applied, welfare judgments are of paramount interest. The first is the analysis of taxes and subsidies. Econometric studies of the impacts of taxes on labor supply, savings, and housing decisions have permitted calculation of the welfare cost or "excess burden" of the tax feature under consideration.[4] Traditionally, such studies have assumed that the taxed activity will be pursued regardless of the existence of the tax.

However, instances in which taxes influence discrete choices are numerous and important. For example, it has been suggested that the federal tax treatment of owner-occupied housing not only increases the quantity demanded of owner-occupied housing services, but also influences whether or not an individual owns a home at all (Rosen [**27**]). For secondary earners, taxes affect not only the number

[1] The work in this paper was supported in part by the National Science Foundation, Grant No. SOC77-07082; the views expressed are those of the authors. We have received useful comments from David Bradford, Peter Diamond, Daniel Feenberg, Jerry Green, Arnold Harberger, Richard Quandt, Robert Willig, and two referees.

[2] For examples and references, see McFadden [**22**].

[3] For example, Domencich and McFadden [**12**], Small [**30**].

[4] See, for example, Aaron [**1**], Harberger [**16**], Boskin [**6**], and Laidler [**20**].

of hours of work, but also whether or not participation in the labor market takes place (Heckman [**18**]). Even for primary workers, taxes may influence not only the hours spent at a given occupation, but the choice between occupations as well.

A second important area is the analysis of quality changes in goods and services. Numerous studies in such areas as transportation, education, health care, child care, and pollution contain explicit or implicit welfare evaluations of public policies which change the quality of some publicly or privately supplied good. In many cases, the good affected is subject to discrete choice: mode of transportation, public or private schools, type of health care, type of child care, and location of recreational activities all serve as examples.

The purpose of the present paper is to demonstrate that the conventional methods of applied welfare economics can be generalized to handle cases in which discrete choices are involved. We think it important for several reasons to set out the generalization carefully. First, there has been some suggestion that conventional welfare change computations may have no relevance in discrete choice cases.[5] Second, as the econometric estimation of discrete choice models of many types gains in popularity, it is useful to have a clear statement regarding their use in applied welfare economics. Finally, the presence of discrete choice introduces some differences in the relation between ordinary and compensated demand curves which alter the way in which empirical approximations should be carried out.

In Section 2 we review the computation of the Hicksian compensated variation for the "standard" case in which there are price-induced changes in quantity demanded by each individual. We also note its relation to the Harberger "excess burden" and to the Marshallian consumer's surplus. In Section 3 it is shown how the computations are performed for circumstances in which discrete choice is involved, and Section 4 extends the result to quality changes. Section 5 discusses in detail the application of the results to stochastic utility models, including the cases of probit and logit analysis. Throughout, the emphasis is on providing rigorous guidelines for carrying out applied work.

2. CONTINUOUS CHOICE

In this section we review the justification for measuring price-induced utility changes as areas to the left of the appropriate compensated demand curves. The basic analytical tool is the expenditure function, which is treated concisely and elegantly in Diamond and McFadden [**11**].

Suppose that a consumer has a twice differentiable, strictly quasi-concave utility function u defined over the commodities x_n and x_1, where x_n is taken to be

[5] For example, Ben-Porath and Bruno [**5**] state that in Israel, the pre-1975 tax structure was "... less a deterrent to work as such than an inducement to search for untaxable *types* of work" (our emphasis). They suggest that "The concept of excess burden is not particularly well defined in this case ..." (p. 289).

the numeraire. The two good case is chosen for convenience; the results generalize easily to an arbitrary number of commodities. The consumer maximizes

$$(2.1) \qquad u = u(x_n, x_1)$$

subject to the budget and nonnegativity constraints

$$(2.2) \qquad x_n + p_1 x_1 = y,$$

$$(2.3) \qquad x_j \geq 0, \quad j = n, 1,$$

where p_1 is the price of good 1, and y is income.

Maximization of (2.1) subject to (2.2) yields the ordinary demand functions

$$(2.4) \qquad x_j = x_j(p_1, y), \quad j = n, 1.$$

We assume an interior solution ($x_j > 0$) with respect to both goods. Substituting (2.4) into (2.1) we define the consumer's indirect utility function

$$(2.5) \qquad v(p_1, y) = u(x_n(p_1, y), x_1(p_1, y))$$

which is known to satisfy Roy's Identity:[6]

$$(2.6) \qquad -\frac{\partial v/\partial p_1}{\partial v/\partial y} = x_1.$$

Provided that the direct utility function is strictly increasing in x_n and is nondecreasing in x_1, v is monotonic increasing in y and can therefore be inverted to yield the expenditure function

$$(2.7) \qquad y = e(p_1, u).$$

The function e therefore indicates how much income is required to achieve the utility level u when the price of good 1 is p_1; it satisfies

$$(2.8) \qquad u = v(p_1, e(p_1, u)).$$

Now suppose that the price of the first good changes from p_1^0 to p_1^f. By definition, the compensating variation associated with the price change is

$$(2.9) \qquad \Delta e = e(p_1^f, u^0) - e(p_1^0, u^0).$$

This expression shows the amount of income the consumer must be given to make him as well off at price p_1^f as at p_1^0. Mohring [**24**] has forcefully argued that it is the appropriate measure for most problems of applied welfare economics.[7]

The problem now is to express (2.9) in terms of the compensated demand function for x_1, which is defined by

$$(2.10) \qquad x_1^c(p_1, u) = x_1(p_1, e(p_1, u)).$$

[6] Roy's Identity follows from comparing the total differentials of (2.2) and (2.5) and using the first-order maximization conditions.

[7] It is employed, for example, by Hause [**17**] and Diamond and McFadden [**11**], both of which demonstrate that the compensating variation measure leads to the well-known Harberger formula for excess burden. Nevertheless, some controversy surrounds its use; see Chipman and Moore [**9**] and Hause [**17**].

This is done by applying Shephard's Lemma:

$$\frac{\partial e(p_1, u)}{\partial p_1} = x_1^c(p_1, u), \tag{2.11}$$

where u is an arbitrarily selected utility level.[8] This equation gives the compensating variation for an infinitesimal change in p_1; to find the compensating variation for a finite change, (2.11) is integrated:

$$e(p_1^f, u^0) - e(p_1^0, u^0) = \int_{p_1^0}^{p_1^f} x_1^c(p_1, u^0)\, dp_1. \tag{2.12}$$

This gives the basic result mentioned at the start of this section; the compensating variation of a price change is the area to the left of the compensated demand curve.

This result is easily aggregated. Define the aggregate compensated demand function for good 1, X_1^c, as the sum of the individual compensated demand functions. X_1^c depends upon prices and upon the utility levels of *all* consumers. Similarly, define the aggregate expenditure function, E, as the sum of the individual expenditure functions at these same utility levels. Then by adding the compensating variations (2.12) for all consumers, we obtain

$$\Delta E = \int_{p_1^0}^{p_1^f} X_1^c(p_1, \{u^i\})\, dp_1, \tag{2.13}$$

where $\{u^i\}$ is the set of utility levels before the change.

For practical purposes, the area to the left of the compensated demand curve in (2.13) is usually calculated from an econometric estimate of the ordinary or Marshallian demand curve.[9] Although the compensated demand function for an *individual* can, under certain conditions, be computed exactly from an econometric estimate of the Marshallian demand (Seade [**28**], Willig [**35**]), the same is not true of *aggregates*. This had led to an approximation procedure, employed by a number of investigators such as Harberger [**16**] and Feldstein [**13**], in which the Slutsky equation is applied to the ordinary aggregate demand curve in order to obtain estimates of compensated price elasticities. This procedure is exact if (a) $\partial x_1/\partial y$ is the same for everyone, and (b) each individual's share of aggregate income is fixed regardless of price and income changes; in this case the Slutsky equation can be aggregated. To the extent that individuals' income slopes are similar, then, this would appear to be a reasonable approximation procedure.

For the special case in which the price change is induced by a tax (or subsidy), (2.13) can be used to calculate the "excess burden" of the tax, i.e., the welfare

[8] Shephard's Lemma follows from differentiating (2.8) with respect to p_1, and applying Roy's Identity.

[9] It has been shown that the area under the ordinary demand curve is itself an exact measure of the utility change under very restrictive conditions on the demand function. See, for example, Chipman and Moore [**10**], Rader [**25**], or Bruce [**8**].

loss brought about by distortions in relative prices. Following Diamond and McFadden [**11**], we define excess burden as

$$\chi = \Delta E - T, \tag{2.14}$$

where T denotes tax receipts. The exact form which equation (2.14) takes in practice depends on the income effects generated by the uses of the tax revenues (or, alternatively, by a set of hypothetical lump-sum taxes of equal yield), and therefore depends on the distribution of these revenue uses or taxes. Although this point is well-known (see Friedman [**15**], Bailey [**2**], Harberger [**16**], and Hause [**17**]), it is worth restating here because its implications for discrete goods, discussed in the next section, are somewhat surprising.

Let α and α^c be the own-price slopes of the aggregate Marshallian and compensated demand functions, respectively; and let ω be the income-slope of the former, viewed as a function of aggregate income $Y \equiv \Sigma_i y^i$. Then the Slutsky approximation discussed above,

$$\alpha^c = \alpha + X_1\omega, \tag{2.15}$$

can be intuitively justified from the observation that $X_1\,dp_1$ is the income compensation required to ameliorate the effect of a price increase dp_1, and hence $\omega X_1\,dp_1$ is the additional consumption induced if income is compensated.

A linear approximation to the compensated demand curve yields

$$\Delta E \simeq X_1^0 \Delta p_1 + \tfrac{1}{2}\alpha^c(\Delta p_1)^2 \tag{2.16}$$

$$= X_1^0 \Delta p_1 + \tfrac{1}{2}[\alpha + X_1^0\omega](\Delta p_1)^2, \tag{2.17}$$

where X_1^0 is the aggregate consumption at initial price p_1^0, and where $\Delta p_1 = p_1^f - p_1^0$. Equation (2.17) can be viewed as the Taylor series approximation to ΔE, of second-order in Δp_1. (Throughout this paper we will be using such second-order approximations. In order to keep the exposition as simple as possible, we will refrain from writing out the expressions for remainder terms that exceed second order. But care is taken to compute fully the second order terms prior to truncation.)

Now consider two alternative assumptions about the uses of the tax revenues T: (a) the *partial* equilibrium assumption that they are used in such a way as to generate no repercussions on demand for good 1, and (b) the general equilibrium assumption that they are distributed in lump sum transfers. We again compute approximations of second order in the price change. Under assumption (a), tax revenues are computed along the Marshallian demand curve:

$$T^P \simeq [X_1^0 + \alpha\Delta p_1]\Delta p_1. \tag{2.18}$$

Under assumption (b), on the other hand, final demand contains an income effect ωT^G, where T^G are the tax revenues, so that

$$T^G \simeq [X_1^0 + \alpha\Delta p_1 + \omega T^G]\Delta p_1. \tag{2.19}$$

Equation (2.19) can be solved for T^G and written as a Taylor series in Δp_1. If the series is truncated after terms that are quadratic in Δp_1, we find[10]

$$(2.20) \quad T^G \simeq [X_1^0 + (\alpha + X_1^0\omega)\Delta p_1]\Delta p_1$$

$$(2.21) \quad = [X_1^0 + \alpha^c \Delta p_1]\Delta p_1.$$

But this is equivalent to computing taxes along the *compensated* demand curve.[11]

Subtracting tax revenues from the compensating variation in (2.16) and rearranging yields the following alternative formulae for excess burden:

(a) Partial equilibrium:

$$(2.22) \quad \chi^p \simeq \tfrac{1}{2}[\alpha^c - 2\alpha](\Delta p_1)^2$$

$$(2.23) \quad = \tfrac{1}{2}[-\alpha + X_1\omega](\Delta p_1)^2;$$

(b) General equilibrium:

$$(2.24) \quad \chi^G \simeq \tfrac{1}{2}[-\alpha^c](\Delta p_1)^2$$

$$(2.25) \quad = \tfrac{1}{2}[-\alpha - X_1\omega](\Delta p_1)^2.$$

The general equilibrium version (2.24) is the famous excess burden triangle usually associated with Harberger.

Note that, whereas the compensating variation is of first order in Δp_1, the excess burden is itself of second-order in Δp_1. Thus, the conditions given by Willig [**35**], under which the compensating variation is adequately approximated by the ordinary consumer's surplus, do not necessarily justify using the ordinary instead of the compensated demand curve for excess burden calculations. Indeed, if the general equilibrium assumptions underlying equation (2.24) prevail, then it is the best approximation (up to second-order terms in Δp_1) of the excess burden, and the fractional error from using α instead of α^c in equation (2.24) is $(\alpha - \alpha^c)/\alpha^c = -X_1\omega/\alpha^c = -\theta\eta/\varepsilon^c$, where θ is the budget share of good 1, η is its income elasticity, and ε^c is its compensated own-price elasticity. This error can be substantial for a good, such as housing, which absorbs a large portion of consumers' incomes.

For a normal good, the excess burden is positive and is smaller in the general than in the partial equilibrium context. This is because the consumption cutback caused by the price distortion is lessened by the income effects arising from the uses of the tax revenues. We will see in the next section that some of the

[10] Proof: From (2.19),

$$T^G \cong \frac{1}{1-\omega\Delta p_1}(X_1^0 + \alpha\Delta p_1)\Delta p_1.$$

The term $1/(1-\omega\Delta p_1)$ can be approximated by $1+\omega\Delta p_1 + (\omega\Delta p_1)^2$. Multiplying this by $(X_1^0 + \alpha\Delta p_1)\Delta p_1$ and truncating terms that are cubic or higher in order yields (2.20).

[11] See Hause [**17**, pp. 1156–1160] for a fuller discussion of the rationale for using the compensated demand curve in computing tax revenue under general equilibrium assumptions. Note also that we are assuming a constant cost technology, i.e., introduction of the tax does not change the producer's price over the relevant region. See also Rohlfs' [**26**] discussion of the adequacy of surplus welfare measures under partial equilibrium assumptions.

ameliorating income effect in the general equilibrium case is lost in discrete good models, making the potential welfare losses from taxes on such goods greater than conventional analysis would imply.

3. DISCRETE CHOICE

In this section, we prove the basic theorem which establishes the validity of using the area to the left of a compensated demand curve for a *discrete* good as a measure of the compensating variation. We take advantage of the notation and general plan of attack used in Section 2 for the continuous goods case. We then show how the use of empirical approximations for computing welfare losses is modified.

Discreteness in demand can be modelled in at least three ways. (a) Commodities may be available in continuous quantities, but in only one of a small number of mutually exclusive varieties. An example is housing. It can be purchased in either the rental or owner mode, but given the tenure choice, a continuous quantity of housing services can be consumed. (b) Goods may be available in discrete units which are so large that most consumers choose only one or two units. Examples include college degrees, transportation mode for work trips, and many consumer durables. (c) Goods may be purchased in discrete units because nonconcavities in utility functions lead the consumer to choose among alternative corner solutions. For example, two television shows aired simultaneously can be consumed in any fractions, but most viewers will prefer to consume all of one and none of the other. Note that many examples could be modelled equally well as cases (a) or (c).

In addition, even with concave utility functions, particular prices and incomes may lead to corner solutions at which a good is not consumed at all. Empirically, this has led to econometric techniques such as Tobit analysis. Although this is not usually considered discrete choice, we mention it here because the issues involved are formally very similar to those of the other cases.

The problem raised by all these cases for the theoretical derivation of the compensating variation is that discreteness introduces a point of discontinuity into the demand functions, and/or a point of nondifferentiability into the indirect utility and expenditure functions. Thus, the derivative in equation (2.11) may be undefined at some "crossover" price. The key to the result in this section is that it is still possible to integrate over (2.11), since the expenditure function is continuous and has right and left derivatives at the point in question.

The formal models for the various cases differ in detail, but the proofs for all are essentially similar. We therefore proceed by considering case (a) in a three-good model in which two of the goods are mutually exclusive. The proofs for the other cases and extensions to more than three goods are outlined in the Appendix.

Consider, then, a consumer with utility function

$$u = u(x_n, x_1, x_2), \tag{3.1}$$

where x_n is the numeraire good. In order for the possibility of zero consumption of good 1 or 2 to make sense, we assume that utility is finite when either x_1 or x_2 is zero. As in the standard case, utility is maximized subject to

$$x_n + p_1x_1 + p_2x_2 = y, \tag{3.2}$$

$$x_j \geqslant 0 \quad (j = 1, 2, n). \tag{3.3}$$

To prevent both x_1 and x_2 from being consumed in positive amounts, we impose the constraint

$$x_1x_2 = 0. \tag{3.4}$$

As in the previous section, we assume interior solutions[12] rather than dealing explicitly with nonnegativity constraints: thus the numeraire and *either* x_1 or x_2 are consumed in positive quantities.

THEOREM 1: *Suppose a consumer maximizes, subject to constraints* (3.2) *through* (3.4), *a twice differentiable, strictly quasi-concave utility function of the form* (3.1). *Assume u is finite whenever x_1 or x_2 is zero, is strictly increasing in x_n, and is nondecreasing in x_1 and x_2. Let $e(p_1, p_2, u)$ be the minimum expenditure required to achieve utility u, and let $u^0 = v(p_1^0, p_2, y)$ be the value of the indirect utility function*[13] *at initial prices and income. Then the compensating variation for a change in price p_1 from p_1^0 to p_1^f is*

$$e(p_1^f, p_2, u^0) - e(p_1^0, p_2, u^0) = \int_{p_1^0}^{p_1^f} x_1^c(p_1, p_2, u^0)\, dp_1, \tag{3.5}$$

where $x_1^c(\cdot)$ is the compensated demand function for good 1 *defined by*

$$x_1^c(p_1, p_2, u^0) = x_1(p_1, p_2, e(p_1, p_2, u^0)). \tag{3.6}$$

PROOF: Constraint (3.4) requires that consumption of either good 1 or good 2 be zero. If $x_2 = 0$, the optimal amount of x_1 is found by maximizing $u(x_n, x_1, 0)$ subject to $x_n + p_1x_1 = y$. The function u is well-behaved when viewed as a function only of x_n and x_1, so this sub-problem is formally identical to the problem of the previous section, and leads to well-defined continuously differentiable indirect utility, expenditure, and compensated demand functions, each conditional on $x_2 = 0$. Denoting these by $\tilde{v}_1(p_1, y)$, $\tilde{e}_1(p_1, u)$, and $\tilde{x}_1^c(p_1, u)$, respectively, we know from (2.11) that

$$\partial\tilde{e}_1/\partial p_1 = \tilde{x}_1^c. \tag{3.7}$$

Similarly, if $x_1 = 0$, the problem of maximizing $u(x_n, 0, x_2)$ yields functions $\tilde{v}_2(p_2, y)$, $\tilde{e}_2(p_2, u)$, and $\tilde{x}_2^c(p_2, u)$ with the property that

$$\partial\tilde{e}_2/\partial p_2 = \tilde{x}_2^c. \tag{3.8}$$

[12] Corner solutions can also be dealt with using the framework developed in this section. See the Appendix for a demonstration.

[13] So long as the numeraire is perfectly divisible, the assumption that u is strictly increasing in x_n and nondecreasing in x_1 and x_2 guarantees that the indirect utility function exists and is strictly increasing in y, and therefore can be inverted to find the expenditure function.

For any income $\bar{y}$, the choice between good 1 and good 2 will be made by comparing $\tilde{v}_1(p_1, \bar{y})$ with $\tilde{v}_2(p_2, \bar{y})$. Let $k(p_1, p_2, \bar{y})$ index the larger of the two, with $k = 1$ in case of a tie. Then the utility achieved is

$$(3.9) \qquad \bar{u} = \tilde{v}_k(p_k, \bar{y}) \equiv \max\{\tilde{v}_1(p_1, \bar{y}), \tilde{v}_2(p_2, \bar{y})\}.$$

The quantity $\bar{y}$ is therefore the income required to achieve utility $\bar{u}$, both unconditionally and conditionally on choice k:

$$(3.10) \qquad \bar{y} = e(p_1, p_2, \bar{u}) = \tilde{e}_k(p_k, \bar{u}).$$

Letting j index *either* good ($j = 1, 2$), the fact that $\tilde{v}_j(p_j, \bar{y}) \leq \bar{u}$ implies

$$(3.11) \qquad \tilde{e}_j(p_j, \bar{u}) \geq \bar{y}, \quad j = 1, 2,$$

since $\tilde{v}_j$ is strictly increasing in $\bar{y}$, and $\tilde{e}_j$ is simply its inverse. But (3.10) and (3.11) together imply that

$$(3.12) \qquad e(p_1, p_2, \bar{u}) = \min_j \tilde{e}_j(p_j, \bar{u}).$$

Since each of the functions $\tilde{e}_j$ is continuously differentiable in price, so is e, except at those prices for which $\tilde{e}_1 = \tilde{e}_2$; and at these points, e is continuous and right and left differentiable.[14] Its price derivatives are therefore bounded and piecewise continuous, and hence integrable.[15] Furthermore,

$$(3.13) \qquad \partial e/\partial p_1 = \begin{cases} \partial \tilde{e}_1/\partial p_1 \equiv \tilde{x}_1^c, & \text{if } k = 1, \\ \partial \tilde{e}_2/\partial p_1 \equiv 0, , & \text{if } k \neq 1, \end{cases}$$

provided the upper and lower expressions are interpreted as the left and right derivatives, respectively, at the point of indifference between the two goods.

It remains only to identify the right-hand side of (3.13) as the compensated demand function, $x_1^c(p_1, p_2, \bar{u})$. When good 1 is chosen (given $p_1, p_2, \bar{u}$), $x_1^c = \tilde{x}_1^c$; when good 2 is chosen, $x_1^c = 0$. Thus, for an infinitesimal change in p_1, the compensating variation (3.13) reduces to

$$(3.14) \qquad \partial e(p_1, p_2, \bar{u})/\partial p_1 = x_1^c(p_1, p_2, \bar{u}).$$

Evaluating (3.14) at utility $u^0 \equiv \max\{\tilde{v}_1(p_1^0, y), \tilde{v}_2(p_2, y)\}$ and integrating over p_1 yields (3.5). *Q.E.D.*

[14] For given p_2 and u, let $y^* = e_2(p_2, u)$. Let p_1^* be the single value of p_1 (if any) at which the consumer switches goods. Thus, $\tilde{e}_1(p_1^*, u) = \tilde{e}_2(p_2, u) = e(p_1^*, p_2, u)$. For $p_1 < p_1^*$, good 1 is chosen and $e = \tilde{e}_1$; for $p_1 > p_1^*$, good 2 is chosen and $e = \tilde{e}_2$. Clearly e is continuous at p_1^*, since $\tilde{e}_1 = \tilde{e}_2$ there. The left derivative of e with respect to p_1, evaluated at p_1^*, is

$$\lim_{p_1 \uparrow p_1^*} \frac{e(p_1, p_2, u) - e(p_1^*, p_2, u)}{p_1 - p_1^*} = \lim_{p_1 \uparrow p_1^*} \frac{\tilde{e}_1(p_1, u) - \tilde{e}_1(p_1^*, u)}{p_1 - p_1^*}$$
$$= (\partial \tilde{e}_1/\partial p_1)|_{p_1^*},$$

since $\tilde{e}_1$ is differentiable. Similarly, the right derivative exists and is equal to $\partial \tilde{e}_2/\partial p_1$.

[15] See any calculus text, e.g., Thomas [**32**, p. 214].

A more heuristic discussion of the theorem may be useful at this point. Suppose an infinitesimal change, dp_1, occurs in the price of good 1. If a positive amount x_1 of good 1 is being consumed, then the welfare loss is $x_1\,dp_1$. If good 1 is not being consumed, i.e., $x_1 = 0$, then the welfare loss is again $x_1\,dp_1$, which in this case equals zero. If the consumer is just at the point of indifference between goods 1 and 2, no welfare loss arises from switching from one good to the other. Therefore, integrating over this point of discontinuity adds nothing to the total for a finite change. In every case, then, the welfare loss from an incremental price change is described by the incremental area to the left of the demand curve. If income is compensated as the price changes, this is equivalent to measuring the area to the left of the compensated demand curve. This intuitive discussion applies equally well to cases (b) and (c), mentioned earlier,[16] and to corner solutions.

As in the ordinary goods case, we define an aggregate compensated demand function for good 1, X_1^c, as the sum of the individual compensated demand functions. It depends upon the prices and the utilities of all consumers. Similarly, define the aggregate expenditure function E as the sum of the individual expenditure functions at arbitrarily selected utility levels. Then, by adding over consumers, we obtain the result that the sum of the individual compensating variations is given by the area to the left of the aggregate compensated demand curve:

$$\Delta E = \int_{p_1^0}^{p_1^f} X_1^c(p_1, p_2, \{u^i\})\,dp_1 \tag{3.15}$$

where u^i is the initial utility level of the ith consumer.

Applying the Theorem

For purposes of applying Theorem 1, it is important to notice that the demand curve in (3.15) is the unconditional demand for good 1, and is not conditional on the choice of good 1. Both the discrete choice itself *and* the quantity demanded conditional on that choice are incorporated in X_1^c.

To make this distinction clear, write the compensated demand function in equation (3.5), for individual i, as

$$x_1^{ci}(p_1, p_2, u^{i0}) = \delta_1^{ci}(p_1, p_2, u^{i0})\tilde{x}_1^{ci}(p_1, p_2, u^{i0}) \tag{3.16}$$

[16] Mäler [**23**, pp. 131–136] demonstrates an even stronger result for case (b), in which the good in question must be purchased in a given quantity or not at all. He shows that, for a *fall* in the price of such a good, the compensating variation is given by the area to the left of its *ordinary* demand curve. This follows from our result because income effects are absent, and thus the ordinary and compensated demand curves are identical. So long as the price remains above the "critical price" p^* at which the consumer purchases the discrete good, no compensation is required to keep him at the initial utility level; and below the critical price, the compensation cannot affect the amount of the discrete good purchased. However, R. Willig has pointed out to us that Mäler is incorrect in stating that the result also holds when the individual is consuming the good, and the price *rises* above p^*. This asymmetry occurs because for the price rise, the compensating income alters the critical price itself, and hence the ordinary demand curve and the relevant compensated demand curve are not identical.

where δ_1^{ci} is a compensated discrete choice index, i.e., δ_1^{ci} is 1 if good 1 is chosen and 0 otherwise, assuming that price changes are compensated in order to permit achievement of initial utility level u^{i0}. The compensated demand *conditional* on choice of good 1, $\tilde{x}_1^{ci}$, is defined as in the above proof. Adding the right-hand sides of equation (3.16) for the N individuals in the economy yields an alternative version of (3.15):

$$(3.17) \qquad \Delta E = \int_{p_1^0}^{p_1^f} \sum_{i=1}^{N} \delta_1^{ci}(p_1, p_2, u^{i0})\tilde{x}_1^{ci}(p_1, p_2, u^{i0})\, dp_1.$$

There are two important problems which must be solved in order to make equation (3.17) useful for applied work. First, an investigator cannot know with certainty whether or not a representative individual will consume a given discrete good: All that can be assigned is the *probability* π_j^i that the good will be purchased, conditional upon a set of measurable characteristics (race, sex, etc.) as well as prices and income. An attractive way to model this is to assume that each individual's utility function is deterministic (as in the preceding section), but that because of factors unobservable to the investigator, the outcome appears random.[17] Thus as we move to applications of our theorem and attach probabilistic interpretations to variables that were heretofore deterministic, we are not moving to a different framework, but are dealing with a special case of the model developed above. Replacing the choice index in (3.17) with this choice probability converts (3.17) to an equation for the *expected* welfare change.[18]

The second problem is that δ_1^{ci} is a *compensated* discrete choice index; therefore, it should be replaced with a compensated choice probability. We provide in the next subsection an approximation procedure, analogous to that for continuous goods, for doing this.

Our method is therefore fully operational provided we can find econometric techniques for estimating the required demand curves. A straightforward procedure would be to estimate the discrete choice and conditional demand functions jointly using maximum likelihood techniques. Alternatively, a consistent recursive procedure has been developed by Heckman [**19**].

Slutsky Effect

A satisfactory approximation procedure for converting econometric estimates into *compensated* demand relations must take into account the fact that neither the Slutsky equation nor the computation of tax revenues is the same for discrete

[17] This seems to have acquired the name "random utility" approach, in contrast to the "constant utility" approach, in which the utility function itself (or equivalently, the choice mechanism) is viewed as having a random component. Operationally, these two formulations are equivalent, i.e. lead to the same kind of estimating equations. Their interpretations are discussed at length by Williams [**34**].

[18] Note that only if the choice probability is independent of price p_1 will the correct answer be obtained by calculating areas for *conditional* demand curves and multiplying them by the probabilities. Thus, for example, Feldstein and Friedman [**14**] are correct in using the latter procedure to calculate welfare effects of changes in the price of health insurance, because in their model the probability of illness is assumed to be exogeneous. However, one must not be misled into thinking their procedure is generalizable to endogenous probabilities.

as for continuous goods, because the nature of the income effects is fundamentally changed. In the continuous case, it is at least reasonable to suppose that all consumers have identical income slopes for good 1; this permits the Slutsky equation to be aggregated, and makes plausible the general equilibrium assumption that tax revenues are redistributed so as to return all consumers to their initial utility levels. In the discrete case, however, we explicitly recognize a group whose consumption of good 1 is zero throughout a range of incomes, and thus the analysis must be modified.

In order to focus on the issue of discreteness *per se*, it is useful to abstract from other differences among individuals by assuming N consumers who differ only in their preferences between goods 1 and 2.[19] Thus, they have identical incomes y, and identical *conditional* Marshallian and compensated demand functions $\tilde{x}_1(p_1, y)$ and $\tilde{x}_1^c(p_1, u)$, respectively. This is, of course, a very restrictive case. However, it is useful in that it highlights the important differences that appear when discreteness is explicitly taken into account. If the assumptions of this section seem too restrictive for a given problem, they can be relaxed, although the results will be less intuitive and computationally more complicated.

The Slutsky equation for this model is

$$\frac{\partial \tilde{x}_1^c}{\partial p_1} = \frac{\partial \tilde{x}_1}{\partial p_1} + \tilde{x}_1 \frac{\partial \tilde{x}_1}{\partial y}. \tag{3.18}$$

Now let $\pi_1(p_1, p_2, \{y^i\})$ be the fraction choosing good 1 at the given prices and incomes. In analogy to the compensated demand function, define the compensated choice probability

$$\pi_1^c(p_1, p_2, \{u^i\}) = \pi_1(p_1, p_2, \{e^i(p_1, p_2, u^i)\}) \tag{3.19}$$

where u^i and e^i represent the utility level and the expenditure function, respectively, for consumer i.

Define the aggregate quantities

$$X_1 = \sum_i x_1^i = N\pi_1\tilde{x}_1, \tag{3.20}$$

$$X_1^c = \sum_i x_1^{ic} = N\pi_1^c\tilde{x}_1^c, \tag{3.21}$$

$$Y = \sum_i y^i = Ny. \tag{3.22}$$

Note that since all incomes y^i are assumed equal, X_1 and π_1 depend on them only through aggregate income Y. Hence we may write

$$\pi_1 = \pi_1(p_1, p_2, Y), \tag{3.23}$$

$$X_1 = X_1(p_1, p_2, Y) = N\pi_1(p_1, p_2, Y)\tilde{x}_1(p_1, p_2, Y/N). \tag{3.24}$$

[19] Assume, for example, that utility for the ith individual is given by

$$u^i(x_n, x_1, x_2) = f(x_n, x_1, x_2) + \varepsilon_1^i\delta_1 + \varepsilon_2^i\delta_2,$$

where $\delta_j = 1$ if x_j is chosen and $\delta_j = 0$ otherwise ($j = 1, 2$), and where ε_1^i and ε_2^i are constants.

Differentiating (3.19) at an initial point for which $x_1^c = x_1$ and $\pi_1^c = \pi_1$, and applying our previous result (3.14), yields the choice-probability analogue to the Slutsky equation:

$$\text{(3.25)} \qquad \frac{\partial \pi_1^c}{\partial p_1} = \frac{\partial \pi_1}{\partial p_1} + \sum_i \frac{\partial \pi_1}{\partial y^i}\frac{\partial e^i}{\partial p_1}$$

$$= \frac{\partial \pi_1}{\partial p_1} + X_1 \frac{\partial \pi_1}{\partial Y}.$$

Equations (3.18) through (3.25) taken together yield a Slutsky-like equation for the aggregate demand functions:[20]

$$\text{(3.26)} \qquad \frac{\partial X_1^c}{\partial p_1} = \frac{\partial X_1}{\partial p_1} + \frac{X_1}{\pi_1}\left[\frac{\partial X_1}{\partial Y} - (1-\pi_1)\frac{X_1}{\pi_1}\frac{\partial \pi_1}{\partial Y}\right].$$

In the special case $\partial \pi_1/\partial Y = 0$, equation (3.26) is the usual aggregate Slutsky equation, except the income effect is divided by π_1 and is thus larger than in the continuous case. The intuition behind this follows from the conceptual experiment implicit in the compensating variation measure. Were it required to maintain utility after a price rise dp_1, it would be necessary to provide compensation

[20] Proof: Differentiate (3.21) to find

$$\text{(3.25a)} \qquad \frac{\partial X_1^c}{\partial p_1} = N\left(\pi_1^c \frac{\partial \tilde{x}_1^c}{\partial p_1} + \tilde{x}_1^c \frac{\partial \pi_1^c}{\partial p_1}\right).$$

Substituting (3.18) and (3.25) into (3.25a) yields

$$\text{(3.25b)} \qquad \frac{\partial X_1^c}{\partial p_1} = N\left[\pi_1^c\left(\frac{\partial \tilde{x}_1}{\partial p_1} + \tilde{x}_1 \frac{\partial \tilde{x}_1}{\partial y}\right) + \tilde{x}_1^c\left(\frac{\partial \pi_1}{\partial p_1} + X_1 \frac{\partial \pi_1}{\partial Y}\right)\right].$$

Note that from (3.20), $\tilde{x}_1 = X_1/(N\pi_1)$, so that $\partial \tilde{x}_1/\partial p_1$ can be written

$$\text{(3.25c)} \qquad \frac{\partial \tilde{x}_1}{\partial p_1} = \frac{1}{N}\left[\frac{1}{\pi_1}\frac{\partial X_1}{\partial p_1} - \frac{X_1}{\pi_1^2}\frac{\partial \pi_1}{\partial p_1}\right].$$

Similarly,

$$\text{(3.25d)} \qquad \frac{\partial \tilde{x}_1}{\partial y} = \frac{1}{N}\left[\frac{1}{\pi_1}\frac{\partial X_1}{\partial y} - \frac{X_1}{\pi_1^2}\frac{\partial \pi_1}{\partial y}\right].$$

Recalling that we are differentiating at an initial point where $X_1 = X_1^c$ and $\pi_1 = \pi_1^c$, and substituting (3.25c), (3.25d), (3.20), and (3.21) into (3.25b) yields

$$\text{(3.25e)} \qquad \frac{\partial X_1^c}{\partial p_1} = \frac{\partial X_1}{\partial p_1} - \frac{X_1}{\pi_1}\frac{\partial \pi_1}{\partial p_1} + \frac{X_1}{N}\left[\frac{1}{\pi_1}\frac{\partial X_1}{\partial y} - \frac{X_1}{\pi_1^2}\frac{\partial \pi}{\partial y}\right] + \frac{X_1}{\pi_1}\left[\frac{\partial \pi_1}{\partial p_1} + X_1 \frac{\partial \pi_1}{\partial Y}\right].$$

From (3.22),

$$\frac{\partial X_1}{\partial y} = N\frac{\partial X_1}{\partial Y} \quad \text{and} \quad \frac{\partial \pi_1}{\partial y} = N\frac{\partial \pi_1}{\partial Y}.$$

Using these facts (3.25e) can be written

$$\text{(3.25f)} \qquad \frac{\partial X_1^c}{\partial p_1} = \frac{\partial X_1}{\partial p_1} + \frac{X_1}{\pi_1}\frac{\partial X_1}{\partial Y} - \frac{X_1^2}{\pi_1^2}\frac{\partial \pi_1}{\partial Y} + \frac{X_1^2}{\pi_1}\frac{\partial \pi_1}{\partial Y}.$$

Rearranging (3.25f) yields (3.26) of the text. *Q.E.D.*

equal to $X_1\, dp_1$ *to that fraction* π_1 *of the population which consumes good* 1. But this would have the same effect on consumption as raising all incomes equally, by an aggregate amount $(X_1/\pi_1)\, dp_1$, since the extra payments to nonconsumers would have no impact (so long as $\partial\pi_1/\partial Y = 0$) on aggregate consumption X_1. Thus, the compensation would cause consumption of good 1 to rise by $(\partial X_1/\partial Y)(X_1/\pi_1)\, dp_1$, which gives the first income effect term in (3.26). The last term arises from the effects of income compensation on the choice probability itself.

Excess Burden

Following the procedure of Section 2, we approximate the demand curves by straight lines with slopes

$$\partial X_1/\partial p_1 = \alpha,$$

$$\partial X_1^c/\partial p_1 = \alpha^c,$$

$$\partial X_1/\partial Y = \omega.$$

We also let

$$\partial\pi_1/\partial Y = \nu.$$

As before, the compensating variation is given by equation (2.16); note, however, that this is no longer equivalent to (2.17).

We next proceed to calculate tax revenues under (a) partial and (b) general equilibrium assumptions, making use of the "Slutsky-like" equation (3.26), which can be written

$$\alpha^c = \alpha + (X_1/\pi_1)\omega - (1-\pi_1)(X_1/\pi_1)^2\nu. \tag{3.27}$$

(a) For the partial equilibrium case, tax revenue is simply given by (2.18), and excess burden by (2.22). Substituting (3.27) into (2.22) yields

$$\chi^P = \tfrac{1}{2}[-\alpha^c + 2(X_1/\pi_1)\omega - 2(1-\pi_1)(X_1/\pi_1)^2\nu](\Delta p_1)^2 \tag{3.28}$$

$$= \tfrac{1}{2}[-\alpha + (X_1/\pi_1)\omega - (1-\pi_1)(X_1/\pi_1)^2\nu](\Delta p_1)^2. \tag{3.29}$$

Note that, in the absence of income effects on the choice probability ($\nu = 0$), the excess burden (3.29) is *larger* than would be calculated from (2.23), if discreteness were ignored.

(b) If tax revenues are returned uniformly in lump sum transfers, equation (2.20) remains valid, but is no longer equivalent to (2.21), corresponding to the fact that the compensation no longer returns each consumer, even approximately, to his initial utility level. Under this regime, the fraction π_1 who paid the tax have their real incomes reduced, while the others have them raised. In neither group are individuals moving along their compensated demand curves. Subtracting (2.20) from (2.16) and applying (3.27) gives the excess burden:

$$\chi^G = \tfrac{1}{2}[\alpha^c - 2\alpha - 2X_1\omega](\Delta p_1)^2$$

$$(3.30) \qquad = \tfrac{1}{2}\left[-\alpha^c + 2\left(\frac{1}{\pi_1} - 1\right)X_1\omega - 2(1-\pi_1)\left(\frac{X_1}{\pi_1}\right)^2 \nu\right](\Delta p_1)^2$$

$$(3.31) \qquad = \tfrac{1}{2}\left[-\alpha + \left(\frac{1}{\pi_1} - 2\right)X_1\omega - (1-\pi_1)\left(\frac{X_1}{\pi_1}\right)^2 \nu\right](\Delta p_1)^2.$$

Comparing (3.31) with (2.25), we see again that, in the absence of income effects on the choice probability, the excess burden is larger than that computed by ignoring discreteness, though it is still smaller than in the partial equilibrium case (3.29).

So in general, if the choice probability is independent of income but the conditional demands have positive income elasticities, the usual approximation procedure which ignores discreteness underestimates the compensating variation and the excess burden of a price rise. There are two reinforcing tendencies causing the result. First, the usual Slutsky correction results in an overestimate of the magnitude of the compensated price elasticity, and hence an underestimate of the compensating variation. Second, the ameliorating effects of tax revenue redistribution on misallocation are less, because some of the distributions are "wasted" on nonconsumers of the good in question. We suspect that this result is a special case of a more general proposition that standard procedures tend to underestimate excess burden (i.e., the compensating variation less tax revenues) for groups of nonidentical consumers.

We conclude this section by compiling, in Table I, the results for computing excess burdens.[21] The formulae have been converted to elasticity form, using the definitions

$$\varepsilon = \frac{p_1}{X_1}\frac{\partial X_1}{\partial p_1},$$

$$\eta = \frac{Y}{X_1}\frac{\partial X_1}{\partial Y},$$

$$\psi = \frac{Y}{\pi}\frac{\partial \pi}{\partial Y},$$

$$\theta = \frac{X_1 p_1}{Y},$$

$$\pi = \pi_1.$$

[21] A sample caculation based upon an actual econometric study is available upon request to the authors.

The expressions given are those which should replace $[-\varepsilon^c]$ in the Harberger formula,

$$\chi^G = \tfrac{1}{2}X_1p_1[-\varepsilon^c](\Delta p_1/p_1)^2,$$

derived from (2.24).

TABLE I

FACTORS FOR COMPUTING EXCESS BURDENS

	Continuous	Discrete
Partial equilibrium	$-\varepsilon+\theta\eta$	$-\varepsilon+\frac{1}{\pi}\theta\eta-\left(\frac{1}{\pi}-1\right)\theta\psi$
General equilibrium	$-\varepsilon-\theta\eta$	$-\varepsilon+\left(\frac{1}{\pi}-2\right)\theta\eta-\left(\frac{1}{\pi}-1\right)\theta\psi$

Observe that when $\pi=1$, the expressions in the second column equal their counterparts in the first. In both relative and absolute terms, the error introduced by ignoring discreteness is small when practically everybody consumes the good.[22] When π tends toward zero, on the other hand, terms involving θ also tend toward zero, whereas those involving θ/π tend to $\tilde{x}_1p_1/y$.[23] Thus, the error introduced by ignoring discreteness, i.e., the difference between terms in Table I multiplied by $\frac{1}{2}X_1p_1(\Delta p_1/p_1)^2$, tends to zero absolutely (though not as a proportion of excess burden) as π approaches zero.

A final issue concerns the realism of the assumed pattern of redistribution of tax revenues, namely that they are returned to the population at large. Equity considerations or interest-group politics frequently lead instead to attempts to target revenue uses to the groups most affected by the tax. If it is possible to target the revenues only to the consumers of the taxed discrete good, the usual formulae would apply without modification. If some targeting occurs but it is incomplete, the excess burden would be somewhere between the "continuous" and "discrete" calculations.

[22] For another consistency check, consider the special case in which π is independent of price and income. In that case, only a fraction π of the population experiences any effective price change. Calling this subpopulation "group A," we note that its price slope is $\alpha^A=\alpha$, and its income slope $\omega^A=\omega/\pi$. Substituting these values into equation (2.17) gives this group's compensating variation:

$$\Delta E^A = X_1^0\Delta p_1+\tfrac{1}{2}[\alpha+X_1^0\omega/\pi](\Delta p_1)^2.$$

Subtracting total tax collections (2.18) or (2.20) yields (3.29) or (3.31), respectively, with $\nu=0$. Thus, the results in the table are consistent, when π is constant, with the result obtained by computing excess burdens for the two groups separately.

[23] $$\theta/\pi=\left(\frac{N\pi p_1\tilde{x}_1}{Ny}\right)/\pi=\tilde{x}_1p_1/y.$$

4. QUALITY CHANGES

Thus far, our focus has been the measurement of price-induced welfare changes. However, in many discrete choice problems the evaluation of quality changes is of primary interest. For example, we may wish to evaluate changes in frequency of bus services in contexts where consumers have a choice between bus and auto; or changes in noise levels when individuals have the options of staying in the affected locale or of moving.

One possibility for dealing with a quality change is to convert it to an equivalent price change, and then to apply the technique discussed in Section 3. Unfortunately, this is possible only in the very special case in which all consumers have constant and identical marginal rates of substitution between the relevant quality variable and the numeraire. For example, this assumption is often made in transportation studies by assuming a single constant value of time for everyone. Demand for a particular transportation service can then be viewed as a function of money plus time price, and consumer surplus techniques are applicable. However, this example illustrates the tenuousness of such an assumption, since both theoretical and empirical considerations suggest that value of time depends upon a variety of factors such as the wage rate.

An alternative tack is to extend the approach taken in Section 3, by adding a quality variable to the model. Suppose that good 1 in the model of the previous section has associated with it a quality variable described by the scalar q_1, which is considered exogenous by consumers. (The variable q_1 could also be interpreted as the level of provision of a public good which is complementary to good 1.) Thus

$$u = u(x_n, x_1, x_2, q_1) \tag{4.1}$$

where, as before, u is assumed to be finite when either $x_1 = 0$ or $x_2 = 0$. We assume further that quality of good 1 does not matter unless good 1 is being consumed:

$$\partial u(x_n, 0, x_2, q_1)/\partial q_1 = 0. \tag{4.2}$$

As in Section 3, the indirect utility function and the expenditure function are well defined, continuous, right and left differentiable in all arguments, and satisfy

$$u = v(p_1, p_2, q_1, e(p_1, p_2, q_1, u)). \tag{4.3}$$

Two alternative formulations of the problem are obtained by implicitly differentiating (4.3) with respect to q_1 or p_1, respectively, keeping in mind that the right and left derivatives may differ at the crossover points.

Taking the *quality* derivative of (4.3) yields

$$\partial e/\partial q_1 = -(1/\lambda)\partial v/\partial q_1, \tag{4.4}$$

where $\lambda \equiv \partial v/\partial y \equiv \partial u/\partial x_n$ is the marginal utility of income. This intuitive formula simply states that the marginal willingness-to-pay for a quality change is given by the marginal utility of quality, converted to monetary units via the marginal utility of income. For problems in which the indirect utility function is explicitly specified, as in Section 5 below, equation (4.4) is extremely useful, particularly if it is reasonable to approximate λ (an empirical quantity, given the normalization implicit in the econometric procedure) by a constant. However, the constancy of λ is in no sense necessary for (4.4) to be valid.

Taking the *price* derivative of (4.3), on the other hand, and applying Roy's Identity, yields Shephard's Lemma, which was the starting point of deriving Theorem 1 of Section 3. Thus, by simply adding q_1 to the list of arguments of all the functions, Theorem 1 is seen to remain valid in the present context. This fact enables us to evaluate quality changes in terms of changes in consumer's surplus, along the lines explored by Bradford and Hildebrandt [**7**] and Willig [**36**] for continuous goods.

To see this, assume, following Bradford and Hildebrandt, that when the price of good 1 becomes high enough, the consumer does not care about its quality, presumably because none of the good is being consumed. More precisely, we assume that the quality derivative of the expenditure function becomes arbitrarily small as the price of good 1 rises:

$$\lim_{p_1^f \to \infty} \partial e(p_1^f, p_2, q_1, u^0)/\partial q_1 = 0. \tag{4.5}$$

Thus, differentiating our previous result, (3.5), with respect to q_1 and letting $p_1^f \to \infty$ yields the following result:

THEOREM 2: *Let the utility function* (4.1) *satisfy* (4.2) *and all the assumptions of Theorem* 1. *Let* $e(p_1, p_2, q_1, u)$, *the minimum expenditure required to achieve utility* u *subject to constraints* (3.2)–(3.4), *satisfy* (4.5). *Then*

$$\frac{\partial}{\partial q_1} e(p_1^0, p_2, q_1, u^0) = -\int_{p_1^0}^{\infty} \frac{\partial}{\partial q_1} x_1^c(p_1, p_2, q_1, u^0)\, dp_1, \tag{4.6}$$

where the derivatives are to be interpreted as left and right derivatives at points of nondifferentiability.

Note that (4.6) is the change in the area to the left of the compensated demand curve as it shifts in response to the change in q_1. This is the result derived for the case of continuous goods by Bradford and Hildebrandt [**7**], using a slightly different assumption on v. Thus, we have demonstrated that the Bradford–Hildebrandt formula remains valid in the discrete goods case.

Equation (4.6) is easily integrated over q_1 to obtain the compensating variation for a quality change from q_1^0 to q_1^f:

$$\Delta e = -\int_{p_1^0}^{\infty} [x_1^c(p_1, p_2, q_1^f, u^0) - x_1^c(p_1, p_2, q_1^0, u^0)]\, dp_1. \tag{4.7}$$

Furthermore, direct aggregation of (4.7) is possible to obtain a formula in terms of the aggregate compensated demand function:

$$\Delta E = -\int_{p_1^0}^{\infty} [X_1^c(p_1, p_2, q_1^f, \{u^i\}) - X_1^c(p_1, p_2, q_1^0, \{u^i\}]\, dp_1. \tag{4.8}$$

5. APPLICATION TO ECONOMETRIC MODELS

McFadden [**21, 22**] has shown that a broad class of discrete choice models can be derived by assuming that each consumer maximizes a utility function with a stochastic term accounting for differences in tastes that are unobservable to the investigator. Since such models underlie the bulk of current empirical work on discrete choice, it is useful to examine the form which the results of the previous two sections take when applied to stochastic utility models, in particular to the popular probit and logit models. Certain especially useful results are obtained in the special case when the marginal utility of income is approximately constant.

In our notation, the assumption behind all these models is that the *conditional* indirect utility function of consumer i for good j, $\tilde{v}_j^i$, is additively separable into three components as follows:[24]

$$\tilde{v}_j^i(p_j, q_j, y^i) = V^i(y^i) + W_j(p_j, q_j, y^i; \underline{S}^i) + \varepsilon_j^i \tag{5.1}$$

where $W_j(\cdot)$ is a "universal" utility function whose form is identical for all consumers, and where ε_j^i is the realization for consumer i of a random variable ε_j which is independent of the arguments of W_j. The vector $\underline{S}^i$ contains observable characteristics of the consumer, and attributes of the discrete goods (e.g., locational attributes) which may vary across consumers.

By assuming a joint probability distribution on $\{\varepsilon_j\}$, we obtain the probability, conditional on prices, quality levels, and observable consumer characteristics, that utility is maximized by choosing good 1:

$$\pi_1^i = \text{prob}\,[\varepsilon_j - \varepsilon_1 < W_1^i - W_j^i \text{ for all } j \neq i], \tag{5.2}$$

where W_j^i denotes the second term in (5.1). Given specific forms for the functions W_j, their parameters (up to a normalization convention) can be estimated from a sample of observed choices by maximizing the likelihood function associated with (5.2).

In order to forecast the aggregate demands, we need to measure the incomes y^i and other characteristics $\underline{S}^i$ of the individuals in the population under consideration. One way to do this is to sample the population, and assume that each sample member i is representative of a group of N^i individuals who are identical with respect to their incomes and *measured* characteristics.[25] The probability π_1^i calculated from (5.2) can therefore be interpreted as a prediction of the fraction of this particular class of consumers who will choose good 1. Assume further that the conditional (uncompensated) demand function $\tilde{x}_1^i$ either is nonstochastic, or contains a random term which is uncorrelated with ε_j of (5.1). The latter will be

[24] The first term in (5.1) does not enter the econometric specification of the discrete choice model, since it is independent of j; it has usually been ignored in the literature. The remaining terms have generally been described as the "utility function" though it is clear from the inclusion of price as an argument that they are part of an *indirect* utility function. A true indirect utility function would have *all* prices as arguments and would not depend on j; hence the qualification "*conditional.*" See Small [**31**] for a fuller discussion of this point.

[25] Domencich and McFadden [**12**, p. 81] discuss an elaboration of this procedure, and derive equation (5.3) for the case of $\tilde{x}_1^i \equiv 1$ (see their equation 4.69).

the case, for example, if the values of $\tilde{x}_1^i$ used in the welfare computations are predicted values from the last stage of Heckman's estimation procedure described earlier. The expected aggregate demand from class i is therefore

$$X_1^i(p_1, p_2, q_1, y^i; \underset{\sim}{S}^i) = N^i \pi_1^i \tilde{x}_1^i. \tag{5.3}$$

Note the parallel with equation (3.20). Furthermore, applying Roy's Identity to (5.1) gives $\tilde{x}_1^i$ in terms of the price derivative of W_1 and the marginal utility of income,

$$\lambda^i \equiv \frac{\partial V^i}{\partial y^i} + \frac{\partial W_1^i}{\partial y^i}.$$

Substituting into (5.3) yields

$$X_1^i(p_1, p_2, q_1, y^i; \underset{\sim}{S}^i) = -(N^i/\lambda^i)\pi_1^i \partial W_1^i/\partial p_1. \tag{5.4}$$

We now proceed to apply Theorem 2 of the previous section in order to compute the expected compensating variation for members of class i arising from a change in the quality of good 1. A similar analysis could be performed, using Theorem 1, for price changes. We make use of the fact that the expectation operator is interchangeable with either differentiation or summation.[26] In the following discussion, we suppress the superscript i and the explicit dependence on $\underset{\sim}{S}^i$, which is assumed to be fixed.

Having specified functional forms for the components W_j of the indirect utility function, and having implicitly normalized by choosing a specific joint probability distribution function for the stochastic term ε_j, we are free to make assumptions about W_j on the basis of purely empirical considerations. We now make three such assumptions, which are likely to be valid in many applications: (a) that the marginal utility of income, λ, is approximately independent of the price and quality of good 1; (b) that the discrete goods are sufficiently unimportant to the consumer so that income effects from quality changes are negligible, i.e. that the compensated demand function in (4.6) is adequately approximated by the Marshallian demand function; and (c) that $\partial W_1/\partial q_1 \to 0$ as $p_1 \to \infty$. Equation (4.6) can therefore be aggregated over members of this consumer group to yield

$$\frac{1}{N}\frac{\partial E}{\partial q_1} = \frac{1}{\lambda}\frac{\partial}{\partial q_1}\int_{p_1^0}^{\infty} \pi_1(p_1, p_2, q_1, y)\frac{\partial W_1(p_1, q_1, y)}{\partial p_1}\, dp_1.$$

But (5.2) implies that π_1 depends on its arguments only through the functions W_1 and W_2. We may therefore make a change of variable, $\omega_1 = W_1(p_1, q_1, y)$, to

[26] Domencich and McFadden [**12**, pp. 94–99], using this same stochastic utility model, compute the expected utility directly from the stochastic specification. They then demonstrate, using our restriction (a) below, that the change in expected utility due to a price change is equal to the conventional consumer's surplus. One virtue of our Theorems 1 and 2 is that they do not depend on any such restriction, but yield the Domencich-McFadden result as a special case. Since our welfare measure is not stochastic at the individual level, we have no need to compute expected utilities. The stochastic element enters instead as unobservable preferences affecting the demand functions used in Theorems 1 and 2, and we therefore need only to take expectations of demands, as in equation (5.3).

write

$$\frac{1}{N}\frac{\partial E}{\partial q_1}=\frac{1}{\lambda}\frac{\partial}{\partial q_1}\int_{\omega_1^0}^{\omega_1^\infty}\pi_1(\omega_1, W_2)\,d\omega_1$$

where $\omega_1^0 = W_1(p_1^0, q_1, y)$, $\omega_1^\infty = W_1(\infty, q_1, y)$. Now using a standard theorem for differentiating a definite integral with respect to its limits (Thomas [**32**, p. 720]) we find

$$\frac{1}{N}\frac{\partial E}{\partial q_1}=\frac{1}{\lambda}\left(\pi_1(\omega_1^\infty, W_2)\frac{\partial\omega_1^\infty}{\partial q_1}-\pi_1(\omega_1^0, W_2)\frac{\partial\omega_1^0}{\partial q_1}\right).$$

But according to assumption (c) above, $\partial\omega_1^\infty/\partial q_1 = 0$. Therefore,

$$\frac{1}{N}\frac{\partial E}{\partial q_1}=-\frac{1}{\lambda}\pi_1(\omega_1^0, W_2)\frac{\partial\omega_1^0}{\partial q_1}.$$

Integrating this expression over q_1 from initial to final values yields

$$(5.5)\qquad (\Delta E)/N = -(1/\lambda)\int_{W_1^0}^{W_1^f}\pi_1(W_1, W_2)\,dW_1$$

where $W_1^0 = W_1(p_1^0, q_1^0, y)$ and $W_1^f = W_1(p_1^0, q_1^f, y)$.[27]

Equation (5.5) is extremely useful for computing welfare effects using discrete choice models estimated from micro data, since it avoids the explicit use of the aggregate demand functions, which are not normally obtained in closed form from such studies. In fact, though equation (5.5) is derived above using the previous results on aggregate demand curves, it can instead be derived directly from the definition (4.3) of the expenditure function.

To see this, recall that the previous results were based on Shepherd's Lemma, obtained by differentiating (4.3) with respect to price. As mentioned in Section 4, one may instead differentiate (4.3) with respect to quality, leading to (4.4). The indirect utility v of (4.4) is equal to $\tilde{v}_1$ for that fraction π_1 of the consumer group which chooses good 1, and is equal to $\tilde{v}_2$ for the rest. Since only $\tilde{v}_1$ depends on q_1, aggregating (4.4) and calculating $\partial\tilde{v}_1/\partial q_1$ from (5.1) yields

$$(5.6)\qquad \partial E/\partial q_1 = -N(\pi_1/\lambda)\partial W_1/\partial q_1.$$

Equation (5.6) is perfectly general, but one must use caution in integrating it, since the income variable which appears as an argument in all the functions is compensated, i.e., is that value which maintains the original utility level. With the assumptions of constant λ and negligible income effects, however, integrating (5.6) yields (5.5) directly.

[27] Equation (5.5) is easily generalized to many simultaneous price and quality changes, provided the Jacobian matrix $(\partial\pi_i/\partial W_j)$ is symmetric. In that case, the following line integral is unique, i.e., path independent (see Silberberg, [**29**]):

$$(5.5a)\qquad (\Delta E)/N = -(1/\lambda)\int_{\underline{W}^0}^{\underline{W}^f}\sum_i \pi_i(\underline{W})\,dW_i$$

where $\underline{W}$ is a vector of components W_i, and takes initial and final values $\underline{W}^0$ and $\underline{W}^f$ respectively.

A final point to notice about equation (5.5) is that it applies equally well to a price change, if W_1^0 and W_1^f are defined as the values taken by W_1 at the initial and final prices, respectively. This may be seen simply by replacing q_1 by p_1 in the above paragraph. Alternatively, the price-change version of (5.5) can be derived directly by integrating (5.4).

In the course of the econometric estimation of the choice model, specific functional forms for the W_j's are assumed, and estimates of the coefficients are obtained. Hence, one can compute W_1 at the initial and final quality levels, and can therefore compute the integral in (5.5). Furthermore, if price is included as a variable in the specification, one has an estimate of $\partial W_1/\partial p_1$. Using this information along with the conditional demand $\tilde{x}_1$, which is often known, λ can be computed by using Roy's Identity.[28] Equation (5.5) therefore represents an operational procedure for calculating welfare effects. We illustrate its use below for the binary probit and logit models.

Probit

In the binary probit model it is assumed that $(\varepsilon_1 - \varepsilon_2)$ is a standard normal variate. The probabilities are therefore given by

$$\pi_1 = \Phi(W_1 - W_2),$$
$$\pi_2 = 1 - \pi_1,$$

where Φ is the cumulative normal distribution function. Formula (5.5) for the compensating variation becomes

$$(5.7)\qquad (\Delta E)/N = -(1/\lambda)\int_{W_1^0}^{W_1^f} \Phi(W_1 - W_2)\, dW_1 = -(1/\lambda)\int_{\omega^0}^{\omega^f} \Phi(\omega)\, d\omega$$

where $\omega^0 = W_1^0 - W_2$ and $\omega^f = W_1^f - W_2$. Given a probit estimation of the functions W_1 and W_2, this quantity can be computed for any price or quality change.[29]

[28] More specifically, suppose that α_p is the coefficient of the price variable in a probit or logit regression. Then $\lambda = -\alpha_p/\tilde{x}_1$, which, as noted above, is an empirical quantity given the normalization implicit in econometric procedure.

[29] The generalization to simultaneous changes in two price and two quality variables is straightforward, since the Jacobian condition $\partial\pi_1/\partial W_2 = \partial\pi_2/\partial W_1$ is satisfied. Equation (5.5a) in footnote 27 thus becomes

$$(5.7a)\qquad (\Delta E)/N = -\frac{1}{\lambda}\int_{W^0}^{W^f} \{\Phi(W_1 - W_2)\, dW_1 + [1 - \Phi(W_1 - W_2)]\, dW_2\} = -\frac{1}{\lambda}\left[\Delta W_2 + \int_{\omega^0}^{\omega^f} \Phi(\omega)\, d\omega\right]$$

where $\Delta W_2 = W_2^f - W_2^0$. Recalling that W_j is an indirect utility function, the first term in (5.7a) is the negative of the willingness to pay for a uniform improvement in both goods of magnitude ΔW_2, whereas the second term gives the appropriate consumer surplus for any improvement in good 1 relative to good 2.

Logit

The logit model arises from the assumption that the stochastic utility components ε_i are independently and identically distributed with the extreme value or double-exponential distribution (McFadden [**21, 22**]). This leads to a formula for the probabilities:

$$\pi_l = \frac{\exp(W_l)}{\sum_{j=1}^{2} \exp(W_j)}, \quad l = 1, 2. \tag{5.8}$$

In this case, the integral in (5.5) can be evaluated explicitly, leading to:

$$(\Delta E)/N = -(1/\lambda)\left[\ln \sum_j \exp(W_j)\right]_{W_1^0}^{W_1^f} \tag{5.9}$$

where the square brackets indicate the difference in the expression inside when evaluated at the initial and final points.[30]

6. CONCLUSION

The analysis and estimation of discrete choice models is currently enjoying a popularity which is unlikely to abate in future years. Ultimately, both researchers and policy makers will be interested in ascertaining the welfare implications of these models. The purpose of this paper has been to set forth rigorous procedures for doing so. It has been shown how, under quite general conditions as well as for the special cases of probit and logit analysis, the usual techniques for measuring welfare effects must be modified for discrete choice problems. Particular attention has been focused on how the standard corrections for income effects might be altered. The results apply to the study of both price and quality changes.

Princeton University

Manuscript received July, 1978; revision received December, 1979.

APPENDIX

A.1 *Proof of Theorem 1 for Different Types of Discreteness*

1. The good may be purchased only in discrete units which are so large that most consumers choose only one or two units.

The utility function is $u(x_n, x_1)$ where $x_n > 0$, and x_1 can take on values of only unity or zero. Utility is maximized subject to the budget constraint $x_n + x_1 p_1 = y$. If $x_1 = 0$, the optimal amount of x_n is trivially equal to y. This subproblem yields the expenditure function conditional on $x_1 = 0$, $\tilde{e}_n(u)$. Similarly, if

[30] Like the Probit model, the Logit model satisfies the Jacobian symmetry conditions, and calculation of (5.5a) for many price and quality changes yields equation (5.9) altered only in that the limits for evaluating the term in the square brackets are the values $\underline{W}^0$ and $\underline{W}^f$ taken by the vector of *all* W_i at initial and final points. The term in square brackets has been identified in the transportation literature as the "inclusive price" or "composite cost" of an alternative composed of several sub-alternatives (Ben-Akiva [**3**]; Williams [**34**]).

$x_1 = 1$, the conditional expenditure function $\tilde{e}_1(p_1, u)$ is found trivially. As in the case analyzed in the text, the point of maximum utility is associated with the minimum of these two expenditure functions:

$$e(p_1, \bar{u}) = \min\{\tilde{e}_n(\bar{u}), \tilde{e}_1(p_1\bar{u})\}.$$

Since $\tilde{e}_n$ and $\tilde{e}_1$ are both continuously differentiable in price (with $\partial\tilde{e}_n/\partial p_1 \equiv 0$) so is e, except at that price at which $\tilde{e}_1 = \tilde{e}_2$, and at this point e is continuous and right and left differentiable. The rest of the argument follows directly that used in the text.

2. Demand functions are continuous, but particular prices and incomes lead to corner solutions at which a good is not consumed at all.

The utility function $u(x_n, x_1)$, where $x_n > 0$, is maximized subject to $x_n + p_1x_1 = y$ and $x_1 \geqslant 0$. For given utility $\bar{u}$, we have two price ranges divided by $p_1^*(\bar{u})$. For $p_1 < p_1^*(\bar{u})$, an interior solution in good 1 exists, and we denote its compensated demand and expenditure functions by $\tilde{x}_n^c$, $\tilde{x}_1^c$, and $\tilde{e}$. For $p_1 \geqslant p_1^*(\bar{u})$, a corner solution holds and good 1 is not consumed; we denote this solution by $\tilde{\tilde{x}}_n^c$ and $\tilde{\tilde{e}}$. The budget constraint requires that these solutions satisfy

$$\text{(A.1)} \qquad \tilde{x}_n^c(p_1, \bar{u}) + p_1\tilde{x}_1^c(p_1, \bar{u}) = \tilde{e}(p_1, \bar{u}), \quad p_1 < p_1^*(\bar{u}),$$

and

$$\text{(A.2)} \qquad \tilde{\tilde{x}}_n^c(\bar{u}) = \tilde{\tilde{e}}(\bar{u}), \quad p_1 \geqslant p_1^*(\bar{u}).$$

The price $p_1^*(\bar{u})$ is defined as the limiting price for the first case, i.e., that price for which

$$\lim_{p_1 \uparrow p_1^*} \tilde{x}_1^c(p_1, \bar{u}) = 0.$$

By assumption, the compensated demand function defined by

$$x_n^c(p_1, \bar{u}) = \begin{cases} \tilde{x}_n^c(p_1, \bar{u}), & p_1 < p_1^*(\bar{u}), \\ \tilde{\tilde{x}}_n^c(\bar{u}), & p_1 \geqslant p_1^*(\bar{u}), \end{cases}$$

is continuous at p_1^*. Therefore, taking limits of equations (A.1) and (A.2) yields

$$\lim_{p_1 \uparrow p_1^*} \tilde{e}(p_1, \bar{u}) = \tilde{\tilde{e}}(\bar{u}).$$

The overall expenditure function is therefore continuous, and the proof of Theorem 1 applies.

3. A good may be purchased in discrete units because nonconcavities in the utility function lead the consumer to choose among alternative corner solutions.

For cases in which discreteness arises from nonconcavity of the utility function, no general theory is available for use in deriving properties of the resulting demand functions. Indeed, so far as we know, no attempt has yet been made to derive formally statistical discrete choice models for such cases, and to do so would be beyond the scope of this paper. Nevertheless, it is not difficult to see that well-behaved examples can be treated within the framework presented in the text. Suppose, for example, that in a three-good world, all the indifference curves between x_1 and x_2 are concave to the origin, but indifference curves between either x_1 or x_2 and the numeraire are convex. Then at every price vector, consumption of either x_1 or x_2 will be zero; hence the constraint $x_1x_2 = 0$ can be added without changing the problem. Furthermore, the assumptions guarantee that $u(x_n, 0, x_2)$ and $u(x_n, x_1, 0)$, viewed as functions of two variables, are well behaved. Thus the proof of Section 3 applies.

A.2 *Proof of Theorem 1 for Arbitrary Numbers of Goods*

1. More than one continuous good. The interpretation of x_n as a vector of goods presents no problems provided that the discussion of the "standard" case in Section 2 generalizes. That this is true is shown in Varian [**33**, pp. 209–211].

2. More than two discrete goods, all mutually exclusive. Utility is given by $u = u(x_n, x_1, x_2 \ldots, x_l)$, where $x_j \geqslant 0 (j = n, 1, \ldots l)$, and where $x_k > 0 (k = 1, \ldots l)$ implies that $x_r = 0$ for $r \neq k$. The budget constraint is $x_n + \Sigma_{k=1}^{l} p_kx_k = y$. If $x_k > 0$, then utility is found by maximizing $u(x_n, 0, \ldots x_k, \ldots, 0)$ subject to $x_n + p_kx_k = y$. The function u is well behaved when viewed as a function only of x_n and x_k, and its maximization leads to a (conditional) continuously differentiable expenditure function $\tilde{e}_k(p_k, u)$. The only difference between this case and that discussed in the text is that there are now l

such subproblems, rather than two. But the idea is the same: utility maximization leads to the expenditure function $e(p_1, \ldots, p_l, \bar{u}) = \min_k \tilde{e}_k(p_k, \bar{u})$. Since each of the $\tilde{e}_k$ is continuously differentiable in price, so is e except at those prices at which $\tilde{e}_l = \tilde{e}_r$, and at such cross-over points e is continuous and right and left differentiable. The rest of the argument follows directly from the proof of Theorem 1.

3. More than one set of mutually exclusive discrete goods. Utility is given by $u(x_n, x_{11}, x_{12}, x_{21}, x_{22}, \ldots x_{l1}, x_{l2})$, where all the arguments in the utility function are nonnegative. The constraints are $x_{k1}x_{k2} = 0$ for all $k = 1, \ldots, l$. The budget constraint is $x_n + \sum_{k=1}^{l}(p_{k1}x_{k1} + p_{k2}x_{k2}) = y$. In this case, we can imagine the individual solving 2^l subproblems of the sort discussed in Theorem 1. Each subproblem arises from the maximizing utility with one argument in each of the pairs equal to zero. This leads to well behaved conditional expenditure functions, the minimum of which is associated with the consumer's optimum. At each vector of "cross-over" prices, the minimum of these functions is continuous and right and left differentiable in each price. The rest of the argument follows as in the text.

REFERENCES

[1] AARON, H.: *Shelter and Subsidies.* Washington, D.C.: The Brookings Institution, 1972.

[2] BAILEY, M. J.: "The Marshallian Demand Curve," *Journal of Political Economy*, 62 (1954), 255–261.

[3] BEN-AKIVA, M.: "Structure of Travel Demand Models," Ph.D. Dissertation, Massachusetts Institute of Technology, 1973.

[4] BEN-AKIVA, M., AND S. LERMAN: "Disaggregate Travel and Mobility Choice Models and Measures of Accessibility," in *Behavioral Travel Modelling*, ed. by D. Hensher and P. Stopher. London: Croom-Helm, 1978.

[5] BEN-PORATH, Y., AND M. BRUNO: "The Political Economy of Tax Reform: Israel 1975," *Journal of Public Economics*, 7 (1977), 285–308.

[6] BOSKIN, M. J.: "Taxation, Saving and the Rate of Interest," *Journal of Political Economy*, 86 (1978), S3–S28.

[7] BRADFORD, D., AND G. HILDEBRANDT: "Observable Public Good Preferences," *Journal of Public Economics*, 8 (1977), 111–131.

[8] BRUCE, N.: "A Note on Consumer's Surplus, the Divisia Index, and the Measurement of Welfare Changes," *Econometrica*, 45 (1974), 1033–1038.

[9] CHIPMAN, J. S., AND J. C. MOORE: "Compensating Variation as a Measure of Welfare Change," mimeo, University of Minnesota, 1976.

[10] ———: "The Scope of Consumer's Surplus Arguments," in *Evolution, Welfare, and Time in Economics*, ed. by A. M. Tang, F. M. Westfield, and J. S. Worley. Lexington, Mass.: D. C. Heath and Company, 1976.

[11] DIAMOND, P., AND D. MCFADDEN: "Some Uses of the Expenditure Function in Public Finance," *Journal of Public Economics*, 3 (1974), 3–22.

[12] DOMENCICH, T. A., AND D. MCFADDEN: *Urban Travel Demand: A Behavioral Analysis*, Amsterdam: North-Holland, 1975.

[13] FELDSTEIN, M. S.: "The Welfare Cost of Capital Income Taxation," *Journal of Political Economy*, 86 (1978), 529–552.

[14] FELDSTEIN, M. S., AND B. FRIEDMAN: "Tax Subsidies, the Rational Demand for Insurance and the Health Care Crisis," *Journal of Public Economics*, 7 (1977), 155–178.

[15] FRIEDMAN, M.: "The Marshallian Demand Curve," *Journal of Political Economy*, 57 (1949), 463–495.

[16] HARBERGER, A. C.: "Taxation, Resource Allocation and Welfare," in *The Role of Direct and Indirect Taxes in the Federal Revenue System*, ed. by J. Due. Washington, D.C.: The Brookings Institution, 1964.

[17] HAUSE, J. C.: "The Theory of Welfare Cost Measurement," *Journal of Political Economy*, 83 (1975), 1145–1182.

[18] HECKMAN, J.: "Shadow Prices, Market Wages and Labor Supply," *Econometrica*, 42 (1974), 679–694.

[19] ———: "Sample Bias as a Specification Error," *Econometrica*, 47 (1979), 153–162.

[20] LAIDLER, D.: "Income Tax Incentives for Owner-Occupied Housing," in *The Taxation of Income from Capital*, ed. by A. C. Harberger and J. M. Bailey. Washington, D.C.: The Brookings Institution, 1969.

[21] McFADDEN, D.: "Conditional Logit Analysis of Qualitative Choice Behavior," in *Frontiers of Econometrics*, ed. by P. Zarembka. New York: Academic Press, 1973.

[22] ———: "Quantal Choice Analysis: A Survey," *Annals of Economic and Social Measurement*, 5 (1976), 363–390.

[23] MÄLER, K.: *Environmental Economics*. Baltimore: Johns Hopkins, 1974.

[24] MOHRING, H.: "Alternative Gain and Loss Measures," *Western Economic Journal*, 9 (1971), 349–368.

[25] RADER, T.: "Equivalence of Consumer Surplus, The Divisia Index of Output, and Eisenberg's Addilog Social Utility," *Journal of Economic Theory*, 13 (1976), 58–66.

[26] ROHLFS, J.: "Evaluation of Changes in a Suboptimal Economy," *Review of Economic Studies*, 63 (1976), 359–362.

[27] ROSEN, H. S.: "Housing Decisions and the U.S. Income Tax: An Econometric Analysis," *Journal of Public Economics*, 11 (1979), 1–24.

[28] SEADE, JESUS: "Consumer's Surplus and Linearity of Engel's Curves," *Economic Journal*, 88 (1978), 511–523.

[29] SILBERBERG, E.: "Duality and the Many Consumer's Surpluses," *American Economic Review*, 62 (1972), 942–952.

[30] SMALL, K. A.: "Bus Priority, Differential Pricing, and Investment in Urban Highways," Ph.D. Dissertation, University of California, Berkeley, 1976.

[31] ———: "Some Notes on Discrete Choice Models and the Scheduling of Activities," mimeo, Dept. of Economics, Princeton University, 1977.

[32] THOMAS, GEORGE B.: *Calculus and Analytic Geometry*. New York: Addison-Wesley, 1960.

[33] VARIAN, H. R.: *Microeconomic Analysis*. New York: W. W. Norton and Company, 1978.

[34] WILLIAMS, H.: "On the Formation of Travel Demand Models and Economic Evaluation Measures of User Benefit," *Environment and Planning*, 9 (1977), 285–344.

[35] WILLIG, R.: "Consumer's Surplus Without Apology," *American Economic Review*, 66 (1976), 589–597.

[36] ———: "Incremental Consumer's Surplus and Hedonic Price Adjustment," *Journal of Economic Theory*, 17 (1978), 227–253.

[11]

DISAGGREGATE TRAVEL AND MOBILITY-CHOICE MODELS AND MEASURES OF ACCESSIBILITY

Moshe Ben-Akiva and Steven R. Lerman

SUMMARY

Existing measures of accessibility are not based on an explicit behavioural theory. This chapter proposes an accessibility measure which is consistent with the application of random-utility models to individuals' decision processes. The proposed measure is the expected maximum utility that a consumer derives from a given situation. The chapter presents the properties and advantages of this measure and its derivation for the special cases of the multinomial logit and probit choice models.

Given the multidimensional nature of the travel and mobility choices, this measure is also shown to provide a logically consistent linkage between component models in a complete model system of travel and mobility choices. The use of this measure is demonstrated for joint and sequential logit models. Finally, the chapter addresses key problem areas in the state-of-the-art of spatial-choice modelling which directly affect the development of measures of accessibility defined over a large set of spatial alternatives.

INTRODUCTION

As Dalvi and Martin (10) point out, the term accessibility is widely used but rarely defined in a rigorous and satisfactory fashion. The existing literature on accessibility is often focused on the development of measures of accessibility, without sufficient thought or insight into precisely what accessibility means. In this chapter, we will define accessibility in a manner directly related to individuals' travel-decision processes. Furthermore, we shall demonstrate that under most commonly encountered conditions, our definition of accessibility can be easily operationalised and used in empirical studies.

The term accessibility, as used in this chapter, refers to some composite measure which describes the characteristics of a group of travel alternatives as they are perceived by a particular individual. In a sense which shall be formalised later in this chapter, accessibility logically depends on the group of alternatives being evaluated and the individual traveller for whom accessibility is being measured. When considered from this persvective, existing measures of accessibility have a distinctly *ad hoc* character.

Consider, for example, the most widely used measure of accessibility proposed by Hansen (15):

$$A_{ik} = \frac{\sum_{j=1}^{n} W_{jk} e^{-\beta c_{ij}}}{\sum_{j=1}^{n} W_{jk}}$$

where:

A_{ik} = the accessibility of zone i to opportunities of type k in zones j=1,...,n;
W_{jk} = a measure of attractiveness of zone j to activities of type k;
c_{ij} = the generalised cost of travel from i to j; and
β = a scale coefficient.

In this measure, there is no consideration of the individual for whom the accessibility is being computed; all individuals in the same zone i have the same level of accessibility, despite the fact that they may perceive the set of travel alternatives (in this case, the destinations j=1,...,n) quite differently. Furthermore, the causal justification for the functional form is relatively arbitrary, and the measurement of attraction is usually some population or employment level.

The underlying justification for these (and virtually all other) measures of accessibility is that the term W_{jk} is in a crude sense a proxy representing how valuable a visit to destination j would be for fulfilling a specific trip purpose k, and the term $e^{-\beta c_{ij}}$ represents the perceived cost of getting to j. While there is nothing intrinsically wrong with this general line of thought, it is clear that the concepts of attraction and impedance as used in these measures are rooted in a relatively naive perspective on how travellers make decisions. This perspective has been largely abandoned in more recent work in travel-demand modelling, yet for reasons which are difficult to explain, the crude measures of accessibility persist.

Other types of accessibility measures such as those used by Dunphy (13) and Sherman, Barber and Kondo (30) rely on isochron analysis. For example, one might use the fraction of regional employment within x minutes by car as a measure of highway accessibility. Such measures have obvious deficiencies, including the arbitrary selection of x and their lack of differentiation between opportunities which are adjacent to the origin and those just within the x minute isochron.

A further shortcoming of existing measures of accessibility is their simplistic underlying assumption about how people travel. All measures of accessibility developed in the past use only the level of service from the origin to potential destinations; they ignore the fact that travellers quite frequently chain together destinations into trip tours. Ideally, the concept of accessibility should incorporate the trip-chaining potential of the available destinations. Some destinations may contribute very little to total accessibility when the home is used as the origin but may in reality be visited quite frequently because they are near other, non-home sites.

The remainder of this chapter will explore the implications of a definition of accessibility which is directly tied to travel demand decisions, and will show how this concept of accessibility can be operationalised. The next section will set forth the formal definition of accessibility and discuss some of the general properties of this measure. Then we will discuss how this definition can be applied in conjunction with existing, disaggregate behavioural travel-demand models. In the following three sections, an example of the use of this measure to construct hierarchical models of choice will be presented. Finally, we will describe some of the unresolved issues implicit in the use of the proposed accessibility measure.

DEFINITION OF ACCESSIBILITY

As discussed above, accessibility can be viewed as the outcome of an operation on a set of travel alternatives. In order to formalise this concept, we shall denote some set of feasible travel alternatives as C_t, where the subscript t denotes the individual for whom the accessibility is being determined. The members of the set C_t are by definition mutually exclusive and collectively exhaustive, and one and only one member can be chosen by t in any single decision. We will assume that there exists a utility that individual t associates with each alternative in C_t, and that the individual selects the member of C_t which maximises that utility. Suppose furthermore that the utilities are random variables, which we shall denote as a vector $U_t=(U_{it},...,U_{nt})$ where n is the number of alternatives in C_t. For the purposes of this chapter it is irrelevant whether one adopts the perspective of the econometrician that the underlying utilities are deterministic but imperfectly observed or the perspective of the mathematical psychologist that the utilities individuals associate with the alternatives are actually random in nature. Manski (24) develops random utility theory from the former perspective, while Luce and Suppes (22) work from the latter.

Under these assumptions, a natural definition of accessibility is simply the utility of the choice situation to the individual t. For any single decision, the individual will select the alternative which maximises his/her utility; thus, a simple definition of accessibility is

$$\max_{i \in C_t} U_{it}$$

657 Chapter 30

However, since the vector U_t is random, this value is not directly measurable. Given the inherent uncertainty in the outcome of the choice process, a reasonable alternative to this measure is *the expected value of the maximum of the entries in* U_t, or $E(\underset{i \varepsilon C_t}{\text{Max}} U_{it})$. This is the value which we shall define as the accessibility of set C_t to individual t.

It is worth noting that under a set of restrictions on the distribution of U_t the expected value of the maximum utility has a direct interpretation as a consumer surplus measure. Several researchers including Harris and Tanner (16) and Williams (34), have used disaggregate choice models and derived this value for specific cases. Neuburger (26) derived the appropriate benefit measure of a gravity model which is the same expression derived for the expected maximum utility in a disaggregate logit model. Lerman (21) used this formulation directly to derive an approximation for the utility of a group of nearly homogeneous alternatives; in this case, the multinomial-logit model was used. Sheffi and Daganzo (29) have explored the properties of this function in the context of the network assignment problem.

While later sections of this chapter will discuss this measure under specific assumptions about C_t and the distribution of U_t, it is useful to explore two properties of this measure and the conditions on the distribution of U_t under which they hold. Consider the following properties:

1 *monotonicity with respect to choice-set size*

$$E\,[\text{Max}\,(U_{1t},\ldots,U_{nt})] \leq E[\text{Max}\,(U_{1t},\ldots,U_{nt},\,U_{n+1,t})]$$

In words, this property implies that the measure does not decrease if a new alternative is added to the choice set.

2 *monotonicity with respect to mean utilities*

If $V_t = (V_{1t},\ldots,V_{nt})$ denotes $E[U_t]$, then

$$\frac{\partial}{\partial V_{it}}\, E[\underset{i \varepsilon C_t}{\text{Max}}\, U_{it}] \geq 0, \text{ for all } i \varepsilon C_t$$

In words, this property implies that the measure of accessibility does not decrease as the mean of any one utility increases, all else held equal.

As will be demonstrated, the first property, monotonicity with respect to choice-set size, holds for all situations in which $E(\underset{i \varepsilon C_t}{\text{Max}} U_{it})$ exists with and without the n + 1 alternative. To prove this, define the random variable k as follows

$$k = \text{Max}\,(U_{1t},\ldots,U_{nt}), \tag{1}$$

and let f(k) denote the probability density function of k. Williams (34) offers an independently developed proof of this proposition. Furthermore, let U* be the utility of some additional alternative, and let f(U*, k) denote the joint probability density function of U* and k. Consider first

$$E[k] = \int_{-\infty}^{\infty} f(k)k\, dk. \quad (2)$$

For reasons that will be clear shortly, this expression will be written as

$$E[k] = \int_{-\infty}^{\infty} k \int_{-\infty}^{\infty} f(U^*,k)\, dU^*\, dk$$

$$= \int_{-\infty}^{\infty} \int_{-\infty}^{k} k\, f(U^*,k)\, dU^*\, dk + \int_{-\infty}^{\infty} \int_{k}^{\infty} kf(U^*,k)dU^*dk. \quad (3)$$

The two integrals in the last expression correspond to the ranges of k and U* such that U*<k and U*$\geq$k, respectively. These are the areas in (U*,k) space for which the additional alternative is not chosen (U*<k) and the additional alternative is chosen (U*$\geq$k).

Now consider

$$E[\text{Max }(U^*,k)] = \int_{-\infty}^{\infty} \int_{-\infty}^{k} k\, f(U^*,k)\, dU^*dk + \int_{-\infty}^{\infty} \int_{k}^{\infty} U^* f(U^*,k)dU^*dk. \quad (4)$$

Comparing expressions (3) with (4), we note that

$$E[\text{Max }(U^*,k)] - E[k] = \int_{-\infty}^{\infty} \int_{k}^{\infty} (U^*-k)\, f(U^*,k)dU^*dk. \quad (5)$$

Furthermore, since over the range of the integral U* is greater than or equal to k (and since f(U*,k) is by definition greater than or equal to zero), the value of the integral must be non-negative. Thus, the addition of an extra alternative cannot decrease the value of the accessibility measure.

A corollary of the above proof is that the expected value of the maximum is greater than or equal to the maximum of the means of the utilities, i.e.

$$E[\text{Max}_{i\varepsilon C_t} U_{it}] \geq \text{Max}_{i\varepsilon C_t} (E[U_{it}]) . \quad (6)$$

A sufficient condition for (6) is that

$$E[\text{Max }(U_{1t},\ldots,U_{nt})] \geq E[U_{1t}], \quad (7)$$

since the order in which utilities are numbered is totally arbitrary. To prove that (7) holds let us define k_j as

$\text{Max}(U_{1t}, U_{2t}, \ldots, U_{jt})$.

We note that

659 Chapter 30

$$E(\mathrm{Max}(U_{1t},\ldots,U_{nt})) = E(\mathrm{Max}\ (k_{n-1},U_{nt})). \tag{8}$$

By the property of monotonicity of choice set size,

$$E[\mathrm{Max}\ (k_{n-1},U_{nt})] \geq E[k_{n-1}]. \tag{9}$$

By recursively using this property, we can show

$$E[k_{n-1}] \geq E[k_{n-2}] \geq \ldots \geq E[k_1], \tag{10}$$

where

$$E(k_1) = E(U_{1t}),$$

thereby proving Equation (6). A simpler proof of (6) was suggested by Charles Manski. Since maximisation is a convex function, Jensen's inequality holds. Expression (6) follows immediately ((27)p. 58).

One might logically expect that the property of monotonicity with respect to mean utilities would also hold in general. Oddly, this is not the case. Consider the binary choice model in which

$$U_{it} = V_{it} + V_{it}\delta_{it}, \tag{11}$$

where δ_{it} is a random variable with zero mean. For notational convenience, we will simplify the utility expressions as follows:

$$U_{1t} = U_1 = V_1 + \delta_1 V_1 \tag{12}$$

$$U_{2t} = U_2 = V_2 + \delta_2 V_2.$$

Assume that δ_1 and δ_2 are the only random components of U_1 and U_2 respectively, and that they are normally distributed. They have means 0, variances σ_1^2 and σ_2^2 respectively and correlation ratio .

This model is a special case of the form used by Hausman and Wise (17) and termed by Lerman and Manski (20) the generalised multinomial probit model. The generalised multinomial probit model applies to any number of alternatives, allows for normally distributed taste variation on each coefficient β in the function $V_{it} = Z_{it}'\beta$, and includes an additional set of normally distributed disturbance terms. The random variables (δ_1 and δ_2) represent taste variation in the population being modelled.

Under these assumptions, Clark (8) has shown that:

$$E[\mathrm{Max}\ (U_1,U_2)] = V_1\ \Phi\left(\frac{V_1-V_2}{a}\right) + V_2\Phi\left(\frac{V_2-V_1}{a}\right) + a\phi\left(\frac{V_1-V_2}{a}\right) \tag{13}$$

where:

$$a^2 = V_1^2\sigma_1^2 + V_2^2\sigma_2^2 - 2\sigma_1\sigma_2\,\rho V_1V_2$$

$\Phi(u)$ denotes the standarised cumulative normal distribution, and

$$\phi(u) = \frac{\partial\Phi(u)}{\partial u}.$$

Noting that $\Phi(-u) = 1-\Phi(u)$, expression (13) can be simplified as

$$V_2 + (V_1-V_2)\quad \Phi\left(\frac{V_1-V_2}{a}\right) + a\ \phi\left(\frac{V_1-V_2}{a}\right). \tag{14}$$

Now consider

$$\frac{\partial E[\text{Max }(U_1,U_2)]}{\partial V_1} = (V_1-V_2)\,\phi\left(\frac{V_1-V_2}{a}\right)\frac{\partial}{\partial V_1}\left(\frac{V_1-V_2}{a}\right) + \Phi\left(\frac{V_1-V_2}{a}\right) +$$

$$a\frac{\partial}{\partial V_1}\ \phi\left(\frac{V_1-V_2}{a}\right) + \frac{\partial a}{\partial V_1}\ \phi\left(\frac{V_1-V_2}{a}\right). \tag{15}$$

Furthermore

$$a\frac{\partial}{\partial V_1}\ \phi\left(\frac{V_1-V_2}{a}\right) = a\phi\left(\frac{V_1-V_2}{a}\right)\left(-\ \frac{V_1-V_2}{a}\right)\frac{\partial}{\partial V_1}\left(\frac{V_1-V_2}{a}\right)$$

$$= -(V_1-V_2)\ \phi\left(\frac{V_1-V_2}{a}\right)\frac{\partial}{\partial V_1}\ \left(\frac{V_1-V_2}{a}\right). \tag{16}$$

Thus, Equation (15) simplifies to:

$$\frac{\partial E[\text{Max }(U_1,U_2)]}{\partial V_1} = \Phi\left(\frac{V_1-V_2}{a}\right) + \frac{\partial a}{\partial V_1}\ \phi\left(\frac{V_1-V_2}{a}\right). \tag{17}$$

Since $\Phi\left(\frac{V_1-V_2}{a}\right)$ and $\phi\left(\frac{V_1-V_2}{a}\right)$ are by definition positive, Equation (17) can only be negative when:

$$\frac{\partial a}{\partial V_1} < -\frac{\Phi\left(\frac{V_1-V_2}{a}\right)}{\phi\left(\frac{V_1-V_2}{a}\right)}. \tag{18}$$

Since,

$$\frac{\partial a}{\partial V_1} = \frac{\partial}{\partial V_1}(V_1{}^2\sigma_1{}^2 + V_2{}^2\sigma_2{}^2 - 2\sigma_1\sigma_2\rho V_1V_2)^{1/2} \tag{19}$$

$$= \frac{1}{a}(V_1\sigma_1{}^2 - \sigma_1\sigma_2\rho\ V_2)$$

661 Chapter 30

it is quite possible for the expression in Equation (19) to satisfy condition 18. For example, suppose the following hold:

$\sigma_1 = \sigma_2 = 1$

$\rho = 0$

$V_1 = -1$

$V_2 = 1.$

In this case

$$\frac{\partial a}{\partial V_1} = \frac{V_1}{a} = \frac{-1}{\sqrt{2}} \cong -.7071 ,$$

while

$$-\frac{\phi\left(\frac{V_1-V_2}{a}\right)}{\Phi\left(\frac{V_1-V_2}{a}\right)} = -\frac{\phi\left(\frac{-2}{\sqrt{2}}\right)}{\Phi\left(\frac{-2}{\sqrt{2}}\right)} \cong -\frac{.07868}{.1468} \cong -.53598.$$

Thus,

$$\frac{\partial\, E[\mathrm{Max}\,(U_1,U_2)]}{\partial V_1} < 0.$$

An interesting question is whether there exists a relatively straightforward set of restrictions on the distribution of the U_t such that the measure of expected maximum utility is monotonic with respect to the mean utilities. One set of useful sufficient conditions was proposed by Williams (34), and Harris and Tanner (16). One way to view conditions on the monotonicity with respect to mean utilities is to consider:

$$\frac{\partial E[k]}{\partial V_{it}} = \frac{\partial}{\partial V_{it}} \int \ldots \int k f(U_t)\, dU_t \ , \qquad (20)$$

where k is as defined in Equation (1).

Moving the derivative inside the integral, we can re-write Equation (20) as:

$$\int \ldots \int \frac{\partial k}{\partial V_{it}} f\,(U_t)\, dU_t + \int \ldots \int k \frac{\partial f(U_t)}{\partial V_{it}} dU_t \qquad (21)$$

Since

$$\frac{\partial k}{\partial V_{it}} = \begin{cases} \frac{\partial U_{it}}{\partial V_{it}} & \text{when } U_{it} \geq U_{jt}, \text{ for all } j \neq i,\ j \in C_t. \\ 0 & \text{otherwise} \end{cases}$$

this expression can be simplified to

$$\int\ldots\int_{k=U_{it}} \frac{\partial U_{it}}{\partial V_{it}} f\,(U_t)\, dU_t + \int\ldots\int k\, \frac{\partial f(U_t)}{\partial V_{it}} dU_t. \tag{22}$$

However, if $\frac{\partial U_{it}}{\partial V_{it}} = 1$, the first integral in Equation (22) is simply the probability that U_{it} is greater than all U_{it}, $j\neq i$, $j\varepsilon C_t$, which is the probability that alternative i is chosen. If we write this probability as $P_{it}(C_t)$, then

$$\frac{\partial E[\underset{i\varepsilon C_t}{\text{Max}}\ U_{it}]}{\partial V_{it}} = P_{it}(C_t) + \int\ldots\int k\, \frac{\partial f(U_t)}{\partial V_{it}} dU_t. \tag{23}$$

Williams has shown that if the distribution $f(U_t)$ is translationally invariant then:*

$$\frac{\partial f(U_t)}{\partial V_{it}} = 0, \tag{24}$$

and therefore, Equation (22) reduces to

$$\frac{\partial E[\underset{i\varepsilon C_t}{\text{Max}}\ U_{it}]}{\partial V_{it}} = P_{it}(C_t). \tag{25}$$

As an obvious consequence of Equation (25), in cases where $\frac{\partial U_{it}}{\partial V_{it}} = 1$ and $\partial f(U_t)/\partial V_{it} = 0$, for all $i\varepsilon C_t$, then

$$\sum_{i\varepsilon C_t} \frac{\partial E[\underset{i\varepsilon C_t}{\text{Max}}\ U_{it}]}{\partial V_{it}} = 1. \tag{26}$$

---

*The property of translational invariance can be best interpreted by noting that condition 24 implies that

$$f(U_t|V_t) = f((U_t+\partial U_t)\,|\,(V_t+\partial V_t)).$$

Thus, increasing the vector of means, V_t, by ∂V_t produces a density function which is the same as before the change in V_t except that it is 'shifted over'. The normal distribution with fixed variance-covariance matrix and the Weibull distribution are both translationally invariant, while the exponential and the gamma distributions are not.

663 Chapter 30

This implies that if we increase the utility of every alternative by some amount ΔV_t then the total accessibility increases by that amount.

For most choice models we can write the utilities as follows:

$$U_{it} = V_{it} + \delta_{it}\, g(V_{it}) + \varepsilon_{it}, \quad (27)$$

where $g(V_{it})$ is any vector of functions, and the vector $_{it}$ and the scalar ε_{it} are unobserved random variables distributed as $f(\delta_t, \varepsilon_t)$. (The notation δ_t denotes a vector consisting of all entries in the vectors δ_{it}, $i\varepsilon C_t$.)

Assuming that

$$\frac{\partial f(\delta_t, \varepsilon_t)}{\partial V_{it}} = 0,$$

Equation (22) can now be written as follows:

$$\frac{\partial E[\underset{i\varepsilon C_t}{\text{Max}}\, U_{it}]}{\partial V_{it}} = \underset{k\, =\, U_{it}}{\int \ldots \int} (1 + \frac{\partial}{\partial V_{it}}\, \delta_{it} g(V_{it}))\, f(\delta_t\, ,\, \varepsilon_t)\, d\delta_t d\varepsilon_t$$

$$= P_{it}(C_t) + \underset{k\, =\, U_{it}}{\int \ldots \int} \frac{\partial}{\partial V_{it}}\, \delta_{it}\, g(V_{it})\, f(\delta_t, \varepsilon_t)\, d\delta_t d\varepsilon_t \quad (28)$$

In the simple case where $g(V_{it})$ and δ_{it} are scalars and

$$g(V_{it}) = V_{it} \quad (29)$$

the restriction that

$$\delta_{it} \geq -1 \quad (30)$$

will result in

$$\frac{\partial E[\underset{i\varepsilon C_t}{\text{Max}}\, U_{it}]}{\partial V_{it}} \geq 0. \quad (31)$$

This case represents a random-utility specification in which δ_{it} represents unobserved taste variations and ε_{it} is the unobserved utility which is independent of V_{it}. It is reasonable to assume that $f(\delta_t)$ is independent of the Vs and that δ_{it} has a lower bound of -1 such that $\partial U_{it}/\partial V_{it}$ is always positive. This requirement implies that the marginal utility of a positive attribute, including the observed and unobserved utilities components, is always positive. The probit model shown earlier assumes a normal distribution of the δs which are therefore not bound to be greater than (-1). Thus, if a random-utility model with unobserved taste variation is carefully specified, such that $\partial U_{it}/\partial V_{it}$ is always positive, the desirable property of monotonicity of the expected maximum utility with the mean utilities is always satisfied.

SOME SPECIAL CASES

Fortunately, the accessibility measure can be derived in closed form for the most widely used individual-choice model, multinomial logit. The logit model is characterised by utilities which satisfy

$$U_{it} = V_{it} + \varepsilon_{it} \qquad (32)$$

where ε_{it} independent from all ε_{it} and every ε has the following cumulative distribution function

$$P(\varepsilon \leq \omega) = e^{-e^{-\mu(\alpha+\omega)}} \qquad (33)$$

Under these assumptions

$$P_{it}(C_t) = \frac{e^{\mu V_{it}}}{\sum_{j \varepsilon C_t} e^{\mu V_{jt}}}. \qquad (34)$$

The Vs are generally defined such that $\mu = 1$. The function in Equation (33) satisfies the condition

$$\frac{\partial f(\varepsilon_t)}{\partial V_{it}} = 0, \quad \text{and} \quad \frac{\partial U_{it}}{\partial V_{it}} = 1.$$

Hence, by Equation (25)

$$\frac{\partial E[\text{Max } U_t]}{\partial V_{it}} = P_{it}(C_t) = \frac{e^{V_{it}}}{\sum_{j \varepsilon C_t} e^{V_{jt}}} \qquad (35)$$

This partial differential equation yields the expression:

$$E[\underset{i \varepsilon C_t}{\text{Max}}\ U_{it}] = \int \frac{e^{V_{it}}}{\sum_{j \varepsilon C_t} e^{V_{jt}}}\, dV_{it}, \qquad (36)$$

665 Chapter 30

which when solved implies that

$$E[\mathrm{Max}\ U_t] = \ln \sum_{j\varepsilon C_t} e^{V_{jt}} + \mathrm{Const.} \tag{37}$$

A more direct approach to derive the expected value of the maximum utility is first to derive the distribution of the maximum utility, defined as k in Equation (1), from the distribution of the vector U_t. For the logit model we obtain ([12]p. 63):

$$P(k \leq \omega) = e^{-e^{-(\alpha_t^* + \omega)}}, \tag{38}$$

where

$$\alpha_t^* = \alpha - \ln \sum_{j\varepsilon C_t} e^{V_{jt}} .$$

The expected value is equal to [14]:

$$E(k) = -\alpha_t^* + \gamma$$

$$= \ln\sum_{j\varepsilon C_t} e^{V_{jt}} - \alpha + \gamma \ , \tag{39}$$

where γ is Euler's constant ($\approx$0.577). Since the selection of the parameter α is arbitrary, a logical value is $\alpha=\gamma$, so that the relevant measure for the logit model is:

$$\ln \sum_{j\varepsilon C_t} e^{V_{jt}}. \tag{40}$$

This expression is simply the natural logarithm of the denominator of the multinomial logit model, and can be derived in a number of other ways. See, for example, Williams [34], Domencich and McFadden [12], Ben-Akiva [5], Lerman [20] or Small [31]. Since the denominator of the logit function is computed in forecasting travel demand anyway, the measurement of accessibility requires little additional computation.

A second case of interest is the situation in which the utility functions have additive disturbances as in Equation (32), but the εs are normally distributed with mean 0 and arbitrary (up to a set of restrictions required for the parameters to be identified) variance-covariance matrix Σ. As noted in the previous section, this assumption leads to the multinomial probit model.

The multinomial probit model has not been used previously because of the computational problems associated with its estimation and application. However, recent work by Lerman and Manski (20), Hausman and Wise (17), Daganzo, Sheffi and Bouthelier (9), and Andrews and Langdon (3) has made probit for multiple alternatives feasible.

Multinomial probit has the advantage over logit of allowing for the possibility that two alternatives have disturbance terms which are not independent. Thus, apparent anomalies such as the 'red bus-blue bus' paradox do not arise. Furthermore, unlike logit, multinomial probit in its most general form permits measurement of taste variation in the population.

There does not exist a closed-form solution for the expected maximum utility, or the accessibility measure, in the case of the multinomial probit. However, it is possible to use a set of formulas (one of which was used in Equation (13)) for the first two moments of the maximum of two normally distributed random variables and the covariance of the maximum with a third normally distributed variable to approximate the accessibility (8). Clark first proposed that his solution for the moments of the maximum of two normally distributed variables be used as an approximation by assuming that the maximum is itself normally distributed. This approximation could then permit solution of

$$E(\mathrm{Max}(U_{1t},\ldots,U_{nt})),$$

by use of a recursive procedure, since

$$\mathrm{Max}(U_{1t},\ldots,U_{n-2t},U_{n-1t},U_{nt}) = \mathrm{Max}(U_{1t},\ldots,U_{n-2t},$$

$$\mathrm{Max}(U_{n-1t},U_{nt})). \tag{41}$$

While Clark recognised that the maximum of two normally distributed variables is obviously not itself normal, some limited empirical evidence indicated that at least for the first moment, it served as a good approximation. Further tests by Daganzo, Sheffi and Bouthelier (9) and subsequently by Manski, Lerman and Albright (23) have provided additional support. The latter group has compared the choice of probabilities for multinomial probit as calculated by simulation techniques with those generated by the Clark approximation, and the results indicate that the absolute error in the Clark algorithm is rarely more than 0.01 or 0.02.

As in the logit model, the value of the accessibility measure for multinomial probit can be computed as part of any forecasting procedure without any major, new computation. In applying the Clark algorithm to finding the choice probability of alternative i, the recursive approximation is used to solve the moments of the maximum utility of all the j ≠ i alternatives. The mean and variance of this maximum (as well as its covariance with the utility of alternative i) are then used in a binary comparison, where the choice probability is simply

$$P[U_{it} \geq \max_{\substack{j \in C_t \\ j \neq i}} U_{jt}].$$

All that is required to compute the expected value of the maximum utility is one extra application of the Clark approximation for the first moment (Equation (13)) to solve for:

$$E[\text{Max} (U_{it}, \underset{\substack{j \in C_t \\ j \neq i}}{\text{Max}} U_{jt})] \, .$$

TRAVEL DEMAND AS A MULTIDIMENSIONAL CHOICE

The previous sections of this chapter dealt with the properties of random-utility choice models and expected maximum utilities in terms of a simple choice of an alternative i from a choice set C_t. In many applications, the members of C_t are choices along a simple dimension such as modes of travel or destinations. However, a complete travel-demand model must consider multiple dimensions of choice that include all household and individual decisions that directly affect trip-making. The set of relevant decisions includes choices with respect to specific trips, such as mode choice and destination choice, and other choices which are so interrelated with actual trip-making choices that it is impossible to separate them from such decisions. For example, the choice of residential location is not in itself a trip-making decision. However, the combination of worker's employment location choice and his or her household's residential location decision has as its consequence a trip choice, i.e. a daily work trip.

For this reason, the general framework from which urban travel-demand models can be derived begins with a partition of all possible household and household-member decisions into two sets, those directly relevant to personal travel and those which can, for practical purposes, be ignored. In formal utility-theory terms, this partition implies that the total utility function for the decision-maker has an additively separable form and that the overall income and time constraints are negligible. Here, this partition produces the following vector of travel-related household decisions:

1 employment location (for all workers)
2 residential location
3 housing type
4 car ownership
5 mode to work (for all workers)
6 frequency (for non-work trips of each purpose)
7 destination (for non-work trips of each purpose)
8 time of day (for all trips)
9 mode (for non-work trips of each purpose)
10 route (for all trips)

For most situations, this vector describes the decisions which a complete travel-demand model must consider. (There are possible exceptions. Frequency and time of day for work trips may be distinct choices or constrained by the work situation. Some decisions may be totally constrained by lack of a driver's license, though the latter may well be part of some decision vectors. Allocation of time to different activities (or purposes) is also suggested as an element of this decision vector in a later section of this chapter.) In theory, each decision may be dependent on the rest. For example, where one chooses to live is obviously linked to the housing type and the level of car ownership one selects. Similarly, shopping-trip destination and mode are likely to be closely linked.

This perspective, if carried through completely, would produce a model of unmanageable dimensions. Since the entire vector of possible choices would result in a virtually limitless choice set, useful models would be impossible to develop. Fortunately, there are some interrelationships among components of this vector which are of a fundamentally different character than others. Some of the decisions, such as residential location choice, have high transaction costs and are consequently stable over fairly long intervals; other choices such as social-trip frequency are altered on a daily basis. Some decisions are more logically represented as being made collectively by the household, while others can be approximated as individual choices. Thus, it is possible to formulate explicit behavioural hypotheses, and establish a structure of the total vector of choices as a logical working hypothesis. Such an explicit structure greatly simplifies the formulation and development of a complete travel-demand model. This structure is termed a *hierarchy of choice*.

Figure 30.1 illustrates one possible choice hierarchy. (See Ben-Akiva (5), Lerman (21) and Adler (1) for more detailed discussions of alternative choice hierarchies.) It defines two distinct sets of choices: the long-run *mobility* decisions of location, housing, car ownership and mode to work and the short-run *travel* choices of frequency, mode, destination, route and time of day for non-work trips. These decisions are assumed to be structured hierarchically, i.e. location and related decisions are made with travel choices indeterminate, and the travel choices are made, conditional on the outcome of the mobility-choice process. *Within each group of choices, decisions are assumed to be made by a joint process in which the full range of possible trade-offs is considered by the household.*

The use of this hierarchical choice structure permits the development of two different models, one for mobility choices and one for travel choices. This set of models can be termed *block conditional*, where the block of mobility and travel choices as single units have a conditional structure, while each block itself has a joint structure. It is important to emphasise that block-conditional or other hierarchical decision structures are based on *explicit behavioural hypotheses* about household or individual behaviour. Different choice hierarchies might be proposed for different decision-makers; since each is essentially an approximation, some hierarchies may prove useful in some situations but may be inappropriate in others. Consider, for example, the hierarchy depicted in Figure 30.2. In this case, employment location has been separated from the remaining mobility choices, which for convenience are termed the mobility bundle. This hierarchy might be appropriate for skilled workers, whose employment location is relatively fixed. A skilled employee must generally switch his employer in order to shift his job location.

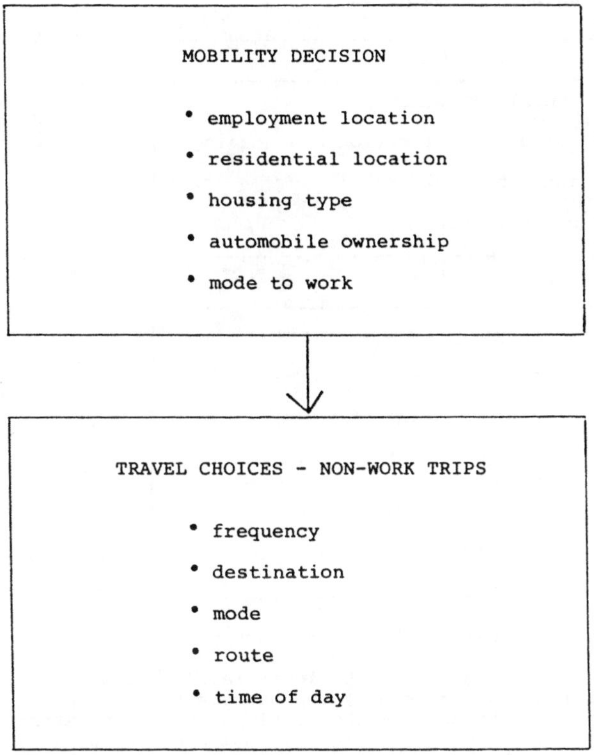

Figure 30.1 A Simple Choice Hierarchy

MODELLING IMPLICATIONS OF A CHOICE HIERARCHY

To illustrate the implications of the choice hierarchy, let us consider some choice j from the set J. Assume that the choice from set J is part of a hierarchy, and that it is preceded by a choice of i from set I and followed by a choice k from set K. (For notational convenience, the subscript t denoting the individual decision-maker will be omitted in the remainder of the chapter.) Given this situation, the entire set of variables which influence the choice from J can be divided into four classes as follows:

1 Those that directly affect the choice of j but do not directly influence the choice of i or k.
2 Those that directly affect the choice of j as well as

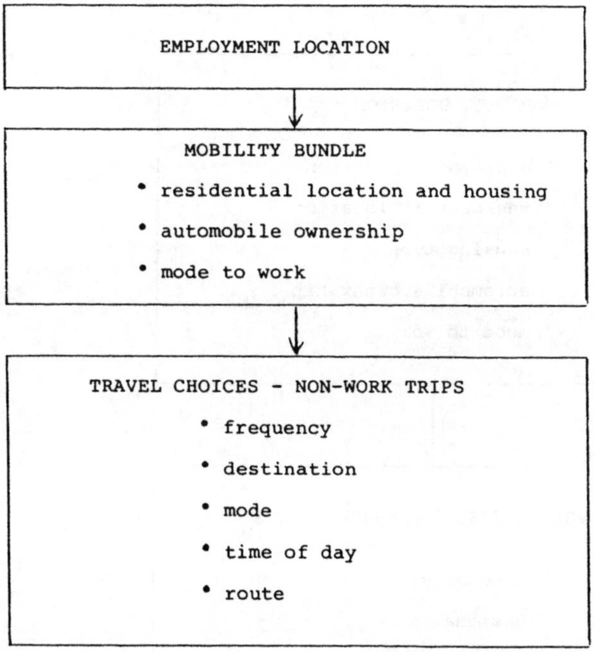

Figure 30.2 A Three-stage Choice Hierarchy

the higher level choice i and the lower level choice k.

3 Those that are determined by the outcome of the higher level choice i and affect the choice of j, such as an attribute of the chosen i which is treated as a socio-economic factor affecting the choice among alternatives in J.

4 Those that express expectations from outcome of the lower level choice from set K; these expectations may vary among alternatives in J and can be treated as attributes of the alternatives in J.

The differences among these variables can be clarified by using the choice hierarchy in Figure 30.2 as an example. The factors affecting the choice of mobility bundle (which corresponds to choice of j) are:

1 Direct attributes of the mobility bundle such as rent or housing price. This variable, in general, has a different value for each alternative location and housing-type combination.

2 Joint attributes of the mobility bundle as well as higher or lower level choices such as level-of-service attributes by transit for the trip to work. This variable is an attribute of an alternative mobility bundle, and is also an attribute

of alternative employment-location alternatives, which corresponds to I.

3 Variables resulting from the employment-location decisions such as a variable indicating whether or not a worker in the household is employed in the central business district. This variable is *predetermined* in the mobility-choice process, and it is an attribute of the household that does not vary among alternative mobility bundles.

4 Variables describing travel decisions made conditional on the mobility choice such as level of service by transit for shopping trips from a given residential zone. This variable depends on how the household will choose to travel for shopping, a decision which is made only conditional on the household's mobility choice. Thus, shopping level of service is said to be *indeterminate* in the mobility decision. This does not imply that it does not enter into the household's evaluation of mobility alternatives; rather, it means that the household does not know the *specific* shopping trips it will make. It does have some *composite* picture of the overall shopping level of service it will obtain for various mobility bundles. For example, if the household were to choose to own two or more cars in its mobility bundle, it would generally have a high composite level of service for shopping associated with suburban locations because it would typically travel by car. Alternatively, if the household chose not to own a car, suburban locations would have poor composite level of service since it would have to shop exclusively by transit.

For a block-conditional model system to be logically consistent, each of these types of variables must be appropriately represented. Specific models must have appropriate linkages to other components of a choice hierarchy in order to reflect the full sensitivity of the whole range of relevant choices to variables influencing travel-related decisions.

In formulating such linkings the construction of variables of the second and fourth types requires further discussion. In modelling the choice from J, attributes which are specific to a combination ijk (i.e. a feasible member of I J K) as in the second type of factors or to a jk combination (i.e. a feasible member of J K) as in the fourth type of factors, must be somehow aggregated over alternative choices in K in order to be included in the model for the choice from J conditional on the choice of i. This requirement and alternative formulations which have been used for such composite attributes are discussed in many references, including Ben-Akiva (5) and Williams (34).

All systems of urban travel-demand models explicitly or implicitly include such composite variables. Examples would be the weighted 'inclusive price' used by CRA (7) and the transit accessibility variable used in a trip-generation model by the Metropolitan Washington Council of Governments (32). However, as noted earlier in this chapter, the definition of accessibility or composite attributes is often arbitrary. The use of expected maximum utilities to define these composite variables has the advantages cited earlier in this chapter as well as the advantage of a consistent formulation of a sequence of models based on maximisation of random utilities.

The assumption of a choice hierarchy for the selection of an alternative from $I \times J \times K$ implies the following decomposition of the utility function:

$$U_{ijk} = U_i + U_{j|i} + U_{k|ij} \tag{42}$$

where

U_{ijk} = the joint utility of an ijk combination,

U_i = the part of the joint utility which is independent of j and k,

$U_{j|i}$ = the part of the joint utility for a choice of j given that i is selected which is independent of k, and

$U_{k|ij}$ = the part of the joint utility for a choice of k given that i and j are selected.

(Note that if U_{ijk} is not separable, then U_i and $U_{j|i}$ are zero, and by definition $U_{k|ij} = U_{ijk}$.) The model for the lower level of the choice hierarchy, the choice of k, can be expressed as follows:

$$P(k|ij) = \text{Prob}[U_{k|ij} \geq U_{k'|ij},\ \forall\ k' \varepsilon K] \tag{43}$$

where

$P(k|ij)$ = the probability of choosing k given that i and j are selected.

The model for the choice of j is:

$$P(j|i) = \text{Prob}[U_{j|i} + \underset{k\varepsilon K}{\text{Max}}\, U_{k|ij} \geq U_{j'|i} + \underset{k\varepsilon K}{\text{Max}}\, U_{k|ij'}, \forall j' \varepsilon J], \tag{44}$$

where

$P(j|i)$ = the probability of choosing j given that i is selected.

Thus, the utility for this choice model is:

$$\tilde{U}_{j|i} = U_{j|i} + \underset{k\varepsilon K}{\text{Max}}\, U_{k|ij}. \tag{45}$$

Similarly, for the choice of i the model can be written as follows:

$$P(i) = \text{Prob}[\tilde{U}_i \geq \tilde{U}_{i'},\ \forall\ i' \varepsilon I], \tag{46}$$

where

$P(i)$ = the marginal probability of choosing i, and

$\tilde{U}_i = U_i + \underset{j\varepsilon J}{\text{Max}}\, \tilde{U}_{j|i}.$

Note that

$$\underset{ijk \in IJK}{\text{Max}} U_{ijk} = \underset{i \in I}{\text{Max}} \tilde{U}_i .$$

Denoting the expected utility components as:

$$E[U_{ijk}] = E[U_i] + E[U_{j|i}] + E[U_{k|ij}]$$

$$= V_i + V_{j|i} + V_{k|ij} \quad (47)$$

we obtain:

$$E[\tilde{U}_{j|i}] = V_{j|i} + E[\underset{k \in K}{\text{Max}} U_{k|ij}] \quad (48)$$

$$E[\tilde{U}_i] = V_i + E[\underset{j \in J}{\text{Max}} \tilde{U}_{j|i}]. \quad (49)$$

This implies that

$$\tilde{V}_{j|i} = V_{j|i} + E[\underset{k \in K}{\text{Max}} U_{k|ij}] \quad (50)$$

and

$$\tilde{V}_i = V_i + E[\underset{j \in J}{\text{Max}} \tilde{U}_{j|i}] \quad (51)$$

are the systematic components of the utilities for the choice models for $P(j|i)$ and $P(i)$, respectively.

We can also derive the disturbances for these choice processes (i.e. the random component of the utility function) as follows:

$$\varepsilon_{k|ij} = U_{k|ij} - V_{k|ij} \quad (52)$$

$$\varepsilon_{j|i} = U_{j|i} - V_{j|i} + \underset{k \in K}{\text{Max}} U_{k|ij} - E[\underset{k \in K}{\text{Max}} U_{k|ij}] \quad (53)$$

$$\varepsilon_i = U_i - V_i + \underset{j \in J}{\text{Max}} \tilde{U}_{j|i} - E[\underset{j \in J}{\text{Max}} \tilde{U}_{j|i}]. \quad (54)$$

Expressing the joint utility function as:

$$U_{ijk} = V_{ijk} + \varepsilon_{ijk}, \quad (55)$$

where

$$V_{ijk} = V_i + V_{j|k} + V_{k|ij}, \quad (56)$$

we obtain:

$$\varepsilon_{ijk} = \varepsilon_i - (\underset{j \in J}{\text{Max}} \tilde{U}_{j|i} - E[\underset{j \in J}{\text{Max}} \tilde{U}_{j|k}])$$

$$+\varepsilon_{j|i} - (\underset{k \in K}{\text{Max}} U_{k|ij} - E[\underset{k \in K}{\text{Max}} U_{k|ij}]) + \varepsilon_{k|ij}. \quad (57)$$

A LOGIT EXAMPLE OF ACCESSIBILITY IN CHOICE HIERARCHIES

If the ε_{ijk}s are independently and identically distributed (i.i.d) as Weibull, we obtain the following joint logit model:

$$P(ijk) = \frac{e^{V_{ijk}}}{\sum_i \sum_j \sum_k e^{V_{ijk}}}. \tag{58}$$

Based on the decomposition of the joint-utility function we can calculate the following conditional and marginal probabilities:

$$P(k|ij) = \frac{e^{V_{k|ij}}}{\sum_{k'} e^{V_{k'|ij}}} \tag{59}$$

$$P(j|i) = \frac{e^{\mu_1 V_{j|i} + \mu_1 \ln \sum_k e^{V_{k|ij}}}}{\sum_{j'} e^{\mu_1 V_{j'|i} + \mu_1 \ln \sum_k e^{V_{k|ij'}}}} \tag{60}$$

$$P(i) = \frac{e^{\mu_2 V_i + (\mu_2/\mu_1) \ln \sum_j e^{\mu_1 V_{j|i} + \mu_1 \ln \Sigma_k e^{V_{k|ij}}}}}{\sum_{i'} e^{\mu_2 V_{i'} + (\mu_2/\mu_1) \ln \sum_j e^{\mu_1 V_{j|i'} + \mu_1 \ln \Sigma_k e^{V_{k|i'j}}}}} \tag{61}$$

where $\mu_1 = \mu_2 = 1$, and were included for reasons that will be clarified below.

From the derivation of the expected maximum utility for the logit model in an earlier section of this chapter we observe that each higher level model includes the expected maximum utility from the lower level. We note that the joint-logit model implies that the three random components are independent and Weibull distributed with the same parameter as follows:

$$\text{Prob}[\varepsilon \leq \omega] = e^{-e^{-\mu(\omega+\alpha)}}$$

where the shift parameter α does not affect the choice probabilities and is not identified, and the scale parameter μ is assumed to equal one. A joint logit model was applied by Ben-Akiva (5), Adler and Ben-Akiva (2), Lerman (21) and others.

If we allow μ_1 and μ_2 to be different from unity but require that:

$$0 < \mu_1 \leq 1$$

$$0 < \mu_2 \leq \mu_1$$

we obtain a sequence of logit models which imply that the three random components are independent and Weibull distributed but with three different parameters: 1, μ_1 and $_2$. This condition is required for the following to hold:

$$\frac{\partial P(j\ k|i)}{\partial V_{k'|ij}} \leq 0 \qquad \text{for } k' \neq k$$

$$\frac{\partial P(i\ j)}{\partial \tilde{V}_{j'|i}} \leq 0 \qquad \text{for } j' \neq j$$

where P(j k|i) is the joint probability that both j and k are selected conditional on i being chosen and P(i j) is the joint probability that both i and j are chosen.

In words, these two conditions imply that:

1 the cross-elasticity of the probability of some choice j and k (given i) with respect to an increase in the utility (given i and j) of alternatives k' ≠ k is negative, and
2 the cross-elasticity of the probability of some choice i and j with respect to an increase in the utility of alternatives j'≠j (given i) is negative.

Except for simple cases with a small number of alternatives it is not feasible in practical applications to estimate this model jointly. A sequential estimation starts with the lowest level choice, a calculation of the estimated expected maximum utility (the natural log of the denominator), estimation of the next higher level choice, and so forth. This model was applied by Ben-Akiva (5), Watanatada and Ben-Akiva (33), Ruiter and Ben-Akiva (28) and Daly and Zachary (11).

McFadden (25) proves that this model can be derived by assuming ϵ_{ijk}s are jointly distributed with the Oliviera distribution function (18). The marginals of this distribution are Weibull distributions. Daly and Zachary (11) noted that since the variance of the Weibull distribution is inversely proportional to its parameter μ, this model represents a decomposition of the alternatives such that the utilities of the lowest stage of the hierarchy have the lowest variance.

To our knowledge, the system developed for the San Francisco Bay Area by Cambridge Systematics (6) is the only complete operational urban travel-forecasting system which has applied such a hierarchical model system with feedback linkages of expected maximum utilities.

DIRECTIONS FOR FUTURE RESEARCH

The expected maximum utility derived from individual travel-choice models is an operational measure of accessibility which has a direct interpretation and also serves to link models in an hierarchical system and as a measure of benefits. However, several problem areas, which arise directly from limitations of the current state-of-the-art of individual travel and mobility choice models, require further research.

The most obvious problem area, which was alluded to earlier in this chapter, is the inclusion of level of service and opportunities for non-home-based trips in an accessibility measure. The only practical approach to modelling non-home-based trips which has been implemented is a conditional structure in which the choice of non-home-based trip is modelled conditional on a home-based trip (19,28). This structure does not take into account the interdependence among the choices with respect to all trip links in a tour (a round trip that starts and ends at home).

This interdependence was observed in several descriptive studies and was recently modelled by Adler (1) in a logit model which considers an entire daily travel pattern as an alternative. An improvement of the level of service for non-home-based trips is likely to result in fewer tours and as a consequence fewer home-based trips. The number of sojourns may increase or stay the same, implying the consolidation of travel patterns into more multiple-stop tours. This indicates that an accessibility measure that is based solely on home-based trips level of service over-estimates the accessibility in areas with fewer opportunities for trip consolidation and under-estimates the accessibilities in areas with more opportunities for multi-stop tours.

A second important problem area in the measurement of accessibility as the expected maximum utility over a large number of spatial alternatives is a lack of natural definition for the set of alternatives and the constraints that define the choice set. For practical reasons, spatial alternatives are always defined as geographical areas which could be taken as an aggregation of some elemental alternatives. If these areas are not homogeneous with respect to the attributes of the elemental alternatives, the measure of accessibility will in general be biased. The direction of the bias depends on the distribution of the attributes within the areas and the form of the accessibility measure. This implies that a careful definition of elemental alternatives and the enumeration of elemental alternatives in each area is an essential part of spatial-choice modelling.

As a consequence of monotonicity of the expected value of the maximum utility with respect to choice-set size, inclusion of irrelevant alternatives in the choice set will always bias upwards the measure of accessibility. One possible approach to the problem of choice-set definition is to explicitly include time allocation in the decision-making process that is modelled. Individuals' allocation of time to various activities can serve as a constraint on total travel time. Bain (4) has developed a simple model which predicts

677 Chapter 30

the individual's decision of whether or not to participate in an activity on a given day and the expected level of participation, measured in allocated time.

Finally, the large number of spatial alternatives make the calculation of any measure of accessibility very costly. A useful approach would be to develop procedures for sampling spatial alternatives which would result in an unbiased measure of accessibility but require less data and computational effort.

REFERENCES

1. Adler, Thomas J. (1976), 'Modelling non-work travel patterns', Ph.D. Dissertation, Department of Civil Engineering, MIT, Cambridge, Massachusetts.
2. Adler, Thomas J. and Ben-Akiva, M., 'Joint-choice model for frequency, destination and travel mode for shopping trips', *Transportation Research Record 569* (1975).
3. Andrews, R.D. and Langdon, M.G., 'An individual cost minimising method of determining modal split between three travel modes', *Transport and Road Research Laboratory Report 698*, Department of the Environment, Crowthorne and Berkshire, UK (1976).
4. Bain, Joseph J. (1976) 'Activity choice analysis time allocation and disaggregate travel demand modelling', S.M. Thesis, Department of Civil Engineering, MIT, Cambridge, Massachusetts.
5. Ben-Akiva, Moshe (1973) 'Structure of passenger travel demand models', Ph.D. Dissertation, Department of Civil Engineering, MIT, Cambridge, Massachusetts.
6. Cambridge Systematics Inc. (1977) Technical report in progress for the Metropolitan Transportation Commission, San Francisco, Cambridge, Massachusetts.
7. Charles River Associates, Inc. (1972) *A Disaggregated Behavioural Model of Urban Travel Demand*, Federal Highway Administration, US Department of Transportation.
8. Clark, Charles E., 'The greatest of a finite set of random variables', *Operations Research* (1961).
9. Daganzo, Carlos R., Bouthelier, F. and Sheffi, Y., 'An efficient approach to estimate and predict with multinomial probit models', mimeograph, Department of Civil Engineering, MIT, Cambridge, Massachusetts (1976).
10. Dalvi, M.Q. and Martin, K.M., 'The measurement of accessibility: some preliminary results', *Transportation*, 5, 1 (1976).
11. Daly, A.J. and Zachary, S., 'Improved multiple choice models', in *Determinants of Travel Choices*, D.A. Hensher and M.Q. Dalvi (eds), Teakfield, Farnborough, UK (1978).
12. Domencich, T. and McFadden, D. (1975) *Urban Travel Demand: A Behavioral Analysis*, North-Holland, Amsterdam.
13. Dunphy, Robert T., 'Transit accessibility as a determinant of automobile ownership', *Highway Research Record 472* (1973).
14. Gumbel, E.J. (1958) *Statistics of Extremes*, Columbia University Press, New York.
15. Hansen, W.G., 'How accessibility shapes land use', *Journal of American Institute of Planners*, 3 (1959).
16. Harris, A.J. and Tanner, J.C., 'Transport demand

models based on personal characteristics', *Transport and Road Research Laboratory Supplementary Report 65 UC*, Department of the Environment, UK (1974).

17. Hausman, Jerry, A. and Wise, David A., 'A conditional probit model for qualitative choice: discrete decisions recognizing interdependence and heterogeneous preferences', *Department of Economics Working Paper No. 173*, Massachusetts Institute of Technology, Cambridge, Massachusetts (1976).

18. Johnson, Norman L. and Kotz, Samuel (1972) *Distributions in Statistics: Continuous Multivariate Distributions*, John Wiley & Sons, Inc., New York.

19. Lerman, Steven R., 'The use of disaggregate choice models in semi-Markov process models of trip chaining behavior', *Center for Transportation Studies Working Paper*, Massachusetts Institute of Technology, Cambridge, Massachusetts (1977).

20. Lerman, Steven R. and Manski, Charles F., 'An estimator for the generalized multinomial probit choice model', *Transportation Research Record* (1978) (in press).

21. Lerman, Steven R., 'A disaggregate behavioral model of urban mobility decisions', *Center for Transportation Studies Report No. 75-5*, Massachusetts Institute of Technology, Cambridge, Massachusetts (1975).

22. Luce, R.D. and Suppes, P., 'Preference, utility and subjective probability', in *Handbook of Mathematical Psychology, Vol. III*, Luce, Bush and Galanter (eds), John Wiley, New York (1965).

23. Manski, Charles F., Lerman, Steven R. and Albright, R., series of technical memos for ongoing project entitled *An Estimator for the Generalized Multinomial Probit Model*, Cambridge Systematics, Inc. (1977).

24. Manski, Charles F. (1973) 'The analysis of qualitative choice', Ph.D. Dissertation, Department of Economics, Massachusetts Institute of Technology, Cambridge, Massachusetts.

25. McFadden, Daniel, 'Quantitative methods for analysing travel behaviour of individuals: some recent developments', (Chapter 13 of the present book).

26. Neuburger, H., 'User benefit in the evaluation of transport and land use plans', *Journal of Transport Economics and Policy*, 5, 1 (1971).

27. Rao, C.R. (1973) *Linear Statistical Inference and Its Applications*, Second Edition, John Wiley and Sons, New York.

28. Ruiter, Earl R. and Ben-Akiva, Moshe, 'A system of disaggregate travel demand models: structure, component models and application procedures', *Cambridge Systematics, Inc. Working Paper*, Cambridge, Massachusetts (1977).

29. Sheffi, Yosef and Daganzo, Carlos, 'Another paradox of traffic flow', *Transportation Research* (1978) (forthcoming).

30. Sherman, L., Barber, B. and Kondo, W., 'Method for evaluating metropolitan accessibility', *Transportation Research Record 499* (1974).

31. Small, Kenneth A., 'Priority lanes on urban radial freeways: an economic simulation', paper presented at the 56th Annual Meeting of the Transportation Research Board, Washington, D.C. (1977).

32. Washington Council of Governments (1974) *Analysis of Zonal Level Trip Generation Relationships*, WCOG Technical Report No. 10.

33. Watanatada, T. and Ben-Akiva, Moshe (1976) *Development*

of an Aggregate Model of Urbanized Area Travel Demand: Detailed Specification of Aggregate Travel Demand Model for Use in TRANS, draft technical report, Center for Transportation Studies, Massachusetts Institute of Technology, Cambridge, Massachusetts.

34. Williams, H.C.W.L., 'On the formation of travel demand models and economic evaluation of user benefit', *Institute for Transport Studies Working Paper 60*, University of Leeds, UK (1976).

[12]

Econometrica, Vol. 45, No. 8 (November, 1977)

THE ESTIMATION OF CHOICE PROBABILITIES FROM CHOICE BASED SAMPLES[1]

BY CHARLES F. MANSKI AND STEVEN R. LERMAN

1. INTRODUCTION

THE CONCERN of this paper is the estimation of the parameters of a probabilistic choice model when choices rather than decision makers are sampled. Existing estimation methods presuppose an exogeneous sampling process, that is one in which a sequence of decision makers are drawn and their choice behaviors observed. In contrast, in choice based sampling processes, a sequence of chosen alternatives are drawn and the characteristics of the decision makers selecting those alternatives are observed.

The problem of estimating a choice model from a choice based sample has substantive interest because data collection costs for such processes are often considerably smaller than for exogeneous sampling. Particular instances of this differential occur in the analysis of transportation behavior. For example, in studying choice of mode for work trips, it is often less expensive to survey transit users at the station and auto users at the parking lot than to interview commuters at their homes. Similarly, in examining choice of destination for shopping trips, surveys conducted at various shopping centers offer significant cost savings relative to home interviews.[2]

While interest in transportation applications provided the original motivation for our work, it has become apparent that choice based sampling processes can be cost effective in the analysis of numerous decision problems. In particular, wherever decision makers are physically clustered according to the alternatives they select, choice based sampling processes can achieve economies of scale not available with exogeneous sampling. Some non-transportation decision problems in which decision makers do cluster as described include the schooling decisions of students, the job decisions of workers, the medical care decisions of patients and the residential location decisions of households.

Realization of the sampling cost benefits of choice based samples presupposes of course that the parameters of the underlying choice model can logically be inferred from such samples and that a tractable estimator with desirable statistical properties can be found. We shall, in this paper, confirm the logical supposition, develop a suitable estimator, and characterize the behavior of existing, exogeneous sampling, estimators in the context of choice based samples. An outline of the presentation and summary of major results follows.

[1] This work was partially supported under contract PO-6-3-0021 from the Federal Highway Administration to Cambridge Systematics, Inc. David Hendry and Daniel McFadden have contributed materially toward resolving questions raised in an earlier draft. We are grateful for their help and encouragement. Responsibility for the contents of the paper is, of course, ours alone.

[2] Comprehensive home interview surveys often cost forty dollars or more per observation. Choice based sampling costs can be as much as an order of magnitude less.

1978 C. F. MANSKI AND S. R. LERMAN

In Section 2 below, we specify a fairly general probabilistic choice model, state the estimation problem of interest, and obtain expressions for the likelihood of an observation under exogeneous and choice based sampling processes. We then specify the prior information available to the analyst. In particular, it is assumed that the analyst knows the fraction of the decision making population selecting each alternative.

Section 3 examines the maximum likelihood estimators appropriate to choice based sampling assuming various amounts of prior information. We conclude that, except in very restricted circumstances, computational intractability renders these estimators impractical.

Section 4 then introduces an alternative estimator which is quite tractable. This method modifies the familiar exogeneous sampling maximum likelihood estimator by weighting each observation's contribution to the log-likelihood. If i is the chosen alternative associated with observation n, then the weight imposed is $Q(i)/H(i)$, where $Q(i)$ is the fraction of the decision making population selecting i and $H(i)$ is the analogous fraction for the choice based sample. We prove the estimator's consistency, state its asymptotic covariance matrix and, for the special case $Q(i)=H(i)$, all i, examine its asymptotic efficiency.

Section 5 proves that the unweighted exogeneous sampling maximum likelihood estimator is generally inconsistent when applied to choice based samples. For most choice models, this inconsistency affects all parameter estimates. Interestingly, however, Daniel McFadden has shown that if the conditional logit model characterizes choice and the model's specification includes a full set of alternative specific dummy variables, then the inconsistency is fully confined to the estimates of the coefficients of these dummies. We report this result and outline McFadden's proof.

Section 6, which closes the paper, remarks on the relevance of our work to the problem of sample design.

The statistical problems introduced by choice based sampling are broadly akin to those encountered whenever a probabilistic model is formulated and observations are drawn based on the values of variables endogeneous to that model. Such problems have been studied in the literature on limited dependent variable regression and in the contingency table field. To our knowledge, an estimator of the type developed here has not previously been proposed.[3]

2. THE SAMPLING OF CHOICES

Consider a continuum of decision makers T each facing the same abstract finite choice set C. A probabilistic choice model is a characterization of behavior associating a probability $Pr(i|t)$ with every pair (i, t) where $i \in C$ and $t \in T$. The

[3] Amemiya [1] gives a rigorous development of maximum likelihood estimation for one class of limited dependent variable regressions. Haberman [5] provides a general treatment of maximum likelihood methods for contingency table analysis. If we let the decision makers be the rows and the set of available alternatives be the columns, observations of choices can be expressed in a two-way contingency table. Set up this way, choice based sampling is an instance of "multi-nomial sampling" with fixed column sums.

expression $Pr(i|t)$ is to be interpreted as the probability that decision maker t will select alternative i from the set C.[4]

For empirical work, decision makers and alternatives are generally given attribute characterizations and parametric structure is imposed on the choice probabilities. Let $z_{ti} \in R^M$, M finite, be a vector of attributes of i as viewed by t, let $z_t = (z_{tj}, j \in C)$, and let $\theta^* \in R^K$, K finite, be a parameter vector. Define an attribute space $Z \subset R^M x \ldots x R^M$ such that $z_t \in Z$, *all* $t \in T$, and define a parameter space $\Theta \subset R^K$ such that $\theta^* \in \Theta$. Then we assume the existence of a function P, defined over $C \times Z \times \Theta$ such that

$$(1) \qquad Pr(i|t) = P(i, z_t, \theta^*)$$

for some $\theta^* \in \Theta$.

The problem of interest is to estimate the parameter vector θ^* given prior specification of Θ, given knowledge of the form of P, and given a sample of observations, each of which is a decision maker t, his choice i, and his attribute matrix z_t. It is obvious but nonetheless important to stress that the properties of any given estimation method may differ under alternative sampling processes. Thus, there is no a priori reason to expect that existing estimators, all of which assume exogeneous sampling, will produce useful estimates in choice based samples.

In preparation for our examination of estimation in choice based samples, we now formally define exogeneous and choice based sampling and state the likelihood of an observation under each regime.

Exogeneous Sampling: Let g be an arbitrary density function over the attribute space Z and let p be the actual density of z in the population T. In exogeneous sampling, the analyst draws a decision maker t characterized by the attributes z_t according to the density g and then observes the choice made by this decision maker from the choice set C. Suppressing the identity of the drawn decision maker (as this is irrelevant to the estimation of θ^*), the likelihood of an observation is thus

$$(2) \qquad \lambda_e(i, z) = P(i, z, \theta^*)g(z).$$

When the analyst's sampling distribution g coincides with the population density p, he is said to draw a random exogeneous sample. Otherwise, his sampling process is said to be stratified.

[4] The assumption of a continuum of decision makers is, of course, a mathematical idealization. The import of the assumption is that it will allow characterization of an attribute space through a density function.

The recent literature on probabilistic choice models generally does not require each decision maker to face the same choice set. The restrictiveness of our assumption is more apparent than real because, for a given decision maker, the choice probabilities for some alternatives may be very low. In making the identical choice set assumption, we are only requiring that each alternative be a logically possible choice for every decision maker. This assumption will allow us to interpret the domain of the choice probability function as a Euclidean space.

McFadden [**15**, **16**], Luce and Suppes [**11**], and Tversky [**20**] each survey aspects of the literature on probabilistic choice. Existing estimation methods, all of which assume exogeneous sampling, include the conditional logit estimator (McFadden [**14**]), the maximum score estimator (Manski [**12**]) and the multinomial probit estimator (Daganzo, Bouthelier and Sheffi [**3**], Hausman and Wise [**6**], and Lerman and Manski [**10**]).

Choice Based Sampling: Let H be an arbitrary probability distribution over the choice set C and let $Q(i)$, $i \in C$ be the actual fractions of the population T selecting each of the available alternatives. In choice based sampling, the analyst draws an alternative i from C with probability $H(i)$, next draws a decision maker at random from that subset of T selecting i and then observes the attribute matrix z associated with that decision maker. The likelihood of an observation is thus

$$\lambda_c(i, z) = \lambda_c(z/i)H(i) = \frac{P(i, z, \theta^*)p(z)}{\int_Z P(i, z, \theta^*)p(z)\, dz} \cdot H(i) \tag{3}$$

where $\lambda_c(z/i)$ is the likelihood of observing z conditioned on drawing a decision maker who has selected i and where the second equality in (3) follows directly from Bayes' Rule. Note that for each $i \in C$, $Q(i) \overset{\text{a.s.}}{=} \int_Z P(i, z, \theta^*)p(z)\, dz$. In line with our terminology for exogeneous samples, we shall term the choice based sampling process random when $H(i) = \int_Z P(i, z, \theta^*)p(z)\, dz$, all $i \in C$, and stratified otherwise. And we point out that $\lambda_e(i, z) = \lambda_c(i, z)$ for all i and z if and only if the two sampling processes are both random.

Beyond the analyst's specification of Θ, functional knowledge of P and sample of observed choice-attribute matrix pairs, we shall assume that the population shares $Q(i)$, $i \in C$, are known. This information, required by the weighted maximum likelihood estimator to be developed, is usually relatively easy to obtain. For example, traffic counts by mode would be sufficient for transportation mode choice studies, college enrollments by school would suffice for an analysis of college going behavior, and a household census by district would provide the requisite data for a study of residential location. Where population shares are not directly available, inexpensive interviews with a random sample of the population T in which the only requested information is the identity of the respondent's chosen alternative could be conducted.[5]

3. CHOICE BASED SAMPLING MAXIMUM LIKELIHOOD (CBSML) ESTIMATORS

Let $y = (i_n, z_n)$, $n = 1, \ldots, \infty$, be a sequence of independent observations drawn via a choice based sampling process. From (3), the log-likelihood of the sample consisting of the first N such observations, evaluated at some $\theta \in \Theta$, is

$$L_{Nc}(y, \theta) = \sum_{n=1}^{N} \log P(i_n, z_n, \theta) - \sum_{n=1}^{N} \log \int_Z P(i_n, z, \theta)p(z)\, dz + \sum_{n=1}^{N} \log (p(z_n) \cdot H(i_n)). \tag{4}$$

Equation (4) forms the basis for two informationally distinct maximum likelihood estimators for θ^*. In particular, given knowledge of the population shares $Q(i)$, $i \in C$, and of the attribute distribution $p(z)$, $z \in Z$, we may maximize (4)

[5] When population share information is estimated using such an auxiliary sample, consistency of the θ^* estimator we develop must be interpreted as requiring that the size of this sample, as well as that of the choice based sample, go to infinity.

The estimator we develop will not require that the distribution $p(z)$ be known.

subject to the set of constraints $Q(i)=\int_Z P(i, z, \theta)p(z)\,dz$, all $i \in C$. With the $p(z)$ known but not the $Q(i)$, an unconstrained maximization of (4) may be performed. Assuming sufficient regularity in the choice model $P(i, z, \theta)$ and in the distributions H and p, both of the above estimators can be shown to yield consistent, asymptotically normal estimates for θ^*. As might be expected, the former estimator has smaller asymptotic variance than does the latter.[6]

Their statistical interest to the side, the various versions of choice based sampling maximum likelihood (CBSML) all suffer a severe computational drawback. That is, each requires numerous evaluations of integrals of the form $\int_Z P(i, z, \theta)p(z)\,dz$. Except in certain special cases, such integrals are quite difficult to work with. Foremost among the favorable cases is the binary choice situation in which decision makers follow the linear probability model, that is $P(i, z, \theta)=(z_i - z_j)\cdot\theta+\frac{1}{2}$ for $(i, j)=C$. There, the relevant integral reduces to a function linear in θ. More realistic binary choice situations yielding at least marginally tractable integrals have been studied by McFadden and Reid **[17]** and by Westin **[21]**. The former authors analyze the combination of a probit choice model and multivariate normal distribution for z while the latter assumes the logit form for $P(i, z, \theta)$ and again a normal $p(z)$. When the choice set size grows beyond two alternatives, performing the numerous required evaluations of the $\int_Z P(i, z, \theta)p(z)\,dz$ function rapidly becomes infeasible. Koppelman's **[9]** study of the problem in the context of three alternative choice sets with conditional logit choice probabilities provides a good feel for the difficulties.

Acknowledgment of the impracticality of CBSML procedures leads one to search for an alternative estimator to be used in the presence of a choice based sample. The next section introduces such an estimator and develops various of its properties.

4. THE WEIGHTED EXOGENEOUS SAMPLING MAXIMUM LIKELIHOOD (WESML) ESTIMATOR

Consider the log-likelihood appropriate to exogeneous sampling. It follows from (2) that for a sample consisting of the first N observations of the sequence y, this function evaluated at any $\theta \in \Theta$ is

$$(5)\qquad L_{Ne}(y, \theta)=\sum_{n=1}^{N}\log P(i_n, z_n, \theta)+\sum_{n=1}^{N}\log g(z_n).$$

Given its simplicity relative to the CBSML estimators, one might inquire whether unconstrained maximization of (5) provides a suitable estimation procedure in the context of choice based sampling. Unfortunately, this is not the case.[7] On the other hand, there exists a straightforward modification of the unconstrained exogeneous sampling maximum likelihood (ESML) criterion which does

[6] These estimators are studied in Manski and McFadden **[13]**.

[7] This will be proved in Section 5. Note that maximization of (5) subject to the constraints $Q(i)=\int P(i, z, \theta)P(z)\,dz$, all $i \in C$, is algebraically identical to the analogous constrained CBSML estimator. Hence, constrained ESML is consistent in choice based samples but, of course, is intractable. Unconstrained ESML is algebraically identical to the estimator we shall propose, and hence is consistent, in one special case. That is the case in which $Q(i)=H(i)$, all $i \in C$.

have desirable computational and statistical properties under choice based sampling. This weighted exogeneous sampling maximum likelihood (WESML) estimator is described presently.

For each $i \in C$, define the function $w(i)$ by $w(i) = Q(i)/H(i)$. Given the analyst's assumed knowledge of the population shares $Q(i)$ and given his ability to calculate the sample shares $H(i)$ directly from the data, the 'weights' $w(i)$ are known non-negative constants. Consider now the weighted exogeneous sampling likelihood function

$$W_N(y, \theta) = \sum_{n=1}^{N} w(i_n) \log P(i_n, z_n, \theta) + \sum_{n=1}^{N} w(i_n) \log g(z_n). \tag{6}$$

Under regularity conditions closely comparable to those required in maximum likelihood estimation, estimates obtained by maximizing (6) are strongly consistent and asymptotically normal. Section A below proves the consistency property. Section B then examines the WESML asymptotic covariance structure.

A. *Consistency of the WESML Estimator*

In order to demonstrate consistency, we shall need the following three lemmas.

LEMMA 1: *Let $g(s, \phi)$ be a real valued function over a space $S \times \Phi$ such that g is integrable with respect to a measure μ over S and $g(s, \phi) \geq 0$, all $s \in S$, $\phi \in \Phi$. Let ϕ^* be an element of Φ such that $g(s, \phi^*) > 0$ for almost every $s \in S$ and $\int_S (g(s, \phi^*) - g(s, \phi))\, d\mu \geq 0$, all $\phi \in \Phi$. Then the expression*

$$f(\phi) = \int_S g(s, \phi^*) \log g(s, \phi)\, d\mu$$

attains its maximum at $\phi = \phi^*$.

PROOF: This is an adaptation of a well-known result from information theory used in some proofs of the consistency of maximum likelihood estimation. See for example, Rao [**18**, p. 59].

LEMMA 2: *Let $f_M(x, \phi)$, $M = 1, \ldots, \infty$ be a sequence of measurable functions on a measurable space X and for each $x \in X$, a continuous function for $\phi \in \Phi$, Φ being compact. Then there exists a sequence of measurable functions $\hat{\phi}_M(x)$, $M = 1, \ldots, \infty$, such that $f_M(x, \hat{\phi}_M(x)) = \sup_{\phi \in \Phi} f_M(x, \phi)$ for all $x \in X$ and $M = 1, \ldots, \infty$.*

Furthermore, if for almost every $x \in X$, $f_M(x, \phi)$ converges to $f(\phi)$ uniformly for all $\phi \in \Phi$ and if $f(\phi)$ has a unique maximum at $\phi^* \in \Phi$, then $\hat{\phi}_M$ converges to ϕ^* for almost every $x \in X$.

PROOF: This is a direct paraphrase of Amemiya [**1**, Lemma 3, p. 1002].

LEMMA 3: *Let μ be a probability measure over a Euclidean space S, let Φ be a compact subset of a Euclidean space, and let $g(s, \phi)$ be a continuous function of ϕ for each $s \in S$ and a measurable function of s for each $\phi \in \Phi$. Assume also that $|g(s, \phi)| \leq \alpha$ for all s and ϕ and some finite α. For any sequence $x = s_1, s_2, \ldots,$ let $f_M(x, \phi) = \sum_{m=1}^{M} g(s_m, \phi)/M$ and let X be the set of all sequences x.*

If sequences x are drawn as random samples from S, then, for almost every realized such sequence, as $M \to \infty$,

$$f_M(x, \phi) \to E(g(s, \phi)) \equiv f(\phi)$$

uniformly for all $\phi \in \Phi$.

PROOF: This law of large numbers for random functions is a slightly strengthened version of Jennrich [**7**, Theorem 2, p. 636].

We may now state a consistency theorem for the WESML estimator.

THEOREM 1: *Assume that choice from a finite choice set C by each member of the continuum of decision makers T is described by the probabilistic choice model $P(i, z_t, \theta^*)$ where the probability is defined for all $i \in C$, $z \in Z$, and $\theta \in \Theta$ and where the sets Z and Θ are both compact. Furthermore assume that P is everywhere positive and is continuous in all of its arguments.*

Let $y = (i_n, z_n)$, $n = 1, \ldots, \infty$ be a realized sequence of observations drawn as a random sample via a choice based sampling process and let Y be the space of all such sequences. Assume that the sampling probabilities $H(i)$ are positive for all $i \in C$.

Let $W_N(y, \theta)$ designate the weighted exogeneous sampling log likelihood function for the first N observations of y, evaluated at θ, and, wherever it exists, let $\hat{\theta}_N(y)$ be a WESML estimate for the sample.

Assume that the function P, the structure of the attribute space Z, and the attribute distribution $p(z)$, $z \in Z$, are such that $D(\theta) \equiv E(w(i) \log P(i, z, \theta))$ possesses a unique maximum over Θ.[8]

Then a $\hat{\theta}_N(y)$ always exists and, as $N \to \infty$, $\hat{\theta}_N(y)$ converges to θ^* for almost every sequence $y \in Y$.

[8] It will be shown in the proof of the theorem that $D(\theta)$ must possess a finite maximum. Hence, the import of the present assumption is the assertion that this maximum is unique. This condition ensures that θ^* is identifiable using our estimator.

It is quite difficult to say anything simultaneously general and practical concerning what combinations of P's, Z's, and p distributions result in an identified model. For example, Rothenberg [**19**] offers non-singularity of the information matrix as a general identification criterion but offers no constructive method for establishing such non-singularity. Bowden [**2**], in a spirit close to ours, examines identification in terms of the uniqueness of the maximum of the expected log-likelihood function.

Meaningful identification conditions can be obtained in the context of particular probabilistic choice models. For example, McFadden's [**14**] conditions ensuring the identifiability of the conditional logit model in exogeneous samples also ensure that weighted conditional logit can identify θ^* in choice based samples.

PROOF: By (6), maximization of $W_N(y, \theta)$ over Θ is equivalent to maximization of the expression

$$D_N(y, \theta) \equiv \sum_{n=1}^{N} w(i_n) \log P(i_n, z_n, \theta)/N.$$

By assumption, $P(i, z, \theta)$ is an everywhere positive, continuous probability function defined over a compact set. Hence, $P(i, z, \theta)$ and $\log P(i, z, \theta)$ are both bounded.[9] Furthermore, since $0 < H(i) < 1$, all $i \in C$, $w(i) = Q(i)/H(i)$ is positive and finite for all $i \in C$. These conditions are more than sufficient to guarantee that $D(\theta)$ exists and is finite for all $\theta \in \Theta$. Hence, by the strong law of large numbers, as $N \to \infty$,

$$(7) \qquad D_N(y, \theta) \overset{\text{a.s.}}{\to} D(\theta) \equiv \int_Z \sum_{i \in C} \frac{P(i, z, \theta^*) \cdot H(i)}{\int_Z P(i, z, \theta^*) p(z)\, dz} \cdot w(i) \log P(i, z, \theta) p(z)\, dz$$

$$\overset{\text{a.s.}}{=} \int_Z \sum_{i \in C} P(i, z, \theta^*) \log P(i, z, \theta) p(z)\, dz.$$

In (7), the first equality follows from (3) and the second from the definition of the weights w.

Observe that for any θ,

$$\int_Z \sum_{i \in C} P(i, z, \theta) p(z)\, dz = 1.$$

Hence, by Lemma 1, $D(\theta)$ is maximized at $\theta = \theta^*$. Moreover, this maximum is, from our identification assumption, unique.

The first part of Lemma 2 ensures that for every $y \in Y$ and for $N = 1, \ldots, \infty$, a WESML estimate $\hat{\theta}_N(y)$ exists. We have previously determined that both $\log P(i, z, \theta)$ and $w(i)$ are bounded, implying that $w(i) \log P(i, z, \theta)$ is bounded and that Lemma 3 is applicable. Thus, the convergence of $D_N(y, \theta)$ to $D(\theta)$ is uniform for almost every $y \in Y$. This result, plus the uniqueness of the maximum of $D(\theta)$ at θ^* fulfill the conditions of the second part of Lemma 2. Hence, as $N \to \infty$, $\hat{\theta}_N$ converges to θ^* almost surely. *Q.E.D.*

B. *The WESML Covariance Structure*

Assume that the conditions of Theorem 1 are met. Also assume that there exists an open set $\Theta_0 \subset R^K$ such that $\theta^* \in \Theta_0 \subset \Theta$ and such that the derivatives $\partial^3 \log P(i, z, \theta)/\partial\theta_j\, \partial\theta_k\, \partial\theta_l$ exist and are continuous for all $i \in C$, $z \in Z$, $\theta \in \Theta_0$, and $j, k, l = 1, \ldots, K$. Then the distribution of $\sqrt{N}(\hat{\theta}_N(y) - \theta^*)$ can be shown to be asymptotically normal with mean 0 and the following covariance matrix:

$$(8) \qquad V = \Omega^{-1} \Delta \Omega^{-1} \qquad \text{where}$$

$$\Omega = \left[-E\left(\frac{\partial^2 w(i) \log P(i, z, \theta)}{\partial\theta\, \partial\theta'} \right)_{\theta^*} \right],$$

$$\Delta = \left[E\left(\frac{\partial w(i) \log P(i, z, \theta)}{\partial\theta} \right)_{\theta^*} \left(\frac{\partial w(i) \log P(i, z, \theta)}{\partial\theta'} \right)_{\theta^*} \right],$$

[9] See Kolmogorov and Fomin [**8**, p. 110 Theorem 2].

and where the expectations E operate over i and z with respect to the distribution given in (3).[10]

Recall that $\lambda_c(i, z) = P(i, z, \theta^*)H(i)p(z)/\int_Z P(i, z, \theta^*)p(z)\,dz$. It follows that the matrix Ω in (8) is almost surely identical to the information matrix for random exogeneous sampling. In the special case of random choice based sampling, $\lambda_c(i, z) = P(i, z, \theta^*)p(z)$, all i and z and $w(i) \overset{\text{a.s.}}{=} 1$, all i, implying that $\Delta \overset{\text{a.s.}}{=} \Omega$. Hence, in this case, matrix V is almost surely identical to the asymptotic covariance structure which results when the sampling process is random exogeneous and the estimation method is unconstrained ESML.

5. THE BEHAVIOR OF ESML ESTIMATES IN CHOICE BASED SAMPLES

Under random choice based sampling, the WESML and unconstrained ESML estimators are identical in every respect. When the choice based sampling process is a stratified one, however, the two estimators are distinct. The following theorem proves that in almost every stratified choice based sampling process, the unconstrained ESML method does not yield consistent estimates for θ^*.

THEOREM 2: *Assume that the conditions of Theorem* 1 *are met. Also assume that the derivatives* $(\partial P(i, z, \theta)/\partial\theta)_{\theta^*}$ *exist and are continuous for all* $i \in C$, $z \in Z$. *Let* $H = (H(i), i \in C)$ *designate any set of choice based sampling probabilities satisfying* $H(i) > 0$, *all* $i \in C$, *and let* Ω *be the space of all such sets* H. *Then the unconstrained ESML criterion*

$$\max_{\theta \in \Theta} \sum_{n=1}^{N} \log P(i_n, z_n, \theta)$$

is inconsistent for θ^* *for almost every* $H \in \Omega$.[11]

PROOF: If the ESML estimator is to be consistent, then

$$F(\theta) \equiv \operatorname*{plim}_{N\to\infty} \sum_{n=1}^{N} \log P(i_n, z_n, \theta) \Big/ N \overset{\text{a.s.}}{=} \sum_{i \in C} \frac{H(i)}{Q(i)} \int_Z P(i, z, \theta^*) \log P(i, z, \theta) p(z)\,dz$$

[10] This covariance matrix is derived in the usual manner. That is, we approximate the first order conditions for the maximization of $W_N(y, \theta)$ by

$$0 = \left(\frac{\partial W_N}{\partial \theta}\right)_{\hat\theta_N} \cong \left(\frac{\partial W_N}{\partial \theta}\right)_{\theta^*} + \left(\frac{\partial^2 W_N}{\partial \theta\, \partial \theta'}\right)_{\theta^*} (\hat\theta_N - \theta^*),$$

observe that

$$\sqrt{N}(\hat\theta_N - \theta^*) \cong \left(-\frac{1}{N}\left(\frac{\partial^2 W_N}{\partial \theta\, \partial \theta'}\right)_{\theta^*}\right)^{-1} \left(\frac{1}{\sqrt{N}}\left(\frac{\partial W_N}{\partial \theta}\right)_{\theta^*}\right),$$

and let $N \to \infty$. The first expression on the right hand side approaches the matrix Ω^{-1}. The second expression approaches a normally distributed vector with mean zero and variance Δ.

[11] Ω is the surface of the unit simplex in $R^{|C|}$, minus end points. The term 'almost every' is to be interpreted with respect to $|C| - 1$ dimensional Lebesque measure over Ω.

must have a unique maximum at $\theta=\theta^*$.[12] Given the existence and continuity assumed for $(\partial P(i, z, \theta)/\partial\theta)_{\theta^*}$, the consistency condition requires that

$$\left(\frac{\partial}{\partial\theta}\sum_{i\in C}\frac{H(i)}{Q(i)}\int_Z P(i, z, \theta^*)\log P(i, z, \theta)p(z)\,dz\right)_{\theta^*}$$

$$=\sum_{i\in C}\frac{H(i)}{Q(i)}\int_Z P(i, z, \theta^*)\left(\frac{\partial \log P(i, z, \theta)}{\partial\theta}\right)_{\theta^*}p(z)\,dz$$

$$=\sum_{i\in C}H(i)\left(\frac{1}{Q(i)}\int_Z\left(\frac{\partial P(i, z, \theta)}{\partial\theta}\right)_{\theta^*}p(z)\,dz\right)=0.^{13}$$

Observe that the above first order conditions form a set of K linear homogeneous equations in H. Identifiability of θ^* implies that $(\partial P(i, z, \theta)/\partial\theta)_{\theta^*}\neq 0$ for at least some subset of Z having positive probability measure. Hence, in general, these equations are non-trivial and restrict H to a linear subspace of $R^{|C|}$.[14] Ω, on the other hand, is the surface of the unit simplex in $R^{|C|}$, minus end points. It follows that the first order conditions will not be satisfied for almost all $H\in\Omega$.[15]

Q.E.D.

It is desirable to go beyond the above theorem and characterize the inconsistency of the ESML estimator. Although we can offer no general analysis of this question, a full characterization has been achieved by McFadden for one choice model. In particular, let

$$P(i, z, \theta^*)=e^{z_i\phi^*+\gamma_i^*}\Big/\sum_{j\in C}e^{z_j\phi^*+\gamma_j^*}$$

where $\theta^*=(\phi^*;\gamma_j^*, j\in C)$. This is the conditional logit form specified to include a full set of alternative specific dummy variables. McFadden's result is as follows.[16]

Assume the regularity conditions imposed in the statement of Theorem 1. Recall the function $F(\theta)$ introduced in the proof of Theorem 2. If there exists a $\tilde{\theta}\in\Theta$ uniquely maximizing $F(\theta)$, the unconstrained ESML estimate will, as $N\to\infty$, almost surely converge to that $\tilde{\theta}$. In the present case, let $\delta_i\equiv$

[12] $Q(i)$ has replaced $\int_Z P(i, z, \theta)p(z)\,dz$ in the denominator of the right most expression and $\overset{\text{a.s.}}{=}$ has replaced = to simplify the ensuing notation. These changes have no substantive effects.

[13] That the derivatives may be passed through the integral follows from the fact that $(\partial \log P(i, z, \theta)/\partial\theta)_{\theta^*}$ is a vector of continuous functions over a compact set and is therefore bounded. We earlier found that $\log P(i, z, \theta)$ is also bounded. These conditions allow us to pass the derivative through the integral. See Fleming [**4**, p. 199, Theorem 18].

[14] The equations restrict H for almost every specification of the model $P(i, z, \theta)$, the distribution $p(z)$, and the vector θ^*, but not every such combination. This slight hedge is necessary in order to admit the possibility that $\int_Z (\partial P(i, z, \theta)/\partial\theta)_{\theta^*}p(z)\,dz=0$, all $i\in C$, through a peculiar juxtaposition of the three factors, P, p, and θ^*.

[15] The conditions are, of course, satisfied when $H(i)=Q(i)$, all $i\in C$, that is the case of random choice based sampling. This follows from the fact that $\Sigma_{i\in C}P(i, z, \theta)=1$ for all $z\in Z$ and all $\theta\in\Theta$.

[16] McFadden's result was communicated to us as part of a comment on an earlier draft of this paper. We thank him for allowing us to report it here.

$\log (H(i)/Q(i))$, all $i \in C$, and observe that

$$F(\theta)=\int_Z \sum_{i\in C} e^{\delta_i}\frac{e^{z_i\phi^*+\gamma_i^*}}{\left(\sum_{j\in C} e^{z_j\phi^*+\gamma_j^*}\right)}\log\frac{e^{z_i\phi+\gamma_i}}{\left(\sum_{j\in C} e^{z_j\phi+\gamma_j}\right)}p(z)\,dz$$

$$=\int_Z \left(\frac{\sum_{j\in C} e^{z_j\phi^*+(\gamma_j^*+\delta_j)}}{\sum_{j\in C} e^{z_j\phi^*+\gamma_j^*}}\right)\left(\sum_{i\in C}\frac{e^{z_i\phi^*+(\gamma_i^*+\delta_i)}}{\left(\sum_{j\in C} e^{z_j\phi^*+(\gamma_j^*+\delta_j)}\right)}\times\log\frac{e^{z_i\phi+\gamma_i}}{\left(\sum_{j\in C} e^{z_j\phi+\gamma_j}\right)}\right)p(z)\,dz.$$

By Lemma 1 and the regularity conditions, the expression

$$\sum_{i\in C}\frac{e^{z_i\phi^*+(\gamma_i^*+\delta_i)}}{\left(\sum_{j\in C} e^{z_j\phi^*+(\gamma_j^*+\delta_j)}\right)}\log\frac{e^{z_i\phi+\gamma_i}}{\left(\sum_{j\in C} e^{z_j\phi+\gamma_j}\right)}$$

is, for every $z \in Z$, maximized at $\tilde{\phi}=\phi^*$, $\tilde{\gamma}_j=\gamma_j^*+\delta_j$, all $j \in C$. Hence, $F(\theta)$ is maximized at this point. Furthermore, this maximum will be unique if sufficient identifiability conditions are imposed. In particular, the conditions given in McFadden **[14]** will ensure uniqueness.

The above demonstrates that if Θ is defined so as to contain the point $(\phi^*; \gamma_j^*+\delta_j, j\in C)$, then unconstrained ESML estimates are consistent for ϕ^*. Such estimates are not consistent for the γ_j^* but instead converge to $\gamma_j^*+\delta_j$. However, given prior knowledge of $Q(j)$, δ_j may be calculated and γ_j^* recovered ex post from the relation $\gamma_j^*=\tilde{\gamma}_j-\delta_j$.

Clearly, the inconsistency of unconstrained ESML in the fully dummied conditional logit model is innocuous. This is an important finding. However, inspection of the proof of the McFadden result makes clear that it depends crucially on the multiplicative separability of the alternative specific terms in the conditional logit specification. Where alternative specific variables enter other than multiplicatively, as for example in probit models, or where they are omitted from the model, the unconstrained ESML inconsistency can be expected to take a more complex form.

6. A REMARK ON SAMPLE DESIGN

The results of this paper have obvious implications for the question of sample design. Where, as is often the situation, costs for choice based sampling are lower than those for exogeneous sampling, at least a prima facie case for a choice based design exists. Two particular designs which may easily be compared are random choice based sampling and random exogeneous sampling. Since the likelihoods for these two processes are identical, the choice between them can be made solely on the basis of relative sampling costs. More generally, however, we must consider how the information content of a sample of given size varies between choice based and exogeneous samples, among particular designs within each class, and with the estimator applied to the sample. These matters, which have not previously attracted attention, deserve considerable study.

Carnegie-Mellon University
and
Massachusetts Institute of Technology

Manuscript received October, 1975; *final revision received December*, 1976.

REFERENCES

[1] AMEMIYA, T.: "Regression Analysis When the Dependent Variable is Truncated Normal," *Econometrica*, 41 (1973), 997–1016.
[2] BOWDEN, R.: "The Theory of Parametric Identification," *Econometrica*, 41 (1973), 1069–1074.
[3] DAGANZO, C., F. BOUTHELIER, AND Y. SHEFFI: "An Efficient Approach to Estimate and Predict with Multi-nomial Probit Models," Xerox, July, 1976.
[4] FLEMING, W.: *Functions of Several Variables*. Reading, Mass.: Addison-Wesley, 1965.
[5] HABERMAN, S.: *The Analysis of Frequency Data*. Chicago: University of Chicago Press, 1974.
[6] HAUSMAN, J., AND D. WISE: "A Conditional Probit Model for Qualitative Choice," Xerox, M.I.T. Department of Economics Working Paper No. 173, April, 1976.
[7] JENNRICH, R.: "Asymptotic Properties of Non-Linear Least Squares Estimators," *Annals of Mathematical Statistics*, 40 (1969), 633–643.
[8] KOLMOGOROV, A., AND S. FOMIN: *Introductory Real Analysis*. Englewood Cliffs, N.J.: Prentice-Hall, 1970.
[9] KOPPELMAN, F.: "Travel Prediction with Models of Individual Choice Behavior," Center for Transportation Studies, M.I.T. Report no. 75–7, 1975.
[10] LERMAN, S., AND C. MANSKI: "An Estimator for the Generalized Multinomial Probit Choice Model," Xerox, August, 1976.
[11] LUCE, R., AND P. SUPPES: "Preference, Utility and Subjective Probability," in *Handbook of Mathematical Psychology*, Vol. III, ed. by R. Luce et al. New York: Wiley, 1965, pp. 249–441.
[12] MANSKI, C.: "Maximum Score Estimation of the Stochastic Utility Model of Choice," *Journal of Econometrics*, 3 (1975), 205–228.
[13] MANSKI, C., AND D. MCFADDEN: "Alternative Estimators and Sample Designs for Discrete Choice Analysis," Xerox, December, 1976.
[14] MCFADDEN, D.: "Conditional Logit Analysis of Qualitative Choice Behavior," in *Frontiers of Econometrics*, ed. by P. Zarembka. New York: Academic Press, 1973, pp. 105–142.
[15] ———: "Quantal Choice Analysis: A Survey," *Annals of Economic and Social Measurement*, 5 (1976), 363–390.
[16] ———: "Economic Applications of Psychological Choice Models," paper presented at the Third World Congress of the Econometric Society, Toronto, August, 1975.
[17] MCFADDEN, D., AND F. REID: "Aggregate Travel Demand Forecasting From Disaggregate Behavioral Models," *Transportation Research Record*, 534 (1975), 24–37.
[18] RAO, C. R.: *Linear Statistical Inference and its Applications*, 2nd. ed. New York: Wiley, 1973.
[19] ROTHENBERG, T.: "Identification in Parametric Models," *Econometrica*, 39 (1971), 577–592.
[20] TVERSKY, A.: "Choice by Elimination," *Journal of Mathematical Psychology*, 9 (1972), 341–367.
[21] WESTIN, R.: "Predictions from Binary Choice Models," *Journal of Econometrics*, 2 (1974), 1–16.

[13]

QUANTITATIVE METHODS FOR ANALYSING TRAVEL BEHAVIOUR OF INDIVIDUALS: SOME RECENT DEVELOPMENTS

Daniel McFadden

SUMMARY

This chapter is concerned with quantitative methods for the analysis of travel behaviour of individuals. It reviews some of the recent developments in model specification, estimation, model evaluation and testing, and aggregation and forecasting. Topics in model specification include the multinomial-probit model and its computation, and generalised-extreme value models and their relation to sequential models. Topics in estimation methods include the use of choice-based samples, sample designs and incomplete choice sets. Model evaluation topics include prediction-success tables and diagnostic tests of specification. Aggregation and forecasting topics include aggregation by the Clark method, synthesis of the distribution of explanatory variables, and the calculus of demand elasticities.

INTRODUCTION

This chapter is concerned with quantitative methods for the analysis of travel behaviour of individuals. It reviews some recent developments in model specification, estimation, model evaluation and testing, and aggregation and forecasting. The reader is assumed to be familiar with the general foundations of disaggregate choice theory (30,31), the historical development and properties of the multinomial logit model (26), and the use of behavioural models in travel-demand analysis (15,38,39).

MODEL SPECIFICATION

The choice models which have received serious consideration in travel-demand applications are multinomial logit (MNL), multinomial probit (MNP), and a sequential - or tree - version of multinomial logit.

The Multinomial-logit Model (MNL)

A typical MNL model for joint choice of mode, destination and auto availability is

$$P_{mda} = e^{v_{mda}} / \sum_{n,c,b} e^{v_{ncb}} \quad (1)$$

where m = mode;
d = destination;
a = auto availability;

and $v_{mda} = \alpha x_{mda} + \beta y_{da} + \gamma z_a$ = utility, with α, β, γ parameter vectors and x_{mda}, y_{da}, z_a variable vectors describing the decision-maker and the alternative. Letting $P_{m|da}$ denote a conditional choice probability and P_m denote a marginal choice probability, we can derive from Equation (1) the formulae:

$$P_{m|da} = e^{v_{mda}} / \sum_{n} e^{v_{nda}} = e^{\alpha x_{mda}} / \sum_{n} e^{\alpha x_{nda}} \quad (2)$$

$$P_{d|a} = \sum_{n} e^{v_{nda}} / \sum_{n,c} e^{v_{nca}} = \sum_{n} e^{\alpha x_{nda}+\beta y_{da}} / \sum_{n,c} e^{\alpha x_{nca}+\beta y_{ca}} \quad (3)$$

$$P_a = \sum_{n,c} e^{v_{nca}} / \sum_{n,c,b} e^{v_{ncb}}$$

$$= \sum_{n,c} e^{\alpha x_{nca}+\beta y_{ca}+\gamma z_a} / \sum_{n,c,b} e^{\alpha x_{ncb}+\beta y_{cb}+\gamma z_b} \quad (4)$$

Define inclusive values

$$I_{da} = \log \sum_{n} e^{\alpha x_{nda}} \; ; \quad (5)$$

$$J_a = \log \sum_{n,c} e^{\alpha x_{nca}+\beta y_{ca}} = \log \sum_{c} e^{I_{ca}+\beta y_{ca}} \; . \quad (6)$$

Then the choice probabilities can be written

$$P_{mda} = P_{m|da} P_{d|a} P_a \; ; \quad (7)$$

$$P_{m|da} = e^{\alpha x_{mda}} / e^{I_{da}} \; ; \quad (8)$$

$$P_{d|a} = e^{I_{da}+\beta y_{da}} / \sum_{c} e^{I_{ca}+\beta y_{ca}} = e^{I_{da}+\beta y_{da}} / e^{J_a} \; ; \quad (9)$$

$$P_a = e^{J_a+\gamma z_a} / \sum_{b} e^{J_b+\gamma z_b} \quad (10)$$

Discussion of the historical development of the MNL model can be found in McFadden (30); the properties of the model, including its derivation from the theory of individual utility maximisation, are given in McFadden (26)

Sequential MNL Models

Next consider the sequential or nested MNL model. A typical *sequential* model differs from the joint MNL model solely in that the coefficients of inclusive values are not constrained to equal one. Hence, the joint MNL model is a linear restriction on any of the sequential models. Specifically, a sequential model is defined by

$$P_{mda} = P_{m|da} P_{d|a} P_a ; \tag{11}$$

$$P_{m|da} = e^{\alpha x_{mda}} / \sum_n e^{\alpha x_{nda}} ; \tag{12}$$

$$I_{da} = \log \sum_n e^{\alpha x_{nda}} ; \tag{5'}$$

$$P_{d|a} = e^{\theta I_{da} + \beta y_{da}} / \sum_c e^{\theta I_{ca} + \beta y_{ca}} ; \tag{13}$$

$$J_a = \log \sum_c e^{\theta I_{ca} + \beta y_{ca}} ; \tag{14}$$

$$P_a = e^{\lambda J_a + \gamma z_a} / \sum_b e^{\lambda J_b + \gamma z_b} . \tag{15}$$

When $\theta = \lambda = 1$, this model is identical to the joint MNL model. More generally, when $\theta \neq 1$, Equations (13) and (14) differ in the two models, and when $\lambda \neq 1$, Equation (15) differs in the two models.

The sequential model was introduced by Domencich and McFadden (15) and studied by Ben-Akiva (3), and is discussed in greater detail below.

The Multinomial-probit Model

A typical model for the mode-destination-auto (mda) choice problem is obtained by assuming that each alternative mda has a utility $u_{mda} = V_{mda} + \lambda_{mda} + \eta_{da} + \nu_a$, where λ_{mda}, η_{da} and ν_{da} summarise the influence of unobserved attributes and taste variations, and are assumed to be jointly normally distributed over the population. If each individual maximises utility, the proportion of the population choosing mda is

$$P_{mda} = \int_{\varepsilon_{mda}=-\infty}^{+\infty} \cdots \int_{\varepsilon_{ncb}=-\infty}^{V_{mda}-V_{ncb}+\varepsilon_{mda}} \cdots \int_{\varepsilon_{MDA}=-\infty}^{V_{mda}-V_{MDA}+\varepsilon_{mda}} n(\varepsilon;0,\Omega)d\varepsilon \quad , \qquad (16)$$

where the number of integrals equals the number of alternatives, $n(\varepsilon;0,\Omega)$ is the multivariate normal density with mean vector 0 and covariance matrix Ω, and $\varepsilon_{mda} = \lambda_{mda} + \eta_{da} + \nu_a$, with the joint normal distribution of λ, η, and ν determining Ω.

The MNP model generalises a classical model of Thurstone (41) for binary choice. Bock and Jones (6) applied the model to the three-alternative case. The model was suggested for transport analysis by Domencich and McFadden (15), and first applied to transport data by Hausman and Wise (20). Further discussion is given below.

Other Choice Models

Several other models deserve passing note. McFadden (27) has proposed a universal, or 'mother', MNL model which can approximate an arbitrary choice model with a function of the form (1), except that V_{mda} functions will depend on the attributes of all alternatives, and not solely on the attributes of mda. This model is useful for testing particular specifications, but is in general inconsistent with utility maximisation.

McLynn (37) has proposed the *fully competitive* model which is a one-parameter mapping of MNL choice probabilities into a second vector of probabilities. This model is in general inconsistent with individual utility maximisation, yet it shares with the MNL model restrictive structural properties which render it implausible in some applications. The McLynn model satisfies 'simple scalability' = 'order independence', which is closely related to the 'independence from irrelevant alternatives' property of the MNL model (see McFadden (28)).

The Generalised Extreme-value Model

McFadden (35) has recently proposed a family of *generalised extreme-value* (GEV) choice models which allow a general pattern of dependence among alternatives and yield a closed form for the choice probabilities. The following result characterises the family:

THEOREM 1. Suppose $G(y_1,\ldots,y_J)$ *is a non-negative, homogeneous-of-degree-one function of* $(y_1,\ldots,y_J) \geq 0$ *. Suppose* $\lim_{y_i \to +\infty} G(y_1,\ldots,y_J) = +\infty$ *for* $i = 1,\ldots,J$ *. Suppose for any distinct* $(i_1,\ldots,i_k)$ *from* $\{1,\ldots,J\}$, $\partial^k G/\partial y_{i_1},\ldots,\partial y_{i_k}$ *is non-negative if* k *is odd and non-positive if* k *is even.*

283 Chapter 13

Then,

$$P_i = e^{V_i} G_i(e^{V_1},\ldots,e^{V_J}) \;/\; G(e^{V_1},\ldots,e^{V_J}) \tag{17}$$

defines a choice model which is consistent with utility maximisation.

The special case $G(y_1,\ldots,y_J) = \sum_{j=1}^{J} y_j$ yields the MNL model. An example of a more general G function satisfying the hypotheses of the theorem is

$$G(y) = \sum_{m=1}^{M} a_m \left(\sum_{i \in B_m} y_i^{\frac{1}{1-\sigma_m}} \right)^{1-\sigma_m}, \tag{18}$$

where $B_m \subseteq \{1,\ldots,J\}$, $\bigcup_{m=1}^{M} B_m = \{1,\ldots,J\}$, $a_m > 0$, and $0 \le \sigma_m < 1$. The parameter $_m$ is an index of the similarity of the unobserved attributes of alternatives in B_m. The choice probabilities for this function satisfy

$$P_i = \sum_{m=1}^{M} P(i|B_m)P(B_m) \tag{19}$$

where $P(i|B_m)$ is the conditional probability that alternative i is chosen, given the event B_m, with

$$P(i|B_m) = \begin{cases} e^{\frac{V_i}{1-\sigma_m}} \Big/ \sum_{j \in B_m} e^{\frac{V_j}{1-\sigma_m}} & \text{if } i \in B_m ; \\ 0 & \text{if } i \notin B_m ; \end{cases} \tag{20}$$

and $P(B_m)$ is the probability of the event B_m, with

$$P(B_m) = a_m \left\{ \sum_{j \in B_m} e^{\frac{V_j}{1-\sigma_m}} \right\}^{1-\sigma_m} \Big/ \sum_{n=1}^{M} a_n \left\{ \sum_{k \in B_n} e^{\frac{V_k}{1-\sigma_n}} \right\}^{1-\sigma_n} . \tag{21}$$

Functions of the form in Equation (18) can also be nested to yield a wider class satisfying the theorem hypotheses. For example, the function

$$G = \sum_{q=1}^{Q} a_q \left(\sum_{m \in D_q} \left(\sum_{j \in B_m} y_j^{\frac{1}{1-\sigma_m}} \right)^{\frac{1-\sigma_m}{1-\delta_q}} \right)^{1-\delta_q} \quad (22)$$

where $\cup B_m = \{1,\ldots,J\}$, satisfies the hypotheses provided $1 > \sigma_m \geq \delta_q \geq 0$ for $m \in D_q$. The choice probabilities for Equation (22) and analogous functions can be written as sums of products of conditional and marginal probabilities, in a manner generalising Equation (19), with each probability element having a multinomial-logit form, and the denominator in each element equalling a representative term in the succeeding element.

Choice probabilities of the form (19) were apparently first derived, for the case of three alternatives and $B_1 = \{1\}$, $B_2 = \{2,3\}$ by Scott Cardell (7). For the case of disjoint B_m, the form (19) has been discovered, independently, by Daly and Zachary (12), Williams (42), and Ben-Akiva and Lerman (4). The demonstration by Daly and Zachary that this choice model is consistent with random utility maximisation is particularly noteworthy in that it permits generalisation of the GEV model and provides a powerful tool for testing the consistency of choice models: suppose alternative i has a utility . $U_i = w_i + y(z_i) + \varepsilon_i$, where $V_i \equiv w_i + y(z_i)$ is the systematic component of utility and $(\varepsilon_1,\ldots,\varepsilon_J)$ is a jointly distributed random vector, with a distribution function not depending on $(w_1,\ldots,w_J)$, but in general depending on $(z_1,\ldots,z_J)$. Suppose the choice probabilities satisfy

$$P_i \equiv P_i(V_1,\ldots,V_J;z_1,\ldots,z_J) = \text{Prob } [V_i + \varepsilon_i \geq V_j + \varepsilon_j \text{ for } j \neq 1]$$

$$\equiv \text{Prob } [V_i - V_j \geq \nu_j - \nu_i \text{ for } j \neq i] , \quad (23)$$

where $\nu_i = \varepsilon_i - \varepsilon_1$. Define the expected value of the maximum of the utilities U_j,

$$\bar{U}(V_1,\ldots,V_J;z_1,\ldots,z_J) = E \text{ Max}_j U_j \quad . \quad (24)$$

285 Chapter 13

Then, the choice probabilities satisfy*

$$P_i(V_1,\ldots,V_J;z_1,\ldots,z_J) = \frac{\partial}{\partial V_i}\bar{U}(V_1,\ldots,V_J;z_1,\ldots,z_J) \quad , \tag{25}$$

and the joint distribution of the differences of the random components of utility, $(\nu_2,\ldots,\nu_J)$, satisfies

$$F(\nu_2,\ldots,\nu_J) = P_1(0,-\nu_2,\ldots,-\nu_J) \quad . \tag{26}$$

Conversely, any choice probability functions $P_i(V_1,\ldots,V_J;z_1,\ldots,z_J)$ which satisfy the necessary and sufficient conditions for $(P_1,\ldots,P_J)$ to be the gradient of a potential** $(\bar{U})$ and for $P_1(0,-\nu_2,\ldots,-\nu_J)$ to be a distribution function,*** satisfy (23), and are consistent with stochastic utility maximisation. The key assumption, and only significant restriction, underlying this result is that the random utilities U_i have linear components w_i with the property that the joint distribution of the stochastic components does not depend on $(w_1,\ldots,w_J)$.****

---

* This condition has been used by Domencich and McFadden (15) and Harris and Tanner (19) to establish a classical identity between social welfare, defined by the expected value (or average over the population) of the maximum utility for each individual, and consumer surplus, defined by the area under the market demand curves, or choice probabilities. The identity can be verified directly by writing out the definition of expected maximum utility and differentiating. The basic assumption required for the social welfare identity is a linear 'transferable' numéraire commodity. A consequence of the additively separable structure of errors specified in (23) is that the choice probabilities are invariant with respect to location; i.e.,

$P_i(V_1 + a,\ldots,V_J + a;z_1,\ldots,z_J) \equiv P_i(V_1,\ldots,V_J;z_1,\ldots,z_J)$.).

** Suppose $P_i(V_1,\ldots,V_J)$ is continuous and continuously differentiable. Then, a necessary and sufficient condition for $(P_1,\ldots,P_J)$ to be the gradient of a potential $(\bar{U})$ is that $\partial P_i/\partial V_j = \partial P_j/\partial V_i$. If P_i is invariant with respect to location, then $\bar{U}$ is homogeneous with respect to location; i.e. $\bar{U}(V_1 + a,\ldots,V_J + a) = \bar{U}(V_1,\ldots,V_J) + a$.

*** See Cramer (11) Sect. 8.4. The key condition for $F(\nu_2,\ldots,\nu_J)$ to be a distribution is that the (J - 1)st difference, $\Delta^{J-1}F$, be non-negative. If F is continuous and almost everywhere J-1 times differentiable, this condition reduces to the requirement that the density $\partial^{J-1}F/\partial\nu_2\ldots\partial\nu_J$ be non-negative.

****Strictly, the condition is that the joint distribution of differences of the random components of utility, $F(\nu_2,\ldots,\nu_J)$, not depend on $(w_1,\ldots,w_J)$.

The GEV model satisfies (25) with $\overline{U} = \log G(e^{V_1},\ldots,e^{V_J})$.

Relation of Sequential MNL and GEV Models

The choice probabilities corresponding to (22) can be specialised to the sequential MNL model described in Equations (11 - 15), as we shall now show. This result establishes that sequential MNL models are consistent with individual utility maximisation for appropriate parameter values, and that the coefficients of inclusive values can be used to obtain estimates of the similarity parameters σ and δ. It is hence possible to estimate some GEV models using sequential MNL models and inclusive values. Further, the GEV class provides a generalisation containing alternative sequential MNL models, and could be estimated directly to test the presence of a sequential or tree structure.

To obtain the sequential model (11 - 15) from Equation (22), index alternatives by mda for mode m, destination d, and auto availability a, and specialise (22) to the form

$$G = \sum_a \left(\sum_d \left(\sum_m y_{mda}^{\frac{1}{1-\sigma}} \right)^{\frac{1-\sigma}{1-\delta}} \right)^{1-\delta}, \quad 0 \leq \sigma \leq \delta < 1 . \tag{27}$$

Assume $V_{mda} = (1-\sigma)\alpha' x_{mda} + (1-\delta)\beta' y_{da} + \gamma' z_a$. Then (17) yields

$$P_{mda} = \frac{e^{\frac{V_{mda}}{1-\sigma}}}{\sum_n e^{\frac{V_{nda}}{1-\sigma}}} \cdot \frac{\left(\sum_n e^{\frac{V_{nda}}{1-\sigma}} \right)^{\frac{1-\sigma}{1-\delta}}}{\sum_c \left(\sum_n e^{\frac{V_{nca}}{1-\sigma}} \right)^{\frac{1-\sigma}{1-\delta}}} \cdot \frac{\left\{ \sum_c \left(\sum_n e^{\frac{V_{nca}}{1-\sigma}} \right)^{\frac{1-\sigma}{1-\delta}} \right\}^{1-\delta}}{\sum_b \left\{ \sum_c \left(\sum_n e^{\frac{V_{ncb}}{1-\sigma}} \right)^{\frac{1-\sigma}{1-\delta}} \right\}^{1-\delta}} \tag{28}$$

$$= \frac{e^{\alpha' x_{mda}}}{\sum_n e^{\alpha' x_{nda}}} \cdot \frac{e^{\beta' y_{da} + \frac{1-\sigma}{1-\delta} I_{da}}}{\sum_c e^{\beta' y_{ca} + \frac{1-\sigma}{1-\delta} I_{ca}}} \cdot \frac{e^{\gamma' z_a + (1-\delta) J_a}}{\sum_b e^{\gamma' z_b + (1-\delta) J_b}}$$

where

$$I_{da} = \log \sum_n e^{\alpha' x_{nda}}$$

$$J_a = \log \sum_c e^{\beta' y_{ca} + \frac{1-\sigma}{1-\delta} I_{ca}} .$$

This is precisely the sequential model (11 - 15), with $\theta = (1-\sigma)/(1-\delta)$ and $\lambda = 1 - \delta$. Hence, we have established that *a sufficient* condition for a nested logit model to be consistent with individual utility maximisation is that the coefficient of each inclusive value lie between zero and one, $0 < \theta , \lambda \leq 1$. (The preceding demonstration for three-level trees is readily generalised to trees of any depth. The simplest proof is by induction.) Application of the Daly-Zachary test shows that this condition is also *necessary* for consistency with random utility maximisation if the domain of $(V_2 - V_1, \ldots, V_J - V_1)$ is unrestricted. When the necessary and sufficient condition $0 < \theta , \lambda \leq 1$ is satisfied, $1 - \theta$ is an index of the similarity of alternative modes, while $1 - \lambda$ is an index of the similarity of alternative destinations.

Computation of the MNP Model

The multinomial-probit model is an appealing conceptual model. It allows consideration of stochastic components for tastes and unobserved attributes within an alternative, and provides a way of specifying the *structure* of dependence between alternatives. However, MNP choice probabilities can be expressed exactly only as multivariate or iterated integrals of dimension J - 1, where J is the number of alternatives. Exact calculation by numerical integration is very fast for J = 2 or 3, moderately costly for J = 4, and impractical on a large scale for $J \geq 5$. One of the more effective direct numerical integration methods, adapted for transport applications, is due to Hausman and Wise (20).

Two recent contributions have provided techniques for approximating MNP choice probabilities at moderate cost. This has made MNP a practical alternative for many transport applications. The first method, due to Manski (25), applies a Monte Carlo procedure directly to the utilities of alternatives. Suppose J + 1 alternatives, with utilities $U_i = V_i + \varepsilon_i$, where $(\varepsilon_1, \ldots, \varepsilon_{J+1})$ is multivariate normal with zero means and covariance matrix $\Sigma = (\sigma_{ij})$. For given values of V_i, vectors $(\varepsilon_1, \ldots, \varepsilon_{J+1})$ from the multivariate distribution can be drawn, and the frequency with which utility is maximised at alternative i recorded. These frequencies approximate the exact MNP probabilities when the number of Monte Carlo repetitions is large. Because this method involves repetitive simple calculations, it can be programmed in computer assembly language to operate quite efficiently. The approach is appealing in its generality - any joint distribution of the unobserved effects can be assumed. In practice, the method is most effective when a relatively good initial approximation to the frequencies is available.

The second approximation method, due to Daganzo,

Bouthelier and Sheffi (13), uses a procedure suggested by Clark (8) to approximate the maximum of bivariate normal variables by a normal variable. When the correlation of the variables is non-negative, this approximation is accurate within a few per cent. Suppose J + 1 alternatives, with utilities $U_i = V_i + \varepsilon_i$ and $(\varepsilon_1,\ldots,\varepsilon_{J+1})$ distributed multivariate normal, zero means and covariance matrix Σ. The probability that the first alternative is chosen is then

$$P_1 = \text{Prob}\ [V_1 + \varepsilon_1 > V_j + \varepsilon_j \quad \text{for } j = 2,\ldots,J+1] \tag{29}$$

$$= \text{Prob}\ [V_1 - V_{J+1} + \varepsilon_1 - \varepsilon_{J+1} > V_j - V_{J+1} + \varepsilon_j - \varepsilon_{J+1}$$

$$\text{for } j = 2,\ldots,J \text{ and } V_1 - V_{J+1} + \varepsilon_1 - \varepsilon_{J+1} > 0]\ .$$

Define $V_j = V_j - V_{J+1}$ and $y_i = \varepsilon_i - \varepsilon_{J+1}$. Then, $(y_1,\ldots,y_J)$ is multivariate normal with mean zero and covariance matrix $\Omega = (\omega_{ij})$, where $\omega_{ij} = \sigma_{ij} + \sigma_{J+1,J+1} - \sigma_{i,J+1} - \sigma_{j,J+1}$. Hence

$$P_1 = \text{Prob}\ [v_1 + y_1 > 0 \text{ and } v_1 + y_1 > v_j + y_j \quad \text{for } j = 2,\ldots,J]$$

$$= \int_{y_1=-v_1}^{\infty} n_1(y_1) N_{(1)}((v_1 - v_j + y_1)\,|\,y_1)\,dy_1 \tag{30}$$

where $n_{Y(X)}(y|x)$ denotes the normal density for the vector of variables indexed by Y, conditioned on the vector of variables indexed by X ; $N_{Y(X)}(y|x)$ denotes the corresponding cumulative distribution function, $N_{Y(X)}(y|x) = \int_{-\infty}^{y} n_{Y(X)}(y'|x)dy'$

and $n_Y(y)$ is the marginal density of the variables indexed by Y. As a shorthand, the set of all indices, or the set of all indices exluding those on which a distribution is conditioned, are omitted. Thus, $N_{(1)}$ means $N_{2,\ldots,J(1)}$. The form (30), involving J integrals, is the basis for exact calculations of P_1. Alternately, write

$$P_1 = \text{Prob}\ [v_1 + y_1 > 0 \text{ and } v_1 + y_1 > \max_{j=2,\ldots,J} (v_j + y_j)]\ . \tag{31}$$

The Clark method considers trivariate normal random variables (X_1,X_2,X_3), and approximates the bivariate distribution of $(X_1,\max(X_2,X_3))$ by a bivariate normal distribution with the same first and second moments. The approximation rests on the fact that these moments for $(X_1,\max(X_2,X_3))$ can be calculated exactly in a straightforward manner. Applied recursively to the expression

$$y_0 = \max(v_2 + y_2, \max(v_3 + y_3, \ldots, \max(v_{J-1} + y_{J-1}, v_J + y_J)\ldots) \tag{32}$$

289 Chapter 13

the method allows the distribution of (y_1, y_0) to be approximated by a bivariate normal distribution $n_1(y_1)n_{0(1)}(y_0|y_1)$, so that Equation (30) is approximated by the univariate integral

$$P_1 = \int_{y_1=-v_1}^{\infty} n_1(y_1)N_{0(1)}(v_1 + y_1|y_1)dy_1 \ , \tag{33}$$

where $N_{0(1)}(y_0|y_1) = \int_{-\infty}^{y_0} n_{0(1)}(y_0'|y_1)dy_0'$. Thus, an MNP choice probability for J + 1 alternatives is approximated by a univariate integral involving a univariate normal density and univariate normal cumulative distribution function (which can be accurately approximated computationally by a series expansion). The approximation requires J - 2 applications of the Clark formula.

Manski (25) has reported good results in maximum-likelihood search methods using the approximation above, with search directions determined by numerical evaluation of derivatives. This suggests that the bias caused by the approximation is relatively stationary for evaluation of probabilities at neighbouring points. This fortuitous conclusion suggests that it is probably unnecessary to obtain analytic derivatives of P_1 with respect to parameters in statistical routines. On the other hand, it is possible that the use of analytic derivatives could decrease computation time. The following argument shows that the Clark procedure can be applied to yield quick approximations to analytic derivatives.

From (30)

$$\frac{\partial P_1}{\partial \theta} = n_1(-v_1)N_{(1)}((-v_j)|-v_1)\frac{\partial v_1}{\partial \theta}$$

$$+ \sum_{j=2}^{J} \frac{\partial(v_1-v_j)}{\partial \theta} \int_{y_1=-v_1}^{\infty} n_{1j}(y_1, v_1-v_j+y_1)N_{(1j)}((v_1-v_k+y_1)|y_1, v_1-v_j+y_1)dy_1 \tag{34}$$

The term $N_{(1)}((-v_j)|-v_1)$ can be approximated by applying the Clark procedure to the conditional distribution. The integrals in the last right-hand term of (34) each have the essential structure of (30), since $n_{1j}(y_1, v_1 - v_j + y_1)$ is proportional to a normal density for y_1 whose mean and variance are computed by a straightforward completion of the square. Then, each integral in this term can be approximated by the corresponding analogue of (33). We conclude that the analytic derivative $\partial P_1/\partial\theta$ can be computed by the evaluation of J univariate integrals, each with the generic form of (33), and each involving J - 3 applications of the Clark procedure. For most problems, where the number of parameters exceeds J, this computation should be considerably faster than numerical computation of the derivatives.

The probability P_1 also depends parametrically on the covariance matrix Ω. The requirement that Ω be positive definite can be imposed by writing $\Omega^{-1} = TT'$, where $T = (\tau_{ij})$ is a lower triangular matrix with positive diagonal elements. Then, $|\Omega|^{-1/2} = \tau_{11} \ldots \tau_{JJ}$. Alternatively, Ω^{-1} may be represented as an unknown non-negative linear combination, with full rank, of known positive semi-definite matrices. Analogues for the parameters of Ω^{-1} of the analytic derivatives above are computationally complex, and their use appears unlikely to improve significantly on numerical differentiation.

The key to the accuracy of the Daganzo-Bouthelier-Sheffi approximation is the accuracy of the Clark procedure. Because the true distribution of the maximum of two normal variates is skewed to the right, one would expect the procedure to tend to under-estimate small probabilities. The approximation will be best when the variates are positively correlated, with widely differing means, and worse when they are negatively correlated with similar means. It may be possible to adjust the Clark formulae empirically to improve their accuracy for computation of small probabilities. Alternately, it would be interesting to explore the possibility of adapting the Clark methodology to other trivariate distribution. In particular, if the generalised extreme-value distribution were utilised, then the only point of approximation would be the initial fit to the multivariate normal density, since maxima of GEV distributed variates are again GEV distributed. This would limit approximation error as J increases, in contrast to the Clark procedure which becomes less accurate with large numbers of alternatives.

STATISTICAL ESTIMATION METHODS AND SAMPLING STRATEGIES

Maximum Likelihood Estimation

The statistical estimation of individual-choice models by the maximum likelihood method is now well established. For random samples of individuals, this procedure can be shown in general to produce estimates with good statistical properties, at least in large samples. The problems remaining in application of maximum likelihood estimation in this context are primarily computational - the issues of rapid computation of choice probabilities, the concavity or unimodality of the log likelihood function, and the relative convergence speed of alternative algorithms.

Estimation of sequential models, with inclusive values obtained using estimates from earlier stages of the model, has been carried out by many investigators such as Domencich and McFadden (15), and Ben-Akiva (3) treating each stage as an independent estimation problem. This procedure neglects the fact that the use of inclusive value measures which are themselves statistics change the asymptotic distribution of the estimators, and leads to biased estimates of the standard errors of the estimators. This problem has been pointed out by Amemiya (1), who provides the corrected asymptotic estimators for the standard errors of the estimates.

Estimation in Choice-Based Samples

Several recent papers have considered the problem of statistical estimation of choice models using data collected by sampling procedures other than random sampling. Of particular interest are *choice-based* samples, utilising data collected from 'on-board' or 'destination' surveys. Such data sources are often available to transport analysts from marketing and operations departments of operating agencies, or can be commissioned at low cost relative to random household surveys. Manski and Lerman (23) have shown that treating choice-based samples as if they were random and calculating estimators appropriate to random samples will generally yield inconsistent estimates. (In an MNL model with alternative-specific dummy variables, the inconsistency is confined to the dummy variable coefficients.) They introduce a weighted likelihood function whose maximisation is shown to yield consistent estimates.

Manski and McFadden* have considered more generally the problem of estimation of discrete choice models under alternative sample designs. The discrete choice problem can be defined by a finite set C of mutually exclusive alternative responses, a space of attributes Z, assumed to be a subset of a finite-dimensional vector space, a generalised probability density, $p(z)$ $[z \in Z]$, giving the distribution of attributes in the population, and a *response probability*, or *choice probability*, $P(i|z,\theta^*)$, specifying the conditional probability of selection of alternative $i \in C$, given attributes $z \in Z$. Prior knowledge of causal structure is assumed to allow the analyst to specify the response model $P(i|z,\cdot)$ up to a parameter vector θ^* contained in a subset Θ of a finite-dimensional vector space. The analyst's problem is to estimate θ^* from a suitable sample of subjects and their associated responses.

The probability of (i,z) pairs in the population is given by

$$f(i,z) = P(i|z,\theta^*)p(z) \quad . \quad [(i,z) \in C \times Z] \tag{35}$$

The analyst can draw observations of (i,z) pairs from $C \times Z$

---

*Manski, C.F. and McFadden, D., 'Alternative estimates and sample designs for discrete choice analysis', Department of Economics, University of California at Berkeley (mimeo)(1978).

according to one of various sampling rules. The problem of interest is first, given any sampling rule, to determine how θ^* may be estimated, and second, to assess the relative advantages of alternative sampling rules and estimation methods.

The data layout can be visualised using a contingency table, as illustrated in Figure 13.1. An observation (i,z) occurs in the population with frequency f(i,z). The row sums give the marginal distributions of attributes p(z), while the column sums give the population shares of responses Q(i). The joint frequency f(i,z) can be written either in terms of the conditional probability of i given z, or choice probability, or in terms of the conditional probability of z given i, as the formulae in the figure illustrate.

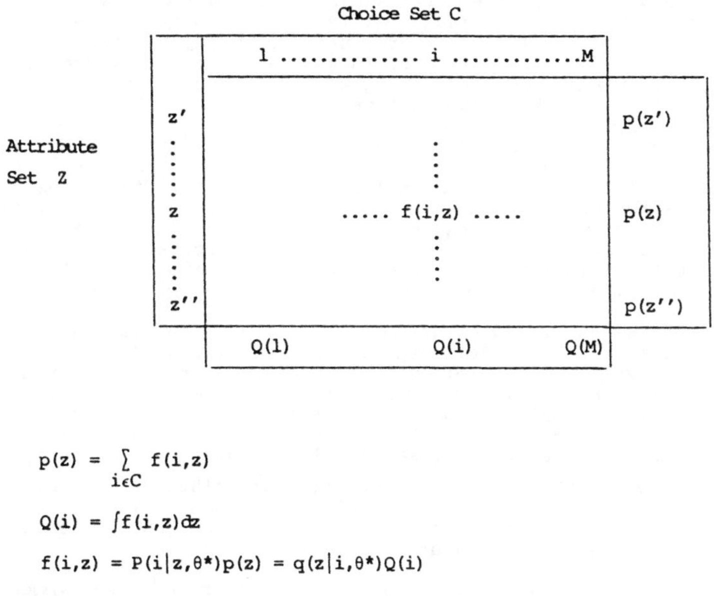

$$p(z) = \sum_{i \epsilon C} f(i,z)$$

$$Q(i) = \int f(i,z)dz$$

$$f(i,z) = P(i|z,\theta^*)p(z) = q(z|i,\theta^*)Q(i)$$

Figure 13.1 Contingency Table Layout of Observations

The feature of the quantal response problem which distinguishes it from the general analysis of discrete data is the postulate that the response probability $P(i|z,\theta^*)$ belong to a known parametric family, and reflects an underlying link from z to i which will continue to hold even if the distribution p(z) of the explanatory variables changes. This postulate is fundamental to the concept of 'scientific explanation'. If the response probability function is invariant over populations with different distributions of attributes, then it defines a 'law' which transcends the character of specific sets of data. Otherwise, the model provides only a device for summarising data, and fails to provide a key ingredient of 'explanation' - predictive power. Alternately, given a population $C \times Z$ with probability distribution specified by $f(i,z)$, one might, in the absence of any knowledge of the process relating i's to z's, obtain a random sample from $C \times Z$ and directly examine the joint distribution $f(i,z)$. This exploratory data analysis approach is exemplified by the literature on associations in contingency tables, where it is assumed only that Z is finite. See, for example, Goodman and Kruskal (16), Haberman (17,18), and Bishop, Fienberg, and Holland (5).

If one believes that the elements of C index conceptually distinct populations of z values, then the natural analytical approach is to decompose $f(i,z)$ into the product $f(i,z) = q(z|i)Q(i)$, where $q(z|i)$ gives the distribution of z within the population indexed by i and $Q(i)$ is the proportion of the population with this index. This is the approach taken in discriminant analysis. There, prior knowledge allows the analyst to specify $q(z|i)$ up to a parametric family, and a sample suitable for estimating the unknown parameters is obtained from the subpopulation i (2,21).

When a well-defined process generates a value from C given any $z \in Z$, then the decomposition $f(i,z) = P(i|z,\theta^*)p(z)$ is appropriate. This decomposition, and the attending focus on the structural relation embodied in $P(i|z,\theta^*)$, is clearly the natural one for the analysis of choice data. A separate and interesting question is whether specific parametric models permit estimation of the parameter vector θ^* of $P(i|z,\theta^*)$ from convenient parameterisations of $f(i,z)$ or $q(z|i)$.

Manski and McFadden attempt to provide a general theory of estimation for quantal response models. The scope of the investigation is as follows: consider the problem of estimating θ^* from stratified samples of (i,z) observations. A stratified sampling process is one in which the analyst establishes an index set B, partitions $C \times Z$ into mutually exclusive and exhaustive measurable subsets $(C \times Z)_b$, $b \in B$, and specifies a suitable probability distribution over B. To obtain an (i,z) observation, he draws a subset of $C \times Z$ according to the specified distribution and then samples at random from within the drawn subset.

Within the class of all stratification rules, two symmetric types of stratification are of particular statistical and empirical interest. In 'exogenous' sampling, the analyst partitions Z into subsets Z_b, $b \in B$, and lets $(C \times Z)_b = C \times Z_b$. In 'endogenous' or 'choice-based' sampling, he partitions C into subsets C_b, $b \in B$, and lets $(C \times Z)_b = C_b \times Z$. Less formally, in exogenous sampling the analyst selects decision-makers and observes their choices while in choice-based sampling the analyst selects alternatives and observes decision-makers choosing them. In Figure 13.1, exogenous sampling corresponds to stratifying on rows, and then sampling randomly from each row, while choice-based sampling corresponds to stratifying on columns, and then sampling randomly from each column.

Manski and McFadden make a detailed statistical examination of maximum likelihood estimation of θ^* in both exogenous and choice-based samples. They find that application of maximum likelihood is wholly classical in exogenous samples. In choice-based samples, however, the form of the maximum likelihood estimate (MLE) depends crucially on whether the analyst has available certain prior information, namely, the marginal distributions $p(z)$, $z \in Z$, or $Q(i)$, $i \in C$, where $Q(i) = \int_Z P(i|z,\theta^*)p(z)dz$

The maximum likelihood estimator of θ in a choice-based sample when p is known and Q is unknown satisfies

$$\max_{\theta\in\Theta} \sum_{n=1}^{N} \log P(i_n|z_n,\theta) - \sum_{n=1}^{N} \int_Z P(i_n|z,\theta)p(z)dz \ . \tag{36}$$

When Q and p are both known, Equation (36) is maximised subject to the constraints

$$Q(i) = \int_Z P(i_n|z,\theta)p(z)dz \ . \tag{37}$$

When p is unknown, the classical conditions for maximum likelihood estimation are not met. However, several alternative non-classical maximum likelihood and pseudo-maximum likelihood methods are available which yield consistent estimators.

When Q is known and p is unknown, Cosslett (9) has shown that the non-classical full-information maximum likelihood estimator satisfies

$$\max_{\theta\in\Theta} \min_{\lambda\geq 0} \sum_{n=1}^{N} \log \left\{ P(i_n|z_n,\theta)\left(\sum_{j\in C} \lambda_j Q(j)\right) \Big/ \left(\sum_{j\in C} \lambda_j P(j|z_n,\theta)\right) \right\} \ . \tag{38}$$

A second estimator, introduced by Manski and Lerman (23) and termed WESML, satisfies

$$\max_{\theta\in\Theta} \sum_{n=1}^{N} w(i_n) \log P(i_n|z_n,\theta) \ , \tag{39}$$

where $w(i) = Q(i)/H(i)$ and $H(i)$ is the sampling frequency for alternative i. Two other consistent estimators, introduced by Manski and McFadden, satisfy

$$\max_{\theta\in\Theta} \left\{ \sum_{n=1}^{N} \log P(i_n|z_n,\theta) - \sum_{n=1}^{N} \log \sum_{j\in C} \frac{Q(j)}{N_j} \sum_{m\in N(j)} P(i_n|z_m,\theta) \right\} \ , \tag{40}$$

where N(j) is the set of observations where alternative j is chosen and N_j is the number of elements in N(j); and

$$\max_{\theta\epsilon\Theta} \sum_{n=1}^{N} \log \left\{ P(i_n|z_n,\theta) \frac{H(i_n)}{Q(i_n)} \Big/ \sum_{j\epsilon C} P(j|z_n,\theta) \frac{H(j)}{Q(j)} \right\} . \tag{41}$$

If both p and Q are unknown in a choice-based sample, then provided an identification condition is satisfied, Manski and McFadden show that the non-classical full-information maximum likelihood estimator satisfies

$$\max_{\theta\epsilon\Theta} \max_{\lambda\geq 0} \sum_{n=1}^{N} \log \left\{ P(i_n|z_n,\theta)\lambda_{i_n} \Big/ \sum_{j\epsilon C} P(j|z_n,\theta)\lambda_j \right\} . \tag{42}$$

An important case in which the identification condition *fails* is the MNL model, where in the absence of a knowledge of Q there is a confounding of the effects of Q and alternative-specific dummies.

A second consistent estimator for this case is obtained by maximising Equation (40), with Q determined as a solution to the equations

$$Q(i) = \sum_{j\epsilon C} Q(j) \frac{1}{N_j} \sum_{m\epsilon N(j)} P(i|z_m,\theta) . \tag{43}$$

Note that one can, with some loss of efficiency, obtain consistent estimates for an information case by using a consistent estimator which ignores some available information. For example, the estimators (38) or (39) could be used in the case both p and Q known, and the estimator (42) could be used in any of the information cases.

Selection of a Sample Design and Estimation Method

Sample designs and estimation methods differ in terms of sampling and computation costs, and precision in parameter estimates and forecasts. Cost comparisons are situation-specific, and only a few general observations can be made. Comparison of the precision of alternative estimators can be made for large samples using the asymptotic covariance matrices of the estimators. In a few cases, the difference of two covariance matrices is positive semi-definite for all possible parameter vectors, and a uniform ranking can be made. More generally, rankings will depend on the true parameter vector and on the true distribution of explanatory variables. Then, rankings of designs and estimators will usually require a Bayesian approach utilising *a priori* beliefs on the distributions of parameters, perhaps based on pilot samples and previous studies. Consider sampling costs. In general, substantial economies can be achieved by stratifications designed to make it easier to locate and observe subjects. For example, exogenous cluster sampling, in which respondents are clustered geographically, reduces interviewer access time. Stratification on other exogenous variables, such as employer, may also reduce location cost. In many applications, choice-based sampling greatly simplifies locating subjects. For example, subjects choosing alternative travel modes can be sampled economically at the site of choice. Choice-based sampling has the greatest potential economy in applications where some responses are rare (e.g. choice of a seldom-used travel mode) or are difficult to observe accurately in an exogenously drawn sample.

Computation costs are comparable in most of the estimation methods considered by Manski and McFadden. The primary component of computation costs is usually the evaluation of response probabilities at each sample point. For some models (e.g. linear), this cost is minimal, for others (e.g. multinomial logit), moderate, and for some (e.g. multinomial probit), substantial.

Sample Designs

Consider the precision of estimates obtained by alternative methods from alternative sample designs. We note first that the level of precision, and possibly the ranking of alternatives, will depend on the prior information available on the marginal distributions p and Q. We shall assume the state of this information is fixed. However, it should be noted that in practice the question of drawing observations on p or Q at some cost in order to utilise more efficient estimators of the response probability function may be an important part of the overall design decision.

Cosslett (9) has investigated the efficiency of alternative choice-based sample designs and estimators for binary probit, logit and arctan models with a single explanatory variable. All three models have form $P(1|z,\theta) = \psi(\theta z)$, where

$$\psi(y) = \begin{cases} \frac{1}{\sqrt{2\pi}} \int_{-\infty}^{y} e^{-x^2/2}\, dx & \text{for probit,} \\ 1/(1 + e^{-y}) & \text{for logit,} \\ \frac{1}{2} + \frac{1}{\pi} \tan^{-1} y & \text{for arctan,} \end{cases} \tag{44}$$

and z is assumed to be normally distributed with mean 2 and variance 1/2. Choice-based sample designs vary in the proportion of the sample H(1) drawn from the subpopulation choosing alternative 1. The optimal sample design for any estimator is determined by the value of H(1) which minimises the asymptotic variance of the estimator.

We concentrate on the case with p unknown and Q known. The maximum likelihood estimator (38) with an optimal sample design provides a standard against which other estimators and sample designs can be measured. Define the *asymptotic efficiency* of an alternative estimator and sample design to

297 Chapter 13

be the asymptotic variance of the maximum likelihood estimator with optimal design, divided by the asymptotic variance of the alternative estimator. Consider as alternative estimators the WESML estimator (39), the Manski-McFadden estimator (41), and the 'conditional' maximum likelihood estimator (42), which does not use information on Q. Table 13.1 gives the asymptotic efficiencies of these estimators for each model for selected values of θ. Three sample designs are considered: 'pseudo-random' sampling in proportion to population shares, H(1) = Q(1); sampling equally from each alternative, H(1) = 1/2; and sampling optimally for the estimator. The optimising values of H(1) for these estimators are also given in the table.

TABLE 13.1 Asymptotic efficiency of choice-based sample designs and estimators[a]

	Pseudo-random design H(1)=Q(1)	Equal shares H(1)=1/2	Optimal design	Optimal value of H(1)
Probit model	%	%	%	%
Q(1) = 0.75[b]				
MLE (38)	87.1	95.0	100.0	0.13
MM (41)	3.1	4.5	4.5	0.46
WESML (39)	3.1	4.4	4.4	0.47
Cond ML (42)	0.4	0.6	0.6	0.49
Q(1) = 0.9				
MLE (38)	62.1	95.2	100.0	0.30
MM (41)	6.3	20.5	21.0	0.42
WESML (39)	6.3	19.1	19.2	0.47
Cond ML (42)	1.3	3.6	3.7	0.45
Q(1) = 0.95				
MLE (38)	40.7	95.5	100.0	0.34
MM (41)	6.1	37.9	39.2	0.39
WESML (39)	6.1	32.0	32.0	0.50
Cond ML (42)	1.6	7.5	7.6	0.43
Q(1) = 0.99				
MLE (38)	9.5	96.9	100.0	0.38
MM (41)	3.4	78.2	81.2	0.38
WESML (39)	3.4	36.8	40.6	0.66
Cond ML (42)	1.4	17.8	17.8	0.46
Q(1) = 0.995				
MLE (38)	4.5	98.4	100.0	0.42
MM (41)	2.6	91.2	92.9	0.41
WESML (39)	2.6	23.4	30.1	0.77
Cond ML (42)	1.4	23.0	23.0	0.49

	Pseudo-random design H(1)=Q(1)	Equal shares H(1)=1/2	Optimal design	Optimal value of H(1)
Logit model	%	%	%	%
$Q(1) = 0.75^b$				
MLE (38)	86.7	94.5	100.0	0.09
MM (41)	2.9	4.0	4.0	0.47
WESML (39)	2.9	4.0	4.0	0.48
Cond ML (42)	0.3	0.4	0.4	0.50
Q(1) = 0.9				
MLE (38)	62.2	94.3	100.0	0.26
MM (41)	5.2	16.1	16.2	0.44
WESML (39)	5.2	15.1	15.1	0.48
Cond ML (42)	0.8	1.8	1.8	0.50
Q(1) = 0.95				
MLE (38)	41.5	94.7	100.0	0.30
MM (41)	4.9	28.9	29.5	0.42
WESML (39)	4.9	24.8	24.8	0.51
Cond ML (42)	0.9	3.4	3.4	0.50
Q(1) = 0.99				
MLE (38)	9.0	95.0	100.0	0.35
MM (41)	2.7	66.5	69.3	0.38
WESML (39)	2.7	31.7	34.4	0.65
Cond ML (42)	0.9	8.9	8.9	0.50
Q(1) = 0.995				
MLE (38)	3.9	95.7	100.0	0.37
MM (41)	2.1	83.4	86.9	0.37
WESML (39)	2.1	20.3	25.6	0.76
Cond ML (42)	1.0	12.9	12.9	0.51
Arctan model				
$Q(1) = 0.75^b$				
MLE (38)	83.5	91.3	100.0	0.00
MM (41)	1.8	2.4	2.4	0.49
WESML (39)	1.8	2.4	2.4	0.49
Cond ML (42)	0.08	0.09	0.09	0.55
Q(1) = 0.9				
MLE (38)	52.9	84.0	100.0	0.00
MM (41)	1.7	4.7	4.7	0.49
WESML (39)	1.7	4.6	4.6	0.51
Cond ML (42)	0.04	0.04	0.05	0.73
Q(1) = 0.95				
MLE (38)	27.0	78.1	100.0	0.00
MM (41)	1.1	5.9	5.9	0.49
WESML (39)	1.1	5.4	5.4	0.53
Cond ML (42)	0.04	0.03	0.04	0.83

299 Chapter 13

	Pseudo-random design H(1)=Q(1)	Equal shares H(1)=1/2	Optimal design	Optimal value of H(1)
	%	%	%	%
Q(1) = 0.99				
MLE (38)	2.2	64.4	100.0	0.00
MM (41)	0.5	11.8	11.9	0.46
WESML (39)	0.5	5.4	5.9	0.65
Cond ML (42)	0.04	0.03	0.05	0.94
Q(1) = 0.995				
MLE (38)	0.8	60.0	100.0	0.00
MM (41)	0.4	21.2	21.2	0.42
WESML (39)	0.4	4.1	5.1	0.74
Cond ML (42)	0.05	0.03	0.07	0.96

a. Adapted from Cosslett [9]. Asymptotic efficiency is defined by the ratio of asymptotic variances, with the optimal choice-based sample design maximum likelihood estimator as the standard. Note that when Q(1) is not observed, the estimators (38), (39) and (41) are not available, and (42) is asymptotically efficient.
b. For the one-parameter model, knowledge of p(z) and Q(1) determines θ; for comparability of models, Q(1) rather than θ has been given.

The results in Table 13.1 suggest the following conclusions:

1 Knowledge of the aggregate share Q(1) is of great value when the maximum likelihood estimator (38) is used, as indicated by the low efficiency of the conditional maximum likelihood estimator (42) which does not utilise this knowledge. Note however, that the information contained in Q(1) will be greatest for a one-variable model without an alternative-specific dummy, and in general the efficiency differential will be smaller.
2 The Manski-McFadden estimator (41) is uniformly more efficient than the WESML estimator (39), but the differential is small when the true parameter value is small. Both (39) and (41) have low efficiency relative to maximum likelihood for small parameter values, but (41) is relatively efficient for large parameter values.
3 The equal shares sample design is generally quite efficient for maximum likelihood estimation, and for all the estimators yields efficiencies comparable to those for the optimal sample designs. The behaviour of optimal H(1) is sensitive to the model and to the parameter value. Hence, in the absence of strong prior knowledge on parameter values, the equal shares sample design is recommended.

Table 13.2 compares the relative efficiencies of a choice-based sample design with equal shares and an exogenous random sample design. For Q(1) known, the choice-based design is always more efficient. For Q(1) unknown, the choice-based design is less efficient for the arctan model, and for small parameter values in the remaining models. Given prior beliefs on the correct model and on the value of Q(1), and given a relative cost r of collecting an observation from an equal shares choice-based sample compared with an exogenous random sample, maximum efficiency subject to a fixed sampling budget will be achieved with the choice-based design if and only if the relative efficiency given in Table 13.2 exceeds r.

TABLE 13.2 Relative efficiency of choice-based sample design (with equal shares) and exogenous random sample design, with maximum likelihood estimators[a]

	Q(1)	Q(1) known	Q(1) unknown
Probit	0.75	1.09	0.19
	0.9	1.53	0.57
	0.95	2.35	1.23
	0.99	10.23	5.30
	0.995	21.73	8.83
Logit	0.75	1.09	0.16
	0.9	1.52	0.35
	0.95	2.28	0.69
	0.99	10.54	3.28
	0.995	24.68	6.26
Arctan	0.75	1.09	0.05
	0.9	1.59	0.02
	0.95	2.90	0.03
	0.99	29.04	0.06
	0.995	75.45	0.10

a. Relative efficiency equals the asymptotic variance of the exogenous random sample maximum likelihood estimator divided by that of the choice-based equal share design maximum likelihood estimator. A ratio exceeding one indicates that the choice-based design is more efficient.

Estimation When Alternatives are Sampled Randomly from the Full Choice Set

A particularly advantageous use of choice-based sampling, either in primary data collection, or in synthesising and reducing existing data sets, is in estimation of the MNL model from data on a strict subset of the full choice set. This method can greatly reduce the magnitude of data to be collected and analysed, with attendant savings in time and cost. The property that a choice model can be estimated consistently using data on a strict subset of the choice set is unique to the MNL model, and is a characterisation of the independence from irrelevant alternatives (IIA) property of this model.

The following summary is drawn from McFadden (35). Let C denote the full choice set. We shall assume it does not vary over the sample; however, this is inessential and can easily be generalised. Let $P(i|C,z,\theta^*)$ denote the true selection probabilities. We assume the choice probabilities satisfy the independence from irrelevant alternatives (IIA) assumption,

$$i \in D \subseteq C \Longrightarrow P(i|C,z,\theta) = P(i|D,z,\theta) \sum_{j \in D} P(j|C,z,\theta) \quad (45)$$

which characterises the MNL model.

Now suppose for each case, a subset D is drawn from the set C according to a probability distribution $\pi(D|i,z)$ which may, but need not, be conditioned on the observed choice i. The observed choice may be either in or out of the set D. Examples of π distributions are: (1) choose a fixed subset D of C, independent of the observed choice; (2) choose a random subset D of C, independent of the observed choice; and (3) choose a subset D of C, consisting of the observed choice i and one or more other alternatives, selected randomly.

We give several examples of distributions of type (3):

(3.1) Suppose D is comprised of i plus a sample of alternatives from the set $C \setminus \{i\}$, obtained by considering each element of this set independently, and including it with probability p. Then, the probability of D will depend solely on the number of elements $K = \#(D)$ it contains, and is given by the binomial formula

$$\begin{aligned} \pi(D|i,z) &= p^{K-1}(1-p)^{J-K} \quad \text{if } i \in D \text{ and } K = \#(D)\,, \\ &= 0 \qquad\qquad\qquad\quad \text{if } i \notin D\,, \end{aligned} \quad (46)$$

where J is the number of alternatives in C. For example, the probability that D will be any two-alternative set containing i as one alternative is $(J-1)p(1-p)^{J-2}$.

(3.2) Suppose D is always selected to be a two-element set containing i and one other alternative selected at random. If J is the number of alternatives in C, then

$$\begin{aligned} \pi(D|i,z) &= \frac{1}{J-1} \quad \text{if } D = \{i,j\} \text{ and } j \neq i\,, \\ &= 0 \qquad\;\; \text{otherwise.} \end{aligned} \quad (47)$$

(3.3) Suppose C has four elements, and

$$\pi(\{1,4\}|4) = \pi(\{1,4\}|1) = \pi(\{2,3\}|2) = \pi(\{2,3\}|3) = 1\,, \quad \text{and } \pi(D|i) = 0 \text{ otherwise}\,. \quad (48)$$

(3.4) Suppose C is partitioned into sets $\{C_1,\ldots,C_M\}$, with J_m elements in C_m, and suppose D is formed by choosing i (from the partition set C_n) and one randomly selected alternative from each remaining partition set. Then,

$$\pi(D|i,z) = J_n / \prod_{m=1}^{M} J_m \quad \text{if } i \in D\text{ , } M = \#(D)\text{ , and } D \cap C_m \neq \emptyset \text{ for } m = 1,\ldots,M, \qquad (49)$$
$$= 0 \quad \text{otherwise.}$$

The π distributions of the type (1), (2) and (3.1) to (3.4) all satisfy the following basic property, which guarantees that if an alternative j appears in an assigned set D, then it has the logical possibility of being an observed choice from the set D, in the sense that the assignment mechanism could assign the set D if a choice j is observed:

Positive conditioning property: *If* $j \in D \subseteq C$ *and* $\pi(D|i,z) > 0$, *then* $\pi(D|j,z) > 0$.

The π distributions (1), (2) and (3.1) to (3.3), but not (3.4), satisfy a stronger condition:

Uniform conditioning property: *If* $i,j \in D \subseteq C$, *then* $\pi(D|i,z) = \pi(D|j,z)$.

A distribution with the uniform conditioning property can be written $\pi(D|i,z) = \phi(D,z)X_D(i)$, where $X_D(i)$ equals one for $i \in D$, and zero otherwise.

Consider a sample n = 1,...,N, with the alternative chosen on case n denoted by i_n, and D_n denoting the choice set assigned to this case from the distribution $\pi(D|i_n,z_n)$. Observations with an observed choice not in the assigned set of alternatives are assumed to be excluded from the sample. Write the multinomial logit model in the form

$$P(i|C,z,\theta) = e^{V_i(z,\theta)} \Big/ \sum_{j\in C} e^{V_j(z,\theta)} \text{ ,} \qquad (50)$$

where $V_i(z,\theta)$ is the strict utility of alternative i.

THEOREM 2. If $\pi(D|i,z)$ *satisfies the positive conditioning property and the choice model is multinomial logit, then maximisation of the modified likelihood function*

$$L_N = \frac{1}{N}\sum_{n=1}^{N} \log \left\{ e^{V_{i_n}(z_n,\theta)+\log \pi(D_n|i_n,z_n)} \Big/ \sum_{j\in D_n^K} e^{V_j(z_n,\theta)+\log \pi(D_n|j,z_n)} \right\} \qquad (51)$$

yields, under normal regularity conditions, consistent estimates of θ^*. *When* $\pi(D|i,z)$ *satisfies the uniform conditioning property, then (51) reduces to the standard likelihood function,*

303 Chapter 13

$$L_N = \frac{1}{N}\sum_{n=1}^{N} \log\left\{ e^{V_{i_n}(z_n,\theta)} \Big/ \sum_{j\in D_n} e^{V_j(z_n,\theta)} \right\} . \tag{52}$$

The theorem above assumes the assigned choice set for an observation may depend on the observed choice set and environment for the observation, but is independent of other observations. More generally, a set of observed choices may be used to define the assigned choice set for each observation. For example, a common procedure is to assign to all observations in a traffic analysis zone the set consisting of all the chosen alternatives observed for this zone. Assume there are N zones, with K_n observations in zone n. If $K_n \to \infty$ for each n, then every alternative in C will eventually be chosen by some subject in a zone, and estimators maximising (52), with assigned sets equal to the set of observed choices for the zone, will have the same asymptotic properties as a maximum likelihood estimator for choice from the full set C. Thus, standard maximum likelihood estimation with assigned choice sets given by the set of chosen alternatives in a zone yields consistent estimates under normal regularity conditions and the usual sampling method where the number of observations in each zone becomes large when the overall sample size becomes large.

In the less common case where the number of zones N becomes large, but the number K of observations in each zone is fixed, the procedure above fails in general to yield consistent estimators. (I have benefited from discussions with Joel Horowitz on this problem.) Let $\lambda(\underset{\sim}{i}_n,\underset{\sim}{z}_n,\theta)$ denote the kernel of the 'likelihood' function for zone n, where $\underset{\sim}{i}_n = (i_{1n},\ldots,i_{Kn})$ and $\underset{\sim}{z}_n = (z_{1n},\ldots,z_{Kn})$ are observed in the zone. Define $D_n = D(\underset{\sim}{i}_n) = \{j \mid j = i_k \text{ for some } k = 1,\ldots,K\}$ and $J(D) = \{\underset{\sim}{j} \mid D = \cup_k\{j_k\}\}$. In the standard case,

$$\lambda(\underset{\sim}{i}_n,\underset{\sim}{z}_n,\theta) = \prod_{k=1}^{K} P(i_{kn} \mid D_n, z_{kn},\theta)$$

$$= e^{\sum_k V_{i_{kn}}(z_{kn},\theta)} \Big/ \sum_{\underset{\sim}{j}\in D_n} e^{\sum_k V_{j_k}(z_{kn},\theta)} .$$

Asymptotically, the likelihood function is the expectation in $\underset{\sim}{z}$ of terms of the form

$$\sum_{D\subseteq C} a(D) \sum_{\underset{\sim}{i}\in J(D)} \frac{e^{\sum_k V_{i_k}(z_k,\theta^*)}}{\sum_{\underset{\sim}{j}\in J(D)} e^{\sum_k V_{j_k}(z_k,\theta^*)}} \log \lambda(\underset{\sim}{i},\underset{\sim}{z},\theta) , \tag{53}$$

where

$$a(D) = \prod_{k=1}^{K} P(D|C,z_k,\theta^*) \sum_{\underset{\sim}{j} \in J(D)} e^{\sum_k V_{j_k}(z_{kn},\theta^*)}$$

Consistency requires that Equation (53) be maximised at $\theta = \theta^*$. When $J(D) \neq D^K$, the standard case fails to give this result. However, consistency can be attained by using a modified likelihood function with the kernel

$$\lambda(\underset{\sim}{i}_n,\underset{\sim}{z}_n,\theta) = e^{\sum_k V_{i_{kn}}(z_{kn},\theta)} \Big/ \sum_{\underset{\sim}{j} \in J(D_n)} e^{\sum_k V_{j_k}(z_{kn},\theta)} .$$

To illustrate the impact of these results, consider a destination choice problem in which individuals face a CBD destination and a large number of suburban destinations. One is interested primarily in whether the CBD destination will be chosen. If an individual chooses the CBD destination, then he is assigned the choice set consisting of the CBD destination and one suburban destination chosen at random. (From the previous analysis, we may choose the suburban destination at random from the subset of suburban destinations chosen by some individual in the home zone of the case in question.) If an individual chooses a suburban destination, he is assigned a choice set consisting of this destination and the CBD destination. Assume J suburban destinations, with probability of selection 1/J for each in the case of a CBD choice. The π distribution is then

$$\begin{aligned} &\pi(\{j,CBD\}|CBD) = 1/J && \text{for } j = 1,\ldots,J , \\ &\pi(\{j,CBD\}|j) = 1 && \text{for } j = 1,\ldots,J , \\ &\pi\ \{D\}|j) = 0 && \text{otherwise.} \end{aligned} \qquad (54)$$

This distribution satisfies the positive conditioning property (but not the uniform conditioning property), and hence consistent estimates can be obtained by maximising (51), which reduces to

$$\text{Max}\ \frac{1}{N} \sum_{n=1}^{N} \left\{ V_{i_n}(z_n,\theta) - \log\left[e^{V_{CBD}(z_n,\theta)+\log J} + e^{V_{j_n}(z_n,\theta)} \right] \right\} \qquad (55)$$

where j_n is the suburban alternative chosen or assigned on observation n, and a term involving log J but independent of θ has been dropped. Alternately, if the model contains a CBD-specific dummy, then unweighted maximum likelihood gives consistent estimates of all parameters except the CBD-specific dummy, and gives a consistent estimate of the true CBD-specific dummy plus log J.

Weighting and Estimation in Composite Samples

Transport samples may be the result of a complex mixture of exogenous and choice-based sampling, or of the amalgamation of surveys conducted using various sampling procedures. The techniques of Manski and Lerman [23], and Manski and McFadden can be adapted to construct consistent estimators from these samples.

Consider first the problem of working with a composite survey, made up of subsamples collected by various procedures. Provided the subsamples are identified and the sampling procedure used for each is known, maximum likelihood estimation of parameters using the combined sample is straightforward: the sample likelihood is the sum of the likelihoods of each of the subsamples, taking into account the sampling process used in each subsample. For example, the likelihood function for an exogenous stratified sample which is 'enriched' by a choice-based sample for minority modes is the sum of an exogenous likelihood function for the first subsample and a choice-based likelihood function for the second subsample. (Cosslett [9] has pointed out that the kernel of the composite sample likelihood will include the marginal distribution p(z).) Maximisation of this composite likelihood function would require modification of most standard computer routines. An alternative consistent estimator which can be calculated using a maximum likelihood programme which allows weighting of the choice variable is the Manski-Lerman estimator (39), with W(i) = 1 for the exogenous subsample and W(i) = Q(i)/H(i) for the choice-based subsample. Interestingly, the result that applying *unweighted* exogenous maximum likelihood estimation to an MNL model and pure choice-based sample produces inconsistency only in the alternative dummy coefficients does *not* carry over to the case of a composite sample when the exogenous subsample is stratified.

Next consider the problem of complex stratifications, such as would result from choice-based subsampling from a large exogenous stratified transport survey. The general theory of estimation from stratified samples of Manski and McFadden can be applied. In the example above, a consistent estimator would be (38), with Q(i) defined to equal the marginal share of alternative i *in the exogenous stratified sample* rather than in the population.

Non-maximum Likelihood Estimation Methods

While maximum likelihood estimators have good asymptotic statistical properties under the conditions normally imposed in transport applications, their finite sample properties are largely unknown. There is some evidence from very limited Monte Carlo studies that maximum likelihood estimators will be unduly sensitive to observations with low calculated probabilities, and hence relatively non-robust with respect to errors in model specification or data measurement which could yield low calculated probabilities for some observed choices. These limited studies suggest that when data grouping is possible, Berkson-Theil estimators may be preferable to maximum likelihood estimators (15, p. 112). However, plausible grouping is rarely possible with transport data. An alternative approach is to develop more 'robust' estimators for individual observations. Manski and McFadden have investigated a class of such estimators, including non-linear least squares (NLLS), which satisfies (for exogenous samples)

$$\underset{\theta\epsilon\Theta}{\text{Min}} \sum_{n=1}^{N} [S_{i_n} - P(i_n|z_n,\theta)]^2 \quad , \tag{56}$$

where S_i is one if i is chosen and zero otherwise. This estimator is consistent, although not as efficient as maximum likelihood estimation, and appears in Monte Carlo studies to be less sensitive than maximum likelihood estimation to outliers caused by data measurement errors. Applications to transport data sets have not, however, resulted in significant differences between maximum likelihood and NLLS estimators.

MODEL EVALUATION AND VALIDATION

Model Evaluation

The transport analyst usually has a number of alternative model specifications he considers to be *a priori* plausible, and wishes to determine empirically which alternative best fits the data. This calls for statistics which measure goodness of fit, and procedures which allow tests of hypothesised specifications.

General goodness-of-fit measures for discrete choice models which are now widely used are the log-likelihood function, the likelihood-ratio index, a multiple-correlation coefficient and a prediction-success index. The likelihood-ratio index ρ^2 is defined by the formula

$$\rho^2 = 1 - L/L_0 \quad , \tag{57}$$

where

$$L = \sum_{n=1}^{N} \sum_{i=1}^{J} S_{in} \log P(i|z_n,\theta) \tag{58}$$

is the log-likelihood function, with the S_{in} equal to one if i is chosen, zero otherwise,

$$L_0 = \sum_{n=1}^{N} \sum_{i=1}^{J} S_{in} \log Q_i \quad , \tag{59}$$

and Q_i equals the sample aggregate share of alternative i. This likelihood-ratio index is defined 'about aggregate shares', and measures the explanatory power of the model beyond that of a simple constant shares model. This index is preferable to a likelihood index 'about zero' reported by

307 Chapter 13

some computer programs, which measures the power of the model beyond that of an *equal* shares model. A similar comment applies to the multiple-correlation coefficient.

When the individual-choice model parameters are estimated by non-linear least squares, an appropriate goodness-of-fit measure is the sum of squared residuals.

$$SS = \sum_{n=1}^{N} \sum_{i=1}^{J} (S_{in} - R_n P_{in}(\hat{\theta}))^2 / R_n \quad , \tag{60}$$

where R_n is the sum of S_{in}. A transformation of this statistic yields a *multiple correlation coefficient* of the form familiar regression analysis,

$$R^2 - 1 - \frac{SS}{SS_0} \quad , \tag{61}$$

where

$$SS_0 = \sum_{n=1}^{N} \sum_{i=1}^{J} (S_{in} - R_n Q_i)^2 / R_n \tag{62}$$

with Q_i the sample aggregate share of mode i as before.*

A third method of assessing the fit of an estimated model is to examine the proportion of successful predictions, by alternative and overall. A *success table* can be defined as illustrated in Table 13.3, with the entry N_{ij} in row i and column j giving the number of individuals who are observed to choose i and predicted to choose j.** Column sums give

---

* While the R^2 index is a more familiar concept to planners who are experienced in ordinary regression analysis, it is not as well behaved a statistic as the ρ^2 measure, for maximum-likelihood estimation. Those unfamiliar with the ρ^2 index should be forewarned that its values tend to be considerably lower than those of the R^2 index and should not be judged by the standards for a 'good fit' in ordinary regression analysis. For example, values of 0.2 to 0.4 for ρ^2 represent an excellent fit.

**The formula for N_{ij} is

$$N_{ij} = \sum_{n=1}^{N} S_{in} P_{jn} \quad .$$

An alternative prediction method is to forecast that the alternative with the highest probability will be chosen.

A dot subscript indicates summation over the corresponding index, e.g.

$$N_{i\cdot} = \sum_j N_{ij} \quad .$$

predicted shares for the sample; row sums give observed shares. The proportion of alternatives successfully predicted, $N_{ii}/N_{\cdot i}$, indicates that fraction of individuals expected to choose an alternative who do in fact choose that alternative. An overall proportion successfully predicted, $(N_{11} + \ldots + N_{JJ})/N_{\cdot\cdot}$, can also be calculated.

		Predicted Choice 1	2 ...	J	Observed Count	Observed Share
Observed Choice	1	N_{11}	N_{12}	N_{1J}	$N_{1\cdot}$	$N_{1\cdot}/N_{\cdot\cdot}$
	2	N_{21}	N_{22}	N_{2J}	$N_{2\cdot}$	$N_{2\cdot}/N_{\cdot\cdot}$
	⋮					
	J	N_{J1}	N_{J2}	N_{JJ}	$N_{J\cdot}$	$N_{J\cdot}/N_{\cdot\cdot}$
Predicted Count		$N_{\cdot 1}$	$N_{\cdot 2}$	$N_{\cdot J}$	$N_{\cdot\cdot}$	1
Predicted Share		$\frac{N_{\cdot 1}}{N_{\cdot\cdot}}$	$\frac{N_{\cdot 2}}{N_{\cdot\cdot}}$	$\frac{N_{\cdot J}}{N_{\cdot\cdot}}$	1	
Proportion Successfully Predicted		$\frac{N_{11}}{N_{\cdot 1}}$	$\frac{N_{22}}{N_{\cdot 2}}$	$\frac{N_{JJ}}{N_{\cdot J}}$	$\frac{N_{11}+\ldots+N_{JJ}}{N_{\cdot\cdot}}$	
Success Index		$\frac{N_{11}}{N_{\cdot 1}} - \frac{N_{\cdot 1}}{N_{\cdot\cdot}}$	$\frac{N_{22}}{N_{\cdot 2}} - \frac{N_{\cdot 2}}{N_{\cdot\cdot}}$	$\frac{N_{JJ}}{N_{\cdot J}} - \frac{N_{\cdot J}}{N_{\cdot\cdot}}$	$\sum_{i=1}^{J} [\frac{N_{ii}}{N_{\cdot\cdot}} - (\frac{N_{\cdot i}}{N_{\cdot\cdot}})^2]$	
Proportional Error in Predicted Share		$\frac{N_{\cdot 1}-N_{1\cdot}}{N_{\cdot\cdot}}$	$\frac{N_{\cdot 2}-N_{2\cdot}}{N_{\cdot\cdot}}$	$\frac{N_{\cdot J}-N_{J\cdot}}{N_{\cdot\cdot}}$		

TABLE 13.3 A Prediction Success Table

Because the proportion successfully predicted for an alternative varies with the aggregate share of that alternative, a better measure of goodness of fit is the prediction-success index,

$$\sigma_i = \frac{N_{ii}}{N_{\cdot i}} - \frac{N_{\cdot i}}{N_{\cdot\cdot}} \quad , \tag{63}$$

where $N_{\cdot i}/N_{\cdot\cdot}$ is the proportion which would be successfully predicted if the choice probabilities for each sampled individual were assumed to equal the observed aggregate shares.* This index will usually be non-negative, with a maximum value of $1 - N_{\cdot i}/N_{\cdot\cdot}$. If an index normally lying between zero and one is desired, Equation (63) can be normalised by $1 - N_{\cdot i}/N_{\cdot\cdot}$.

An overall prediction success index is

$$\sigma = \sum_{i=1}^{J} \frac{N_{\cdot i}}{N_{\cdot\cdot}} \sigma_i = \sum_{i=1}^{J} \left(\frac{N_{ii}}{N_{\cdot\cdot}} - \left(\frac{N_{\cdot i}}{N_{\cdot\cdot}}\right)^2 \right) . \tag{64}$$

Again, this index will usually be non-negative, with a maximum value of

$$1 - \sum_{i=1}^{J} \left(\frac{N_{\cdot i}}{N_{\cdot\cdot}} \right)^2 ,$$

and can be normalised to have a maximum value of one if desired.

In tests of model specification, one is often concerned with questions such as whether certain variables enter the determination of choice, and whether certain coefficients are equal. For example, the question of whether in-vehicle travel time is generic, or homogeneous-effect, can be formulated as the hypothesis that the coefficients of alternative-specific travel times are all equal. Such problems, where the null hypothesis is a subset of a specified universe of alternatives, can be tested conveniently using likelihood ratios, as described in Theil ((40) p. 396), and McFadden (26). Specification tests which are less easily performed using classical statistical methods are those in which the model corresponding to the universe of alternatives cannot be specified or estimated. Examples are the question of which of two alternative measures of travel time better explain mode choice, and tests of a particular model specification such as MNL against mutually exclusive alternatives such as MNP. Methods of statistical decision theory can be applied to some of these problems; an exposition is beyond the scope of this chapter.

---

*In a model with alternative-specific dummies and the estimation data set, estimation of parameters imposes the condition $N_{i\cdot} = N_{\cdot i}$. If one predicted the choice probabilities for each individual to equal aggregate shares, then $N_{\cdot i}/N_{\cdot\cdot}$ would be the proportion successfully predicted to choose i. This represents a 'chance' prediction rate for a model in which no variables other than alternative-specific dummies enter. Thus, σ_i measures the net contribution to prediction success of variables other than the alternative-specific dummies.

Diagnostic Tests for the MNL Model

The MNL model has significant advantages over most alternative choice models in terms of simplicity and computational efficiency, and its independence from irrelevant alternatives (IIA) property greatly facilitates estimation and forecasting. On the other hand, the IIA restriction may be invalid in some applications, resulting in erroneous forecasts. Hence, the validity of the IIA property should be tested in each application. McFadden, Tye and Train* have developed a series of diagnostic tests for this property; the major findings are summarised in Chapter 1 of the present volume. One is a test of the MNL model against a 'universal' alternative, approximated by an MNL-like form in which attributes of all alternatives can enter the 'utility' of each alternative - this is the 'universal' logit model. A second test is based on the implications of the IIA property that the model can be estimated consistently from a random sample of the set of all available alternatives, as discussed earlier. A third class of tests examines residuals from the fitted MNL model, i.e. the differences of indicators of observed choices and the estimated probabilities of these choices. Under the hypothesis that the MNL specification is correct, these residuals will have specific mean, variance and correlation properties which can be utilised in statistical tests.

AGGREGATION AND FORECASTING

Aggregate Forecasts

An important use of individual-choice models is in policy analysis of the impacts of alternative transport plans on operating strategies. Evaluation of these impacts usually requires forecasts of the behaviour of the aggregate population, or of specific market segments. Given an estimated choice model $P(i|z,\theta)$, the aggregate share of alternative i satisfies

$$Q(i) = \int_Z P(i|z,\theta)p(z)dz \qquad (65)$$

where p(z) is the probability distribution of the explanatory variables in the population. For a market segment, this formula applies, with p(z) interpreted as the distribution of explanatory variables in the segment.

A variety of methods have been proposed for the evaluation of (65) in applications; the most practical and flexible appears to be a 'Monte Carlo' procedure in which Q(i) is approximated by

*McFadden, D., Tye, W. and Train, K., 'Diagnostic tests for the independence from irrelevant alternatives property of the multinomial logit model', *Urban Travel Demand Forecasting Project Working Paper No. 7616*, Institute of Transportation Studies, University of California, Berkeley (1976).

$$Q(i) = \frac{1}{N} \sum_{i=1}^{N} P(i|z_n,\theta) \quad , \qquad (66)$$

where $\{z_n\}$ is a sample drawn randomly from p(z). The points z_n may be from a representative sample of the population, or may themselves be synthesised from incomplete data sources, as described below. The formula (66) can be modified to accommodate non-uniform sampling weights. For computational purposes, it is often useful to group sample points into strata with homogeneous choice probabilities. Discussions of this and alternative aggregation procedures and their properties can be found in Koppelman (22) and McFadden (34).

Aggregation by the Clark Method

In general, direct evaluation of (65) requires numerical integration over the set Z, which may be of relatively high dimension. This may be impractical even if the choice probabilities are relatively easy to compute, and the problem is compounded if evaluation of the choice probabilities is expensive.

An approach which eliminates the intermediate calculation of choice probabilities has been suggested in a specific context by McFadden and Reid (36), and generalised by Manski and Daganzo. Suppose individuals maximise utility, with utility functions $u_i = \beta' z_i + \varepsilon_i$ for alternative i. Given a probability distribution p(z) for $z = (z_1,\ldots,z_J)$ and a distribution of $(\varepsilon_1,\ldots,\varepsilon_J)$, one can construct the probability distribution of $(u_1,\ldots,u_J)$ resulting from *joint* variation of z and the ε_i. The distribution of $(u_1,\ldots,u_J)$ is obtained as a multivariate *convolution* of the probability densities of z and of $(\varepsilon_1,\ldots,\varepsilon_J)$. For some probability distributions, such as the multivariate normal case considered below, the distribution of the convolution is known. More generally, if $\phi(t_1,\ldots,t_{JK})$ is the characteristic function of the distribution of $z = (z_{11},\ldots,z_{K1},\ldots,z_{1J},\ldots,z_{KJ})$, and $\psi(t_1,\ldots,t_J)$ is the characteristic function of the distribution of $(\varepsilon_1,\ldots,\varepsilon_J)$, with z and $(\varepsilon_1,\ldots,\varepsilon_J)$ assumed independent, then $(u_1,\ldots,u_J)$ with $u_i = \beta' z_i + \varepsilon_i$ has the characteristic function $\gamma(t_1,\ldots,t_J) = \psi(t_1,\ldots,t_J)\phi(t_1\beta_1,\ldots,t_1\beta_K,t_2\beta_1,\ldots,t_J\beta_1, \ldots,t_J\beta_K)$, or more compactly, $\gamma(t) = \psi(t)\phi(t \otimes \beta')$. The density of $(u_1,\ldots,u_J)$ can then be obtained from the inversion formula $h(u_1,\ldots,u_J) = (2\pi)^{-J}\int e^{-itu}\gamma(t)dt$. Using this expression in (67), one could carry out the computation of Q(i) with a numerical integration of dimension at most 2J, for an extremely broad class of distributions of z and ε. Application of approximation methods to the combined integral may then allow rapid computation of aggregate probabilities, even for complex choice models. Let $H(u_1,\ldots,u_J)$ denote the cumulative distribution of $(u_1,\ldots,u_J)$ and H_i its derivative with respect to u_i,

$$Q(i) = \text{Prob}\,\{u_i \geq u_j \text{ for } j = 1,\ldots,J\} \tag{67}$$

$$= \int_{u=-\infty}^{+\infty} H_i(u,u,\ldots,u)du \ .$$

Evaluation of this integral requires only a single numerical integration when H_i can be obtained analytically, and at most a J-dimensional numerical integration is required to compute Q(i) when the density of H is analytic.

The procedure outlined above can be applied with particular convenience to the case where z and ε are assumed multivariate normal. This assumption, which yields the MNP model of individual choice, implies $(u_1,\ldots,u_J)$ is multivariate normal, with mean of u_i equal to $\beta'\bar{z}_i$ where $\bar{z}$ is the mean of z, and covariances $\omega_{ij} = \beta'\Sigma_{ij}\beta + \sigma_{ij}$, where σ_{ij} = cov $(\varepsilon_i,\varepsilon_j)$ and Σ_{ij} = cov (z_i,z_j). Then, Q(1) can be obtained from a formula analogous to (30) for this multivariate normal distribution. The Clark approximation method discussed above then permits rapid computation of approximate aggregate shares. Further, application of the Clark formulae to the computation of analytic derivatives of Q(i) with respect to $\bar{z}$, in a manner analogous to that described in (34), would allow rapid approximation of aggregate elasticities.

The Distribution of Explanatory Variables

The computation of aggregate shares or elasticities requires knowledge of the distribution of the explanatory variables in the population, or in a market segment of the population. A random sample from the population of sufficient size, say from a major population survey, can meet this data requirement. However, it is often difficult to obtain current data of this type. Forecasts at future dates present a further problem, since the distribution of explanatory variables used in the forecasts should take into account shifts in explanatory variables over time.

Cosslett, Duguay, Jung and McFadden (10) have proposed a method of synthesising the distribution of explanatory variables at any forecast date, integrating available data sources plus information on trends. The method is particularly useful when current random survey data is unavailable, and can be applied in most urban areas using only US census data. The method utilises a classical statistical procedure for completing contingency tables, called *iterative proportional fitting*, due to Deming and Stephan (14). This procedure allows the integration of marginal information from US census tract statistics, Public Use Samples, and the Urban Transportation Planning Package. Parametric models of some variable interactions, simple trend models for shifts in the distribution over time, and exogenous forecasts for some explanatory variables allow projection of the synthesised distribution to future dates. Sampling from the constructed distribution yields a synthesised random sample for the urban area at the forecast date.

Calculus for Demand Elasticities

Demand elasticities encapsulate considerable information on transport demand response, and are valuable tools for policy analysis. For the multinomial logit (MNL) model, the elasticities can be expressed in relatively simple formulae. However, great care must be taken to avoid mechanical use of these formulae, and to see that the computation performed corresponds to the policy question asked. The first rules set out below hold for any choice model. We use the notation P_i for the choice probability for alternative i, and z_k^i for the kth component of the vector of attributes of alternative i.

Rule 1 - aggregation over market segments. *Aggregate elasticity equals the sum of segment elasticities, weighted by segment shares of the market.* If P_i^ℓ is the choice probability for segment ℓ, $\overline{P}_i$ is the aggregate choice probability, and q_ℓ is the proportion of the population in segment ℓ, then

$$\left(\frac{z_k^j}{\overline{P}_i}\frac{\partial \overline{P}_i}{\partial z_k^j}\right) = \sum_\ell q_\ell \left(\frac{z_k^j}{P_i^\ell}\frac{\partial P_i^\ell}{\partial z_k^j}\right) . \tag{68}$$

(Note: This is a relevant elasticity only if a policy will result in equal percentage changes for each market segment.)

Rule 2 - aggregation over alternatives. *Elasticity for a compound alternative equals the sum of component alternative elasticities, weighted by the component shares of the compound alternative.* Let $\overline{P} = \sum_i P_i$ be the choice probability for a compound alternative (e.g. 'all transit'). Then,

$$\left(\frac{z_k^j}{\overline{P}}\frac{\partial \overline{P}}{\partial z_k^j}\right) = \sum_i \left(\frac{P_i}{\overline{P}}\right)\left(\frac{z_k^j}{P_i}\frac{\partial P_i}{\partial z_k^j}\right) . \tag{69}$$

(Note: This is a relevant elasticity only if a policy will result in equal percentage changes for each component alternative.)

Rule 3 - component effect. *The elasticity with respect to a component of a variable equals the elasticity with respect to the variable times the component's share in the variable.* Suppose $z_k^j = w_k^j + y_k^j$. Then

$$\frac{y_k^j}{P_i}\frac{\partial P_i}{\partial y_k^j} = \left(\frac{y_k^j}{z_k^j}\right)\left(\frac{z_k^j}{P_i}\frac{\partial P_i}{\partial z_k^j}\right) . \quad (70)$$

(Note: It is particularly important in policy analysis to look only at components influenced by a policy, such as the transit fare component of total trip cost or the bus on-vehicle time component of a multi-mode trip total on-vehicle time.)

Rule 4 - multiple effect. *The elasticity with respect to a policy that causes an equal percentage change in several variables equals the sum of the elasticities with respect to each variable.* Suppose a policy changes z_k^j to $z_k^j(1 + t)$ for several j. Then,

$$\frac{1}{P_i}\frac{\partial P_i}{\partial t} = \sum_j \left(\frac{z_k^j}{P_i}\frac{\partial P_i}{\partial z_k^j}\right) . \quad (71)$$

Since t is a proportional change, the left-hand side of this equation is in elasticity form. Alternately, suppose $z_k^j = w_k^j + y_k$ for several j, and a policy changes y_k. Then,

$$\frac{y_k}{P_i}\frac{\partial P_i}{\partial y_k} = \sum_j \left(\frac{y_k}{z_k^j}\right)\left(\frac{z_k^j}{P_i}\frac{\partial P_i}{\partial z_k^j}\right) . \quad (72)$$

This formula is obtainable from a combination of Rules 3 and 4.

Often, combinations of these rules will be required to obtain the most relevant elasticity for a policy calculation. For example, suppose transit alternatives are disaggregated by access mode, and the impact of a fare increase is to be assessed. The answer is given by combining Rules 2, 3 and 4 to obtain the formula

$$\begin{pmatrix}\text{Elasticity}\\ \text{of transit}\\ \text{patronage}\\ \text{with respect}\\ \text{to fare}\end{pmatrix} = \sum_i \sum_j \begin{pmatrix}\text{Patronage on}\\ \text{mode i as a}\\ \text{proportion of}\\ \text{total transit}\\ \text{patronage}\end{pmatrix} \cdot \begin{pmatrix}\text{Fare on}\\ \text{mode j as a}\\ \text{proportion}\\ \text{of total}\\ \text{cost on j}\end{pmatrix} \cdot \begin{pmatrix}\text{Elasticity of}\\ \text{mode i patronage}\\ \text{with respect to}\\ \text{total cost on}\\ \text{mode j}\end{pmatrix} \quad (73)$$

where i and j are summed over the transit access modes.

Consider elasticities for the sequential model defined earlier. Taking $\theta = \lambda = 1$, these elasticities will also hold for the joint MNL model.

$$\frac{x_{ncbk}}{P_{m|da}}\frac{\partial P_{m|da}}{\partial x_{ncbk}} = \alpha_k z_{ndak}\,(\delta_{mn} - P_{n|da})\,\delta_{cd}\,\delta_{ab} \quad (74)$$

where x_{ndak} is component k of x_{nda} and $\delta_{mn} = 1$ if $m = n$, 0 otherwise, etc.

$$\frac{x_{ncbk}}{P_{d|a}} \frac{\partial P_{d|a}}{\partial x_{ncbk}} = \theta\alpha_k x_{ncak} P_{n|ca}(\delta_{cd} - P_{c|a})\delta_{ab} \quad , \tag{75}$$

$$\frac{y_{cbk}}{P_{d|a}} \frac{\partial P_{d|a}}{\partial y_{cbk}} = \beta_k y_{cak}(\delta_{cd} - P_{c|a})\delta_{ab} \quad , \tag{76}$$

where y_{cak} is component k of y_{ca}.

$$\frac{x_{mdbk}}{P_a} \frac{\partial P_a}{\partial x_{mdbk}} = \lambda\theta\alpha_k x_{mdbk} P_{m|db} P_{d|b}(\delta_{ab} - P_b) \quad ; \tag{77}$$

$$\frac{y_{dbk}}{P_a} \frac{\partial P_a}{\partial y_{dbk}} = \lambda\beta_k y_{dbk} P_{d|b}(\delta_{ab} - P_b) \quad ; \tag{78}$$

$$\frac{z_{bk}}{P_a} \frac{\partial P_a}{\partial z_{bk}} = \gamma z_{bk}(\delta_{ab} - P_b) \quad . \tag{79}$$

Other elasticities are readily derived from these formulae using Rules 1 - 4 and the definitions of conditional and marginal probabilities. For example, $P_{da} = P_{d|a}P_a$ implies

$$\frac{x_{mca}}{P_{da}} \frac{\partial P_{da}}{\partial x_{mca}} = \frac{x_{mca}}{P_{d|a}} \frac{\partial P_{d|a}}{\partial x_{mca}} + \frac{x_{mca}}{P_a} \frac{\partial P_a}{\partial x_{mca}} \quad , \tag{80}$$

and the preceding formulae can be substituted in the right-hand side of this expression. Another example is the joint probability $P_{mda} = P_{m|da}P_{d|a}P_a$, which satisfies

$$\frac{x_{ncbk}}{P_{mda}} \frac{\partial P_{mda}}{\partial x_{ncbk}} = \alpha_k x_{ncbk} \Big\{\delta_{mn}\delta_{cd}\delta_{ab} + \delta_{cd}\delta_{ab}(\theta - 1)P_{n|cb} + \theta\delta_{ab}(\lambda - 1)P_{n|cb}P_{c|b} - \theta\lambda P_{ncb}\Big\} \quad . \tag{81}$$

As a check, one sees that for $\theta = \lambda = 1$, this reduces to the conventional MNL elasticity formula.

CONCLUSION

This chapter has surveyed selected recent developments in quantitative methods for travel-demand analysis. This subject has developed rapidly in the past few years on a wide spectrum of topics. As a result, the transport analyst now has available a greatly expanded 'bag of tools' with which to address policy problems. Experience makes it clear that quantitative methods are not a panacea for solving the problems of transport policy analysis. On the other hand, the use of techniques of modern mathematics and statistics relax one of the constraints which has limited the analyst in attacking a full range of transport issues. A review of the state of the art of quantitative methods in transport demand forecasting suggests that the task of establishing a firm analytic and statistical foundation for the subject has just begun.

REFERENCES

1. Amemiya, T. 'Specification and estimation of a multinomial logit model', *Institute of Mathematical Studies in the Social Sciences Technical Report 211*, Stanford University, Stanford, California (1976).

2. Anderson, T.W. (1958) *An Introduction to Multivariate Statistical Analysis*, Wiley, New York.

3. Ben-Akiva, M., 'Structure of passenger travel demand models', *Transportation Research Record No. 526* (1973).

4. Ben-Akiva, M. and Lerman, S., 'Disaggregate travel and mobility choice models and measures of accessibility', (Chapter 30 of the present book).

5. Bishop, Y., Fienberg, S. and Holland, P. (1975) *Discrete Multivariate Analysis*, Massachusetts Institute of Technology Press, Cambridge, Massachusetts.

6. Bock, R.D. and Jones, L.V. (1968) *The Measurement and Prediction of Judgement and Choice*, Holden-Day, San Francisco.

7. Cardell, S. (1975), personal communication.

8. Clark, C., 'The greatest of a finite set of random variables', *Operations Research*, 9, pp. 145-62 (1961).

9. Cosslett, S., 'Efficient estimation of choice probabilities from choice-based samples', *Alfred P. Sloan Foundation Workshop in Transportation Economics*, Department of Economics, University of California, Berkeley (1977).

10. Cosslett, S., Duguay, G.E., Jung, W.S. and McFadden, D., 'Synthesis of household transportation survey data: the SYNSAM methodology', *Urban Travel Demand Forecasting Project, Working Paper No. 7705*, Institute of Transportation Studies, University of California, Berkeley (1977).

11. Cramer, H. (1946), *Mathematical Methods of Statistics*, Princeton University Press, Princeton, New Jersey.

12. Daly, A. and Zachary, S., 'Improved multiple choice models', in *Determinants of Travel Choice*, D.A. Hensher and M.Q. Dalvi (eds), Teakfield, Farnborough, England (1978).

13. Daganzo, D., Bouthelier, F. and Sheffi, Y., 'An efficient approach to estimate and predict with multinomial probit models', Department of Civil Engineering, Massachusetts Institute of Technology (unpublished) (1976).

14. Deming, W. and Stephan, F., 'On a least square adjustment of a sampled frequency table when the expected marginal totals are known', *Annals of Mathematical Statistics*, 11, pp. 427-44 (1940).

15. Domencich, R. and McFadden, D. (1975) *Urban Travel Demand: A Behavioral Analysis*, North-Holland, Amsterdam.

16. Goodman, L. and Kruskal, W., 'Measures of association for cross-classification', *Journal of the American Statistical Association*, 49, pp. 732-64 (1954).

17. Haberman, S. (1974) *The Analysis of Frequency Data*, University of Chicago Press, Chicago, Illinois.

18. Haberman, S., 'Log-linear fit for contingency tables', *Applied Statistics*, 21, pp. 218-25 (1974).

19. Harris, A. and Tanner, J., 'Transport demand models based on personal characteristics', *Transport and Road Research Laboratory Supplementary Report 65 UC* (1974).

20. Hausman, J.A. and Wise, D.A., 'A conditional probit model for qualitative choice: discrete decisions recognizing interdependence and heterogeneous preferences', *Econometrica*, 46(2), pp. 403-26 (1978).

21. Kendall, D. and Stuart, K. (1976) *Advanced Theory of Statistics*, Vol. 3, Hafner, New York.

22. Koppelman, F. (1975) 'The Structure of Aggregated Prediction Models', Ph.D. Dissertation, Department of Civil Engineering, Northwestern University, Evanston, Illinois.

23. Manski, C. and Lerman, S., 'The estimation of choice probabilities from choice-based samples', *Econometrica*, 46(1) (1978).

24. Manski, C., 'Maximum score estimation of the stochastic utility model of choice', *Journal of Econometrics*, 3, pp. 205-28 (1975).

25. Manski, C., 'Multinomial probit model', internal memorandum, Cambridge Systematics, Inc., Cambridge, Massachusetts (1976).

26. McFadden, D., 'Conditional logit analysis of qualitative choice behavior', in *Frontiers in Econometrics*, P. Zarembka (ed.), Academic Press, New York (1974).

27. McFadden, D., 'On independence, structure, and simultaneity in transportation demand analysis', *Urban Travel Demand Forecasting Project, Working Paper No. 7511A*, Institute of Transportation Studies, University of California, Berkeley (1975).

28. McFadden, D., 'Economic applications of psychological choice models', *Urban Travel Demand Forecasting Project, Working Paper No. 7519*, Institute of Transportation Studies, University of California, Berkeley (1975).

29. McFadden, D., 'The revealed preferences of a government bureaucracy: evidence', *Bell Journal of Economics*, 7, pp. 55-72 (1976).

30. McFadden, D., 'Quantal choice analysis: a survey', *Annals of Economic and Social Measurement*, 5 (1976).

31. McFadden, D., 'A comment on discriminant "versus" logit analysis', *Annals of Economic and Social Measurement*, 5 (1976).

32. McFadden, D., 'The theory and practice of disaggregate demand forecasting for various modes of urban transportation', *Urban Travel Demand Forecasting Project, Working Paper 7623*, Institute of Transportation Studies, University of California, Berkeley (1976).

33. McFadden, D., 'Properties of the multinomial logit (MNL) model', *Urban Travel Demand Forecasting Project, Working Paper No. 7617*, Institute of Transportation Studies, University of California, Berkeley (1976).

34. McFadden, D., 'The mathematical theory of demand models', in *Behavioral Travel Demand Models*, P.R. Stopher and A.H. Meyburg (eds), Lexington Books, Lexington (1976).

35. McFadden, D., 'Modeling the choice of residential location', in *Spatial Interaction Theory and Planning Models*, A. Karlqvist, L. Lundquist, F. Snickers, J. Weibull (eds), North-Holland, Amsterdam (1978).

36. McFadden, D. and Reid, F., 'Aggregate travel demand forecasting from disaggregated behavioral models', *Transportation Research Board Record No. 534* (1975).

37. McLynn, J. (1973) *A Technical Note on a Class of Fully Competitive Modal Choice Models*, DTM Corp., Bethesda, Maryland (1973).

38. Stopher, P.R. and Meyburg, A.H. (1975) *Urban Transportation Planning and Modelling*, Lexington Books, Lexington.

39. Stopher, P.R. and Meyburg, A.H. (eds) (1976) *Behavioral Travel Demand Models*, Lexington Books, Lexington.

40. Theil, H. (1971) *Principles of Econometrics*, Wiley, New York.

41. Thurstone, L., 'A law of comparative judgment', *Psychological Review*, 34, pp. 273-86 (1927).

42. Wiliams, H.C.L., 'On the formation of travel demand models and economic evaluation measures of user benefit', *Environment and Planning A*, 9, pp. 285-344 (1977).

[14]

Testing Disaggregate Travel Demand Models by Comparing Predicted and Observed Market Shares

JOEL L. HOROWITZ

ABSTRACT

An intuitively appealing and popular method for testing a disaggregate choice model of travel demand, such as a logit model, consists of comparing the model's predictions of the market shares of travel alternatives in population groups with observations of these shares. Excessively large differences between the predicted and observed shares indicate that the model being tested is incorrect. In current practice, the decision whether differences between predictions and observations are large is made judgmentally, thereby raising the possibility that a correct or approximately correct model will be rejected because of the effects of random sampling errors. A statistical test is described that enables one to distinguish between the effects of random sampling errors and those of true model errors when predicted and observed market shares are compared. Five easily programmable steps for implementing the test are given, and commercially available software that can help with the computations is identified. A numerical example of the application of the test is presented, and the role of the test in practical model development is discussed.

An intuitively appealing way of testing any model of travel behavior is to compare its predictions with actual observations. In the case of disaggregate choice models, such as logit and probit models, that predict individuals' choices among sets of discrete alternatives, this approach to testing often consists of comparing predictions of market shares of alternatives in population groups with observations of the actual market shares in the same groups. Large differences between predicted and observed shares constitute grounds for rejecting the model. For example, to test a model of mode choice the population of interest might be grouped according to characteristics such as income, automobile ownership, location of residence or work, and so forth. The model's predictions of the proportions of individuals in each group that use each mode would be compared with the observed proportions. The model would be rejected as incorrect if the differences between the predicted and observed proportions were excessively large.

In current practice, the decision whether differences between predictions and observations are excessive is made judgmentally. This is unsatisfactory because differences between predicted and observed market shares are subject to random sampling errors. These errors are not relevant to the question of whether the model under consideration is correct. However, depending on the details of the model, selection of population groups, and size of the data set being used, they can produce differences between predictions and observations that are large by reasonable judgmental standards, even if the model being tested is correct. In other words, when predictions and observations are compared judgmentally, random sampling errors may cause a correct model to be rejected.

To minimize the likelihood of this undesirable outcome, it is necessary to have a method for distinguishing between random sampling errors and true model errors in comparisons of predicted and observed market shares. In the terminology of statistics, it is necessary to have a test of the statistical significance of differences between predictions and observations. The main objectives of this paper are to describe such a test and to present a numerical example illustrating its use. Subsidiary objectives are to discuss briefly two important questions relating to the use of the test. These are as follows:

1. In carrying out the test, should the data used for testing (i.e., for computing predicted and observed market shares) be independent of the data used for model estimation or should all of the available data be used for both estimation and testing?
2. The test based on comparisons of predicted and observed market shares is only one of several procedures that are available for testing disaggregate choice models. How should one choose among these procedures in practical, empirical work?

The remainder of this paper is organized as follows. The test statistic is described in the next section and the first question posed previously is answered. Then the numerical example of the use of the test statistic is presented. In the final section the second question posed previously is answered and some concluding comments are presented.

THE TEST STATISTIC

The most frequently used form of disaggregate choice model is the multinomial logit model with a linear-in-parameters utility function. Therefore, to minimize the complexity of the discussion, it will be assumed here that the model being tested has this form. The test statistic for a general choice model is given by Horowitz (1).

In the multinomial logit model with a linear-in-parameters utility function, the probability $P(i|m,\theta)$ that individual m chooses alternative i from a set of I available alternatives is (2,3)

$$P(i|m,\theta) = (\exp X'_{mi}\,\theta)/\sum_k (\exp X'_{mk}\,\theta) \qquad (1)$$

where X'_{mk} (k = 1, ..., I) is a row vector of explanatory variables evaluated for individual m and alternative k, θ is a column vector of constant parameters, and the sum in the denominator is over all available alternatives. In practice, the values of the parameters θ usually are not known a priori and must be estimated by fitting the model to data. In accordance with usual practice, it is assumed in this paper that θ is estimated by the method of maximum likelihood using a disaggregate data set consisting of observations of the choices and X-values corresponding to M randomly selected individuals. This data set will be called the estimation data set. Let $\hat{\theta}$ denote the estimated values of the parameters θ. Then the estimated probability that individual m chooses alternative i is $P(i|m,\hat{\theta})$.

Derivation

Suppose that the model is to be tested by using a test data set consisting of observations of the choices and X-values corresponding to N randomly selected individuals. The test data set is assumed to be either the same as the estimation data set (in which case N = M) or independent of it. Let the individuals in the test data set be organized into J mutually exclusive groups (J > 1) either randomly or according to the values of characteristics such as income, automobile ownership, location of residence or work, and so on and let N_j denote the number of individuals assigned to group j (j = 1, ..., J). Let $z_{ni} = 1$ if individual n in the test data set chose alternative i and let $z_{ni} = 0$ otherwise. Then the observed market share of alternative i in population group j of the test data set ($\hat{Q}_{ij}$) is

$$\hat{Q}_{ij} = \sum_{\substack{n \text{ in} \\ \text{group } j}} (z_{ni}/N_j) \tag{2}$$

The predicted market share of alternative i in population group j according to the estimated model ($\hat{P}_{ij}$) is

$$\hat{P}_{ij} = \sum_{\substack{n \text{ in} \\ \text{group } j}} P(i|n,\hat{\theta})/N_j \tag{3}$$

The difference between the predicted and observed shares ($\hat{D}_{ij}$) is $\hat{Q}_{ij} - \hat{P}_{ij}$ or

$$\hat{D}_{ij} = \sum_{\substack{n \text{ in} \\ \text{group } j}} [z_{ni} - P(i|n,\hat{\theta})]/N_j \tag{4}$$

$\hat{D}_{ij}$ contains two sources of random error that cause it to differ from zero in general, even if the model $P(i|n,\theta)$ with suitably chosen parameter values is correct. First, the individuals in the test data set are sampled randomly, so their choice indicators z_{ni} are random. Second, the estimated parameter values $\hat{\theta}$ are random because they depend on the choices of the randomly selected individuals in the estimation data set. To develop a test statistic that enables one to distinguish between the effects on $\hat{D}_{ij}$ of random sampling errors and those of true errors in the model, it is necessary to know how large the sampling errors might cause $\hat{D}_{ij}$ to be if the model being tested is in fact correct. [Throughout this paper, the term "large" refers to both large positive and large negative values of $\hat{D}_{ij}$.] This in turn requires knowledge of the probability distribution of the random variable $\hat{D}_{ij}$ for the case of testing a correct model.

To obtain this distribution, let θ_0 denote the true (but unknown) values of the parameters. In other words, $P(i|n,\theta_0)$ is a correct model. Then as discussed by Chernoff (4), $P(i|n,\theta)$ is given approximately by

$$P(i|n,\hat{\theta}) = P(i|n,\theta_0) + \sum_k P(i|n,\theta_0)(X'_{ni} - X'_{nk}) \times P(k|n,\theta_0)(\hat{\theta} - \theta_0) \tag{5}$$

where the sum on the right-hand side is over all of the available alternatives. Substituting Equation 5 into 4 yields

$$\hat{D}_{ij} = \sum_{\substack{n \text{ in} \\ \text{group } j}} \left\{ [z_{ni} - P(i|n,\theta_0)]/N_j \right\} - K'_{ij}(\hat{\theta} - \theta_0) \tag{6}$$

where K'_{ij} is the row vector defined by

$$K'_{ij} = \sum_{\substack{n \text{ in} \\ \text{group } j}} \sum_k P(i|n,\theta_0)(X'_{ni} - X'_{nk}) P(k|n,\theta_0)/N_j \tag{7}$$

The first term on the right-hand side of Equation 6 gives the effect on $\hat{D}_{ij}$ of random variations in the z_{ni}'s. This term is normally distributed with a mean of zero by virtue of the central limit theorem and the mean value of z_{ni} of $P(i|n,\theta_0)$. The second term in the right-hand side of Equation 6 gives the effect on $\hat{D}_{ij}$ of random sampling errors in the estimated parameter values. This term also is normally distributed with mean zero because $\hat{\theta}$ is normally distributed with mean θ_0 when $\hat{\theta}$ is obtained by the method of maximum likelihood (5). [The N_j values and the term K'_{ij} that multiplies $\hat{\theta} - \theta_0$ in Equation 6 can be treated as constants in samples of practical size.] Because sums and differences of normally distributed random variables are normally distributed, it follows that for each i and j, $\hat{D}_{ij}$ has the normal distribution with a mean of zero when the model being tested is correct.

To complete the derivation of the probability distribution of $\hat{D}_{ij}$, it is necessary to calculate the variance of $\hat{D}_{ij}$. Before doing this, however, it is important to observe that there are IJ different values of $\hat{D}_{ij}$, one for each alternative-population group pair. To conclude that the model being tested is incorrect, it is necessary for these IJ values to be excessively large collectively rather than individually. As will be seen, carrying out a test of the sizes of the $\hat{D}_{ij}$'s considered collectively requires knowledge of the covariances of $\hat{D}_{ij}$'s corresponding to different alternative-population group pairs as well as knowledge of the variances of individual $\hat{D}_{ij}$'s. Thus it is necessary to obtain the covariance terms $\text{cov}(\hat{D}_{ij},\hat{D}_{rs})$ for each combination of pairs ij and rs.

It can be seen from Equation 6 that each $\hat{D}_{ij}$ contains two parts, one associated with random variations in the z_{ni}'s (i.e., the first term on the right-hand side of Equation 6) and one associated with random variations in $\hat{\theta}$ (i.e., the second term on the right-hand side of Equation 6). Let A_{ijrs} denote the covariance of the first term on the right-hand side of Equation 6 and let B_{ijrs} denote the covariance of the second term. Then as shown by Horowitz (1),

$$A_{ijrs} = \sum_{\substack{n \text{ in} \\ \text{group } j}} [P(i|n,\theta_0)\delta_{ir} - P(i|n,\theta_0)P(r|n,\theta_0)]\delta_{js}/N_j^2 \tag{8}$$

where $\delta_{ir} = 1$ if i = r, $\delta_{ir} = 0$ if i = r, and δ_{js} is defined similarly. B_{ijrs} is given by (1)

$$B_{ijrs} = K'_{ij} V K_{rs} \tag{9}$$

where V is the covariance matrix of the parameter estimates $\hat{\theta}$. Note that A_{ijrs} is associated with random variations in the z_{ni}'s, whereas B_{ijrs} is associated with random variations in $\hat{\theta}$.

The covariance $\text{cov}(\hat{D}_{ij}, \hat{D}_{rs})$ can be obtained by combining A_{ijrs} and B_{ijrs} in the appropriate way. Consider first the case of independent estimation and test data sets. In this case the two terms on the right-hand side of Equation 6 are independent (because they are computed using different data sets), so $\hat{D}_{ij}$ is the difference of two independent random variables. Therefore, $\text{cov}(\hat{D}_{ij}, \hat{D}_{rs})$ is simply the sum of the covariances arising from the independent components of $\hat{D}_{ij}$ and $\hat{D}_{rs}$ (5). In other words,

$$\text{cov}(\hat{D}_{ij}, \hat{D}_{rs}) = A_{ijrs} + B_{ijrs} \tag{10}$$

when the estimation and test data sets are independent.

Derivation of $\text{cov}(\hat{D}_{ij}, \hat{D}_{rs})$ for the case in which the estimation and test data sets are the same is more complicated because $\hat{\theta}$ depends on the z_{ni}'s in this case, which causes the two terms on the right-hand side of Equation 6 to be correlated. Horowitz has shown (1) that when the estimation and test data sets are the same, $\text{cov}(\hat{D}_{ij}, \hat{D}_{rs})$ is the difference between A_{ijrs} and B_{ijrs}. Thus,

$$\text{cov}(\hat{D}_{ij}, \hat{D}_{rs}) = A_{ijrs} - B_{ijrs} \tag{11}$$

when the estimation and test data sets are the same.

To obtain a statistic that tests whether the $\hat{D}_{ij}$'s considered collectively are larger than can be explained by random sampling errors, it is convenient to organize the $\hat{D}_{ij}$'s into a vector and the covariances $\text{cov}(\hat{D}_{ij}, \hat{D}_{rs})$ into a matrix. The appropriate vector is given in row vector form by

$$\hat{D}' = (\hat{D}_{11}, \hat{D}_{21}, \ldots, \hat{D}_{I1}, \hat{D}_{12}, \hat{D}_{22}, \ldots, \hat{D}_{I2}, \ldots, \hat{D}_{1J}, \hat{D}_{2J}, \ldots, \hat{D}_{IJ}) \tag{12}$$

Let $\hat{D}$ denote the corresponding column vector. The appropriate matrix is most conveniently defined in terms of submatrices. Define the I x I submatrix S_{js} (j,s = 1, ..., J) by

$$S_{js} = \begin{bmatrix} \text{cov}(\hat{D}_{1j}, \hat{D}_{1s}) & \text{cov}(\hat{D}_{1j}, \hat{D}_{2s}) \ldots \text{cov}(\hat{D}_{1j}, \hat{D}_{Is}) \\ \text{cov}(\hat{D}_{2j}, \hat{D}_{1s}) & \text{cov}(\hat{D}_{2j}, \hat{D}_{2s}) \ldots \text{cov}(\hat{D}_{2j}, \hat{D}_{Is}) \\ & \ldots \\ \text{cov}(\hat{D}_{Ij}, \hat{D}_{1s}) & \text{cov}(\hat{D}_{Ij}, \hat{D}_{2s}) \ldots \text{cov}(\hat{D}_{Ij}, \hat{D}_{Is}) \end{bmatrix} \tag{13}$$

Then the desired IJ x IJ covariance matrix S is

$$S = \begin{bmatrix} S_{11} & S_{12} & \ldots & S_{1J} \\ S_{21} & S_{22} & \ldots & S_{2J} \\ & & \ldots & \\ S_{J1} & S_{J2} & \ldots & S_{JJ} \end{bmatrix} \tag{14}$$

This matrix contains all the covariances $\text{cov}(\hat{D}_{ij}, \hat{D}_{rs})$ organized in a way that is conformable with the vector $\hat{D}$. In matrix notation $E(\hat{D}\hat{D}') = S$. If the estimation and test data sets are independent, the elements of S are given by Equation 10. If the estimation and test data sets are the same, the elements of S are given by Equation 11.

The matrix S is singular (i.e., its determinant is zero) owing to the existence of exact linear relations among the $\hat{D}_{ij}$'s. For example, for any population group j

$$\sum_{i=1}^{I} \hat{D}_{ij} = 0 \tag{15}$$

because the sums over all alternatives of the predicted and observed market shares must both equal 1. Thus, the elements of $\hat{D}$ are normally distributed with mean zero and singular covariance matrix S when the model being tested is correct.

Define the random variable C by

$$C = \hat{D}' S^- \hat{D} \tag{16}$$

where S^- is any matrix satisfying

$$SS^- S = S \tag{17}$$

S^- is called a generalized inverse of S and, as will be explained shortly, can be computed from S using standard computer software. C is a collective indicator of the sizes of the $\hat{D}_{ij}$'s. Roughly speaking, if the $\hat{D}_{ij}$'s are large, C is large, and if the $\hat{D}_{ij}$'s are small, C is small. Moreover, C has a known probability distribution when the model being tested is correct. Specifically, C has the chi-square distribution with degrees of freedom equal to the rank of S (6). As a result, C can be used to test whether the differences between the predicted and observed market shares are larger than can be explained by random sampling errors. If the $\hat{D}_{ij}$'s differ from zero only because of random sampling errors, with probability $1 - \alpha$ the value of C will be less than the $1 - \alpha$ quantile of the chi-square distribution with degrees of freedom equal to the rank of S. Therefore, if the value of C exceeds the $1 - \alpha$ quantile of this distribution, the model being tested is rejected at the α significance level (i.e., either the model being tested is incorrect or an event of probability α has occurred). By choosing a small enough value of α (values of 0.05 and 0.01 are used frequently in practice), one ensures that there is little likelihood of rejecting a correct model because of the effects of random sampling errors.

Two problems remain to be solved before the test based on the C statistic of Equation 16 (hereafter called the C test) can be implemented in practice. First, the elements of the matrix S depend on the unknown true parameter values θ_0 and on the covariance matrix V of the parameter estimates (see Equations 7-9). A means must be found for estimating these quantities. Second, a method is needed for computing the matrix S^-. The first problem can be solved by using the parameter estimates $\hat{\theta}$ in place of the unknown true values θ_0 in Equations 7 and 8. The matrix V can be estimated by the inverse of the Fisher information matrix of the estimation data set evaluated at the parameter values $\hat{\theta}$ (2,5). This estimate of V is one of the standard outputs of many logit estimation computer programs.

The matrix S^- can be obtained in several different ways. One is by using a commercially available software package for computing generalized inverses of matrices. For example, the operator GINV in the SAS procedure MATRIX computes the generalized inverse of a matrix that is supplied as input to the procedure (7). Another way to compute S^- is by using the eigenvalues and eigenvectors of S. Let W be the matrix whose columns are the eigenvectors of S and let λ_k (k = 1, ..., IJ) denote the corresponding eigenvalues of S. The λ's and the matrix W can be obtained using commercially available computer software such as the subroutine EIGRS of the International Mathematical and Statistical Library (IMSL) (8) or the operator EIGEN in the SAS MATRIX procedure. For each k define λ_k^* by $\lambda_k^* = 1/\lambda_k$ if $\lambda_k = 0$ and $\lambda_k^* = 0$ otherwise. Then the matrix whose (p,q) element is

$$S^-_{pq} = \sum_k \lambda_k^* W_{pk} W_{qk} \tag{18}$$

is a generalized inverse of S (5). A singular matrix has infinitely many generalized inverses, and not all procedures for computing generalized inverses yield the same results. However, any generalized inverse can be used in carrying out the C test.

Implementation

The results of the preceding discussion can be organized into five steps for comparing predicted and observed market shares by means of a C test. These steps, which can easily be programmed for implementation by computer, are as follows:

1. Use the method of maximum likelihood to estimate the values of the parameters $\hat{\theta}$ of the model to be tested and the covariance matrix V of the parameter estimates.
2. Organize the test data set into the desired population groups. For each alternative i and group j, compute the observed market share $\hat{Q}_{ij}$ (Equation 2), the predicted market share $\hat{P}_{ij}$ (Equation 3), and the difference $\hat{D}_{ij}$ between the observed and predicted shares. Organize the elements $\hat{D}_{ij}$ into the vector $\hat{D}$ (Equation 12).
3. Using the estimate of V and the estimated parameter values $\hat{\theta}$ in place of θ_0, compute the quantities A_{ijrs}, B_{ijrs}, and $\text{cov}(\hat{D}_{ij},\hat{D}_{rs})$ (Equations 7-9 and either 10 or 11, depending on whether the estimation and test data sets are independent or the same). Organize the quantities $\text{cov}(\hat{D}_{ij},\hat{D}_{rs})$ into the matrix S (Equations 13 and 14). Determine the rank of S. An easy way to do this is by computing the eigenvalues of S using one of the methods described earlier. The rank of S equals the number of nonzero eigenvalues.
4. Compute S^- using one of the methods described earlier.
5. Compute the test statistic C (Equation 16). Reject the model under consideration at the α significance level if the value of C exceeds the $1 - \alpha$ quantile of the chi-square distribution with degrees of freedom equal to the rank of S.

A numerical example illustrating the application of these steps is given later is this paper.

Division of Data

A statistical test can identify an incorrect model with high probability only if the effects of random sampling errors on the test statistic are less than those of errors in the model. In other words, to maximize a test's power (or ability to identify erroneous models) it is necessary to minimize the effects of random sampling errors.

In the case of the C test, Equations 10 and 11 indicate that the effects of random sampling errors are likely to be smaller when the estimation and test data sets are the same than when they are independent. There are two reasons for this. First, recall that the covariance components A_{ijrs} and B_{ijrs} respectively represent the effects on the $\hat{D}_{ij}$'s of random sampling errors in the z_{ni}'s and the parameter estimates $\hat{\theta}$. Equations 10 and 11 show that the latter errors are added to the former when the estimation and test data sets are independent, whereas the latter are subtracted from the former when the estimation and test data sets are the same. This causes the sampling errors in the $\hat{D}_{ij}$'s to be smaller when the estimation and test data sets are the same than when they are independent. Second, use of independent estimation and test data sets means that only part of the available data is used in each of the two stages, estimation and testing, whereas all of the data is used in both stages when the estimation and test data sets are the same. This also makes the random sampling errors in the $\hat{D}_{ij}$'s smaller when the estimation and test data sets are the same than when they are independent.

Because the random sampling errors in the $\hat{D}_{ij}$'s are smaller when the estimation and test data sets are the same than when they are independent, the power of the C test usually is larger when the same data are used for estimation and testing than when independent data sets are used. [A more formal presentation of this argument is given elsewhere (1).] In summary, when a model is tested by comparing predicted and observed market shares in population groups, all the available data should be used for both estimation and testing whenever this is feasible (i.e., whenever the full data set is not too large for use in model estimation). The data should not be divided into separate estimation and test data sets.

A NUMERICAL EXAMPLE

The example consists of testing the logit model of mode choice. The modes are automobile and transit. The data used in the example consist of 500 observations of choices and the relevant explanatory variables. The observations were generated by simulation from a logit mode-choice model specified as in Equation 1 with

$$X'_{mi}\,\theta_0 = -0.0865T_{mi} - (0.24881C_{mi}/Y_m) + 3A_m R_i - 4.5R_i \tag{19}$$

where

- i = automobile or transit,
- T_{mi} = individual m's travel time (min) by mode i,
- C_{mi} = individual m's travel cost (cents) by mode i,
- Y_m = individual m's annual income ($10,000s),
- A_m = number of automobiles owned by individual m's household, and
- R_i = 1 if mode i is automobile and 0 if mode i is transit.

[Those who wish to work through this example in detail may obtain a copy of the data set and the FORTRAN program that generated it from the author on request.]

The logit model that is tested in the example has the specification

$$X'_{mi}\,\theta = \theta_1 T_{mi} + (\theta_2 C_{mi}/Y_m) + \theta_3 R_i \tag{20}$$

This model is incorrect because it does not include the variable $A_m R_i$. To maximize the probability that the C test will identify the model of Equation 20 as incorrect, the same data set will be used for both estimation and testing.

The C test will now be implemented by carrying out the five steps given in the previous section.

Step 1

The maximum-likelihood estimates of the parameters of the model of Equation 20 and the estimate of the covariance matrix V are given in Table 1. Note that the signs of the time and cost coefficients are consistent with expectation and that the t-statistics of these coefficients are satisfactory. Thus, neither the signs nor the t-statistics suggest that the model is incorrect. The nonsignificance of the estimated coefficient of R_i does not indicate that the model is incorrect because there are no strong a priori expectations concerning the importance of this variable.

Step 2

Two population groups are used in this example: Group 1 consists of individuals whose households own one car, and group 2 consists of individuals whose households own two cars. All individuals in the data set used in the example are from one-car or two-car households. The values of the $\hat{Q}_{ij}$'s, $\hat{P}_{ij}$'s, and $\hat{D}_{ij}$'s are shown in Table 2. Organizing the D_{ij} values into the vector $\hat{D}$ yields

$$\hat{D} = \begin{bmatrix} -0.1124 \\ 0.1124 \\ 0.0942 \\ -0.0942 \end{bmatrix} \quad (21)$$

TABLE 1 Estimation Results for the Logit Model of Equation 20

Parameter	Estimated Value	t-Statistic
θ_1	-0.05056	-2.494
θ_2	-0.2148	-9.382
θ_3	0.3194	1.158

$$V = \begin{bmatrix} 0.4110 & -0.3542 & 4.318 \\ -0.3542 & 0.5242 & -2.388 \\ 4.318 & -2.388 & 76.08 \end{bmatrix} \times 10^{-3}$$

TABLE 2 Values of Q_{ij}, P_{ij}, and D_{ij} for the Numerical Example

i (Mode)[a]	j (Group)	$\hat{Q}_{ij}$	$\hat{P}_{ij}$	$\hat{D}_{ij}$
1	1	0.3465	0.4588	-0.1123
2	1	0.6535	0.5412	0.1123
1	2	0.6618	0.5676	0.0942
2	2	0.3382	0.4324	-0.0942

[a] Mode 1 is automobile, and mode 2 is transit.

Step 3

The row vectors K'_{ij} defined in Equation 7 are

$$K'_{11} = (-0.9799,\ 0.4670,\ 0.09388) \quad (22a)$$

$$K'_{21} = (0.9799,\ -0.4670,\ -0.09388) \quad (22b)$$

$$K'_{12} = (-0.8070,\ 0.2279,\ 0.08145) \quad (22c)$$

$$K'_{22} = (0.8070,\ -0.2279,\ -0.08145) \quad (22d)$$

The covariance terms A_{ijrs}, B_{ijrs}, and $\text{cov}(\hat{D}_{ij},\hat{D}_{rs})$ are shown in Table 3. Organizing the quantities $\text{cov}(\hat{D}_{ij},\hat{D}_{rs})$ into the matrix S yields

$$S = \begin{bmatrix} 0.2033 & -0.2033 & -0.1704 & 0.1704 \\ -0.2033 & 0.2033 & 0.1704 & -0.1704 \\ -0.1704 & 0.1704 & 0.1429 & -0.1429 \\ 0.1704 & -0.1704 & -0.1429 & 0.1429 \end{bmatrix} \times 10^{-3} \quad (23)$$

The eigenvalues of S were computed using the subroutine EIGRS of the IMSL and are (0, 0, 0, 6.923 x 10^{-3}). Because there is only one nonzero eigenvalue, the rank of S is 1.

Step 4

The generalized inverse of S as computed from Equation 18 is

$$S^{-} = \begin{bmatrix} 424.2 & -424.2 & -355.6 & 355.6 \\ -424.2 & 424.2 & 355.6 & -355.6 \\ -355.6 & 355.6 & 298.0 & -298.0 \\ 355.6 & -355.6 & -298.0 & 298.0 \end{bmatrix} \quad (24)$$

Step 5

The test statistic C is computed by substituting Equations 21 and 24 into Equation 16. The result is C = 62.15. The 0.95 quantile of the chi-square distribution with 1 degree of freedom is 3.841. Because the computed value of C exceeds this, the model of Equation 20 is rejected as incorrect at the 0.05 significance level.

CONCLUSIONS

Testing a disaggregate choice model by comparing predicted and observed market shares has much intuitive appeal, but it is not the only way in which these models can be tested. A large number of test procedures based on likelihood ratio tests, Lagrangian multiplier tests, and the likelihood ratio index goodness-of-fit statistic are also available (9,10). It is worthwhile to consider how one might choose among these tests in practical model development.

An important difference between the C test discussed in this paper and the other tests is that the other tests require the analyst to specify an alternative model (e.g., a logit model with a different specification of the utility function $X'_{mi}\theta$) against which the model under consideration is to be tested. In effect, these tests attempt to determine whether the alternative model fits the available data better than the model under consideration does, in which case the model under consideration is rejected as being incorrect. In contrast, the C test does not require specification of an alternative

TABLE 3 Covariance Terms for the Example

A_{ijrs}

		s = 1, r=1	s = 1, r=2	s = 2, r=1	s = 2, r=2
j = 1	i = 1	4.117×10^{-4}	-4.117×10^{-4}	0	0
	i = 2	-4.117×10^{-4}	4.117×10^{-4}	0	0
j = 2	i = 1	0	0	2.995×10^{-4}	-2.995×10^{-4}
	i = 2	0	0	-2.995×10^{-4}	2.995×10^{-4}

B_{ijrs}

		s = 1, r=1	s = 1, r=2	s = 2, r=1	s = 2, r=2
j = 1	i = 1	2.084×10^{-4}	-2.084×10^{-4}	1.704×10^{-4}	-1.704×10^{-4}
	i = 2	-2.084×10^{-4}	2.084×10^{-4}	-1.704×10^{-4}	1.704×10^{-4}
j = 2	i = 1	1.704×10^{-4}	-1.704×10^{-4}	1.566×10^{-4}	-1.566×10^{-4}
	i = 2	-1.704×10^{-4}	1.704×10^{-4}	-1.566×10^{-4}	1.566×10^{-4}

$\mathrm{cov}(\hat{D}_{ij}, \hat{D}_{rs})$

		s = 1, r=1	s = 1, r=2	s = 2, r=1	s = 2, r=2
j = 1	i = 1	2.033×10^{-4}	-2.033×10^{-4}	-1.704×10^{-4}	1.704×10^{-4}
	i = 2	-2.033×10^{-4}	2.033×10^{-4}	1.704×10^{-4}	-1.704×10^{-4}
j = 2	i = 1	-1.704×10^{-4}	1.704×10^{-4}	1.429×10^{-4}	-1.429×10^{-4}
	i = 2	1.704×10^{-4}	-1.704×10^{-4}	-1.429×10^{-4}	1.429×10^{-4}

model. In effect, it tests the model under consideration against all alternatives simultaneously.

The ability of a test against a specific alternative to identify an erroneous model and the relative power of the C test and a test against a specific alternative depend on the choice of the alternative. As is discussed elsewhere (1,11), a test of an erroneous model against an alternative that is a good approximation to the correct model is likely to be much more powerful than a C test. However, a test against an alternative that is a poor approximation to the correct model can be less powerful than a C test.

These considerations suggest that the C test and tests against specific alternatives are complements, rather than substitutes, and that both types of tests should be carried out during the process of developing empirical models. A practical approach to this begins by formulating several alternatives to the model currently under consideration. The developer of an empirical model can virtually always do this. Although there can be no assurance that any of these alternatives is correct or approximately correct (if there could be such assurance, the tests being discussed here would be unnecessary), one or more of the alternatives may nonetheless provide a powerful test of the current model if the model is seriously erroneous (9). Accordingly, the current model should be tested against the alternatives using likelihood ratio tests or other appropriate procedures (9,10). However, it is not possible to test a model against all reasonable alternatives, and failure to reject the current model in tests against specific alternatives may be the result of a poor choice of alternatives rather than an indication that the current model is correct. Therefore, if the current model is not rejected in tests against specific alternatives, a C test should be carried out. The C test amounts to a test of the current model against all remaining alternatives and may have a higher probability of detecting errors in the current model than do the tests against specific alternatives if the specific alternatives are themselves highly erroneous.

ACKNOWLEDGMENT

The work reported in this paper was supported in part by a cooperative agreement between UMTA and the University of Iowa.

REFERENCES

1. J.L. Horowitz. Testing Probabilistic Discrete Choice Models of Travel Demand by Comparing Predicted and Observed Aggregate Choice Shares. Transportation Research, in press (1985).
2. T.A. Domencich and D. McFadden. Urban Travel Demand: A Behavioral Analysis. American Elsevier, New York, 1975.
3. D.A. Hensher and L.W. Johnson. Applied Discrete-Choice Modelling. Croom Helm, London, 1981.
4. H. Chernoff. Large-Sample Theory: Parametric Case. Annals of Mathematical Statistics, Vol. 27, 1956, pp. 1-22.

5. C.R. Rao. Linear Statistical Inference and Its Applications, 2nd ed. Wiley, New York, 1973.
6. C.R. Rao and S.K. Mitra. Generalized Inverse of Matrices and Its Applications. Wiley, New York, 1971.
7. SAS User's Guide: Statistics. SAS Institute, Inc., Cary, N.C., 1982.
8. The IMSL Library. IMSL, Inc., Houston, Texas, 1982.
9. J. Horowitz. Specification Tests for Probabilistic Choice Models. Transportation Research, Vol. 16A, 1982, pp. 383-394.
10. J.L. Horowitz. Evaluation of Usefulness of Two Standard Goodness-of-Fit Indicators for Comparing Non-Nested Random Utility Models. In Transportation Research Record 874, TRB, National Research Council, Washington, D.C., 1982, pp. 19-25.
11. A. Wald. Tests of Statistical Hypotheses Concerning Several Parameters When the Number of Observations Is Large. Transactions of the American Mathematical Society, Vol. 54, 1943, pp. 426-487.

[15]

TRANSPORTATION SCIENCE, Vol. 11, No. 4, November 1977

Multinomial Probit and Qualitative Choice: A Computationally Efficient Algorithm

CARLOS F. DAGANZO

University of California, Berkeley

FERNANDO BOUTHELIER and YOSEF SHEFFI

Massachusetts Institute of Technology, Cambridge, Massachusetts

Even though multinomial probit models have many attractive theoretical features and have been proposed for diverse choice problems (such as modal split and route choice in the transportation field), they have never been used in practice due to the lack of an adequate numerical technique for their application. The purpose of this paper is to introduce such a technique and to demonstrate the feasibility of forecasting with multinominal probit models. Our limited computational experience with the proposed numerical technique indicates that it is accurate, and can be efficiently applied to large choice problems.

1. INTRODUCTION

Travel demand analyses often require prediction of human choice from among a set of alternatives. This set of alternatives (the choice set) varies with the scope of the problem. For instance, a set of zones (which are usually spatially aggregated into centroids) is the choice set for trip distribution or land use, whereas a set of routes or modes is the choice set for traffic assignment or modal split.

Traditionally, each of these aspects of travel demand forecasting has been handled with a specific technique of its own; the techniques used, however, have always explicitly or implicitly assumed that humans behave rationally. In one of the most popular approaches to modelling rational human behavior, one assumes that humans select the alternative which they believe exhibits the largest utility. This approach is typified in the transportation field by the so-called "all or nothing" traffic assignment techniques[1] which allocate all the traffic between an origin-destination pair to the shortest route (i.e., the alternative with the largest utility).

It has been long recognized, however, that, with such a deterministic approach, observed and predicted patterns differ substantially because similar persons often make different choices. That humans make different choices was first recognized in route selection models by means of empirical traffic-diversion curves.[2] This phenomenon was later included in modal split models[3, 4] and, more recently, in a variety of models for traffic assignment,[5] trip distribution,[6] and combination of these.

The uncertainty associated with the way in which humans behave can be captured by the so-called random utility models, of which all of the above applications are special cases. The two basic postulates of these models are that the perceived utility, U_i, of alternative i, can be expressed as

$$U_i = V_i + \xi_i, \tag{1}$$

in which V_i is the observed (or measured) utility and ξ_i is an error term (which is modelled as a random variable); and that choice makers choose the alternative with the highest *perceived* utility.

The measured utility, V_i, is usually specified as a function of some key attributes of the alternative and some socioeconomic characteristics of the choice maker. The attractiveness of an alternative to choice makers with the same measured utility is not necessarily the same because of the choice makers' inherent inaccurate perception of V_i and because of many unquantifiable factors not included in V_i. The error terms, ξ_i, are included to capture such discrepancies; they are modelled as random variables in order to ensure that not all individuals from a group of people with same measured utilities $(V_1, \cdots, V_n)$ select the alternative with the highest measured utility. An overview of random utility models and their application to choice problems can be found in reference 7.

The probability of choosing the ith alternative, p_i, from a set of n is thus

$$p_i = P_r[U_i > U_j, \forall j \neq i], \tag{2}$$

i.e.,

$$\begin{aligned} p_i &= P_r[\xi_j < V_i - V_j + \xi_i, \forall j \neq i] \\ &= \int_{-\infty}^{\infty} P_r[\xi_i \epsilon [t, t + dt) \text{ and } \xi_j \epsilon (-\infty, t + V_i - V_j), \forall j \neq i]. \end{aligned} \tag{3}$$

Letting $F(t_1, \cdots, t_n)$ denote the distribution function of the error terms, $\xi = (\xi_1, \cdots, \xi_n)$, and $F_i(t_1, \cdots, t_n)$ its partial derivative with respect to t_i (assumed to exist), one can rewrite (3) as

$$p_i = \int_{-\infty}^{\infty} F_i(\cdots, t + V_i - V_j, \cdots)\, dt. \tag{4}$$

If the error terms ξ are independently identically distributed (i.i.d.) Gumbel variates, (4) reduces to[8–10]:

$$p_i = e^{V_i} / \sum_{j=1}^{n} e^{V_j}. \tag{5}$$

This is the well known multinomial logit (MNL) formula of choice theory and the above derivation provides its theoretical justification. Equation (5), however, must be used with extreme care as the i.i.d. error terms can produce paradoxical results when, for example, the alternatives are not evaluated independently. In route choice problems, specifically, (5) gives unrealistic results[11] since routes which overlap heavily are not likely to be evaluated independently by rational decision makers.[12, 13]

Multinomial probit (MNP) models provide a more attractive alternative to the MNL models of (5) as they are based on the hypothesis that the error terms, ξ, are multivariate normal (MVN) distributed with zero mean and covariance matrix, Σ. In some instances, it can even be shown that an MNP model is theoretically justified and one can derive the functional structure of the covariance matrix.[13]

Unfortunately, (4) is not easy to compute for MNP models and only very small problems have been successfully tackled to date. Hausman and Wise[14] evaluate the multiple integral (4) by series of expansions of the integrand. Although the error introduced by the series approximation seems to be small, the method is computationally cumbersome. The dimensionality of the integral in (4) increases linearly with the number of alternatives and this makes the method unfeasible for several alternatives (say more than 3). More recently and almost simultaneously Lerman and Manski[15] and Daganzo, Bouthelier, and Sheffi[16] developed two alternate approaches to calculate (4). Lerman and Manski[15] proposed to use Monte Carlo simulation to calculate the probability of choice. The method is attractive because it can theoretically approximate the probabilities of choice of any random utility model (not just the MNP model) for any number of alternatives. The simulation technique, however, is seriously biased when the probabilities of choice are small, is not suited for optimization purposes in the neighborhood of the optimum, and is very expensive.

This paper further develops and evaluates the numerical technique originally proposed by Daganzo, Bouthelier, and Sheffi.[16] The technique is based on approximate recursive formulas[17] to (4) and, as shown below, is sufficiently accurate and fast to be successfully applied to choice problems of realistic size.

The relative merits of the simulation approach and the approximation methods described in this paper are discussed in Appendix II.

2. THE APPROXIMATION FORMULA: CLARK'S METHOD

CLARK[17] has developed analytic formulas to approximate the distribution of max $(U_1, \cdots, U_n)$, where the n random variables, U_j, have an unrestricted joint normal distribution. He has discussed the application of the formulas to nonnormal distributions and the accuracy of the approximation for special cases.

For $n = 3$, Clark obtained formulas for the exact values of the first four moments about zero, $(\nu_1 \cdots \nu_4)$, of the maximum of U_1 and U_2, max (U_1, U_2), and the coefficient of linear correlation of max (U_1, U_2) and U_3. He then approximated the maximum of two normal random variables by a normal random variable, i.e.:

$$\max (U_1, U_2) \sim N(\nu_1; \nu_2 - \nu_1^2). \qquad (6)$$

This made it possible to obtain the approximate distribution of the maximum of 3 (and more) variables with the following recursive formula:

$$\max (U_1, U_2, \cdots, U_{n-1}, U_n) = \max [\max (U_1, \cdots, U_{n-1}), U_n]. \quad (7)$$

Thus, after $n - 1$ iterations, one can obtain the approximate mean and variance, $\mu_{\max}$ and $\sigma^2_{\max}$, of the greatest value and the following approximation to its distribution:

$$\max (U_1, \cdots, U_n) \sim N(\mu_{\max}; \sigma^2_{\max}). \qquad (8)$$

Due to the error introduced by (6) the results obtained are approximations to the actual values. The magnitude of the error varies with the number of random variables taken into consideration. Table I displays the accuracy levels reported by Clark in his paper.

Clark had developed these recursive formulas to predict the mean and variance of project duration in PERT networks with random activity durations.

In this context the formulas are quite accurate and are used in practice. For choice theory, however, a reasonable good approximation of the shape of the distribution function of max $\{U_1, \cdots, U_n\}$ is also needed since, as it will become clear in the next section, choice probabilities are determined by the general shape of the distribution of max $\{U_1, \cdots, U_n\}$. When $U_1, \cdots, U_n$ are mutually independent, the exact distribution function of

TABLE I

The Expected Value of the Greatest of n Independent Standardized Normal Variables

n	E [max $(Z_1, \cdots, Z_n)$]	Approximation	Differences
2	0.5642	0.5642	0
3	0.8463	0.8476	+0.0013
4	1.0294	1.0310	+0.0016
5	1.1630	1.1643	+0.0013
6	1.2672	1.2679	+0.0007
7	1.3522	1.3522	0
8	1.4236	1.4230	−0.0006
9	1.4850	1.4837	−0.0013
10	1.5388	1.5367	−0.0021

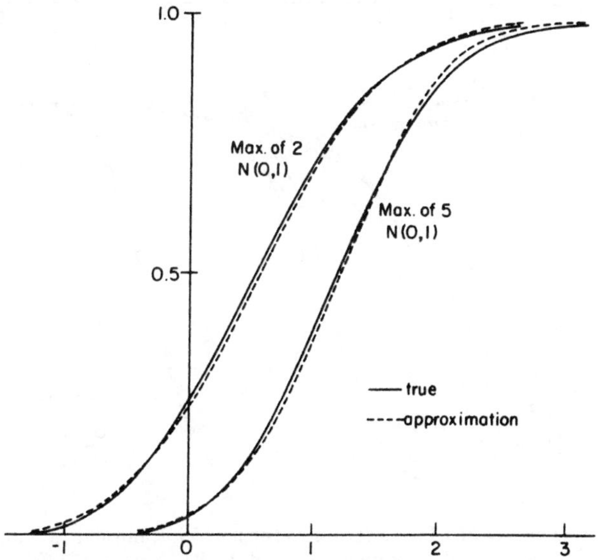

Fig. 1. Accuracy of Clark's formulas for i.i.d. normal random variables.

max $\{U_1, \cdots, U_n\}$ can be obtained by multiplying the cumulative distribution functions of $U_1, U_2 \cdots U_n$. This enables us to assess the accuracy of (8) more thoroughly. Figure 1 displays the true and approximate distribution functions of max $\{U_1, \cdots, U_n\}$ for $n = 2$ and $n = 5$ and for i.i.d. standard normal variables. Figure 2, A and B, illustrates that the accuracy of the approximation improves when the means of the random variables are different and drops when the variances become very different.

When $U_1 \cdots U_n$ are not mutually independent, one can no longer use a simple numerical approach to calculate the distribution function of max $(U_1, \cdots, U_n)$. Nevertheless, the existence of positive correla-

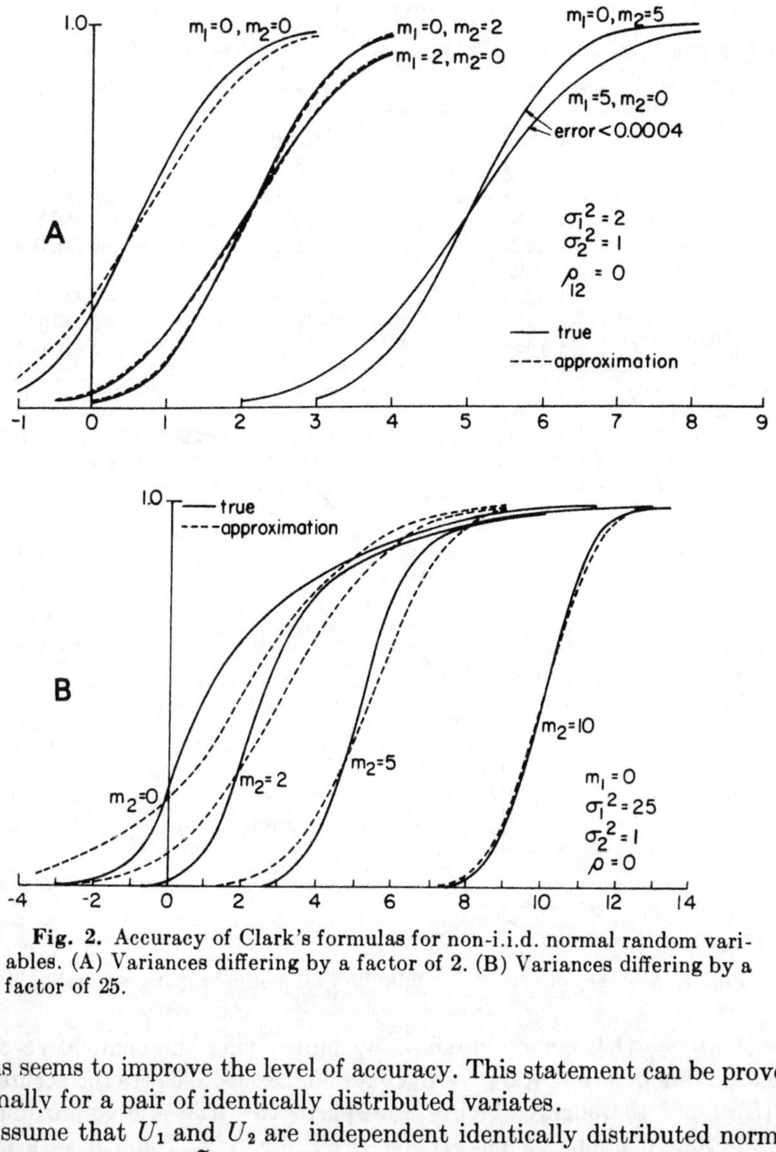

Fig. 2. Accuracy of Clark's formulas for non-i.i.d. normal random variables. (A) Variances differing by a factor of 2. (B) Variances differing by a factor of 25.

tions seems to improve the level of accuracy. This statement can be proven formally for a pair of identically distributed variates.

Assume that U_1 and U_2 are independent identically distributed normal variables and write $\tilde{F}_U(x)$ and $F_U(x)$, respectively, for the approximate and exact distribution function of max $\{U_1, U_2\}$.

If we let $\epsilon_U = F_U(x) - \tilde{F}_U(x)$ and $\epsilon_U^* = \sup_x \{| \epsilon_U(x) |\}$, we have the following:

PROPOSITION. *If W_1 and W_2 are bivariate normal random variables marginally distributed like U_1 and U_2 and with corr $(W_1, W_2) = \rho > 0$, the maxi-*

mum absolute error when using the normal approximation to the distribution function of max $\{W_1, W_2\}$, ϵ_W^*, *is no greater than* ϵ_U^*.

Proof. Let $E(U_1) = E(U_2) = m$ and var $(U_1) =$ var $(U_2) = \sigma^2$. The following change of variable yields a bivariate random variable, $W = (W_1, W_2)$ distributed as required in the proposition:

$$W_1 = \sqrt{1-\rho}\,(U_1 - m) + \sqrt{\rho}\,\sigma Z + m \tag{9a}$$

$$W_2 = \sqrt{1-\rho}\,(U_2 - m) + \sqrt{\rho}\,\sigma Z + m \tag{9b}$$

where Z is an independent standard normal variate. The distribution of max $\{W_1, W_2\}$ can be obtained if we take into account that

$$\max\{W_1, W_2\} = \sqrt{1-\rho}\,[\max(U_1, U_2) - m] + \sqrt{\rho}\,\sigma Z + m. \tag{10}$$

It is:

$$\Pr[\max\{W_1, W_2\} \leqq x]$$

$$= \int_{-\infty}^{\infty} \Pr\left[\max\{U_1, U_2\} \leqq \frac{x - m - \sqrt{\rho}\,\sigma t}{\sqrt{1-\rho}} + m\right]\phi(t)\,dt,$$

where $\phi(t) = (2\pi)^{-1/2}\exp\{-x^2/2\}$ is the density function of Z.

Using the above mentioned function, we have:

$$F_W(x) = \int_{-\infty}^{\infty} F_U(Ax + Bt + C)\phi(t)\,dt$$

where $A = \dfrac{1}{\sqrt{1-\rho}}$, $B = -\sqrt{\dfrac{\rho}{1-\rho}}\,\sigma$ and $C = m\left(1 - \dfrac{1}{\sqrt{1-\rho}}\right)$. In order to obtain $\tilde{F}_W(x)$, we note that $\tilde{F}_U(x)$ and $\tilde{F}_W(x)$ are normally distributed and have the same means and variances, respectively, as $F_U(x)$ and $F_W(x)$ (Clark's formulas are exact the first time around). Obviously, then, if max (U_1, U_2) was $\tilde{F}_U(x)$ distributed, the left hand side of (10) would also be normally distributed (it is a linear combination of normal variates) with exact mean and variance, i.e., it would be $\tilde{F}_W(x)$ distributed. Consequently, applying the change of variable defined by (10) to $\tilde{F}_U(x)$ one can write:

$$\tilde{F}_W(x) = \int_{-\infty}^{\infty} \tilde{F}_U(Ax + Bt + C)\phi(t)\,dt,$$

and subtracting this from the above expression for $F_W(x)$ one gets:

$$\epsilon_W(x) = \int_{-\infty}^{\infty} \epsilon_U(Ax + Bt + C)\phi(t)\,dt \leqq \int_{-\infty}^{\infty} \epsilon_U^*\phi(t)\,dt = \epsilon_U^*$$

which proves the proposition.

Since the normal approximation is very accurate except perhaps when the means of the two variables are equal, the correlation is zero or negative and the variances very different (an almost pathological combination of conditions infrequently encountered in practice) we conclude that Clark's formulas appear to be sufficiently accurate for our purposes.

In addition to this analytical evidence, we also report in the sequel of the paper that in our runs with simulated data, the differences between the estimated and true parameter values were never statistically significant. Appendix II also contains a satisfactory comparison with simulated results.

3. PREDICTION WITH MULTINOMIAL PROBIT MODELS

LET US now derive the probabilities of choice for an MNP model and illustrate the technique with a numerical example.

From (2), the probability of choosing the last alternative, p_n, is given by:

$$p_n = P_r[U_n > \max(U_1, \cdots, U_{n-1})]. \qquad (11)$$

From the numerical technique described in Section 2, it is possible to compute approximately:

$$\mu_{-n} = E(\max(U_1, \cdots, U_{n-1}))$$

$$\sigma_{-n}^2 = \mathrm{Var}(\max(U_1, \cdots, U_{n-1}))$$

$$\sigma_{-n,n}^2 = \mathrm{Cov}(\max(U_1, \cdots, U_{n-1}), U_n)$$

and thus (remembering that $E(U_n) = V_n$)

$$p_n = P_r[\max(U_1, \cdots, U_{n-1}) - U_n < 0]$$

$$\simeq \Phi[(V_n - \mu_{-n})/\sqrt{(\sigma_n^2 + \sigma_{-n}^2 - 2\sigma_{-n,n}^2)}\,]$$

where $\Phi(x)$ is the standard normal distribution function.

It must be noted that (especially for large n) the order in which the $n - 1$ first random variables are selected to compute μ_{-n}, σ_{-n}^2, and $\sigma_{-n,n}^2$ may affect the final value for p_n. However, Daganzo, Bouthelier, and Sheffi[16] have applied the MNP technique discussed in this paper to a route choice problem with ten alternatives (in different order) and this phenomenon was not of practical significance.

We now illustrate numerically some properties of MNP models with a typical transportation choice problem involving two transit alternatives (say buses and streetcars) and the private auto. We assume that the two transit alternatives are not evaluated independently as, naturally, humans will have similar biases towards both of them. That is,

$$U \sim \text{MVN}\left(\begin{bmatrix} V_1 \\ V_2 \\ V_3 \end{bmatrix}; \begin{bmatrix} \sigma_1^2 & \sigma_{12}^2 & 0 \\ \sigma_{12}^2 & \sigma_2^2 & 0 \\ 0 & 0 & \sigma_3^2 \end{bmatrix}\right).$$

Figure 3 illustrates that the probabilities of choice depend quite markedly on the variance-covariance structure of the error terms, ξ_i, and that consequently use of MNL should be restricted to situations where the error terms can be reasonably expected to be independent and identically distributed. The limiting case with $\rho = 1$ corresponds to the well-known "red bus-blue bus paradox" in connection with (5) and, as expected, MNP exhibits reasonable behavior.

4. ESTIMATION

IN ORDER TO forecast with MNP models it is necessary to infer the values of V and Σ with statistical techniques. One starts by specifying the model; that is, by postulating, a set of functional relationships which define the measured utilities, V_i, and the elements of the covariance matrix, σ_{lm}^2, in terms of a vector of attributes of the alternatives and the choice-maker (time, cost, income, etc. . . .), v, and of some unknown vectors of parameters, α,

$$V_i = V_i(v; \alpha); \qquad i = 1, \cdots, n \tag{12.a}$$

$$\sigma_{lm}^2 = \sigma_{lm}^2(v; \alpha); \, l, m = 1, \cdots, n \tag{12.b}$$

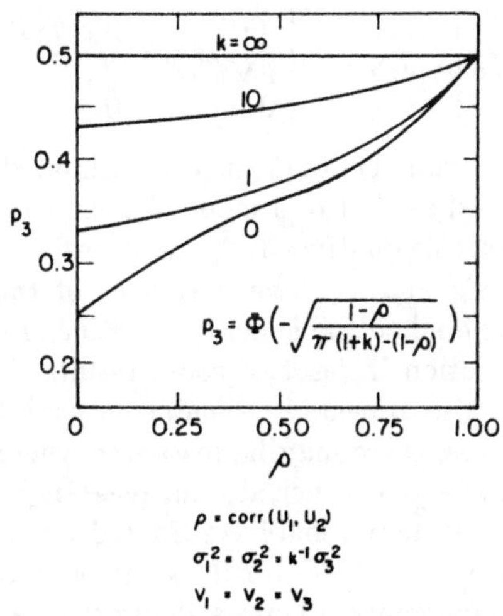

Fig. 3. The effect of correlation on the probability of choosing a third alternative, p_3.

The problem is then to find the values of the parameters α that best fit the available data. Each observation consists of a set of attribute levels for each one of the alternatives and an observed choice.

The maximum likelihood technique is the most efficient method known to deal with this problem and it consists of determining values of α , $\hat{\alpha}$, which maximize the likelihood function $L(\alpha)$:

$$L(\alpha) = \prod_{j=1}^{N} p_{C^{(j)}}(v^{(j)}, \alpha) \qquad (13)$$

where $C^{(j)}$ is the choice taken by the jth observation (part of our data), N is the sample size, $v^{(j)}$ is the vector of attribute levels for the jth observation (part of our data) and $p_{C^{(j)}}(v^{(j)}, \alpha)$ is the probability of the observed choice. $p_{C^{(j)}}$ can be calculated by means of (12) and the recursive formulas described in Section 2.

Equation (13) (or its logarithm) can be maximized with the help of efficient nonlinear programming algorithms. Since for our particular problem, it is quite time consuming to compute (13), an optimal step gradient search technique which computes (13) a minimum number of times was tailored to our problem. It is basically a feasible direction steepest ascent algorithm which performs a one-dimensional Fibbonacci search at each iteration.

We illustrate the technique with a very simple example with three alternatives and two parameters. The simplicity of the example will enable us to display the results graphically and to illustrate the essential points.

Simulated data (Appendix I) has been used instead of real data to verify the accuracy of the method. The model is specified as follows:

$$V = \begin{bmatrix} -T_1 \\ -T_2 \\ -T_3 \end{bmatrix} \qquad \Sigma = \theta \begin{bmatrix} T_1 & \rho\sqrt{T_1T_2} & 0 \\ \rho\sqrt{T_1T_2} & T_2 & 0 \\ 0 & 0 & T_3 \end{bmatrix} \qquad (14)$$

where θ and ρ are the parameters that must be estimated. The specification of (14) can be visualized as that of a mode choice problem between auto, shared ride, and transit (alternatives 1, 2, and 3, respectively) with known generalized costs T_1, T_2, and T_3. The variances of the error term were assumed to be proportional to the generalized costs, T_i, which seemed to be a reasonable assumption in light of some results that apply to route choice.[13] Although it also appears reasonable to have the same constant θ, for all the alternatives, there may be instances where this is not so (in the case of auto vs. taxi—plus other alternatives—it is clear that since a fare must be paid, cost is more reliably estimated for taxi than for auto).

The algorithm was applied twice with two poor initial starting points to test the speed of convergence. Figure 4 shows the resulting convergence pattern.

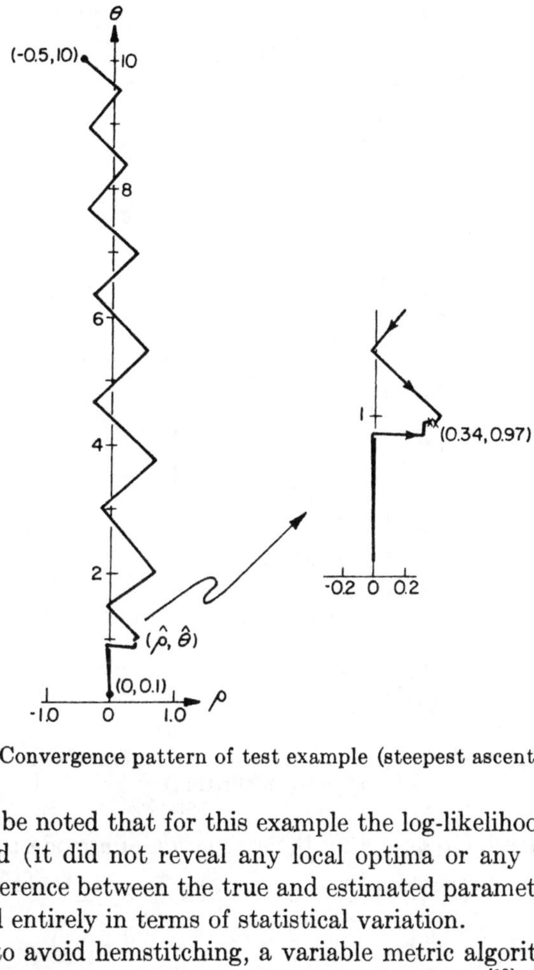

Fig. 4. Convergence pattern of test example (steepest ascent algorithm).

It should be noted that for this example the log-likelihood function was well-behaved (it did not reveal any local optima or any "valleys") and that the difference between the true and estimated parameters value could be explained entirely in terms of statistical variation.

In order to avoid hemstitching, a variable metric algorithm which uses Davidson-Fletcher-Powell's (DFP) updating formula[18] for the inverse Hessian of the likelihood function was developed. The number of steps for convergence was substantially reduced as can be seen from Figure 5. Variable metric algorithms, thus, seem very attractive, especially since the savings are more noticeable with more parameters and the additional cost per step incurred by the Hessian updating calculations is negligible compared to the cost of one step.

5. COMPUTATIONAL COSTS

The special structure of the recursive formulas used for the evaluation of the objective function plus the strategy used for the search technique led us to the following "a priori" formula for central processing unit

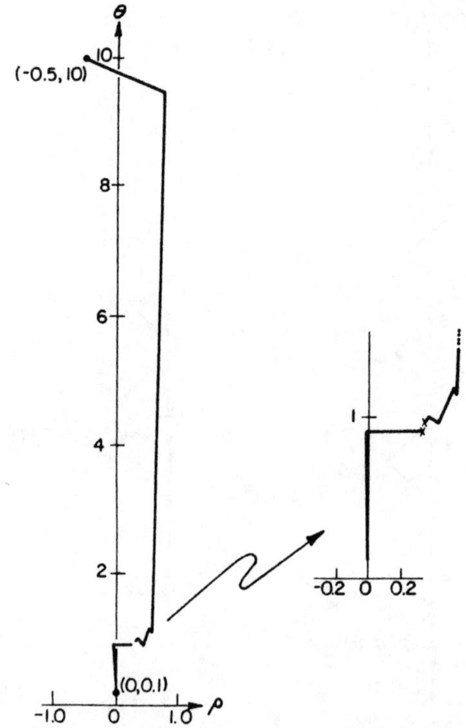

Fig. 5. Convergence pattern of the test example (variable metric algorithm).

(c.p.u.) execution time required by the estimation of a model:

$$T = NS(P + \beta_C)((A - 2)(A + 3))\alpha_C$$

where

N is the sample size
A is the number of alternatives
P is the number of parameters
S is the number of steps performed by the search algorithm

and α_C and β_C are two parameters which depend on the type of machine used.

Limited testing on an IBM 370 computer yielded values of

$$\beta_C = 10$$

$$\alpha_C = \tfrac{1}{2} \times 10^{-5} \text{ min},$$

i.e.,
$$T = NS(P + 10)\,\frac{(A - 2)(A + 3)}{6} \times 10^{-5} \text{ min.} \qquad (16)$$

Equation (16) applies to both, the gradient search and the variable metric methods; the number of steps, S, is, in the latter case, comparable with the number of unknown parameters. Thus, a problem with 5 alternatives, 10 unknown parameters, and 1,000 data points, which runs 5 steps, would use about 4 min of c.p.u. time. Small problems are solved very efficiently. For instance, estimation of a problem with 3 alternatives, 4 parameters, and 100 data points in 4 steps takes less than 4 sec of c.p.u. time. Table II displays the c.p.u. times of the 3 experiments that were performed.

Prediction of the final probabilities of choice from a calibrated model is very inexpensive as even larger problems with more than 10 alternatives require less than 10 sec to perform all calculations and data manipulations.

In order to verify the computation requirements, an example of realistic size with 5 alternatives, 500 data points, and 9 parameters was exercised. The specification of the utilities for each 1 of the 5 alternatives is similar to the specification selected by Lerman and Ben-Akiva for an auto-ownership study,[19] namely:

$$
\begin{aligned}
V_0 &= \beta_6 \log (I) + \beta_7(\mathrm{DIST}) + \beta_8 (\mathrm{CBD}) \\
V_1 &= \beta_1 + \beta_5 A + \beta_6 \log (I\text{-}1000) + 2\beta_8 (\mathrm{CBD}) \\
V_2 &= \beta_2 + 2\beta_5 A + \beta_6 \log (I\text{-}2000) + 3\beta_8 (\mathrm{CBD}) \\
V_3 &= \beta_3 + 3\beta_5 A + \beta_6 \log (I\text{-}3000) + 4\beta_8 (\mathrm{CBD}) \\
V_4 &= \beta_4 + 4\beta_5 A + \beta_6 \log (I\text{-}4000) + 5\beta_8 (\mathrm{CBD})
\end{aligned}
$$

where V_i is the measured utility of owning i cars ($i < 4$), V_4 is the measured

TABLE II

Predicted and Observed Computation Times

Experiments	1	2	3
Data set size (N)	50	50	500
Number of steps (S)	4	14	5
Number of parameters (P)	2	2	2
Number of alternatives (A)	3	3	3
Predicted time (T) (in thousandths of minute)	24	84	300
Actual time (time)	27	107*	270

* The predicted time and the actual time differ in this case because all 14 steps were longer than average due to the artificial remoteness of the initial values. When the starting point is far away from the optimum value, the initial steps are longer and the undimensional Fibonacci search performed at each iteration requires more function evaluations.

utility derived from owning four or more cars and:

A = 1/number of licensed drivers in household (if NLD = 0, $A = 0$)
I = annual income of household in dollars
DIST = distance from household to transit
CBD = 1 if work place is CBD; 0 otherwise.

Since the MNL log-likelihood function is concave for specifications linear in the parameter and the MNL formula can be approximated by an MNP with independent error terms (at least for three or four alternatives), it is reasonable to expect that the log-likelihood function for MNP models is also concave if the error terms are independent. Because of this and in light of the well-behaved example reported in the previous section, we decided to select a highly nonlinear specification for the covariance matrix to see if this would have an effect on the unimodality of the log-likelihood function. The covariance matrix of the error terms, Σ, was taken to be

$$\underset{i \leq j}{\sigma_{ij}} = \beta_9[| V_1 | + | V_2 - V_1 | + \cdots + | V_1 - V_{i-1} |]$$

Note that Σ corresponds to a case where the marginal perceived utilities are independent multivariate normal random variables with zero mean. Their variance-covariance matrix is:

$$\text{var} - \text{cov}\,(\xi_0; \xi_1 - \xi_0; \xi_2 - \xi_1; \xi_3 - \xi_2; \xi_4 - \xi_3)$$

$$= \begin{bmatrix} V_0 & 0 & 0 & 0 & 0 \\ 0 & | V_1 - V_0 | & 0 & 0 & 0 \\ 0 & 0 & | V_2 - V_1 | & 0 & 0 \\ 0 & 0 & 0 & | V_3 - V_2 | & 0 \\ 0 & 0 & 0 & 0 & | V_4 - V_3 | \end{bmatrix}.$$

Simulated data (which enable us to know the true parameter values) were used and two different computer runs with different starting points performed. The results are summarized in Table IIIa. The starting point for Run #1 was $\beta_i = 1, \forall i$, while the starting point of Run #2 used the values of the parameters with which data were simulated. In both cases, the DFP search method was used and the search converged (in 9 and 2 steps, respectively) but at different points; that is, for this particular example, the likelihood function exhibits multiple optima. The awkward highly nonlinear) specification of the variance-covariance matrix may be the cause of this result. Note in particular that the null-hypothesis:

$$H_0: \beta = \beta_0 \text{ (the simulated values)}$$

cannot be rejected by the likelihood ratio test at any reasonable level of significance and this further verifies the accuracy of the method.

TABLE IIIa

	PAR1	PAR2	PAR3	PAR4	PAR5	PAR6	PAR7	PAR8	PAR9	LIKELIHOOD
S.P.*	1	1	1	1	1	1	1	1	1	−1,275.9
1	0.48	2.30	0.53	0.45	0.92	1.20	1.31	−0.69	2.45	−625.4
2	0.76	2.16	0.46	0.48	0.93	1.24	1.39	−0.89	2.44	−614.6
3	0.93	2.21	0.36	0.49	0.94	1.26	1.38	−0.89	2.45	−611.3
4	1.20	2.30	0.31	0.40	0.95	1.30	1.37	−0.88	2.45	−606.3
5	1.53	2.68	0.17	0.33	0.99	1.53	1.88	−0.81	2.11	−599.2
6	1.89	3.18	0.56	0.72	1.04	1.87	1.99	−0.88	1.93	−594.1
7	1.89	3.11	0.61	0.86	1.19	2.66	1.97	−0.72	2.15	−592.4
8	1.75	3.05	0.57	0.98	1.46	4.61	1.37	−0.73	2.04	−587.9
9	1.71	3.02	0.57	0.96	1.87	4.82	1.36	−0.75	2.00	−587.2
S.P.*	2	3.5	4.0	4.1	1.0	10.0	1.0	−0.5	0.6	−563.9
1	1.94	3.47	3.99	4.08	0.99	10.01	1.00	−0.52	0.61	−561.9
2	1.89	3.47	4.00	4.09	0.99	10.01	1.01	−0.52	0.66	−560.3

* Starting points.

TABLE IIIb

Experiment	#1	#2
Number of steps	9	2
Predicted time (min)	3.22	0.76
Actual time (min)	3.45	0.757

Note, also, that the actual computation times for Runs #1 and #2 shown in Table IIIb were correctly predicted by Equation (16).

From our limited experience with the model, it appears that, unless a very distant initial point is selected, the number of iterations for convergence will be roughly equal to the number of unknown parameters. The cost of estimation, thus, appears to be about 5 times more expensive than a conventional MNL routine, but can be greatly reduced by using only a fraction of the data (say 100 data points) until an optimum is located and then proceeding (with the updated Hessian as an input) with the whole data set. With large data sets, this simple strategy may reduce the cost of estimation by an order of magnitude.

Further reductions in the computation time can be achieved by relaxation of the very strict convergence criterion used in our research and (if it is established that the log-likelihood function is "well behaved") by replacing the one dimensional searches by quasi-Newton steps.[18]

Although the log-likelihood function of a multinomial probit seems to be unimodal for the case of a diagonal variance-covariance matrix (independent probit). Further research is needed when dealing with more general variance-covariance matrices. Most likely, though, experience with the models will dictate advantageous specifications of the variance-covariance matrix.

6. DISCUSSION

THIS PAPER has attempted to demonstrate the feasibility and desirability of using multinomial probit models for estimation and prediction of human choice behavior.

Section 2 introduced and evaluated a very powerful recursive technique which is used to compute the probabilities of choice and forms the basis for the numerical analysis of MNP models which follows.

Section 3 illustrated the most salient features of a model with three alternatives and one correlation term. From the analysis there, it can be seen that when correlations are present probit models reproduce what is generally considered to be a reasonable behavior.

The purpose of Section 4 was twofold, first to demonstrate the computational feasibility of the estimation package; and second, to assess the convergence characteristics in order to pinpoint areas where "fine tuning" of the search algorithm may increase its efficiency. Variable metric algorithms which approximate the inverse Hessian at each iteration were shown to greatly reduce the number of steps before convergence. Only two parameters were used to allow graphical display of the information. The two runs with very different starting points yielded the same optimum which seemed to show that the likelihood function is well-behaved.

The computational results in Section 5 show that the estimation and prediction of MNP models are entirely feasible; the technique seems to be statistically efficient (note, for instance, that with only 500 data points the global optimum for the example in Section 5 was remarkably close to the true parameter values), reasonably cheap and, even as it exists now, it can cope with all but, perhaps, the largest choice problems.

APPENDIX I

Data Generation Procedure

Data for the estimation of the model described in Section 4 were generated using standard pseudo-random number generators.

For each data point (500 of them) three generalized costs were sampled from three independent normal distributions,

$$T_1 \sim N(15, 4.0)$$

$$T_2 \sim N(13, 3.5)$$

$$T_3 \sim N(18.5, 4.1),$$

and, then, in order to determine the corresponding choice, the error terms, ξ, were sampled from the following MVN distribution,

$$\xi \sim \text{MVN}\left(\begin{bmatrix} 0 \\ 0 \\ 0 \end{bmatrix}; \begin{bmatrix} T_1 & 0.5\sqrt{T_1T_2} & 0 \\ 0.5\sqrt{T_1T_2} & T_2 & 0 \\ 0 & 0 & T_3 \end{bmatrix}\right),$$

that corresponds to $\rho = 0.5$, $\theta = 1$ in the text.

This is done by generating three independent standard normal variates $Z = (Z_1, Z_2, Z_3)$ which are linearly combined to yield ξ:

$$\xi_1 = Z_1\sqrt{T_1}$$

$$\xi_2 = (0.5Z_1 + 0.866Z_2)\sqrt{T_2}$$

$$\xi_3 = Z_3\sqrt{T_3}.$$

The ξ's so generated are distributed as stated above since

$$\begin{bmatrix} \sqrt{T_1} & 0 & 0 \\ 0.5\sqrt{T_2} & 0.866\sqrt{T_2} & 0 \\ 0 & 0 & \sqrt{T_3} \end{bmatrix} \times \begin{bmatrix} \sqrt{T_1} & 0.5\sqrt{T_2} & 0 \\ 0 & 0.866\sqrt{T_2} & 0 \\ 0 & 0 & \sqrt{T_3} \end{bmatrix}$$

$$= \begin{bmatrix} T_1 & 0.5\sqrt{T_1T_2} & 0 \\ 0.5\sqrt{T_1T_2} & T_2 & 0 \\ 0 & 0 & T_3 \end{bmatrix}.$$

They are then added to the T's and the alternative with the smallest perceived generalized cost is selected.

The first 50 data points which were used for the test example described in Section 4 are given in Table IV.

APPENDIX II

Comparative Simulation Experiments

To further test the methods in this paper, we compared some of the results obtained from this approximation method with those obtained from a Monte Carlo simulation similar to the one proposed by Lerman and Manski.[15]

Monte Carlo simulation, however, has some deficiencies which must be explored before one uses it to test the approximation. First, the choice probability is estimated by sampling the error terms and determining the probability of choice according to the following formula[15]:

$$F = \frac{\text{NWIN} + 1}{\text{NTOT} + \text{NALT}}$$

TABLE IV

Attribute Values T1, T2 and T3 and Choice C, for the Sample

T1	T2	T3	C	T1	T2	T3	C
16.481	16.196	23.890	2	15.237	14.345	19.984	2
15.123	11.373	14.182	2	10.840	11.071	10.188	1
19.469	8.822	20.819	2	16.841	11.224	13.417	2
18.847	15.649	21.280	2	13.913	16.991	26.618	3
12.578	10.671	18.335	2	13.089	9.822	19.162	2
11.513	20.582	27.838	1	16.626	10.725	15.285	3
10.651	15.537	17.418	1	13.477	15.509	24.421	2
8.359	15.675	21.050	1	20.851	14.557	19.800	2
11.679	12.668	23.104	1	11.365	12.673	22.212	2
23.237	10.356	21.346	2	13.296	10.076	17.810	2
13.236	16.019	10.087	3	15.417	14.103	21.050	1
20.052	16.861	14.168	3	15.938	11.180	19.851	2
18.917	14.764	21.564	2	19.034	14.125	19.764	2
18.200	6.868	19.095	2	10.466	12.841	18.540	1
10.777	16.554	15.938	1	15.799	16.979	13.074	3
20.003	6.377	9.314	2	12.713	15.105	13.629	2
19.768	8.523	18.960	2	16.908	10.958	19.713	2
8.151	13.845	17.643	2	17.098	6.853	14.502	2
22.173	18.045	15.535	1	18.608	14.286	18.301	2
13.134	11.067	19.108	2	11.059	10.812	20.121	1
14.051	14.247	15.764	1	15.641	10.754	24.669	2
14.685	10.811	12.361	3	7.822	18.949	16.904	1
11.666	10.758	16.445	1	12.824	5.697	19.183	2
17.211	15.201	17.059	3	11.852	12.147	15.672	2
13.930	16.227	22.024	1	15.557	8.307	22.286	2

where

NWIN = number of replications for which the alternative actually chosen had the greatest perceived utility.

NTOT = total number of replications.

NALT = number of alternatives.

F = estimated probability of choice.

The above formula is convenient to use (instead of F = NWIN/NTOT) because it ensures that no matter how small NWIN is, $\log F > -\infty$. The formula, however, introduces some bias in the estimation of F. This bias may be negligible for large values of NWIN but introduces serious errors when the number of successes is very small (this is especially important for problems with large numbers of alternatives and/or when we are away from the optimum in the estimation process).

To avoid this problem (since we are interested in high accuracy) the formula F = NWIN/NTOT was used instead. However, for the data displayed in Table IV (with $\theta = 0.1$ and $\rho = 0$) and after 10,000 replications no success was found (NWIN = 0) for data points 18, 19, and 29. This forced us to restrict our experiments to values near the optimum.

The second problem with simulation is that efficiency requires that the number of trials (NTOT) should not be fixed. For example, Lerman and Manski replicate until a relative precision criterion is met; namely:

$$\text{NTOT} \geq \frac{1 - F}{F \cdot \lambda}$$

where λ is a tolerance level.

This procedure, however, introduces a bias in the estimate, F, since this estimate is not independent of the number of rounds performed. On the other hand, we did not alter this procedure because the biases seem to be small and the cost of fixing NTOT was too high.

The log-likelihood function was evaluated for the three alternative examples of Section 4 at $\rho = 0.34$ and $\theta = 0.91$ using simulation. We obtained the following result:

	Log-likelihood
Simulation	−32.98
Approximation	−33.07

The larger example in Section 5 was not analyzed because the cost of simulation in that case would have been too large and the parameters obtained in Run #2 were very close to the true values anyway. Despite the very large number of replications (which drove the cost of simulation—in c.p.u. time—past 1,000 times the cost of the approximation) the difference in values (0.09) can be entirely explained in terms of the variability of the simulation results since the standard deviation of the simulated log-likelihood was approximately 0.07. We note parenthetically that this variability (which is very large for smaller number of replications) makes it very difficult to use simulation as an optimization tool in the proximity of the optimum.

The comparison of the simulation and approximation methods thus revealed that at a considerably larger cost to simulation, the results of both methods are very close. This seems to indicate that the approximation method is accurate (as is to be expected from the results in Section 2) and that the biases of the simulation method are not large if one sets F = NWIN/NTOT.

REFERENCES

1. COMSIS CORP., *Traffic Assignment: Methods, Applications, Products*, Federal Highway Administration, U.S. Department of Transportation, Washington, D.C., 1973.
2. M. E. CAMPBELL, "Route Selection and Traffic Assignment," Highway Research Board Correlation Service, mimeo, 1950.
3. P. R. STOPHER, "A Probability Model of Travel Mode Choice for the Work Journey," *Highway Res. Rec. No. 283*, 57–65 (1969).
4. T. E. LISCO, "The Value of Commuter's Travel Time: A Study in Urban Transportation," unpublished Ph.D. dissertation, University of Chicago, 1967.
5. H. VON FALKENHAUSEN, "Traffic Assignment by a Stochastic Model," in *Proceedings of the Fourth International Conference on Operational Research*, pp. 415–421, 1966.
6. CHARLES RIVER ASSOCIATES, INC., *A Disaggregate Behavioral Model of Urban Travel Demand*, Federal Highway Administration, U.S. Department of Transportation, Washington, D.C., 1972.
7. C. F. MANSKI, "The Analysis of Qualitative Choice," unpublished Ph.D. thesis, Massachusetts Institute of Technology, 1973.
8. H. BEILNER AND F. JACOBS, "Probabilistic Aspects of Traffic Assignment," in *Traffic Flow and Transportation*, G. F. Newell (Ed.), pp. 183–194, Elsevier, New York, 1972.
9. D. MCFADDEN, "The Measurement of Urban Travel Demand," *J. Public Econ.* **3**, 303–328 (1974).
10. M. E. BEN-AKIVA, "Structure of Passenger Demand Models," *Trans. Res. Rec. No. 526*, 26–42 (1974).
11. M. SCHNEIDER, "Probability Maximization in Networks," in *Proceedings of the International Conference on Transportation Research*, Bruges, Belgium, pp. 748–755, 1973.
12. M. FLORIAN AND B. FOX, "On the Probabilistic Origin of Dial's Multipath Traffic Assignment Model," *Trans. Res.* **10**, 339–341 (1976).
13. C. F. DAGANZO AND Y. SHEFFI, "On Stochastic Models of Traffic Assignment, *Trans. Sci.* **11**, 253–274 (1977).
14. J. A. HAUSMAN AND D. A. WISE, "A Conditional Probit Model for Qualitative Choice: Discrete Decisions Recognizing Interdependence and Heterogeneous Preference," Paper presented at the Third World Congress of the Econometric Society, 1975.
15. S. R. LERMAN AND C. F. MANSKI, "An Estimator for the Generalized Multinomial Probit Choice Model," August 1976, Paper presented at the 1977 Transportation Research Board meeting.
16. C. F. DAGANZO, F. BOUTHELIER, AND Y. SHEFFI, "An Efficient Approach to Estimate and Predict with Multinomial Probit Models," August 1976, Paper presented at the 1977 Transportation Research Board meeting.

17. C. Clark, "The Greatest of a Finite Set of Random Variables," *Opns. Res.* **9**, 145–162 (1961).
18. M. Avriel, *Nonlinear Programming: Analysis and Methods*, Chapter 11, Section 2, Prentice-Hall, Englewood Cliffs, N. J., 1976.
19. S. R. Lerman and M. Ben-Akiva, "A Disaggregate Behavioral Model of Auto Ownership," Paper presented for presentation at the Transportation Research Board Annual Meeting, Washington, D.C., January 1975.

(Received, April 1977; revised, October 1977)

[16]

Econometrica, Vol. 57, No. 5 (September, 1989), 995–1026

A METHOD OF SIMULATED MOMENTS FOR ESTIMATION OF DISCRETE RESPONSE MODELS WITHOUT NUMERICAL INTEGRATION

BY DANIEL MCFADDEN[1]

This paper proposes a simple modification of a conventional method of moments estimator for a discrete response model, replacing response probabilities that require numerical integration with estimators obtained by Monte Carlo simulation. This *method of simulated moments* (MSM) does not require precise estimates of these probabilities for consistency and asymptotic normality, relying instead on the law of large numbers operating across observations to control simulation error, and hence can use simulations of practical size. The method is useful for models such as high-dimensional multinomial probit (MNP), where computation has restricted applications.

KEYWORDS: Method of moments, simulation, multinomial probit, discrete response.

1. INTRODUCTION

A CLASSICAL METHOD of moments estimator θ_{mm} of an unknown parameter vector θ^* minimizes the (generalized) distance from zero of empirical moments

$$\sum_{\text{observations}} \begin{bmatrix}\text{Instrument}\\ \text{Vector}\end{bmatrix}\left(\begin{bmatrix}\text{Observed}\\ \text{Response}\end{bmatrix} - \begin{bmatrix}\text{Expected}\\ \text{Response at } \theta_{mm}\end{bmatrix}\right).$$

For some problems, the expected response function may be difficult to express analytically or to compute, but relatively easy to simulate. When this function is replaced by an unbiased simulator such that the simulation errors are independent across observations and sufficiently regular in θ, the variance introduced by simulation will be controlled by the law of large numbers operating across observations, making it unnecessary to consistently estimate each expected response. This is the basis for the estimation method developed in this paper, the *method of simulated moments* (MSM).[2]

This paper focuses on application of MSM to discrete response models, particularly the multinomial probit (MNP) model. However, the method is more general and can be applied to most moment estimation problems. In a related paper, Pakes and Pollard (1989) have independently proposed minimum distance

[1] This research grows out of joint work with Kenneth Train on the estimation of choice models containing variables measured with error. I have particularly benefited from discussions with Ariel Pakes and David Pollard, who pointed out a lacuna in my original analysis of this problem. I have shortened the proof of the main theorem by adapting arguments from Pakes and Pollard's independent investigation of the asymptotic behavior of simulation experiments. I have also benefited from suggestions made by Chunrung Ai, Moshe Ben-Akiva, Chris Cavanagh, Vassilis Hajivassiliou, Robert Hall, James Heckman, Hidehiko Ichimura, Charles Manski, Dan Nelson, Peter Phillips, and Paul Ruud. This research was supported in part by National Science Foundation Grant No. SES-8606349.

[2] The idea of simulating response probabilities from an underlying latent variable model, generating the response probabilities by stochastic integration, is standard in the area of computer simulation; see Hammersley and Handscomb (1964), Fishman (1973), and Lerman and Manski (1981). This literature has concentrated on simulating the response probabilities to a level of accuracy that enables their use in standard maximum likelihood procedures.

estimators using simulation, and have established their statistical properties using combinatorial empirical process methods. Most of the statistical results in this paper could also be obtained by application of their methods.

Section 2 of this paper gives definitions and notation for discrete response models. Section 3 defines the MSM estimator and previews the conditions under which it is consistent asymptotically normal (CAN). Section 4 discusses issues of computation and statistical efficiency. Sections 5–7, respectively, discuss applications of the method to discrete panel data with autoregressive errors, to discrete response models with measurement errors in explanatory variables, and to nonnormal discrete response problems. Section 8 contains the theorem and lemmas referred to in the text, and their proofs.

2. DEFINITIONS AND NOTATION

Define $C=\{1,\dots,m\}$ to be a set of mutually exclusive and exhaustive alternatives. A latent variable model for response from C is defined by

$$(1)\qquad u_i=\alpha x_i,\quad i\in C,$$

where α is a row vector of individual weights distributed randomly in the population, x_i is a column vector of measured attributes of alternative i, and response i is observed if $u_i\geqslant u_j$ for $j\in C$ (with zero probability of ties). Let d_i denote a response indicator, equal to one for the observed response, zero otherwise.

Assume $\alpha=a(\theta,\eta)$ is a smooth parametric function of a random vector η, with unknown parameter vector θ taking true value θ^*. Let $g(\eta)$ denote the density of η. Let $\beta(\theta)$ and $\Omega(\theta)$ denote the mean and covariance matrix of $a(\theta,\eta)$. In applications, it is often convenient to work with a Cholesky factor of Ω: let $\Gamma(\theta)$ be an upper triangular matrix satisfying $\Gamma'\Gamma=\Omega$.

Define $X_C=(x_1,\dots,x_m)$ and $u_C=(u_1,\dots,u_m)$. The response probability for alternative i, $P_C(i|\theta,X_C)$, equals the probability of drawing a latent vector u_C with $u_i\geqslant u_j$ for $j\in C$, given X_C. Define

$$u_{C-i}=(u_1-u_i,\dots,u_{i-1}-u_i,u_{i+1}-u_i,\dots,u_m-u_i),$$
$$X_{C-i}=(x_1-x_i,\dots,x_{i-1}-x_i,x_{i+1}-x_i,\dots,x_m-x_i).$$

Then u_{C-i} has a multivariate density $g_U(u_{C-i}|\theta,X_C)$ with mean βX_{C-i} and covariance matrix $X_{C-i}'\Omega X_{C-i}$, induced by the transformation $u_{C-i}=a(\theta,\eta)X_{C-i}$ of the random vector η. The response probability $P_C(i|\theta,X_C)$ equals the nonpositive orthant probability of u_{C-i},

$$(2)\qquad P_C(i|\theta,X_C)=\int 1(u_{C-i}\leqslant 0)g_U(u_{C-i}|\theta,X_C)\,du_{C-i}$$
$$=\int 1(a(\theta,\eta)X_{C-i}\leqslant 0)g(\eta)\,d\eta,$$

where $1(Q)$ denotes an indicator function for the event Q.

When α is multivariate normal, one obtains the MNP model. For this model, α can be written

$$(3) \qquad \alpha = a(\theta, \eta) \equiv \beta(\theta) + \eta\Gamma(\theta),$$

with η a row vector of independent standard normal variates.

In economic applications, the latent variables u_i often have the interpretation of utility or profit, and $P_C(i|\theta, X_C)$ is the choice probability for a population of optimizing agents. The attributes x_i are functions of observed characteristics of the alternatives and of the decision-makers, with αx_i interpreted as an approximation to a general economic function of observed characteristics and of the deep parameter θ. Alternative-specific dummy variables may be included in x_i; the associated components of α can be interpreted as alternative-specific additive disturbances.

Let $n = 1, \ldots, N$ index a random sample from the population, yielding observations (d_{Cn}, X_{Cn}) with $d_{Cn} = (d_{1n}, \ldots, d_{mn})$ and $X_{Cn} = (x_{1n}, \ldots, x_{mn})$. The log likelihood of the sample is

$$L(\theta) = \sum_{n=1}^{N} \sum_{i \in C} d_{in} \ln P_C(i|\theta, X_{Cn}).$$

The associated score is

$$(4) \qquad \partial L(\theta)/\partial\theta = \sum_{n=1}^{N} \sum_{i \in C} W_{in}[d_{in} - P_C(i|\theta, X_{Cn})],$$

where

$$(5) \qquad W_{in} = \partial \ln P_C(i|\theta, X_{Cn})/\partial\theta.$$

Equation (4) is derived using the identity

$$0 \equiv \sum_{i \in C} \partial P_C(i|\theta, X_C)/\partial\theta \equiv \sum_{i \in C} [\partial \ln P_C(i|\theta, X_C)/\partial\theta] P_C(i|\theta, X_C).$$

The primary impediment to practical maximum likelihood estimation of θ for the MNP model is computation of the $(m-1)$ dimensional orthant probabilities for u_{C-i} to obtain $P_C(i|\theta, X_C)$. Direct numerical integration is practical for $m \leqslant 4$ using a method of Owen (1956), modified by Hausman and Wise (1978), or expansions due to Dutt (1976). Otherwise, unless α has a factor-analytic covariance structure with less than four factors, it is usually impractical to carry out the large number of numerical integrations required to iteratively solve (4). Lerman and Manski (1981) suggest a Monte Carlo procedure for estimating $P(i|\theta, X_C)$ that can be applied to MNP models with large m, but find that it requires an impractical number of Monte Carlo draws to estimate small probabilities and their derivatives with acceptable precision. Daganzo (1980) has developed approximate maximum likelihood estimators for MNP using a normal approximation to maxima of normal variates suggested by Clark (1961). This approach has the drawbacks that the accuracy of the approximation cannot be refined with increasing sample size, and the method can be inaccurate when components have unequal variances; see Horowitz, Sparmonn, and Daganzo (1981).

3. THE METHOD OF SIMULATED MOMENTS

The conventional method of moments estimator of a $k \times 1$ parameter vector θ (with domain Θ) in the discrete response model $P_C(i|\theta, X_C)$ satisfies

$$\theta_{mm} = \arg\min_\theta (d - P(\theta))'W'W(d - P(\theta)), \tag{6}$$

where $d - P(\theta)$ denotes the $mN \times 1$ vector of residuals $d_{in} - P_C(i|\theta, X_{Cn})$ stacked by observation and by alternative within observation, and where W is a $K \times mN$ array of instruments of rank $K \geqslant k$. The instruments may depend on θ, but are evaluated at some fixed θ_0 in forming first-order conditions for solution of (6). The instrument array (5), evaluated at θ^* (or at a consistent estimator of θ^*), yields a method of moments estimator asymptotically equivalent to the maximum likelihood estimator for θ, and hence asymptotically efficient. If computation makes exact calculation of the efficient instruments impractical, (5) nevertheless provides a template for instruments that with relatively crude approximations to P and its $mN \times k$ array of derivatives P_θ will yield moderately efficient estimators. Computation of instruments is discussed further in Section 4. In the remainder of this section, I will assume W is a given fixed instrument array.

Under mild regularity assumptions, sufficient conditions for classical method of moments estimation to be CAN are the following:

(i) *The instruments are asymptotically correlated with the score; i.e., the array* $\bar{R} = \lim N^{-1}WP_\theta(\theta^*)$ *is of maximum rank.*

(ii) *The conditional expectation of the residuals* $d - P(\theta)$, *given the instruments, is zero if and only if* $\theta = \theta^*$.

The *method of simulated moments* (MSM) avoids the computation of $P(\theta)$ required for (6), replacing it with a simulator $f(\theta)$ that is (asymptotically) conditionally unbiased, given W and d, independent across observations, and "well behaved" in θ. An example is the *simple frequency simulator* calculated from the latent variable model (1) by independently drawing, for each observation, one or more vectors η from the density $g(\eta)$, and then for any trial θ calculating $u_{in} = a(\theta, \eta)x_{in}$ and counting the frequency with which the u_{in} for each alternative is maximized. The MSM estimator is given by any argument θ_{sm} satisfying[3]

$$\begin{aligned}(d - f(\theta_{sm}))'W'W(d - f(\theta_{sm})) \\ \leqslant \inf_{\theta \in \Theta} (d - f(\theta))'W'W(d - f(\theta)) + o(1).\end{aligned} \tag{7}$$

This definition assures the existence of a MSM estimator even if the infimum cannot be attained.

[3] A sequence of numbers a_N is $O(1)$ if it is bounded in magnitude by a convergent sequence, and is $o(1)$ if it converges to zero. A sequence of random variables Z_n is $O_p(1)$ if, given $\varepsilon > 0$, there exists δ such that $\text{Prob}(|Z_N| > \delta) < \varepsilon$ for all N. The sequence is $o_p(1)$ if Z_N converges in probability to zero.

Sufficient conditions for the MSM estimator to be CAN are given formally in Theorem 1. They involve the same regularity assumptions and conditions on instruments as classical method of moments estimators, and in addition place two critical restrictions on the simulator $f(\theta)$:

(iii) *The simulation bias* $B(\theta) = N^{-1/2}W(Ef(\theta) - P(\theta))$, *where the expectation is conditioned on* W *and* d, *is either zero, or else satisfies*

$$(8) \qquad \sup_{\theta \in \Theta} |B(\theta)| = o(1).$$

(iv) *The simulation residual process* $\zeta(\theta) = N^{-1/2}W(f(\theta) - Ef(\theta))$ *is uniformly stochastically bounded and equicontinuous in* θ; *i.e.*,

$$(9) \qquad \sup_{\theta \in \Theta} |\zeta(\theta)| = O_p(1),$$

$$(10) \qquad \sup_{\theta \in A_N} |\zeta(\theta) - \zeta(\theta^*)| = o_p(1),$$

where, for a given $\delta > 0$, $A_N = \{\theta | N^{1/2}|\theta - \theta^*| \leqslant \delta\}$.

If $f(\theta)$ is an unbiased simulator of $P(\theta)$ for all θ, and the random numbers used to compute $f(\theta)$ are independent of the observed responses and of any simulation used in the construction of the instrument array, then (iii) is satisfied. The simulation residuals $\zeta(\theta)$ are by construction the normalized sum over observations of independent identically distributed terms that are independent of d and uniformly bounded, with $E(\zeta(\theta)| W) = 0$ for each θ. Then $\zeta(\theta)$ is an *empirical process* in θ that by a standard central limit theorem is pointwise asymptotically normal. Elementary arguments (Lemma 4) establish that if $f(\theta)$ is smooth for θ in a compact domain, then (iv) holds. However, (iv) can also be satisfied by simulators that have "well-behaved" discontinuities (Lemma 8), such as the simple frequency simulator. To satisfy (iv), a simulator must avoid "chatter" as θ varies; this will generally require that the Monte Carlo random numbers used to construct $f(\theta)$ *not* be redrawn when θ is changed.

4. COMPUTATIONAL ISSUES AND STATISTICAL EFFICIENCY

Practical use of the MSM estimator requires that the Monte Carlo simulation of the probabilities and their derivatives be practical and "well behaved"; that easily calculated, moderately efficient instruments W be available; that iterative algorithms to compute the estimators be fairly stable and efficient; and that estimators for the asymptotic covariance matrix of the estimators be computable.

Simulators for the Response Probabilities

I have given the example of a *simple frequency simulator* $f(\theta)$ for the discrete response model generated from the latent variable model (1): Count the frequency $f_C(i|\theta, X_{Cn})$ with which component i of $u_{Cn} = a(\theta, \eta)X_{Cn}$ is largest, where the η are one or more Monte Carlo random vectors from the density $g(\eta)$, independent across observations and fixed for the duration of the analysis. This simulator is unbiased for all θ, but has discontinuities at values of θ where there are ties for the maximum component of u_{Cn}. For the MNP model, the frequency simulator is computed economically from (3) by drawing standard normal vectors η and calculating $u_{Cn} = (\beta(\theta) + \eta\Gamma(\theta))X_{Cn}$.

It is also possible to construct a *smooth unbiased simulator* $f(\theta)$. This simplifies the iterative computation of the estimator, and its statistical analysis. Let $\gamma(u_{C-i})$ denote a density chosen for the simulation that has the nonpositive orthant as its support. Then (2) can be rewritten as

$$(11) \qquad P_C(i|\theta, X_C) \equiv \int h(u_{C-i}, \theta, X_{C-i})\gamma(u_{C-i})\,du_{C-i},$$

where $h(u_{C-i}, \theta, X_{C-i}) = g_U(u_{C-i}|\theta, X_C)/\gamma(u_{C-i})$. Average $h(u_{C-i}, \theta, X_{C-i})$ for an observation, using one or more Monte Carlo draws from $\gamma(u_{C-i})$ that are taken independently across observations and fixed for different θ. This gives a smooth positive unbiased estimator of $P_C(i|\theta, X_C)$, provided γ is chosen so that h is dominated by a function H independent of θ with $\int H\gamma\,du_{C-i}$ finite. The density γ can be chosen to facilitate Monte Carlo draws and reduce simulation variance. For example, if γ is independent exponential in each component, then random variates from this distribution can be calculated from logarithms of uniform (0, 1) random numbers. Choices of γ that make h flatter can reduce simulation error, as in Monte Carlo importance sampling. For MNP,

$$\begin{aligned} &h(u_{C-i}, \theta, X_{C-i}) \\ &\quad = n(u_{C-i} - \beta(\theta)X_{C-i}, X'_{C-i}\Gamma(\theta)'\Gamma(\theta)X_{C-i})/\gamma(u_{C-i}), \end{aligned}$$

where $n(v, A)$ denotes a multivariate normal density centered at zero with covariance matrix A. When γ is exponential, this h is uniformly bounded.

The estimation of the asymptotic covariance matrix of the MSM estimator, as well as approximation of efficient instruments, requires simulation of derivatives of the response probabilities with respect to θ. From (11), these derivatives can be written

$$(12) \qquad \partial P_C(i|\theta, X_C)/\partial\theta \equiv \int h_\theta(u_{C-i}, \theta, X_{C-i})\gamma(u_{C-i})\,du_{C-i},$$

where h_θ denotes the vector of derivatives of h with respect to θ. Then, a smooth unbiased simulator of (12) can be constructed in the same manner as was done for (11). Lemma 10 details this construction for MNP.

A potential drawback of smooth simulators based on (11) is that they are not constrained to sum up to one for $i \in C$. An alternative class of *kernel-smoothed frequency simulators* satisfy summing-up, but are only asymptotically unbiased. The idea underlying these simulators is that (2) can be approximated by an integral

$$(13) \qquad \tilde{P}_C(i|\theta, X_C) = \int \mathbb{K}(a(\theta, \eta)X_{C-i}/b_N)g(\eta)\,d\eta,$$

where $\mathbb{K}(u_{C-i}/b_N)$ is a smooth approximation that approaches the indicator function $1(u_{C-i} \leqslant 0)$ as $b_N \to 0$. Let $\mathbb{K}_i(y_1, \ldots, y_m) \equiv \mathbb{K}(y_{C-i})$. I require that $\Sigma_{i \in C} \mathbb{K}_i(u_C/b_N) \equiv 1$. The multinomial logit function $\mathbb{K}_i(y_C) = e^{y_i}/\Sigma_{j \in C} e^{y_j}$ is one example in this class. Smooth simulators satisfying summing-up for $i \in C$ are obtained by averaging $\mathbb{K}_i(a(\theta, \eta) X_C/b_N)$ over a common Monte Carlo sample from $g(\eta)$.

Kernel-smoothed simulators can be derived from a perturbation of the latent variable model (1),

$$(14) \qquad \tilde{u}_C = u_C + \nu_C b_N,$$

where ν_C is a vector whose components are independently distributed with a distribution function Ψ, and b_N is a scalar chosen for the simulation. This formulation can be interpreted as a *mixture* of (1) and a contaminating distribution. Assume Ψ has a finite moment generating function $\mu(t)$ for t in a neighborhood of zero. Define the smooth function

$$(15) \qquad \mathbb{K}_i(y_1, \ldots, y_m) = \int \Bigl(\prod_{j \neq i} \Psi(y_i - y_j + v) \Bigr) \Psi'(v)\, dv.$$

This kernel will be most practical when Ψ is chosen so that $\mathbb{K}_i$ has an easily calculated closed form. The response probability implied by (14), obtained by first conditioning on u_C and integrating out ν_C, coincides with the approximation (13) when the smoothing function (15) is used. This simulator is nonnegative, and is strictly positive if the support of Ψ is the real line. Lemma 3 shows that a sufficient condition for it to be asymptotically unbiased is that b_N satisfy $N^{\varepsilon + 1/2} b_N \to 0$ for some $\varepsilon > 0$. If the simulators for all $i \in C$ are constructed from common Monte Carlo draws, then they satisfy summing-up. Choosing Ψ to be type I extreme value distributed yields the multinomial logit form, and (13) is a multivariate normal mixture of logits. This model, with the mixture interpreted as the result of taste variations in the population, has been of independent interest as a discrete choice model; see Westin (1974) and McFadden (1984).

A *polynomial kernel* such as $\Psi(v) = [6 + 5v + (2 - |v|)v^3]/12$ for $|v| \leqslant 1$ is computationally economical, yielding a closed form for $\mathbb{K}_i$. One advantage of this kernel is that it limits the number of alternatives for which calculations must be done. If an observation has every component of u_{C-i} greater than $2b_N$ in magnitude, then $\mathbb{K}_i(u_C/b_N)$ coincides with $1(u_{C-i} \leqslant 0)$ and the kernel-smoothed frequency simulator coincides with the simple frequency simulator. The probability of the converse is of the order $O(b_N)$. Then, in a sample of size N with r Monte Carlo draws per observation, the expected number of alternatives for which further calculation is required to obtain the simulator and corresponding instruments is bounded by $(r+1)N + mrNO(b_N) \leqslant (r+1)N + o(mrN^{-\varepsilon - 1/2})$. This makes the calculation practical even if the number of alternatives is large.

For MNP, a variant due to Stern (1987) of the kernel-smoothed frequency simulator is unbiased. The idea is that the normal latent variable model can be decomposed into a mixture of two normal vectors, one of which is scaled standard normal. Thus, it is unnecessary to contaminate the model to achieve mixing, permitting an unbiased simulator. Rewrite (1) as $u_C \equiv \bar{u}_C + \nu b_N$, with ν a standard normal vector independent of $\bar{u}_C \sim N(\beta X_C, A'A)$, where A is upper triangular and $A'A \equiv X_C'\Gamma'\Gamma X_C - b_N I$. This can be done if b_N is small enough so that $X_C'\Gamma'\Gamma X_C - b_N I$ is positive definite. It is adequate for the asymptotic properties of MSM using this simulator that b_N be constant in open neighborhoods of Γ. Then, b_N can be set for each observation and estimation iteration by calculating a Cholesky factor of $X_C'\Gamma'\Gamma X_C$ at the trial Γ and choosing b_N less than the smallest diagonal element of this factor. As in (14), conditioning on $\bar{u}_C$,

$$P_C(i|\theta, X_C) = \int \mathbb{K}_i((\beta X_C + \eta A)/b_N) g(\eta)\, d\eta, \tag{16}$$
$$\mathbb{K}_i(y_1, \ldots, y_m) = \int \left(\prod_{j \neq i} \Phi(y_i - y_j + v) \right) \Phi'(v)\, dv,$$

with g the multivariate standard normal density and Φ the univariate standard normal distribution. An average of $\mathbb{K}_i$ in (16) over Monte Carlo draws from g yields an unbiased positive smooth *Stern frequency simulator*. Adding-up holds for an observation if common draws are used for all $i \in C$.

For MNP, construction of economical simulators is aided by the use of spherical transformations. The expression (11), and the specializations of (12) given in Lemma 10, involve simulation of integrals of the generic form

$$Q = \int_{u \geq 0} \left(\prod_{j=1}^{m} u_j^{k_j} \right) n(u + \mu, \Lambda)\, du,$$

where $\Sigma_{j=1}^{m} k_j$ is 0, 1, or 2, $\mu = \beta X_{C-i}$, and $\Lambda = X_{C-i}' \Omega X_{C-i}$. Make the transformation $r = (\Sigma_{j=1}^{m} u_j^2)^{1/2}$ and $s_j = u_j / r$. Define

$$C(n, a, b) = \int_0^\infty r^n e^{-(r - b/a)^2 a/2}\, dr;$$

this is proportional to a parabolic cylinder function (Spanier and Oldham (1987)), and satisfies the recursion

$$C(0, a, b) = (2\pi/a)^{1/2} \Phi(b/a^{1/2}),$$
$$C(1, a, b) = C(0, a, b) b/a + e^{b^2/2a}/a, \tag{17}$$
$$C(n, a, b) = C(n-1, a, b) b/a + C(n-2, a, b)(n-1)/a \quad (n \geq 2).$$

Then, a *cylinder simulator* is defined from the form

$$Q = c_0 E_s c_1 C\left(\sum_{j=1}^{m} k_j + m - 1, a, b \right) \left(\prod_{j=1}^{m} s_j^{k_j} \right), \tag{18}$$

where s is distributed uniformly on the intersection of the unit sphere and the nonnegative orthant, and

$$a = s'(X'_{C-i}\Omega X_{C-i})^{-1}s,$$
$$b = -\beta X_{C-i}(X'_{C-i}\Omega X_{C-i})^{-1}s,$$
$$c_0 = (2\pi)^{1/2}2^{-3m/2}|\Omega|^{-1/2}\Gamma(m/2)^{-1},$$
$$c_1 = \exp\Big(-\big[\beta X(X'\Omega X)^{-1}X'\beta' - \big(\beta X(X'\Omega X)^{-1}s\big)/s'(X'\Omega X)^{-1}s\big]/2\Big),$$

with $X = X_{C-i}$, and c_0 independent of X and s. To generate uniform draws from the distribution of s, draw a standard normal random vector u, and take

$$s_j = |u_j| \Bigg/ \left(\sum_{j=1}^{m} u_j^2\right)^{1/2}.$$

Then, (18) is simulated by drawing one or more s, and for each s using the recursion (17) to calculate C. A further refinement is to use control variates for C; Moran (1984) suggests several. Peter Phillips and Vasillis Hajivassiliou suggested the use of spherical transformations for this problem, and Dan Nelson developed many of the details.

The spherical transformation can also be used to calculate a *conditional chi-square frequency simulator* for MNP that is economical, unbiased, and smooth. Let s be a uniform draw from the unit sphere in $\mathbb{R}^K$, and let λ^2 be an independent random variable with a chi-square distribution with K degrees of freedom, denoted $H_K(\lambda^2)$. Then, the latent variable model for MNP can be written $u_C = (\beta + \lambda s\Gamma)X_C$. Given s, an easy computation yields a partition of $[0, +\infty]$ into intervals $[\lambda_j, \lambda_{j+1}]$, $j = 0, \ldots, m$, on which each of the components of u_C is maximum. (Some of the intervals may be degenerate.) The probability of response i, given s, is $P_C(i|\theta, X_C, s) = H_K(\lambda^2_{j+1}) - H_K(\lambda^2_j)$, where j is the ascending rank of $s\Gamma x_i$ in the vector $s\Gamma X_C$. The λ_j are smooth in θ for almost all X_C, so $P_C(i|\theta, X_C, s)$ is also smooth. The simulator is an average of the $P_C(i|\theta, X_C, s)$ for r random draws of s. An advantage of this method is that it simultaneously provides, for all alternatives, simulators satisfying summing-up.

The accuracy of simulators for MNP that are based on spherical transformations can be improved substantially by use of antithetic variates. Deák (1980) gives an effective procedure: For uniform draws from the unit sphere in $\mathbb{R}^K$, first draw a random basis $s^1, \ldots, s^K$. This can be done by drawing K standard normal vectors and applying a Gram-Schmidt orthonormalization. Then use the $2K$ vectors $\pm s^j$, or the $2K(K-1)$ vectors $(\pm s^i \pm s^j)$ for $i < j$, as directions for the simulation. To generate a denser set of antithetic points for any integer $T > 1$, take each pair s^i and s^j with $i < j$ and construct the directions $(\pm s^i \cos \pi t/2T \pm s^j \sin \pi t/2T)$ for $t = 1, \ldots, T-1$. Combined with the points $\pm s^i$, this gives $4(T+1)$ evenly spaced points on each great circle, for a total of $2K + 2TK(K-1)$ directions.

Numerical experiments on the algorithms discussed in this section suggest that for MNP with 5 to 20 alternatives, the conditional chi-square simulator combined with the Deák construction of antithetic directions is the fastest and most accurate.[4]

Choice of Instruments

Consider the question of suitable instruments. The classical method of moments estimator is asymptotically efficient if and only if, except for stochastically negligible terms, W is proportional to $\partial \ln P(\theta^*)/\partial\theta$. Since the asymptotic efficiency of MSM relative to the classical moments estimator can be controlled by the number of Monte Carlo draws used to simulate $P(\theta)$, the issue is how to construct W to obtain good asymptotic efficiency for MSM without excessive computation.

Simulation of (12) based on Monte Carlo draws from the density $\gamma(u)$ yields smooth unbiased estimates of the derivatives. Since the smooth simulator (11) of $P_C(i|\theta, X_C)$ is positive, the ratio of the simulators of (12) and (11) provides an approximation to the ideal instruments $\partial \ln P_C/\partial\theta$. The number of draws per observation must go to infinity with sample size if the ideal instruments are to be estimated consistently, permitting MSM to be asymptotically efficient. However, modestly efficient instruments can be obtained with relatively few draws. It is essential for the asymptotic statistics of the MSM estimator that simulators of the response probabilities and their derivatives used to construct instruments be *independent* of the simulator $f(\theta)$ used in the moment condition (7). For instrument construction, use of common draws from γ to simulate the numerator and denominator of $(\partial P_C/\partial\theta)/P_C$ at each observation may improve the efficiency of the instruments.

In general, starting from any $K\times mN$ array of instruments Z^0, a standard argument from nonlinear generalized least squares shows that the asymptotic minimum variance estimator in the class using linear combinations of instruments in Z^0 is attained by $W = P_\theta(\theta^*)'Z'(Z\hat{P}Z')^{-1}Z$, where $P_\theta(\theta^*)$ is the $mN\times k$ array of derivatives $\partial P_C(i|\theta, X_{Cn})/\partial\theta$, evaluated at θ^*, $\hat{P} = \text{diag } P(\theta^*)$, and

$$Z_{in} = Z_{in}^0 - \sum_{j\in C} Z_{jn}^0 P_C(j|\theta^*, X_{Cn}).$$

If $Z^0 = \partial \ln P(\theta^*)/\partial\theta$, then $W = \partial \ln P(\theta^*)/\partial\theta$. Approximations to θ^* and to the functions P and P_θ yield approximations to the minimum variance instruments that can be constructed from Z^0.

[4] A program to perform these calculations, in either GAUSS or FORTRAN, is available from the author.

Iterative Estimation Methods

A practical estimation procedure is first to use relatively crude instruments, defined independently of θ, to iterate to an initial consistent estimator $\hat{\theta}$, second to simulate the ideal instruments using (11) and (12) evaluated at $\hat{\theta}$, and third to carry out one or more iterations using these approximately ideal instruments. Good candidates for crude instruments are low-order polynomials in the explanatory variables: If the model is identified, then there are always polynomials in X_{C-i} that have an asymptotic correlation matrix with $\partial P_C(i|\theta, X_C)/\partial\theta$ that is of full rank. For example, in the MNP case, X_{C-i} and $X_{C-i}X_{C-i}'$ will usually be adequate first-round instruments for $\partial \ln P_C(i|\theta, X_C)/\partial\beta$ and $\partial \ln P_C(i|\theta, X_C)/\partial\Gamma$; from Lemma 10, these are a superset of the ideal instruments when $\beta = 0$ and Γ consists of an identity submatrix corresponding to alternative-specific dummy variables and a zero submatrix corresponding to the remaining variables. In the third step when smooth simulators are being used, one Newton-Raphson iteration from $\hat{\theta}$ achieves the maximum asymptotic efficiency attainable from the second-round instruments.

Consider iterative algorithms for calculation of MSM estimators. When smooth simulators are used for $f(\theta)$ in (11), and the instruments W are defined independently of θ, then estimates can be computed by Newton-Raphson iteration or a similar second-order method applied to minimize the criterion

$$(19) \qquad (d-f(\theta))'W'W(d-f(\theta)).$$

This criterion may be irregular; in particular, kernel-smoothed frequency simulators may have local flats. Then, optimization methods that use nonlocal information, such as simulated annealing, may be more reliable; see Press et al. (1986).

When a simple frequency simulator is used, (19) is piecewise constant in θ, and nonlocal methods must be used in iteration. I have tried random search algorithms and pseudo-gradient methods that adaptively approximate slopes using long baselines; the former have performed better. For discrete response models that can be parameterized in terms of mean and variance, such as MNP, convergence can be accelerated using a method due to Manski: Suppose r simulations are made per observation, and that starting from a trial θ_0, a search direction $\Delta\theta$ has been determined. Consider (19) as a function of $\theta_0 + \lambda\,\Delta\theta$, with λ a step size to be determined. The value λ_{nj} at which there is a jump in (19) from draw j and observation n is easily calculated. Then, it is practical to enumerate the values of (19) at all the jump points λ_{nj} and choose a global minimum along this search direction.

Generally, iteration using smooth simulators is faster than that using frequency simulators. However, in applications where the number of alternatives is very large, the burden of computing $f(\theta)$ or approximations to the optimal instruments for all alternatives may be excessive. In such cases, a frequency simulator $f(\theta)$ with r repetitions will be nonzero for at most r alternatives, and the instruments need be computed only for these alternatives plus the observed one.

For example, a single Monte Carlo draw for each observation requires calculation of the instruments only for the observed and drawn alternatives, and gives half the efficiency of the classical method of moments estimator, no matter how large the set of possible alternatives. Comparable reductions in computation can be achieved using a kernel-smoothed frequency simulator with a kernel of bounded support.

Estimators for the Asymptotic Covariance Matrix

A standard result, obtained by expansion of the first-order condition, is that the asymptotic covariance matrix of a classical method of moments estimator is

$$\Sigma_{mm} = (\bar{R}'\bar{R})^{-1}\bar{R}'G_{mm}\bar{R}(\bar{R}'\bar{R})^{-1},$$

where

$$\bar{R} = \lim_{N\to\infty} N^{-1}WP_\theta(\theta^*),$$

$$G_{mm} = \lim_{N\to\infty} N^{-1}\sum_{n=1}^{N}\left\{\sum_{i\in C} P_C(i|\theta^*, X_{Cn})W_{in}W_{in}' - W_{\cdot n}W_{\cdot n}'\right\},$$

with $W_{\cdot n} = \Sigma_{i\in C}P_C(i|\theta^*, X_{Cn})W_{in}$. The asymptotic covariance matrix of a CAN method of simulated moments estimator has an almost identical form,

$$\Sigma_{sm} = (\bar{R}'\bar{R})^{-1}\bar{R}'G_{sm}\bar{R}(\bar{R}'\bar{R})^{-1}, \tag{20}$$

where $G_{sm} = G_{mm} + G_{ss}$, with

$$G_{ss} = \lim_{n\to\infty} N^{-1}\sum_{n=1}^{N}\sum_{i,j\in C} W_{in}W_{jn}'E(Y_{in}Y_{jn}),$$

and $Y_{in} = f_{in}(\theta^*) - P_{Cn}(i|\theta^*, X_{Cn})$. The term G_{ss} is the contribution of the simulation to the asymptotic variance.

If $f(\theta)$ is the simple frequency simulator obtained by r independent Monte Carlo draws for each observation, then $G_{ss} = r^{-1}G_{mm}$ and $\Sigma_{sm} = (1 + r^{-1})\Sigma_{mm}$. In this case, one draw per observation gives fifty percent of the asymptotic efficiency of the corresponding classical method of moments estimator, and nine draws per observation gives ninety percent relative efficiency. Use of Monte Carlo variance reduction techniques such as antithetic variates, or use of smooth simulators, may improve further the relative efficiency of MSM.

Consider estimation of Σ_{sm}. I establish in Lemma 9 that a consistent estimator of G_{sm} is

$$\hat{G}_{sm} = N^{-1}\sum_{n=1}^{N}\sum_{i,j\in C} W_{in}(d_{in} - f(i|\theta_{sm}, X_{Cn}))(d_{jn} - f(j|\theta_{sm}, X_{Cn}))W_{jn}'. \tag{21}$$

The matrix $\bar{R} = \lim N^{-1}WP_\theta(\theta^*)$ is consistently estimated by

$$\hat{R} = N^{-1}W\hat{P}_\theta, \tag{22}$$

where $\hat{P}_\theta$ is an unbiased simulator of the array P_θ from (12), evaluated at θ_{sm}. The simulator $\hat{P}_\theta$ must be independent of any simulation used in the construction of W. The consistency of $\hat{R}$ continues to hold with any consistent estimator $\hat{\theta}$ in place of θ_{sm}.

5. DISCRETE PANEL DATA WITH AUTOREGRESSIVE ERRORS

Consider longitudinal discrete response data (d_{tn}, x_{tn}) for subjects $n = 1, \ldots, N$ observed over $t = 1, \ldots, T$ periods, where $d_{tn} = \pm 1$ indicates a binary response, and x_{tn} is a vector of explanatory variables. This problem has 2^T alternative response patterns, large for long panels. A latent variable model that could generate such data is

$$u_{tn} = \beta x_{tn} + \varepsilon_{tn},$$

$$d_{tn} = \operatorname{sign}(u_{tn}),$$

with $\varepsilon_{tn} = \xi_n + \nu_{tn}$, ξ_n a normal subject-specific disturbance, ν_{tn} a normal first-order autoregressive disturbance, and ξ, ν independent of each other and independent across subjects. Define λ^2 to be the proportion of the variance in the autoregressive error, and ρ the serial correlation. The probability of the observed response is

$$P(d_n | X_n, \beta, \lambda, \rho) = \Pr(\{\xi_n, \nu_{1n}, \ldots, \nu_{Tn} | d_{tn} \cdot \operatorname{sign}(\beta x_{tn} + \xi_n + \nu_{tn}) > 0\}),$$

where $d_n = (d_{1n}, \ldots, d_{Tn})$ and $X_n = (x_{1n}, \ldots, x_{Tn})$. If ε_{tn} is stationary, with variance normalized to one, then

$$\text{(23)} \qquad \varepsilon_{tn} = (1 - \lambda^2)^{1/2} \eta_{0n} + \lambda \left((1 - \rho^2) \sum_{j=0}^{t-2} \rho^j \eta_{t-j,n} + \rho^{t-1} \eta_{1n} \right),$$

where the η_{jn} are independent standard normal variates.

Full maximum likelihood estimation of this model requires T-dimensional numerical integration to evaluate $P(d_n | X_n, \beta, \lambda, \rho)$, which is computationally impractical for $T > 4$. Ruud (1981) has developed practical consistent estimators using partial likelihoods for small numbers of adjacent periods; see also Chamberlain (1984). The MSM method, starting from initially consistent estimators, offers a computationally practical method that may increase efficiency. A simple frequency simulator or a kernel-smoothed frequency simulator with a polynomial kernel, with a small number of repetitions, requires simulation of the instruments for a small number of alternatives per subject, even for large T.

Hajivassiliou and McFadden (1987) have investigated another approach to this problem which consistently simulates the score $\partial \ln P(d_n | \theta, X_n)/\partial\theta$ for each observation. Estimators with good relative efficiency can then be obtained by iterating to a root of the sample score. A first method for this simulation is to use panel data analogues of (11) and (12), with many Monte Carlo repetitions, to estimate consistently the denominator and numerator of $[\partial P(d_n | \theta, X_n)/\partial\theta] / P(d_n | \theta, X_n)$.

A second *acceptance/rejection* method yields *unbiased* simulators of the score. As in the case of the basic MSM estimator, this permits consistent estimation of θ^* through the operation of the law of large numbers over observations. Consistent simulation of the score for each observation is not required. Let $g_U(u|\theta, X_n)$ denote the density of $(u_{1n},\ldots, u_{Tn})$ induced by the model, given the density of the disturbances. Then, the response probability and the score satisfy

$$P(d_n|\theta, X_n) = \int_{Q_n} g_U(u|\theta, X_n)\, du,$$

$$\begin{aligned}\partial \ln P(d_n|\theta, X_n)/\partial\theta &= \int_{Q_n} [\partial g_U(u|\theta, X_n)/\partial\theta]\, du/P(d_n|\theta, X_n)\\ &= \int_{Q_n} [\partial \ln g_U(u|\theta, X_n)/\partial\theta]\, g_U(u|\theta, X_n, Q_n)\, du\end{aligned}$$

where $Q_n = \{u|\mathrm{sign}(u) = d_n\}$, and $g_U(u|\theta, X_n, Q_n)$ is the *conditional* density of u given Q_n. The acceptance-rejection algorithm starts with a density $\gamma(u)$ such that (i) it is easy to draw Monte Carlo samples from $\gamma(u)$, and (ii) there is a known constant M such that $M \geqslant \sup_{Q_n} g_U(u|\theta, X_n)/\gamma(u)$. Draw a pair of points (u, y) with u from $\gamma(u)$ and, independently, y from the uniform density on $[0, M]$. If $u \in Q_n$ and $y \leqslant g_U(u|\theta, X_n)$, accept the variate u; otherwise, reject this pair and draw again. The density of the accepted u is $g_U(u|\theta, X_n, Q_n)$; this is verified by an application of Bayes law. Averaging $\partial \ln g_U(u|\theta, X_n)/\partial\theta$ over the accepted u yields an unbiased simulator of the score. The main drawback of this method is that many draws may be necessary to get accepted u.

MSM estimation of discrete panel data models extends readily to more general time-series covariance structures, so long as it is practical to Cholesky-factor and invert the covariance matrix to obtain a representation analogous to (23) for the ε_{tn} in terms of independent normal variates, and so long as it is practical to construct instrument arrays for the deep parameters of the problem. The MSM estimator can also be applied to models with general state dependence, provided the initial value problem (Heckman (1981)) can be handled. For example, consider the model

$$\begin{aligned}&u_{tn} = \beta x_{tn} + \psi d_{t-1,n} + \xi_n + \nu_{tn},\\ &d_{tn} = \mathrm{sign}(u_{tn}),\end{aligned} \tag{24}$$

with ξ_n a subject-specific disturbance and ν_{tn} independent across t. If the disturbances are normal, and ν_{tn} has unit variance, then

$$P(d_n|x_n, d_{0n}, \beta, \xi_n) = \prod_{t=1}^{T} \Phi(d_{tn}(\beta x_{tn} + \psi d_{t-1,n} + \xi_n)). \tag{25}$$

Suppose the conditional distribution of ξ_n given x_n and d_{0n} can be assumed to depend only on d_{0n}; this is justified if x_n is independent of the past history of the

x process. Suppose the *inverse* $G^{-1}(p|d_{0n})$ of the cumulative distribution function $p = G(\xi_n|d_{0n})$ is placed in a flexible parametric family that spans the true inverse distribution. Then the response probabilities are given by the expectation of (25) with respect to ξ, which can be simulated economically from G^{-1}. Adding serial correlation to the disturbances ν_{tn} in (24) makes (25) a T-dimensional integral, whose simulation by MSM can be handled jointly with simulation of the expectation with respect to ξ.

6. DISCRETE RESPONSE MODELS WITH MEASUREMENT ERROR

Suppose discrete response for a random sample $n = 1, \ldots, N$ satisfies a latent variable model

$$\begin{aligned} u_n &= \beta z_n + \varepsilon_n, \\ d_n &= H(u_n), \end{aligned} \tag{26}$$

where H maps the row vector u_n into m discrete categories with d_n an indicator for the observed category, and $H^{-1}(d_n)$ the set of u_n yielding the observed category. To simplify notation, assume β is a scalar; generalization merely requires that the construction below be carried out component by component. Suppose z_n is not observed directly, but is related to a vector of observations x_n by

$$x_n = z_n \Lambda + \xi_n,$$

where $\xi_n \sim N(0, \Psi)$, independent of ε. We interpret the x as observations on z measured with error, or as indicators for z. In form, this is a multiple indicator or factor-analytic latent variable model, with Λ giving the factor loadings.

Suppose in the population $z_n \sim N(\mu, \Gamma)$, independent of ξ_n. Then the conditional distribution of z given x, suppressing subscripts, is

$$z \sim N\big(\mu + (x - \mu\Lambda)(\Lambda'\Gamma\Lambda + \Psi)^{-1}\Lambda'\Gamma, \Gamma - \Gamma\Lambda(\Lambda'\Gamma\Lambda + \Psi)^{-1}\Lambda'\Gamma\big).$$

If the $\varepsilon \sim N(0, \Omega)$ in (26), then

$$\begin{aligned} u \sim N\big(&\beta\mu + \beta(x - \mu\Lambda)(\Lambda'\Gamma\Lambda + \Psi)^{-1}\Lambda'\Gamma, \\ &\beta^2\big[\Omega + \Gamma\Lambda(\Lambda'\Gamma\Lambda + \Psi)^{-1}\Lambda'\Gamma\big]\big) \end{aligned}$$

and the response probabilities given x are of MNP form. The MSM estimator for the general MNP model can be adapted directly to this problem, the main practical difficulty being calculation of the derivatives of the Cholesky factor of the covariance matrix with respect to the deep parameters in order to calculate a relatively efficient instrument matrix.

A number of variants of the measurement error model (26) may be encountered in applications, including variables measured with error that are common to several alternatives or interact with alternative-specific dummies, multiple variables measured with possibly correlated errors, and simultaneity between the latent variables and observed indicators. These may alter the details of the density of z given x and the density of u, but give the same basic structure for the response probabilities and MSM estimator. It is also possible to treat measurement error in discrete response models such as multinomial logit by allowing the ε to have an appropriate distribution. For the logit example, MSM estimation can be used by simulating the expectations of the logit formulas with respect to the conditional distribution of the true explanatory variables. These topics are studied in greater detail in McFadden (1986a, 1986b) and Train, McFadden, and Goett (1987).

7. NONNORMAL DISCRETE RESPONSE MODELS

This paper has focused on estimation of the MNP model. However, the MSM estimator can be applied to any latent variable model in which unbiased estimates of the response probabilities can be obtained economically by Monte Carlo methods. For example, in the latent variable model (1) it may be reasonable to assume that some components of α are always nonnegative, giving monotonicity. This could be modeled by taking the density of α to be multivariate truncated normal, or by giving some components nonnegative densities such as gamma. This complicates the analytic representation of response probabilities, but is readily accommodated in Monte Carlo draws from the latent variable model to obtain frequency estimators.

The MSM estimator also permits analysis of discrete response data generated by more complex partial observation functions than the maximum indicator appearing in (1). For example, consider data on ranks of alternatives. With the exception of the multinomial logit model, it is impossible to obtain analytically tractable expressions for probabilities of more than the first few ranks in terms of response probabilities; see Falmange (1978), Barbara and Pattanaik (1985), and McFadden (1986a). However, Monte Carlo drawings from the latent variable model provides unbiased frequency estimators of the ranking probabilities that can be used in MSM estimation.

8. STATISTICAL PROPERTIES OF MSM ESTIMATORS

The conditions under which MSM estimators are consistent asymptotically normal (CAN) are stated formally and proved in this section. I use the following notation, mostly collected from Sections 2 and 3 of the paper:

$C=\{1,\dots,m\}$: the set of possible responses.

$u_i=\alpha x_i$ or $u_C=\alpha X_C$: a latent variable model, $i\in C$, with $X_C=(x_1,\dots,x_m)$ a $\bar{K}\times m$ array, $u_C=(u_1,\dots,u_m)$, $\alpha=a(\theta,\eta)$ a $1\times\bar{K}$ vector function, with θ a $k\times 1$ parameter vector with true value θ^*, and η a random vector with density $g(\eta)$ and associated measure g, independent of X_C. Let $X_{C-i}=(x_1-x_i,\dots,x_{i-1}-x_i,x_{i+1}-x_i,\dots,x_m-x_i)$, and $u_{C-i}=(u_1-u_i,\dots,u_{i-1}-u_i,u_{i+1}-u_i,\dots,u_m-u_i)$.

$p(X_C)$: density for X_C, with associated measure p.

$g_U(u_{C-i}|\theta,X_C)$: the density of u_{C-i} induced by the transformation $u_{C-i}=a(\theta,\eta)X_{C-i}$ of the random vector η.

$d_i=1(u_{C-i}\leqslant 0)$: observed response ($=$ indicator for maximum u_i).

$P_C(i|\theta, X_C)$: probability of η such that $a(\theta, \eta)X_C$ is maximized at i, given X_C; the *discrete response probability*.

$f_C(i|\theta, X_C)$: a simulator for $P_C(i|\theta, X_C)$.

W_i: $K \times 1$ instrument vector, determined as a function $W_i = w_i(\theta, X_C)$, with $K \geqslant k$.

$n = 1, \ldots, N$: a random sample.

d, $P(\theta)$, $f(\theta)$: $mN \times 1$ vectors formed by stacking d_i, $P_C(i|\theta, X_C)$, or $f_C(i|\theta, X_C)$ by alternative, then by observation.

$W = W(\theta)$: $K \times mN$ array formed by stacking W_{in}.

$P_\theta(\theta)$: $mN \times k$ array of derivatives of $P(\theta)$.

θ_{sm}: any vector satisfying $\|W(\theta_0)(d - f(\theta_{sm}))\| \leqslant \inf_\theta \|W(\theta_0)(d - f(\theta))\| + O(1)$, and θ_0 either prespecified or estimated.

$R_N(\theta)$, $R(\theta)$, $\bar{R}$: $K \times k$ array of sample covariances, $R_N(\theta) = WP_\theta(\theta)/N$, $R(\theta) = \lim R_N(\theta)$, $\bar{R} = R(\theta^*)$.

The response probabilities are invariant under monotone transformations of the latent variable model. Hence, without loss of generality, we may normalize $x_1 \equiv 0$, so X_C is contained in a $\bar{K}(m-1)$ dimensional space. Further, α may be defined without loss of generality to have a compact range: Given a latent variable model $u_C = \alpha X_C$, the transform $\tilde{\alpha} = \alpha/(1 + \|\alpha\|)$ has a range contained in $[-1, 1]^{\bar{K}}$, and the model $\tilde{u}_C = \tilde{\alpha} X_C$ yields the same response probabilities.

The first assumptions made require X_C and θ to have regular domains, and guarantee a zero probability that the latent variables for different alternatives are equal, so the response probabilities are well-defined without additional tie-breaking rules:

ASSUMPTION A1: *The parameter space Θ is a compact convex subset of $\mathbb{R}^k$, and θ^* is in the interior of Θ.*

ASSUMPTION A2: *The domain $\mathbb{X}$ of the attributes X_C is a compact subset of a $\bar{K}(m-1)$ dimensional space.*

ASSUMPTION A3: *The random vector η is finite-dimensional with domain $\mathbb{N}$, is independent of X_C, and has a finite mean. The function $\alpha = a(\theta, \eta)$ is continuous on $\Theta \times \mathbb{N}$, and is twice differentiable in θ with these derivatives continuous on $\Theta \times \mathbb{N}$.*

ASSUMPTION A4: *For an open set $\mathbb{X}_0 \subseteq \mathbb{X}$ with $p(\mathbb{X}_0) = 1$, the subset $\mathbb{N}(\theta, X_C)$ of $\mathbb{N}$ such that $a(\theta, \eta)X_C$ is distinct in every component has probability one for each $\theta \in \Theta$.*

The last assumption is usually imposed in the definition of discrete response models, and can be derived from more basic structural conditions. The following lemma covers common applications, including MNP. When the model contains alternative-specific random effects, the array A_{22} in this result is a $(m-1)$ dimensional identity matrix.

LEMMA 1: *Suppose* A1 *and* A2. *Suppose there is a partition*

$$X_C = \begin{pmatrix} 0 & A_{12} \\ 0 & A_{22} \end{pmatrix}$$

such that A_{22} *is* $(m-1)\times(m-1)$ *and almost surely nonsingular. Suppose* $\alpha = a(\theta,\eta) \equiv \beta(\theta) + \eta\Gamma(\theta)$ *is twice continuously differentiable in* θ. *Suppose* α *is partitioned commensurately with* X_C, *so*

$$[\alpha^1 \quad \alpha^2] = [\beta^1(\theta) \quad \beta^2(\theta)] + [\eta^1 \quad \eta^2]\begin{bmatrix} \Gamma_{11} & \Gamma_{12} \\ 0 & \Gamma_{22} \end{bmatrix}. \tag{27}$$

Suppose Γ_{22} *is nonsingular for* $\theta \in \Theta$. *Suppose the density of* η^2 *conditioned on* η^1 *is uniformly bounded and continuous, with support* $\mathbb{R}^{m-1}$, *and suppose* η *has a finite mean. Then* A3 *and* A4 *hold.*

PROOF: $\alpha X_C = \beta X_C + [0, \eta^1(\Gamma_{11}A_{12} + \Gamma_{12}A_{22}) + \eta^2\Gamma_{22}A_{22}]$. With probability one, the term $\eta^2\Gamma_{22}A_{22}$ has a continuous density with support $\mathbb{R}^{m-1}$, given η^1, implying that the probability of a hyperplane where components of αX_C are tied is zero. *Q.E.D.*

The next assumption guarantees that the response probabilities are well-behaved:

ASSUMPTION A5: *The probability* $P_C(i|\theta, X_C)$ *is positive, and twice differentiable in* θ, *and the probability and its derivatives are continuous, on* $\Theta \times \mathbf{X}$.

The following result gives a sufficient condition for A5 which holds in particular for the MNP model with alternative-specific dummies:

LEMMA 2: *Suppose the hypotheses of Lemma* 1, *with* A_{22} *always nonsingular. Then* A5 *holds.*

PROOF: By the symmetry of the problem in alternatives, it is sufficient to consider $P_C(1|\theta, X_C) = \Pr(\alpha X_C \leqslant 0|X_C)$. Using the decomposition of Lemma 1, $\alpha X_C = [0, s] \leqslant 0$ implies

$$\eta^2 = [s - \beta^1 A_{12} - \beta^2 A_{22} - \eta^1(\Gamma_{11}A_{12} + \Gamma_{12}A_{22})](\Gamma_{22}A_{22})^{-1}. \tag{28}$$

Then, given η^1, the set $B(\eta^1)$ of η^2 satisfying $\alpha X_C \leqslant 0$ is the intersection of $m-1$ linearly independent half-spaces, with each bounding hyperplane twice continuously differentiable in (θ, X_C). Hence,

$$P_C(1|\theta, X_C) = \int_{\eta^1}\int_{B(\eta^1)} g_{2.1}(\eta^2|\eta^1)\, d\eta^2 g_1(\eta^1)\, d\eta^1$$

is twice continuously differentiable in (θ, X_C). Since $g_{2.1}$ has support $\mathbb{R}^{m-1}$, the probability is positive. *Q.E.D.*

The next assumptions concern the instruments and identification of θ^*:

ASSUMPTION A6: *The function $W_i = w_i(\theta, X_C)$ determining the instruments is continuous, bounded, and twice continuously differentiable on $\Theta \times \mathbf{X}$. (Let M_w denote a bound on w_i and its θ derivative, uniform in i, θ, X_C.)*

ASSUMPTION A7: *The instruments identify θ^*, with*

$$(29) \qquad \omega(\theta, \tilde{\theta}) \equiv \int_{\mathbf{X}} \sum_{i \in C} w_i(\tilde{\theta}, X_C)[P_C(i|\theta, X_C) - P_C(i|\theta^*, X_C)]\, dp(X_C)$$

equal to zero if and only if $\theta = \theta^*$, for any $\tilde{\theta} \in \Theta$.

ASSUMPTION A8: *$\bar{R}$ is of maximum rank.*

To satisfy A6, instruments constructed by simulation require the use of smooth simulators such as (11) and (12). If A5 holds and the instruments equal the score of the log likelihood evaluated at each trial θ, $w_i(\theta, X_C) \equiv \partial \ln P_C(i|\theta, X_C)/\partial\theta$, then $\tilde{\theta} = \theta$ and ω reduces to

$$\omega(\theta, \tilde{\theta}) = \int_{\mathbf{X}} \sum_{i \in C} P_C(i|\theta^*, X_C)[\partial \ln P_C(i|\theta, X_C)/\partial\theta]\, dp(X_C),$$

the expected score of an observation under maximum likelihood estimation. For this case, A7 requires that θ^* be the only critical point of the expected log likelihood, a standard identification condition. Also, in this case, $\bar{R}$ equals the information matrix evaluated at θ^*, which is symmetric and nonnegative definite, and by A7 is definite at some point in every neighborhood of θ^*. Then A8 adds only a regularity requirement. In the case of more general instruments, A7 and A8 are standard assumptions for the identification and regularity of classical method of moments estimators. Hence, the identification conditions for MSM are the same as for the corresponding classical method of moments estimator. If crude instruments independent of θ are used to obtain an initially consistent estimator, then ω in (29) is independent of $\tilde{\theta}$. If approximations to the ideal instruments are calculated, starting from an initially consistent estimator, then it is sufficient that A7 hold for $\tilde{\theta}$ in a neighborhood of θ^*.

The next assumptions concern the simulator $f_C(i|\theta, X_C)$:

ASSUMPTION A9: *Vectors $(\eta_{1n}, \ldots, \eta_{rn})$ are drawn, by simple random sampling or otherwise, independently of W and d, and independently for different n, so that each η has marginal density $g(\eta)$. The simulator $f_C(i|\theta, X_{Cn})$ is a uniformly bounded function of θ, X_{Cn} and $(\eta_{1n}, \ldots, \eta_{rn})$.*

ASSUMPTION A10: *For the simulator $f_C(i|\theta, X_{Cn})$, the simulation bias converges to zero uniformly in θ as $N \to \infty$; i.e., $B(\theta) = N^{-1/2}W(Ef(\theta) - P(\theta))$, where the* *expectation is conditioned on W and d, satisfies*

(8) $$\sup_{\theta \in \Theta} |B(\theta)| = o(1).$$

ASSUMPTION A11: *For the simulator* $f_C(i|\theta, X_{Cn})$, *the simulation residual process* $\zeta(\theta) = N^{-1/2}W(f(\theta) - Ef(\theta))$ *is uniformly stochastically bounded and equicontinuous in* θ; *i.e.,*

(9) $$\sup_{\theta \in \Theta} |\zeta(\theta)| = O_p(1);$$

and for each $\delta > 0$, *defining* $A_N = \{\theta | N^{1/2}|\theta - \theta^*| \leqslant \delta\}$,

(10) $$\sup_{\theta \in A_N} |\zeta(\theta) - \zeta(\theta^*)| = o_p(1).$$

The main result on the asymptotic properties of MSM estimators is given in the theorem below. Following the proof of this theorem, I examine the conditions under which various frequency simulators, including the simple frequency simulator and smooth simulators, will satisfy A11.

THEOREM 1: *Suppose the MSM estimator* θ_{sm} *defined by* (7) *satisfies Assumptions* A1 *to* A11. *Then* θ_{sm} *is consistent, with* $N^{1/2}(\theta_{sm} - \theta^*)$ *converging in distribution to a normal vector with mean zero and covariance matrix* $\Sigma_{sm} = (\overline{R}'\overline{R})^{-1}\overline{R}'G_{sm}\overline{R}(\overline{R}'\overline{R})^{-1}$, *with* $\overline{R} = \lim N^{-1}WP_\theta(\theta^*)$ *and* $G_{sm} = \lim N^{-1}EW(d - f(\theta^*))(d - f(\theta^*))'W'$.

PROOF: The argument parallels that of Pakes and Pollard (1989). The vector $W(d - f(\theta))$ entering the defining condition (7) for the MSM estimator can be decomposed into four terms,

(30) $$\begin{aligned} N^{-1/2}W(d - f(\theta)) \equiv {} & [\zeta(\theta^*) - \zeta(\theta)] - B(\theta) \\ & + [N^{-1/2}W(d - f(\theta^*)) + B(\theta^*)] \\ & - [N^{-1/2}W(P(\theta) - P(\theta^*))]. \end{aligned}$$

The asymptotic properties of the estimator are argued by applying conditions (8) to (10) to the first two terms in (30), and applying the following arguments to the last two terms:

[a] By construction of the simulator, $N^{-1/2}W(d - f(\theta^*)) + B(\theta^*)$ has expectation zero, given W. Random sampling and the independence of the simulators across observations, plus the implication from A6 that $W(d - f(\theta))$ is uniformly bounded, imply by the Lindeberg-Feller central limit theorem that this expression converges in distribution to a multivariate normal vector Z with mean zero and covariance matrix G_{sm}.

[b] The expression $\omega_N(\theta) \equiv N^{-1}W(P(\theta) - P(\theta^*))$ converges uniformly in probability to a smooth function $\omega(\theta)$ with the properties that $\omega(\theta) = 0$ if and

only if $\theta = \theta^*$, and that $\bar{R} \equiv \omega_\theta(\theta^*) = \lim \omega_{\theta N}(\theta^*)$ is of rank k. To establish this result, note that continuous differentiability and compactness imply $|\omega_N(\theta) - \omega_N(\tilde{\theta})| \leqslant M|\theta - \tilde{\theta}|$, where $M \geqslant \max_\Theta |R(\theta)|$. Given $\varepsilon > 0$, extract a finite covering of Θ with neighborhoods of radius less than $\varepsilon/3M$; let Θ_ε denote the finite set of centers of these neighborhoods. Then choose N_ε sufficiently large so that for $N > N_\varepsilon$, $\Pr\{\max_{\Theta_\varepsilon} |\omega_N(\theta) - \omega(\theta)| > \varepsilon/3\} < \varepsilon$. By construction of Θ_ε, for each $\theta \in \Theta$, there is a $\tilde{\theta} \in \Theta_\varepsilon$ such that $|\omega_N(\theta) - \omega(\theta)| \leqslant |\omega_N(\tilde{\theta}) - \omega(\tilde{\theta})| + 2\varepsilon/3$. Hence, $\Pr\{\max_\Theta |\omega_N(\theta) - \omega(\theta)| > \varepsilon\} < \varepsilon$. Regularity condition A8 implies $R(\theta^*)$ nonsingular.

Consider first the consistency of θ_{sm}. Argument [a] implies $N^{-1/2}W(d - f(\theta^*)) = O_p(1)$. Hence, (7) satisfies

$$
\begin{aligned}
(31) \qquad & N^{-1}(d - f(\theta_{sm}))'W'W(d - f(\theta_{sm})) \\
& \leqslant N^{-1} \inf_\Theta (d - f(\theta))'W'W(d - f(\theta)) + O(N^{-1}) \\
& \leqslant [N^{-1/2}W(d - f(\theta^*))]'[N^{-1/2}W(d - f(\theta^*))] + O(N^{-1}) \\
& = O_p(1),
\end{aligned}
$$

implying $N^{-1/2}W(d - f(\theta_{sm})) = O_p(1)$. Then, multiplying (30) by $N^{-1/2}$ and using (8), (9), and argument [b], one has $\omega_N(\theta_{sm}) = o_p(1)$. But ω_N converges uniformly outside each neighborhood of θ^* to a function bounded away from zero. Hence, the probability that θ_{sm} is contained in any neighborhood of θ^* approaches one, proving consistency.

Next, I argue that $N^{1/2}(\theta_{sm} - \theta^*)$ is stochastically bounded. From (30), the condition $N^{-1/2}W(d - f(\theta^*)) = O_p(1)$ from argument [a], (8), (9), and (31) implies

$$O_p(1) = N^{-1/2}W(P(\theta_{sm}) - P(\theta^*)).$$

A Taylor's expansion[5] yields

$$
\begin{aligned}
& N^{-1/2}W(P(\theta_{sm}) - P(\theta^*)) \\
& \quad = [N^{-1}WP_\theta(\theta^*) + O(\theta_{sm} - \theta^*)] N^{1/2}(\theta_{sm} - \theta^*).
\end{aligned}
$$

Then $N^{-1}WP_\theta(\theta^*) = \bar{R} + o_p(1)$ and $\theta_{sm} = \theta^* + o_p(1)$ imply

$$O_p(1) = [\bar{R} + o_p(1)] N^{1/2}(\theta_{sm} - \theta^*).$$

Since $\bar{R}$ is of rank k, this implies $N^{1/2}(\theta_{sm} - \theta^*) = O_p(1)$.

Finally, consider the asymptotic normality of the MSM estimator. An asymptotically normal statistic $\tilde{\theta}$ is defined, and then θ_{sm} is shown to be asymptotically equivalent to it. Let $\tilde{\theta} = \theta^* + (\bar{R}'\bar{R})^{-1}\bar{R}'N^{-1}W(d - f(\theta^*))$. Argument [a] implies $N^{1/2}(\tilde{\theta} - \theta^*) = (\bar{R}'\bar{R})^{-1}\bar{R}'Z + o_p(1) = O_p(1)$. Then $N^{1/2}(\tilde{\theta} - \theta^*)$ is asymptotically normal with covariance matrix $(\bar{R}'\bar{R})^{-1}\bar{R}'G_{sm}\bar{R}(\bar{R}'\bar{R})^{-1}$. Also, (10) implies $\zeta(\theta^*) - \zeta(\tilde{\theta}) = o_p(1)$. Substituting $\tilde{\theta}$ in (30) and applying the argument above

[5] In this and following proofs, a Taylor's expansion of a vector of functions will mean a component by component expansion, with remainders representable as expansion terms evaluated at intermediate arguments that differ across components.

with $\tilde{\theta}$ in place of θ_{sm} implies

$$(32)\qquad N^{-1/2}W(d-f(\tilde{\theta})) = Z - \left[\bar{R} + O(\tilde{\theta}-\theta^*)\right]N^{1/2}(\tilde{\theta}-\theta^*) + o_p(1)$$
$$= \left[I - \bar{R}(\bar{R}'\bar{R})^{-1}\bar{R}'\right]Z + o_p(1).$$

From (32), (10), argument [b], a Taylor's expansion of $P(\tilde{\theta}) - P(\theta_{sm})$, and the result that $N^{-1}WP_\theta(\theta_{sm}) = \bar{R} + o_p(1)$,

$$(33)\qquad \Delta \equiv N^{-1/2}W(f(\tilde{\theta}) - f(\theta_{sm}))$$
$$= N^{-1/2}W(P(\tilde{\theta}) - P(\theta_{sm})) + \zeta(\tilde{\theta}) + B(\tilde{\theta}) - \zeta(\theta_{sm}) - B(\theta_{sm})$$
$$= N^{-1/2}W(P(\tilde{\theta}) - P(\theta_{sm})) + o_p(1) = \bar{R}N^{1/2}(\tilde{\theta} - \theta_{sm}) + o_p(1)$$
$$= \bar{R}(\bar{R}'\bar{R})^{-1}\bar{R}'Z + o_p(1).$$

Rewrite condition (7) characterizing θ_{sm} as

$$(34)\qquad N^{-1}(d-f(\tilde{\theta}))'W'W(d-f(\tilde{\theta})) + o_p(1)$$
$$\geqslant N^{-1}(d-f(\theta_{sm}))'W'W(d-f(\theta_{sm}))$$
$$= N^{-1}(d-f(\tilde{\theta}))'W'W(d-f(\tilde{\theta}))$$
$$+2N^{-1/2}(d-f(\tilde{\theta}))'W'\Delta + \Delta'\Delta.$$

From (32) and (33), $N^{-1/2}(d-f(\tilde{\theta}))'W'\Delta = o_p(1)$, and (34) implies $\Delta'\Delta = o_p(1)$. But then $\Delta \equiv \bar{R}N^{1/2}(\tilde{\theta} - \theta_{sm}) + o_p(1) = o_p(1)$, implying θ_{sm} and $\tilde{\theta}$ are asymptotically equivalent. *Q.E.D.*

The next result establishes sufficient conditions for a kernel-smoothed frequency simulator to satisfy the asymptotic unbiasedness condition (8):

LEMMA 3: *Suppose the assumptions of Lemma* 1 *hold, with A_{22} always nonsingular. Suppose a kernel-smoothed frequency simulator with a kernel of the form* (15). *Assume the distribution function Ψ has a finite moment generating function in a neighborhood of the origin. Assume $N^{\varepsilon+1/2}b_N \to 0$ for some $\varepsilon > 0$. Then* A10 *holds.*

PROOF: Let $\mu(t)$ be the moment generating function of Ψ. There exists $\tau > 0$ such that $\Psi(v) \leqslant e^{\tau v}\mu(-\tau)$ for all $v < 0$ and $1 - \Psi(v) \leqslant e^{-\tau v}\mu(\tau)$ for all $v > 0$. If $c \equiv \max_{j\neq i}(y_j - y_i)/2 > 0$, then $\mathbb{K}_i(y_1, \ldots, y_m) = \int_{v\leqslant c}(\prod_{j\neq i}\Psi(v + y_i - y_j))\Psi'(v)\,dv + \int_{v>c}(\prod_{j\neq i}\Psi(v + y_i - y_j))\Psi'(v)\,dv \leqslant e^{-\tau c}\mu(-\tau) + e^{-\tau c}\mu(\tau)$, with the first term the result of bounding Ψ at negative arguments, and the second the result of bounding the probability at positive arguments. If $c < 0$, a similar argument yields $\mathbb{K}_i(y_1, \ldots, y_m) \geqslant (1 - e^{-\tau|c|}\mu(\tau))^m \geqslant 1 - me^{-\tau|c|}\mu(\tau)$. Let $\mathbb{K}(y_{C-i}) \equiv \mathbb{K}_i(y_C)$. Define $I(A) = \int_A|\mathbb{K}(u_{C-i}/b_N) - 1(u_{C-i} \leqslant 0)|g_U(u_{C-i}|\theta, X_C)\,du_{C-i}$. Define A_1 to be the set of u_{C-i} less than $-Mb_N$ in every component, A_2 to be the set of u_{C-i} greater than Mb_N in at least one component, with M a positive constant, and $A_3 = \mathbb{R}^{m-1} - A_1 - A_2$. Then, the bounds on $\mathbb{K}$ imply $I(A_1) \leqslant e^{-\tau M}\mu(\tau)m$ and $I(A_2) \leqslant e^{-\tau M}(\mu(\tau)+\mu(-\tau))$. Further, $I(A_3) \leqslant \Sigma_{j \neq i} \Pr(|u_j - u_i| \leqslant Mb_N)$. But (28) holds when the second partition is of dimension one and s is the value of a single component $u_j - u_i$ of u_{C-i}. Then, letting M_γ be a uniform bound on the conditional density of η^2 given η^1, $\Pr(|u_j - u_i| \leqslant Mb_N) \leqslant 2Mb_N M_\gamma$. Therefore, $I(A_3) \leqslant 2mMb_N M_\gamma$. Then, $N^{1/2}|\tilde{P}_C(i|\theta, X_C) - P_C(i|\theta, X_C)| \leqslant N^{1/2}(I(A_1) + I(A_2) + I(A_3)) \leqslant N^{1/2}(e^{-\tau M}\mu(\tau)m + e^{-\tau M}(\mu(\tau)+\mu(-\tau)) + 2mMb_N M_\gamma)$. Choose $M = \tau^{-1}\ln N$. Then, the right-hand side of the last inequality goes to zero if $N^{1/2}(\ln N)b_N \to 0$. The condition $N^{1/2+\epsilon}b_N \to 0$ implies the required limit. *Q.E.D.*

The stochastic boundedness and equicontinuity conditions in A11 can be demonstrated for *smooth* simulators by the following argument:

LEMMA 4: *If A1 to A9 hold, and the simulator $f(\theta)$ is uniformly bounded and twice continuously differentiable, then* (9) *and* (10) *hold.*

PROOF: A second-order Taylor's expansion of ζ about θ^* yields

$$\zeta(\theta) - \zeta(\theta^*) = \zeta_\theta(\theta^*)(\theta - \theta^*) + (1/2)\left[N^{-1/2}\zeta_{\theta\theta}\right] \operatorname{vec}\left(\left[(\theta-\theta^*)\right]\left[N^{1/2}(\theta-\theta^*)\right]'\right), \tag{35}$$

where $\zeta_{\theta\theta}$ is a $K \times k^2$ array of second derivatives evaluated at points between θ and θ^*. The array ζ_θ satisfies $E(\zeta_\theta(\theta^*)) = 0$, with independence across observations, so a central limit theorem implies $\zeta_\theta(\theta^*) = O_p(1)$. The contribution of each observation to the array $\zeta_{\theta\theta}$ is uniformly bounded, so $N^{-1/2}\zeta_{\theta\theta} = O_p(1)$. Hence, (35) implies, for $A_N = \{\theta | N^{1/2}|\theta - \theta^*| \leqslant \delta\}$,

$$\sup_{\theta \in A_N} |\zeta(\theta) - \zeta(\tilde{\theta})| = O_p(1) \cdot O_p(N^{-1/2}),$$

establishing (10).

I next establish (9), using a "chaining" argument. Given an integer i, cover $[0,1]^k$ with 2^{ki} cubes with sides 2^{-i}, and let Θ_i be a set containing one point selected from each cube that intersects Θ. For $\theta \in \Theta$, define $\theta_i = \theta_i(\theta)$ to be the nearest point in Θ_i; then $|\theta - \theta_i(\theta)| < 2^{-i}$ and $|\theta_{i+1}(\theta) - \theta_i(\theta)| < 2^{-i}$. From this construction,

$$|\zeta(\theta)| \leqslant |\zeta(\theta_1)| + \sum_{i=1}^{\infty} |\zeta(\theta_{i+1}) - \zeta(\theta_i)|.$$

I shall need Bernstein's inequality, which states that independent identically distributed random variables Y_i with $EY_i = 0$ and $|Y_i| \leqslant c$ satisfy

$$P\left\{\sum_{i=1}^{N} Y_i > t\right\} \leqslant \exp\left[-t^2/(2N\sigma^2 + 2ct/3)\right],$$

for $t > 0$, where $\sigma^2 = EY_i^2$; see Giné and Zinn (1986), Lemma 3.2, and also Pollard (1984) and Shorack and Wellner (1986). Replace t by $N^{1/2}t$ and use

$\sigma^2 \leqslant c^2$ to obtain

$$P\left\{N^{-1/2}\left|\sum_{i=1}^{N} Y_i\right| > t\right\} \leqslant 2\exp\left[-t^2/(2c^2 + 2ct/3N^{1/2})\right].$$

Let $M \geqslant 1$ be a uniform bound for $\Sigma_{i\in C}W_{in}(f_C(i|\theta, X_{Cn}) - Ef_C(i|\theta, X_{Cn}))$ and for its derivative with respect to θ. Note that $\Sigma_{i=1}^{\infty} i2^{-i-3} = 1/4$. Then, for any constant C satisfying the bound $C > 48M + 8kM \ln 2$,

$$P\left\{\sup_{\Theta} |\zeta(\theta)| > C\right\} \tag{36}$$

$$\leqslant P\{|\zeta(\theta_1)| > C/2\} + \sum_{i=1}^{\infty} P\left\{\sup_{\Theta} |\zeta(\theta_{i+1}(\theta)) - \zeta(\theta_i(\theta))| > i2^{-i-3}C\right\}$$

$$\leqslant P\{|\zeta(\theta_1)| > C/2\} + \sum_{i=1}^{\infty} 2^{ki} \sup_{\Theta} P\{|\zeta(\theta_{i+1}(\theta)) - \zeta(\theta_i(\theta))| > i2^{-i-3}C\} \tag{37}$$

$$\leqslant 2\exp\left[-C^2/4(2M^2 + MC/3)\right] + \sum_{i=1}^{\infty} 2^{ki} 2\exp\left[-C^2 i^2 4^{-i-3}/(2M^2 4^{-i} + 2M2^{-i}Ci2^{-i-3}/3)\right] \tag{38}$$

$$\leqslant 2\exp[-C/4M] + \sum_{i=1}^{\infty} 2\exp[-iC/8M] \leqslant 5\exp[-C/8M]. \tag{39}$$

The inequalities (36) and (37) hold since left-hand-side events are contained in the union of the right-hand-side events, while (38) follows by application of the Bernstein inequality, and (39) by use of the bound on C and manipulation of the exponential terms. Given $\varepsilon > 0$, C can then be chosen sufficiently large to make the right-hand side of (39) less than ε. This proves (9). *Q.E.D.*

The following results establish conditions under which simulators can have jumps, but these jumps are sufficiently "well-behaved" so (9) and (10) are satisfied. The simple frequency simulator in the MNP model, in particular, is shown to satisfy these sufficient conditions.

ASSUMPTION A12: *Define $\varphi_C(i|\theta, X_{Cn})$ to be the simple frequency in the r draws for observation n of the event that $a(\theta, \eta_{jn})X_{Cn}$ is maximized at component i. Assume the simulator $f_C(i|\theta, X_{Cn})$ is a uniformly bounded function of θ, X_{Cn}, and $(\eta_{1n}, \ldots, \eta_{rn})$ satisfying*

$$\left|f_C(i|\theta, X_{Cn}) - f_C(i|\tilde{\theta}, X_{Cn})\right| \leqslant M_\varphi\left|\varphi_C(i|\theta, X_{Cn}) - \varphi_C(i|\tilde{\theta}, X_{Cn})\right| + M_f|\theta - \tilde{\theta}|^\lambda \tag{40}$$

for some M_φ, M_f, $\lambda > 0$, and all θ, $\tilde{\theta} \in \Theta$ and $X_{Cn} \in \mathbf{X}$.

Condition (40) requires that the simulator be at least as smooth in θ as the simple frequency simulator. Condition (40) is satisfied trivially by either the frequency simulator, or by a smooth simulator. If the simulator is differentiable at non-jump points, then $\lambda = 1$; the assumption also allows $0 < \lambda < 1$, corresponding to "polynomial" nondifferentiability. A simulator satisfying (40) will be termed λ-Lipschitz in neighborhoods without jumps.

The next result characterizes the regularity in θ of the simulated moments, and guarantees that with probability one, the condition defining θ_{sm} has a solution with $|W(d - f(\theta_{sm}))| \leqslant mM_w M_\varphi / r$. Then, any bounded sequence $a_N = O(1)$ on the right-hand side of the definition (7) of a MSM estimator that satisfies $a_N \geqslant (mM_w M_\varphi / r)^2$ implies existence of the estimator.

LEMMA 5: *Suppose* A1–A9 *and* A12. *Then, almost surely,* $W(d - f(\theta))$ *is uniformly* λ*-Lipschitz in* θ *except for a closed subset* Θ_0 *of* Θ *with Lebesgue measure zero, and the jumps in this function on* Θ_0 *are bounded by* $mM_w M_\varphi / r$.

PROOF: Define $I(\theta, X_C, \eta) = 0$ if the components of $a(\theta, \eta) X_C$ are all distinct, and $I(\theta, X_C, \eta) = 1$ otherwise. For each $\theta \in \Theta$, A4 implies

$$0 = \int_{\mathbf{N}} \int_{\mathbf{X}} I(\theta, X_C, \eta) \, dg(\eta) \, dp(X_C),$$

and hence

$$0 = \int_{\Theta} \int_{\mathbf{N}} \int_{\mathbf{X}} I(\theta, X_C, \eta) \, dg(\eta) \, dp(X_C) \, d\theta. \tag{41}$$

Applying Fubini's Theorem to (41), there exists a set $\mathbf{X}_1 \subseteq \mathbf{X}$ with probability measure one; for $X_C \in \mathbf{X}_1$, a set $\mathbf{N}(X_C) \subseteq \mathbf{N}$ with probability measure one; and, for $(X_C, \eta) \in \mathbf{X}_1 \times \mathbf{N}(X_C)$, a set $\Theta_1(X_C, \eta) \subseteq \Theta$ of full Lebesgue measure on which $I(\theta, X_C, \eta) = 0$. The continuity of $a(\theta, \eta)$ in θ implies that if $I(\theta, X_C, \eta) = 0$, then this is also true in a neighborhood of θ, so $\Theta_1(X_C, \eta)$ is open.

The function $W(d - f(\theta))$ is defined by N independent draws X_{Cn} with density $p(X_C)$, and for each n, r draws $(\eta_{1n}, \ldots, \eta_{rn})$, each with marginal density $g(\eta)$. Hence, with probability one, $X_{Cn} \in \mathbf{X}_1$ and $\eta_{jn} \in \mathbf{N}(X_{Cn})$ for $j = 1, \ldots, r$ and $n = 1, \ldots, N$, implying $\Theta_N = \bigcap_{n=1}^{N} \bigcap_{j=1}^{r} \Theta_1(X_{Cn}, \eta_{jn})$ is an open set of full measure. But, by A12, $f_C(i | \theta, X_C)$ is uniformly λ-Lipschitz with constant M_f on Θ_N.

Suppose $\theta \notin \Theta_N$, so $\theta \notin \Theta_1(X_{Cn}, \eta_{jn})$ for some (n, j). With probability one, θ is contained in $\Theta_1(X_{Cn'}, \eta_{j'n'})$ for $(n', j') \neq (n, j)$. Hence, using (40), the discontinuity in $|W(d - f(\theta))|$ is at most $mM_w M_\varphi / r$ with probability one. *Q.E.D.*

Assumption A4 implies that the set of η for which there are ties in the components of $a(\theta, \eta) X_C$ has probability zero for all θ and almost all X_C. The next assumption requires that the geometry of $a(\theta, \eta)$ be such that the exceptional set $\mathbf{N}(\theta, X_C)^c$ of η where ties occur varies smoothly in (θ, X_C). Define the

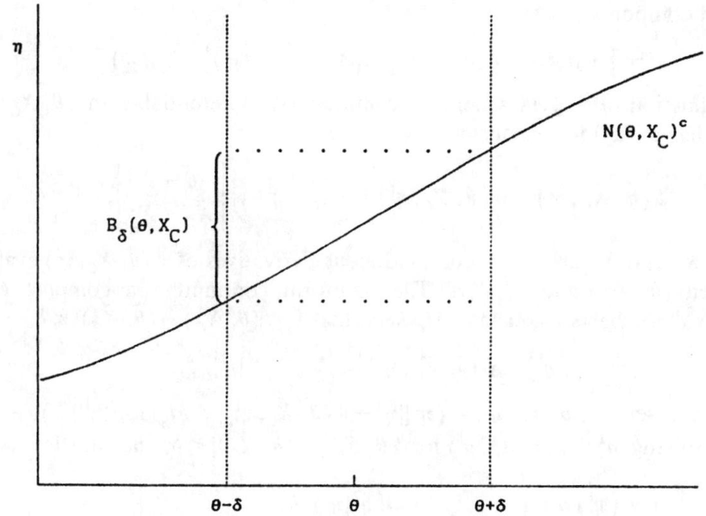

FIGURE 1

set

(42) $$B_\delta(\theta, X_C) = \left\{\eta \mid \eta \in \mathbb{N}(\tilde{\theta}, X_C)^c \text{ for some } |\tilde{\theta} - \theta| \leqslant \delta\right\}.$$

Figure 1 illustrates the construction of $B_\delta(\theta, X_C)$. The following argument establishes that $B_\delta(\theta, X_C)$ is closed, and hence measurable, for $(\theta, X_C) \in \Theta \times \mathbf{X}_0$: If $\eta^j \in B_\delta$ and $\eta^j \to \eta^0$, then $\eta^j \in \mathbb{N}(\theta^j, X_C^j)^c$, a closed set, for some (θ^j, X_C^j) in a closed δ neighborhood of (θ, X_C), by A3. Hence, using the continuity of $a(\theta, \eta)X_C$ in (θ, X_C), $\eta^0 \in \mathbb{N}(\theta^0, X_C^0)^c$ for each limit point (θ^0, X_C^0) of (θ^j, X_C^j).

ASSUMPTION A13: *There exists* M_g *and* $\lambda > 0$ *such that for* $X_C \in \mathbf{X}_0$ *and almost all* $\theta \in \Theta$, *the set* $B_\delta(\theta, X_C)$ *has* $g(B_\delta(\theta, X_C)) \leqslant M_g \delta^\lambda$.

The assumption requires that the measure of the set of η yielding ties for θ in a δ-neighborhood shrink toward zero at a "polynomial rate" as δ goes to zero. This condition holds if the set-valued function $\mathbb{N}(\theta, X_C)^c$ is transversal at θ or if there is at most a polynomial singularity. The next result shows that with regularity conditions, the case $a(\theta, \eta) = \beta(\theta) + \eta\Gamma(\theta)$ satisfies A13; this assumption then holds in particular for the MNP model.

LEMMA 6: *Suppose the hypotheses of Lemma* 1, *with* A_{22} *always nonsingular, and* A6–A9. *Then* A13 *holds.*

PROOF: Suppose a tie between alternatives 1 and 2, so $\alpha x_2 = 0$. Using the notation of (27) and (28), partition $\alpha_1 = (\alpha_1, \alpha_3, \ldots, \alpha_m)$ and let α_2 denote the second component. Then,

$$\eta^2 = \left[-\beta^1 A_{12} - \beta^2 A_{22} - \eta^1 (\Gamma_{11} A_{12} + \Gamma_{12} A_{22}) \right] (\Gamma_{22} A_{22})^{-1}.$$

The function $\eta^2 = \psi(\theta, X_C, \eta^1)$ is continuously differentiable in (θ, X_C), and hence has a Taylor's expansion

$$\psi(\tilde{\theta}, \tilde{X}_C, \eta^1) - \psi(\theta, X_C, \eta^1) = \left[\lambda_1 + \eta^1 \lambda_2 \right] \begin{bmatrix} \tilde{\theta} - \theta \\ \tilde{X}_C - X_C \end{bmatrix},$$

where λ_1 and λ_2 are vectors of continuous derivatives of $\psi(\theta, X_C, \eta^1)$ evaluated between (θ, X_C) and $(\tilde{\theta}, \tilde{X}_C)$. Then uniform continuity on compact $\Theta \times \mathbf{X}$ implies there exists a constant M_ψ such that for $|(\theta, X_C) - (\tilde{\theta}, \tilde{X}_C)| \leqslant \delta$,

$$|\psi(\tilde{\theta}, \tilde{X}_C, \eta^1) - \psi(\theta, X_C, \eta^1)| \leqslant M_\psi (1 + |\eta^1|)\, \delta.$$

Then the set $\mathbb{N}_2(\tilde{\theta}, \tilde{X}_C, \eta^1) = \{ \eta^2 \,|\, |\eta^2 - \psi(\tilde{\theta}, \tilde{X}_C, \eta^1)| \leqslant M_\psi (1 + |\eta^1|)\, \delta \}$ contains all η^2 solving $\eta^2 = \psi(\tilde{\theta}, \tilde{X}_C, \eta^1)$ for $|(\theta, X_C) - (\tilde{\theta}, \tilde{X}_C)| \leqslant \delta$, and satisfies

$$\int_{\eta^1} g_1(\eta^1)\, d\eta^1 \int_{\mathbb{N}_2(\theta,\, X_C,\, \eta^1)} g_{2.1}(\eta^2 | \eta^1)\, d\eta^2$$

$$\leqslant M_\psi (1 + E|\eta^1|)\, \delta M_\gamma \equiv 2 M_g \delta / m(m-1),$$

where M_γ bounds $g_{2.1}$. There are $m(m-1)$ possible combinations of tied alternatives, each of which can with permutations of components of X_C, α, and η and relocation of X_C be put in the form above. The sum of the bounds for each combination gives A13. *Q.E.D.*

Given $\varepsilon > 0$, a finite family of random functions F_ε is said to *bracket* a family of random functions F if for each $Y \in F$ there exist $\underline{Y}, \overline{Y} \in F_\varepsilon$ such that $\underline{Y} \leqslant Y \leqslant \overline{Y}$ and $E(\overline{Y} - \underline{Y}) < \varepsilon$. The logarithm of the number of elements in the smallest set F_ε that brackets F, denoted $H(\varepsilon)$, is called *metric entropy with bracketing*. The following result establishes stochastic equicontinuity conditions for families whose metric entropy does not rise too rapidly as ε falls.

LEMMA 7: *Assume F is a uniformly bounded family of measurable random functions. Assume F satisfies $\int_0^1 H(\varepsilon^2)^{1/2}\, d\varepsilon$ finite, where H is the metric entropy with bracketing. Suppose $Y \Rightarrow y_1, Y \Rightarrow y_2, \ldots$ denote independent identically distributed realizations of deviations from the mean, $Y - EY$, for $Y \in F$. Define $\|Y\| = E|Y - EY|$. Then for every $\lambda > 0$,*

$$\lim_{\delta \to 0} \limsup_{N \to \infty} \Pr \left\{ \sup_{\substack{Y \in F \\ Y \Rightarrow y_n}} \sup_{\substack{Y' \in F \\ \|Y' - Y\| \leqslant \delta \\ Y' \Rightarrow y_n'}} N^{-1/2} \left| \sum_{n=1}^{N} (y_n - y_n') \right| > \lambda \right\} = 0. \tag{43}$$

PROOF: Dudley (1984), Theorem 6.2.1, establishes (43). I use a restatement from Alexander (1987), Theorem 2.1. *Q.E.D.*

The next result establishes that the simulation residuals satisfy stochastic equicontinuity and boundedness conditions sufficient for the MSM estimator to be CAN. The critical step is to show that these residuals satisfy the assumption on metric entropy required by Lemma 7.

LEMMA 8: *Suppose A1–A9, A12–A13. Then A11 holds.*

PROOF: Assume $\Theta \in [0,1]^k$. For any integer j, cover $[0,1]^k$ with 2^{kj} cubes with sides 2^{-j}, and for each $X_C \in \mathbf{X}_0$, let $\Theta_j(X_C)$ be a set containing one point selected from each cube that intersects Θ. By A13, the selection can be made so that $g(B_\delta(\theta, X_C)) \leqslant M_g \delta^\lambda$ for $\theta \in \Theta_j(X_C)$. Define $\theta_j(\theta) \equiv \theta_j(\theta, X_C)$ to be a point in $\Theta_j(X_C)$ nearest to θ; then $|\theta - \theta_j(\theta)| \leqslant 2^{-j} \equiv \delta_j$.

Let $Y(\theta, X_C) = \Sigma_{i \in C} W_i f_C(i|\theta, X_C)$. Define $q_j(\theta, X_C)$ to be the number of draws η_s for $s = 1, \ldots, r$ with $\eta_s \in B_{\delta_j}(\theta, X_C)$. Using the notation of (40), and λ satisfying A12 and A13, define

$$Y_j^0(\theta, X_C) = mM_w\Big(M_f|\theta - \theta_j(\theta)|^\lambda + M_\varphi q_j(\theta, X_C)/r\Big).$$

Then, by A13, $\mathrm{E}q_j(\theta, X_C) \leqslant rg(B_{\delta_j}(\theta, X_C))$, implying

$$\begin{aligned} EY_j^0(\theta, X_C) &\leqslant mM_w M_f|\theta - \theta_j(\theta)|^\lambda + mM_w M_\varphi g\big(B_{\delta_j}(\theta, X_C)\big) \\ &\leqslant mM_w\big(M_f + M_\varphi M_g\big)\,\delta_j^\lambda \equiv M_0\delta_j^\lambda. \end{aligned}$$

From (40),

$$\begin{aligned} &\big|Y(\theta, X_C) - Y\big(\theta_j(\theta), X_C\big)\big| \\ &\quad\leqslant mM_w\Big(M_f|\theta - \theta_j(\theta)|^\lambda\Big) + mM_w M_\varphi \max_{i \in C}\big|\varphi_C(i|\theta, X_C) \\ &\qquad\qquad - \varphi_C\big(i|\theta_j(\theta), X_C\big)\big| \\ &\quad\leqslant mM_w\Big(M_f|\theta - \theta_j(\theta)|^\lambda + M_\varphi q_j(\theta, X_C)/r\Big). \end{aligned}$$

Hence, $\underline{Y}_j(\theta, X_C) \equiv Y(\theta_j(\theta), X_C) - Y_j^0(\theta, X_C) \leqslant Y(\theta, X_C) \leqslant \overline{Y}_j(\theta, X_C) \equiv Y(\theta_j(\theta), X_C) + Y_j^0(\theta, X_C)$. Given $\varepsilon > 0$, choose j to be the smallest integer such that $2^{-\lambda j} < \varepsilon$. Then the 2^{kj+1} functions $\underline{Y}_j$ and $\overline{Y}_j$ bracket $Y(\theta, X_C)$, $\theta \in \Theta$. This implies that the metric entropy with bracketing for $F = \{Y(\theta, X_C)|\theta \in \Theta\}$ satisfies $H(\varepsilon) \leqslant (kj + 1)\ln 2 \leqslant (-\ln \varepsilon)k/\lambda + (k+1)\ln 2$, and hence $\int_0^1 H(\varepsilon^2)^{1/2}\,d\varepsilon \leqslant \int_0^1 H(\varepsilon^2)\,d\varepsilon \leqslant (k+1)\ln 2 - 2(k/\lambda)\int_0^1 \ln \varepsilon\,d\varepsilon < \infty$. This establishes the assumptions of Lemma 7, so (43) holds.

For any $\delta > 0$, forming the expectation of (40) and using A12, $|\theta - \tilde{\theta}| < \delta$ implies $E|Y(\theta, X_C) - Y(\tilde{\theta}, X_C)| < mM_w(M_f + M_\varphi M_g)\,\delta \equiv M_0\delta$. Hence, (43) can be written in the form

$$\lim_{\delta \to 0}\ \limsup_{N \to \infty}\ \Pr\big\{|\zeta(\theta) - \zeta(\tilde{\theta})| > \lambda\big\} = 0. \tag{44}$$

Taking $\delta = 2^{-j}$, $j = 1, 2, \ldots$, one has $|\theta - \tilde{\theta}| < \delta$ for $N \geqslant 4^j$ and $N^{1/2}|\theta - \tilde{\theta}| < 1$. Then (44) implies (10).

Next prove (9). From (44), given $\lambda > 0$, there exists $\delta > 0$ such that

$$\limsup_{N \to \infty} \Pr\left\{ \sup_{\theta \in \Theta} \sup_{\substack{\tilde{\theta} \in \Theta \,\& \\ |\theta - \tilde{\theta}| \leqslant \delta}} |\zeta(\theta) - \zeta(\tilde{\theta})| > \lambda \right\} < \lambda.$$

Choose any $\theta_0 \in \Theta$. A central limit theorem implies there exists M_0 such that $\sup_N \Pr\{|\zeta(\theta_0)| > M_0\} < \lambda$. But any $\theta \in \Theta$ can be written $\theta = \theta_0 + \Sigma_{j=0}^{J}(\theta_{j+1} - \theta_j)$ with $\theta_j = (j/J)\theta + (1 - j/J)\theta_0$ and J the smallest integer exceeding $1/\delta$. Then,

$$\Pr\{|\zeta(\theta)| > M_0 + \lambda J\}$$

$$\leqslant \Pr\left\{|\zeta(\theta_0)| > M_0 \,\&\, |\zeta(\theta_{j+1}) - \zeta(\theta_j)| < \lambda,\ j = 0, \ldots, J\right\} < \lambda.$$

Then (9) holds. *Q.E.D.*

In this lemma, the construction holds even if the number of repetitions r is a random function of θ, X_C, and N. Then, in particular, the lemma holds for simulators formed by acceptance/rejection methods with random stopping rules, and for consistent simulators where r increases with sample size.

Let $\hat{\theta}_N$ be a sequence in Θ and assume that the instruments are evaluated at $\hat{\theta}_N$ for each N. The $\hat{\theta}_N$ might be nonstochastic, or a sequence of initially consistent estimators, or might equal the MSM estimator θ_{sm}. In the last case, θ_{sm} solves

$$\|W(\theta_{sm})(d - f(\theta_{sm}))\| \leqslant \inf_\theta \|W(\theta_{sm})(d - f(\theta))\| + O(1).$$

Lemma 8 holds in all these cases.

The next result establishes the consistency of the estimators (21) and (22) of the components of the asymptotic covariance matrix of the MSM estimator.

LEMMA 9: *Assume A1–A11. Assume $\hat{P}_\theta(\theta)$ is a simulator of $P_\theta(\theta)$ that is twice continuously differentiable in θ, such as the smooth simulator* (12) *with the density γ chosen so that the function $h_\theta(u_{C-i}, \theta, X_{C-i})$ is dominated by an integrable function (i.e., some $H(u_{C-i}, X_{C-i})$ satisfies $|h_\theta| \leqslant H$ and $\int H(u_{C-i}, X_{C-i})\gamma(u_{C-i})\,du_{C-i}$ finite). Then the estimator $\hat{\Sigma}_{sm}$ for Σ_{sm} given in* (21) *is consistent, as is the estimator $\hat{R} = N^{-1}W\hat{P}_\theta$ for $\bar{R}$ given in* (22), *with $\hat{P}_\theta$ evaluated at θ_{sm} or any consistent estimator of θ^*.*

PROOF: To show (21), note first that this expression with θ^* in place of θ_{sm} converges to G_{sm} by a law of large numbers; see part [a] of the proof of Theorem 1. Second, by (8)–(10), terms involving the difference of $f(\theta^*)$ and $f(\theta_{sm})$ are $o_p(1)$. The argument for (22) is the same, but it is necessary to use versions of (8)–(10) for $\hat{P}_\theta$. These hold for smooth simulators by Lemma 4. *Q.E.D.*

Expressions for the derivatives of the response probabilities with respect to the parameters θ, in a form suitable for application of simulation methods, are needed for the construction of instruments, and consistent estimation of the MSM covariance matrix. They are also needed for Newton-Raphson type iterative search for the estimators. For multinomial probit, Paul Ruud has suggested a characterization of the derivatives of the response probability with respect to β and Γ. Applying the chain rule to $\beta(\theta)$ and $\Gamma(\theta)$ yields derivatives of the response probabilities with respect to the deep parameters θ. These equations provide a template for construction of good crude instruments for MNP. Note that these equations require simulation of only the first and second order censored moments of the multivariate distribution, which can be done efficiently using cylinder function simulators.

LEMMA 10: *Assume the MNP model, generated by the latent variable model* (1) *with α satisfying* (3). *Then, the derivatives of the response probabilities with respect to the parameters β, Γ are*

$$\begin{aligned}\partial P_C(i|\theta, X)/\partial\beta &= X(X'\Omega X)^{-1}\int_{u\leqslant 0}(u-\beta X)n(u-\beta X, X'\Omega X)\,du\\ &\equiv X(X'\Omega X)^{-1}\int_{u\leqslant 0}(u-\beta X)h(u,X,\theta)\gamma(u)\,du,\end{aligned}$$

and

$$\begin{aligned}&\partial P_C(i|\theta, X)/\partial\Gamma\\ &\quad= \Gamma X(X'\Omega X)^{-1}\left\{\int_{u\leqslant 0}[(u-\beta X)'(u-\beta X)-X'\Omega X]\right.\\ &\qquad\qquad\left.\cdot n(u-\beta X, X'\Omega X)\,du\right\}(X'\Omega X)^{-1}X'\\ &\quad\equiv \Gamma X(X'\Omega X)^{-1}\left\{\int_{u\leqslant 0}[(u-\beta X)'(u-\beta X)-X'\Omega X]\right.\\ &\qquad\qquad\left.\cdot h(u,X,\theta)\gamma(u)\,du\right\}(X'\Omega X)^{-1}X',\end{aligned}$$

where $\Omega=\Gamma'\Gamma$, $X=X_{C-i}$, and $h(u,X,\theta)$ is the ratio of the multivariate normal density to a Monte Carlo sampling distribution $\gamma(u)$ on the nonpositive orthant.

PROOF: Consider the normal density

$$n(u-\mu,\Lambda) = (2\pi)^{-1/2}|\Lambda|^{-1/2}e^{(u-\mu)'\Lambda^{-1}(u-\mu)/2},$$

with $\Lambda = X'\Gamma'\Gamma X$ and $\mu = \beta X$. The following matrix differentiation formulas are derived by writing out terms from the familiar expressions $\partial \ln|A|/\partial A = A^{-1}$ and $\partial A^{-1}/\partial A = -A^{-1}\otimes A^{-1}$ (which hold when A is symmetric, but identity of cross-terms is not imposed in the differentiation):

$$\partial \ln |X'\Gamma'\Gamma X| / \partial \Gamma = 2\Gamma X(X'\Gamma'\Gamma X)^{-1}X',$$

$$\partial\left(z'(X'\Gamma'\Gamma X)^{-1}z\right)/\partial \Gamma = -2\Gamma X(X'\Gamma'\Gamma X)^{-1}zz'(X'\Gamma'\Gamma X)^{-1}X'.$$

The derivatives of $\ln n(u-\beta X, X'\Gamma'\Gamma X)$ are then

$$\partial \ln n/\partial \beta = X(X'\Gamma'\Gamma X)^{-1}(u-\beta X)',$$

$$\partial \ln n/\partial \Gamma = -\Gamma X(X'\Gamma'\Gamma X)^{-1}X' + \Gamma X(X'\Gamma'\Gamma X)^{-1}(u-\beta X)'(u-\beta X)(X'\Gamma'\Gamma X)^{-1}X'.$$

Q.E.D.

Department of Economics, Massachusetts Institute of Technology, Cambridge, MA 02139, U.S.A.

Manuscript received October, 1987; final revision received September, 1988.

REFERENCES

ALEXANDER, K. (1987): "The Central Limit Theorem for Empirical Processes on Vapnic-Cervonenkis Classes," *The Annals of Probability*, 15, 178–203.

BARBERA, S., AND P. PATTANAIK (1986): "Falmagne and the Rationalizability of Stochastic Choices in Terms of Random Orderings," *Econometrica*, 54, 707–715.

CHAMBERLAIN, G. (1984): "Panel Data," in *Handbook of Econometrics*, Vol. 2, ed. by Z. Griliches and M. Intriligator. Amsterdam: North Holland, 1247–1320.

CLARK, C. (1961): "The Greatest of a Finite Set of Random Variables," *Operations Research*, 9, 145–162.

DAGANZO, C. (1980): *Multinomial Probit*. New York: Academic Press.

DEÁK, I. (1980): "Three Digit Accurate Multiple Normal Probabilities," *Numerische Mathematik*, 35, 369–380.

DEVROYE, L. (1986): *Non-Uniform Random Variate Generation*. New York: Springer.

DUDLEY, R. (1984): "A Course on Empirical Processes," Ecole d'Été de Probabilités de Saint-Flour, XII-1982, *Lecture Notes in Mathematics* 1097. New York: Springer, 1–142.

DUTT, J. (1976): "Numerical Aspects of Multivariate Normal Probabilities in Econometric Models," *Annals of Economic and Social Measurement*, 5, 547–562.

FALMANGE, J. (1978): "A Representation Theorem for Finite Random Scale Systems," *Journal of Mathematical Psychology*, 18, 52–72.

FISHMAN, G. (1973): *Concepts and Methods of Digital Simulation*. New York: Wiley.

GINÉ, E., AND J. ZINN (1986): "Lectures on the Central Limit Theorem for Empirical Processes," Probability and Banach Spaces, *Lecture Notes in Mathematics*, 1221. New York: Springer, 50–113.

HAJIVASSILIOU, V., AND D. MCFADDEN (1987): "The Debt Repayment Crises of LDC's: Estimation by the Method of Simulated Moments," Yale Univ., Working Paper.

HAMMERSLEY, J., AND D. HANDSCOMB (1964): *Monte Carlo Methods*. London: Methuen.

HAUSMAN, J., AND D. WISE (1978): "A Conditional Probit Model for Qualitative Choice: Discrete Decisions Recognizing Interdependence and Heterogeneous Preferences," *Econometrica*, 46, 403–426.

HECKMAN, J. (1981): "The Incidental Parameters Problem and the Problem of Initial Conditions in Estimating a Discrete Time-Discrete Data Stochastic Process," in *Structural Analysis of Discrete Data with Econometric Applications*, ed. by C. Manski and D. McFadden. Cambridge: MIT Press, 179–195.

HENDRY, D. (1984): "Monte Carlo Experimentation in Econometrics" in *Handbook of Econometrics*, Vol. 2, ed. by Z. Griliches and M. Intriligator. Amsterdam: North Holland, 937–976.

HOROWITZ, J., J. SPARMONN, AND C. DAGANZO (1981): "An Investigation of the Accuracy of the Clark Approximation for the Multinomial Probit Model," *Transportation Science*, 16, 382–401.

LERMAN, S., AND C. MANSKI (1981): "On the Use of Simulated Frequencies to Approximate Choice Probabilities," in *Structural Analysis of Discrete Data with Econometric Applications*, ed. by C. Manski and D. McFadden. Cambridge: MIT Press, 305–319.

MCFADDEN, D. (1984): "Econometric Analysis of Qualitative Response Models," in *Handbook of Econometrics*, Vol. 2, ed. by Z. Griliches and M. Intriligator. Amsterdam: North Holland, 1395–1457.

——— (1986a): "The Choice Theory Approach to Marketing Problems," *Marketing Science*, 5, 275–297.

——— (1986b): "Discrete Response to Unobserved Variables for Which There are Multiple Indicators," MIT, Working Paper.

MORAN, P. (1984): "The Monte Carlo Evaluation of Orthant Probabilities for Multivariate Normal Distributions," *Australian Journal of Statistics*, 26, 39–44.

OWEN, D. (1956): "Tables for Computing Bivariate Normal Probabilities," *Annals of Mathematical Statistics*, 27, 1075–1090.

PAKES, A., AND D. POLLARD (1989): "The Asymptotic Distribution of Simulation Experiments," *Econometrica*, 57, 1027–1057.

POLLARD, D. (1984): *Convergence of Stochastic Processes*. New York: Springer.

——— (1985): "New Ways to Prove Central Limit Theorems," *Econometric Theory*, 1, 295–314.

PRESS, W., B. FLANNERY, S. TEUKOLSKY, AND W. VETTERLING (1986): *Numerical Recipes*. Cambridge: Cambridge University Press.

RUUD, P. (1981): "Misspecification Errors in Limited Dependent Variable Models," MIT, PhD Dissertation.

RUUD, P., AND D. MCFADDEN (1987): "Estimation of Limited Dependent Variable Models from the Regular Exponential Family by the Method of Simulated Moments," Univ. of California, Berkeley, Working Paper.

SHORACK, G., AND J. WELLNER (1986): *Empirical Processes with Applications to Statistics*. New York: Wiley.

SPANIER, J., AND K. OLDHAM (1987): *An Atlas of Functions*. Washington: Hemisphere.

STERN, S. (1987): "A Method for Smoothing Simulated Moments of Probabilities in Multinomial Probit Models," University of Virginia, Working Paper.

TRAIN, K., D. MCFADDEN, AND A. GOETT (1987): "Consumer Attitudes and Voluntary Rate Schedules for Public Utilities," *Review of Economics and Statistics*, forthcoming.

WESTIN, R. (1974): "Predictions from Binary Choice Models," *Journal of Econometrics*, 2, 1–16.

[17]

Transpn. Res.-B Vol. 21B, No. 4, pp. 251–267, 1987
Printed in Great Britain.
0191-2615/87 $3.00+.00

ESTIMATING "TREE" LOGIT MODELS

ANDREW DALY
Hague Consulting Group bv, Laan van Meerdervoort 32, 2517 AL Den Haag, The Netherlands

(*Received* 28 *January* 1986; *in revised form* 3 *June* 1986)

Abstract—The existence of the "tree" generalisation of the multinomial logit model, its consistency with theories of "rational" human behaviour, as well as the advantages offered in terms of more realistic modelling by this model form, have all been known for some time. Although a few studies have applied tree logit models, however, applications have been restricted by practical and theoretical difficulties in the estimation of these models, in particular with the sequential estimation that has normally been necessary. This paper presents a new estimation procedure, employing the maximum likelihood criterion, for the estimation of tree logit models. The procedure is based on a simple notation for the tree structure and is believed to be original. It offers the possibility of estimating simultaneously all the parameters of general tree logit structures, without restriction on the number of levels but allowing the user to impose constraints of parameter equality where required. Results are presented indicating both the usefulness of the method in deriving improved models, relative to the more familiar sequential estimations, and its practicality and speed of operation on main-frame, minicomputers and microcomputers.

INTRODUCTION

Models of the "logit" form have been widely applied for the analysis of qualitative data, particularly in the field of transportation planning, where they have frequently been used to predict travellers' choices of travel mode, etc. A systematic development of logit modelling for this application was given by Domencich and McFadden (1975), including the establishment of consistency between the logit model and individual utility maximisation, subject to appropriate assumptions. The reader is referred to Domencich and McFadden (or one of the many other presentations; Ben-Akiva and Lerman, 1985, is one of the most recent) for an exposition of the logit model.

The limitations of the multinomial logit form were already known in the mid-70s, and in particular the "IIA" assumption of "independence of irrelevant alternatives" (effectively a restriction on the cross-elasticities) was widely questioned. The model form studied in this paper, the "structured", "hierarchical", "sequential", "nested" or "tree" logit model†, which does not require the IIA assumption (but which does imply some, less severe, restrictions on cross-elasticities), was already known in 1975, but was distrusted because of its unknown relationship to individual utility maximisation. This relationship was clarified by several authors immediately after 1975 (Williams, 1977; Daly and Zachary, 1978; McFadden, 1979) and an international conference in 1977 concluded that tree logit "warranted immediate implementation" (Westin and Manski, 1979). McFadden (1979, 1981) defines the tree logit model, gives its properties, and sets it in its context among related choice models.

Since 1977, however, applications of tree logit have been the exception rather than the rule. A major reason for this has been the lack of computer software for the efficient estimation of tree logit models. "Sequential" estimators for tree logit models have generally been used, i.e. estimations are made at the lowest levels of the models first and, conditional on those estimates, estimations are made subsequently at the higher levels of the model. Although it is known that these sequential estimates are consistent (i.e. as the amount of data increases, they converge to the true parameter values), they are *inefficient* both in the sense that information is omitted in the estimation of the lowest level and in the sense that the amount of calculation needed to pass information between the initial and subsequent estimates is excessive. A further problem is that simple computer programs give incorrect results for tree models as regards the estimates of accuracy in the upper levels of the model. Finally, the tree logit model is quite complicated to specify and exploit; McFadden (1981, Sections 5.17 and 5.22) indicates the theoretical complexity, but many of the problems are practical.

†The five terms are used interchangeably and apparently arbitrarily in the literature. In this paper we shall use the term "tree" logit, for reasons that are explained below.

Despite these problems, sequential estimation has been used in a small number of studies, sometimes involving large systems of models (e.g. Daly and Van Zwam, 1981; a particularly clear description of one of the several parts of this work that involved tree logit structures is given by Sobel, 1980). The practical difficulties encountered in sequential estimation do not seem to be widely appreciated. First, it is often difficult to derive acceptable results (e.g. coefficients with the right sign) in the first-round estimation, because of the greatly reduced amount of information in the data and because a very particular group of observations have to be used. Second, the calculation of the "logsums" that are needed to summarise the first-round submodels in subsequent estimations is somewhat tedious and difficult to check. Third, the need to make two or more separate estimation runs is itself time-consuming and makes it difficult to impose constraints that may be desirable (e.g. consistency of coefficients of cost variables throughout the model system; Hensher's (1986) ingenious "stacking" procedure allows equality constraints to be imposed in some but not all cases). Fourth, because of the statistical inefficiency, the results that are obtained by the process are less accurate then they need to be; it appears in some practical situations that these errors may importantly affect policy conclusions drawn from the models. Finally, correction of the variance estimates in the higher levels of the tree requires software which is neither widely available nor cheap to run.

It is clear that "full-information" simultaneous estimation of the whole model would both give better answers, by being statistically more efficient, and save time and resources by eliminating time-consuming and error-prone calculation. The lack of appropriate computer software has, however, restricted full-information estimation to a small number of studies only. Moreover, the estimation procedures used in these few studies have been in themselves problematic and expensive.

For example, Daly and Zachary (1978) conducted full-information estimation of a simple tree logit model, but were unable to give error estimates for the parameter values. Their work used a general no-derivative optimisation routine, a very expensive method for optimisation of a function for which derivatives can be calculated. In that study, the full-information estimates that were derived were negligibly different from the sequential estimates.

Unpublished work by Cosslett (reported by McFadden, 1981) also presented full-information estimates for tree logit models. In this work there were important differences from the sequential estimates, but there were also indications of specification problems.

More recently, Small and Brownstone (1982) developed a program in APL to derive full-information estimates for simple tree models. APL is a convenient language in which to program some problems, but not known for the computational efficiency of its compilers. It was not surprising that they felt the cost of the full-information estimation was so great that sequential estimation should be used to derive initial values for starting the APL estimation and that the first-iteration approximation (also known to be a consistent estimator) could be used in lieu of the fully-converged estimates. These authors found significant inefficiencies in the sequential estimators, including the possibility of finding a *lower* likelihood value than in the corresponding multinomial logit model (i.e. the multinomial model with the same specification of the alternatives and their utilities, but with no tree structure).

Hensher (1986) doubts the value of the first-iteration approximation, particularly when sequential estimation is used to derive the starting point of that iteration. He reports results with full-information estimation, using an optimisation routine employing first and (approximate) second derivatives, thus allowing him to derive error estimates. The paper referenced describes only two-level structures, but his method can be extended to three levels (personal communication). He comments "with improvements in software and speed of computation. . . (full-information estimation) will no longer be seen as the preferred but computationally unwieldy alternative, indeed it is likely that. . . (sequential estimation) will take on the status of the unwieldy alternative." His empirical results show that tree logit is a necessary model generalisation for his data set, but that sequential estimation seems (on his data) to provide estimates quite different from the full-information estimates. Hensher also raises the issues of finding good initial values for the estimation (both to obtain rapid convergence and to ensure that the global optimum is found) and of determining appropriate specifications for a model which is structurally different from the familiar multinomial logit model: these issues are discussed subsequently.

Ortúzar (1983) concluded that tree logit gave significantly better results on his data than multinomial logit models. He also concluded, however, that multinomial models should be used for initial "screening" of the data, then sequential estimation of tree logit to derive the "best" model. The model development strategy in his work was constrained by the number of options that could be investigated with the software available. He did not attempt full-information estimation, presumably because he did not have appropriate software.

It is clear from the above discussion that the application of model forms more realistic than multinomial logit has been found to be highly desirable but has been severely hampered by the lack of appropriate software for the estimation of tree logit, which is the most practical generalisation of the multinomial form. Authors using sequential estimation have reported results of better quality than multinomial logit, while authors using full-information estimation have achieved still better estimates. Both groups, however, have esperienced difficulty with the practical aspects of the work, particularly the cost and time consumed by estimation. In several cases, inferior results have been accepted because of the time and cost needed to produce better ones.

This paper presents a new and efficient method for full-information estimation of tree logit models with general structure and a number of levels limited only by processing capacity, which has been implemented in a fast FORTRAN program. It is clear from the summary of the literature that the execution speed of the method is vital to its acceptability: speed is achieved by a novel system of notation, suitable for programming in FORTRAN (a computer language for which many efficient compilers exist), which is explained in the following section. Estimation of the parameters of the model is achieved by maximising the likelihood function; this function is derived and the maximisation algorithm explained in Section 2. The third section presents some results obtained in applications for transportation planning in Sweden and in The Netherlands. In conclusion, the relevance of this method to logit modelling in general is discussed and recommendations derived for subsequent work.

1. NOTATION FOR TREE LOGIT MODELS

The notation required for derivation of the tree logit model from individual utility maximisation is extremely complicated (see McFadden, 1981). However, in this paper our concern is not with the justification and derivation of the model but with its use in practice. For this purpose the specification of the "probability model" (Daly, 1984) is sufficient. That is, the model is expressed only in terms of the predicted probabilities for each of the alternatives, the form in which the data is addressed. The behavioural theory (utility maximisation, etc.) on which the model is based is not treated here.

In the literature, a two-level tree logit model is defined for a given individual by the following equations, giving the probability p_{ij} of the choice of the combination i, j, with i at the "higher" level and j at the "lower":

$$p_{ij} = p_i \cdot p_{j|i}, \qquad (1)$$

$$p_{j|i} = \exp(V_{j|i}) \Big/ \sum_{k \in C(i)} \exp(V_{k|i}), \qquad (2)$$

$$p_i = \exp(V_i) \Big/ \sum_{l \in R} \exp(V_l), \qquad (3)$$

$$V_{j|i} = X_{j|i}, \qquad (4)$$

$$V_i = X_i + h_i \log \sum_{k \in C(i)} \exp(V_{k|i}), \qquad (5)$$

where $C(i)$ is a set of "lower-level" alternatives that each form part of the "higher-level" alternative i, R is the set of "higher-level" alternatives, and $X_{j|i}$ and X_i are the measured attractiveness of alternative j (conditional on i) and i itself, respectively. The theory which connects tree models with utility maximisation implies that $0 < h_i \leq = 1$ for all composite alternatives i. The extension of the model to more levels if required is clear; constraints on h_i

then apply at all levels. Although there is no requirement from the utility theory for h_i to be equal for different alternatives, this will often be necessary to be consistent with intuition in particular situations.

The problem is that the specification (1–5) is unwieldy and difficult to formalise for programming, particularly if generalised to more than two levels and irregular structures, where the alternatives available may vary across individuals. The following notation has been developed to deal with these difficulties.

A "qualitative choice model" is defined by a probability distribution function over a finite set C (the "alternatives"). The crucial characteristic is that the probabilities given by the model should indeed sum to 1.

The multinomial logit model giving the probability of choosing alternative r from the choice set C is defined by the function l:

$$l(r, C) = \exp V_r \Big/ \left(\sum_{c \in C} \exp V_c \right) \tag{6}$$

or, more conveniently,

$$\log l(r, C) = V_r - \log \sum_{c \in C} \exp V_c, \tag{7}$$

where V_c measures the attractiveness or utility of alternative c. Usually V is a parametrised function of measured attributes of the alternative; estimation of the unknown parameters within V is typically one of the main aims of the analysis. Note that

$$\sum_{c \in C} l(c, C) = 1$$

so that l defines a true qualitative choice model under the definition introduced above.

The tree logit model is introduced by defining a larger (but still finite) set S of "choice elements", of which the set of alternatives C is a subset. It is within the set of choice elements that the tree structure is defined. These choice elements are comprised of single alternatives or sets of alternatives, the larger elements being "higher" in the hierarchy and containing a number of smaller, "lower-level" elements. To function as choice elements, the members of S must not exhibit partial overlaps; i.e. given any two choice elements, then either they must be totally disjoint, or one must contain the other entirely.

More formally, we could define successively higher levels in the hierarchy as each being aggregations of the alternatives at the next lower level into a smaller set of nonempty, disjoint and exhaustive sets. The lowest level comprises the original alternatives, and at the highest level there is only one set, the "root", which contains all the choice possibilities. These successive aggregations of the alternatives form the choice elements in the slightly less formal discussion which follows. For simplicity of notation, the "root" is not considered to be one of the choice elements.

On a set of choice elements S, hierarchy functions t may be defined:

$$t\colon S \longrightarrow S \cup \{s_0\}. \tag{8}$$

These hierarchy functions are to be interpreted so that $t(s) = s'$ means that choice element s is a part of the more general element s'. The fact that the aggregations are disjoint and exhaustive means that t can always be defined and is unique. The dummy element s_0, "above" the "highest" level within S, has the function that $t(s) = s_0$ when s is not part of any more general element, i.e. s_0 is the "root" element.

A specific function t induces for each element s two subsets of S: its "ancestors" $A(s, t)$ and its "siblings" $B(s, t)$, defined by

$$A(s, t) = \{s, s' = t(s), s'' = t(s'), \ldots, s^n | t(s^n) = s_0\}, \tag{9}$$

$$B(s, t) = \{b | t(b) = t(s)\}. \tag{10}$$

Note that the definitions have been formulated so that s is itself a member of both $A(s, t)$ and $B(s, t)$; the root element is intended to be excluded from A by the definition of A as a subset of S, which excludes the root.

The function t can be called a "tree" if the sequences of ancestors A contain no cycles (repetitions) for any s. The finiteness of S then implies that all sequences A terminate at elements whose only ancestors are the common ancestor or root s_0. The formalisation of S as a series of aggregations of the alternatives ensures that t will in fact define a tree in this sense.

The essence of the notation being introduced is that the functions t contain *all* the structural information. This follows from the fact that all hierarchical structures of successive aggregation of alternatives can be represented by a function t and that all functions t satisfying the "tree" condition define a hierarchy of this form.

One means of ensuring for a specific function t that are no cycles is to index S by identifying a unique number $i(s)$ in the range $1, \ldots, |S|$ with each element of S, and the number $|S| + 1 = i(s_0)$ with s_0. Then if, with this indexing, $i(t(s)) > i(s)$ for every s in S, we can be certain that the function t is a "tree" as defined (i.e. has no cycles). When t is in fact a tree function, it will always be possible to set up an indexing meeting this constraint. For computational purposes, it is in any case necessary to set up an indexing of the elements, and having done so it is convenient to refer to the element by its index, i.e. to blur the distinction between s and $i(s)$. In the remainder of the paper it will be assumed that an indexing with this property exists for every set of elements, and the precise distinction between elements and their indexes will be ignored, so that we can formulate the restriction on tree functions as $t(s) > s$.

In practice an indexing has to be constructed for every specific situation, but this is not difficult to achieve as there are many possibilities which meet the tree function constraint. A simple and logical way is to draw out a diagram showing the choice elements and their relationship graphically; examples of diagrams of this type are given below. From this diagram, all the elementary alternatives can be numbered first, then the choice elements at the next higher level, and so on up the tree. Other possibilities for numbering are shown in the examples below.

Given an indexing of a set S of choice elements and a tree function t, the tree logit model is then defined by the formula

$$f(r, t) = \prod_{a \in A(r,t)} l(a, B(a, t)) \tag{11}$$

or, again more conveniently

$$\log f(r, t) = \sum_{a \in A(r,t)} \log l(a, B(a, t)) \tag{12}$$

$$= \sum_{a \in A(r,t)} \left(V_a - \log \sum_{b \in B(a,t)} \exp V_b \right) \tag{13}$$

using eqn (7) to substitute for l.

Simple algebra will show that this formula defines a qualitative choice model (i.e. the probabilities f add up to 1) over the set of "elementary" or noncomposite elements E, defined by

$$E = \{e | t(s) \neq e, \quad \text{for any } s \in S\}. \tag{14}$$

That is, if we take the alternatives C to be the elementary elements E we may use the tree logit formula (13) to define a qualitative choice model. Simple algebra will also show that the tree logit model defined by (11) or (13) is indeed a formulation of the nested logit model as defined in the literature and in eqns (1–5), provided that

$$V_s = X_s + h_s \log \sum_{t(r)=s} \exp V_r, \tag{15}$$

where X_s is the measured attractiveness of choice element s (the second term being present only for composite choice elements) and provided that h_s lies between 0 and 1. Note that there is again no reason from utility for h_s to be equal for different alternatives, although this may well be required for other reasons in particular situations (see the examples).

In fact, the formula (12) defines a qualitative choice model over other subsets C of S (specifically, any set C for which the predicted probabilities always add up to 1). This formulation, in which observed choices may be groupings of elementary choices, can be useful (Ben-Akiva *et al.*, 1984). Formulations of this type can be generated graphically by drawing a line through the choice elements represented graphically in a tree so as to divide the tree into upper and lower parts; the elements along the line then have the property that their choice probabilities add up to 1. In the remainder of this paper it will however be assumed that the tree logit model is defined over elementary alternatives only (i.e. $C = E$).

The advantage of this notation for the user is that he or she has only to define the function t in eqn (8). No further definitions are required as far as the structure of the model is concerned. For the computer, the function (13), which follows immediately from the definition of t, turns out to be amenable to efficient computation, as will be seen in the following section. This function and its name are drawn from the analogy with transportation network processing, where a "tree" giving shortest routes through the network from a given origin may be defined simply by specifying the "back node" or ancestor of each of the network nodes. (This analogy explains the choice of name for the model. McFadden, 1981, uses an essentially equivalent though less compact notation; concentrating more on the utility structure than on the choice probabilities, he terms the model "tree extreme value.")

To summarise, to define a tree logit model it is sufficient to define the tree function (8). For computation, the function t is used to derive the sets A and B for each node, from which the choice probability may be calculated by eqn (13).

Two examples may help to illustrate the economy of the definition using tree functions. Results of estimating models which apply these two specific structures are presented in Section 3.

Example 1: *Four-alternative mode choice model*

For this structure, we can number the choice elements as follows:

1-Car driver	$t(1) = 5$
2-Car passenger	$t(2) = 5$
3-Public transport	$t(3) = 6$
4-Slow modes	$t(4) = 6$
5-Composite car	$t(5) = 6$

(See Fig. 1.) Note the use of the number 6 to index the tree root. This numbering corresponds to the standard suggested in the theoretical presentation above. The sets A and B can be derived automatically for each alternative from t:

$$\begin{array}{ll} A(1) = 1, 5 & B(1) = 1, 2 \\ A(2) = 2, 5 & B(2) = 1, 2 \\ A(3) = 3 & B(3) = 3, 4, 5 \\ A(4) = 4 & B(4) = 3, 4, 5 \\ A(5) = 5 & B(5) = 3, 4, 5. \end{array}$$

Normally, of course, the user would not have to derive these sets.

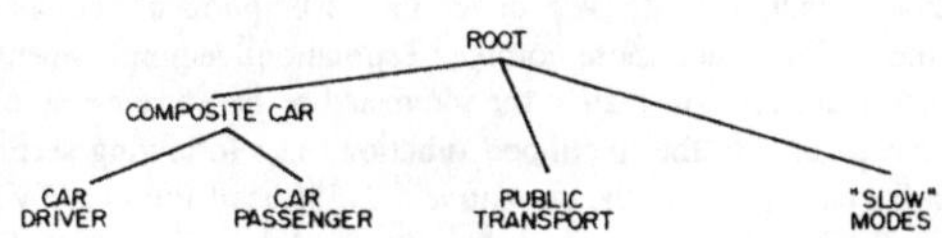

Fig. 1.

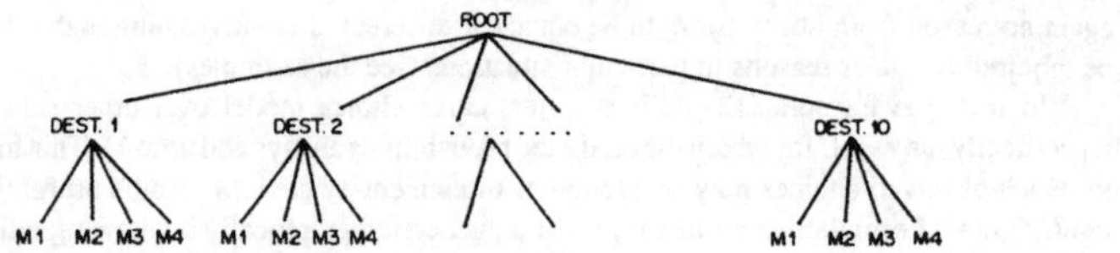

Fig. 2.

Example 2: Mode and destination choice model

Ten destinations are included in the (sampled) set for the estimation of this model. (See Fig. 2.) For each destination, up to four modes may be available.

This structure can be indexed as follows:

Choice element 1: $M1,D1$ $t(1) = 5$
Choice element 2: $M2,D1$ $t(2) = 5$
Choice element 3: $M3,D1$ $t(3) = 5$
Choice element 4: $M4,D1$ $t(4) = 5$
Choice element 5: composite $D1$ $t(5) = 51$
Choice element 6: $M1,D2$ $t(6) = 10$
⋮ ⋮
Choice element 49: $M4,D10$ $t(49) = 50$
Choice element 50: composite $D10$ $t(50) = 51$.

Again the sets A and B follow automatically:

$A(1) = 1, 5 \quad B(1) = 1, 2, 3, 4$
⋮ ⋮
$A(5) = 5 \quad B(5) = 5, 10, \ldots, 45, 50$
⋮ ⋮

In this structure, because of the symmetry with respect to destinations, it is intuitive to require h_s to be equal for the relevant alternatives s (i.e. 5, 10, etc.). Here, the numbering does not follow the standard suggested, but remains consistent with the requirement that $t(s) > s$ for all s.

Note that in both examples, the structure is completely defined when the function t is specified.

2. ESTIMATION OF THE MODEL

The tree logit model is estimated using the maximum likelihood criterion, which is the most common criterion used for estimating logit models of all types. The likelihood function is maximised using a modified Newton-Raphson procedure, which requires the calculation of first and second derivatives. The simple notation derived in the previous section allows the calculation of *exact* second derivatives, as well as the approximate derivatives which are used in preliminary stages of the optimisation. Some studies in the literature use *only* the approximate derivatives, which give less rapid optimisation and less accurate information on the parameter estimation errors.

The likelihood function is derived under the assumption of reasonably straightforward sampling procedures. The much more complex estimations required when data is collected in more sophisticated ways are not treated; the interested reader is referred to Cosslett (1981) for the necessary amendments to the likelihood function. The following section outlines the procedures used for the calculation of the derivatives, and is itself followed by a section describing the way in which these derivatives are employed to find the optimum of the function. Finally, some details are given about the programming of the estimation.

2.1 *Derivatives of the likelihood function*

Under suitable assumptions about the sampling used to select observations for analysis (e.g. that sampling is "exogenous", not dependent on the specific choice made by the individual), the likelihood function for the tree logit model is proportional to

$$L(g, t) = \prod_{0=obs} f(r_o, t), \tag{16}$$

where g is a vector of unknown parameters contained in the attractiveness functions V (i.e. g includes the structural parameters h), r_o is the alternative observed to be chosen by individual 0, and the function f is as given in eqn (11). To simplify analysis, it is sufficient to maximise the log-likelihood, equivalent to maximising

$$L^*(g, t) = \sum_{0=obs} \log f_o = \sum_{0=obs} f^*_o, \tag{17}$$

where

$$f^*_o = \sum_{a \in A(ro,t)} \left(V_{ao} - \log \sum_{b \in B(a,t)} \exp (V_{bo}) \right), \tag{18}$$

substituting the form of eqn (13) for log f.

Maximisation over t (i.e. the *structure* of the model) presents a problem, since the function is discrete in its nature. The only reliable method at present is to evaluate the maximum of the likelihood over g for a number of different specifications of t and choose the t function that gives the largest likelihood maximum. This was the method employed by Sobel (1980), where a large number of evaluations were made; while this problem cannot be solved immediately, the difficulties caused would clearly be reduced by the provision of a more efficient means of maximisation over g (i.e. the *parameters* of the model) such as proposed here. Some shortcuts can be taken in determining t on the basis of *a priori* reasoning, but as will be seen in the empirical tests presented in Section 3, such shortcuts can be dangerous. For the remainder of this section attention will be focussed on the easier problem of optimisation with respect to g. The function t will be assumed to be fixed and will be dropped from the formulae to simplify the notation.

Differentiating eqn (18) with respect to the parameters g, (and dropping the subscript 0 for clarity) we obtain

$$f^*_i = \sum_{a \in A(r)} \left(V_{a,i} - \sum_{b \in B(a)} l(b, B(a)) V_{b,i} \right), \tag{19}$$

where $V_{b,i}$ denotes the differential of V_b with respect to the ith component of g, and l is as defined in eqn (6) (i.e. the multinomial logit model). This can be written more simply as

$$f^*_i = \sum_{a \in A(r)} (V_{a,i} - V_{B(a),i}), \tag{20}$$

where

$$V_{B(a),i} = \sum_{b \in B(a)} l(b, B(a)) V_{b,i}. \tag{21}$$

Differentiating once more we obtain (using double subscripts ij to indicate second derivatives)

$$f^*_{ij} = \sum_{a \in A(r)} \left(V_{a,ij} - V_{B(a),ij} + V_{B(a),i} V_{B(a),j} - \sum_{b \in B(a)} l(b, B(a)) V_{b,i} V_{b,j} \right). \tag{22}$$

The third and fourth terms in eqn (22) are analogous to those derived in multinomial logit models, and form, as in that case, a negative definite matrix (summation over the sequence A and over observations does not affect this property). It is the nonlinear part of V, the part that gives V a nonzero second derivative, seen in the first and second terms of (22), thay may cause nondefiniteness in the second derivative matrix. In multinomial logit, V is normally specified as linear in g, but in the case of tree logit the function V for composite alternatives is essentially nonlinear in g (even if X is linear) because of its form containing the logsum from lower levels, as can be seen by differentiating eqn (15) twice, which yields the results

$$V_{a,i} = X_{a,i} + h_a V_{S(a),i} \tag{23}$$

and

$$V_{a,ij} = X_{a,ij} + h_a\left(V_{S(a),ij} - V_{S(a),i}V_{S(a),j} + \sum_{b\in S(a)} l(b, B(a))V_{b,i}V_{b,j}\right), \tag{24}$$

where $S(a)$ is the set of choice elements b such that $t(b) = a$.

Because of this essential nonlinearity in V, which causes the third and fourth terms in (24) to remain even if X is linear, it is necessary to plan for nondefinite matrices f^*_{ij} and the corresponding difficulty of optimisation of the likelihood function.

2.2 *The optimisation algorithm*

One of the most efficient optimisations of reduced log likelihood functions of the form (17) is given by the Newton-Raphson procedure using the first and second derivatives of the function. Many practical logit estimation packages use this procedure, which yields as a major by-product at the optimum the covariance matrix of the estimates. In multinomial logit models with utility functions linear in the unknowns, the matrix of second derivatives is always negative definite (provided the function is well-conditioned, i.e. no singularity arises). However in the tree logit case, this definiteness of the matrix is not guaranteed (as indicated in the previous section), and the simple Newton-Raphson procedure cannot be guaranteed to work.

This case is analogous to the estimation of models in which the V functions are nonlinear in the unknowns because of the presence of "size" or "attraction" variables, which was studied by Daly (1982). In that paper, an algorithm was developed from an idea of Berndt *et al.* (1974), which proposes the use of a substitute matrix, the sample estimator of the covariance using the first derivatives. The Daly algorithm employs the substitute matrix only when the (more accurate) true matrix is indefinite, and employs an approximate "look-ahead" procedure to further reduce the number of times the data is processed.

Several years of experience with this algorithm have established its effectiveness in estimating large systems of models (Cambridge Systematics, 1983). Minor improvements in the parameters controlling the algorithm have been made, but major amendments have not proved necessary. The same optimisation algorithm is used for tree logit and has proved effective in this case also.

Note that the ability to specify the analytical form of the *true* second derivative matrix is a substantial advantage of the tree notation. Experience shows that the Berndt *et al.* approximation can exhibit substantial divergences from the true matrix. These inaccuracies slow convergence of the algorithm (by distorting the step direction and length) and impede an accurate interpretation of the results of the estimation by distorting the parameter error estimates.

Providing the algorithm is started in a feasible region for the parameters, it appears to find the region of definiteness of the second derivative matrix within three or four iterations at most. Note that the existence of a region of definiteness around the "true" value, which is at least a local optimum, is guaranteed in expectation given certain conditions of regularity (e.g. Edwards, 1972, Chap. 7). Problems of multiple optima reported by other researchers have not been encountered in estimations based on real data.

At the optimum, the value of L^* is available to conduct a number of tests that may be useful in assessing the quality of the model. In particular, likelihood ratio tests are commonly used. Further the so-called ρ^2 (rho-squared) statistics are available, which indicate the overall quality of the model. Two such statistics are commonly calculated, ρ_0^2, which relates the likelihood at the optimum to what would be achieved by a model attributing equal probability to all (available) alternatives, and ρ_c^2, relating the optimum to a model in which constants are fitted to take account of the different aggregate numbers choosing each alternative, but no other parameters are present. These statistics are not affected by the change from multinomial to tree logit.

At the optimum we also have $L_i^* = 0$, for all i. Examination of the form of eqns (17) and (18) *suggests* that, as in multinomial logit, optimality implies that the observed average value for a measured variable contained in V will also be the average value predicted over the sample by the model. In particular, this equality would maintain the very useful property that when alternative-specific constants are included in the model the predicted numbers choosing the alternatives match the observed numbers. Further study of this point is required, and may well show that this property is *asymptotic*—i.e. that equality is attained only for very large data sets.

The covariance matrix of the estimates is also available at the optimum. No problems arise in applying this matrix directly to draw inferences about the distribution of the values of the parameters (in contrast to the sequential estimation). In particular, confidence limits may be obtained and (approximate) t tests may be made for the significance of variables. A test of particular importance in this context is whether the value of a structural parameter is different from 1, since equality to 1 implies that the structure can be simplified. The statistic t_1, representing the number of standard errors by which the parameter differs from 1, can be useful in this context, as a generalisation of the usual t-statistic, which might acquire the analogous label t_0.

2.3 *Programming considerations*

Given the use of the efficient algorithm for the solution of the optimisation problem described in the previous subsection, the major programming consideration is the calculation of the likelihood function itself and its derivatives. These are simply accumulated over the observations and it suffices to specify the calculations for a single observation. This involves the evaluation of eqns (18), (20) and (22); intrinsic to these equations are the conditional probabilities l given by eqn (7) and the derivatives of V given by (23) and (24).

The procedure adopted, which has been incorporated in a computer program, depends heavily on the function t defining the tree structure and on the indexing of the alternatives so that $t(s) > s$ for all $s \in S$.

For each observation, an initial loop calculates the values of X and V for each element of S. This is done in the order prescribed by the indexing of S, so that V is calculated for an element only *after* the calculations are complete for all elements of which it is an "ancestor".

A second loop then calculates, for each element s, again in the order of the indexing, the value of $l(s, B(s))$, and then the derivatives from eqns (23) and (24). Again this is possible because the calculations are complete for all lower elements before their ancestors are treated. These results are used in turn to calculate the derivatives (20) and (22). Finally, if the element is an ancestor of the chosen alternative, the likelihood itself is updated as provided in eqn (18).

If these calculations are compared in detail with what is necessary to make equivalent calculations for a multinomial logit model, it appears that the calculations for each choice element in tree logit are in principle almost identical to the calculations for each alternative in multinomial logit, provided no attempt is made to exploit the structure of the utility functions (i.e. the fact that some variables are not relevant for some alternatives). Thus the calculation time relative to the "corresponding" multinomial logit is increased by (approximately) the ratio of composite elements to elementary elements in S. In addition there is of course an overhead connected with the indexing of the structure by the function t.

In *linear* multinomial logit, it may be possible to take advantage of the structure of a specific model, particularly when "structural" zeroes are present (often when a particular component is not relevant to a particular alternative). This specific structure may be exploited to prepare a very fast program for simple models. However, for tree logit, for models containing mainly "generic" variables (i.e. where most components of utility are nonzero for most alternatives) and for models with other forms of nonlinearity in the utility functions (e.g. models containing "size" variables), the advantage of exploiting the structure is less significant. The comparability of the tree logit calculations with those of multinomial logit applies only to programs *not* exploiting specific structure. Most programs used in practice for multinomial logit take no account of specific model structure, although this *can* be automated.

The provision has been retained in the program developed for tree logit estimations to incorporate "size" variables at points in the tree structure specified by the user. Strictly, this facility is not necessary, since size variables are equivalent to an additional level in the tree structure, with constants as the only characterisation of the alternatives.† However, it was considered more convenient for the user to be able to define size variables at the "natural" points in the model, and the facility has been incorporated in the program. The functions for X are therefore nonlinear in general and the derivatives of V correspondingly more complicated.

Further flexibility has been given in the program to specify "ordinary" variables (i.e. those in which the function X is linear) freely throughout the tree. This flexibility is necessary because the selection of variables to appear in the "utility" of an elementary alternative may not be obvious *a priori*. This is particularly true in the case of "dummy" variables (taking the values 0 and 1), when it may be known that a variable affects a lower level choice, and it is thus attached to the "utility" of one of the alternatives, chosen arbitrarily. However, the sign of the parameter that is estimated for that variable is affected by the (arbitrary) choice of alternative to which it is attached, and the sign of the contribution of the variable through the logsum to higher-level choices is also affected. These arbitrary effects, which can be large in practice, can be eliminated either by defining the variable in question to be part of the utility (with different parameters) for all the lower-level choices, or by attaching the variable (again with a different parameter) to the "utility" of the composite choice element at the next higher level.

To maintain transferability between different makes of computer, and to take advantage of the efficient compilers widely available, the program has been written in standard FORTRAN to implement the procedures outlined in this section. The following section presents some of the experience that has been gained in its use.

3. PRACTICAL EXPERIENCE AND RESULTS OBTAINED

The FORTRAN program described in the previous section has been implemented on a mainframe, a minicomputer and on a microcomputer. In none of these installations were there any unusual problems with the programming implementation of the procedures. The results obtained to date are described below.

3.1 *Swedish results*

Tree logit models were estimated to describe the choice of mode and destination for shopping trips in the city of Jönköping. Previously, a multinomial model had been estimated (with an improved version of the program developed by Daly, 1982), for the four modes and for a sample of up to ten destinations, using the method of McFadden (1978) for sampling the destination alternatives. The model contained 16 parameters, plus a single "size" variable, and was estimated on a sample of 885 observed trips. The multinomial logit program had required 9:02 minutes of CPU time on a Vax 11/750 minicomputer to reach convergence after six iterations.

Convergence is defined throughout by the criterion convergence is achieved when the length of the "step" made between two iterations, normalised by the *standard error* of the parameter estimate in each dimension, is less than 0.01. In a sense, the criterion is that the computational error should be less than 1% of the statistical error. It is greatly preferable to relate convergence to the estimation error of a parameter than to the parameter value, as is often done, because when a parameter is close to zero convergence can be unnecessarily delayed and when the parameter is large spurious convergence can be reported. All runs were started with all parameters zero, except the structural parameter (where applicable) which was started at 1.

As a test of the new program, it was first run with the trivial tree structure in which $t(s) = s_0$ for all elementary alternatives, i.e. the multinomial logit model again. This run required 8:13 min to reach the same optimum, also in six iterations, making more-or-less the same steps. The timings of the two runs are not strictly comparable, because the new program was compiled with an improved version of the FORTRAN compiler, but it does seem possible to conclude that the "overhead" caused by referencing the t function is moderate.

†The equivalence between size variables and an additional level in the tree is deeper than simply that of the mathematical form exploited by Ben-Akiva *et al.* (1984), who to estimated a tree model with constants only at the lower level using a multinomial logit algorithm which allowed for size variables. Daly (1982) and Ben-Akiva and Watanatada (1978) give more details.

The second test was of a model based on the tree structure of Example 2 in Section 1, with mode choice being modelled conditional on destination choice, as is generally thought to be appropriate. This run required 13 iterations to converge, taking a time of 27:48 CPU minutes. Because of the introduction of the non-trivial tree structure, the run contained an average of 11.97 elements of S per observation, compared with 8.60 for the trivial case. The time per iteration per element increased by 15%, probably due to the presence of one additional parameter, the structural parameter. This parameter had an estimated value of 1.28 (outside the theoretically acceptable range of zero to one), while the total log likelihood improved from -1405.9 to -1402.9. Either by a χ^2 test on the likelihood ratio, or by a direct test on the significance of the parameter difference from 1, there was a significant improvement in the fit to the data by the generalisation; however, the model is unacceptable because of the value of the structural parameter.

Because of this unacceptable result, a third test was made with the tree structure "inverted:" destination choice modelled as dependent on mode choice. This run had an average of 12.60 elements of S per observation, and required 12 iterations and 31:21 minutes of CPU to converge. The time per iteration per element increased by 33% relative to the trivial structure. However, the likelihood value improved to -1393.2 and the structural parameter had the acceptable value of 0.63. Likelihood ratio or direct tests show in this case a very significant difference of the structural parameter from 1.

This result, which shows a very significant improvement in fit to the data by adopting a structure contrary to the accepted wisdom but not at all intuitively unacceptable, was quite unexpected. It is not known whether other models have been estimated, sequentially or with full-estimation estimates, with this structure, but this result certainly suggests that it would be worthwhile for this structure to be tried in other circumstances. It is likely that it would have been impossible for reasons of time to attempt to estimate the structure without the availability of an efficient full-information estimation procedure. The entire process from deciding to attempt the inverted structure to obtaining the result took about two hours, including the time taken to correct several data processing errors; a sequential estimation of the same model might have required two days, even assuming that reasonable first-round estimations could have been obtained.

The parameters obtained by the tree logit estimator in this case were very similar to those yielded by the multinomial model, except for general scaling because of the presence of the structural parameter. Attempts had been made to estimate the tree structure (mode *below* destination) sequentially, but these had been abandoned because of the failure to obtain satisfactory signs for time and cost parameters in the lower-level (mode choice) estimation.

The results obtained for the timing of the runs were satisfactory as regards the per-iteration results: part of the increase is predictable, in terms of the increased number of elements of S and the additional parameter; the unpredictable increase seems small. As regards the increased number of iterations, the results are less satisfactory. A detailed examination showed that part of the problem was caused by initial difficulty in finding the region of definiteness of the matrix, which caused the algorithm to adopt the less efficient substitute matrix instead of the true second derivatives. This problem could be greatly alleviated by using the multinomial model to generate good starting values. However, there was also some inefficiency in final convergence; minor subsequent corrections may well have eliminated this second problem. On the whole, the timings given by these tests are entirely acceptable and indicate that the program is suitable for routine use.

3.2 *Netherlands results*

A major recent study in The Netherlands (Gunn and Pol, 1985) has transferred the "Zuidvleugel" models (Cambridge Systematics, 1983) to the region around Utrecht in the centre of the country. During this study the issue of the appropriate structure of the mode choice models received particular attention. The Zuidvleugel models had been estimated in 1979–80 using sequential methods for the tree logit models, at that time the best practicable procedure. During the transfer (in 1984) it was natural to reconsider the estimation procedure and in particular the approximation of sequential estimation.

The structure applied in the Zuidvleugel system was that shown in Example 1 above, in which car driver and car passenger were treated as "lower-level" choices, subordinate to a "higher" level model predicting the choice between car (both forms), public transport and slow modes. The sequential estimation analysis on which this structure had been based is largely as reported by Sobel (1980). Further structural issues concerned the various "slow" modes (walk, cycle and moped) and the relationship of mode choice to other choices, such as destination and travel frequency. These issues are not treated here.

A special difficulty in these models is the *cost* of the car mode, and the extent to which part of this might properly be incorporated in the utility of the car passenger. In the Zuidvleugel model system, the estimations had given different results for different purposes: in some cases, the cost was not found to be significant at the higher level, in other cases it was missing at the lower level. The net result was that the elasticity of demand for car passenger travel (or, more specifically, the elasticity of car occupancy) with respect to the price of petrol was unsatisfactory, particularly for longer journeys. The much greater number of long journeys in the Utrecht data gave an opportunity to estimate this elasticity more reasonably, provided that the structural issue could be solved.

The cause of the structural problem appeared to be in the model specification and estimation procedure. At the lower level, the only travellers whose behaviour was informative were those who had *both* car modes available. This implied possession of a licence, which eliminated most of those who were actually car passengers. Thus the parameters estimated at the lower level were based on a rather small and biased group of observations. The estimation at the higher level, and in particular the estimation of the hierarchy parameter itself, was thus distorted by these incorrect lower-level estimates. Multinomial models estimated on the Utrecht data with the four modes all considered at the *same* level appeared to give more reasonable results and had been adopted provisionally, but it was difficult to determine whether the more complex structure should in fact be abandoned because of the confusing effect of the inefficient sequential estimation. The availability of the tree logit estimator gave an opportunity to resolve this problem.

A series of tests was therefore made using two of the models in the system: those for home-work travel and those for home-personal business. The models incorporated destination choice as well as mode choice (although that is not the issue considered here) and were therefore large, requiring a mainframe computer for any estimation procedure. For each of the two travel purposes, sequential estimations and simple multinomial logit models were compared with the full-information tree logit estimator.

Work travel

For the work purpose models, the results obtained are shown in Table 1. These results are based on a data set of 716 observations, choosing among four modes and a random sample of destinations using McFadden's method (1978). The variables, of which there were 22, are specified in the same way for each of the estimations.

In these models, the cost variable was attached to both car modes with the same parameter (i.e. it is estimated at the higher level) which explains the stability of the results for that parameter but which does not give reasonable elasticity estimates, since increasing car cost will *not* be predicted to cause an increase in car occupancy.

Another notable feature of the results is that although the structural parameter is markedly different from 1 in the sequential estimation, the model is actually *worse* in terms of its fit to the data than the multinomial estimation. This implies that the gain in fit obtained from the structural generalisation is less than the loss suffered by inefficient estimation of the lower-level parameters. Moreover, the estimate of standard error of the structural parameter in the sequential case, which is known in general to be biased downwards (this is confirmed by the results), leads to a gross overestimation of the importance of the tree structure.

Table 1. Work purpose mode choice

Estimation Procedure	Log-Likelihood	Structural Parameter (std. error)	Cost Parameter (std. error)
Sequential	−2214.5	0.16 (0.11)	−0.24 (0.02)
Multinomial	−2213.8	1.00 (fixed)	−0.25 (0.02)
Tree Logit	−2212.7	0.58 (0.26)	−0.24 (0.02)

Table 2. Personal business mode choice

Estimation Procedure	Log-Likelihood	Structural Parameter (std. error)	Cost Parameter (std. error)
Sequential	− 1633.9	1.01 (0.09)	− 1.36 (0.62
Multinomial	− 1600.6	1.00 (fixed)	− 2.26 (0.27)
Tree Logit	− 1597.5	1.78 (0.46)	− 1.45 (0.38)

The comparison of the tree model with the multinomial model shows that the true value of the structural parameter is probably different from 1. However, the multinomial model seems reliable and in this case its simplicity would probably outweigh the moderate improvement in fit given by the tree model.

Personal business travel

The results obtained from the personal business model are rather different, as shown in Table 2. Again the variable definitions were kept constant and the model represented choice among four modes and a random sample of destinations; there were 970 observations.

These results are still less satisfactory for the sequential estimation procedure, which is shown to be very much worse than the multinomial logit. A more detailed examination reveals that this loss of fit is caused by poor estimation of the lower-level parameters, a number of which are changed in sign between the sequential and other estimations.

The lower-level estimation showed the cost parameter to be significant for the choice between driver and passenger submodes, with the "correct" sign, as shown in Table 2. In the multinomial model the parameter for "cost," attached to car driver and to public transport, was, however, larger. In the tree model, the parameter returned to a lower value, but the structural parameter took the (theoretically unacceptable) value of 1.78, so that the marginal effect of the car driver's cost in the higher-level choice is much greater than indicated by the parameter value of 1.45. It seems reasonable to hypothesise that the effect of cost is greater for the choice among car, public transport and slow modes than for the choice between the car modes; this difference could be associated with the passenger (effectively) bearing part of the cost. Thus the unacceptable structural parameter value is in a sense a diagnosis of the specification problem. However, in the sequential estimation the problem is concealed.

A further explanation of the value of the structural parameter may be that the structure adopted for this model is in fact wrong—i.e. destination choice might be better modelled at a lower level than mode choice, as in the Swedish example. The attribution of the relative magnitudes of these effects remains speculation, however.

A correct procedure for this model would be to allow both car modes *and* public transport to have separate cost parameters, and to estimate these parameters in a context in which all modes were considered. The models implemented in practical applications have in fact been estimated in this way. For further sophistication, the tree structure could be considered if required, as could structures in which mode and destination choice were reversed.

The general conclusion from these results appears to be that the practical difficulty of obtaining reliable models from sequential estimation is quite severe. An important cause of this unreliability is the small size and biased nature of the data available for lower-level estimation. The multinomial model appears to perform quite well, and might be preferred to sequential estimation on grounds of simplicity even if the fit to the data appeared slightly inferior. In some cases the fit to the data of the simpler model is, however, actually better. In the models implemented for forecasting based on this work, a multinomial model with improved specification, which *did* give a reasonable elasticity of car occupancy with respect to petrol prices, was used.

3.3 *Microcomputer results*

The program described in this paper has also been implemented for microcomputers. To data, tests have been primarily concerned with establishing the performance of the program rather than with studying aspects of the tree logit structure. Nevertheless, the results are interesting in indicating the convenience and practicality of the method and its computational implementation.

The program has been implemented for "industry-standard" micros. The results given refer to a machine with 256K bytes of core, a clock speed of 8 MHz, and using floppy-disk drives. No specialised chip for mathematical processing was used. Superior performance is obtainable (and has been obtained in further tests) from a machine with a hard-disk drive, or could be achieved by installing a specialised chip, without spending more than U.S. $3000. The micro imposed no new restrictions on the problem size.†

An artificial data set was developed for testing the program. The "data" simulates the choices of 1000 individuals, each choosing from three alternatives in a tree structure. Choices are generated by random sampling, based on utility functions incorporating eight variables, of which two are "size" variables. This data set is typical in size of many small models used in practice. Iterations of the tree logit program for this data required about six minutes each, for a total of 18–36 minutes to reach convergence, depending on the starting values.

A further test was made on a real data set, applying the tree program but with trivial tree structure. This data represented travel mode choice from five modes (with varying availability) with 15 unknown parameters for 975 individuals. This data required 13–14 minutes per iteration on the floppy-disk system, reduced to just under 11 minutes per iteration on the hard-disk machine. It could be expected that the implementation of a non-trivial tree structure on this data would increase the run time by 20–40%.

These results indicate that sophisticated logit modelling is possible on microcomputers, without requiring enormous investment in hardware or excessive waiting for results. Many mainframe systems are not capable of giving results in less than two hours. The models tested are typical in size of many small- or medium-sized models used in practice, but the micro is not yet capable of tackling the largest models such as those described in Sections 3.1 and 3.2.

The overhead imposed by the sophistication of handling the tree structure is quite large. The travel mode choice data set was also estimated on the floppy-disk system using a program specifically designed to exploit the structure of simple models (i.e. those without tree structure or size variables). This program was able to iterate in two minutes. However, it must be stressed that the performance of this latter program is exceptional: a commercial package required 26–30 minutes per iteration for the same data on the same machine, without offering the possibility of generalising the multinomial model.

4. CONCLUSIONS

Many researchers have found the "tree" logit model to be desirable for analyses of travel demand. However, their work has been hampered by the absence or inefficiency of software. Often approximate procedures of unknown reliability have been used because of the impossibility or excessive cost of accurate, full-information estimation.

This paper has presented an efficient full-information estimation method for models of the tree logit form. The method proposed allows general tree structures with multiple levels to be specified and estimated comparatively simply. The method has been implemented in FORTRAN in a computer progam.

Results have been presented which demonstrate the practicality of the procedure and program. These results also throw some light on the specification properties of tree logit models, which are still poorly understood. The results are also of practical value to studies in Sweden and The Netherlands.

The findings support Hensher's (1986) conclusion that the "sequential . . . logit model is not in general an empirically desirable intermediate step in the development of efficient estimates." The inefficiency of the sequential estimation is so great in some cases that the fit to the data is *worse* than that given by the multinomial logit model (a possibility also reported by Small and Brownstone, 1982). In this context, the information given by sequential estimation on the

†The microcomputers used were Olivetti M24 machines, using the 8086 chip and otherwise closely compatible with the IBM PC or XT, except for the higher clock speed. MicroSoft FORTRAN (version 3.20) was used. Further details of the micro implementation and the tests made are available from the author.

structure of the model can be quite misleading, even if allowance is made for the biased estimation error in the structural parameter. This can be of vital importance when the structure adopted *a priori* is wrong, particularly since the operational difficulty of sequential estimation often precludes the testing of alternative structures. Empirical testing suggests that *a priori* structures may in fact often be in error.

Given the computational efficiency of the method proposed, there seems little reason to wish to make an intermediate step using sequential estimation. The first-iteration approximation also seems unnecessarily risky. If an intermediate step seems absolutely necessary, for example in very large models, the multinomial logit model appears to give quite reasonable results. In particular, this model can be estimated exceptionally quickly by programs taking automatic advantage of the specific structure and linearity of the utility functions.

There remains uncertainty about the appropriate criteria for specifying tree logit models. Two problems may be isolated.

(i) Care must be exercised in determining where in the tree structure to insert particular variables. When variables are relevant to the choice *among* lower-level alternatives, it should be realised that these variables may also be relevant to the choice *between* those lower-level alternatives as a group and others at the higher level, and that the representation by the "logsum" may be inadequate.

(ii) The appropriate methods for defining the structures of tree models are still not clear. While *a priori* reasoning may be of some help, results suggest that intuition may be an imperfect guide. The ultimate need is an efficient method for optimising the tree function t.

It is hoped that this paper will facilitate the acquisition of further experience with the application of tree logit models, and that the methodological and modelling problems mentioned can be addressed during that work.

Acknowledgements—The financial support of Stockholms Läns Landsting and of the Dienst Verkeerskunde, Rijkswaterstaat, The Netherlands Ministry of Transport and Public Works, is gratefully acknowledged. I am also grateful to my colleagues Steven Pitschke and Ger Hungerink for their help in programming, to Staffan Algers and Staffan Widlert of S.L.L. for their help with the Jönköping model, and my colleauge Hugh Gunn for his help with the Utrecht model. I remain responsible for any bugs, other mistakes or errors of interpretation.

REFERENCES

Ben-Akiva M., Bergman M. J., Daly A. J. and Ramaswamy R. (1984) Modelling inter-urban route choice behaviour. *Proc. Ninth International Symposium on Transportation and Traffic Theory*, 299–330. VNU Science Press, Utrecht.

Ben-Akiva M. and Watanatada T. (1978) Application of a continuous spatial choice logit model, presented to N.B.E.R.-N.S.F. Conference on Decision Rules and Uncertainty, Carnegie-Mellon University.

Ben-Akiva M. and Lerman S. R. (1985) *Discrete Choice Analysis*. MIT Press, Cambridge, Mass.

Berndt E. U., Hall B. H., Hall R. E. and Hausman J. A. (1974) Estimation and inference in non-linear structural models. *Ann. Econ. Social Measurement* **3/4**, 653–665.

Cambridge Systematics Europe b.v. (1983) *Travel Demand Models, Zuidvleugel Study Report 7*. Rijkswaterstaat, Ministry of Transport and Public Works, The Netherlands.

Cosslett S. (1981) Efficient estimation of discrete choice models, in *Structural Analysis of Discrete Data with Econometric Applications* (Edited by C. F. Manski and D. McFadden). MIT Press, Cambridge, Mass.

Daly A. J. (1982) Estimating choice models containing attraction variables. *Transpn. Res.* **16B**, 5–15.

Daly A. J. (1984) Applicability of disaggregate behavioural modelling. *Transpn. Res.* **16A**, 363–370.

Daly A. J. and Zachary S. (1978) Improved multiple choice models, in *Determinants of Travel Choice* (Edited by D. A. Hensher and M. Q. Dalvi). Saxon House, Sussex.

Daly A. J. and Van Zwam H. H. P. (1981) Travel demand models for the Zuidvleugel study, *Proc. Summer Annual Meeting*. P.T.R.C. Education and Research Services Ltd., London.

Domencich T. A. and McFadden D. (1975) *Urban Travel Demand*. North-Holland, Amsterdam.

Edwards A. W. F. (1972) *Likelihood*. Cambridge University Press.

Gunn H. F. and Pol H. D. P. (1985) Model transferability: the potential for increasing cost effectiveness, presented to Conference on Behavioural Research for Transport Policy, Noordwijk, The Netherlands.

Hensher D. A. (1986) Sequential and full information maximum likelihood estimation of a nested logit model (to be published).

McFadden D. (1978) Modelling the choice of residential location. *Transpn. Res. Rec.* **673**, 72–77.

McFadden D. (1979) Quantitative models for analysing travel behaviour of individuals, in *Behavioural Travel Modelling* (Edited by D. Hensher and P. R. Stopher). Croom Helm, London.

McFadden D. (1981) Econometric models of probabilistic choice, in *Structural Analysis of Discrete Data with Econometric Applications* (Edited by D. McFadden and C. F. Manski). MIT Press, Cambridge, Mass.

Ortúzar J. de D. (1983) Nested logit models for mixed-mode travel in urban corridors. *Transpn. Res.* **17A**, 283–299.
Small K. A. and Brownstone D. (1982) Efficient estimation of nested logit models: an application to trip timing. Research Memorandum No. 296, Economic Research Program, Princeton University.
Sobel K. L. (1980) Travel demand forecasting with the nested multinomial logit model. *59th Annual Meeting of the Transpn. Res. Board*, Washington D. C., January 1980.
Williams H. C. W. L. (1977) On the formation of travel demand models and economic measures of user benefit. *Environment and Planning* **9A**, 285–344.
Westin R. D. and Manski C. F. (1979) Theoretical and conceptual developments in demand modelling, in *Behavioural Travel Modelling* (Edited by D. A. Hensher and P. R. Stopher). Croom Helm, London.

[18]

PERGAMON

Transportation Research Part B 36 (2002) 1–17

TRANSPORTATION RESEARCH PART B

www.elsevier.com/locate/trb

Specification and estimation of the nested logit model: alternative normalisations ☆

David A. Hensher [a], William H. Greene [b,*]

[a] *Faculty of Economics and Business, Institute of Transport Studies, The University of Sydney, Sydney, NSW 2006, Australia*

[b] *Department of Economics, Stern School of Business, New York University, 44 West 4th Street, Mec 7-80, New York, NY 10012, USA*

Received 9 November 1999; received in revised form 5 March 2000; accepted 13 March 2000

Abstract

The nested logit model is currently the preferred extension to the simple multinomial logit (MNL) discrete choice model. The appeal of the nested logit model is its ability to accommodate differential degrees of interdependence (i.e., similarity) between subsets of alternatives in a choice set. The received literature displays a frequent lack of attention to the very precise form that a nested logit model must take to ensure that the resulting model is invariant to normalisation of scale and is consistent with utility maximisation. Some recent papers by F.S. Koppelman, C.H. Wen [Transp. Res. B 32 (5) (1998a) 289; Transp. Res. Record 1645 (1998b) 1] and G.L. Hunt [Nested logit models with partial degeneracy, Department of Economics, University of Maine, December 1998 (revised)] have addressed some aspects of this issue, but some important points remain somewhat ambiguous.

When utility function parameters have different implicit scales, imposing equality restrictions on common attributes associated with different alternatives (i.e., making them generic) can distort these differences in scale. Model scale parameters are then 'forced' to take up the real differences that should be handled via the utility function parameters. With many variations in model specification appearing in the literature, comparisons become difficult, if not impossible, without clear statements of the precise form of the nested logit model. There are a number of approaches to achieving this, with some or all of them available as options in commercially available software packages. This article seeks to clarify the issue, and to establish the points of similarity and dissimilarity of the different formulations that appear in the literature.

☆ A number of individuals have contributed to discussions leading up to the preparation of this paper. We are indebted to John Bates, Gary Hunt, Frank Koppelman, Andrew Daly, and two referees. Any remaining errors are our own.

* Corresponding author. Tel.: +1-212-998-0876; fax: +1-212-995-4218.

E-mail addresses: davidh@its.usyd.edu.au (D.A. Hensher), wgreene@stern.nyu.edu (W.H. Greene).

0191-2615/01/$ - see front matter
PII: S0191-2615(00)00035-7

1. Introduction

The *nested logit* (NL) model is the preferred specification of a discrete choice model when analysts move beyond the multinomial logit (MNL) model. [See Ortuzar (2000) for an historical perspective on nested logit models.] Despite the increasing availability of other less restrictive models (in terms of the way that the random components of the utility expressions for each alternative are handled) such as *heteroscedastic extreme value*, *mixed logit*, *random parameter logit*, *covariance heterogeneity logit* and *multinomial probit* – see Louviere et al. (2000, Chapter 6, Appendix B) for a review – there remain reasons why the NL model will continue to be estimated. For example, the NL model is relatively easy to estimate, and, with its closed-form structure, it is easy to implement in the simulation of market shares before and after a policy change.

Specialists involved in the development of NL models, especially the active set of individuals researching estimation methods and developing software, have recently entered into a dialogue on the model specifications required in using software to ensure that the estimation is consistent with utility maximisation, and how one should handle degenerate branches (i.e., those with only a single alternative). Much of the discussion has taken place by email, however, the sentiment of the dialogue is partially represented in a series of recent papers by Koppelman and Wen (1998a, 1998b) and Hunt (1998). The objective of this article is to gather the presentation into a single transparent notation and to illustrate how one sets up an NL model to obtain outputs consistent with McFadden's NL model for utility maximisation, a derivative of his generalised extreme value (GEV) model (McFadden, 1981).

2. A common notation for NL models

We propose the following notation as a method of unifying the different forms of the NL model. [1] Each observed (or representative) component of the utility expression for an alternative (usually denoted as V_k for the kth alternative) is defined in terms of four parts – the parameters associated with the explanatory variables, β, an alternative-specific constant, α_k, a scale parameter, θ, and the explanatory variables, $\mathbf{x}$. The utility of alternative k for individual t is

$$U_{tk} = g_k(\alpha_k, \beta'\mathbf{x}_{tk}, \varepsilon_{tk}) = g_k(V_{tk}, \varepsilon_{tk}) = \alpha_k + \beta'\mathbf{x}_{tk} + \varepsilon_{tk}, \tag{1}$$

$$\text{Var}[\varepsilon_{tk}] = \sigma^2 = \kappa/\theta^2. \tag{2}$$

The scale parameter, θ, is proportional to the inverse of the standard deviation of the random component in the utility expression, [2] σ, and is a critical input into the set up of the NL model (Ben-Akiva and Lerman, 1985; Louviere et al., 2000). Under the assumptions now well established in the literature, utility maximisation in the presence of random components which have

[1] A referee pointed out that the notation used is a standard that already exists. One may wish to disagree with this position (remembering a failed attempt 15 years ago to agree on common nomenclature in the transport research community). It is, however, still necessary to set out this standard herein.

[2] We have used θ here to avoid any confusion with its equivalent in various models below where we use λ, μ and γ.

independent (across choices and individuals) extreme value distributions produces a simple closed form for the probability that choice k is made, known as the MNL model;

$$\text{Prob}[U_{tk} > U_{tj} \quad \forall j \neq k] = \frac{\exp(\alpha_k + \beta'\mathbf{x}_{tk})}{\sum_{l=1}^{K} \exp(\alpha_l + \beta'\mathbf{x}_{tl})}. \tag{3}$$

Under these assumptions, the common variance of the assumed i.i.d. random components is lost. The same observed set of choices emerges regardless of the (common) scaling of the utilities. Hence, the latent variance is normalised at one, not as a restriction, but of necessity for identification.

One justification for moving from the MNL model to an NL model is to recognise (or at least test for) the possibility that the standard deviations (or variances) of the random error components in the utility expressions are different across groups of alternatives in the choice set. This arises because the sources of utility associated with the alternatives are not fully accommodated in V_k. The missing sources of utility may differentially impact on the random components across the alternatives, resulting in different variances. To accommodate the possibility of differential variances, we must explicitly introduce the scale parameters into each of the utility expressions. (If all scale parameters are equal, then the NL model 'collapses' back to a simple MNL model.) Hunt (1998) discusses the underlying conditions that produce the NL model as a result of utility maximisation within a partitioned choice set.

The notation for a three-level NL model covers the majority of applications. The literature suggests that very few analysts estimate models with more than three levels, and two levels are the most common. However, it will be shown below that a two-level model *may* require a third level (in which the lowest level is a set of dummy nodes and links) simply to ensure consistency with utility maximisation (which has nothing to do with a desire to test a three-level NL model). It is also common for a nested structure to have a branch with only one alternative. This is referred to as a *degenerate branch*. This requires careful definition in estimation. We will return to this point below.

It is useful to represent each level in an NL tree by a unique descriptor. For a three-level tree (Fig. 1), the top level will be represented by *limbs*, the middle level by a number of *branches* and the bottom level by a set of *elemental alternatives*, or *twigs*. We have $k = 1, \ldots, K$ elemental alternatives, $j = 1, \ldots, J$ branch composite alternatives and $i = 1, \ldots, I$ limb composite alternatives.

We use the notation $k|ji$ to denote alternative k in branch j of limb i and $j|i$ to denote branch j in limb i.

Define parameter vectors in the utility functions at each level as follows: β for elemental alternatives, γ for branch composite alternatives, and δ for limb composite alternatives. The branch-level composite alternative involves an aggregation of the lower-level alternatives. As discussed below, a branch specific scale parameter $\mu(j|i)$ will be associated with the lowest level of the tree. Each elemental alternative in the jth branch will actually have scale parameter $\mu'(k|ji)$. Since these will, of necessity, be equal for all alternatives in the same branch, the distinction by k is meaningless. As such, we collapse these into $\mu(j|i)$. The parameters $\lambda(j|i)$ will be associated with the branch level. The inclusive value (IV) parameters at the branch level will involve the ratios $\lambda(j|i)/\mu(j|i)$. The IV parameters associated with the IV variable in a branch, calculated from the natural logarithm of the sum of the exponentials of the V_k expressions at the elemental alternative level directly below a branch (Eq. (4)),

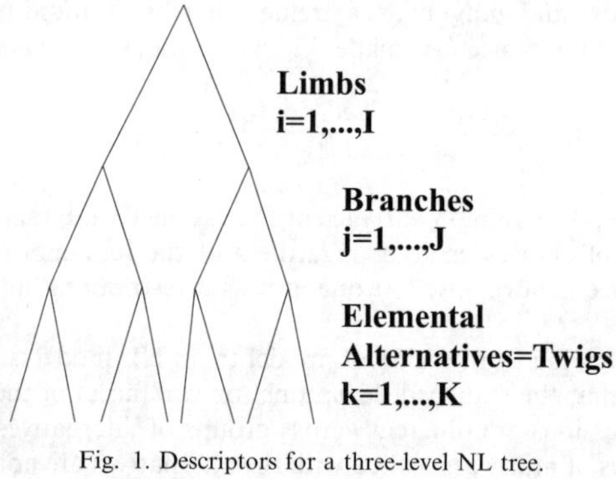

Fig. 1. Descriptors for a three-level NL tree.

$$\mathrm{IV}(j|i) = \log \sum_{l=1}^{K|ji} \exp\left(\alpha_{l|ji} + \beta'\mathbf{x}(l|ji)\right) \tag{4}$$

have associated parameters defined as the $\lambda(j|i)/\mu(h|i)$, but, as noted, some normalisation is required. Normalisation is simply the process of setting one or more scale parameters equal to unity, while allowing the other scale parameters to be estimated. Some analysts do this without acknowledgment of which normalisation they have used, which makes the comparison of reported results between studies difficult. One approach restricts the numerator of $\lambda(j|i)/\mu(j|i)$ to be equal to one and the other so restricts the denominator.

The literature is vague on the implications of choosing the normalisation of $\lambda(j|i) = 1$ vs. $\mu(j|i) = 1$. It is important to note that the notation $\mu'(m|ji)$ used below refers to the scale parameter for each elemental alternative. However, since a NL structure is specified to test for the presence of identical scale within a subset of alternatives, it comes as no surprise that all alternatives partitioned under a common branch have the same scale parameter imposed on them. Thus, $\mu'(k|ji) = \mu(j|i)$ for every $k = 1, \ldots, K|ji$ alternatives in branch j in limb i.

We now set out the probability choice system (PCS) defined for later purposes as a three-level PCS (Eq. (5)),

$$P(k, j, i) = P(k|j, i) \times P(j|i) \times P(i). \tag{5}$$

In introducing alternative normalisations, we emphasise that there is one model normalised in different ways. When we normalise $\mu(j|i)$ to one, we refer to random utility model 1 (RU1), and when we normalise $\lambda(j|i)$ to one, we refer to Random Utility Model 2 (RU2). We ignore the subscripts for an individual.

2.1. Random Utility Model 1 (RU1)

The choice probabilities for the *elemental alternatives* are defined as

$$P(k|j, i) = \frac{\exp\left[\alpha_{k|ji} + \beta'\mathbf{x}(k|ji)\right]}{\sum_{l=1}^{K|j,i} \exp\left[\alpha_{l|ji} + \beta'\mathbf{x}(l|ji)\right]} = \frac{\exp\left[\alpha_{k|ji} + \beta'\mathbf{x}(k|ji)\right]}{\exp\left[\mathrm{IV}(j|i)\right]}, \tag{6}$$

where $k|ji$ = elemental alternative k in branch j of limb i, $K|ji$ = number of elemental alternatives in branch j of limb i, and the inclusive value for branch j in limb i is

$$\mathrm{IV}(j|i) = \log \sum_{l=1}^{K|ji} \exp[\alpha_{l|ji} + \beta'\mathbf{x}(l|ji)]. \tag{7}$$

The *branch-level* probability is

$$P(j|i) = \frac{\exp\{\lambda(j|i)[\gamma'\mathbf{y}(j|i) + \mathrm{IV}(j|i)]\}}{\sum_{m=1}^{J|i} \exp\{\lambda(m|i)[\gamma'\mathbf{y}(m|i) + \mathrm{IV}(m|i)]\}} = \frac{\exp\{\lambda(j|i)[\gamma'\mathbf{y}(j|i) + \mathrm{IV}(j|i)]\}}{\exp[\mathrm{IV}(i)]}, \tag{8}$$

where $j|i$ = branch j in limb $i, J|i$ = number of branches in limb i, and

$$\mathrm{IV}(i) = \log \sum_{j=1}^{J|i} \exp\{\lambda(j|i)[\gamma'\mathbf{y}(j|i) + \mathrm{IV}(j|i)]\}. \tag{9}$$

Finally, the *limb level* is defined by

$$P(i) = \frac{\exp\{\rho(i)[\delta'\mathbf{z}(i) + \mathrm{IV}(i)]\}}{\sum_{n=1}^{I} \exp\{\rho(n)[\delta'\mathbf{z}(n) + \mathrm{IV}(n)]\}} = \frac{\exp\{\rho(i)[\delta'\mathbf{z}(i) + \mathrm{IV}(i)]\}}{\exp(\mathrm{IV})}, \tag{10}$$

where I = number of limbs in the three-level tree and

$$\mathrm{IV} = \log \sum_{i=1}^{I} \exp\{\rho(i)[\delta'\mathbf{z}(i) + \mathrm{IV}(i)]\}. \tag{11}$$

RU1 has been described e.g., by Koppelman and Wen (1998a) and Bates (1999) as corresponding to a non-normalised nested logit (NNNL) specification, since the parameters are scaled at the lowest level, i.e., for $\mu'(k|j,i) = \mu(j|i) = 1$. Thus, note in this NNNL context, that there is no explicit scaling in (6) and (7) at the lowest level.

2.2. Random utility model 2 (RU2)

Suppose, instead, we normalise the upper-level parameters and allow the lower-level scale parameters to be free. The *elemental alternatives-level* probabilities will be

$$\begin{aligned} P(k|ji) &= \frac{\exp[\mu'(k|ji)[\alpha_{k|ji} + \beta'\mathbf{x}(k|ji)]]}{\sum_{l=1}^{K|j,i} \exp[\mu'(l|ji)[\alpha_{l|ji} + \beta'\mathbf{x}(l|ji)]]} = \frac{\exp[\mu'(k|ji)[\alpha_{k|ji} + \beta'\mathbf{x}(k|ji)]]}{\exp[\mathrm{IV}(j|i)]} \\ &= \frac{\exp\left[\mu(j|i)[\alpha_{k|ji} + \beta'\mathbf{x}(k|ji)]\right]}{\sum_{l=1}^{K|ji} \exp[\mu(j|i)[\alpha_{l|ji} + \beta'\mathbf{x}(l|j,i)]]} = \frac{\exp[\mu(j|i)[\alpha_{k|ji} + \beta' x(k|ji)]]}{\exp[\mathrm{IV}(j|i)]} \end{aligned} \tag{12}$$

(with the latter equality resulting from the identification restriction $\mu'(k|ji) = \mu'(m|ji) = \mu(j|i)$) and

$$\mathrm{IV}(j|i) = \log \sum_{l=1}^{K|ji} \exp\{\mu(j|i)[\alpha_{l|ji} + \beta'\mathbf{x}(l|ji)]\}. \tag{13}$$

The *branch level* is defined by:

$$p(j|i) = \frac{\exp\left\{\rho(i)\left[\gamma'\mathbf{y}(j|i) + \frac{1}{\mu(j|i)}\mathrm{IV}(j|i)\right]\right\}}{\sum_{m=1}^{J|i}\exp\left\{\rho(i)\left[\gamma'\mathbf{y}(m|i) + \frac{1}{\mu(m|i)}\mathrm{IV}(m|i)\right]\right\}} = \frac{\exp\left\{\rho(i)\left[\gamma'\mathbf{y}(j|i) + \frac{1}{\mu(j|i)}\mathrm{IV}(j|i)\right]\right\}}{\exp[\mathrm{IV}(i)]} \tag{14}$$

and

$$\mathrm{IV}(i) = \log\sum_{m=1}^{J|i}\exp\left\{\rho(i)\left[\gamma'\mathbf{y}(m|i) + \frac{1}{\mu(m|i)}\mathrm{IV}(m|i)\right]\right\}. \tag{15}$$

The *limb level* is defined by

$$P(i) = \frac{\exp\left[\delta'\mathbf{z}(i) + \frac{1}{\rho(i)}\mathrm{IV}(i)\right]}{\sum_{n=1}^{I}\exp\left[\delta'\mathbf{z}(n) + \frac{1}{\rho(n)}\mathrm{IV}(n)\right]} = \frac{\exp\left[\delta'\mathbf{z}(i) + \frac{1}{\rho(i)}\mathrm{IV}(i)\right]}{\exp(\mathrm{IV})}, \tag{16}$$

$$\mathrm{IV} = \log\sum_{i=1}^{I}\exp\left[\delta'\mathbf{z}(i) + \frac{1}{\rho(i)}\mathrm{IV}(i)\right]. \tag{17}$$

It is typically assumed that it is arbitrary as to which scale parameter is normalised. (See Hunt, 1998 for a useful discussion.) Most applications normalise the scale parameters associated with the branch-level utility expressions (i.e., $\lambda(j|i)$) at 1 as in RU2 above, then allow the scale parameters associated with the elemental alternatives $[\mu(j|i)]$ and hence the IV parameters in the branch composite alternatives to be unrestricted. It is implicitly assumed that the empirical results are identical to those that would be obtained if RU1 were instead the specification (even though parameter estimates are numerically different). *But, within the context of a two-level partition of a nest estimated as a two-level model, unless all attribute parameters are alternative-specific, this assumption is only true if the non-normalised scale parameters are constrained to be the same across nodes within the same level of a tree (i.e., at the branch level for two levels, and at the branch level and the limb level for three levels).* This latter result actually appears explicitly in some early studies of this model, e.g. Maddala (1983, p. 70) and Quigley (1985), but is frequently ignored in more recent applications. Note that in the common case of estimation of RU2 with two levels (which eliminates γ(i)) the 'free' IV parameter estimated will typically be $1/\mu(j|i)$. Other interpretations of this result are discussed in Hunt (1998).

2.3. Conditions to ensure consistency with utility maximisation

The previous section set out a uniform notation for a three-level NL model, choosing a different level in the tree for normalisation (i.e., setting scale parameters to an arbitrary value, typically unity). We have chosen levels one and two, respectively, for the RU1 and RU2 models. We are now ready to present a range of alternative empirical specifications for the NL model, some of which satisfy utility maximisation either directly from estimation or by some simple transformation of the estimated parameters. Compliance with utility maximisation requires that any monotonically increasing transformation of the utility functions of all elemental alternatives leave unaffected the ranking of the choice probabilities of the alternatives (McFadden, 1981). We limit the discussion to a two-level NL model and initially assume that all branches have at least two elemental alternatives. The important case of a degenerate branch (i.e., only one elemental alternative) is treated separately later.

3. An empirical illustration

To investigate the implications of alternative model specifications, we have estimated nine two-level models, using data collected in 1986 on non-business interurban trips between Sydney, Canberra and Melbourne. A total of 210 travellers chose a mode of transport from four alternatives – plane, car, train and bus. Details of the data are provided in Econometric Software (1998) and Louviere et al. (2000). The utility functions for the four alternatives are specified as follows:

$$U_{\text{Train}} = \alpha_{\text{Train}} + \beta_{\text{GC}}\text{GC}_{\text{Train}} + \beta_H \text{Hinc} + \beta_T \text{Ttime}_{\text{Train}} + \varepsilon_{\text{Train}},$$
$$U_{\text{Bus}} = \alpha_{\text{Bus}} + \beta_{\text{GC}}\text{GC}_{\text{Bus}} + \beta_H \text{Hinc} + \beta_T \text{Ttime}_{\text{Bus}} + \varepsilon_{\text{Bus}},$$
$$U_{\text{Plane}} = \alpha_{\text{Plane}} + \beta_{\text{GC}}\text{GC}_{\text{Plane}} + \beta_H \text{Hinc} + \beta_T \text{Ttime}_{\text{Plane}} + \varepsilon_{\text{Plane}},$$
$$U_{\text{Car}} = \beta_{\text{GC}}\text{GC}_{\text{Car}} + \varepsilon_{\text{Car}}.$$

The variables in the utility functions in addition to the alternative-specific constants are GC = Generalised cost (in dollars) out-of-pocket fuel cost for car or fare for plane, train and bus + time cost (the latter defined for main mode plus access and egress times excluding transfer time); Hinc = household income per annum (in $000's); Ttime = Transfer time (in minutes) the time spent waiting for and transferring to plane, train, bus.

Table 1 presents full information maximum likelihood (FIML) estimates of a two-level NNNL model. The tree structure for Table 1 has two branches, PUBLIC = (Train, Bus) and OTHER = (Car, Plane). In the PCS for this model, household income enters the probability of the branch choice directly in the utility for OTHER. Inclusive values from the lowest level enter both utility functions at the branch level. Table 2 presents FIML estimates of a two-level partially degenerate NL model. The tree structure for the models in Table 2, save for Model 7 which has an artificial third level, is FLY (Plane) and GROUND (Train, Bus, Car).

Estimates for both the NNNL model and the utility maximising (GEV-NL) parameterisations are presented. In the case of the GEV model parameterisation, estimates under each of the two normalisations (RU1 : $\mu = 1$ and RU2 : $\lambda = 1$) are provided as are estimates with the IV parameters restricted to equality within a level of the tree and unrestricted.

Eight models are summarised in Table 1 and six models in Table 2. Since there is only one limb, we drop the limb indicator from $\lambda(j|i)$ and denote it simply as $\lambda(j)$.

Model 1: RU1 with scale parameters equal within a level $[\lambda(1) = \lambda(2)]$.

Model 2: RU1 with scale parameters unrestricted within a level $[\lambda(1) \neq \lambda(2)]$.

Model 3: RU2 with scale parameters equal within a level (not applicable for a degenerate branch) $[\mu(1) = \mu(2)]$.

Table 1
Summary of alternative model specifications for a non-degenerate NL model[a]

Variables	Alternative	Model 1: RU1	Model 2: RU1	Model 3: RU2	Model 4: RU2	Model 5: NNNL[c]	Model 6: NNNL[c]	Model 8: RU1[b]	Model 9: RU2
Train constant	Train	4.542 (6.64)	3.757 (5.8)	5.873 (5.8)	6.159 (5.7)	3.6842 (2.34)	3.757 (5.8)	17.396 (2.2)	2.577 (3.8)
Bus constant	Bus	3.924 (5.83)	2.977 (4.4)	5.075 (6.0)	5.380 (5.8)	3.218 (2.18)	2.977 (4.4)	19.523 (2.4)	2.892 (3.73)
Plane constant	Plane	5.0307 (6.81)	4.980 (6.7)	6.507 (5.7)	6.154 (5.2)	3.681 (2.34)	4.980 (6.7)	4.165 (3.3)	4.165 (3.5)
Generalised cost ($)	All	−0.01088 (−2.6)	−0.0148 (−3.5)	−0.01407 (−2.6)	−0.01955 (−3.2)	−0.01169 (−1.8)	−0.0148 (−3.5)		
Transfer time (mins.)	All excl car	−0.0859 (−7.4)	−0.0861 (−7.3)	−0.1111 (−5.5)	−0.1064 (−5.2)	−0.0637 (−2.5)	−0.0861 (−7.3)		
Hhld income ($000s)	other	0.03456 (3.2)	0.0172 (2.9)	0.0447 (4.0)	0.0426 (3.8)	0.0426 (3.8)	0.0416 (3.4)	0.04269 (4.24)	0.04269 (3.8)
Generalised cost ($)	Air							0.00492 (0.56)	0.00492 (0.60)
Generalised cost ($)	Train							−0.0943 (−3.0)	−0.0139 (−2.8)
Generalised cost ($)	Bus							−0.1065 (−2.9)	−0.0158 (−2.9)
Generalised cost ($)	Car							−0.0143 (−2.5)	−0.0143 (−3.0)

Transfer time (min)	Air							−0.1048 (−6.2)	−0.1048 (−7.1)
Transfer time (min)	Train							−0.0787 (−2.5)	−0.0116 (−1.9)
Transfer time (min)	Bus							−0.1531 (−3.5)	−0.0227 (−1.9)
Inclusive value Parameters:									
IV other	Other	1.293 (5.3)	2.42 (4.6)	0.773 (3.8)	0.579 (3.3)	0.969 (3.2)[c]	2.42 (4.6)	1.00 (fixed)	1.00 (fixed)
IV public transport [d]	Public transport	1.293 (5.3)	1.28 (5.1)	0.773 (3.8)	1.03 (3.2)	1.724 (3.3)[c]	1.28 (5.1)	0.148 (2.0)	6.75 (1.9)
Log-likelihood		−190.178	−184.31	−190.178	−188.43	−188.43	−184.31	−177.82	−177.82
Direct elasticities:									
	Plane	−0.544	−0.797	−0.544	−0.666	−0.666	−0.797	0.228	0.228
	Car	−0.651	−1.081	−0.651	−0.762	−0.762	−1.081	−0.799	−0.799
	Train	−0.629	−0.854	−0.629	−0.910	−0.910	−0.854	−0.188	−1.27
	Bus	−0.759	−1.014	−0.759	−1.174	−1.174	−1.014	−0.343	−2.32

[a] Tree structure: other {plane, car} vs. public transport {train, bus} except for Model 5 which is OTHER {planem (plane), carm(car)} vs. public transport {trainm (train), busm (bus)}. *Note*: there is no Model 7 in order to keep equivalent model numbering in Tables 1 and 2.

[b] Model 8 with all alternative-specific attributes produces the exact parameter estimates, overall goodness-of-fit and elasticities as the NNNL model (and hence it is not reported).

[c] Standard errors are uncorrected.

[d] = IV parameters in Model 5 based on imposing equality of IV for (other, trainm, busm) and for (public transport, planem,carm).

Table 2
Summary of alternative model specifications for a partial degeneracy NL model[a]

Variables	Alternatives	Model 1: RU1	Model 2: RU1	Model 4: RU2	Model 5: NNNL[b]	Model 6: NNNL[b]	Model 7: RU2
Train constant	Train	5.070 (7.6)	5.065 (7.7)	2.622 (5.9)	9.805 (3.4)	5.065 (7.7)	4.584 (2.7)
Bus constant	Bus	4.145 (6.7)	4.096 (6.7)	2.143 (5.5)	8.015 (3.3)	4.096 (6.7)	3.849 (2.7)
Plane constant	Plane	5.167 (4.3)	6.042 (5.04)	2.672 (3.0)	9.993 (3.8)	6.042 (5.04)	5.196 (2.7)
Generalised cost ($)	All	−0.0291 (−3.6)	−0.0316 (−3.9)	−0.0151 (4.32)	−0.0564 (2.8)	−0.0316 (−3.9)	−0.0187 (−2.4)
Transfer time (min)	All excl car	−0.1156 (8.15)	−0.1127 (−7.9)	−0.0598 (−5.9)	−0.2236 (3.7)	−0.1127 (−7.9)	−0.0867 (−2.7)
Hhld income ($000s)	Fly	0.02837 (1.4)	0.0262 (1.5)	0.0143 (1.35)	0.01467 (1.4)	0.01533 (1.6)	0.02108 (1.4)
Party size	Auto						0.4330 (2.0)
Inclusive value Parameters:							
IV	Fly	0.517 (4.1)	0.586 (4.2)	1.00(0.67×10^{15})[c]	1.00(0.67×10^{15})[c]	0.586 (4.2)	Not applicable
IV	Ground	0.517 (4.1)	0.389 (3.1)	1.934 (5.0)[c]	0.517 (5.0)	0.389 (3.1)	
IV	Auto						Not applicable
IV	Public transport						1.26 (2.3)
IV	Other						0.844 (2.1)
IV	Land PT						Not applicable
Log-likelihood		−194.94	−193.66	−194.94	−194.94	−193.66	−194.27
Direct elasticities:							
	Plane	−0.864	−1.033	−0.864	−0.864	−1.033	−0.859
	Car	−1.332	−1.353	−1.332	−1.332	−1.353	−0.946
	Train	−1.317	−1.419	−1.317	−1.317	−1.419	−1.076
	Bus	−1.650	−1.878	−1.650	−1.650	−1.878	−1.378

[a] Tree structure: fly {plane} vs. ground {train, bus, car}. *Note*: Model 3 is not defined for a degenerate branch model when the IV parameters are forced to equality. Forcing a constraint on Model 4 (i.e., equal IV parameters) to obtain Model 3 produced exactly the same results for all the parameters. This is exactly what should happen. Since the IV parameter is not identified, no linear constraint that is imposed that involves this parameter is binding. Model 7 tree is other{fly (plane) vs. auto (car)} vs. Land PT{ public transport (train, bus}).

[b] Standard errors are uncorrected.

[c] = IV parameters in Model 5 based on imposing equality of IV for (ground, airm). It is not applicable for (fly, trainm, busm, carm) since fly is degenerate.

Model 4: RU2 with scale parameters unrestricted within a level [$\mu(1) \neq \mu(2)$].

Model 5: NNNL model with dummy nodes and links to allow unrestricted scale parameters in the presence of generic attributes to recover parameter estimates that are consistent with utility maximisation. This is equivalent up to scale with RU2 (model 4).

Model 6: NNNL model with no dummy nodes/links and different scale parameters within a level. This is a typical NL model implemented by many practitioners (and is equivalent to RU1 (Model 2)).

Model 7: RU2 with unrestricted scale parameters and dummy nodes and links to comply with utility maximisation (for partial degeneracy). Since Model 7 is identical to Model 8 in Table 1, it is presented only in Table 2.

Models 8 and 9: For the non-degenerate NL model (Table 1), these are RU1 and RU2 in which all parameters are alternative-specific and scale parameters are unrestricted across branches.

All results reported in Tables 1 and 2 are obtained using LIMDEP Version 7 (Revised, December 1998) (Econometric Software, 1998). The IV parameters for RU1 and RU2 that LIMDEP reports are the μ's and the λ's that are shown in the equations above. These μ's and λ's are proportional to the reciprocal of the standard deviation of the random component. The t-values in parenthesis for the NNNL model require correction to compare with RU1 and RU2. Koppelman and Wen (1998b) provide the procedure to adjust the t-values. For a two-level model, the corrected variance and hence standard error of estimate for the NNNL model is

$$\mathrm{Var}[\hat{\beta}_{\mathrm{RU}}] = \beta_{\mathrm{NN}}^2 \mathrm{Var}[\hat{\mu}_{\mathrm{NN}}] + \mu_{\mathrm{NN}}^2 \mathrm{Var}[\hat{\beta}_{\mathrm{NN}}] + 2\mu_{\mathrm{NN}}\beta_{\mathrm{NN}} \mathrm{Cov}[\hat{\mu}_{\mathrm{NN}}, \hat{\beta}_{\mathrm{NN}}]. \tag{18}$$

3.1. The case of generic attribute parameters

Beginning with the non-degenerate case, it can be seen in Table 1 that the GEV parameterisation estimates with IV parameters unrestricted (Models 2 and 4) are *not* invariant to the normalisation chosen. Not only is there no obvious relationship between the two sets of parameter estimates, the log-likelihood function values at convergence are not equal (−184.31 vs. −188.43) illustrating the fact that the normalisation has not been handled properly. When the GEV parameterisation is estimated subject to the restriction that the IV parameters be equal (Models 1 and 3), invariance is achieved across normalisation after accounting for the difference in scaling. The log-likelihood function values at convergence are equal (−190.178), and the IV parameter estimates are inverses of one another ($1/0.773 = 1.293$, within rounding error). Multiplying the utility function parameter estimates at the elemental alternatives level (i.e., $\alpha_{\mathrm{Plane}}, \alpha_{\mathrm{Train}}, \alpha_{\mathrm{Bus}}$, GC, Ttime) by the corresponding IV parameter estimate in one normalisation (e.g., Model 1) yields the utility function parameter estimates in another normalisation (e.g., Model 3). For example, in Model 3, $(1/1.293) \times 5.873$ for Train constant $= 4.542$ in Model 1.

The points made above about invariance, or the lack of it, scaling, and the equivalence of GEV and NNNL under the appropriate set of parametric restrictions are also illustrated in Table 2 for the case of a partially degenerate NL model structure. However, an additional and important result emerges for the partial degeneracy case. If the IV parameters are unrestricted, the GEV model "estimate" of the parameter on the degenerate partition IV is unity under the $\lambda = 1$ normalisation. This will always be the case because of the cancellation of the IV parameter and the lower-level scaling parameter in the GEV model in the degenerate partition. The results will be invariant to whatever value this parameter is set to. To see this, consider the results for the unrestricted GEV model presented as Model 4 in Table 2. The IV parameter is "estimated" to be 1.934, and if we were to report Model 3, all of the other estimates would be the same as in Model 4 and the log-likelihood function values at convergence are identical (−194.94). In a degenerate branch, whatever the value of $(1/\mu)$ is, it will cancel with the lower-level scaling parameter, μ, in the degenerate partition marginal probability. If we select $\mu = 1$ for normalisation (in contrast to λ) in the presence of a degenerate branch, the results will produce restricted (Model 1) or unrestricted (Model 2) estimates of λ which, unlike μ, do not cancel out in the degenerate branch. (Hunt (1998) pursues this issue at length.)

To illustrate the equivalence of behavioral outputs for RU1 and RU2, Tables 1 and 2 present the weighted aggregate direct elasticities for the relationship between the generalised cost of alternative *kji* and the probability of choosing alternative $k|ji$. As expected the results are identical for RU1 (Model 1) and RU2 (Model 3) when the IV parameters are equal across all branches at a level in the GEV model. The elasticities are significantly different from those obtained from Models 2 and 4, although Models 4 and 5 produce the same results (see below). Model 6 (equivalent to Model 2) is a common model specification in which parameters of attributes are generic and scale parameters are unrestricted within a level of the NL model with no constraints imposed to recover the utility maximisation estimates.

3.2. Allowing different scale parameters across nodes in a level in the presence of generic and/or alternative-specific attribute parameters between partitions

When we allow the IV parameters to be unrestricted in the RU1 and RU2 GEV models and in the NNNL model we fail to comply with normalisation invariance, and for Models 2 and 6 we also fail to produce consistency with utility maximisation. RU1 (Model 2) fails to comply with utility maximisation because of the absence of explicit scaling in the utility expressions for elemental alternatives. We obtain different results on overall goodness-of-fit and the range of behavioural outputs such as elasticities.

For a given nested structure and set of attributes there can only be one utility maximising solution. This presents a dilemma, since we often want the scale parameters to vary between branches and/or limbs or at least test for non-equivalence. This is after all, the main reason why we seek out alternative nested structures. Fortunately there is a solution, depending on whether one opts for a specification in which some or all of the parameters are generic or whether they are all alternative-specific. Models 5 to 9 are alternative specifications.

If all attributes between partitions are unrestricted (i.e., alternative-specific), unrestricted scale parameters are compliant with utility maximisation under all specifications (i.e., RU2 = 1, RU2 and NNNL). Intuitively, the fully alternative-specific specification avoids any artificial 'transfer' of information from the attribute parameters to the scale parameters that occurs when restrictions are imposed on parameter estimates. Models 8 and 9 in Table 1 are totally alternative-specific. The scale parameters for Models 8 and 9 are the inverse of each other. That is, for the unrestricted IV, 0.148 in Model 8 equals (1/6.75) in Model 9. The alternative-specific parameter estimates associated with attributes in the public transport branch for Model 8 can be recovered from Model 9 by a scale transformation. For example, 0.148×17.396 for the train constant equals 2.577 in Model 9. The estimated parameters are identical in Models 8 and 9 for the 'other' modes since their IV parameter is restricted to equal unity in both models. This demonstrates the equivalence up to scale of RU1 and RU2 when all attribute parameters (including IV) are unrestricted.

When we impose the generic condition on an attribute associated with alternatives in different partitions of the nest, Koppelman and Wen (1998a,b) (and Daly in advice to ALOGIT (Hague Consulting Group, 1995) subscribers) have shown how one can recover compliance with utility maximisation in an NNNL model under the unrestricted scale condition (within a level of the NL model) by adding dummy nodes and links below the bottom level and imposing cross-branch equality constraints as illustrated in Fig. 2. Intuitively, what we are doing is allowing for differences in scale parameters at each branch but preserving the (constant) ratio of the IV parameters between two levels through the introduction of the scale parameters at the elemental level; the latter requires the additional lower level in an NNNL specification. The NNNL specification does not allow unrestricted values of scale at the elemental level, unlike RU2, for example. Preserving a constant ratio through cross-over equality constraints between levels in the nest satisfies the necessary condition of choice probability invariance to the addition of a constant in the utility expression of all elemental alternatives.

Adding an extra level is not designed to investigate the behavioural implications of a three-level model; rather it is a 'procedure' to reveal the scale parameters at upper levels where they have not been identified. This procedure is fairly straightforward for two branches (see Model 5 in Tables 1 and 2). With more than two branches, one has to specify additional levels for each branch. The number of levels grows quite dramatically. However, there is one way of simplifying this procedure, if we recognise that the ratio of the scale parameters between adjacent levels must be constant. Thus, for any number of branches, consistency with utility maximisation requires that the product of all the ratios of scale parameters between levels must be identical from the root to all elemental alternatives. To facilitate this, one can add a single link below each real alternative with the scale of that link set equal to the product of the scales of all scale parameters not included in the path to that alternative. For example, in the case of three branches with scales equal to

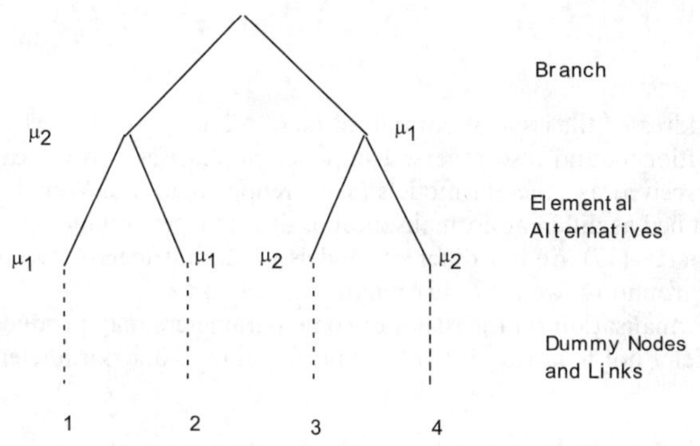

Fig. 2. Estimating a two-level model to allow for unrestricted scale parameters within a level.

λ_1, λ_2 and λ_3; the scale below the first branch would be $(\lambda_2 \times \lambda_3)$, below the second branch it would be $(\lambda_1 \times \lambda_3)$ and below the third branch it would be $(\lambda_1 \times \lambda_2)$.

Model 5 is estimated as an NNNL model with the addition of a lower level of nodes and links with cross-branch equality constraints on the scale parameters. For example, in Table 1, the tree structure is as follows: {Other [planem (plane), carm (car)], Public Transport [trainm (train), busm (bus)]}. The cross-over constraint for two branches sets the scale parameters to equality for {*Other*, trainm, busm} and {*Public Transport*, planem, carm}. The Model 5 (Table 1) produces results which are identical to RU2 (model 4) in respect of goodness-of-fit and elasticities; with all parameter estimates equivalent up to scale. Since we have two scale parameters in Model 5, the ratio of each branches IV parameters to their equivalent in Model 4 provides the adjustment factor to translate Model 5 parameters into Model 4 parameters (or vice versa). For example, the ratio of $0.579/0.969 = 1.03/1.724 = 0.597$. If we multiply the train-specific constant in Model 4 of 6.159 by 0.597, we obtain 3.6842, the train-specific constant in Model 5. This is an important finding, because it indicates that

> the application of the RU2 specification with unrestricted scale parameters in the presence of generic parameters across branches for the attributes is identical to the results obtained by estimating the NNNL model with an extra level of nodes and links.

RU2 thus avoids the need to introduce the extra level. [3] The equivalent findings are shown in Table 2 where the scale ratio is 3.74. Intuitively one might expect such a result given that RU2 allows the scale parameters to be freely estimated at the lower level (in contrast to RU1 where they are normalised to 1.0). One can implement this procedure under an exact RU2 model specification to facilitate situations where one wishes to allow scale parameters at a level in the nest to be different across branches in the presence or absence of a generic specification of attribute parameters. *The estimation results in Model 4 are exactly correct and require no further adjustments.* The procedure can also be implemented under an NNNL specification (with an extra level of nodes and links) (Model 5). The elasticities, marginal rates of substitution, goodness-of-fit are identical in Models 4 and 5. The parameter estimates are identical up to the ratio of scales.

4. Conclusions

This paper has addressed the issue of normalisation of NL models which is a common source of confusion for practitioners and researchers. The paper emphasises two critical points:

1. What may be perceived as different models (as in Koppelman and Wen 1998a,b) are instead, appropriately defined as different normalisation of the same general model. Thus, it is seen that our (6)–(11) and (12)–(17) are not different models at all, but merely two formulations of the one model built around (4) and the surrounding discussion
2. The impact of normalisation on the scales of some parameters may produce internal inconsistency of the model if not handled properly. Typically, if the same parameter appears in several

[3] From a practical perspective, this enables programs like NLOGIT that limit the number of levels which can be jointly estimated to use all levels for real behavioural analysis.

nests, normalisation from the bottom (RU1) may cause problems, as the parameter will be scaled differently in each nest.

The empirical applications and discussion herein have identified the model specification required to ensure compliance with the necessary conditions for utility maximisation.

This can be achieved for a *GEV-NL model* by either

- setting the IV parameters to be the same at a level in the nest in the presence of generic parameters, or
- implementing the RU2 specification and allowing the IV parameters to be free in the presence of generic attribute parameters between partitions of a nest, or
- setting all attribute parameters to be alternative-specific between partitions, allowing IV parameters to be unrestricted.

This can be achieved for a NNNL model by either

- setting the scale parameters to be the same at a level in the nest (for the non-normalised scale parameters) and rescaling all estimated parameters associated with elemental alternatives by the estimated IV parameter, or
- allowing the IV parameters to be free, and adding an additional level at the bottom of the tree through dummy nodes and links, and constraining the scale parameters at the elemental alternatives level to equal those of the dummy nodes of all other branches in the total NL model, or
- setting all attribute parameters to be alternative-specific between partitions, allowing IV parameters to be unrestricted.

The statement is made in Koppelman and Wen (1998a,b) (attributed to Daly (1987)), that the non-normalised form is not consistent with RUM. In view of the preceding, we see that this is not necessarily correct; at best, the statement is imprecise. With the proper normalisation of the model, we see that the NNNL model is, indeed, consistent with RUM.

Appendix A. Random utility model 3 (RU3)

John Bates, in correspondence to the authors questions the usefulness of RU2 (our preferred specification) as an appropriate model of utility maximisation (Bates 1999). He states:

> I am altogether less clear as to the purpose of RU2. The presence of $\mu \neq 1$ at the bottom of the structure signifies that the coefficients are not being scaled at the lowest level. In moving up one level, the logsums are deflated by μ and then a new IV parameter γ is applied. At the top level, the scaling factor is set to 1 and the logsum is deflated by γ. While this appears to scale the parameters at the top of the structure, it does not seem to me to correspond directly with UMNL (utility maximising nested logit). The reason is that the "final" alternatives are still constrained to be located at the bottom of the structure.

Bates' point is well taken. He proposes an alternative specification of the model which he argues is more appropriate. We lay out his model and show that what he has proposed is identical to RU2 with a minor transformation of the parameters. This explains the finding in his example, that though the parameter estimates he presents for a model differ from LIMDEP's RU2 counterparts, the log-likelihood functions are the same.

Bates' proposed alternative specification of the model is as follows:

$$P(k\lfloor j,i) = \frac{\exp\left[\frac{1}{\lambda(j|i)\omega(i)}[\alpha_{k\lfloor ji} + \beta'\mathbf{x}(k\lfloor ji)]\right]}{\sum_{m=1}^{K\lfloor ji}\exp\left[\frac{1}{\lambda(j|i)\omega(i)}[\alpha_{m\lfloor ji} + \beta'\mathbf{x}(m\lfloor ji)]\right]},$$

$$\mathrm{IV}(j|i) = \lambda(j|i)\omega(i)\log\sum_{m=1}^{K\lfloor ji}\exp\left[\frac{1}{\lambda(j|i)\omega(i)}[\alpha_{m\lfloor j,i} + \beta'\mathbf{x}(m\lfloor ji)]\right],$$

$$P(j|i) = \frac{\exp\left[\frac{1}{\omega(i)}[\gamma'\mathbf{y}(j|i) + \mathrm{IV}(j|i)]\right]}{\sum_{m=1}^{J|i}\exp\left[\frac{1}{\omega(i)}[\gamma'\mathbf{y}(m|i) + \mathrm{IV}(m|i)]\right]},$$

$$P(i) = \frac{\exp[\delta'\mathbf{z}(i) + \mathrm{IV}(i)]}{\sum_{n=1}^{I}\exp[\delta'\mathbf{z}(n) + \mathrm{IV}(n)]},$$

$$\mathrm{IV}(i) = \rho(i)\log\sum_{m=1}^{J|i}\exp\left[\frac{1}{\omega(i)}[\delta'\mathbf{y}(m|i) + \mathrm{IV}(m|i)]\right].$$

This appears to be a different formulation, but it is not. To see this, note first that since $\lambda(j|i)$ is a free parameter in the model that appears only in the scaling parameter for the elemental utility functions, we may write the model in terms of the compound parameter $\phi(j|i) = \lambda(j|i)\omega(i)$ and, moreover, since MLEs are invariant to transformation, write this as simply $\mu(j|i) = 1/\phi(j|i) = 1/[\lambda(j|i)\omega(i)]$. Inserting this into Bates' $P(k\lfloor j,i)$ produces the counterpart for RU2, so the probabilities are identical and, moreover, the slope parameters, β, are the same in the two models. The inclusive values appear to be different, but this is misleading. Now, let $\rho(i) = 1/\omega(i)$ and make the substitutions for $\omega(i)$ and the necessary changes in $\mathrm{IV}(j|i)$ in $P(j|i)$. What emerges, once again, is RU2, so $P(j|i)$ is also identical. No new parameters are introduced by $P(i)$, so the direct substitution of $\rho(i) = 1/\omega(i)$ produces the now expected result.

References

Bates, J., 1999. More thoughts on nested logit, John Bates Services, Oxford (mimeo), January.

Ben-Akiva, M., Lerman, S.R., 1985. Discrete Choice Analysis: Theory and Application to Travel Demand. MIT Press, Cambridge.

Daly, A., 1987. Estimating 'tree' logit models. Transportation Research B 21 (4), 251–267.

Econometric Software, 1998. Limdep Version 7 for Windows, Econometric Software, New York and Sydney, December revision.

Hague Consulting Group, 1995. ALOGIT. User's Guide, Hague Consulting Group, Den Haag.

Hunt, G.L., 1998. Nested logit models with partial degeneracy. Department of Economics, University of Maine, December (revised).

Koppelman, F.S., Wen, C.H., 1998a. Alternative nested logit models: structure, properties and estimation. Transportation Research B 32 (5), 289–298.

Koppelman, F.S., Wen, C.H., 1998b. Nested logit models: which are you using? Transportation Research Record 1645, 1–7.

Louviere, J.J., Hensher, D.A., Swait, J., 2000. Stated Choice Methods: Analysis and Applications in Marketing, Transportation and Environmental Valuation. Cambridge University Press, Cambridge, in press.
Maddala, J.S., 1983. Limited Dependent and Qualitative Variables in Econometrics. Cambridge University Press, New York.
McFadden, D.L., 1981. Econometric models of probabilistic choice. In: Manski, C.F., McFadden, D.L. (Eds.), Structural Analysis of Discrete Data, MIT Press, Cambridge, MA, pp. 198–271.
Ortuzar, Juan de Dios, 2000. A short note on the history of nested logit models. Transportation Research, in press.
Quigley, J., 1985. Consumer Choice of Dwelling, Neighborhood, and Public Services. Regional Science and Urban Economics 15, 41–63.

[19]

Pergamon

Transpn Res. B, Vol. 32, No. 5, pp. 289–298, 1998

Printed in Great Britain
0191-2615/98 $19.00+0.00

PII: S0191-2615(98)000803-4

ALTERNATIVE NESTED LOGIT MODELS: STRUCTURE, PROPERTIES AND ESTIMATION

FRANK S. KOPPELMAN* and CHIEH-HUA WEN

Department of Civil Engineering and Transportation Center, Northwestern University, 2415 Sheridan Road, Evanston, Illinois 60208, U.S.A.

(Received 19 March 1997; in revised form 30 October 1997)

Abstract—Two distinctly different nested logit models have been widely used in both research and applications. The differences, not widely recognized, between these models will substantially influence estimation results, behavioral interpretation and policy analysis. The McFadden nested logit model is derived from random utility theory; the Daly or non-normalized nested logit model is based on probability relationships and is not consistent with utility maximization. This paper describes and compares the model structure and properties of these different nested logit models identifying important differences between the different model structures. An empirical application demonstrates that the different nested logit models produce dramatically different results with respect to nesting structure and the relative importance of utility components. Thus, the selection of one or another of the nested logit models has important consequences for model interpretation and prediction with consequent impacts on policy analysis. The authors prefer the McFadden model because of its basis in utility theory, intuitively reasonable elasticity relationships and a clear interpretation of utility function parameters across alternatives. © 1998 Elsevier Science Ltd. All rights reserved

Keywords: nested logit, discrete choice, travel demand, intercity rail

1. INTRODUCTION

Discrete choice analysis is used to model the choice of one among a set of mutually exclusive alternatives. The multinomial logit (MNL) model (McFadden, 1973), the most widely used discrete choice model, is based on principles of utility maximization and has the advantages of simple mathematical structure and ease of estimation. However, it has the property that the relative probabilities of each pair of alternatives are independent of the presence or characteristics of all other alternatives. This property, known as the independence of irrelevant alternatives (IIA), implies that the introduction or improvement of any alternative will have the same proportional impact on the probability of each other alternative. This representation of choice behavior will result in biased estimates and incorrect predictions in cases which violate the IIA property. Extreme examples of non-IIA cases include the addition of a second bus service identical to an existing service, except for a change in vehicle color, to existing competition between a single bus alternative and private rail (the red bus, blue bus problem) or the addition of a classical CD to an existing choice between another classical CD and a jazz CD. Less extreme, but more realistic examples include mode choice between public transit (bus and light rail) and private vehicle (drive alone and shared ride) (Ortuzar, 1983) or route choice among alternatives which include common road segments (Yai *et al.*, 1997).

The most widely known relaxation of the MNL model is the nested (NL) or hierarchical (HL) logit model which allows interdependence between the pairs of alternatives in a common group (McFadden, 1978; Ben-Akiva and Lerman, 1985; Börsch-Supan, 1990a). The utility maximizing nested logit (UMNL) model is a special case of the generalized extreme value (GEV) model (McFadden, 1978, 1981) which ensures that it is consistent with utility maximization, provided that the logsum parameters are bounded appropriately. An alternative, is the non-normalized nested logit (NNNL) by Daly (1987), which is identical to the McFadden model except that the model does not include the inverse of each logsum parameter in the utility function of the

*Author for correspondence. Fax: (847) 491-4011; e-mail: f-koppelman@nwu.edu

alternatives in the corresponding nest. This apparently small difference has a dramatic impact on the properties and behavior of this model. Most importantly, the NNNL model is not consistent with utility maximization.* Estimation and application of these different NL models will, in general, result in different utility function parameters, different nesting structures and different travel forecasts; these differences may be substantial enough to impact capital investment and operating decisions.

This paper compares these alternative NL models to identify their important differences and presents an empirical example which demonstrates the extent of these differences which are not widely recognized by users of NL models. The remainder of this paper is organized as follows. Section 2 presents the formulation and properties for the alternative NL models. Section 3 describes the estimation structure for both NL models. Section 4 discusses the empirical example and demonstrates the magnitude of the empirical differences in one case. Section 5 provides a summary and implications for model application.

2. ALTERNATIVE NL MODELS

2.1. Model formulation

2.1.1. The utility maximizing nested logit (UMNL) model. McFadden's UMNL model is a member of the GEV family, and is consistent with utility maximization (McFadden, 1978). A GEV model can be derived from any function, $G(Y_1, Y_2, \ldots, Y_n)$, $Y_1, Y_2, \ldots, Y_n \geqslant 0$, which is a non-negative, linear homogeneous function† which approaches infinity as any Y_i, $i = 1, 2, \ldots, n$ does and has mth cross-partial derivatives which are non-negative for odd m and non-positive for even m. If G satisfies these conditions, the probability of choosing alternative i is given by

$$P_i = \frac{Y_i G_i(Y_1, Y_2, \ldots, Y_n)}{G(Y_1, Y_2, \ldots, Y_n)} \tag{1}$$

where G_i is the first derivative of G with respect to Y_i. A two-level UMNL model is obtained from the G function:

$$G(Y_1, Y_2, \ldots, Y_n) = \sum_{m=1}^{M} \left(\sum_{n \in N_m} Y_n^{\frac{1}{\mu_m}} \right)^{\mu_m} \tag{2}$$

where N_m is the set of alternatives in nest m and μ_m is an index of the dissimilarity of alternatives included in nest m.‡ The UMNL model is consistent with utility maximization if the conditions, $0 < \mu_m \leqslant 1$,§ are satisfied for all μ_m. If $\mu_m = 1$ for all m, the NL collapses to the MNL.

To ensure positive Y_i, the transformation $Y_i = \exp(V_i)$ is adopted, where V_i represents the observable components of the utility for each alternative ($U_i = V_i + \varepsilon_i$, $i = 1, 2, \ldots, n$). The probability that alternative n is chosen can be written as

$$P_n = P_{n/m} \times P_m \tag{3}$$

where

$$P_{n/m} = \frac{e^{V_n/\mu_m}}{\sum_{n' \in N_m} e^{V_{n'}/\mu_m}} \tag{4}$$

*Except for the special case when the logsum parameters are equal across all nests at the same level.

†McFadden's original formulation requires the function to be linear homogeneous of degree one; however, Ben-Akiva and Lerman (1985) refer to an unpublished report by Ben-Akiva and Francois (1983) which demonstrates that the function can be homogeneous of any degree.

‡Dissimilarity implies the absence of correlation between the error distribution of pairs of alternatives within a nest. The correlation between pairs of alternatives equals $(1 - \mu_m^2)$.

§Values of logsum parameters greater than one can be consistent with utility maximization over a limited portion of the real space which may be relevant in cases where the range of attribute variables is limited during both estimation and prediction (Börsch-Supan 1990a; Kling and Herriges, 1995; Herriges and Kling, 1986).

$$P_m = \frac{e^{\mu_m \Gamma_m}}{\sum_{m'=1}^{M} e^{\mu_{m'}/\Gamma_{m'}}} \tag{5}$$

and

$$\Gamma_m = \ln \sum_{n' \in N_m} e^{V_{n'}/\mu_m} \tag{6}$$

V_n is the utility associated with alternative n in nest m, $P_{n/m}$ is the conditional probability of choosing alternative n conditional on choosing nest m, P_m is the marginal probability of choosing nest m of which n is a member; N_m is the set of all alternatives included in nest m, Γ_m is the logsum variable of nest m* and μ_m is the logsum or inclusive value (IV) parameter. Thus, V_m, the utility of nest m is equal to $\mu_m \Gamma_m$.†

All alternatives may be considered to be in a nest; in the case of a single alternative in a nest, the nest is considered degenerate and the logsum parameter, μ_m, will equal one. If only one alternative is available in each nest, the model collapses to the multinomial logit

$$P_i = \frac{e^{V_i}}{\sum_{m=1}^{M} e^{V_m}} \tag{7}$$

2.1.2. The Daly non-normalized nested logit (NNNL) model. Daly's (1987) NNNL model is defined by the following equations:

$$P_n = P_{n/m} \times P_m \tag{8}$$

where

$$P_{n/m} = \frac{e^{V_n}}{\sum_{n' \in N_m} e^{V_{n'}}} \tag{9}$$

$$P_m = \frac{e^{\mu_m \Gamma_m}}{\sum_{m'=1}^{M} e^{\mu_{m'} \Gamma_{m'}}} \tag{10}$$

$$\Gamma_m = \ln \sum_{n' \in N_m} e^{V_{n'}} \tag{11}$$

where the notation is the same as that used in the McFadden NL model. The only difference between the models is that the Daly model excludes the inverse of the IV parameters, μ_m, in the utility function of the elemental alternatives in each nest [as can be seen by comparing eqns (9) and (11) to eqns (4) and (6)].‡

The NNNL model is equivalent to the UMNL model only when the $\mu_m = \mu$, for all m in both models. In this case, the utility function parameters in both models will be equal up to the scale

*Γ_m represents the expected value of the maximum of the random utilities of alternatives in nest m.
†Additional variables which apply to all nested alternatives may be included in V_m however, this can be identically represented by adding these variables to each alternative in the nest.
‡Also, the inclusion of variables common to all alternatives in a nest at the level of the elemental alternatives is not equivalent to including these variables at the level of the nest in the Daly formation.

factor, μ. However, when $\mu_m \neq \mu$, for any m, the NNNL model is neither equivalent to the UMNL model nor consistent with utility maximization.* As a result, the behavioral interpretation of the NNNL model is based solely on the logic of marginal and conditional choice probabilities and the interpretation of the utility parameters across alternatives is obscure. In particular, the utility value of generic variables, such as time or cost, for different alternatives will depend on the IV parameter associated with the nest of which the alternative is a member. While there are conditions under which it would be interesting to consider different utility values of some attributes across alternatives (e.g. the value of travel time on a mode may depend on the extent to which the traveler can use his/her in-vehicle time for other purposes), it is always interesting to test such model specifications against the hypothesis that the utility value of time is constrained to be equal across alternatives. This constraint is even more likely to be relevant for the utility value of money spent on travel by each alternative.

2.2. *Relationship among alternatives*

Both nested logit models allow the user to consider the existence of different competitive relationships between groups of alternatives in a common nest. Such differences indicate that the effect of a change in an attribute of an alternative on the probability of that alternative depends on whether it is or is not in a nest and on other alternatives depends on whether they are or are not in a common nest. One way to describe these differences is in terms of direct- and cross-elasticities of the choice probabilities of the same or other alternatives with respect to a change in the attributes of an alternative. The direct- and cross-elasticities for the MNL and the two NL models are shown in Table 1. All of the elasticity terms are proportional to the magnitude of the variable which changes and the parameter associated with that variable. The direct-elasticities are differentiated between alternatives which are or are not in a nest and the cross-elasticities are differentiated between pairs of alternatives which are or are not in a common nest. The direct- and cross-elasticities of the MNL model depend exclusively on the probability of the mode which is subject to change. Thus, the MNL cross-elasticities are identical across alternatives and produce the commonly observed equal proportional effect of the addition, deletion or change of any alternative on all other alternatives.

The direct elasticities for alternatives not in any nest are structurally identical to the MNL direct-elasticities for both NL models.† The UMNL model direct-elasticities for alternatives in a nest are greater than the corresponding direct elasticity for alternatives not in a nest; this relationship is consistent with the idea that alternatives in a nest face a more competitive choice context than do alternatives not in any nest. However, the NNNL direct-elasticities are smaller for alternatives in a nest than the corresponding direct-elasticity for alternatives which are not in any nest. These NNNL model differences are counter-intuitive in that they imply that similarity of an alternative to other alternatives reduces the effect of a change in that alternative on its own choice probability relative to the case where that alternative is not in any nest. The magnitude of the difference in direct-elasticities between alternatives in or not in a nest increases as the IV parameter, μ_m, decreases from one to zero for both models.

The cross-elasticities between pairs of alternatives for the two NL models are differentiated between pairs which are or are not in the same nest. The cross-elasticities for pairs of alternatives which are not in the same nest are structurally identical to that for the MNL case for the UMNL model. The corresponding cross-elasticities for the NNNL model differ from the MNL model by the scale parameter, μ_m. The cross-elasticities between pairs of alternatives in a common nest are greater for both NL models than the corresponding cross-elasticities for alternatives not in the same nest. This result is consistent with the notion that cross-elasticities between pairs of alternatives within a nest should be larger than cross-elasticities between pairs of alternatives not in the same nest. In both cases, the cross-elasticities are equal to those for the MNL when μ_m is equal to one.

*The NNNL model does not satisfy the necessary condition that the addition of a constant value to all elemental alternatives has no effect on the choice probabilities of the alternatives (Daly and Zachary, 1978; McFadden, 1981).

†The empirical value of the elasticities will differ from the MNL model if the utility function parameters change as a result of a change in the nesting structure. For this reason, Section 4 includes empirical comparison between the direct-elasticities for alternatives in or not in a nest and the cross-elasticities between alternatives which are or are not in the same nest within each model.

Table 1. Direct- and cross-elasticities of the MNL, UMNL and NNNL models

Model structure	Direct-elasticity (change in P_n due to change in X_n)	Cross-elasticity (change in $P_{n'}$ due to change in X_n)
MNL model	$(1 - P_n)\beta X_n$	$-P_n\beta X_n$
McFadden NL model	n not in nest $(1 - P_n)\beta X_n$	n and n' not in same nest $-P_n\beta X_n$
	n in nest m $[(1 - P_n) + (\frac{1}{\mu_m} - 1)(1 - P_{n/m})]\beta X_n$	n and n' in nest m $-[P_n + (\frac{1}{\mu_m} - 1)P_{n/m}]\beta X_n$
Daly NL model	n not in nest $(1 - P_n)\beta X_n$	n and n' not in same nest, n in nest m $-\mu_m P_n\beta X_n$
	n in nest m $[(1 - P_n) + (\mu_m - 1)P_{n/m}(1 - P_m)]\beta X_n$	n and n' in nest m $-[P_n + (1 - \mu_m)P_{n/m}(1 - P_m)]\beta X_n$

3. MODEL ESTIMATION

Maximum likelihood techniques are used to estimate parameters of the MNL and both NL models. The log-likelihood for discrete outcomes is of the form

$$L = \sum_q \sum_i \delta_{qi} \ln P_{qi} \tag{12}$$

where δ_{qi} is 1 if individual q chooses alternative i and 0 otherwise, P_{qi} is the probability that individual q chooses alternative i. The likelihood function for the two-level NL model is

$$L = \sum_q \sum_i \delta_{qi} \ln P_{qi} = \sum_q \left(\sum_{m=1}^{M} \delta_{qm} \ln P_{qm} + \sum_{n \in N_m} \delta_{q,nm} \ln P_{q,n/m} \right) \tag{13}$$

where δ_{qm} is 1 if individual q chooses nest m and 0 otherwise, P_{qm} is the probability that individual q chooses nest m, $\delta_{q,nm}$ is 1 if individual q chooses alternative n in the nest m and 0 otherwise, and $P_{q,n/m}$ is the probability that individual q chooses alternative n in the nest m.

The log-likelihood function of the UMNL model is defined by the following equation:

$$L = \sum_q \left\{ \sum_{m=1} \delta_{qm} \left[\mu_m \Gamma_m - \ln\left(\sum_{m'=1} e^{\mu_{m'} \Gamma_{m'}} \right) \right] + \sum_{n \in N_m} \delta_{q,nm} \left[\frac{V_n}{\mu_m} - \ln\left(\sum_{n' \in N_m} e^{\frac{V_{n'}}{\mu_m}} \right) \right] \right\} \tag{14}$$

The log-likelihood function of the NNNL model is

$$L = \sum_q \left\{ \sum_{m=1}^{M} \delta_{qm} \left[\mu_m \Gamma_m - \ln\left(\sum_{m'=1} e^{\mu_{m'} \Gamma_{m'}} \right) \right] + \sum_{n \in N_m} \delta_{q,nm} \left[V_n - \ln\left(\sum_{n' \in N_m} e^{V_{n'}} \right) \right] \right\} \tag{15}$$

The difference between these log-likelihood functions is that the log-likelihood of the conditional probability (the last term in each equation) includes the inverse of the scale parameter in the UMNL model but not in the NNNL model. The differences between these equations will result in different estimations for all of the model parameters. The simplification in the NNNL eqn (15), due to the elimination of μ_m^{-1}, appears to make the NNNL model less difficult to estimate than the UMNL model. This enables software for the NNNL model to accommodate a large number of levels in the tree structure, an important capability in some contexts.

Estimation of both NL models should use full information maximum likelihood to increase estimation efficiency and allow the user to impose constraints on utility function parameters in different nests in the structure (Brownstone and Small, 1989; Hensher, 1991). Commercial software packages have been developed to estimate either the UMNL model, the NNNL model or both. These include ALOGIT (Hague Consulting Group, 1988, 1992 and 1995), HieLoW

(Bierlaire, 1995; Bierlaire and Vandevyvere, 1995), HLOGIT (Börsch-Supan, 1990b) and LIMDEP (Econometric Software, 1996). The model equations included in software documentation should provide the user with a clear statement of the formulations which are estimated by each package. It is particularly important to recognize that software designed to estimate the NNNL model may be used to estimate the UMNL model by inclusion of dummy nodes and links in the NNNL structure and constraining the IV parameters at such nodes appropriately.* This approach, illustrated in the Fig. 1, where the addition of a dummy link (dashed line) and node and imposition of equality constraints on the IV parameters, enables the estimation of the UMNL model. The resultant utility function parameters will be scaled by μ. The utility function scaling to match the original tree structure can be calculated by multiplication of the parameters by the scale adjustment. The standard errors of the corrected parameter can be obtained by using Cramer's approximation (Ben-Akiva and Lerman, 1985, p.298). This approach can be applied to any tree structure by adding dummy links and logsum parameters so that the product of the logsum parameters between the root and each elemental alternative is identical.

4. EMPIRICAL EXAMPLE

The following empirical example demonstrates the differences between the estimation results for the UMNL and NNNL models.† The data used in this study was assembled by VIA rail in 1989 to estimate the demand for high-speed rail in the Toronto–Montreal corridor and to support future decisions on rail service improvements in the corridor (Forinash and Koppelman, 1993). The choice set includes four intercity travel modes; air, train, bus and car.‡ 2779 individuals who have all four modes available were selected. The distribution of choices in the data set is: train (463, 16.66%), air (1039, 37.39%), bus (10, 0.36%) and car (1267, 45.59%).

The utility function specification includes mode-specific constants, frequency, travel cost, and out- of-vehicle and in-vehicle travel times. The estimation results for the MNL and the two NL

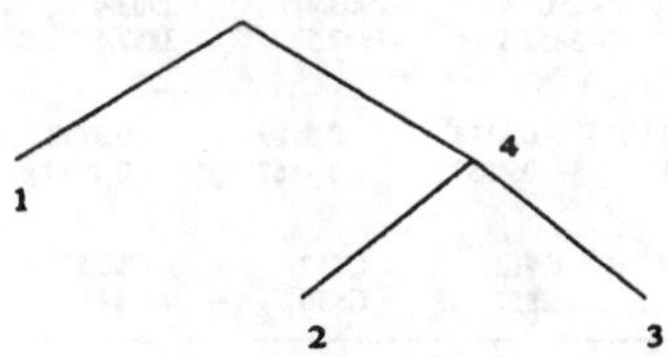

(a) The nested structure for the simple tree

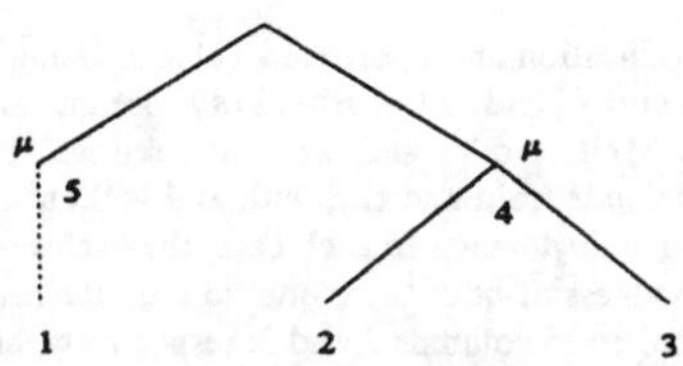

(b) The modified nested structure for the simple tree

Fig. 1. Estimation of single node UMNL model using software designed to estimate the UMNL model (a) or software designed to estimate the NNNL model (b).

*Software packages differ in their ability to incorporate this approach. The user should ensure that he/she can use particular software for this purpose through examination of the documentation, testing and/or verification from the software provider.

†The reported models were estimated using Gauss (Aptech Systems, 1993) based programs developed at Northwestern University's Transportation Center and verified with HLOGIT for the McFadden model and ALOGIT for Daly model.

‡Screening of observations without a full set of alternatives does not impact the substantive results reported in this paper.

Table 2. The estimation results of the MNL, UMNL and NNNL models

Variables	Estimated parameters (standard errors)					
	MNL model	UMNL model		NNNL model		
		Train–car nested	Air–car nested	Train–bus, Air–car nested	Air–train nested	Air–bus nested
	1	2	3	4	5	6
Mode constants						
Air	7.7876	7.5014	6.6186	7.0342	7.2664	11.8620
	(0.599)	(0.549	(0.666)	(0.815)	(0.659)	(0.869)
Train	5.8532	5.9698	5.2677	5.7050	5.6265	7.4589
	(0.348)	(0.334)	(0.382)	(0.377)	(0.439)	(0.302)
Car	4.1751	4.3288	3.9762	3.8376	3.5905	5.8149
	(0.414)	(0.388)	(0.397)	(0.463)	(0.446)	(0.270)
Bus (base)						
Frequency	0.0940	0.0932	0.0731	0.0967	0.0976	0.1631
	(0.005)	(0.004)	(0.007)	(0.005)	(0.005)	(0.014)
Travel cost	−0.0455	−0.0423	−0.0312	−0.0372	−0.0422	−0.0639
	(0.004)	(0.004)	(0.005)	(0.006)	(0.004)	(0.004)
In-vehicle time	−0.0100	−0.0094	−0.0094	−0.0126	−0.0097	−0.0027
	(0.001)	(0.001)	(0.001)	(0.001)	(0.001)	(0.001)
Out-of-vehicle-time	−0.04265	−0.0400	−0.0366	−0.0512	−0.0496	−0.0471
	(0.003)	(0.003)	(0.003)	(0.004)	(0.004)	(0.004)
Logsum	–	80.8204	0.7400	0.7267[a]	0.7955	0.4764
	–	(0.068)	(0.071)	(0.069)	(0.041)	(0.049)
				0.7896[b]		
				(0.083)		
Log-likelihood						
At convergence	−1983.3	−1980.6	−1977.6	−1976.5	−1970.1	−1938.8
At market share	−2903.4	−2903.4	−2903.4	−2903.4	−2903.4	−2903.4
At zero	−3852.5	−3852.5	−3852.5	−3852.5	−3852.5	−3852.5
Likelihood ratio index						
vs market share	0.3169	0.3178	0.3189	0.3192	0.3215	0.3322
vs zero	0.4852	0.4859	0.4867	0.4870	0.4886	0.4967
Value of time (hours)						
In-vehicle time	C$13	C$13	C$17	C$20	C$14	C$3
Out-of-vehicle time	C$56	C$57	C$70	C$83	C$71	C$44

[a]Logsum parameter for train and bus net.
[b]Logsum parameter for air and car nest.

models with a common utility specification are reported in Table 2. Using the UMNL model, four of the 25 possible nested structures had all dissimilarity parameters within the zero-one range, significantly rejected the MNL model and were not rejected by other UMNL structures. Of the four models, two include train and car, with and without bus, and two include air and car, with and without bus, in a single nest. In each case, the exclusion of bus in the nest has very little effect on the overall goodness of fit of the model so only the results for the models with train-car and with air-car are reported in columns 2 and 3, respectively, of Table 2.

Using the NNNL model, four structures had all dissimilarity parameters within the zero-one range, significantly rejected the MNL model and were not rejected by other NNNL structures. Of these, two included air and train in a nest, with and without bus; as for the McFadden model, the exclusion of bus has almost no effect on the model goodness of it and this model is dropped. The remaining models include train and bus, and air and car in separate nests (model 4), air and train (model 5) and air and bus (model 6) in a single nest. The model with air-bus in a nest has the best fit; however, the air-bus nest is illogical and the value of in-vehicle time implied by this model, $3 per hour, is unreasonably low. The log-likelihood values of the other NNNL models are somewhat greater than those for all of the McFadden models. This result raises the question of whether the NNNL model should be used despite the problem with respect to utility maximization and

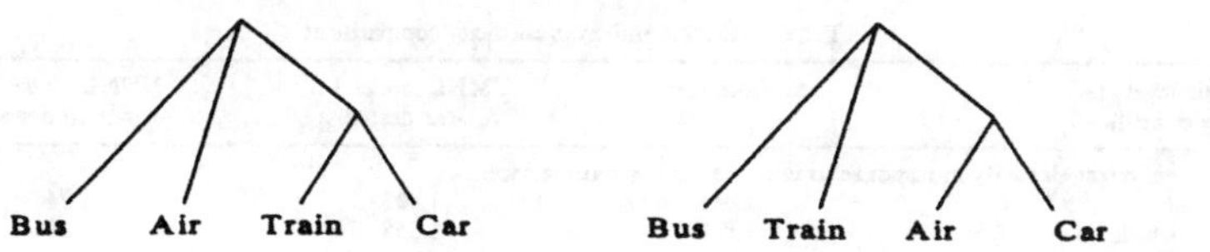

(a) Empirically identified nested model structures using the UMNL model

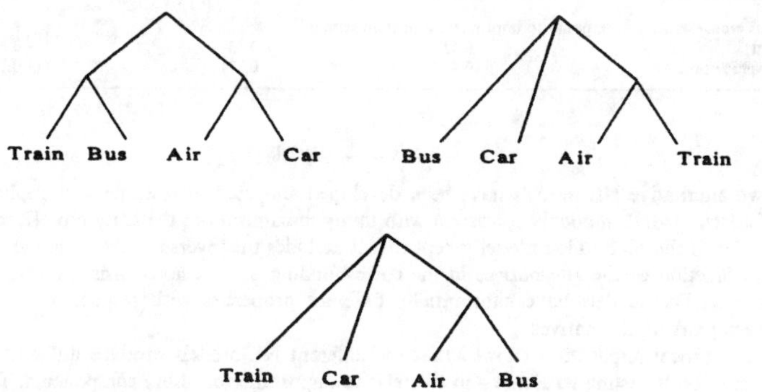

(b) Empirically identified nested model structures using the NNNL model

Fig. 2. Comparison of nesting structures obtained using the McFadden and Daly NL models.

interpretation. Our view is that preference be given to adopting the model with a strong theoretical foundation* and interpretability.

The estimation results for the McFadden and Daly models are very different. The preferred models in each case have different nesting structures (see Fig. 2) which implies different patterns of competitiveness among the alternatives. The direct elasticities of train and the cross- elasticities of air, car and bus with respect to a change in train cost and in-vehicle time are reported in Table 3 for UMNL model 3 and NNNL model 5. The emphasis in this table is placed on changes in train service because the original study was directed toward consideration of major improvements in rail service in the corridor. The direct elasticities for train and the cross- elasticities of each other mode with respect to changes in train service differ substantially between these models. These differences are due to differences in the preferred nesting structures, scale parameters and utility function parameters including differences in the relative values of level of service parameters (as indicated by the different values of time reported in Table 2). The cross- elasticities of the air, car and bus modes to changes in train service, an indication of the extent to which train improvements will impact air and bus revenues and reduce congestion at air terminals and on roadways, also differ substantially across models.

These results confirm that the use of the different NL model structures may lead to substantial differences in estimation results and the subsequent forecasts of train ridership and the sources of train riders under proposed futures. These differences may lead to very different decisions about whether and what service improvements to make.

*Screening of observations without a full set of alternatives does not impact the substantive results reported in this paper.

Table 3. Direct- and cross-elasticity comparisons

Train level of service attribute	MNL model	UMNL model 3 Air-car nested	NNNL model 5 Air-train nested
(a) Train direct-elasticity in response to improvement in train service			
Cost	2.045	1.402	1.744
In-vehicle time	1.809	1.555	1.614
(b). Air cross-elasticity in response to improvement in train service			
Cost	−0.486	−0.334	−0.603
In-vehicle time	−0.430	−0.371	−0.558
(c) Car cross-elasticity in response to improvement in train service			
Cost	−0.486	−0.334	−0.392
In-vehicle time	−0.430	−0.371	−0.362
(d) Bus cross-elasticity in response to improvement in train service			
Cost	−0.486	−0.334	−0.392
In-vehicle time	−0.430	−0.371	−0.362

5. CONCLUSIONS

Two alternative NL models have been developed and used in research and applications. The McFadden UMNL model is consistent with utility maximization; the Daly NNNL model, which is similar to the McFadden model except that it excludes the inverse of the scale parameter in the utility function of the alternatives in the corresponding nest, is not consistent with utility maximization. The models have substantially different properties with respect to competitiveness between pairs of alternatives.

An empirical application showed that the different NL models produce different results with respect to both nesting structure and the relative importance of utility components. This confirms the important differences which can result from the selection of the UMNL or NNNL models. We recommend use of the McFadden model because it is based on utility maximization, has intuitively reasonable elasticities and provides a clear interpretation of parameters across alternatives.

Acknowledgements—This research was supported, in part, by NSF Grant DMS-9313013 to the National Institute of Statistical Sciences and, in part, by a Dissertation Year Fellowship to the second author from The Transportation Center, Northwestern University. The quality of this paper was enhanced by suggestions, comments and critiques by Chandra Bhat, Christopher Fornash, James Ryan, Andrew Daly, Tom Adler, Carlos Daganzo and three anonymous referees.

REFERENCES

Aptech Systems (1993) *GAUSS: User's Guide*. Aptech Systems.

Ben-Akiva, M. and Francois, B. (1983) μ Homogeneous generalized extreme value model. Working paper, Department of Civil Engineering, MIT, Cambridge.

Ben-Akiva, M. and Lerman, S. R. (1985) *Discrete Choice Analysis: Theory and Application to Travel Demand*. The MIT Press, Cambridge.

Bierlaire, M. (1995) *A Robust Algorithm for the Simultaneous Estimation of Hierarchical Logit Models*. Technical Report, Department of mathematics, FUNDP, Namar, Belgium.

Bierlaire, M. and Vandevyvere, Y. (1995) *HieLoW: the Interactive User's Guide*. Transportation Research Group, FUNDP, Namur.

Börsch-Supan, A. (1990a) On the compatibility of nested logit models with utility maximization. *Journal of Econometrics* **32**, 371–387.

Börsch-Supan, A. (1990b) *HLOGIT Documentation*.

Brownstone, D. and Small, K. A. (1989) Efficient estimation of nested logit model. *Journal of Business and Economic Statistics* 7, 67–74.

Daly, A. (1987) Estimating 'tree' logit models. *Transportation Research* **21B**, 251–267.

Daly, A. and Zachary, S. (1978) Improved multiple choice models. In *Determinants of Travel Choice*, eds. D. A., Hensher and M. Q., Dalvi. Saxon House, Sussex.

Forinash, C. V. and Koppelman, F. S. (1993) Application and interpretation of nested logit models of intercity mode choice. *Transportation Research Record* 1413, 98–106.

Econometric Software (1996) *LIMDEP V7.0*. Econometric Software, Bellport NY.

Hague Consulting Group (1988) *ALOGIT: User's Guide*. HCG, The Hague.

Hague Consulting Group (1992) *ALOGIT: User's Guide*. HCG, The Hague.

Hague Consulting Group (1995) *ALOGIT: User's Guide*. HCG, The Hague.

Hensher, D. A. (1991) Efficient estimation of hierarchical logit mode choice model. *Proceedings of the Japanese Society of civil Engineering* **425**, 17–28.

Herriges, J. A. and Kling, C. L. (1996) Testing the consistency of nested logit models with utility maximization. *Economics Letters* **50**, 33–39.

Kling, C. L. and Herriges, J. A. (1995) An empirical investigation of the consistency of nested logit models with utility maximization. *American Journal of Agricultural Economics* **77**, 875–884.

McFadden, D. (1973) Conditional logit analysis of qualitative choice behavior. In *Frontiers in Econometrics*, ed. P. Zarembka. Academic Press, New York.

McFadden, D. (1978) Modeling the choice of residential location. *Transportation Research Record* **672**, 72–77.

McFadden, D. (1981) Econometric models of probabilistic choice. In *Structural Analysis of Discrete Data*, eds. C. F. Manski and D. McFadden. The MIT Press, Cambridge MA.

Ortuzar, J. D. (1983) Nested logit models for mixed-mode travel in urban corridors. *Transportation Research* **17A**, 283–299.

Yai, T., Iwakura, S. and Morichi, S. (1997) Multinomial probit with structured covariance for route choice behavior. *Transportation Research* **31B**, 195–207.

Journal of Econometrics 43 (1990) 373–388. North-Holland

ON THE COMPATIBILITY OF NESTED LOGIT MODELS WITH UTILITY MAXIMIZATION*

Axel BÖRSCH-SUPAN

University of Mannheim, D-6800 Mannheim, West Germany

The paper examines the relationship between the nested multinomial logit (NMNL) model and rational consumer behavior. We show that the Daly–Zachary–McFadden (DZM) condition of the validity of stochastic utility maximization in NMNL models is unnecessarily strong and leads too often to rejection of NMNL models with large dissimilarity parameters. In many cases, the distribution of the stochastic utility components in the NMNL model can be modified in a way that preserves the NMNL choice probabilities on a subset of R^I, where I is the number of alternatives in the choice set. On this subset, the DZM condition can be violated without violating the restrictions of stochastic utility maximization.

1. Introduction

Discrete choice models are increasingly popular in applied econometric work. Most popular is the multinomial logit (MNL) model which is easy to compute even for a large number of alternatives, but suffers from the 'independence of irrelevant alternatives'. The multinomial probit (MNP) model avoids this restriction but is computationally infeasible for problems with more than a few alternatives. McFadden (1978) introduced the nested multinomial logit (NMNL) model as a compromise between functional flexibility and computational feasibility. This model has since enjoyed a larger number of applications particularly in the analysis of transportation policies.

In general, all of the above models have structural microeconomic interpretations as demand functions derived from stochastic utility maximization [McFadden (1981)]. For the NMNL model, however, certain restrictions on the parameters that control the correlation among unobserved attributes have to be satisfied for this interpretation to hold. This is frequently not the case in practical applications.

The aforementioned parameter conditions (the Daly–Zachary–McFadden [DZM] condition) essentially guarantee the nonnegativity of the density function that characterizes the NMNL model. The frequent violation of the DZM

*This paper owes much to many very helpful discussions with Dan McFadden and the comments by two anonymous referees. All remaining errors are mine. The research was conducted at the J.F. Kennedy School of Government at Harvard University. Partial financial support by the National Science Foundation is gratefully acknowledged.

0304-4076/90/$3.50

condition may be interpreted as a weakness of the specification of this density function, i.e., the functional form of the NMNL model. Because in all discrete choice models the underlying density function should just be viewed as an approximation to something much more complicated, we propose a slight modification of the NMNL model that extends its applicability to many cases in which the DZM condition does not hold.

This modification consists of constructing an underlying distribution function for the stochastic component of the choice model which is nonnegative in R^I and coincides with the distribution function of the NMNL model on a subset of R^I, where I is the number of alternatives in the choice set. On this subset, the DZM condition can be violated without violating the restrictions of stochastic utility maximization. This set can be characterized by signs of derivatives of choice probabilities. For two-level NMNL models with few alternatives per branch, the sign conditions reduce to very simple expressions.

The paper proceeds in three steps. First, we briefly review the hypothesis of stochastic utility maximization and the NMNL model. Second, we illustrate the above-mentioned construction in a simple example. Finally, we generalize this construction to a broad class of discrete choice models and apply the results on two-level NMNL models.

2. Stochastic utility maximization

We assume a sample of T consumers, each choosing among I discrete alternatives. Each alternative i provides utility u_{it} to consumer t. Utility u_{it} consists of a deterministic component v_{it} (usually specified as a linear combination $\sum_{k=1,\dots,K} X_{it}^k \beta^k$ of K characteristics X_{it}^k with β to be estimated) and an additive disturbance ε_{it}:

$$u_{it} = v_{it} + \varepsilon_{it}. \tag{1}$$

A consumer is said to maximize his stochastic utility [McFadden (1981)] if he prefers alternative i over alternative j if and only if

$$u_{it} > u_{jt}. \tag{2}$$

Relations (1) and (2) imply the probability that consumer t chooses alternative i from the set of all I alternatives:

$$P_i(v_t) = \int_{\varepsilon_{it}=-\infty}^{\infty} \int_{\{\varepsilon_{jt} | \varepsilon_{jt} < \varepsilon_{it} + v_{it} - v_{1t},\ j=1,\dots,I,\ j \neq i\}} \mathrm{d}F(\varepsilon_t), \tag{3}$$

where F denotes the joint c.d.f. of $\varepsilon_t = (\varepsilon_{1t},\ldots,\varepsilon_{It})$, assumed to be i.i.d. across consumers, and $v_t = (v_{1t},\ldots,v_{It})$.

For F multivariate normal, eq. (3) defines the choice probabilities of the multinomial probit (MNP) model; for F extreme value distributed and i.i.d. across alternatives, eq. (3) generates the multinomial logit (MNL) model.

Eq. (3) shows that a discrete choice model can equivalently be specified by the c.d.f. F of the stochastic utility components ε_i, $i = 1,\ldots,I$, or a set of choice probabilities $\{P_i | i = 1,\ldots,I\}$. We will call F the generating function of the P_i. Any c.d.f. will generate a discrete choice model. However, the multiple integral in eq. (3) may be impractical to evaluate as in the case of multinomial probit models for more than four alternatives. In turn, any set of choice probabilities that satisfies a set of compatibility conditions defines a stochastic utility maximization model with an implied joint distribution of the stochastic utility components. These compatibility conditions are [Williams (1977), Daly and Zachary (1979), McFadden (1981)]:

$$P_i(v) \geq 0, \quad \sum_{i=1,\ldots,I} P_i(v) = 1, \quad P_i(v) = P_i(v+\alpha) \quad \text{for all} \quad \alpha \in R, \tag{4}$$

$$\partial P_i(v)/\partial v_j = \partial P_j(v)/\partial v_i, \tag{5}$$

$$\partial^{(I-1)} P_i(v)/\partial v_1 \ldots [\partial v_i] \ldots \partial v_I \geq 0.^1 \tag{6}$$

Condition (4) represents the basic requirements of nonnegativity and adding-up of the I choice probabilities as well as the dependence of the comparison only on the differences in utilities ('translation invariance'). Condition (5) guarantees the integrability of the P_i and is a straightforward analogue to the Slutsky condition in continuous demand analysis. Condition (6) is the essential requirement for the implied distribution function to be properly defined, i.e., to have a nonnegative density function.

3. The nested multinomial logit model

In the nested multinomial logit model [NMNL, McFadden (1978)], the I alternatives are grouped in K subsets, each consisting of $I(k)$ alternatives.[2]

[1] The square brackets denote a term to be left out.

[2] More levels of nesting can be introduced to impose a hierarchical structure of correlations on the choice set. To simplify the notation, only two-level models are considered in this paper. However, the theory outlined below applies to NMNL models of all levels.

We will denote such a hierarchical choice model ('tree') by $T(I(1),\ldots, I(K))$. The choice can be visualized as first among the K subsets, then among the $I(k)$ alternatives in the chosen subset k. The NMNL choice probabilities can be decomposed into

$$P_i(v) = Q_k(v) \cdot P_{i|k}(v), \tag{7}$$

where Q_k denotes the marginal choice probability of subset k and $P_{i|k}$ the conditional probability of choosing alternative i among the $I(k)$ alternatives in subset k. Q_k and $P_{i|k}$ have the familiar functional form of simple conditional logit choice probabilities [McFadden (1978)]:

$$P_i(v) = \frac{\exp(v_i/\theta_k)}{\mathrm{E}(k)} \cdot \frac{\mathrm{E}(k)^{\theta_k}}{\sum_{j=1,\ldots,K} \mathrm{E}(j)^{\theta_j}}. \tag{8}$$

Here $\mathrm{E}(k) = \sum_{i=J(k),\ldots,J(k)+I(k)-1} \exp(-v_i/\theta_k)$ denotes the exponent of the so-called inclusive value of subset k, $J(k)$ the index of the first alternative in this subset, and θ_k the so-called dissimilarity parameter of subset k. In terms of the c.d.f. in eq. (3), the NMNL model parametrizes the generating function F by the dissimilarity parameters θ_k:

$$F_{\mathrm{NMNL}}(\varepsilon;\theta) = \exp\left\{ - \sum_{k=1}^{K} \left[\sum_{i=1}^{I(k)} \exp(-\varepsilon_i)^{1/\theta_k} \right]^{\theta_k} \right\}. \tag{9}$$

Each θ_k not equal to one introduces a nonzero correlation among the disturbances ε_i within subset k. Therefore, the NMNL model overcomes the assumption of i.i.d. disturbances across alternatives, the so-called 'independence of irrelevant alternatives', that is the major disadvantage of the MNL model.

The compatibility of the NMNL model with the stochastic utility maximization hypothesis can be established by verifying conditions (4) through (6). Only condition (6) is restrictive and equivalent to

$$0 < \theta_k \leq 1, \qquad k = 1,\ldots, K, \tag{10}$$

if condition (6) is to be valid for *all* deterministic utility components $v \in R^I$

[McFadden (1979), Daly and Zachary (1979), referred to as DZM condition]. Only if condition (10) is satisfied is the generating function F a proper cumulative distribution function.

The dissimilarity parameters θ_k are usually estimated from the data by maximum likelihood methods. The second inequality in condition (10) is quite frequently violated in empirical analysis.[3] A violation may be interpreted as a misspecification of choice model (3), for instance an unsuitable choice of the generating function F. On the other hand, the requirement that condition (6) holds for all $v \in R^I$ may be overly restrictive because economic theory usually restricts the set of data points that are sensible for a specific application of the choice model to a subset of R^I.

4. A three-alternative example

The following example shows the potential for a reconciliation of NMNL models with the stochastic utility maximization hypothesis. We will illustrate the effect of $\theta_k > 1$ in the simplest case of a three-alternative NMNL model in which the first two alternatives constitute a group, denoted by $T(2,1)$. This model is generated by the cumulative distribution function

$$F(\varepsilon) = \exp\left\{ -\left[\exp(-\varepsilon_1/\theta) + \exp(-\varepsilon_2/\theta)\right]^{\theta} - \exp(-\varepsilon_3)\right\}. \tag{11}$$

Because of translation invariance [condition (4)], we can reduce F to the two-dimensional space of differences without losing information. Define the differences $\eta_1 = \varepsilon_2 - \varepsilon_1$ and $\eta_2 = \varepsilon_3 - \varepsilon_1$. Their joint distribution function is

$$G(\eta) = \frac{\left(1 + \exp(-\eta_1/\theta)\right)^{\theta - 1}}{\left(1 + \exp(-\eta_1/\theta)\right)^{\theta} + \exp(-\eta_2)}. \tag{12}$$

We define as pseudo-density the function $g = \partial^2 G/\partial\eta_1\partial\eta_2$,

$$g(\eta) = \frac{\left(1 + \exp(-\eta_1/\theta)\right)^{\theta}}{\left(1 + \exp(-\eta_1/\theta)\right)^{\theta} + \exp(-\eta_2)}$$

$$\cdot \exp(-\eta_2) \cdot \exp(-\eta_1/\theta) \cdot \Delta, \tag{13}$$

[3]Examples are: McFadden, Talvitie, and Associates (1977), Coslett (1978), Small and Brownstone (1982), Hensher (1984), Börsch-Supan (1985).

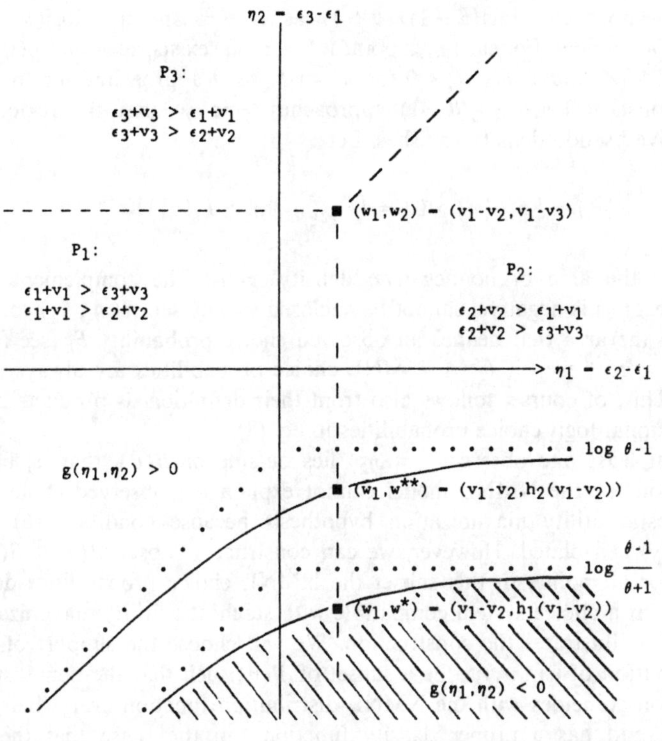

Fig. 1. Choice probabilities at deterministic utility (v_1, v_2, v_3) and density function of the trinary NMNL model defined by $F(\varepsilon_1, \varepsilon_2, \varepsilon_3) = \exp\{-[\exp(-\varepsilon_1/\theta) + \exp(-\varepsilon_2/\theta)]^\theta - \exp(-\varepsilon_3)\}$.

where the discriminant term Δ,

$$\Delta = \frac{2(1+\exp(-\eta_1/\theta))^\theta}{(1+\exp(-\eta_1/\theta))^\theta + \exp(\eta_2)} - \frac{\theta-1}{\theta} = 2\cdot Q_1 - \frac{\theta-1}{\theta}, \qquad (14)$$

signs the pseudo-density $g(\eta)$.

If $\theta < 1$, then $\Delta > 0$ and $g(\eta)$ represents a proper density function. However, if $\theta > 1$, then

$$g(\eta) > 0 \Leftrightarrow \eta_2 > h_1(\eta_1) = \log\frac{\theta-1}{\theta+1} - \theta\log\left[1 + \exp\left(-\frac{\eta_1}{\theta}\right)\right]. \qquad (15)$$

The function $h_1(\eta_1)$ defined by $g(\eta_1, \eta_2) = 0$ is plotted in fig. 1. For $\theta > 1$,

$h_1(\eta_1)$ approaches $\log[(\theta-1)/(\theta+1)]$ as $\eta_1 \to \infty$ and $\eta_1 - \log[(\theta-1)/(\theta+1)]$ as $\eta_1 \to -\infty$. For each η_1, a point $w^* = h_1(\eta_1)$ exists, such that $g(\eta_1, \eta_2) \geq 0$ for $\eta_2 \geq w^*$ and $g(\eta_2, \eta_2) < 0$ for $\eta_2 < w^*$. As θ approaches one from above, the constant $\log(\theta - 1/\theta + 1)$ approaches $-\infty$ so that the region with a negative pseudo-density vanishes. Let

$$B(\theta) = \{\eta | g(\eta) \geq 0\} = \{(\eta_2, \eta_2) | \eta_2 \geq h_1(\eta_1)\} \tag{16}$$

denote the area of nonnegative 'density' $g(\eta)$. The complement of $B(\theta)$ [where $g(\eta)$ is negative] cannot be enclosed by any set of (η_1, η_2) corresponding to the area that defines an observed choice probability P_i (see fig. 1). In other words, even if $\theta > 1$, NMNL choice probabilities are always nonnegative. This, of course, follows also from their definition as products of simple conditional logit choice probabilities in eq. (8).

If at least one observed (η_1, η_2) lies outside of $B(\theta)$, that is, below the function h_1, the NMNL model cannot explain the observed choices by the stochastic utility maximization hypothesis because condition (6) (positive density) is violated. However, we can construct a subset $A(\theta) \subset B(\theta)$, such that for all points in this subset the NMNL choice probabilities do indeed represent a choice system compatible with stochastic utility maximization.

Fig. 1 illustrates the construction. We will choose the support of the new distribution of (η_1, η_2) to be a subset of $B(\theta)$ such that the new distribution function coincides with the NMNL distribution function everywhere on that subset and has a proper density function – in the sense that the density function is nonnegative in the entire domain R^I and integrates to one.

For each point (η_1, η_2), define

$$L(\eta_1, \eta_2) = \int_{-\infty}^{\eta_2} g(\eta_1, y)\,\mathrm{d}y. \tag{17}$$

Because of (15) and (16), $L(\eta_1, \eta_2) < 0$ for $\eta_2 < h_1(\eta_1)$. For each η_1, the continuity of $g(\eta)$ implies the existence of a point $w^{**} = h_2(\eta_1)$ such that $L(\eta) \geq 0$ for $\eta_2 \geq w^{**}$. Evaluating $L(\eta_1, \eta_2)$ yields

$$L(\eta) > 0 \Leftrightarrow \eta_2 > h_2(\eta_1) = \log(\theta - 1) - \theta \log[1 + \exp(-\eta_1/\theta)]. \tag{18}$$

The set $A(\theta)$, defined by

$$A(\theta) = \{\eta | L(\eta) \geq 0\} = \{(\eta_1, \eta_2) | \eta_2 \geq h_2(\eta_1)\}, \tag{19}$$

is the region where the NMNL model can be reconciled with utility maximization. Define a modified density function

$$g^*(\eta) = g(\eta) \quad \text{if} \quad \eta \in A(\theta), \qquad = 0 \quad \text{otherwise.} \tag{20}$$

This amounts to offsetting the 'negative mass' outside $B(\theta)$ with the positive mass in $B(\theta)\setminus A(\theta)$ in a way that preserves the NMNL choice probabilities in $A(\theta)$:

$$\begin{aligned} P_1(\eta_1, \eta_2) &= \int_{x=-\infty}^{\eta_1} \int_{y=-\infty}^{\eta_2} g^*(x, y)\,\mathrm{d}y\,\mathrm{d}x \\ &= \int_{x=-\infty}^{\eta_1} \left(\int_{y=-\infty}^{h_2(\eta_1)} g^*(x, y)\,\mathrm{d}y + \int_{y=h_2(\eta_1)}^{\eta_2} g^*(x, y)\,\mathrm{d}y \right) \mathrm{d}x \\ &= \int_{x=-\infty}^{\eta_1} \left(L(\eta_1, h_2(\eta_1)) + \int_{y=h_2(\eta_1)}^{\eta_2} g(x, y)\,\mathrm{d}y \right) \mathrm{d}x \\ &= \int_{x=-\infty}^{\eta_1} \int_{y=-\infty}^{\eta_2} g(x, y)\,\mathrm{d}y\,\mathrm{d}x \quad \text{if} \quad (\eta_1, \eta_2) \in A(\theta). \end{aligned}$$

For points in $A(\theta)$, the new choice model defined by g^* is equivalent to the NMNL model. For points outside of $A(\theta)$, the choice probabilities will in general be different from those of the NMNL model because in $B(\theta)\setminus A(\theta)$ $0 = g^* \leq g$ and elsewhere $g \leq g^* = 0$. However, g^* is a proper density function in the entire domain R^I.

There are, of course, many other ways to construct supports that yield proper density functions. For instance, renormalizing $g(\eta_1, \eta_2)$ in $B(\theta)$ yields the largest possible support and a continuous density function [g^* is discontinuous on the boundary of $A(\theta)$]. However, the attractiveness of the proposed construction is that it exactly reproduces NMNL choice probabilities on its support. The possibility of this construction therefore reconciles the use of NMNL choice probabilities even if $\theta > 1$ as long as all relevant data is contained in $A(\theta)$.[4]

[4]Relevant data points include all observed and projected deterministic utility components v_i. In general, the v_i will be linear combinations $X_i\beta$ of characteristics X_i for alternative i, see eq. (1). The coefficients β will be estimated from a data set (d_i, X_i) that includes the dependent indicator variable for alternative i, d_i.

Because of

$$L(v)=\int_{y=-\infty}^{v_2} g(v_1,y)\,\mathrm{d}y$$

$$=\frac{\partial}{\partial v_1}\int_{x=-\infty}^{v_1}\int_{y=-\infty}^{v_2} g(x,y)\,\mathrm{d}y\,\mathrm{d}x$$

$$=\frac{\partial}{\partial v_1}P_1(v_1,v_2),$$

the inclusion of (v_1, v_2) in $A(\theta)$ can easily be checked by evaluating the first derivative of a choice probability:

$$\frac{\partial}{\partial v_1}P_1(v_1,v_2)=C\cdot\left(Q_1(v_1,v_2)-\frac{1-\theta}{\theta}\right),\qquad C>0. \tag{21}$$

Therefore, the above compatibility condition can also be interpreted as a restriction on the admissable choice probabilities that is satisfied whenever the choice probability of the first subset is sufficiently large. Eq. (21) also implies that the set $A(\theta)$ is not empty in the three-alternative, two-subset nested choice model $T(2,1)$ with $0<\theta<\infty$.

5. General case

The above construction can be generalized. We first prove a local compatibility theorem that is valid for any discrete choice model.

Theorem 1. *Let* $\{P_i | i=1,\ldots,I\}$ *define a system of choice probabilities satisfying the adding-up and translation invariance conditions* (4) *and* (5), *but not necessarily the global nonnegativity condition* (6).

Let $A=[a_1,b_1]\times\cdots\times[a_I,b_I]$ *be an I-dimensional interval.*

If for all $v\in A$ *the choice probabilities* $\{P_i(v)|i=1,\ldots,I\}$ *have nonnegative mixed partial derivatives of any order up to* $I-1$, *then these choice probabilities define a discrete choice model compatible with stochastic utility maximization even when the generating function F is not a proper c.d.f. because its associated pseudo-density f is negative in the complement of A.*

Proof. Let $v=(v_1,\ldots,v_I)$ be a point in A. Because of translation invariance [condition (4)], we can map v, A, and F into the $(I-1)$-dimensional space of differences relative to the first alternative:

$$w_i = v_1 - v_i, \qquad i = 2, \dots, I,$$

$$C = [c_2, d_2] \times \cdots \times [c_I, d_I],$$

$$c_i = \min(a_i - b_1, b_i - a_1), \quad d_i = \max(a_i - b_1, b_i - a_1), \quad i = 2, \dots, I,$$

$$G_1(w_2, \dots, w_I) = \int_{-\infty}^{\infty} D_1 F(z, w_2 + z, \dots, w_I + z)\, \mathrm{d}z.$$

With these definitions [McFadden (1981, eq. (5.3))],

$$\begin{aligned} P_1(v) &= P_1(0, v_2 - v_1, \dots, v_I - v_1) \\ &= G^1(v_1 - v_2, \dots, v_1 - v_I) = G^1(w) \end{aligned} \tag{22}$$

and

$$\begin{aligned} P_1(v) &= \int_{\varepsilon_1 = -\infty}^{\infty} \int_{\varepsilon_2 = -\infty}^{\varepsilon_1 + v_1 - v_2} \cdots \int_{\varepsilon_I = -\infty}^{\varepsilon_1 + v_1 - v_I} f(\varepsilon)\, \mathrm{d}\varepsilon \\ &= \int_{\eta_2 = -\infty}^{w_2} \cdots \int_{\eta_I = -\infty}^{w_I} g^1(\eta)\, \mathrm{d}\eta. \end{aligned} \tag{23}$$

Consider the first choice probability for $w \in C$. Only points with $w_i < d_i$ are relevant. Define

$$g^{1,*}(w) = \begin{cases} g^1(w) \quad \text{if} \quad w_i > c_i \quad \text{for all} \quad i = 2, \dots, I, \\ \dfrac{\partial^{I-2}}{\partial w_2 \dots [\partial w_j] \dots \partial w_I} P_1(w) \\ \qquad\qquad \text{if} \quad w_j = c_j, \quad w_i > c_i \quad \text{for} \quad i = 2, \dots, I, \quad i \neq j, \\ \dots \\ \dfrac{\partial}{\partial w_j} P_1(w) \quad \text{if} \quad w_i = c_i \quad \text{for} \quad i = 2, \dots, I, \quad i \neq j, \quad w_j > c_j, \\ P_1(w) \quad \text{if} \quad w_i = c_i \quad \text{for all} \quad i = 2, \dots, I, \\ 0 \quad \text{if} \quad w_i < c_i \quad \text{for at least one} \quad i = 2, \dots, I. \end{cases} \tag{24}$$

The derivatives of the choice probabilities are nonnegative by assumption, consequently, $g^{1,*} \geq 0$.

Furthermore,

$$
\begin{aligned}
P_1(v) &= \int_{\eta_2=-\infty}^{w_2} \cdots \int_{\eta_I=-\infty}^{w_I} g^1(\eta)\,\mathrm{d}\eta \\
&= \int_{-\infty}^{c_2} \cdots \int_{-\infty}^{c_I} g^1(\eta)\,\mathrm{d}\eta \\
&\quad + \int_{c_2}^{w_2}\int_{-\infty}^{c_3} \cdots \int_{-\infty}^{c_I} g^1(\eta)\,\mathrm{d}\eta + \cdots + \int_{-\infty}^{c_2} \ldots \int_{-\infty}^{c_{I-1}} \int_{c_I}^{w_I} g^1(\eta)\,\mathrm{d}\eta \\
&\quad + \cdots + \\
&\quad + \int_{c_2}^{w_2} \ldots \int_{c_{I-1}}^{w_{I-1}} \int_{-\infty}^{c_I} g^1(\eta)\,\mathrm{d}\eta + \cdots + \int_{-\infty}^{c_2} \int_{c_3}^{w_3} \ldots \int_{c_I}^{w_I} g^1(\eta)\,\mathrm{d}\eta \\
&\quad + \int_{c_2}^{w_2} \cdots \int_{c_I}^{w_I} g^1(\eta)\,\mathrm{d}\eta \\
&= P_1(c) + \int_{c_2}^{w_2} \frac{\partial}{\partial w_2} P_1(\eta_2, w_3, \ldots, w_I)\,\mathrm{d}\eta_2 + \cdots \\
&\quad + \int_{c_I}^{w_I} \frac{\partial}{\partial w_I} P_1(w_2, \ldots, w_{I-1}, \eta_I)\,\mathrm{d}\eta_I \\
&\quad + \cdots + \\
&\quad + \int_{c_3}^{w_3} \ldots \int_{c_I}^{w_I} \frac{\partial^{(I-2)}}{\partial w_3 \ldots \partial w_I} P_1(w_2, \eta_3, \ldots, \eta_I)\,\mathrm{d}\eta_3 \ldots \mathrm{d}\eta_I + \cdots \\
&\quad + \int_{c_2}^{w_2} \ldots \int_{c_{I-1}}^{w_{I-1}} \frac{\partial^{(I-2)}}{\partial w_2 \ldots \partial w_{I-1}} P_1(\eta_2, \ldots, \eta_{I-1}, w_I)\,\mathrm{d}\eta_2 \ldots \mathrm{d}\eta_{I-1} \\
&\quad + \int_{c_2}^{w_2} \cdots \int_{c_I}^{w_I} g^1(\eta)\,\mathrm{d}\eta \\
&= \int_{-\infty}^{w_2} \cdots \int_{-\infty}^{w_I} g^{1,*}(\eta)\,\mathrm{d}\eta,
\end{aligned}
$$

which shows that the choice model based on $g^{1,*}$ generates the same choice probability of the first alternative as the original choice model based on g^1. Analogous arguments show the possibility of defining density functions that preserve the other choice probabilities. These definitions trivially coincide in the complement of A. It remains to be shown that the definitions are compatible with each other in the interior and at the boundary of A. Using the Slutsky condition (5), this follows from[5]

$$\frac{\partial}{\partial w_1}\cdots\left[\frac{\partial}{\partial w_i}\right]\frac{\partial}{\partial w_j}\frac{\partial}{\partial w_I}\int_{\eta_1=-\infty}^{w_1}\left[\int_{\eta_i=-\infty}^{w_i}\right]$$

$$\times\cdots\int_{\eta_I=-\infty}^{w_I} g^{i,*}(\eta)\,\mathrm{d}\eta$$

$$=\frac{\partial}{\partial w_1}\cdots\left[\frac{\partial}{\partial w_i}\right]\cdots\frac{\partial}{\partial w_j}\cdots\frac{\partial}{\partial w_I}P_i(w)$$

$$=\frac{\partial}{\partial w_1}\cdots\frac{\partial}{\partial w_i}\cdots\left[\frac{\partial}{\partial w_j}\right]\cdots\frac{\partial}{\partial w_I}P_j(w)$$

$$=\frac{\partial}{\partial w_1}\cdots\frac{\partial}{\partial w_i}\cdots\left[\frac{\partial}{\partial w_j}\right]\cdots\frac{\partial}{\partial w_I}\int_{\eta_1=-\infty}^{w_1}\cdots\left[\int_{\eta_j=-\infty}^{w_j}\right]$$

$$\times\cdots\int_{\eta_I=-\infty}^{w_I} g^{j,*}(\eta)\,\mathrm{d}\eta.$$

Hence f^*, defined by

$$g^{1,*}(\eta_2,\ldots,\eta_I)=\int_{-\infty}^{\infty} D_1 f^*(z,\eta_i+z,\ldots,\eta_I+z)\,\mathrm{d}z,$$

is a well-defined function that generates the same choice probabilities in A as the original f. Because the original model satisfied the adding-up condition (4), f^* integrates to one. Nonnegativity was shown above. Hence f^* is also a proper density function which finishes the proof. Q.E.D.

[5]The square brackets denote terms to be left out. The argument shown applies to the interior points of $A(\theta)$. Leaving out one or more integrations yields the compatibility of the derivatives in definition (24).

For practical purposes, it has to be checked whether the nonnegativity condition of Theorem 1 is satisfied in an interval which contains all relevant deterministic utility components. In general, this involves evaluating all mixed partial derivatives of all choice probabilities up to order $I-1$, a number that increases combinatorially.

However, in the case of the nested multinomial logit model, the tree-like structure yields much more convenient conditions that involve derivatives of the choice probabilities of order less than the number of alternatives in each subset. Also, these derivatives have simple functional forms, namely mixed polynomials in the marginal choice probabilities of these subsets. Taking first derivatives, we obtain a generalization of eq. (21) that applied to the simple trinary model $T(2,1)$.

Theorem 2. In two-level NMNL models, a necessary criterion for the nonnegativity condition in Theorem 1 are sufficiently large marginal choice probabilities of the subsets of similar alternatives:

$$Q_k \geq (1-\theta_k)/\theta_k, \qquad k=1,\ldots,K. \tag{25}$$

Proof. Using the definitions in eq. (8),

$$\frac{\partial P_{J(k)}}{\partial y_{J(k)+1}} = \frac{\partial}{\partial y_{J(k)+1}} \frac{\mathrm{E}(k)^{\theta_k-1}}{\sum\limits_{j=1,\ldots,K} \mathrm{E}(j)^{\theta_j}}$$

$$= \exp(-y_{J(k)+1}/\theta_k)\cdot \frac{\mathrm{E}(k)^{\theta_k-2}}{\sum \mathrm{E}(j)^{\theta_j}} \cdot \left\{ \frac{1-\theta_k}{\theta_k} + \frac{\mathrm{E}(k)^{\theta_k}}{\sum \mathrm{E}(j)^{\theta_j}} \right\},$$

and the term in curled parentheses equals (25). Q.E.D.

As opposed to the case of the three-alternative, one-subset model $T(2,1)$, the condition in Theorem 2 is generally not sufficient. Furthermore, the K criteria in (25) may be conflicting for models with $K>1$. For instance, in the four-alternative, two-subset model $T(2,2)$, we obtain

$$Q_1 \geq (1-\theta_1)/\theta_1 \quad \text{and} \quad Q_2 = (1-Q_1) \geq (1-\theta_2)/\theta_2,$$

which cannot be satisfied if $\theta_1=\theta_2>2$.

Theorem 2 shows that it is not always possible to find a subset of data points in which the NMNL model can be reconciled with stochastic utility maximization. The following theorem presents a necessary and sufficient criterion for the nonnegative condition in Theorem 1.

Theorem 3. *Let $T(I(1),\ldots,I(K))$ denote a two-level nested multinomial logit model with K subsets of $I(k)$ alternatives. Let $g_I(1),\ldots,I(K)$ denote the pseudo-density function that generates the model $T(I(1),\ldots,I(K))$. Let $v=(v_1,\ldots,v_I)$ be a point in the interval $A\subset R^I$. The nonnegativity condition of Theorem 1 is satisfied if and only if all members in the set*

$$\{g_{n_1,\ldots,n_K}(Q_1(v),\ldots,Q_K(v);\theta_1,\ldots,\theta_K)$$
$$|0\le n_1\le I(1),\ldots,0\le n_K\le I(K)\} \tag{26}$$

are nonnegative at the marginal choice probabilities $Q_1(v),\ldots,Q_K(v)$. Moreover, the functions $g_{n_1,\ldots,n_K}$ are signed by mixed polynomials $h_{n_1,\ldots,n_K}$ in $Q_1,\ldots,Q_K$ of degree $I(1)-1,\ldots,I(K)-1$.

Proof. The proof is a simple, but tedious exercise of evaluating all derivatives in eq. (24), continuing the proof of Theorem 2. Note that the mixed derivatives

Table 1

Density-signing polynomials for some typical nested multinomial logit models.

NMNL-model	Density	Nontrivial derivatives
$T(2,1)$	h^1_{21}	h^1_2
$T(2,1,1)$	h^1_{211}	h^1_{21}, h^1_2
$T(2,2)$	h_{22}	$h^1_{21}, h^2_{21}, h^1_2, h^2_2$
$T(3,1)$	h^1_{31}	h^1_{21}, h^1_3, h^1_2
$T(3,2)$	h^{12}_{32}	$h^1_{31}, h_{22}, h^1_{21}, h^2_{21}, h^1_3, h^1_{21}, h^2_{21}$
$T(3,3)$	h_{33}	$h^{12}_{32}, h^{21}_{32}, h^1_{31}, h^2_{31}, h_{22}, h^1_{21}, h^2_{21}, h^1_3, h^1_2, h^2_2$

$h^i_2=h_2(Q_i,\theta_i)=Q_i+\tau_i$

$h^i_{21}=h_{21}(Q_i,\theta_i)=2\cdot Q_i+\tau_i$

$h^i_{211}=h_{211}(Q_i,\theta_i)=3\cdot Q_i+\tau_i$

$h^i_3=h_3(Q_i,\theta_i)=2\cdot Q_i^2+3\cdot\tau_i\cdot Q_i+\tau_i\cdot\sigma_i$

$h^i_{31}=h_{31}(Q_i,\theta_i)=6\cdot Q_i^2+6\cdot\tau_i\cdot Q_i+\tau_i\cdot\sigma_i$

$h_{22}=h_{22}(Q_1,Q_2,\theta_1,\theta_2)=6\cdot Q_1\cdot Q_2+2\tau_2\cdot Q_1+2\tau_1\cdot Q_2+\tau_1\cdot\tau_2$

$$h^{ij}_{32}=h_{32}(Q_i,Q_j,\theta_i,\theta_j)=24\cdot Q_i^2\cdot Q_j+6\cdot\tau_j\cdot Q_i^2+18\cdot\tau_i\cdot Q_i\cdot Q_j+6\cdot\tau_i\cdot\tau_j\cdot Q_i$$
$$+2\cdot\tau_i\cdot\sigma_i\cdot Q_j+\tau_i\cdot\sigma_i\cdot\tau_j$$

$$h_{33}=h_{33}(Q_1,Q_2,\theta_1,\theta_2)=120\cdot Q_1^2\cdot Q_2^2+72\cdot\tau_2\cdot Q_1^2\cdot Q_2+72\cdot\tau_1\cdot Q_1\cdot Q_2^2+54\cdot\tau_2\cdot\tau_1\cdot Q_1\cdot Q_2$$
$$+6\cdot\tau_1\cdot\sigma_1\cdot Q_2^2+6\cdot\tau_2\cdot\sigma_2\cdot Q_1^2+6\cdot\tau_1\cdot\sigma_1\cdot\tau_2\cdot Q_2+6\cdot\tau_2\cdot\sigma_2\cdot\tau_1\cdot Q_1$$
$$+\tau_1\cdot\sigma_1\cdot\tau_2\cdot\sigma_2$$

for $\tau_i=(\theta_i-1)/\theta_i$, $\sigma_i=(\theta_i-2)/\theta_i$

with respect to y_i and y_j are always nonnegative unless alternatives i and j belong in a common subset. Finally, repeated application of $\partial Q_k/\partial y_i = \exp(-y_i/\theta_m)\cdot \mathrm{E}(m)^{-1}\cdot\{Q_k(Q_m-\delta_{km})\}$ (Theorem 2) yields the signing part $h_{n_1,\ldots,n_K}$. Here, m denotes the subset of alternative i and $\delta_{km}=1$ for $k=m$, 0 otherwise. Q.E.D.

Theorem 3 reduces the evaluation of all mixed derivatives up to order $I-1$ of I choice probabilities to the evaluation of a much smaller set of mixed polynomials in the marginal probabilities of choosing subsets of similar alternatives. This set of mixed polynomials can be identified as the set of pseudo-density functions of all NMNL models that are generated by deleting one or more alternatives from the original model. Table 1 presents the sets of polynomials for some typical nested multinomial logit models.

6. Conclusions

We showed that the Daly–Zachary–McFadden condition of the validity of stochastic utility maximization in nested multinomial logit models is unnecessarily strong. Therefore we may too often reject NMNL models because of their large dissimilarity parameters.

Theorem 1 presents a weaker validity condition for large class of discrete choice systems that can be invoked when the domain of estimated and projected deterministic utilities can be restricted to a subset of R^I.

Theorem 3 applies this condition to NMNL models. Here, the condition has a convenient form that involves mixed polynomials in the marginal choice probabilities with degrees equal to the numbers of alternatives in each relevant subset minus one. Moreover, Theorem 2 provides a simple necessary condition for Theorem 1. It reveals that nested NMNL models with large dissimilarity parameters are only compatible with stochastic utility maximization when the marginal choice probabilities of subsets of similar alternatives are sufficiently large.

References

Börsch-Supan, Axel, 1985, Tenure choice and housing demand, in: Konrad Stahl and Raymond Struyk, eds., U.S. and German housing markets: Comparative economic analyses (Urban Institute Press, Washington, DC) 55–105.

Coslett, Stephen R., 1978, Efficient estimation of discrete choice models from choice based samples, Unpublished Ph.D. dissertation (University of California at Berkeley, CA).

Daly, Andrew and S. Zachary, 1979, Improved multiple choice models, in: David Hensher and Q. Dalvi, eds., Identifying and measuring the determinants of mode choice (Teakfield, London) 335–357.

Hensher, David A., 1984, Full information maximum likelihood estimation of a nested logit mode-choice model, Working paper no. 13, Dimensions of automobile demand project (Macquire University, North Ryde).

McFadden, Daniel, A. Talvitie, and Associates, 1977, Demand model estimation and validation: Urban travel demand forecasting project, Final report (Institute for Transportation Studies, University of California at Berkeley, CA).

McFadden, Daniel, 1978, Modelling the choice of residential location, in: A. Karlgvist, ed., Spatial interaction theory and residential location (North-Holland, Amsterdam) 75–96.

McFadden, Daniel, 1979, Quantitative methods for analyzing travel behavior of individuals: Some recent developments, in: David Hensher and P. Stopher, eds., Behavioral travel modeling (Croom Helm, London).

McFadden, Daniel, 1981, Econometric models of probabilistic choice, in: Charles F. Manski and Daniel McFadden, eds., Structural analysis of discrete data with econometric applications (MIT Press, Cambridge, MA) 198–272.

Small, Kenneth A. and David Brownstone, 1982, Efficient estimation of nested logit models: An application to trip timing, Economic research program research memorandum no. 296 (Princeton University, Princeton, NJ).

Williams, H., 1977, On the formation of travel demand models and economic evaluation measures of user benefit, Environment Planning A 9.

[21]

Transpn. Res.-B, Vol. 25B, No. 1, pp. 1-12, 1991
Printed in Great Britain.

0191-2615/91 $3.00+.00

ESTIMABILITY IN THE MULTINOMIAL PROBIT MODEL

DAVID S. BUNCH
Graduate School of Management, University of California, Davis, Davis, CA 95616, U.S.A.

(*Received* 11 *July* 1989; *in revised form* 15 *February* 1990)

Abstract – Random utility models often involve terms which represent alternative-specific errors, and the main attractive feature of the multinomial probit (MNP) model is that it allows a rather general covariance structure for these errors. However, since observed choices only reveal information regarding utility differences, and since scale cannot be determined, not all parameters in an arbitrary MNP specification may be identified. This paper examines identification restrictions that arise in the linear-in-parameters multinomial probit framework, and provides discussion and recommendations for estimation and analysis of probit normalizations.

1. INTRODUCTION

Recent advances in computational methods for estimating multinomial probit models have stimulated renewed interest on this topic: for example, McFadden (1989) and Pakes and Pollard (1989) suggest simulation methods which may lead to practical probit estimation codes for more than four alternatives. In addition, Kamakura (1989) demonstrates, via a simulation study, that the Mendell-Elston approximation to the multivariate normal CDF is more accurate than the Clark method, and may provide an alternative solution to the problem. Bunch and Kitamura (1989) corroborate Kamakura's results in a study using empirical data, and discuss improved algorithms for maximum likelihood estimation.

This paper considers another important practical issue, the problem of formulating multinomial probit (MNP) model specifications for which the parameters are estimable. A discussion of parameter estimability issues and some illustrative examples appear in section 3.1 of Daganzo (1979); however, the topic is difficult and no general comprehensive theory is offered by Daganzo, nor do we believe one is likely to be offered in the near future. The discussion and conclusions presented here focus on the linear-in-parameters MNP model with taste variation and correlated random errors. This framework is quite flexible and is consistent with many specifications discussed in the literature.

The identification difficulties which arise are primarily due to the random errors, which are usually associated with the effect of unobserved attributes on a choice object's utility. A general model specification includes the possibility of correlations among the utilities of objects which might share unobserved attributes. Unfortunately, information about the underlying utilities is available only through observation of discrete choices, which depend on *differences* of utilities. This, plus the issue of scaling, lead to restrictions on the number of estimable parameters.

The material presented here overlaps that of Dansie (1985) and Albright, Lerman, and Manski (1977), and is perhaps well-known to some (certainly not all) workers in the field. However, the extent to which this is true is unclear. Bunch and Kitamura (1989) give a brief review of empirical applications, and a significant proportion of them were found to contain model specification errors. This is important since misspecified models potentially compound the already troublesome computational difficulties inherent in computing MNP estimates, and could be a contributing factor to the relative dearth of successful empirical applications of MNP in the published literature.

2. LINEAR-IN-PARAMETERS MULTINOMIAL PROBIT MODELS

In this paper we will consider a standard discrete choice modeling situation in which an individual drawn at random from a population makes a choice from a set of J mutually exclusive alternatives. A common example in the transportation literature is the choice of mode for the work commute, where $J = 3$ or 4 and the alternatives consist of car, train, bus, shared ride, etc. Following McFadden (1981, 1989), assume that the utility of alternative j for individual n, U_{nj}, is given by the general form

$$U_{nj} = X_{nj}^T \alpha_n, \; j = 1, \ldots, J, \tag{1}$$

where X_{nj} *is a* K-vector of explanatory variables which may be a function of the attributes of alternative j and individual n. The K-vector α_n contains the taste weights for individual n, and may be rewritten as $\alpha_n = \theta + \delta_n$, where θ is the mean taste weight for the population and δ_n is the (unobserved) random deviation from the mean for individual n. (Ideally, θ and the distribution of δ_n would vary as an explicit function of the observed characteristics of the individual, but this consideration is usually suppressed for simplicity.)

In theory, utility should be a function of generic (or "real") attributes, and should not depend on nominal attributes such as the labels "car," "bus," etc. In practical applications it is also desirable for the model to include only generic variables, since the model may then be used more effectively in forecasting, especially for testing the effect of adding new choice alternatives. However, it has generally been observed that including alternative-specific dummy variables significantly improves the fit of discrete choice models. One interpretation is that unobserved attributes are often empirically correlated with the nominal labels of the alternatives (McFadden *et al.*, 1977). For example, the attributes "lack of flexibility," or "lack of comfort," might be correlated with the nominal label "bus."

Equation (1) readily accommodates the inclusion of dummy variables, which is the approach taken by Albright, Lerman, and Manski (1977). Alternatively, we may assume that X_{nj} in eqn (1) includes only generic variables, and add the additional terms μ_j and ϵ_{nj}, where μ_j is the mean of the alternative-specific errors, and ϵ_{nj} represents a random deviation from the mean. The ϵ_{nj} term may be regarded to include both the effects of unobserved attributes and any other sources of observation-specific random error. This gives the following model, expressed now in vector notation:

$$U_n = X_n^T(\theta + \delta_n) + \mu + \epsilon_n, \tag{2}$$

where $U_n, \mu, \epsilon_n \in \Re^J$, $\theta, \delta_n \in \Re^K$, and $X_n \in \Re^{K \times J}$. To get a multinomial probit model, one adds the theoretically appealing assumption that the random terms have multivariate normal distributions:

$$\delta_n \sim MVN(0, \Sigma_\delta), \; \Sigma_\delta \in \Re^{K \times K} \text{ and } \epsilon_n \sim MVN(0, \Sigma_\epsilon), \; \Sigma_\epsilon \in \Re^{J \times J}. \tag{3}$$

Note that in this formulation the δ and ϵ terms are assumed to be independent, which is slightly more restrictive that the model implied by eqn (1). This framework is consistent with Hausman and Wise (1978).

Now, the probability that individual n selects alternative j is given by the MNP model:

$$P(j \mid V_U(\theta, \mu, X_n), \Sigma_U(\Sigma_\delta, \Sigma_\epsilon, X_n)) = \text{Prob}[U_{nj} > U_{ni} \text{ for all } i \neq j] \tag{4a}$$

$$= \int_{u_j=-\infty}^{\infty} \int_{u_1=-\infty}^{u_j} \cdots \int_{u_{j-1}=-\infty}^{u_j} \int_{u_{j+1}=-\infty}^{u_j} \cdots \int_{u_J=-\infty}^{u_j} \phi(u \mid V_U, \Sigma_U) du_1 \cdots du_J \tag{4b}$$

where

$$V_U(\theta, \mu, X_n) = X_n^T\theta + \mu,$$

$$\Sigma_U(\Sigma_\delta, \Sigma_\epsilon, X_n) = X_n^T \Sigma_\delta X_n + \Sigma_\epsilon,$$

and $\phi(x \mid m, S)$ is the multivariate normal density function with mean m and covariance S. If we assume that Σ_δ and Σ_ϵ are positive definite then it is straightforward to show that

$\Sigma_U(\Sigma_\delta, \Sigma_\epsilon, X_n)$ is also positive definite, which is desirable for establishing regularity conditions: see Daganzo (1979), or, hereafter, "Daganzo."

The purpose of this paper is to discuss the issues and problems of specifying the linear-in-parameters MNP model so that all the parameters are estimable. A primary concern is specification of Σ_ϵ, which is especially important since most published applications of MNP focus exclusively on estimating the effects of observation-specific errors (i.e. they assume (2) with $\delta_n = 0$).

3. REDUCTION OF DIMENSION

As has been often noted, one of the difficulties with MNP is that it requires evaluation of the multivariate integral (4b), which does not have a closed form solution. The usual first step is to reduce the dimension of the integral from J to J-1 using the transformation discussed by Daganzo (1979, pp. 43–44 and pp. 94–95). Assume that we wish to compute $P(j \mid V_U(\theta, \mu, X), \Sigma_U(\Sigma_\delta, \Sigma_\epsilon, X))$ and define $\Delta_j \in \Re^{J-1 \times J}$ by

$$\Delta_j = \begin{array}{c} \\ 1 \\ 2 \\ 3 \\ \vdots \\ j-1 \\ j \\ \vdots \\ J-2 \\ J-1 \end{array} \left[\begin{array}{cccccccccc} 1 & 2 & 3 & \cdots & j-1 & j & j+1 & \cdots & J-1 & J \\ 1 & 0 & 0 & \cdots & 0 & -1 & 0 & \cdots & 0 & 0 \\ 0 & 1 & 0 & \cdots & 0 & -1 & 0 & \cdots & 0 & 0 \\ 0 & 0 & 1 & & 0 & -1 & 0 & \cdots & 0 & 0 \\ \vdots & \vdots & \vdots & & \vdots & \vdots & \vdots & & \vdots & \vdots \\ 0 & 0 & 0 & & 1 & -1 & 0 & & 0 & 0 \\ 0 & 0 & 0 & & 0 & -1 & 1 & & 0 & 0 \\ \vdots & \vdots & \vdots & & \vdots & \vdots & \vdots & & \vdots & \vdots \\ 0 & 0 & 0 & \cdots & 0 & -1 & 0 & \cdots & 1 & 0 \\ 0 & 0 & 0 & \cdots & 0 & -1 & 0 & \cdots & 0 & 1 \end{array} \right] . \tag{5}$$

The transformation $Z = \Delta_j U$ applied to (4) gives

$$\begin{aligned} P(j \mid V_U(\theta, \mu, X), \Sigma_U(\Sigma_\delta, \Sigma_\epsilon, X)) &= \text{Prob}\,[U_i - U_j < 0, i \neq j] \\ &= \Phi(0 \mid V_Z, \Sigma_Z) \end{aligned} \tag{6}$$

where

$$V_Z = \Delta_j V_U = \Delta_j(X^T\theta + \mu) = \Delta_j X^T\theta + \Delta_j\mu, \tag{7a}$$

$$\Sigma_Z = \Delta_j \Sigma_U \Delta_j^T = \Delta_j(X^T \Sigma_\delta X + \Sigma_\epsilon)\Delta_j^T = \Delta_j X^T \Sigma_\delta X \Delta_j^T + \Delta_j \Sigma_\epsilon \Delta_j^T; \tag{7b}$$

$Z, V_Z \in \Re^{J-1}$, $\Sigma_Z \in \Re^{(J-1)\times(J-1)}$, and Φ is the cumulative distribution function for the (J – 1)-dimensional multivariate normal distribution.

Define $m_j \in \Re^{J-1}$ by $m_j = \Delta_j\mu$ and $C_j \in \Re^{(J-1)\times(J-1)}$ by $C_j = \Delta_j\Sigma_\epsilon\Delta_j^T$, where C_j is symmetric. Consider the matrix $M_j \in \Re^{(J-1)\times(J-1)}$ which is obtained by taking Δ_j and deleting the Jth column; M_j is of full rank (i.e. rank $J - 1$). Next, without loss of generality choose alternative J as the "reference alternative." It is straightforward to show that $\Delta_j = M_j\Delta_J$ for all j, and hence $m_j = M_j m_J$ and $C_j = M_j C_J M_j^T$ for all j. It follows that (7) may be rewritten as

$$V_Z = \Delta_j X^T\theta + M_j m_J, \tag{8a}$$

$$\Sigma_Z = \Delta_j X^T \Sigma_\delta X \Delta_j^T + M_j C_J M_j^T, \tag{8b}$$

and thus choice probabilities evaluated via (6) may *always* by expressed in terms of m_J and C_J, which together contain $(J - 1) + J(J - 1)/2$ parameters. It follows that μ and Σ_ϵ together only have $(J - 1) + J(J - 1)/2$ identifiable parameters. As an illustration, consider the case $J = 3$ and $j = 2$, which gives (taking into account the symmetry of Σ_ϵ):

$$m_2 = \begin{bmatrix} \mu_1 - \mu_2 \\ \mu_3 - \mu_2 \end{bmatrix} = \begin{bmatrix} 1 & -1 \\ 0 & -1 \end{bmatrix} \begin{bmatrix} \mu_1 - \mu_3 \\ \mu_2 - \mu_3 \end{bmatrix} = M_2 m_3,$$

and

$$C_2 = \begin{bmatrix} \sigma_{11} - 2\sigma_{21} + \sigma_{22} & \sigma_{21} - \sigma_{31} - \sigma_{32} + \sigma_{22} \\ \sigma_{21} - \sigma_{31} - \sigma_{32} + \sigma_{22} & \sigma_{33} - 2\sigma_{31} + \sigma_{22} \end{bmatrix}$$

$$= \begin{bmatrix} 1 & -1 \\ 0 & -1 \end{bmatrix} \begin{bmatrix} \sigma_{11} - 2\sigma_{31} + \sigma_{33} & \sigma_{21} - \sigma_{31} - \sigma_{32} + \sigma_{33} \\ \sigma_{21} - \sigma_{31} - \sigma_{32} + \sigma_{33} & \sigma_{22} - 2\sigma_{32} + \sigma_{33} \end{bmatrix} \begin{bmatrix} 1 & 0 \\ -1 & -1 \end{bmatrix}$$

$$= M_2 C_3 M_2^T,$$

where the σ_{ij}'s denote the elements of Σ_ϵ.

In addition to these considerations, it turns out that one can also rescale the problem so as to eliminate another parameter. Specifically, evaluation of $\Phi(0 \mid kV_Z, k^2\Sigma_Z)$ gives the same result as evaluating $\Phi(0 \mid V_Z, \Sigma_Z)$, for $k > 0$. Hence, suitable selection of k can eliminate one more parameter. This leads to the assertion that the model (3) has a total of $K + K(K + 1)/2 + J + J(J - 1)/2 - 2$ identifiable parameters. Since θ, μ, Σ_δ, and Σ_ϵ together have $K + K(K + 1)/2 + J + J(J + 1)/2$ parameters, this implies that $J + 2$ parameters are inestimable and must be fixed via some normalization. (The fact that Σ_ϵ has only $J(J - 1)/2$ identifiable parameters was noted by Daganzo, who also recognized that one could sometimes eliminate another parameter by rescaling. Albright, Lerman, and Manski (1977) state the above result for the number of free parameters, referring the reader to technical memoranda.)

Note that for the binary probit model with no taste variation (i.e. $J = 2$ and $\delta = 0$), there are K taste weights, $J - 1$ alternative specific dummy variables, and $J(J - 1)/2 - 1 = 0$ free parameters in Σ_ϵ. Although this is generally known, even experienced investigators publishing in refereed journals can miss this point; for example, in a study of travel mode choice Johnson and Hensher (1982) erroneously assume that Σ_ϵ has one free parameter. In studies involving more complex MNP models, other authors have completely missed the requirements described above, and assume that all the parameters are in principle estimable. See, for example, Currim (1982) and van Lierop (1986). For a brief review of MNP empirical applications which includes further discussion, see Bunch and Kitamura (1989).

These restrictions have implications for practical estimation of MNP models. Recall that Daganzo discusses MNP in a slightly more general framework by considering the MNP function $P(j \mid V(\theta, A), \Sigma(\theta, A))$, where θ is a general parameter vector and A is a matrix of attributes. (Note, however, that many of his examples fit in the linear-in-parameters framework.) In discussing the practical issues of parameter estimation, he recommends that $\Sigma(\theta, A)$ be specified so as to be positive definite over all feasible values of θ, since otherwise it "would not represent a covariance matrix and the program would not return meaningful values." Daganzo recommends two possibilities:

(i) express $\Sigma(\theta, A)$ as a product of a matrix and its transpose (i.e. $\Sigma(\theta, A) = C(\theta, A)C(\theta, A)^T$),
(ii) express $\Sigma(\theta, A)$ as a function of θ and A directly, placing simple bounds on θ so as to ensure positive definiteness.

We may regard $C(\theta, A)$ to be lower triangular with positive diagonal elements (i.e. the Cholesky factorization of $\Sigma(\theta, A)$). For the case we are considering here, either of these approaches could be difficult when choosing a specification for Σ_U. Directly writing $\Sigma_U = CC^T$ is not practical if taste variation is included in the model. One could express each of Σ_δ and Σ_ϵ in terms of Cholesky factorizations, but this could be tricky for Σ_ϵ (or, Σ_U in the case of fixed tastes) since we have at most $J(J - 1)/2$ free parameters to work with in Σ_ϵ. For most of the following discussion, we will assume that we wish to choose a normalization which utilizes all available parameters.

Albright, Lerman, and Manski (1977), which we denote "ALM" in the sequel, deal with the issue by choosing one normalization from "among the alternative formally equivalent normalizations." First, they choose to express both Σ_δ and Σ_ϵ in terms of Cholesky factorizations. Next, they choose to fix J parameters by setting the last row (and column) of Σ_ϵ, and correspondingly, the last row of its Cholesky factorization, to zero. Finally, they choose to fix the scale of the specification by constraining the diagonal elements of Σ_ϵ so that (trace Σ_ϵ)/J equals the variance of the standard Weibull distribution. (This was done to facilitate comparisons between MNP and multinomial logit estimates.) Note that this is inconsistent with Daganzo's recommendation in the no-taste-variation case: this specification of Σ_ϵ, while a valid covariance matrix, is only positive semi-definite and hence violates Daganzo's regularity conditions.

In fact, ALM are doing slightly more than simply choosing an "arbitrary normalization": they are choosing to work directly in $(J-1)$-space, estimating C_J so that C_J is constrained to be positive definite (which implies that C_j for all $j \neq J$ must also be positive definite). This is a more general approach than choosing to perform the estimation using arbitrarily constrained formulations in the original J-dimensional space.

As an example, consider the case $J = 3$. For simplicity, we suppress the scaling issue at this stage: one can assume that scale has been fixed via elimination of a parameter component from either θ, μ, or Σ_δ. For $J = 3$ Σ_ϵ has $3(3-1)/2 = 3$ free parameters. The ALM normalization (with no rescaling) is given by:

$$\Sigma_\epsilon^{\mathrm{ALM}} = \begin{bmatrix} \sigma_{11} & \sigma_{21} & 0 \\ \sigma_{21} & \sigma_{22} & 0 \\ 0 & 0 & 0 \end{bmatrix}. \tag{9}$$

Another possible normalization, which assumes independence of the random errors, is given by a diagonal covariance matrix:

$$\Sigma_\epsilon^{\mathrm{D}} = \begin{bmatrix} \sigma_{11} & 0 & 0 \\ 0 & \sigma_{22} & 0 \\ 0 & 0 & \sigma_{33} \end{bmatrix}, \tag{10}$$

with $\sigma_{11}, \sigma_{22}, \sigma_{33} > 0$ to ensure positive definiteness. Now, suppose that a maximum likelihood estimation routine produces an estimate for C_J and returns the following result:

$$C_J = \begin{bmatrix} 1.5 & -0.4 \\ -0.4 & 1.2 \end{bmatrix}. \tag{11}$$

Then the ALM normalization is simply

$$\Sigma_\epsilon^{\mathrm{ALM}} = \begin{bmatrix} 1.5 & -0.4 & 0 \\ -0.4 & 1.2 & 0 \\ 0 & 0 & 0 \end{bmatrix}. \tag{12}$$

However, the corresponding $\Sigma_\epsilon^{\mathrm{D}}$ is computed to be:

$$\Sigma_\epsilon^{\mathrm{D}} = \begin{bmatrix} 1.9 & 0 & 0 \\ 0 & 1.6 & 0 \\ 0 & 0 & -0.4 \end{bmatrix}, \tag{13}$$

which is clearly not a valid covariance matrix. Problems could arise if the estimation routine were attempting to directly estimate the diagonal normalization: a boundary solution would probably be the result.

It seems clear that the best course to follow is to first estimate C_J, and to then explore the various possible normalizations by performing transformations between C_J and Σ_ϵ. If any particular specification is inappropriate, it will show up as an invalid covariance matrix without jeopardizing the performance of the estimation routine. In addition, the possibility of accidentally choosing an inestimable normalization will be minimized, since the process of analyzing the transformation will reveal the mistake. This is discussed next.

4. TRANSFORMATIONS

As above, assume for now that fixing the scale is not an issue. In addition, assume that the specifications we are considering are fairly simple, (i.e. parameters do not appear simultaneously across θ, μ, Σ_δ, Σ_ϵ). (Although this restriction is not necessary, it greatly simplifies the analysis and discussion.) In what follows, it will often be convenient to regard symmetric matrices as vectors in packed storage form (e.g. when $J = 3$ then $\Sigma_\epsilon \in \Re^{J(J+1)/2}$ with $\Sigma_\epsilon = (\sigma_{11}, \sigma_{21}, \sigma_{22}, \sigma_{31}, \sigma_{32}, \sigma_{33})^T$, and $C_J \in \Re^{(J-1)J/2}$ with $C_J = (c_{11}, c_{21}, c_{22})^T$).

Suppose that $\beta \in \Re^{(J-1)J/2}$ denotes the vector of "identified" parameters. Then candidate normalizations may be represented as mappings from $\Re^{(J-1)J/2}$ to $\Re^{J(J+1)/2}$. For example, consider the ($J = 3$) ALM normalization in eqn (9) which in matrix form can be written as

$$\Sigma_\epsilon^{\text{ALM}} = \begin{bmatrix} \beta_1 & \beta_2 & 0 \\ \beta_2 & \beta_3 & 0 \\ 0 & 0 & 0 \end{bmatrix}. \tag{14}$$

In packed form this particular normalization may be represented by the (linear) mapping

$$\begin{bmatrix} \beta_1 \\ \beta_2 \\ \beta_3 \\ 0 \\ 0 \\ 0 \end{bmatrix} = h_1(\beta) = \begin{bmatrix} 1 & 0 & 0 \\ 0 & 1 & 0 \\ 0 & 0 & 1 \\ 0 & 0 & 0 \\ 0 & 0 & 0 \\ 0 & 0 & 0 \end{bmatrix} \begin{bmatrix} \beta_1 \\ \beta_2 \\ \beta_3 \end{bmatrix} = H_1\beta. \tag{15}$$

Recall that the "observable" parameters reside in $C_J \in \Re^{(J-1)J/2}$ (in packed form), which is obtained through the mapping $g(\cdot)$ from $\Re^{J(J+1)/2}$ to $\Re^{(J-1)J/2}$, defined below. Define the function $f(\beta) = g(h(\beta))$ which maps $\Re^{(J-1)J/2}$ to itself. Then the identification problem reduces to verifying that $f(\cdot)$ represents a unique invertible transformation between β and C_J. The relevant requirement from the Inverse Function Theorem – see Apostol (1974) – is that the Jacobian determinant of f be different from zero.

To illustrate, consider the simple class of $J = 3$) normalizations which are restricted so that either $\sigma_{ij} = 0$ or $\sigma_{ij} = \sigma_{kl}$. This includes both of the previous examples:

$$\Sigma_1 = \begin{bmatrix} \beta_1 & \beta_2 & 0 \\ \beta_2 & \beta_3 & 0 \\ 0 & 0 & 0 \end{bmatrix} \Rightarrow h_1(\beta) = \begin{bmatrix} \beta_1 \\ \beta_2 \\ \beta_3 \\ 0 \\ 0 \\ 0 \end{bmatrix} = \begin{bmatrix} 1 & 0 & 0 \\ 0 & 1 & 0 \\ 0 & 0 & 1 \\ 0 & 0 & 0 \\ 0 & 0 & 0 \\ 0 & 0 & 0 \end{bmatrix} \beta = H_1\beta \tag{16}$$

and

$$\Sigma_2 = \begin{bmatrix} \beta_1 & 0 & 0 \\ 0 & \beta_2 & 0 \\ 0 & 0 & \beta_3 \end{bmatrix} \Rightarrow h_2(\beta) = \begin{bmatrix} \beta_1 \\ 0 \\ \beta_2 \\ 0 \\ 0 \\ \beta_3 \end{bmatrix} = \begin{bmatrix} 1 & 0 & 0 \\ 0 & 0 & 0 \\ 0 & 1 & 0 \\ 0 & 0 & 0 \\ 0 & 0 & 0 \\ 0 & 0 & 1 \end{bmatrix} \beta = H_2\beta. \quad (17)$$

Some additional possibilities are:

$$\Sigma_3 = \begin{bmatrix} \beta_1 & \beta_2 & 0 \\ \beta_2 & \beta_1 & \beta_3 \\ 0 & \beta_3 & \beta_1 \end{bmatrix} \Rightarrow h_3(\beta) = \begin{bmatrix} \beta_1 \\ \beta_2 \\ \beta_1 \\ 0 \\ \beta_3 \\ \beta_1 \end{bmatrix} = \begin{bmatrix} 1 & 0 & 0 \\ 0 & 1 & 0 \\ 1 & 0 & 0 \\ 0 & 0 & 0 \\ 0 & 0 & 1 \\ 1 & 0 & 0 \end{bmatrix} \beta = H_3\beta, \quad (18)$$

$$\Sigma_4 = \begin{bmatrix} \beta_1 & \beta_2 & 0 \\ \beta_2 & \beta_3 & 0 \\ 0 & 0 & \beta_3 \end{bmatrix} \Rightarrow h_4(\beta) = \begin{bmatrix} \beta_1 \\ \beta_2 \\ \beta_3 \\ 0 \\ 0 \\ \beta_3 \end{bmatrix} = \begin{bmatrix} 1 & 0 & 0 \\ 0 & 1 & 0 \\ 0 & 0 & 1 \\ 0 & 0 & 0 \\ 0 & 0 & 0 \\ 0 & 0 & 1 \end{bmatrix} \beta = H_4\beta, \quad (19)$$

$$\Sigma_5 = \begin{bmatrix} \beta_1 & \beta_2 & 0 \\ \beta_2 & \beta_1 & 0 \\ 0 & 0 & \beta_3 \end{bmatrix} \Rightarrow h_5(\beta) = \begin{bmatrix} \beta_1 \\ \beta_2 \\ \beta_1 \\ 0 \\ 0 \\ \beta_3 \end{bmatrix} = \begin{bmatrix} 1 & 0 & 0 \\ 0 & 1 & 0 \\ 1 & 0 & 0 \\ 0 & 0 & 0 \\ 0 & 0 & 0 \\ 0 & 0 & 1 \end{bmatrix} \beta = H_5\beta, \quad (20)$$

$$\Sigma_6 = \begin{bmatrix} \beta_1 & \beta_2 & \beta_3 \\ \beta_2 & \beta_1 & \beta_3 \\ \beta_3 & \beta_3 & \beta_1 \end{bmatrix} \Rightarrow h_6(\beta) = \begin{bmatrix} \beta_1 \\ \beta_2 \\ \beta_1 \\ \beta_3 \\ \beta_3 \\ \beta_1 \end{bmatrix} = \begin{bmatrix} 1 & 0 & 0 \\ 0 & 1 & 0 \\ 1 & 0 & 0 \\ 0 & 0 & 1 \\ 0 & 0 & 1 \\ 1 & 0 & 0 \end{bmatrix} \beta = H_6\beta. \quad (21)$$

The function $g(\cdot)$ which maps Σ_r to C_j may be defined by the linear transformation G given by

$$g(\Sigma_r) = \begin{bmatrix} 1 & 0 & 0 & -2 & 0 & 1 \\ 0 & 1 & 0 & -1 & -1 & 1 \\ 0 & 0 & 1 & 0 & -2 & 1 \end{bmatrix} \begin{bmatrix} \sigma_{11} \\ \sigma_{21} \\ \sigma_{22} \\ \sigma_{31} \\ \sigma_{32} \\ \sigma_{33} \end{bmatrix} = G\Sigma_r, \quad (22)$$

and hence for this class of normalizations $f(\beta) = g(h(\beta)) = GH\beta$ is the composite of two linear transformations. Application of the chain rule gives the Jacobian of f, $Df = Dg \circ Dh = GH$. It follows that

$$Df_1 = \begin{bmatrix} 1 & 0 & 0 \\ 0 & 1 & 0 \\ 0 & 0 & 1 \end{bmatrix}, \qquad Df_2 = \begin{bmatrix} 1 & 0 & 1 \\ 0 & 1 & 1 \\ 0 & 0 & 1 \end{bmatrix},$$

$$Df_3 = \begin{bmatrix} 2 & 0 & 0 \\ 2 & 0 & -2 \\ 1 & 1 & -1 \end{bmatrix}, \qquad Df_4 = \begin{bmatrix} 1 & 0 & 1 \\ 0 & 1 & 1 \\ 0 & 0 & 2 \end{bmatrix},$$

$$Df_5 = \begin{bmatrix} 1 & 0 & 1 \\ 0 & 1 & 1 \\ 1 & 0 & 1 \end{bmatrix}, \qquad Df_6 = \begin{bmatrix} 2 & 0 & -2 \\ 1 & 1 & -2 \\ 2 & 0 & -2 \end{bmatrix}.$$

The Jacobians Df_1 through Df_4 are of full rank, and hence the β's are identifiable for the corresponding specifications. In contrast, Df_5 and Df_6 are not of full rank, and the β's are not identifiable in Σ_5 and Σ_6. Thus, one may not arbitrarily choose any normalization which appears to have the correct number of free parameters. It is also essential to verify that the transformation implied by the normalization is invertible, a point which has been overlooked until recently.

In particular, consider Σ_5. If the scaling of this specification is fixed by dividing by β_1, the resulting normalization is

$$\Sigma_5' = \begin{bmatrix} 1 & \beta_2' & 0 \\ \beta_2' & 1 & 0 \\ 0 & 0 & \beta_3' \end{bmatrix}. \tag{23}$$

This unidentified normalization appears in Daganzo (1979), is quoted by Currim (1982), and is used in a simulation study by Horowitz *et al.* (1982). The fact that Σ_5' is unidentified was pointed out by Dansie (1985).

The above approach is general and is easily extended to $J > 3$. For example, consider a mode choice problem with $J = 4$ where the choice set is {drive alone, carpool, train, bus}. There are $4(4 - 1)/2 = 6$ identifiable parameters in Σ_ϵ, and two possible candidate normalizations are:

$$\Sigma_6 = \begin{bmatrix} \beta_1 & \beta_2 & 0 & 0 \\ \beta_2 & \beta_3 & 0 & 0 \\ 0 & 0 & \beta_4 & \beta_5 \\ 0 & 0 & \beta_5 & \beta_6 \end{bmatrix}, \tag{24}$$

and

$$\Sigma_7 = \begin{bmatrix} \beta_1 & \beta_2 & \beta_3 & \beta_3 \\ \beta_2 & \beta_1 & \beta_4 & \beta_4 \\ \beta_3 & \beta_4 & \beta_5 & \beta_6 \\ \beta_3 & \beta_4 & \beta_6 & \beta_5 \end{bmatrix}. \tag{25}$$

For Σ_6, the assumption is that each of the alternatives has an error term with a different variance, and that there is correlation of unobserved attributes between the pairs {drive alone, car pool} and {train, bus}, respectively. Error terms for {drive, carpool} are assumed to be uncorrelated with error terms for {train, bus}. In contrast, for Σ_7 the error terms for {drive, carpool} are assumed to be correlated with the error terms for {train, bus}, and each of these pairs is assumed to have the same variance. A straightforward application of the procedure developed above reveals that Σ_6 is identified, where as Σ_7 is not.

5. SCALING

Although one can generally consider fixing the scale of (2) by dividing through by a coefficient parameter, the standard practice in published MNP applications is to incorporate scaling in the specification of Σ_ϵ. This seems more intuitive, and is based on what are probably more acceptable assumptions. The identification results for the examples of the previous section still hold if one chooses to include scaling, as a consequence of the simple structure that was assumed.

If thinking about the specification in J-space, one could divide Σ_ϵ by a constant multiple of one of the (nonzero) variance components, leaving one or more constant terms on the diagonal. (If one is keeping track, a corresponding adjustment would take place for θ and μ, multiplying them by the positive square root of the same expression.) Alternatively, one could consider the "observable" parameters to live in $(J - 1)$-space, and divide all the elements of C_j by c_{11} $(=\sigma_{11} - 2\sigma_{1j} + \sigma_{jj})$ so that the estimated parameters reside in a symmetric $(J - 1)$-dimensional matrix with a "1" in the upper left-hand corner. The matrix C_j may be constrained to be positive definite through a convenient Cholesky factorization B_j with $J(J - 1)/2 - 1$ free parameters (i.e. $C_j = B_j B_j'$) where:

$$B_j = \begin{bmatrix} 1 & 0 & 0 & \cdots & 0 \\ b_{21} & b_{22} & 0 & \cdots & 0 \\ b_{31} & b_{32} & b_{33} & \cdots & 0 \\ \vdots & \vdots & \vdots & \vdots & \vdots \\ b_{J1} & b_{J2} & b_{J3} & \cdots & b_{JJ} \end{bmatrix}. \qquad (26)$$

Transformations which directly incorporate scaling, defined using the spaces $\Re^{J(J+1)/2-1}$ and $\Re^{(J-1)J/2-1}$, may be studied using the ideas of the previous section, although the exercise is more tedious and a bit less intuitive. It should be clear that one can readily move from one normalization to another via C_j, and rescale when it is convenient. This is illustrated in the next section.

6. NUMERICAL EXAMPLES

A major application of choice models in transportation is the estimation of commuter mode choice. Most applications of this type have used the logit model, but two major examples using linear-in-parameters MNP are Hausman and Wise (1978) and the report by Albright, Lerman, and Manski. Both use a data set collected in Washington, D.C. in which the choices are {car, shared-ride, bus}.

Hausman and Wise (HW) use a subset containing 100 observations, and restrict themselves to models for which the most general specification assumes uncorrelated random errors (i.e. that Σ_δ and Σ_ϵ are diagonal). The generic attributes are trip cost divided by personal income, in-vehicle travel time, and out-of-vehicle travel time. The choice probabilities are evaluated using numerical integration.

In contrast, ALM use 1353 observations, and estimate a quite general specification which allows for correlated random errors. They use essentially the same generic attributes as HW, but include two mode-specific variables on available autos per licensed driver. They evaluate choice probabilities via Clark's approximation – see Daganzo (1979).

An interesting feature of these reported results is that both obtain estimates for a fully-specified Σ_ϵ matrix. In fact, the two specifications are essentially those given by eqns (9) and (10) above, but with the following adjustments for scaling purposes:

$$\Sigma_\epsilon^{\text{ALM}} = \begin{bmatrix} \sigma_{11} & \sigma_{21} & 0 \\ \sigma_{21} & w - \sigma_{11} & 0 \\ 0 & 0 & 0 \end{bmatrix},$$

$$\Sigma_\epsilon^{\text{HW}} = \begin{bmatrix} 1 & 0 & 0 \\ 0 & \sigma_{22} & 0 \\ 0 & 0 & \sigma_{33} \end{bmatrix}.$$

Based on the discussion in the previous two sections, one can transform the HW and ALM results into various identifiable normalizations for comparison purposes. Table 1 includes such a comparison using the (identified) normalizations discussed above. There are no striking differences between the two sets of results, even though they were obtained with different sample sizes and different assumptions regarding taste variation. It is clear from this example that, depending upon the modeling assumptions one is willing to make, different interpretations involving the effect of unobserved variables are possible.

However, recall from the example in eqns (11) through (13) that in some situations candidate normalizations could be rejected if they produce invalid covariance matrices. This is illustrated in Bunch and Kitamura (1989), in which trinomial probit models of car ownership are estimated using the approach recommended here. A comparison of various normalizations is made, with some being rejected as invalid.

7. MORE PARSIMONIOUS SPECIFICATIONS

In the section on transformations we limited ourselves to normalizations which utilize all available parameters; however, this is not necessary and one might wish to consider more parsimonious specifications involving fewer parameters. In this case the relationships between C_j and Σ_ϵ may still be examined, but the researcher must give careful thought to what is being assumed.

For example, the specification Σ_5 (or, equivalently, Σ_5') is unidentified. Dansie (1985) shows that the three covariance matrices

$$\Sigma_A = \begin{bmatrix} 1 & \sigma_{21} & 0 \\ \sigma_{21} & 1 & 0 \\ 0 & 0 & \sigma_{33} \end{bmatrix}$$

$$\Sigma_B = \begin{bmatrix} 1 & \sigma_{21} & 0 \\ \sigma_{21} & 1 & 0 \\ 0 & 0 & 1 \end{bmatrix}$$

$$\Sigma_C = \begin{bmatrix} 1 & 0 & 0 \\ 0 & 1 & 0 \\ 0 & 0 & \sigma_{33} \end{bmatrix}$$

are equivalent, but that only the second two are identified, with one free parameter. As a consequence, he recommends estimating the model using a one-parameter C_j matrix given by

Table 1. Alternative Σ_ϵ normalization for MNP mode choice results

Albright, Lerman, and Manski	Hausman and Wise
$\begin{bmatrix} 1 & 0.45 & 0 \\ 0.45 & 1.21 & 0 \\ 0 & 0 & 0 \end{bmatrix}$	$\begin{bmatrix} 1 & 0.50 & 0 \\ 0.50 & 1.51 & 0 \\ 0 & 0 & 0 \end{bmatrix}$
$\begin{bmatrix} 1 & 0 & 0 \\ 0 & 1.38 & 0 \\ 0 & 0 & 0.82 \end{bmatrix}$	$\begin{bmatrix} 1 & 0 & 0 \\ 0 & 2.02 & 0 \\ 0 & 0 & 1.00 \end{bmatrix}$
$\begin{bmatrix} 1 & -0.21 & 0 \\ -0.21 & 1 & -0.34 \\ 0 & -0.34 & 1 \end{bmatrix}$	$\begin{bmatrix} 1 & -0.51 & 0 \\ -0.51 & 1 & -0.51 \\ 0 & -0.51 & 1 \end{bmatrix}$
$\begin{bmatrix} 1 & -0.39 & 0 \\ -0.39 & 1.53 & 0 \\ 0 & 0 & 1.53 \end{bmatrix}$	$\begin{bmatrix} 1 & -1.04 & 0 \\ -1.04 & 3.08 & 0 \\ 0 & 0 & 3.08 \end{bmatrix}$

$$C_J = \begin{bmatrix} 1 & \rho \\ \rho & 1 \end{bmatrix}$$

This is equivalent to assuming that, whatever the normalization may look like, we expect that the variance of $\epsilon_1-\epsilon_3$ equals the variance of $\epsilon_2-\epsilon_3$. Note that many normalizations may satisfy this requirement. In particular, if the estimation routine produces a result with $\rho < 0$, then neither of the two normalizations Σ_B and Σ_C will be valid covariance matrices; of course others could be found which are.

8. SUMMARY

The linear-in-parameters multinomial probit framework in eqn (2) includes a random error vector which in general has a covariance matrix Σ_ϵ, but unfortunately not all the covariance parameters are identified. Section 4 develops the arguments which give the number of estimable parameters, and recommends that estimation be performed in terms of a matrix C_J. Multiple normalizations may correspond to the same estimated C_J, but some may not produce valid covariance matrices. Choosing a particular (valid) normalization is essentially a *modeling decision*, as illustrated via the examples in section 4. This feature of MNP is often overlooked in the sweeping laudatory descriptions of the model, which extol the generality of the approach versus more highly restrictive models such as multinomial logit. In fact, users of probit must in the final analysis make modeling assumptions which are analogous to choosing among various alternative tree structures in the nested multinomial logit or tree extreme value models.

To perform this exercise, however, knowledge of the number of estimable parameters is still not enough. Arbitrarily selected specifications for Σ_ϵ which contain the prescribed number of estimable parameters may not be identified, since the transformation between the parameters in the specification and the "observable" C_J parameters may not be unique and invertible. Examples are given which demonstrate that an analysis is essential for ensuring valid results. Specification errors are common in the literature and these issues appear to not be generally understood. The results presented here provide useful guidelines for those practitioners seeking to apply probit models.

Acknowledgements—This work was supported in part by the USDOT through the Region Nine Transportation Center at University of California, Berkeley. The author thanks Joel Horowitz for providing a copy of the Albright, Lerman, and Manski (1977) report, and Ryuichi Kitamura, David M. Rocke, and an anonymous referee for helpful discussions and comments on an earlier draft of this paper.

REFERENCES

Albright R. L., Lerman S. R., and Manski C. F. (1977) Report on the development of an estimation program for the multinomial probit model. Preliminary report prepared for the Federal Highway Administration, October, p. 54.

Apostol T. M. (1974) *Mathematical Analysis*, (Second edition). Addison-Wesley, Reading, MA.

Bunch D. S., and Kitamura R. (1989) Multinomial probit estimation revisited: Testing of new algorithms and evaluation of alternative model specifications for trinomial models of household car ownership. Transportation Research Group Research Report UCD-TRG-RR-4, University of California, Davis, CA.

Currim I. S. (1982) Predictive testing of consumer choice models not subject to independence of irrelevant alternatives. *J. Marketing Res.*, **19**, 208–222.

Daganzo C. (1979) *Multinomial Probit: The Theory and Its Application to Demand Forecasting*. Academic Press, New York.

Dansie B. R. (1985) Parameter estimability in the multinomial probit model. *Transpn. Res. B*, **19B**, 526–528.

Hausman J. A., and Wise D. A. (1978) A conditional probit model for qualitative choice: Discrete decisions recognizing interdependence and heterogeneous preferences. *Econometrica*, **46**, 403–426.

Horowitz J. L., Sparmann J. M., and Daganzo C. F. (1982) An investigation of the accuracy of the Clark approximation for the multinomial probit model. *Transpn. Sci.*, **16**, 3, 382–401.

Johnson L. and Hensher D. (1982) Application of multinomial probit to a two-period panel data set. *Transpn. Res. A*, **16A**, 5/6, 457–464.

Kamakura W. (1989) The estimation of multinomial probit models: A new calibration algorithm, *Transpn. Sci*, **23**(4), 253–265.

van Lierop W. (1986) *Spatial Interaction Modeling and Residential Choice Analysis*. Gower Publishing, Aldershot, England.

McFadden D. (1981) Econometric models of probabilistic choice. In C. F. Manski and D. McFadden, (Eds.) *Structural Analysis of Discrete Data with Econometric Applications*, pp. 198–272. MIT Press, Cambridge, MA.

McFadden D. (1989) A method of simulated moments for estimation of discrete response models without numerical integration. *Econometrica*, 57(5), 995–1026.

McFadden D., Tye W., and Train K. (1977) An application of diagnostic tests for the independence from irrelevant alternatives property of the multinomial logit model. *Trnspn. Res. Rec.*, 637, 39–46.

Pakes A. and Pollard D. (1989) Simulation and the asymptotics of optimization estimators. *Econometrica*, 57(5), 1027–1057.

[22]

Statistical Comparison of Non-Nested Probabilistic Discrete Choice Models

JOEL L. HOROWITZ

The University of Iowa, Iowa City, Iowa

The development of empirical probabilistic discrete-choice models frequently entails comparing two non-nested models (i.e., models with the property that neither can be obtained as a parametric special case of the other) to determine which is most likely to provide a correct explanation of a particular choice situation. Conventional statistical procedures, such as the likelihood ratio test, do not apply to comparisons of non-nested models. This paper describes three procedures for carrying out such comparisons and explores the ability of each to distinguish between correct and incorrect models. The procedures are: tests against a composite model, the Cox test of separate families of hypotheses, and comparisons based on the likelihood ratio index goodness-of-fit statistic. A modification of the likelihood ratio index is proposed that corrects for the effects of differences in the numbers of estimated parameters in the compared models. The abilities of the various procedures to reject incorrect models and accept correct ones are explored analytically and through numerical experiments. It is shown analytically that, in large samples, the modified likelihood ratio index has greater ability to distinguish between correct and incorrect models than do composite model procedures. The results of the numerical experiments suggest that the modified likelihood ratio index also has greater ability to distinguish between correct and incorrect models than does the Cox test. The numerical results give encouraging indications of the ability of the modified likelihood ratio index to choose the correct model in comparisons of models whose choice probabilities differ by at least 10–15%.

1. INTRODUCTION

Travel decisions frequently entail choices among discrete sets of alternatives, such as frequencies, destinations, modes, and routes of

Transportation Science
Vol. 17, No. 3, August 1983

0041-1655/83/1703-0319 $01.25

travel, and a large proportion of travel behavior research is oriented toward predicting the outcomes of such choices. A convenient behavioral and mathematical framework for making these predictions is provided by a class of mathematical models called probabilistic discrete-choice models. These models predict the probabilities that a randomly selected individual chooses each of the available alternatives as functions of a set of explanatory variables consisting of attributes of the individual and the alternatives. The multinomial logit,[1, 2] multinomial probit,[3–5] and generalized extreme value[6] models are three well-known examples of probabilistic discrete choice models. See DOMENCICH AND MCFADDEN[1] and HENSHER AND JOHNSON[7] for discussions of the behavioral foundations of these models in the context of travel analysis.

In practice, the functional relations constituting a probabilistic discrete choice model are not known *a priori* and must be estimated by fitting a model to randomly sampled observations of choice and the explanatory variables. The fitting process usually takes place in two steps. In the first step, the functional form of the relation between the choice probabilities and the explanatory variables is specified up to a finite set of constant parameters. In the second step, the values of the parameters are estimated statistically from the observations. The method of maximum likelihood usually is used for this purpose. The statistical theory upon which this estimation procedure is based assumes that the first step is carried out without error. It is well known that if this assumption is true and certain broad regularity conditions are satisfied, then the maximum likelihood estimates of the parameter values have desirable statistical properties, including consistency, asymptotic unbiasedness, and asymptotic efficiency. One important consequence of these properties is that the estimated model converges to the true one as the size of the estimation sample approaches infinity.

In practice, of course, the correct functional forms of the relations between the choice probabilities and the explanatory variables are not known *a priori*, even up to a set of constant parameters. Not surprisingly, specification of incorrect functional relations in the first step of the model estimation process invalidates the statistical theory upon which the second step is based and can lead to models that produce highly erroneous forecasts.[8–10] Accordingly, in practice the development of an empirical discrete choice model, like the development of most other statistically based models, usually includes comparing differently specified models with one another in order to distinguish models that likely are incorrectly specified from ones that may be correctly specified.

Consider a comparison of two models.[1] It is useful to formulate such a

[1] The discussion in this paper will be concerned mainly with two-model comparisons, the problem of comparisons among many models being left largely to future research. However,

comparison as a statistical hypothesis test. In other words, one model is designated as the null model and is compared with the other model using a procedure that has desirable statistical properties (e.g., a high probability of rejecting a seriously erroneous null model and a low probability of rejecting a correct one). Rejection of the null model then implies that this model is likely to be incorrect (although not necessarily that the alternative model is likely to be correct).

Two-model hypothesis tests can be divided into two classes: those involving nested models, and those involving non-nested models. In nested models, the null model can be obtained as a special case of the alternative model by assigning appropriate values to some subset of the alternative model's parameters. In non-nested models, this cannot be done; given the values of either model's parameters, it is not possible to choose values of the other model's parameters so that the two models become identical. (A more precise definition of non-nestedness and examples of non-nested models will be given in Section 2.) Tests of nested discrete choice models usually are carried out by means of likelihood-ratio tests or the asymptotically equivalent Wald and Lagrangian multiplier tests. (See SILVEY[11] and RAO[12] for discussions of these tests.) Subject to regularity conditions, these tests have been shown to have certain optimal asymptotic statistical properties relating to their power.[13] Numerical experiments with the tests have indicated that they have good ability to distinguish between correct and seriously erroneous models in the nested case.[10, 14, 15]

The situation regarding comparisons of non-nested models is considerably less clear than that for nested models. Although, as will be discussed in Section 3, several procedures for comparing non-nested discrete choice models are available, virtually nothing is known about their ability to distinguish between correct and incorrect models. This paper reports the results of research aimed at helping to remedy this situation. The paper develops analytic results concerning the ability of several existing procedures for comparing non-nested models to reject erroneous models and accept correct ones, and it presents the results of a set of numerical experiments that further explore and illustrate the properties of the procedures.

The remainder of the paper is organized as follows. Sections 2 and 3 provide background information that is needed to develop the main results of the paper. Section 2 defines the concepts of correct models and non-nestedness mathematically and formulates the problem of comparing two non-nested models. Section 3 describes a variety of existing comparison procedures for non-nested models. The main results of the paper are

---

certain multimodel generalizations of the two-model procedures discussed here will be identified.

presented in Sections 4 and 5. Section 4 develops the analytic results concerning the abilities of the comparison procedures to distinguish between correct and incorrect models, and Section 5 presents the results of the numerical experiments. Section 6 presents the conclusions of this research.

2. BASIC CONCEPTS AND DEFINITIONS

LET AN INDIVIDUAL face a set of J mutually exclusive alternatives, one of which must be chosen. Let C denote the set of all available alternatives, and let $\underline{X}_j$ denote a column vector of observed attributes of the individual and alternative $j \in C$.[2] Define the matrix $\underline{X}$ by $\underline{X} = (\underline{X}_1, \cdots, \underline{X}_J)$. A probabilistic discrete choice model (referred to hereafter simply as a choice model) consists of a functional relation $P(j \mid \underline{X}, \underline{\alpha})$ specifying the probability that a randomly selected individual chooses each alternative $j \in C$ in terms of the observed attributes $\underline{X}$ and a finite vector of constant parameters $\underline{\alpha}$. For example, in the familiar linear-in-parameters multinomial logit model

$$P(j \mid \underline{X}\, \underline{\alpha}) = \exp(\alpha' \underline{X}_j) / \textstyle\sum_{k=1}^{J} \exp(\alpha' \underline{X}_k). \qquad (1)$$

2.1. Definition of a Correct Choice Model

Let observations be made on a set of attributes $\underline{X}$, and let $P(j \mid \underline{X}, \underline{\alpha})$ be a choice model for the choice set C.[3] $P(j \mid \underline{X}, \underline{\alpha})$ will be called a correct model if there is a value of $\underline{\alpha}$, say $\underline{\alpha}_0$, such that the probability that a randomly selected individual chooses alternative j satisfies:

$$\Pr(j \text{ is chosen} \mid \underline{X}) = P(j \mid \underline{X}, \underline{\alpha}_0). \qquad (2)$$

It is important to note that the correctness of a particular choice model depends on the set of observed attributes of individuals and alternatives. In other words, a model is correct or incorrect conditional on the set of observed attributes. For example, let $\underline{X}^*$ denote a subset of the attributes $\underline{X}$, and let $P(j \mid \underline{X}^*, \underline{\alpha}^*)$ denote a choice model that depends only on attributes in $\underline{X}^*$. Then it may be true that for a suitable $\underline{\alpha}^*$ value

$$\Pr(j \text{ is chosen} \mid \underline{X}^*) = P(j \mid \underline{X}^*, \underline{\alpha}^*) \qquad (3)$$

for a randomly chosen individual. However, if observations are made on

[2] It will be assumed throughout this paper that all individuals have the same choice set C. If one or more alternatives in C are, in fact, unavailable to an individual, these can be thought of as having positive but negligibly small probabilities of being chosen by this individual.

[3] In the remainder of this paper, the same symbol will be used to denote both the set of observed attributes or explanatory variables of a model and the matrix in which the values of these variables are stored. The sense in which the symbol is used will be clear from the context.

the entire attribute set $\underset{\sim}{X}$, then $P(j \mid \underset{\sim}{X}^*, \underset{\sim}{\alpha}^*)$ is a correct model only if

$$\Pr(j \text{ is chosen} \mid \underset{\sim}{X}) = P(j \mid \underset{\sim}{X}^*, \underset{\sim}{\alpha}^*). \tag{4}$$

In other words, the attributes in $\underset{\sim}{X}$ that are not also in $\underset{\sim}{X}^*$ must be irrelevant to the choice being modeled.

In practical modeling, it often is necessary to exclude certain variables from a model, even though they are included among the available data and affect choice. For example, practical considerations may make it necessary to exclude the variable "age of the traveler" from a mode choice model, even if age is included among the available data and is believed to affect choice. A model from which relevant variables are excluded *a priori* is correct according to the definition given here if it satisfies Equation 2 when $\underset{\sim}{X}$ consists of the included variables and if the model and the excluded variables are not used in the same analysis. For example, the excluded variables cannot be used to define population strata that will be studied with the model from which the variables are excluded. Nor can the excluded variables be used as explanatory variables of models that will be compared with or used with the model from which the variables are excluded. In other words, a variable that is treated as if it were unobserved *is* unobserved for the purposes of the current discussion, even if the variable is available for observation in the sense of being included among the available data.

The following example illustrates the relation between a model's correctness and the set of observed attributes:

Example. Let there be two alternatives in C and assume that observations can be made on two attributes, $\underset{\sim}{x} = (x_1, x_2)'$ and $\underset{\sim}{y} = (y_1, y_2)'$, where x_i and $y_i (i = 1, 2)$ denote the attributes for alternative i. Suppose that the following binomial probit choice model is correct:

$$P(1 \mid \underset{\sim}{x}, \underset{\sim}{y}) = \Phi[(x_1 - x_2) + (y_1 - y_2)] \tag{5a}$$

$$P(2 \mid \underset{\sim}{x}, \underset{\sim}{y}) = 1 - P(1 \mid \underset{\sim}{x}, \underset{\sim}{y}) \tag{5b}$$

where Φ denotes the cumulative standard normal distribution function. Now suppose that y_1 and y_2 are normally distributed independently of each other and of $\underset{\sim}{x}$ with mean zero and unit variance. Then the marginal choice probabilities $P(1 \mid \underset{\sim}{x})$ and $P(2 \mid \underset{\sim}{x})$ are given by:

$$P(1 \mid \underset{\sim}{x}) = \Phi[(x_1 - x_2)/\sqrt{3}] \tag{6a}$$

$$P(2 \mid \underset{\sim}{x}) = 1 - P(1 \mid \underset{\sim}{x}). \tag{6b}$$

If only the attributes $\underset{\sim}{x}$ are treated as being observed, then Equations 6 constitute a correct choice model. However, if the attributes $\underset{\sim}{y}$ also are treated as being observed (for example, if Equations 5 are compared with Equations 6 or if $\underset{\sim}{y}$ is used to define population strata whose choices will be studied), then this model no longer is correct, even though it is true that for a randomly selected individual:

$$\Pr(1 \text{ is chosen} \mid \underset{\sim}{x}) = P(1 \mid \underset{\sim}{x}) \tag{7a}$$

$$\Pr(2 \text{ is chosen} \mid \underset{\sim}{x}) = P(2 \mid \underset{\sim}{x}). \tag{7b}$$

The subsequent discussion deals with comparisons of choice models that may have different sets of explanatory variables. Let $P(j \mid \underset{\sim}{X}_P, \underset{\sim}{\alpha})$ and $Q(j \mid \underset{\sim}{X}_Q, \underset{\sim}{\beta})$ denote two such models. $\underset{\sim}{X}_P$ and $\underset{\sim}{X}_Q$ may consist of identical attributes, contain a common subset of attributes, or contain no attributes in common. Let $\underset{\sim}{X}$ denote all attributes that are included in either $\underset{\sim}{X}_P$ or $\underset{\sim}{X}_Q$. All of the attributes $\underset{\sim}{X}$ must be observed to make it possible for empirical realizations of the models P and Q to be developed and compared. Therefore, if the two models are compared and model P is correct, then:

$$\Pr(j \text{ is chosen} \mid \underset{\sim}{X}) = P(j \mid \underset{\sim}{X}_P, \underset{\sim}{\alpha}) \tag{8a}$$

for a suitable $\underset{\sim}{\alpha}$ value. If model Q is correct, then

$$\Pr(j \text{ is chosen} \mid \underset{\sim}{X}) = P(j \mid \underset{\sim}{X}_Q, \underset{\sim}{\beta}) \tag{8b}$$

for a suitable $\underset{\sim}{\beta}$ value. Equations 8 constitute hypotheses that can be tested if appropriate statistical procedures are available. These equations form the basis of the tests of non-nested models that are discussed in this paper.

2.2. Some Useful Notation

Suppose that $P(j \mid \underset{\sim}{X}_P, \underset{\sim}{\alpha})$ and $Q(j \mid \underset{\sim}{X}_Q, \underset{\sim}{\beta})$ are two choice models whose explanatory variables $\underset{\sim}{X}_P$ and $\underset{\sim}{X}_Q$ may or may not include common elements. As before, let $\underset{\sim}{X}$ denote all of the explanatory variables that are included in either model. Let $p_x(\underset{\sim}{X})$ denote the joint probability density function of these variables in the population under consideration.[4] Let $f(j, \underset{\sim}{X} \mid \underset{\sim}{\alpha})$ and $g(j, \underset{\sim}{X} \mid \underset{\sim}{\beta})$, respectively, denote the joint distribution functions of the choice variable j (j being a discrete variable that indicates which alternative is chosen) and explanatory variables $\underset{\sim}{X}$ with the models P and Q. In other words:

$$f(j, \underset{\sim}{X} \mid \underset{\sim}{\alpha}) = P(j \mid \underset{\sim}{X}_P, \underset{\sim}{\alpha}) p_x(\underset{\sim}{X}) \tag{9a}$$

$$g(j, \underset{\sim}{X} \mid \underset{\sim}{\beta}) = Q(j \mid \underset{\sim}{X}_Q, \underset{\sim}{\beta}) p_x(\underset{\sim}{X}). \tag{9b}$$

[4] To simplify the discussion, it will be assumed that explanatory variables are continuous and that the population is sampled through simple random sampling. The generalization to discrete explanatory variables is obvious. Stratification on the explanatory variables can be treated by defining p_x to be the distribution of attributes under the stratified sampling rule.

Given any function $h(j, \underset{\sim}{X})$, let $E_f(h \mid \underset{\sim}{\alpha})$ and $V_f(h \mid \underset{\sim}{\alpha})$ denote the mean and variance of h with respect to the distribution function $f(j, \underset{\sim}{X} \mid \underset{\sim}{\alpha})$ if these quantities exist. Thus:

$$E_f(h \mid \underset{\sim}{\alpha}) = \sum_{j \in C} \int_X h(j, \underset{\sim}{X}) f(j, \underset{\sim}{X} \mid \underset{\sim}{\alpha})\, d\underset{\sim}{X} \tag{10a}$$

$$V_f(h \mid \underset{\sim}{\alpha}) = \sum_{j \in C} \int_X [h(j, \underset{\sim}{X}) - E_f(h \mid \underset{\sim}{\alpha})]^2 f(j, \underset{\sim}{X} \mid \underset{\sim}{\alpha})\, d\underset{\sim}{X}, \tag{10b}$$

where the integrals are over all values of the explanatory variables. Define $E_g(h \mid \underset{\sim}{\beta})$ and $V_g(h \mid \underset{\sim}{\beta})$ is an analogous way.

2.3. Definition of Non-Nested Models

Let A and B be subsets of Euclidean spaces whose dimensionalities equal those of $\underset{\sim}{\alpha}$ and $\underset{\sim}{\beta}$, respectively, and suppose that $\underset{\sim}{\alpha}$ and $\underset{\sim}{\beta}$ in the models P and Q of Equations 9 are required to satisfy $\underset{\sim}{\alpha} \in A$, $\underset{\sim}{\beta} \in B$. Let $\underset{\sim}{\alpha}^*$ and $\underset{\sim}{\beta}^*$, respectively, denote the large-sample limits of the maximum likelihood estimates of $\underset{\sim}{\alpha}$ and $\underset{\sim}{\beta}$. The models P and Q are defined to be non-nested if

$$E_f[\log f(j, \underset{\sim}{X} \mid \underset{\sim}{\alpha}^*) - \log g(j, \underset{\sim}{X} \mid \underset{\sim}{\beta}) \mid \underset{\sim}{\alpha}^*] > 0 \tag{11a}$$

for all $\underset{\sim}{\beta} \in B$ and

$$E_g[\log g(j, \underset{\sim}{X} \mid \underset{\sim}{\beta}^*) - \log f(j, \underset{\sim}{X} \mid \underset{\sim}{\alpha}) \mid \underset{\sim}{\beta}^*] > 0 \tag{11b}$$

for all $\underset{\sim}{\alpha} \in A$. This definition will be satisfied by models P and Q if there exists a set of $(j, \underset{\sim}{X})$ values whose probability of occurrence with either model exceeds zero and such that $P(j \mid \underset{\sim}{X}_P, \underset{\sim}{\alpha}) \neq Q(j \mid \underset{\sim}{X}_Q, \underset{\sim}{\beta}^*)$ and $Q(j \mid \underset{\sim}{X}_Q, \underset{\sim}{\beta}) \neq P(j \mid \underset{\sim}{X}_P, \underset{\sim}{\alpha}^*)$ for all $\underset{\sim}{\alpha} \in A$ and $\underset{\sim}{\beta} \in B$ whenever $(j, \underset{\sim}{X})$ is in this set.

Example. Let P and Q be the binomial logit models defined by:

$$P(1) = 1/[1 + \exp(\alpha_1 x + \alpha_2 y)] \tag{12a}$$

$$Q(1) = 1/[1 + \exp(\beta_1 x + \beta_2 y^2)] \tag{12b}$$

where the α's and β's are constant parameters, x and y are the explanatory variables, $P(1)$ stands for $P(1 \mid x, y, \alpha_1, \alpha_2)$, and $Q(1)$ is defined analogously. Suppose that the α's and β's are restricted to the interval $[-1, 1]$ and that x and y are independently normally distributed with mean zero and unit variance. Then if α_2^* and β_2^* both are nonzero, models P and Q are non-nested. If $\alpha_2^* = 0$, the definition of non-nestedness is not satisfied, since $P(1 \mid x, y, \alpha_1^*, \alpha_2^*)$ then can be obtained from $Q(1 \mid x, y, \beta_1, \beta_2)$ by setting $\beta_1 = \alpha_1^*$ and $\beta_2 = \alpha_2^* = 0$. Similarly, if $\beta_2^* = 0$, the definition of non-nestedness is not satisfied.

3. PROCEDURES FOR COMPARING NON-NESTED MODELS

THREE CLASSES of statistical procedures for comparing non-nested choice models are described in this section: comparisons against composite models, the Cox test of separate families of hypotheses, and comparisons based on the likelihood ratio index goodness-of-fit statistic. Although none of the procedures are new, several of them are not widely known, particularly in the field of choice modeling. They are described here to provide a basis for the discussion in Sections 4 and 5.

The discussion in this section and in Section 4 assumes that certain regularity conditions are satisfied. These conditions are stated in Section A.1 of the Appendix. The regularity conditions include the requirement that the models being compared be non-nested. Many of the results presented in this section and Section 4 are not applicable to comparisons of nested models.

3.1. Comparisons Against Composite Models

One way to compare two non-nested models is by embedding them in a more general, or composite, model of which each is a parametric special case. The original models are then tested against the composite using likelihood ratio tests. Rejection of one model and acceptance of the other is interpreted as indicating that the rejected model is incorrectly specified, whereas the accepted model may be correctly specified and should be retained for further consideration.

Example. The binary logit models of Equations 12 can be obtained as parametric special cases of the following composite binary logit model:

$$\Pi(1) = 1/[1 + \exp(\gamma_0 x + \gamma_P y + \gamma_Q y^2)], \qquad (13)$$

where the γ's are constant parameters. If $\gamma_Q = 0$, model P is obtained, and if $\gamma_P = 0$, model Q is obtained.

See HOROWITZ,[15] COX,[16, 17] ATKINSON,[18] and QUANDT[19] for discussions of other formulations of composite models.

There are four possible outcomes of a test of two non-nested models against a composite model. These are listed in Table I. As was previously noted, the first two outcomes in Table I would indicate that one of the models should be rejected as being incorrect and that the other should be retained as a possibly correct model. The third outcome would indicate that the two non-nested models cannot be distinguished with the test procedure and data being used. The fourth outcome would indicate that both models are incorrect unless it is believed strongly that one of the two models is, in fact, correct. In the latter case, the test would provide no information on which model is more likely to be correct.

It is a straightforward matter to generalize the foregoing tests based on

TABLE I

Possible Outcomes of Comparisons Based on Composite Models or the Cox Test of Separate Families of Hypotheses

Outcome	Model P	Model Q
1	Accept	Reject
2	Reject	Accept
3	Accept	Accept
4	Reject	Reject

composite models to permit comparisons of more than two non-nested models. See, for example, Atkinson.[18]

3.2. The Cox Test of Separate Families of Hypotheses[16, 17]

Let $L_{Nf}(j, \underline{X} \mid \underline{\alpha})$ denote the log-likelihood function of a simple random sample of size N on the variates $(j, \underline{X})$ under the hypothesis that the joint distribution function of $(j, \underline{X})$ is $f(j, \underline{X} \mid \underline{\alpha})$. *Let* $L_{Ng}(j, \underline{X} \mid \underline{\beta})$ denote the log-likelihood function of such a sample under the hypothesis that the true joint distribution of $(j, \underline{X})$ is $g(j, \underline{X} \mid \underline{\beta})$. Then, if $j^{(n)}$ and $\underline{X}^{(n)}$, respectively, denote the nth observed values of j and $\underline{X}$, L_{Nf} and L_{Ng} are given by:

$$L_{Nf}(j, \underline{X} \mid \underline{\alpha}) = \textstyle\sum_{n=1}^{N} \log f(j^{(n)}, \underline{X}^{(n)} \mid \underline{\alpha}) \tag{14a}$$

$$L_{Ng}(j, \underline{X} \mid \underline{\beta}) = \textstyle\sum_{n=1}^{N} \log g(j^{(n)}, \underline{X}^{(n)} \mid \underline{\beta}). \tag{14b}$$

Let $\hat{\underline{\alpha}}$ and $\hat{\underline{\beta}}$, respectively, denote the values of $\underline{\alpha}$ and $\underline{\beta}$ that maximize L_{Nf} and L_{Ng}. Given any $\underline{\alpha}$ value, define $\underline{\beta}_{\alpha}$ by:

$$E_f[\log g(j, \underline{X} \mid \underline{\beta}_{\alpha}) \mid \underline{\alpha}] = \max_{\beta} E_f[\log g(j, \underline{X} \mid \underline{\beta}) \mid \underline{\alpha}], \tag{15a}$$

and for any $\underline{\beta}$ value define $\underline{\alpha}_{\beta}$ by:

$$E_g[\log f(j, \underline{X} \mid \underline{\alpha}_{\beta}) \mid \underline{\beta}] = \max_{\alpha} E_g[\log f(j, \underline{X} \mid \underline{\alpha}) \mid \underline{\beta}]. \tag{15b}$$

Finally, let the distribution functions f and g be related to the non-nested choice models $P(j \mid \underline{X}_P, \underline{\alpha})$ and $Q(j \mid \underline{X}_Q, \underline{\beta})$ as in Equations 9.

In the Cox test of separate families of hypotheses,[16, 17] one model is designated as the null hypothesis and is tested against the other model (the alternative hypothesis) using the test statistic

$$t_{Nf} = N^{-1/2}\{L_{Nf}(j, \underline{X} \mid \hat{\underline{\alpha}}) - L_{Ng}(j, \underline{X} \mid \hat{\underline{\beta}}) - E_f[L_{Nf}(j, \underline{X} \mid \hat{\underline{\alpha}}) - L_{Ng}(j, \underline{X} \mid \hat{\underline{\beta}}) \mid \hat{\underline{\alpha}}]\} \tag{16a}$$

if model P is the null hypothesis and

$$t_{Ng} = N^{-1/2}\{L_{Ng}(j, \underline{X} \mid \hat{\underline{\beta}}) - L_{Nf}(j, \underline{X} \mid \hat{\underline{\alpha}}) - E_g[L_{Ng}(j, \underline{X} \mid \hat{\underline{\beta}}) - L_{Nf}(\mid j, \underline{X} \mid \hat{\underline{\alpha}}) \mid \hat{\underline{\beta}}]\} \tag{16b}$$

if model Q is the null hypothesis. If model P with parameter values $\underset{\sim}{\alpha} = \underset{\sim}{\alpha}_0$ is correct, then t_{Nf} is asymptotically normally distributed with mean zero. The asymptotic variance of t_{Nf} is:

$$\begin{aligned} V_f(t_{Nf} \mid \underset{\sim}{\alpha}_0) &= V_f[\log f(j, \underset{\sim}{X} \mid \alpha_0) - \log g(j, \underset{\sim}{X} \mid \underset{\sim}{\beta}_{\underset{\sim}{\alpha}_0}) \mid \underset{\sim}{\alpha}_0] \\ &\quad - E_f\{[\partial \log f(j, X \mid \alpha_0)/\partial\alpha'][\log f(j, \underset{\sim}{X} \mid \underset{\sim}{\alpha}_0) - \log g(j, \underset{\sim}{X} \mid \underset{\sim}{\beta}_{\underset{\sim}{\alpha}_0})] \mid \underset{\sim}{\alpha}_0\} \\ &\quad \cdot V_f(\hat{\underset{\sim}{\alpha}} \mid \underset{\sim}{\alpha}_0) E_f\{[\partial \log f(j, X \mid \alpha_0)/\partial\alpha][\log f(j, \underset{\sim}{X} \mid \underset{\sim}{\alpha}_0) \\ &\qquad - \log g(j, \underset{\sim}{X} \mid \underset{\sim}{\beta}_{\underset{\sim}{\alpha}_0})] \mid \underset{\sim}{\alpha}_0\}, \end{aligned} \tag{17}$$

where

$$V_f(\hat{\underset{\sim}{\alpha}} \mid \underset{\sim}{\alpha}_0) = -\{E_f[\partial^2 \log f(j, X \mid \underset{\sim}{\alpha}_0)/\partial\underset{\sim}{\alpha}\,\partial\alpha' \mid \underset{\sim}{\alpha}_0]\}^{-1} \tag{18}$$

and the notation $\partial \log f(j, X \mid \underset{\sim}{\alpha}_0)/\partial\underset{\sim}{\alpha}$ signifies that the derivative is evaluated at $\underset{\sim}{\alpha} = \underset{\sim}{\alpha}_0$. If model Q with parameters $\underset{\sim}{\beta} = \underset{\sim}{\beta}_0$ is correct, then t_{Ng} is asymptotically normally distributed with mean zero and a variance $V_g(t_{Ng} \mid \underset{\sim}{\beta}_0)$ that can be obtained from Equations 17 and 18 by exchanging f with g and $\underset{\sim}{\alpha}$ with $\underset{\sim}{\beta}$.

Although the values of $\underset{\sim}{\alpha}_0$, $\underset{\sim}{\beta}_0$, $\underset{\sim}{\beta}_{\underset{\sim}{\alpha}_0}$ and $\underset{\sim}{\alpha}_{\underset{\sim}{\beta}_0}$ cannot be determined in practical empirical work, consistent estimates of $V_f(t_{Nf} \mid \underset{\sim}{\alpha}_0)$ and $V_g(t_{Ng} \mid \underset{\sim}{\beta}_0)$ can be obtained by estimating $\underset{\sim}{\alpha}_0$ and $\underset{\sim}{\beta}_0$ with $\hat{\underset{\sim}{\alpha}}$ *and* $\hat{\underset{\sim}{\beta}}$, estimating $\underset{\sim}{\beta}_{\underset{\sim}{\alpha}_0}$ with $\underset{\sim}{\beta}_{\hat{\alpha}}$, the $\underset{\sim}{\beta}$ value that maximizes the expression

$$\textstyle\sum_{n=1}^{N} f(j^{(n)}, \underset{\sim}{X}^{(n)} \mid \hat{\underset{\sim}{\alpha}}) \log g(j^{(n)}, \underset{\sim}{X}^{(n)} \mid \underset{\sim}{\beta}), \tag{19}$$

and estimating $\underset{\sim}{\alpha}_{\underset{\sim}{\beta}_0}$ in the analogous way. In addition, the expectation in Equation 16a can be estimated by

$$\textstyle\sum_{n=1}^{N} \sum_{j=1}^{J} P(j \mid \underset{\sim}{X}_P^{(n)}, \hat{\underset{\sim}{\alpha}}) \log[P(j \mid \underset{\sim}{X}_P^{(n)}, \hat{\underset{\sim}{\alpha}})/Q(j \mid \underset{\sim}{X}_Q^{(n)}, \underset{\sim}{\beta}_{\hat{\alpha}})] \tag{20}$$

with an analogous expression for the expectation in (16b). Thus the models P and Q can be tested against one another by evaluating t_{Nf} and t_{Ng} and accepting or rejecting each model according to whether t_{Nf} (in the case of model P) or t_{Ng} (in the case of model Q) are significantly different from zero at a suitable significance level. For example, model P is rejected at the η significance level if $|t_{Nf}| > z_{\eta/2}(\hat{V}_f)^{1/2}$, where $z_{\eta/2}$ is the $1 - \eta/2$ quantile of the standard normal distribution and $\hat{V}_f$ is the estimated variance of t_{Nf}.

The Cox test of separate families of hypothesis, like the tests based on composite models, can yield the four outcomes shown in Table I. In addition, if either or both of the models being compared is rejected, it may be possible to infer useful diagnostic information from the signs of the corresponding test statistics. See Cox[17] for details. The Cox test of separate families does not generalize readily to tests involving more than two models.

3.3. The Likelihood Ratio Index

Let $L_{NP}(j \mid \underset{\sim}{X}_P, \underset{\sim}{\alpha})$ denote the conditional log likelihood function of a random sample of observations of choices, given the values of the explanatory variables $\underset{\sim}{X}_P$ and the model specification $P(j \mid \underset{\sim}{X}_P, \underset{\sim}{\alpha})$. L_{NP} is given by:

$$L_{NP}(j \mid \underset{\sim}{X}_P, \underset{\sim}{\alpha}) = \sum_n \log P(j^{(n)} \mid \underset{\sim}{X}_P^{(n)}, \underset{\sim}{\alpha}). \tag{21}$$

The likelihood ratio index for the model P, ρ_{P^2}, is defined by:

$$\rho_P^2 = 1 - L_{NP}(j \mid \underset{\sim}{X}_P, \hat{\underset{\sim}{\alpha}})/L^*, \tag{22}$$

where $\hat{\underset{\sim}{\alpha}}$ is the maximum likelihood estimate of $\underset{\sim}{\alpha}$ and L^* is a quantity that is independent of the model P. Typical L^* values are the conditional log likelihood of a model in which all available alternatives have equal probabilities of being chosen and the conditional log likelihood of a model in which the probability that an alternative j is chosen equals the proportion of sampled individuals who chose that alternative.[1-3, 20] The expressions for L^* in these two cases are:

$$L^* = \begin{cases} -N \log J \text{ (equal probabilities)} \\ \sum_{j=1}^{J} N_j \log(N_j/N) \text{ (observed proportions)} \end{cases} \tag{23}$$

where J is the number of alternatives in the choice set and N_j is the number of sampled individuals who chose alternative j. The likelihood ratio indices corresponding to these two forms of L^* will be referred to here as the "equal probabilities" and "observed proportions" forms.

The likelihood ratio index in either form constitutes a goodness-of-fit statistic for choice models that is analogous to the coefficient of multiple determination R^2 in regression models. The larger the value of ρ^2 for a given model, the better the model fits the given data. Therefore, two or more non-nested choice models can be compared by computing the values of ρ^2 for each model and accepting the model with the largest ρ^2 value.[5] This procedure is equivalent to accepting the model that yields the largest log likelihood value when the parameters equal their maximum likelihood estimates, and it yields results that are independent of the form of the likelihood ratio index.

A disadvantage of the likelihood ratio index as a means of discriminating between models is that it does not compensate for the tendency of a model's log likelihood value and, therefore, its ρ^2 value to increase when the number of estimated parameters increases. This tendency is inde-

[5] As in the earlier discussion, acceptance here means that the accepted model may be correct and should be retained for further consideration, not that the model has been proven to be correct.

pendent of whether the variables associated with the added parameters are relevant to the choice situation being considered. A modification of the likelihood ratio index that compensates for the effects of changing the number of estimated parameters will be proposed in Section 4.

There are only two possible outcomes of a two-model comparison based on the likelihood ratio index. One model must be rejected and the other accepted. Of course, acceptance of a model in such a comparison does not necessarily imply that the model is correct. However, it will be shown in Section 4 that a small difference between the modified equal-probabilities ρ^2 values of two models can indicate with high probability that the model with the lower ρ^2 value is incorrect.

4. THE POWER OF THE TESTS

THIS SECTION develops analytic results concerning the abilities of the foregoing procedures to distinguish between correct and incorrect choice models. Three types of results are developed. First, expressions are derived for the probabilities that the procedures will reject an incorrect model in a comparison with a correct one. The expression pertaining to the likelihood ratio index is used to suggest a modification of ρ^2 that compensates for the effects of differences in the numbers of estimated parameters in the compared models. Second, lower and upper bounds are obtained for the probabilities that comparisons of correct and incorrect models based on the composite model procedure or on the Cox test of separate families of hypotheses will yield the outcome "reject the incorrect model and accept the correct one." (In comparisons based on the likelihood ratio index, this outcome is equivalent to rejecting the incorrect model.) The outcome "reject the incorrect model and accept the correct one" is of particular interest, because among the possible outcomes of a comparison of a correct and an incorrect model it is the only one which indicates unambiguously that the correct model is preferable to the incorrect one. Finally, the ability of the likelihood ratio index (as modified to take account of differences in the numbers of estimated parameters in the compared models) to reject incorrect models and accept correct ones is explored. It is shown that with moderate size samples (and subject to the validity of certain asymptotic approximations) small differences in the values of the equal-probability form of this index indicate with high probability that the model with the lower index value is incorrect. Moreover, in a comparison of a correct model with an incorrect one, either form of the modified likelihood ratio index yields asymptotically a higher probability of the outcome "reject the incorrect model and accept the correct one" than do tests against composite models.

4.1. The Probability of Rejecting an Incorrect Model

Let $P(j \mid \underline{X}_P, \underline{\alpha})$ be the incorrect model and $Q(j \mid \underline{X}_Q, \underline{\beta})$ be the correct model. As before, let $\underline{X}$ denote the explanatory variables of both models combined, and let $f(j, \underline{X} \mid \underline{\alpha})$ and $g(j, \underline{X} \mid \underline{\beta})$ be the probability distribution functions defined in Equations 9. Let $\underline{\beta}_0$ denote the true value of the parameter vector $\underline{\beta}$, and for any $\underline{\beta}$, let $\underline{\alpha}_{\beta}$ be defined as in equation (15b). Finally, let R_P denote the event "reject model P."

Consider, first, comparisons based on composite models. Let models P and Q be parametric special cases of a composite model $\Pi\ (j \mid \underline{X}, \gamma)$. In other words, models P and Q can be obtained from Π by appropriately constraining the components of the parameter γ. If model P is tested against model Π with a likelihood ratio test, the test statistic has asymptotically the noncentral chi-square distribution with degrees of freedom d equal to the number of components of γ that are constrained by the hypothesis that P is the correct model.[13] The noncentral parameter, Z_N, for a sample of size N is given by:

$$Z_N = 2NE_g[\log Q(j \mid \underline{X}_Q, \underline{\beta}_0) - \log P(j \mid \underline{X}_P, \underline{\alpha}_{\beta_0}) \mid \underline{\beta}_0] \quad (24)$$

Let $\chi^2\ (\eta, d)$ denote the $1 - \eta$ quantile of the central chi-square distribution with d degrees of freedom. A likelihood ratio test of model P against model Π rejects P at the η significance level if the test statistic, λ_N, exceeds $\chi^2(\eta, d)$. Let $F(z; Z_N, d)$ denote the probability that a noncentral chi-square variate with noncentral parameter Z_N and d degrees of freedom is less than or equal to z. Then the probability that model P is rejected at the η significance level is given asymptotically by:

$$\Pr[R_P] = \Pr[\lambda_N > \chi^2(\eta, d)] \quad (25a)$$

$$= 1 - F[\chi^2(\eta, d); Z_N, d]. \quad (25b)$$

Now consider the Cox test of separate families of hypotheses. It is shown in Section A.2 of the Appendix that if the null hypothesis is false and the alternative hypothesis is true, then the test statistic t_{Nf} is asymptotically normally distributed with the following mean:

$$\begin{aligned} E_g(t_{Nf} \mid \underline{\beta}_0) = N^{1/2}\{ & E_g[\log f(j, \underline{X} \mid \underline{\alpha}_{\beta_0}) \\ & - \log g(j, \underline{X} \mid \underline{\beta}_0) \mid \underline{\beta}_0] - E_f[\log f(j, \underline{X} \mid \underline{\alpha}_{\beta_0}) \\ & - \log g(j, \underline{X} \mid \underline{\beta}_\alpha^*) \mid \underline{\alpha}_{\beta_0}]\}, \end{aligned} \quad (26)$$

where $\underline{\beta}_\alpha^*$ is $\underline{\beta}_\alpha$ evaluated at $\underline{\alpha} = \underline{\alpha}_{\beta_0}$. $E_g(t_{Nf} \mid \underline{\beta}_0)$ is always negative. The asymptotic variance of t_{Nf} under the alternative hypothesis is given by:

$$\begin{aligned} V_g(t_{Nf} \mid \underline{\beta}_0) = V_g[&\log f(j, \underline{X} \mid \underline{\alpha}_{\beta_0}) \\ & - \log g(j, \underline{X} \mid \underline{\beta}_0) \mid \underline{\beta}_0] + 2\, \underline{s}' \underline{V}^{-1} \underline{r} + \underline{s}' \underline{V}^{-1} \underline{D} \underline{V}^{-1} \underline{s}, \end{aligned} \quad (27)$$

where $\underset{\sim}{s}$, $\underset{\sim}{r}$, $\underset{\sim}{V}$, and $\underset{\sim}{D}$ are defined as follows

$$\underset{\sim}{s} = E_f\{\partial \log f(j, \underset{\sim}{X} \mid \underset{\sim}{\alpha}_{\beta_0})/\partial\underset{\sim}{\alpha}[\log f(j, \underset{\sim}{X} \mid \underset{\sim}{\alpha}_{\beta_0}) - \log g(j, \underset{\sim}{X} \mid \underset{\sim}{\beta}_{\alpha}{}^*)] \mid \underset{\sim}{\alpha}_{\beta_0}\} \tag{28a}$$

$$\underset{\sim}{r} = E_g\{\partial \log f(j, \underset{\sim}{X} \mid \underset{\sim}{\alpha}_{\beta_0})/\partial\underset{\sim}{\alpha}[\log f(j, \underset{\sim}{X} \mid \underset{\sim}{\alpha}_{\beta_0}) - \log g(j, \underset{\sim}{X} \mid \underset{\sim}{\beta}_0)] \mid \underset{\sim}{\beta}_0\} \tag{28b}$$

$$\underset{\sim}{V} = E_g[\partial^2 \log f(j, \underset{\sim}{X} \mid \underset{\sim}{\alpha}_{\beta_0})/\partial\underset{\sim}{\alpha}\partial\underset{\sim}{\alpha}' \mid \underset{\sim}{\beta}_0] \tag{28c}$$

$$\underset{\sim}{D} = E_g\{[\partial \log f(j, \underset{\sim}{X} \mid \underset{\sim}{\alpha}_{\beta_0})/\partial\underset{\sim}{\alpha}][\partial \log f(j, \underset{\sim}{X} \mid \underset{\sim}{\alpha}_{\beta_0})/\partial\underset{\sim}{\alpha}'] \mid \underset{\sim}{\beta}_0\} \tag{28d}$$

Recall that when the null model P is tested against the alternative model Q, the variance of t_{NF} is estimated by substituting $\hat{\underset{\sim}{\alpha}}$ and the expression (19) estimate of $\underset{\sim}{\beta}_{\hat{\alpha}}$ into Equation 17. If, in fact, model P is incorrect and model Q is correct, then the resulting variance estimate will converge almost surely to $V_f(t_{NF} \mid \underset{\sim}{\alpha}_{\beta_0})$ as $N \to \infty$. Therefore, the probability that model P is rejected at the η significance level is asymptotically equal to $\Pr\{|t_{Nf}| > z_{\eta/2}[V_f(t_{Nf} \mid \underset{\sim}{\alpha}_{\beta_0})]^{1/2}\}$. Since the asymptotic distribution of t_{Nf} under the alternative hypothesis is normal with mean and variance given by Equations 26 and 27, the asymptotic probability of rejecting the incorrect model P at the η significance level in a test against the correct alternative model Q is:

$$\Pr(R_P) = 1 - \Phi\{[z_{\eta/2}(V_f(t_{Nf} \mid \underset{\sim}{\alpha}_{\beta_0}))^{1/2} - E_g(t_{Nf} \mid \underset{\sim}{\beta}_0)]/[V_g(t_{Nf} \mid \underset{\sim}{\beta}_0)]^{1/2}\} + \Phi\{[-z_{\eta/2}(V_f(t_{Nf} \mid \underset{\sim}{\alpha}_{\beta_0}))^{1/2} - E_g(t_{Nf} \mid \underset{\sim}{\beta}_0)]/[V_g(t_{Nf} \mid \underset{\sim}{\beta}_0)]^{1/2}\}. \tag{29}$$

Finally, consider comparisons based on the likelihood ratio index. Regardless of which form of the index is used, $\rho_Q{}^2 - \rho_P{}^2$ exceeds zero, implying that model P is rejected, if and only if the quantity $N^{-1/2}\Delta L_{gf}$ defined by

$$N^{-1/2}\Delta L_{gf} = N^{-1/2}[L_{Ng}(j, \underset{\sim}{X} \mid \hat{\underset{\sim}{\beta}}) - L_{Nf}(j, \underset{\sim}{X} \mid \hat{\underset{\sim}{\alpha}})] \tag{30}$$

also exceeds zero. However, if model Q is correct, then $N^{-1/2}L_{Ng}(j, \underset{\sim}{X} \mid \hat{\underset{\sim}{\beta}})$ is asymptotically distributed as $N^{-1/2}L_{Ng}(j, \underset{\sim}{X} \mid \underset{\sim}{\beta}_0)$, and $N^{-1/2}L_{Nf}(j, \underset{\sim}{X} \mid \hat{\underset{\sim}{\alpha}})$ is asymptotically distributed as $N^{-1/2}L_{Nf}(j, \underset{\sim}{X} \mid \underset{\sim}{\alpha}_{\beta_0})$.[17]. Therefore, $N^{-1/2}\Delta L_{gf}$ is asymptotically distributed as $N^{-1/2}[L_{Ng}(j, \underset{\sim}{X} \mid \underset{\sim}{\beta}_0) - L_{Nf}(j, \underset{\sim}{X} \mid \underset{\sim}{\alpha}_{\beta_0})]$. Since the latter quantity is the sum of independently and identically distributed random variables, it follows from the Lindeberg-Levy theorem that this quantity and, hence, $N^{1/2}\Delta L_{gf}$ are asymptotically normally distributed with the following mean and variance:

$$E_g(N^{-1/2}\Delta L_{gf} \mid \underset{\sim}{\beta}_0) = N^{1/2}E_g[\log g(j, \underset{\sim}{X} \mid \underset{\sim}{\beta}_0) - \log f(j, \underset{\sim}{X} \mid \underset{\sim}{\alpha}_{\beta_0}) \mid \underset{\sim}{\beta}_0] \tag{31a}$$

$$V_g(N^{-1/2}\Delta L_{gf} \mid \underset{\sim}{\beta}_0) = V_g[\log g(j, \underset{\sim}{X} \mid \underset{\sim}{\beta}_0) - \log f(j, \underset{\sim}{X} \mid \underset{\sim}{\alpha}_{\beta_0}) \mid \underset{\sim}{\beta}_0]. \tag{31b}$$

Equations 31 enable the probability distribution function of $N^{1/2}\Delta L_{gf}$ to be approximated with arbitrary accuracy by making N sufficiently large. However, if the choice probabilities of models P and Q are not greatly different, the quality of the approximation can be improved by including in Equation 31a an additional term from the asymptotic expansion of the mean of $N^{1/2}\Delta L_{gf}$. This term enables the approximate distribution function of $N^{-1/2}\Delta L_{gf}$ to reflect the tendency of a model's log likelihood to increase as the number of estimated parameters increases. It is shown in Section A.3 of the Appendix that the appropriate additional term is $(k_Q - k_P)/2N^{1/2}$, where k_Q and k_P, respectively, are the numbers of estimated parameters in models Q and P. With this term included, Equation 31a becomes

$$E_g(N^{-1/2}\Delta L_{gf} \mid \underline{\beta}_0) = N^{1/2}E_g[\log g(j, \underline{X} \mid \underline{\beta}_0) - \log f(j, X \mid \underline{\alpha}_{\beta_0}) \mid \underline{\beta}_0] + (k_Q - k_P)/2N^{1/2}. \tag{32}$$

Although the second term on the right-hand side of Equation 32 obviously is negligibly small when N sufficiently large, the term can be important at moderate values of N if the choice probabilities associated with models P and Q are not greatly different.

The asymptotic cumulative distribution function of $N^{-1/2}\Delta L_{gf}$ is now given by:

$$\Pr(N^{-1/2}\Delta L_{gf} \leq z) = \Phi\{[z - E_g(N^{-1/2}\Delta L_{gf} \mid \underline{\beta}_0)]/[V_g(N^{-1/2}\Delta L_{gf} \mid \underline{\beta}_0)]^{1/2}\} \tag{33}$$

where E_g is given by Equation 32 and V_g is given by Equation 31b. The probability that a comparison based on the likelihood ratio index rejects model P in a comparison with model Q is:

$$P(R_P) = \Phi\{[E_g(N^{-1/2}\Delta L_{gf}) \mid \underline{\beta}_0)]/[V_g(N^{-1/2}\Delta L_{gf} \mid \underline{\beta}_0)]^{1/2}\}. \tag{34}$$

Equation 32 implies that the likelihood ratio index will tend to favor the model with the larger number of parameters, regardless of whether that model is correct. This problem can be dealt with by defining a modified likelihood ratio index, $\bar{\rho}^2$, as follows:

$$\bar{\rho}_P{}^2 = 1 - [L_{NP}(j \mid X_P, \hat{\underline{\alpha}}) - k_P/2]/L^* \tag{35}$$

for model P and analogously for model Q. Model P is rejected in favor of model Q if $\bar{\rho}_Q{}^2 > \bar{\rho}_P{}^2$. Using this criterion, the probability of rejecting model P is:

$$\Pr(R_P) = \Phi\{[E_g(^{-1/2}\Delta L_{gf} \mid \underline{\beta}_0) - (k_Q - k_P)/2N^{1/2}]/[V_g(N^{-1/2}\Delta L_{gf} \mid \underline{\beta}_0)]^{1/2}\}. \tag{36}$$

It can be seen from Equations 31b and 32 that $\Pr(R_P)$ in Equation 36 does not depend on k_Q or k_P. Hence, the use of $\bar{\rho}^2$ corrects (asymptotically) the tendency of ρ^2 to favor the model with the larger number of estimated parameters.[6] Because of this advantage of $\bar{\rho}^2$ over ρ^2, the discussion of the properties of likelihood-ratio-index comparisons in the remainder of this section and in Section 4 will be concerned only with $\bar{\rho}^2$ unless otherwise noted.

4.2. The Probability of Rejecting the Incorrect Model and Accepting the Correct One

Let A_Q denote the event "accept model Q." Then the event "reject the incorrect model and accept the correct one" corresponds to $R_P \cap A_Q$. In a comparison of models P and Q using any form of the likelihood ratio index, $R_P = A_Q$. Therefore, the probability of rejecting the incorrect model and accepting the correct one is the same as the probability of rejecting the incorrect one. In comparisons based on composite models or the Cox test of separate families of hypotheses, $R_P \neq A_Q$ owing to the possibility that both models may be rejected or both may be accepted.

An upper bound on $\Pr(R_P \cap A_Q)$ for composite models or the Cox test can be obtained by noting that:

$$\Pr(R_P \cap A_Q) = \Pr(R_P | A_Q) \Pr(A_Q) \leq \Pr(A_Q) \tag{37}$$

and that

$$\Pr(R_P \cap A_Q) = \Pr(A_Q | R_P) \Pr(R_P) \leq \Pr(R_P). \tag{38}$$

Therefore,

$$\Pr(R_P \cap A_Q) \leq \min[\Pr(R_P), \Pr(A_Q)], \tag{39}$$

A lower bound on $\Pr(R_P \cap A_Q)$ can be obtained by noting that:

$$\Pr(R_P \cap A_Q) = \Pr(R_P) + \Pr(A_Q) - \Pr(R_P \cup A_Q) \tag{40a}$$

$$\geq \Pr(R_P) + \Pr(A_Q) - 1. \tag{40b}$$

Therefore,

$$\Pr(R_P) + \Pr(A_Q) - 1 \leq \Pr(R_P \cap A_Q) \leq \min[\Pr(R_P), \Pr(A_Q)]. \tag{41}$$

$\Pr(R_P)$ is given (asymptotically) by Equation 25b for a comparison based on a composite model and by Equation 29 for a comparison based on the Cox test of separate families of hypotheses. $\Pr(A_Q)$ is equal to $1 - \eta$, where η is the significance level of the comparison.

[6] The correction is asymptotic, even though it approaches zero as $N \to \infty$, because it is based on a large-sample approximation to the probability distribution of $\bar{\rho}$. See Section A.3 of the Appendix for details.

4.3. Further Properties of the Likelihood Ratio Index and Composite Model Methods

A simplification of the foregoing results that permits additional insight into the abilities of the composite model comparison method and the modified likelihood ratio index to distinguish between correct and incorrect models can be obtained in the following way. For any $(j, \underline{X})$ define $\delta(j, \underline{X})$ by:

$$\delta(j, \underline{X}) = g(j, \underline{X} \mid \underline{\beta}_0) - f(j, \underline{X} \mid \underline{\alpha}_{\beta_0}). \tag{42}$$

Assume that N is large (so that asymptotic theory applies) but that $N^{1/2} \mid \delta(j, \underline{X}) \mid^2$ is close to zero for all $(j, \underline{X})$ except, possibly, a set of $(j, \underline{X})$ values whose probability of occurrence is zero (i.e., for almost all $(j, \underline{X})$). This implies that models P and Q are close to one another in the sense that $P(j \mid \underline{X}_P, \underline{\alpha}_{\beta_0}) - Q(j \mid \underline{X}_Q, \underline{\beta}_0)$ can differ substantially from zero only on a set of $(j, \underline{X})$ values whose probability of occurrence is close to zero. Expand $\log g(j, \underline{X} \mid \underline{\beta}_0) - \log f(j, \underline{X} \mid \underline{\alpha}_{\beta_0})$ in a Taylor series about $\delta(j, \underline{X}) = 0$ to obtain:

$$\begin{aligned}\log g(j, \underline{X} \mid \underline{\beta}_0) - \log f(j, \underline{X} \mid \underline{\alpha}_{\beta_0}) &= \delta(j, \underline{X})/g(j, \underline{X} \mid \underline{\beta}_0) \\ &+ (\tfrac{1}{2})[\delta(j, \underline{X})/g(j, \underline{X} \mid \underline{\beta}_0)]^2 + \text{terms of order } \delta^3.\end{aligned} \tag{43}$$

Define μ_{gf} by:

$$\mu_{gf} = E_g\{[\delta(j, \underline{X})/g(j, \underline{X} \mid \underline{\beta}_0)]^2 \mid \underline{\beta}_0\}, \tag{44}$$

and define Z_N as in Equation 24. Note that $E_g[\delta(j, \underline{X})/g(j, \underline{X} \mid \underline{\beta}_0) \mid \underline{\beta}_0]$ is zero and that Equation 24 is unchanged if Q and P, respectively, are replaced with g and f. Therefore, by substituing Equation 43 into Equations 24, 32, and 31b the following results are obtained:

$$Z_N = N\mu_{gf} + \text{terms of order } NE_g(\delta^3 \mid \underline{\beta}_0) \tag{45}$$

$$\begin{aligned}E_g(N^{-1/2}\Delta L_{gf} \mid \underline{\beta}_0) &= (\tfrac{1}{2})N^{1/2}\mu_{gf} + (k_Q - k_P)/2N^{1/2} \\ &+ \text{terms of order } N^{1/2}E_g(\delta^3 \mid \underline{\beta}_0)\end{aligned} \tag{46a}$$

$$V_g(N^{-1/2}\Delta L_{gf} \mid \underline{\beta}_0) = \mu_{gf} + \text{terms of order } E_g(\delta^3 \mid \underline{\beta}_0). \tag{46b}$$

The higher order terms in Equations 45 and 46 can be dropped to any desired degree of accuracy by making $N^{1/2} \mid \delta(j, \underline{X})\mid^2$ sufficiently small for almost all $(j, \underline{X})$. Therefore, Equation 25b becomes:

$$\Pr[R_P] = 1 - F[\chi^2(\eta, d); N\mu_{gf}, d] \tag{47}$$

and Equation 33 becomes

$$\Pr[N^{-1/2}\Delta L_{gf} \leq z] = \Phi\{[z - (\tfrac{1}{2})N^{1/2}\mu_{gf} - (k_Q - k_P)/2N^{1/2}]/\mu_{gf}^{1/2}\} \tag{48}$$

if $N^{1/2} \mid \delta(j, \underline{X})\mid^2$ is sufficiently small.

If $N^{1/2}|\delta(j, \underset{\sim}{X})|^2$ is not small, then the right hand sides of Equations 25b and 47 both converge to one as $N \to \infty$, and the right hand sides of Equations 33 and 48 both converge to zero as $N \to \infty$. Therefore, Equations 47 and 48 are valid asymptotically regardless of the size of $N^{1/2}|\delta(j, \underset{\sim}{X})|^2$.[7]

Equations 47 and 48 now will be used to explore the abilities of the composite model method and the modified likelihood ratio index to reject incorrect models and accept correct ones. The modified equal-probabilities likelihood ratio index will be discussed first.

Let z be any positive number, and consider the probability that the modified equal-probabilities likelihood ratio index yields the outcome $\bar{\rho}_P{}^2 - \bar{\rho}_Q{}^2 > z$. If this outcome occurs, a comparison of models P and Q indicates erroneously that model Q is incorrect and that model P may be correct. The outcome $\bar{\rho}_P{}^2 - \bar{\rho}_Q{}^2 > z$ with the modified equal-probabilities likelihood ratio index occurs if and only if

$$N^{-1/2}\Delta L_{gf} < (k_Q - k_P)/2N^{1/2} - zN^{1/2}\log J \tag{49}$$

Therefore, Equation 48 yields the following result:

$$\Pr[\bar{\rho}_P{}^2 - \bar{\rho}_Q{}^2 > z] = \Phi[-zN^{1/2}\mu_{gf}^{-1/2}\log J - (N\mu_{gf})^{1/2}/2]. \tag{50}$$

The right-hand side of Equation 50 is maximized at

$$\mu_{gf} = 2z \log J. \tag{51}$$

Therefore,

$$\Pr(\bar{\rho}_P{}^2 - \bar{\rho}_Q{}^2 > z) \le \Phi[-(2Nz \log J)^{1/2}]. \tag{52}$$

Inequality (52) provides an asymptotic upper bound on the probability that the modified equal-probabilities likelihood ratio index for a correct model will be less than that for an incorrect model by an arbitrary amount $z > 0$. Table II shows values of the right-hand side of inequality (52) for several different values of N, z, and J. Note that $\Phi[-(2Nz \log J)^{1/2}]$ is a decreasing function of J. Therefore, the tabulated results imply that if $N \ge 250$ and the equal-probabilities $\bar{\rho}^2$ values of two non-nested models differ by 0.01 or more, the model with the lower $\bar{\rho}^2$ value almost certainly is incorrect. Moreover, depending on the values of N and J, $\bar{\rho}^2$ differences that are considerably less than 0.01 may imply that the model with the lower $\bar{\rho}^2$ value is incorrect.[8]

[7] The argument leading to this conclusion is essentially that used by Wald[13] to derive the asymptotic distribution of the likelihood ratio statistic under the alternative hypothesis. The argument can be made rigorous by considering a comparison of model P with a sequence of alternative models Q_N whose associated distribution functions $g_N(j, \underset{\sim}{X} | \underset{\sim}{\beta}_N)$ have the property that $N^{1/2}|f - g_N|$ remains finite for almost all $(j, \underset{\sim}{X})$ as $N \to \infty$.

[8] Equation 50 and inequality (52) may seem to suggest the following alternative comparison procedure based on the modified likelihood ratio index: Given $z > 0$, accept model P

TABLE II

Values of $\Phi\,[-(2Nz \log J)^{1/2}]$ Corresponding to Various N, z, and J Values

N	z	J	$\Phi\,[-(2Nz \log J)^{1/2}]$
100	0.005	2	0.20
	0.010	2	0.12
	0.005	3	0.15
	0.010	3	0.07
250	0.005	2	0.09
	0.010	2	0.03
	0.005	3	0.05
	0.010	3	0.01
500	0.005	2	0.03
	0.010	2	0.004
	0.005	3	0.01
	0.010	3	0.0005
1000	0.005	2	0.004
	0.010	2	0.0001
	0.005	3	0.0005
	0.010	3	0.0

Equations 47 and 50 together can be used to show that asymptotically the modified equal-probabilities and observed-proportions likelihood ratio indices both yield larger probabilities of rejecting the incorrect model and accepting the correct one than do comparisons based on composite models. Suppose, initially, that $d = 1$ in the test against a composite model. A noncentral chi-square variate with one degree of freedom is equivalent to the square of a normal variate. The mean of this normal variate equals the square root of the noncentral parameter, and its variance is one. Therefore, if $d = 1$, Equation 47 can be written as:

$$\Pr[R_P] = 1 + \Phi[-(N\mu_{gf})^{1/2} - z_{\eta/2}] - \Phi[-(N\mu_{gf})^{1/2} + z_{\eta/2}], \quad (53)$$

and inequality (39) becomes asymptotically:

$$\Pr[R_P \cap A_Q] \leq \min\{1 - \eta,\, 1 + \Phi[-(N\mu_{gf})^{1/2} - z_{\eta/2}] - \Phi[-(N\mu_{gf})^{1/2} + z_{\eta/2}]\} \quad (54)$$

and reject model Q if $\bar{\rho}_{P^2} - \bar{\rho}_{Q^2} > z$; accept model Q and reject model P if $\bar{\rho}_{Q^2} - \rho_P^{\,2} > z$; and make no decision if $|\bar{\rho}_{P^2} - \bar{\rho}_{Q^2}| \leq z$. However, it is easy to show that the probability of a correct decision with this procedure is maximized when $z = 0$, in which case the alternative procedure is the same as the standard procedure described in the text. The purpose of inequality (52) is to provide a practical guide to the confidence one can place in a rejection decision based on $\bar{\rho}^2$, rather than to suggest an alternative rejection criterion. Unlike the other power function formulas presented here, this guide can be used without knowledge of the correct model.

for a comparison based on a composite model. If $d > 1$, then:

$$1 - F[\chi^2(\eta, d); N\mu_{gf}, d] < 1 - F[\chi^2(\eta, 1), N\mu_{gf}, 1]. \tag{55}$$

(see Reference [21]). Therefore, inequality (54) still holds. For the modified equal-probabilities and observed proportions likelihood ratio indices, $\Pr(R_P \cap A_Q)$ is equal to $\Pr(\bar{\rho}_Q^2 - \bar{\rho}_P^2 > 0)$. Therefore asymptotically

$$\Pr(R_P \cap A_Q) = 1 - \Phi[-(N\mu_{gf})^{1/2}/2]. \tag{56}$$

for the modified likelihood ratio indices.

Numerical evaluation of the right-hand sides of inequality (54) and Equation 56 has indicated that for any positive values of $N\mu_{gf}$ and η the right-hand side of (56) exceeds that of (54).[9] The relative magnitudes of the right-hand sides of (54) and (56) depend only on the properties of the cumulative normal distribution function and not on those of the composite model and likelihood ratio index comparison methods. Assuming on the basis of the numerical results that the right-hand side of (56) always is greater than that of (54) when $N\mu_{gf}$ and η are positive, it follows that asymptotically $P(R_P \cap A_Q)$ is larger for the modified likelihood ratio index method than it is for the composite model method.

5. NUMERICAL EXPERIMENTS

THE OBJECTIVES of the numerical experiments were to illustrate numerically the abilities of the different comparison procedures to distinguish correct models from incorrect ones and, particularly, to investigate the relative abilities of the Cox test of separate families of hypotheses and the other procedures to make such distinctions. In each experiment a true choice model Q and a non-nested incorrect model P were specified. Using the methods described in Section 4, the values of $\Pr(R_P)$ and $\Pr(R_P \cap A_Q)$ corresponding to various sample sizes then were computed for the following comparison procedures: the composite utility method, the Cox test of separate families of hypotheses, and the modified likelihood ratio index. The results presented here are independent of whether the equal-probabilities or observed proportions form of the likelihood ratio index is used. Moreover, since the models P and Q used in the experiments have equal numbers of estimated parameters, the results apply to both the modified and unmodified likelihood ratio indices. However, if the models P and Q had different numbers of estimated parameters but yielded choice probabilities similar to those obtained here, then the results given here for the likelihood ratio index would apply to the modified but not necessarily to the unmodified form of this index.[10]

[9] This result can easily be obtained analytically if $(N\mu_{gf})^{1/2} + z_{\eta/2}$ is sufficiently large to make $\Phi[-(N\mu_{gf})^{1/2} - z_{\eta/2}]$ negligibly small.

[10] An alternative and, possibly, more familiar method for evaluating $\Pr(R_P)$ and $\Pr(R_P \cap A_Q)$ is Monte Carlo simulation. This method was not used here owing to its large computational costs and the availability of the analytic results in Section 4.

In all experiments, the correct and incorrect models were three-alternative logit models. The experiments were conducted in three groups: A, B, and C. In group A, the systematic components of the correct and incorrect utility functions for each alternative j ($j = 1, 2, 3$) were specified as:

$$\bar{U}_{Qj} = 0.5x_j \tag{57a}$$

$$\bar{U}_{Pj} = \alpha y_j, \tag{57b}$$

where x_j and y_j are explanatory variables. In group B, the utility functions were:

$$\bar{U}_{Qj} = 0.5x_{1j} + 0.5x_{2j} \tag{58a}$$

$$\bar{U}_{Pj} = \alpha_1 y_{1j} + \alpha_2 y_{2j}. \tag{58b}$$

In group C the utility functions were:

$$\bar{U}_{Qj} = 0.5x_{1j} + 0.5x_{2j} \tag{59a}$$

$$\bar{U}_{Pj} = \alpha_1 y_{1j} + \alpha_2 x_{2j}. \tag{59b}$$

The x variables were assumed to be discretely uniformly distributed over 50 values in group A and 50 pairs of values in groups B and C. The procedure used to generate these values is described in Section A.4 of the Appendix. The y variables were assumed to be related to the corresponding x variables by

$$y = x + \epsilon. \tag{60}$$

For each x value, ϵ was obtained by independent random sampling from the normal distribution $N(0, \sigma_\epsilon^2)$, where the value of σ_ϵ varied from 0.025 to 0.40, depending on the experiment. Thus, the correct and incorrect models differed in that the incorrect model contained at least one incorrect explanatory variable in place of a correct variable.

Important characteristics of the correct and incorrect models used in the experiments are summarized in Table III. In preparing this table, the values of the α parameters were set equal to the large-sample limits of their maximum likelihood estimates (i.e., $\alpha = \alpha_{\beta_0}$). In all of the experiments, the correct and incorrect explanatory variables are highly correlated, and the large-sample limits of the equal-probabilities ρ^2 values for the correct and incorrect models are close. The differences between the choice probabilities of the correct and incorrect models are small at the lower end of the range of σ_ϵ values but increase to levels that could be of considerable practical significance toward the upper end of this range.

Tables IV–VI show the abilities of the three comparison procedures to distinguish between the correct and incorrect models with sample sizes of 250, 500, and 1000. The 0.05 significance level was used in the composite

TABLE III

Characteristics of Correct and Incorrect Models in the Numerical Experiments

Experiment[a]		Correlation Coefficients[b]		Equal-Probabilities ρ^2 Values[c]		Differences between Choice Probabilities of Correct and Incorrect Models[d]			
						Absolute		Fractional	
	σ_ϵ	x_1y_1	x_2y_2	Correct model	Incorrect model	Max	RMS	Max	RMS
1A	0.025	0.9997	—	0.2272	0.2270	0.018	0.0060	0.071	0.024
2A	0.050	0.9990	—		0.2263	0.036	0.011	0.115	0.043
3A	0.100	0.996	—		0.2246	0.068	0.025	0.289	0.091
4A	0.200	0.986	—		0.2196	0.144	0.041	0.492	0.168
5A	0.400	0.954	—		0.1921	0.295	0.090	1.761	0.433
1B	0.025	0.9997	0.9998	0.2272	0.2268	0.028	0.0085	0.100	0.033
2B	0.050	0.9987	0.9994		0.2262	0.052	0.015	0.183	0.063
3B	0.100	0.994	0.998		0.2232	0.092	0.029	0.427	0.131
4B	0.200	0.980	0.988		0.2095	0.206	0.062	1.010	0.283
5B	0.400	0.929	0.956		0.1776	0.374	0.109	2.346	0.524
1C	0.025	0.9997	—	0.2272	0.2270	0.018	0.006	0.069	0.023
2C	0.050	0.9990	—		0.2266	0.033	0.011	0.122	0.0428
3C	0.100	0.995	—		0.2246	0.071	0.025	0.276	0.090
4C	0.200	0.982	—		0.2200	0.128	0.040	0.502	0.165
5C	0.400	0.916	—		0.1973	0.300	0.082	1.721	0.400

[a] Experiments are labeled A, B, or C according to the group to which they belong.

[b] x_1 and y_1 refer to the first variables of $\bar{U}_Q$ and $\bar{U}_P$, and x_2 and y_2 refer to the second variables. Alternatives are not distinguished in the correlation coefficients.

[c] ρ^2 values are compared as large-sample limits.

[d] The choice probabilities for the incorrect model are computed with the α parameters set equal to the large-sample limits of their maximum likelihood estimates (i.e., $\alpha = \alpha_{\beta_\infty}$). RMS means "root-mean-square." The fractional differences between the choice probabilities for the correct and incorrect models are computed as $(P\text{-}Q)/P$.

TABLE IV

Results of Group A Numerical Experiments[a]

Experiment	Sample Size	Probability of Rejecting Incorrect Model			Probability of Rejecting Incorrect Model and Accepting Correct Model				
					Composite model		Cox test		
		Composite model	Cox test	Likelihood ratio index	Lower bound	Upper bound	Lower bound	Upper bound	Likelihood ratio index
1A	250	0.06	0.06	0.56	0.01	0.06	0.01	0.06	0.56
	500	0.07	0.07	0.58	0.02	0.07	0.02	0.07	0.58
	1000	0.09	0.09	0.61	0.04	0.09	0.04	0.09	0.61
2A	250	0.08	0.08	0.61	0.03	0.08	0.03	0.08	0.61
	500	0.12	0.12	0.65	0.07	0.12	0.07	0.12	0.65
	1000	0.19	0.19	0.70	0.12	0.19	0.12	0.19	0.70
3A	250	0.22	0.22	0.72	0.17	0.22	0.17	0.22	0.72
	500	0.37	0.39	0.80	0.32	0.37	0.34	0.39	0.80
	1000	0.66	0.66	0.88	0.61	0.66	0.61	0.66	0.88
4A	250	0.52	0.53	0.85	0.47	0.52	0.48	0.53	0.85
	500	0.84	0.82	0.93	0.79	0.84	0.77	0.82	0.93
	1000	0.99	0.98	0.98	0.94	0.95	0.93	0.95	0.98
5A	250	1.00	0.99	0.99	0.95	0.95	0.94	0.95	0.99
	500	1.00	1.00	1.00	0.95	0.95	0.95	0.95	1.00
	1000	1.00	1.00	1.00	0.95	0.95	0.95	0.95	1.00

[a] The 0.05 significance level is used in the composite model procedure and the Cox test. Bounds on the probabilities that these tests yield inconclusive results (i.e., accept both models) can be computed from: upper (lower) bound = 0.95 − lower (upper) bound on probability of rejecting the incorrect model and accepting the correct model.

TABLE V

Results of Group B Numerical Experiments[a]

Experiment	Sample Size	Probability of Rejecting Incorrect Model			Probability of Rejecting Incorrect Model and Accepting Correct Model				
					Composite model		Cox test		
		Composite mode	Cox test	Likelihood ratio index	Lower bound	Upper bound	Lower bound	Upper bound	Likelihood ratio index
1B	250	0.06	0.07	0.58	0.01	0.06	0.02	0.07	0.58
	500	0.08	0.09	0.61	0.03	0.08	0.04	0.09	0.61
	1000	0.11	0.13	0.66	0.06	0.11	0.08	0.13	0.66
2B	250	0.09	0.12	0.64	0.04	0.09	0.07	0.12	0.64
	500	0.14	0.19	0.70	0.09	0.14	0.14	0.19	0.70
	1000	0.24	0.32	0.77	0.19	0.24	0.27	0.32	0.77
3B	250	0.24	0.32	0.77	0.19	0.24	0.27	0.32	0.77
	500	0.43	0.56	0.85	0.38	0.43	0.51	0.56	0.85
	1000	0.80	0.84	0.93	0.75	0.80	0.79	0.84	0.93
4B	250	0.81	0.89	0.94	0.76	0.81	0.84	0.89	0.94
	500	0.99	0.99	0.99	0.94	0.95	0.94	0.95	0.99
	1000	1.00	1.00	1.00	0.95	0.95	0.95	0.95	1.00
5B	250	1.00	1.00	1.00	0.95	0.95	0.95	0.95	1.00
	500	1.00	1.00	1.00	0.95	0.95	0.95	0.95	1.00
	1000	1.00	1.00	1.00	0.95	0.95	0.95	0.95	1.00

[a] The 0.05 significance level is used in the composite model procedure and the Cox test. Bounds on the probabilities that these tests yield inconclusive results (i.e., accept both models) can be computed from: upper (lower) bound = 0.95 − lower (upper) bound on probability of rejecting the incorrect model and accepting the correct model.

TABLE VI

Results of Group C Numerical Experiments[a]

Experiment	Sample Size	Probability of Rejecting Incorrect Model			Probability of Rejecting Incorrect Model and Accepting Correct Model				
					Composite model		Cox test		
		Composite model	Cox test	Likelihood ratio index	Lower bound	Upper bound	Lower bound	Upper bound	Likelihood ratio index
1C	250	0.06	0.06	0.56	0.01	0.06	0.01	0.06	0.56
	500	0.07	0.07	0.58	0.02	0.07	0.02	0.07	0.58
	1000	0.09	0.09	0.61	0.04	0.09	0.04	0.09	0.61
2C	250	0.08	0.08	0.60	0.03	0.08	0.00	0.08	0.60
	500	0.12	0.12	0.65	0.07	0.12	0.07	0.12	0.65
	1000	0.20	0.19	0.70	0.15	0.20	0.14	0.19	0.70
3C	250	0.21	0.22	0.72	0.16	0.21	0.17	0.22	0.72
	500	0.36	0.39	0.80	0.31	0.36	0.34	0.39	0.80
	1000	0.64	0.66	0.88	0.59	0.64	0.62	0.66	0.88
4C	250	0.50	0.54	0.84	0.45	0.50	0.49	0.54	0.84
	500	0.81	0.81	0.92	0.76	0.81	0.76	0.81	0.92
	1000	0.99	0.98	0.98	0.94	0.95	0.93	0.95	0.98
5C	250	0.99	0.98	0.98	0.94	0.95	0.93	0.95	0.98
	500	1.00	1.00	1.00	0.95	0.95	0.95	0.95	1.00
	1000	1.00	1.00	1.00	0.95	0.95	0.95	0.95	1.00

[a] The 0.05 significance level is used in the composite model procedure and the Cox test. Bounds on the probabilities that these tests yield inconclusive results (i.e., accept both models) can be computed from: upper (lower) bound = 0.95 − lower (upper) bound on probability of rejecting the incorrect model and accepting the correct model.

model procedure and the Cox test of separate families of hypothesis. In all of the experiments, the likelihood ratio index gives a larger probability of rejecting the incorrect model and accepting the correct one than do the other comparison methods. The dominance of the likelihood ratio index is particularly great when the choice probabilities of the correct and incorrect models are close (experiments 1, 2, and 3 of each group). This is because in these cases, the composite model procedure and the Cox test have high probabilities of accepting both models, whereas the likelihood ratio index always indicates that one model is preferable to the other.

The probabilities that the composite model procedure and the Cox test of separate families of hypotheses yield correct decisions depend on the significance level that is used, and varying the significance level would change the results reported for these procedures in Table IV–VI. However, it has already been shown analytically in the case of the composite model procedure (see the discussion following Equation 56) and it has been found in the numerical experiments in the case of the Cox test that varying the significance levels of these tests does not alter the dominance of the modified likelihood ratio index in terms of the probability of yielding a correct decision.[11]

It may seem obvious that a procedure such as the modified likelihood ratio index, which always must accept one model and reject the other, will have a higher correct-decision probability than the composite model procedure and Cox test, which can yield uninformative results. However, it should be borne in mind that the relative magnitudes of the correct-decision probabilities for the various tests depend on the parameters of the probability distributions of the test statistics as well as on the possible test outcomes. It is easy to identify hypothetical values of these parameters that would cause the correct-decision probability of the likelihood ratio index to be less than that of either of the other tests. The analytic results presented in Section 4 demonstrate that such parameter values cannot occur in the case of the composite model procedure, and the results of the numerical experiments suggest that such values do not occur in the case of the Cox test. However, this is a consequence of the functional relations governing the parameter values, not of the possibility of uninformative outcomes in the composite model procedure and the Cox test.

Not surprisingly, with all of the comparison methods the probability of

[11] It is worth noting that although the modified likelihood ratio index has the highest probability of accepting the correct model and rejecting the incorrect one, it does not necessarily have the lowest probability of rejecting the correct model. For example, in Tables IV–VI, the probability that the modified likelihood ratio index rejects the correct model varies between 0 and 0.44, depending on the experiment, whereas the probabilities that the composite model procedure and Cox test reject the correct model are 0.05.

rejecting the incorrect model and accepting the correct one increases as the sample size and the differences between the two models' choice probabilities increase. In samples whose size is at least 250–500, the likelihood ratio index rejects the incorrect model and accepts the correct one with reasonably high probability (e.g., 0.80 or more) whenever the root-mean square (RMS) percentage difference between the choice probabilities of the two models exceeds 10–15%.

In the group A and group C experiments, where the chi-square test in the composite model procedure has one degree of freedom, there are no clear differences between the abilities of this procedure and the Cox test to reject the incorrect model and accept the correct one. However, in the group B experiments, where there are two degrees of freedom in the chi-square test, the performance of the Cox test is often better (e.g., in experiments 2B and 3B, and in experiment 4B with $N = 250$) and is never worse than that of the composite model procedure. This reflects the tendency of the chi-square test to lose power as the number of degrees of freedom increases (see Equation 55). It is likely that the tendency of the Cox test to dominate the composite model procedure becomes more marked as the number of degrees of freedom in the chi-square test increases beyond two.

In Monte Carlo studies involving comparisons of non-nested linear regression models with equal numbers of parameters, ANEURYN-EVANS AND DEATON[22] found that acceptance of the model with the larger log-likelihood value gave a higher probability of rejecting the incorrect model and accepting the correct one than did the Cox test. This finding is analogous to the dominance of the likelihood ratio index found here. In Monte Carlo studies with two-variable linear regression models, PESARAN[34] found that the Cox test had a higher probability of rejecting the incorrect model and accepting the correct one than did a composite model comparison. However, Pesaran used small samples (the largest had 80 observations), and the differences between the performances of the Cox test and the composite model procedure diminished greatly as the sample size increased. The two methods gave quite similar results with a sample size of 80. Thus, Pesaran's results seem reasonably consistent with the finding here that asymptotically the performances of the Cox test and the composite model procedure are similar when there is one degree of freedom in the chi-square test.

6. CONCLUSIONS

THE RESULTS presented here suggest that the likelihood ratio index, as modified to take account of differences between the numbers of estimated parameters in the models under consideration, provides a powerful method for comparing non-nested discrete-choice models. Assuming that the asymptotic approximations used here are reasonably accurate in samples of several hundred or more observations, very small differences in the values of the modified equal-probabilities likelihood ratio index for two models indicate with high probability that the model with the lower value is incorrect. Moreover, if one of the models being compared is correct, the modified likelihood ratio index in either the equal probabilities or the observed proportions form yields a higher probability of rejecting the incorrect model and accepting the correct one than does the composite model method. The results of the numerical experiments suggest that the modified likelihood ratio index also dominates the Cox test of separate families of hypotheses in this respect. In addition, the numerical experiments have given encouraging indications of the ability of the modified likelihood ratio index to choose the correct model in comparisons of models whose choice probabilities differ by at least 10–15%.

A situation that has not been treated in this paper but that is important in practice is the comparison of two models which may both be incorrect. In this situation, the ability of the composite model method and the Cox test to reject both models may give these methods an advantage over the modified likelihood ratio index. The modified likelihood ratio index could reject both models only in comparisons with a third model that approximates the correct model more closely than to the two original models.[12] Of course, any advantage of the composite model method or the Cox test in this situation would be obtained at the cost of a reduced probability of rejecting the incorrect model and accepting the correct one if one of the two models is correct. Presumably, the probability of choosing the best model if one of the two is a good approximation to the correct model also would be reduced. Further research will be required to clarify the nature of such trade-offs and the general usefulness of the composite model method and the Cox test in situations where both models may be incorrect.

APPENDIX

A.1 Regularity Conditions

In the case of comparisons based on a composite model, the composite is assumed to satisfy standard regularity conditions for maximum likelihood estimation. (See, for example Reference [12], Section 5f.) In the case of comparisons based on the Cox test of separate families of hypotheses or the likelihood ratio index, the following straightforward extensions of the standard conditions are assumed to hold.

Condition 1. The quantities j, $\underline{X}$, $\underline{\alpha}$, and $\underline{\beta}$ are contained in compact subsets of Euclidean spaces with the appropriate dimensionalities. Denote these subsets by C, S, A, and B, respectively.

[12] Aneuryn-Evans and Deaton[22] also have suggested the possible usefulness of the Cox test in situations where both models may be incorrect.

Condition 2. For all $j \in C$, $\underline{X} \in S$, $\underline{\alpha} \in A$ and $\underline{\beta} \in B$, $f(j, \underline{X} \mid \underline{\alpha}) > 0$ and $g(j, \underline{X} \mid \underline{\beta}) > 0$.

Condition 3. For each $j \in C$ and $\underline{X} \in S$ and for every $\underline{\alpha}$ and $\underline{\beta}$ interior to A and B, $f(j, \underline{X} \mid \underline{\alpha})$ and $g(j, \underline{X} \mid \underline{\beta})$ are three times continuously differentiable with respect to the components of $\underline{\alpha}$ and $\underline{\beta}$, respectively.

Condition 4. Given any $\underline{\alpha}_0 \in A$ and $\underline{\beta}_0 \in B$, the functions $E_f[\log f(j, \underline{X} \mid \underline{\alpha}) \mid \underline{\alpha}_0]$ and $E_g[\log f(j, \underline{X} \mid \underline{\alpha}) \mid \underline{\beta}_0]$ have unique maxima with respect to $\underline{\alpha} \in A$. The functions $E_f[\log g(j, \underline{X} \mid \underline{\beta}) \mid \underline{\alpha}_0]$ and $E_g[\log g(j, \underline{X} \mid \underline{\beta}) \mid \underline{\beta}_0]$ have unique maxima with respect to $\underline{\beta} \in \underline{B}$.

Either conditions $5f$ through $7f$ or conditions $5g$ through $7g$ must be satisfied. Only conditions $5f$ through $7f$ will be stated explicitly. Conditions $5g$ through $7g$ can be obtained by exchanging f with g and $\underline{\alpha}$ with $\underline{\beta}$ in $5f$ through $7f$.

Condition 5f. The sampling distribution of $(j, \underline{X})$ is $f(j, \underline{X} \mid \underline{\alpha}_0)$ for some $\underline{\alpha}_0$ that is interior to A. (In other words, $P(j \mid \underline{X}_P, \underline{\alpha}_0)$ is the correct model.)

Condition 6f. $\underline{\beta}_{\underline{\alpha}_0}$ is interior to B, and $\underline{\alpha}_{\underline{\beta}}^*$ is interior to A. (These quantities are defined in Equations 15 of the text.)

Condition 7f. The matrices $E_f[\partial^2 \log f(j, \underline{X} \mid \underline{\alpha}_0)/\partial \underline{\alpha} \partial \underline{\alpha}' \mid \underline{\alpha}_0]$ and $E_f[\partial^2 \log g(j, \underline{X} \mid \underline{\beta}_{\underline{\alpha}_0})/\partial \underline{\beta} \partial \underline{\beta}' \mid \underline{\alpha}_0]$ are positive definite.

Condition 8. Models P and Q are non-nested in the sense defined in Section 1 of the text.

Conditions 1 through 5 ensure that the maximum likelihood estimates of the parameters $\underline{\alpha}$ and $\underline{\beta}$ converge almost surely to unique points $\underline{\alpha}^* \in A$ and $\underline{\beta}^* \in B$. In other words, $\underline{\alpha}$ and $\underline{\beta}$ are asymptotically identifiable. If the sampling distribution of $(j, \underline{X})$ is $f(j, \underline{X} \mid \underline{\alpha}_0)$, then $\underline{\alpha}^* = \underline{\alpha}_0$ and $\underline{\beta}^* = \underline{\beta}_{\underline{\alpha}_0}$. These results are straightforward extensions of Theorem 6 of JENNRICH.[24] In addition, condition 4 guarantees that $\underline{\beta}_{\underline{\alpha}}^*$ (as defined in connection with Equation 26 of the text) is unique. Analogous results hold if the sampling distribution of $(j, \underline{X})$ is $g(j, \underline{X} \mid \underline{\beta}_0)$.

Conditions 3, 5, 6 and 7 make possible certain Taylor series expansions that are used in deriving the asymptotic distributions of the Cox separate families test statistic and the likelihood ratio index. These conditions also ensure that the maximum likelihood estimates of $\underline{\alpha}$ and $\underline{\beta}$ are asymptot ically normally distributed.

Condition 8 is required to establish that the Cox separate families test statistic and the quantity $N^{-1/2}\Delta L_{gf}$ defined in Equation 30 of the text (as well as the analogous quantity $N^{-1/2}\Delta L_{fg}$) are asymptotically normally distributed. $N^{-1/2}\Delta L_{gf}$ is used in establishing the asymptotic properties of the likelihood ratio index.

A.2. The Asymptotic Distribution of t_{Nf} when Model Q is Correct

The derivation given here is an extension of that given by Cox[17] for the case where model P is correct. Because the two derivations are very similar, the development here is given in outline form only. See Cox[17] for details.

If Model Q is correct, then asymptotically

$$N^{-1/2}[L_{Nf}(j, \underline{X} \mid \hat{\underline{\alpha}}) - L_{Ng}(j, \underline{X} \mid \hat{\underline{\beta}})] = N^{-1/2}[L_{Nf}(j, \underline{X} \mid \underline{\alpha}_{\beta_0}) - L_{Ng}(j, \underline{X} \mid \underline{\beta}_0), \tag{A1}$$

where terms of order $N^{-1/2}$ in probability have been dropped (Reference [17], Equation 12).

Note that $\hat{\underline{\alpha}} \to \underline{\alpha}_{\beta_0}$ as $N \to \infty$. Therefore, in terms of the notation of this paper Equation 15 of Cox[17] can be written as:

$$\begin{aligned} N^{-1/2}E_f[L_{Nf}(j, \underline{X} \mid \hat{\underline{\alpha}}) - L_{Ng}(j, \underline{X} \mid \hat{\underline{\beta}}) \mid \hat{\underline{\alpha}}] &= N^{1/2}E_f[\log f(j, \underline{X} \mid \underline{\alpha}_{\beta_0}) - \log g(j, \underline{X} \mid \underline{\beta}_{\underline{\alpha}}^*) \mid \underline{\alpha}_{\beta_0}] \\ &+ N^{1/2}E_f\{[\partial \log f(j, \underline{X} \mid \underline{\alpha}_{\beta_0})/\partial \underline{\alpha}'] \\ &\cdot [\log f(j, \underline{X} \mid \underline{\alpha}_{\beta_0}) - \log g(j, \underline{X} \mid \underline{\beta}_{\underline{\alpha}}^*)] \mid \underline{\alpha}_{\beta_0}\}(\hat{\underline{\alpha}} - \underline{\alpha}_{\beta_0}). \end{aligned} \tag{A2}$$

In addition, Equation 4 of Cox[17] can be written as:

$$N^{1/2}(\hat{\underline{\alpha}} - \underline{\alpha}_{\beta_0}) = -[N^{-1}\partial^2 L_{Nf}(j, \underline{X} \mid \underline{\alpha}_{\beta_0})/\partial \underline{\alpha} \partial \underline{\alpha}']^{-1}[N^{-1/2}\partial L_{Nf}(j, \underline{X} \mid \underline{\alpha}_{\beta_0})/\partial \underline{\alpha}]. \tag{A3}$$

As $N \to \infty$, the first term in brackets on the right-hand side of Equation A3 converges almost surely to $E_g[\partial^2 \log f(j, \underline{X} \mid \underline{\alpha}_{\beta_0})/\partial \underline{\alpha} \partial \underline{\alpha}' \mid \underline{\beta}_0]$. Therefore, asymptotically

$$N^{1/2}(\hat{\alpha} - \underline{\alpha}_{\beta_0}) = -\{E_g[\partial^2 \log f(j, \underline{X} \mid \underline{\alpha}_{\beta_0})/\partial \underline{\alpha} \partial \underline{\alpha}' \mid \underline{\beta}_0]\}^{-1} \cdot [N^{-1/2}\partial L_{Nf}(j, \underline{X} \mid \underline{\alpha}_{\beta_0})/\partial \underline{\alpha}]. \tag{A4}$$

Upon substituting Equations A1, A2, and A4 into Equation 16a of the text, the following asymptotic equation for t_{Nf} is obtained:

$$\begin{aligned} t_{Nf} = {} & N^{-1/2}[L_{Nf}(j, \underline{X} \mid \underline{\alpha}_{\beta_0}) - L_{Ng}(j, \underline{X} \mid \underline{\beta}_0)] \\ & - N^{1/2}E_f[\log f(j, \underline{X} \mid \underline{\alpha}_{\beta_0}) - \log g(j, \underline{X} \mid \underline{\beta}_{\underline{\alpha}}^*) \mid \alpha_{\beta_0}] \\ & + N^{1/2}E_f\{[\partial \log f(j, \underline{X} \mid \underline{\alpha}_{\beta_0})/\partial \alpha'] \\ & \cdot [\log f(j, \underline{X} \mid \underline{\alpha}_{\beta_0}) - \log g(j, \underline{X} \mid \underline{\beta}_{\underline{\alpha}}^*) \mid \underline{\alpha}_{\beta_0}\} \\ & \cdot \{E_g[\partial^2 \log f(j, \underline{X} \mid \underline{\alpha}_{\beta_0})/\partial \underline{\alpha} \partial \underline{\alpha}' \mid \underline{\beta}_0]\}^{-1} \\ & \cdot N^{-1/2}\partial L_{Nf}(j, \underline{X} \mid \underline{\alpha}_{\beta_0})/\partial \underline{\alpha}. \end{aligned} \tag{A5}$$

The first and third terms on the right-hand side of Equation A5 each can be written as sums of N independently and identically distributed random variables. Therefore, these terms are asymptotically normally distributed by virtue of the Lindeberg-Levy theorem. The second term on the right-hand side of Equation A5 is a constant. Therefore, t_{Nf} is asymptotically normally distributed. By taking the mean of the right-hand side of Equation A5, Equation 26 of the text is obtained. The variance of the right-hand side of Equation A5 is given by Equation 27 of the text.

A.3. The Asymptotic Mean of $N^{-1/2}\Delta L_{gf}$

Assume that model Q is correct. Expand $N^{-1/2}L_{Nf}(j, \underline{X} \mid \underline{\alpha}_{\beta_0})$ in a Taylor series about $\underline{\alpha} = \hat{\underline{\alpha}}$, keeping terms through order $N^{-1/2}$ in probability. Since $\partial L_{Nf}(j, \underline{X} \mid \hat{\underline{\alpha}})/\partial \underline{\alpha}$ is zero, the following result is obtained:

$$N^{-1/2}L_{Nf}(j, \underline{X} \mid \underline{\alpha}_{\beta_0}) = N^{-1/2}L_{Nf}(j, \underline{X} \mid \hat{\underline{\alpha}}) + (½)N^{1/2}(\hat{\underline{\alpha}} - \underline{\alpha}_{\beta_0})'[N^{-1}\partial^2 L_{Nf}(j, \underline{X} \mid \underline{\alpha})/\partial\underline{\alpha}\partial\underline{\alpha}'](\hat{\underline{\alpha}} - \underline{\alpha}_{\beta_0}). \tag{A6}$$

Asymptotically, $N^{-1}\partial^2 L_{Nf}(j, \underline{X} \mid \hat{\underline{\alpha}})/\partial\underline{\alpha}\partial\underline{\alpha}'$ can be replaced with $E_g[\partial^2 \log f(j, \underline{X} \mid \underline{\alpha}_{\beta_0})/\partial\underline{\alpha}\partial\underline{\alpha}' \mid \underline{\beta}_0]$. Therefore, the terms of Equation A6 can be rearranged to yield

$$N^{-1/2}L_{Nf}(j, \underline{X} \mid \hat{\underline{\alpha}}) = N^{-1/2}L_{Nf}(j, \underline{X} \mid \underline{\alpha}_{\beta_0}) - (½)N^{1/2}(\hat{\alpha} - \underline{\alpha}_{\beta_0})' E_g[\partial^2 \log f(j, X \mid \underline{\alpha}_{\beta_0})/\partial\underline{\alpha}\partial\underline{\alpha}' \mid \underline{\beta}_0](\hat{\underline{\alpha}} - \underline{\alpha}_{\beta_0}). \tag{A7}$$

Similarly, $N^{-1/2}L_{Ng}(j, \underline{X} \mid \hat{\underline{\beta}})$ is given through order $N^{-1/2}$ in probability by:

$$N^{-1/2}L_{Ng}(j, \underline{X} \mid \hat{\underline{\beta}}) = N^{-1/2}L_{Ng}(j, \underline{X} \mid \underline{\beta}_0) - (½)N^{1/2}(\hat{\underline{\beta}} - \underline{\beta}_0)' E_g[\partial^2 \log g(j, \underline{X} \mid \underline{\beta}_0)/\partial\underline{\beta}\partial\underline{\beta}' \mid \underline{\beta}_0](\hat{\underline{\beta}} - \underline{\beta}_0). \tag{A8}$$

It follows that to order $N^{-1/2}$ in probability

$$\begin{aligned} N^{-1/2}\Delta L_{gf} &= N^{-1/2}[L_{Ng}(j, X \mid \underline{\beta}_0) - L_{Nf}(j, \underline{X} \mid \underline{\alpha}_{\beta_0})] \\ &+ (1/2)N^{-1/2}\{-N^{1/2}(\hat{\underline{\beta}} - \underline{\beta}_0)' E_g[\partial^2 \log g(j, \underline{X} \mid \underline{\beta}_0)/\partial\underline{\beta}\partial\underline{\beta}' \mid \underline{\beta}_0] \\ &\cdot N^{1/2}(\hat{\underline{\beta}} - \underline{\beta}_0) + N^{1/2}(\hat{\alpha} - \underline{\alpha}_{\beta_0})' \\ &\cdot E_g[\partial^2 \log f(j, \underline{X} \mid \underline{\alpha}_{\beta_0})/\partial\underline{\alpha}\partial\underline{\alpha}' \mid \underline{\beta}_0] N^{1/2}(\hat{\underline{\alpha}} - \underline{\alpha}_{\beta_0})\}. \end{aligned} \tag{A9}$$

The first term in the braces in Equation A9 is asymptotically equivalent to the likelihood ratio test statistic of the hypothesis $\underline{\beta} = \underline{\beta}_0$ in model Q (see, for example, Reference [12], Section 6e). Therefore, this term is asymptotically chi-square distributed with k_Q degrees of freedom, and its asymptotic mean is k_Q. The second term in braces, when multiplied by

-1, would be asymptotically equivalent to the likelihood ratio test statistic of the hypothesis $\alpha = \alpha_{\beta_0}$ in model P if model P with parameter α_{β_0} and model Q with parameter $\underline{\beta}_0$ coincided. Thus, the mean of the second term would be $-k_P$. Since models P and Q do not coincide, the actual mean of the second term is $-k_P$ plus a correction term which has the same order of magnitude as $g(j, \underline{X} \mid \underline{\beta}_0) - f(j, \underline{X} \mid \alpha_{\beta_0})$ as $N \to \infty$. Denote this correction term by $0(g - f)$. Note that

$$E_g N^{-1/2}[L_{Ng}(j, \underline{X} \mid \underline{\beta}_0) - L_{Nf}(j, \underline{X} \mid \alpha_{\beta_0}) \mid \underline{\beta}_0] \\ = N^{1/2} E_g[\log g(j, \underline{X} \mid \underline{\beta}_0) - \log f(j, \underline{X} \mid \alpha_{\beta_0}) \mid \underline{\beta}_0]. \tag{A10}$$

Therefore, asymptotically

$$E_g(N^{1/2}\Delta L_{gf}) = N^{1/2} E_g[\log g(j, \underline{X} \mid \underline{\beta}_0) - \log f(j, \underline{X} \mid \alpha_{\beta_0}) \mid \underline{\beta}_0] \\ + (k_Q - k_P)/2N^{1/2} + N^{-1/2} 0(g - f). \tag{A11}$$

Define $\delta(j, \underline{X})$ as in Equation 42 of the text, and consider a sequence of models g such that $\delta(j, \underline{X})$ is of order $N^{-1/2}$ as $N \to \infty$ for almost all $(j, \underline{X})$. (In practical terms, this corresponds to N being large and $N^{1/2} \mid \delta(j, \underline{X}) \mid^2$ being small, as in the discussion following Equation 42. Note that $N^{1/2} \mid \delta(j, \underline{X}) \mid$ is not necessarily small.) Then the first two terms on the right-hand side of Equation A11 are of order $N^{-1/2}$, whereas the third term is of order N^{-1}. (The order of magnitude of the first term can be obtained from Equation 42 of the text.) Therefore, to lowest nonvanishing order in N, $E_g(N^{-1/2}\Delta L_{gf} \mid \underline{\beta}_0)$ is given by Equation 32 of the text.

Now suppose that as $N \to \infty$, $N^{1/2} \mid \delta(j, \underline{X}) \mid \to \infty$ on some set of $(j, \underline{X})$ values whose probability of occurrence exceeds zero. Then the first term on the right-hand side of Equation A11 is of order $N^{1/2}$ as $N \to \infty$, whereas the other terms are of order $N^{-1/2}$. Hence, to lowest nonvanishing order in N, $E_g(N^{-1/2}\Delta L_{gf} \mid \underline{\beta}_0)$ is given by Equation 31a of the text. This differs from Equation 32 only by terms of order $N^{-1/2}$. Therefore, as $N \to \infty$, $E_g(N^{-1/2}\Delta L_{gf} \mid \beta_0)$ approaches the right-hand side of Equation 32 regardless of the size of $\delta(j, \underline{X})$.

A.4. Generating the Explanatory Variables for Models Q in the Numerical Experiments

The values of the variables were generated through a process that produced correct-model choice probabilities which were distributed throughout the interval [0.05, 0.95]. The process consisted of repeating the following sequence of steps 50 times.

1. Select a permutation of the alternatives 1, 2, and 3 by cycling through the sequence (1, 2, 3), (2, 3, 1), (3, 1, 2). Label the selected permutation $[j(1), j(2), j(3)]$.

2. Select $Q_{j(1)}$ randomly from the uniform distribution on the interval [0.05, 0.90].

3. Select $Q_{j(2)}$ randomly from the uniform distribution on the interval $[0.05, 0.95 - Q_{j(1)}]$.

4. Set $Q_{j(3)}$ equal to $1.0 - Q_{j(1)} - Q_{j(2)}$.

5. Set the explanatory variables associated with alternative 1 equal to zero. Set $\bar{U}_{Q2}$ and $\bar{U}_{Q3}$ equal to the values that are consistent with the choice probabilities $Q_{j(1)}$, $Q_{j(1)}$, and $Q_{j(3)}$.

6. If there is only one explanatory variable (group A experiments), set x_j (j = 2, 3) equal to the value that is consistent with $\bar{U}_{Qj}$.

7. If there are two explanatory variables, select the value of x_{1j}(j = 2, 3) through independent random sampling from the normal distribution with mean zero and standard deviation 2.0. Set x_{2j} equal to the value that is consistent with the values of x_{1j} and $\bar{U}_{Qj}$.

ACKNOWLEDGMENTS

I THANK Margaret Zentner for her help in developing the computer programs used in the numerical experiments.

REFERENCES

1. T. A. DOMENCICH AND D. MCFADDEN, *Urban Travel Demand: A Behavioral Analysis*, American Elsevier, New York, 1975.
2. D. MCFADDEN, "Analysis of Qualitative Choice Behavior," in *Frontiers in Econometrics*, P. Zarembka (ed.), Academic Press, New York, 1974.
3. C. DAGANZO, *Multinomial Probit: The Theory and Its Application to Demand Forecasting*, Academic Press, New York, 1979.
4. C. F. DAGANZO, F. BOUTHELIER AND Y. SHEFFI, "Multinomial Probit and Qualitative Choice: A Computationally Efficient Algorithm," *Trans. Sci.* **11,** 338–358 (1977).
5. J. A. HAUSMAN AND D. A. WISE, "A Conditional Probit Model for Qualitative Choice: Discrete Decisions Recognizing Interdependence and Heterogeneous Preferences," *Econometrica* **46,** 403–426 (1978).
6. D. MCFADDEN, "Modeling the Choice of Residential Location," *Trans. Res. Rec. No. 673*, 72–77 (1978).
7. D. A. HENSHER AND L. W. JOHNSON, *Applied Discrete-Choice Modelling*, Croom Helm, London, 1981.
8. J. HOROWITZ, "Sources of Error and Uncertainty in Behavioral Travel Demand Models," in *New Horizons in Behavioral Travel Research*, W. Brog, A. Meyburg and P. Stopher (eds.), D. C. Heath, Lexington, Mass., 1981.
9. J. HOROWITZ, "Sampling, Specification and Data Errors in Probabilistic Discrete-Choice Models," in *Applied Discrete-Choice Modelling*, D. A. Hensher and L. W. Johnson (eds.), Croom Helm, London, 1981.
10. J. HOROWITZ, "The Accuracy of the Multinomial Logit Model as an Approx-

imation to the Multinomial Probit Model of Travel Demand," *Trans. Res.* **14B,** 331–341 (1980).

11. S. D. SILVEY, "The Lagrangian Multiplier Test," *Ann. Math. Stat.* **30,** 389–407 (1959).
12. C. R. RAO, *Linear Statistical Inference and Its Applications*, Ed. 2, John Wiley & Sons, New York, 1973.
13. A. WALD, "Tests of Statistical Hypotheses Concerning Several Parameters When the Number of Observations is Large," *Transact. Am. Math. Soc.* **54,** 426–487 (1943).
14. J. HOROWITZ, "Testing the Multinomial Logit Model Against the Multinomial Probit Model without Estimating the Probit Parameters," *Trans. Sci.* **15,** 153–163 (1981).
15. J. L. HOROWITZ, "Specification Tests for Probabilistic Choice Models," *Trans. Res.* **16A,** 383–394 (1982).
16. D. R. COX, "Tests of Separate Families of Hypotheses," in *Proceedings of the Fourth Berkeley Symposium on Mathematical Statistics and Probability*, Vol. I. pp. 105–123, J. Neyman (ed.), University of California Press, Berkeley, Calif., 1961.
17. D. R. COX, "Further Results on Tests of Separate Families of Hypotheses," *J. Roy. Stat. Soc.* **24B,** 406–424 (1962).
18. A. C. ATKINSON, "A Method of Discriminating between Models," *J. Roy. Stat. Soc.* **32B,** 323–353 (1970).
19. R. E. QUANDT, "A Comparison of Methods for Testing Non-Nested Hypotheses," *Rev. Econ. Stat.* **56,** 92–99 (1974).
20. T. J. TARDIFF, "A Note on Goodness-of-Fit Statistics for Probit and Logit Models," *Transportation* **5,** 377–388 (1976).
21. S. D. GUPTA AND M. D. PERLMAN, "Power of the Noncentral F-Test: Effect of Additional Variates on Hotelling's T^2-Test," *J. Am. Stat. Assoc.* **69,** 174–180 (1974).
22. G. ANEURYN-EVANS AND A. DEATON, "Testing Linear Versus Logarithmic Regression Models," *Rev. Econ. Stud.* **47,** 275-291 (1980).
23. M. H. PESARAN, "On the General Problem of Model Selection," *Rev. Econ. Stud.* **41,** 153–171 (1974).
24. R. I. JENNRICH, "Asymptotic Properties of Non-Linear Least Squares Estimators," *Ann. Math. Stat.* **40,** 633–643 (1969).

[23]

PERGAMON

Transportation Research Part E 37 (2001) 143–161

TRANSPORTATION RESEARCH PART E

www.elsevier.com/locate/tre

Confidence intervals to bound the value of time

Paula Armstrong, Rodrigo Garrido, Juan de Dios Ortúzar *

Department of Transport Engineering, Pontificia Universidad Católica de Chile, Casilla 306, Código 105, Santiago 22, Chile

Abstract

The derivation of a subjective value of time (SVT) requires finding the marginal rate of substitution between travel time and cost in a travel choice model. In the typical case of models with linear-in-parameters utility functions, the SVT is equal to the ratio between the parameters of travel time and cost. However, since model estimation yields an estimator of the true values of their parameters (with a certain probability distribution), the computed SVT is also an estimator with another probability distribution; then, it is important to devise a method to incorporate the randomness of the estimated SVT in project evaluation. In this paper, we consider this problem rigorously and propose methods to replace the typical SVT point estimates by the construction of confidence intervals for a certain probability level. This allows, in addition, to estimate the SVT limits (lower and upper) which may be used in sensitivity analyses of the calculation of project revenues in transport infrastructure investment. The paper proposes two forms for building these intervals: the *t*-test and the LR-test, and discusses the construction of intervals for Multinomial Logit (MNL), Hierarchical Logit (HL) and Box–Cox Logit (BCL) models. We use two samples where the values of the level-of-service attributes have been measured with an unusually high degree of precision. Other methods proposed in the literature are also studied (simulation of multivariate normal variates (MVNS), SVT normal approximation (NA), and re-sampling techniques) using the above data, and their advantages and disadvantages are analysed. In addition, the effects of different modelling elements on the size and quality of the constructed intervals are scrutinised, such as model specification, sample size and individual income. Finally, the proposed methods are compared and recommendations about the use of each one in practice are indicated.

Keywords: Value of time; Confidence interval; Discrete choice

* Corresponding author. Tel.: +56-2-686 4822; fax: +56-2-553 0281.
E-mail address: jos@ing.puc.cl (J. de D. Ortúzar).

1366-5545/01/$ - see front matter
PII: S1366-5545(00)00019-3

1. Introduction

In order to estimate the willingness-to-pay for savings in travel time (what is normally referred to as the subjective value of time – SVT – in the classic transport microeconomic literature, see for example, Jara-Diáz, 1999) modellers need to measure the trade-offs between travel time and cost faced by a target population represented by a statistical sample (e.g., individuals commuting from certain suburbs to the CBD). In fact, the SVT can be shown to correspond to the marginal rate of substitution between travel time (t_i) and travel cost (C_i) at constant utility.

In practice, the SVT is derived normally from discrete choice models based on random utility theory (Ben-Akiva and Lerman, 1985). As the systematic or representative utility function traditionally assumed in these models is linear and additive in the (fixed) marginal utility parameters, under this assumption the SVT corresponds to the ratio between the estimated parameters θ_t and θ_c of the attributes travel time and cost (see for example, Gaudry et al., 1989):

$$\mathrm{SVT} = \frac{\theta_t}{\theta_c}. \tag{1}$$

However, as estimates of the "true" model parameters, θ_t and θ_c are not really constants, but random variables with a certain probability density function (PDF), the "SVT point estimate" in (1) is also a random variable with an unknown PDF. Therefore, it was considered appropriate (Garrido and Ortúzar, 1993) to examine the consequences of replacing this single value by the construction of a confidence interval given a certain level of confidence.

Thus the basic objectives of this paper is to propose practical methods to build these confidence intervals and to test their properties in practice. The rest of the paper is structured as follows. Section 2 discusses various methods to construct confidence intervals for the SVT; Section 3 examines the impact of model structure and functional form in the characteristics of the constructed intervals. Section 4 discusses the main properties of some alternative methods suggested in the literature, and Section 5 summarises our main conclusions.

2. Confidence intervals for the subjective value of time

It is well known that the maximum likelihood estimation method yields parameters that are asymptotically distributed multivariate normal (Ben-Akiva and Lerman, 1985). Consequently, the SVT point estimate (1) is a random variable governed by an unknown PDF (the probability distribution for the ratio between two normally distributed variables is unknown a priori). Some things are known in special cases; for example, the ratio between two independently distributed standard normal variables follows a Cauchy PDF (Arnold and Brockett, 1992), but this is unstable since it has an indefinite variance and its mean does not have an analytical expression. Also, the ratio between two bivariate normal variables with non-zero correlation follows another unstable PDF, even more cumbersome than the Cauchy function (see Fieller, 1933).

Given these facts, it is highly likely that the ratio between the parameters θ_t and θ_c, which are components of a general multivariate normal population, be governed by an unstable PDF. It is necessary then to find an econometric procedure to make statistical inference on this ratio without resorting to the direct use of the associated PDF.

2.1. Proposed methods

2.1.1. The asymptotic t-test

The asymptotic *t*-test is generally used to prove if a normally distributed parameter is significantly different from zero. Ben-Akiva and Lerman (1985) present an extension of this test for a linear combination of the parameters. As θ_t and θ_c are asymptotically distributed normal, the following null hypothesis can be postulated:

$$H_0 : \theta_t - \mathrm{VT}\theta_c = 0, \tag{2}$$

where VT represents the SVT point estimate. The confidence interval is given by the set of VT values for which it is not possible to reject H_0 at a given level of significance. The corresponding test statistic is (Garrido and Ortúzar, 1993)

$$t = \frac{\theta_t - \mathrm{VT}\theta_c}{\sqrt{\mathrm{Var}(\theta_t - \mathrm{VT}\theta_c)}}. \tag{3}$$

This expression distributes normal for linear models and asymptotically normal for non-linear models like the Multinomial Logit (MNL) (see Ben-Akiva and Lerman, 1985). Garrido and Ortúzar (1993) also derived the upper and lower bounds for the interval as follows:

$$V_{S,I} = \left(\frac{\theta_t}{\theta_c}\frac{t_c}{t_t}\right)\frac{(t_t t_c - \rho t^2)}{(t_c^2 - t^2)} \pm \left(\frac{\theta_t}{\theta_c}\frac{t_c}{t_t}\right)\frac{\sqrt{(\rho t^2 - t_t t_c)^2 - (t_t^2 - t^2)(t_c^2 - t^2)}}{(t_c^2 - t^2)}, \tag{4}$$

where t_t and t_c correspond to the *t*-statistics for θ_t and θ_c, respectively; t is the critical value of t given the degree of confidence required and sample size and ρ is the coefficient of correlation between both parameter estimates. Expression (4) is a real number only if the radical argument is non-negative; it can be shown that this condition is met when the parameters θ_t and θ_c are statistically significant (so that t_c and t_t are greater than t). This condition assures positive upper and lower bounds.

It can be observed that the confidence interval derived from this formulation is not symmetrical with respect to the SVT point estimate (θ_t/θ_c), and that the interval's mid-point is greater than θ_t/θ_c as well. Another feature is that the value of ρ has a strong influence on the size of the interval. In fact, the bigger the values of ρ, the narrower the interval and vice versa, all other things being equal. In addition, the more significant the *t*-statistics are, the narrower the intervals (for details, see Armstrong, 1998).

It is also important to note that for large samples the following equality holds:

$$\lim_{\substack{N\to\infty \\ t_t t_c \to \infty}} V_{S,I} = \mathrm{VT}, \tag{5}$$

which agrees with the intuition that the larger the sample size, the smaller the interval size should be. We will come back to all these results in Section 3.

2.1.2. The likelihood ratio test

This method is based on imposing the linear restriction (2) to the maximum likelihood estimation process and comparing the statistical efficiency of the estimation with respect to the unrestricted case. The procedure consists in searching for values of VT for which the linear restriction is valid given a certain significance level. The null hypothesis is still the same as in the previous case but the test is performed according to the following statistic:

$$LR = -2[l(\theta_r) - l(\theta)], \tag{6}$$

where $l(\theta_r)$ and $l(\theta)$ represent the logarithm of the likelihood function for the restricted and unrestricted models respectively (see Ortúzar and Willumsen, 1994). LR is distributed χ^2 with one degree of freedom (corresponding to the single restriction imposed).

To illustrate this procedure, let us consider the following systematic utility function to be estimated:

$$V_{iq} = \theta_t t_{iq} + \theta_c C_{iq} + \sum_k \theta_k Z_{kiq}, \tag{7}$$

where t_{iq} and C_{iq} are the travel time and cost for the individual q, respectively, Z_{kiq} the attributes (different from travel time and cost) for individual q, and θ_k are their corresponding parameters. Replacing the ratio of θ_t and θ_c by VT into (7), the following utility function is obtained:

$$V_{iq} = \theta_c(\mathrm{VT}t_{iq} + C_{iq}) + \sum_k \theta_k Z_{kiq}. \tag{8}$$

Eqs. (7) and (8) allow the computation of the unrestricted, $l(\theta)$, and restricted, $l(\theta_r/\mathrm{VT})$, log-likelihood functions, respectively. Clearly, if the SVT is equal to VT, then $l(\theta) = l(\theta_r/\mathrm{VT})$, but different values of VT will yield different values of the restricted log-likelihood function. This method requires a search for the maximum and minimum values of VT for which the following inequality holds:

$$-2[l(\theta_r/\mathrm{VT}) - l(\theta)] \leqslant \chi^2_{1,1-\alpha}. \tag{9}$$

Appendix A presents an optimisation procedure to obtain the upper and lower bounds of the SVT confidence intervals in this case.

An advantage of this method over the previous one is that it is not restricted to linear utility functions. However, the process of constructing the intervals is more tedious than in the previous case because it requires an iterative procedure to obtain each limit (see Appendix A).

2.2. Methods suggested in the literature

At the start of this research project (Garrido and Ortúzar, 1993), there was no scientific literature on the topic of confidence intervals for the SVT. However, in the last few years, some work on this subject has been presented and we summarise it below.

2.2.1. Multivariate normal simulation

Ettema et al. (1997) discuss a general method to construct confidence intervals for the SVT in cases where the parameters of travel time and cost are even allowed to interact with other segmentation variables (the procedure also considers Jackknife estimation to derive intervals corrected from the repeated observations problem in SP data). Simulation is used to simultaneously calculate the parameters from a multivariate normal distribution, defined by the covariance matrix of the estimated travel time and cost parameters given by ALOGIT (Daly, 1992). Values for these are generated a sufficiently large number of times (ideally 1000) and the confidence interval is constructed on the basis of the mean and variance estimates of the generated sample; it is possible to simulate values for the parameters of travel time, waiting time, walking time and cost simultaneously. Finally, by simply calculating the 0.025 and 0.975 percentiles, the limits of the confidence interval at the 95% level are obtained.

An important characteristic of this method is that it does not need to introduce additional assumptions (other than normality for the maximum likelihood estimators). In addition to being a method applicable to any type of utility function specification, it considers the variance of the parameters and the correlation between them. The results of Ettema et al. (1997) suggest that when correlation increases, the size of the intervals decrease indicating that when correlation is not considered we may obtain extreme results.

2.2.2. SVT normal approximation

Yadlin (1997) constructs confidence intervals simply assuming that a continuous function of normal variates does follow a normal PDF. Thus, the SVT would be asymptotically distributed normal with mean equal to the ratio between θ_t and θ_c (the SVT point estimate), and variance given by

$$\mathrm{Var}(\mathrm{SVT}) = \frac{1}{N\theta_c^2}\left[\sigma_t^2 + \frac{\theta_t}{\theta_c}\left(\frac{\theta_t}{\theta_c}\sigma_c^2 - 2\rho\sigma_t\sigma_c\right)\right], \tag{10}$$

where N is the sample size, σ_t and σ_c are the standard errors of the estimates of θ_t and θ_c, and all the other elements are previously defined. This method is very simple and produces very narrow confidence intervals. However, it is based on a continuous function (i.e., θ_c can never take the zero value) and it assumes that the interval mid-point is equal to VT, but this does not happen in practice for samples of normal size as we will see below.

2.2.3. Re-sampling methods

In this case, numerous subsamples from an original sample are generated, and models are estimated (with the same specification) for each one of them. Thus, numerous values of the SVT are obtained allowing to approximate its probability distribution. Finally, the limits of the 95% confidence interval are computed by determining the SVT values that correspond to the cumulative probability being equal to the percentiles 0.025 and 0.975.

This method has at least one drawback: the original sample must be large enough to be divided into various subsamples of reasonable size; otherwise, artificial subsamples must be generated, but this procedure would implicitly force the SVT estimates to be very close to those obtained from the original sample yielding a very small range of values. However, re-sampling methods exist. The Jackknife and Bootstrap techniques (Shao and Tu, 1995) are now widely used in practice and their use has been recommended when an analytical solution does not provide unbiased estimators of a given parameter and its variance. The Jackknife method creates subsamples by deleting observations from the original sample, whereas the Bootstrap generates subsamples randomly (with repetition) with the same number of observations as the original sample.

Unfortunately, different combinations of observations generate different modelling results; in addition, the generation of all possible combinations (2^N) is practically infeasible.

In spite of these problems and only as an example, we will present some results obtained with the Jackknife method for 100 random re-samplings eliminating five individuals every time.

3. Impact of various modelling elements on the SVT confidence intervals

3.1. Data available for the study

The data set available for our study consisted of information on commuter mode choice for the morning peak in two corridors of Santiago (Las Condes-CBD, with 697 observations and San Miguel-CBD with 677 observations). The data was collected in the mid-1980s and is rather special in the unusually high level of precision achieved during the measurement of the level-of-service attributes. The data set has been described in detail elsewhere (see for example Daly and Ortúzar, 1990) and is used as the test-bed of the TRIO set of models (Gaudry et al., 1994).

The choice set includes five pure modes (Car-driver, Car-passenger, Shared taxi, Metro and Bus) and four combinations of Metro with the other modes. The main level-of-service attributes considered were in-vehicle travel time (IVT), walking time (WKT), waiting time (WT) and travel cost divided by either the expenditure rate (C/g) or by the wage rate (C/w). All these variables should have a negative effect on the representative utility function. In the expenditure rate model, g was defined as the ratio between income and the total time available for consumption (i.e., total time − working time, see Jara-Díaz and Ortúzar, 1989); in the wage rate specification, w was approximated by the ratio between income and working time (see Train and McFadden, 1978).

Additionally, the following socio-economic variables were considered: SEX, dummy variable that takes the value one for males and zero otherwise, AUTLIC, car competition variable, defined as the ratio between the number of cars and the number of driver licenses in the household with a ceiling of one. SEX is included in the modes Car-passenger, Shared taxi and Kiss and Ride and we expect a negative sign (these are modes more favoured by females); AUTLIC is included in the modes Car-driver and Park and Ride and we expect a positive sign for it.

To carry out some test on the effect of income on SVT and its associated confidence intervals, we stratified the complete sample by family income (FI) (taking care to express all income and cost figures in money of the same year).

3.2. Model structure

To analyse the effect of model structure on the size of the SVT confidence intervals (as it has being known for many years that this affects the SVT point estimate, see Gaudry et al., 1989), we estimated the following model structures: MNL, Hierarchical Logit (HL) with two versions: HL-1, which considers a public transport nest including all modes except Car-driver and Car-passenger, and HL-2, which also incorporates a private transport nest (grouping both car-based modes); and finally a Box–Cox Logit model (BCL). The first three structures were estimated using ALOGIT and the BCL using TRIO.

Table 1
Wage rate models for the Las Condes-CBD corridor

Model	MNL	HL-1	HL-2	BCL	λ
IVT	−0.0832	−0.1011	−0.1031	−0.0940	1.000
	(−4.80)	(−5.60)	(−5.50)	(−4.12)	na
WKT	−0.1608	−0.1964	−0.2014	−0.8200	0.012
	(−8.30)	(−9.10)	(−8.20)	(−8.25)	(0.06)
WT	−0.2389	−0.3250	−0.3268	−0.3600	0.057
	(−2.10)	(−2.60)	(−2.60)	(−2.33)	(0.09)
C/w	−0.0209	−0.0158	−0.0163	−0.2000	0.330
	(−2.80)	(−2.20)	(−2.20)	(−3.00)	(1.45)
SEX	−0.6419	−0.7226	−0.7412	−0.2900	1.000
	(−1.80)	(−2.10)	(−2.10)	(−1.36)	na
AUTLIC	2.317	2.1640	2.2210	2.3000	1.000
	(5.50)	(5.60)	(5.40)	(5.38)	na
Logsum[a]	na	0.48	0.51 0.79	na	
		(5.88)	(3.85) (1.41)		
$l(C)$	−1084.3243	−1084.3243	−1084.3243	−1027.94	
$l(\theta)$	−951.308	−938.577	−965.640	−930.102	
$\bar{\rho}^2$	0.1227	0.1344	0.1095	0.095	
LR(C)	266.0	291.5	237.4	195.7	

[a] t-test against one (rather than zero); na: not applicable.

Wage rate specification models for the first corridor are presented in Table 1; in the case of the BCL model, the values of the transformation parameters (λ) are given in addition to the values of the normal parameters and their t-test. All signs were as expected and most parameters were statistically significant at the 95% level (only models MNL and BCL presented t-test of 1.80 and 1.36 for the coefficient of SEX, which implies a level of confidence equivalent to 93% and 83%, respectively). All models are significantly different from the market shares model (see Ortúzar and Willumsen, 1994) since their likelihood ratio test, LR(C), is greater than 12.59 (the critical value of χ^2 with six degrees of freedom at the 95% confidence level). Finally, the best overall goodness-of-fit was obtained in the case of model Hl-1.

Some practitioners have suggested that a Box–Cox specification could replace the estimation of a HL model to tackle the problem of correlation between options. [1] To test this issue a sequential approach was used: first the BCL transformation parameters (λ) were applied to the respective level-of-service variables in the data set, and then a HL model (HL-BC), with identical hierarchical structure to that of model HL-1, was estimated with the transformed data.

This sequential estimation achieved a log-likelihood value at convergence of 961.804 (i.e., worse than those of the models in Table 1) and significant parameters with suitable signs. It is very important to note that the public transport logsum coefficient turned out to be significantly different from one (0.62). This implies that model BCL *does not* capture the effect of correlation

[1] The argument is as follows: non-linear effects that a MNL cannot capture might be picked up by a HL and the user led to believe that there is correlation among some options; a similar argument has been put forward by Börsch-Supan (1990) to justify use of the HL in the presence of heteroscedasticity (see Munizaga et al., 2000).

Table 2
SVT confidence intervals by the *t*-test method for the MNL

Variable	Travel time (Ch$/min)	Walking time (Ch$/min)	Waiting time (Ch$/min)
Upper limit	14.22	26.96	45.71
Lower limit	1.89	4.19	0.57
SVT point estimate	3.98	7.70	11.44
t(SVT)	2.42	2.65	1.68
ρ	0.033	−0.070	0.037
t	−4.80	−8.30	−2.10

Table 3
SVT confidence intervals by the LR-test method for the MNL

Variable	Travel time (Ch$/min)	Walking time (Ch$/min)	Waiting time (Ch$/min)
Upper limit	13.12	25.54	42.40
Lower limit	1.90	4.14	0.95
SVT point estimate	3.98	7.70	11.44
t(SVT)	2.42	2.65	1.68
ρ	0.033	−0.070	0.037
t	−4.80	−8.30	−2.10

Table 4
SVT confidence intervals by the *t*-test method for model HL-1

Variable	Travel time (Ch$/min)	Walking time (Ch$/min)	Waiting time (Ch$/min)
Upper limit	53.84	104.07	177.92
Lower limit	2.96	6.26	4.66
SVT point estimate	6.40	12.44	20.58
t(SVT)	2.05	2.14	1.68
ρ	−0.019	−0.109	0.009
t	−5.60	−9.10	−2.60

between options and/or that this persists over and above the non-linear effects allowed for by this specification. The latter suggests the convenience of using a hierarchical structure whenever correlation is expected to be present.

3.2.1. *SVT confidence intervals*

The *t*-test and LR-test methods were used first to estimate SVT confidence intervals for the MNL (see Tables 2 and 3). All results are given in Chilean $ (Ch$) of 1985 [2] per minute. Given the similarity of their results, only the first (and easier) method was used to construct intervals for the HL models (see Tables 4–6). Each table presents the upper and lower bounds of the intervals, the SVT point estimate (of each time variable) and its *t*-ratio, [3] *t*(SVT), the correlation

[2] At the time of the survey, 1 US$ = 160 Ch$.

[3] Constructed based on a first-order expansion of a Taylor series for the SVT around the point estimate (see Ortúzar and Willumsen, 1994, p. 416).

Table 5
SVT confidence intervals by the t-test method for model HL-2

Variable	Travel time (Ch$/min)	Walking time (Ch$/min)	Waiting time (Ch$/min)
Upper limit	55.11	108.97	182.07
Lower limit	3.82	6.14	4.54
SVT point estimate	6.32	12.34	20.03
t(SVT)	2.04	2.13	1.68
ρ	0.018	−0.027	0.015
t	−5.5	−8.20	−2.60

Table 6
SVT confidence intervals by the t-test method for model HL-BC

Variable	Travel time (Ch$/min)	Walking time (Ch$/min)	Waiting time (Ch$/min)
Upper limit	1.99	64.33	219.75
Lower limit	0.39	13.19	24.40
SVT point estimate	0.82	25.83	84.96
t(SVT)	2.40	2.74	1.58
ρ	0.002	−0.15	0.035
t	−4.50	−5.50	−2.80

coefficient (ρ) between the time and cost parameters, and the t-ratio of each time coefficient in the estimated model.

In order to understand these results, it is first important to mention that the mean wage rate of the sample was 8.06 Ch$/min; therefore, the SVT values in Tables 2–6 appear unusually high in relation to common knowledge (i.e., they are much higher than income). The only exception is in the case of in-vehicle travel time in the HL-BC model of Table 6, whose confidence interval is also narrower; but this pattern is not followed in the cases of walking and waiting time. Nevertheless, it is important to remark that SVT point estimates higher than income have been found in Chile before (see Gaudry et al., 1989). More importantly, it has been argued that values conforming to the standard norm (of SVT being smaller than income) in the literature may be, in many occasions, a statement of the "willingness-to-conform" syndrome enunciated by Talvitie (1980). In fact, if non-reported SVTs are computed from the published work of even very respected authors, one can often find also unusually high values in this sense (see for example McFadden et al., 1977; Swait and Ben-Avika, 1987).

Secondly, it is clear that the SVT point estimates (and their confidence intervals) vary strongly with model specification. In particular, the confidence intervals derived from the HL-BC model differ markedly from those obtained with the other models. Nevertheless, no general conclusions should be derived from this specification until more cases are analysed; at this stage, it is only possible to indicate that the effects of the correlation coefficient ρ and of the t-ratios are indeed as expected. It can be seen also that waiting times present confidence intervals wider than walking times and that the latter are also wider than those for in-vehicle travel times (the SVT point estimates for these attributes are also ranked in the same order). This is a consistent finding for all model structures tested.

Thirdly, although no direct relation has been established between the *t*-test and LR-test methods, it seems clear not only that the SVT confidence intervals derived with the former are slightly wider, but that the confidence intervals derived with the latter method are usually contained within the former. Finally, it has been shown empirically that the confidence interval derived from the *t*-test method is indeed asymmetrical with respect to the SVT point estimate, and that the interval mid-point is greater than the SVT point estimate.

3.2.2. Income effects on the SVT confidence intervals

Theoretically, individual income affects the subjective valuation of time. To test this in practice, we derived confidence intervals for expenditure rate MNL models, where the whole sample (i.e., both corridors) was stratified according to FI; we used three income strata (i.e., FI $\leqslant$ Ch\$70 000; Ch\$70 000<FI<Ch\$125 000; FI $\geqslant$ Ch\$125 000).Table 7 presents the estimation results for these three groups. All the models presented correct signs and significant parameters, except for the parameter of SEX, for the average and low income groups. Again, all estimated models outperformed the market shares model, since their LR(*C*) tests were greater than 12.59 (χ^2 critical value). Table 7 also shows that the individuals with high income have an expenditure rate almost 2.5 times that of the individuals with medium income, and these in turn have an expenditure rate twice that of the low income individuals.

Table 7
MNL models for different FI levels

Parameter	Low income	Medium income	High income
IVT	−0.0865 (−3.9)	−0.1177 (−5.6)	−0.0872 (−3.9)
WKT	−0.0844 (−3.9)	−0.1142 (−5.3)	−0.1400 (−6.8)
WT	−0.3601 (−3.7)	−0.2252 (−2.7)	−0.5066 (−5.2)
C/*g*	−0.0251 (−3.9)	−0.0243 (−2.9)	−0.0180 (−2.1)
SEX	−0.3325 (−1.0*)	−0.4604 (−1.5*)	−1.1121 (−3.8)
AUTLIC	2.0783 (2.4)	2.3211 (3.8)	2.0984 (4.2)
Car-driver	−2.6014 (−3.2)	−2.5143 (−4.4)	−1.9462 (−4.1)
Car-passenger	−2.6662 (−6.7)	−2.5760 (−7.4)	−1.7090 (−5.6)
Shared taxi	−1.6571 (−4.2)	−1.6462 (−4.7)	−1.2930 (−3.5)
Metro	1.5940 (4.1)	1.7410 (5.0)	3.0861 (8.7)
P&R	−2.8822 (−3.6)	−2.8433 (−5.1)	−1.2313 (−2.6)
K&R	−1.6790 (−4.7)	−1.7120 (−4.7)	−0.0517 (−0.2*)
Shared taxi – Metro	−1.6000 (−4.0)	−1.6352 (−4.6)	−0.4864 (−1.3*)
Bus – Metro	−0.8685 (−2.6)	−1.3212 (−4.1)	−0.3967 (−1.1*)
L(*C*)	−1.027.936	−1.027.936	−1.027.936
$l(\theta)$	−414.915	−524.482	−594.741
ρ^2	0.596	0.490	0.421
LR(*C*)	1226.0	1006.9	866.4
Expenditure rate (Ch\$/min)	7.53	2.95	1.31

* Not significant at 95% of confidence.

Table 8
Confidence intervals built with the *t*-test method

		SVT (Ch$/min)		
		Low income	Medium income	High income
IVT	Lower limit	2.01	7.29	13.32
	Upper limit	10.22	45.58	575.55
	Size	8.21	38.30	562.22
	Middle value	6.11	26.44	294.43
	SVT point estimate	4.53	14.34	36.36
WKT	Lower limit	2.16	6.98	27.54
	Upper limit	9.06	44.05	881.12
	Size	6.90	37.07	853.59
	Middle value	5.61	25.52	454.33
	SVT point estimate	4.42	13.91	58.40
WT	Lower limit	8.30	7.19	101.38
	Upper limit	41.26	91.15	2932.13
	Size	32.96	83.96	2830.75
	Middle value	24.78	49.17	1516.76
	SVT point estimate	18.86	27.44	211.33

Table 8 presents detailed information about the SVT confidence intervals computed with the *t*-test method (the LR-test method gave almost identical values, so they are not reported). As expected, individuals with high FI (more than Ch$125 000/month) value travel, walking and waiting times more than the other two groups; for example, in the case of in-vehicle time, the SVT point estimate ranges between 4.53 and 36.36 Ch$/min, whereas the confidence interval mid-points show an even bigger variation with income (from 6.11 to 294.43 Ch$/min).In addition, both the upper bound and the interval size also grow with income (see Fig. 1.).

Finally, it is worth noting that the medium and low income groups yield confidence intervals for walking time which are contained within the in-vehicle time interval. This is due to the unusual fact that these groups actually value in-vehicle time more than walking time.

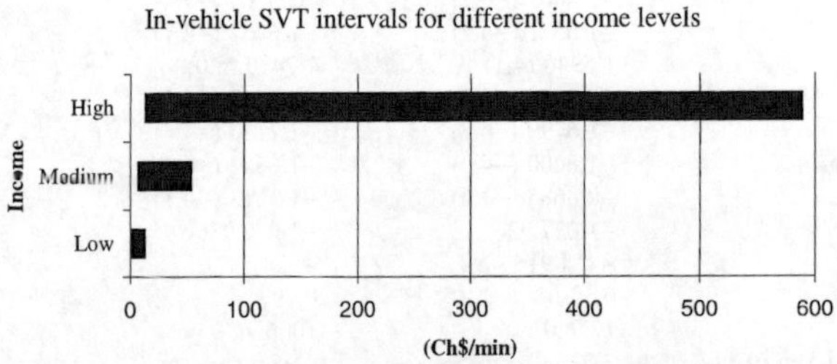

Fig. 1. Travel time confidence interval for different FI levels.

The above implies that when using a single value of time to evaluate projects that may affect different socio-economic groups, the willingness-to-pay of the relevant individuals may end up not being correctly assessed. Of course this does not mean that the savings of time of individuals with different income levels should be valued differently from a social point of view; but it is important to stress that high income people appear to be willing to pay even more than lower income people, than what their SVT point estimates suggest (the high income SVT intervals are almost 70 times ampler than those of low income people and around 15 times bigger than those of medium income individuals). Finally, it can be concluded that low income people are most sensitive to small changes in travel costs, as expected.

3.2.3. Impact of sample size on the confidence intervals

To analyse the sensitivity of the SVT intervals to changes in sample size, we calculated the SVT point estimate, and the mode, median and mean of the distribution using a simulation procedure. The simulation parameters were obtained from the MNL presented in Table 1.

The simulation procedure consists of generating a sample of artificial individuals and making them choose one of the available alternatives based on the specified utility function given the attributes and their parameters (see Williams and Ortúzar, 1982). Once the representative utility (for each alternative and individual) has been computed, a random term is added to form the corresponding random utility function. The random term is generated from an identical and independent Gumbel PDF, with zero mean and standard deviation equal to $\pi/\sqrt{6}$ (i.e., that required by the MNL). The utilities for each option are compared and that alternative with the highest one is assumed to be chosen. Thus, the artificial sample (simulated data) comprises attribute values for each alternative in the choice set plus the chosen option for each simulated observation. Then MNL models with the same specification are estimated using this artificial sample, and SVT confidence intervals for in-vehicle travel, walking and waiting times are constructed. However, only the case of in-vehicle time is reported here, since the behaviour of the three sets of confidence intervals were very similar (see Armstrong, 1998 for details).

The simulation/estimation procedure was carried out for generated samples of different size, from 697 observations (the original sample size) to 10,455 observations (15 times the original sample size). Table 9 presents the SVT confidence intervals estimated with the *t*-test method. The effect of sample size on the confidence intervals can be observed in Fig. 2. As expected, the figure shows that when sample size increases, the limits of the intervals tend to the SVT point estimate; although the latter is always smaller than the interval's middle value, their difference tends to decrease as the number of observations increase. It is interesting to note that the limits of the intervals do not show the same pattern when sample size increases, the upper level pattern being particularly irregular. Although it is not clear what causes this phenomenon, we feel that it could be due to the fact that the values of the lower limit are smaller and represent less percentage variation; as the upper limits have higher values, a small percentage variation may produce a large change in its absolute value.

Table 9
Variation of SVT confidence intervals for in-vehicle time with sample size

Sample size	Lower bound	Upper bound	SVT point estimate	Middle value	Interval size
697	6.99	21.23	11.83	14.13	14.23
1394	9.11	22.00	13.77	15.58	12.89
2091	9.85	20.24	13.84	15.05	10.38
2788	12.08	23.27	16.39	17.66	11.20
3485	12.29	22.50	16.32	17.38	10.21
4182	13.32	23.80	17.48	18.58	10.49
4879	13.28	22.39	16.99	17.84	9.11
5576	12.96	20.94	16.32	16.95	7.98
6273	12.01	18.75	14.87	15.36	6.71
6970	12.54	19.14	15.36	15.86	6.64
7667	12.22	18.19	14.80	15.19	5.97
8364	12.08	17.59	14.52	14.83	5.51
9061	12.11	17.27	14.41	14.69	5.16
9758	12.04	16.92	14.23	14.48	4.91
10455	12.08	16.81	14.20	14.45	4.73

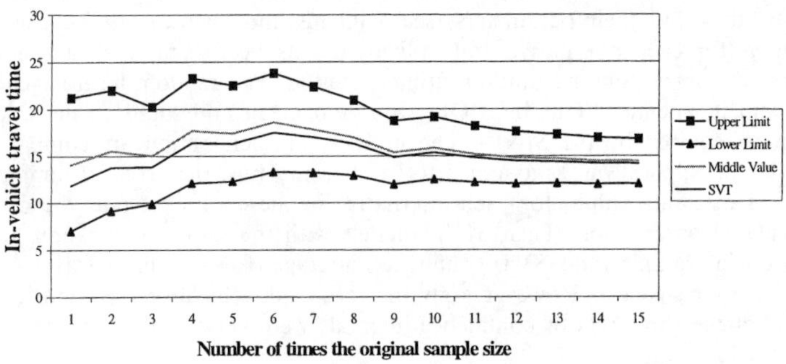

Fig. 2. Variation of SVT confidence intervals for in-vehicle time with sample size.

4. Other methods for building confidence intervals

SVT confidence intervals were built according to the following additional methods: simulation of multivariate normal variates (MVNS), SVT normal approximation (NA) and re-sampling techniques (i.e., the Jackknife method). The results are shown in Table 10 together with those obtained from our proposed methods. The MVNS is arguably the closest method to reality, as it reproduces precisely what happens when the ratio of two normal variables is taken. This method allows calculating not only the mean and the standard deviation of the ratio between θ_t and θ_c, but also its median and its mode (see Table 11); it is informative to note that the SVT point estimate (14.51) is very similar to the median in Table 11.

Table 10
Intervals for the SVT of travel time constructed with different methods

	MVNS	NA	Jackknife	*t*-test	LR-test
Lower limit	7.52	14.49	14.30	7.38	7.40
Upper limit	36.45	14.53	14.83	33.49	32.88
Size	28.93	0.04	0.53	26.12	25.48
SVT point estimate	14.51	14.51	14.51	14.51	14.51
Middle value	21.99	14.51	14.57	20.44	20.14

Table 11
Statistics for the SVT constructed by the MVNS method

Mean	Median	Mode	Standard deviation
15.27	14.16	17.34	32.60

It is clear that the various methods produce intervals that differ greatly in some cases. Nevertheless, on the one hand the NA and Jackknife approaches give similar results, and on the other, the MVNS and our two methods also give very close results. It is also interesting to note that the order of the statistics presented in Table 11 implies that if the SVT point estimate (14.51) was used for project evaluation purposes, the value of time could be underestimated as the latter value is clearly smaller than the middle value of the confidence interval.

The NA method needs the assumption that (for large size samples) the ratio between θ_t and θ_c follows a normal PDF with the SVT point estimate as the mean (14.51) and expression (10) as the variance (0.01). As can be seen in Table 10, in this case, the computed interval came out very narrow; the range being smaller than 1% of the expenditure rate; this is due to the small variance given by expression (10). However, an interval so narrow is not necessarily good. In fact, this interval does not even contain the median obtained from the MVNS method. In addition, the interval is symmetrical with respect to the SVT point estimate, which is unusual for the typical sample sizes used in practice.

Although the re-sampling method produced intervals with a very narrow range, this was due to the fact that each re-sample involved eliminating (randomly) five observations from the original sample, and this produced in turn very small variations in the SVT point estimates. We did not test the effects of deleting more observations, but had already observed that it was not feasible to test all possible deleting combinations. For these reasons and given our prior experience with re-sampling methods (Ortúzar et al., 2000), we are left with no choice but to insist in our call to be very careful when using these methods.

Finally, we have already mentioned that the *t*-test and LR-test SVT confidence intervals were very similar to those derived with the simulation of multivariate normal variables (MVNS) method. In fact, it can be seen above that both the lower and upper limits of the proposed methods are slightly smaller than those corresponding to the MVNS approach, and the same happens with the interval's mid-point. [4]

[4] In fact, only the limits of the interval for waiting time vary a little, in particular the lower one which exceeds 1% of the expenditure rate.

5. Final conclusions

The PDF of the SVT (calculated as the ratio of maximum likelihood parameters in discrete choice models with a linear utility function) is both unstable and unknown. Therefore it is not practical to derive directly a confidence interval for the SVT.

5.1. On confidence interval building methods

We proposed two methods for constructing confidence intervals for the SVT: the *t*-test and the LR-test. Our theoretical analysis allowed us to conclude that the interval's mid-point should be greater than the SVT point estimate, and that smaller confidence intervals should be derived from more significant parameters. Additionally, as the correlation between the time and cost coefficients becomes more positive, the range of the intervals tend to decrease. This corroborates the findings of Watson et al. (2000) who found that negative correlation between the time and cost variables (which maps onto positive correlation between the time and cost parameter estimates [5]) increased the level of precision of estimates of the point SVT. This suggests that when considering the value of time estimation, it would be useful to generate data sets that allow us to obtain positively correlated coefficients in the model estimation process.

The proposed methods were compared with three other approaches postulated in the literature. We found that intervals vary with the method used. The SVT NA method is the simplest to implement (because it only requires a simple formula for the variance), but our results indicate that the method is not appropriate: not only are the intervals obtained too narrow but they are also symmetrical, by construction, with respect to the SVT point estimate. The Jackknife method cannot be recommended either; on the one hand, it is a complicated procedure difficult to implement in practice, which takes a long computing time. On the other, it tends to produce a narrow range of values for the SVT, and although results vary with the number of observations deleted to create each re-sample, it is just not feasible to consider all possible deleting combinations. Finally, the simulation of MVNS is the method that clearly represents the case studied more accurately. However, it is tedious and requires considerable computing effort to be implemented.

Since the results obtained with the *t*-test and LR-test methods proved very similar to those derived by the MVNS method, we can confidently conclude that these methods provide an easy and practical way to obtain good confidence intervals for the SVT. Although, the first method is easier to implement than the LR-test, the latter is more versatile since it can be used for different functional forms of the representative utility. Thus, we recommend using one or the other depending on the context being studied.

5.2. On the impact of some modelling elements in the confidence intervals

SVT and their confidence intervals (both bounds and size) vary strongly with model specification; in other words, they are strongly dependent on the functional form assumed for

[5] We thank Jeremy Toner for pointing this out to us.

the representative utility, and on the model structure. Our empirical results corroborate that the mean values of the intervals are always greater than the SVT point estimates. Therefore, if the latter are used as values of time in project evaluation, we would be undervaluing how much the individuals actually value their time. For this reason, we recommend building confidence intervals for the SVT and carrying out sensitivity analyses using the values contained in them.

The intervals with narrower range for the in-vehicle, walking and waiting SVTs are always derived from the model with the specification that adjusts better to the data and presents more significant estimators. It is instructive to note that in our experiments the SVT of waiting time was always greater than that of walking time, and this one is always greater than that for in-vehicle travel time. The size of the intervals was also arranged in the same order.

The confidence intervals obtained from Box–Cox specifications differ from those obtained for more traditional specifications. Nevertheless, we believe it is necessary to estimate a greater number of this type of models to draw general conclusions. In this line, and from the estimation of a BCL model with a hierarchical structure, we were able to confirm empirically that when correlation is present, models of the Box–Cox type are not capable to take it into account, hence we recommend to use hierarchical structures when necessary.

The level of income of the individuals affects considerably the size and bounds of the confidence intervals. As income increases the SVT point estimates also grow, but the variation of the intervals' mid-point is much more drastic and the range of values increases considerably. Therefore, people with greater income would be prepared to pay even more than low income people for a reduction in travel, walking or waiting time than what the SVT point estimate would indicate. Our results also confirm the expectation that people with low income are more sensitive to small changes in the cost of travel.

Finally, as a result of a theoretical and empirical analysis we concluded that the limits of the confidence interval tend to the SVT point estimate as sample size increases. The SVT point estimate is always smaller than the interval's mid-point, and only tends to become equal to it for a large number of observations. In fact, the SVT point estimate tends to coincide with the median rather than the mean. On the other hand, the limits of the interval do not have a monotonic tendency with sample size increases, this effect being stronger for the upper bound.

Acknowledgements

We want to thank the Chilean Fund for the Development of Scientific and Technological Research (FONDECYT) for the support given to this research during many years.

Appendix A

Consider the following minimisation problem:

$$
\begin{array}{ll}
\text{Min} & \text{VT} \\
\text{subject to} & \\
 & -2[l(\theta_r/\text{VT}) - l(\theta)] \leqslant \chi^2_{1,1-\alpha} \\
 & \qquad\qquad\qquad\quad \text{VT} \geqslant 0
\end{array}
\tag{A.1}
$$

where VT is the optimisation variable; $l(\theta)$, and $l(\theta_r/\text{VT})$, are the unrestricted and restricted log-likelihood functions of a discrete choice model with the following systematic utility function:

$$V_{iq} = \theta_t t_q + \theta_c C_q + \sum_j \theta_j Z_{jq} \tag{A.2}$$

with the restricted version given by

$$V_{iq} = \theta_c(\text{VT}t_q + C_q) + \sum_j \theta_j Z_{jq}, \tag{A.3}$$

where t_q and C_q are the travel time and cost for individual q, respectively; Z_{jq} are attributes (different from travel time and cost) for individual q and θ_j are their corresponding parameters.

To solve the mathematical program (A.1), the following binary search strategy can be applied:

Algorithm (*SVT lower bound*).

begin

Estimate the unrestricted model and compute the values of $l(\theta)$ and $V^* = \hat{\theta}_t/\hat{\theta}_c$.

k = 0; Tol = 1000; Inf = 0; Sup = V^*;

While(Tol > ε)

begin

$\text{VT}[k] = \frac{Inf+Sup}{2}$;

$\text{LR}[k] = -2\{l(\theta_r/\text{VT}[k]) - l(\theta)\}$;

If ($\text{LR}[k] < \chi^2_{1,1-\alpha}$) **then**

begin

Sup = VT[k];

$\text{VT}[k+1] = \frac{Inf+Sup}{2}$;

end

else

begin

Inf = $V[k]$;

$V[k+1] = \frac{Inf+Sup}{2}$;

end

$\text{Tol} = |\text{LR}[k+1] - \chi^2_{1,1-\alpha}|$;

$k = k + 1$;

end

end

In this algorithm $\hat{\theta}_t$ and $\hat{\theta}_c$ represent the maximum likelihood estimates of θ_t and θ_c; ε is an arbitrary tolerance limit; $\chi^2_{1,1-\alpha}$ represents the value of the Chi-squared distribution for a significance level α, and one degree of freedom.

An analogous approach can be followed to obtain the upper bound.

References

Arnold, B., Brockett, P., 1992. On distributions whose component ratios are Cauchy. The American Statistician 46, 25–26.

Armstrong, P.M., 1998. Intervalos de Confianza para Delimitar el Valor del Tiempo. MSc Thesis, Department of Transport Engineering, Pontificia Universidad Católica de Chile, Santiago (in Spanish).

Ben-Akiva, M., Lerman, S.R., 1985. Discrete Choice Analysis: Theory and Application to Travel Demand. MIT Press, Cambridge, MA.

Börsch-Supan, A., 1990. Recent developments in flexible discrete choice models: nested logit analysis versus simulated moments probit analysis. In: M.M. Fisher, P. Nijkamp, Y.Y. Papageorgiou (Eds.), Behavioural Modelling of Spatial Choices and Processes. North-Holland, Amsterdam.

Daly, A.J., 1992. ALOGIT 3.2 User's Guide. Hague Consulting Group, The Hague.

Daly, A.J., Ortúzar, J. de D., 1990. Forecasting and data aggregation: theory and practice. Traffic Engineering and Control 31, 632–643.

Ettema, D., Gunn, H., De Jong, G., Lindveld, K., 1997. A simulation method for determining the confidence interval of a weighted group average value of time. In: Proceedings of the 25th European Transport Forum, Brunel University, England.

Fieller, E., 1933. The distribution of the index in a normal bivariate population. Biometrika XXIV, 428–440.

Garrido, R.A., Ortúzar, J. de D., 1993. The Chilean value of time study: methodological developments. In: Proceedings of the 21st PTRC Summer Annual Meeting, University of Manchester Institute of Science and Technology, England.

Gaudry, M.J.I., Duclos, L.P., Dufort, F., Liem, T., 1994. TRIO reference manual, version 2.0. Publication 903, Centre de Recherche sur les Transports, Université de Montréal.

Gaudry, M.J.I., Jara-Díaz, S.R., Ortúzar, J. de D., 1989. Value of time sensitivity to model specification. Transportation Research B 23, 151–158.

Jara-Díaz, S.R., 1999. In: Gunn, H.F. (Ed.), Income, leisure and the value of time from discrete choice models. The Value of Time, PTRC Education and Research Services, London.

Jara-Díaz, S.R., Ortúzar, J. de D., 1989. Introducing the expenditure rate in the estimation of mode choice models. Journal of Transport Economics and Policy XXIII, 293–308.

McFadden, D., Talvitie, A.P., Associates, 1977. Demand model estimation and validation. Special Report UCB-ITS-SR-77-9, Institute of Transportation Studies, University of California, Berkeley.

Munizaga, M.A., Heydecker, B.G., Ortúzar, J. de D., 2000. Representation of heteroscedasticity in discrete choice models. Transportation Research B 3, 219–240.

Ortúzar, J. de D., Willumsen, L.G., 1994. Modelling Transport, second ed. Wiley, Chichester.

Ortúzar, J. de D., Roncagliolo, D.A., Velarde, U.C., 2000. Interactions and independence in stated preference modelling. In: J. de D. Ortúzar (Ed.), Stated Preference Modelling Techniques, Perspectives 4, PTRC Education and Research Services, London.

Shao, J., Tu, D., 1995. The Jackknife and the Bootstrap. Springer, New York.

Swait, J., Ben-Akiva, M.E., 1987. Empirical test of a constrained choice discrete model: mode choice in Sao Paulo, Brazil. Transportation Research B 21, 103–116.

Talvitie, A.P., 1980. A look at the conceptual foundations of the transportation planning process. In: Proceedings of the International Conference on Research and Applications of Disaggregate Travel Demand Models, University of Leeds, England.

Train, K.E., McFadden, D., 1978. The goods/leisure trade-off and disaggregate work trip mode choice models. Transportation Research 12, 349–353.

Watson, S.M., Toner, J.P., Fowkes, A.S., Wardman, M., 2000. Efficiency properties of orthogonal stated preference designs. In: Ortúzar, J. de D. (Ed.), Stated Preference Modelling Techniques. Perspectives 4, PTRC Education and Research Services, London.

Williams, H.C.W.L., Ortúzar, J. de D., 1982. Behavioural theories of dispersion and the mis-specification of travel demand models. Transportation Research B 16, 167–219.

Yadlin, M., 1997. Private communication.

[24]

PERGAMON

Transportation Research Part B 37 (2003) 681–698

TRANSPORTATION RESEARCH PART B

www.elsevier.com/locate/trb

A latent class model for discrete choice analysis: contrasts with mixed logit

William H. Greene [a], David A. Hensher [b,*]

[a] *Department of Economics, Stern School of Business, New York University, 44 West 4th Street, New York, NY 10012, USA*

[b] *Faculty of Economics and Business, School of Business, Institute of Transport Studies, University of Sydney, Sydney, NSW 2006, Australia*

Received 23 April 2002; received in revised form 31 August 2002; accepted 3 September 2002

Abstract

The multinomial logit model (MNL) has for many years provided the fundamental platform for the analysis of discrete choice. The basic model's several shortcomings, most notably its inherent assumption of independence from irrelevant alternatives have motivated researchers to develop a variety of alternative formulations. The mixed logit model stands as one of the most significant of these extensions. This paper proposes a semi-parametric extension of the MNL, based on the latent class formulation, which resembles the mixed logit model but which relaxes its requirement that the analyst makes specific assumptions about the distributions of parameters across individuals. An application of the model to the choice of long distance travel by three road types (2-lane, 4-lane without a median and 4-lane with a median) by car in New Zealand is used to compare the MNL latent class model with mixed logit.

1. Introduction

Although the multinomial logit model (MNL) has provided the foundation for the analysis of discrete choice modeling, its basic limitations, most notably its assumption of independence from irrelevant alternatives (IIA) have motivated researchers to consider alternative specifications. The mixed logit model (McFadden and Train, 2000; Hensher and Greene, in press) is probably the most significant among a number of recent innovations in terms of the range of behavior it can

* Corresponding author. Tel.: +61-2-9351-0071; fax: +61-2-9351-0888.
E-mail addresses: wgreene@stern.nyu.edu (W.H. Greene), davidh@its.usyd.edu.au (D.A. Hensher).
URL: http://www.stern.nyu.edu/~wgreene

0191-2615/03/$ - see front matter
doi:10.1016/S0191-2615(02)00046-2

accommodate and its overall flexibility. The latent class model (LCM) proposed in this paper is in some respects a semiparametric variant of the MNL that resembles the mixed logit model. It is somewhat less flexible than the mixed logit model in that it approximates the underlying continuous distribution with a discrete one, however, it does not require the analyst to make specific assumptions about the distributions of parameters across individuals. Thus, each model has its limitations and virtues. This paper will compare the two models in the context of an application to the choice of long distance travel by three road types (2-lane, 4-lane without a median and 4-lane with a median) by car in New Zealand.

2. The latent class model

The LCM for the analysis of individual heterogeneity has a history in several literatures. (See Heckman and Singer, 1984 for theoretical discussion.) However, a review of the literature suggests that the vast majority of the received applications have been in the area of models for counts using the Poisson or negative binomial models. See Nagin and Land (1993) for an application and Greene (2001) for a survey of the literature. The model has had limited application to the analysis of discrete choice among multiple alternatives. Two exceptions are Swait (1994) and Bhat (1997).

The underlying theory of the LCM posits that individual behavior depends on observable attributes and on latent heterogeneity that varies with factors that are unobserved by the analyst. We propose to analyze this heterogeneity through a model of discrete parameter variation. Thus, it is assumed that individuals are implicitly sorted into a set of Q classes, but which class contains any particular individual, whether known or not to that individual, is unknown to the analyst. The central behavioral model is a logit model for discrete choice among J_i alternatives, by individual i observed in T_i choice situations,

$$\text{Prob}[\text{choice } j \text{ by individual } i \text{ in choice situation } t \,|\, \text{class } q] = \frac{\exp(\mathbf{x}'_{it,j}\boldsymbol{\beta}_q)}{\sum_{j=1}^{J_i} \exp(\mathbf{x}'_{it,j}\boldsymbol{\beta}_q)} = F(i,t,j\,|\,q). \tag{1}$$

The number of observations and the size of the choice set may vary by individual. In principle, the choice set could vary by choice situation as well. The probability for the specific choice made by an individual can be formulated in several ways; for convenience, we allow y_{it} to denote the specific choice made, so that the model provides

$$P_{it|q}(j) = \text{Prob}(y_{it} = j\,|\,\text{class} = q). \tag{2}$$

For convenience, we simplify this further to $P_{it|q}$. We have used a generic notation for the density of the random variable of interest to suggest that this formulation will provide a means of extending the LCM to other frameworks, though we restrict our attention herein to the discrete choice model. Note that this is a ‘panel data’ sort of application in that we assume that the same individual is observed in several choice situations.

We assume that given the class assignment, the T_i events are independent. (This is a possibly strong assumption, especially given the nature of the sampling design used in our application—a stated choice experiment in which the individual answers a sequence of survey questions. In fact, there might well be correlation in the unobserved parts of the random utilities. The latent class does not readily extend to autocorrelation, so we have left this aspect for further research.) Thus, for the given class assignment, the contribution of individual i to the likelihood would be the joint probability of the sequence $\mathbf{y}_i = [y_{i1}, y_{i2}, \ldots, y_{iT}]$. This is

$$P_{i|q} = \prod_{t=1}^{T_i} P_{it|q}. \tag{3}$$

The class assignment is unknown. Let H_{iq} denote the prior probability for class q for individual i (we consider posterior probabilities below). Various formulations have been used (see Greene, 2001). For this application, a particularly convenient form is the multinomial logit:

$$H_{iq} = \frac{\exp(\mathbf{z}_i'\theta_q)}{\sum_{q=1}^{Q} \exp(\mathbf{z}_i'\theta_q)}, \quad q = 1, \ldots, Q, \quad \boldsymbol{\theta}_Q = \mathbf{0}, \tag{4}$$

where $\mathbf{z}_i$ denotes a set of observable characteristics which enter the model for class membership. Roeder et al. (1999), using this same formulation, denote $\mathbf{z}_i$ the 'risk factors'. The Qth parameter vector is normalized to zero to secure identification of the model (Greene, 2003, Chapter 21). There may be no such covariates, in which case, the only element in $\mathbf{z}_i$ would be the constant term, '1', and the latent class probabilities would be simple constants which, by construction, sum to one. The likelihood for individual i is the expectation (over classes) of the class-specific contributions:

$$P_i = \sum_{q=1}^{Q} H_{iq} P_{i|q}. \tag{5}$$

The log likelihood for the sample is

$$\ln L = \sum_{i=1}^{N} \ln P_i = \sum_{i=1}^{N} \ln \left[\sum_{q=1}^{Q} H_{iq} \left(\prod_{t=1}^{T_i} P_{it|q} \right) \right]. \tag{6}$$

Maximization of the log likelihood with respect to the Q structural parameter vectors, $\boldsymbol{\beta}_q$ and the $Q-1$ latent class parameter vectors, $\boldsymbol{\theta}_q$ is a conventional problem in maximum likelihood estimation. Greene (2001) discusses the mechanics and various aspects of estimation. In comparison to more familiar maximum likelihood problems, this is a relatively difficult optimization problem, though not excessively so. For a given choice of Q, the choice of good starting values seems to be crucial. The asymptotic covariance matrix for the full set of parameter estimators is obtained by inverting the analytic second derivatives matrix of the log likelihood function.

An issue to be confronted is the choice of Q, the number of classes. This is not a parameter in the interior of a convex parameter space, so one cannot test hypotheses about Q directly. If there is a known Q^* that is greater than the 'true' Q, then it is possible to 'test down' to Q by using, for example likelihood ratio tests. A model with $Q+1$ classes encompasses one with Q if the parameters in any two of the $Q+1$ classes are forced to equality. This does move the problem up one level, since the Q^* must now be assumed known, but testing down from a specified Q^* is straightforward. ('Testing up' from a small Q (one) is not valid, since the estimates obtained for any model that is too small are inconsistent.) Roeder et al. (1999) suggest using the Bayesian information criterion

$$\text{BIC(model)} = \ln L + \frac{(\text{model size}) \ln N}{N}. \tag{7}$$

With the parameter estimates of $\boldsymbol{\theta}_q$ in hand, the prior estimates of the class probabilities are $\widehat{H}_{iq}$. Using Bayes theorem, we can obtain a posterior estimate of the latent class probabilities using

$$\widehat{H}_{q|i} = \frac{\widehat{P}_{i|q}\widehat{H}_{iq}}{\sum_{q=1}^{Q} \widehat{P}_{i|q}\widehat{H}_{iq}}. \tag{8}$$

The notation $\widehat{H}_{q|i}$ is used to indicate the person-specific estimate of the class probability, conditioned on their estimated choice probabilities, as distinct from the unconditional class probabilities which enter the log likelihood function. A strictly empirical estimator of the latent class within which the individual resides would be that associated with the maximum value of $\widehat{H}_{q|i}$. We may also use these results to obtain posterior estimates of the individual-specific parameter vector

$$\hat{\boldsymbol{\beta}}_i = \sum_{q=1}^{Q} \widehat{H}_{q|i}\hat{\boldsymbol{\beta}}_q. \tag{9}$$

The same result can be used to estimate marginal effects in the logit model;

$$\sigma_{km,itj|q} = \frac{\partial \ln F(i,t,j|q)}{\partial x_{it,km}} = x_{it,km}[1(j=k) - F(i,t,k|q)]\beta_{m|q} \tag{10}$$

for the effect on individual i's choice probability j in choice situation t of attribute m in choice probability k. The posterior estimator of this elasticity is

$$\hat{\sigma}_{km,tj|i} = \sum_{q=1}^{Q} \widehat{H}_{q|i}\hat{\sigma}_{km,ji|q}. \tag{11}$$

An estimator of the average of this quantity over data configurations and individuals would be

$$\hat{\bar{\sigma}}_{km,j} = \frac{1}{N}\sum_{i=1}^{N}\frac{1}{T_i}\sum_{t=1}^{T_i}\hat{\sigma}_{km,tj|i}. \tag{12}$$

3. The mixed logit model

The MLM is similar to the LCM, but embodies several important differences as well. The central equation for the choice probability is

$$\text{Prob[choice } j \text{ by individual } i \text{ in choice situation } t] = \frac{\exp(\mathbf{x}'_{it,j}\boldsymbol{\beta}_i)}{\sum_{j=1}^{J_i}\exp(\mathbf{x}'_{it,j}\boldsymbol{\beta}_i)} = P_{it}\,|\,\boldsymbol{\beta}_i. \tag{13}$$

The K model parameters are continuously distributed across individuals with

$$\boldsymbol{\beta}_i = \boldsymbol{\beta} + \boldsymbol{\Delta}\mathbf{z}_i + \boldsymbol{\Gamma}\mathbf{v}_i, \tag{14}$$

where $\mathbf{z}_i$ may be a vector of individual characteristics that affect the mean of the random parameter distribution and $\boldsymbol{\Delta}$ is the associated parameter matrix. The underlying random effect, $\mathbf{v}_i$ is characterized by

$$E[\mathbf{v}_i] = \mathbf{0}, \quad \text{Var}[\mathbf{v}_i] = \boldsymbol{\Sigma} = \text{diag}[\sigma_1, \ldots, \sigma_k] \tag{15}$$

and where σ_k is a *known* constant. The variances and covariances of the joint distribution of $\boldsymbol{\beta}_i$ are parametrized in the unknown lower triangular matrix $\boldsymbol{\Gamma}$ which is to be estimated. Since $\boldsymbol{\Gamma}$ is unknown, the assumption that σ_k is known is of no consequence. Where parameters are marginally normally distributed, for example, $\sigma_k = 1$ while if they have a logistic distribution, $\sigma_k = \pi^2/3$. The variance of the distribution of the parameters is

$$\boldsymbol{\Omega} = \boldsymbol{\Gamma}\boldsymbol{\Sigma}\boldsymbol{\Gamma}'. \tag{16}$$

As before, T_i observations are made on each individual. The conditional contribution to the likelihood is

$$P_i \mid \mathbf{v}_i = \prod_{t=1}^{T_i} P_{it} \mid \mathbf{v}_i. \tag{17}$$

In order to form the unconditional likelihood, it is necessary to integrate $\mathbf{v}_i$ out of the joint probability. Thus,

$$P_i = \int_{\mathbf{v}_i} P_i \mid \mathbf{v}_i h(\mathbf{v}_i)\, d\mathbf{v}_i, \tag{18}$$

where $h(\mathbf{v}_i)$ is the density of the standardized random vector $\mathbf{v}_i$. This integral will generally be intractable, even if $\mathbf{v}_i$ is not a mixture of distributions, which it may be. Recent applications have surmounted this difficulty by maximizing the simulated log likelihood function

$$\ln L_s = \sum_{i=1}^{N} \ln\left[\frac{1}{R} \ln P_i \mid \mathbf{v}_{ir}\right], \tag{19}$$

where $\mathbf{v}_{ir}$ is a simulated random draw from the assumed distribution. See Gourieroux et al. (1994) and Train (2003) for discussion and extensive analysis of maximum simulated likelihood estimation. One of the large virtues of the mixed logit model is that in the simulated likelihood function, one is not limited to the normal distribution; indeed, the components in $\mathbf{v}_i$ may be drawn from different distributions. They are independent, so the draws may be constructed individually. Thus, for example, one might wish to restrict a parameter to be positive or restrict the variation to a pre-specified range.

The mixed logit model also provides a person-specific posterior estimator of the parameter vector. With estimates of the structural parameters, $\boldsymbol{\beta}$, $\boldsymbol{\Delta}$, $\boldsymbol{\Gamma}$ in hand, let

$$\hat{\boldsymbol{\beta}}_{ir} = \hat{\boldsymbol{\beta}} + \hat{\boldsymbol{\Delta}}\mathbf{z}_i + \hat{\boldsymbol{\Gamma}}\mathbf{v}_{ir} \tag{20}$$

denote a draw from the individual-specific distribution. Then, the posterior estimate of the individual-specific parameter vector is

$$\hat{\boldsymbol{\beta}}_i = \frac{\frac{1}{R}\sum_{r=1}^{R}(\widehat{P}_i\,|\,\mathbf{v}_{ir})\hat{\boldsymbol{\beta}}_{ir}}{\frac{1}{R}\sum_{r=1}^{R}(\widehat{P}_i\,|\,\mathbf{v}_{ir})}. \tag{21}$$

The elasticities for a given choice situation can also be estimated

$$\hat{\sigma}_{km,tj|i} = \frac{\frac{1}{R}\sum_{r=1}^{R}(\widehat{P}_i\,|\,\mathbf{v}_{ir})(\hat{\sigma}_{km,tj|i}\,|\,\mathbf{v}_{ir})}{\frac{1}{R}\sum_{r=1}^{R}(\widehat{P}_i\,|\,\mathbf{v}_{ir})}. \tag{22}$$

One might then average these over individuals to characterize the sample.

4. A comparison of LCM and MLM

4.1. Empirical setting

To illustrate the behavioral contrasts of the latent class and mixed logit models, we draw on a study undertaken in New Zealand in 2000 in which a sample of car drivers undertaking a long-distance trip were surveyed with the intent of establishing their preferences for road environments. The drivers were sampled from residents of six cities/regional centers in New Zealand. [1] The main survey was executed as a laptop-based face-to-face interview in which each respondent was asked to complete the survey in the presence of an interviewer.

The centerpiece of the survey was a stated choice experiment. The choice experiment presented four alternatives to a respondent:

A. The current road the respondent is/has been using;
B. A hypothetical 2-lane road;
C. A hypothetical 4-lane road with no median;
D. A hypothetical 4-lane road with a wide grass median.

There are two choice responses, one including all four alternatives and the other excluding the current road option. All alternatives are described by six attributes except alternative A, which does not have toll cost. Toll cost is set to zero for alternative A since there are currently no toll roads in New Zealand. The attributes in the stated choice experiment are

1. Time on the open road which is free flow (in minutes);
2. Time on the open road which is slowed by other traffic (in minutes);
3. Percentage of total time on open road spent with other vehicles close behind (i.e. tailgating) (%);
4. Curviness of the road (a four-level attribute—almost straight, slight, moderate, winding);

[1] Auckland, Hamilton, Palmerston North, Wellington, Christchurch, and Dunedin on both the North and South Islands.

5. Running costs (in dollars);
6. Toll cost (in dollars).

Each sampled respondent evaluated 16 stated choice (SC) profiles, making two choices: the first involving choosing amongst three labelled SC alternatives and the current revealed preference (RP) alternative, and the second choosing amongst the three SC alternatives. [2] A total of 274 effective interviews [3] with car drivers were undertaken producing 4384 car driver cases for model estimation (i.e. 274 $*$ 16 treatments). The experimental design is a 4^6 profile in 32 runs. That is, there are two versions of 16 runs each. The design was chosen to minimize the number of dominants in the choice sets. Within each version, the order of the runs was randomized to control for order effects. For example, the levels proposed for alternative B should always be different from those of alternatives C and D.

In 32 runs it is straightforward to construct the following main effects plan: $4^9\ 2^4$. No interactions can be estimated without imposing some correlation. To obtain the 4^6 design, six columns in four levels were extracted from the nine columns available in the plan. This formed the base and the levels were manipulated to eliminate dominant alternatives in the choice sets. This is achieved, for example, by changing 0,1,2,3 to 2,1,0,3. Given that there are four levels and six attributes, a lot of designs can be produced. It is not difficult to produce a few of them and keep the one with the minimum number of dominant alternatives. In the present case the result of this procedure yielded a design with only one choice set presenting a dominant alternative. The dominant alternative has been used in a 2-lane road. Therefore all respondents who prefer driving on a 4-lane road might not see it as being a dominant alternative, because although all attributes of the 2-lane road are better, they may still be willing to trade them off for a 4-lane road. This produces a design that should conform well with the specifications of the study. [4] One of the two-level variables has been used to create the versions.

The four levels of the six attributes that were chosen are as follows:

- Free flow travel time: −20%, −10%, +10%, +20%;
- Time slowed down: −20%, −10%, +10%, +20%;
- Percent of time with vehicles close behind: −50%, −25%, +25%, +50%;
- Curviness: almost, straight, slight, moderate, winding;
- Running costs: −10%, −5%, +5%, +10%;

[2] The development of the survey instrument occurred over the period March to October 2000. Many variations of the instrument were developed and evaluated through a series of pre-pilot and pilot tests.

[3] We also interviewed truck drivers but they are excluded from the current empirical illustrations (see Hensher and Sullivan, in press for the truck models).

[4] The SC design is generic. The mean, range and standard deviation across 2-lane, 4-lane no median and 4-lane with median are identical. Although the attribute levels seen across the alternatives on each screen are different the design levels overall are identical. An alternative-specific design would be more complex since one can have different ranges across alts and would really require more choices or loss of explanatory capability on 16 sets from full 64. This generic structure has produced a generic specification for the design attributes that are treated in estimation as having random parameters.

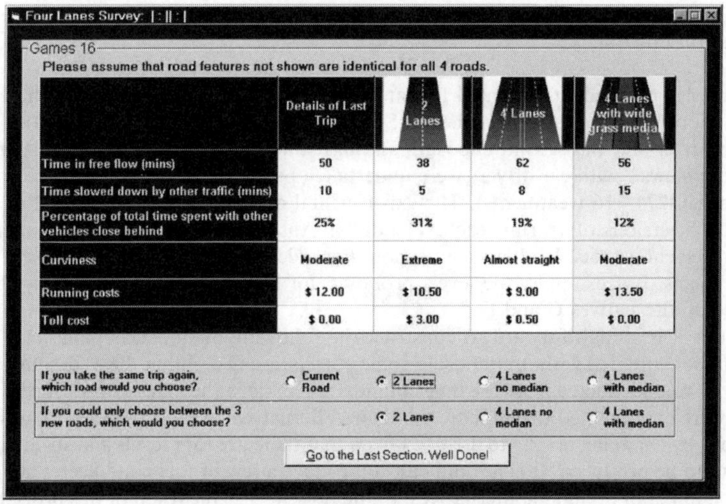

Fig. 1. An example of a stated choice screen.

- Toll cost for car and double for truck if trip duration is
  - 1 h or less: 0, 0.5, 1.5, 3,
  - between 1 h and 2 h 30 min: 0, 1.5, 4.5, 9,
  - more than 2.5 h: 0, 2.5, 7.5, 15.

The design attributes together with the choice responses and contextual data provide the information base for model estimation. An example of a stated choice screen is shown in Fig. 1. Further details are given in Hensher and Sullivan (in press). Herein we focus only on models where individuals choose amongst the three SC alternatives.

4.2. Empirical results

A series of choice models were estimated to arrive at the preferred LCM and MLM, summarized in Table 1 in which the travel time components were aggregated into a single measure. [5] We have specified travel time to have alternative-specific parameter estimates on the argument that the marginal utility of time is not independent of the circumstances under which travel occurs. This is analogous to distinguishing travel time on public transport in contrast to the car. The travel time attributes are defined as random parameters in the mixed logit model. We have selected a triangular distribution and imposed the constraint that the parameter estimates across the

[5] Estimators for both models are provided by NLOGIT Version 3.0 (Econometric Software, Inc., 2003).

Table 1
Estimated discrete choice models (t ratios in parentheses)

Attribute	Alternative	MNL	MLM	LCM		
				Class 1	Class 2	Class 3
Travel time[a]	2-lane (2L)	−0.00541	−0.0233	−0.00885	−0.0090	−0.0051
		(−5.9)	(−19.9)	(−3.0)	(−6.9)	(−5.5)
Travel time	4-lane w/out median (4NM)	−0.00475	−0.0188	−0.01119	−0.0068	−0.0063
		(−5.3)	(−19.7)	(−4.4)	(−6.6)	(−6.2)
Travel time	4-lane with median (4WM)	−0.00375	−0.0193	−0.00348	−0.0062	−0.00424
		(−4.4)	(−19.6)	(−1.4)	(−5.6)	(−4.3)
Percent time being tailgated (%)	All	−0.01061	−0.01418	−0.00976	−0.0308	−0.0039
		(−6.1)	(−7.1)	(−2.6)	(−15.2)	(−1.6)
Total trip cost (toll plus running cost)[b]	All	−0.1292	−0.1889	−0.1565	−0.0741	−0.2447
		(−25.70)	(−27.9)	(−15.9)	(−13.6)	(−43.3)
4NM constant	4NM	0.22029	0.01778	2.0259	0.9637	−0.3533
		(2.8)	(0.2)	(7.9)	(8.6)	(−4.9)
4WM constant	4WM	0.72072	0.5982	3.0696	0.6770	−0.2886
		(10.3)	(5.7)	(12.9)	(5.3)	(−4.8)
Travel time standard deviation	2L	–	0.0233	–	–	–
			(19.9)			
Travel time standard deviation	4NM	–	0.0188	–	–	–
			(19.7)			
Travel time standard deviation	4WM	–	0.0193	–	–	–
			(19.6)			
Latent class probability		–	–	0.31722	0.2703	0.4124
				(10.5)	(8.4)	(12.3)
Log-likelihood[c]		−4095.2	−3594.6		−3532.9	
Pseudo-R^2		0.0999	0.2531		0.2645	

[a] Travel time is in minutes.
[b] Cost is in dollars.
[c] 4384 observations, 16 observations per person.

distribution cannot change sign. In particular, we set the spread of the triangular distribution to 1.0. Given the definition of the profile of the betas under a triangular distribution as $\beta_i + \text{scale} \times \beta_i \times t$ where t is the underlying random variable with the triangular distribution that ranges from −1 to +1. With the scale t equal to 1.0, the range of β_i is transformed to the interval 0 to $2\beta_1$.

Three latent classes were selected as the best fit from 2, 3, 4 and 5 classes. To facilitate comparisons we restricted the set of attributes and their generic vs alternative-specific specification to a common condition. Comparing different models is always a challenging task given the many domains of contrast. Behavioral outputs such as choice elasticities, willingness to pay valuations (e.g. value of travel time savings) and choice probability profiles offer useful means of comparison in addition to the set of statistical measures of fit. From the results in Table 1, based on the log likelihood values, we can safely reject the MNL model in favor of either the mixed logit or latent class model. (The MNL is a special case of both models.) Since the mixed logit and latent class models are not nested the comparison on a likelihood ratio test is not appropriate.

Table 2
Implied values of travel time savings (willingness to pay) ($NZ per person hour) ns = not statistically significant (estimates in parentheses for MLM are the standard deviation values)

Alternative	MNL	MLM	LCM		
			Class 1	Class 2	Class 3
2-lane (2L)	2.52	7.36 (3.01)	3.39	7.33	1.26
4-lane w/out median (4NM)	2.20	6.06 (2.41)	4.30	5.53	1.55
4-lane with median (4WM)	1.74	6.11 (2.48)	1.34 (ns)	5.02	1.04

Evaluating the absolute parameter estimates across models is not informative because of scale differences (Louviere et al., 2000). [6] However contrasts of willingness to pay indicators and elasticities is very informative. We present summaries of the implied values of travel time savings (VTTS) in Table 2 and kernel density estimators for the empirical estimates in Fig. 2. [7] The mean estimates of VTTS differ a great deal across the three latent classes for LCM although the variation is surprisingly similar to the profile for MLM for two lanes with mean values higher and lower than the mean for MLM. Class 2 has almost the same mean estimate as MLM for two lanes. In contrast, all class mean VTTS are lower in four lanes (with and without the median) for LCM compared to the mean for mixed logit, although the VTTS distribution in mixed logit for four lanes captures the mean and two standard deviations for all three classes in LCM. Overall the latent class model has revealed three segments of apparent low (class 3), medium (class 1) and high

[6] Note as well that the models are parametrized differently. The MLM is somewhat more parsimonious in its characterization of the underlying distribution. The LCM assumes a fixed parameter vector in each class, with the overall mean being a function of how these are mixed by the class probabilities. These, in turn, may depend on covariates, $\mathbf{z}_i$ and parameters $\boldsymbol{\theta}_j$. The mixed logit model, in contrast, parametrizes the mean of the underlying distributions with a constant and (possibly) person-specific levels, $\Delta\mathbf{z}_i$ and covariance matrix $\boldsymbol{\Gamma\Gamma}'$. Thus, either might have the deeper parametrization, depending on the application. An important implication is that it is not useful to compare these models based on parameter estimates. It will be much more meaningful to base any comparison on model predictions such as choice probabilities, elasticities, simulations, and so on. Another important difference between the models concerns correlation across the choice situations. The latent class model assumes that the choices are independent draws from the distribution. The mixed logit model holds the random vector $\mathbf{v}_i$ the same in all choice situations, which induces the correlation across choice settings. Once again, this is part of the deeper parametrization of the mixed model versus the less detailed specification of the latent class model.

[7] The kernel density function for a single attribute is computed using the following formula:

$$\hat{f}(z_j) = \frac{1}{n}\sum_{i=1}^{n}\frac{K\lfloor(z_j - x_i)/h\rfloor}{h}, \quad j = 1,\ldots,M$$

computed for a specified set of values z_j, $j = 1,\ldots,M$. z_j is a partition of the range of the attribute. Each value requires a sum over the full sample of n values. The kernel function, $K[\cdot]$ may take any of a number of forms. For example, the logit kernel is $K[z] = \Lambda(z)[1 - \Lambda(z)]$, the normal is $K[z] = \phi(z)$ (normal density). The other essential part of the computation is the smoothing (bandwidth) parameter h. Large values of h stabilize the function, but tend to flatten it and reduce the resolution. Small values of h produce greater detail, but also cause the estimator to become less stable. The bandwidth used in our application is a typical one, $h = 0.9Q/n^{0.2}$ where $Q = \min(\text{standard deviation, range}/1.5)$. The number of points must be specified. The set of points z_j is (for any number of points) defined by formula: $z_j = z_L + j[(z_U - z_L)/M]$, $j = 1,\ldots,M$, $z_L = \min(x) - h$ to $z_U = \max(x) + h$. The procedure produces an $M \times 2$ matrix in which the first column contains z_j and the second column contains the values of $\hat{f}(z_j)$ and plot of the second column against the first—this is the estimated density function.

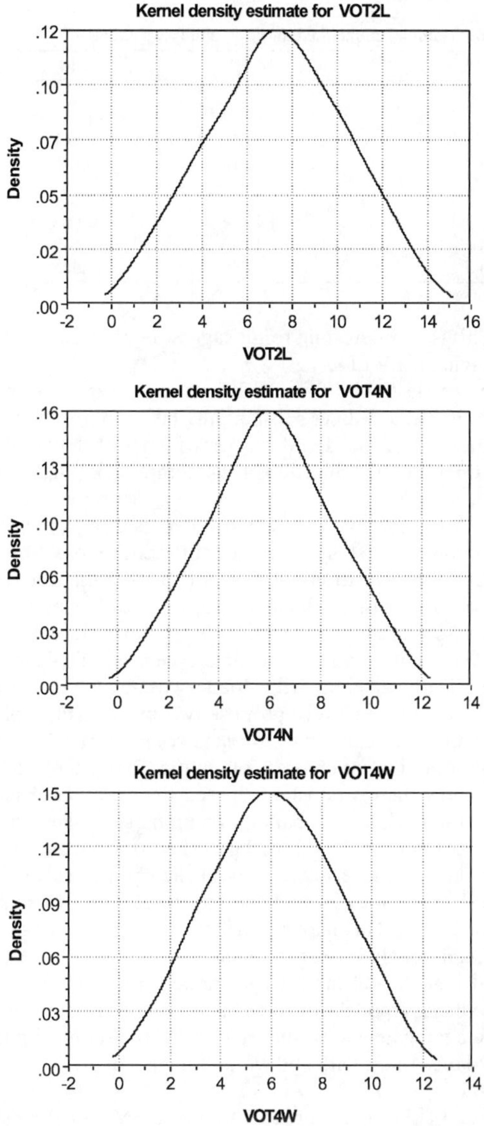

Fig. 2. Value of travel time savings distributions for mixed logit (triangular distribution).

Table 3
Implied direct share elasticities (sample enumerated and probability weighted)

Alternative	MNL	MLM	LCM
(i) Travel time			
2-lane (2L)	−0.483	−1.096	−0.474
4-lane w/out median (4NM)	−0.357	−0.861	−0.471
4-lane with median (4WM)	−0.210	−0.740	−0.187
(ii) Travel cost			
2-lane (2L)	−2.134	−2.009	−2.498
4-lane w/out median (4NM)	−1.818	−1.807	−1.745
4-lane with median (4WM)	−1.396	−1.455	−1.194

(class 2) mean VTTS. This is an interesting result suggesting that the latent influences are to some extent related to an individual's VTTS.

Summaries of the choice elasticities for travel time and travel cost are given in Table 3. The choice (share) elasticities in Table 3 differ substantially between mixed logit and latent class logit, especially for travel time. Indeed the LCM suggests far less behavioral response sensitivity to changes in travel times than does the mixed logit. By comparison, the total cost choice elasticities are relatively similar. In both MLM and LCM for both attributes the elasticities decline as we move from two lanes to four lanes with a median. There is directional consistency.

Another useful behavioral contrast is the profiles of the choice probabilities for each alternative under the MLM and LCM specifications. A kernel density estimator is used to graph the distributions non-parametrically for mixed logit (Fig. 3) and latent class logit (Fig. 4).

An assessment of Figs. 3 and 4 suggest that the choice probability ranges for the latent class and mixed logits are somewhat similar with the possible exception of 2-lane. However the shapes of the distributions are markedly different with 4-lane without a median displaying the greatest similarity. To illuminate the differences we propose two profiles: (a) a plot of the choice probabilities for mixed logit and latent class logit for each respondent's choice set (Fig. 5), and (b) a graphing of the ratio of the equivalent choice probabilities for each respondent choice set (Fig. 6).

The graphs in Fig. 5 show the relationship between the choice probabilities under MLM and LCM most vividly. The 4-lane choice probabilities map most closely, especially 4-lane without a median which are tight around the 45 degree line. The OLS models accompanying the graphs show that over 77% of the variance associated with the choice probability for LCM for 4-lane without a median explains the choice probability for mixed logit. In contrast only 35.7% of the variance is explained for 2-lane. This may be attributable to the least-favored 2-lane alternative From this evidence we can conclude that the relationship between the predicted choice probabilities under the mixed logit model (and a constrained triangular distribution on the random parameters) and the latent class model (for three latent classes) is relatively weak at the individual respondent level. At the aggregate choice shares level for the sampled population, the respective shares respectively for 2-lane, 4-lane with and without a median are MLM: 0.233, 0.315, 0.451 and LCM: 0.317, 0.270, 0.412.

When we take the ratio of the choice probabilities of LCM to MLM (Fig. 6) we find that the distribution around 1.0 is skewed to the left for 2-lane, and slightly to the right for 4-lane with and without a median. The majority of the ratios lie in the 0 to 2 band. Again there is a noticeable

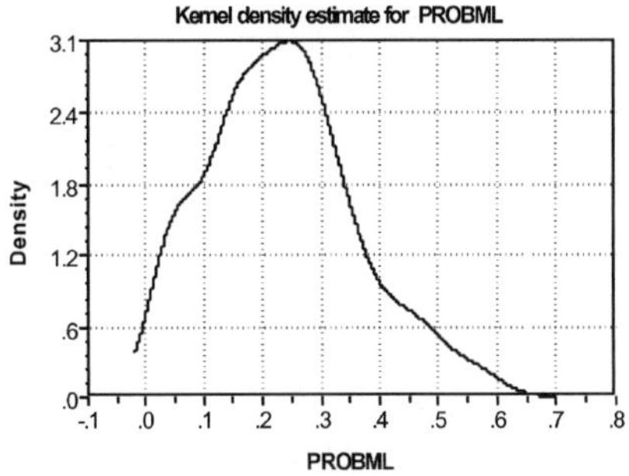

(i) 2 Lane

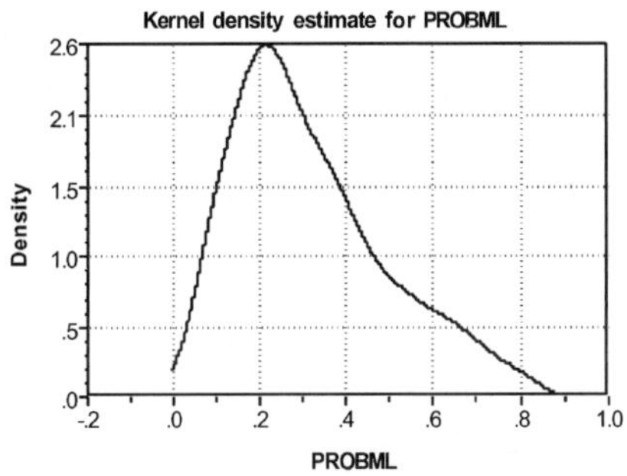

(ii) 4 Lanes without a median

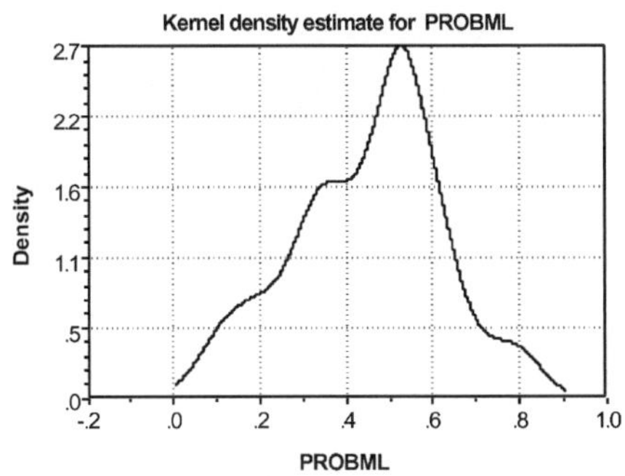

(iii) 4 Lane with Median

Fig. 3. Kernel densities for choice probabilities for the mixed logit (triangular distribution).

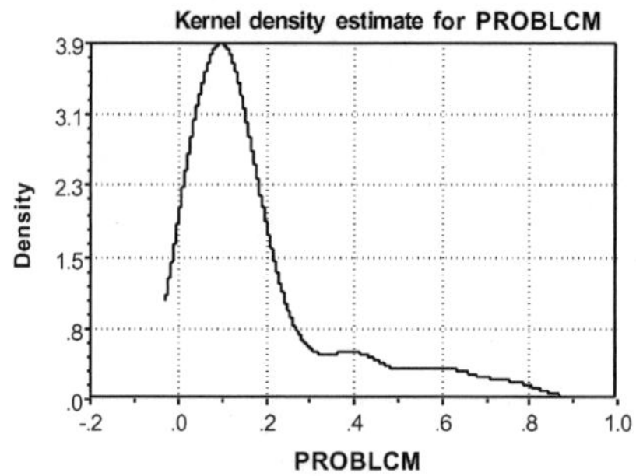

(i) 2 Lane

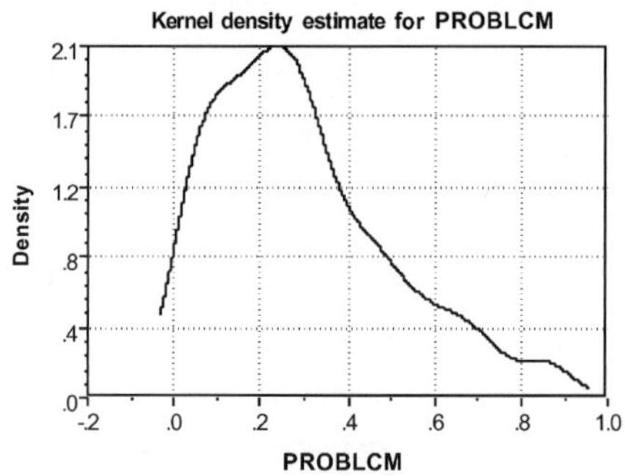

(ii) 4 Lane without median

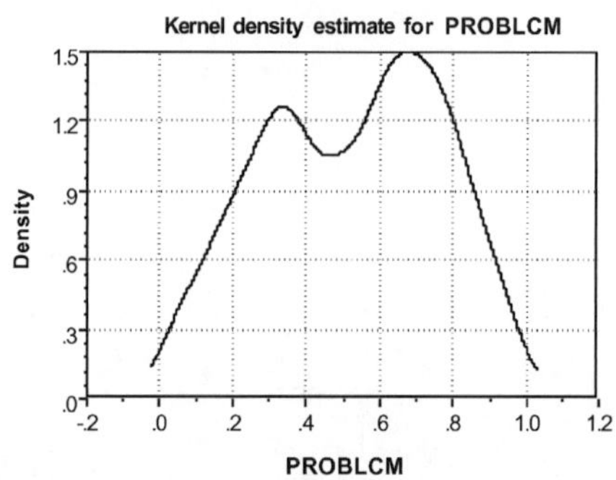

(iii) 4 Lane with Median

Fig. 4. Kernel densities for the choice probabilities for the latent class model.

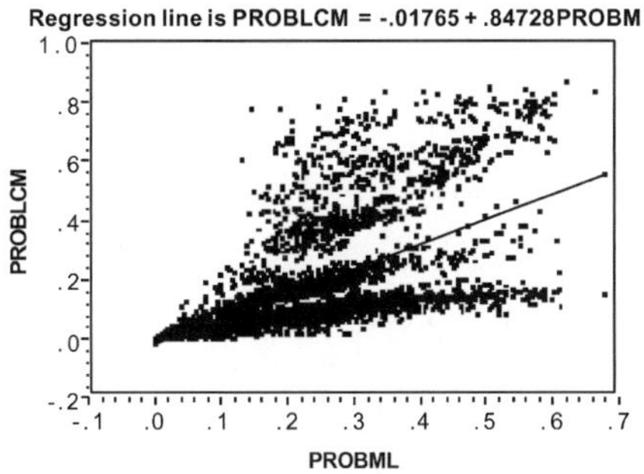

(i) 2 Lane ($R^2 = 0.357$)

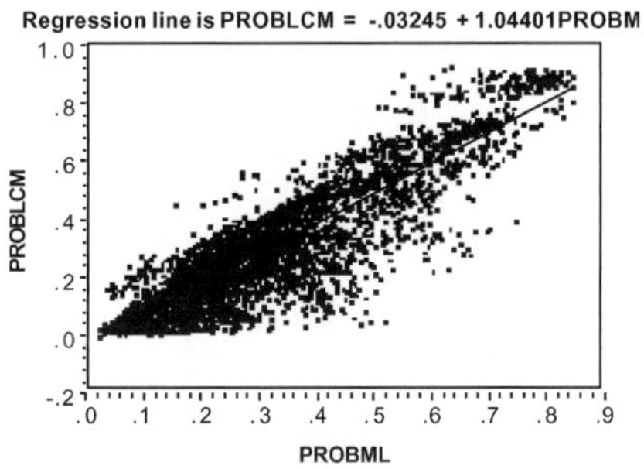

(ii) 4 Lane without median ($R^2 = 0.775$)

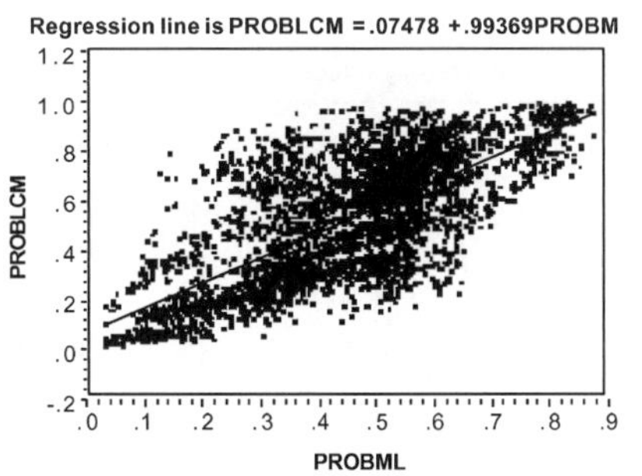

(iii) 4 Lane with Median ($R^2 = 0.4950$)

Fig. 5. Comparison of probability profiles of LCM and MLM.

variation around equality of choice probabilities leading us to conclude that each model is representing the choice responses quite differently for the majority of the sample. In the main,

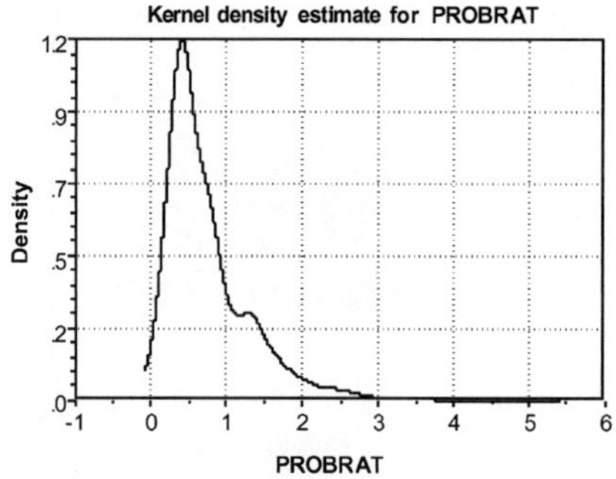

(i) 2 Lane

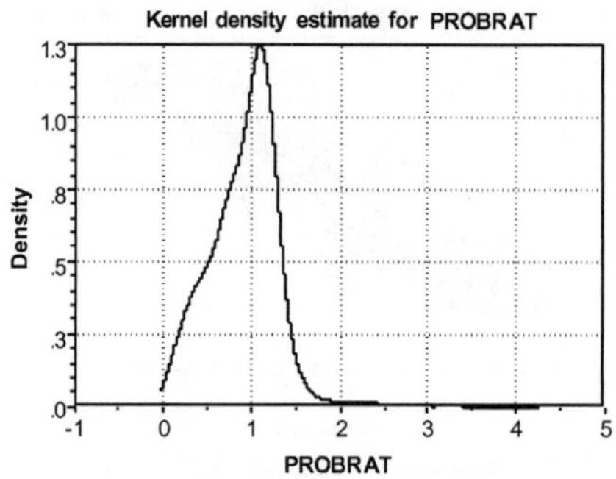

(ii) 4 Lane without median

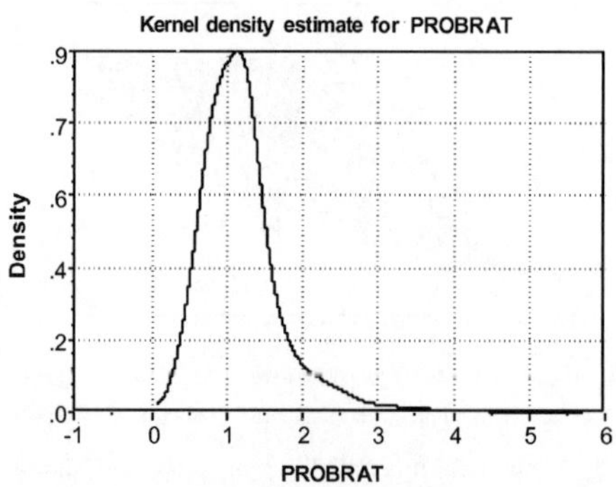

(iii) 4 lane with median

Fig. 6. Comparison of probability profiles of LCM and MLM ratios.

Table 4
Comparison of sensitivity to 50% increase in travel time

Alternative	MNL	MLM	LCM
(i) 2-lane increase in travel time			
2-lane (2L)	−4.639	−9.266	−3.004
4-lane w/out median (4NM)	1.625	3.817	1.349
4-lane with median (4WM)	3.014	5.449	1.654
(ii) 4-lane without median increase in travel time			
2-lane (2L)	1.545	3.949	1.841
4-lane w/out median (4NM)	−4.813	−10.839	−6.254
4-lane with median (4WM)	3.268	6.890	4.413
(iii) 4-lane with median increase in travel time			
2-lane (2L)	2.376	5.967	1.229
4-lane w/out median (4NM)	2.769	7.975	2.819
4-lane with median (4WM)	−5.145	−13.942	−4.048

Note: The 50% increase is applied to each alternative separately. Absolute change in choice share.

the kernel plots of these ratios suggests the broad similarity of the predictions from the two models.

Finally, we compare the change in absolute choice shares in response to a change in the level of attributes across the sample. We have chosen a 50% increase in travel time, assessed for each alternative, one at a time. The results (in Table 4) show a greater change in absolute choice shares after full sample enumeration for mixed logit than latent class logit. As expected, this is consistent with the choice elasticity evidence in Table 3.

5. Conclusions

This paper has contrasted a mixed logit model with a latent class logit model. The objective was to seek some understanding of the relative merits of both modeling strategies, each regarded as an advanced interpretation of discrete choice models. Both models offer alternative ways of capturing unobserved heterogeneity and other potential sources of variability in unobserved sources of utility. Like any empirical evidence, our judgments are conditioned on a single data set's performance under alternative behavioral assumptions.

It might be desirable to decide that one approach is unambiguously preferred to the other, but this is not possible. Each has its own merits. The latent class model has the virtue of being a semiparametric specification, which frees the analyst from possibly strong or unwarranted distributional assumptions about individual heterogeneity. The mixed logit model, while fully parametric, is sufficiently flexible that it provides the modeler a tremendous range within which to specify individual, unobserved heterogeneity. To some extent, this flexibility offsets the specificity of the distributional assumptions. We do find that both models allow the analyst to harvest a rich variety of information about behavior from a panel, or repeated measures data set.

We regard the (stated choice) data set as of high quality in terms of it delivering a substantial amount of variability that can be explained by both models. Overall it is a marked statistical improvement over multinomial logit. Which model is superior on all behavioral measures of performance is inconclusive despite stronger statistical support overall for the latent class model (on this occasion). The inconclusiveness is an encouraging result since it motivates further research involving more than one specification of the choice process. Based on the empirical evidence herein, both mixed logit and latent class logit offer attractive specifications. We encourage a greater effort to compare and contrast such advanced models as one approach to searching for rules on stability in explanation and prediction.

Acknowledgement

The comments of a referee have assisted greatly in the revision on earlier versions.

References

Bhat, C.R., 1997. An endogenous segmentation mode choice model with an application to intercity travel. Transportation Science 31, 34–48.

Gourieroux, C., Monfort, A., Trognon, A., 1994. Pseudo maximum likelihood methods: applications to Poisson models. Econometrica 52, 701–720.

Greene, W., 2001. Fixed and random effects in nonlinear models. Working paper EC-01-01, Stern School of Business, Department of Economics.

Greene, W., 2003. Econometric Analysis, fifth ed. Prentice Hall, Englewood Cliffs, forthcoming.

Heckman, J., Singer, B., 1984. Econometric duration analysis. Journal of Econometrics 24, 63–132.

Hensher, D.A., Greene, W.H., in press. Mixed logit models: state of practice, Transportation.

Hensher, D.A., Sullivan, C., in press. Willingness to pay for road curviness and road type for long distance travel in New Zealand, Transportation Research E.

Louviere, J.J., Hensher, D.A., Swait, J.F., 2000. Stated Choice Methods and Analysis. Cambridge University Press, Cambridge.

McFadden, D., Train, K., 2000. Mixed MNL models for discrete response. Journal of Applied Econometrics 15, 447–470.

Nagin, D., Land, K., 1993. Age, criminal careers, and population heterogeneity: specification and estimation of a nonparametric mixed Poisson model. Criminology 31, 327–362.

Roeder, K., Lynch, K., Nagin, D., 1999. Modeling uncertainty in latent class membership: a case study in criminology. Journal of the American Statistical Association 94, 766–776.

Swait, J., 1994. A structural equation model of latent segmentation and product choice for cross-sectional revealed preference choice data. Journal of Retail and Consumer Services 1 (2), 77–89.

Train, K., 2003. Discrete Choice Methods with Simulation. Cambridge University Press, Cambridge.

[25]

Transpn Res.-A Vol. 14A, pp. 367-378
© Pergamon Press Ltd., 1980. Printed in Great Britain

0191-2607/80/1201-0367/$02.00/0

THE EFFECT OF FUEL ECONOMY STANDARDS ON THE U.S. AUTOMOTIVE MARKET: AN HEDONIC DEMAND ANALYSIS

J. HAYDEN BOYD and ROBERT E. MELLMAN
Charles River Associates Incorporated, Boston, MA 02116, U.S.A.

Abstract—Both federal Corporate Average Fuel Economy (CAFE) regulations and market forces resulting from sharply higher gasoline prices are forcing auto manufacturers to dramatically improve the fuel economy of cars built for sale in the United States. Because these fuel economy improvements are being accompanied by significant changes in other car attributes that are believed to be important determinants of consumer choice among car models, there is currently considerable uncertainty about the likely effects on the automotive market. This paper analyzes market demand for automobile attributes, including those that are likely to be affected by fuel economy improvements, and presents estimates of dollar market valuations of key attributes. Market share effects of various assumed changes in car prices are analyzed in order to gain insight into competition among car models and the sensitivity of new car fleet average fuel economy to possible manufacturer or size-class-specific pricing strategies. Effects of gasoline price changes are also analyzed. These analyses make use of the hedonic demand model (also known as the "random coefficients logit model"), an extension of the multinomial logit probability choice model which explicitly incorporates variations in consumer tastes across the car-buying population. A data base measuring attributes and observed market shares of some 150 car models and submodels for the 1977 and 1978 model years is used.

INTRODUCTION AND SUMMARY

New cars available to the American consumer are expected to continue to change significantly in the 1980s in response to Corporate Average Fuel Economy (CAFE) regulations and higher fuel prices. Planning by the National Highway Traffic Safety Administration (NHTSA) assumes that automotive manufacturers, for the most part, will continue to offer the same range of "car concepts" as today. These car concepts include the current range of size classes from subcompact cars which seat 4 persons, to full size cars which seat 6 persons, as well as luxury and specialty variations across the size classes. Fuel efficiency improvements are projected to result from body redesign, material substitution, engine/drivetrain improvements and other technological changes. The cars of the 1980s are expected by NHTSA and by most industry observers to be smaller and lighter, but to offer substantially the same range of passenger and cargo capacities as today's cars (see U.S. Department of Transportation, 1977).

One can infer probable consumer reaction to the downsized cars of the 1980s by understanding consumers' valuations of those attributes of automobiles that will be changed in response to the CAFE regulations and higher fuel prices. This paper reports on the results of research designed to explain actual market shares in terms of consumers' choices among cars with varying attributes, such as price, fuel economy, reliability, luxury, styling and performance. It also explores how those market shares might change in response to possible changes in attributes. A primary methodological tool used is the hedonic demand model developed by Charles River Associates (CRA). The model is an extension of the multinomial logit probability choice model which incorporates random coefficients to account for variations in tastes across the car-buying population.

In interpreting the results reported in this paper, more significance should be placed on broad qualitative results than on the precise quantitative estimates of consumer valuations of automobile attributes and market responses to attribute changes. Several methodological and empirical considerations lead to this caveat. While it is likely that the analysis uses (or has tried) measures for most of the general attributes valued by consumers, no feasible sample of quantifiable attributes can hope to capture the entire complexity of the automobile market and of consumers' choices among competing makes and models. While we believe they are the best possible given the data publicly available, quantifications of many attributes are necessarily imprecise. A number of specifications of the model (i.e. combinations of attributes simultaneously analyzed) yielded predicted shares that fit actual shares well, but no fit was perfect; also, some coefficients displayed low levels of statistical significance. In addition, valuation estimates for most attributes appear to be higher than *a priori* expectations.

Despite these caveats, a number of relevant conclusions appear to hold true across alternative model specifications and alternative measures of individual vehicle attributes. Among the conclusions relevant to understanding the market impacts of fuel economy improvements are the following:

(1) The car market is heterogeneous and complex, with purchase decisions determined by personal evaluations of millions of individual buyers of the various "combinations of attributes" embodied in the various completing makes and models offered in the market by different manufacturers. This heterogeneity of consumer

tastes and the large number of relevant attributes implies that small changes in fuel economy or other attributes of a model do not lead to large changes in market share. For this reason, market shares of the various manufacturers tend to be relatively stable over time.

(2) The traditional American large car is purchased at least as much for reasons of luxury, styling proportions and acceleration performance as for exterior size, weight, passenger space and cargo volume. All of these attributes are correlated with size, but the former attributes proved to be significant predictors of market shares in our analysis, while the latter attributes did not.

(3) Aside from fuel savings and possible changes in purchase price, fuel economy gains can be expected to lead to changes in other car attributes which might reduce perceived value to consumers. Valued attributes which might be so reduced include "style" (i.e. the longer, lower, wider look), acceleration, luxury and reliability. Therefore, consumer acceptance of 1980 cars, and changes in consumer welfare due to changes in auto attributes, will depend critically on the degree to which manufacturers can, at reasonable costs, maintain traditional big car style, luxury, performance and reliability in more fuel-efficient automobiles.

(4) Consumers perceive fuel economy to be a valuable automobile attribute and make tradeoffs between lifetime fuel cost and purchase price.

(5) Assuming that the range of car types available (and their attributes) remains fixed, the model predicts that although large gasoline price changes greatly effect relative sales shares of many individual car models, they do not greatly affect the average fleet fuel economy of all new cars sold. The model similarly predicts that average new car fleet fuel economy is relatively insensitive to increasing price differentials between larger and smaller car size classes. These results suggest that the fuel savings from gasoline price increases or vehicle price changes will come primarily from supply-side improvements in the fuel economy of cars in each size class (and perhaps from changes in driving habits), rather than from market shifts among size classes of cars.

THEORY OF THE HEDONIC DEMAND MODEL

Automobiles may be thought of as bundles of attributes desired by consumers, such as fuel economy, durability, style, performance, luxury and low price. Different makes and models are distinguished by the different amounts of the various attributes they offer. Consumers make choices among the various makes and models so as to maximize their utility, choosing the make and model with the bundle of attributes considered superior to those of all other makes and models. A car's market share, and thus its competitive success, is determined by the number of buyers who consider that car's combination of price and other attributes to be superior to those of other cars. The hedonic demand model (described more completely in Boyd and Mellman, 1980) is an extension of the multinomial logit model which uses this theoretical approach to analyze market shares of individual makes and models of automobiles.

The individual logit model

The starting point for the Hedonic demand model is a multinomial logit model of an individual's choice among alternative car makes and models. The Hedonic demand model postulates that the utility derived by individual i from choosing car j is

$$U^*_{ij} = U_{ij} + \epsilon_{ij}, \tag{1}$$

where

$$U_{ij} = \sum_{a=1}^{A} \beta_{ia} X_{ja}. \tag{2}$$

The term U_{ij} is the systematic component of utility which depends on the A observed attributes which are quantified and included in the model specification. The amount of attribute a offered by car j is given by X_{ja}. The β_{ia} parameters may be interpreted as "tastes" for the attributes. The stochastic error term ϵ_{ij} is interpreted as the component of utility which cannot be estimated because it depends on unobserved attributes.

We assume that individual i chooses that car j which yields the highest level of utility U^*_{ij}. Because of the stochastic component ϵ_{ij}, it is not possible to predict with certainty exactly which car will be chosen. Rather, the task is to predict the probability that each car will be chosen by this particular individual. If the ϵ_{ij} follow an independent Weibull distribution,† then, as Domencich and McFadden (1975) have shown, the probability p_{ij} that car j will yield the highest utility to individual i, and thus be chosen, is given by:

$$p_{ij} = \exp\left(\sum_{a=1}^{A} \beta_{ia} X_{ja}\right) \Big/ \sum_{k=1}^{J} \exp\left(\sum_{a=1}^{A} \beta_{ia} X_{ka}\right). \tag{3}$$

Equation (3) is the individual logit model.

Application of the logit model to disaggregate data

In principle each individual in the market could have a unique set of β_{ia}'s. Thus, the individual logit model in eqn (3) needs further development to be estimated econometrically. A common approach is to broaden the specification of the utility function to a form U_{ij} $(X_{j1}, \ldots X_{jA}; S_{i1}, \ldots S_{iC})$ which depends explicitly both upon automobile attributes X_{ja} and upon household characteristics S_{ic}. This approach requires data on each sample household i and assumes that all households have identical logit model parameters. Among other things, this assumption implies that households with identical observed characteristics have identical tastes for observed attributes. Thus it is necessary to choose specifications $U_{ij}(X; S)$ such that the assumption of constant tastes is satisfactory.

The Hedonic demand model

The Hedonic demand model is a different development of the individual logit model which is particularly ap-

†The Weibull distribution is nearly identical to the normal distribution except in the extreme tails.

propriate for econometric estimation on aggregate market shares data, where it is not reasonable to assume that tastes are uniform across the car-buying population. The Hedonic demand model postulates a probability distribution of tastes (i.e. the β's) and estimates the parameters of that distribution. While any well-behaved probability density function could be used, the results reported herein assume that the β's are distributed independently and log-normally.

The predicted market share or aggregate probability P_j of car-model j can be thought of as the summation of the individual choice probabilities in eqn (3). Using integral notation

$$P_j = \int_{-\infty}^{\infty}\int_{-\infty}^{\infty}\cdots\int_{-\infty}^{\infty}\left[\frac{\exp\left(\sum_{a=1}^{A}\beta_a X_{ja}\right)}{\sum_{k=1}^{K}\exp\left(\sum_{a=1}^{A}\beta_a X_{ka}\right)}\right] f(\beta)\,\mathrm{d}\beta_1\,\mathrm{d}\beta_2\ldots\mathrm{d}\beta_A, \quad (4)$$

where $f(\beta)$ is the probability density function over the random β_a's.

In practice, we approximated this integral by a Monte Carlo simulation:

$$P_j = N^{-1}\sum_{n=1}^{N}\left[\frac{\exp\left(\sum \beta_{an}X_{ja}\right)}{\sum_{k=1}^{k}\exp\left(\Sigma\,\beta_{an}X_{ka}\right)}\right], \quad (5)$$

where

$$\beta_{an} = \exp\left(\mu_a + R_{an}\sigma_a\right). \quad (6)$$

The R_{an} are $N \times A$ independent normal random variables with mean zero and standard deviation unity. The parameters to be estimated in the model are the μ_a's and σ_a's, respectively the log mean and log standard deviation parameters.

Aggregate logit model

If all individuals are assumed to have the same tastes for the attributes, then the Hedonic demand model becomes simply the aggregate logit model:

$$P_j = \exp\left(\sum_{a=1}^{A}\beta_a X_{ja}\right)\Big/\sum_{k=1}^{K}\exp\left(\sum_{a=1}^{A}\beta_a X_{ka}\right). \quad (7)$$

Both the individual and aggregate logit models (eqns 3 and 7) display two properties which, while in many instances valid at the individual level, are inappropriate at the aggregate market level. It is the assumption of constant tastes (i.e. constant β's) across the car-buying population which causes these properties to be inappropriately preserved at the aggregate level. The Hedonic demand model, because it allows tastes to vary, displays neither of these properties.

The first property is the "independence of irrelevant alternatives", which means that the predicted shares of any two cars depend only on the attributes of those two cars and not on the attributes of other cars. From eqn (7) the ratio of predicted shares of any two cars is:

$$P_j/P_m = \exp\left(\sum_{a=1}^{A}\beta_a X_j\right)\Big/\exp\left(\sum_{a=1}^{A}\beta_a X_m\right). \quad (8)$$

Thus the logit model predicts that the introduction into the choice equation of a new car, such as the Ford Fiesta, will reduce all other cars' market shares in proportion. Similarly, it predicts that a reduction in the price of one car (or, more generally, any change in attributes which increases its utility) will reduce the predicted market shares of all other cars in proportion.

The second property of the logit model which is undesirable for aggregate market shares analyses is the property of equal cross elasticities. Again from eqn (7), it can be seen that the elasticity of the predicted share of model j with respect to a change in attribute b of model m is the same for all j:

$$e_{jm} = \frac{\partial P_j}{\partial X_{mb}}\frac{X_{mb}}{P_j} = -P_m\beta_b X_{mb}. \quad (9)$$

Because the logit model predicts that all cross elasticities are equal, it cannot be used to analyze substitutability (i.e. relative cross elasticities) among cars.

Thus, the assumption of constant tastes in the logit model implies that logit simulations or forecasts of market shares based on changes in automobile attributes (or on changes in the car-models offered by manufacturers) are likely to be biased. The Hedonic demand model, because it explicitly incorporates variations in tastes across the car-buying population, is not subject to this source of bias. However, the Hedonic demand model still requires that the assumptions of the logit model be satisfactory at the individual level.

Despite its theoretical shortcomings, the fit of the aggregate logit model was not dramatically worse than that of the Hedonic demand model, assuming equivalent specifications. The logarithms of the coefficients of the logit model were found to provide good starting values in the estimation of the corresponding Hedonic demand model μ parameters. Because the logit model is much less expensive to estimate, it was used to screen a number of alternative specifications to find the ones considered most promising for estimation using the Hedonic demand model.

THE ESTIMATION DATA BASE

Both the aggregate logit and Hedonic demand models were estimated on a model-year 1977 data base that contains total U.S. sales and attributes of 153 automobile submodels. In addition, some analyses not described in this paper were performed using a model-year 1978 data base containing 162 submodels. To reduce problems with overlap in sales of cars from adjacent model-years, market shares for each model-year were calculated based on sales from November–August. The data base includes all car-models with significant sales. Within each make/model, submodels consisting of the most popular station wagon version (where offered) and various engine/transmission combinations for non-station wagons were included.

Automobile attributes

A survey of the marketing and economic literature of automobile demand, and of the relevent data sources, is reported in Boyd and Mellman (1980). The survey revealed a reasonable consensus about those general automobile attributes that are determinants of consumer choice among competing makes and models. The data base described below contains a number of specific quantifications of most of these general attributes. A special effort was made to acquire data and to construct attribute variables and measure attributes likely to be desired by consumers, as opposed to using readily available data on specifications, dimensions, and the like.

Attributes measured in physical dimensions, such as vehicle weight and horesepower, are taken from the standard trade references—the *Automotive News Almanac* issue, *Ward's Automotive Yearbook*, and *Ward's Automotive Reports*. More subjective measures such as reliability, quality of ride, and comfort are taken from the *Consumer Reports* ratings of makes and models of cars.

The more important attributes contained in the estimation data base are described below:

PRICE Attribute

The purchase price used is the price in dollars of the standard two door (or lowest priced) version of the submodel, corrected for certain differences in standard equipment. Lacking data on actual transaction prices, we used the average of sticker price and dealer cost.

PRICE50 Attribute

This variable is computed by adding PRICE to the cost of 50,000 miles of gasoline at \$.70 per gallon, undiscounted, based on EPA composite metro-highway rating. A similar variable using 30,000 miles of gasoline cost was also tried.

MPGCOST Attribute

This attribute measures fuel consumption in gallons per hundred miles, based on EPA composite metro-highway fuel economy rating.

ACCEST Attribute

This attribute is the estimated acceleration rating, measured by 60 divided by 0–60 mph estimated acceleration time in seconds. Acceleration was estimated as a function of the ratio of horsepower to weight.

NOISE Attribute

NOISE is the *Consumer Reports* interior noise level rating, ranging from 1 (very high) to 5 (very low). It is a proxy for luxury and refinement. Other proxies tried included front seat comfort, ride quality, automatic transmission, and various composite variables consisting of these variables and NOISE. While those other proxies gave generally good results, specifications including NOISE fit the 1977 data somewhat better. Those results are reported here. However, a composite variable consisting of a weighted sum of NOISE and *Consumer Reports* ratings for front seat comfort and ride was later found to give somewhat more consistent results across model years 1977 and 1978. (Weights were derived from the first moment of a principal components analysis of the three variables.)

STYL1 Attribute

This attribute is a proxy for style, and seeks to capture the essence of the "longer, lower, wider" look. It is defined as the sum of exterior length and width, divided by exterior height.

Other styling proxies were also tried. STYL2, the ratio of exterior length to the sum of front and rear seat leg room, was designed to measure the proportions of the "long hood" look. Specifications including this attribute fitted the data somewhat less well than similar specifications including STYL1. STYL3, the ratio of exterior width to interior front seat shoulder room, was designed to capture the degree to which the sides of the car were rounded and streamlined. STYL3 was found not to vary significantly across car models.

None of these "style" proxies, of course, captures all of the relevant esthetic qualities that distinguish one car from another. However, they are related to the basic constraints within which stylists must work, and each is related negatively to "package efficiency" which in turn is related positively to fuel efficiency.

REPAIR Attribute

This attribute is the sum of the *Consumer Reports* frequency of repair ratings for the model for the previous five years, ranging from 5 (much worse than average) to 25 (much better than average).

HANDLING Attribute

This attribute is the *Consumer Reports* normal handling rating. It ranges from 1 (very poor) to 5 (very good).

Other Attributes

We were not able to discover a measure of interior volume or spaciousness that yielded statistically significant results and positive estimated valuation. Candidates tried included front and rear seat passenger space, several measures of cargo volume (including measures which differentiated station wagons from other cars), and individual interior measurements (front leg room, shoulder room, etc.). None of these attributes were found to yield significant and positive coefficients on either 1977 or 1978 data. However, a specification not reported here which was estimated on a subset of car models which excluded station wagons and specialty cars did yield a significant and positive coefficient on passenger space.

Car weight or exterior size (length times width) did not yield significant positive coefficients, nor did these variables add significant explanatory power to specifications that included a luxury proxy such as NOISE.

AN OVERVIEW OF THE 1977 AUTO MARKET

Table 1, depicting 1977 market shares by six *Consumer Reports* size classes, shows that domestic manufacturers are predominant in compact, mid-size, full size, luxury and speciality cars, and that imports are strongest in the subcompact class. A similar pattern emerges for *Consumer Reports* size classes in 1978. General Motors, while not especially strong in the smaller size classes, captures 60% or more of the market in the larger size classes.

Table 2 shows how sales weighted average values of automobile attributes vary across size classes for model year 1977. Average values of PRICE, MPGCOST, STYL1, ACCEST and NOISE all tend to be larger for larger size classes, while average REPAIR and HANDLING show no consistent pattern of variation with size class. These results indicate that while larger cars tend to be more expensive and thirstier, they tend also to be more stylish, more powerful performers, and more luxurious.

In 1978, EPA began to classify models into nine size categories based on interior roominess (three classes of station wagons, five classes of sedans, and one class of two-seaters). *Consumer Reports* changed its size classification system by eliminating the Intermediate category. Although the two systems categorize models differently, 1978 tabulations similar to those reported in Table 2 using both systems indicate the same pattern as in 1977 of increasing price, fuel consumption, style, luxury and performance with increasing size.

ATTRIBUTE VALUATION ESTIMATES

Consumer valuations for an automotive attribute may be derived from probability choice models by comparing the relative influence of price and attribute on consumer choice. In this section we present the estimated parameters of several alternative specifications of the logit and Hedonic demand models, and derive the attribute valuations implied by these estimates.

Parameter estimates

Table 3 compares parameter estimates for three corresponding specifications, denoted A, B and C, of the logit and Hedonic demand models. Model year 1977 data were used. For convenience in comparing logit and

Table 1. 1977 market shares by size class

	Sub-Compact	Compact	Mid-Size	Full-Size	Luxury	Specialty
Share of Total Sales	22.9	18.8	17.1	20.5	5.2	15.6
Share of Class Size						
General Motors	19.9	27.7	66.9	67.0	67.5	61.7
Ford	17.7	29.4	23.0	24.0	30.7	19.3
Chrysler	5.0	31.9	8.9	9.0		10.8
"Big 3" Subtotal	42.5	88.9	98.7	100.0	98.2	91.8
AMC	1.8	6.5	1.3			
Datsun	10.8	1.4				3.5
Honda	9.9					
Toyota	19.8					
Volkswagen	9.7					2.2
Other Import	5.4	3.2			1.8	2.5

[1]Sales November 1976 through August 1977.

SOURCE: CRA data base.

Table 2. Sales-weighted average values of attributes by size class, 1977

Size Class	PRICE	MPGCOST	REPAIR	STYL1	ACCEST	NOISE	HANDLING
Subcompact	3,390	3.60	17.1	4.38	3.85	2.76	4.33
Compact	3,930	5.25	11.2	5.00	3.92	3.43	3.97
Intermediate	4,190	5.77	17.3	5.43	4.18	3.95	4.67
Full-Size	4,630	5.96	17.5	5.34	4.35	4.54	4.52
Luxury	8,560	6.56	18.0	5.52	4.50	4.47	4.05
Specialty	4,700	5.72	13.8	5.45	4.27	3.78	4.60
All Size Classes	4,360	5.24	15.7	5.10	4.12	3.70	4.58

SOURCE: CRA data base.

Table 3. Logit and Hedonic demand model parameter estimates, 1977
("t" Statistics in Parentheses)

	SPECIFICATION A				SPECIFICATION B				SPECIFICATION C			
	Logit		Hedonics		Logit		Hedonics		Logit		Hedonics	
Attribute	Parameter	Log Parameter	Median[1]	Std. Dev.[2]	Parameter	Log Parameter	Median[1]	Std. Dev.[2]	Parameter	Log Parameter	Median[1]	Std. Dev.[2]
PRICE	.000286 (4.21)	-8.16	-7.94 (-22.09)	1.18 (4.62)								
MPGCOST	.339 (2.95)	-1.08	-1.28 (-2.87)	.001 (--)								
PRICE50					.000361 (5.89)	-7.92	-7.75 (-36.07)	.796 (3.83)	.000341 (5.08)	-7.98	-7.80 (-30.76)	.804 (3.41)
REPAIR	.0374 (2.71)	-3.29	-4.10 (-1.98)	.999 (.49)	.0432 (3.20)	-3.14	-3.86 (-1.93)	.905 (.36)	.0402 (2.95)	-3.21	-3.99 (-2.01)	.961 (.44)
STYLE	1.37 (5.53)	.318	.569 (2.09)	.622 (1.85)	.947 (5.60)	-.0542	.230 (.631)	.765 (1.91)	1.05 (6.11)	.0514	.337 (1.00)	.708 (1.80)
ACCEST	.375 (2.93)	-.981	-1.75 (-1.71)	1.34 (1.79)	.302 (2.40)	-1.20	-2.11 (-1.89)	1.56 (2.05)	.281 (2.13)	-1.27	-2.05 (-1.71)	1.46 (1.75)
NOISE	.462 (5.46)	-.772	-2.63 (-.80)	2.34 (.93)	.525 (6.24)	-.645	-9.67 (-1.08)	.961 (1.16)	.391 (3.74)	-.938	-1.72 (-.78)	1.45 (.83)
HANDLING									.209 (1.74)	-1.56	-2.27 (-.50)	1.12 (.25)
χ^2			8.888				8.672				8.110	

[1]Estimated mean and median of natural logarithm of taste distribution.

[2]Estimated standard deviation of natural logarithm of taste distribution.

SOURCE: CRA estimates.

Hedonic demand model results, the natural logarithms of the logit parameter estimates are also given. While logit and median Hedonic demand model parameters are generally of the same order of magnitude for equivalent specifications, there are some significant variations in the estimates of the two models.

A likelihood ratio test is used to ascertain whether the use of the Hedonic demand model, which adds the taste variance parameters to the logit model, significantly improves the fit of estimated car model and submodel market shares to actual shares. If L_H and L_L are the Hedonics and logit log likelihoods, it can be shown that the quantity $2 \times (L_H - L_L)$ has the chi-square distribution, with degrees of freedom equal to the number of taste deviation parameters estimated. For each of the three specifications, the improved fit is significant at approximately the 0.10–0.20 level.

Student's "t" statistics are shown in parentheses below each parameter estimate. All logit coefficients are significant in the table. The Hedonic demand model standard deviation parameter estimates are significant for the price attributes and for ACCEST and STYL1. This indicates a significant dispersion in tastes for these three attributes. The "t" statistics for the median Hedonic demand model parameters do not have the same natural interpretation as the "t" statistics for the logit and Hedonic demand standard deviation parameters, since a zero logarithm does not imply a zero taste parameter.

Attribute valuations

Table 4 reports the attribute valuations implied by the parameter estimates reported in Table 3. The logit model attribute valuation for the ith attribute is defined as

$$V_{Li} = \beta_i/\beta_p,$$

where β_{Li} is the logit parameter for the ith attribute and β_p is the logit price parameter. The median Hedonic demand model attribution, given the assumption that the taste parameters are distributed log-normally across the car-buying population, is defined as

$$V_{Hi} = \exp(\mu_i - \mu_p)$$

where μ_i and μ_p are respectively the estimated means of the natural logarithms of the taste parameters for attribute i and price. The mean Hedonic demand model attribute valuation is defined as

$$V'_{Hi} = \exp(\mu_i - \mu_p + 0.5(\sigma_i^2 + \sigma_p^2))$$

where σ_i and σ_p are respectively the estimated standard deviations of the natural logarithm of the distributions of the taste parameters for attribute i and for price.

Turning first to fuel consumption, the mean Hedonic demand model valuation of MPGCOST in Specification A implies that the average new car buyer is willing to pay approx. 220,000 miles worth of gasoline savings at $0.70 per gallon (undiscounted) in higher purchase price for mpg gains. This result is somewhat higher than a *priori* expectations. The median miles implied by Hedonics and the miles implied by logit also seem unreasonably high at 110,000 and 170,000 miles respectively. Given the statistical range of uncertainty in the estimates, the Hedonics results are not necessarily inconsistent with the proposition that consumers trade off lifetime fuel cost and purchase price in choosing among competing models, other things being equal.

Depending on the specification, mean Hedonic demand values for REPAIR range from $100 to $150. This result implies that an improvement in frequency of repair from average (REPAIR = 15) to better than average (REPAIR = 20) would be worth about $500–$750. The logit estimates are roughly equivalent.

The mean Hedonic valuation for the styling proxy STYL1 ranges from $5370 to $12,100, depending on the specification. Comparing the highest and lowest values for this "longer-lower-wider" attribute in the 1977 data

Table 4. Logit and Hedonics attribute valuation estimates, 1977

	Specification A			Specification B			Specification C		
		Hedonics			Hedonics			Hedonics	
Attribute	Logit	Median	Mean	Logit	Median	Mean	Logit	Median	Mean
PRICE	Base	Base	Base						
MPGCOST	1190.[1]	778.[1]	1563.						
PRICE50				Base	Base	Base	Base	Base	Base
REPAIR	131.[1]	46.3	153.	120.[1]	48.6	100.6	118.[1]	45.3	99.
STYLE	4810.[1]	4950.	12051.[2]	2630.[1]	2910.	5369.[2]	3080.[1]	3430	6064.[2]
ACCEST	1310.[1]	486.	2403.[2]	837.[1]	280.	1294.[2]	824.[1]	316.	1257.[2]
NOISE	1620.[1]	201.	6278.	1450.[1]	881.	1922.	1150.[1]	440.	1734.
HANDLING							612.	253.	650.

[1]Logit parameter for this attribute is significant at 0.25 level.

[2]Hedonics variance parameter for this attribute is significant at 0.10 level.

SOURCE: CRA estimates using 1977 data base.

base, the lower end of this range implies consumer willingness to pay about $12,000 for the difference in proportions between the Renault LeCar (STYL1 = 3.7) and the Lincoln Continental Mark V (STYL1 = 5.8), or about $6400 for the difference in proportions between a Volkswagen Rabbit (STYL1 = 3.9) and a downsized Chevrolet Impala (STYL1 = 5.1). The parameter measuring the standard deviation in tastes for this attribute was significantly different from zero.

Mean Hedonic valuations for the performance attribute ACCEST range from $1260 to $2400; logit valuations are similar. This implies a willingness to pay about $1400–$2800 for the difference in horsepower-to-weight between a Ford Mustang 4 and V-8, or between a Chevrolet Chevette and a full size Chevrolet V-8. This result is higher than the typical price of higher performance represented by the cost of optional engines. The parameter measuring the standard deviation in tastes for this attribute was significantly different from zero, based on 1977 data.

While logit estimates on the 1978 data base generally confirmed the sign and approximate magnitude and statistical significance of valuations on most attributes, the positive and significant valuation for ACCEST was not replicated on the 1978 data.

Estimated mean Hedonic valuations for the luxury proxy NOISE varied from $1700 to $6300 for the three specifications; however, estimated mean and median valuations varied greatly from one another and across specifications. Because the estimated variation in tastes was especially large for Specification A, the estimated median valuation was substantially less than the mean for this specification. The NOISE coefficient also varied significantly between similar logit specifications estimated on 1977 and 1978 data.

Taking $2000 as an order-of-magnitude representative valuation, the difference in luxury between the average 1977 full size and subcompact car (4.53 and 2.76 in Table 2) is worth approx. $3600. These results imply that the degree of luxury and refinement is an important attribute to new car buyers. However, further experimentation with alternative luxury proxies would be useful. Preliminary experiments with a weighted combination of NOISE, front seat comfort, and ride quality uses have yielded encouraging results.

The attribute HANDLING is included in one specification. The mean Hedonics valuation of $650 represents the average willingness to pay for an improvement of one on a five-point rating scale.

IMPLICATIONS FOR MARKET ACCEPTANCE OF MORE FUEL ECONOMIC VEHICLES

The results reported above indicate that consumers do value improvements in fuel economy. However, improvements in fuel economy will potentially change vehicle attributes other than fuel economy, attributes that our results indicate are also valued by consumers in the marketplace. Thus, consumer acceptance of cars of the 1980s, and the impact on their welfare of the expected gains in average fuel efficiency, will depend critically on the ability of manufacturers to maintain traditional levels of style, luxury, performance and reliability in larger cars as they are downsized. Unfortunately, in each case maintenance of these attributes can be in conflict with fuel efficiency improvements.

For example, the downsized cars of the 1980s are expected to be more efficient in their packaging of people and cargo. This improved package efficiency is likely to result in cars which will be shorter, narrower and higher than cars of the 1970s. This change in proportions reverses a styling trend that has persisted since at least the 1920s. As Harley Earl, who as General Motors' chief stylist played a major role in American automotive design, put it in 1954 (as quoted in Sloan, 1972):

> My primary purpose for 28 years has been to lengthen and lower the American automobile, at times in reality and always at least in appearance. Why? Because my sense of proportion tells me that oblongs are more attractive than squares...

Our results—positive and significant valuations on STYL1—confirm the market's acceptance of Earl's sense of proportion. While individual manufacturers in the 1980s will of course continue to have varying degrees of success in producing attractive designs within given proportions, our results suggest that overall the reduction in STYL1 may lead to lower product content as perceived by car buyers.

Other attributes valued by consumers are also potentially in conflict with fuel efficiency gains. Decreasing power-to-weight ratio and thus acceleration results in lower fuel consumption, other things equal.† Maintaining luxury (quietness, comfort, smooth ride) at reasonable costs as cars become lighter and smaller will be technologically more difficult than if cars were not being downsized. Similarly, new car designs are usually associated with lower reliability compared to older designs. However, this is a problem of transition to more fuel efficient cars rather than, as for the other attributes, a long-run problem.

FIT TO PREDICTED AND ACTUAL MARKET SHARES

While the logit and Hedonic demand models were both able to replicate actual market shares fairly well, as is common in econometric work the fit was by no means exact. In general, errors in predicted shares of individual submodels tended to partially cancel out when predicted and actual shares were aggregated into broader categories, such as manufacturer or size class shares. This result is consistent with the belief that while the broad quantified attributes used in the analysis capture major factors relevant to consumer choice among car models, individual car models nonetheless differ in other significant attributes not included in the analysis.

As indicated in Table 5, the Hedonic demand model (Specification A) slightly overpredicts the market shares of the smaller domestic manufacturers and slightly underpredicts the shares of the two larger corporations.

†NHTSA planning assumes, however, that manufacturers will reduce both weight and power in proportion so as to achieve equivalent performance (U.S. Department of Transportation, 1977, pp. 2-22 & 3).

Table 5. Comparison of actual and estimated 1977 market shares by manufacturer using Hedonic demand model, Specification A

Manufacturer	Actual	Estimated	Estimated-Actual
General Motors[2]	47.96	47.69	(.27)
Ford Motor Co.[2]	23.01	21.38	(1.63)
Chrysler[2]	12.18	15.08	2.90
AMC	1.86	2.74	.89
Datsun	3.27	4.58	1.31
Honda	2.26	1.25	(1.01)
Toyota	4.55	3.37	(1.18)
Volkswagen	2.57	1.07	(1.50)
Total Domestic[2]	85.01	86.89	1.88
Total Foreign[3]	14.99	13.11	(1.88)

[1]Based on sales from November 1976 through August 1977.
[2]Includes captive imports.
[3]Excludes captive imports.
SOURCE: CRA data base and CRA estimates.

However, the rank ordering of the four firms is correct, and model results are not grossly inaccurate.

Table 6 presents estimated vs actual total U.S. market shares by size class, again using Specification A of the Hedonic demand model. The full size and luxury car class shares are estimated closely, but the specialty car market share estimate is much lower than the actual share. The model also allocates some part of the compact class share to the subcompact and intermediate classes. The calculated new car sales weighted fleet fuel economy is very nearly the same whether actual or predicted shares are used in the calculation.

MARKET EFFECTS OF AUTOMOBILE ATTRIBUTE CHANGES

We next examine the effects of changes in the prices or other attributes of one or more car models on predicted market shares of car models, manufacturers and size classes. This analysis sheds light on the ability of manufacturer price and product policies to influence market shares, and on the possible efficacy of government automotive CAFE or fuel tax policies in influencing the market behavior of automotive consumers.

Price elasticities and cross elasticities

Insight into the degree to which individual car models compete with one another can be gained by examining their elasticities and cross elasticities of market share. Calculated price elasticities and the closest competitors (as measured by highest cross elasticities) are displayed in Table 7 for several selected submodels. The 1977 elasticities and cross elasticities were calculated numerically using Specification A of the Hedonic demand model (see Table 3). Attributes included in this specification are purchase price, fuel consumption,

Table 6. Comparison of actual and estimated 1977 market shares by automobile size using Hedonic demand model, Specification A

Auto Size	Actual	Estimated	Estimated-Actual
Subcompact	22.94	26.63	3.70
Compact	18.81	14.81	(4.00)
Intermediate	17.05	21.07	4.02
Full-Size	20.47	21.88	1.41
Luxury	5.19	5.40	.21
Specialty	15.55	9.68	(5.25)
Average Miles per Gallon	19.072	10.084	.012

[1]Based on sales from November 1976 through August 1977.
SOURCE: CRA data base and CRA estimates.

Table 7. Computed price elasticities of market share for selected submodels and derived competing models, 1977

Selected Submodel[1]	Price Elasticity[2]	Derived Competing Models[3]
Datsun B-210 M4	-7.57	Honda Civic, Toyota Corolla, Mazda GLC, Dodge Colt, Ford Pinto
Chevrolet AB*	-3.53	Pontiac,* Buick,* Oldsmobile,* Chrevrolet Chevelle, Dodge Colt
Volkswagen Rabbit M4	-3.17	Dodge Colt, Datsun B-210, Honda Civic, Mazda GLC, Toyota Corolla
Oldsmobile Cutlass A8	-2.26	Chevolet Monza, Chevrolet Nova, Datsun 280Z, Chrysler Cordoba, Oldsmobile Omega
Ford Mustang A4	-2.56	Mazda GLC, Datsun B-210, Toyota Corolla, Chevrolet Vega, Ford Pinto
Ford A8*	-2.06	Ford LTD II, Mercury Cougar, Dodge,* Plymouth,* Mercury*
Plymouth Volare A8	-2.90	Ford Pinto, Toyota Corolla, Chevrolet Vega, AMC Gremlin, Datsun B-210
Cadillac A8*	-1.60	Buick Riviera, Buick,* Pontiac,* Oldsmobile,* Chevrolet*

Notes and Source on following page.

*Full-Size.

[1]All are nonstation wagons.

[2]Elasticity of market share with respect to price, as computed using Hedonic Demand Model.

[3]Models corresponding to submodels with highest cross-elasticities as estimated using Hedonic Demand Model (submodel designations and duplicate models suppressed).

Abbreviations:

M: Manual transmittion
A: Automatic transmission
4, 6, 8: Number of engine cylinders.

SOURCE: Simulations using CRA Hedonic Demand Model, specification A.

frequency of repair, STYL1, estimated acceleration, and interior noise rating.

The results conform generally, but not in all cases, to *a priori* expectations. Elasticities are generally high in absolute value for cars with many good substitutes and lower for cars with fewer good substitutes. The car models predicted to be the closest competitors, based on highest cross elasticities, appear to be reasonable in most cases.

Simulation exercises

Next, we use the Hedonic demand model to analyze the market effects of changes that affect groups of car models. Three such simulations are reported herein: a change in price differentials between large and small car classes, a change in price by a single manufacturer, and an increase in the price of gasoline. As in the previous section, Specification A of the Hedonic demand model is used. All the simulations assume that only the specified change occurs and that other attributes of the makes and models offered in 1977 remain unchanged. In addition, the estimated change in market shares does not take account of any production constraints.

Large and small car price differentials

The first simulation is designed to test the sensitivity of industry fuel economy to an industry wide strategy designed to increase the differential between large and small cars. Market forces might lead to increasing differentials between large and small cars as fuel economy standards become more binding on domestic manufacturers. The simulation assumes that the price of large cars (intermediate, full size and luxury) is increased by 10% and that the price of subcompacts is reduced by 10%; compact and specialty car prices remain the same.

The estimated effect of this change, as shown in Table 8, is to increase the share of subcompacts by some 21% and to reduce the share of the larger size classes. Weighted average fuel economy of all new cars sold improves by 2.4%. All domestic manufacturers lose market share in this secenario, and all importers except Mercedes-Benz gain.

Change in price by a single manufacturer

The second simulation, summarized in Table 9, examines the extent to which one manufacturer can increase market share by across-the-board price cuts.

Table 8. Simulated effect of increased differential between small and large car prices, 1977

Size Class	Assumed Price Change (Percent)	Estimated Market Share (Percent) Baseline	Scenario
Subcompact	- 10	26.63	32.18
Compact	0	14.81	14.69
Intermediate	+ 10	21.07	17.89
Full-Size	+ 10	21.88	19.70
Luxury	+ 10	5.40	4.86
Specialty	0	10.20	10.68
Fuel Economy		19.084 mpg	19.536 mpg

SOURCE: Similation using CRA Hedonic Demand Model, specification A.

Table 9. Simulated effect of price reduction on Chrysler compact and larger models, 1977

Manufacturer	Assumed Price Change (Percent)	Estimated Market Share (Percent) Baseline	Scenario
Chrysler	-10[1]	15.08	17.88
GM	0	47.69	46.23
Ford	0	21.38	20.61
AMC	0	2.74	2.63
Imports[2]	0	13.11	12.65
Average Fuel Economy		19.084 mpg	18.895 mpg

[1]Except for subcompacts (Dodge Colt and Plymouth Arrow).

[2]Excludes captive imports.

SOURCE: Simulation using CRA Hedonic Demand Model, specification A.

Chrysler prices (except for its captive imports) are assumed to fall by 10%.

Chrysler's estimated market share increases by some 19% in this simulation, from 15.1 to 17.9% of the market.† The share of other domestic manufacturers and of almost all importers falls by varying amounts. Average fuel economy falls because the Chrysler models that gain sales in this scenario are less fuel efficient on average than the other models that lose sales.

Gasoline price increases

The final simulation reported here is designed to estimate the effect of a doubling of gasoline prices. This simulation was performed by doubling each submodel's MPGCOST attribute.

†Note that the model in the base case tends to overpredict Chrysler's share, which was only 12.18% in the November 1976–August 1977 period used for the 1977 model year analysis.

Table 10 reports the results. As might be expected, large cars lose estimated market shares while subcompacts gain, and domestic manufacturers lose share while imports gain. Average fuel economy increases by about 6.3%.

Market implications

These results imply that the market for new automobiles is relatively stable, in the sense that relative market shares of size classes or of individual manufacturers are somewhat insensitive to rather large perturbations in gasoline prices or in class or manufacturer average purchase prices. They also imply that shifts in market shares from more to less fuel efficient cars in response to feasible changes in new car prices or gasoline prices are likely to have only modest short-run impacts on fleet average fuel economy. Changes in fuel economy within size classes remain as the option available to manufacturers to meet the CAFE standards of the 1980s.

Table 10. Simulated effect of doubling of gasoline prices, 1977

	Estimated Market Share (Percent)	
Size Class	Baseline	Scenario
Subcompact	26.63	35.20
Compact	14.81	14.33
Intermediate	21.07	18.15
Full-Size	21.88	18.93
Luxury	5.40	4.16
Specialty	10.20	9.22
Manufacturer		
GM	47.69	46.85
Ford	21.38	20.37
Chrysler	15.08	12.46
AMC	2.74	2.38
Subtotal -- Domestic[1]	86.89	82.06
Datsun	4.58	6.08
Toyota	3.37	4.37
Honda	1.25	1.96
Volkswagen	1.07	1.61
Other Imports	2.84	3.92
Subtotal -- Imports[2]	13.11	17.94
Fuel Economy	19.08	20.29

[1]Includes captive imports.

[2]Excludes captive imports.

SOURCE: Simulation using CRA Hedonic Demand Model, specification A.

Acknowledgements—This paper is based in large measure on research conducted at Charles River Associates Incorporated (CRA), sponsored by the U.S. Department of Transportation, National Highway Traffic Safety Administration, Contract Number DOT-HS-01786. The results of this research are reported more fully in Boyd and Mellman (1980). Advice and assistance from Scott Cardell, Jerry Hausman and Timothy Tardiff are gratefully acknowledged.

REFERENCES

Boyd J. H. and Mellman R. E. (1980) *Impact of Automotive Fuel Economy Standards on Competition in the Automotive Industry*. Charles River Associates, Boston, Mass.

Domencich T. A. and McFadden D. (1975) *Urban Travel Demand: A Behavioral Analysis, A Charles River Associates Research Study*. North Holland/American Elsevier, Amsterdam. Chap. 4.

Sloan A. P. (1972) *My Years with General Motors*, Anchor Edn, pp. 318–319. Doubleday, New York.

U.S. Department of Transportation, National Highway Traffic Safety Administration (1977) *Data and Analysis for* 1981–84. *Passenger Automobile Fuel Economy Standards, Document* 2; *Automotive Design and Technology*, Vol. 1, Feb. 28.

[26]

Transpn Res.-A Vol. 14A, pp. 423–434
© Pergamon Press Ltd., 1980. Printed in Great Britain

0191-2607/80/1201-0423/$02.00/0

MEASURING THE SOCIETAL IMPACTS OF AUTOMOBILE DOWNSIZING

N. Scott Cardell
Department of Economics, Harvard University, Cambridge, MA 02139, U.S.A.

and

Frederick C. Dunbar
National Economic Research Associates, Inc., 80 Broad Street, New York, NY 10004, U.S.A.

Abstract—This paper uses an innovative cost-benefit methodology to evaluate various strategies aimed at reducing automobile gasoline consumption. These strategies are the current Corporate Average Fuel Economy (CAFE) regulations and various pricing instruments including gasoline taxes and MPG based vehicle taxes. We conclude that the social costs of CAFE are substantially higher (probably on the order of $20 billion per year) than the social costs of gasoline taxes in achieving comparable oil import reductions. That is, forcing consumers to buy undesirable cars is more onerous to them than simply raising fuel prices and allowing them to make their own adjustments. Also, it is questionable whether CAFE has positive net social benefits even allowing liberal estimates of the social benefits of oil conservation. The methodological advance in this cost-benefit analysis is the use of a probability choice model of auto-purchase behavior to allow for both changes in the non-price attributes of consumer goods, and also the dispersion of preferences for these attributes among consumers.

BACKGROUND

The National Highway Traffic Safety Administration (NHTSA) is responsible for writing and enforcing the Corporate Average Fuel Economy regulations (CAFE). CAFE implements the applicable sections of Title V: "Improving Automotive Efficiency of the Motor Vehicle Information and Cost Savings Act" (15 U.S.C. 1901 *et seq.*), as amended. CAFE is designed to improve substantially the average corporate fuel economy of motor vehicles sold in the United States.

In order to comply with CAFE, corporations are expected to make relatively large design changes in the motor vehicles they sell. These include reduced vehicle weight and other modifications which will affect motor vehicle prices and their performance, handling and perceived luxury characteristics.

Changes such as these will obviously affect the benefits which consumers feel they are receiving when they buy a car. The typical new car sold under CAFE will get better gas mileage, but may be perceived to be less desirable than the typical current car with regard to such factors as ride quality, crash-worthiness, acceleration, interior space and overall comfort while driving.

An evaluation of CAFE should consider the benefits received in terms of reduced oil imports, the social costs which would occur if alternative strategies were pursued to achieve these benefits and, finally, the costs which CAFE itself will impose on consumers. This paper addresses the latter one of these issues. In particular, a key issue in evaluating the impacts of CAFE on vehicle users is that many attributes of new cars will change, in addition to price, and consequently traditional consumer surplus measures are of limited usefulness in quantifying consumer impacts.

Below, we develop, and present the results of, a method for computing some of the required cost-benefit measures for evaluating CAFE which take account both of the changes in nonprice attributes of cars and of the variation in consumer preferences observed in the new car buying population.

COST-BENEFIT ANALYSIS WITH PROBABILITY CHOICE MODELS

Recently, transportation researchers have shown how probability choice models of travel behavior can give conceptually elegant and easily computed summary measures of user impacts. For example, Williams (1977) has shown how multinomial logit, generalized to account for correlated error terms, can be used to compute precise measures of consumer surplus in the traditional four-step urban transportation planning system process. Ben-Akiva and Lerman (1977) demonstrated how these measures of consumer surplus correspond to a rigorously defined measure of accessibility, which itself is a primary objective of transportation planning and policy. Sheffi (1977) has shown how these measures can be computed from random coefficient multinomial probit models to determine how projects improve network performance. Dunbar (1980) compares the relative accuracy of those measures in the context of transportation planning.

Below, we give an intuitive explanation of consumer surplus measures in discrete choice situations. This explanation is sketched mainly in verbal form, and is supported by the above cited literature which formally derives equations for computing the change in consumer surplus with a multinomial logit (MNL) model. Following this is a discussion of extensions of the MNL model which will be necessary in the present study. Specifically the Hedonic Demand Model is used to show how monetized measures of consumer impacts can be derived from an auto choice model.

AN INTUITIVE EXPLANATION

There are differences in conceptualization of consumer

surplus between probability-choice behavior and traditional economic demand theory. If probability-choice theory is in fact a good representation of the individual automobile ownership process, then some of the arguments against cost-benefit analysis which are based on traditional economic theory are not valid. To see this, we explore the concept in the probability choice framework.

In auto make and model decisions, households consider many attributes of automobiles besides the price. Consumer impact measurements must account for the value of these attributes as they are affected by CAFE. The typical probability choice model is designed to deal with just such situations. It assumes that for each individual and each auto type modeled (subcompact, compact, etc.) it is possible to formulate a linear combination of these attributes and purchase price into a single measure. Although given different names in different papers, we will call this measure the composite price index, I_j, for auto type j. This composite price is dimensionless; it is the negative of the quantity most often defined as utility in the transportation literature, although identical probability choice models can be developed from other precepts. Here we presume that what people do not want in a car (high purchase price, noise, high turning radius, etc.) are positive contributions which increase the composite price of the car and those things which people do want (acceleration, interior size, etc.) are offsets to this price.

If the design changes caused by CAFE restrict the availability of some automobile attributes, they in effect increase the composite price which must be paid to obtain these attributes. For example, if CAFE causes a reduction in the acceleration and the interior size which can be obtained at current dollar purchase prices, consumers will find their composite prices increased. Depending on the importance a consumer places on each auto attribute, he or she may respond to these changes in three ways: first, pay more money to purchase the original amount of the desirable attributes (for example, it may be supposed that some purchasers of high cost luxury cars will be able to afford the purchase price increase necessary to continue to own these cars, even if their gas mileage is far from the CAFE standards), second, reduce the level of attributes obtained by spending the previous amount of money to purchase a different, less desirable (at least with regard to these attributes) automobile; finally, choose some combination of these two strategies. To the extent the consumer chooses the second or third alternative, he or she will receive an offsetting benefit (reduced composite price) from the reduced operating cost associated with the better gas mileage. He or she may also get increased benefits from other attributes such as a smaller turning radius.

If the new combination of attributes which is chosen was available as an automobile on the market before implementation of CAFE, it must be the case that the consumer was better off before CAFE (by revealed preference). Thus, the net effect of these changes is to make the consumer worse off. Alternatively, if new technology or changes in marketing strategy by the corporations result in new combinations of alternatives being offered as automobiles on the market, the consumer may be made better off by the change. A marketing strategy may be for corporations to subsidize small car sales in order to bring down their corporate average miles per gallon. They would presumably pay for these subsidies by increased charges for their larger automobiles. In any event, trying to measure all of these offsetting effects obviously requires more than the simple price-quantity demand curve usually used in consumer surplus arguments. This is because the nature of the good purchased has changed. It is here that the concept of composite price and use of probability-choice models can provide an alternative if they are applicable. A more formal discussion follows.

The composite price must correspond to a plausible behavioral model when it is constructed. It should include all attributes of automobiles which affect consumers' purchase decisions. The relative importance of these attributes should be measured by weights with values such that the automobile with the lowest composite price is the one actually chosen. That is, if for any given individual there are N attributes h_{ij} for auto type j with weights or coefficients θ_i, then for

$$I_j = \sum_{i=1}^{N} \theta_i h_{ij} \tag{1}$$

the θ_i have values such that if

$$I_j < I_k \tag{2}$$

then auto type j is chosen for any two auto types k and j, j not equal to k. If the θ_i meet this test, then they show the trade-offs in individual makes across auto attributes.

If such a composite price index satisfying the above behavioral criteria could be estimated *with certainty* for all individuals, then we would be able to construct very simple and powerful cost-benefit measures. Suppose a policy changes the attributes of various auto types. Then the monetized per new car value of the change in consumer surplus across a population of individuals is simply:

$$\$\Delta CSC = \sum_{t=1}^{T} \left\{ \frac{I'_{jt} - I''_{kt}}{\theta_{ot}} \right\} \tag{3}$$

where $\$\Delta CSC$ = change in consumer surplus in dollars, assuming certainty, I'_{jt} = composite price index of the auto chosen by the tth individual after the change in attributes, I''_{kt} = composite price index of the auto chosen by the tth individual after the change in attributes (j may equal k), and θ_{ot} = coefficient on auto purchase price in the composite price for the tth individual.

The division by θ_{ot} serves to monetize an otherwise dimensionless number, so that $\$\Delta CSC$ is measured in dollars.

The multidimensional nature of composite price is crucially important for the present study. To see this, suppose that as a result of CAFE, corporations change their cars by reducing automobile weight, reducing the interior size, and switching engines to increase miles per gallon. The weights which a consumer places on these factors are used in the composite price to capture all (under certainty) of the adjustments which would be made in driving patterns and habits as a result of the changes. The consumer would presumably find increased gas mileage desirable while reduced weight and interior size would probably be found undesirable. As a result of these changes, the consumer might drive more or fewer miles than in the automobile owned previously. Any changes in the miles driven, however, are fully considered in the way he or she calculates their composite price. (These changes are not, however, observable. Calculating changes in miles driven requires a different analytical approach.)

Thus the monetized change in the composite price under certainty fully measures the individual's perception of the change in his or her status in dollar terms.

A practical difficulty exists with this simplified model. Our powers of observation do not allow us to determine with certainty eqn (1) for each individual. As in more traditional econometric analysis, this difficulty is overcome by specifying statistical models and estimating the parameters thereof. In the present case, we made probabilistic statements about individual behavior using well-defined probability choice models.

The most common probability choice model uses the multinomial logit (MNL) functional form. In terms of composite prices, this model can be written as:

$$P_{jt} = \frac{e^{-I_{jt}}}{\sum_{m=1}^{M} e^{-I_{mt}}} \tag{4}$$

where P_{jt} = probability of an individual t choosing the jth among M alternatives.

Probability choice models add realism to auto choice models but they complicate the mathematical derivation of changes in consumer surplus. The previously cited literature shows how consumer surplus changes are calculated from probability-choice models generally, and from MNL specifically. Fortunately, as shown in this literature, the change in consumer surplus from an MNL model is a relatively simple function:

$$\$\Delta CSL = \sum_{t=1}^{T} \frac{1}{\theta_{ot}} \left(\ln\left(\sum_{m=1}^{M} e^{-I''_{mt}} \right) - \ln\left(\sum_{m=1}^{M} e^{-I'_{mt}} \right) \right) \tag{5}$$

where $\$\Delta CSL$ = change in consumer surplus over a population of T individuals in dollar terms, under the assumption that MNL is the correct estimator.

Equation (5) measures the change in the log of the denominators from eqn (4) after the policy-induced changes in attributes. Notice that it resembles eqn (3) except that all auto types are represented, including those not chosen. However, if an auto type has a low probability of being chosen because it has a relatively large composite price for individual t, then its contribution to $\$\Delta CSL_t$ is relatively slight.

In general eqn (5) weighs the change in composite price by the probability of an alternative being chosen. To see this, suppose that a policy only changes the composite price of a single auto type j:

$$\$\Delta CSL = \sum_{t=1}^{T} \frac{1}{\theta_{ot}} (\ln(P''_{jt} e^{-I''_{jt}}) - \ln(P_{jt} e^{-I'_{jt}})) \tag{6}$$

where P' and P'' are given by eqn (4) with I' and I'', respectively, substituted for I. This nonlinear weighting scheme is a plausible method for computing changes in user benefits, since changes in popular auto types do count more than changes in types which attract only a small share of consumers, and large changes in composite price count more than small changes.

An intuitive explanation of eqn (5) is as follows. In contrast to the traditional consumer surplus calculation, the consumer's well-being in a probability choice model does not revolve around how many units of the good he or she purchases at a given price. Instead, all consumers purchase one unit of the good, but each version of the good has a different composite price.

In most cost-benefit studies, the goal is to measure the total consumer surplus to the economy if the policy change is implemented. However, important difficulties may arise in calculating consumer welfare changes. Some difficulties involve the theoretical concept of consumer surplus itself, and some have to do with attempting to aggregate individual consumers' surpluses to obtain an overall measure of consumer impacts.

With regard to the former, the principal problem arises because a change in price and quantity of a good changes the remaining income available to spend on other goods. This will in general change the overall level of the consumer's utility function in a way not exactly equal to the measure of consumer surplus. (Domencich and McFadden, 1975) demonstrate how this effect could be resolved theoretically in the context of a multinomial logit model of consumer behavior.) Some authors have felt that this taints the concept of consumer surplus in traditional analyses to the extent that it is actively misleading. Nonetheless, consumer surplus continues to be used in applied welfare economics. Recently, a rigorous justification of this practical application was given by Willig (1976). He derives limits on the amount which measured consumer surplus can deviate from the true measure of the change in utility, and provides numerical tables which can be used to calculate the difference. Even more importantly, he notes that in almost all applications, this difference is so small that it can be neglected. That is, the uncertainty with regard to how much correction is necessary to consider the income effect is less than the uncertainty surrounding estimation of the demand curve itself (see, Willig, 1976). Based on what we now know, this conclusion should be generally valid for the present study. Even though the present study addresses purchase of automobiles, for which each purchase is a relatively large amount in dollars, the total proportion of income is likely to remain small. Thus, income effects are probably not much more important here than in a typical case addressed by Willig.

The problem of aggregating individuals is reviewed in the next section, but before presenting this we should note two conclusions from the discussion so far. First, computation of consumer impacts requires little extra effort if a probability choice framework is already being used in auto demand analysis. All of the information needed to compute $\$\Delta CSL$, using either eqns (5) or (6), is available from the auto demand estimation and forecasting exercise. The second issue involves the reasonableness of using changes in consumer surplus as a measure of consumer impacts caused by CAFE. With recent advances in behavioral modeling, many of the old arguments against using cost-benefit analysis have lost their validity. In particular, the probability choice models can consider a wide range of auto attributes and choices which affect user well-being. Thus, they explicitly consider many of the changes which cannot be modeled using the simple price-quantity paradigm.

INDIVIDUAL TASTE VARIATION

If all consumers had the same taste coefficients, θ, we would expect them all to purchase the same type of car, except for minor random effects which comprise the Weibull distributed error term in the MNL model. In reality, different people purchase cars with widely varying attributes, so that the description thus far cannot be a satisfactory way to model the automobile choice. This issue requires extending the MNL model.

The issue of variation in consumer choice of automobiles can be addressed in at least two ways. The first is to assume that there are different segments of the population, with different tastes among these segments, but the same taste within a segment. Thus, there may be a "low income" taste for gas mileage and a "high income" taste for gas mileage. Similarly, there may be a variation in taste for acceleration and overall performance depending on the age of the consumer. An alternative specification is to allow tastes to vary continuously throughout the population. This may or may not include separate estimations for different population segments. However, even within a segment (if this is estimated separately), consumers are assumed to vary in their preferences. Obviously, this latter approach is more realistic.

For a more formal discussion, consider the following. Assume each consumer makes choices according to the MNL model specified by eqn (4); however, the composite price index, I_{jt}, varies among consumers because the weight on any attribute h_{ij} in the inclusive cost can vary across individuals. In formal terms, we consider for individual t the composite price of the jth auto type to be the following vector product (restating eqn (1)):

$$I(h_j|\theta_t) = \theta_t h_j \tag{7}$$

where there are N elements for each of the θ_t and h_j vectors and each element corresponds to an identifiable automobile attribute which consumers value in their purchase decisions.

If the θ_t were assumed to be constant across the population, then the inclusive cost would have no explanatory power for observed variations in auto buying patterns (see, Cardell, Dobson and Dunbar 1978). This is because virtually everyone in the population can choose among the same set of automobile offerings. Given that there is no variation in h_j across individuals, differences among automobile attributes by auto type cannot be used to estimate the θ_t if they are assumed constant across all individuals. Stated another way, observed market shares for automobile types cannot be explained by assuming both h_j and θ_t are constant across consumers because if this were true, only the auto type with the lowest composite price would be predicted to be purchased. Because the h_j are constant across consumers of all j, and because there are significant market shares for a wide variety of auto types, it must be the case that either θ_t varies across individuals, or there is an extremely large stochastic component in auto purchases. The former seems much more likely.

One method of inducing variations in the $I(h_j|\theta_t)$ across individuals is to use demographic variables in the composite price. Lave and Train (1976, 1979) have employed this approach in their MNL model of auto choice behavior. When the model is estimated, the individual attributes of autos are made functions of demographic variables:

$$g_{jti} = g_i(h_{ji}, s_{ti}) \tag{8}$$

where g_{jti} = the ith transformed attribute of the jth auto type for individual t, h_{ji} = the ith attribute of the jth auto type, and s_{ti} = the socioeconomic characteristic of individual t used to transform the ith attribute of autos.

Examples of g_{jti} include car cost divided by income and car weight times age of the respondent.

In order to perform an impact evaluation with attributes defined according to eqn (8), the s_{ti} must remain constant before and after the CAFE-induced change in attributes. The initial values of θ are estimated according to the following function form:

$$I(h_j|\theta, s_t) = \theta g(h_j, s_t) \tag{9}$$

where θ and $g(h_j, s_t)$ are vectors in auto attribute space. The θ vectors in eqn (9) are assumed constant across all decisionmakers. Variations in weights on observed auto attributes are attained by combining the estimated θs with the demographic variables:

$$\theta g(h_j, s_t) = \lambda(s_t) h_j. \tag{10}$$

Examples would be: (1) if $g(h_j, s_t)$ is car price divided by income, then $\lambda(s_t)$ is the estimated θ-weight (on car price divided by income) divided by income; and (2) if $g(h_j, s_t)$ is car weight times age of respondent, then $\lambda(s_t)$ is the θ-weight (on car weight times age of respondent) multiplied by age of respondent. The monetized change in consumer surplus arising from this model is then approximated by:

$$\$\Delta CSL = \sum_{t=1}^{T} \frac{1}{\lambda_o(s_{to})} \left(\ln\left(\sum_j e^{-\lambda(s_t)h_j^n} \right) - \ln\left(\sum_j e^{-\lambda(s_t)h_j^i} \right) \right) \tag{11}$$

where h_j' = auto attribute vector for the jth auto type before CAFE, h_j'' = auto attribute vector for the jth auto type after CAFE, and $\lambda_o(s_{to})$ = the transformed θ-weight on auto price.

Though the introduction of demographic variables allows the estimation of an MNL model, there is reason to believe that demographics should not be the sole determinant of market shares. It is likely that substantial differences in auto preferences exist within demographic market segments. The Hedonic Demand Model (HDM) approach is designed to forecast auto choices under these conditions.

The HDM assumes that the θ-weights in eqn (7) differ across individuals according to a statistical density function whose moments (i.e. mean, variance and higher ones if appropriate) can be estimated from a suitable database. As the distribution of θ is not directly observed, it is assumed to follow a specific density function, such as the lognormal in the case of existing HDM estimates. If it is also assumed that individual probability-choice decisions follow a specific rule, such as multinomial logit (eqn (4)), then the moments of the distribution of θ can be estimated by maximizing a likelihood function of observed choices with respect to the moments of θ.

The change in consumer surplus with the HDM model is as follows:

$$\$\Delta CSH = T\int\ldots\int \frac{1}{\theta_o}\ln\left[\frac{\sum_{m=1}^{M} e^{-I(h_m''|\theta)}}{\sum_{m=1}^{M} e^{-I(h_m'|\theta)}}\right] f(\theta\colon \mu,\Sigma)d\theta \tag{12}$$

where $f(\theta\colon \mu,\Sigma)$ = probability density function for the multivariate distribution of weights on auto attributes, μ = mean value of the θ vector, Σ = variance–covariance matrix of θ vector, θ_o = weight on auto price, h_m' = value of attributes for the mth auto type before CAFE, and h_m'' = value of attributes for the mth auto type after CAFE.

Essentially, the multiple integral in eqn (12) performs the same function as the summation in eqn (5). Unfortunately, it is a rather complex integral with order equal to the number of attributes in the inclusive cost. However, the techniques required for evaluating eqn (12) are the same as those used in estimating or in forecasting with the HDM and, consequently, only a small incremental computational burden is required to measure consumer impacts.

MONETIZED MEASURES OF CAFE IMPACTS

In this section, we use eqn (12) to compute the average consumer surplus resulting from CAFE regulations; we also compute the consumer surplus change for the median consumer using a simplified computation which does not require solution of a complex integral.

To perform these computations, we make the simplifying assumption that auto manufacturers will comply with CAFE by easing out their low mile per gallon makes and models. We make this assumption because the actual configuration of cars and their attribute in 1985 is not entirely knowable and because it eases somewhat the computational burden. In terms of 1977 makes and models, this assumption is roughly equivalent to reducing the choice set to the subcompact size class to achieve the 1985 fuel regulations.

In actuality, automobile manufacturers will pursue a strategy of making design changes to existing classes of cars which will increase mpg, and add to their purchase price. If the costs per vehicle of pursuing this strategy are less than restricting the choice set, then the computation of consumer surplus change using the HDM applied to the restricted choice set is an upper bound of the social cost of the CAFE regulations.

The version of the HDM which we are using is estimated on 1977 market data and is presented in the Appendix. For average consumer surplus, taking account of the wide dispersion of tastes in the auto market, eqn (12) is used to perform the consumer surplus computation.

It is also useful to consider the impact of CAFE on the median consumer as this differs considerably from the average impact. To perform this calculation we can assume that we are dealing with a single individual, in which case, eqn (12) reduces to eqn (5). The median consumer is defined as an individual who has the median value for each taste parameter.

As further simplification, the assumption that manufacturers implement CAFE by phasing out low mpg auto classes allows us to compute the monetized consumer impact for median individual t as follows:

$$\$\Delta CSL_t = \frac{1}{\theta_{ot}}\ln\left[\frac{\sum_{m=1}^{M_2} e^{-I_{mt}}}{\sum_{m=1}^{M_1} e^{-I_{mt}}}\right] \tag{13}$$

$$= \frac{1}{\theta_{ot}}\ln(P(M_2|t))$$

where M_1 = number of auto types available before CAFE, M_2 = number of auto types available after CAFE, and $P(M_2|t)$ = probability that individual t would choose an auto from the choice set $(1\ldots M_2)$ before CAFE, θ_{ot} = 0.4137 per \$1000 of new car transaction price using the HDM estimates in the Appendix.

Table 1 presents the estimates of changes in consumer surplus which would occur if various auto size classes were removed from the market in 1977. Forecasts of market shares under alternative choice set reduction scenarios are presented in the Appendix. Car types in Table 1 are arranged according to their existing fuel economy ratings, also shown. Thus, if luxury cars had been eliminated from the choice set, the median new car buyer would have experienced a loss of \$100 and the average loss would have been \$359. If full-size cars follow, the median consumer surplus loss is \$754 and the average loss is \$1891. If only subcompacts remain then the median consumer loss is \$3079 and the average loss is \$7398.

The disparity between the median and average change in consumer surplus is a result of the variation in taste feature of the HDM. In particular, the parameter which

Table 1. Impacts of removing 1977 vehicle size classes from the new car market to achieve 1985 CAFE regulations

		Market Share		Cumulative Change In Consumer Surplus per New Vehicle From Restricted Choice Set			
Vehicle Class	Average MPG[2]	By Class	Cumulative	Median[3]	Average	National Aggregate (billions)[4]	Reduced Choice Set Cumulative Average MPG[5]
Subcompact	27.78	.2753	.2753	$3079	$7398	$82.75	26.43
Compact	19.05	.1819	.4572	1901	4462	49.91	22.85
Speciality[1]	17.48	.0443	.5015	1560	3827	42.80	22.24
Mid-Size	17.33	.2256	.7271	754	1891	21.15	20.27
Full-Size	16.78	.2312	.9583	100	359	4.02	19.23
Luxury	15.24	.0417	1.0000	-0-	-0-	-0.0-	19.07

[1] "Specialty" cars are principally sporty types, such as the Ford Mustang or Datsun 280Z.

[2] Sales weighted harmonic average within class.

[3] Approximate calculation: see text

[4] Based on 1977 U.S. Passenger Car Retail Sales of 11.185 million vehicles. See Motor Vehicle Manufacturers Association, *MVMA Motor Vehicle Facts and Figures '79*, (Detroit: 1979), p.22.

[5] Harmonic average of sales weighted MPG using HDM market shares after cumulatively reducing the choice set. The last figure, 19.07, is the average for all sales in 1977. If luxury cars were excluded from the market, the HDM forecasts that the market shares of remaining offerings would result in 19.23 average MPG. If all but subcompacts were excluded the forecast market shares of makes and models in this category would yield a 26.43 average MPG.

measures the variance in utility associated with new car price was relatively large. This implies that there was a substantial portion of the new car market which attached very high value to autos in the larger size classes and is willing to pay much more for cars with these attributes than is the normal, market-clearing price. Note that the ratio of the average to the median consumer surplus loss declines with auto size indicating that this dispersion in taste is less for market segments which buy the types of cars which will be least affected by CAFE.

These estimates are for new cars purchased and are net of any offsetting savings due to lower fuel costs. The reductions in fuel costs are considered in the composite prices and inclusive costs because fuel cost is one of the attributes on which the model is estimated (see the Appendix). Also, given that a car will last around 10 years, the actual annualized loss to consumers will be much less than that which is presented in Table 1.

In discussing the reasonableness of these results consideration should be given to the parameter estimates of the model as described in the Appendix. In general, the model appears to be valid in describing consumer behavior in 1977. However, the question arises as to whether 1985 consumers will display the same characteristics as their 1977 counterparts.

Whether tastes on auto attributes will be similar in 1985 and beyond is something on an open question. The compression of auto features which affect fuel economy may itself change owners' preferences toward vehicle attributes such that what is now most highly prized, especially in perceived luxury characteristics, will no longer be as important. Also, national demographic trends such as smaller family sizes would affect the demand for attributes in autos. Finally, and probably most importantly, the 1977 data do not reflect the most recent round of gasoline price increase; consequently, in order to refine the estimated changes in consumers surplus, it would be advisable to reestimate the model on recent automobile sales data. Alternatively, relatively few differences emerged in a comparison of 1974 and 1977 parameter estimates of the HDM indicating that secular changes in tastes will happen relatively slowly if at all (see, Toder, Cardell and Burton 1978).

Even with these caveats, the welfare losses implied by the CAFE regulations appear to be large. In 1977, the only vehicle class meeting the 1985 fuel economy restrictions was the subcompact group. Immediate imposition of the regulations would have implied a welfare decrease of approximately $83 billion according to the results of the HDM. Also, the sales weighted mpg under this restriction is forecast by the HDM to be less than 27.5 mpg indicating that even such a restriction policy would have difficulty achieving the 1980 CAFE targets.

Consumer surplus changes of this magnitude indicate that there is considerable scope for manufacturers to use strategies other than simply reducing the range of their vehicle offerings. The actual fuel economy program of manufacturers also consists of altering vehicle characteristics within a size class. That is, design changes are attempted which minimize the change in vehicle attributes of importance to consumers other than fuel economy. These efforts are not without substantial cost, however. Industry sources have indicated that a one mile per gallon increase, holding the other vehicle attributes constant, adds $200 to the cost of manufacturing each vehicle in 1978 dollars. Capital costs alone can be conservatively estimated to be $100 per unit mpg increment per vehicle (see, Federal Task Force, 1976). Making the extremely conservative assumption that incremental costs do not increase as mpgs increase. This implies a cost increase of about $1800 to produce the 1977 mix of attributes achieving the 1985 fuel economy regulations. This computation is based on using a sales weighted harmonic average to achieve the CAFE standards as is mandated in the regulations. Using an arithmetic average would lower the overall cost increase.

The difference between the cost of making "existing" cars more fuel efficient and the welfare loss of restricting consumers' choices to the subcompact class is on the order of $62 billion using 1977 as the base model year. That is, given 1977 sales and prices, the strategy of making design changes to existing vehicle types which will minimize attribute changes other than fuel economy could cost consumers about $20.13 billion in terms of higher prices. Though this is still a high cost, it is substantially less than restricting market offerings and suggests that vehicle manufacturers will pursue this strategy.

Either approach, or their combination, entails high social costs. Consequently, there is reason to wonder whether alternative strategies could be devised which would accomplish the same energy policy goals but would entail less social cost. This subject is considered in the following section.

THE COST OF USING ENERGY PRICES TO ACHIEVE THE SAME POLICY TARGET

A variety of strategies can be used to achieve the policy goal of reduced oil consumption. In the transportation sector, most of the policy instruments involve either rationing fuel supply with price ceilings or changing the demand for fuel by restricting auto use and by improving alternative modes of travel. In terms of the welfare of transportation consumers, it can usually be shown that these strategies will make people worse off than using prices to achieve fuel conservation (or other social) aims (Dunbar, 1978, see also, Dorfman and Harrington, 1979). However, the use of increased prices to ration gasoline consumption has been expressly limited in federal legislation. Also, the ill-fated "gas guzzler" tax has been soundly rejected in favor of, probably, more costly regulations.

Below, we analyze the effects of gasoline taxes to conserve fuel and the effects of a neutral automobile tax which penalizes low mpg cars and subsidizes high mpg cars. The approach to evaluating a gas tax relies on traditional consumer surplus arguments. In contrast, the mpg based vehicle tax analysis uses the HDM.

Gasoline price strategies

Pricing strategies to conserve gasoline can take several forms. The simplest, and most politically unacceptable, approach is to decontrol oil and refined product prices; it is unlikely, however, that such a strategy would result in gasoline consumption declines of the magnitude which will be induced by CAFE regulations. Also, it is unlikely that even decontrolled prices would cover the social costs of gasoline consumption (see, Stobaugh 1979). In such a situation, it is appropriate for the government to intervene and establish a more appropriate price mechanism. Two classes of methods can be used: A. government taxes and tariffs can be imposed which will increase the pump price of gasoline and decrease demand to the socially desired level; or B. quotas on, and rationing of, supplies can be implemented with a market mechanism imposed to adjust prices. On the basis of the aggregate level of consumer welfare impacts there is usually little reason for policy-makers to prefer one type of mechanism over the other.

In choosing among pricing strategies, the major issue is the distributional effects of alternative schemes (see, Burrows and Domencich, 1970). The use of taxes and tariffs on oil products will determine how the increased prices to consumers are distributed back to the population. Similarly, if ration coupons are used when the government constrains both supply and the pump price, and if ration coupons can be traded among households, then an explicit market mechanism will reallocate the increased prices among consumers in terms of income for fuel conservers and higher costs for fuel users.

We can presume that to achieve a given (reduced) consumption level, the cost per gallon of gasoline to the eventual consumer will be similar under a regime which uses any of these mechanisms. Hence, except for administrative costs and distributional issues, we can evaluate all of them using traditional cost-benefit analysis.

For ease of exposition, we consider the issue of how to measure the welfare loss from a gasoline tax which might have the same effect as CAFE. Consider first an individual consumer who drives a car which gets the average 1977 miles per gallon of 18.6 (U.S. Department of Transportation, 1978). Suppose this consumer shows a demand function for gasoline of the form

$$Q = Ap^{\alpha} \tag{14}$$

where Q = the demand for gasoline in gallons, A = a constant term, p = the price of gasoline in dollar per gallon, and α = the elasticity of demand for gasoline.

Suppose the consumer drives 10,000 miles per year (see, Shonka, 1979) and has the long-run elasticity of gasoline −0.659, as estimated by CRA (see, Charles River Associates, 1975). This long-run elasticity allows consumers to adjust their auto type in response to a change in the price of gasoline. Thus this long-run elasticity provides comparability with changes likely from CAFE which modify the attributes of cars. Ten thousand miles at 18.6 miles per gallon implies an annual gasoline demand per vehicle of 537.6 gal. Assuming 65 cents per gallon as the 1977 price for gasoline (Shonka, 1979), the value of A is computed as 404.7.

The next issue is to define a fuel conservation target. We use one which is implied by the NHTSA regulations for 1985; that is, the amount of gasoline that would be consumed at 1977 prices if a car got 27.5 mpg and was driven the same amount (10,000 miles per year). We neglect the problems that the rated mpg will be higher than on-road mpgs, that fuel-efficient cars may be driven more or less than current types of cars, and that the diffusion of fuel efficient cars into the national fleet will take place over an extended period of time. All of these assumptions imply that the policy target is 363.6 gal per vehicle per year.

We now return to the issue of what the price would have to be to reduce consumption to this amount if a tax were imposed on gasoline. The above assumptions imply a price on gasoline of almost $1.18 per gallon in 1977 prices.

Given that we know the relative price range, the change in consumer surplus is given by

$$\$\Delta CST = \int_{p'}^{p''} Ap^{\alpha}dp$$
$$= (A/(1+\alpha))(p''^{1+\alpha} - p'^{1+\alpha}) \qquad (15)$$

where $\$\Delta CST$ = the change in consumer surplus due to a tax.

Based on the above assumptions, $\$\Delta CST$ equals almost $230. Part of this change in consumer surplus goes to the taxing authority. This amount equals the new quantity purchased (363.6 gal) times the change in price (approx. 53 cents) which equals just over $191. Thus the total welfare loss per vehicle per year is just over $38. This is 16.7% of the total change in consumer surplus. In terms of national aggregates, these per vehicle annual averages times the number of 1977 passenger car registrations (112.97 millions (see, MVMA, 1979)) yield $25.98 billion for the change in consumer surplus and $4.29 billion for the net welfare loss.

These computations are in terms of the manifest fuel reduction goals of CAFE and not in terms of the actual on-road fuel economy which will be achieved. McNutt *et al.* (1978) have shown that the post-CAFE automobile will have substantially lower on-road fuel economy than is rated. However, manufacturers will only be required to satisfy certified miles per gallon ratings and will not be regulated on the basis of actual consumer experience. Using data on model years 1974–77, the McNutt *et al.* results show that incremental changes in on-road fuel economy will only be 53 per cent of the incremental changes in rated fuel (see, McNutt testimony, 1980). In order to be comparable to the CAFE regulations, the fuel conservation target of the gasoline tax should be adjusted to account for actual on-road gasoline consumption rather than the hypothetical gasoline consumption computed from certified miles per gallon ratings. Taking 53% of the increment between gasoline consumption at 18.6 and 27.5 mpg and adding this to the manifest policy target of 363.6 gal per vehicle per year yields 455.8 gal per vehicle per year as the new target. Even this gas tax target is more stringent than the CAFE fuel consumption target because McNutt used 1975 as his base year and showed that the 1977 fuel economy ratings overstated actual experience; McNutt's computations imply 1985 new car actual on-road mpg of 21.3 mpg whereas our adjustments imply an on-road mpg of 23.3 for 1985 new cars.

The change in consumer surplus and the welfare loss from a gasoline tax to achieve this reduced target was computed using the same procedures and data as before. The implied price to the consumer of gasoline in 1977 would be 83 cents per gallon, or 28% higher than existed, to reduce consumption, from 537.6 to 455.8 gallons per vehicle per year. This entails an estimated change in consumer surplus of $89 per vehicle owned of which $82 is annual tax and $7 is net welfare loss. In terms of 1977 national aggregates, the change in consumer surplus is $10.06 billion and the net welfare loss is $0.80 billion.

In general, the gasoline tax is associated with substantially lower consumer net welfare losses than the CAFE program to achieve the same or higher levels of oil conservation.

Effects of an mpg based vehicle tax

A tax on new car sales which penalizes low mpg cars and subsidizes high mpg is another pricing strategy which could be applied instead of technology regulation. Such a tax allows consumers more choice in their vehicle purchase decision than restricting market offerings through CAFE and, it can be reasoned, would entail a lower consumer surplus loss than would occur if 1985 CAFE standards were implemented.

A neutral tax, one where tax receipts equal buyer subsidies, centered around the 1985 standard of 27.5 mpg and proportional to the rated gallons per mile of vehicles would have the following formula:

$$\text{Vehicle Tax} = (\text{Tax Rate})\left(\frac{1}{\text{mpg}} - \frac{1}{27.5}\right) \qquad (16)$$

The HDM can be used to solve for the Tax Rate which would have induced a fleet average of 27.5 mpg in 1977 new car sales. Then, using eqn (12), the changes in consumer surplus associated with such a tax rate can be calculated.

These computations were, in fact, performed yielding the following estimates:

Tax Rate = $406.805

Change in Consumer Surplus per Vehicle = $2478

Market share forecasts under this scenario are presented in the Appendix.

A notion of the magnitude of the tax which would be imposed can be gained by noting that the fleetwide sales-weighted harmonic average mpg of vehicles sold in 1977 was about 19 mpg and, consequently, the tax on the average car sold in 1977 would be $6540. Alternatively, buyers of the 1977 Honda offerings, rated at about 36 mpg, would have received a $3400 rebate. The tax on an incremental mpg around the fleet average of 19 mpg is $1070 and around the target of 27.5 mpg is $520.

Obviously, taxes of this magnitude would induce substantial manufacturer response in terms of configuring the mpg ratings of their products. In this regard, it is noteworthy that the very conservative $1800 per vehicle cost estimate of manufacturing the 1977 fleet in conformance with 1985 CAFE standards, is relatively close to the consumer surplus loss of a vehicle mpg-based tax

Table 2. Estimates of cost and benefits of alternative oil consumption strategies under 1977 conditions

	Estimate in Billions of Dollars	
Category of Cost/Benefit	Gross National Consumer Welfare Cost	Net National Welfare Gain[1]
CAFE Regulations	20.13 to 82.75	-4.07 to -75.93
Tax Strategies:		
New Car MPG	27.72	-11.66 to -20.90
Gasoline	.80	15.26 to 6.02

[1] Net National Welfare Gain estimates are calculated by deducting Gross National Consumer Costs from Stobaugh's estimate of national benefits from reduced oil imports, assuming all reduction in gasoline consumption comes from imported oil (see text).

scheme. This suggests that manufacturers may choose a combination of design changes and price incentives to achieve the 1985 standards.

SUMMARY AND CONCLUSION

This paper has demonstrated a methodology for consumer impact analysis which takes account of policies that affect nonprice attributes of consumer goods and takes account of dispersions of tastes which are normally observed in consumer markets. As such, the approach is an advance over the more traditional use of consumer surplus in evaluating public policy which makes the somewhat restrictive assumptions that both the goods being sold and the consumers are homogeneous.

In order to perform a complete cost-benefit analysis, it would be necessary to compute the social benefits of meeting the CAFE oil consumption reduction targets. Though a thorough and independent tabulation of the benefits of lower oil imports is beyond the scope of this paper, it is worthwhile to present Stobaugh's (1979) highly publicized results on this issue. Using liberal assumptions regarding GNP multipliers associated with increased imports and conservative estimates of price elasticities of crude oil associated with increased consumption, Stobaugh estimates that the net welfare loss of an extra barrel of imported oil is in the range of $31–$73 in 1979. Adjusting his results for 1977 prices ($12.50 per barrel instead of $15.00 per barrel) and multiplying by the annual barrels of oil which would have been saved in 1977 had the 1985 CAFE regulations been in effect (0.22 billion barrels) implies net national benefits in the range of $6.82–16.06 billions.

Given the magnitude of uncertainty regarding both CAFE social costs and oil import reduction benefits, it is difficult to present a definitive statement on the relative net national welfare gains among alternative fuel conservation strategies. Table 2 collects the computations from the preceding sections and presents ranges of estimates of net social benefits of using CAFE regulations and of using taxation policies. Even given the magnitude of uncertainty, two conclusions emerge: first, even with liberal estimates of the 1977 gains from reduced oil imports and with conservative estimates of incremental vehicle manufacture cost, CAFE regulations are not obviously in the public interest; second, gasoline taxes are a more effective instrument for reducing oil imports than are auto industry regulations.

Viewed from a somewhat different perspective, the results indicate that the use of CAFE rather than gasoline taxes to achieve oil import reductions cost consumers on the order of $20 billion per year. This can be interpreted as the "shadow price" on political constraints to using more cost-effective energy policy.

In the short time period between the most recently available data for performing this analysis (1977) and now (March 1980), the prices of gasoline have increased substantially and, consequently, both the consumer valuation of miles per gallon in new cars and the social benefits of reduced oil imports may have also changed substantially. Though these events raise the possibility that the net welfare gains of CAFE will be positive, this possibility is by no means certain. Moreover, even if the estimated range of net social welfare gains to CAFE is made more favorable by recent events, it is unlikely that these regulations will ever compare favorably with fuel price strategies to achieve reduced oil import goals.

The evaluation of CAFE-type regulations is by no means a dormant issue. Legislation was recently introduced to mandate CAFE of 40 mpg by 1995. We conclude that both the opportunity and the means exist to compare the cost-effectiveness of new CAFE regulations to alternative energy policies and that the social welfare losses of implementing cost-ineffective energy policies clearly justify such a comparison.

Acknowledgements—Much of the research reported herein was funded by the National Highway Traffic Safety Administration under contract to Charles River Associates, Inc. The authors gratefully acknowledge the assistance of A. Lawrence Kolbe and Robert Mellman. However, neither NHTSA, CRA nor these individuals are responsible for opinions or errors reported herein.

REFERENCES

Ben-Akiva M. and Lerman S. (1977) Disaggregate Travel Mobility Choice Models and Measures of Accessibility. *3rd Int. Conf. on Behavioral Travel Modeling*, Adelaide, Australia.

Burrows J. C. and Domencich T. A. (1970) *An Analysis of the United States Oil Import Quota*. D. C. Heath, Lexington, Mass.

Cardell, N. S., Dobson, R. and Dunbar, F. (1978) Consumer research implications of random coefficient models. In *Advances in Consumer Research* (Edited by Hunt H. K.), Vol. V Association for Consumer Research, Ann Arbor.

Charles River Associates Incorporated (1975) *The Effects of Automotive Fuel Conservation Measures on Automotive Air Pollution*. Charles River Associates, Cambridge, Mass.

Domencich T. A. and McFadden D. (1975) *Urban Travel Demand: A Behavioral Analysis*, pp. 94–99. North-Holland, Amsterdam.

Dorfman N. and Harrington I. (1979) Evaluating the Cost and Benefits of Plans to Reduce Gasoline Queues. Center for Transportation Studies, Massachusetts Institute of Technology.

Dunbar F. C. (To be published) Relative accuracy of user benefit measures. *Transpn Res. Record.*

Dunbar F. C. (To be published) The impacts of transportation control plans. *Transpn Res.*

Electric Power Research Institute (1977) *Methodology for Predicting the Demand for New Electricity-Using Goods*, EA-593, Project 488-1, *Final Rep.* Electric Power Research Institute, Palo Alto, California.

John R., *et al.* (1978) Mandated Fuel Economy Standards as a Strategy for Improving Motor Vehicle's Fuel Economy. Symposium on Technology, Government and the Future of the Automobile Industry. Harvard Business School, Cambridge, Mass.

Lave, C. A. and Train, K. (1976) *Prog. Rep. No.* 2, Description of Auto Choice Model. Energy Research and Development Administration, Washington, D.C.

Lave C. A. and Train, K. (1979) A disaggregate model of auto-type choice. *Transpn Res.* **13A**, 1–9.

McNutt B. D., *et al.* (1978) A Comparison of Fuel Economy Results from EPA Tests on Actual In-Use Experience, 1974–79 Model Year Cars. U.S. Department of Energy. Washington, D.C.

McNutt B. (4 Feb. 1980). Testimony before the House Subcommittee on Environment, Energy and Natural Resources, reported in EPA Plans to crack down on loopholes in MPG Test. *Automotive News.*

Motor Vehicle Manufacturer's Association (1979) *MVMA Motor Vehicle Facts and Figures* '79. Detroit, Michigan, 22.

Samuelson P. A. (1965) *Foundations of Economic Analysis*, pp. 195–202. Atheneum, New York.

Sheffi Y. (1977) Measures of network performance. *Int. Symp. on Travel Supply Models*, Montreal, Canada.

Shonka D. B. (Ed.) (1979) *Transportation Energy Conservation Data Book: Edition* 3, pp. 71–102. Oak Ridge National Laboratory, Oak Ridge, Tennessee.

Stobaugh R. (1979) After the peak: the threat of imported oil. In *Energy Future: Report of the Energy Project at the Harvard Business School* (Edited by Stobaugh R. and Yergin D.) Random House, New York.

Toder E. J., Cardell N. S. and Burton E. (1978) *Trade Policy and the U.S. Automobile Industry*. Praeger, New York.

U.S. Federal Task Force (2 Sept. 1976) *Motor Vehicle Goals Beyond* 1980, Vol. I, 29, Vol. 2, 6, 6B 1–2.

U.S. Department of Transportation, National Highway Traffic Safety Administration (1978). Automotive Fuel Economy Program, 2*nd Ann. Rep. ot the Congress.*

Williams H. C. W. L. (1977) On the formulation of travel demand models and economic evaluation measures of user benefit. *Environment and Planning* **19**.

Willig R. D. (Sept. 1976). Consumer's surplus without apology. *Am. Econ. Rev.* **66**(4), 589–597.

APPENDIX

The Hedonic Demand Model

The Hedonic Demand Model (HDM) used in this paper is described in more detail below. The HDM, as now implemented, is a probability choice model with variable coefficients. The model is used here to predict the effects of changes in automobile characteristics on automobile purchases and consumers. The HDM forecasts the market shares of individual car makes and models and these are summed to forecast the shares of automobile size classes. There are a total of 153 individual car makes and models (for the year 1977) whose market shares are forecast in the results presented in this study.

A complete description of the model including its theoretical underpinnings and estimation procedure is presented in Electric Power Institute (1977).

The input data include new car sales and attributes affecting consumer choice. The current version of the HDM uses six vehicle attributes defined as follows:

Price refers to the price of the standard two-door (or lowest price) version of the auto make and model. This price definition is used both because data are not available on average car price with options by submodel and because the quality of some options, such as trim packages, are difficult to measure. The logic behind the price definition is that within submarkets, options can be added to any submodel at comparable prices. Base price should thus be a proxy for actual quality-adjusted price. The transaction price is assumed to be halfway between the sticker price and the dealer price for all models.

Fuel Economy is defined as 100 divided by the DOE/EPA composite fuel economy measurement for the submodel.

Acceleration is measured by 60 divided by the 0-to-60 time in seconds. The 0-to-60 time is approximated by an estimated algorithm and depends on the horsepower to weight ratio of the submodel.

Luxury is based on Consumer Reports ratings of noise and ride, which range in quality from one (very poor) to five (excellent). The luxury variable is defined for each submodel as: $3 \times \text{Noise} + 2 \times \text{Ride} + 1 \times \text{Auto} - 6$, where auto is a dummy variable taking the value of one for cars with an automatic transmission. Without inclusion of this dummy variable, the model would see that automatic transmissions produce poorer fuel economy at higher prices with *no* gain in any other included attribute.

Frequency of Repair is measured by Consumer Reports incidence of repair ratings summed over the 1972–76 period. For each year the rating ranges from 1 to 5, so this variable can take values from 5 to 25.

Interior Space is defined as front and rear seat leg room times shoulder room times a constant. Experimentation with alternative specifications showed that the interior headroom variable added no explanatory power. We hypothesized that the public likes the long, low look and is not willing to pay extra for headroom. Perhaps, in a specification in which headroom and car height were included separately, headroom would get a positive valuation and height a negative consumer valuation. This hypothesis has not yet been tested.

Table A1 summarizes the statistical information on the estimated marginal rates of substitution between characteristics and price. The distribution of consumer tastes for auto attributes is assumed to be log-normal. The parameters reported in Table A1 were computed by

Table A1. Hedonic demand model parameter estimates

Characteristics	Median	Mean
	---(Dollars per Unit)---	
Fuel Economy	$162.350	$ 275.635
Acceleration	296.363	1994.397
Luxury	417.438	708.720
Frequency of Repair	61.127	103.781
Passenger Space	42.475	72.113

taking exponents of the normal distributions of the logs of attributes. As the distributions are log-normal, the mean and median of the distributions are not the same.

Each parameter is for the distribution of monetized consumer valuation of the attribute. That is, if β_i is the unit free consumer valuation on price, then the mean monetized valuation on attribute i is the expected value of β_i/β_p.

The median values of the distributions in Table B1 give the marginal value of an additional unit of attribute in dollars. These are interpreted as follows:

The *fuel economy* coefficient of $162 per unit indicates that the median consumer will pay a dollar amount for better fuel economy which is less than the dollar savings on about the first 30,000 miles of travel. Given the conventional wisdom that new car buyers have a high discount rate, the implied three-year payback period on an investment in fuel economy is tenable. Note, however, that the absence of car weight as an explanatory variable may cause the fuel economy coefficient to be underestimated. Weight is highly negatively correlated with fuel economy and is desired by consumers (holding other characteristics including fuel economy constant) for reasons of safety and driving stability. We can expect that the inclusion of curb weight in a future model specification will lead to a positive valuation of that characteristic and a higher estimate of fuel economy valuation.

The *acceleration* coefficient of $296 indicates that the median consumer will pay about $147 for the difference in acceleration between an average 1977 subcompact car and an average full-size car. The acceleration coefficient is roughly the market cost of an optional larger engine on any car model and is an entirely reasonable coefficient estimate. Note that the mean value of this coefficient is much higher than the median indicating a large dispersion of taste for acceleration.

The *luxury* estimate of $417 implies that much of the difference in price among size classes is accounted for by luxury, and that consumers really want the quiet, smooth ride of a bigger car rather than interior space *per se.* While we believe that luxury is important to consumers, we nonetheless expect that a more fully specified auto demand model would lower the current estimate somewhat.

The estimate of the coefficient of the *frequency of repair* variable indicates that a car with a good repair record is worth about $305 more to the median consumer than a car with an average repair record, which in turn is worth about $305 more than a car with a poor repair record. This coefficient estimate seems reasonable.

The parameter estimate for *interior passenger space* is $42 per cubic foot. This implies, for example, that the median consumer valuation on the difference in interior space between the standard size Chevrolet and the next model in the Chevrolet line (the Chevelle in 1977) is approx. $400. In the more extreme comparison between the standard sized Chevrolet and the Honda Civic, the median consumer valuation is $1700. This may be a somewhat low valuation of this attribute but not inordinately so.

In summary, we believe that a completely specified model will give a somewhat higher consumer weighting to fuel economy and interior space and a lower valuation to luxury.

Another way of judging the model is to look at the fit of the model to sales by major classes of cars. For example, the estimated domestic car market share is 85.01% while the actual share is 83.77%. The model performs well on this test.

Table A2. Market shares by size class, 1977 actual and estimated

	Actual		Estimated
	---	(Percent)	---
Class 1 (subcompact)	22.94%		27.53%
Class 2 (compact)	18.81		18.19
Class 3 (intermediate)	17.05		22.56
Class 4 (full)	20.47		23.12
Class 5 (luxury)	5.19		4.17
Class 6 (specialty)	15.55		4.43

Table A3. 1977 New vehicle market share forecasts with hedonic demand model applied to policy scenarios

Vehicle Class	Market Shares of Remaining Vehicle Classes After Higher MPG Vehicle Classes From the Market				Market Shares After Imposition of MPG Tax Causing Fleet Average 27.5 MPG
	-(Percent)-				-(Percent)-
Subcompact	28.41	36.44	52.72	57.76	72.89
Compact	19.00	25.48	38.19	42.24	8.73
Specialty	4.64	6.22	9.09	-0.0-	3.32
Mid-Size	23.60	31.86	-0.0-	-0.0-	6.26
Full-Size	24.36	-0.0-	-0.0-	-0.0-	7.07
Luxury	-0.0-	-0.0-	-0.0-	-0.0-	1.73

Table A2 presents estimated vs. actual total U.S. market shares by size class. The model performs relatively well in explaining shares of standard cars by size class, but the specialty car market share estimate is much lower than the specialty class actual share. This can be attributed to the absence of a styling taste variable in the current HDM specification. The model also appears to allocate some part of the compact class share to the subcompact class. However, with the exception of the specialty class estimate we believe the model performs relatively well in estimating size-class shares.

Another measure that can be used to indicate the accuracy of the model's size-class estimation it its accuracy in forecasting sales-weighted 1977 new car fleet miles per gallon. For the months of the sample (November 1976–August 1977) the actual new car average miles per gallon is 19.072; the average miles per gallon estimated with market shares from the model would be 19.062. The model is correct to within one-tenth of 1%.

As a final test of the HDMs performance, we present the forecasts of 1977 market shares under the alternative policy scenarios apecified in the body of this paper. These results are presented in Table A3. The model performs relatively well in this regard. Most consumers are shown to have a tendency to move to the next size class when their own class of vehicle is removed from the market. When only compacts and subcompacts remain, there is a definite trend toward higher priced imports in the subcompact category inasmuch as these are positioned closer to existing specialty cars.

On the whole, the HDMs performance indicates that is well suited to the problem of evaluating automobile related policy issues.

[27]

MIXED LOGIT WITH REPEATED CHOICES: HOUSEHOLDS' CHOICES OF APPLIANCE EFFICIENCY LEVEL

David Revelt and Kenneth Train*

Abstract—Mixed logit models, also called random-parameters or error-components logit, are a generalization of standard logit that do not exhibit the restrictive "independence from irrelevant alternatives" property and explicitly account for correlations in unobserved utility over repeated choices by each customer. Mixed logits are estimated for households' choices of appliances under utility-sponsored programs that offer rebates or loans on high-efficiency appliances.

I. Introduction

MIXED logit (also called random-parameters logit) generalizes standard logit by allowing the parameter associated with each observed variable (e.g., its coefficient) to vary randomly across customers. The moments of the distribution of customer-specific parameters are estimated. Variance in the unobserved customer-specific parameters induces correlation over alternatives in the stochastic portion of utility. As a result, mixed logit does not exhibit the restrictive forecasting patterns of standard logit (i.e., it does not exhibit independence from irrelevant alternatives). Mixed logit also allows efficient estimation when there are repeated choices by the same customers, as occurs in our application.

Mixed logits have taken different forms in different applications; their commonality arises in the integration of the logit formula over the distribution of unobserved random parameters. The early applications (Boyd and Mellman (1980), Cardell and Dunbar (1980)) were restricted to situations in which explanatory variables do not vary over customers, such that the integration, which is computationally intensive, is required for only one "customer" using aggregate share data rather than for each customer in a sample. Advances in computer speed and in our understanding of simulation methods for approximating integrals have allowed estimation of models with explanatory variables varying over customers. Ben-Akiva et al. (1993), Ben-Akiva and Bolduc (1996), Bhat (1996), and Brownstone and Train (1996) apply a mixed-logit specification like that given below but without repeated choices. Other empirical studies (Berkovec and Stern (1991), Bolduc et al. (1993), and Train et al. (1987)) have specified choice probabilities that integrate a logit function over unobserved terms, but with these terms representing something other than random parameters of observed attributes. In all cases except Ben-Akiva et al. (1993) and Train et al. (1987), the integration is performed through simulation, similar to that described below. These two exceptions used quadrature, which was feasible in their cases because only one- or two-dimensional integration was required in their specifications.

Terminology for these models varies. "Random-coefficients logit" or "random-parameters logit" has been used for obvious reasons (Ben-Akiva and Lerman (1985), Bhat (1996), Train (1996)). The term "error-components logit" is useful since it emphasizes the fact that the unobserved portion of utility consists of several components and that these components can be specified to provide realistic substitution patterns rather than to represent random parameters *per se* (Brownstone and Train, 1996). "Mixed logit" reflects the fact that the choice probability is a mixture of logits with a specified mixing distribution (Brownstone and Train (forthcoming), McFadden and Train (1997), Train (forthcoming)). This term encompasses any interpretation that is consistent with the functional form. We use "mixed logit" in the current paper because of this generality, even though our specification is motivated through a random-parameters concept. Ben-Akiva and Bolduc (1996) use the term "probit with a logit kernel" to describe models where the customer-specific parameters are normally distributed. This term is instructive since it points out that the distinction between pure probits (in which utility is normally distributed) and mixed logits with normally distributed parameters is conceptually minor.

II. Specification

A person faces a choice among the alternatives in set J in each of T time periods or choice situations. The number of choice situations can vary over people, and the choice set can vary over people and choice situations. The utility that person n obtains from alternative j in choice situation t is $U_{njt} = \beta'_n x_{njt} + \epsilon_{njt}$ where x_{njt} is a vector of observed variables, coefficient vector β_n is unobserved for each n and varies in the population with density $f(\beta_n|\theta^*)$ where θ^* are the (true) parameters of this distribution, and ϵ_{njt} is an unobserved random term that is distributed iid extreme value, independent of β_n and x_{njt}. Conditional on β_n, the probability that person n chooses alternative i in period t is standard logit:

$$L_{nit}(\beta_n) = \frac{e^{\beta'_n x_{nit}}}{\sum_j e^{\beta'_n x_{njt}}}. \quad (1)$$

The unconditional probability is the integral of the conditional probability over all possible values of β_n, which depends on the parameters of the distribution of β_n:

$$Q_{nit}(\theta^*) = \int L_{nit}(\beta_n) f(\beta_n|\theta^*)\, d\beta_n.$$

For maximum likelihood estimation we need the probability of each sampled person's sequence of observed choices. Let $i(n,t)$ denote the alternative that person n chose in period t.

Received for publication March 18, 1996. Revision accepted for publication October 9, 1997.

* University of California, Berkeley.

Conditional on β_n, the probability of person n's observed sequence of choices is the product of standard logits:[1]

$$S_n(\beta_n) = \prod_t L_{ni(n,t)t}(\beta_n).$$

The unconditional probability for the sequence of choices is

$$P_n(\theta^*) = \int S_n(\beta_n) f(\beta_n | \theta^*)\, d\beta_n. \qquad (2)$$

Note that there are two concepts of parameters in this description. The coefficient vector β_n is the parameters associated with person n, representing that person's tastes. These tastes vary over people; the density of this distribution has parameters θ^* representing, for example, the mean and covariance of β_n. The goal is to estimate θ^*, that is, thepopulation parameters that describe the distribution of individual parameters.

The log-likelihood function is $LL(\theta) = \Sigma_n \ln P_n(\theta)$. Exact maximum likelihood estimation is notpossible since the integral in equation (2) cannot be calculated analytically. Instead, we approximate the probability through simulation and maximize the simulated log-likelihood function. In particular, $P_n(\theta)$ is approximated by a summation over randomly chosen values of β_n. For a given value of the parameters θ, a value of β_n is drawn from its distribution. Using this draw of β_n, $S_n(\beta_n)$—the product of standard logits—is calculated. This process is repeated for many draws, and the average of the resulting $S_n(\beta_n)$'s is taken as the approximate choice probability:

$$SP_n(\theta) = (1/R) \sum_{r=1,...,R} S_n(\beta_n^{r|\theta})$$

where R is the number of repetitions (i.e., draws of β_n), $\beta_n^{r|\theta}$ is the r-th draw from $f(\beta_n|\theta)$, and $SP_n(\theta)$ is the simulated probability of person n's sequence of choices. By construction $SP_n(\theta)$ is an unbiased estimator of $P_n(\theta)$ whose variance decreases as R increases. It is smooth (i.e., twice-differentiable) which helps in the numerical search for the maximum of the simulated log-likelihood function. It is strictly positive for any realization of the finite R draws, such that the log of the simulated probability is always defined.[2]

The simulated log-likelihood function is constructed as $SLL(\theta) = \Sigma_n \ln(SP_n(\theta))$, and the estimated parameters are those that maximize SLL.[3] Lee (1992) and Hajivassiliou and Ruud (1994) derive the asymptotic distribution of the maximum simulated likelihood estimator based on smooth probability simulators with the number of repetitions increasing with sample size. Under regularity conditions, the estimator is consistent and asymptotically normal. When the number of repetitions rises faster than the square root of the number of observations, the estimator is asymptotically equivalent to the maximum likelihood estimator. Note that, even though the simulated probability is an unbiased estimate of the true probability, the log of the simulated probability with fixed number of repetitions is not an unbiased estimate of the log of the true probability. The bias in SLL decreases as the number of repetitions increases. We use 500 repetitions in our estimation.[4]

The simulated score for each person is

$$SS_n(\theta) \equiv \frac{\partial \ln SP_n(\theta)}{\partial \theta} = \left[\frac{1}{SP_n(\theta)}\right]\left[\frac{1}{R}\right] \times \sum_r S_n(\beta_n^{r|\theta}) \times \left[\sum_t \sum_j (d_{njt} - L_{njt}^{r|\theta}) \frac{\partial \beta_n^{r|\theta\prime} X_{njt}}{\partial \theta}\right] \qquad (3)$$

[1] Our specification assumes that the person's tastes, as represented by β_n, are the same for all choice situations. The model can be generalized to allow the coefficient vector to vary over t as well as n. Our data consist of repeated choices within a survey, such that the assumption of β_n constant over choices seems reasonable.

[2] The simulated probabilities for a sequence of choices sum to one over all possible sequences. Similarly, simulated choice probabilities in each time period (that is, simulated versions of $Q_{nit}(\tau)$) sum to one over alternatives, which is useful in forecasting.

[3] Software to estimate mixed logits is available on K. Train's home page at http://elsa.berkeley.edu/~train.

[4] Other estimation procedures could be applied. The method of simulated moments (MSM) (McFadden, 1989) has the advantage of being consistent with a fixed number of repetitions when the weights in the moment condition are independent of the residuals; however, it is inefficient unless the ideal weights are used. When the ideal weights are simulated with the same draws as the probabilities, then MSM is equivalent to our procedure with maximum simulated likelihood (MSL): the weights and residuals are not independent, and the procedure is not consistent for a fixed number of repetitions. Simulating the weights separately from the probabilities (i.e., using separate draws for each) provides a consistent and asymptotically efficient estimator. However, anecdotal evidence indicates that the finite sample properties of this estimator are poor (Hajivassiliou, personal communication). Furthermore, MSM requires simulation of the probability of each possible sequence of responses, which in our situation would involve calculation of over 300,000 probabilities for each customer. Method of simulated scores (Hajivassiliou and McFadden (forthcoming)) is consistent if an unbiased simulator for the score is used; however, an unbiased score simulator is difficult to develop. The score takes the form $(1/P)dP/d\theta$. An unbiased simulator for $dP/d\theta$ is readily available; however, obtaining an unbiased simulator of $(1/P)$ is difficult. In particular, the reciprocal of an unbiased simulator of P is not unbiased for $1/P$. Usually, MSS estimators are called asymptotically unbiased, meaning that their bias disappears when the number of repetitions increases without bound, which is the same as MSL. Our procedure using MSL is a MSS estimator with $(1/P)$ simulated as the reciprocal of the simulated probability.

A reviewer suggested an alternative procedure that has desirable characteristics. First, obtain a consistent estimate using, e.g., MSM with exogenous weights or MSS with an unbiased score simulator. Then, apply one bhhh step to this consistent estimator. This estimator is efficient when the number of repetitions increases without bound along with sample size, the same as MSL. However, the asymptotic properties can perhaps be attained more readily with this approach than with MSL. In particular, since only one bhhh step is used (i.e., one iteration in MSL), the number of repetitions can be increased enormously for this one step while still utilizing the same computer time as with MSL. In our application, we used 500 repetitions, and approximately twenty iterations were needed to reach convergence. The alternative procedure could use 10,000 repetitions for its one iteration. The difficulty, of course, would be obtaining the initial consistent estimate. MSM is infeasible in our setting, since, as stated, it would involve simulation of hundreds of thousands of probabilities for each customer. In other settings, however, MSM could be utilized; importantly, the inefficiency that arises from nonideal weights would not be a concern since the MSM estimator is followed by a bhhh step using a very large number of repetitions.

where $d_{njt} = 1$ if person n chose alternative j in period t and zero otherwise, and $L_{njt}^{r|\theta}$ is the logit formula (1) evaluated with $\beta_n^{r|\theta}$. The score is easy to compute, which speeds the iteration process. We found that calculating the Hessian from formulas for the second derivatives resulted in computationally slower estimation than using the bhhh or other approximate-Hessian procedures.

In general, the coefficient vector can be expressed as $\beta_n = b + \eta_n$, where b is the population mean, and η_n is the stochastic deviation that represents the person's tastes relative to the average tastes in the population. Then $U_{njt} = b' x_{njt} + \eta'_n x_{njt} + \epsilon_{njt}$. In contrast to standard logit, the stochastic portion of utility $(\eta'_n x_{njt} + \epsilon_{njt})$ is in general correlated over alternatives and time due to the common influence of η_n. Mixed logit does not exhibit the independence from irrelevant alternatives property of standard logit, and very general patterns of correlation over alternatives and time (and hence very general substitution patterns) can be obtained through appropriate specification of variables and parameters. In fact, McFadden and Train (1997) show that any random-utility model can be approximated to any desired degree of accuracy with a mixed logit through appropriate choice of explanatory variables and distributions for the random parameters.[5] In the application below, we estimate models with normal and log-normal distributions for elements of β_n; other distributions are of course possible.

III. Application

Demand-side management (DSM) programs by electric utilities have relied heavily on rebates as a mechanism for promoting energy efficiency. As the electricity industry moves toward greater competition, the feasibility of rebates is questionable. Low-interest loan programs are being considered as alternatives. Potentially, loans can provide an incentive for efficiency (and so serve the goals of DSM) and yet generate profits as long as the interest rates on the loans are above the firm's cost of capital.

Using data from Southern California Edison (SCE), we estimate the impact of rebates and loans on residential customers' choice of efficiency level for refrigerators. Since loans have not been offered by SCE in the past, and since there has been little variation in rebate levels, data on actual purchases by SCE customers do not provide the information that is needed to estimate choice models with loan terms and rebate levels as explanatory variables. Stated-preference data were collected to estimate such models. In particular, a sample of SCE's residential customers was presented in a survey with a series of choice experiments. In each experiment, two or three refrigerators with different efficiency levels were described, with a rebate, loan, or no incentive offered on the high-efficiency units. The customer was asked which appliance he/she would choose. For customers who had bought a refrigerator within the last three years, these stated-preference data were supplemented, insofar as possible, with information on the efficiency level of the refrigerator that the customer actually purchased. Mixed logits are estimated on the stated-preference data; the models are then adjusted, or "calibrated," to reflect the limited revealed-preference data. The calibrated models are then used to forecast the impact of various loan programs.

In the stated-preference choice experiments, each sampled customer was offered a series of binary choices, followed by a series of trinary choices. For the binary choices, the purchase price and operating cost of a standard-efficiency and a high-efficiency refrigerator were described, and the customer was asked to choose between them. The high-efficiency unit was offered without any incentive, with a rebate, or with a financing package detailing the interest rate, amount borrowed, repayment period, and monthly payment. Trinary choices were then offered to the customer. In these experiments, the customer was offered three high-efficiency units: one with no incentive, one with a rebate, and one with financing. The purchase price and operating cost of the units differed, such that the unit with no incentive was not dominated. In total, responses to 6,081 choice experiments were obtained from 401 surveyed customers, with each customer providing responses to twelve binary choice experiments and up to four trinary experiments. The 6,081 experiments consist of the following types: 1,604 pair a standard unit with a high-efficiency unit that has no incentive; 1,626 pair a standard unit with a high-efficiency unit on which a rebate is available; 1,602 pair a standard unit with a high-efficiency unit on which a loan is offered; and 1,249 include three high-efficiency units with no incentive, a rebate, and a loan.[6]

The choice experiments were designed to provide plausible attributes, orthogonal over experiments, and with no

[5] This result differs critically and is stronger than the "mother logit" theorem, which states that any choice model can be approximated by a model that takes the form of a standard logit (McFadden (1975)). In the mother logit theorem, any choice model can be expressed as a standard logit if attributes of one alternative are allowed to enter the "representative utility" of other alternatives. However, when cross-alternative attributes are entered, the logit model is no longer a random utility model (i.e., it is not consistent with utility maximizing behavior), since the utility of one alternative depends on the attributes of other alternatives. In the theorem regarding mixed logit, any random utility model can be approximated by a mixed logit without entering cross-alternative variables, or, more precisely, while still maintaining consistency with utility-maximizing behavior.

[6] A note concerning identification is warranted. In the binary choice experiments, the variance in β_n induces heteroskedasticity in the difference in utility between the two alternatives. The parameters of the distribution of β_n, i.e., θ, are identified by the heteroskedasticity over experiments (that is, by the variation in the variance in the utility-difference). In the trinary experiments, the variance in β_n induces heteroskedasticity and covariance in the two utility-differences (that is, in the utility for two of the alternatives minus the utility for the remaining alternative.) Essentially, each person has a variance in utility differences in a binary situation, and two variances and a covariance between two utility-differences in a trinary situation. If these terms were fixed over people and normalized to account for the arbitrary scale of utility, then estimation of at most two parameters would be possible with trinary experiments and none with binary experiments. However, with mixed logit, these terms vary over people in a way that depends on θ and the variables; θ is thereby identified even in binary experiments and even when its dimension is greater than two in trinary experiments.

experiment containing a dominated alternative. The variables that enter the models below are:

(a) *Price of the refrigerator, net of any rebate, in hundreds of dollars.* (For a standard-efficiency unit and high-efficiency units without a rebate, this variable is the price of the unit. For high-efficiency units with a rebate, it is the price of the unit minus the rebate.[7])
(b) *Savings, in hundreds of dollars.* This variable is zero for the standard unit and, for the high-efficiency units, is the annual dollar reduction in operating cost that the unit provides relative to the standard unit. (That is, savings in any experiment is the operating cost of the standard unit minus the operating cost of the high-efficiency unit.)
(c) *Amount borrowed, in hundreds of dollars.* This variable is zero for standard units and for high-efficiency units for which no loan is offered. For high-efficiency units on which a loan is offered, this variable is the maximum dollar amount that the customer is allowed to borrow. The percent of the purchase price that the customer is able to borrow varies over experiments.
(d) *Interest rate, in digits* (i.e., 4% interest is entered as 0.04). This variable is zero for standard units and for high-efficiency units for which no loan is offered. For high-efficiency units with a loan available, the variable is the interest rate that is offered for the loan. The interest rate varies over experiments.
(e) *Efficiency dummy.* This variable takes the value of zero for standard units and one for high-efficiency units.
(f) *Rebate dummy,* taking the value of one for high-efficiency units on which a rebate is provided, and zero otherwise.
(g) *Finance dummy,* taking the value of one for high-efficiency units for which a loan is provided, and zero otherwise.

The means of these variables over the choice experiments are given in table 1. Details of the survey design and variables are provided in SCE (1994).

A. *Model Estimation*

We specify the price coefficient to be fixed while allowing the other coefficients to vary. The willingness to pay for each attribute (which is the ratio of the attribute's coefficient to the price coefficient) is thereby distributed in the same way as the attribute's coefficient, which is convenient for interpretation of the model.[8]

TABLE 1.—MEANS OF EXPLANATORY VARIABLES

Price of standard-efficiency refrigerator	875.94
Price of high-efficiency refrigerator	1127.89
Annual savings in operating cost for high-efficiency units relative to standard	116.89
Rebate (when rebate is offered)	125.75
Amount borrowed (when loan is offered)	698.50
Interest rate (when loan is offered)	0.0505

We first specify all the nonprice coefficients to be independently normally distributed. The coefficient vector is expressed as $\beta_n = b + W\mu_n$ in which W is a diagonal matrix whose elements are standard deviations (with the top-left element being zero, for the price coefficient), and μ_n is a vector of independent standard normal deviates. For simulation, draws of μ_n are obtained from a pseudorandom number generator, and the corresponding draws of β_n are calculated for any given values of the means b and standard deviations W. With this specification, the derivatives that enter the score (3) are $\partial\beta_n^{r|\theta\prime} x_{njt}/\partial b_k = x_{k,njt}$ and $\partial\beta_n^{r|\theta\prime} x_{njt}/\partial W_k = \mu_k^r x_{k,njt}$, where the subscript k denotes the k-th element. Subsequent models allow correlation among the coefficients and specify log-normal distributions for some of the coefficients.

Table 2 provides the estimation results for this model, along with the results for a standard logit model. The mean coefficients in the mixed logit are consistently larger than the fixed coefficients in the standard logit model. This result reflects the fact that the mixed logit decomposes the unobserved portion of utility and normalizes parameters on the basis of part of the unobserved portion. Suppose true utility is given by the mixed logit: $U_{njt} = b'x_{njt} + \mu_n' Wx_{njt} + \epsilon_{njt}$. The parameters b are normalized such that ϵ_{njt} has the appropriate variance for an extreme value error. The standard logit model treats utility as $U_{njt} = b'x_{njt} + \xi_{njt}$ with b normalized such that ξ_{njt} has the variance of an extreme value deviate. The extreme value term in the standard logit model incorporates any variance in the parameters. In the mixed logit, the variance in parameters is treated explicitly as a separate component of the error ($\mu_n' Wx_{njt}$) such that the remaining error (ϵ_{njt}) is "net" of this variance. Since the variance in the error term in the standard logit is greater than the variance in the extreme value component of the error term in the mixed logit, the normalization makes the parameters in the standard logit model smaller in magnitude than those in the mixed logit. The fact that the parameters rise by a factor of three or more implies that the random

[7] When the rebate enters as a separate variable, rather than subtracted from price, its mean coefficient is similar in magnitude and opposite in sign to the mean coefficient of price. The hypothesis cannot be rejected at reasonable significance levels that the rebate is considered a reduction in price.

[8] When all coefficients are allowed to vary in the population, identification is empirically difficult, for the reasons given by Ruud (1996). In particular, if the stochastic portion of utility is dominated by the random parameters such that the iid extreme-value term has little influence, then the scaling of utility by the variance of the extreme-value term becomes unstable and an additional scaling is needed. At an extreme, where the extreme-value term has no influence (i.e., zero variance), the simulated probability becomes an accept/reject simulator, and a scaling of the remaining utility (that is, utility without the extreme-value term) is required. We chose the price coefficient to be fixed, since, as stated, this restriction allows easy derivation of the distribution of the willingness to pay. Models with all coefficients varying did not converge in any reasonable number of iterations, as expected by Ruud's observation.

TABLE 2.—STANDARD AND MIXED LOGIT WITH ALL NORMALLY DISTRIBUTED COEFFICIENTS

		Standard Logit Estimates	*Mixed Logit Estimates*
Price net of rebate	Coefficient	−0.379	−1.23
		(0.0360)	(0.108)
Savings	Mean coefficient	0.807	3.03
		(0.0609)	(0.345)
	Standard deviation of coefficient	—	2.24
			(0.281)
Amount borrowed	Mean coefficient	0.0701	0.392
		(0.0176)	(0.066)
	Standard deviation of coefficient	—	0.489
			(0.057)
Interest rate	Mean coefficient	−6.87	−48.5
		(4.03)	(10.09)
	Standard deviation of coefficient	—	44.4
			(7.53)
Efficiency dummy	Mean coefficient	1.33	3.70
		(0.101)	(0.421)
	Standard deviation of coefficient	—	3.20
			(0.398)
Rebate dummy	Mean coefficient	0.229	0.022
		(0.109)	(0.212)
	Standard deviation of coefficient	—	1.30
			(0.204)
Finance dummy	Mean coefficient	−0.0175	0.156
		(0.264)	(0.621)
	Standard deviation of coefficient	—	0.284
			(0.475)
Likelihood ratio index		0.275	0.461
Willingness to pay in higher purchase price, calculated at estimated mean coefficients, for:			
	\$1 extra savings	2.13	2.46
	\$1 extra of amount borrowed	0.19	0.32
	1% reduction in interest rate	18.13	39.43

Notes: Standard errors in parentheses.
Price, savings, and amount borrowed are in hundreds of dollars. Interest rates are in digits (e.g., 4% is entered as 0.04).

parameters constitute a very large share of the variance in unobserved utility.

In the mixed logit, the estimated standard deviations of coefficients are highly significant, indicating that parameters do indeed vary in the population. Also, the likelihood ratio index[9] rises substantially from allowing the parameters to vary, indicating that the explanatory power of the mixed logit is considerably greater than with standard logit.[10] The magnitudes of the estimated standard deviations are reasonable relative to the estimated means. For example, the distribution of the savings coefficient has an estimated mean of 3.03 and an estimated standard deviation of 2.24. Given the estimated price coefficient, the model implies that the willingness to pay for \$1.00 of annual savings, on the margin, is normally distributed in the population with mean of \$2.46 and standard deviation of \$1.81—which is a fairly substantial variation in willingness to pay. The standard logit model implies a willingness to pay of \$2.12. If customers consider refrigerators to have a 10-year lifespan, and expect no real growth in energy prices, a willingness to pay of \$2.12 implies a discount rate of 46%, and \$2.46 implies a discount rate of 39%.[11] These implicit discount rates, while high relative to interest rates, are consistent with previous findings on residential customers' choice of refrigerator efficiency levels (e.g., Cole and Fuller (1980), McRae (1980), Meier and Whittier (1983)).

The mixed logit implies that approximately 9% of the population place a negative coefficient on savings. This implication could reflect reality or could be an artifact of the assumption of normally distributed coefficients. It is possible that some customers are highly skeptical of energy-conservation claims and become more mistrustful the greater the claim of savings is. In this case, negative coefficients for savings reflect the mistrust of these customers and are an accurate representation of reality. On the other hand, the assumption of a normal distribution implies that some share of the population has negative coefficients for savings, whether or not this is true. This issue is addressed below with a model that specifies a log-normal distribution for the coefficients of savings and other variables.

The parameters associated with the amount borrowed imply that the mean willingness to pay for being able to borrow an extra dollar is \$0.32 and the standard deviation is \$0.40. Interest rates are denoted in digits (e.g., an interest rate of 9% is denoted as 0.09). The mean willingness to pay for a 1% reduction in interest rate is therefore \$39 with a standard deviation of \$36. For both the interest rate and amount borrowed, the variation in coefficients is fairly substantial, implying that different people respond quite differently to loan terms.

An efficiency dummy enters the utility of high-efficiency refrigerators, whether or not an incentive is offered on the

[9] The likelihood ratio index is a measure of goodness-of-fit, defined as 1-[SLL(θ_e)/SLL(0)], where SLL(θ_e) is the value of the simulated log-likelihood function at the estimated parameters, and SLL(0) is the value with all parameters equal to zero. The index ranges from zero (for a model that is no better than chance, such that SLL(θ_e) = SLL(0)) to 1 (for a "perfect" model that provides a simulated probability of one to the chosen sequence of choices of each sampled decision-maker, such that SLL(θ_e) = 0).

[10] Atherton and Train (1995) estimated a nested logit model on these data, with the high-efficiency options nested together. As such, their model is analogous to a mixed logit with fixed coefficients for all variables except the efficiency dummy, whose coefficient varies randomly over customers and, importantly, over time for each customer. (The random coefficient for the efficiency dummy induces correlation in the stochastic portion of utility over the high-efficiency options (namely, refrigerators with rebates, loans, or no incentive), without inducing correlation with the utility of a standard refrigerator—as in the nested logit. The nested-logit model treats the stochastic portion of utility as independent over repeated choices, which requires assuming that each customer's coefficient for the efficiency dummy is independent over choice situations.) The mixed logit in table 2 obtains a considerably higher log-likelihood than the nested logit of Atherton and Train. This is expected of course, since, in the mixed logit, the standard deviations in the coefficients of variables other than the efficiency dummy are highly significant. One could construct nested-logit models that have richer correlation patterns than in Atherton and Train. Brownstone and Train (1996) compare probit with mixed logit using data on households' choice of cars.

[11] The discount rate is calculated by solving for d in WTP = $[1/(1+d)] + [1/(1+d)^2] + \ldots + [1/(1+d)^{10}]$ where WTP is the willingness to pay for \$1 of extra savings annually, and the lifespan of the refrigerator is assumed to be ten years.

unit. Its mean coefficient indicates that, on average, customers choose the high-efficiency unit in the choice experiments more readily than can be explained by the price, savings, and other financial matters. The standard deviation indicates that 88% of the population have a "high-efficiency preference." This "preference" is largely an artifact of the experiments, with customers perhaps feeling that the interviewer wants them to say they would purchase the high-efficiency unit, or would think well of them if they did. When the model is calibrated against revealed-choice data below, the mean drops considerably. However, it is still significantly different from zero, indicating that there is some preference for high-efficiency units, independent of price and savings, even in customers' actual choices. This preference might indicate that customers think that high-efficiency is correlated with higher quality, greater durability, less noise, or other desirable attributes.

Rebates can be viewed by customers in a variety of ways independent of the reduction in price that they provide. Customers seem to be skeptical of information from their energy utility, including information about the supposed savings that high-efficiency appliances provide (Constantzo et al. (1986); Bruner and Vivian (1979); Craig and McCann (1978)). For some customers, the offer of a rebate lends credibility to the savings claim: these customers interpret the rebate as evidence that the utility is willing to "put its money where its mouth is" (Train, 1988). For these customers, the rebate dummy has a positive coefficient. Other customers might see the rebate as the opposite kind of signal, namely, as a sign that the appliances are too poor to sell on their own merit. These customers have a negative coefficient for the rebate dummy. Table 2 indicates that the mean coefficient for the rebate dummy is slightly positive but not significantly different from zero, while the standard deviation is fairly large and highly significant. These results indicate that customers hold a wide variety of views about rebates, with about as many seeing the rebates as a negative signal as those who see it as a positive signal. Note that the standard logit model masks this reality: its slightly positive coefficient for the rebate dummy would be interpreted as indicating that customers, in general, view rebates as a slightly positive signal, while in reality, many customers view rebates as a negative signal (and many view it as a strong positive signal). It is simply that the customers who take the rebate as a negative signal nearly balance the customers who take it as a positive signal, such that the mean effect is only slightly positive.

The coefficient of the financing dummy obtains an insignificant mean and standard deviation: the hypothesis that customers examine loans only on the basis of their financial terms cannot be rejected. The difference in how customers respond to loans versus rebates is plausible. Rebates are a "giveaway"; customers naturally wonder about the motivation for the giveaway and tend to read a signal into it even if there is none. Loans are not a giveaway; the customer realizes that the lender makes money from the

TABLE 3.—MIXED LOGIT WITH DEMOGRAPHIC VARIABLES

		Parameter Estimates
Price net of rebate for respondents with	Some college, income <$25,000	−1.17
		(0.184)
	Some college, income $25,000–$50,000	−1.49
		(0.196)
	Some college, income >$50,000	−1.54
		(0.100)
	No college, income <$25,000	−0.399
		(0.181)
	No college, income $25,000–$50,000	−0.530
		(0.159)
	No college, income >$50,000	−2.40
		(0.326)
Savings	Mean coefficient	3.35
		(0.376)
	Standard deviation of coefficient	2.79
		(0.321)
Amount borrowed	Mean coefficient	0.348
		(0.108)
	Standard deviation of coefficient	0.504
		(0.074)
Interest rate	Mean coefficient	−47.8
		(13.4)
	Standard deviation of coefficient	52.6
		(8.65)
Efficiency dummy	Mean coefficient	3.99
		(0.446)
	Standard deviation of coefficient	3.41
		(0.449)
Rebate dummy	Mean coefficient	−0.146
		(0.188)
	Standard deviation of coefficient	0.775
		(0.217)
Finance dummy	Mean coefficient	0.275
		(0.771)
	Standard deviation of coefficient	0.222
		(0.607)
Number of respondents		375
Likelihood ratio index		0.471

Notes: See table 2 for definitions of variables. Standard errors in parentheses.

loans. The customer need not read a signal into the offer of loans, since the motivation for the offer is clear. Several variations on this basic model were estimated to explore particular issues. These models are described below.

The estimates in table 2 indicate that parameters vary greatly in the population. However, the specification does not include observed characteristics of the customer. Variations in parameters that are related to observed characteristics can be captured in standard logit models through interaction of customer characteristics with attributes of the alternatives. The question arises, therefore: to what extent can the variation in parameters that is evidenced in table 2 be captured through the inclusion of customer characteristics? Table 3 presents a model that includes the income and the education level of the customer interacted with the price of the refrigerator. This specification follows Atherton and Train (1995) and was obtained after extensive testing with the demographic variables that were available from the survey. In this model, willingness to pay for each attribute varies with income and education, since the price variable is interacted with these factors. The standard deviations are still large and significant, which indicates that the willingness to pay varies more than is captured by the income and education of customers. There are probably other potentially observable characteristics that relate to willingness to pay; the fact that only education and income enter this model reflects the limited nature of the sociodemographic information that was available from the survey.

The model in table 2 specifies the coefficients to be independently distributed while, in reality, one would generally expect correlation. For example, customers who are especially concerned about savings in their monthly energy bill might also be concerned about interest rates, particularly since the loan payments will appear on their monthly energy bill. To investigate these possibilities, we specify $\beta_n \sim N(b,\Omega)$ for general Ω. The coefficient vector is expressed $\beta_n = b + L\mu_n$ where L is a lower-triangular Choleski factor of Ω, such that $LL' = \Omega$. We estimate b and L, and calculate standard errors for elements of Ω with the derivative rule.[12] The ratios of estimated means are very similar to those in table 2, with similar levels of significance; their magnitudes are somewhat higher, reflecting the fact that allowing for covariances captures more variance in the unobserved portion of utility, such that ϵ has less variance and the normalization raises the parameters. The estimates of b and L are not reported, since the estimates of b have the same interpretation as for table 2, and the estimates of L have no meaning in themselves. Table 4 gives the estimated covariance matrix, t-statistics for the estimated covariance matrix, and point estimates for the correlation matrix. Five covariances have t-statistics over 1.6.

(i) The savings coefficient is negatively correlated with the coefficient of the efficiency dummy. This estimate implies that customers who value savings highly tend not to be motivated by the label of high-efficiency independent of savings.

(ii) The savings coefficient is negatively correlated with the rebate dummy coefficient, implying that customers who value savings highly tend not to be motivated by rebates beyond the reduction in price that the rebates provide.

(iii and iv) The efficiency dummy coefficient is positively correlated with the coefficient of amount borrowed and negatively with the finance dummy coefficient. Customers who like high-efficiency per se (independent of savings) like being able to borrow and are not motivated by the offer of a loan independent of its terms.

(v) The coefficients of the rebate and finance dummies are positively correlated: customers who are motivated by rebates beyond the reduction in price that the rebates provide are also motivated by the offer of a loan beyond the terms of the loan.

[12] The general result is: for $\psi = f(\rho)$, $\mathrm{Var}(\psi) = (\partial\psi/\partial\rho)' \,\mathrm{Var}(\rho)\, (\partial\psi/\partial\rho)$ where ψ and ρ are vectors. In our case, ρ is the vector composed of the elements of L, ψ is the vector composed of the elements of Ω, and f is LL′ expressed in vector form.

TABLE 4.—COVARIANCES AMONG COEFFICIENTS IN MIXED LOGIT

COEFFICIENTS OF: 1. SAVINGS
2. AMOUNT BORROWED
3. INTEREST RATE
4. EFFICIENCY DUMMY
5. REBATE DUMMY
6. FINANCE DUMMY

Estimated Covariance Matrix:					
12.12	−0.890	−115.4	−5.300	−1.205	5.259
		−10.46	1.371	−0.004	−1.259
		6,032.00	113.2	19.16	−88.12
			17.92	0.3740	−12.20
				3.074	4.375
					18.11
T-Statistics for Estimated Covariances:					
4.09	1.36	1.59	2.57	1.96	1.39
	3.22	0.50	2.96	0.02	1.45
		2.88	1.33	0.75	0.77
			3.97	0.26	1.94
				3.41	1.90
					1.52
Correlation Matrix:					
1.0	−0.26	−0.43	−0.35	−0.20	0.35
	1.0	−0.14	0.32	−0.002	−0.30
		1.0	0.34	0.14	−0.27
			1.0	0.05	−0.68
				1.0	0.59
					1.0

The normal distribution allows coefficients of both signs. For some variables, such as savings, it is reasonable to expect that all customers have the same sign for their coefficients. We estimate a model with log-normal distributions for the coefficients of savings, amount borrowed, and interest rates. The coefficients for the efficiency, rebate, and finance dummies are kept as normals, since these coefficients can logically take either sign for a given individual. Let k denote an element of β_n that has a log-normal distribution. This coefficient is expressed $\beta_{nk} = \exp(b_k + s_k\mu_{nk})$ where μ_{nk} is an independent standard normal deviate. The parameters b_k and s_k, which represent the mean and standard deviation of $\log(\beta_{nk})$, are estimated. The median, mean, and standard deviation of β_{nk} are $\exp(b_k)$, $\exp(b_k + (s_k^2/2))$, and mean $* \sqrt{(\exp(s_k^2) - 1)}$, respectively. Savings and amount borrowed enter directly, such that all customers' coefficients are positive, and the negative of interest rates is entered such that all customers' coefficients of interest rate are negative. Table 5 gives the estimation results. The results are similar qualitatively to those obtained with all normal distributions. Each of the three log-normal distributions has median and mean that bracket the mean that is obtained with a normal distribution. For example, from table 5, the estimated median willingness to pay for savings is \$1.81 with an estimated mean of \$3.23, while the

TABLE 5.—MIXED LOGIT WITH LOG-NORMAL DISTRIBUTION FOR COEFFICIENTS OF SAVINGS, AMOUNT BORROWED, AND INTEREST RATE

		Parameter Estimates	Median and Mean for Log-Normally Distributed Coefficients, Calculated at Estimated b and s	
			Median	Mean
Price net of rebate	Coefficient	−1.22 (0.0964)		
Savings	b	0.79 (0.152)	2.20	3.95
	s	1.08 (0.165)		
Amount borrowed	b	−1.17 (0.244)	0.310	0.686
	s	1.26 (0.24)		
Interest rate (neg.)	b	3.78 (0.301)	43.82	73.7
	s	1.02 (0.227)		
Efficiency dummy	Mean coefficient	3.43 (0.337)		
	Standard deviation of coefficient	2.47 (0.285)		
Rebate dummy	Mean coefficient	0.199 (0.188)		
	Standard deviation of coefficient	1.13 (0.214)		
Finance dummy	Mean coefficient	−0.191 (0.533)		
	Standard deviation of coefficient	0.479 (0.586)		
Likelihood ratio index		0.448		
Willingness to pay in extra purchase price, calculated at mean and median coefficients, for	$1 extra savings		1.80	3.24
	$1 extra amount borrowed		0.25	0.56
	1% reduction in interest rate		35.92	60.41

Notes: See table 2 for definitions of variables. Standard errors in parentheses.

mean/median with a normal distribution is $2.46.[13] It is interesting to note that the log-likelihood value is lower for the model with log-normal distributions than the comparable model (see table 2) with all normally distributed coefficients. A possible reason is discussed in footnote fourteen. For calibration and simulation, we utilize both models.

B. *Calibration to Revealed-Preference Data*

Once estimated, the models are calibrated to the limited revealed-preference data that were available. Each surveyed customer was asked whether he/she had purchased a refrigerator during the last three years. Those who responded in the positive were asked to locate the serial number or other identifying information for the unit that they purchased. With this information, we determined, using product specification sheets, the efficiency level of the refrigerator. Program files were then used to determine which of the customers who had purchased a high-efficiency refrigerator had received a rebate. In combination, this information identified whether the customer had chosen standard-efficiency, high-efficiency without a rebate, or high efficiency with a rebate. The information was obtained for 163 of the 401 surveyed customers. Of course, since financing had not been offered by SCE's programs, a high-efficiency unit with utility financing was not available.

Actual choices are expected to differ from stated choices for two primary reasons. First, customers might have a tendency to say that they would purchase a high-efficiency refrigerator more readily than they actually do. This would evidence itself in the coefficient for the high-efficiency dummy being higher with the stated-preference data than is true for actual choices. Second, any time or effort that the customer must expend to receive a rebate, or any lack of awareness about the program, is not reflected in the stated-preference data. In the hypothetical situation, the customer is informed about the rebate and does not have to do anything to receive it. As a result, the estimated coefficient for the rebate dummy is expected to be higher in the stated-preference models than in reality. To account for these issues, the parameters associated with the efficiency and rebate dummies were reestimated on the revealed-preference data, holding the other parameters at the values obtained with the stated-preference data. The results are given in table 6. As expected, the mean and standard deviation of the efficiency dummy coefficient drop considerably—the mean from 3.70 to 0.785, and the standard deviation from 3.20 to 0.213 for the model with all normally distributed coefficients, and comparable amounts for the model with log-normal distributions for some coefficients. The mean of the rebate dummy coefficient decreases, but the standard deviation increases. This result is consistent with rebates being more burdensome to obtain in the real world

TABLE 6.—CALIBRATION TO REVEALED-PREFERENCE DATA

		Parameter Estimates	
		Model with all normals	Model with log-normals and normals
Efficiency dummy	Mean coefficient	0.785 (0.182)	0.713 (3.64)
	Standard deviation of coefficient	0.213 (2.86)	0.397 (0.322)
Rebate dummy	Mean coefficient	−3.70 (7.31)	−3.01 (2.17)
	Standard deviation of coefficient	2.84 (8.30)	2.03 (1.70)
Number of respondents		163	163
Likelihood ratio index		0.122	0.121

Note: Standard errors in parentheses.

[13] Convergence was very slow with the log-normal distributions, taking nearly a hundred iterations. We reparameterized the likelihood function and gradient to operate in the means and standard deviations of the log-normal distributions themselves, but this reparameterization did not materially reduce the number of iterations.

than in the hypothetical experiments, and the value that people place on the time and hassle required to obtain the rebate varying considerably across customers. In simulation, the mean and standard deviation of the financing dummy coefficient are adjusted by the same amount by which the calibration adjusted the rebate dummy's mean and standard deviation. This adjustment reflects the presumption that the hassle associated with obtaining rebates will also occur for obtaining a loan.

Our calibration procedure that adjusts only the distribution of constants is analogous to the procedure used by Atherton and Train (1995), which adjusts the constants and nesting parameter in a nested logit (the nesting parameter in their model is equivalent to the variance of the efficiency dummy in our mixed logit). This correspondence allows us to compare our forecasts with those of Atherton and Train. Other procedures that could be pursued are estimation of the model on the combined stated- and revealed-preference data with mixed or Bayesian procedures that weight the two sources of data, or estimation on the revealed-preference data of a scale parameter that adjusts all the parameters obtained on the stated-preference data (e.g., Swait and Louviere (1993), Hensher and Bradley (1993)).

C. *Predictions*

We use the calibrated models to predict the effect of DSM programs. Consider first the impact of the rebate program. From the mixed logit with all normal coefficients, 15.8% of refrigerator purchasers obtained a rebate, 46.1% purchased a standard-efficiency unit, and 38.1% purchased a high-efficiency unit but did not obtain a rebate. The average rebate is $64. With no DSM program (i.e., without the option of purchasing a high-efficiency unit with a rebate), 54.6% of customers are predicted to purchase a standard unit with the other 45.4% buying a high-efficiency unit without a rebate. These predictions imply that the rebates reduced the standard efficiency share from 54.6% to 46.1%, such that the rebate program is predicted to have induced 8.5% of buyers to switch from a standard- to a high-efficiency refrigerator. The cost per induced switch is therefore $119 ($64 × 0.158/0.085). Predictions from the model with log-normal distributions are essentially identical.

Consider now the impact of loan programs. Table 7 presents predictions under various interest rates for loans offered on the full price of high-efficiency units. Zero interest loans are predicted to attract about 40% of refrigerator purchasers, which is far greater participation than the rebate program. Compared to no program, such loans would induce 22.6% of buyers to switch from standard to high efficiency, which is nearly three times greater than the rebate program's impact. The average loan in this scenario is $1,031, such that cost to the utility is $64 at a 6% cost of funds and a two-year repayment period—the same as the average rebate. The cost per induced switch is $112, which is

TABLE 7.—PREDICTED CHOICES OF REFRIGERATOR BUYERS WHEN LOANS ARE OFFERED ON HIGH EFFICIENCY UNITS

	Mixed Logit with All Normal Distributions			Mixed Logit with Log-Normal and Normal Distributions		
Interest Rate	Standard Efficiency	High Efficiency Without Loan	High Efficiency With Loan	Standard Efficiency	High Efficiency Without Loan	High Efficiency With Loan
0%	0.320	0.283	0.397	0.317	0.280	0.403
2%	0.354	0.314	0.332	0.361	0.319	0.320
4%	0.381	0.336	0.283	0.387	0.342	0.272
6%	0.402	0.351	0.246	0.405	0.357	0.238
8%	0.418	0.362	0.220	0.419	0.370	0.212
10%	0.430	0.370	0.201	0.430	0.379	0.191
12%	0.438	0.375	0.186	0.439	0.387	0.174

slightly lower than the rebate program. The total outlay by the utility is higher with the loans than with the rebates, since participation is greater.

The utility earns a profit on loans when the interest rate is above its cost of funds. At 8% interest, 19% to 22% of refrigerator purchasers are predicted to obtain the loans, depending on which model is used in prediction. At 12% interest, the predicted share is 14% to 17%. In all scenarios, more than half of the customers who obtain loans would have purchased a standard unit without the loans. So, a loan program that finances the entire price of the high-efficiency unit at a rate that allows the utility to make a profit is predicted to induce 8.4% to 13% of customers to switch from a standard- to a high-efficiency unit. The loans have a larger impact than the rebates and also generate profit for the firm: a "win-win" situation.[14]

[14] The loans could also induce customers to buy larger refrigerators than they otherwise would. This effect would reduce the energy savings but increase consumer surplus.

An interesting phenomenon arises when predicting the effect of loans that cover the incremental price of the high-efficiency unit (i.e., the price of the high-efficiency unit minus the standard unit's price) rather than the full price. For interest rates above 4%, the mixed logit with normally distributed coefficients predicts the share of customers who obtain a loan to rise as the interest rate rises. Recall that this model implies that 14% of the population have positive coefficients for interest rates. When the amount borrowed is only the incremental price and the interest rate is above 4%, the share of customers obtaining loans is so small that the tail of the distribution dominates. The customers who supposedly like to pay interest are primarily the ones predicted to obtain loans, and for these customers a rise in the interest rates makes the loans more attractive. This phenomenon does not occur when the amount borrowed is sufficiently high to make the loans attractive to a large share of the population. In short, when predicted shares are small, the tails of the distribution drive the results, and so the plausibility of the tails is important; when predicted shares are large, the tails are less determinative, and the distribution can be treated as a reasonable approximation.

With the log-normal distribution, the share obtaining loans necessarily decreases as the interest rate rises. It is important to note that the basic issue does not disappear with a log-normal distribution, it is just made less obvious. The basic issue is that an unrestricted distribution necessarily gives implausible results for some share of the population. With the normal distribution, the implausibility of, for example, positive interest rate coefficients, is obvious. However, the normal distribution also provides implausibly large coefficients of the correct sign, which might not be so obvious (or, more precisely, the cutoff for what is plausible cannot be so easily discerned.) The log-normal avoids the obvious problem with the

Atherton and Train (1995) performed the same kind of predictions with their nested logit model. They obtain practically the same shares for the base situation of the rebate program. This is expected, since both models were calibrated to this base situation on the same revealed-preference data. In predicting beyond the base situation, Atherton and Train (A-T) predict essentially the same shares as we do for the situation without a DSM program; however, their model predicts about half as many participants as our model for the loan programs. The reasons for these results are directly traceable to the specification of the models. The change in shares from the base situation to the no-DSM situation is determined primarily by the correlation between the stochastic portion of utility for a rebated high-efficiency unit and that of a nonrebated high-efficiency unit. (If the correlation is zero, then the shares for standard and nonrebated high-efficiency units increase nearly proportionately when the rebated high-efficiency unit is eliminated as an option, as required in a logit model with the independence from irrelevant alternatives property.) Both the nested logit model of A-T and our mixed logit include a correlation between the utilities of these alternatives; the two models obtain similar forecasts as a result. The predicted share for a loan program depends largely on the coefficients of the loan-related variables (amount borrowed, interest rate, and finance dummy), since these coefficients determine how attractive the loans are to people. A-T have fixed coefficients for these variables, which can be considered to reflect the tastes of the average person. The mixed logit reflects the distribution of tastes and obtains large standard deviations for the loan-related coefficients, indicating a wide divergence of tastes. Stated loosely, the results from the two models indicate that while the loans do not appeal greatly to the average tastes, a sizable share of the population have tastes such that the loans are attractive.

These predictions should not be overinterpreted. An important limitation is the implicit assumption that only the utility offers loans on appliance purchases, whereas in reality retailers offer credit and customers can use their credit cards. These loans are available for standard-efficiency units as well as high-efficiency units. To induce buyers to switch from standard- to high-efficiency units when loans are available on both, better loan terms must be offered on the high-efficiency units. The interest rates on credit cards and retailers' loans are fairly high, certainly above the utilities' cost of funds. However, whether the difference represents a premium for nonpayment and management, which the utility must also bear, is a critical issue. In this context, the analysis can perhaps best be taken simply as a indication that loans might be an avenue to generate profits and greater energy efficiency, and that attention to this potential by utilities and regulators is warranted.

normal but retains and actually exacerbates the less obvious problem (since its upper tail is thicker.) This difference at the high end might be the reason the model with all normal distributions obtains a higher log-likelihood value than the model with log-normals. A distribution with an bounded support, such as the beta distribution, might be worth exploring.

REFERENCES

Atherton, T., and K. Train, "Rebates, Loans, and Customers' Choice of Appliance Efficiency Level: Combining Stated- and Revealed-Preference Data," *Energy Journal*, Vol. 16, No. 1 (1995), 55–69.

Ben-Akiva, M., and D. Bolduc, "Multinomial Probit with a Logit Kernel and a General Parametric Specification of the Covariance Structure," working paper, Department of Civil Engineering, MIT (1996).

Ben-Akiva, D. Bolduc, and M. Bradley, "Estimation of Travel Choice Models with Randomly Distributed Values of Time," *Transportation Research Record* 1413 (1993), 88–97.

Ben-Akiva, M., and S. Lerman, *Discrete Choice Analysis*, Cambridge, MA: MIT Press (1985).

Berkovec, J., and S. Stern, "Job Exit Behavior of Older Men," *Econometrica*, Vol. 59, No. 1 (1991), p 189–210.

Bhat, C., "Accommodating Variations in Responsiveness to Level-of-Service Measures in Travel Model Choice Modeling," working paper, Department of Civil Engineering, University of Massachusetts at Amherst (1996).

Bolduc, D., B. Fortin, and M.-A. Fournier, "The Impact of Incentive Policies on the Practical Location of Doctors: A Multinomial Probit Analysis," Cahier de recherche numero 93-05 du Groupe de Recherche en Politique Economique (1993), Department d'economique, University Laval, Quebec, Canada, G1K 7P4.

Boyd, J., and R. Mellman, "The Effect of Fuel Economy Standards on the U.S. Automotive Market: An Hedonic Demand Analysis," *Transportation Research*, Vol. 14A, No. 5–6 (1980), 367–378.

Brownstone, D., and K. Train, "Forecasting New Product Penetration with Flexible Substitution Patterns," *Journal of Econometrics* (forthcoming).

Bruner, R., and W. Vivian, *Citizen Viewpoints on Energy Policy*, Ann Arbor: University of Michigan, Institute of Public Studies (1979).

Cardell, N., and F. Dunbar, "Measuring the Societal Impacts of Automobile Downsizing," *Transportation Research*, Vol. 14A, No. 5–6 (1980), 423–434.

Cole, H., and R. Fuller, "Residential Energy Decision Making: An Overview with Emphasis on Individual Discount Rates and Responsiveness to Household Income and Prices," Hittman Associates report, Columbia, MD (1980).

Constantzo, M., D. Archer, E. Aronson, and T. Pettigrew, "Energy Conservation Behavior: The Difficult Path from Information to Action," *American Psychologist* 41 (1986), 521–528.

Craig, C., and J. McCann, "Assessing Communication Effects on Energy Conservation," *Journal of Consumer Research* 5 (1978), 82–88.

Hajivassiliou, V., and D. McFadden, "The Method of Simulated Scores for the Estimation of LDV Models," *Econometrica* (forthcoming).

Hajivassiliou, V., and P. Ruud, "Classical Estimation Methods for LDV Models Using Simulation," *Handbook of Econometrics*, Vol. IV, R. Engle and D. McFadden (Eds.), Elsevier Science B.V., New York (1994).

Hensher, D., and M. Bradley, "Using Stated Response Data to Enrich Revealed Preference Discrete Choice Model," *Marketing Letters*, Vol. 4, No. 2 (1993), 39–152.

Lee, L., "On Efficiency of Methods of Simulated Moments and Maximum Simulated Likelihood Estimation of Discrete Response Models," *Econometric Theory* 8 (1992), 518–552.

McFadden, D., "On Independence, Structure, and Simultaneity in Transportation Demand Analysis," working paper no. 7511, Urban Travel Demand Forecasting Project, Institute of Transportation and Traffic Engineering, University of California, Berkeley (1975).

——— "A Method of Simulated Moments for Estimation of Discrete Choice Models without Numerical Integration," *Econometrica* 57 (1989) 995–1026.

McFadden, D., and K. Train, "Mixed Multinomial Logit Models for Discrete Response," working paper, Department of Economics, University of California, Berkeley (1997).

McRae, D., "Rational Models for Consumer Energy Conservation," in Burby and Marsden (Eds.), *Energy and Housing*, Oelgeschleger: Gunn and Hain Publishers (1980).

Meier, A., and J. Whittier, "Consumer Discount Rates Implied by Purchases of Energy-Efficient Refrigerators," *Energy*, Vol. 8, No. 12 (1983), 957–962.

Ruud, P., "Approximation and Simulation of the Multinomial Probit Model: An Analysis of Covariance Matrix Estimation," working paper, Department of Economics, University of California, Berkeley (1996).

Southern California Edison, *Customer Decision Study: Analysis of Residential Customer Equipment Purchase Decisions*, report prepared by Cambridge Systematics (1994).

Swait, K., and J. Louviere, "The Role of the Scale Parameter in the Estimation and Use of Multinomial Logit Models," *Journal of Marketing Research* 30 (1993), 305–314.

Train, K., "Incentives for Energy Conservation in the Commercial and Industrial Sectors," *Energy Journal*, Vol. 9, No. 3 (1988), 113–128.

——— "Recreation Demand Models with Taste Differences Over People," *Land Economics*, Vol. 74, No. 2 (1998), 230–239.

——— forthcoming, "Mixed Logit Models for Recreation Demand," in C. Kling and J. Herriges (Eds.), *Valuing the Environment Using Recreation Demand Models*, Elgar Press.

Train, K., D., McFadden, and A. Goett, "Consumer Attitudes and Voluntary Rate Schedules for Public Utilities," *Review of Economics and Statistics*, Vol. LXIX, No. 3 (1987) 383–391.

[28]

JOURNAL OF APPLIED ECONOMETRICS
J. Appl. Econ. **15**: 447–470 (2000)

MIXED MNL MODELS FOR DISCRETE RESPONSE

DANIEL McFADDEN* AND KENNETH TRAIN
Department of Economics, University of California, Berkeley, CA, 94720-3880, USA

SUMMARY

This paper considers mixed, or random coefficients, multinomial logit (MMNL) models for discrete response, and establishes the following results. Under mild regularity conditions, any discrete choice model derived from random utility maximization has choice probabilities that can be approximated as closely as one pleases by a MMNL model. Practical estimation of a parametric mixing family can be carried out by Maximum Simulated Likelihood Estimation or Method of Simulated Moments, and easily computed instruments are provided that make the latter procedure fairly efficient. The adequacy of a mixing specification can be tested simply as an omitted variable test with appropriately defined artificial variables. An application to a problem of demand for alternative vehicles shows that MMNL provides a flexible and computationally practical approach to discrete response analysis. Copyright © 2000 John Wiley & Sons, Ltd.

1. INTRODUCTION

Define a *mixed multinomial logit (MMNL)* model as a MNL model with *random coefficients* α drawn from a cumulative distribution function $G(\alpha;\theta)$:

$$P_C(i \mid \boldsymbol{x}, \theta) = \int L_C(i; \boldsymbol{x}, \alpha) \cdot G(\mathrm{d}\alpha; \theta) \text{ with } L_C(i; \boldsymbol{x}, \alpha) = e^{x_i \alpha} / \sum_{j \in C} e^{x_j \alpha} \tag{1}$$

In this setup, $\mathbf{C} = \{1, \ldots, J\}$ is the choice set; the x_i are $1 \times K$ vectors of functions of observed attributes of alternative i and observed characteristics of the decision maker, with $\boldsymbol{x} = (x_1, \ldots, x_J)$; α is a $K \times 1$ vector of random parameters; $L_C(i; \boldsymbol{x}, \alpha)$ is a MNL model for the choice set $\mathbf{C}$; and θ is a vector of deep parameters of the mixing distribution G. The random parameters α may be interpreted as arising from taste heterogeneity in a population of MNL decision makers. If the x_i contain alternative-specific variables, then the corresponding components of α can be treated as alternative-specific random effects. Alternately, the model may simply be interpreted as a flexible approximation to choice probabilities generated by a random utility model. The mixing distribution G may come from a continuous parametric family, such as multivariate normal or log normal, or it may have a finite support. When G has finite support, MMNL models are also called *latent class* models. Equation (1) describes a single decision, but extension to dynamic choice models with multiple decisions is straightforward, by mixing over the parameters of a product of MNL models for each component decision.

* Correspondence to: Daniel McFadden, Department of Economics, University of California, Berkeley, CA 94720-3880, USA; e-mail: mcfadden@econ.berkeley.edu

Contract/grant sponsor: E. Morris Cox Fund.

Received 30 November 1998
Revised 15 May 2000

The MMNL model was introduced by Boyd and Mellman (1980) and Cardell and Dunbar (1980), although an earlier literature had considered the mathematically similar problem of aggregating the MNL model over a distribution of explanatory variables; see Talvitie (1972), Westin (1974), McFadden and Reid (1975), and Westin and Gillen (1978). There is a lengthy literature investigating various aspects of the MMNL model; see Beggs (1988), Börsch-Supan (1990), Brownstone and Train (1999), Chavas and Segerson (1986), Dubin and Zeng (1991), Enberg, Gottschalk, and Wolf (1990), Follman and Lambert (1989), Formann (1992), Gonul and Srinivasan (1993), Jain, Vilcassim, and Chintagunta (1994), Montgomery, Richards, and Braun (1986), Reader (1993), Revelt and Train (1998), Steckel and Vanhonacker (1988), Train, McFadden, and Goett (1987), and Train (1998, 1999). Chesher and Santos-Silva (1995) have developed specification tests for MMNL that are relatives of ones proposed here. This paper establishes the following results:

- Under mild regularity conditions, MMNL models are random utility maximization (RUM) models, and any discrete choice model derived from a RUM model has choice probabilities that can be approximated as closely as one pleases by a MMNL model (Section 2).
- Numerical integration or approximation by simulation is usually required to evaluate MMNL probabilities. *Maximum Simulated Likelihood* (MSLE) or *Method of Simulated Moments* (MSM) can be used to estimate the MMNL model (Section 3).
- The adequacy of a mixing specification can be tested simply as an omitted variable test with appropriately defined artificial variables (Section 4).
- An application to a problem of demand for alternative vehicles shows that MMNL provides a flexible and computationally practical approach to discrete response analysis (Section 5).

2. A GENERAL APPROXIMATION PROPERTY OF MMNL

Economic theory often suggests that discrete responses are the result of optimization of payoffs to decision makers: utility for consumers, profit for firms. The following discussion will be phrased in terms of utility-maximizing consumers. When unobserved heterogeneity in the population of consumers is accounted for, this will lead to a class of response models based on *random utility maximization* (RUM). A resource allocation to a consumer will specify quantities of goods and leisure, and for our particular interest the attributes of a discrete alternative, such as an automobile model. We will consider two sources of unobserved heterogeneity: features of alternatives that are not recorded by the analyst, and unmeasured consumer characteristics that determine preferences.

Let $q = (g, l, z, \zeta)$ denote a consumer's resource allocation, where z is a vector of observed attributes and ζ is a vector of unobserved attributes of a discrete alternative, g is a vector of quantities of other goods, and l is leisure. Assume that the domain of q is a compact rectangle in a finite-dimensional Euclidean space. Consumers have a vector of observed characteristics s and a vector of unobserved characteristics ς; with (s,ς) determining preferences over resource allocations. Assume that the domain of (s,ς) is a compact subset of a finite-dimensional Euclidean space. This is not a substantive restriction for discrete choice analysis when the number of choice alternatives is bounded. Assume that consumer preferences over resource allocations, $\succeq_{s,\varsigma}$, are complete and transitive, with the continuity property that if a sequence of allocations and consumer characteristics converges, $(q^{1\prime}, q^{2\prime}, s', \varsigma') \to (q^1, q^2, s, \varsigma)$, and satisfies $q^{1\prime} \succeq_{s',\varsigma'} q^{2\prime}$, then $q^1 \succeq_{s,\varsigma} q^2$. For fixed (s,ς), this is the standard continuity condition on preferences. Our condition extends this to require that consumers with similar characteristics will also have similar preferences. Together, these assumptions imply that preferences can be represented by a utility function $U(g, l, z, \zeta, s, \varsigma)$ that is continuous in its arguments; see Appendix Lemma 1.

We next consider the stochastic properties of unobserved elements in this formulation of the consumer's problem. Let $(\Omega, \mathcal{W}, \pi)$ denote a fundamental probability space, where $\mathcal{W}$ is the σ-field of measurable subsets and π is a probability measure. Let $\mathbf{T}$ denote a subset of $\mathbb{R}^m$, and $X : \Omega \times \mathbf{T} \rightarrow \mathbb{R}^n$ denote a *continuous random field*; i.e., for each $t \in \mathbf{T}$, $X(\cdot, t)$ is a random vector, measurable with respect to $\mathcal{W}$, and for a set of ω occurring with probability one, $X(\omega, \cdot)$ is a continuous function on $\mathbf{T}$. We will often suppress the dependence of the random field on ω, and write it as $X(t)$. A continuous random field has $\lim_{t' \rightarrow t} X(t') = X(t)$ with probability one, implying that $X(t')$ converges in distribution to $X(t)$ as $t' \rightarrow t$. The CDF of $X(t)$ is $F(x, t) = \pi(\{\omega \in \Omega \mid X(\omega, t) \leqslant x\})$. We say that X has a *regular canonical representation* if there exists a continuous function $h : [0, 1]^n \times \mathbf{T} \rightarrow \mathbb{R}^n$ and a uniformly distributed continuous random field $\varepsilon : \Omega \times \mathbf{T} \rightarrow [0, 1]^n$ such that $X(t) = h(\varepsilon(t), t)$ with probability one.[1] We show in the Appendix that a continuous random field whose CDF admits a positive continuous density has a regular canonical representation. For example, if $X(t)$ is a mean-zero Gaussian continuous random field with a definite covariance matrix $\Omega(t)$, and Φ denotes the standard normal CDF, then $\Omega(t)$ has a continuous Cholesky factor $\Lambda(t)$ and the mapping $\varepsilon(t) = \Phi(\Lambda(t)^{-1} X(t))$ is a uniformly distributed continuous random field that inverts to the regular canonical representation $X(t) = \Lambda(t)\Phi^{-1}(\varepsilon(t))$.

A primitive postulate of preference theory is that tastes are established prior to assignment of resource allocations. Then, the distribution of ς cannot depend on q, although in general it will depend on s. We assume that $\varsigma = \varsigma(s)$ is a continuous random field with a regular canonical representation, and write it as $\varsigma(s) = h_0(\upsilon(s), s)$, where $\upsilon(s)$ is a uniformly distributed continuous random field. Then consumers with similar observed characteristics will have similar distributions of unobserved characteristics. Another primitive postulate of consumer theory is that the description of a resource allocation does not depend on consumer characteristics. Thus, consumers' tastes and perceptions do not enter the 'objective' description of a resource allocation, although they will obviously enter the consumer's evaluation of the allocation. This postulate implies that the distribution of ξ cannot depend on (s, ν), although it may depend on z. We will assume that ζ is specified as a continuous random field with a regular canonical representation, and write it as $\zeta(z) = h(\varepsilon(z), z)$, where $\varepsilon(s)$ is a uniformly distributed continuous random field. Then discrete alternatives that are similar in their observed attributes will have similar distributions of unobserved attributes. Substituting the transformations h_0 and h into the definition of U, we can consider a *canonical random utility model* $U(g, l, z, s, \varepsilon(z), \upsilon(s))$ that is continuous in its arguments, with $\varepsilon(z)$ and $\upsilon(s)$ independently uniformly distributed continuous random fields.

Economic consumers make choices subject to dollar and time budgets. For discrete choice, if assigned a discrete alternative z, the consumer will choose goods g and leisure l to maximize utility subject to these budgets. If the alternative requires time $t = \tau(z)$, the consumer's 24-hour/day time budget is $24 = l^* + e + t$, where e is hours worked and l^* is hours of pure leisure. If only a portion λ of the time t devoted to the alternative is equivalent to work, then $l = l^* + (1 - \lambda)t$ is the effective leisure entering the utility function. Suppose the consumer faces a dollar budget

$$a + w \cdot e = p \cdot g + c \tag{2}$$

[1] A random field ε is *uniformly distributed* if $\varepsilon(t)$ has a uniform distribution on $[0,1]^n$ for each $t \in \mathbf{T}$; see Appendix Lemma 3.

where a is non-wage income, c is the cost of the discrete alternative, w is the wage, and p is the vector of goods prices. For the assigned alternative, maximum utility then satisfies

$$U'(a-c, p, w, t\lambda, z, s, \varepsilon(z), \upsilon(s)) = \max_{e,g} U(g, 24-e-t\lambda, z, s, \varepsilon(z), \upsilon(s))$$
$$\text{subject to } a + w{\cdot}e = p{\cdot}g + c$$

This is a *conditional indirect utility function*, given the discrete alternative.[2] With a monotone transformation, we can assume that the range of utility is contained in the unit interval. For economic applications, it will be important to distinguish the market variables a, p, and w, which can be altered by economic policy, from the observed consumer characteristics included in s. Similarly, the market cost c of the discrete alternative which can be altered by policy is distinguished from z, while t is a component of z. An important implication of these distinctions is that for each realization of $\varepsilon(z)$ and $\upsilon(s)$, the conditional indirect utility function is characterized by the standard economic properties that it is increasing in $a-c$, non-increasing in (p,w), and homogeneous of degree zero and quasi-convex in $(a-c, p, w)$. It will be convenient as a shorthand in the following analysis to redefine z and s to absorb the market variables, and write the conditional indirect utility function as $U(z, s, \varepsilon(z), \upsilon(s))$, keeping in mind that $\varepsilon(z)$ and $\upsilon(s)$ will not depend on the market variable components of z and s. Let $\mathbf{Z}$ and $\mathbf{S}$ denote the domains of z and s, respectively, and note that they are assumed to be compact subsets of finite-dimensional spaces.

Consider choice over finite sets of discrete alternatives $\mathbf{C} = \{z_1, \ldots, z_J\}$, distinguished by the consumer (and the observer) in terms of their observed attributes z_j which may include 'brand names' or other alternative-specific identifiers that influence the consumer's evaluation. We will interpret $\mathbf{C}$ as an ordered sequence, and denote the family of possible J-element choice sets by $\mathcal{C}_J \subset \mathbf{Z}^J$. By construction, all the elements of $\mathbf{C} \in \mathcal{C}_J$ must be distinct. We assume that $\mathcal{C}_J$ is compact; this excludes cases where alternatives are observationally indistinguishable in the limit. We assume that there is an upper bound $\mathbf{J}^*$ on the number of elements in a choice set. Then $\mathcal{C}^* = \mathcal{C}_2 \cup \cdots \cup \mathcal{C}_{J^*}$ is the universe of possible choice sets. We assume that proper subsets of possible choice sets are also possible; in particular, if $\mathbf{C} \in \mathcal{C}_J$ contains elements z' and z'', then $\{z', z''\} \in \mathcal{C}_2$. For brevity, $\mathbf{C} = \{z_1, \ldots, z_J\}$ will sometimes be written as $\mathbf{C} = \{1, \ldots, J\}$.

In a well-specified RUM model, there will be zero probability of ties in a choice set $\mathbf{C} = \{z_1, \ldots, z_J\}$, so that a realization $\upsilon = \upsilon(s)$ and $\varepsilon_j = \varepsilon(z_j)$ for $j = 1, \ldots, J$ of the random elements in the model almost surely determines a unique choice. When U is continuously differentiable, a sufficient condition for this is that the Jacobian

$$\begin{bmatrix} \partial U(z_1, s, \varepsilon_1, \upsilon)/\partial \upsilon & \partial U(z_1, s, \varepsilon_1, \upsilon)/\partial \varepsilon_1 & \cdots & 0 \\ \cdots & \cdots & \cdots & \cdots \\ \partial U(z_J, s, \varepsilon_J, \upsilon)/\partial \upsilon & 0 & \cdots & \partial U(z_J, s, \varepsilon_J, \upsilon)/\partial \varepsilon_J \end{bmatrix}$$

have rank at least $J-1$, and that the support of $(\upsilon, \varepsilon_1, \ldots, \varepsilon_J)$ contain the space spanned by the Jacobian. Ways to guarantee no ties include taste factors (determined by υ) of the required dimension that interact with a full-rank array of alternative attributes, or a full set of alternative-specific effects (determined by the ε_j), or some combination. The following result establishes that

[2] The conditional indirect utility function (3) is modified in obvious ways if the consumer cannot choose work hours e, the time requirement t for the discrete alternative is absent, or time required for consumption of other goods enters the time budget.

MNL mixtures can closely approximate a very broad class of RUM models that have zero probability of ties:

Theorem 1. Let $z \in \mathbf{Z}$, with $\mathbf{Z}$ compact, denote the vector of observed attributes of a discrete alternative, and $s \in \mathbf{S}$, with $\mathbf{S}$ compact, denote the vector of observed characteristics of the consumer. Suppose discrete choices are made from choice sets $\mathbf{C} = \{z_1, \ldots, z_J\}$, with at most J^* alternatives, contained in a compact universe C^* in which all alternatives are distinct. Let $\mathbf{z} = (z_1, \ldots, z_J)$, and as a shorthand let $\mathbf{C} = \{1, \ldots, J\}$. Suppose discrete responses maximize a canonical conditional indirect utility function $U^*(z_j, s, \varepsilon_j, \upsilon)$ that is a bounded continuous function of its arguments, where $\varepsilon_j = \varepsilon(z_j)$ and $\upsilon = \upsilon(s)$ are uniformly distributed continuous random fields. Assume there is zero probability of ties. Let $P^*_{\mathbf{C}}(i \mid \mathbf{z}, s)$ denote the choice probabilities generated by maximization of U^* over $\mathbf{C}$. If η is a small positive scalar, then there exists a continuous function $x = x(z, s)$ of dimension $1 \times k$ for some integer k, with $\mathbf{x} = (x(z_1, s), \ldots, x(z_J, s))$, and a random utility model with choice probabilities $P_{\mathbf{C}}(i \mid \mathbf{x}, \theta)$ of the MMNL form (1), such that $P^*_{\mathbf{C}}(i \mid \mathbf{z}, s)$ and $P_{\mathbf{C}}(i \mid \mathbf{x}, \theta)$ differ by at most η for all $s \in \mathbf{S}$ and $\mathbf{z} \in C^*$.

The proof is given in the Appendix. The construction in the proof shows that the random coefficients α in equation (1) can be taken to be continuous polynomial transformations of the uniformly distributed continuous random fields $\varepsilon(z)$ and $\upsilon(s)$, and from the earlier discussion the indexing of these fields will exclude economic market variables. Then, the distribution of α will not depend on observed variables except through the correlations across similar alternatives. One implication of the theorem is that MMNL can be used to approximate computationally difficult parametric random utility models simply by taking the distributions underlying these models, suitably scaled, as the mixing distributions. These can be interpreted as simulation approximations using a MNL kernel. For multinomial probit models, Brownstone and Train (1999) and Ben-Akiva and Bolduc (1996) find in Monte Carlo experiments that MMNL gives approximations that are as accurate and quick as direct simulation alternatives such as the Geweke–Hajivassiliou–Keane (GHK) simulator; see Hajivassiliou and Ruud (1994).

The theorem is stated for a single choice, but applies by reinterpretation to multiple or dynamic choice applications by treating each possible portfolio of choices as a distinct alternative. Alternately, the theorem extends easily to a time series of serially correlated RUM models approximated by serially correlated mixtures of a product of MNL models for the individual decisions: MMNL probabilities for a sequence of choices i_t from sets $\mathbf{C}_t$ for $t = 1, \ldots, T$ will have the form $P_{\mathbf{C}}(i_1, \ldots, i_T \mid \mathbf{x}, \theta) = \int \Pi_{t \leqslant T} L_{C_t}(i_t; \mathbf{x}_t, \alpha) \cdot G(\mathrm{d}\alpha; \theta)$, where $L_{C_t}(i_t; \mathbf{x}_t, \alpha)$ is a MNL probability for period t choice, with $\mathbf{x}_t$ a vector of functions of alternative attributes and consumer characteristics that may include state dependence on historical choices, and G is a distribution that can in general include the effects of unobserved heterogeneity and serial correlation. When both state dependence and unobserved heterogeneity are present, this model suffers from Heckman's initial values problem, and a latent class form of the model with G depending on initial state can be interpreted as the Heckman–Singer semiparametric treatment for this problem; see Heckman (1981), Heckman and Singer (1984, 1986), and Heckman, Lochner, and Taber (1998). In particular, a MMNL model in this form can approximate a dynamic choice model generated by a RUM model with a multivariate normal distribution of unobserved factors.

In the proof of the theorem, a polynomial approximation to the true random utility function is perturbed by adding scaled i.i.d. Extreme Value Type I disturbances ν, yielding MNL as the base model to which mixing is applied. At this step, one could have used other distributions for the ν, although most alternatives are not as computationally tractable as MNL. For example, one might take the ν to be scaled i.i.d. standard normal. When the mixing distribution is multivariate normal, this can be interpreted as the method for simulation of the MNP model proposed by Stern (1994). Adopting i.i.d. standard normals for the base model adds one dimension of numerical integration, and requires computation of a product of univariate normal CDF's for each integration point and each decision maker. This requires more computation than a MNL base model; see Train (1995). One can use classical orthogonal polynomials, Fourier series, neural nets, or wavelets as a *basis* $x_k(z, s), k = 1, 2, \ldots$ for the approximation. Judicious choice of a basis can make the approximation more parsimonious and easier to identify econometrically than simple polynomials, and may make it easier to impose or check monotonicity and quasi-convexity properties of a conditional indirect RUM. In applications, it is often desirable to make the leading terms in the basis expressions that occur in standard parametric economic consumer models such as a Stone–Geary specification. Then, a satisfactory approximation may be achieved without a large number of additional terms.

There are two approximation results available in the literature that are somewhat different from Theorem 1. Discrete choice models continuous in their arguments can be approximated by MNL models in which the scale value of each alternative is a general function of all variables for all choices; see McFadden (1984). This approximation, sometimes called 'mother logit', does not require that the discrete choice model come from a random utility model, and the MNL approximation is not guaranteed to be consistent with RUM. Thus, this approximation can be useful for testing a RUM/MNL specification against alternative models that are not necessarily RUM, but is not useful for approximations within the RUM family. Dagsvik (1994) establishes, for a general class of RUM that have a representation in which the random effect is additive and independent of (z, s), that the random utility process can be approximated by a generalized extreme value process. Specialized to the current problem, this shows that this class of random utility models can be approximated by generalized Extreme Value RUM. This is a powerful theoretical result, but its practical econometric application is limited by the difficulty of specifying, estimating, and testing the consistency of relatively abstract generalized Extreme Value RUM.

One limitation of Theorem 1 is that it provides no practical indication of how to choose parsimonious mixing families, or how many terms are needed to obtain acceptable approximations to $P_C(i \mid \mathbf{z}, s)$. However, Monte Carlo studies indicate that fairly simple mixing structures, with random coefficients following a factor analytic structure of relatively low dimension, and relatively simple mixing families, such as latent class models with relatively few classes, are sufficiently flexible to capture quite complex patterns of heterogeneity; see Bolduc, Fortin and Gordon (1996) and Brownstone and Train (1999). The specification tests described in Section 4 are one practical adaptive approach to obtaining satisfactory approximations. In principle, one can combine a method of sieves for specification of the x_i variables with a latent class structure for the mixing distribution G to develop a fully non-parametric approach to estimation of random utility models for discrete choice.

A second limitation of the theorem is that while it guarantees the existence of a satisfactory MMNL approximation, it leaves open the possibility that identification conditions for regular maximum likelihood estimates of the MMNL model may fail, or that estimates may blow up. The first possibility is the usual local and global identification problem, reduced but not eliminated by judicious choice of the basis and careful global search in estimation. The second possibility of estimates blowing up arises if the linear approximation and mixing distribution happen to be *exact*, so that the true random utility model satisfies $U^*(z_i, s, \varepsilon, \upsilon) \equiv x_i \cdot \alpha$ with x_i a vector of polynomials in z_i and s and α distributed $G(\alpha; \theta)$. Then by scaling down the i.i.d. Extreme Value perturbations to $U^*(z_i, s, \varepsilon, \upsilon)$, one can make the MMNL approximation converge to $P^*_C(i \mid \mathbf{z}, s)$. This corresponds to approaching the maximum likelihood by scaling the MNL coefficients by a factor $\psi \to \infty$ in $P_C(i \mid \mathbf{x}, \theta, \psi) = \int L_C(i \mid \mathbf{x}, \alpha \cdot \psi) \cdot G(\mathrm{d}\alpha; \theta)$; a finite maximand does not exist. This is rarely a practical problem, since any specification of x and G adopted in an application will almost certainly miss features of the true random utility model, and ψ will be determined by a search to achieve a best approximation to the influence of these omitted factors. Alternatively, if the exact model contains additive i.i.d. Extreme Value I components, the problem cannot arise. Suppose a random utility model $U^*(z, s, \varepsilon, \upsilon)$ and $\mathbf{C} = \{z_1, \ldots, z_J\}$. Let $F(u \mid \mathbf{z}, s)$ be the CDF of $(U^*(z_1, s, \cdot), \ldots, U^*(z_J, s, \cdot))$. A necessary and sufficient condition for additive i.i.d. Extreme Value I components is that $F(-\log(t_1), \ldots, -\log(t_J))$ have the properties of a multivariate Laplace Transform: derivatives of all orders with

$$(-1)^{n_1+\cdots+n_J} \cdot \partial^{n_1+\cdots+n_J} F(-\log(t_1), \ldots, -\log(t_J)) / \partial^{n_1} t_1 \ldots \partial^{n_J} t_J \geqslant 0$$

See Appendix Lemma 4. In practice, it is difficult to find CDFs satisfying this condition, and difficult to test the condition, so that the likely possibility that the model is not exact is the best guarantee for convergence of estimators.

3. SIMULATION OF THE MMNL MODEL

A tractable empirical form for the MMNL model $P_C(i \mid \mathbf{x}, \theta) = \int L_C(i; \mathbf{x}, \alpha) \cdot G(\mathrm{d}\alpha; \theta)$ is obtained by taking $\alpha = \beta + \Lambda\zeta$, where β is a $K \times 1$ vector of 'mean' coefficients, Λ is a $K \times M$ matrix of factor loadings, with exclusion restrictions for identification, and ζ is an $M \times 1$ vector of factor levels that are independently distributed with a 'standard' density $f(\zeta)$. (This specification includes models with alternative-specific random effects: take x_j to include alternative-specific dummies and introduce factors that load on these dummies.) Let vec(B) denote the operation that stacks the columns of an array B into a vector, define $\gamma = \mathrm{vec}(\Lambda')$, let $\theta' = (\beta', \gamma')$ denote the vector of parameters of this model, and let θ_0 denote the true value of θ. Define $x_C(\zeta) = \Sigma_{j \in C} x_j \cdot L_C(j; \mathbf{x}, \beta + \Lambda\zeta)$ and let $x_{iC}(\zeta) = x_i - x_C(\zeta)$. Let $\mathbf{E}_{\zeta \mid i}$ denote an expectation with respect to the density of ζ conditioned on the event that i is chosen; i.e., the density $L_C(i; \mathbf{x}, \beta + \Lambda\zeta) \cdot f(\zeta) / \int L_C(i; \mathbf{x}, \beta + \Lambda\zeta) \cdot f(\zeta) \mathrm{d}\zeta$. Then $P_C(i \mid \mathbf{x}, \theta) = \mathbf{E}_\zeta L_C(i; \mathbf{x}, \beta + \Lambda\zeta)$, $\nabla_\beta \log P_C(i \mid \mathbf{x}, \theta) = \mathbf{E}_{\zeta \mid i} x_{iC}(\zeta)'$ and $\nabla_\gamma \log P_C(i \mid \mathbf{x}, \theta) = \mathrm{vec}(\mathbf{E}_{\zeta \mid i}\, \zeta x_{iC}(\zeta))$.

3.1. Simulation of the MMNL Probabilities and Their Derivatives

If the integral $P_C(i \mid \mathbf{x}, \theta) = \mathbf{E}_\zeta L_C(i; \mathbf{x}, \beta + \Lambda\zeta)$ can be obtained analytically, or by computationally feasible numerical integration of low dimension, then conventional maximum likelihood can be used to estimate θ. Otherwise, it is possible to simulate $P_C(i \mid \mathbf{x}, \theta)$ and its derivatives, and use these simulation approximations for statistical inference. Make Monte Carlo draws ζ_p, $p = 1, \ldots, r$, from $f(\zeta)$. Let $\mathbf{E}_r$ denote an empirical expectation with respect to a simulation sample of size r. Then,

$$P^r_C(i \mid \mathbf{x}, \theta) = \sum_{p=1}^{r} L_C(i; \mathbf{x}, \beta + \Lambda\zeta_p) \equiv \mathbf{E}_r L_C(i; \mathbf{x}, \beta + \Lambda\zeta) \tag{4}$$

is a positive, unbiased estimator of $P_C(i \mid \mathbf{x}, \theta)$ that is continuous and continuously differentiable to all orders in θ. The derivatives of log $P_C(i \mid \mathbf{x}, \theta)$ involve conditional expectations $\mathbf{E}_{\zeta \mid i} b(\zeta) \equiv \{\mathbf{E}_\zeta b(\zeta) \cdot L_C(i; \mathbf{x}, \beta + \Lambda\zeta)\}/P_C(i \mid \mathbf{x}, \theta)$ for various functions $b(\zeta)$. These expectations are simulated by

$$E_{r \mid i} b(\zeta) \equiv \{\mathbf{E}_r b(\zeta) \cdot L_C(i; \mathbf{x}, \beta + \Lambda\zeta)\}/P^r_C(i \mid \mathbf{x}, \theta) \tag{5}$$

which is again continuously differentiable to all orders in θ. This can be interpreted as importance sampling with draws from $f(\zeta)$ as the comparison density. The simulator $\mathbf{E}_{r \mid i} b(\zeta)$ is not unbiased in general because of the appearance of the simulator $P^r_C(i \mid \mathbf{x}, \theta)$ in the denominator. Similarly, the simulator log $P^r_C(i \mid \mathbf{x}, \theta)$ of log $P_C(i \mid \mathbf{x}, \theta)$ is not unbiased because of the non-linear transformation. However, all the simulators above are consistent when $r \to \infty$. It is possible to get unbiased, but no longer continuous, estimates of $E_{r \mid i} b(\zeta)$ using an acceptance/rejection procedure that accepts draws that would produce i as the choice. Some computations require the second derivatives of log $P_C(i \mid \mathbf{x}, \theta)$; these are given in Appendix Lemma 5. In applications, these second derivatives can alternately be obtained by numerical differentiation of the formulas for the first derivatives.

In the statistical procedures to be discussed next, it will be critical that the simulators satisfy a condition of *stochastic equicontinuity*, which requires that they not 'chatter' as θ changes. This is easily accomplished by keeping the draws ζ_p fixed during iterative procedures that adjust θ; this can be done by storing the ζ_p or by regenerating them from fixed seeds.

3.2. Maximum Simulated Likelihood Estimation (MSLE)

Maximum Simulated Likelihood Estimation (MSLE) finds an estimator θ_N that maximizes the simulated log likelihood, $\mathbf{E}_N \log P^r_C(i \mid \mathbf{x}, \theta)$, with $\mathbf{E}_N$ denoting empirical expectation for a random sample of size N. Hajivassiliou and McFadden (1997) show that under mild regularity conditions, a stochastic equicontinuity property, and $r \cdot N^{-1/2} \to \infty$ as $N \to \infty$, the MSLE estimator θ_N is asymptotically equivalent to the classical maximum likelihood estimator. However, estimators that are relatively free of simulation bias in moderate samples are likely to require r considerably larger than $N^{1/2}$. Monte Carlo draws need not be independent across observations, or across the simulators of different derivatives that may be used in iterative search for θ_N. It is also possible to allow dependence across the different simulation draws, provided there is sufficient mixing for them to satisfy a central limit property. In particular, Train (1999) has found that patterned pseudo-random numbers such as Halton sequences give estimators that in Monte Carlo studies give lower mean square errors than independent random draws. We give an estimator for the asymptotic covariance matrix of θ_N only for the case of independent simulators across observations. Define the arrays

$$\Gamma_N(\theta) = -\mathbf{E}_N\nabla_{\theta\theta'} \log P^r_C(i\,|\,\mathbf{x},\theta) \text{ and } \Delta_N(\theta) = \mathbf{E}_N\{\nabla_\theta \log P^r_C(i\,|\,\mathbf{x},\theta)\}\{\nabla_\theta \log P^r_C(i\,|\,\mathbf{x},\theta)\}' \quad (6)$$

As $r \to \infty$, both $\Gamma_N(\theta_N)$ and $\Delta_N(\theta_N)$ converge to $\Omega_N(\theta_o) = \mathbf{E}_N\{\nabla_\theta \log P_C(i\,|\,\mathbf{x},\theta_o)\}\{\nabla_\theta \log P_C(i\,|\,\mathbf{x},\theta_o)\}'$, so that $\Gamma_N(\theta_N)^{-1}$ and $\Delta_N(\theta_N)^{-1}$ are consistent estimators of the asymptotic covariance estimator. However, for finite r, $\Delta_N(\theta_N)$ is larger than $\Gamma_N(\theta_N)$ due to simulation noise, and $\Delta_N(\theta_N)$ decreases as r increases. Consequently, $\Delta_N(\theta_N)^{-1}$ may substantially underestimate the covariance of the estimator when r is finite, and may suggest erroneously that increasing r decreases the precision of the estimator. For this reason, we recommend the *robust asymptotic covariance matrix estimator* $\Gamma_N(\theta_N)^{-1}\Delta_N(\theta_N)\Gamma_N(\theta_N)^{-1}$ that is associated with quasi-maximum likelihood estimation; see Newey and McFadden (1994, p. 2160).

3.3. Method of Simulated Moments

Let d_i denote an indicator that is one when i is chosen, zero otherwise, and let $\mathbf{d} = (d_1, \ldots, d_J)$. A classical method of moments estimator for θ can be based on the condition that the *generalized residual* $d_i - \mathbf{E}_\zeta L_C(i;\mathbf{x},\beta+\Lambda\zeta)$, evaluated at the true parameters, is orthogonal in the population to any *instrument vector* $W_i(\mathbf{x},\theta)$ that has the dimension of θ. Write this moment as

$$\mathrm{m}(\theta;\mathbf{d},\mathbf{x}) = \sum_{i\in C}\{d_i - \mathbf{E}_\zeta L_C(i;\mathbf{x},\beta+\Lambda\zeta)\}\cdot W_i(\mathbf{x},\theta) \quad (7)$$

Define $s_i(\theta;\mathbf{x}) \equiv \nabla_\theta \log P_C(i\,|\,\mathbf{x},\theta)$. When $W_i(\mathbf{x},\theta) = s_i(\theta;\mathbf{x})$, $m(\theta;\mathbf{d},\mathbf{x})$ reduces to the score of an observation and the classical method of moments estimator coincides with the maximum likelihood estimator. However, any instrument vector $W_i(\mathbf{x},\theta)$ whose covariance matrix with $s_i(\theta;\mathbf{x})$ is of maximum rank can be used to obtain estimators that are consistent and $N^{1/2}$ asymptotically normal, but in general less than fully efficient. A Method of Simulated Moments (MSM) estimator for MMNL is obtained by replacing $P_C(i\,|\,\mathbf{x},\theta)$ in the generalized residual by the *unbiased* simulator $P^r_C(i\,|\,\mathbf{x},\theta)$ and using *statistically independent* simulators (as necessary) to obtain the instrument vector $W_i(\mathbf{x},\theta)$ for a simulator $m^r(\theta;\mathbf{d},\mathbf{x})$ of $m(\theta;\mathbf{d},\mathbf{x})$. The MSM estimator θ_N is a root of $\mathbf{E}_N m^r(\theta;\mathbf{d},\mathbf{x})$. McFadden (1989, 1996) shows that under mild regularity conditions, including stochastic equicontinuity, the MSM estimator θ_N is consistent and asymptotically normal. It is not necessary for this result that r increase with N, so long as the simulators of the generalized residuals are independent or satisfy a weaker condition that is sufficient for a central limit theorem to operate across observations. The array $\Psi_N(\theta_N)^{-1}\Sigma_N(\theta_N)\Psi_N(\theta_N)^{-1}$ consistently estimates the asymptotic covariance matrix of θ_N, where

$$\Psi_N(\theta) = -\mathbf{E}_N\sum_{i\in C}\{\nabla_\theta P^r_C(i\,|\,\mathbf{x},\theta)\}W'_i = -\mathbf{E}_N\sum_{i\in C}\left\{\mathbf{E}_r\begin{bmatrix} x_{iC}(\zeta)' \\ \mathrm{vec}(\zeta x_{iC}(\zeta))\end{bmatrix} L_C(i;\mathbf{x},\beta+\Lambda\zeta)\right\}W'_i$$

$$\Sigma_N(\theta) = \mathbf{E}_N\left\{\sum_{i\in C} W_i P^r_C(i\,|\,\mathbf{x},\theta)W'_i - \left[\sum_{i\in C} W_i P^r_C(i\,|\,\mathbf{x},\theta)\right]\left[\sum_{i\in C} W_i P^r_C(i\,|\,\mathbf{x},\theta)\right]'\right\}$$

The MSLE method is asymptotically efficient, but the computational advantages of the MSM method may offset the loss of statistical efficiency. The more highly correlated $W_i(\mathbf{x},\theta)$ with $s_i(\theta_0;\mathbf{x})$, the more efficient the MSM estimator. An obvious candidate for $W_i(\mathbf{x},\theta)$ is the simulated score $s^r_i(\theta;\mathbf{x})$. Large r will be needed to simulate $s_i(\theta_0;\mathbf{x})$ accurately and achieve high efficiency. However, it is possible to obtain a computationally convenient instrument vector that is fairly highly correlated with $s_i(\theta; \mathbf{x})$, and will as a consequence yield moderately efficient MSM estimates at low computational cost. Using the approach of Talvitie (1972), make a second-order Taylor's expansion of the multinomial logit function $L_C(i; \mathbf{x}, \beta + \Lambda\zeta)$ in ζ around $\zeta = 0$, and take the expectation of this approximation with respect to ζ,

$$\mathbf{E}_\zeta L_C(i; \mathbf{x}, , \beta + \Lambda\zeta) \approx L_C(i; \mathbf{x}, \beta)\cdot\{1 + \tfrac{1}{2}\mathrm{tr}(\Lambda' Q_{ic}\Lambda)\} \tag{8}$$

where $Q_{iC} = x'_{iC}x_{iC} - \Sigma_{j\in C}L_C(j; \mathbf{x}, \beta)x'_{jC}x_{jC}$ and $x_{iC} = x_i - \Sigma_{j\in C}x_jL_C(j; \mathbf{x}, \beta)$. Because the Taylor expansion is not uniformly convergent, this is a poor approximation to the MMNL response probability itself. However, it provides an easily computed approximation to $s_i(\theta_o; \mathbf{x})$: Make a linear approximation log $\{1 + \frac{1}{2}\mathrm{tr}(\Lambda' Q_{iC}\Lambda)\} \approx \frac{1}{2}\mathrm{tr}\{\Lambda' Q_{iC}\Lambda\}$, and take the gradient of the log of equation (8) with respect to θ, ignoring the dependence of Q_{iC} on β, to obtain $W_i(\mathbf{x}, \theta)' = [x_{iC}\mathrm{vec}(Q_{iC}\Lambda)']$. For preliminary estimation, β can be set to simple MNL coefficient estimates and Λ can be any matrix of full column rank that respects the exclusion restrictions present in the model. Limited Monte Carlo evidence suggests that use of these easily computed instruments will often yield MSM estimators with asymptotic efficiencies over 90%.[3]

4. SPECIFICATION TESTING

Because the MMNL model requires use of simulation methods, it is useful to have a specification test based solely on MNL model estimates that determine if mixing is needed. The next result describes a Lagrange Multiplier test for this purpose. This test has the pivotal property that its asymptotic distribution, under the null hypothesis that the correct specification is MNL, does not depend on the parameterization of the mixing distribution under the alternative.

Theorem 2. Consider choice from a set $\mathbf{C} = \{1, \ldots, J\}$. Let x_i be a $1 \times K$ vector of attributes of alternative i. From a random sample $n = 1, \ldots, N$, estimate the parameter α in the simple MNL model $L_C(i; \mathbf{x}, \alpha) = e^{x_i\alpha}/\Sigma_{j\in C}e^{x_j\alpha}$ using maximum likelihood; construct artificial variables

$$z_{ti} = \tfrac{1}{2}(x_{ti} - x_{tC})^2 \text{ with } x_{tC} = \sum_{j\in C} x_{tj}\cdot L_C(j; \mathbf{x}, \hat{\alpha}) \tag{9}$$

for selected components t of x_i, and use a Wald or Likelihood Ratio test for the hypothesis that the artificial variables z_{ti} should be omitted from the MNL model. This test is asymptotically equivalent to a Lagrange multiplier test of the hypothesis of no mixing against the alternative of a MMNL model $P_C(i \mid \mathbf{x}, \theta) = \int L_C(i; \mathbf{x}, \alpha)\cdot G(d\alpha; \theta)$ with mixing in the selected components t of α. The degrees of freedom equals the number of artificial variables z_{ti} that are linearly independent of x.

The proof is given in the Appendix. To examine the operating characteristics of the test, we carried out two simple Monte Carlo experiments for choice among three alternatives, with random utility functions $u_i = \alpha_1 x_{1i} + \alpha_2 x_{2i} + \varepsilon_i$. The disturbances ε_i were i.i.d. Extreme Value Type I. In the first experiment, the covariates were distributed as described below:

[3] These instruments are similar to instruments for the multinomial probit model proposed independently by Ruud (1996).

Variable	Alternative 1	Alternative 2	Alternative 3
x_1	$\pm\frac{1}{2}$ w.p. $\frac{1}{2}$	0	0
x_2	$\pm\frac{1}{2}$ w.p. $\frac{1}{2}$	$\pm\frac{1}{2}$ w.p.	0

The parameter $\alpha_2 = 1$ under both the null and the alternative. The parameter $\alpha_1 = 0.5$ under the null hypothesis, and under the alternative $\alpha_1 = 0.5 \pm 1$ w.p. $\frac{1}{2}$. We carried out 1000 repetitions of the test procedure for a sample of size $N = 1000$ and choices generated alternately under the null hypothesis and under the alternative just described, using likelihood ratio tests for the omitted variable z_{1i}. The results are given below:

Nominal significance level	Actual significance level	Power against the alternative
10%	8·2%	15·6%
5%	5·0%	8·2%

The nominal and actual significance levels of the test agree well. The power of the test is low, and an examination of the estimated coefficients reveals that the degree of heterogeneity in tastes present in this experiment gives estimated coefficients close to their expected values. Put another way, this pattern of heterogeneity is difficult to distinguish from added extreme value noise.

In the second experiment, the covariates are distributed as shown below:

Variable	Alternative 1	Alternative 2	Alternative 3
x_1	$\pm\frac{1}{2}$ w.p. $\frac{1}{2}$	$\pm\frac{1}{2}$ w.p. $\frac{1}{2}$	0
x_2	$\pm\frac{1}{2}$ w.p. $\frac{1}{2}$	$\pm\frac{1}{2}$ w.p. $\frac{1}{2}$	0

The utility function is again $u_i = \alpha_1 x_{1i} + \alpha_2 x_{2i} + \varepsilon_i$. Under the null hypothesis, $\alpha_1 = \alpha_2 = 1$, while under the alternative $(\alpha_1, \alpha_2) = (2, 0)$ w.p. $\frac{1}{2}$ and $(0, 2)$ w.p. $\frac{1}{2}$. Again, 1000 repetitions of the tests are made for $N = 1000$ under the null and the alternative; the results are given below:

Nominal significance level	Actual significance level	Power against the alternative
10%	9·7%	52·4%
5%	3·9%	39·8%

In this case where mixing is across utility functions of different variables, the test is moderately powerful. It remains the case in this example that the estimated coefficients in the MNL model without mixing are close to their expected values.

4.1. Testing the Adequacy of a Mixing Distribution

Suppose one has estimated a MMNL model in which the MNL parameters $\alpha = \beta + \Lambda\zeta$ are mixed by a base density $f(\zeta)$, and the object is to test whether *additional* mixing is needed to describe the sample. The choice probability under the alternative is

$$P_C(i\,|\,\mathbf{x}, \theta, \lambda) = \int\left\{\int L_C(i; \mathbf{x}, \beta + \Lambda\zeta + \lambda^{1/2} \odot \nu)\cdot f(\zeta)\mathrm{d}\zeta\right\}\cdot h(\nu)\mathrm{d}\nu \tag{10}$$

where β is a $K \times 1$ vector, Λ is a factor loading matrix, ν is $K \times 1$ with mean zero and unit variances, λ is a $k \times 1$ vector of variances, $K - T$ of which are maintained at zero, $\lambda^{1/2}$ denotes the component-wise square root, and $\odot$ denotes the component by component direct product. The null hypothesis is that the data are generated by this model with $\lambda = 0$; i.e., a mixed MNL model with latent factors ζ determining the choice probabilities, versus the alternative that up to T additional factors, with density $h(.)$, are needed. The following theorem, proved in the Appendix, gives a Lagrange Multiplier test for this hypothesis:

Theorem 3. Suppose the base model $P_C(i\,|\,\mathbf{x}, \theta) = \int L_C(i; \mathbf{x}, \beta + \Lambda\zeta)\cdot f(\zeta)\mathrm{d}\zeta$ has been estimated by MSLE, using Monte Carlo draws ζ^k from $f(\cdot)$ for $k = 1, \ldots, r$. Construct the quantities

$$x_C^k = \sum_{j\in C} x_j\cdot L_C(j; \mathbf{x}, \beta + \Lambda\zeta^k),\ z_{ti}^k = \tfrac{1}{2}(x_{ti} - x_{tC}^k)^2,\ z_{tC}^k = \sum_{j\in C} z_{tj}^k\cdot L_C(j; \mathbf{x}, \beta + \Lambda\zeta^k)$$

$$v_i = \frac{1}{r\cdot P_C^r(i\,|\,\mathbf{x}, \theta)}\cdot\sum_{k=1}^{r}(x_i - x_C^k)\cdot L_C(i; \mathbf{x}, \beta + \Lambda\zeta^k)$$

$$w_i = \frac{1}{r\cdot P_C^r(i\,|\,\mathbf{x}, \theta)}\sum_{k=1}^{r}\mathrm{vec}(\zeta^k(x_i - x_C^k))'L_C(i; \mathbf{x}, \beta + \Lambda\zeta^k)$$

$$y_{ti} = \frac{1}{r\cdot P_C^r(i\,|\,\mathbf{x}, \theta)}\sum_{k=1}^{r}(z_{ti} - z_{tC}^k)\cdot L_C(i; \mathbf{x}, \beta + \Lambda\zeta^k)$$

where all parameters are set to the base model estimates. A regression over alternatives and observations of the integer 1 on the variables v_i, w_i, and y_{ti} for $t = 1, \ldots, T$ and an F-test for the significance of the variables in this regression is asymptotically equivalent to a Lagrange Multiplier test of the hypothesis of no additional mixing in the coefficients of x_{ti} for $t = 1, \ldots, T$.

In light of the Monte Carlo results in the base case of no mixing, one can expect this test to have relatively low power. Hence, for use as a diagnostic for model specification, one will want to err on the side of admitting too much potential heterogeneity, and use a rejection region with a large nominal significance level.

5. AN APPLICATION: DEMAND FOR ALTERNATIVE VEHICLES

The State of California suffers from air pollution generated by conventional gasoline-powered vehicles, and the State is in the process of mandating quotas for alternative-fuelled vehicles: methanol, compressed natural gas (CNG), or electric. An important policy question is consumer acceptance of these alternative vehicles, and the extent to which subsidies will be necessary to stimulate consumer demand to the levels required by the quotas. Brownstone *et al.* (1996) have carried out a conjoint analysis study of preferences between alternative vehicles. The study has 4654 respondents, each of whom was asked to choose among six alternatives. The alternatives were described in terms of the variables defined in Table I. We do not alter the variable transformations used in the original study, but note that the dependence of their specification on the price of an alternative and on income fails the quasi-convexity condition for conditional

Table I. Variable definitions

Variable	Definition
Price/log(income)	Purchase price (in thousands of dollars) divided by log(household income in thousands)
Range	Hundreds of miles vehicle can travel between refuellings/rechargings
Acceleration	Tens of seconds required to reach 30 mph from stop
Top speed	Highest attainable speed in hundreds of MPH
Pollution	Tailpipe emissions as fraction of those for new gas vehicle
Size	0=mini, 0·1=subcompact, 0·2=compact, 0·3=mid-size or large
'Big enough'	1 if household size $\succeq$ and vehicle is mid or large
Luggage space	Fraction of luggage space in comparable new gas vehicle
Operating cost	Cost per mile of travel (tens of cents): home recharging for electric vehicle, station refuelling otherwise
Station availability	Fraction of stations that can refuel/recharge vehicle
Sports utility vehicle	1 if sports utility vehicle, 0 otherwise
Sports car	1 if sports car
Station wagon	1 if station wagon
Truck	1 if truck
Van	1 if van
EV	1 if electric vehicle (EV)
Commute <5 & EV	1 if electric vehicle and commute <5 miles/day
College & EV	1 if electric vehicle and some college education
CNG	1 if compressed natural gas (CNG) vehicle
Methanol	1 if methanol vehicle
College & Methanol	1 if methanol vehicle and some college education

indirect utility that comes from economic consumer theory. An experimental design was used to select the offerings of six alternatives from 120 possible profiles, distinguished by four fuels (gasoline, methanol, CNG, electric), five sizes (mini, subcompact, compact, midsize, large), and six body types (regular car, sports car, truck, van, station wagon, sports utility vehicle).

Table II gives a MMNL model estimated by Brownstone and Train (1999). This model includes four random effects, associated with the following variables: Dummy for non-EV, Dummy for non-CNG, Size, and Luggage Space. The segment of the table headed 'Variables' gives estimates of the β parameters, and the segment headed 'Random Effects' gives the factor loading Λ on standard normal factors, with an independent factor for each of the random effects above. Then, the coefficients are estimates of the standard deviations of these random effects. The estimation uses 250 replications per observation, and MSLE. The parameter estimates show strong random effects, with magnitudes large enough to suggest that they are capturing correlation structure in unobservables in addition to variation in tastes. The variables and random effects included in this model are the result of a classical selection procedure that estimated alternative MMNL models and used a likelihood ratio test to select from them. A likelihood ratio test at the 5% level shows that this model fits significantly better than a simple MNL model (given in Table III). The table gives estimates of the standard errors of the coefficients for 250 replications, and also for 50 replications. The columns headed 'Asymptotic' give standard errors using $\Delta_N(\theta_N)^{-1}$. As noted in Section 3, while this estimator is consistent, for moderate r it can underestimate covariances and lead to the perverse conclusion that standard errors increase when the number of simulation draws rises. The columns headed 'Robust' give standard errors using the recommended covariance matrix estimator $\Gamma_N(\theta_N)^{-1}\Delta_N(\theta_N)\Gamma_N(\theta_N)^{-1}$. The 'Robust' standard errors fall with number of repetitions, as expected. In general, using the 'Asymptotic' covariance formula with 250 replications results in a 10–20% underestimate of standard errors of coefficients, compared to the 'Robust' formula.

Table III, Model 1, is a simple MNL model $L_C(i; \mathbf{x}, \beta)$ fitted to the data; these estimates are taken from Brownstone and Train (1999). Model 2 adds the artificial variables defined in Theorem 2; i.e. given the base MNL model $L_C(i; \mathbf{x}, \beta)$ and $x_C = \Sigma_{j\in C} x_j \cdot L_C(j; \mathbf{x}, \beta)$, with β set equal to its MNL estimator, define the artificial variables $z_{ti} = \frac{1}{2}(x_{ti} - x_{tC})^2$ for variables t where heterogeneity is suspected, and estimate the MNL model with the original x variables and the additional artificial variables. The list of artificial variables may include variables t which have the coefficient β_t constrained to zero in the base MNL model; these are interpreted as pure random effects. A likelihood ratio test at the 5% significance level rejects the null hypothesis of no mixing. The individual T-statistics for the artificial variables are not necessarily a reliable guide to

Table II. Mixed logit for alternative-fuelled vehicle choice

	Parameter estimates	Standard error: 250 replications		Standard error: 50 replications	
		Asymptotic	Robust	Asymptotic	Robust
Variables					
Price/log(income)	−0·264	0·0435	0·0452	0·0412	0·0525
Range	0·517	0·0581	0·0685	0·0511	0·1022
Acceleration	−1·062	0·1859	0·1990	0·1738	0·2519
Top speed	0·307	0·1150	0·1184	0·1131	0·1188
Pollution	−0·608	0·1392	0·1420	0·1357	0·1546
Size	1·435	0·5082	0·4991	0·4945	0·5156
'Big enough'	0·224	0·1126	0·1166	0·1113	0·1220
Luggage space	1·702	0·4822	0·5854	0·4314	0·8971
Operating cost	−1·224	0·1593	0·2069	0·1393	0·2998
Station availability	0·615	0·1452	0·1536	0·1410	0·1757
Sports utility vehicle	0·901	0·1484	0·1486	0·1482	0·1493
Sports car	0·700	0·1625	0·1513	0·1626	0·1518
Station wagon	−1·500	0·0674	0·0645	0·0674	0·0659
Truck	−1·086	0·0556	0·0520	0·0555	0·0556
Van	−0·816	0·0558	0·0468	0·0557	0·0471
EV	−1·032	0·4249	0·5022	0·3777	0·6035
Commute <5 & EV	0·372	0·1660	0·1763	0·1608	0·1927
College & EV	0·766	0·2182	0·2374	0·2073	0·2796
CNG	0·626	0·1482	0·1670	0·1391	0·2139
Methanol	0·415	0·1464	0·1474	0·1440	0·1534
College & Methanol	0·313	0·1243	0·1256	0·1223	0·1308
Random effects					
Non-EV	2·464	0·5414	0·7184	0·4428	1·0252
Non-CNG	1·072	0·3773	0·4109	0·2781	0·5711
Size	7·455	1·8194	2·0408	1·5538	2·4734
Luggage Space	5·994	1·2483	1·6617	1·0483	2·7719
Log likelihood	−7375·34				

Note: Parameter estimates are from Brownstone and Train (1999); standard error estimates are from this study.

the location of significant mixing, due to lack of independence, and to the possibility of correlation across alternatives in unobserved attributes. However, the results (based on *T*-statistics exceeding one in magnitude) suggest that there may be taste variation in the following variable coefficients: Non-EV, Non-CNG, Size, Luggage space, Operating Cost, and Station Availability. The first four of these were included in the Brownstone–Train model in Table II; the last two are additional factors where mixing may be present. Our specification testing procedure

Table III. Multinomial logit model

Variables	Model 1 Parameter estimate	SE	Model 2 Parameter estimate	SE
Price/log(income)	−0·185	0·027	−0·4240	0·0298
Range	0·350	0·027	0·5036	0·0447
Acceleration	−0·716	0·111	−0·9771	0·1263
Top speed	0·261	0·080	0·3592	0·0814
Pollution	−0·444	0·100	−0·6567	0·1161
Size	0·935	0·311	1·4179	0·3430
'Big enough'	0·143	0·076	0·2248	0·0845
Luggage space	0·501	0·188	1·0161	0·2574
Operating cost	−0·768	0·073	−1·1447	0·0897
Station availability	0·413	0·097	0·6350	0·1074
Sports utility vehicle	0·820	0·144	0·8806	0·1458
Sports car	0·637	0·156	0·6869	0·1580
Station wagon	−1·437	0·065	−1·5229	0·0663
Truck	−1·017	0·055	−1·0776	0·0551
Van	−0·799	0·053	−0·8272	0·0542
EV	−0·179	0·169	−0·6979	0·2384
Commute <5 & EV	0·198	0·082	0·3102	0·0840
College & EV	0·443	0·108	0·6863	0·1145
CNG	0·345	0·091	0·4216	0·1056
Methanol	0·313	0·103	0·4886	0·1105
College & Methanol	0·228	0·089	0·3070	0·0903
Artificial variables				
Price/log(income)			0·0019	0·0927
Range			−0·0349	0·0551
Acceleration			−1·3728	2·1388
Top speed			−0·2071	0·6383
Pollution			0·0977	0·6764
Size			21·5773*	9·5000
'Big enough'			0·2837	0·3832
Luggage space			3·8731*	3·4638
Operating cost			4·2245*	0·8369
Station availability			0·6741*	0·3781
EV			2·3476*	0·5704
CNG			1·2364*	0·4798
Log likelihood	−7391·83		−7356·61	

Notes: Model 1 is from Brownstone and Train (1999).
*denotes the artificial variables with $|T| > 1$.

Table IV. Mixed multinomial logit model

	Parameter estimates	SE
Variables		
Price/log(income)	−0·3622	0·0669
Range	0·6753	0·0965
Acceleration	−1·2688	0·2591
Top speed	0·4027	0·1553
Pollution	−0·7929	0·1980
Size	1·7351	0·6694
'Big enough'	0·2695	0·1468
Luggage space	2·2631	0·6426
Operating cost	−1·8056	0·2912
Station availability	0·7029	0·1896
Sports utility vehicle	0·9234	0·1498
Sports car	0·7270	0·1645
Station wagon	−1·5246	0·0681
Truck	−1·1195	0·0559
Van	−0·8191	0·0564
EV	−1·5733	0·5819
Commute <5 & EV	0·4793	0·2242
College & EV	1·0534	0·3114
CNG	0·7709	0·2018
Methanol	0·5435	0·1922
College & Methanol	0·3849	0·1542
Random effects		
Non-EV	3·3802	0·7647
Non-CNG	1·1042	0·4990
Size	8·0788	2·7021
Luggage space	7·6220	1·7153
Operating cost	4·4532	0·8014
Station availability	1·3987	0·5730
Log likelihood	−7358·93	

is easier and quicker than the Brownstone–Train method. All the factors identified in their search were picked up by our procedure, as were some additional candidates.

Table IV gives a MMNL model which includes the six random effects identified as possibly significant by the artificial variable test in Table III, using T-statistics greater than one in magnitude as the selection criterion. The MMNL estimates show that there is significant mixing in each of these factors. Likelihood ratio tests show that this model is a significant improvement on the model in Table II. Further exploration with additional factors in the MMNL model finds that there are several factor combinations that will fit as well or marginally better than the model in Table IV, and that some of these combinations will place weight on factors that were excluded by the artificial variable selection procedure, and will lower the significance of some of the factors previously included. These results reflect the inherent difficulty of identifying the factor structure of unobserved utility from observed data on discrete choices, but may also indicate more conventional specification issues such as omitted observed variables or interactions.

6. CONCLUSIONS

This paper has established that MMNL models, estimated using MSLE or MSM, provide a flexible and computationally practical econometric method for economic discrete choice that is postulated to come from utility maximization. First, a general approximation property is established. Second, estimation of parametric MMNL models by MSLE or MSM is shown to provide estimates with good statistical properties, and easily computed fairly efficient instruments are provided for MSM. Third, simply computed specification tests are developed that allow one to test for the presence of mixing, or for the presence of omitted mixing factors. Finally, an application to the demand for alternatively-fuelled vehicles shows that the method can detect and estimate significant mixing effects which can have a strong effect on the pattern of substitutability across alternatives.

APPENDIX: PROOFS OF THEOREMS

Lemma 1. Suppose consumers with tastes defined by points s in a compact topological space $\mathbf{S}$ have preferences over objects z in a compact topological space $\mathbf{Z}$, with $z' \succeq_s z''$ meaning z' is at least as good as z'' for a consumer with tastes s. Suppose $\succeq_s$ is complete and transitive, and has the continuity property that if a sequence of triples (z'^k, z''^k, s^k) converges to a limit (z'^0, z''^0, s^0) and satisfies $z'^k \succeq_{s^k} z''^k$, then $z'^0 \succeq_s z''^0$. Then there exists a utility function $U(z, s)$, continuous in its arguments, that represents $\succeq_s$ for $s \in \mathbf{S}$.

Proof: A standard construction for fixed s due to Rader and Debreu defines a utility function $U(z, s)$ which is continuous in z for each s; see Barten and Bohm (1982, pp. 388–390). But the level sets $\{(z', s') \mid U(z', s') \geqslant U(z, s)\}$ and $\{(z', s') \mid U(z', s') \leqslant U(z, s)\}$ are then closed by the hypothesized continuity property, implying that U is continuous on $\mathbf{Z} \times \mathbf{S}$.

Lemma 2. Consider a random variable X with CDF F. Define $F(x^-) = \lim_{\varepsilon \searrow 0} F(x - \varepsilon)$ and the right-continuous inverse $F^{-1}(p) = \sup\{x \in \mathbb{R} \mid F(x) \leqslant p\}$ for $p \in (0, 1)$. Define the random variable $Z = U \cdot F(X) + (1 - U) \cdot F(X^-)$, where U is a uniformly distributed random variable on [0,1] that is independent of X. Define $X^* = F^{-1}(Z)$. Then Z is uniformly distributed on (0,1), the function F^{-1} is almost surely continuous, and $X^* = X$ almost surely. If, in addition, F is strictly increasing, then F^{-1} is continuous and $X^* \equiv X$.

Proof: Define $\mathbf{A} = \{x \in \mathbb{R} | F(x + \varepsilon) = F(x)$ for some $\varepsilon > 0\}$, and $\mathbf{B} = F(\mathbf{A})$. The set $\mathbf{A}$ is a countable union of disjoint half-open intervals of the form $[a,b)$ with $F(a) = F(b^-)$, so that $\mathbf{A}$ occurs with probability zero. For $c \in (0, 1)$, let $x = F^{-1}(c)$. Then, for all $\varepsilon > 0$, $F(x - \varepsilon) \leqslant F(x^-) \leqslant c \leqslant F(x) < F(x + \varepsilon)$. Hence, the event $\{Z \leqslant c\}$ occurs if and only if one of the disjoint events $\{X < x\}$ or $\{X = x$ & $F(x^-) + U \cdot [F(x) - F(x^-)] < c\}$ occurs. But $P(X < x) = F(x^-)$ and $P(X = x$ & $F(x^-) + U \cdot [F(x) - F(x^-)] < c) = c - F(x^-)$, implying $P(Z \leqslant c) = c$. Thus, Z is uniformly distributed on (0,1). If $x \notin \mathbf{A}$ and $F(x^-) \leqslant c \leqslant F(x)$, then $F^{-1}(c) = x$. Then, in the event $X \notin \mathbf{A}$, which occurs with probability one, one has $X = X^* \equiv F(Z)$. Finally, $F^{-1}(p)$ is a monotone right-continuous function that is also left-continuous except at jumps when $p \in \mathbf{B}$, a countable set that contains Z with probability zero. Then, F^{-1} is almost surely continuous. If F is strictly increasing, then $\mathbf{A}$ and $\mathbf{B}$ are empty. ■

Let $(\Omega, \mathcal{W}, \pi)$ denote a probability space, $\mathbf{T}$ a subset of $\mathbb{R}^m$, and $X : \Omega \times \mathbf{T} \to \mathbb{R}^n$ a random field, measurable with respect to $\mathcal{W}$ for each $t \in \mathbf{T}$, and almost surely measurable on $\mathbf{T}$. We say that X admits a *coordinate conditional probability structure* at t if there exist conditional CDF functions

$F_i(x_i \mid x_1, \ldots, x_{i-1}, t)$, measurable in their arguments, such that for all $y \in \mathbb{R}^n$, the CDF of $X(t)$ can be written

$$F(y,t) = \int_{-\infty}^{y_1} \int_{-\infty}^{y_2} \cdots \int_{-\infty}^{y_n} F_1(\mathrm{d}x_1 \mid t) \cdot F_2(\mathrm{d}x_2 \mid x_1, t) \cdot \ldots \cdot F_n(\mathrm{d}x_n \mid x_1, \ldots, x_{n-1}, t)$$

This condition follows from Fubini's theorem if $F(x, t)$ has a density $f(x, t)$, and will hold automatically if F is built up from conditional CDF functions. It can fail in pathological cases; see Billingsley (1986, p. 458).

Lemma 3. Suppose X is a random field from $\mathbf{T} \subseteq \mathbb{R}^m$ into $\mathbb{R}^n$ that admits a coordinate conditional probability structure for each $t \in \mathbf{T}$. Then there exists a uniformly distributed random field $Z : \Omega \times \mathbf{T} \to [0,1]^n$ and measurable functions $h_i : [0,1]^i \times \mathbf{T} \to \mathbb{R}$ for $i = 1, \ldots, n$ such that $X_i(t) = h_i(Z_1(t), \ldots, Z_i(t), t)$ almost surely. If in addition, there is a rectangle $\mathbf{X} \subseteq \mathbb{R}^n$ such that $X(t)$ has a density $f(x, t)$ that is continuous in its arguments and strictly positive on the interior of $\mathbf{X}$, with $F(\mathbf{X}, t) = 1$, then the h_i are continuous in their arguments and Z is a continuous random field.

Proof: For $n = 1$, Lemma 2 gives the result for each $t \in \mathbf{T}$ that $X_1(t) = h_1(z_1(t), t)$ almost surely. Proceed by induction. Suppose the result has been established for $n - 1$, with $Z_i(t)$ independently distributed uniformly on [0,1] for $i = 1, \ldots, n-1$ and $X_i(t) = h_i(Z_1(t), \ldots, Z_i(t), t)$ almost surely. Apply Lemma 2 to the random variable $X_n(t)$ with measurable conditional distribution function $F_n(x_n \mid h_1(Z_1(t), t), \ldots, h_{n-1}(Z_1(t), \ldots, Z_{n-1}(t), t), t)$. This yields a function satisfying $X_n(t) = h_n(Z_1(t), \ldots, Z_n(t), t)$ almost surely. This completes the induction step. Finally, since X is a random field, almost sure continuity assures that the pointwise construction for each $t \in \mathbf{T}$ is measurable in t.

When X has a positive continuous density $f(x, t)$ on the interior of the rectangle $\mathbf{X}$, the conditional CDF $F_i(x_i \mid x_1, \ldots, x_{i-1}, t)$ is strictly increasing in x_i and continuous in all its arguments, so that an implicit function theorem implies that the inverse function $x_i = F_i^{-1}(z_i \mid x_1, \ldots, x_{i-1}, t)$ is continuous in all its arguments, giving the last result of the lemma. ■

Lemma 4. A necessary and sufficient condition for a random utility function over J alternatives with a multivariate CDF $F(u)$ to have a representation $U = W + \varepsilon$, where the components of ε are independent of W and independent identically distributed Extreme Value I, is that $F(-\log(t_1), \ldots, -\log(t_J))$ be a multivariate Laplace Transform; i.e. F treated as a function of $(t_1, \ldots, t_J)$ is analytic and has derivatives satisfying the sign condition

$$(-1)^{n_1+\cdots+n_J} . \partial^{n_1+\cdots+n_J} F(-\log(t_1), \ldots, -\log(t_J)) / \partial^{n_1} t_1 \ldots \partial^{n_J} t_J \geqslant 0$$

Proof: Suppose U has the representation. Then, F must satisfy the convolution formula

$$F(u_1, \ldots, u_J) = \int_{-\infty}^{+\infty} \exp(-(e^{-u_1+w_1} + \cdots + e^{-u_J+w_J})) \cdot G(\mathrm{d}w)$$

where G is the CDF of W. Make the transformations $t_k = \exp(-u_k)$ and $V_k = \exp(W_k)$, and let H be the CDF of V. Then,

$$F(-\log(t_1), \ldots, -\log(t_J)) = \int_0^{+\infty} \exp(-(t_1 \nu_1 + \cdots + t_J \nu_J)) \cdot H(\mathrm{d}\nu)$$

This is a multivariate Laplace Transform. Conversely, if $F(-\log(t_1), \ldots, -\log(t_J))$ is a multivariate Laplace Transform, then it satisfies $F(-\infty) = 0$, $F(+\infty) = 1$, and from the derivative property of Laplace Transforms, $\partial^J F/\partial u_1 \ldots \partial u_J \geqslant 0$, so that it is a multivariate CDF; see Feller (1966, p. 415). ■

Lemma 5. If $P_C(i \mid \mathbf{x}, \theta) = \mathbf{E}_\zeta L_C(i; \mathbf{x}, \beta + \Lambda\zeta)$ is given by equation (5), then

$$\begin{aligned} \nabla_{\beta\beta'} \log P_C(i \mid \mathbf{x}, \theta) = {} & \mathbf{E}_{\zeta \mid i}\{x_{iC}(\zeta)' x_{iC}(\zeta) - \Sigma_{j \in C} x_{jC}(\zeta)' x_{jC}(\zeta) L_C(j; \mathbf{x}, \beta + \Lambda\zeta)\} \\ & -\{\nabla_\beta \log P_C(i \mid \mathbf{x}, \theta)\}\{\nabla_\beta \log P_C(i \mid \mathbf{x}, \theta)\}' \end{aligned}$$

$$\begin{aligned} \nabla_{\gamma\beta'} \log P_C(i \mid \mathbf{x}, \theta) = {} & \mathbf{E}_{\zeta \mid i}\{\mathrm{vec}(\zeta x_{iC}(\zeta)) x_{iC}(\zeta) - \Sigma_{j \in C} \mathrm{vec}(\zeta x_{jC}(\zeta)) x_{jC}(\zeta) L_C(j; \mathbf{x}, \beta + \Lambda\zeta)\} \\ & -\{\nabla_\gamma \log P_C(i \mid \mathbf{x}, \theta)\}\{\nabla_\beta \log P_C(i \mid \mathbf{x}, \theta)\}' \end{aligned}$$

$$\begin{aligned} \nabla_{\gamma\gamma'} \log P_C(i \mid \mathbf{x}, \theta) = {} & \mathbf{E}_{\zeta \mid i}\{\mathrm{vec}(\zeta x_{iC}(\zeta)) \mathrm{vec}(\zeta x_{jC}(\lambda))' - \Sigma_{j \in C} \mathrm{vec}(\zeta x_{jC}(\lambda)) \mathrm{vec}(\zeta x_{jC}(\lambda))' L_C(j; \mathbf{x}, \beta + \Lambda\zeta)\} \\ & -\{\nabla_\gamma \log P_C(i \mid \mathbf{x}, \theta)\}\{\nabla_\gamma \log P_C(i \mid \mathbf{x}, \theta)\}' \end{aligned}$$

Proof: Direct computation. ■

Proof of Theorem 1: Consider the random utility model $U^*(z, s, \varepsilon(\omega, z), \upsilon(\omega, s))$, where $\varepsilon(\omega, z) \in [0, 1]^p$ and $\upsilon(\omega, s) \in [0, 1]^r$ are uniformly distributed continuous random fields defined for ω in a fundamental probability space $(\Omega, \mathcal{W}, \pi)$. For $(z', z'') \in \mathcal{C}_2$ and $s \in \mathbf{S}$, define the set

$$\mathbf{A}_k(z', z'', s) = \{\omega \in \Omega \mid |U^*(z', s, \varepsilon(\omega, z'), \upsilon(\omega, s)) - U^*(z'', s, \varepsilon(\omega, z''), \upsilon(\omega, s))| \geqslant 5/k\}$$

The continuity of U^* and the measurability of the random fields implies that $\mathbf{A}_k(z', z'', s)$ is measurable. This set is monotone increasing as $k \to \infty$ to the set of ω for which the alternatives $(z', z'') \in \mathcal{C}_2$ are not tied. By hypothesis, this set has probability one, implying that there exists $k = k(z', z'', s)$ such that $\pi(\mathbf{A}_k(z', z'', s)) > 1 - \eta/4J^*$.

The uniform continuity of U^* on $\mathbf{Z} \times \mathbf{S} \times [0, 1]^p \times [0, 1]^r$ implies that given $k(z', z'', s)$, there exists $\delta(z', z'', s) > 0$ such that in a neighbourhood of this radius U^* varies by less than $1/k(z', z'', s)$. The almost certain continuity of $\varepsilon(\omega, z)$ and $\upsilon(\omega, s)$ imply that the set

$$\begin{aligned} \mathbf{B}_m(z', s) = \{\omega \in \Omega \mid & \sup_{|z^* - z'| < 1/m} |\varepsilon(\omega, z^*) - \varepsilon(\omega, z')| + \sup_{|s^* - s| < 1/m} |\upsilon(\omega, s^*) \\ & - \upsilon(\omega, s)| < \delta(z', z'', s)\} \end{aligned}$$

and the corresponding set $\mathbf{B}_m(z'', s)$, are monotone increasing as $m \to \infty$ to limiting sets that occur with probability one. Then there exists $m = m(z', z'', s)$ such that $\pi(\mathbf{B}_m(z', s)) > 1 - \eta/4J^*$ and $\pi(\mathbf{B}_m(z'', s)) > 1 - \eta/4J^*$. Therefore with probability at least $1 - 3\eta/4J^*$,

$\omega \in \mathbf{A}_k(z', z'', s) \cap \mathbf{B}_{ml}(z', s) \cap \mathbf{B}_{ml}(z'', s)$, implying that for $(z^{*\prime}, z^{*\prime\prime}, s^*)$ in an open neighbourhood of $(z', z'', s) \in \mathcal{C}_2 \times \mathbf{S}$ of radius $\delta(z', z'', s)$, one has

$$| U^*(z^{*\prime}, s^*, \varepsilon(\omega, z^{*\prime}), \upsilon(\omega, s^*)) - U^*(z^{*\prime\prime}, s^*, \varepsilon(\omega, z^{*\prime\prime}), \upsilon(\omega, s^*)) | \geqslant 1/k$$

These neighbourhoods cover the compact set $\mathcal{C}_2 \times \mathbf{S}$. Therefore, there exists a finite subcovering. Let k^* be the larger of $-\log(\eta/4J^*)$ and the maximum value of $k(z', z'', s)$ for the centres of the finite subcover. We have now established that each point $(z^{*\prime}, z^{*\prime\prime}, s^*) \in \mathcal{C}_2 \times \mathbf{S}$ falls in some neighbourhood in a finite cover with centre (z', z'', s), and satisfies $| U^*(z^{*\prime}, s^*, \varepsilon(\omega, z^{*\prime}), \upsilon(\omega, s^*)) - U^*(z^{*\prime\prime}, s^*, \varepsilon(\omega, z^{*\prime\prime}), \upsilon(\omega, s^*)) | \geqslant 3/k(z', z'', s) \geqslant 3/k^*$ on a set of ω that occurs with probability at least $1 - 3\eta/4J^*$.

The continuous function U^* has a Bernstein–Weierstrauss polynomial approximation U^{*k} on $\mathbf{Z} \times \mathbf{S} \times [0, 1]^{p+r}$ that satisfies $| U^* - U^{*k} | \leqslant 1/k^*$. Consider a choice set $\mathbf{C} = \{z_1, \ldots, z_J\} \in \mathcal{C}^*$ and let $\mathbf{z} = (z_1, \ldots, z_J)$. Form $U^k(z_i, s, \varepsilon(z_i), \upsilon(s)) = U^{*k}(z_i, s, \varepsilon(z_i), \upsilon(s)) + \nu_i/k^{*2}$, where the ν_i are i.i.d. Extreme Value Type I random variables. Consider the event of a preference reversal between U^* and U^k for a pair $(z_i, z_j) \subseteq \mathbf{C}$ and $s \in \mathbf{S}$; i.e. the set of $\omega \in \Omega$ and $\nu \in \mathbb{R}^2$ such that $U^*(z_i, s, \varepsilon(\omega, z_i), \upsilon(\omega, s)) > U^*(z_j, s, \varepsilon(\omega, z_j), \upsilon(\omega, s))$ and $U^k(z_i, s, \varepsilon(\omega, z_i), \upsilon(\omega, s)) < U^k(z_j, s, \varepsilon(\omega, z_j), \upsilon(\omega, s))$. If $| U^*(z_i, s, \varepsilon(\omega, z_i), \upsilon(\omega, s)) - U^*(z_j, s, \varepsilon(\omega, z_j), \upsilon(\omega, s)) | > 3/k^*$, then

$$\begin{aligned} 0 &> U^k(z_i, s, \varepsilon(\omega, z_i), \upsilon(\omega, s)) - U^k(z_j, s, \varepsilon(\omega, z_j), \upsilon(\omega, s)) \\ &= U^{*k}(z_i, s, \varepsilon(\omega, z_i), \upsilon(\omega, s)) - U^{*k}(z_j, s, \varepsilon(\omega, z_j), \upsilon(\omega, s)) + (\nu_i - \nu_j)/k^{*2} \\ &\geqslant U^*(z_i, s, \varepsilon(\omega, z_i), \upsilon(\omega, s)) - U^*(z_j, s, \varepsilon(\omega, z_j), \upsilon(\omega, s)) - 2/k^* + (\nu_i - \nu_j)/k^{*2} \\ &\geqslant 1/k^* + (\nu_i - \nu_j)/k^{*2} \end{aligned}$$

and hence $\nu' - \nu'' < -1/k^*$. The probability of this last event is $(1 + e^{k^*})^{-1} < \eta/4J^*$, and from the previous argument the probability that the conditioning event does not occur is at most $3\eta/4J^*$. Then the probability of a preference reversal at (z_i, z_j, s) is at most η/J^*. Therefore, the probability of the event that the alternative in $\mathbf{C}$ that maximizes U^k differs from the alternative that maximizes U^* is at most $\eta J/J^* \leqslant \eta$.

Write the polynomial approximation U^k in the form $U^k(z, s, \varepsilon(z), \upsilon(s)) = x(z, s)\cdot\alpha(z, s) + \nu/k^{*2}$, where $x(z, s)$ is a vector of the z and s components of the terms in the polynomial and $\alpha(z, s)$ is a vector of the corresponding $\varepsilon(z)$ and $\upsilon(s)$ components. Finally, for a choice set $\mathbf{C} = \{z_1, \ldots, z_J\} \in \mathcal{C}^*$, define $\alpha = (\alpha(z_1, s), \ldots, \alpha(z_J, s))$ and $x_i = (0, \ldots, 0, x(z_i, s), 0, \ldots, 0)$, so that $U^k(z_i, s, \varepsilon_i) = x_i\cdot\alpha + \nu_i/k^{*2}$. This is a MMNL model of the form of equation (1), and the construction guarantees that with probability at least $1 - \eta$, U^* and U^k are maximized at the same alternative in $\mathbf{C}$. Therefore, $P^*_{\mathbf{C}}(i \mid \mathbf{z}, s)$ from U^* and $P_{\mathbf{C}}(i \mid \mathbf{x}, \theta)$ from U^k differ by at most η. ■

Proof of Theorem 2: Write the MMNL model as $P_C(i \mid \mathbf{x}, \theta, \lambda) = \int L_C(i; \mathbf{x}, \beta + \lambda^{1/2} \odot \zeta)\cdot G(\mathrm{d}\zeta; \theta)$, where β and λ are vectors of parameters, $\lambda^{1/2}$ is the vector of square roots of the components of λ, ζ is a vector of random variables that has mean zero, component variances of one, and full rank over the specified components r, and $\lambda^{1/2} \odot \zeta$ denotes the component-by-component direct product. The parameterization $\lambda^{1/2}$ is chosen to circumvent the problem that a natural parameterization in terms of the standard deviations of the mixing density leads to a score that is identically zero under the null, as in Lee and Chesher (1986), McFadden (1987), and Newey and McFadden (1994). Then

$$\nabla_\beta P_C(i \mid \mathbf{x}, \theta, \lambda) = \int L_C(i; \mathbf{x}, \beta + \lambda^{1/2} \odot \zeta) \cdot (x_i - x_C) \cdot G(\mathrm{d}\zeta; \theta)$$

$$\text{with } x_C = \Sigma_{j \in C} x_j \cdot L_C(j; \mathbf{x}, \beta + \lambda^{1/2} \odot \zeta)$$

$$\nabla_{\lambda_t} P_C(i \mid \mathbf{x}, \theta, \lambda) = \tfrac{1}{2} \cdot \lambda^{-1/2} \cdot \int L_C(i; \mathbf{x}, \beta + \lambda^{1/2} \odot \zeta) \cdot (x_i - x_C) \cdot \zeta_t \cdot G(\mathrm{d}\zeta; \theta)$$

Taking the limit as the $\lambda_t \to 0$, and using L'Hôpital's rule on $\nabla_{\lambda_t} P_C(i \mid \mathbf{x}, \theta, \lambda)$, one obtains

$$\nabla_\beta P_C(i \mid \mathbf{x}, \theta, \lambda) = L_C(i; \mathbf{x}, \beta_e) \cdot (x_i - x_C) \text{ and } \nabla_{\lambda_t} \log P_C(i \mid \mathbf{x}, \theta) = L_C(i; \mathbf{x}, \beta_e) \cdot (z_{ti} - z_{tC})$$

where $z_{ti} = \frac{1}{2}(x_{ti} - x_{tC})^2$ and $z_{tC} = \Sigma_{j \in C} z_{tj} \cdot L_C(j; \mathbf{x}, \hat{\alpha})$. The sample mean of $\nabla_\beta \log P_C(i \mid \mathbf{x}, \theta)$ is zero at the maximum likelihood estimator β_e of the simple MNL model, and the Lagrange Multiplier statistic tests whether the vector of sample means of $\nabla_{\lambda_t} \log P_C(i \mid \mathbf{x}, \theta)$ for the selected t are zero. As in McFadden (1987), this test is equivalent to a Lagrange Multiplier test for the null hypothesis that the variables z_{ri} have zero coefficients in the MNL model, and thus asymptotically equivalent to a Likelihood Ratio or Wald test for this hypothesis. ■

Proof of Theorem 3: Consider $P_C(i \mid \mathbf{x}, \theta) = \int \{\int L_C(i; \mathbf{x}, \beta + \Lambda\zeta + \lambda^{1/2} \odot \nu) \cdot f(\zeta) \mathrm{d}\nu\} H(\mathrm{d}\nu)$. Differentiating, $\nabla_\beta P_C(i \mid \mathbf{x}, \theta) = \int \{\int (x_i - x_C) L_C(i; \mathbf{x}, \beta + \Lambda\zeta + \lambda^{1/2} \odot \nu) \cdot f(\zeta) \mathrm{d}\nu\} H(\mathrm{d}\nu)$, $\nabla_{\Lambda'} P_C(i \mid \mathbf{x}, \theta) = \int \{\int \zeta (x_i - x_C) L_C(i; \mathbf{x}, \beta + \Lambda\zeta + \lambda^{1/2} \odot \nu) \cdot f(\zeta) \mathrm{d}\nu\} H(\mathrm{d}\nu)$, and $\nabla_{\lambda_t} P_C(i \mid \mathbf{x}, \theta) = \frac{1}{2}\lambda_t^{-1/2} \int \{\int (x_{ti} - x_{tC}) L_C(i; \mathbf{x}, \beta + \Lambda\zeta\lambda^{1/2} \odot \nu) \cdot f(\zeta) \mathrm{d}\zeta\} \cdot \nu_t \cdot H(\mathrm{d}\nu)$, with $x_C \equiv x_C(\zeta) = \Sigma_{j \in C} x_j L_C(j; \mathbf{x}, \beta + \Lambda\zeta + \lambda^{1/2} \odot \nu)$. To evaluate the last derivative under the null, use L'Hôpital's rule. The derivative of $2\lambda_t^{1/2} \nabla_{\lambda_t} P_C(i \mid \mathbf{x}, \theta)$ with respect to λ_t is

$$\tfrac{1}{2}\lambda_t^{-1/2} \int \left\{ \int (x_{ti} - x_{tC})^2 L_C(i; \mathbf{x}, \beta + \Lambda\zeta + \lambda^{1/2} \odot \nu) \cdot f(\zeta) \mathrm{d}\zeta \right\} \cdot \nu_t^2 \cdot H(\mathrm{d}\nu)$$

$$-\tfrac{1}{2}\lambda_t^{-1/2} \int \left\{ \int \sum\nolimits_{j \in C} x_{tj} (x_{tj} - x_{tC}) L_C(j; \mathbf{x}, \beta + \Lambda\zeta + \lambda^{1/2} \odot \nu) L_C(i; \mathbf{x}, \beta + \Gamma\eta + \lambda^{1/2} \odot \nu) \cdot f(\zeta) \mathrm{d}\zeta \right\} \cdot \nu_t^2 \cdot H(\mathrm{d}\nu)$$

$$= \tfrac{1}{2}\lambda_t^{-1/2} \int \left\{ \int (z_{ti} - z_{tC})^2 L_C(i; \mathbf{x}, \beta + \Lambda\zeta + \lambda^{1/2} \odot \nu) \cdot f(\zeta) \mathrm{d}\zeta \right\} \cdot \nu_t^2 \cdot H(\mathrm{d}\nu),$$

with $z_{ti} \equiv z_{ti}(\zeta) = (x_{ti} - x_{tC}(\zeta))^2/2$ and $z_{tC} \equiv z_{tC}(\zeta) = \Sigma_{j \in C} z_{tj}(\zeta) \cdot L_C(j \mid \mathbf{x}, \beta + \Lambda\zeta + \lambda^{1/2} \odot \nu)$. Hence, at $\delta = 0$,

$$P_C(i \mid \mathbf{x}, \theta) = \int L_C(i; \mathbf{x}, \beta + \Lambda\zeta) \cdot f(\zeta) \mathrm{d}\zeta,$$

$$\nabla_\beta P_C(i \mid \mathbf{x}, \theta) = \int (x_i - x_C(\zeta)) L_C(i; \mathbf{x}, \beta + \Lambda\zeta) \cdot f(\zeta) \mathrm{d}\zeta,$$

$$\nabla_{\Lambda'} P_C(i \mid \mathbf{x}, \theta) = \int \zeta (x_i - x_C(\zeta)) L_C(i; \mathbf{x}, \beta + \Lambda\zeta) \cdot f(\zeta) \mathrm{d}\zeta, \text{ and}$$

$$\nabla_{\lambda_t} P_C(i \mid \mathbf{x}, \theta) = \int (z_{ti}(\zeta) - z_{tC}(\zeta)) L_C(i; \mathbf{x}, \beta + \Lambda\zeta) \cdot f(\zeta) \mathrm{d}\zeta.$$

For comparison, suppose one had the base model in variables x and wanted to test whether additional variables z_{ti} belong in the model. The model under the alternative is

$P_C(i \mid \mathbf{x}, \mathbf{z}, \theta, \alpha) = \int L_C(i; \mathbf{x}, \mathbf{z}(\zeta), \beta + \Lambda\zeta, \alpha) \cdot f(\zeta) d\zeta$. The derivatives under the null hypothesis $\alpha = 0$ are the same as before for $\nabla_\beta P_C(i \mid \mathbf{x}, \mathbf{z}, \theta, \alpha)$ and for $\nabla_{\Lambda'} P_C(i \mid \mathbf{x}, \mathbf{z}, \theta, \alpha)$. Finally, $\nabla_\alpha P_C(i \mid \mathbf{x}, \mathbf{z}, \theta, \alpha) = \int (z_i(\zeta) - z_C(\zeta)) L_C(i; \mathbf{x}, \beta + \Lambda\zeta) \cdot f(\zeta) d\zeta$, also as before. Therefore, a LM test for the hypothesis $\lambda = 0$ is equivalent to a LM test for the hypothesis $\alpha = 0$ for the auxiliary variables $z_i(\zeta)$. This test is readily computed by first estimating the base model using a simulation procedure with specified starting seeds, then regressing (over observations and alternatives) the integer 1 on the scores $\nabla_\beta \log P^r_C(i \mid \mathbf{x}, \theta)$, $\mathrm{vec}(\nabla_{\Lambda'} \log P^r_C(i \mid \mathbf{x}, \theta))$, and $\nabla_{\lambda_t} \log P^r_C(i \mid \mathbf{x}, \theta)$ for $t = 1, \ldots T$, and testing whether the sum of squared residuals is significant according to a chi-square distribution with T degrees of freedom. ■

ACKNOWLEDGEMENTS

We are indebted to the E. Morris Cox fund for research support, and to Moshe Ben-Akiva, David Brownstone, Denis Bolduc, Andre de Palma, and Paul Ruud for useful comments. This paper was first presented at the University of Paris X in June 1997.

REFERENCES

Barten A, Bohm V. 1982. Consumer theory. In *Handbook of Mathematical Economics*, Vol. II, Arrow K, Intriligator M (eds). North-Holland: Amsterdam.

Beggs J. 1988. A simple model for heterogeneity in binary logit models. *Economics Letters* **27**: 245–249.

Ben-Akiva M, Bolduc D. 1996. Multinomial probit with a logit kernel and a general parametric specification of the covariance structure, MIT Working Paper.

Billingsley P. 1986. *Probability and Measure*. Wiley: New York.

Bolduc D, Fortin B, Gordon S. 1996. Multinomial probit estimation of spatially interdependent choices. *International Regional Science Review*, forthcoming.

Boyd J, Mellman J. 1980. The effect of fuel economy standards on the U.S. automotive market: a hedonic demand analysis. *Transportation Research* **14A**(5–6): 367–378.

Borsch Supan A. 1990. Recent developments in flexible discrete choice models: nested logit analysis versus simulated moments probit analysis. In *Spatial Choices and Processes. Studies in Regional Science and Urban Economics*, Vol. 21, Fischer M *et al.* (eds). North-Holland: Amsterdam; 203–217.

Brownstone D, Bunch D, Golob T, Ren W. 1996. Transactions choice model for forecasting demand for alternative-fueled vehicles. *Research in Transportation Economics* **4**: 87–129.

Brownstone D, Train K. 1999. Forecasting new product penetration with flexible substitution patterns, *Journal of Econometrics* **28**: forthcoming.

Cardell N, Dunbar F. 1980. Measuring the societal impacts of automobile downsizing. *Transportation Research* **14A**(5–6): 423–434.

Chavas J, Segerson K. 1986. Singularity and autoregressive disturbances in linear logit models. *Journal of Business and Economic Statistics* **4**: 161–169.

Chesher A, Santos-Silva J. 1995. Taste variation in discrete choice models, University of Bristol Working Paper.

Chintagunta P. 1992. Estimating a multinomial probit model of brand choice using the method of simulated moments. *Marketing Science* **11**: 386–407.

Dagsvik J. 1994. Discrete and continuous choice, max-stable processes, and independence from irrelevant attributes. *Econometrica* **62**: 1179–1205.

Dubin J, Zeng L. 1991. The heterogeneous logit model, Caltech Social Science Working Paper: 759.

Enberg J, Gottschalk P, Wolf D. 1990. A random effects logit model of work welfare transitions. *Journal of Econometrics* **43**: 63–75.

Feller W. 1966. *An Introduction to Probability Theory and its Applications*, Vol. II. Wiley: New York.

Follman D, Lambert D. 1989. Generalized logistic regression by nonparametric mixing. *Journal of the American Statistical Association* **84**: 295–300.

Formann A. 1992. Linear logistic latent class analysis for polytomous data. *Journal of the American Statistical Association* **87**: 476–486.

Gonul F, Srinivasan K. 1993. Modeling multiple sources of heterogeneity in multinomial logit models. *Marketing Science* **12**: 213–229.

Hajivassiliou V, Ruud P. 1994. Classical estimation methods for LDV models using simulation. In *Handbook of Econometrics*, Vol. IV, Engle R, McFadden D (eds); 2384–2441.

Hajivassiliou V, McFadden D. 1997. The method of simulated scores with application to models of external debt crises. *Econometrica* **66**: 273–286.

Heckman J. 1981. Statistical models for discrete panel data. In *Structural analysis of Discrete Data with Econometric Applications*, Manski C, McFadden D (eds). MIT Press: Cambridge; 114–178.

Heckman J. 1981. The incidental parameters problem and the problem of initial conditions in estimating a discrete time–discrete data stochastic process. In *Structural analysis of Discrete Data with Econometric Applications*, Manski C, McFadden D (eds). MIT Press: Cambridge; 179–196.

Heckman J, Singer B. 1984. A method for minimizing the impact of distributional assumptions in econometric models for duration data. *Econometrica* **52**: 271–320.

Heckman J, Singer B. 1986. Econometric analysis of longitudinal data. In *Handbook of Econometrics*, Vol. III, Griliches Z, Intriligator M (eds). North-Holland: Amsterdam; 1689–1763.

Heckman J, Lochner L, Taber C. 1998. Explaining rising wage inequality: explorations with a dynamic general equilibrium model of labor earnings with heterogeneous agents. *Review of Economic Dynamics* **1**: 1–58.

Jain D, Vilcassim N, Chintagunta P. 1994. A random coefficients logit brand choice model applied to panel data. *Journal of Business and Economic Statistics* **12**: 317–328.

Lee LF, Chesher A. 1986. Specification testing when score test statistics are identically zero. *Journal of Econometrics* **31**: 121–149.

McFadden D, Reid F. 1975. Aggregate travel demand forecasting from disaggregated behavioral models. *Transportation Research Record: Travel Behavior and Values* **534**: 24–37.

McFadden D. 1984. Econometric analysis of qualitative response models. In *Handbook of Econometrics*, Vol. II, Griliches Z, Intriligator M (eds). North Holland: Amsterdam.

McFadden D. 1987. Regression-based specification tests for the multinomial logit model. *Journal of Econometrics* **34**: 63–82.

McFadden D. 1996. Lectures in simulation-assisted statistical inference. University of California, Berkeley, Working Paper.

McFadden D. 1989. A method of simulated moments for estimation of discrete choice models without numerical integration. *Econometrica* **57**: 995–1026.

McFadden D, Ruud P. 1994. Estimation by simulation. *Review of Economics and Statistics* **76**: 591–608.

Montgomery M, Richards T, Braun H. 1986. Child health, breast feeding, and survival in Malaysia: a random effects logit approach. *Journal of the American Statistical Association* **81**: 297–309.

Newey W, McFadden D. 1994. Large sample estimation and hypothesis testing. In *Handbook of Econometrics*, Vol. IV, Engle R, McFadden D (eds). North Holland: Amsterdam; 2111–2245.

Reader S. 1993. Unobserved heterogeneity in dynamic discrete choice models. *Environment and Planning A* **25**: 495–519.

Revelt D, Train K. 1998. Mixed logit with repeated choices: households' choices of appliance efficiency level. *Review of Economics and Statistics* **80**: 1–11.

Ruud P. 1996. Approximation and simulation of the multinomial probit model: an analysis of covariance matrix estimation, UC Berkeley Working Paper.

Steckel J, Vanhonacker W. 1988. A heterogeneous conditional logit model of choice. *Journal of Business and Economic Statistics* **6**: 391–398.

Stern S. 1994. Two dynamic discrete choice estimation problems and simulation method solutions. *Review of Economics and Statistics* **76**: 695–702.

Talvitie A. 1972. Comparison of probabilistic modal-choice models. *Highway Research Board Record* **392**: 111–120.

Train K. 1995. Simulation methods for probit and related models based on convenient error patitioning. Working Paper 95-237, Department of Economics, University of California, Berkeley.

Train K. 1998. Recreation demand models with taste differences over people. *Land Economics* **74**: 230–239.
Train K. 1999. Halton sequences for mixed logit. Dept. of Economics, Univ. of California, Berkeley.
Train K, McFadden D, Goett A. 1987. Consumer attitudes and voluntary rate schedules for public utilities. *Review of Economics and Statistics* **69**: 383–391.
Westin R. 1974. Predictions from binary choice models. *Journal of Econometrics* **2**: 1–16.
Westin R, Gillen D. 1978. Parking location and transit demand: a case study of endogenous attributes in disaggregate mode choice models. *Journal of Econometrics* **8**: 75–101.

[29]

ELSEVIER

Journal of Econometrics 89 (1999) 109–129

JOURNAL OF
Econometrics

Forecasting new product penetration with flexible substitution patterns

David Brownstone[a], Kenneth Train[b,*]

[a] *Department of Economics, University of California, Irvine, USA*

[b] *Department of Economics, University of California, Berkeley, 549 Evans Hall # 3880, Berkeley, CA 94720-3880, USA*

Abstract

We describe and apply choice models, including generalizations of logit called 'mixed logits,' that do not exhibit the restrictive 'independence from irrelevant alternatives' property and can approximate any substitution pattern. The models are estimated on data from a stated-preference survey that elicited customers' preferences among gas, electric, methanol, and CNG vehicles with various attributes. © 1999 Elsevier Science S.A. All rights reserved.

JEL classification: C15; C35; L62; R41

Keywords: Mixed logit; Random-coefficients logit; Probit; Simulation

1. Introduction

By far the most popular econometric models for forecasting demand for new products are logit and nested logit (McFadden, 1973, 1978; Ben-Akiva and Lerman, 1985). While computationally convenient, these models exhibit the well-known and restrictive 'independence from irrelevant alternatives,' or iia, property. Logit exhibits the property over all alternatives while nested logit exhibits it over alternatives within each nest. This property states that the ratio of the probabilities for any two alternatives is independent of the existence and

* Corresponding author. E-mail: train@econ.berkeley.edu; web site: http://else.berkeley.edu/~train

PII: S0304-4076(98)00057-8

attributes of any other alternative. As a result of this property, the models necessarily predict that a change in the attributes of one alternative (or the introduction of a new alternative, or the elimination of an existing alternative) changes the probabilities of the other alternatives proportionately, such that the ratios of probabilities remain the same. This substitution pattern can be unrealistic in many settings. For example, consider the introduction of electric cars, as examined, e.g., by Train (1980, 1986) and Brownstone et al. (1996). The logit model predicts that, among households with the same observed characteristics, the electric vehicle will draw the same proportion of households from large luxury gas cars as from small gas cars. However, if the electric car is similar in size to a subcompact gas car, one might expect the electric car to draw disproportionately from different classes of vehicles, with, for example, households who would have chosen a subcompact gas car switching more readily to the electric car than households who would have chosen a large gas car. More fundamentally, identification of the correct substitution pattern is an empirical issue, and the iia property of logit and nested logit imposes a particular substitution pattern rather than allowing the data analysis to find and reflect whatever substitution pattern actually occurs.

In this paper, we describe and estimate models for new product forecasting that can represent very general patterns of substitution. We first provide a general specification that distinguishes several types of models, particularly mixed logits with various structures and probits. These specifications have been known (citations given below), though perhaps not described in the same manner. More importantly, there have been few applications, particularly of mixed logits. We apply the models to data from a stated-preference survey on households' choices among gas, methanol, CNG, and electric vehicles.

2. Specification

A person faces a choice among J alternatives. Without loss of generality, the person's utility from any alternative can be decomposed into a nonstochastic, linear-in-parameters part that depends on observed data, a stochastic part that is perhaps correlated over alternatives and heteroskedastic over people and alternatives, and another stochastic part that is independently, identically distributed (iid) over alternatives and people. In particular, the utility from alternative i is denoted $U_i = \beta' x_i + [\eta_i + \varepsilon_i]$ where x_i is a vector of observed variables relating to alternative i and the person; β is a vector of parameters to be estimated which are fixed over people and alternatives; η_i is a random term with zero mean whose distribution over people and alternatives depends in general on underlying parameters and observed data relating to alternative i; and ε_i is a random term with zero mean that is iid over alternatives, does not depend on underlying parameters or data, and is normalized to set the scale of utility.

Stacking the utilities, we have: $U = \beta'X + [\eta + \varepsilon]$ where $V(\varepsilon) = \alpha I$ with known (i.e., normalized) α and $V(\eta)$ is general and can depend on underlying parameters and data. For standard logit, each element of ε is iid extreme value, and, more importantly, η is zero, such that the unobserved portion of utility (i.e., the term in brackets) is independent over alternatives. This independence gives rise to the iia property and its restrictive substitution patterns. We consider below models that allow correlation and heteroskedasticity.

2.1. Mixed logit: General distribution for η and extreme value for ε

Let each element of ε be iid extreme value as for standard logit; however, allow any distribution for η. Denote the density of η as $f(\eta|\Omega)$ where Ω are the fixed parameters of the distribution. Given the value of η, the conditional choice probability is simply logit, since the remaining error term is iid extreme value

$$L_i(\eta) = \exp(\beta' x_i + \eta_i) \Big/ \sum_j \exp(\beta' x_j + \eta_j). \tag{1}$$

Since η is not given, the (unconditional) choice probability is this logit formula integrated over all values of η weighted by the density of η

$$P_i = \int L_i(\eta) f(\eta|\Omega)\, d\eta. \tag{2}$$

Models of this form are called 'mixed logit' since the choice probability is a mixture of logits with f as the mixing distribution. The probabilities do not exhibit iia and different substitution patterns are attained by appropriate specification of f.

The choice probability cannot be calculated exactly because the integral does not have a closed form in general. The integral is approximated through simulation. For a given value of the parameters Ω, a value of η is drawn from its distribution. Using this draw, the logit formula $L_i(\eta)$ is calculated. This process is repeated for many draws, and the average of the resulting $L_i(\eta)$'s is taken as the approximate choice probability:

$$\mathrm{SP}_i = (1/R) \sum_{r=1,\ldots,R} L_i(\eta^r), \tag{3}$$

where R is the number of replications (i.e., draws of η), η^r is the rth draw, and SP_i is the simulated probability that the person chooses alternative i. By construction, SP_i is an unbiased estimate of P_i for any R; its variance decreases as R increases. It is strictly positive for any R, such that $\ln(\mathrm{SP}_i)$ is always defined, which is important when using SP_i in a log-likelihood function (as below). It is smooth (i.e., twice differentiable) in parameters and variables, which helps in the calculation of elasticities and especially in the numerical search for the maximum of the likelihood function. The simulated probabilities sum to one over alternatives, which is useful in forecasting.

The choice probabilities depend on parameters β and Ω, which are to be estimated. Adding subscript n to index sampled individuals and denoting the chosen alternative for each person by i, the log-likelihood function $\sum_n \ln(P_{ni})$ is approximated by the simulated log-likelihood function $\sum_n \ln(\mathrm{SP}_{ni})$ and the estimated parameters are those that maximize the simulated log-likelihood function.[1] Lee (1992) and Hajivassiliou and Ruud (1994) derive the asymptotic distribution of the maximum simulated likelihood estimator based on smooth probability simulators with the number of replications increasing with sample size. Under regularity conditions, the estimator is consistent and asymptotically normal. When the number of replications rises faster than the square root of the number of observations, the estimator is asymptotically equivalent to the maximum likelihood estimator.

The earliest applications of mixed logit were apparently the automobile demand models of Boyd and Melman (1980) and Cardell and Dunbar (1980). These researchers used aggregate, market-share data rather than customer-specific choice data. As a result, the computationally difficult integration for the choice probabililities (which in their case where shares) needed to be performed only once rather than for each customer in a sample. Recent applications (cited below) have used customer-specific data. These applications have placed various structures on the mixed logit specification, or, more precisely, on the specification of f. In Section 3 below, as in Train (1995) and Ben-Akiva and Bolduc (1996), we specify an error-components structure: $U_i = \beta' x_i + \mu' z_i + \varepsilon_i$ where μ is a random vector with zero mean that does not vary over alternatives and has density $g(\mu|\Omega)$ with parameters Ω; z_i is a vector of observed data related to alternative i; and ε_i is iid extreme value. This is a mixed logit with a particular structure for η, namely, $\eta_i = \mu' z_i$. The terms in $\mu' z_i$ are interpreted as error components that induce heteroskedasticity and correlation over alternatives in the unobserved portion of utility: $E([\mu' z_i + \varepsilon_i]\,[\mu' z_j + \varepsilon_j]) = z_i' V(\mu) z_j$. Even if the elements of μ are uncorrelated such that $V(\mu)$ is diagonal, the unobserved portion of utility is still correlated over alternatives.

In this specification, the choice probabilities are simulated by drawing values of μ from its distribution and calculating $\eta_i = \mu' z_i$. Insofar as the number of error components (i.e., the dimension of μ) is smaller than the number of alternatives

[1] Note that even though SP_i is unbiased for P_i, $\ln(\mathrm{SP}_i)$ is a biased estimator of $\ln(P_i)$ for finite R, such that simulator induces bias in the log-likelihood function. This bias decreases as R increases and, as stated, when R increases faster than the square root of the number of observations, disappears asymptotically. While we utilize maximum simulated likelihood (MSL) estimation, as do all the empirical studies cited below, other forms of parameter estimation could be applied, such as method of simulated moments (MSM), method of simulated scores, or Gibbs resampling. See, e.g., McFadden and Ruud (1994).

(the dimension of η), placing an error-components structure on a mixed logit reduces the dimension of integration and hence simulation that is required for calculating the choice probabilities.

Different patterns of correlation, and hence different substitution patterns, are obtained through appropriate specification of z_i and g. For example, an analog[2] to nested logit is obtained as follows. The alternatives are grouped into K nests, labeled $k = 1, \ldots, K$. For nest k, define a dummy variable d_i^k that equals 1 if alternative i is in nest k, and zero otherwise. Define z_i as the vector composed of these dummy variables: $z_i = \{d_i^1, \ldots, d_i^K\}'$. Finally, specify μ to be a vector of K iid deviates, such that $V(\mu)$ is diagonal with elements σ_k, $k = 1, \ldots, K$. Then the unobserved portion of utility is correlated for any two alternatives within a nest and uncorrelated for alternatives in different nests: for any $i \neq j$, $E[(\mu' z_i + \varepsilon_i)(\mu' z_j + \varepsilon_j)] = \sigma_k$ if i and j are in nest k, and $= 0$ if i and j are in different nests. The pattern of correlation is therefore the same as in a nested logit. Constraining the elements of μ to have the same variance, i.e., $\sigma_k = \sigma$ for all k, is analogous to restricting the correlations within a nested logit model to be the same for all nests.[3] In both cases, the correlation is the same within all nests. Overlapping nests can be handled by allowing alternatives to enter more than one nest in the definition of z_i.

Mixed logits with error-components are more general than their specification and our illustration with nested logit might immediately suggest. Importantly, McFadden and Train (1997) show that any random utility model can be approximated arbitrarily closely by a mixed logit with an error-components structure and appropriate choice of the z_i's and g. This result differs critically and is stronger than the 'mother logit' theorem, which states that any choice model can be approximated by a model that takes the form of a standard (i.e., non-mixed) logit (McFadden, 1975; Train, 1986, pp. 21–24.) In the mother logit theorem, any choice model can be expressed as a standard logit if attributes of one alternative are allowed to be entered in the 'representative utility' other alternatives. However, when cross-alternative attributes are entered, the logit model is no longer a random utility model (i.e., is not consistent with utility maximizing behavior and cannot be used for welfare analysis) since the utility of one alternative depends on the attributes of other alternatives. In the theorem

[2] By 'analog' we mean that the mixed logit contains the same pattern of correlation as a nested logit, namely, equal correlation between all pairs of alternatives within a nest and no correlation over alternatives in different nests. The models are not exactly the same because the distributions are different: unobserved utility in a nested logit follows a generalized extreme value distribution which cannot be obtained exactly as the sum of several random variables. However, as mentioned below, the proof of McFadden and Train (1996) indicates that a mixed logit can approximate a nested logit arbitrarily closely.

[3] In the terminology of nested logit models, this is equivalent to restricting the 'log-sum coefficients' to be the same for all nests.

regarding mixed logits, any random utility model can be approximated by a mixed logit with an error-components structure without entering cross-alternative variables, or, more precisely, while still maintaining the mixed logit as a random utility model.

Most recent empirical work with mixed logits has been motivated by a random-parameters, or random-coefficients, specification (Allenby and Lenk, 1994;[4] Bhat, 1996a, b; Mehndiratta, 1996; Revelt and Train, 1998; Train, 1998). The difference between a random-parameters and an error-components specification is entirely interpretation. In the random-parameters specification, the utility from alternative i is $U_i = b'x_i + \varepsilon_i$ where coefficients b are random with mean β and deviations μ. Then $U_i = \beta' x_i + [\mu' x_i + \varepsilon_i]$, which is an error-components structure with $z = x$. Elements of x that do not enter z can be considered variables whose coefficients do not vary in the population. And elements of z that do not enter x can be considered variables whose coefficients vary in the population but with zero means.

Other types of mixed logits have also been used. Elrod (1988) and Erdem (1995) provide a factor-analytic structure to η. This specification is the same as the error-components described above with the important difference that the z_i's are estimated (subject to normalization) rather than being observed variables. Ben-Akiva and Bolduc (1996) specify a 'general autoregressive' error structure, under which each η_i is correlated with each other η_j for all $j \neq i$ with the covariance being proportional to weights associated with each i–j pair. This set-up is particularly useful for spatial choice models (such as destination choice for travel and shipping), with the weight for any two locations reflecting the distance between the them.

Ben-Akiva and Bolduc (1996) use the term 'probit with a logit kernel' to describe any model where η is normally distributed but the elements of ε are iid extreme value. This term is instructive since it points out that the distinction between pure probit models (with all components of the error being normal) and mixed logits with a normal mixing distribution (where all error components are normal except the final component which is iid extreme value) is conceptually minor and might be empirically indistinguishable. Unlike pure probits, however, mixed logits can represent situations where η is not normal, as might arise when random coefficients must take a particular sign (such as a price coefficient that must be negative for all people) such that the unrestricted range of the normal is inappropriate.

2.2. *Mixed probits: General distribution for η and standard normal for ε*

When the elements of ε are iid standard normal, then a family of models arises that is analogous to that discussed above for extreme value ε and with estimation performed by the same type of simulation. However, a mixed probit

[4] Allenby and Lenk include autocorrelated additive error terms in addition to random parameters.

requires one additional dimension of simulation relative to a mixed logit (Train, 1995.) In particular, the probability of alternative i conditional on η is $\text{Prob}(\beta' x_i + \eta_i + \varepsilon_i > \beta' x_j + \eta_j + \varepsilon_j \forall j \neq i) = \text{Prob}(\varepsilon_j - \varepsilon_i < \beta'(x_i - x_j) + \eta_i - \eta_j \; \forall j \neq i)$. In a mixed logit, this probability is the logit formula; however, in a mixed probit, it is a multi-dimensional integral since $\varepsilon_j - \varepsilon_i$ is correlated over j's due to the common influence of ε_i. Conditional on η and ε_i, the conditional choice probability for a mixed probit, labeled $M_i(\eta, \varepsilon_i)$, is a product of univariate cumulative normals, which is easy to calculate: $M_i(\eta, \varepsilon_i) = \Pi_{j \neq i} \Phi(\beta'(x_i - x_j) + \eta_i - \eta_j + \varepsilon_i)$, where Φ is the standard normal distribution. The choice probabilities for a mixed probit are therefore simulated as $\text{SP}_i = (1/R) \sum_{r=1,\ldots,R} M_i(\eta^r, \varepsilon_i^r)$.[5] Conditioning on ε_i adds an extra dimension of simulation relative to mixed logit; therefore, unless there is a reason to expect ε to be normal instead of extreme value, assuming ε to be extreme value seems preferable on pragmatic grounds for general distributions of η.

2.3. *Pure probits: Normal η and standard normal for ε*

When η is normal as well as ε, then the model is a pure probit and simulation methods that have been developed for probits can be utilized. The model can be characterized as $U_i = \beta' x_i + \xi_j$ where the vector of unobserved utility components $\xi = (\xi_1, \ldots, \xi_J)'$ is distributed normal with zero mean and covariance matrix Λ. Given our notation, $\xi_i = \eta_i + \varepsilon_i$, and any of the structures given above can be placed on η (provided the distributions are normal), which gives a structure to Λ. Hajivassiliou et al. (1992) describe and compare, using Monte Carlo methods, several probit simulators. These simulators differ structurally from the simulator described above for mixed logits. In particular, the probit simulators are based on draws of ξ (or more precisely, on draws of the difference between ξ_j for each non-chosen alternative and ξ_i for the chosen alternative) while the mixed logit simulator is based on draws of the random terms that compose η. The probit simulators draw from a $(J-1)$-dimensional distribution of utility differences, while the mixed logit simulator draws from a mixing distribution whose dimension is determined by the specification of the model.

Hajivassiliou et al. (1992) found the GHK simulator (due to Geweke, 1991; Hajivassiliou and McFadden, 1990; Keane, 1990) performed better than other probit simulators for the specifications that they examined. To our knowledge, there has been no comparison of probit simulators with the simulator for mixed logit with normal η. (As stated above, these are essentially the same models, with the only difference being that the iid term is normal in the pure probit and extreme value in this version of the mixed logit.) We provide a comparison on our data set. However, the advantages and limitations of

[5] This is essentially the Stern (1992) simulator generalized to allow for non-normal distributions of η.

each depend on the specific situation. For example, in situations where the dimension of the mixing distribution is less than the number of alternatives (as in Train, 1998, which had 59 alternatives and seven error components), the mixed logit simulator might have an advantage simply because the simulation is over fewer dimensions. The opposite occurs when the dimension of the mixing distribution exceeds the number of alternatives (as in Revelt and Train, 1998).

In the following section we estimate: (1) a mixed logit with an error-components structure and normally distributed η, (2) a pure probit with the same structure, and (3) a mixed logit with some elements of η being non-normal. Before describing the models, we describe the data that were used in estimation.

3. Estimated models

3.1. Data

We utilize the survey data collected and described by Brownstone et al. (1996) on households' attitudes and preferences regarding alternative-fuel vehicles. Their sample was identified using pure random digit dialing, geographically stratified into 79 areas covering most of urbanized California. An initial computer-aided telephone interview (CATI) was completed for each of 7387 households. This initial CATI collected information on household structure, vehicle inventory, housing characteristics, basic employment and commuting for all adults, and the household's intended next vehicle transaction.

The data from the initial CATI were used to produce a customized mail-out questionnaire for each sampled household. This questionnaire contained a stated preference (SP) discrete-choice experiment. SP data have been used extensively in marketing and demand studies, especially for new products for which historic data on market choices are unavailable (see, e.g., Green and Srinivasan, 1990; Hensher, 1992; Louviere, 1994.) An example SP task from the questionnaire is given in Fig. 1. Three hypothetical vehicles with different fuel types were described, each of which was available in either of two different body types. The respondents was asked to choose among the six options.[6] There were four possible fuel types (gasoline, compressed natural gas, methanol, and electric), three of which appeared in each SP question. There were 10–12

[6] Respondents were also asked to state their second choice. We did not utilize the second-choice data in our analysis. Logit models estimated on the first and second choice responses yielded essentially the same parameter estimates with only slightly smaller standard errors. Also, the inclusion of two choices for each respondent makes the estimation of mixed logits and pure probits somewhat more complicated (so as to incorporate the correlation in unobserved factors over the two choices) and increases the computer time required for estimation by considerably more than twice. See Revelt and Train (1998) and Train (1998) for estimation of mixed logits with repeated choices for each decisionmaker.

Suppose that you were considering purchasing a vehicle and the following three vehicles were available: (assume that gasoline costs $1.20 per gallon)

	Vehilce A	Vehilce B	Vehicle C
Fuel Type	Electric Runs on electricity only	Natural Gas (CNG) Runs on CNG only	Methanol Can also run on gasoline
Vehicle Range	80 miles	120 miles	300 miles on methanol
Purchase Price	$21,000 (includes home charge unit)	$19,000 (includes home refueling unit)	$23,000
Home refueling time	8 hrs for full charge (80 miles)	2 hrs to fill empty tank (120 miles)	Not available
Home refueling cost	2 cents per mile (50 mpg gasoline equivalent)	4 cents per mile (25 mpg gasoline equivalent)	
Service station refueling time	10 min. for full charge (80 mi.)	10 min. to fill empty CNG tank (120 mi.)	6 min. to fill empty tank (300 mi.)
Service station fuel cost	10 cents per mile (10 mpg gasoline equivalent)	4 cents per mile (25 mpg gasoline equivalent)	4 cents per mile (25 mpg gasoline equivalent)
Service station availability	1 recgarge station for every 10 gasoline stations	1 CNG station for every 10 gasoline stations	Gasoline available at current stations
Acceleration Time to 30 mph	6 seconds	2.5 seconds	4 seconds
Top speed	65 miles per hour	80 miles per hour	80 miles per hour
Tailpipe emissions	'Zero' tailpipe emissions	25% of new 1993 gasoline car emissions when run on CNG	Like new 1993 gasoline cars when run on methnaol
Vehicle size	Like a compact car	like a sub-compact car	Like a mid-size car
Body types	Car or truck	Car or van	Car or truck
Luggage space	Like a comparable gasoline vehcile	Like a comparable gasoline vehicle	Like a comparable gasoline vehicle

Given these choices, which vehicle would you purchase? (please circle one choice)

1) Vehicle "A" (car)
2) Vehicle "A" (truck)
3) Vehicle "B" (car)
4) Vehicle "B" (van)
5) Vehicle "C" (car)
6) Vehicle "C" (truck)

Fig. 1. Vehicle choice survey question.

attributes per vehicle per choice set, depending upon the fuel type of the vehicle. Four levels were used to cover the range of most attributes. Variation in the attribute levels was obtained through an orthogonal main effects design. Respondents were specially instructed to treat all non-listed attributes (e.g., maintenance costs and safety) as identical for all vehicles in the choice set.

4747 households successfully completed the mail-out portion of the survey, which constitutes a 66% response rate among the households that completed the initial CATI. A comparison with Census data reveals that the sample is slightly biased toward home-owning larger households with higher incomes. Of these 4747 respondents, 4654 had sufficient non-missing information to use in model estimation.

The variables that enter the model are defined in Table 1. The choice of variables to enter the nonstochastic portion of utility was determined though exploration and testing with a standard logit model. Most of the variables are self-explanatory; however, a few notes are required. (i) Dividing price by the natural log of income provides a higher log-likelihood for the logit model than: not dividing by income, dividing by untransformed income, or dividing by the square root of income (with price and income always measured in thousands of dollars.) The price coefficient for a respondent with median income is essentially the same under any of these specifications. (ii) The questionnaire described to the respondent the cost of recharging/refueling the vehicle at a station, as well as, for electric and compressed natural gas (CNG) vehicles, the cost of refueling at home. We found that station refueling cost is not significant for electric vehicles and home refueling cost is not significant for CNG vehicles. Consistent with these findings, the variable that enters the model is defined as home refueling cost for electric vehicles and station refueling cost for non-electric vehicles. (iii) When a separate constant is included for each size class, with the constant for the mini class normalized to zero, the estimated coefficients obtain the following pattern nearly exactly: the coefficient for compacts is twice that of subcompacts, and the coefficients for mid-sized and large vehicles are equal to each other and are three times that of subcompacts. The size variable that enters the model is a parsimonious representation of this result: 0 for mini, 1 for subcompact, 2 for compact, and 3 for mid-size and large (multiplied by 0.1 for scaling.)[7]

3.2. Standard logit and mixed logit estimates

Column 1 of Table 2 gives the estimated parameters and standard errors for a standard logit model. Column 2 presents a mixed logit with the same specification for the non-stochastic portion of utility plus four error components. The first and second error components are iid normal deviates that enter the utility for each non-electric vehicle and each non-CNG vehicle, respectively. These error components are motivated by the nested logit specification of Bunch and Bradley (1995), which contains nests for non-electric and non-CNG vehicles. The third and fourth error components relate to the dimensions of the vehicle. In particular, the third error component is a normal deviate multiplied by the size variable described above, and the fourth error component is a normal deviate

[7] Interating to the maximum of the objective function with quasi-Newton Raphson procedures, as we use, is faster when variables are scaled such that the elements of the diagonal of the Hessian have approximately the same magnitude.

Table 1
Variable definitions

Variable names	Definitions
Price/ln(income)	Purchase price in thousands of dollars, divided by the natural log of household income in thousands
Range	Hundreds of miles that the vehicle can travel between refuelings/rechargings
Acceleration	Seconds required to reach 30 mph from stop, in tens of seconds (e.g., 3 s is entered as 0.3)
Top speed	Highest speed that the vehicle can attain, in hundreds of miles/h (e.g., 80 mph is entered as 0.80)
Pollution	Tailpipe emissions as fraction of comparable new gas vehicle
Size	0 = mini, 0.1 = subcompact, 0.2 = compact, 0.3 = mid-size or large
'Big enough'	1 if household size is over 2 and vehicle size is 3; 0 otherwise
Luggage space	Luggage space as fraction of comparable new gas vehicle
Operating cost	Cost per mile of travel, in tens of cents per mile (e.g., 5 cents/mile is entered as 0.5.) For electric vehicles, cost is for home recharging. For other vehicles, cost is for station refueling
Station availability	Fraction of stations that have capability to refuel/recharge the vehicle
Sports utility vehicle	1 for sports utility vehicle, zero otherwise
Sports car	1 for sports car, zero otherwise
Station wagon	1 for station wagon, zero otherwise
Truck	1 for truck, zero otherwise
Van	1 for van, zero otherwise
Constant for EV	1 for electric vehicle, zero otherwise
Commute $< 5 \times$ EV	1 if respondent commutes less than five miles each day and vehicle is electric; zero otherwise
College $\times$ EV	1 if respondent had some college education and vehicle is electric; zero otherwise
Constant for CNG	1 for compressed natural gas vehicle, zero otherwise
Constant for methanol	1 for methanol vehicle, zero otherwise
College $\times$ methanol	1 if respondent had some college education and vehicle is methanol; zero otherwise
Non-EV	1 if vehicle is not electric; zero if electric
Non-CNG	1 if vehicle is not CNG; zero if CNG

multiplied by the luggage space variable. To be precise, the stochastic portion of utility for alternative i is defined as $[\sum_{k=1-4}\sigma_k(\varsigma_k z_{ki})] + \varepsilon_i$ where ς_k is iid standard normal, z_{ki} are the four variables described above, and ε_i is iid extreme value. The parameters $\sigma_1, \ldots, \sigma_4$ are estimated; each denotes the standard deviation of the normal deviate that generates that error component. In simulating the choice probability for a respondent, four numbers are drawn from a random-number generator for the standard normal distribution; the four 'variables' $\varsigma_1 z_{1i}$–$\varsigma_4 z_{4i}$ are created; and the conditional probability is evaluated with coefficients $\sigma_1, \ldots, \sigma_4$ for the four 'variables.' This process is repeated for numerous draws and the conditional probabilities are averaged to obtain the simulated probability. We used 250 draws in estimation of the mixed logit model.[8]

The error components enter significantly. Gas and methanol vehicles enter both the no-EV and non-CNG error components, unlike electric and CNG vehicles which enter only one. The covariance in the stochastic portion of utility is therefore greater for gas and methanol vehicles than other pairs of fuels. CNG vehicles enter the non-EV component, which has a larger coefficient than the non-CNG component; the covariance between the stochastic portion of utility for CNG vehicles with that for gas and methanol vehicles is larger than for electric vehicles with gas and methanol vehicles. Stated succinctly, the following pairs are given in order of decreasing covariance: a gas vehicle paired with a methanol vehicle, gas or methanol paired with CNG, gas or methanol paired with electric, CNG paired with electric.

The error component associated with the variable 'size' induces covariance across size classes. Since the variable is largest for mid-size and large vehicles, the covariance is largest for these. The covariance decreases for mid-size or large vehicles paired with either compact, subcompact, and mini vehicles, respectively. Similarly, the error component associated with luggage space induces greater covariance for pairs of vehicles with greater luggage space. As a referee pointed out for us, significant variation in the value of luggage space is expected, since

[8] Different draws are taken for different respondents. McFadden (1989) indicates the importance, in the context of method of simulated moments estimation, of taking different draws for each observation: with different draws for each observation, the simulation error in the simulated probability is uncorrelated over observations and tends to cancel out when the simulated probability is averaged over observations. With maximum simulated likelihood (MSL) estimation, the average of the log of the simulated probability is utilized rather than the average of the untransformed probabilities. Since the log of the simulated probability is not an unbiased estimate of the log of the true probability, the canceling-out can only be shown to occur in MSL when the number of replications is sufficiently large as to effectively eliminate the bias. However, some type of canceling probably occurs even with fewer replications. Lee (1992) describes the properties of MSL estimators when the same draws are used for all observations.

households that use the vehicle for commuting would generally place a lower value on luggage space than those who use the vehicle primarily for vacations and out-of-town trips. The luggage space variable probably also served as a second indication of vehicles' overall dimensions. Respondents were told the size class of each vehicle as well as the luggage space relative to a comparable gas vehicle. Respondents could easily consider the luggage space information as an indication of relative dimensions of the vehicle within the fairly broad size classes. For example, if a respondent is told that an electric vehicle is a mini with

Table 2
Models of vehicle choice

	Standard logit		Mixed logit A	
	Estimate	Std. error	Estimate	Std. error
Variables				
Price/ln(income)	− 0.185	0.027	− 0.264	0.043
Range	0.350	0.027	0.517	0.058
Acceleration	− 0.716	0.111	− 1.062	0.186
Top speed	0.261	0.080	0.307	0.115
Pollution	− 0.444	0.100	− 0.608	0.139
Size	0.935	0.311	1.435	0.508
'Big enough'	0.143	0.076	0.224	0.113
Luggage space	0.501	0.188	1.702	0.482
Operating cost	− 0.768	0.073	− 1.224	0.159
Station availability	0.413	0.097	0.616	0.145
Sports utility vehicle	0.820	0.144	0.901	0.148
Sports car	0.637	0.156	0.700	0.162
Station wagon	− 1.437	0.065	− 1.500	0.067
Truck	− 1.017	0.055	− 1.086	0.056
Van	− 0.799	0.053	− 0.816	0.056
Constant for EV	− 0.179	0.169	− 1.032	0.425
Commute < 5 × EV	0.198	0.082	0.372	0.166
College × EV	0.443	0.108	0.766	0.218
Constant for CNG	0.345	0.091	0.626	0.148
Constant for methanol	0.313	0.103	0.415	0.146
College × methanol	0.228	0.089	0.313	0.124
Error components				
Non-EV			2.464	0.541
Non-CNG			1.072	0.377
Size			7.455	1.819
Luggage space			5.994	1.248
Log-likelihood	− 7391.83		− 7375.34	

Table 2 Continued

	Probit		Mixed logit B		
	Estimate	Std. error	Estimate		Std. error
Variables					
Price/ln(income)	– 0.184	0.031	– 0.286	– 5.999	0.172
Range	0.371	0.044	0.588	– 0.877	0.126
Acceleration	– 0.761	0.136	– 1.046	– 0.302	0.190
Top speed	0.207	0.082	0.361	– 1.364	0.335
Pollution	– 0.414	0.098	– 0.695	– 0.711	0.234
Size	0.983	0.363	1.541		0.533
'Big enough'	0.164	0.080	0.246	– 1.748	0.495
Luggage space	1.333	0.371	1.563		0.463
Operating cost	– 0.894	0.121	– 1.318	– 0.071	0.135
Station availability	0.434	0.103	0.674	– 0.741	0.236
Sports utility vehicle	0.594	0.103	0.897		0.149
Sports car	0.448	0.114	0.698		0.163
Station wagon	– 1.085	0.049	– 1.508		0.067
Truck	– 0.798	0.041	– 1.094		0.056
Van	– 0.614	0.042	– 0.819		0.056
Constant for EV	– 1.058	0.359	– 0.905		0.418
Commute $< 5 \times$ EV	0.294	0.136	0.359		0.163
College $\times$ EV	0.615	0.181	0.770		0.218
Constant for CNG	0.465	0.108	0.621		0.152
Constant for methanol	0.315	0.101	0.476		0.154
College $\times$ methanol	0.203	0.086	0.335		0.128
Error components					
Non-EV	2.232	0.435	2.289		0.553
Non-CNG	0.707	0.300	0.971		0.412
Size	5.187	1.434	6.808		2.072
Luggage space	4.823	0.935	5.380		1.293
Log-likelihood	– 7368.74			– 7375.19	

75% of the luggage space of a mini gas car, the respondent could logically think that the electric vehicle is smaller than a mini gas car–a mini–mini, so to speak.

The estimated parameters that enter the non-stochastic portion of utility are generally larger in magnitude in the mixed logit than the standard logit. This phenomenon is expected. The scale of utility is determined by the normalization of the iid term ε. In a standard logit, all stochastic terms are absorbed (as well as possible, given that they are not, in reality, all iid) into this one error term. The variance of this error term is larger in the standard logit model than in a mixed logit since, in the mixed logit, some of the variance in the stochastic portion of utility is captured in η rather than ε. Utility is scaled so that ε has the variance of an extreme value. Since the variance before scaling is larger in the standard logit than the mixed logit, utility (and hence the parameters) are scaled down in the standard logit relative to the mixed logit. This is the same result as obtained by Revelt and Train (1998).

The ratios of estimated parameters, which are the economically meaningful statistic, are very similar in the standard logit and mixed logit models. For example, the ratio of the first two coefficients (for price and range) is 0.529 in the standard logit and 0.511 in the mixed logit. The ratio of the second to the third coefficients (range and acceleration) is 0.489 in both models. Bhat (1996a) and Train (1998) also found the ratios of coefficients not to differ significantly between a standard and mixed logit, while Bhat (1996b) found fairly substantial differences.

3.3. Pure probit estimates

The third column of Table 2 presents the estimated parameters of a pure probit model. This model has the same specification as the mixed logit in column 2 except that the final term in the stochastic portion of utility, ε, consists of iid standard normal terms rather than iid extreme value. The choice probabilities are simulated with the GHK simulator. This simulator requires more computer time per replication than the mixed logit simulator; to keep the computer time manageable we reduced the number of replications to 50.[9]

The ratios of estimated parameters are similar in the pure probit model to those in the standard and mixed logits. The scale of the estimated parameters is

[9] We performed an experiment to compare the relative accuracy (or, more precisely, the simulation variance) of the GHK probit simulator and the mixed logit simulator. We calculated the simulated log-likelihood function at the estimated parameters in Table 2 separately ten times using ten different sets of random draws (i.e., different seeds for the random number generator.) We clocked the time required for each calculation and computed the variance in the simulated log-likelihood value over these ten sets of draws. The GHK probit simulator with 50 replications took an average of 51.0 seconds for each calculation of the simulated log-likelihood function and obtained a variance of 26.9 in the value of the simulated log-likelihood over the ten sets of draws. The mixed logit simulator with 50 replications took 19.8 seconds and obtained a variance of 35.3. The GHK probit simulator therefore had lower variance than the mixed logit simulator with the same number of replications. However, the mixed logit simulator took considerably less computer time. A mixed logit simulator with 125 replication took 48.1 seconds (which is about the same as the GHK probit simulator with 50 replications) and obtained a variance of 11.6 (which is less than half that of the GHK probit simulator with 50 replications.) These results suggest that: for a given number of replications the GHK probit simulator has somewhat less variance than the mixed logit simulator, while for a given amount of computer time, the mixed logit simulator has considerably lower variance.

about the same as in the standard logit. This is due to two counteracting factors. First, as described above for the mixed logit, the incorporation of part of the stochastic portion of utility into η rather than ε causes the parameters to rise in magnitude, since the parameters are scaled by the variance of ε. Second, the variance of a standard normal is smaller than that of an extreme value; therefore, utility is scaled down further in a probit model where ε is standard normal than in a logit model where ε is extreme value. In our application, it is simply a coincidence that these two factors have approximately the same impact, though in opposite directions, such that the probit parameters are similar in magnitude to the standard logit parameters. It is interesting to note that we did not use the logit parameters directly as starting values for the probit model but instead used the scaled logit parameters (i.e., the logit parameters divided by 1.6 to account for the difference in the variance between standard normal and extreme value). The iteration process moved the parameters back to the approximate scale of the original logit parameters. At convergence, the probit obtained a higher simulated log-likelihood value than the mixed logit. However, the difference is within the range expected simply from simulation variance.[10]

3.4. Mixed logit with additional error components

The fourth column of Table 2 presents a mixed logit with more error components than the mixed logit in column 2 and the pure probit. These extra error components do not have normal distributions; as a result, there is no pure probit analog to this model. The motivation and specification of this model require some discussion. We wanted to try a fairly complete random-parameters specification, in which households' tastes regarding each attribute of vehicles vary in the population. We first estimated a model in which each of the following variables was assumed to have a coefficient that is distributed independently normally in the population with mean and standard deviation being estimated: price/ln(income), range, acceleration, pollution, size, big enough, luggage space, operating cost, station availability, the EV constant, and the CND constant. (Note that the mixed logit in column 2 could be interpreted as having random parameters for size, luggage space, EV constant, CNG constant.) In this specification, only one extra coefficient, beyond those four in the mixed logit model of

[10] Using the method described in the previous footnote, the simulation variance in the log-likelihood value for the probit with 50 replications is estimated as 26.9, and that for the mixed logit with 250 replications as 2.19. The simulation variance for the difference is therefore 29.1, such that the standard deviation is 5.4. The difference in simulated log-likelihood values is 7375.34-7368.74 = 6.6, which is 1.2 times the standard deviation of 5.4.

column 2, obtained a statistically significant standard deviation. More importantly, the model produced counter-intuitive forecasts under some scenarios. For example, the predicted share of households choosing a large, expensive gas car was predicted to rise in response to a 20% rise in the price of large gas cars. This phenomenon is a natural (though undesirable) consequence of having the coefficients of attributes take a normal distribution when in reality all households can be expected to have the same sign for their coefficients. For example, the price coefficient is necessarily negative for all households; and yet the normal distribution for this coefficient necessarily implies that some households have positive coefficients. In forecasting, the households with positive price coefficients prefer a vehicle more when its price rises. If the share of households with positive price coefficients is large compared to the share of households choosing a given vehicle, then the model can predict that a price increase raises demand. This phenomenon occurs not just for price but for any attribute whose coefficient is given a normal distribution and yet has an expected sign for all households. The phenomenon was evidenced in one of the models of Revelt and Train (1998) in forecasting the impact of rising interest rates on households' decisions to take loans. Pure probits with a random-parameters specification are, by their nature, susceptible to it.

The solution is to specify a density that is strictly positive only on one side of zero. For the model in column 4, we assume log-normal distributions for the coefficients of price/ln(income), range, acceleration, top speed, pollution, big enough, operating cost and station availability. Since the log-normal distribution gives positive coefficients, variables whose coefficients are necessarily negative (price/ln(income), acceleration, pollution, and operating cost) are entered as the negative of the variable. The four variables that enter the error components of the mixed logit in column 2, could logically take different signs by different households; these are therefore assumed to have normal distributions, as in the mixed logit model in column 2.

The kth coefficient with a log-normal distribution is specified as $\exp(b_k + s_k v_k)$, where v_k is iid standard normal and s_k and b_k are parameters. The mean coefficient is $\exp(b_k + (s_k^2/2))$ and the standard deviation of the coefficient is the mean multiplied by $\sqrt{(\exp(s_k^2) - 1)}$. In preliminary analysis, models with unrestricted b_k's and s_k's failed to converge, with one or more of the s_k's becoming so large that $\exp(b_k + s_k v_k)$ exceeded the numerical limit of the software. We therefore constrained the parameters such that the standard deviation of each log-normally distributed coefficient was equal to its mean. (Mechanically, we constrained each s_k to be 0.8326.) This constraint is appealing, since it results in a model with no more parameters than in the mixed logit in column 2 or the pure probit, and yet contains variation in the stochastic portion of utility over more attributes than in these models. The simulated log-likelihood value for this model is nearly the same as that for the mixed logit without the extra variation. While the extra variation does not improve the fit of the model, it changes the substitution patterns that are forecast by the model. The differences are explored below.

Table 2 gives two sets of estimates for the variables with log-normally distributed coefficients. On the right is the estimate of b_k for each coefficient; the standard error is for the estimate of b_k. On the left is the mean coefficient implied by the point estimate of b_k and the constrained value of s_k (multiplied by -1 if the negative of the variable was entered.). The left-hand number is comparable to the estimates in the previous columns for other models. The ratios of these estimates are similar to those in the other three models; the scale is similar to that of the mixed logit in column 2. If indeed the ratios of coefficients are adequately captured by a standard logit model, as our results and those of Bhat (1996a) and Train (1998) indicate, then the extra difficulty of estimating a mixed logit or a probit need not be incurred when the goal is simply estimation of willingness to pay, without using the model for forecasting.

3.5. Substitution patterns

The substitution patterns that are implied by the models can be compared through several examples. Suppose a small electric car is introduced to a base situation consisting of gas cars that range in size from small to large. The standard logit model, because of the iia property, implies that the new electric car will draw proportionately from all sizes of the gas cars. In contrast, the mixed logits and probit predict that the electric car will draw more proportionately from smaller gas cars than from larger gas cars. This more realistic substitution pattern is the consequence of the error component relating to size. It is particularly important for policy analysis. For example, electric cars are seen as a way of reducing gas consumption and tailpipe emissions. The predicted reductions are lower when households are predicted, realistically, to switch from small gas cars more readily than from large gas cars.

Suppose now that a large methanol car is added to the small electric and various sizes of gas cars. The logit model of course predicts proportionate switching. The mixed logits and probit predict disproportionate switching, with greater switching from the larger gas cars than the smaller gas cars, and with greater switching from the gas cars than the electric car. The later difference is due to the fact that the same error components enter for methanol and gas, indicating a similarity in households' views of these two types of fuel (relative to electric). This difference is reasonable, since refueling with methanol is essentially the same as refueling with gas, whereas the procedures for recharging an electric car are quite different.

The distinction between the two mixed logits is illustrated by considering the predicted impact of a rise in the price of large gas cars. As always, the standard logit predicts that households switch proportionately to each of the other size classes. The two mixed logits and the probit predict that households switch more readily to mid-size cars than to smaller cars, as one would expect in reality. However, the two mixed logits imply a different amount of switching in total. In particular, the mixed logit in column 4 of Table 2 predicts considerably less switching away from large cars in reaction to a price increase, than the mixed logit in column 2 or the probit. Recall that this model, unlike the other mixed logit or the probit, includes variation in the price coefficient over households. Households who place relatively little importance on price have a greater tendency to buy an expensive large car. And these households, since their price coefficient is relatively small, do not react to price increases as readily as a household with average price coefficient. As a result, the mixed logit with variation in the price coefficient would predict a smaller share of customers switching away from large cars when the price is raised. This example illustrates the flexibility of mixed logits to represent various substitution patterns.[11]

Acknowledgements

David Bunch and Tom Golob collected the data and conducted preliminary analyses upon which our analysis relies. We are grateful to them for allowing us to use the data. They are not, of course, responsible for any errors or representations that we made in this paper.

References

Allenby, G., Lenk, P., 1994. Modeling household purchase behavior with logistic normal regression. Journal of the American Statistical Association 89, 1218–1231.

Ben-Akiva, M., Bolduc, D., 1996. Multinomial probit with a logit kernel and a general parametetric specification of the covariance structure. Working paper, Department of Economics, MIT.

Ben-Akiva, M., Lerman, S., 1985. Discrete Choice Analysis. MIT Press, Cambridge, MA.

Bhat, C., 1996a. Accommodating variations in responsiveness to level-of-service measures in travel mode choice modeling. Working paper, Department of Civil Engineering, University of Massachusetts at Amherst.

Bhat, C., 1996b. Incorporating observed and unobserved heterogeneity in urban work travel mode choice modeling. Working paper, Department of Civil Engineering, University of Massachusetts at Amherst.

Boyd, J., Melman, R., 1980. The effect of fuel economy standards on the U.S. automotive market: An hedonic demand analysis. Transportation Research 14A, 367–378.

[11] GAUSS software to estimate mixed logits is available for downloading, along with a users' manual and sample runs, from Train's web site at http://elsa.berkeley.edu/ ~ train.

Brownstone, D., Bunch, D., Golob, T., Ren, W., 1996. Transactions choice model for forecasting demand for alternative-fuel vehicles. Research in Transportation Economics 4, 87–129.

Bunch, D., Bradley, M., 1995. Personal vehicle survey model results: Modeling reactions to hypothetical future alternative and conventional fuel vehicles. Working paper, Graduate School of Management, University of California, Davis.

Cardell, N., Dunbar, F., 1980. Measuring the societal impacts of automobile downsizing. Transportation Research 14A, 423–434.

Erdem, T., 1995. A dynamic analysis of market structure based on panel data. Working paper, Haas School of Business, University of California, Berkeley.

Elrod, T., 1988. Choice map: Inferring a product market map from observed choice behavior. Marketing Letters 2, 253–266.

Geweke, J., 1991. Efficient simulation from the multivariate normal and Student-t distributions subject to linear constraints. Computer Science and Statistics. Proceedings of the 23rd Symposium on the Interface. American Statistical Association, Alexandria, VA.

Green, P., Srinivasan, V., 1990. Conjoint analysis in marketing research: New developments and directions. Journal of Marketing 54, 3–19.

Hajivassiliou, V., McFadden, D., 1990. A method of simulated scores for the estimation of LDV models. Cowles Foundation Discussion paper #967, Yale University.

Hajivassiliou, V., McFadden, D., Ruud, P., 1992. Simulation of multivariate normal rectangle probabilities and their derivatives: theoretical and computational results. Cowles Foundation Discussion paper #1021, Yale University.

Hajivassiliou, V., Ruud, P., 1994. Classical estimation methods for LDV models using simulation. In: Engle, R., McFadden, D., (Eds.), Handbook of Econometrics, vol. IV. Elsevier, New York.

Hensher, D., 1992. Stated-preference analysis of travel choices: The state of the practice. Transportation 21, 107–133.

Keane, M., 1990. Four essays in empirical macro and labor economics. Ph.D. Dissertation, Brown University.

Lee, L., 1992. On efficiency of methods of simulated moments and maximum simulated likelihood estimation of discrete response models. Econometrica 8, 518–552.

Louviere, J., 1994. Comjoint analysis. In: Bagozzi, R. (Ed.), Advanced Methods of Marketing Research. Blackwell Publishers, Cambridge, MA.

McFadden, D., 1973. Conditional logit analysis of qualitative choice behavior. In Zarembka, P. (Ed.), Frontiers in econometrics. Academic Press, New York.

McFadden, D., 1975. On independence, structure and simultaneity in transportation demand analysis. Working paper # 7511, Urban Travel Demand Forecasting Project, Institute of Transportation and Traffic Engineering, University of California, Berkeley.

McFadden, D., 1978. Modeling the choice of residential location. In Karquist, A. et al. (Eds.), Spatial Interaction Theory and Planning Models. North-Holland, Amsterdam.

McFadden, D., 1989. A method of simulated moments for estimation of the multinomial probit without numerical integration. Econometrica 57, 995–1026.

McFadden, D., Train, K., 1997. Mixed MNL models of discrete choice. Working paper, Department of Economics, University of California, Berkeley.

McFadden, D., Ruud, P., 1994. Estimation by simulation. Review of Economics and Statistics 76, 591–608.

Mehndiratta, S., 1996. Time-of-day effects in inter-city business travel. Ph.D. Thesis, Department of Civil Engineering, University of California, Berkeley.

Revelt, D., Train, K., 1998. Mixed logit with repeated choices: Households' choices of appliance efficiency level. Review of Economics and Statistics, 80 (4).

Stern, S., 1992. A method for smoothing simulated moments of discrete probabilities in multinomial probit models. Econometrica 60, 943–952.

Train, K., 1980. The potential market for non-gasoline-powered automobiles. Transportation Research 14A, 405–414.

Train, K., 1986. Qualitative Choice Analysis. MIT Press, Cambridge, MA.

Train, K., 1995. Simulation methods for probit and related models based on convenient error partitioning. Working paper, Department of Economics, University of California, Berkeley.

Train, K., 1998. Recreation demand models with taste differences over people. Land Economics, 74(2) 230–239.

[30]

PERGAMON

Transportation Research Part B 35 (2001) 677–693

TRANSPORTATION RESEARCH PART B

www.elsevier.com/locate/trb

Quasi-random maximum simulated likelihood estimation of the mixed multinomial logit model

Chandra R. Bhat *

Department of Civil Engineering, University of Texas at Austin, ECJ 6.806, Austin, TX 78712-1076, USA

Received 19 May 1999; received in revised form 10 January 2000; accepted 21 January 2000

Abstract

This paper proposes the use of a quasi-random sequence for the estimation of the mixed multinomial logit model. The mixed multinomial structure is a flexible discrete choice formulation which accommodates general patterns of competitiveness as well as heterogeneity across individuals in sensitivity to exogenous variables. The estimation of this model has been achieved in the past using the pseudo-random maximum simulated likelihood method that evaluates the multi-dimensional integrals in the log-likelihood function by computing the integrand at a sequence of pseudo-random points and taking the average of the resulting integrand values. We suggest and implement an alternative quasi-random maximum simulated likelihood method which uses cleverly crafted non-random but more uniformly distributed sequences in place of the pseudo-random points in the estimation of the mixed logit model. Numerical experiments, in the context of intercity travel mode choice, indicate that the quasi-random method provides considerably better accuracy with much fewer draws and computational time than does the pseudo-random method. This result has the potential to dramatically influence the use of the mixed logit model in practice; specifically, given the flexibility of the mixed logit model, the use of the quasi-random estimation method should facilitate the application of behaviorally rich structures in discrete choice modeling.

Keywords: Mixed multinomial logit model; Maximum simulated likelihood estimation; Pseudo-random sequences; Quasi-random sequences; Polynomial-based cubature; Discrete choice analysis

1. Introduction

The econometric field has seen the increasing use of models that involve analytically intractable criterion functions during the estimation and inference process. The criterion function depends on

* Tel.: +1-512-471-4535; fax: +1-512-475-8744.
E-mail address: bhat@mail.utexas.edu (C.R. Bhat).

0191-2615/01/$ - see front matter
PII: S0191-2615(00)00014-X

the inference approach adopted and may take the form of a log-likelihood function (for the maximum likelihood inference approach), a pseudo-log likelihood function (for the pseudo-maximum likelihood inference approach), or a conditional moment function (for the Generalized Methods of Moments inference approach). The analytic intractability of the criterion function in all these instances usually arises because of the presence of multi-dimensional integrals.

The increasing use of models with analytically intractable criterion functions may be attributed to two reasons. First, analysts are formulating and estimating models which do not impose a priori behavioral restrictions on the mechanism underlying the decision process being examined. Many analytically tractable models, though elegant and simple in structure, maintain restrictions which are difficult to justify. For example, in a discrete choice context, the multinomial logit model has a simple form, but is saddled with the independent from irrelevant alternatives (IIA) property. Relaxing such rigid behavioral restrictions tends to lead to analytically intractable models. Second, the tools available for data processing have seen dramatic improvement over the past few years. This has made possible the implementation of numerical methods to evaluate multi-dimensional integrals in criterion functions.

The numerical methods to evaluate multi-dimensional integrals may be categorized into three broad groups: (a) multi-dimensional polynomial-based cubature methods, (b) Monte Carlo simulation methods, and (c) quasi-Monte Carlo simulation methods. We discuss each of these approaches in the subsequent paragraphs.

The multi-dimensional polynomial-based cubature methods are extensions of the one-dimensional quadrature principle. The theory of integration formulas in cubature methods are closely related to the theory of orthogonal polynomials (see Stroud, 1971). However, the construction of efficient integration formulas based on polynomial interpolation for multi-dimensional integration is substantially more difficult than for single dimensional integration. An important reason is that the theory of orthogonal polynomials is considerably more complex in more than one variable than in just one variable (see Cools, 1992; Cools and Rabinowitz, 1993). Consequently, polynomial interpolation-based integration is not generally considered for multi-dimensional integration, though it is the method of choice for one-dimensional integration. The one qualification to the above statement is when the region of integration is "nice" (say, the s-cube or the s-sphere) and when the multi-dimensional integral can be transformed into the product of s single integrals for which well-known Gaussian quadrature formulas exist. In such situations, one can construct product formulas from s one-dimensional Gauss formulas each of which use N points. The resulting product formula will contain N^s points. Unfortunately, this number (N^s) increases very rapidly with N and s (for example, with 15 one-dimensional evaluation points and just three-dimensions for integration, the total number of points for the product formula climbs to 3375!). Consequently, product formulas of one-dimensional Gauss formulas are unable to compute integrals with sufficient precision and speed for optimization of the criterion function in higher than two-dimensions (see Hajivassiliou and Ruud, 1994; Sloan and Joe, 1994, Chapter 1).

The Monte Carlo simulation method (or "the method of statistical trials") to evaluating multi-dimensional integrals entails computing the integrand at a sequence of "random" points and computing the average of the integrand values. The basic principle is to replace a continuous average by a discrete average over randomly chosen points. By the strong law of large numbers, convergence is almost sure in this method. The Monte Carlo simulation method has a long history, dating back to the work of Metropolis and Ulam (1949). The concept has been known even before that, though the practical viability of the method had to wait till the turn to the computer era in the early 1950s (Halton, 1970 presents an exhaustive review of the history of the method). Of course, in actual implementation, truly random sequences are not available; instead, deterministic pseudo-random sequences which appear random when subjected to simple statistical tests are used (see Niederreiter, 1995 for a discussion of pseudo-random sequence generation). This pseudo-Monte Carlo (or PMC) method has a slow asymptotic convergence rate with the expected integration error of the order of $N^{-0.5}$ (N being the number of pseudo-random points drawn from the s-dimensional integration space). Thus, to obtain an added decimal digit of accuracy, the number of draws needs to be increased hundred fold. Also, the PMC method does not distinguish between nicely behaved smooth integrands and poorly behaved non-smooth integrands. That is, smooth functions are not integrated any more accurately or efficiently than non-smooth functions (this is really the other side of the coin of the oft-touted advantage of the PMC method that it works for any integrand with a finite variance; see Spanier and Maize, 1994).

The quasi-Monte Carlo method is similar to the Monte Carlo method in that it evaluates a multi-dimensional integral by replacing it with an average of values of the integrand computed at discrete points. However, rather than using pseudo-random sequences for the discrete points, the quasi-Monte Carlo approach uses "cleverly" crafted non-random and more uniformly distributed sequences within the domain of integration. The underlying idea of the method is that it is really inconsequential whether the discrete points are truly random; of primary importance is the even distribution (or maximal spread) of the points in the integration space. The sequences used in the quasi-Monte Carlo (or QMC) method are labeled as quasi-random sequences, though this is a misnomer since randomness plays no part in the construction of the sequences. The convergence rate for quasi-random sequences is, in general, faster than for pseudo-random sequences. In particular, the theoretical upper bound for the integration error in the QMC method is of the order of N^{-1}, where N is the number of quasi-random integration points. [1]

To summarize, quasi-MC sequences are more uniformly distributed than random sequences (a uniformly distributed sequence can loosely be described as one which assigns to each sub-interval of the integration domain its "fair" percentage of points). Mathematicians use a measure called "discrepancy" to assess the uniformity of a sequence; lower discrepancy values implies greater uniformity. The discrepancy is directly related to the integration error bound and is of order $N^{-0.5}$ for the random sequences and of order N^{-1} for the quasi-random sequences. The lower discrepancy of the quasi-random sequences results in lower integration error and faster convergence rates. This is especially the case for well behaved and smooth integrands. Thus, for a given error tolerance level, the quasi-random simulation of integrals for smooth integrands

[1] The afore-mentioned convergence result for the QMC method holds only for integrands with bounded variation in the sense of Hardy and Krause; this requirement of the integrand is more restrictive than the finite variance requirement in the Monte Carlo method. But for most practical purposes, the restriction is not of a serious nature (see Niederreiter, 1995 or Morokoff and Caflisch, 1995 for a more detailed theoretical discussion). Also, the reader should note that the convergence result provided here is an upper bound; in the average case, Wozniakowski (1991) has shown a much faster convergence rate for QMC sequences. Further, Owen (1997, 1998) has shown recently that some scrambled versions of QMC sequences have a convergence rate of the order of N^{-3}.

requires significantly less number of simulation points or "draws" relative to the PMC method (see Morokoff and Caflisch, 1995; Press et al., 1992, Chapter 7; Bratley and Fox, 1988; Bratley et al., 1992). [2]

The appeal of the QMC method should be clear from the above discussion. The generation and application of QMC sequences for multi-dimensional integration has been the subject of intensive research in recent years in mathematics and physics (see, for example, Sloan and Wozniakowski, 1998; Owen, 1998; Mullen et al., 1995; Kocis and Whiten, 1997). Krommer and Ueberhuber (1994) provide an extensive review of quasi-random sequences. Against this backdrop of literature extolling the much faster convergence rate and superior accuracy of QMC methods over the PMC method, is the surprising lack of use of these methods in econometric model estimation. While the use of simulation techniques in model estimation has been the focus of much recent econometric work, almost all of this literature is based on the PMC method. Econometricians have refined the PMC method using variation reduction techniques such as stratified sampling, importance sampling, and antithetic variates (see, for example, Hajivassiliou et al., 1996); however, these are not specific to the PMC method and are as equally applicable to QMC methods (see Spanier and Maize, 1994).

The objective of this paper is to compare the performance of the polynomial-based cubature method (or simply the cubature method), the PMC method, and the QMC method using numerical experiments. The comparison is conducted in the context of the maximum simulated likelihood estimation of a mixed multinomial logit (MMNL) model. We use the MMNL model form in the numerical analysis for two reasons. First, the MMNL model is a very flexible discrete choice structure. As our review later indicates, it is becoming the method of preference to accommodate unobserved taste variations and general error variance-covariance matrices. Second, the integrands involved in the maximum likelihood estimation of the MMNL model have a multinomial logit structure, which is a very nicely behaved, continuous, and smooth function. Thus, the use of the QMC method would appear to be particularly suitable for the MMNL model. In contrast, all previous applications of the MMNL structure have used the PMC method, except for a very recent use of the QMC method in Bhat (1999a). If our numerical experiments indeed show that the QMC method is very efficient in the MMNL context, it could lead to the more widespread use of the flexible MMNL model.

There are several quasi-random sequences that may be employed in the QMC simulation method. Among these sequences are those that belong to the family of r-*adic* expansion of integers: the Halton, Faure, and Sobol sequences (see Bratley et al., 1992 for a good review). In this paper, we will use the Halton sequence in the QMC simulation because of its conceptual simplicity.

The rest of this paper is structured as follows. Section 2 discusses the structure of the mixed multinomial logit model. Section 3 presents the methodology to estimate the mixed logit model

[2] Theoretically speaking, the discrepancy of a quasi-random sequence also depends on the dimensionality of the integration, with the discrepancy (or integration error) increasing with dimensionality. However, in practice, studies (for example, see Papageorgiou and Traub, 1997 or Paskov, 1997) have shown the integration error to be independent of the number of dimensions. Sloan and Wozniakowski (1998) have recently examined the reasons for this superior empirical performance of the quasi-random sequences for high dimensionality of integration.

using the cubature method, the PMC method, and the QMC method. Section 4 describes the design for the numerical experiments. Section 5 identifies the performance criteria used in comparing alternative methods and presents the experimental results. The final section closes the paper.

2. Mixed multinomial logit model

The MMNL model is a generalization of the well-known multinomial logit (MNL) model. It involves the integration of the multinomial logit formula over the distribution of unobserved random parameters. It takes the structure shown below:

$$P_{qi}(\theta) = \int_{-\infty}^{+\infty} L_{qi}(\beta) f(\beta \mid \theta) \mathrm{d}(\beta), \quad L_{qi}(\beta) = \frac{\mathrm{e}^{\beta' x_{qi}}}{\sum_j \mathrm{e}^{\beta' x_{qj}}}, \tag{1}$$

where P_{qi} is the probability that individual q chooses alternative i, x_{qi} a vector of observed variables specific to individual q and alternative i, β represents parameters which are random realizations from a density function $f(\cdot)$, and θ is a vector of underlying moment parameters characterizing $f(\cdot)$.

The MMNL model structure of Eq. (1) can be motivated from two very different (but formally equivalent) perspectives. Specifically, a MMNL structure may be generated from an intrinsic motivation to allow flexible substitution patterns across alternatives (error-components structure) or from a need to accommodate unobserved heterogeneity across individuals in their sensitivity to observed exogenous variables (random-coefficients structure).

The error-components structure partitions the overall random term associated with each alternative's utility into two components: one component which allows the unobserved error terms to be non-identical and non-independent across alternatives, and the other which is specified to be independent and identically (type I extreme-value) distributed across alternatives. Specifically, consider the following utility function for individual q and alternative i:

$$U_{qi} = \gamma' y_{qi} + \zeta_{qi} = \gamma' y_{qi} + \mu' z_{qi} + \epsilon_{qi}, \tag{2}$$

where $\gamma' y_{qi}$ and ζ_{qi} are the systematic and random components of utility, and ζ_i is further partitioned into two components, $\mu' z_{qi}$ and $\epsilon_{qi} \cdot z_{qi}$ is a vector of observed data associated with alternative i, some of whose elements might also appear in the vector y_{qi}. μ is a random vector with zero mean. The component $\mu' z_{qi}$ induces heteroscedasticity and correlation across unobserved utility components of the alternatives. The emphasis in the error-components structure is to allow a flexible substitution pattern among alternatives in a parsimonious fashion. This is achieved by the "clever" specification of the variable vector z_{qi} combined with (usually) the specification of independent normally distributed random elements in the vector μ. Defining $\beta = (\gamma', \mu')'$ and $x_{qi} = (y'_{qi}, z'_{qi})'$ we obtain the MMNL model structure for the choice probability of alternative i for individual q. Applications of the error-components formulation include Brownstone and Train (1999) and Bhat (1998a, 1999b).

The random-coefficients structure allows heterogeneity in the sensitivity of individuals to exogenous attributes. The utility that an individual q associates with alternative i is written as

$$U_{qi} = \beta'_q x_{qi} + \epsilon_{qi}, \tag{3}$$

where x_{qi} is a vector of exogenous attributes, β_q is a vector of coefficients that varies across individuals with density $f(\beta)$, and ϵ_{qi} is assumed to be an independently and identically distributed (across alternatives) type I extreme value error term. With this specification, the unconditional choice probability of alternative i for individual q is given by the mixed logit formula of Eq. (1). While several density functions may be used for $f(\cdot)$, the most commonly used is the normal distribution. A log-normal distribution may also be used if, from a theoretical perspective, an element of beta has to take the same sign for every individual (such as a negative coefficient for the travel time parameter in a travel mode choice model). Applications of the random-coefficients formulation include Revelt and Train (1998), Train (1998), Bhat (1998b,1999a,b) and Ben-Akiva and Bolduc (1996).

The reader will note that the error-components specification in Eq. (2) and the random-coefficients specification in Eq. (3) are structurally equivalent. Specifically, if β_q is distributed with a mean of γ and deviation μ, then Eq. (3) is identical to Eq. (2) with $x_{qi} = y_{qi} = z_{qi}$. However, this apparent restriction for equality of Eqs. (2) and (3) is purely notational. Elements of x_{qi} that do not appear in z_{qi} can be viewed as variables whose coefficients are deterministic in the population, while elements of x_{qi} that do not enter in y_{qi} may be viewed as variables whose coefficients are randomly distributed in the population with mean zero.

In the numerical experiments in this paper, we use a random-coefficients interpretation of the mixed-logit structure. However, the results from the experiments should be generalizable to any model structure with a mixed-logit form.

3. Estimation methodology

This section discusses the details of the estimation procedure for the random-coefficients mixed-logit model using each of the three methods: the cubature method, the PMC method, and the QMC method.

Consider Eq. (3) and separate out the effect of variables with fixed coefficients (including the alternative specific constant) from the effect of variables with random coefficients

$$U_{qi} = \alpha_{qi} + \sum_{k=1}^{K} \beta_{qk} x_{qik} + \epsilon_{qi}, \tag{4}$$

where α_{qi} is the effect of variables with fixed coefficients. Let $\beta_{qk} \sim N(\mu_k, \sigma_k)$ so that $\beta_{qk} = \mu_k + \sigma_k s_{qk} (q = 1, 2, \ldots, Q;\ k = 1, 2, \ldots, K)$. [3] $s_{qk} (q = 1, 2, \ldots, Q;\ k = 1, 2, \ldots, K)$ is a standard normal variate. Further, let $V_{qi} = \alpha_{qi} + \sum_k \mu_k x_{qik}$.

[3] In this notation, we are implicitly assuming that the elements of the β_{qk} vector are independent of one another. Even if they are not, a simple Choleski decomposition can be undertaken so that the resulting integration involves independent normal variates (see Revelt and Train, 1998).

The log-likelihood function for the random-coefficients logit model may be written as

$$\begin{aligned}\mathscr{L} &= \sum_q \sum_i y_{qi} \log P_{qi} \\ &= \sum_q \sum_i y_{qi} \log \left\{ \int_{s_{q1}=-\infty}^{s_{q1}=+\infty} \int_{s_{q2}=-\infty}^{s_{q2}=+\infty} \cdots \int_{s_{qK}=-\infty}^{s_{qK}=+\infty} \frac{e^{V_{qi}+\sum_k \sigma_k s_{qk} x_{qik}}}{\sum_j e^{V_{qj}+\sum_k \sigma_k s_{qk} x_{qjk}}} \mathrm{d}\Phi(s_{q1}) \mathrm{d}\Phi(s_{q2}) \cdots \mathrm{d}\Phi(s_{qK}) \right\},\end{aligned} \tag{5}$$

where $\Phi(\cdot)$ represents the standard normal cumulative distribution function and

$$y_{qi} = \begin{cases} 1 & \text{if the } q\text{th individual chooses alternative } i \\ 0 & \text{otherwise.} \end{cases} \quad (q = 1, 2, \ldots Q,\ i = 1, 2, \ldots, I) \tag{6}$$

The cubature method, the PMC method, and the QMC method represent three different ways of evaluating the multi-dimensional integral involved in the log-likelihood function.

3.1. Polynomial-based cubature method

To apply the cubature method, define $\varpi_k = s_{qk}/\sqrt{2}$ for all q. Then, the log-likelihood function in Eq. (5) takes the following form:

$$\begin{aligned}\mathscr{L} = \sum_q \sum_i y_{qi} \log \Bigg\{ \left(\frac{1}{\sqrt{\pi}}\right)^K \int_{\varpi_1=-\infty}^{\varpi_1=+\infty} \int_{\varpi_2=-\infty}^{\varpi_2=+\infty} \cdots \int_{\varpi_K=-\infty}^{\varpi_K=+\infty} \\ \times \frac{e^{V_{qi}+\sqrt{2}\sum_k \sigma_k \varpi_k x_{qik}}}{\sum_j e^{V_{qj}+\sqrt{2}\sum_k \sigma_k \varpi_k x_{qjk}}} e^{-\varpi_1^2} e^{-\varpi_2^2} \cdots e^{-\varpi_K^2} \mathrm{d}\varpi_1 \mathrm{d}\varpi_2 \cdots \mathrm{d}\varpi_K \Bigg\}\end{aligned} \tag{7}$$

The above integration is now in an appropriate form for application of a multi-dimensional product formula of the Gauss–Hermite quadrature (see Stroud, 1971).

3.2. Pseudo-random Monte Carlo (PMC) method

This technique approximates the choice probabilities by computing the integrand in Eq. (5) at randomly chosen values for each s_{qk}. Since the s_{qk} terms are independent across individuals and variables, and are distributed standard normal, we generate a matrix s of standard normal random numbers with Q^*K elements (one element for each variable and individual combination) and compute the corresponding individual choice probabilities for a given value of the parameter vector to be estimated. We then repeat this process R times for the given value of the parameter vector and approximate the integrand by averaging over the computed choice probabilities in the different draws. This results in an unbiased estimator of the actual individual choice probabilities. It's variance decreases as R increases. It also has the appealing properties of being smooth (i.e., twice differentiable) and being strictly positive for any realization of the finite R draws. The parameter vector is estimated as the vector value that maximizes the simulated log-likelihood function. Under rather weak regularity conditions, the PMC estimator is consistent, asymptotically efficient, and asymptotically normal (see Hajivassiliou and Ruud, 1994; Lee, 1992). However, the estimator will generally be a biased simulation of the maximum likelihood (ML) estimator because of the logarithmic transformation of the choice probabilities in the log-likelihood function. The bias decreases with the variance of the probability simulator; that is, it decreases as the number of repetitions increase.

An important point in implementation of the PMC method is that the same matrix s of standard normal random numbers has to be used across iterations of the likelihood function maximization for each of the R repetitions. This can be achieved by re-setting the seed to the same pre-determined value at the beginning of each likelihood (and gradient) function evaluation. This seed is automatically updated for each repetition within a single likelihood (and gradient) function evaluation, and is updated to the same value for any repetition across function evaluations by assigning the same initial seed value at each function evaluation.

3.3. Quasi-random Monte Carlo (QMC) method

The quasi-random Halton sequence is designed to span the domain of the S-dimensional unit cube uniformly and efficiently (the interval of each dimension of the unit cube is between 0 and 1). In one-dimension, the Halton sequence is generated by choosing a prime number $r(r \geqslant 2)$ and expanding the sequence of integers $0, 1, 2, \ldots g, \ldots G$ in terms of the base r

$$g = \sum_{l=0}^{L} b_l r^l, \quad \text{where } 0 \leqslant b_l \leqslant r-1 \text{ and } r^L \leqslant g \leqslant r^{L+1}. \tag{8}$$

Thus, $g(g = 1, 2, \ldots G)$ can be represented by the *r-adic* integer string $b_1 \ldots b_1 b_0$. The Halton sequence in the prime base r is obtained by taking the radical inverse of $g(g = 1, 2, \ldots G)$ to the base r by reflecting through the radical point:

$$\varphi_r(g) = 0.b_0 b_1 \ldots b_L (\text{base } r) = \sum_{l=0}^{L} b_l r^{-l-1}. \tag{9}$$

The sequence above is very uniformly distributed in the interval (0, 1) for each prime r. The Halton sequence in K-dimensions is obtained by pairing K one-dimensional sequences based on K pairwise relatively prime integers, $r_1, r_2, \ldots, r_S$ (usually the first K primes)

$$\Psi_g = \left(\varphi_{r_1}(g), \varphi_{r_2}(g), \ldots, \varphi_{r_S}(g)\right). \tag{10}$$

The Halton sequence is generated number-theoretically rather than randomly and so successive points at any stage "know" how to fill in the gaps left by earlier points, leading to a uniform distribution within the domain of integration. This is illustrated in Fig. 1, where we have plotted 1000 points from a two-dimensional uniform pseudo-random sequence and correspondingly 1000 points generated by a two-dimensional Halton sequence. The "clumping" of points in the pseudo-random sequence is clearly noticeable, while the Halton sequence has a much more even spread.

The simulation technique to evaluate the integral in the log-likelihood function of Eq. (5) involves generating the K-dimensional Halton sequence for a specified number of "draws" R for each individual. To avoid correlation in simulation errors across individuals, we make separate

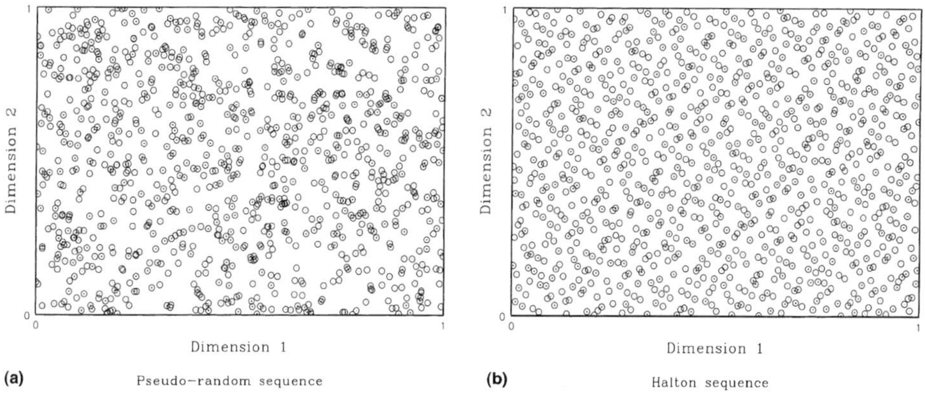

Fig. 1. 1000 draws in two-dimensions from the uniform distribution.

independent draws of R Halton numbers in K-dimensions for each individual. We achieve this by generating a Halton "matrix" Y of size $G \times K$, where $G = R * Q + 10$ (Q is the total number of individuals in the sample). We then discard the first ten terms in each dimension because the integrand may be sensitive to the starting point of the Halton sequence (see Morokoff and Caflisch, 1995; Bratley et al., 1992). This leaves a $(R * Q) \times K$ Halton matrix which is partitioned into Q sub-matrices of size $R \times K$, each sub-matrix representing the R Halton draws in K-dimensions for each individual (thus, the first R rows of the Halton matrix Y are assigned to the first individual, the second R rows to the second individual, and so on). It is important to note that storing a matrix of size $(R * Q) \times K$ in memory may not require substantial memory space since typically the number of repetitions R in the QMC estimation method is not high. Alternatively, one could store the matrix on disk and extract the appropriate $Q * K$ matrix corresponding to each draw as needed during the likelihood function iterations.

The Halton sequence is uniformly distributed over the multi-dimensional cube. To obtain the corresponding multivariate normal points over the multi-dimensional domain of the real line, we take the inverse standard normal distribution transformation of Y. By the integral transform result, provides the Halton points for the multi-variate normal distribution (see Fang and Wang, 1994, Chapter 4). The integrand in Eq. (5) is computed at the resulting points in the columns of the matrix X for each of the R draws for each individual and then the simulated likelihood function is developed in the usual manner as the average of the values of the integrand across the R draws.

4. Experimental design

The data used in the numerical experiments are obtained from an intercity mode choice survey conduced by VIA Rail (the Canadian national rail carrier) in 1989 to develop travel demand models to forecast future intercity travel in the Toronto-Montreal corridor. We extracted the level-of-service information for each of three modes (car, air and train) and for the trip of each of 2000 weekday-business travelers from the data. The reason for using actual level-of-service data in the experiments is to ensure that the simulation data resemble field data. However, the choice process is generated by simulating the normally distributed random coefficients on the level-of-service parameters. Thus, the experimental data may be characterized as "pseudo-simulated" data, with independent variables obtained from an actual field survey, but the choice being generated using an experimental design.

Five level-of-service variables are included in the x_{qi} vector of Eq. (3): line-haul cost, access cost, in-vehicle time, access time, and terminal time. To examine the performance of the three alternative numerical estimation methods (i.e., the cubature method, the PMC method and the QMC method) vis-a-vis the dimensionality of the integration, we started the experiments by allowing the parameter on line-haul cost to be randomly (normal) distributed and maintaining fixed coefficients on other variables (this leads to one-dimensional integration). Subsequently, we generated new choice data by also allowing the coefficient on access cost to be randomly (normal) distributed (leading to a two-dimensional integration). This process of adding random coefficients was continued till all the level-of-service variables are random (leading to five-dimensional integration). Thus, we generated five data sets, each data set representing a specific number of underlying random coefficients in the choice process.

The mean (and standard deviations) of the coefficients adopted in the data generating process are as follows: line-haul cost (−4.5 and 3), access cost (−6.0 and 4.5), in-vehicle time (−1 and 0.75), access time (−3 and 2.25), and terminal time (−2 and 1.5). The alternative specific constants were assumed to be 3.5 (for the air mode) and −0.3 (for the train mode), with the car mode being the base (the alternative specific constant values and the mean values of the level-of-service coefficients used in the experiments were informed by a multinomial logit estimation on the original data; the standard deviations used were obtained as roughly three-fourths of the mean values). The reader will note that the standard deviation of a level-of-service coefficient applies only if that coefficient is allowed to be random; if it is fixed in a particular experiment, the corresponding standard deviation is zero.

The utility for each mode is computed based on Eq. (3) after generating values for β_q for each individual from the normal distribution and for ϵ_{qi} from the standard type I extreme value distribution. Then, the brand with the highest computed utility value is identified as the chosen brand in the experiments.

5. Computational results and comparative performance

5.1. Background

The three numerical estimation methods were implemented using the GAUSS matrix programming language. The log-likelihood function and the gradients of the function with respect to relevant parameters were coded. Estimations were carried out using an Intel pentium II 300 MHz.

processor with 128 MB of RAM. The parameters used to generate the data were used as the common starting point for all estimations. This allows a comparison of time to convergence across estimations.

For the estimations involving one and two-dimensional integration, we used the results from the 20 point cubature method as the benchmark for comparing the performance of alternative methods. For estimations in three to five-dimensions, we obtained benchmark results using the PMC method with 20,000 draws. While there may be simulation error even when using 20,000 draws, it is expected that this error would be very small.

For one-dimensional integration, cubature estimation using 20 points can be achieved very quickly and so we did not estimate models with lower number of cubature points. For two-dimensional integration, we estimated models with 2, 4, and 10-point cubature. For three-dimensional integration, we obtained results using 2- and 4-point cubature. For higher dimensions, we estimated models with only 2-point cubature (more than 2 points of cubature dramatically increases computational time).

PMC estimation was based on four different numbers of draws: 250, 500, 1000, and 2000. We used 250 draws as the minimum, though it is generally preferable to use higher number of pseudo-random draws to reduce simulation variance. We did not go beyond 2000 draws because computation time starts to increase quite substantially beyond this many number of draws.

We estimated models with 25, 50, and 75 Halton points for one and two-dimensional integration. For higher dimensions, we also estimated models with 100 and 125 Halton points.

5.2. Performance criteria and evaluation results

To evaluate the performance of different methods, we used measures that indicate the ability of each method to recover the "true" parameters and the choice probabilities as obtained in the benchmark estimation. The evaluation of the proximity of estimated and true parameters was based on the root mean square error as well as the mean absolute error ratio across parameters. The evaluation of the ability to reproduce true choice probabilities was similarly based on the root mean square error and mean absolute error ratio of computed choice probabilities (vis-a-vis true choice probabilities) across modes and across individuals. Thus, four measures of performance are used. These measures, and the time required for convergence of the maximum likelihood iterations, were compared across methods.

Tables 1–5 present the error measures for different dimensions of integration. In all the tables, the error measures tend to become smaller as the number of cubature points or the number of draws increase. For the PMC and QMC methods, this is not always the case. For example, the parameter-based error measures increase between 500 and 1000 draws for the PMC method in three-dimensions (Table 3). Similarly, the parameter-based error measures increase between 75 and 100 draws for the QMC method in three-dimensions. These minor aberrations are not surprising because of the way that draws are assigned to individuals. For example, in the case of 75 Halton draws, the procedure involves drawing $75 * N$ Halton points and assigning each set of 75 points to each individual. Thus, the first 75 points get assigned to the first individual, the second 75 points to the second individual, and so on. For 100 Halton draws, 100*N Halton points are obtained and each set of 100 is assigned to an individual as before. Thus, in the sampling scheme,

Table 1
Maximum simulated likelihood estimation results for one dimensional integration

Evaluation basis	Performance measure	Pseudo-random Monte Carlo (PMC) estimation				Quasi-random Monte Carlo (QMC) estimation		
		Number of draws				Number of draws		
		250	500	1000	2000	25	50	75
Parameters	MAPE[a]	2.435	1.255	0.577	0.548	1.429	0.382	0.143
	RMSE[b]	0.089	0.047	0.024	0.021	0.050	0.007	0.004
Choice probabilities	MAPE	3.681	2.524	1.782	1.302	3.680	1.722	0.877
	RMSE	0.010	0.007	0.005	0.004	0.010	0.004	0.002
Time to convergence (min)		40.8	71.8	143.0	330.3	6.1	9.4	14.5

[a] Mean Absolute Percentage Error (MAPE).
[b] Root Mean Square Error.

Table 2
Maximum simulated likelihood estimation results for two-dimensional integration

Evaluation basis	Performance measure	Polynomial-based cubature estimation			Pseudo-random Monte Carlo (PMC) estimation				Quasi-random Monte Carlo (QMC) estimation		
		Number of cubature points			Number of draws				Number of draws		
		2	4	10	250	500	1000	2000	25	50	75
Parameters	MAPE	17.640	6.923	0.867	6.857	1.237	1.632	1.114	2.891	1.315	0.695
	RMSE	0.485	0.194	0.026	0.233	0.049	0.041	0.042	0.144	0.037	0.016
Choice probabilities	MAPE	6.162	2.356	1.815	4.852	3.218	2.331	1.784	4.851	2.517	1.652
	RMSE	0.015	0.009	0.004	0.014	0.010	0.007	0.005	0.014	0.007	0.004
Time to convergence (min)		1.6	5.9	146.3	42.8	103.4	200.5	345.3	7.0	13.6	16.8

Table 3
Maximum simulated likelihood estimation results for three-dimensional integration

Evaluation basis	Performance measure	Polynomial-Based cubature		Pseudo-random Monte Carlo (PMC) estimation				Quasi-random Monte Carlo (QMC) estimation				
		Number of cubature points		Number of draws				Number of draws				
		2	4	250	500	1000	2000	25	50	75	100	125
Parameters	MAPE	5.186	4.185	10.604	3.253	5.021	2.651	6.292	5.117	2.542	3.736	0.585
	RMSE	0.167	0.123	0.322	0.106	0.163	0.063	0.148	0.100	0.088	0.098	0.013
Choice probabilities	MAPE	3.532	1.815	5.403	3.649	2.626	1.787	5.846	3.565	2.599	1.768	1.411
	RMSE	0.012	0.006	0.015	0.011	0.008	0.005	0.017	0.010	0.008	0.005	0.004
Time to convergence (min)		3.0	65.0	48.4	99.5	193.0	409.0	7.4	14.2	21.3	32.7	35.7

Table 4
Maximum simulated likelihood estimation results for four-dimensional integration

Evaluation basis	Performance measure	Polynomial-based cubature estimation	Pseudo-random Monte Carlo (PMC) estimation				Quasi-random Monte Carlo (QMC) estimation				
		Number of cubature points	Number of draws				Number of draws				
		2	250	500	1000	2000	25	50	75	100	125
Parameters	MAPE	17.563	18.970	10.036	11.975	9.044	21.189	29.171	18.248	10.796	4.32
	RMSE	0.736	0.517	0.225	0.253	0.213	0.478	0.758	0.426	0.223	0.167
Choice probabilities	MAPE	5.113	5.493	4.133	2.857	2.129	7.499	4.373	3.655	2.586	2.071
	RMSE	0.015	0.017	0.012	0.009	0.006	0.022	0.012	0.010	0.007	0.006
Time to convergence (min)		8.5	60.6	113.7	236.3	455.0	10.4	23.3	30.3	35.8	44.9

Table 5
Maximum simulated likelihood estimation results for five-dimensional integration

Evaluation basis	Performance measure	Polynomial-Based Cubature Estimation	Pseudo-random Monte Carlo (PMC) estimation				Quasi-random Monte Carlo (QMC) estimation				
		Number of cubature points	Number of draws				Number of draws				
		2	250	500	1000	2000	25	50	75	100	125
Parameters	MAPE	41.77	37.121	13.435	18.354	14.17	56.685	52.433	29.000	12.804	6.657
	RMSE	0.742	0.687	0.360	0.306	0.221	0.945	0.791	0.424	0.240	0.134
Choice probabilities	MAPE	4.862	6.665	4.771	3.332	2.418	8.812	5.073	3.905	3.090	2.283
	RMSE	0.014	0.020	0.014	0.010	0.007	0.025	0.014	0.010	0.008	0.007
Time to convergence (min)		26.9	73.7	121.7	283.7	501.0	14.5	24.0	36.1	47.9	59.3

moving from 75 to 100 draws does not imply maintaining the same 75 draws for each individual and supplementing this with an additional 25 draws. It involves a fresh set of points for each individual, and therefore, there is always a small chance that fewer draws might provide better results than a larger fresh set of draws. The important point to note, however, is that these are minor aberrations to the more stable general trend of reduced errors with higher draws.

The results for one-dimensional integration (Table 1) indicate that with as few as 50 Halton draws, the error measures from the QMC method are smaller than from 1000 draws of the PMC method; those from 75 Halton draws are much smaller than from 2000 pseudo-random draws. Besides, the times to convergence for the QMC method are considerably lesser than for the PMC method. As indicated earlier, we are not presenting cubature results in one-dimension because it is easy to estimate one-dimensional integrals with a high number of cubature points. The benchmark used for one-dimensional integration is 20 points, and this estimation takes just 7.5 min. Obviously, the cubature method is the preferred method for one-dimensional integration, but its effectiveness drops significantly beyond one-dimensional integration (as we will see later). The QMC method, on the other hand, does not take significantly longer than the cubature method and is also much more effective in higher dimensions.

The maximum simulated likelihood estimation results for the mixed logit model with two-dimensional integration are provided in Table 2. Polynomial-cubature methods with 2 and 4 points converge quickly, but the associated error measures are rather large. The cubature technique is quite accurate with 10 points, though it requires about 2.5 h for convergence. However, 10 point cubature is superior to the 2000 draw PMC method both in terms of accuracy as well as convergence time. Among all the three methods, the Halton method comes out as being a clear winner; with as few as 75 draws, it is able to recover the true parameters and choice probabilities more accurately and in substantially less time than 10 point cubature or a 2000-draw PMC method.

In the case of three-dimensional integration, cubature-based estimation of the mixed logit with more than 4 points becomes very expensive. Between the PMC and QMC methods, the QMC method with as few as 75 draws is better than the PMC method with 1000 draws. Also, the QMC method with 125 draws is far superior to the PMC method with 2000 draws, and takes less than one-tenth the time required by the 2000-draw PMC method.

Similar results may be observed for the estimation of the mixed logit model in four and five-dimensions. A particularly important point in 4- and 5-dimensions is that the cubature method beyond 2 points becomes very time-intensive, and estimation with just 2 points leads to very substantial errors.

Overall, the QMC method dominates the other two methods in performance. Also, it takes substantially lesser time for convergence. This is a valuable finding. It suggests that the estimation of the mixed logit model using the Halton method is very efficient and practical.

6. Summary and conclusions

This paper proposes the use of a QMC method (specifically, the Halton method) for the estimation of the flexible mixed logit model for discrete choice analysis. The QMC method uses "cleverly" crafted non-random and uniformly distributed sequences in the domain of integration.

The basic idea of the method is that it is really inconsequential whether the discrete points are truly random; of primary importance is the even distribution (or maximal spread) of the points in the integration space.

The results from our simulation experiments indicate that the QMC method out-performs the polynomial-cubature and PMC methods for mixed logit model estimation. In less than or equal to three-dimensions, simulation estimation with as few as 75 Halton draws provides considerably better accuracy than with 2000 pseudo-random draws. In higher dimensions (4–5), 100 Halton draws provide about the same level of accuracy as 2000 pseudo-random draws and 125 Halton draws provides much better accuracy at about one-tenth the time required for convergence using 2000 pseudo-random draws.

The experimental result have the potential to dramatically influence the use of the mixed logit model in practice. Given the flexibility of the mixed logit model to accommodate very general patterns of competition among alternatives and/or random coefficients, the use of the QMC simulation method of estimation should facilitate the application of behaviorally rich structures for discrete choice modeling.

The author is currently pursuing the comparison of potentially more efficient quasi-random sequences than the Halton sequence used in the current paper.

Acknowledgements

This research was supported by National Science Foundation grants DMS 9208758 and DMS 9313013 to the National Institute of Statistical Sciences (NISS). The author would also like to thank Frank Koppelman and three referees for valuable comments on an earlier version of the paper.

References

Ben-Akiva, M., Bolduc, D., 1996. Multinomial probit with a logit kernel and a general parametric specification of the covariance structure, working paper, Department of Civil and Environmental Engineering, Massachusetts Institute of Technology, Cambridge, MA and Département d'économique, Université Laval, Sainte-Foy, Qc, Canada.

Bhat, C.R., 1998a. Accommodating flexible substitution patterns in multi-dimensional choice modeling: formulation and application to travel mode and departure time choice. Transportation Research 32B, 425–440.

Bhat, C.R., 1998b. Accommodating variations in responsiveness to level-of-service measures in travel mode choice modeling. Transportation Research 32A, 495–507.

Bhat, C.R., 1999a. A multi-level cross-classified model for discrete response variables. Transportation Research, accepted.

Bhat, C.R., 1999b. Incorporating observed and unobserved heterogeneity in urban work travel mode choice modeling.Transportation Science (forthcoming).

Bratley, P., Fox, B.L., 1988. Implementing Sobol's quasi-random sequence generator. ACM Transactions on Mathematical Software 14, 88–100.

Bratley, P., Fox, B.L., Niederreiter, H., 1992. Implementation and tests of low-discrepancy sequences. ACM Transactions on Modeling and Computer Simulation 2, 195–213.

Brownstone, D., Train, K., 1999. Forecasting new product penetration with flexible substitution patterns. Journal of Econometrics 89, 109–129.

Cools, R., 1992. A survey of methods for constructing cubature formulae. In: Espelid, T.O., Genz, A.C. (Eds.), Numerical Integration: Recent Development, Software and Application. Kluwer Academic Publishers, Dordrecht, pp. 1–24.

Cools, R., Rabinowitz, P., 1993. Monomial cubature rules since Stroud: a compilation. Journal of Computational and Applied Mathematics 43, 309–326.

Fang, K.-T., Wang, Y., 1994. Number-Theoretic Methods in Statistics. Chapman & Hall, London.

Halton, J.H., 1970. A retrospective and prospective survey of the Monte Carlo method. SIAM Review 12, 1–63.

Hajivassiliou, V.A., McFadden, D., Ruud, P., 1996. Simulation of multivariate normal rectangle probabilities and their derivatives: theoretical and computational results. Journal of Econometrics 72, 85–134.

Hajivassiliou, V.A., Ruud, P.A., 1994. Classical estimation methods for LDV models using simulation. In: Engle, R.F., McFadden, D.L. (Eds.), Handbook of Econometrics 4, 2383–2441.

Kocis, L., Whiten, W.J., 1997. Computational investigation of low-discrepancy sequences. ACM Transactions on Mathematical Software 23, 266–294.

Krommer, A.R., Ueberhuber, C.W., 1994. Numerical integration on advanced computer systems. Springer, Berlin.

Lee, L.-F., 1992. On the efficiency of methods of simulated moments and maximum simulated likelihood estimation of discrete response models. Econometric Theory 8, 518–552.

Metropolis, N.C., Ulam, S.M., 1949. The Monte Carlo method. Journal of the American Statistical Association 44, 335–341.

Morokoff, W.J., Caflisch, R.E., 1995. Quasi-Monte Carlo integration. Journal of Computational Physics 122, 218–230.

Mullen, G.L., Mahalanabis, A., Niederreiter, H., 1995. Tables of (T,M,S)-net and (T,S)-sequence parameters. In: Niederreiter, H., Shiue, J.-S. (Eds.), Monte Carlo and Quasi-Monte Carlo Methods in Scientific Computing. Springer, New York, pp. 58–86.

Niederreiter, H., 1995. New developments in uniform psuedo-random number and vector generation. In: Niederreiter, H., Shiue, J.-S. (Eds.), Monte Carlo and Quasi-Monte Carlo Methods in Scientific Computing. Springer, New York, pp. 94–112.

Owen, A.B., 1997. Scrambled net variance for integrals of smooth functions. The Annals of Statistics 25, 1541–1562.

Owen, A.B., 1998. Latin supercube sampling for very high dimensional simulations. ACM Transactions on Modeling and Computer Simulation 8, 71–102.

Papageorgiou, A., Traub, J.F., 1997. Faster evaluation of multidimensional integrals. Risk 9, 63–65.

Paskov, S.H., 1997. New methodology for valuing derivatives. In: Pliska, S., Dempster, M. (Eds.), Mathematics of Derivative Securities. Isaac Newton Institute, Cambridge University Press, Cambridge.

Press, W.H., Teukolsky, S.A., Nerlove, M., 1992. Numerical Recipes in C: The Art of Scientific Computing. Cambridge University Press, Cambridge, MA.

Revelt, D., Train, K., 1998. Mixed logit with repeated choices: households' choices of appliance efficiency level. Review of Economics and Statistics (forthcoming).

Sloan, I.H., Joe, S., 1994. Lattice Methods for Multiple Integration. Clarendon Press, Oxford.

Sloan, J.H., Wozniakowski, H., 1998. When are quasi-Monte Carlo algorithms efficient for high dimensional integrals? Journal of Complexity 14, 1–33.

Spanier, J., Maize, E.H., 1994. Quasi-random methods for estimating integrals using relatively small samples. SIAM Review 36, 18–44.

Stroud, A.H., 1971. Approximate Calculation of Multiple Integrals. Prentice-Hall, Englewood Cliffs, NJ.

Train, K., 1998. Recreation demand models with taste differences over people. Land Economics 74, 230–239.

Wozniakowski, H., 1991. Average case complexity of multivariate integration. Bulletin of the American Mathematical Society 24, 185–194.

[31]

Transportation **30**: 133–176, 2003

The Mixed Logit model: The state of practice

DAVID A. HENSHER[1] & WILLIAM H. GREENE[2]
[1] *Institute of Transport Studies, Faculty of Economics and Business, The University of Sydney, NSW 2006, Australia (E-mail: Davidh@its.usyd.edu.au);* [2] *Department of Economics, Stern School of Business, New York University, New York, USA (E-mail: wgreene@stern.nyu.edu)*

Key words: empirical distributions, Mixed Logit, model specification, random parameters, valuation

Abstract. The mixed logit model is considered to be the most promising state of the art discrete choice model currently available. Increasingly researchers and practitioners are estimating mixed logit models of various degrees of sophistication with mixtures of revealed preference and stated choice data. It is timely to review progress in model estimation since the learning curve is steep and the unwary are likely to fall into a chasm if not careful. These chasms are very deep indeed given the complexity of the mixed logit model. Although the theory is relatively clear, estimation and data issues are far from clear. Indeed there is a great deal of potential mis-inference consequent on trying to extract increased behavioural realism from data that are often not able to comply with the demands of mixed logit models. Possibly for the first time we now have an estimation method that requires extremely high quality data *if* the analyst wishes to take advantage of the extended behavioural capabilities of such models. This paper focuses on the new opportunities offered by mixed logit models and some issues to be aware of to avoid misuse of such advanced discrete choice methods by the practitioner.

1. Introduction

The logit family of models is recognised as the essential toolkit for studying discrete choices. Starting with the simple binary logit model we have progressed to the multinomial logit model (MNL) and the nested logit (NL) model, the latter becoming the most popular of the generalised logit models (see Koppelman & Sethi 2000; Carrasco & Ortuzar 2002 for an overview). The theoretical progress occurred primarily between the mid-1960s through to the late 1970s with practical applications lagging by at least five years. Although more advanced choice models such as the Generalised Extreme Value (GEV) and multinomial probit (MNP) models existed in conceptual and analytical form in the early 1970s, parameter estimation was seen as a practical barrier to their empirical usefulness. During the 1980s we saw a primary focus on refinements in MNL and NL models as well as a greater understanding of their behavioural and empirical strengths and limitations (including the data requirements to assist in minimising violation of the underlying behavioural properties of the random component of the utility expression for each alternative). A number of software packages offered a relatively user-friendly capability to estimate MNL and NL models.[1]

With increasing recognition of some of the behavioural limitations of the closed-form MNL and NL models and the appeal of more advanced models that were analytically complex to estimate beyond three alternatives, together with the complex open-form[2] representation of the choice probability expression, researchers focussed on finding ways to numerically estimate these models. The breakthrough came with the development of simulation methods (e.g. simulated maximum likelihood estimation) that enabled the open-form models such as multinomial probit and mixed logit to be estimated with relative ease. Papers by McFadden (1985), Börsch-Supan and Hajvassiliou (1990), Geweke et al. (1994), McFadden and Ruud (1994), to name a few, all reviewed in Stern (1997), established methods to simulate the choice probabilities and estimating all parameters, by drawing pseudo-random realisations from the underlying error process (Börsch-Supan & Hajivassiliou 1990).

With estimation methods now more tractable and integrated into the popular software packages, in the mid-1990s we started seeing an increasing number of applications of mixed logit models and an accumulating knowledge base of experiences in estimating such models with available and new data sets. A close reading of this literature however revealed a concern about the general failure of advice to the analyst of many of the underlying (often not revealed) challenges that modellers experienced in arriving at a preferred model. The balance of this paper focuses on some of the most recent experiences of a number of active researchers estimating mixed logit models. Sufficient knowledge has been acquired in the last few years to be able to share some of the early practical lessons.

2. An intuitive description of mixed logit[3]

Like any random utility model of the discrete choice family of models, we assume that a sampled individual ($q = 1, \ldots, Q$) faces a choice amongst I alternatives in each of T choice situations.[4] The individual is assumed to consider the full set of offered alternatives in choice situation t and to choose the alternative with the highest utility. The (relative) utility associated with each alternative i as evaluated by each individual q in choice situation t is represented in a discrete choice model by a utility expression of the general form in Equation (1).

$$U_{itq} = \boldsymbol{\beta}_q'\mathbf{x}_{itq} + \varepsilon_{itq}, \qquad (1)$$

$\mathbf{x}_{itq}$ is a vector of explanatory variables that are observed by the analyst (from any source) and include attributes of the alternatives, socio-economic characteristics of the respondent and descriptors of the decision context and choice task itself (e.g. task complexity in stated choice experiments as defined by number of choice situations, number of alternatives, attribute ranges, data collection method etc.) in choice situation t. The components $\boldsymbol{\beta}_q$ and ε_{itq} are not observed by the analyst and are treated as stochastic influences.

Within a logit context we impose the condition that ε_{itq} is independent and identically distributed (IID) extreme value type 1. The IID assumption is restrictive in that its does not allow for the error components of different alternatives to be correlated. We would want to be able to take this into account in some way. One way to do this is to partition the stochastic component additively into two parts. One part is correlated over alternatives and heteroskedastic, and another part is IID over alternatives and individuals as shown in Equation (2) (ignoring the t subscript for the present);

$$U_{iq} = \boldsymbol{\beta}_q'\mathbf{x}_{iq} + [\eta_{iq} + \varepsilon_{iq}], \tag{2}$$

where η_{iq} is a random term with zero mean whose distribution over individuals and alternatives depends in general on underlying parameters and observed data relating to alternative i and individual q; and ε_{iq} is a random term with zero mean that is IID over alternatives and does not depend on underlying parameters or data.

The Mixed Logit class of models assumes a general distribution for η_{iq} and an IID extreme value type 1 distribution for η_{iq}.[5] That is, η_{iq} can take on a number of distributional forms such as normal, lognormal, or triangular. Denote the density of η_{iq} by $f(\eta_{iq}|\boldsymbol{\Omega})$ where $\boldsymbol{\Omega}$ are the fixed parameters of the distribution. For a given value of η_{iq}, the conditional probability for choice i is logit, since the remaining error term is IID extreme value:

$$L_{iq}(\boldsymbol{\beta}_q|\eta_{iq}) = \frac{\exp(\boldsymbol{\beta}_q'\mathbf{x}_{iq} + \eta_{iq})}{\sum_j \exp(\boldsymbol{\beta}_q'\mathbf{x}_{jq} + \eta_{jq})}. \tag{3}$$

The unconditional choice probability would be this logit formula integrated over all values of η_{iq} weighted by the density of η_{iq} as shown in Equation (4):

$$P_{iq}(\boldsymbol{\beta}_q|\boldsymbol{\Omega}) = \int_{\eta_{iq}} L_{iq}(\boldsymbol{\beta}_q|\eta_{iq})\, f(\eta_{iq}|\boldsymbol{\Omega})\eta_{iq}. \tag{4}$$

Models of this form are called *mixed logit* because the choice probability P_{iq} is a mixture of logits with f as the mixing distribution. The probabilities do not exhibit the questionable independence from irrelevant alternatives property

(IIA), and different substitution patterns may be obtained by appropriate specification of f. This is handled in two ways. The first, known as the random parameters specification, involves specifying each element of $\boldsymbol{\beta}_q$ associated with an attribute of an alternative as having both a mean and a standard deviation (i.e. it is treated as a random parameter instead of a fixed parameter[6]). The second, known as the error components approach, treats the unobserved information as a single separate error component in the random component (as done above in Equations (3) and (4).)

The standard deviation of an element of the $\boldsymbol{\beta}_q$ parameter vector, which we denote β_{qk}, accommodates the presence of preference heterogeneity in the sampled population. While one might handle this heterogeneity in the context of a fixed β_{qk} parameter through data segmentation (e.g., a different model for each trip length range, age, gender and income of each traveller – see Rizzi & Ortuzar 2002) and/or attribute segmentation (e.g., separate β_{qk}s for different trip length ranges), in contrast to treating it all as random, the challenge of these (deterministic) segmentation strategies is in picking the right segmentation criteria and range cut-offs that account for statistically significant sources of preference heterogeneity. The random parameters representation of preference heterogeneity is more general. However such a specification carries a challenge in that these parameters have a distribution that is unknown. Selecting such a distribution has plenty of empirical challenges. As shown in Hensher and Greene (2002), the concern that one might not know the location of each individual's preferences on the distribution can be accommodated by retrieving estimates of individual-specific preferences by deriving the individual's conditional distribution based (within-sample) on their choices (i.e. prior knowledge). Using Bayes Rule, we first define the conditional choice probability as in Equation (5):

$$\mathbf{H}_{iq}(\boldsymbol{\beta}_q|\boldsymbol{\Omega}) = \frac{L_{iq}(\boldsymbol{\beta}_q)g(\boldsymbol{\beta}_q|\boldsymbol{\Omega})}{P_{iq}(\boldsymbol{\beta}_q|\boldsymbol{\Omega})}, \tag{5}$$

where $L_{iq}(\boldsymbol{\beta}_q)$ is now the likelihood of an individual's choice if they had this specific $\boldsymbol{\beta}_q$, $\boldsymbol{\Omega}$ is the set of parameters in the underlying distribution of $\boldsymbol{\beta}_q$, $g(\boldsymbol{\beta}_q|\boldsymbol{\Omega})$ is the distribution in the population of $\boldsymbol{\beta}_q$s, and $P_{iq}(\boldsymbol{\Omega})$ is the choice probability function defined in open-form as:

$$P_{iq}(\boldsymbol{\Omega}) = \int_{\boldsymbol{\beta}_q} L_{iq}(\boldsymbol{\beta}_q)g(\boldsymbol{\beta}_q|\boldsymbol{\Omega})\, d\boldsymbol{\beta}_q, \tag{6}$$

[See Train (2003)]. This shows how one can estimate the person specific choice probabilities as a function of the underlying parameters of the distribution of the random parameters.

The choice probability in Equation (4) or (6) cannot be calculated exactly because the integral does not have a closed form in general. The integral is approximated through simulation. For a given value of the parameters $\mathbf{\Omega}$, a value of $\boldsymbol{\beta}_q$ is drawn from its distribution. Using this draw, the logit formula (3) for $L_{iq}(\boldsymbol{\beta}_q)$ is calculated. This process is repeated for many draws, and the mean of the resulting $L_{iq}(\boldsymbol{\beta}_q)$'s is taken as the approximate choice probability giving Equation (7).

$$SP_{iq}(\mathbf{\Omega}) = (1/R) \textstyle\sum_{r=1}^{R} L_{iq}(\boldsymbol{\beta}_{qr}), \tag{7}$$

R is the number of replications (i.e., draws of $\boldsymbol{\beta}_{qr}$), $\boldsymbol{\beta}_{qr}$ is the rth draw, and SP_{iq} is the simulated probability that an individual chooses alternative i.[7] It remains to specify the structure of the random vector $\boldsymbol{\beta}_q$. For example, in our application of this model, we will use the structure $\boldsymbol{\beta}_q = \boldsymbol{\beta} + \boldsymbol{\Delta}\mathbf{z}_q + \boldsymbol{\Gamma}\mathbf{v}_q$ where the fixed underlying parameters are $\mathbf{\Omega} = (\boldsymbol{\beta}, \boldsymbol{\Delta}, \boldsymbol{\Gamma})$, $\boldsymbol{\beta}$ is the fixed mean of the distribution, $\mathbf{z}_q$ is a set of person-specific characteristics, $\boldsymbol{\Delta}$ is a matrix of parameters, $\mathbf{v}_q$ is a vector of uncorrelated random variables with variances on the diagonals of $\boldsymbol{\Sigma}$, and $\boldsymbol{\Gamma}$ is a lower triangular matrix which, because $\text{Var}[\boldsymbol{\beta}_q] = \boldsymbol{\Gamma\Sigma\Gamma}'$, allows free correlation of the parameters. Thus, a "draw" from the distribution of $\boldsymbol{\beta}_q$ consists of a "draw" from the distribution of $\mathbf{v}_q$ which is then used to compute $\boldsymbol{\beta}_q$ as shown above.

The simulation method was initially introduced by Geweke (and improved by Keane, McFadden, Börsch-Supan and Hajivassiliou – see Geweke et al. 1994; McFadden & Ruud 1994) to compute random variates from a multivariate truncated normal distribution. Although it fails to deliver unbiased multivariate truncated normal variates (as initially suggested by Ruud and detailed by Börsch-Supan and Hajivassiliou (1990)), it does produce unbiased estimates of the choice probabilities. The cumulative distribution function in their research is assumed to be multivariate normal and characterised by the covariance matrix $\mathbf{M}$. The approach is quick and generated draws and simulated probabilities depend smoothly on the parameters $\boldsymbol{\beta}$ and $\mathbf{M}$. This latter dependence enables one to use conventional numerical methods such as quadratic hill climbing or gradient methods to solve the first order conditions for maximising the simulated likelihood function (Equation (7)) across a sample of $q = 1, \ldots, Q$ individuals; hence the term maximum simulated likelihood (MSL) (Stern 1997).

After model estimation, there are many results for interpretation. An early warning – parameter estimates typically obtained from a random parameter or error components specification should not be interpreted as stand-alone parameters but must be assessed jointly with other linked parameter estimates. For example, the marginal utility of travel time is a function of the mean parameter, an allowance for trip length (as a segment descriptor) and a random term varying across individuals (the latter defined as the standard deviation parameter). This most general formula will be written out with due allowance for the distributional assumption on the random parameter (see Section 4.2.6).

Thus far, the specification has assumed that the attributes of alternatives are independent. If we allow for attribute (i.e. alternative) correlation, then the random components in the preceding will be replaced with mixtures of the random components of the several parameters. (See Sections 4.5 and 4.6 for more details on how to specify cross parameter correlation in the mixed logit model.)

This overview of mixed logit models provides a framework within which we can investigate a number of important issues of practical significance. We have classified these into seven key empirical issues:

1. Selecting the random parameters;
2. Selecting the distribution of the random parameters;
3. Selecting the number of points on the distributions;
4. Preference heterogeneity around the mean of a random parameter;
5. Accounting for observations drawn from the same individual: correlated choice situations;
6. Accounting for correlation between parameters;
7. Willingness to pay challenges.

The differences between these key empirical issues will be explained in the following sections but before we do so we need to summarise details of the data sets that are used to illustrate the various issues. We have deliberately selected more than one data set since each data set offers evidence that adds more insights than are obtained from any one data set.

3. Data sources used to illustrate specific issues

We will use three data sets to illustrate the range of specification, estimation and application issues in the various models. Given the focus on mixed logit models we briefly summarise their informational content and cross-reference to other sources for further details.

3.1. *A Stated choice experiment for long distance car travel (Data Set 1)*

A survey of long-distance road travel was undertaken in 2000, sampling residents of six cities/regional centres in New Zealand (i.e. Auckland, Hamilton, Palmerston North, Wellington, Christchurch, and Dunedin on both the North and South Islands). The main survey was executed as a laptop-based face-to-face interview in which each respondent was asked to complete the survey in the presence of an interviewer at their residence. Each sampled respondent evaluated 16 stated choice situations, making two choices: the first involving choosing amongst three labelled SC alternatives and the current RP alternative, and the second choosing amongst the three SC alternatives A total of 274 effective interviews[8] with car drivers were undertaken producing 4,384 car driver cases for model estimation (i.e. 274 × 16 treatments). The choice experiment presents four alternatives to a respondent:

A. The current road the respondent is/has been using
B. A hypothetical 2 lane road
C. A hypothetical 4 lane road with no median
D. A hypothetical 4 lane road with a wide grass median

There are two choice responses, one including all four alternatives and the other excluding the current road option. All alternatives are described by six attributes except alternative A, which does not have toll cost. Toll cost is set to zero for alternative A since there are currently no toll roads in New Zealand. The attributes in the stated choice experiment are:

1. Time on the open road which is free flow (in minutes)
2. Time on the open road which is slowed by other traffic (in minutes)
3. Percentage of total time on open road spent with other vehicles close behind (i.e. tailgating) (%)
4. Curviness of the road (a four-level attribute – almost straight, slight, moderate, winding)[9]
5. Running costs (in dollars)
6. Toll cost (in dollars)

These six attributes have four levels which, were chosen as follows:

• Free Flow Travel Time:	–20%, –10%, +10%, +20%
• Time Slowed Down:	–20%, –10%, +10%, +20%
• Percent of time with vehicles close behind:	–50%, –25%, +25%, +50%
• Curviness:	almost straight, slight, moderate, winding
• Running Costs:	–10%, –5%, +5%, +10%
• Toll cost ($) for car and double for truck if trip duration is:	
– 1 hours or less	0, 0.5, 1.5, 3
– between 1 hour and 2 hours 30 minutes	0, 1.5, 4.5, 9
– more than 2 and a half hours	0, 2.5, 7.5, 15

The experimental design is a 4^6 profile in 32 choice situations. That is, there are two versions of 16 choice situations each. The design has been chosen to minimise the number of dominants in the choice situations. Within each version the order of the choice situations has been randomised to control for

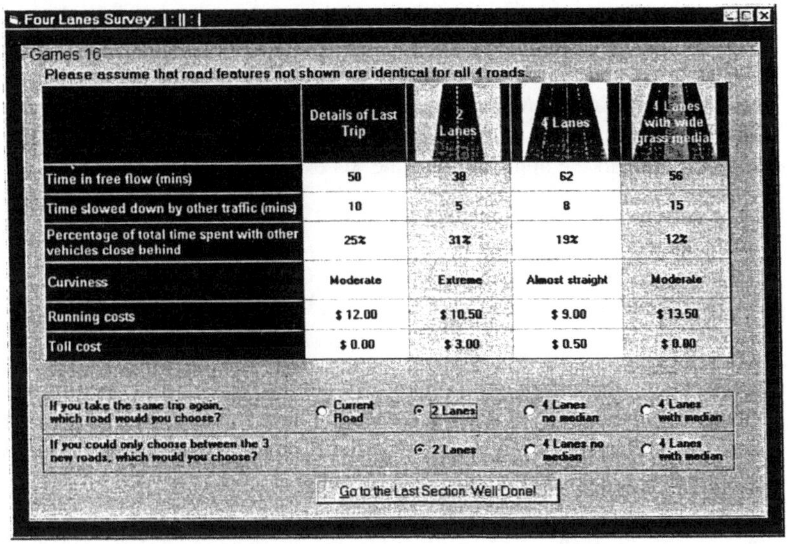

Figure 1. An example of a stated choice screen for data set 1.

order effect. For example, the levels proposed for alternative B should always be different from those of alternatives C and D.

The design attributes together with the choice responses and contextual data provide the information base for model estimation. An example of a stated choice screen is shown in Figure 1. Further details are given in Hensher and Sullivan (2003). Herein we focus only on models where individuals choose amongst the three SC alternatives.

3.2. *A stated choice experiment for urban commuting (Data Set 2)*

A survey of a sample of 143 commuters was undertaken in late June and early July 1999 in urban New Zealand sampling residents of seven cities/regional centres (i.e. Auckland, Wellington, Christchurch, Palmerston North, Napier/Hastings, Nelson and Ashburton on both the North and South Islands). The main survey was executed as a laptop-based face-to-face interview in which each respondent was asked to complete the survey in the presence of an interviewer. Each sampled respondent evaluated 16 choice situations, choosing amongst two SC alternatives and the current (revealed preference) alternative. The 143 interviews represent 2,288 cases for model estimation (i.e. 143 × 16 treatments).

The stated choice experimental design is based on two unlabelled alternatives (A and B) each defined by six attributes each of four levels (i.e. 4^{12}): free flow travel time, slowed up travel time, stop/crawling travel time, uncertainty of travel time, running cost and toll charges. Except for toll charges, the levels are *proportions* relative to those associated with a current trip identified prior to the application of the SC experiment:

Free flow travel time:	–0.25, –0.125, 0.125, 0.25
Slowed up travel time:	–0.5, –0.25, 0.25, 0.5
Stop/crawling travel time:	–0.5, –0.25, 0.25, 0.5
Uncertainty of travel time:	–0.5, –0.25, 0.25, 0.5
Car running cost:	–0.25, –0.125, 0.125, 0.25
Toll charges ($):	0, 2, 4, 6

The levels of the attributes for both SC alternatives were rotated to ensure that neither A nor B would dominate the current trip, and to ensure that A and B would not dominate each other. For example, if free flow travel time for alternative A was better than free flow travel time for the current trip, then we structured the design so that at least one among the five remaining attributes would be worse for alternative A relative to the current trip; and

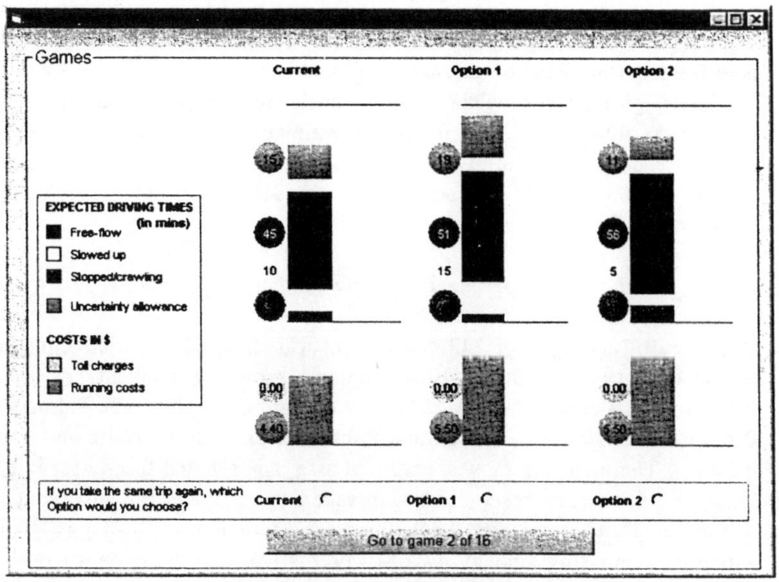

Figure 2. An example of a stated choice screen for data set 2.

likewise for the other potential situations of dominance. The fractional factorial design has 64 rows. We allocated four blocks of 16 "randomly" to each respondent, defining block 1 as the first 16 rows of the design, block 2 the second set of 16 etc. The assignment of levels to each SC attribute conditional on the current trip levels is straightforward. A stated choice screen is shown in Figure 2. Further details are provided in Hensher (2001a, b).

3.3. *A stated choice study of urban route choice for light commercial vehicles (Data Set 3)*

A stated choice experiment was designed as part of a study undertaken in 2001 in the Sydney metropolitan area to update values of travel time savings for car commuters, car non-commuters, light commercial vehicles and heavy trucks. We have selected the light commercial vehicle sub-sample of 60 interviews and 16 choice situations. The transport manager was interviewed together with the driver where the driver was an employee. Where the driver was the owner, he was the only person interviewed. The attributes in the design, their levels and range are summarised below:

Variables	Number of levels	Range
1- Free flow travel time	4	% variation from the current
2- Slowed down travel time	4	% variation from the current
3- Uncertainty in travel time	4	% variation from the current
4- Running costs	4	% variation from the current
5- Toll costs	4	$0 (free road) to $16
6- Toll Payment: Electronic/Tag	2	Present / absent
7- Toll Payment: Cash	2	Present / absent
8- Toll Payment: Electronic/Licence plate recognition (no tag required)	2	Present / absent

Attributes 1 to 5 are based on the values for the current trip, while attributes 6 to 8 are uniquely for the SC alternatives. Running costs have been specified as 10 litres/100 km with fuel at 97 c/litre for light commercial vehicles. In the design of the choice experiment, important considerations that needed to be accounted for were:

A. Toll should range from $0 to $16.
B. A longer trip should involve higher toll alternatives.
C. For a current trip without a toll, SC alternatives involving a toll should mostly be faster than the current trip.

D. We assume that the faster the road, the higher the toll; the lower the running costs, the lower the free-flow time; and the lower the slowed down time the lower the uncertainty.

To address issue D, four nests were built. The first one is for very fast, very expensive roads. The second is for fast and expensive roads. The third is for a normal speed road and normal costs while the fourth one is for relatively inexpensive and slow roads. These nests set a starting point around which the trip attributes will vary to create SC alternatives. A starting point is set for attributes 1 to 5. These starting points are:

	Free-flow time	Slowed down time	Uncertainty	Running costs	Toll costs
Nest 1	–70%	–70%	–70%	–35%	$13.5
Nest 2	–50%	–50%	–50%	–25%	$9.5
Nest 3	–30%	–30%	–30%	–15%	$5.5
Nest 4	–10%	–10%	–10%	–5%	$1.5

An index variable in the experimental design shows which nest the SC alternative should be built from. Then around the starting points of that nest, the route attributes 1 to 5 are varied on four levels as:

	Free-flow time	Slowed down time	Uncertainty	Running costs	Toll costs
Level 1	+6%	+6%	+3%	+6%	+$1.5
Level 2	+2%	+2%	+1%	+2%	+$0.5
Level 3	–2%	–2%	–1%	–2%	–$0.5
Level 4	–6%	–6%	–3%	–6%	–$1.5

With these variations, the SC alternatives using the first nest presents values of free-flow travel time ranging from –76% to –64% of current free-flow and slowed down times, from –73% to –67% of uncertainty, from –41% to –29% of running costs and from $15 to $12 of toll. To account for the toll amount paid for the current trip, another coefficient is used to offer realistic SC alternatives. For different toll levels, the variations allowed within each nest are derived. The overall design has 32 choice situations that are blocked in two versions of 16 choice situations. Each choice situation presents two stated choice alternatives and the current trip. A SC screen is shown in Figure 3.

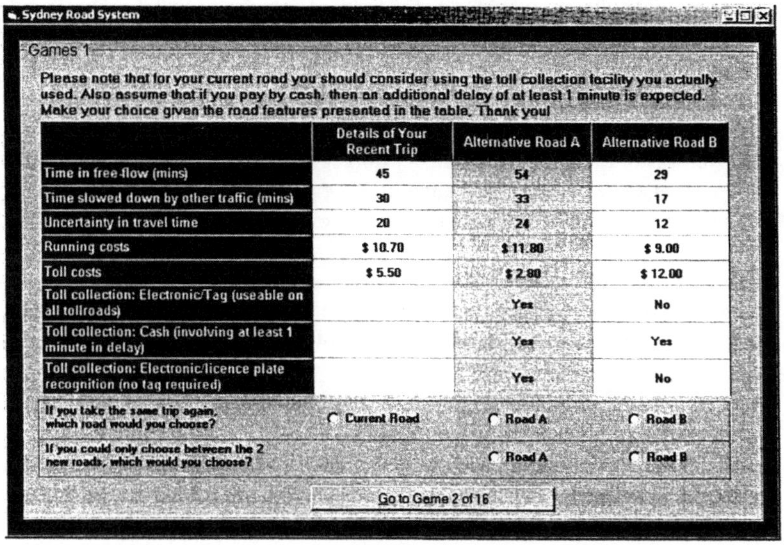

Sydney Road System

Games 1

Please note that for your current road you should consider using the toll collection facility you actually used. Also assume that if you pay by cash, then an additional delay of at least 1 minute is expected. Make your choice given the road features presented in the table. Thank you!

	Details of Your Recent Trip	Alternative Road A	Alternative Road B
Time in free-flow (mins)	45	54	29
Time slowed down by other traffic (mins)	30	33	17
Uncertainty in travel time	20	24	12
Running costs	$ 10.70	$ 11.80	$ 9.00
Toll costs	$ 5.50	$ 2.80	$ 12.00
Toll collection: Electronic/Tag (useable on all tollroads)		Yes	No
Toll collection: Cash (involving at least 1 minute in delay)		Yes	Yes
Toll collection: Electronic/licence plate recognition (no tag required)		Yes	No
If you take the same trip again, which road would you choose?	Current Road	Road A	Road B
If you could only choose between the 2 new roads, which would you choose?		Road A	Road B

Go to Game 2 of 16

Figure 3. An example of a stated choice screen for data set 3.

4. Model specification issues

4.1. *Selecting the random parameters*

The random parameters provide a rich array of preference information. They define the degree of preference heterogeneity through the standard deviation of the parameters and through interactions between the mean parameter estimate and deterministic segmentation criteria (the latter including other attributes of alternatives, socio-economic and contextual descriptors and even descriptors of the data collection method and instrument). They are also the basis for accommodating correlation across alternatives and across choice situations.

It is important to allocate a good proportion of time estimating models in which many of the attributes of alternatives are considered as having random parameters. The possibility of different distributional assumptions (see Section 4.2) for each attribute should also be investigated, especially where sign is important. The findings will not necessarily be independent of the number of random draws in the simulation (see Equation (7) and Section 4.3). Establishing the appropriate set of random parameters requires consideration of the number (and type) of draws, the distributional assumptions and, in the case of multiple choice situations per individual, whether correlated choice situations are accounted for (see Sections 4.5 and 4.6). These interdependencies may make for a lengthy estimation process.

Estimation of a multinomial logit model is an essential starting point for establishing candidate attributes and their (deterministic) functional form,[10] However it is of limited value in the a priori selection of random parameterised attributes unless extensive segmentation on each attribute occurs.

To assist in the establishment of candidate random parameters, the Lagrange Multiplier test proposed in McFadden and Train (2000) provides one statistical basis for accepting/rejecting the preservation of fixed parameters in the model. Brownstone (2001) provides a succinct summary of the test. These tests work by constructing artificial variables as in Equation (8).

$$z_{in} = (x_{in} - \overline{x}_i)^2, \text{ with } \overline{x}_i = \Sigma_j x_{jn} P_{jn}, \tag{8}$$

and P_{jn} is the conditional logit choice probability. The conditional logit model is then re-estimated including these artificial variables, and the null hypothesis of no random coefficients on attributes x is rejected if the coefficients of the artificial variables are significantly different from zero. The actual test for the joint significance of the z variables can be carried out using either a Wald or Likelihood Ratio test statistic. These Lagrange Multiplier tests can be easily carried out in any software package that estimates the conditional logit model. Brownstone suggests that these tests are easy to calculate and appear to be quite powerful omnibus tests; however, they are not as good for identifying which error components to include in a more general mixed logit specification. Another test (suggested by a referee) is to assume all parameters are random and then examine their estimated standard deviations, using a zero-based t-test for individual parameters and the likelihood-ratio test to establish the overall contribution of the additional information. While appealing, this is very demanding for a large number of explanatory variables and might be problematic in establishing the model with a full set of random parameters.

4.2. *Selecting the distribution of the random parameters*

If there is one single issue that can cause much concern it is the influence of the distributional assumptions of random parameters.[11] The layering of selected random parameters can take a number of predefined functional forms, the most popular being normal, triangular, uniform and lognormal. The lognormal form is often used if the response parameter needs to be a specific (non-negative) sign. A uniform distribution with a (0, 1) bound is sensible when we have dummy variables.

Distributions are essentially arbitrary approximations to the real behavioural profile. We select specific distributions because we have a sense that the "empirical truth" is somewhere in their domain. All distributions in common practice unfortunately have at least one major deficiency – typically with respect to sign and length of the tail(s). Truncated or constrained distributions appear to be the most promising direction in the future given recent concerns (see Section 4.2.4). For example, we might propose a generalised constrained triangular in which the spread of the distribution is allowed to vary within 10% of the mean. The normal is a well-known distribution. The uniform, triangular and log-normal are less well known and are documented below.

4.2.1. *Uniform distribution*
The spread of the uniform distribution (i.e. the distance up and down from the mean) and the standard deviation are different and while both can be used, the former is preferred in representing the uniform distribution. Suppose s is the spread, such that the time parameter is uniformly distributed from (mean – s) to (mean + s). Then the parameter is distributed as (mean parameter estimate + $s(2u - 1)$) where u is the standard uniformly distributed [0, 1] underlying variable. Since the distribution of u is uniform from 0 to 1, $2u - 1$ is uniform from -1 to $+1$; then multiplying by s gives a uniform +/– s from the mean. The standard deviation can be derived from the spread by dividing s by $\sqrt{3}$.

4.2.2. *Triangular distribution*
For the triangular distribution, the density function looks like a tent: a peak in the centre and dropping off linearly on both sides of the centre. Let c be the centre and s the spread. The density starts at $c - s$, rises linearly to c, and then drops linearly to $c + s$. It is zero below $c - s$ and above $c + s$. The mean and mode are c. The standard deviation is $s/\sqrt{6}$; hence the spread is the standard deviation times $\sqrt{6}$. The height of the tent at c is $1/s$ (such that each side of the tent has area $s \times (1/s) \times (1/2) = 1/2$, and both sides have area $1/2 + 1/2 = 1$, as required for a density). The slope is $1/s^2$. See Evans et al. (1993) for formal proofs.

4.2.2. *Lognormal distribution*
The lognormal distribution is very popular for the following reasoning. The central limit theorems explain the genesis of a normal curve. If a large number of random shocks, some positive, some negative, change the size of a particular attribute, x, in an additive fashion, the distribution of that attribute will tend to become normal as the number of shocks increases. But if these shocks act multiplicatively, changing the value of x by randomly distributed proportions instead of absolute amounts, the central limit theorems applied to $Y = \ln(x)$

tend to produce a normal distribution. Hence x has a lognormal distribution. The substitution of multiplicative for additive random shocks generates a positively skewed, leptokurtic, lognormal distribution instead of a symmetric, mesokurtic normal distribution. The degree of skewness and kurtosis of the two-parameter lognormal distribution depends only on the variance of the normal distribution, and so if this is low enough, the lognormal approximates the normal distribution. Lognormals are appealing in that they are limited to the non-negative domain; however they typically have a very long right-hand tail which is a disadvantage (especially for willingness-to-pay calculations – see Section 4.7). It is this large proportion of "unreasonable" values that often casts doubt on the appropriateness of the lognormal.

In parameter estimation, experience has demonstrated that entering an attribute in a utility expression specified with a random parameter that is lognormally distributed, and which is expected a priori to produce a negative mean estimate, typically causes the model to either not converge or converge with unacceptably large mean estimates (see Section 4.5). The trick to overcome this is to reverse the sign of the attribute prior to model estimation (i.e. define the negative of the attribute instead of imposing a sign change on the estimated parameter). The logic is as follows. The lognormal has a nonzero density only for positive numbers. So to ensure that an attribute has a negative parameter for all sampled individuals, one has to enter the negative of the attribute. A positive lognormal parameter for the negative of the attribute is the same as a negative lognormal parameter on the attribute itself.

4.2.4. *Imposing constraints on a distribution*

In practice we often find that any one distribution has strengths and weaknesses. The weakness is usually associated with the spread or standard deviation of the distribution at its extremes including behaviourally unacceptable sign changes for the symmetrical distributions. The lognormal has a long upper tail. The normal, uniform and triangular may give the "wrong" sign to some parameter depending on the standard deviation. One appealing "solution" is to make the spread or standard deviation of each random parameter a function of the mean. For example, the usual specification in terms of a normal distribution is to define $\beta_i = \beta + sv_i$ where v_i is the random variable. The constrained specification would be $\beta_i = \beta + \beta v_i$ so that the standard deviation equals the mean (recall, the standard deviation of v_i is one) or $\beta_i = \beta + z\beta v_i$ where z is the coefficient of variation taking any positive value. We would generally expect z to lie in the 0–1 range since a standard deviation greater than the mean estimate *typically* results in behaviourally unacceptable parameter estimates. (This is not part of the stochastic specification, however. If z is not set in advance, and is treated instead as a parameter to estimate, then this is the same as allowing the standard deviation of β_i to be unrestricted. In our analysis, we experimented with different values of z, but the most useful one is the unit value discussed in the next paragraph.)

This constraint specification can be applied to any distribution. In particular, however, for a triangular with mean = spread, if $z = 1$, then the density starts at zero, rises linearly to the mean, and then declines to zero again at twice the mean. It is peaked, as one would expect. It is bounded below at zero, bounded above at a reasonable value that is estimated, and is symmetric such that the mean is easy to interpret. This is appealing for handling willingness to pay parameters which must be positive. Also with $\beta_i = \beta + \beta v_i$, where v_i has support from −1 to +1, the sign of β is unconstrained. A negative coefficient on v_i simply reverses all the signs of the draws, but does not change the interpretation. In this instance, the range of variation would be restricted to the interval (2β, 0). For example, this might constrain a price coefficient to be negative.

4.2.5. *Discrete distributions*

The set of continuous distributions presented above impose a priori restrictions. An alternative is a discrete distribution. Such a distribution may be viewed as a nonparametric estimator of the random distribution. Using a discrete distribution that is identical across individuals is equivalent to a latent segmentation model with the probability of belonging to a segment being only a function of constants (See Ch. 10 of Louviere et al. (2000) for a discussion on such models.) However allowing this probability to be a function of individual attributes is equivalent to allowing the points characterising the nonparametric distribution to vary across individuals. In this paper, we focus on a continuous distribution for the random components. Greene and Hensher (2003) contrast a latent class model with mixed logit.

4.2.6. *An empirical comparison of the analytical distributions*

In most empirical studies, one tends to get similar means and comparable measures of variance for normal, uniform and triangular distributions. With the lognormal, however, the evidence tends to shift around a lot. The mean of a normal, uniform or triangular, typically lies between the mode and mean of the lognormal. In Table 1 we present some typical findings on a key behavioural output – the value of travel time savings (VTTS) using Data Set 1, noting that the standard deviation is used in the normal and lognormal distributions and the spread in the uniform and triangular distributions. The VTTS is given as the ratio of the marginal utilities of time and cost. Herein the cost parameter (marginal utility) has been assumed to be non-random and the marginal utility of time is allowed to vary with trip length and has a random component. The results in Table 1 are derived using the following formulae:

Lognormal:

$$mlvotl = \frac{-60 \times (\exp(-5.40506 - 0.0075148 \times tripl + 2.36613 \times n_a))}{-0.1048};$$

Normal:

$$mlvotn = \frac{60 \times (-0.012575 + 0.00002840 \times tripl + 0.00881228 \times n_b)}{-0.10355};$$

Triangular:

$$mlvott = \frac{60 \times (-0.0125428 + 0.000028117 \times tripl + 0.0203768 \times t)}{-0.103448};$$

where t is obtained from a standard uniform $V = U[0, 1]$ by $t = \sqrt{2V} - 1$ if $V < 0.5$ else $t = 1 - \sqrt{2(1 - V)}$;

Uniform:

$$mlvotu = \frac{60 \times (-0.0120956 + 0.0000258667 \times tripl + 0.0128616 \times (2u_c - 1))}{-0.1032216}$$

Table 1. A comparison of estimates of values of travel time savings (Data Set 1)

		Mean	Standard deviation or spread
Value of Travel Time Savings ($ per person hour)			
Lognormal	*mlvotl*	14.759	165.4
Normal	*mlvotn*	4.665	5.361
Triangular	*mlvott*	4.629	5.107[a]
Uniform	*mlvotu*	4.628	4.592[a]
Using Standard Deviation instead of Spread:			
Triangular	*mlvotts*	4.636	2.588[b]
Uniform	*mlvotus*	2.451	2.001[b]

Note: the standard deviation of the triangular distribution is $0.0203768/\sqrt{6}$; the standard deviation of a uniform distribution is $0.0128616/\sqrt{3}$. In the last column, 'a' indicates that we have calculated the standard deviation for the descriptive statistics based on the application of the spread formula, and 'b' indicates that we used the standard deviation formula.

where *tripl* is trip length in minutes, 60 is the conversion from dollars per minute to dollars per hour, *n* has a standard normal distribution, *u* has a uniform distribution and *t* has a triangular distribution. The VTTS for each individual has been estimated by repeated (250) random draws for n_a, n_b, t and u_c and the mean and standard deviation (or spread) derived.

The moments for the normal, triangular and uniform are quite similar (including the overall goodness of fit of the associated models not reported); the lognormal is noticeably different with an unacceptably large standard deviation. The lognormal however guarantees non-negative VTTS whereas the other three (unconstrained distributions) almost certainly imply some negative VTTS revealed in Figure 4. (See Section 4.2.7 for a discussion of how the figures are produced.) In this application, the percentage of VTTS that are negative for normal, triangular and uniform are respectively 19.21%, 39.33% and 37.92%.[12] These percentages are obtained from a cumulative frequency distribution of VTTS.

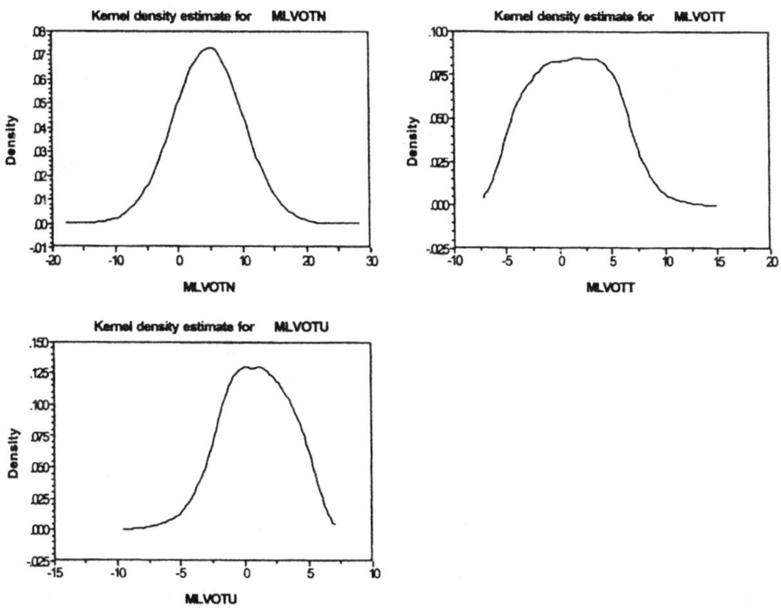

Figure 4. Incidence of negative VTTS for normal, triangular and uniform distributions.

4.2.7. *Revealing empirical distributions in assisting the search for analytical distributions*

Selecting an analytical distribution that has desirable behavioural properties is not an easy task as already indicated above. Indeed the real distribution may be bi-modal or multi-modal with the consequence that none of the popular distributions are suitable. Given the uncertainty in picking an appropriate analytical distribution for the random parameters, an empirical perspective can be useful. That is, can we inform the choice of distribution by reference to parameter estimation at the individual level? This involves establishing unique (mean) parameter estimates for each sampled individual and then plotting the distribution (simply calculating a standard deviation or spread fails to reveal the shape of the distribution).

To illustrate this, given a sufficiently rich data set (such as Data Set 2) in which we have multiple observations on each sampled individual (common in stated choice experiments), we might estimate a multinomial logit model for each sampled individual using a 16 choice situation. The derived individual-specific parameter estimates can be plotted non-parametrically using kernel densities (defined below and in Greene 2002) to reveal information about their distribution across the sampled population. Examining the empirical distribution of the individual-specific parameters gives clues about structure and ways that this structure might be incorporated back into a mixed logit model.

Establishing the true distribution empirically is however a challenge because of the biases that can exist in real data, be it revealed or stated choice data. When individual-specific models are to be estimated, the variability in attribute levels across the choice situations becomes even more crucial. Stated choice designs with limited variability (especially if the variability is a fixed range relative to a current alternative) can create problems in achieving asymptotically efficient parameter estimates. It is not uncommon to find unacceptably large *t*-values and incorrect signs in models estimated using a single individuals data on a number of choice situations. For example, in data set 2 with individual models estimated on 16 choice situations and 10 degrees of freedom, up to 80% of the sampled individuals had one parameter that was not statistically significant (sometimes including a wrong sign).[13] We suspect this is largely the product of limited variability in the attribute levels offered in the stated choice experiments across the choice situations at the individual respondent level.[14] Improved variability can be achieved by a number of strategies such as increasing the number of levels in a wide range, and sampling across alternative attribute ranges for a given attribute with a common number of levels (e.g. four levels) across the choice situations. It could also be accommodated by pooling subsets of individuals provided one can establish agreed segmentation criteria (e.g. trip length, personal income). The selection of an appropriate strategy is complex and is under-researched.

Our proposed approach involves estimating $Q + 1$ models (where Q is the 143 individuals in the sample). Except for a model involving the entire sample, each of the other models is distinguished by the removal of a different individual.[15] The difference in the numerical value of the parameter estimates for a model based on the full sample (143) and each of the models based on 142 individuals provides the contribution (incremental marginal utility) of a specific individual to the overall sample mean parameter estimate and hence the profile of individual preference heterogeneity. Data Set 2 is used to illustrate this procedure.

The matrix of parameter estimates for 143 models are plotted to establish the empirical profile for each attribute's marginal utility (i.e. preference heterogeneity). The kernel density estimator is a useful device since it can describe the distribution of a parameter non-parametrically, that is, without any assumption of the underlying analytical distribution. The kernel density is a modification of the familiar histogram used to describe the distribution of a sample of observations graphically. The disadvantages of the histogram that are overcome with kernel estimators are, first that histograms are discontinuous whereas (our models assume) the underlying distributions are continuous and, second, the shape of the histogram is crucially dependent on the assumed widths and placements of the bins. Intuition suggests that the first of these problems is mitigated by taking narrower bins, but the cost of doing so is that the number of observations that land in each bin falls so that the larger picture painted by the histogram becomes increasingly variable and imprecise. The kernel density estimator is a "smoothed" plot that shows, for each selected point, the proportion of the sample that is "near" it. (Hence, the name "density.") Nearness is defined by a weighting function called the kernel function, which will have the characteristic that the farther a sample observation is from the selected point, the smaller will be the weight that it receives.

The kernel density function for a single attribute is computed using formula (9).

$$f(z_j) = \frac{1}{n} \sum_{i=1}^{n} \frac{K[(z_j - x_i) / h]}{h}, j = 1, \ldots, M. \tag{9}$$

The function is computed for a specified set of values of interest, z_j, $j = 1, \ldots, M$ where z_j is a partition of the range of the attribute. Each value requires a sum over the full sample of n values, x_i, $i = 1, \ldots, n$. The primary component of the computation is the kernel, or weighting function, $K[.]$ which take a number of forms. For example, the normal kernel is $K[z] = \phi(z)$ (normal density). Thus, for the normal kernel, the weights range from $\phi(0) = 0.399$ when $x_i = z_j$ to values approaching zero when x_i is far from z_j. Thus, again, what the kernel density function is measuring is the proportion of the sample of values that is close to the chosen z_j.

The other essential part of the computation is the smoothing (bandwidth) parameter, h to ensure a good plot resolution. The bandwidth parameter is exactly analogous to the bin width in a common histogram. Thus, as noted earlier, narrower bins (smaller bandwidths) produce unstable histograms (kernel density estimators) because not many points are "in the neighbourhood" of the value of interest. Large values of h stabilise the function, but tend to flatten it and reduce the resolution – imagine a histogram with only two or three bins, for example. Small values of h produce greater detail, but also cause the estimator to become less stable. An example of a bandwidth is given in formula (10), which is a standard form used in several contemporary computer programs (e.g., Stata, LIMDEP):

$$h = 0.9Q/n^{0.2} \text{ where } Q = \min(\text{standard deviation, range}/1.5) \quad (10)$$

A number of points have to be specified. The set of points z_j is (for any number of points) defined by formula (11).

$$z_j = z_{\mathrm{LOWER}} + j \times [(z_{\mathrm{UPPER}} - z_{\mathrm{LOWER}})/M],$$
$$j = 1, \ldots, M \; z_{\mathrm{LOWER}} = \min(_x) - h \text{ to } z_{\mathrm{UPPER}} = \max(x) + h \quad (11)$$

The procedure produces an $M \times 2$ matrix in which the first column contains z_j and the second column contains the values of $f(z_j)$ and plot of the second column against the first – this is the estimated density function. Using the kernel density to graphically describe the empirical distributions for three parameters – free flow time, slowed down time and toll cost. (Figure 5), we can establish the empirical shape of each distribution. A close inspection of the properties of each distribution (i.e. kurtosis and skewness) suggest approximate analytical distributions. For example, the toll cost attribute looks lognormal, in contrast the free flow parameter appears normal, while the slowdown parameter's longish right tail and symmetry to the left of the tail qualifies for neither a normal nor a lognormal distribution. These empirical distributions have thus guided the analyst to the domain of the normal and lognormal in this instance. One useful follow-up strategy is to regress the 143 parameter estimates across the sample of individuals against contextual variables such as socio-economic characteristics to see if there is any possible relationship between location on the distribution for a parameter estimate and these contextual influences. If there is evidence for example that the longish tail in slowdown time can be "explained" by high vs low income then maybe the interaction of slowdown time with a number of income ranges would establish a revised (possibly normal) distribution over the low and high income ranges respectively.

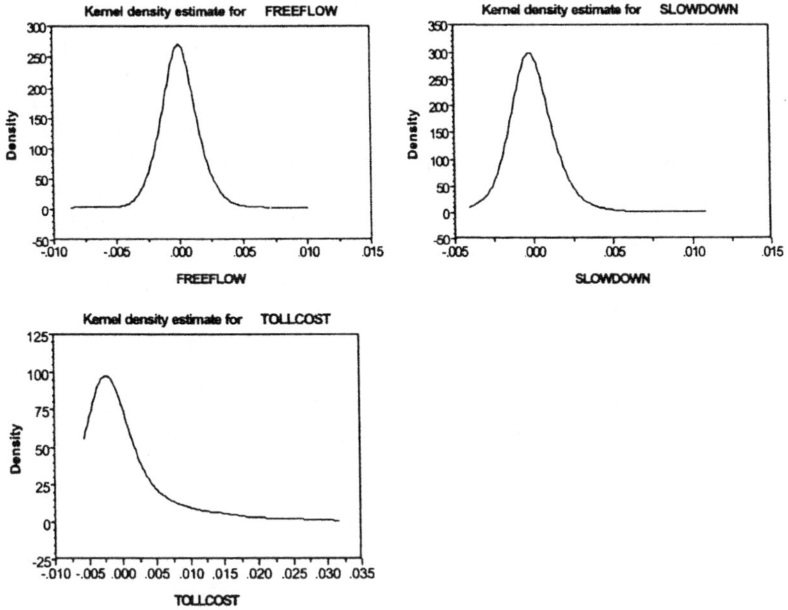

Figure 5. Empirical distributions (Data Set 2) for 143 individuals derived non-parametrically for three parameters.

4.3. *Selecting the number of points for the simulations*

The number of draws required to secure a stable set of parameter estimates varies enormously. In general, it appears that as the model specification becomes more complex in terms of the number of random parameters and the treatment of preference heterogeneity around the mean, as well as correlation of attributes and alternatives, the number of required draws increases for a given type of draw (e.g. Halton intelligent draws). There is no standard number but experience suggests that a choice model with three alternatives and one or two random parameters (with no correlation between the attributes and no decomposition of heterogeneity around the mean) can produce stability with as low as 25 *intelligent* draws (e.g., Halton sequences – see Bhat (2001) and Train (2003) for discussion), although 100 appears to be a "good" number. The best test however is to estimate models over a range of draws (e.g. 25, 50, 100, 250, 500, 1,000 and 2,000 draws). Confirmation of stability/precision for *each and every model* is very important. Table 2 with only one random parameter provides a series of runs from 25 to 2,000 intelligent draws (car drivers in Data Set 1). The results stabilise after about 500 draws, which is probably more than are necessary, especially given only one dimension of integration. Given the usual scale considerations in comparing model parameter estimates, the ratio of the mean to its standard deviation for the random parameter, total time, is informative in showing how the stability of the relationship of the first two moments of the distribution settles down. In this application, the range of the ratio across the entire range of draws is sufficiently similar to not send out alarm bells about some unacceptable change in the shape or spread of the distribution. This is particularly important when deriving empirical distributions for willingness to pay indicators such as VTTS.

One might ask why the analyst does not simply select a larger number of draws in recognition of the greater likelihood of arriving at the appropriate set of stable parameter estimates? The reason why a smaller number of draws is a relevant consideration is essentially practical – the ability to explore alternative model specifications relatively quickly before estimating the preferred model on a large number of draws. Even with fast computers, it can take hours of run time with many random parameters, large sample sizes and thousands of draws. To know when parameter stability cuts in is of immense practical virtue, enabling the analyst to search for improved models in a draw domain that is less likely to mislead the inferential process.

Bhat (2001) and Train (1999) found that the simulation variance in the estimated parameters was lower using 100 Halton numbers than 1,000 random numbers. With 125 Halton draws, they both found the simulation error to be half as large as with 1,000 random draws and smaller than with 2,000 random draws. The estimation procedure is much faster (often 10 time faster). Hensher (2000) investigated Halton sequences involving draws of 10, 25, 50, 100, 150 and 200 (with three random generic parameters) and compared the findings in the context of VTTS with random draws. In all models investigated Hensher concluded that a small number of draws (as low as 25) produces model fits and mean VTTS that are almost indistinguishable. This is a phenomenal development in the estimation of complex choice models. However before we can confirm that we have found the "best" draw strategy, researchers are finding that other possibilities may be even better. For example, research by Sandor and Train (2002) investigating random, Halton, Niederreiter and orthogonal array latin hypercube draws finds the results "often perplexing" with purely random draws sometimes doing much better than they should and sometimes all the various types of draws doing much worse than they should. What are we missing in simulation variance of the estimates? Perhaps the differences in estimates with different draws is due to the optimisation algorithm?[16] Recent research by Bhat (in press) on the type of draws vis-a-vis the dimensionality of integration suggests that the uniformity of the standard

Table 2. Mixed Logit Models

Attributes	Alternative	Mixed Logit (lognormal random parameter) Number of Intelligent Draws						
(i) With Heterogeneity in Mean		**25**	**50**	**100**	**250**	**500**	**1000**	**2000**
Random Parameters:								
Total time	All	–4.9174 (–7.0)	–5.2996 (–5.6)	–5.416 (–5.9)	–5.232 (–6.1)	–5.158 (–6.1)	–5.1043 (–6.1)	–5.1279 (6.2)
Fixed Parameters:								
Total cost	All	–0.1294 (–48)	–0.1294 (–48)	–0.1295 (–48)	–0.1296 (–48)	–0.1296 (–48)	–0.1296 (–48)	0.1296 (–48)
Tailgate percentage	All	–0.01138 (–9.4)	–0.01134 (–9.3)	–0.01135 (–9.4)	–0.01135 (–9.4)	–0.01134 (–9.4	–0.01134 (–9.4)	–0.01135 (–9.4)
Non–winding vs winding curviness	2–lane	0.3036 (2.3)	0.3085 (2.3)	0.3080 (2.3)	0.3073 (2.3)	0.3066 (2.3)	0.3066 (2.3)	0.30687 (2.3)
Non–winding vs winding curviness	4–lane	0.5652 (10)	0.5707 (10.3)	0.5703 (10.3)	0.5712 (10.3)	0.5711 (10.2)	0.5709 (10.3)	0.5708 (10.3)
Constant	4 no median	0.1179 (1.0)	0.1200 (0.94)	0.1196 (0.9)	0.1175 (0.9)	0.1169 (0.9)	0.1168 (0.9)	0.1173 (0.9)
Constant	4 with median	0.7569 (5.9)	0.7491 (5.9)	0.7484 (5.9)	0.7461 (5.9)	0.7453 (5.9)	0.7453 (5.9)	0.7458 (5.9)
Heterogeneity in mean:								
Travel time: Trip length	All	–0.006375 (–2.3)	–0.00913 (–2.0)	–0.00757 (–1.85)	–0.00799 (–1.97)	–0.00789 (–2.0)	–0.00796 (–2.1)	–0.00788 (–2.0)
Std Deviation of parameter distribution								
Total time	All	1.6085 (7.2)	2.2926 (5.9)	2.0946 (6.1)	1.9103 (5.5)	0.1.8348 (5.0)	1.7969 (4.8)	1.8097 (5.2)
Adjusted ρ^2		0.167	0.1669	0.1675	0.1679	0.1679	0.1679	0.1679
Log-likelihood		–4009.9	–4008.1	–4005.3	–4003.4	–4003.4	–4003.3	–4003.4
Random parameter mean/ standard deviation(*)		3.057	2.31	2.59	2.74	2.81	2.84	2.83

(ii) Without Heterogeneity in Mean		25	50	100	250	500	1000	2000
Random Parameters:								
Total time	All	–6.519	–6.637	–7.5291	–7.2502	–7.251	–7.2154	–7.1899
		(–17.3)	(–14.6)	(–9.1)	(10.0)	(–9.6)	(–9.5)	(–9.6)
Fixed Parameters:								
Total cost	All	–0.1297	–0.1296	–0.1297	–0.1298	–0.1298	–0.1299	–0.1299
		(–48)	(–48)	(–48)	(–48)	(–48)	(–48)	(–48)
Tailgate percentage	All	–0.01136	–0.01134	–0.01137	–0.01136	–0.01136	–0.01136	–0.01136
		(–9.4)	(9.4)	(–9.4)	(–9.4)	(–9.4)	(–9.4)	(9.4)
Non–winding vs winding curviness	2–lane	0.3037	0.3045	0.3078	0.3071	0.3067	0.3065	0.3064
		(2.3)	(2.3)	(2.3)	(2.3)	(2.3)	(2.3)	(2.3)
Non–winding vs winding curviness	4–lane	0.566	0.5667	0.5714	0.5714	0.5718	0.5717	0.5717
		(10.3)	(10.3)	(10.3)	(10.3)	(10.3)	(10.3)	(10.3)
Constant	4 no median	0.1195	0.1196	0.1185	0.1170	0.1163	0.1161	0.1160
		(0.9)	(0.9)	(0.9)	(0.9)	(0.9)	(0.9)	(0.9)
Constant	4 with median	0.7473	0.7475	0.7466	0.7452	0.7444	0.7441	0.7434
		(6.0)	(6.0)	(5.9)	(6.0)	(5.9)	(5.9)	(5.9)
Std Deviation of parameter distribution								
Total time	All	2.057	2.0763	2.6516	2.321	2.310	2.279	2.248
		(10.9)	(9.0)	(5.9)	(5.9)	(5.2)	(5.0)	(4.9)
Adjusted ρ^2		0.1658	0.1661	0.1669	0.1673	0.1673	0.1673	0.1673
Log–likelihood		–4013.9	–4012.5	–4008.7	–4007.0	–4007.1	–4007.1	–4007.1
Random parameter mean/ standard deviation		3.168	3.212	2.839	3.124	3.139	3.166	3.198

* This ratio does not account for the trip length effect around the mean but is useful in gauging how the ratio varies.
All travel times are in minutes and costs are in dollars. *T*–values in brackets Source: Data Set 1.

Halton sequence breaks down in high dimensions because of the correlation in sequences of high dimension. Bhat proposes a scrambled version to break these correlations, and a randomised version to compute variance estimates. These examples of recent research demonstrate the need for ongoing inquiry into simulated draws, especially as the number of attributes with imposed distributions increases.[17]

4.4. *Preference heterogeneity around the mean of a random parameter*

Introducing an interaction between the mean estimate of the random parameter and a covariate is equivalent to revealing the presence or absence of preference heterogeneity around the mean parameter estimate.[18] This is not the same as the standard deviation of the parameter estimate associated with a random parameter. If the interaction is not statistically significant then we can conclude that there is an absence of preference heterogeneity around the mean on the basis of the observed covariates. This does not imply that there is no preference heterogeneity around the mean, but simply that we have failed to reveal its presence. This then means that the analyst relies fully on the mean and the standard deviation of the parameter estimate, with the latter representing all sources of preference heterogeneity.

To illustrate the role of preference heterogeneity around the mean, we contrast the findings in Table 2 with and without heterogeneity around the mean where the heterogeneity is defined by trip length. The presence of a statistically significant interacting covariate reduces the role of the "non-interactive" component of the mean estimate for travel time. When combined with this mean estimate in the current application it produces a relativity between the overall mean and the parameter estimate of the standard deviation that is slightly higher when heterogeneity around the mean is represented by trip length. Given each sampled individual's trip length, the ratio is 3.55 with heterogeneity and 3.19 without heterogeneity. The interest in this relativity is attributed to the desire to reduce the standard deviation or spread of the parameter estimate in order to establish sensible estimates across the entire distribution (which is not always possible with unconstrained distributions). What we find here is that the sources of preference heterogeneity are represented to some small extent by the decomposition of the mean but much remains within the random component. This highlights the growing need to focus research on the variability in the random component (Louviere et al. 2002) and a recognition that potential sources of variability are associated with many sources (such as the study design) often not captured by the attributes of alternatives and characteristics of respondents.

4.5. *Accounting for observations drawn from the same individual: correlated choice situations*

Observations drawn from the same individual, as in stated choice experiments, are a common source of data for mixed logit estimation. In part this link is the result of a recognition that SC data are usually much richer than revealed preference (RP) data and hence SC data open up real opportunities to enhance the behavioural capability of the mixed logit model.

The presence of multiple observations on stated choice responses for each sampled individual means that the potential for correlated responses across observations is a violation of the independence of observations assumption in classical choice model estimation. This correlation can be the product of many sources including the commonality of socio-economic descriptors that do not vary across the choice situations for a given sampled individual and the sequencing of offered choice situations that results in mixtures of learning and inertia effects, amongst other possible influences on choice response.

Mixed logit models, through the relaxation of the IIA property, enable the model to be specified in such a way that the error components in different choice situations from a given individual are correlated. To motivate this point and show in particular that correlation and preference heterogeneity are related and hence a key as to how mixed logits handle correlation across choice situations, think of the unobserved sources of utility and how they might be treated. Consider a simple random utility model, in which there are heterogeneous preferences for observed and unobserved attributes of offered alternatives:

$$U_{itq} = \alpha_{iq} + \gamma_q p_{itq} + \beta_q x_{itq} + \varepsilon_{itq} \tag{12}$$

where most terms are defined in Section 2 except for p_{itq} which denotes price, and x_{itq} denotes observed attribute of i (which for complete generality varies across individuals and choice situations). α_{iq} denotes the individual-specific intercept for alternative i, arising from q's preferences for unobserved attributes of i. γ_q and β_q are individual-specific utility parameters that are intrinsic to the individual and hence invariant over choice situations. The ε_{itq} can be interpreted as task-specific shocks to q's tastes, which for convenience are assumed to be independent over choice situations, alternatives and individuals.

Suppose we estimate an MNL model, incorrectly assuming that the intercept and slope parameters are homogeneous in the population. The random component in this model will be

$$w_{itq} = \hat{\alpha}_{iq} + \hat{\gamma}_q p_{itq} + \hat{\beta}_q x_{itq} + \varepsilon_{itq} \tag{13}$$

where ^ denotes the individual-specific deviation from the population mean. Observe that (from the analyst's perspective) the variance of this random component for individual q in choice situation t is

$$\mathrm{var}(w_{itq}) = \sigma^2_{\alpha i} + \sigma^2_{\gamma} p^2_{itq} + \sigma^2_{\beta} x^2_{itq} + \sigma^2_{\varepsilon} \tag{14}$$

(assuming that the parameters are uncorrelated) and the covariance between choice situations t and $t - 1$ is

$$\mathrm{cov}(w_{itq}, w_{i,t-1,q}) = \sigma^2_{\alpha i} + \sigma^2_{\gamma} p^2_{itq} p_{i,t-1,q} + \sigma^2_{\beta} x_{itq} x_{i,t-1,q} \tag{15}$$

Equations (14) and (15) (which both assume independence between the various random effects) reveal two interesting consequences of ignoring preference heterogeneity. First, the error variance *will* differ across choice situations as the price p and attribute x are varied. If one estimates an MNL model with a constant error variance, this will impact the intercept and slope parameters across choice situations – in essence, the underlying variance will show up elsewhere in the model if it is not properly specified to begin with. For example, in an SC experiment context this could lead to a false conclusion that there are order effects in the process generating responses.[19]

Second, Equation (15) shows how preference heterogeneity can induce correlated errors across choice situations. This is revealed through the parameterisation of the interactions between the prices and the other attributes in two choice situations. *That heterogeneity is a special type of correlation amongst choice situations is not well understood.* To obtain efficient estimates of choice model parameters one should include a specification of the heterogeneity structure in the model. Daniels and Hensher (2000) and Bhat and Castelar (2002) indicate that the inter-alternative error correlation could be confounded with unobserved preference heterogeneity if the latter is not explicitly taken into account. One such way is to specify the parameters associated with each attribute (including price) as random,[20] which is exactly the intent of the mixed logit model.[21] As long as one recognises that the preference heterogeneity must treat all alternatives across all choice situations defining an individual's choice responses (i.e. 16 in data sets 1, 2 and 4) then correlation is automatically accommodated through the explicit modelling of preference heterogeneity present across all choice situations as defined by the underlying covariance matrix for the random parameters. This correlation is not likely to be autoregressive for "instantaneous" stated choices since it is not the product of a long period of accumulated experience commonly attributed to state dependence. Rather it is recognition in a very short time span of the sharing of preference heterogeneity between choice situations that is evaluated by the same individual. The discussion herein assumes that each attribute specified with a random parameter is independent of other such specified attributes in a given choice situations (within and between alternatives). This restriction, discussed in the next section, can be relaxed and tested.

4.6. *Accounting for correlation between parameters*

All data sets, regardless of the number of choice situations per sampled individual, may have unobserved effects that are correlated amongst alternatives in a given choice situation. One way to recognise this is to permit correlation of random parameters of attributes that are common across alternatives. This engenders a covariance matrix with off-diagonal estimates identifying the dependency (through representing the variance of each random parameter as an error component) of one attribute on another within and between alternatives (depending on whether the attribute parameters are generic or alternative-specific). It also has interesting ramifications for the correlated choice situation issue in the previous section.

Let us define the utility expression for each alternative as before (see Equation (1)): $U_{itq} = \boldsymbol{\beta}'_q x_{itq} + \varepsilon_{itq}$. Since $\boldsymbol{\beta}_q$ is random, it can be rewritten as $\boldsymbol{\beta}_q = \boldsymbol{\beta} + \mathbf{u}_q$ where $\boldsymbol{\beta}$ is fixed (i.e. the mean) and $\mathbf{u}_q$ is the deviation from the mean. Then $U_{itq} = \boldsymbol{\beta}' x_{itq} + (\mathbf{u}'_q \mathbf{x}_{itq} + \varepsilon_{itq})$. There is correlation over alternatives because $\mathbf{u}_q$ is the same for all alternatives. That is, each individual's preferences are used in the evaluation of the alternatives. For example, suppose $\mathbf{x}_{itq}$ contains a single element, x_{itq}. It follows that $\text{Cov}[(\mathbf{u}'_q \mathbf{x}_{itq} + \varepsilon_{itq}), (\mathbf{u}'_q \mathbf{x}_{isq} + \varepsilon_{isq})]$ equals $\sigma^2(u_q) x_{itq} x_{isq}$ where $\sigma^2(u_q)$ is the variance of u_q. In addition, however, there is also correlation over choice situations for each alternative because u_q is the same in each choice situation. Again another way of stating this is that each individual uses the same preferences to evaluate (relative) utilities in each choice situation (or time period). Thus $\text{Cov}[(u_q x_{itq} + \varepsilon_{itq}), (u_q x_{isq} + \varepsilon_{isq})]$ equals $\sigma^2(u_q) x_{itq} x_{isq}$. The behavioural implication is that random preferences induce correlation over alternatives *and* choice situations.

Thus both correlated alternatives and choice situations usually go hand in hand (assuming that one identifies the set of choice situations associated with each individual).[22] Correlation over alternatives and not over choice situations could however be established by specifying utility as $U_{itq} = \boldsymbol{\beta}'_{tq} \mathbf{x}_{itq} + \varepsilon_{isq}$ where $\boldsymbol{\beta}_{tq}$ represents preferences instead of β_q. Thus preferences vary over individuals and over choice situations with β_{tq} independent over choice situations for each individual. This is likely to be an unreasonable assumption for most situations. In particular, although for an individual preferences might vary over choice situations, it is doubtful that they are independent across these choice situations. In general, the mixed logit model can accommodate (i) correlation over alternatives and not over choice situations by assuming

β_{tq} is IID over choice situations, or (ii) correlation across choice situations but not over alternatives by fixing all of the parameters except those representing the alternative-specific constants (ASC's), and assuming that ASC parameters are IID over alternatives but the same for each individual across the choice situations.

Table 3 illustrates (using Data Set 1) the presence of correlated alternatives due to correlated random parameters that are both lognormally distributed. When we have more than one random parameter and we permit correlated random parameters then the standard deviations are no longer independent. To assess this we have to decompose the standard deviation parameters into their attribute-specific (e.g. travel time) and attribute-interaction (e.g. time × cost) standard deviations. The Cholesky decomposition is the method to do this (and is described fully in Section 4.7). The mixed logit model is extended to accommodate this case by allowing the set of random parameters to have an unrestricted covariance matrix. The nonzero off-diagonal element of this matrix carries the cross parameter correlations. The correlation matrix associated with Table 3 gives a correlation of 0.7799 between time and cost random parameters.

Table 3. An example of evidence of correlated alternatives

Attributes	Alternative	Mixed Logit (lognormal random parameter) *t*-values in brackets.	
Total time (mins)	All	−3.84218	(−15.9)
Total cost ($)	All	−0.756144	(−6.5)
Tailgate percentage	All	−0.012579	(9.9)
Constant	4 no median	0.42995	(17.4)
Constant	4 with median	1.1500	(63.1)
Heterogeneity in mean:			
Travel time: Trip length	All	−0.010399	(−7.8)
Travel cost: Trip length	All	−0.006197	(−11.5)
Cholesky matrix of random parameters:[a]			
Total time (L11)	All	1.8812	(12.8)
Total cost (L22)	All	0.882167	(18.6)
Time:Cost (L21)	All	1.0989	(12.3)
Adjusted ρ		0.2245	
Log-likelihood		−3730.8	

[a] The variance of the random parameter distribution is written in Cholesky factorization form, $\Sigma = \Gamma\Gamma'$.Γ is a lower triangular matrix. Rather than estimate Σ directly, we estimate the parameters in Γ then compute Σ as above. The values in Γ are reported. Further discussion appears in Section 4.7. The estimated elements of Σ are $\sigma_{11} = 1.8812^2$, $\sigma_{21} = 1.8812\ (1.0989) = 2.0672$, and $\sigma_{22} = 0.882167^2 + 1.0989^2 = 1.4091^2$. The implied correlation is 2.0672/(1.8812 (1.4091)) = 0.7799.

4.7. *Willingness to pay challenges*

Although selecting distributions for individual parameters is challenge enough, it is compounded when interest focuses on ratios of random parameters, as in the derivation of estimates of willingness to pay (WTP). For example, the ratio of two triangular parameters has a discontinuous distribution with either distribution having a singularity unless the range is forced to exclude zero. Infinite mean and variance occurs in both cases however. The ratio of two normals has the same problem with the singularity at zero for the denominator.

In deriving WTP estimates based on random parameters one can use all the information in the distribution or just the mean and standard deviation. The former is preferred but is more complicated. Simulation is used in the former case, drawing from the estimated covariance matrix for the parameters. To explain the two approaches, suppose we have a model with a fixed cost parameter β_1, and another attribute whose parameter is normally distributed with mean β_2 and standard deviation β_3. Then the willingness to pay for the attribute is distributed normally with mean β_2/β_1 and standard deviation β_3/β_1. We can use the point estimates of β_1, β_2, and β_3 to calculate these ratios. This approach takes the point estimates as given and ignores the sampling variance in these point estimates. To incorporate the sampling variation, let $\boldsymbol{\beta}$ be the vector with elements β_1, β_2, and β_3. The estimation process yields an estimated asymptotic covariance matrix for all the estimated parameters. One extracts the part for $\boldsymbol{\beta}$ (call it **W**), which is a 3 by 3 symmetric matrix. We now wish to draw random observations from the normal distribution which has mean $\boldsymbol{\beta}$ and covariance matrix **W**. The Cholesky decomposition provides a convenient way to do so.

The matrix **W** is decomposed into the product **LL′** where **L** is a lower triangular matrix. Then, the sample we seek can be drawn by first obtaining a set of three independent standard normal draws in a vector $\boldsymbol{\mu}$, which is simple since the three draws can be drawn independently. Then, the desired vector is computed as $\boldsymbol{\beta} + \mathbf{L}\boldsymbol{\mu}$. Thus, we generate draws of β_1, β_2, and β_3 as $\hat{\boldsymbol{\beta}} + \mathbf{L}\boldsymbol{\mu}$ where $\boldsymbol{\mu}$ is a three by one vector of IID standard normal deviates drawn from a random number generator and $\hat{\boldsymbol{\beta}}$ is the point estimate of $\boldsymbol{\beta}$. For each draw, calculate β_2/β_1 and β_3/β_1, which are the mean WTP and the standard deviation in WTP implied by those draws. Do this for many draws. Then calculate the mean and standard deviation of β_2/β_1 over these draws. That provides the estimated mean WTP and the standard error in this estimated mean. Also calculate the mean and standard deviation of β_3/β_1 over these draws to get the estimated standard deviation of WTP and the standard error of this estimate.

To accommodate the entire distribution of WTP (rather than just the mean and standard deviation), take a draw of β_1, β_2, and β_3 as described above (as

$\hat{\beta} + \mathbf{L}\boldsymbol{\mu}$. For this draw, one takes numerous draws of WTP, with each draw constructed as $(\beta_2 + \beta_3^{\mu})/\beta_1$. Repeat for many draws of β_1, β_2, and β_3, to get many sets of draws of WTP. Then, you can calculate whatever you want to know about WTP from the combined set of WTP draws; e.g., you can calculate the probability that WTP exceeds some amount. Using the four lane data for car drivers (Data Set 1) we estimated three models (Table 4) and report the VTTS outputs using the formulae set out just before Table 1. The first model treats travel time as a random parameter, the second model treats travel cost as a random parameter, and the third model allows both travel time and cost to have random parameters. The random parameters are assumed to be correlated in the third model and hence the Cholesky decomposition is used to identify the standard deviations (or spread).[23]

A lognormal distribution was imposed on all random parameters with sign reversal of the attributes associated with these parameters. The VTTS (per person hour) distributions produce quite different means and standard deviations. For the full sample they range from a mean of \$4.77 for travel cost as a random parameter to \$5.76 for travel time as a random parameter and \$23.40 when both time and cost are random parameters. Since the lognormal distribution has a very long tail (see Table 6), it is often suggested that the last few percentiles could be removed to at least ensure that the mean is a better representation of the majority of the individuals (recognising this unfortunate feature of a lognormal). When we remove the highest two percentile, the mean and standard deviation change significantly, especially for the model with two random parameters (compare 6 and 7 based on M3). The authors' experience with a number of data sets suggests a phenomenon that is not unique to a specific data set but widespread. It is not until one investigates the WTP outputs that the critical influence of the actual distributions is highlighted.[24] Armstrong et al. (2001) discuss this issue in the context of confidence intervals.

The concern with arbitrarily removing part of a distribution for whatever reason[25] suggests that constrained distributions may make better sense. To illustrate the implications of imposing a constraint on the lognormal distribution we have estimated a series of models using Data Set 3. We have constrained the standard deviation to be 0.75, 1.0, 1.5 and 2.0 of the mean.[26] The results are summarised in Table 6 and Figure 8. The distributions still have a long tail with mean estimates of VTTS declining (from 19.09 to 15.08) as we move from 0.75 of the mean to twice the mean. This initially might seem odd given that a more constrained standard deviation should reduce the mean; however this is only correct if the distribution is in the numerator. The calculation of VTTS herein uses the cost variable as the random parameter (i.e. the denominator), and hence the result is as expected. What is particularly noticeable is that the mean estimate of the random parameter increases

Table 4. Three Mixed Logit Models with Alternative Random Parameters for WTP calculation.

Attributes	Alternative	Mixed Logit (lognormal random parameter)		
		M1 (time = RP)	M2 (cost = RP)	M3 (time and cost = RP)
Total time (mins)	All	–4.7136 (–7.67)	–0.004874 (–6.4)	–3.84218 (–15.9)
Total cost ($)	All	–0.12743 (–49.1)	–0.9469 (–7.3)	–0.756144 (–6.5)
Tailgate percentage	All	–0.010856 (–9.0)	–0.012145 (–9.7)	–0.012579 (–9.9)
Constant	4 no median	0.3199 (13.2)	0.4117 (16.7)	0.42995 (17.4)
Constant	4 with median	0.9418 (53.2)	1.1213 (61.3)	1.1500 (63.1)
Heterogeneity in mean:				
Travel time: Trip length	All	–0.0061335 (–2.4)	–	–0.010399 (–7.8)
Travel cost: Trip length	All	–	–0.054599 (–9.9)	–0.006197 (–11.5)
Std Deviation. of parameter distribution				
Total time	All	1.4876 (7.35)	–	1.8812 (12.8)*
Total cost	All	–	1.2578 (15.5)	0.882167 (18.6)*
Time:Cost	All	–	–	1.0989 (12.3)*
Adjusted ρ^2		0.1526	0.2152	0.2245
Log-likelihood		–4078.3	–3776.9	–3730.8
Value of Travel Time Savings ($ per person hour) based on full sample of 4384 observations				
MLVOTT	All	5.762 (20.7)		
MLVOTC	All		4.773 (11.542)	
MLVOTTC	All			23.463 (320.0)
Value of Travel Time Savings ($ per person hour) based on truncated sample post-estimation (removing last 2 percentile):				
MLVOTT	All	4.066 (6.72)		
MLVOTC	All		4.0247 (6.25)	
MLVOTTC	All			9.087 (22.4)

Notes: T-values in brackets. parameters with an asterisk are from the Cholesky matrix. (Data Set 1).

Table 5. Full Sample cumulative distribution of value of travel time savings

Range ($/person hour)	MLVOTT	MLVOTC	MLVOTTC
0–1	0.3897	0.3352	0.4450
1.01–2	0.5605	0.5300	0.5601
2.01–3	0.6577	0.6461	0.6247
3.01–4	0.7237	0.7165	0.6706
4.01–5	0.7673	0.7687	0.7007
5.01–6	0.8006	0.8082	0.7288
6.01–7	0.8225	0.8390	0.7505
7.01–8	0.8429	0.8593	0.7679
8.01–9	0.8597	0.8761	0.7834
9.01–10	0.8733	0.8910	0.7967
10.01–15	0.9196	0.9356	0.8410
15.01–20	0.9441	0.9583	0.8681
20.01–50	0.9840	0.9916	0.9338
50.01–100	0.9949	0.9980	0.9637
100.01–200	0.9989	0.9995	0.9803
200.02–300	0.9993	0.9998	0.9879
300.01–400	0.9995	1.000	0.9916
400.01–500	0.9997		0.9942
500.01–1000	1.000		0.9973
Over 1000			1.000

Sample Size: 16 choice situations per individual times 274 individuals times 3 alternatives (Data Set 1).

Table 6. Implications of constrained lognormal distributions on value of travel time savings ($ per driver hour) (2,976 observations) (Data Set 3).

VTTS distribution	Mean	Standard distribution	Minimum	Maximum	Goodness of fit
Unconstrained	12.60	19.67	0.18	462.7	-740.61
SD = 0.75 of mean	19.09	22.09	0.61	420.59	-761.54
SD = mean	18.68	25.13	0.40	533.58	-750.59
SD = 1.5 of mean	15.57	23.10	0.26	525.14	-745.51
SD = 2.0 of mean	15.08	25.31	0.18	623.99	-742.79

substantially to almost compensate for the constrained standard deviation, resulting in far less of an impact on the overall average VTTS. While we are capable of imposing such a series of constraints, there appears to be no strong theoretical basis for doing so. Distributions are analytical constructs however and hence the imposition of such constraints is no better or worse than an unconstrained distribution unless there is a theoretical/behavioural rationale. Except for the sign of the WTP, we appear to have no theoretical arguments to support one distribution over another. Practitioners are likely

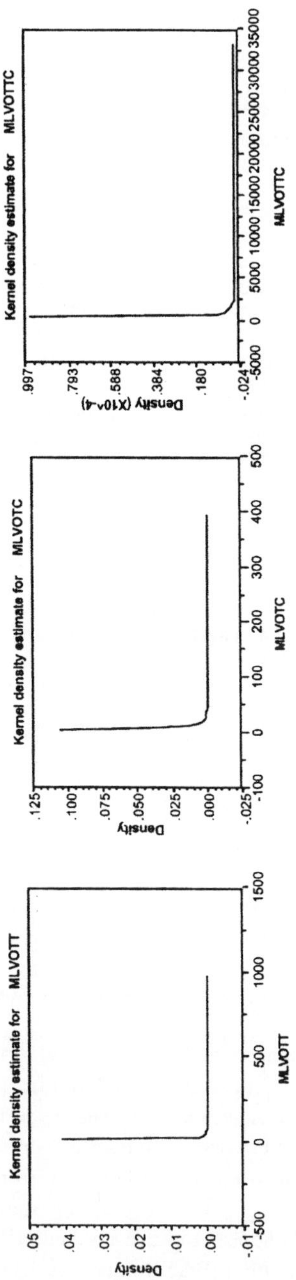

Figure 6. Full sample distribution of VTTS.

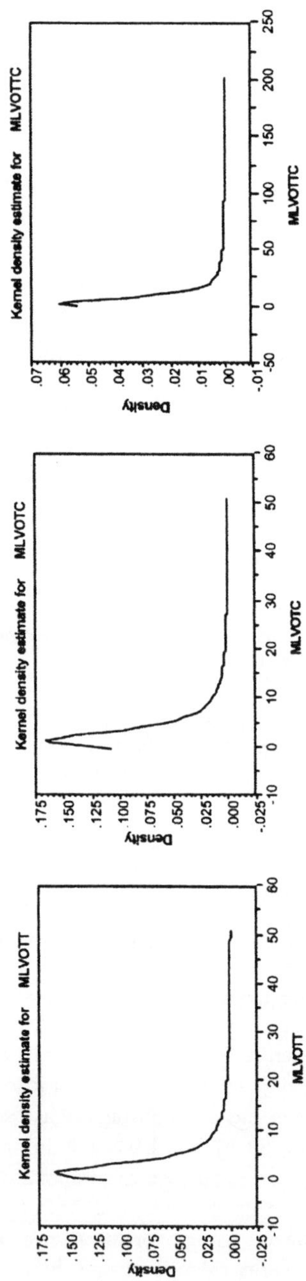

Figure 7. Removing last two percentile (Data Set 1).

168

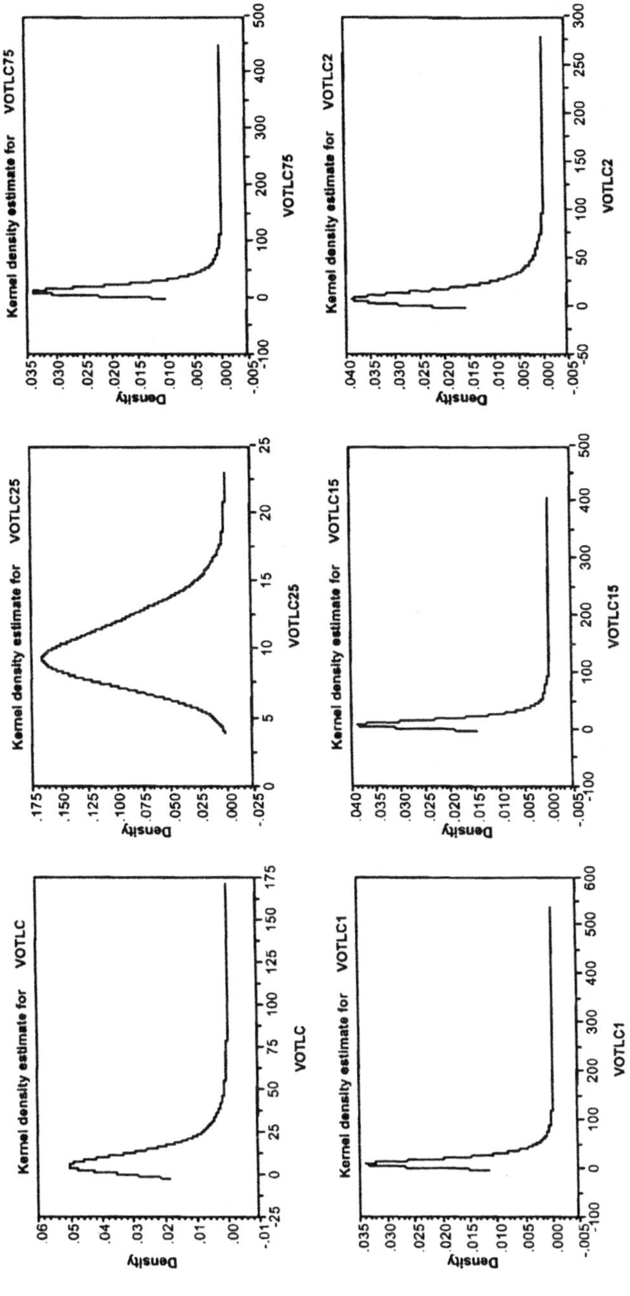

Figure 8. Constrained Distributions Relative to unconstrained distribution (VOTLC) (Data Set 3).

to remain sceptical of WTP measures based on such long tails as typified by the lognormal. The alternative may well be greater consideration of segmentation of attributes in order to establish a discrete set of fixed parameters along a line (essentially points on an undefined distribution). The disadvantage of this is that one might select the set of thresholds and segment criteria that are inadequate representations of the heterogeneity in the variance structure of the unobserved effects.

To investigate the implications of constraints on distributions other than the lognormal, we estimated a model using the triangular distribution, imposing constraints on the spread for Data Set 3. Setting the spread to 1.0 guarantees a non-negative sign. Any other value will lead to both signs. The reason is as follows. Define as before β_i + scale$\beta_i t$ where t is the triangular distribution that ranges from –1 to +1. If the scale equals 1.0, the range is 0 to 2 β_1. We found that the mean VTTS for spread equal to 1.0 is $7.62 (with a range $4.93 to $14.1). Thus the entire distribution is within the positive VTTS range in contrast to the unbounded spread with a mean of $2.51 and a range from –$5,848 to $3,112 (although 99% of values are in the range –$200 to $240). Figure 9 graphs these two distributions. We conclude on the basis of this evidence that a lower bounded triangular distribution has appeal in that it eliminates the long tail common to a lognormal while ensuring the behaviourally correct sign of WTP. This initial inquiry into constrained distributions suggests a major topic for ongoing research.[27]

5. Conclusions

The continuing challenges we face with mixed logit models are derived in the main from the quality of the data. Mixed logit certainly demands better quality data than MNL since it offers an extended framework within which

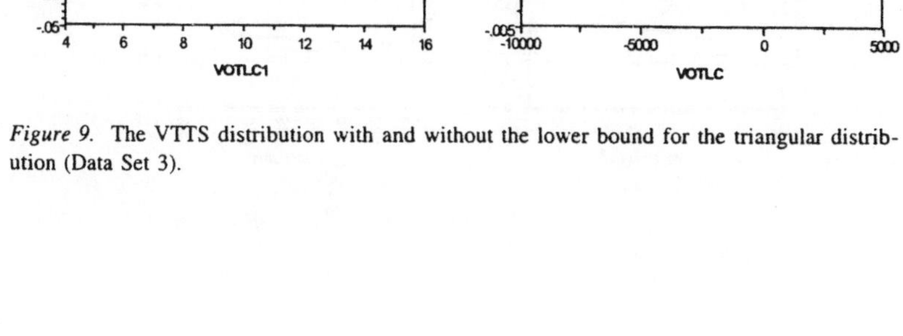

Figure 9. The VTTS distribution with and without the lower bound for the triangular distribution (Data Set 3).

to capture a greater amount of true behavioural variability in choice making. Broadly speaking the mixed logit model aligns itself much more with reality than most discrete choice models with every individual having their own inter-related systematic and random components for each alternative in their perceptual choice set(s).

As discrete choice models become less restrictive in their behavioural assumptions, the possibility of identifying sources of preference heterogeneity associated with the mean and variance of systematic and random components increases. Ultimately we want to improve on our modelling capability to improve the predictability of a model when individuals are faced with changes in the decision environment as represented by a set of attributes of alternatives, characteristics of decision makers and other contextual effects (which can include task complexity for data collection, especially stated choice experiments). The sources of explanatory power reside within the systematic and random components in potentially complex ways and can be captured by both the mean and the variance of parameters representing observed and unobserved effects. The mixed logit model certainly opens up new opportunities to research these behavioural phenomena.

Acknowledgements

We are indebted to Ken Train for the many hours we have discussed the challenges facing modellers estimating mixed (or random parameter) logit models. Jordan Louviere, David Brownstone and David Bunch also provided a platform to test ideas. Chandra Bhat provided informative comments on an earlier draft. The very extensive comments of three referees are greatly appreciated. Although we did not agree with every suggestion by the referees, in the main we complied. We recognise the huge effort each referee made to assist the authors in materially improving this paper.

Notes

1. Although there were a number of software tools available prior to the late 1980s, the majority of analysts used LIMDEP (Econometric Software), Alogit (Hague Consulting Group), Quail (Brownstone) and Blogit (Hensher & Johnson 1981). Today LIMDEP/NLOGIT and Alogit continue to be the main software packages for MNL and NL estimation with SSP also relatively popular although its development is limited. Hlogit (Börsch-Supan) and Hielow (Bierlaire) are used by a small number of researchers. GAUSS is increasing in popularity as a software language and application template for advanced discrete choice models.
2. This is in contrast to the closed form models such as MNL and NL whose probabilities can be evaluated after estimation without further analytical or numerical integration.

3. It is also referred to in various literatures as random parameter logit (RPL), mixed multinomial logit (MMNL), kernel logit, hybrid logit and error components logit.
4. A single choice situation refers to a set of alternatives (or choice set) from which an individual chooses one alternative. They could also rank the alternatives but we focus on first preference choice. An individual who faces a choice situation on more than one occasion (e.g. in a longitudinal panel) or a number of choice sets, one after the other as in stated choice experiments, is described as facing a number of choice situations. Louviere et al. (2000) provide a useful introduction to discrete choice methods that use data derived from repeated choice situations, commonly known as stated choice methods.
5. The proof in McFadden and Train (2000) that mixed logit can approximate any choice model including any multinomial probit model is an important message. The reverse cannot be said: the multinomial probit model cannot approximate all mixed logit models since the multinomial probit relies critically on normal distributions. If a random term in utility is not normal, then mixed logit can handle it and multinomial probit cannot. The description of mixed logit follows that given by Brownstone and Train (1999).
6. A fixed parameter essentially treats the standard deviation as zero such that all the behavioural information is captured by the mean.
7. By construction, SP_i is an unbiased estimate of P_i for any R; its variance decreases as R increases. It is strictly positive for any R, so that $\ln SP_i$ is always defined in a log-likelihood function. It is smooth (i.e., twice differentiable) in parameters and variables, which helps in the numerical search for the maximum of the likelihood function. The simulated probabilities sum to one over alternatives. Train (1998) provides further commentary on this.
8. We also interviewed truck drivers but they are excluded from the current empirical illustrations (See Hensher and Sullivan (2003) for the truck models).
9. One referee raised a concern about a respondent's ability to interpret degree of curviness. This issue is discussed in detail in Hensher and Sullivan (2003). In the current paper the focus is on the use of a range of data sets to illustrate the diversity of issues that mixed logit models have to address.
10. Regardless of what is said about advanced discrete choice models, the MNL model should always be the starting point for empirical investigation. It remains a major input into the modelling process, helping to ensure that the data are clean and that sensible results (e.g. parameter signs and significance) can be obtained from models that are not "cluttered" with complex relationships (see Louviere et al. 2000).
11. One can use different distributions on each attribute. The reason you can do this is that you are not using the distributional information in constructing the estimator. The variance estimator is based on the method of moments. Essentially, one is estimating the variance parameters just by computing sums of squares and cross products. In more detail (in response to a student inquiry) Ken Train comments that it is possible to have underlying parameters jointly normal with full covariance and then transform these underlying parameters to get the parameters that enter the utility function. For example, suppose $V = \alpha_1 x_1 + \alpha_2 x_2$. We can say that β_1 and β_2 are jointly normal with correlation and that $\alpha_2 = \exp(\beta_2)$ and $\alpha_1 = \beta_1$. That gives a lognormal and a normal with correlation between them. The correlation between α_2 and α_2 can be calculated from the estimated correlation between β_1 and β_2. Alternatively one can calculate it by simulating many α_1s and α_2s from many draws of β_1s and β_2s from their estimated distribution and then calculate the correlation between the α_1s and α_2s. This can be applied for any distributions. Let α_2 have density $g(\alpha_2)$ with cumulative distribution $G(\alpha_2)$, and let α_1 be normal. $F(\beta_2|\beta_1)$ is the normal CDF for β_2 given β_1. Then α_2 is calculated as $\alpha_2 = G^{-1}(F(\beta_2|\beta_1))$. For some Gs there will be limits on the correlation that can be attained between α_1 and α_2 using this procedure.
12. If the analyst uses the standard deviation instead of the spread in the formula for uniform

and triangular distributions (Table 1) the mean and standard deviation for VTTS across the sample changes quite markedly (except in this case the mean for the triangular is very similar by coincidence).

13. A referee indicated that he had tested many data sets and had never experienced more than a few individuals (less than 10%) with similar findings. We would encourage the referee to share these findings although we suspect that the referee is not estimating individual models but undertaking some descriptive classification of responses based on some rules of expected response. We are unaware of any research in transportation that has focussed on the matter of empirical distributions from stated choice situations.
14. This is in itself an important finding, suggesting that a wider range is generally preferred to a narrower range (within limits of meaningfulness to the respondent). Although one usually pools data across the sample, the analysis at the individual level should reveal important behavioural properties of the design configuration. The recovery of parameters is an important feature of the pilot stage of any stated choice study and was undertaken on this data set. However typically such estimation is not individual-specific but sample-specific. What we have discovered is that the pivoting of the attribute levels around the current levels, which is intuitively appealing, has a potential downside of limiting the variability profile of the attributes across the alternatives in a choice situation and across choice situations for each respondent. A way around this is to have a range of attribute ranges (e.g. for a 4 level attribute we might have +25%, +10%, –10%, +25% and +59%, +20%, –20% and –50%). Current research by Louviere, Hensher, Street and Anderson is developing a template for a generic design that provides precision of estimates for each and every sampled individual.
15. This idea has been around for sometime and has been mentioned in various contexts by David Hensher, Pierre Uldry and Jordan Louviere. The technique when used to study sampling variation of parameter estimates is known as the "jackknife" procedure.
16. Sandor and Train (2002) identify draws where one never gets to the maximum of the likelihood function, with a wide area where the algorithms converge indicating a close enough solution. Depending on the path by which this area is approached (which will differ with different draws), the convergence point differs. As a result, there is a greater difference in the convergence points than there is in the actual maximum.
17. A referee cited ongoing research by Garrido and Silva in Chile on this important issue.
18. Adding in a set of covariates that interact with the mean of the estimate of a random parameter for any distribution that does not require some non-linear transformation is equivalent to interacting a covariate with the random parameter attribute and adding it in as a fixed parameter. A direct comparison with multinomial logit can *t* be made. To compare the multinomial logit model with the mixed logit model under a lognormal form, one can transform the mixed logit lognormal parameter estimates to generate the mean and standard deviation of the utility parameters at different levels of the covariate.
19. Order effects are due to the order of the choice sets offered to a respondent. Randomising the order across the sample should remove the potential for significant order effects.
20. Some empirical evidence (e.g. Daniels & Hensher 2000) suggests that once unobserved heterogeneity is taken into account via a random effects specification such as ML or RPL, serial correlation may be negligible or absent. That is, serial correlation may be spurious due to the failure to account for unobserved heterogeneity.
21. But more importantly, if preference heterogeneity is present it is not merely a statistical nuisance requiring correction. Rather, one should model the heterogeneity in order to obtain accurate choice model predictions, because the presence of heterogeneity will impact on the marginal rates of substitution between attributes, and lead to IIA violations.
22. The only circumstance in which you can distinguish correlated choice situations from correlated alternatives is by ignoring the dependency between choice situations or assume that it does not exist.

23. In order to allow for correlation between the parameters, we can write the entire vector of correlated parameters $\boldsymbol{\beta}_q = \boldsymbol{\beta}_{mean} + \boldsymbol{\Gamma\Sigma}\mathbf{v}_q$ where $\mathbf{v}_q$ is the set of random draws from the assigned distribution (note, these need not be the same for all parameters), $\boldsymbol{\Sigma}$ is the diagonal matrix of scale (or "spread") factors that appears above, and $\boldsymbol{\Gamma}$ is a lower triangular matrix. The diagonal elements of $\boldsymbol{\Gamma}$ are constrained to be equal to one.) Then, the actual covariance matrix of the random terms that enters the parameters is $\boldsymbol{\Gamma\Sigma S\Sigma\Gamma}'$ where $\mathbf{S}$ is a diagonal matrix with diagonal elements equal to 1.0 for normally distributed parameters, $\sqrt{6}$ for uniformly distributed parameters, and $\sqrt{3}$ for the triangularly distributed parameters and $\boldsymbol{\Sigma}$ is an unrestricted diagonal matrix of standard deviations. In this case, it can be seen that each parameter is equal to its mean plus a mixture of the random terms which enter some or all of the other parameters. (Since $\boldsymbol{\Gamma}$ is triangular and $\boldsymbol{\Sigma}$ is diagonal, β_{i1} is a function of v_1 only, β_{i2} is a function of v_{i1} and v_{i2} and so on.) This allows the parameters to be freely correlated and have an unrestricted scale as well while insuring that the covariance matrix that we estimate is positive definite at all times.
24. This is not to suggest that it is an unimportant issue for prediction.
25. For the normal, uniform and triangular, the negative region for VTTS is often quite substantial, indeed often exceeding 2 percentiles.
26. When you allow for correlation amongst attributes, the scale factor is no longer proportional to the inverse of the standard deviation of the distribution as in simpler models such as nested logit. The standard deviation as the square root of the sum of squares of the elements in a row of the Cholesky matrix, cannot be equivalenced to one of the parameters.
27. There are a number of views in the research community about ways of handling the information in distributions. These include using only the mean from a lognormal instead of the simulated distribution and selecting a more symmetrical distribution such as the triangular but constraining it to the non-negative range (as we have done in the text). The evidence herein suggests little gain from constraining a lognormal distribution; however promoting the use of only the mean (including any parameterisation of heterogeneity around the mean) from a lognormal is controversial since relevant information is being discarded. The possibility of eliminating the extreme values where they are small in number remains appealing if one wishes to use a lognormal.

References

Armstrong P, Garrido R & Ortuzar J de D (2001) Confidence intervals to bound the value of time. *Transportation Research* 37E: 143–161.

Ben-Akiva M & Bolduc D (1996) Multinomial probit with a logit kernel and a general parametric specification of the covariance structure. *Working paper*, Department of Civil and Environmental Engineering, MIT.

Bhat CR (2000) Flexible model structures for discrete choice analysis. In: Hensher DA & Button KJ (eds) *Handbook of Transport Modelling*, Volume 1, of Handbooks in Transport (pp 71–90). Oxford: Pergamon Press.

Bhat CR (2001) Quasi-random maximum simulated likelihood estimation of the mixed multinomial logit model. *Transportation Research* 35B: 677–695.

Bhat CR (in press) Simulation estimation of mixed discrete choice models using randomised and scrambled Halton sequences. *Transportation Research.*

Bhat CR & Castelar S (2002) A unified mixed logit framework for modeling revealed and stated preferences: formulation and application to congestion pricing analysis in the San Francisco Bay Area. *Transportation Research* 36B: 593–616.

Boersch-Supan A & Hajvassiliou V (1990) Smooth unbiased multivariate probability simulators for maximum likelihood estimation of limited dependent variable models. *Journal of Econometrics* 58: 347–368.

Brownstone D (2001) Discrete choice modelling for transportation. In Hensher DA (ed) *Travel Behaviour Research: The Leading Edge* (pp 97–124). Oxford: Pergamon Press.

Brownstone D & Train K (1999) Forecasting new product penetration with flexible substitution patterns. *Journal of Econometrics* 89: 109–129.

Brownstone D, Bunch DS & Train K (2000) Joint mixed logit models of stated and revealed preferences for alternative-fuel vehicles. *Transportation Research* 34B: 315–338.

Carrasco JA & Ortuzar J de D (2002) Review and assessment of the nested logit model. *Transport Reviews* 22: 197–218.

Daniels R & Hensher DA (2000) Valuation of environmental impacts of transportation projects: the challenge of self-interest proximity. *Journal of Transport Economics and Policy* 34 (May): 189–214.

DeShazo JR & Fermo G (2002) Designing choice sets for stated preference methods: the effects of complexity on choice consistency. *Journal of Environmental Economics and Management* 44: 123–143.

Evans M, Hastings N & Peacock B (1993) *Statistical Distributions*. New York: John Wiley and Sons.

Geweke J, Keane M & Runkle D (1994) Alternative computational approaches to inference in the multinomial probit model. *Review of Economics and Statistics* LXXVI: 609–632.

Greene WH (2002) *Econometric Analysis*, 5th edition. Englewood Cliffs: Prentice Hall.

Greene WH & Hensher DA (2003) A latent class model for discrete choice analysis: contrasts with mixed logit. *Transportation Research B*.

Halton JH (1960) On the efficiency of certain quasi-random sequences of points in evaluating multidimensional integrals. *Numerische Math* 2: 84–90 and corrigenda 196.

Hensher DA (2001a) Measurement of the valuation of travel time savings. *Journal of Transport Economics and Policy (Special Issue in Honour of Michael Beesley)* 35: 71–98.

Hensher DA (2001b) The valuation of commuter travel time savings for car drivers in New Zealand: evaluating alternative model specifications. *Transportation* 28, 101–118.

Hensher DA & Greene WH (2002) Taking advantage of priors in estimation and posteriors in application to reveal individual-specific parameter estimates in mixed logit models. *Institute of Transport Studies Working Paper*. The University of Sydney, September.

Hensher, D.A. and Johnson, L.W. (1981) Applied Discrete Choice Modelling, Croom Helm (London) and Wiley (New York).

Hensher DA, Louviere JJ & Swait J (1999) Combining sources of preference data. *Journal of Econometrics* 89: 197–221.

Hensher DA & Sullivan C (2003) Willingness to pay for road curviness and road type for long distance travel in New Zealand. *Transportation Research D*.

Huber J & Train K (2001) On the similarity of classical and Bayesian estimates of individual mean partworths. *Marketing Letters* 12 (August): 259–270.

Koop G & Poirier DJ (1993) Bayesian analysis of logit models using natural conjugate priors. *Journal of Econometrics* 56: 323–340.

Koppelman F & Sethi V (2000) Closed-form discrete-choice models. In: Hensher DA & Button KJ (eds) *Handbook of Transport Modelling*, Volume 1, of Handbooks in Transport (pp 211–222). Oxford: Pergamon Press.

Louviere JJ & Hensher DA (2001) Combining sources of preference data. In: Hensher DA (ed) *Travel Behaviour Research: The Leading Edge* (pp 125–144). Oxford: Pergamon Press.

Louviere JJ, Hensher DA & Swait JF (2000) Stated Choice Methods and Analysis. Cambridge: Cambridge University Press.

Louviere J, Carson R, Ainslie A, Cameron T, DeShazo JR, Hensher D, Kohn R, Marley T & Street D (2002) Dissecting the random component of utility, Workshop Report for the Asilomar Invitational Choice Symposium, California. *Marketing Letters* 13(3): 177–194.

McFadden D (2001) Disaggregate Behavioural Travel Demand's RUM Side – A 30 years retrospective. In: Hensher DA (ed) *Travel Behaviour Research: The Leading Edge* (pp 17–64). Oxford: Pergamon Press.

McFadden D & Ruud PA (1994) Estimation by simulation. *Review of Economics and Statistics* LXXVI(4): 591–608.

McFadden D & Train K (2000) Mixed MNL models for discrete response. *Journal of Applied Econometrics* 15: 447–470.

Revelt D & Train K (1998) Mixed Logit with repeated choices: households' choices of appliance efficiency level. *Review of Economics and Statistics* 80: 1–11.

Rizzi LI & Ortuzar J de D (2002) Stated preference in the valuation of interurban road safety. *Accident Analysis and Prevention*, in press.

Sandor Z & Train K (2002) *Quasi-random Simulation of Discrete Choice Models*. Department of Economics, University of California at Berkeley, Berkeley.

Stern S (1997) Simulation-based estimation. *Journal of Economic Literature* XXXV (December), 2006–2039.

Swait J & Adamowicz W (2001) Choice complexity and decision strategy selection. *Journal of Consumer Research* 28: 135–148.

Train K (1997) Mixed logit models for recreation demand. In: Kling C & Herriges J (eds) *Valuing the Environment Using Recreation Demand Models*. New York: Elgar Press.

Train K (1998) Recreation demand models with taste differences over people. *Land Economics* 74: 230–239

Train K (1999) *Halton Sequences for Mixed Logit. Working paper*. Department of Economics, University of California, Berkeley.

Train K (2001) A comparison of hierarchical Bayes and maximum simulated likelihood for mixed logit, Paper presented at the *Asilomar Invitational Choice Symposium*, California, June.

Train K (2003), Discrete Choice Methods with Simulation. Cambridge: Cambridge University Press.

About the author

David Hensher is Professor of Management, and Director of the Institute of Transport Studies at The University of Sydney. David is a Fellow of the Academy of Social Science in Australia and Immediate Past President of the International Association of Travel Behaviour Research. David is on the editorial boards of 10 of the leading transport journals and Area Editor of *Transport Reviews*. David has recently been appointed by one of the worlds most prestigious academic publishing houses – Elsevier/Pergamon Press – as series and volume editor of a new handbook series "Handbooks in Transport". He has published extensively (over 250 papers) in the leading international transport journals and key journals in economics as well as five books. His most recent books are *Transport: An Economics and Management Perspective* (with Ann Brewer – Oxford University Press), and *Stated Choice Methods* (with Jordan Louviere and Joffre Swait – Cambridge University Press).

William Greene is currently Professor of Economics and Entertainment and Media Faculty Fellow, Department of Economics, Stern School of Business, New York University. Fields of interest are applied econometrics, production economics, panel data and economics of the entertainment industry. Chairman of the economics department at Stern from 1995 to 2001, director of the Ph.D. program from 1988 to 1994.

176

Previously Professor of Economics, Cornell University, 1976–1982. Other employment includes visiting lectureships at Oxford, Indiana, University of York, the Chicago Federal Reserve Bank, University of Lund, and consulting to Resource Consultants, Inc., Ortho Biotech, National Economic Research Associates, The U.S. Navy, The World Health Organization and others. Author of software LIMDEP and NLOGIT, textbook Econometric Analysis and approximately 50 articles primarily in applied econometrics and econometric methods in Econometrica, Journal of Econometrics, Review of Economics and Statistics, Transport Research and others. Associate editor for The Journal of Productivity Analysis and the Journal of Economic Education.

[32]

Marketing Letters 8:3 (1997): 307–322

Current Issues in Discrete Choice Modeling

MICHAEL P. KEANE
1035 Management and Economics, University of Minnesota, 271 19th Avenue South, Minneapolis, MN 55455

Abstract

Until recently, computational constraints forced researchers in the discrete choice area to limit themselves to very simple statistical models, such as the multinomial logit (MNL), in which choice probabilities could be evaluated quickly on a computer. But the MNL only makes sense as a behavioral model under very special circumstances. Recent advances in computation make it possible to estimate richer behavioral models that generate very complex choice probability expressions. This paper discusses a number of possible avenues for future research in the discrete choice area in light of these developments.

Key words: discrete choice, brand choice, choice dynamics, stated preference, contingent valuation, purchase quantity, new products

I. Introduction

Discrete choice models have been widely used in marketing, transportation, economics and many other areas to study both revealed and stated preference data. The most commonly used discrete choice model has of course been the multinomial logit (see McFadden (1974)). The appeal of the multinomial logit (MNL) arose from the fact that it is simple to estimate. Choice probabilities and their derivatives take a simple closed form, so that the likelihood for the MNL can be quickly constructed and easily maximized using modern digital computers.

The problem with MNL is that it makes very strong assumptions about consumer behavior. The assumption that has received the most attention is the independence of irrelevant alternatives (IIA) property, which says that if a new alternative is added to a choice set then choice probabilities for all existing alternatives fall proportionately. Despite the fact that this and other behavioral assumptions underlying MNL are untenable in many contexts, researchers were still willing to use MNL because attempts to relax its behavioral assumptions would typically lead to models that were computationally intractable. Specifically, such attempts would typically lead to choice models in which the choice probabilities took the form of high dimensional integrals with no closed form, as occurs, for example, in the multinomial probit model (MNP).

Today we live in a rather different world. The speed of digital computers has increased dramatically since 1974. This alone would make it feasible to estimate discrete choice models in which choice probabilities have no closed form, provided the integrals that must be evaluated numerically are below a certain dimension (say 4). But in addition, there have been important advances in estimation technology. The most important of these is the development of highly accurate smooth probability simulators (see McFadden (1989), Keane (1993, 1994), Borsch-Supan and Hajivassiliou (1993)). These allow (approximate) likelihood functions for discrete choice models to be constructed far more quickly than would be possible using numerical integration.

In my view, most researchers in marketing, transportation, economics and other areas where discrete choice models are widely used have not yet grasped the full import of these events. Most interpret them to mean that it is now possible to relax IIA and estimate MNP or other generalizations of MNL. The real meaning is far more profound. Given current technology, it is no longer necessary to adopt what might be called a "statistical" approach to empirical work in the discrete choice area—that is, the common practice of starting with a particular *statistical* model that one knows is tractable (like MNL or now MNP), and then adopting (ex-post) whatever explicit or implicit behavioral assumptions are needed to fit the research question at hand into that framework.

Given current technology, it is often feasible to adopt a "theory-based" approach to discrete choice modeling. Given a research question, one starts by writing down an appealing *theoretical* model of the choice behavior of interest. Then, given assumptions about the distributions of the stochastic terms in that model, one obtains expressions for choice probabilities—and hence a *statistical* model that may be estimated. Since one's starting point was to write down a theoretical model that captures the salient features of the particular choice behavior under study, there is no reason to expect that the statistical model so obtained will resemble any textbook model like MNL or MNP. But in many instances, it will still be possible to use modern simulation technology to evaluate the required choice probability expressions and form the appropriate likelihood.

A good example is work on welfare program participation by Keane and Moffitt (1996). We start with a utility based optimizing model of the behavior of single women with children confronted by the complex array of constraints presented by the set of programs that make up the US welfare system. The expressions for program participation probabilities derived from this theoretical model are quite complex—in fact, the limits of integration in the expressions cannot be expressed analytically. Nevertheless, it is straightforward to use simulation techniques to evaluate the choice probabilities and form the likelihood.

In my view, a major obstacle to progress in building our understanding of choice behavior is that many researchers continue to adopt a statistical modeling approach. And many of the research papers that are being published simply apply new statistical methods to discrete choice data—rather than attempting to develop and estimate new and interesting theoretical models of behavior. More careful attention must be paid to behavioral theory if we hope to make further progress. In this paper I discuss a number of issues in the discrete choice modeling area that are currently attracting attention, focussing on theory-based approaches to modeling. The topics are: joint modeling of brand choice and the timing and volume of purchases, modeling demand for new products, error structures in choice models, and contingent valuation.

II. Joint modeling of brand choice, purchase timing and purchase quantity: static case

A number of authors have estimated statistical models for both the purchase timing and brand choice processes. For example, Zufryden (1977) specifies an Erlang distribution of interpurchase times in a category and a beta distribution of conditional brand choice probabilities, while Jeuland et al (1980) alter the statistical model by adopting a Dirichlet distribution for purchase probabilities. Shoemaker et al (1977) introduce correlation between interpurchase times and brand choice probabilities. Models with a no-purchase option are also purchase timing models (e.g., Bucklin and Lattin (1991) specify a MNL for brand choice, nested in a logit for purchase in the category).

Other authors jointly estimate statistical models of brand choice and purchase quantity (e.g., Krishnamurthi and Raj (1988) estimate switching regressions for purchase quantity where a MNL for brand choice determines if the left hand side is observed). Also, Guadagni and Little (1983) and Keane (1996) estimate MNL and MNP models (respectively) with brand/size combinations as alternatives, thus incorporating an aspect of quantity choice, but ignoring purchase of multiple units.

Recently, some authors have considered all three of the timing, brand and quantity decisions. Gupta (1988) specifies a separate statistical model for each. But Chiang (1991) and Chintagunta (1993) set all three within a single utility maximization problem. They appeal to the Hanemann (1984) result that when brands are perfect substitutes and quantity is infinitely divisible, there is a separation of brand choice and quantity decisions. The timing/brand choice part reduces to a multinomial choice model with a no-purchase option, and a quantity regression can be estimated in a separate step. Achieving this separation is important because, with multiple brands, the number of feasible brand/quantity combinations quickly becomes astronomical, and it is not computationally feasible to search over all combinations to find the optimal choice.

The Chiang (1991) and Chintagunta (1993) papers are laudable in that they attempt to apply a "theory-based" approach by starting from an optimizing model of consumer behavior. However, they err in applying the Hanemann (1984) results in cases where they do not apply—the former to coffee that comes in 16 oz units and the latter to yogurt which comes in 6 and 8 oz units. Even if all brands are perfect substitutes in utility, if quantity is discrete one does not achieve a separation between timing/brand choice and quantity decisions.

To illustrate, suppose utility is linear in the quantity of two alternative brands in one category, and logarithmic in a composite other commodity. Substituting a static budget constraint into the utility function one obtains the expression $U = \alpha b_1 + \beta b_2 + \ln(Y - p_1 b_1 - p_2 b_2)$, where b_j is quantity of brand j, p_j is its price, Y is income, and α and β are parameters capturing preferences for the two brands. If quantity is infinitely divisible, the consumer will make a purchase in the category if and only if $p_1 < \alpha Y$ or $p_2 < \beta Y$. Conditional on purchase, the consumer buys only brand 1 if $\alpha/p_1 > \beta/p_2$, and only brand two otherwise (i.e., he/she buys only the brand that provides the most utils per dollar). For example, suppose that $\alpha = 0.2$, $\beta = 0.095$, $p_1 = 2$, $p_2 = 1$ and $Y = 20$. Then the consumer will choose to buy only brand one, and he/she will set $b_1 = 5$. But now suppose that the brands can only be bought in units of 2 (i.e., 2, 4, 6, etc.). Then the optimal choice is to buy *both* brands, and to set $b_1 = 4$ and $b_2 = 2$. The timing/brand choice and purchase quantity decisions do not separate.

Thus, the computational problem of dealing with discrete quantity choice problems remains open. At present, there is no alternative to exogenously imposing constraints that keep the size of the choice set tractable, such as that agents cannot chose more than one brand on a purchase occasion. Research on behaviorally appealing approaches to this problem is needed.

Another important question is whether the decision to buy in a category and the brand choice/quantity decision are best thought of as flowing from the same utility maximization problem. For example, if store visits are costly, the decision to buy in a category may be made prior to seeing prices, in-store promotions, etc., followed by a separate in-store brand/quantity choice problem. Note that brand choice models that use shopping occasions as the "time" line (by including a no-purchase option) implicitly assume that the category purchase decision, but not the store visit decision, is influenced by prices or promotions of brands in the category. In contrast, models that use purchase occasions as the "time" line (excluding the no-purchase option), implicitly assume that the store visit and category purchase decisions are not influenced by the prices or promotions of brands in the category. It would be interesting to develop and estimate theoretical models of consumer behavior that are explicit about the stage of the choice process at which prices and promotions are observed.

III. Purchase timing, brand choice and quantity decisions of forward-looking consumers

If consumers are forward-looking, and there exist intertemporal linkages in preferences or constraints, then current demand will depend not just on current prices but also on expected future prices. That is, consumers solve a dynamic rather than a static optimization problem.

Intertemporal linkages may arise even for a perishable good like walleye pike, which must be eaten soon after being caught. Suppose I go to the store and see that the price of walleye is higher today than normal, so I expect it to drop next week. If my preferences for walleye are additively separable over time, and if I cannot save, then I still face a static choice problem—only the current price matters to my decision, not the price I expect next week. But, if by passing up walleye this week I can save money for next week or raise my marginal utility of walleye consumption next week, the fact that I expect next week's price to be lower may give me an incentive to defer the purchase.

For storable consumer goods and durable goods intertemporal linkages are obviously important. In the former case an obvious source of intertemporal linkage is inventories. In the latter case it is that the good, once purchased, provides a flow of consumption over a long period of time. In either case, consumers will have an incentive to time purchases so they buy when the price is "low" relative to expected future prices. This is easy to say, and introspection suggests that we all engage in such behavior. But forward-looking behavior is very difficult to formalize in a model. The whole area of modeling expectations is extremely difficult, both conceptually and operationally.

Economists often assume that agents form expectations "rationally." Here, the technical meaning of rational is to form expectations in a manner that is consistent with the "true" model. When applied to a storable consumer good like detergent, this means consumers know the process that generates detergent price fluctuations, and form expectations of future prices optimally given that process. The computational demands of pursuing the rational expectations approach in discrete choice models are formidable. In such models, consumers behave *as if* they solve complex dynamic programming (DP) problems to determine optimal choices. Hence, the researcher must also solve a DP problem to determine consumers' choice probabilities. An example is the recent paper by Erdem and Keane (1996). The statistical model that arises from our theoretical model requires many hours of supercomputer time to estimate, despite that fact that we used simulation and interpolation techniques to approximate both the DP solution and the resultant choice probabilities.

While the "full blown optimization" approach exemplified by the Erdem and Keane paper is now feasible for many problems, many researchers will want to adopt less computationally intensive alternatives, while still allowing for effects of expected future prices on current demand. Some alternatives are: 1) assume expectations are formed adaptively, so expected future prices are a simple function of past prices, 2) attempt to measure expectations directly and include them in the model, 3) assume that agents make choices using relatively simple rules-of-thumb, 4) assume that agents have short-time horizons or only re-optimize on rare occasions (thus simplifying DP problems).

The problem with such simplifications, as well as with purely statistical models that ignore entirely issues of how agents form expectations and form decision rules, is that they can run a-foul of the "Lucas critique of econometric policy evaluation," due to Marschak (1952) and Lucas (1976). To understand the Lucas critique, consider the following simple example. Suppose after a few years of shopping I realize that my favorite supermarket always cuts the price of my favorite detergent, say Era, from $4.00 to $3.50 per 32oz during one week of every month. Most other shoppers at the store realize this too. So those who like Era adopt a decision rule that says: "Only buy Era if the price is $3.50, and then buy enough so that my inventory will last at least 7 weeks (the longest possible time until the next sale)." There are some random deviations from this rule (e.g., sometimes people may have big positive usage shocks that cause them to stock out and deviate from the rule), but it is the dominant pattern of behavior. If one were to estimate a MNL model for detergent choice in the store, the price elasticity of demand for Era would appear to be enormous.

Now, suppose the store changes its policy, and starts to charge $4.00 for Era all the time. The MNL model would predict that sales of Era would fall drastically—in fact, almost to zero. But what would really happen? The shoppers who like Era would let 7 weeks go by and then be surprised to find that the price was still $4.00 in week 8. At this point, it seems implausible that sales of Era would really drop to almost zero. Rather, some shoppers would buy Era anyway because they prefer it sufficiently to other brands.

Some would indeed switch brands. Some would check out prices in a different store, and perhaps even switch stores. All the regular Era shoppers would realize that the pricing policy had changed and start to develop a new decision rule. Clearly the MNL model estimated on the data from the old monthly price cut regime will have little hope of predicting what will happen under the new constant price regime. This inability of statistical models to predict effects of regime shifts is the basic idea of the Lucas critique.

To successfully forecast behavior after a regime change one needs to model how agents tailor their decision rules to particular regimes. One needs a so-called "structural" model whose parameters are "primitives" of agents' preferences, information processing systems, etc., which remain *fixed* across regimes. Then, given any regime, one can solve for the optimal decision rules of agents in that regime. In other words, the goal is a model that is generalizable across regimes.

Only a "full blown optimization" approach in which agents *choice of decision rule* is modeled can achieve this goal. In contrast models with fixed rule-of-thumb decision rules would break down after the regime shift in the detergent example. One such model is a "reference price" model, in which current demand depends in a *fixed* way on deviations of current prices from average or "reference" prices (see Winer (1986)). In the detergent example, if such a model was estimated on data from the monthly price cut regime, it would predict almost zero demand for Era when price equals "reference" price. It would therefore predict a drop in Era sales to almost zero in the constant price regime.

Nevertheless, simple statistical models which incorporate expectations (e.g., reference price and other rule-of-thumb type models) may be very useful for predicting responses to "marginal" changes within fixed regimes. If a statistical model is estimated on historical data in which prices are drawn from a certain stochastic process, that model could be reliably used to forecast demand tomorrow given a particular realization from the same process. It is only if we attempt to use the model to forecast the effect of a fundamental change in the stochastic process for price that we run a-foul of the Lucas critique. Despite these concerns, some authors have recently applied control theory to derive optimal pricing or advertising rules for retailers while taking statistical representations of consumers' decision rules as invariant to pricing or advertising policy (e.g., Chintagunta and Vilcassim (1992), Kopalle and Winer (1996)). Such attempts ignore the basic message of the Lucas critique that decision rules will change when policy rules change.

It is worth stressing that problem raised by the Lucas critique is really an identification problem: If we observed data from many regimes, we could fit a purely statistical model to the data, perhaps using regime indicators as explanatory variables, and successfully use the model to predict changes in behavior across different regimes. So one response to the critique is to collect more data.

Finally, note that the rational expectations assumption is not *de rigueur* in structural modeling. Given costs of computation, it may well be optimal for agents to form expectations in simpler ways. The optimal expectation formation mechanism may depend both on the regime and more fundamental primitives that characterize the consumer's information processing costs and capabilities. Obviously, these are difficult issues that lie at the cutting-edge of research in the social and behavioral sciences.

IV. Modeling demand for new products

In thinking about demand for new products, it is useful to differentiate them along two dimensions. First, is the new product only marginally different from existing products, or does it represent a fundamental change? Second, are there "network externalities" associated with the adoption of the new product?

An example of a new product that is only marginally different from existing products is a new HMO that has a different monthly premium and covers different fractions of prescription expenses than existing HMOs. In this case, it would be possible to estimate a choice model on existing market or "revealed preference" (RP) data, which exhibits variation in the attributes of interest, and use the model to predict demand for the new product.

Data from stated preference (SP) choice experiments can also be used to estimate such models (see Louviere (1988) or Hensher (1994)). In an SP experiment, respondents are presented with a series of artificial choice sets. A set of attributes of the alternatives is defined and varied across the sets. Thus, in contrast to market data, the researcher controls the attribute variation in the data (Bunch et al (1996) provide evidence on the statistical efficiency of various experimental designs). As pointed out by Adamowicz et al (1994), there are often cases where attributes are collinear in market data, making it difficult or impossible to predict the effect of independent variation in an attribute. In such cases SP data has a key advantage over market data.

However, there are important potential problems with the use of SP data. Most obviously, respondents have no incentive to make choices in an SP experiment in the same way they would in the market. Furthermore, even if people do respond as if they applied their true utility weights to the attributes presented in the experiment, the SP choice situation is typically somewhat different from a market choice situation. Some aspects of the market choice context, such as search costs, are absent in the SP experiment. And in the experiment alternatives are defined solely by the attributes presented, while in market data there may be attributes observed (or perceived) by the consumer but unobserved by the researcher, and these will be pushed into the choice model error terms.

Despite these potential problems, a number of recent papers have obtained a rather striking result that lends credence to the use of SP experiments. In a large number of cases in which both RP and SP data have been used to fit MNL models for the same good, researchers have not rejected the hypothesis that the estimated utility weights are proportional in the RP and SP choice models. Examples are Adamowicz et al (1994), Ben-Akiva and Morikawa (1990), and Hensher and Bradley (1993). These researchers generally find that the only significant difference between the MNL models estimated on RP and SP data is the variance (or "scale") of the error term (see Swait and Louviere (1993) for a discussion of tests of this hypothesis).

A difficult question is why the process generating responses to SP choice experiments should resemble that generating market choice behavior. In the papers mentioned above, the choice tasks are all of a simple variety that is familiar to consumers (e.g., choose among several varieties of detergent based on price and other attributes). Respondents may get utility from demonstrating they can make rational price/quality tradeoffs in such situations. Or, the researchers may have successfully "framed" the choice tasks so that respondents believe it is in their interest to reveal accurately how they value attributes (because, say, that information will be used to design new products). An interesting avenue for future research is to conduct SP experiments of varying designs so as to discover conditions under which response patterns do and do not resemble those in market data.

If the scale of the error term does indeed differ between RP and SP choice models it creates a problem when applying the SP model to predict market share for a new product. To deal with this, utility weights estimated from the SP data should be scaled proportionately so as to set predicted market shares as close as possible to those in the historical market data. This scaled model can then be used to forecast market shares after the new product introduction.

Another issue is how to optimally combine RP and SP data to more efficiently estimate choice model parameters. Given the processes assumed to be generating the RP and SP data (e.g., the MNL in the papers cited above), one can form the correct likelihood for the combined data. Each choice observation, whether from the market or SP data, contributes one term to the likelihood. There is no reason to apply weights to the observations. However, if consumers' respond as if their preference weights are the same in the RP and SP data, consumer heterogeneity will generate dependence across responses that must be accounted for in forming the likelihood. There has also been work on how to incorporate SP data on stated attribute importance with market choice data in order to obtain more efficient estimates of choice model parameters (see McFadden (1986) and Harris and Keane (1996)).

Now consider the problem of predicting market share for a fundamentally new product. Examples of products that were fundamentally different when first introduced are lap-top computers and cellular phones. Prior to their introduction all computers and phones had the attribute "not mobile," and these products introduced variability on that dimension for the first time.

Such "fundamental change" may create an identification problem. Market data cannot be used to estimate the effect of varying an attribute that is invariant in the market, unless we have a model that specifies how that attribute maps into some more fundamental determinant of utility. In a structural or utility based approach this is often the case. For example, the welfare program participation model of Keane and Moffitt (1996) can be used to predict how changes in aspects of program rules that are invariant in the data would affect participation decisions, provided the rule changes affect agents' income conditional on participation. But if the model only specifies that certain attributes affect utility, without specifying any more fundamental mechanism through which they do so, then those attributes must vary in the data in order to identify their effect on choice.

Because of the identification problem in market data, SP experiments may often be the only means to predict demand for a fundamentally different product. But fundamental changes also create problems for SP experiments, because of the difficultly of conveying to participants the meaning of a change along a dimension that is invariant in their experience. One approach is to use computer simulation or virtual reality techniques that help consumers understand the innovation (see Weinberg (1992) and Urban et al (1996)).

There is considerable scope for experimentation in this area. Another problem is that the SP model will again need to be scaled to historical market choice data. And we cannot test whether the utility weight for the fundamentally changed attribute "scales."

Finally I turn to the issue of forecasting demand for a new product when there are network externalities. A network externality arises when the utility I get from adopting a product depends on how many other people adopt it. An example is the decision to adopt a new word processing package from a startup software company (as opposed to an update from a major vendor). If I am alone in adopting the new package, I face several problems. For example, I will not be able to send documents electronically to others to print, since they will lack the necessary software. And I will not be able to obtain support for the package locally, since I will be the only person using it.

Thus, only certain segments of consumers will adopt the new package initially: those who do not need to send documents electronically to others, those who are good at deciphering software manuals, those with great confidence that many other people will soon adopt the new package, etc. Later, after some consumers have already adopted, a wider group of consumers may be willing to adopt, etc. This suggests using a sequence of SP choice experiments to predict demand for the new product at different stages of its life cycle. The state of adoption could be part of the framing of the choice task. That is: 1) no one has yet adopted the product, no support is available, etc., 2) a certain fraction of the population has adopted and a certain level of support is available, etc. At some point one finds the level of prior adoption such that the same fraction of consumers would choose to adopt, and this is the steady state adoption level.

Given this series of conditional choice models, one must translate the predicted growth in market shares across models into real time. This is a difficult problem. One possibility is to find a previously introduced product that is in some sense similar (including similar initial and steady state adoption levels), and assume the diffusion time path will be the same. Also, one could introduce questions about timing of adoption into the SP choice task, so as to obtain the information needed to predict, given an initial market share, how much time would pass before a certain fraction of additional people adopt. In the Urban et al (1996) study on the electric car, "managerial judgement" was used to predict the number of recharging stations available at different points in time. But this seems to skirt the issue, since the state of infrastructure by any point in time will depend on cumulative adoption decisions up to that point, which is what the choice model is meant to predict.

In principle, market data could also be used to forecast demand for a new product that entails a network externality, provided the product is only marginally different from other such products introduced in the past (e.g. an improved word processing package that is not fully compatible with older versions). But, while historical data on consumers' past adoption decisions for similar products could be collected, such data appears to be rare at the individual level. Further, the type of panel data needed to model the dynamics of adoption as described above appears to be nonexistent. Thus, at present SP choice experiments appear to be the only practical option in this context.

Finally, note that demand for new products may depend crucially on expectations. Prices of many new products drop systematically with time, so expected future prices will affect current demand. And in cases of network externalities, expected future infrastructure will matter too.

V. Error structures in choice models

The "error term" in discrete choice models has often been treated as noise or intrinsic randomness in behavior arising from unknown and unspecified sources. This is misguided. It is important to interpret the error term in the light of behavioral models. To illustrate the kind of misunderstanding that can arise from failure to do so, consider a simple random utility model, in which there are heterogeneous preferences for observed and unobserved brand attributes:

$$U_{ijt} = \alpha_{ij} + P_{ijt}\gamma_i + X_{ijt}\beta_i + \epsilon_{ijt} \tag{1}$$

Here, U_{ijt} is the utility that i receives given choice of alternative j on occasion t. In market data, t could index time, store visits, or purchase occasions. In an SP experiment, t would index choice tasks. P_{ijt} denotes price, and X_{ijt} denotes an observed attribute of j (which for complete generality I allow to vary over people and choice occasions). The α_{ij} denotes the person specific intercept for alternative j, which can be interpreted as arising from i's preferences for unobserved attributes of j. The γ_i and β_i are individual specific utility parameters which are intrinsic to the consumer and hence invariant over choice occasions. The ϵ_{ijt} can be interpreted as occasion specific shocks to i's tastes, which for convenience I assume to be independent over choice occasions, alternatives and consumers.

Suppose I estimate a multinomial choice model, falsely assuming that the intercept and slope parameters are *homogeneous* in the population. The error term in this model will be

$$w_{ijt} = \hat{\alpha}_i + P_{ijt}\hat{\gamma}_i + X_{ijt}\hat{\beta}_i + \epsilon_{ijt} \tag{2}$$

where ˆ denotes the individual specific deviation from the population mean. Observe that (from the analyst's perspective) the variance of this error term for person i on choice occasion t is

$$\text{Var}(w_{ijt}) = \sigma_\alpha^2 + P_{ijt}^2\sigma_\gamma^2 + X_{ijt}^2\sigma_\beta^2 + \sigma_\epsilon^2 \tag{3}$$

and the covariance between choice occasions t and $t-1$ is

$$\text{Cov}(w_{ijt}, w_{ij,t-1}) = \sigma_\alpha^2 + P_{ijt}P_{ij,t-1}\sigma_\gamma^2 + X_{ijt}X_{ij,t-1}\sigma_\beta^2 \tag{4}$$

Equations (3) and (4) reveal two interesting consequences of ignoring heterogeneity in preferences. First, the error variance will differ across choice occasions as the price P and attribute X are varied. If one estimates a MNL model with a constant error variance, this will show up as variation in the intercept and slope parameters across choice occasions. In an SP experiment context, this could lead to a false conclusion that there are order effects in the process generating responses.

Second, equation (4) shows how preference heterogeneity leads to serially correlated errors. That heterogeneity is a special type of serial correlation is apparently not well understood in the marketing and transportation literatures. To obtain efficient estimates of choice model parameters one should include a specification of the heterogeneity structure in the model. But more importantly, if preference heterogeneity is present it is not merely a statistical nuisance requiring correction. Rather, one must model the heterogeneity in order to obtain accurate choice model predictions, because the presence of heterogeneity will alter cross-price elasticities, lead to IIA violations, etc. This is just one example of how paying attention to the behavioral source of the error terms in a choice model leads to new insights into how the model should be estimated, interpreted and applied.

VI. Contingent valuation

Contingent valuation (CV) is a specific SP data technique in which the researcher attempts to uncover the demand function for a particular good. This is typically done either by asking a sample of consumers how much they are willing to pay for the good (the "open-ended" approach), or by presenting consumers with various different prices, and asking if they would buy the good at those prices (the "referendum" approach). The fraction of consumers willing to buy at each price traces out the demand curve. Referendum CV is a special case of an SP choice experiment in which price is the only attribute varied, so only the complete attribute bundle the good represents can be valued.

As with SP choice experiments, a key advantage of CV over studies based on market data is that it can be used to predict demand for goods that are fundamentally different from any that are currently being traded in markets. As a result, CV has been widely used to predict demand for public goods. An example of such a good would be the Porcupine Caribou herd, whose existence provides utility (i.e., "existence value") to many people.

Recently, CV has received a great deal of attention because of its use in litigation (such as the highly publicized Exxon Valdez case) to assess existence values of public goods damaged in environmental accidents. As a result, the National Oceanic and Atmospheric Administration (NOAA) recently formed a distinguished panel of economists to evaluate the use of CV in determining existence values. Arrow et al (1993) concluded that if a number of stringent design criteria were met, then "CV studies convey useful information," although the report also suggests that few if any existing CV studies meet all these criteria. One key criterion which the panel emphasized was that "the payment scenario should be convincingly described, preferably in a referendum context, because most respondents will have had experience with referendum ballots."

The NOAA panel recommendation of the referendum format has raised controversy, with researchers taking different positions on whether that format is more incentive compatible and/or psychometrically reliable than the open-ended format. Consider first the issue of incentives to misstate preferences. Suppose a CV study deals with a wolf conservation program. In an open-ended format, respondents are asked how much they would be willing to pay in taxes to implement the program. Suppose a respondent wants to see the conservation program implemented, and believes that the higher the mean response to the CV question the more likely is implementation. However, he/she does not believe that the mean response will affect either the form of the program finally implemented or the cost in taxes (i.e., the respondent has a set belief about what the program will really cost). In that case, the respondent has an incentive to report the highest possible willingness to pay, subject to the constraint that the response look reasonable so it is not discarded as an outlier. Analogously, in a referendum format, such a respondent would have an incentive to answer "yes, I would vote for the referendum" no matter how high a tax was quoted in the question.

As Green et al (1995) note, if the above scenario is changed only in that the respondent believes the probability of program implementation depends not on the mean response to the CV question, but rather on the fraction of respondents who indicate support for the program (either by stating a willingness to pay that exceeds cost, or answering yes in the referendum format when the stated cost is greater than or equal to true cost), then the respondent has an incentive to be truthful in *either* format. For example, suppose the respondent is truly willing to pay $100 for the program. It is then optimal for him/her to express a willingness to pay of exactly $100, regardless of format, because this insures that he/she is voting "Yes" contingent on the true program cost being less than or equal to $100, and "No" otherwise. (An interesting question is how the respondent should respond in the referendum format if expressing a willingness to pay of *exactly* $100 is not an option).

Thus, Green et al (1995) argue that the referendum format should not be preferred to the open-ended format on a priori incentive compatibility grounds. However, if one wants an incentive compatible design the real issue is which format makes it easiest to frame the question in an incentive compatible way. If one wants respondents to believe that the probability of implementation depends on the fraction of respondents who vote yes, it seems easiest to do this in the referendum format.

It is worth noting, however, that the NOAA panel did not prefer referendum CV because of incentive compatibility concerns (that was a minor point in the report) but rather stressed the fact that "most respondents will have had experience with referendum ballots," making it a task with which respondents are familiar. We do not yet understand why and under what conditions choice behavior in SP choice tasks resembles revealed preference behavior in the "scaling" sense described in section IV, but at this point it appears likely that familiarity of the task is important—since agents have little or no economic incentive to work hard on the task, the cognitive burden had better be small!

Green et al (1995) also argue that the emphasis on incentive compatibility in CV surveys is misplaced, since few respondents will believe they can affect either the probability of program implementation or cost. They argue that avoidance of various psychometric biases is likely to be the more important consideration in choosing between referendum and open-ended formats. For instance, they present evidence that in referendum CV the quoted program costs act as "anchors," such that respondent's valuations move toward the anchor with which they are presented.

A potential explanation for anchoring is that it is a learning phenomenon. If we ask people what they are "willing to pay" for a government program, those who support it might respond by forming a guess of what it *should* cost, if implemented cost effectively. And costs quoted in a referendum CV survey may be used as indicators of true program cost. As Hanemann (1994) notes, a related response behavior is observed in experiments where open-ended designs have been applied to market goods, in which "people are more likely to tell you what the good costs than what it is worth to them." This is not surprising. Why should I be "willing to pay" more for a market good than the going market price, even if at a higher market price I would still buy the good?

A key issue, in all SP task design is that the attributes and prices presented be believable. In a CV task respondents may not believe the government can provide a certain environmental amenity at a certain price, and in an SP choice task they may not believe a manufacturer could provide a certain product attribute. In an SP task where the choice is among software packages, I would ignore an indication that one had an easy to read manual (since that's impossible), and in a CV task I would not believe the state government could restore the Minnesota river to pristine condition with a $10 increase in state taxes. It is not obvious how people might respond in such contexts.

A key criticism of CV is that it is subject to "embedding" effects, whereby people exhibit implausibly low marginal willingness to pay for increments to environmental amenities (see McFadden (1994)). Such behavior may stem from scenario implausibility. For example, suppose a person says that are willing to pay $100 to clean up the Minnesota river, but he/she indicates they are unwilling to pay much more for a program to clean up all the rivers in the state. The respondent may simply be skeptical of the government's ability to successfully implement the larger project.

CV has also been criticized on the grounds that respondents pay insufficient attention to opportunity costs. But this is also true in SP choice experiments. For example, in Urban et al (1996), the percentage of people indicating they would purchase a GM electric car dropped substantially when other alternatives were presented explicitly. With market goods it is often possible to deal with such problems by "scaling" an SP choice model so its predictions align with observed market shares for previously existing products. But as the NOAA panel noted, a fundamental problem in the case of public goods is that there may be no market data available to make such adjustments.

But it is sometimes possible to compare CV estimates of demand for existence of public goods to revealed preference data. For example, there have been actual referenda on proposals to conserve forests. And some people are willing to pay a premium to help preserve existence of natural resources by buying products like tuna caught in dolphin friendly nets or recycled paper. A major research program is needed to compare behavior in SP and CV choice tasks with behavior in market contexts. Much work along these lines has already been done (e.g., Carson et al (1996), Cameron (1992), Bishop and Heberlein (1979), Davis (1963) and the SP studies cited in section IV). But we are a long way from having general rules for adjusting SP and CV choice models so they can reliably predict behavior in market contexts—even when no market data exist to aid in calibration.

Finally, the referendum CV format posses a number of interesting statistical problems, which are discussed at length in Hanemann and Kanninen (1996). An important theme of their work is that simple logit and probit models of the type usually estimated in the CV literature rarely satisfy the restrictions of economic theory. This harkens back to my point in section I that particular statistical models should not be the starting point for analysis of choice behavior. Rather, one should start from sensible behavioral models and then work out the statistical models that emerge.

VII. Conclusion

Recent advances in computation make it possible to estimate behavioral models that generate very complex choice probability expressions. I argue that this should lead to a fundamental change in mind-set among researchers in the discrete choice area. Given a research question, one should start by developing an appealing theoretical model of the behavior of interest, and then derive the implied statistical model. Given modern technology, it will often be possible to press ahead with estimation even if the statistical model so obtained is quite complex. This contrasts with the traditional approach (often necessitated by computational limitations) of trying to find a way to fit the research question into a logit or other simple statistical framework, regardless of whether the behavioral assumptions in the framework are sensible or appealing in the context under study.

In this paper I have considered several possible avenues for future research opened up by these advances. These include: 1) joint modeling of the process by which consumers decide on store visits, purchase in a category and brand choice, so as to shed light on the role played by price and promotion activity at each stage of the process, 2) modeling consumers' choice of purchase decision rules in alternative price setting environments, 3) combining stated and revealed preference data to estimate richer models of the demand for new and existing products, 4) estimation of models which rich structures of preference heterogeneity across consumers, and 5) estimation of models of the behavioral processes underlying responses in SP and CV choice tasks. It is very exciting to be working in the discrete choice area at a time when so many possibilities are opening up.

Acknowledgments

This paper was prepared in collaboration with the participants in the workshop "Current Issues in Discrete Modeling" at the Third International Symposium on Choice Behavior held in Harrison, NY on June 14–17, 1996. Participants in the workshop were Jordan Louviere (co-chair), Wiktor Adamowicz, David Bunch, Richard Carson, Michael Hanemann, David Hensher, Bernard Pailthorpe and Joffre Swait. It should be stressed however, that the views expressed here are my own and not necessarily those of the workshop participants. Helpful comments by the editor and three anonymous referees are appreciated.

References

Adamowicz, W., Louviere, J., and M. Williams (1994), "Combining Revealed and Stated Preference Methods for Valuing Environmental Amenities," *Journal of Environmental Economics and Management*, 26, 271–292.

Arrow, K., Solow, R., Portney, P., Leamer, E., Radner, R. and H. Schuman (1993), "Report of the NOAA Panel on Contingent Valuation," *Federal Register*, 58:10, 4601–4614.

Ben-Akiva, M. and T. Morikawa (1990), "Estimation of Switching Models from Revealed Preferences and Stated Intentions," *Transportation Research A*, 24A:6, 485–495.

Bishop, R. and T. Heberlein (1979), "Measuring Values of Extra-Market Goods: Are Indirect Measures Biased?," *American Journal of Agricultural Economics*, 61:5, 926–930.

Borsch-Supan, A. and V. Hajivassiliou (1993), "Smooth Unbiased Multivariate Probability Simulators for Maximum Likelihood Estimation of Limited Dependent Variable Models," *Journal of Econometrics*, 58, 347–368.

Bucklin, R. and J. Lattin (1991), "Purchase Incidence and Brand Choice," *Marketing Science*.

Bunch, D., Louviere, J. and D. Anderson (1996), "A Comparison of Experimental Design Strategies for Choice-Based Conjoint Analysis with Generic-Attribute Multinomial Logit Models," manuscript, Graduate School of Management, University of California at Davis.

Cameron, T. (1992), "Combining Contingent Valuation and Travel Cost Data for the Valuation of Nonmarket Goods," *Land Economics*, 68:3, 302–317.

Carson, R., Flores, N., Martin, K., and J. Wright (1996), "Contingent Valuation and Revealed Preference Methodologies: Comparing the Estimates for Quasi-Public Goods," *Land Economics*, 72, 80–89.

Chiang, J. (1991), "A Simultaneous Approach to the Whether, What and How Much to Buy Questions," *Marketing Science*, 10:4, 297–315.

Chintagunta, P. (1993), "Investigating Purchase Incidence, Brand Choice and Purchase Quantity Decisions of Households," *Marketing Science*, 12:2, 184–208.

Chintagunta, P. and N. Vilcassim (1992), "An Empirical Investigation of Advertising Strategies in a Dynamic Duopoly," *Management Science*, 38:9, 1230–1244.

Davis, R. (1963), "Recreation Planning as an Economic Problem," *Natural Resources Journal*, 3, 239–249.

Erdem, T. and M. Keane (1996), "Decision-making Under Uncertainty: Capturing Dynamic Brand Choice Processes in Turbulent Consumer Goods Markets," *Marketing Science*, 15, 1–20.

Green, D., Jacowitz, K., Kahneman, D., and D. McFadden (1995), "Referendum Contingent Valuation, Anchoring, and Willingness to Pay for Public Goods," Working Paper, University of California–Berkeley.

Guadagni, P. and J. Little (1983), "A Logit Model of Brand Choice Calibrated on Scanner Data," *Marketing Science*, 2, 203–238.

Gupta, S. (1988), "Impact of Sales Promotions on When, What and How Much to Buy," *Journal of Marketing Research*, 25, 342–355.

Hanemann, W. M. (1984), "Discrete/Continuous Models of Consumer Demand," *Econometrica*, 52, 541–561.

Hanemann, W. M. and B. Kanninen (1996), "The Statistical Analysis of Discrete Response CV Data." In I. Bateman and K. Willis (eds.) *Valuing Environmental Preferences: Theory and Practice of the Contingent Valuation Method in the US, EC and Developing Countries*, Oxford: Oxford University Press.

Harris, K. and M. Keane (1996), "A Model of Health Plan Choice: Inferring Preferences and Perceptions from a Combination of Stated and Revealed Preference Data," *Journal of Econometrics*, forthcoming.

Hensher, D. (1994), "Stated Preference Analysis of Travel Choices: The State of the Practice," *Transportation*, 21.

Hensher, D. and M. Bradley (1993), "Using Stated Response Choice Data to Enrich Revealed Preference Discrete Choice Models," *Marketing Letters*, 4:2, 139–151.

Jueland, A., Bass, F. and G. Wright (1980), "A Multibrand Stochastic Model Compounding Heterogeneous Erlang Timing and Multinomial Choice Processes," *Operations Research*, 28:2, 255–277.

Keane, M. (1993). Simulation Estimation for Panel Data Models with Limited Dependent Variables. *The Handbook of Statistics*, G. S. Maddala, C. R. Rao and H. D. Vinod editors, North Holland publisher.

Keane, M. (1994). A Computationally Practical Simulation Estimator for Panel Data. *Econometrica*, 62:1, 95–116.

Keane, M. (1996), "Modeling Heterogeneity and State Dependence in Consumer Choice Behavior," *Journal of Business and Economic Statistics*, forthcoming.

Keane, M. and R. Moffitt (1996), "A Structural Model of Multiple Welfare Program Participation and Labor Supply," *International Economic Review*, forthcoming.

Kopalle, P. and R. Winer (1996), "A Dynamic Model of Reference Price and Expected Quality," *Marketing Letters*, 7:1, 41–52.

Krishnamurthi, L. and S. P. Raj (1988), "A Model of Brand Choice and Purchase Quantity Price Sensitivities," *Marketing Science*, 7:1, 1–17.

Louviere, J. (1988), "Analyzing Decision Making: Metric Conjoint Analysis." Beverly Hills: Sage.

Lucas, R. (1976), "Econometric Policy Evaluation: A Critique," *Carnegie-Rochester Conference Series on Public Policy*, 1, pp. 19–46.

Marschak, J. (1952), "Economic Measurements for Policy and Prediction." In *Studies in Econometric Method*, W. C. Hood and T. J. Koopmans (eds.), New York: Wiley, pp. 1–26.

McFadden, D. (1974), "Conditional Logit Analysis of Qualitative Choice Behavior." In P. Zarembka (ed.), *Frontiers in Econometrics*, New York: Academic Press, 105–142.

McFadden, D. (1989), "A Method of Simulated Moments for the Estimation of Discrete Response Models without Numerical Integration," *Econometrica*, 57:5, 995–1026.

McFadden, D. (1989), "The Choice Theory Approach to Market Research," *Marketing Science*, 5, 275–297.

McFadden, D. (1994), "Contingent Valuation and Social Choice," *American Journal of Agricultural Economics*, 76, 689–708.

Shoemaker, R., Staelin R., Kadane J., and F. Shoaf (1977), "Relation of Brand Choice and Purchase Timing Behavior," *Journal of Marketing Research*, 14, 458–468.

Swait, J. and J. Louviere (1993), "The Role of the Scale Parameter in the Estimation and Comparison of Multinomial Logit Models," *Journal of Marketing Research*, 30, 305–314.

Urban, G., Weinberg, B. and J. Hauser (1996), "Premarket Forecasting of Really-New Products," *Journal of Marketing*, 60, 47–60.

Weinberg, B. (1996), "An Information-Acceleration-Based Methodology for Developing Preproduction Forecasts for Durable Goods: Design, Development and Initial Validation," Ph.D. dissertation, Sloan School of Management, MIT.

Winer, R. (1986) "A Reference Price Model of Brand Choice for Frequently Purchased Products," *Journal of Consumer Research*, 13, 250–256.

Zufryden, F. (1977), "A Composite Heterogeneous Model of Brand Choice and Purchase Timing Behavior," *Management Science*, 24:2, 121–136.

Available online at www.sciencedirect.com
ScienceDirect
ELSEVIER
Journal of Econometrics 141 (2007) 683–703
JOURNAL OF Econometrics
www.elsevier.com/locate/jeconom

Masking identification of discrete choice models under simulation methods

Lesley Chiou[a,*], Joan L. Walker[b]

[a]Department of Economics, Occidental College, 1600 Campus Road, Los Angeles, CA 90041, USA
[b]Center for Transportation Studies, Boston University, 675 Commonwealth Avenue, Boston, MA 02215, USA

Available online 8 December 2006

Abstract

We present examples based on actual and synthetic datasets to illustrate how simulation methods can mask identification problems in the estimation of discrete choice models such as mixed logit. Simulation methods approximate an integral (without a closed form) by taking draws from the underlying distribution of the random variable of integration. Our examples reveal how a low number of draws can generate estimates that appear identified, but in fact, are either not theoretically identified by the model or not empirically identified by the data. For the particular case of maximum simulated likelihood estimation, we investigate the underlying source of the problem by focusing on the shape of the simulated log-likelihood function under different conditions.

JEL classification: C15; C25

Keywords: Simulation methods; Discrete choice; Identification

1. Introduction

Over the past decade, simulation methods have grown in popularity as advancements in computational speed have allowed researchers to estimate increasingly richer models of consumer and firm behavior. In particular, the literature on consumer choice theory has spread rapidly with the development of numerical techniques such as maximum simulated likelihood and the method of simulated moments (for example, Berry et al., 1995;

*Corresponding author. Tel.: +1 323 259 2875; fax: +1 323 259 2704.
E-mail addresses: lchiou@oxy.edu (L. Chiou), joanw@bu.edu (J.L. Walker).

0304-4076/$ - see front matter
doi:10.1016/j.jeconom.2006.10.012

Brownstone and Train, 1999; Goolsbee and Petrin, 2003). While simulation allows estimation of more flexible models, we examine how simulation noise can mask identification problems inherent in the model or data. We explore the issue within the context of mixed logit and maximum simulated likelihood estimation through the use of both synthetic and real data. Furthermore, we investigate the underlying source of the problem by examining the shape of the simulated log-likelihood function under different conditions. While we examine the particular case of maximum simulated likelihood estimation, the caveats presented in this paper could apply to other estimation strategies that employ simulation methods.

Simulation methods rely on approximating an integral (that does not have a closed form) through Monte Carlo integration. Draws are taken from the underlying distribution of the random variable of integration and used to calculate the numeric integral. Poor approximations of numerical techniques have important implications for the interpretation of the estimates and any resulting conclusions or welfare calculations. We show how the practice of applying maximum simulated likelihood estimation can generate misleading results even under 1000 pseudo-random, Halton, or shuffled Halton draws. Most empirical work on mixed logit models typically apply 200–300 draws.

We present examples of mixed logit models where employing a "low" number of draws to construct the simulated integral can generate estimates that are not identified by the model or the data. In each of the examples, we estimate the model under different types of simulation draws: random, Halton, and shuffled Halton. We consider two types of identification problems: theoretical and empirical unidentification. Theoretical unidentification occurs when the model cannot be estimated in principle (regardless of the data at hand). Empirical unidentification occurs when the data cannot support the model even though the model may be estimable in principle.

The first example utilizes a dataset on consumers' choices of telephone plans. It demonstrates how a model that is not theoretically identified can appear to result in identified estimates at a low number of draws. A classic symptom of unidentification, a singular Hessian, does not emerge until a much higher number of draws is employed. In the second set of examples, we generate synthetic datasets to investigate the source of empirical unidentification by examining the shape of the simulated log-likelihood functions under varying numbers of draws and identification conditions. The last two examples use an actual dataset on consumer choices across retail stores and a synthetic dataset to consider empirical unidentification under more complex specifications.

Limited research exists on the empirical identification of discrete choice models under simulation methods. Ben-Akiva and Bolduc (1996) and Walker (2001) note that an identification problem can arise when a low number of draws are used, and they and others (e.g., Hensher and Greene, 2003) emphasize the necessity of verifying the stability of parameter estimates as the number of draws are increased. Walker (2001) and Walker et al. (2006) examine the theoretical framework for the identification of mixed logit models and support their findings with empirical examples. In contrast, this paper focuses primarily on the issue of empirical unidentification by explicitly examining the properties and transformation of the log-likelihood function over a range of number of draws.

The next section presents the theoretical framework of the mixed logit model and describes the estimation procedure. The remaining sections discuss the empirical examples and illustrate the sensitivity of the estimates with respect to simulation.

2. The mixed logit model

2.1. Consumer preferences

In this discrete choice model, the utility that consumer n, $n = 1, \ldots, N$ where N is the sample size, receives from choosing alternative i, $i = 1, \ldots, J_n$ is given by

$$U_{ni} = X_{ni}\beta_n + \varepsilon_{ni}, \tag{1}$$

where X_{ni} is a $(1 \times K)$ vector of observable characteristics for alternative i and consumer n and β_n is a $(K \times 1)$ vector of consumer n's tastes over the attributes of alternative i. The random coefficient β_n contains a subscript n to indicate that preferences over the characteristics of an alternative may vary among individuals in the population. The term ε_{ni} captures consumer n's idiosyncratic and unobservable taste for alternative i. Under a logit model, ε_n (consisting of ε_{ni}, $i = 1, \ldots, J_n$) is an i.i.d. extreme value random vector. The random coefficient β_n can assume any distributional form (see Train, 2003, for further information). McFadden and Train (2000) demonstrate that any random utility model can be "approximated to any degree of accuracy by a mixed logit model with the appropriate choice of variables" and distribution of the random coefficient.

A consumer chooses the alternative that gives her the highest utility. More specifically, the set of values A_{ni} of the idiosyncratic error ε_{ni} that induces consumer n to choose alternative i is given by

$$A_{ni} = \left\{ \varepsilon_{ni} : U_{ni}(X_{ni}, \beta_n, \varepsilon_{ni}) \geqslant \max_{j=1,\ldots,J_n} U_{nj}(X_{nj}, \beta_n, \varepsilon_{nj}) \right\}, \tag{2}$$

where j indexes all possible alternatives in consumer n's choice set. Conditional on the utility parameters β_n, the probability that consumer n chooses alternative i is given by the standard logit formula:

$$L_{ni}(\beta_n) = \int_{A_{ni}} f(\varepsilon)\,\mathrm{d}\varepsilon, \tag{3}$$

$$L_{ni}(\beta_n) = \frac{\exp(X_{ni}\beta_n)}{\sum_{j=1}^{J_n} \exp(X_{nj}\beta_n)}, \tag{4}$$

where $f(\cdot)$ is the density of the extreme value distribution. By convention, the parameters of the distribution of ε_{ni} are normalized to set the level and scale of the utility function (Train, 2003). The location parameter of each extreme value error ε_{ni} is zero, and the scale is set to 1 so that $\mathrm{Var}(\varepsilon_{ni}) = \pi^2/6$.

Since β_n is not observed, the unconditional probability of consumer n choosing alternative i is obtained by integrating out β_n over its population distribution:

$$P_{ni}(\theta) = \int L_{ni}(\beta) g(\beta|\theta)\,\mathrm{d}\beta, \tag{5}$$

where $g(\cdot)$ is the density of the distribution of β_n over the population and θ is the vector of parameters of the distribution. For instance, if the joint distribution of the $(K \times 1)$ vector β_n is multi-variate normal, then θ would represent the mean and parameters of the covariance matrix of the joint distribution. The vector θ is an unknown to be estimated.

2.2. Maximum simulated likelihood estimation

To estimate the mixed logit model under maximum simulated likelihood, we construct the log-likelihood by calculating each individual's probability P_{ni} of making her observed choice. When the integral in the expression for P_{ni} does not have a closed form, the probability is often evaluated numerically by taking R draws $\beta^{(r)}$ (with $r = 1,2, \ldots, R$) from the population density $g(\beta)$ and calculating $L_{ni}(\beta^{(r)})$ for each draw. The average of $L_{ni}(\beta^{(r)})$ over R draws gives the simulated probability:

$$\hat{P}_{ni}(\theta) = \frac{1}{R}\sum_{r=1}^{R} L_{ni}(\beta^{(r)}). \tag{6}$$

This simulated probability is an unbiased estimator whose variance decreases as the number of draws R increases; it is smooth (twice-differentiable) and sums to one over all alternatives (Train, 2003). Since it is strictly positive, its logarithm is defined.

The simulated log-likelihood $SL(\theta)$ of the sample is the sum of the logarithm of the simulated probabilities for each consumer making her observed choice:

$$SL(\theta) = \sum_{n=1}^{N}\sum_{j=1}^{J_n} d_{nj} \log \hat{P}_{nj}(\theta), \tag{7}$$

where d_{nj} equals 1 if consumer n chose alternative j and 0 otherwise.

It is a well-known fact that although the simulated log-likelihood function is consistent when the number of draws increases with the sample size, it is simulated with a downward bias under a finite number of draws (Börsch-Supan and Hajivassiliou, 1993). Our paper focuses on a different phenomenon: namely, how the shape of the simulated log-likelihood is affected by the number of draws.

2.3. Methods of generating draws for simulation

We focus on three common procedures for generating draws from a density. The most straightforward approach obtains draws through a pseudo-random number generator available in most statistical software.

An alternative approach creates draws based on a deterministic Halton sequence (Halton, 1960). Train (1999, 2003) provide an explanation and an example of the construction of a Halton sequence. In general, a Halton sequence can be created from any prime number p. The unit interval [0,1] is divided into p equally sized segments, and the endpoints or "breaks" of these segments form the first p numbers in the Halton sequence. Successive numbers in sequence are generated by further subdividing each segment into p equally sized segments and adding the breaks in a particular order.

The resulting Halton draws achieve greater precision and coverage for a given number of draws than random draws, since successive Halton draws are negatively correlated and therefore tend to be "self-correcting" (Train, 2003). In fact, Bhat (2001) demonstrates that for a particular mixed logit model, 100 Halton draws provided results that were more accurate than 1000 random draws.

Since each Halton sequence is constructed from a prime number, each dimension of simulation corresponds to a different sequence or prime. For instance, if β_n is a 2×1 vector where the two components are independently distributed, then the first component of the vector is generated from a Halton sequence based on the prime 2, and the second component is generated from a Halton sequence based on the prime 3. Higher dimensions of simulation require using higher primes. Unfortunately, under higher primes, Halton draws can become highly correlated, leading to "poor multi-dimensional coverage" (Walker, 2001; Hess and Polak, 2003b).

To ameliorate the poor coverage of Halton draws for higher dimensions, researchers have adopted modified procedures such as shuffled and scrambled Halton draws. Hess and Polak (2003a, b) describe the construction of the shuffled sequence, which creates multi-dimensional sequences from randomly shuffled versions of the one-dimensional standard Halton sequence. They find that the shuffled Halton sequence typically outperforms the standard Halton and scrambled Halton sequences.

3. A simple example of theoretical unidentification

3.1. Telephone services

As a way of introducing the problem of interest, we present an example of a model that is not theoretically identified, and we show estimation results in which an identification problem is masked at low numbers of simulation draws.

This example uses a dataset of households' choices over telephone services. The choice set comprises five alternatives, which are categorized into two groups: flat and measured. The three flat alternatives consist of a fixed monthly charge for unlimited calls within a specified geographic area, and the two measured alternatives include a reduced fixed monthly charge for a limited number of calls as well as usage charges for additional calls. A consumer's tastes over the five alternatives are assumed to be correlated within groups (or nests). Consumer n's utility from choosing telephone service i is given by

$$U_{ni} = X_{ni}\alpha + NEST_i\,\beta_n + \varepsilon_{ni}. \tag{8}$$

X_{ni} is a (1×5) vector consisting of four alternative-specific constants and the log of the cost of the service, and α is the (5×1) vector of associated taste parameters. The variable $NEST_i$ is a (1×2) vector of dummies for each nest. The parameter β_n is a (2×1) vector consisting of $\beta 1_n$ distributed $N(0, \sigma_1^2)$ and $\beta 2_n$ distributed $N(0, \sigma_2^2)$ where $\beta 1_n$ and $\beta 2_n$ are independent. More detail on the dataset and model can be found in Train et al. (1987) and Walker (2001).

Walker (2001) discusses conditions for identification of the model and shows that only the value $(\sigma_1^2 + \sigma_2^2)$ is identified. That is, when exactly two nests exist, only one nesting parameter is identified and to estimate the model an identifying constraint must be imposed, e.g., $\sigma_1 = \sigma_2$, $\sigma_1 = 0$, or $\sigma_2 = 0$.

Table 1 shows the estimation results[1] for a specification that does not include the necessary identifying constraint. Even without a necessary identifying restriction, the estimation procedure generates estimates that appear identified under a low number of

[1]All estimation results in this paper were estimated using either (1) BIOGEME using the DONLP2 optimization routine (see Bierlaire et al., 2004, and http://roso.epfl.ch/biogeme) or (2) a MATLAB implementation of Kenneth Train's GAUSS code using a BHHH-algorithm (Berndt et al., 1974) to compute the Hessian (for further information, see Chiou, 2005). Both estimation programs were shown to produce similar results.

Table 1
The demand for telephone service

Draws	2000 Random		5000 Random		1000 Halton		2000 Halton	
Parameter	Estimate	Std. error	Estimate	Std. error	Estimate	Std. error	Estimate	Std. error
Alternative specific constants	−3.81	(0.66)	−3.81	(0.66)	−3.80	(0.67)		
Budget measured (1)	−3.01	(0.61)	−3.01	(0.61)	−3.01	(0.61)	Singular	
Standard measured (2)	−1.09	(0.30)	−1.09	(0.30)	−1.09	(0.30)		
Local flat (3)	−1.19	(0.85)	−1.19	(0.85)	−1.19	(0.85)		
Extended flat (4)	−3.25	(0.53)	−3.26	(0.53)	−3.25	(0.53)		
Log cost								
σ_1	0.81	(0.81)	3.07	(1.06)	2.65	(0.85)		
σ_2	2.91	(0.94)	0.24	(1.20)	1.51	(0.69)		
$(\sigma_1^2+\sigma_2^2)^{1/2}$	3.02		3.08		3.05			
Simulated log-likelihood	−472.73		−472.66		−473.02			
Number of observations	434		434		434		434	

Note: Uses robust standard errors.

draws (1000 Halton, 5000 pseudo-random). A large number of simulation draws (in this case, 2000 Halton draws) are necessary before resulting in a singular Hessian.

Not realizing the identification condition can lead to incorrect conclusions drawn from hypothesis tests based on standard errors. Since the parameter estimates and standard errors are poorly approximated under a low number of draws, they are a function of the specific draws and the starting values that are used. For example, the 2000 pseudo-random draw results for the telephone dataset would lead the modeler to incorrectly conclude that there is no correlation within the first nest (measured), but there is correlation within the second nest (flat). However, the estimation results under 5000 pseudo-random draws lead to the opposite conclusion (correlation among the measured alternatives but not among the flat alternatives).

4. Empirical unidentification and the log-likelihood function

In this section, we use extremely simple, synthetic datasets to examine the source of the empirical unidentification by investigating the properties of the simulated log-likelihood function as the number of draws increase. We show that regardless of whether the model is empirically identified, the simulated log-likelihood for mixed logit is always globally concave under only one draw because the model is analogous to a standard logit. When a model is not empirically identified, the simulated log-likelihood function begins to flatten and exhibit a singular Hessian only as the number of draws increases. The obfuscation of the identification problem occurs in the intermediate cases where the log-likelihood still exhibits the concavity as when only one draw is used. For the discussion, we consider two examples of the most common ways in which mixed logit is applied: first error components with a nesting formulation and then random coefficients on continuous explanatory variables.

4.1. Random coefficient on a nest dummy

We consider a simplified case where only one parameter is estimated. The discrete choice model consists of five alternatives that are divided into two nests, and the first three alternatives comprise Nest 1. Consumer n's utility of choosing alternative i is given by

$$U_{ni} = NEST1_i\beta_n + \varepsilon_{ni}, \tag{9}$$

where $NEST1$ is a dummy for whether alternative i lies in Nest 1. We specify the random coefficient β_n with a normal distribution, N(0, σ^2); thus only one parameter σ must be estimated. Strictly speaking, the resulting standard deviation is calculated as $\sqrt{\sigma^2}$, and therefore the sign of the estimated coefficient σ is irrelevant. As the number of draws approaches infinity, the simulated log-likelihood will be symmetric about zero.

We generate the synthetic data according to the true value $\sigma = 2.0$ by creating observations for N consumers. For each consumer, we calculate the utility of each alternative by taking a single draw of β_n from the N(0, σ^2) distribution and ε_{ni} from the extreme value distribution; the consumer chooses the alternative with the highest utility.

Table 2 reports the estimates of the standard deviation σ when the dataset contains only $N = 50$ observations. Under lower number of draws, the estimation procedure converges to a non-singular Hessian, but under a higher number of draws, the empirical unidentification becomes apparent. Figs. 1 and 2 graph the simulated log-likelihood as a function of the parameter σ for a varying number of random and Halton draws.

As shown in Figs. 1 and 2, the simulated log-likelihood is always concave when only one draw is used. In general, including only one draw in the simulation is equivalent to estimating a standard logit model with an additional variable included in the utility equation. Consider a model with a single explanatory variable X_{ni} and a random coefficient β_n. We express consumer n's utility from alternative i as $U_{ni} = X_{ni}\beta_n + \varepsilon_{ni}$. If the number of draws R is equal to one, then the simulated probability of consumer n choosing alternative i is

$$\hat{P}_{ni} = \frac{\exp(X_{ni}\beta_n)}{\sum_{j=1}^{J_n}\exp(X_{nj}\beta_n)}. \tag{10}$$

In the estimation procedure, the random coefficient for a single draw is decomposed as $\beta_n = \bar{\beta} + \sigma\upsilon_n$ where υ_n, $n = 1, \ldots, N$, are independent draws from a standard normal distribution. The coefficients to be estimated are $\bar{\beta}$ and σ, which are the population mean and standard deviation for the random taste. Substituting this expression into (10), we obtain:

$$\hat{P}_{ni} = \frac{\exp(X_{ni}(\bar{\beta} + \sigma\upsilon_n))}{\sum_{j=1}^{J_n}\exp(X_{nj}(\bar{\beta} + \sigma\upsilon_n))} = \frac{\exp(X_{ni}\bar{\beta} + X_{ni}\upsilon_n\sigma)}{\sum_{j=1}^{J_n}\exp(X_{nj}\bar{\beta} + X_{nj}\upsilon_n\sigma)} = \frac{\exp(X_{ni}\bar{\beta} + W_{ni}\sigma)}{\sum_{j=1}^{J_n}\exp(X_{nj}\bar{\beta} + W_{nj}\sigma)}. \tag{11}$$

where $W_{ni} = X_{ni}\upsilon_n$ is defined as a "new" variable created from X_{ni} and the particular draw for the consumer n. This is the standard logit formula where fixed parameters $\bar{\beta}$ and σ are estimated over the variables X_{ni} and W_{ni}. Since the standard logit model is globally concave (Train, 2003), estimation will always return a non-singular Hessian.

In our example, a draw υ_n is taken from a N(0,1) distribution, and β_n is calculated as $\beta_n = \sigma\upsilon_n$. The "new" variable is $\upsilon_n NEST1_i$. In other words, we can reinterpret the utility function as

$$U_{ni} = \sigma(NEST1_i\,\upsilon_n) + \varepsilon_{ni}, \tag{12}$$

Table 2
Empirical unidentification with a random coefficient on a nest dummy

	True value	1 Random	10 Random	35 Random	100 Random	1000 Random	1 Halton	10 Halton	35 Halton	100 Halton
σ	2.0	0.065	0.763	4.556	No convergence	No convergence	0.168	21.456	No convergence	No convergence
		(0.254)	(0.848)	(9.050)			(0.279)	(101.142)		
Simulated log-likelihood		−80.44	−80.26	−78.58	—	—	−80.32	−78.73	—	—
Number of observations		50	50	50	50	50	50	50	50	50

Notes: Standard error in parentheses. Uses non-robust standard errors.

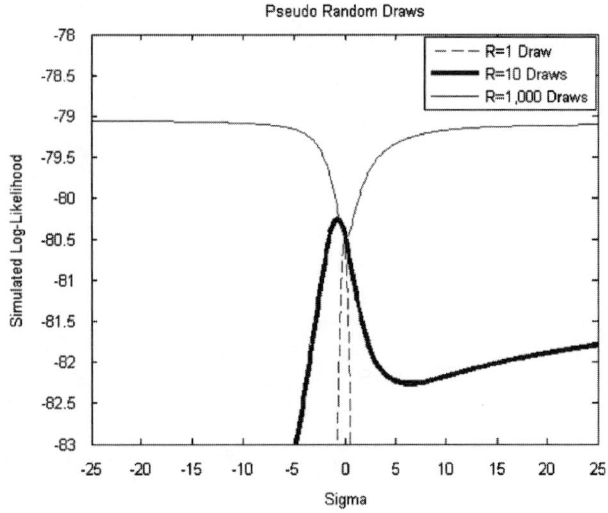

Fig. 1. Unidentified model with random coefficient on a nest dummy (50 observations, random draws).

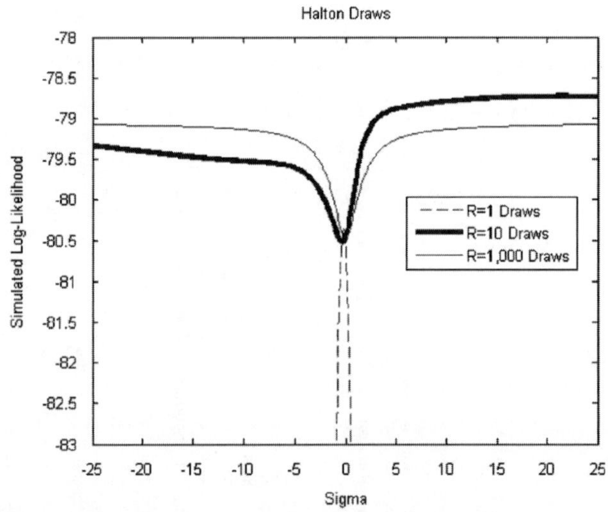

Fig. 2. Unidentified model with random coefficient on a nest dummy (50 observations, Halton draws).

where σ is a fixed coefficient on the variable $\upsilon_n NEST1_i$. Not surprisingly, the local maximum when 1 draw is used occurs near the origin, since the purely random draw has no explanatory power.

On the other hand, the singularity of the Hessian is evident under 1000 random draws. In Fig. 1, the simulated log-likelihood function rises away from 0, reflecting that the true value of σ is not zero, but the log-likelihood function flattens at higher magnitudes of σ. The data cannot empirically distinguish among the higher magnitudes of σ. In the

Table 3
Empirical identification with a random coefficient on a Nest dummy

	True value	1 Random	10 Random	100 Random	1000 Random	1 Halton	10 Halton	100 Halton
σ	2.0	0.003	0.152	1.770	2.378	0.004	2.112	2.464
		(0.020)	(0.064)	(0.223)	(0.319)	(0.020)	(0.274)	(0.336)
Simulated Log-likelihood		−16094.37	−16092.56	−16071.31	−16052.96	−16094.36	−16059.71	−16049.65
Number of observations		10,000	10,000	10,000	10,000	10,000	10,000	10,000

Notes: Standard error in parentheses. Uses non-robust standard errors.

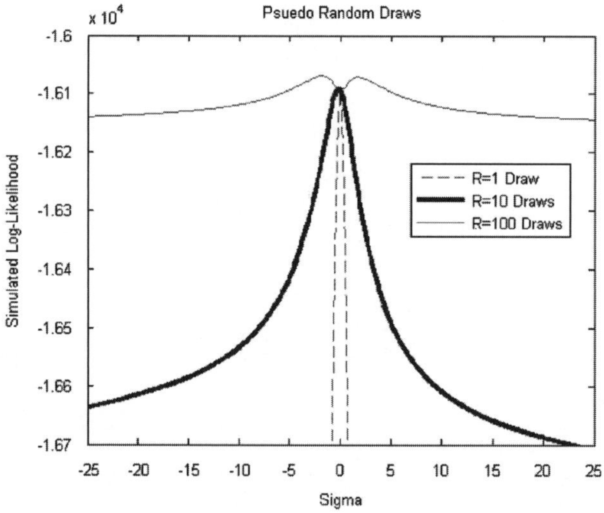

Fig. 3. Identified model with random coefficient on a nest dummy (10,000 observations, random draws).

intermediate case of 10 random draws, the simulated log-likelihood still exhibits a single peak as in the case of 1 draw. The local concavity gives rise to a convergence of the maximization routine.

Due to the efficiency of Halton draws relative to random draws, the Halton draws achieve the same unidentification properties at a lower threshold. In Table 2, the singularity of the Hessian occurs at 35 Halton draws whereas 35 random draws still generate a local maximum. Moreover, the large standard error of 101.142 under 10 Halton draws suggests the presence of an identification problem.

Table 3 reports the estimates of the standard deviation σ when the dataset contains $N = 10,000$ observations. In contrast to the previous case of only 50 observations, the dataset of 10,000 observations is sufficient to empirically identify the model. The parameter estimates stabilize and approach the true value of $\sigma = 2.0$ as the number of draws increases. Figs. 3 and 4 graph the simulated log-likelihood as a function of the parameter σ for a varying number of random and Halton draws, indicating a unique maximum (disregarding the sign) even for large number of draws.

4.2. Random coefficients on continuous variables

The dataset generated for this example uses three alternatives ($i = 1, 2, 3$) and two explanatory variables ($X1$ and $X2$). Unlike the previous example with a nest dummy, the two explanatory variables here are drawn from a continuous distribution. The utility function is as follows:

$$U_{ni} = X1_{ni}\beta_{1n} + X2_{ni}\beta_{2n} + \varepsilon_{ni}. \qquad (13)$$

The parameters β_{1n} and β_{2n} are independently and identically distributed N(0,σ_k), resulting in two parameters to estimate: σ_1 and σ_2. As with the previous case, two different synthetic datasets were generated that produced an empirically unidentified and identified

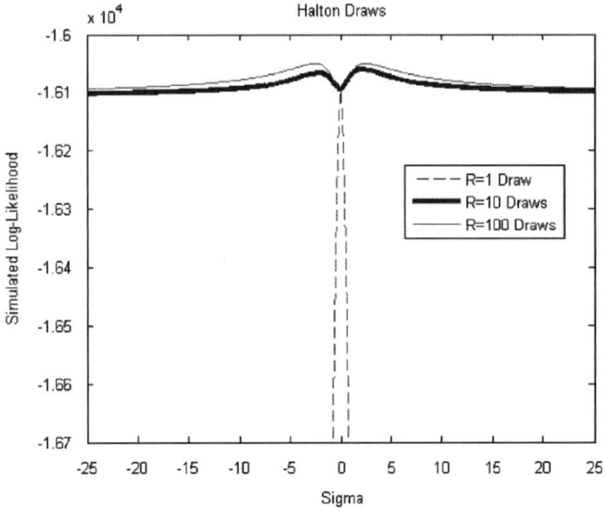

Fig. 4. Identified model with random coefficient on a nest dummy (10,000 observations, Halton draws).

model. The true values used for the parameters were $\sigma_1 = 1$ and $\sigma_2 = 1$. For the unidentified model, 100 observations were generated, and $X1$ and $X2$ were drawn from a bivariate normal distribution (variance of each equal to 1.0, covariance equal to 0.5, and non-zero means). The identified model used an identical specification except that 10,000 observations were generated, and the covariance of $X1$ and $X2$ was set to 0.[2]

For this example, only pseudo-random draws were used. Table 4 provides the results for the unidentified model. Fig. 5 plots the maximum of the simulated log-likelihood over σ_2 with respect to a given value of σ_1 for 1 draw, 5 draws, and 500 draws. First note that the model is, indeed, unidentified as indicated by the exploding parameter estimates and flat log-likelihood function when 500 draws are used in estimation. However, note that for a low number of draws (5, in this case), the simulated log-likelihood exhibits two local maxima on each side of zero, and therefore estimation of the model with 5 draws results in a seemingly identified model.

Table 5 and Fig. 6 report an analogous set of results for an identified model estimated with 10,000 observations. The model is identified as indicated by stable parameter estimates for 1000 and 2000 draws; these estimates are also close to the true values used to generate the synthetic data.

4.3. Discussion of simulated log-likelihood analysis

The simulated log-likelihood functions for mixed logit models are not as well behaved as a standard logit model; mixed logit likelihood functions are not globally concave and are sensitive to poor approximations of the simulated probabilities for low number of draws.

[2] $Cov(X1,X2)$ was set to 0.0 in order to be able to visually see curvature in the log-likelihood plots in Fig. 2. However, 10,000 observations using the same specification as the "unidentified example" (i.e., with $Cov(X1,X2) = 0.5$) is, indeed, identified.

Table 4
Empirical unidentification with random coefficients on continuous variables

	True value	1 Random	5 Random	500 Random
σ_1	1.0	0.002	0.698	5972.361
		(0.017)	(0.222)	(67105.679)
σ_2	1.0	0.042	−0.305	2147.465
		(0.066)	(0.212)	(24133.121)
Simulated log-likelihood		−109.6	−94.1	−85.5
Number of observations		100	100	100

Notes: Standard error in parentheses. Uses robust standard errors.

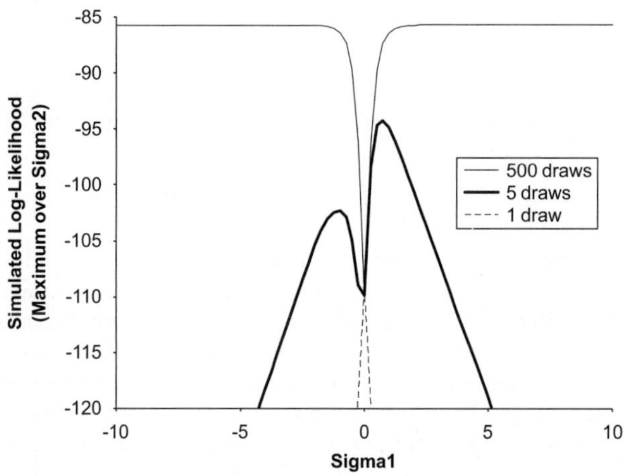

Fig. 5. Unidentified model with random coefficient on normally distributed variable (100 observations, random draws). *Note*: This figure plots the maximum of the simulated log-likelihood over Sigma2 for a given value of Sigma1.

Table 5
Empirical identification with random coefficients on continuous variables

	True value	1 Random	25 Random	1000 Random	2000 Random
σ_1	1.0	0.000	−0.496	0.909	0.920
		(0.002)	(0.020)	(0.123)	(0.127)
σ_2	1.0	−0.001	0.123	0.866	0.877
		(0.007)	(0.059)	(0.178)	(0.181)
Simulated Log-likelihood		−10,986	−10,083	−9917	−9911
Number of observations		10,000	10,000	10,000	10,000

Notes: Standard error in parentheses. Uses robust standard errors.

The results from these simple examples show that for a small number of draws, an empirically unidentified model can appear identified. It is only after a sufficient number of draws is used that the shape of the log-likelihood reveals the singularity of the Hessian.

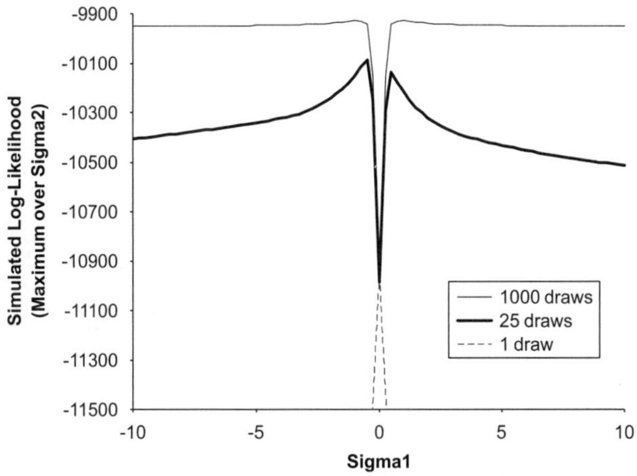

Fig. 6. Identified model with random coefficient on normally distributed variable (10,000 observations, random draws). *Note*: This figure plots the maximum of the simulated log-likelihood over Sigma2 for a given value of Sigma1.

5. Examples of empirical unidentification

The simple examples from the previous section were used to explore the source of empirical unidentification and to demonstrate the behavior of the log-likelihood function under different numbers of draws and under different conditions of identification. This section considers estimation results for more realistic datasets, including one real dataset regarding households' purchases of DVDs and one synthetic dataset.

5.1. Retail stores

In the first example, we apply data from Chiou (2005) to examine a household's choice of retail store to purchase a DVD. We estimate a consumer's choice of store conditional on the purchase of a DVD. The consumer's choice set consists of retail stores from the top 15 chains that sell DVDs, and each retail store is classified under one of five store types: mass merchant, video specialty, electronics, music, and online. Consumer n's utility from traveling to store i to purchase her chosen video is given by

$$U_{ni} = X_{ni}\alpha + \sum_{k=1}^{5} TYPE_{ik}\,\beta_{nk} + \varepsilon_{ni}, \tag{14}$$

where X_{ni} contains interactions of observable store and consumer characteristics (such as price, distance to store, income, education), and $TYPE_i$ is a vector of store type dummies. The explanatory variables in vector X_{ni} do not have random coefficients ($\alpha_n \equiv \alpha$ for all n); the vector X_{ni} contains variables for which tastes are constant across the population. In contrast, consumers' marginal utilities over store types vary by unobservable consumer characteristics. More specifically, the coefficients (β_n) on the store type dummies are assumed to be independently and normally distributed. The random coefficients can be expressed as

$$\beta_{nk} = \bar{\beta}_k + \sigma_k \upsilon_{nk} \quad \text{with } k = 1, 2, \ldots, 5, \tag{15}$$

where k indexes the store's type, and υ_{nk} are independent standard normal variables. The coefficients $\bar{\beta}_k$ and σ_k are the population mean and standard deviation for the marginal utility of store type k. Note that the standard deviations are allowed to differ by store type. The unknown parameters to be estimated are α, $\bar{\beta}$ and σ_k (for $k = 1,2, \ldots, 5$). For further details on the data, specification, and estimation procedure, refer to Chiou (2005).[3]

Table 6 presents the results under 1, 100, 200, and 1000 draws with pseudo-random, Halton, and shuffled Halton draws.[4] Although the model specification is theoretically identified, the results with high numbers of draws indicate that the parameters are not empirically identified by the data. Nonetheless, optimizations from 200 random or 100 Halton draws converge and generate estimates that appear identified. Without checking the robustness of the estimates to varying number of draws, the unidentification issue would not be apparent. For instance, under 200 random draws, the mean and standard deviation of the population distribution of tastes over video specialists are 19.391 (6.381) and 1.501 (0.446), and the coefficients are significant at the 1% level. Similarly, under 100 Halton draws, the mean and standard deviation of the random coefficient on video specialists are 19.576 (8.817) and 1.244 (0.507).

The identification issue becomes readily apparent under 100 shuffled Halton draws; the optimization routine does not converge as parameter estimates explode. The results suggest that shuffled Halton draws expose the identification issue at a lower number of draws relative to other types of draws.

5.2. Synthetic data

The above retail and synthetic datasets consist of relatively simple specifications. In this section, we present an example to illustrate how simulation difficulties become more apparent as additional complexities are introduced into the model. The example uses a dataset that consists of 2000 observations, each making a choice among 4 alternatives. The utility function is given by

$$U_{ni} = X_{ni}\beta_n + \varepsilon_{ni}, \tag{16}$$

where X_{ni} is a (1×8) vector containing 3 alternative specific constants and 5 explanatory variables. The explanatory variables are drawn from a multivariate normal distribution (means ranging from 1 to 3, variances approximately equal to 1, and covariances ranging from 0.0 to 0.6). The random coefficient β_n is (8×1), and each parameter is independent and normally distributed, $N(\bar{\beta}_k, \sigma_k^2)$. This specification provides for alternative specific variances as well as taste heterogeneity with respect to the five explanatory variables. The variance for the fifth explanatory variable was set to 0.0, based on the conventional wisdom to fix at least one parameter in estimation. The true values of the parameters used for data generation are provided in Table 7, along with estimation results.

[3]Chiou (2005) estimates a mixed nested logit which is analogous to constraining the standard deviations of the marginal utilities across all store types to be equal.

[4]The shuffling procedure is not valid when there is only 1 draw. See Hess and Polak (2003b) for the shuffled Halton procedure.

Table 6
Retail stores

		Parameter	1 Draw		100 Draws		200 Draws		1000 Draws	
			Estimate	Std. error	Estimate	Std. error	Estimate	Std. error	Estimate	Std. error
Random	Mass									
	Mean	$\bar{\beta}_1$	5.281	(0.656)	19.515	(7.510)	20.488	(6.386)		
	Std. dev.	σ_1	0.032	(0.040)	0.419	(0.375)	0.038	(0.547)		
	Video									
	Mean	$\bar{\beta}_2$	4.672	(0.677)	18.530	(7.504)	19.391	(6.381)	No convergence	
	Std. dev.	σ_2	0.004	(0.056)	1.209	(0.405)	1.501	(0.446)		
	Electronics									
	Mean	$\bar{\beta}_3$	2.077	(0.851)	16.026	(7.582)	17.262	(6.439)		
	Std. dev.	σ_3	0.086	(0.133)	0.878	(0.930)	0.487	(1.636)		
	Music									
	Mean	$\bar{\beta}_4$	5.631	(0.671)	19.726	(7.516)	20.816	(6.391)		
	Std. dev.	σ_4	0.069	(0.048)	1.317	(0.351)	0.967	(0.373)		
	Online									
	Mean	$\bar{\beta}_5$	0	—	0	—	0	—		
	Std. dev.	σ_5	0.021	(0.140)	8.873	(3.406)	8.737	(2.818)		
	Simulated Log-likelihood		−5254.20		−5229.80		−5231.59			

Halton	Mass							
	Mean	$\bar{\beta}_1$	5.282	(0.657)	20.559	(8.812)		
	Std. dev.	σ_1	0.020	(0.040)	0.183	(0.934)		
	Video							
	Mean	$\bar{\beta}_2$	4.681	(0.678)	19.576	(8.817)	No convergence	No convergence
	Std. dev.	σ_2	0.095	(0.054)	1.244	(0.507)		
	Electronics							
	Mean	$\bar{\beta}_3$	2.084	(0.852)	17.437	(8.854)		
	Std. dev.	σ_3	0.002	(0.182)	0.057	(6.371)		
	Music							
	Mean	$\bar{\beta}_4$	5.639	(0.673)	20.739	(8.827)		
	Std. dev.	σ_4	0.023	(0.050)	1.358	(0.393)		
	Online							
	Mean	$\bar{\beta}_5$	0	—	0	—		
	Std. dev.	σ_5	0.042	(0.126)	9.442	(4.361)		
	Simulated log-likelihood		−5253.91		−5236.63			
Shuffled Halton			—		No convergence		No convergence	No convergence
Number of observations			3132		3132		3132	3132

Note: Uses non-robust standard errors.

Table 7
Synthetic results

	Parameter	True value	250 Draws		1000 Draws		2000 Draws	
			Estimate	Std. error	Estimate	Std. error	Estimate	Std. error
Random	ASC1_Mean	0.10	−0.032	(0.154)	−0.244	(0.500)	−0.559	(0.656)
	ASC1_StDev	1.00	0.067	(0.722)	−1.133	(1.296)	1.944	(1.582)
	ASC2_Mean	0.10	−0.094	(0.370)	−0.581	(0.817)	−0.080	(0.543)
	ASC2_StDev	1.00	−0.838	(1.051)	2.024	(1.594)	−1.132	(1.880)
	ASC3_Mean	0.20	0.066	(0.220)	0.029	(0.228)	−0.350	(0.742)
	ASC3_StDev	1.00	0.428	(1.038)	0.320	(1.160)	1.996	(2.206)
	Var1_Mean	0.05	0.006	(0.043)	0.002	(0.051)	0.021	(0.068)
	Var1_StDev	0.50	0.430	(0.120)**	0.571	(0.198)**	0.747	(0.438)
	Var2_Mean	0.05	0.118	(0.048)**	0.140	(0.065)**	0.154	(0.092)
	Var2_StDev	0.50	0.382	(0.129)**	0.411	(0.198)**	0.424	(0.262)
	Var3_Mean	0.05	0.054	(0.047)	0.066	(0.071)	0.104	(0.090)
	Var3_StDev	0.50	0.490	(0.103)**	0.634	(0.249)**	0.751	(0.384)
	Var4_Mean	0.10	0.020	(0.046)	0.009	(0.059)	0.032	(0.068)
	Var4_StDev	0.50	0.338	(0.139)**	0.494	(0.221)**	0.474	(0.292)
	Var5_Mean	0.02	0.084	(0.045)*	0.119	(0.064)*	0.111	(0.080)
	Sim. log-likelihood		−2726.07		−2725.08		−2724.91	
Halton	ASC1_Mean	0.10	−0.410	(0.654)	−0.901	(1.544)	−0.402	(0.665)
	ASC1_StDev	1.00	−1.442	(1.504)	3.210	(4.805)	−1.414	(1.552)
	ASC2_Mean	0.10	−0.097	(0.762)	−0.540	(1.718)	−0.094	(0.506)
	ASC2_StDev	1.00	0.927	(2.609)	2.892	(5.654)	0.897	(1.666)
	ASC3_Mean	0.20	−0.003	(0.421)	−0.881	(1.650)	0.055	(0.286)
	ASC3_StDev	1.00	−0.687	(2.021)	3.780	(5.558)	0.296	(2.605)
	Var1_Mean	0.05	0.004	(0.050)	0.045	(0.124)	0.003	(0.048)
	Var1_StDev	0.50	0.546	(0.276)**	1.222	(1.659)	0.532	(0.231)
	Var2_Mean	0.05	0.129	(0.079)*	0.240	(0.318)	0.124	(0.062)
	Var2_StDev	0.50	0.374	(0.180)**	0.630	(0.843)	0.378	(0.181)
	Var3_Mean	0.05	0.081	(0.071)	0.159	(0.236)	0.081	(0.072)
	Var3_StDev	0.50	0.613	(0.310)**	1.148	(1.489)	0.620	(0.305)
	Var4_Mean	0.10	0.023	(0.055)	0.046	(0.109)	0.020	(0.053)
	Var4_StDev	0.50	−0.400	(0.294)	−0.858	(1.341)	0.390	(0.231)
	Var5_Mean	0.02	0.101	(0.078)	0.181	(0.275)	0.097	(0.062)
	Sim. Log-likelihood		−2725.88		−2725.64		−2726.30	
Shuffled Halton	ASC1_Mean	0.10	−0.746	(0.561)	−0.814	(1.362)		
	ASC1_StDev	1.00	2.204	(1.066)**	2.423	(3.090)		
	ASC2_Mean	0.10	−0.116	(0.402)	−0.312	(0.667)		
	ASC2_StDev	1.00	−1.061	(1.138)	1.674	(2.129)	No convergence	
	ASC3_Mean	0.20	0.008	(0.269)	−0.092	(0.617)		
	ASC3_StDev	1.00	−0.778	(0.897)	1.163	(2.805)		
	Var1_Mean	0.05	0.001	(0.054)	0.010	(0.065)		
	Var1_StDev	0.50	0.596	(0.202)**	0.698	(0.556)		
	Var2_Mean	0.05	0.140	(0.065)**	0.150	(0.113)		
	Var2_StDev	0.50	0.380	(0.187)**	0.435	(0.302)		
	Var3_Mean	0.05	0.102	(0.069)	0.114	(0.129)		
	Var3_StDev	0.50	0.716	(0.216)**	0.830	(0.696)		

Table 7 (*continued*)

	Parameter	True value	250 Draws		1000 Draws		2000 Draws	
			Estimate	Std. error	Estimate	Std. error	Estimate	Std. error
	Var4_Mean	0.10	0.024	(0.058)	0.022	(0.068)		
	Var4_StDev	0.50	−0.431	(0.194)**	0.486	(0.403)		
	Var5_Mean	0.02	0.105	(0.060)*	0.124	(0.101)		
	Sim. log-likelihood		−2725.07		−2726.13			
Number of observations			2000		2000		2000	

**Significant at 5% level of significance.
*Significant at 10% level of significance.
Note: Uses robust standard errors.

The estimation results appear identified and statistically significant (particularly on the distribution for the random coefficients) for 250 draws, whether they are pseudo-random, Halton, or shuffled Halton. The parameter estimates appear to be fairly stable at 1000 draws, but the standard errors rise significantly, resulting in insignificant parameter estimates in all but the pseudo-random case and suggesting a problem. At 2000 shuffled Halton draws, the model does not converge as the parameters began to explode with successive iterations. The results also indicate that the pseudo-random case is heading in this direction (albeit more slowly) in that successive increases in draws result in increasing standard errors. The Halton results do not exhibit such a trend, and this may be due to either starting values (therefore resulting in different local maximum) or because of correlations among the Halton sequences for this 8-dimensional integral.

6. Conclusion

With advancements in computational speed, simulation techniques have vastly improved the ability to estimate complex models to answer a myriad of questions. However, the implementation of simulation can often mask problems of identification. A low number of draws can result in estimates that appear identified, but in fact are not identified either theoretically by the model or empirically by the data.

To highlight the issue, we present examples of maximum simulated likelihood estimation of mixed logit models under actual and synthetic datasets. Although each of these models was unidentified, estimation with too few draws resulted in coefficients that appeared identified. The first was a telephone dataset that was theoretically unidentified, but the problem was masked at 5000 pseudo-random draws and 1000 Halton draws. The second was a model using a retail dataset of DVD store purchases, which was empirically unidentified, but the problem was masked at 200 pseudo-random draws and 100 Halton draws. The third was a model using a synthetic dataset that was empirically unidentified, but the problem was masked at 2000 pseudo-random draws, 2000 Halton draws, and 1000 shuffled Halton draws. These estimation results also provide further evidence of the benefit of variance reduction methods such as shuffled Halton, which were shown to uncover identification issues at a lower number of draws.

The important lesson is that it is critical not to stop at 200 draws, whether pseudo-random, Halton, or shuffled Halton. No general rule of thumb exists for what constitutes a "high" or "low" number of draws as it depends on the data, specification and type of draw. One has to verify the stability of the parameter estimates as well as the standard errors as the number of draws increases.

In addition to the empirical results, the underlying source of these issues was investigated by examining the shape of the log-likelihood function under varying numbers of draws and different identifying conditions. We demonstrate that under one draw, the mixed logit model is equivalent to a standard logit model, and, therefore, the simulated log-likelihood is globally concave and always uniquely identified. Thus, for an unidentified model, the simulated log-likelihood is globally concave under one draw, and only a sufficient number of draws reveals the flatness of the likelihood function and results in either exploding parameter estimates or a singular Hessian.

While we examined the case of mixed logit models under maximum simulated likelihood, the findings can be extended to other discrete choice models and simulation estimators. This applies, for example, to mixed logit under method of simulated moments as well as generalized extreme value models under maximum simulated likelihood. The number of draws affects the precision of the numerical integration and, therefore, the simulated log-likelihood. The obfuscation that leads to masked identification occurs for any situation in which the model is estimable under one draw regardless of whether the model is identified or not.

Acknowledgements

The authors would like to thank Moshe Ben-Akiva, Denis Bolduc, Victor Chernozhukov, Glenn Ellison, John Geweke, Nancy Rose, and anonymous referees for their insights into this work.

References

Ben-Akiva, M., Bolduc, D., 1996. Multinomial probit with a logit kernel and a general parametric specification of the covariance structure. Working paper, Massachusetts Institute of Technology.

Berndt, E., Hall, B., Hall, R., Hausman, J., 1974. Estimation and inference in nonlinear structural models. Annals of Economics and Social Measurement 3/4, 653–665.

Berry, S., Levinsohn, J., Pakes, A., 1995. Automobile prices in market equilibrium. Econometrica 63 (4), 841–890.

Bhat, C., 2001. Quasi-random maximum simulated likelihood estimation of the mixed multinomial logit model. Transportation Research B 35, 677–693.

Bierlaire, M., Bolduc, D., Godbout, M.-H., 2004. An introduction to BIOGEME (Version 1.0). Working paper, Ecole Polytechnique Federale de Lausanne.

Börsch-Supan, A., Hajivassiliou, V., 1993. Smooth unbiased multivariate probability simulators for maximum likelihood estimation of limited dependent variable models. Journal of Econometrics 58, 347–368.

Brownstone, D., Train, K., 1999. Forecasting new product penetration with flexible substitution patterns. Journal of Econometrics 89, 109–129.

Chiou, L., 2005. Empirical analysis of retail competition: spatial differentiation at Wal-Mart, Amazon.com, and their competitors. Working paper, Occidental College.

Goolsbee, A., Petrin, A., 2003. The consumer gains from direct broadcast satellites and the competition with cable television. Econometrica 72, 351–381.

Halton, J., 1960. On the efficiency of evaluating certain quasi-random sequences of points in evaluating multi-dimensional integrals. Numerische Mathematik 2, 84–90.

Hensher, D., Greene, W., 2003. The mixed logit model: the state of practice. Transportation 30, 133–176.

Hess, S., Polak, J.W., 2003a. A comparison of scrambled and shuffled Halton sequences for simulation based estimation. Centre for Transport Studies Working paper, Centre for Transport Studies, Imperial College London.

Hess, S., Polak, J.W., 2003b. An alternative to the scrambled Halton sequence for removing correlation between standard Halton sequences in high dimensions. Paper presented at the European Regional Science Conference, Jyväskylä.

McFadden, D., Train, K., 2000. Mixed MNL models of discrete response. Journal of Applied Econometrics 15, 447–470.

Train, K., 1999. Halton sequences for mixed logit. Working paper, University of California, Berkeley.

Train, K., 2003. Discrete choice methods with simulation. Cambridge University Press, New York.

Train, K., McFadden, D., Ben-Akiva, M., 1987. The demand for local telephone service: a fully discrete model of residential calling patterns and service choices. RAND Journal of Economics 18 (1), 109–123.

Walker, J.L., 2001. Extended discrete choice models: integrated framework, flexible error structures, and latent variables. Ph.D. dissertation, Massachusetts Institute of Technology, Department of Civil and Environmental Engineering.

Walker, J.L., Ben-Akiva, M., Bolduc, D., 2006. Identification of parameters in normal error components logit mixture models. Journal of Applied Econometrics, forthcoming.

[34]

PETER E. ROSSI and GREG M. ALLENBY*

The authors present a Bayesian approach to the estimation of household parameters. Applied to the standard logit model, the procedure produces household-level estimates of all model parameters, enabling researchers to identify differences in household reaction to all variables in the marketing mix. Simulated data are used to study the small-sample performance of the estimator. The estimator can be easily implemented with standard algorithms used to maximize likelihood functions. In application to tuna scanner panel data, strong evidence of heterogeneity in price, display, and feature response (slope) parameters is detected. Approaches that fail to take into account slope heterogeneity are shown to underestimate the value of feature advertising and in-store displays in this dataset. In addition, the household price sensitivity estimates are strongly related to coupon usage and demonstrate how the estimates can be used to implement a targeted household drop.

A Bayesian Approach to Estimating Household Parameters

A fundamental assumption of marketing is that consumers differ in their preferences and reactions to promotional variables such as price and advertising. Researchers have proposed a wide variety of models of household behavior as a basis for developing and evaluating marketing policies. At the same time, a wealth of information on household purchase behavior has become available in scanner panel datasets. However, attempts to use household-level models with panel data have been frustrated by the lack of statistical procedures that are flexible enough to generate household-level estimates for all model parameters. We introduce a new approach to estimating household parameters that yields estimates of household preference and reaction to promotional variables.

Our household-level estimates can be used to address two important issues. First, household estimates can be used to tailor marketing strategies to specific households. We give an example in which direct mail coupon drops targeted to price-sensitive households are used instead of traditional blanket mailings. Second, market-wide response to promotional variables can be estimated by aggregating the estimated responses across households. Estimates of aggregate market response can be severely biased unless adjustments are made for differences among households. In our analysis of scanner panel data, estimates of market response to in-store display and newspaper advertising double in size when adjustments are made for the distribution of heterogeneity.

The challenge facing the modeler using scanner panel data is to devise a flexible estimation procedure that incorporates heterogeneity of a general form while simultaneously reckoning with the small amount of data per household. Typically, no more than 25 or so purchases a year are observed for each panel household, even though there might be more than 500 households in the panel. As we discuss in detail subsequently, most current procedures meet this modeling challenge by assuming that some of the model parameters are constant across all households (Guadagni and Little 1983) or at least some subset of households (Currim 1981; Kamakura and Russell 1989). An alternative approach is to assume that household parameters come from a common distribution. This approach, referred to as a random effects specification, estimates the distribution of parameters over

*Peter E. Rossi is Associate Professor, Graduate School of Business, University of Chicago. Greg M. Allenby is Assistant Professor, College of Business, The Ohio State University.

The authors appreciate helpful comments by Bob Blattberg, Peter Dickson, Kris Helsen, Jim Ginter, and Mary Sullivan. In addition, the editor and anonymous *JMR* reviewers made invaluable suggestions for improvement of drafts of the article. The authors are listed in reverse alphabetical order.

Journal of Marketing Research
Vol. XXX (May 1993), 171–82

the population but does not directly produce household parameter estimates. A random effects model for the intercepts of a logit model is investigated by Chintagunta, Jain, and Vilcassim (1991). Our analysis of scanner data suggests that it is very important to allow for different slopes as well as intercepts across the population of households.

All current approaches to modeling heterogeneity in short panels rely on some sort of *a priori* restrictions on the extent of variation in the parameters across households. For example, Kamakura and Russell (1989) assume that households within a segment share common parameter values. We solve the problem of scarcity of household information by using prior information about the likely range of choice probabilities and parameter values. Our approach incorporates prior information through a Bayesian method that yields different parameter estimates for each household. An interpretable and flexible reference prior is used to form the household Bayes estimates. Moreover, our Bayesian household estimates can be obtained by simple modifications of current maximum likelihood algorithms.

In the next section, we review and critique present procedures in more detail. The proposed Bayesian procedures are then introduced and evaluated with both simulated and actual scanner panel data. The simulation experiments serve to assess the sampling properties of the proposed procedures and to compare them with alternatives. We then use an ERIM scanner panel dataset from A. C. Nielsen to illustrate the procedure and provide new evidence on the bias induced by slope heterogeneity and the relation between price sensitivity and coupon usage. Finally, we examine the predictive performance of the procedure and offer concluding remarks.

REVIEW AND CRITIQUE OF PRESENT PROCEDURES

Approaches to estimating parameters in models of consumer behavior can be grouped into two broad classes, (1) those that estimate parameters for each household (i.e., a fixed effect model) and (2) those that assume the household parameters are distributed according to a probability distribution and estimate the parameters of that distribution (random effects models).

The Random Effects Approach

A natural and conceptually appealing approach to modeling heterogeneity across households is to assume that the parameters vary according to a probability distribution. This general approach is called a random effects model. The advantage of the random effects model comes from the radical reduction in the number of parameters achieved by assuming a distribution of heterogeneity. Suppose the basic statistical model has k parameters. If we start with N households, the random effects approach replaces the $N \times k$ household-level parameters with a smaller number of parameters that describe the heterogeneity (or mixture) distribution.

Key to the success of the random effects approach is the proper choice of the heterogeneity distribution. There is a tradeoff between flexibility and parsimony. The analyst would like to specify a very general form for the distribution to avoid specification errors that might arise from assuming an incorrect form. An alternative approach advocated by Kamakura and Russell (1989) is the finite mixture model, which approximates the continuous distribution of heterogeneity by a discrete distribution. That model assumes a fixed number of homogeneous segments and estimates segment parameters and segment sizes simultaneously.[1] Our view is that the question of whether the distribution of heterogeneity is discrete (with a small number of mass points) or continuous should be answered from the data. Our procedures for estimating household parameters, which do not assume a fixed number of segments or any particular form for the heterogeneity distribution, can shed light on this issue.

Perhaps the most severe limitation of all random effects models is that they are not well suited for the estimation of household parameters. For some marketing decisions such as a chainwide pricing decision, knowledge of the distribution of heterogeneity is sufficient for correct prediction of aggregate market response. However, this knowledge is not adequate for designing customized marketing instruments, which are increasingly being used to target specific households. Examples include direct mail and point-of-purchase couponing. Given the technological revolution in the collection of purchasing data from a wide variety of sources, household-specific marketing instruments should become even more common in the near future.

Fixed Effects Models

Difficulties in estimating fixed effects models at the household level have prevented the investigation of heterogeneity in all model parameters. Heterogeneity is typically modeled by including demographic variables or variables that measure past buying behavior as covariates (Allenby and Rossi 1991a; Guadagni and Little 1983). These variables, which alter the intercepts for each household, are useful in studying the heterogeneity of consumer preference for different brands. However, there is evidence that the standard set of household demographic data is inadequate to capture heterogeneity. In addition, it is implausible that heterogeneity is limited to the intercepts.

[1]In purely formal terms, this mixture model is identical to a random effects model in which the population distribution of the parameters over households is discrete with probability mass on a small number of points in the parameter space. In fact, if the nonparametric approach of Chintagunta, Jain, and Vilcassim (1991; Vilcassim and Jain 1991) were generalized to include all model parameters, it would yield a likelihood identical to that of the Kamakura and Russell mixture model. The difference is a matter of interpretation.

If long panels were available, there would be nothing to keep us from using the method of maximum likelihood to estimate a parameter vector for each household. However, in reality, scanner panel households rarely make more than 25 purchases a year. Furthermore, each household rarely purchases all available brands during its time in the panel. These problems of insufficient data combined with household heterogeneity cause great difficulty. The MLE does not exist for many household purchase histories. Specifically, if households are observed choosing only a subset of brands, some of the choice model parameters cannot be identified. In the ERIM tuna data we examined, only two households of 777 were observed to have purchased all brands in the choice set at some point in their panel history. For a household with an incomplete purchase history, the maximum likelihood procedure will set some of the parameters to infinity to drive the fitted probabilities to zero for the brands that have not been purchased.[2] We do not set the parameters at infinity in practice, of course, but merely shut down the routine that maximizes the likelihood after a specified tolerance level is reached. This method results in what are called extended maximum likelihood estimates (algorithm 3 of Clarkson and Jennrich 1991). In a sense, these extended maximum likelihood estimates are inconsistent with the basic choice model as applied to sets of brands of the same product. We believe it is fundamentally incorrect to infer on the basis of only a few observations that the household will never purchase certain brands regardless of the prices of the other brands.

Though we would not infer that a household has a limited choice set on the basis of only a few observations, we do not rule out the conceptual possibility of limited choice or "consideration sets." According to the consideration set concept (see Hauser and Wernerfelt 1989; Roberts and Lattin 1991), some households have a limited choice set outside of which they will never purchase regardless of the price of outside alternatives. For example, some households may never purchase tuna packed in oil even if it were available at zero price. Typically, consideration sets are constructed from past purchase behavior and then used to specify a reduced set of brands for a logit model. Our panel dataset provides evidence that this practice is not appropriate. If we develop a consideration set based on the first two thirds of each household's purchase history, 17% of the households purchase outside the consideration set in the final third of the data. This finding is not caused by short panel histories. If we limit attention to households with 15 or more purchases, more than 20% purchase outside a consideration set. Fundamentally, with only 10 or so purchase observations, it is impossible to say whether a household has zero choice probability for an item or merely has small probability of choice.

Bayesian Approaches to Fixed Effects Estimation

All current fixed and random effects approaches to modeling heterogeneity with short panels rely on some sort of *a priori* restrictions on the extent of variation in the parameters across households. We propose an alternative Bayesian method that introduces additional information through a prior distribution. We use a prior constructed from a pooled sample in which all households are assumed to have the same choice model parameters. The data for each household move the parameter estimates away from the pooled estimates in a natural Bayesian updating process.

As an illustration of our approach, consider the Bayesian analysis of the data from household i facing m choice alternatives. Let $l_i(\theta \mid \text{Data}_i)$ denote the likelihood for household i and θ denote the model parameters. For the standard logit model, $l_i(\theta \mid \text{Data}_i) = \Pi_t p_{i1t}^{z_{i1t}} p_{i2t}^{z_{i2t}} \ldots p_{ikt}^{z_{ikt}}$ where $p_{ikt} = \exp[\mathbf{x}_{ikt}'\theta]/\Sigma_j \exp[\mathbf{x}_{ijt}'\theta]$, $\mathbf{z}_{it}$ denotes the vector of multinomial outcomes for household i on purchase occasion t, and $\mathbf{x}_{ijt}$ corresponds to the covariates for household i, alternative j, and purchase occasion t. We postulate a prior distribution over θ, denoted π. This prior is combined with the likelihood to form the posterior for household i.

$$\pi_i(\theta \mid \text{Data}_i) \propto l_i(\theta \mid \text{Data}_i)\, \pi(\theta) \tag{1}$$

It is common for Bayes estimators to be constructed by using the mean of the posterior distribution. The sampling properties (as measured by bias, variance, mean squared error) of the Bayes estimator can be analyzed and compared with those of other proposed estimators such as the MLE.

Any Bayesian analysis depends on a convenient and reasonable representation of the prior information. In our case, the prior specification is doubly important because the sample size is small and hence the prior will influence the estimator. Indeed, as discussed subsequently, the prior is important to achieve parameter identification on the household level when the household is observed to choose from a subset of the available choices. On an intuitive level, we propose that prior information be used to ensure that households always have a positive, but possibly small, probability of choosing any alternative. Researchers who endorse a consideration set approach will find this assumption to be a limitation of our analysis. The prior information is coupled with household sample information to form the household estimate.

A Formal Bayesian Approach

Bayesian approaches to parameter estimation have been criticized on two grounds. Critics argue that the prior

[2] Though the maximum of the likelihood may not exist formally for any finite parameter value, Haberman (1974) has noted that it is still possible to define an "extended" maximum likelihood value by finding the supremum of the likelihood. Clarkson and Jennrich (1991) discuss algorithms for "computing" the extended maximum likelihood estimates in the case of linear-in-the-parameters models and grouped or repeated data.

distribution is often difficult to specify and Bayes estimators can be difficult to compute. We propose simple methods of avoiding these problems.

We propose a general method of constructing prior distributions that does not dominate the information contained in the household likelihood. The resulting default or "reference" prior is designed for situations in which the investigator is reluctant to explicitly specify a prior distribution. This default procedure can be used in nearly any situation, including the analysis of new choice models for which likely ranges of parameters may not yet be known.

The prior distribution is assumed to be multivariate normal with mean ($\bar{\theta}$) and covariance (Σ) based on pooled estimates of model parameters. The normal form of the prior can be justified as an approximate posterior distribution from some previous data analysis. For samples of moderate and large size, Zellner and Rossi (1984) show that a normal approximation to the logit posterior distribution is highly accurate. Because we use the entire panel sample to assess the prior, we are justified in using the normal approximation. It is only when the individual-household likelihood function is introduced that we must worry about the accuracy of normal approximations.

In the spirit of an empirical Bayes approach, information across households is used to estimate or elicit parameters of the prior. All households are pooled into one large sample under the assumption that all parameters are equal across households. The pooled likelihood is then maximized to yield the pooled MLE, $\hat{\Theta}$, and the estimated variance-covariance matrix $\hat{\Phi}$. The prior mean is set equal to the MLE ($\bar{\theta} = \hat{\Theta}$), whereas the prior covariance matrix is set proportional to $\hat{\Phi}$.

At this point, we have reduced the problem of specifying a complete prior distribution to the choice of the scaling of the prior covariance matrix. We interpret the scaling parameter of the prior as the size of an imaginary sample (see McCulloch and Rossi 1991 for a detailed justification of this idea). In general, our prior with a sample size parameter of ν is MVN($\bar{\theta} = \hat{\Theta}$, $\Sigma = N/\nu\hat{\Phi}$). For example, the prior covariance matrix can be scaled to represent a sample of size one by setting ν to one.[3] A prior set with a sample size parameter of one imparts only a modest amount of prior information to keep the parameter estimates from drifting off to infinity. For a prior with a sample size of one, the household-level estimates will be determined largely by the data for that household only. Hence households with only a small number of purchase occasions will have very imprecise parameter estimates. Setting the prior sample size to larger numbers will produce estimates that are "shrunk" toward the pooled estimate, especially for households with a very small number of observations. As the prior sample size is increased beyond the number of observations for a household, the household estimates will converge to the homogeneous or pooled model estimates. In the application section we investigate the prior sensitivity and provide estimates of the posterior standard deviation for various priors and various numbers of purchase observations.

Some researchers may regard the sensitivity of the household parameter estimates to prior tightness as a weakness of our approach. We believe the flexibility and interpretability of our prior are strong points. Very small prior sample sizes will put little weight on the information contained in the purchase records of other households in formulating a household estimate. Large prior sample sizes result in household estimates that put more weight on the information from other households and, thus, assume more commonality or homogeneity in the population of households. In many applications it will be useful to specify truly informative priors that are fairly tight. There are no automatic procedures for choosing the prior sample size parameter that will perform well in all situations. The user must carefully consider the prior and perform prior sensitivity analysis.

Calculating the Formal Approach Estimates

Household parameter estimates are obtained by combining the prior with the household likelihood to form the household posterior as indicated in equation 1. One popular Bayes estimator is the mean of the posterior distribution. However, there is no analytic expression for the posterior mean. These posteriors are based on multinomial likelihoods that are nonlinear in the parameters. We approximate the posterior mean by the posterior mode.[4]

The posterior mode represents a compromise between the sample information represented in the household likelihood and the prior information. The MLE, if it ex-

[3]The amount of Fisher or expected information in a sample of size one can be computed easily from an estimate of the information in a sample of size N. We recognize that the information matrix for a random sample of size N is simply N $\Phi_1(\theta)$ where Φ_1 is the average information contained in one observation. We deflate the estimate of the information matrix of the pooled sample so that it is an estimate of the expected information in one observation by multiplying each element of the matrix by $1/N$.

[4]The posterior mean is commonly used as an estimator. We use the posterior mode as an approximation to the posterior mean. A more accurate estimate might be constructed by using approximations proposed by Tierney and Kadane (1986) instead. Poirier and Koop (1991) show that though the Tierney and Kadane methods will enhance accuracy, there is only a minor improvement over the posterior mode. The posterior mode is the maximum of the function formed by summing the log likelihood and the log prior. It is important to note that the log of the normal prior is strictly concave and has a unique maximum. In addition, the log likelihood is bounded above by zero. In the case of the standard logit model, the log likelihood is also strictly concave. Thus, the posterior mode is guaranteed to exist and to be unique. The same is not true of the log likelihood itself, which may not have a unique maximum.

ists, will be "shrunk" toward the prior mean vector. It is important to note that the posterior mode will always exist even when the household MLE does not. The role of the normal prior is twofold, (1) to provide a centering point toward which the sample information is shrunk and (2) to ensure the existence of a posterior mode. In practice, we use a relatively diffuse prior so that the sample information for each household will greatly influence the posterior mean. The damped tails of the normal prior will achieve identification even in the cases in which the likelihood has no unique maximum. The normal prior keeps the parameters from drifting off to infinity and keeps the associated fitted probabilities from approaching too close to zero or one.

Standard maximization routines can be used to calculate the posterior mode for each household. The code used to find the maximum of a logit likelihood function can be modified with little effort to produce our Bayesian household-level estimates. To see this, recall that from equation 1 the log of the posterior is simply the sum of the log likelihood and log prior, $\log(\pi_i(\theta \mid \text{Data}) = \log(l_i) + \log(\pi(\theta))$. Thus, the objective function, gradient, and hessian from the standard likelihood analysis need to be modified only by adding a second term that comes from the prior. Equations 2, 3, and 4 give the exact formulas.

$$\log(\pi(\theta|\text{Data})) = L(\theta) - 1/2(\theta - \bar{\theta})' \Sigma^{-1}(\theta - \bar{\theta}) + K \tag{2}$$

$$g_\pi = g_L - \Sigma^{-1}(\theta - \bar{\theta}) \tag{3}$$

$$H_\pi = H_L - \Sigma^{-1} \tag{4}$$

$\bar{\theta}$ is the prior mean, which we take to be the MLE based on the pooled sample of all households, and Σ is the prior variance-covariance matrix; g_π, g_L are the gradients of the posterior and log likelihood, respectively; and H_π and H_L are the hessians of the posterior and log likelihood.[5] Finally, K is the log of the integrating constant of the posterior distribution. The i subscripts have been dropped for simplicity. Every standard optimizer (such as NPSOL or GQOPT) requires that the user supply objective function, gradient, and (sometimes) hessian routines. It is a simple matter to add code from the preceding equations. Self-contained FORTRAN code and UNIX compilation scripts are available on request from the authors.

Having laid out the theory and computation methods for our Bayesian approach, we now apply the approach to both actual and simulated panel data. We compare the Bayesian approach with present methods of adjusting for heterogeneity.

[5]For the small sample sizes encountered in scanner panel data, standard estimates of the hessian such as the outer product approximation used in the BHHH quasi-newton method can be very inaccurate. For the standard logit model, the exact hessian is simple to compute and we have used the exact hessian in deriving the posterior modes used throughout the article. We also made comparisons with the outer product method and verified the inaccuracy of the outer product approximation.

PERFORMANCE OF THE ESTIMATORS IN SMALL SAMPLES

Because we are proposing a new method for fixed effects models, it is important to demonstrate that this method has acceptable sampling properties and improves on the best available methods. After summarizing the results of simulation experiments designed to investigate the ability of our method to recover household parameters, we compare our method with the only available method that allows for estimation of fixed effects in all parameters household by household—the extended maximum likelihood estimates.

We chose five different values of the parameter vector to represent both brand loyalty and switcher behavior (see Allenby and Rossi 1993 for details). For each of these five groups, we simulated 100 replicate household panel histories. This procedure enabled us to compute the sampling distribution of our Bayes estimates for each different type of household. The simulation results provide both an absolute and a relative comparison of the performance of the Bayes estimators as measured by mean squared error.

Figure 1 shows the root mean squared error for our Bayesian procedure and the extended MLE for a sample size of 10. It is remarkable that, even with as few as 10 observations per household, the Bayes estimators move away from the prior mean and have root mean squared errors less than one. The results indicate that the Bayes estimators perform dramatically better than the extended MLE, averaging anywhere from a twofold to a 20-fold reduction in root mean squared error. What is important to note is that the Bayes estimators uniformly dominate the extended MLE across different parameter settings. We previously obtained similar results with more complicated choice models (Allenby and Rossi 1993).

Figure 1

ROOT MSE OF BAYES AND ML ESTIMATORS: ONE-PRICE LOGIT

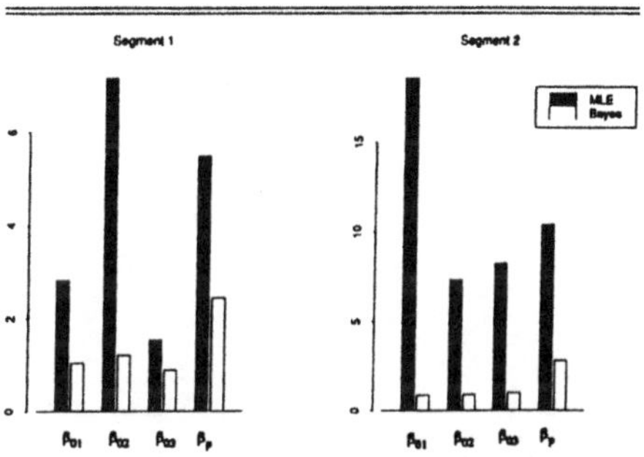

APPLICATION TO SCANNER PANEL DATA

We explored the Bayesian estimator with actual scanner panel data. Our goals were both substantive and methodological. On the substantive side, we investigated the extent of household heterogeneity detected in the data. In particular, we emphasized the importance of detection and measurement of heterogeneity in *nonintercept* parameters such as price, display, and feature response. Methodologically, we assessed the predictive performance of our estimators and compared them with traditional loyalty-based adjustments advocated previously (Allenby and Rossi 1991b; Guadagni and Little 1983).

The scanner panel dataset consists of household tuna purchases in three grocery chains in Springfield, Missouri. Seven tuna UPCs from four brands, which account for more than 87% of the total category volume, are included in the dataset. The brand names are Chicken of the Sea, Starkist, 3 Diamond, and a house brand. The nationally distributed brands include both water- and oil-packed tuna, but only the water-packed house brand was included for analysis. The tuna panel data serve well to test the performance of our techniques with very short panels. The median number of purchase occasions in our data is eight per household with 25% of the households reporting six or fewer purchase occasions and 75% reporting 11 or fewer purchase occasions. There are 777 households, observed over a maximum of 2.5 years, in the dataset. In addition to information on competitive pricing, display and feature information is captured in the dataset.

Comparison With the MLE and Prior Sensitivity

Before we discuss our substantive findings for ERIM panel purchases of tuna, we use the panel data to shed further light on the performance of our procedure in relation to estimating logits for each household. In addition, we illustrate the sensitivity of the household estimates to the choice of the prior tightness parameter (the sample size parameter, ν). Table 1 gives household estimates of the price coefficient for 15 randomly selected

Table 1

COMPARISON OF PRICE COEFFICIENTS[a]

(Guadagni and Little estimates: $\beta = -5.958$, standard error of $\beta = .129$)

Household	*No. of observations*	*Individual logit[b]*	*Bayesian approach with reference prior sample size of[c]*				
			1	*2*	*5*	*10*	*100*
1	7	−40.84	−8.62	−7.80	−7.08	−6.74	−6.13
			(4.41)	(3.83)	(3.08)	(2.51)	(.99)
2	5	−45.27	−9.32	−8.44	−7.53	−7.00	−6.11
			(7.26)	(5.52)	(3.80)	(2.83)	(1.01)
3	3	−6.01	−9.62	−8.40	−7.14	−6.67	−6.09
			(3.85)	(2.99)	(1.88)	(1.46)	(.72)
4	10	−116.7	−9.57	−8.32	−7.19	−6.66	−6.06
			(2.11)	(2.05)	(1.90)	(1.73)	(.90)
5	6	−25.22	−10.0	−8.09	−6.72	−6.25	−6.00
			(8.15)	(6.01)	(4.06)	(3.01)	(1.05)
6	35	−8.21	−6.26	−6.23	−6.19	−6.15	−6.05
			(.98)	(.98)	(.97)	(.94)	(.72)
7	7	−21.16	−7.29	−6.69	−6.19	−6.01	−5.95
			(2.64)	(2.56)	(2.35)	(2.09)	(.99)
8	12	−44.65	−6.68	−5.89	−5.20	−4.95	−5.39
			(2.32)	(2.09)	(1.75)	(1.50)	(.77)
9	8	−6.51	−11.5	−9.64	−8.35	−7.35	−6.10
			(5.47)	(4.41)	(3.39)	(2.62)	(1.00)
10	10	−5.27	−11.9	−10.7	−8.92	−7.80	−6.29
			(1.29)	(1.28)	(1.21)	(1.07)	(.64)
11	18	−4.91	−6.62	−6.53	−6.35	−6.20	−5.97
			(3.91)	(3.51)	(2.98)	(2.48)	(1.01)
12	5	−25.19	−6.12	−6.03	−5.98	−5.94	−5.96
			(5.47)	(4.18)	(2.97)	(2.31)	(.91)
13	9	−14.85	−10.8	−9.64	−8.41	−7.71	−6.25
			(4.36)	(3.73)	(2.95)	(2.38)	(.98)
14	14	−5.78	−4.52	−4.81	−5.24	−5.56	−5.95
			(2.83)	(2.72)	(2.45)	(2.13)	(.97)
15	14	−52.65	−21.4	−15.6	−10.4	−8.36	−6.33
			(7.24)	(5.28)	(3.57)	(2.55)	(.99)

[a]Posterior standard deviation is in parentheses.

[b]Logit model includes display, feature, and brand intercepts for a total of nine parameters. It is estimated using convergence tolerance = 1.0×10^{-7}; note that the standard errors for the individual logits are not defined because of a singular hessian (incomplete histories).

[c]Price coefficient prior standard deviations = 11.01, 7.79, 4.92, 3.48, 1.10.

households. The second column lists the number of purchase occasions for each household. As emphasized previously, many households had only a small number of occasions whereas some households had a large number. The third column gives the estimates of individual logit models using the extended MLE procedure outlined previously. The fourth through seventh columns report the estimates based on priors of varying degrees of tightness, from a one-obeservation prior to a 100-observation prior. Below the Bayes estimates are approximate posterior standard deviations, calculated from the inverse of the posterior hessian.

The table clearly shows the problem with the extended MLE. Recall that for households with incomplete choice histories, the standard MLE is undefined for all model parameters (not just the intercepts). All households but two in our panel have incomplete purchase histories based on our choice set of seven. The extended MLE procedure initiates the search for a maximum and terminates after the percentage change in the likelihood is below a specified tolerance. The extended MLEs of the intercepts and price coefficient drift off to infinity. Many of the point estimates of the price coefficient are absurdly large (with a smaller tolerance, we could drive them all beyond any specified number). In addition, the identification problem renders the hessian of the likelihood singular and there are no asymptotic standard errors to report for the extended MLE.

Table 1 also illustrates the sensitivity of the Bayes estimates to the prior. For a prior sample size of 100, all estimates are close to the prior mean (the Guadagni and Little estimate of −6.0), whereas the estimates for a prior sample size of one are very variable. For small prior sample sizes and households with a small number of purchase occasions, some posterior standard deviations are large.[6] This finding merely indicates that if there is little information in the sample for the household and the investigator is not willing to impart strong prior information, estimating household parameters will be difficult. In our view, the one-observation prior is overly diffuse for many applications. The prior standard deviation is 11.01, which means that the prior mass is spread over the interval −39 to 27. Most analysts would agree that the price coefficient is unlikely to be positive and that values of −20 or smaller would imply overly sensitive switching behavior. A more reasonable prior, which is still diffuse but rules out these unrealistic values, corresponds to the reference prior size of five. In the analysis reported next, we use the five-observation prior on the grounds that it more reasonably represents our information. In addition, as we show, Bayes estimates based on the five-observation prior outpredict estimates based on one- and two-observation priors.

Measured Parameter Heterogeneity

The household estimates computed by our formal Bayesian approach reflect the considerable amount of household heterogeneity in all model parameters. Our logit model is a standard one-price logit (using log price and display and feature dummy variables equal to one if the item is displayed anywhere in the store or featured in a major ad in the local newspaper). Summary statistics on the distribution of logit model log price, display, and feature coefficients across households follow.

Coefficient	*Mean*	*S.D.*	*Sampling error component*
Price	−6.85	1.78	.54 (30%)
Display	.34	.71	.30 (42%)
Feature	.57	.67	.14 (21%)

The mean of the price slope distribution is −6.85 with a large standard deviation of 1.78. The feature slope coefficient shows even more heterogeneity with a larger standard deviation in relation to the mean.

A legitimate criticism of these standard deviation estimates is that sampling error may cause them to be inflated. To see this point, suppose there were no heterogeneity at all in slope parameters. Estimation error will induce variation in the distribution of estimates unrelated to the true heterogeneity. To gauge the seriousness of this problem, we estimate the proportion of parameter variation attributable to sampling error. We use the asymptotic covariance matrix from the pooled model and inflate the sample variance to account for the much smaller average sample size for each individual household. The right column in the preceding table gives these estimates of the standard deviation in the absence of heterogeneity. In parentheses are the estimated percentages of the total variation that can be ascribed to sampling error. Clearly sampling error alone cannot account for the observed variation in slope coefficients. Less than half of the variation is due to sampling error. In addition, the proportion of total variation explained by sampling error is lowest for the feature variable, suggesting greater heterogeneity in household response for features than in that for displays and promotions. This finding seems reasonable in light of the varied subscription and reading habits of households in the population. Also note that these estimates of the proportion of variation due to sampling error are overstated, because the Bayesian estimator certainly has better sampling performance than the MLE.

It is logical to ask whether the heterogeneity in the response coefficients can be related to measured demographic variables. If so, interaction terms could be added to the models to capture this heterogeneity without re-

[6] The posterior standard deviations computed in Table 1 are based on standard asymptotic approximations. To check this asymptotic approximation, we computed estimates of the exact finite sample posterior standard deviations using numerical integration. We used an importance sampling method that has become standard in the Bayesian econometrics and statistics literature (see Zellner and Rossi 1984). Though there are some differences between the exact and approximate standard deviations, there is no systematic pattern in which the exact finite sample results tend to be larger or smaller than the asymptotic approximation.

sorting to more complicated fixed effects or random effects models. We regressed our estimated price coefficients against the log of household income, log of family size, and dummy variables for household head college education and retirement status. This fairly standard set of variables accounts for less than 2% of the total variation in the price coefficients across households. This finding is consistent with those of previous research that show loyalty measures dramatically improve the fit of choice models even after demographic variables are entered.

Figure 2 is a histogram of the price coefficients estimated for the one-price logit model. There is considerable household heterogeneity in price sensitivity. Furthermore, the distribution is clearly unimodal and reasonably symmetric, suggesting that there is no evidence of distinct segments of price sensitive and insensitive households.

Implications for Couponing Behavior

In tuna and other product categories, both store and manufacturer coupons are used as a method of stimulating sales. Coupons may provide a means to price discriminate between price sensitive and price insensitive consumers as advanced by Narasimhan (1984). Because our procedures generate household-level estimates of price sensitivity, a first step toward a better understanding of couponing behavior would be to relate price sensitivity estimates to coupon usage by the households. Using the logit model's price coefficient, we sorted the households in ascending order from the most price sensitive to the least. We then looked at whether or not the households used coupons during the entire panel period. Thirty-eight percent of the households in the first and highest quartile of the price coefficient distribution used at least one coupon whereas only 20% of those in the lowest quartile used coupons. This finding strengthens the view that couponing can be used to attract price sensitive consumers. In addition, it provides independent corroboration of the quality of our price coefficient estimates; note that coupon usage data were not used to compute the price coefficients.

Figure 2
DISTRIBUTION OF LOGIT PRICE COEFFICIENT ESTIMATES

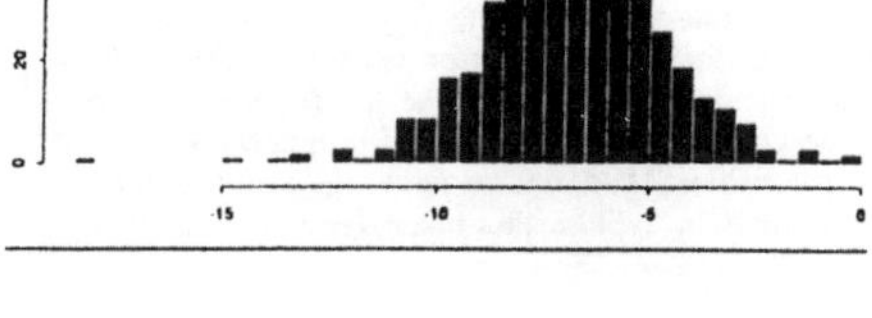

One potentially valuable use for our estimated model coefficients would be to target a coupon distribution at specific households. For example, consider the ideal drop of coupons for the Chicken of the Sea brand. We expect a strong response from households that show loyalty toward other brands and yet are price sensitive. Ideally, we would like to distribute coupons to such households. Within the standard logit parameterization, we can implement this drop by targeting households for which the intercept of some other brand exceeds the intercept of Chicken of the Sea oil or water items and whose price coefficients rank above the third quartile level. Of the 777 households, 109 fit into this category of households potentially most responsive to a Chicken of the Sea coupon drop. To estimate the potential gains from targeting, we compare the response to a targeted drop to the 109 susceptible households with that from a blanket coverage of all households in our sample. For illustrative purposes, we consider a 30-cent coupon for Chicken of the Sea tuna in water. Note that the identification of a target group of households could be approached by estimating a finite mixture model, identifying a "coupon-susceptible" segment, and then using a classification rule to assign households to this segment. This procedure is fundamentally different from the one advocated here. An interesting avenue for future research would be to examine the relative efficiencies of these procedures for generating the target population.

To estimate the effects on eventual sales from a coupon drop is a difficult task. Some fraction of the households will not be aware of the coupon. In addition, some cost of exercising the coupon must be factored into the net effect of the coupon. For the purposes of our calculations, we assumed that for households that are aware of the coupon and willing to use it, the coupon acts as a temporary price cut in the full amount of the coupon. To gauge the difference in the response of the two sets of households to the coupon, we computed the average predicted probability of purchase of Chicken of the Sea tuna in water at the modal price of 89 cents and compared it with the predicted probability of purchase at the reduced price net of the coupon. For the population of all households, the median predicted probability increased from .35 to .67 after the coupon drop. For the targeted population, the predicted probability of purchase increased from .20 to .71. Thus, under the targeted coupon distribution, we will persuade many households that otherwise might not purchase Chicken of the Sea to switch from other brands. A major advantage of the targeting over blanket coverage is that price discounts will not be given away to households that are very likely to purchase Chicken of the Sea without the discount.

The ultimate profitability of these sorts of targeted couponing strategies depends on many factors (see Blattberg and Neslin 1990, chapter 10, for an excellent overview of couponing costs). With current direct mail technology, the cost of reaching the targeted population is probably substantially greater than that of reaching the entire population with a newspaper insert or blanket mailing. However, the costs of targeting will certainly decline in the future with the advent of point-of-purchase couponing and improved technology. For high ticket items, the benefits of targeting may far exceed the cost differential. The key to the implementation of these strategies is the availability of historical data on household purchases coupled with techniques for producing household-level parameters.

Implications of Heterogeneity for Aggregate Market Response

The distribution of estimated parameters across households is interesting, but tracing the implications of this heterogeneity for managerial decision making is not straightforward. In this section, we examine the implications of heterogeneity for the computation of aggregate market share responses to changes in price, display, or feature. Expected aggregate market share is simply the sum over all households of the purchase probabilities divided by the number of households. Because there is a large number of households, expected and actual market shares will be very close by the law of large numbers. Aggregate chain or store-level pricing decisions are made, in part, on the basis of estimates of the derivative of market share with respect to various marketing mix variables. Manufacturers want to know how their market share will respond to price promotions, displays, or features. The derivative of market share is the sum of the derivatives of the probabilities of purchase for each household.

$$\frac{\partial \text{ Mkt Share}(k)}{\partial \mathbf{x}_j} = \sum_{i=1}^{N} \sum_{t=1}^{T_i} \frac{\partial}{\partial \mathbf{x}_j} \Pr(k|\mathbf{x} = \mathbf{x}_{it}, \boldsymbol{\theta}_i)/N^* \tag{5}$$

Here **x** is the vector of marketing mix variables, log price, display, and feature. N^* is the total number of observations in the panel. In equation 5, we sum over both households and time, thus averaging the response over the distribution of prices faced by the households and eliminating the need to pick a point at which to compute the elasticity.

Estimates of aggregate market share derivatives are influenced dramatically by the degree and type of heterogeneity allowed in the $\boldsymbol{\theta}$ vector. Table 2 gives estimated derivatives for various estimation procedures in the one-price logit model. In the first column are derivatives based on a pooled $\boldsymbol{\theta}$ estimate that is common across all households (the case of no heterogeneity). The second column allows for intercept heterogeneity by use of the Allenby/

Table 2

COMPARISON OF MARKET SHARE DERIVATIVES FOR ALTERNATIVE HETEROGENEITY ADJUSTMENT PROCEDURES

	Pooled estimates: common slope/intercept	*Allenby/ Rossi adjustment*	*Bayes estimator: 5-observation prior*
Log price			
COS-W	−.91	−.79	−.74
STK-W	−.73	−.65	−.58
3DIA-W	−.13	−.13	−.11
HSE-W	−.25	−.23	−.21
COS-O	−.57	−.49	−.48
STK-O	−.38	−.34	−.30
3DIA-O	−.060	−.055	−.048
Display			
COS-W	.038	.042	.071
STK-W	.031	.034	.054
3DIA-W	.0055	.0067	.012
HSE-W	.010	.012	.019
COS-O	.024	.025	.044
STK-O	.016	.018	.030
3DIA-O	.0026	.0046	.0041
Feature			
COS-W	.075	.066	.11
STK-W	.060	.055	.081
3DIA-W	.011	.011	.020
HSE-W	.020	.019	.028
COS-O	.047	.041	.074
STK-O	.031	.029	.045
3DIA-O	.0050	.0046	.0087

Rossi procedure for constructing a loyalty measure. The price elasticities show an approximately 10% reduction whereas the display and feature derivatives show little change. The role of heterogeneity can be better understood from the expression for the derivative in the case of the standard logit model: $\partial\Pr/\partial\log \text{price} = \beta_p \Pr(1 - \Pr)$. Pr denotes the choice probability locus viewed as a function of price. Adjusting for intercept heterogeneity increases the common price coefficient estimate from −5.38 to −5.95. Adjusting for both slope and intercept increases the average price response further to −6.85. This procedure would tend to increase the size of the price elasticity through the first term. In contrast, allowing the intercepts to vary from household to household and increasing responsiveness to price has the effect of making the fitted probabilities more flexible and the probabilities move toward zero or one, which tends to lower the magnitude of the elasticity. In the case of the price elasticity, it is the latter effect that dominates.

In the third column of Table 2 are market share derivatives for the Bayes household estimates that allow for heterogeneity in both the intercept and the slope with respect to price, feature, and display. Allowing for slope heterogeneity has dramatic effects on the size of the derivatives, particularly for the feature variables. The estimated response to features nearly doubles when slope heterogeneity is allowed. An investigator who fails to take into account heterogeneity will seriously undervalue feature advertising in this dataset. The fact that the feature derivative estimates are most influenced by heterogeneity is consistent with our previous finding of more heterogeneity in the feature slopes than in the other model slopes.

Predictive Performance

We now compare the predictive performance of procedures that allow intercept heterogeneity only through the use of loyalty measures with our Bayesian methods that accommodate heterogeneity in all parameters. Predictive performance is not the only or the ultimate test of a model or estimation procedure. As is well known, particular models may forecast well simply because of a reduction in the number of parameters even though the predictions may be biased. Perhaps even more important is the realization that superior predictive performance in data similar to the data used for prediction does not mean that the model will predict well after a change in policy (such as a change in the pricing policy). Further, very simple models that predict well may not yield sufficiently rich detail to explain or better understand individual household behavior. Our goal in examining predictive performance is to ensure that we have not paid too high a price in predictive performance for the very rich detail of household behavior available through our method.

Measuring predictive performance in the choice setting is difficult and controversial. To provide a balanced view of performance, we report three standard measures and introduce a new measure. In addition to predictive log likelihood, hit rates, and residual mean absolute deviation, we report the average probability for "hits."

The predictive log likelihood is a very conservative measure of performance. It assesses a high penalty for low predicted probabilities in cases when the household is observed to make purchases. These highly penalized "misses" tend to overshadow improvements in the probability of "hits" due to the Bayesian approach. One can argue that from the point of view of policy evaluation, a few misses on the household level are not nearly as important as more accurate prediction of the bulk of household response to new pricing or advertising policies. For this reason, many researchers advocate the use of a hit rate—the percentage of time that observed choices have the highest fitted probability. Hit rate is a more balanced measure that does not penalize incorrect predictions as heavily as predictive log likelihood. A defect of the hit rate measure is that it does not provide an assessment of the confidence with which the correct predictions are made. What is most desirable is a procedure that produces very high fitted probabilities for the choices made. To assess the predicted probabilities for the alternatives chosen, we introduce the average probability for hits as a supplement to the hit rate. Finally, we compute the average absolute value of the "residuals" (MAD), where the residual is defined as the choice vector (vector of ones and zeros) minus the predicted probabilities.

Table 3 reports the results of predictive tests. The dataset is broken into thirds, with the final third reserved for predictive testing. The first third of the data is used to fit a model without a loyalty parameter. Two different varieties of loyalty measures are employed to allow for intercept heterogeneity. We consider both the Guadagni and Little (1983) and the Allenby and Rossi (1991b) approaches. To further bolster our choice of the five-observation prior, we consider Bayes estimates based on the one-, two-, five-, 10-, and 100-observation priors. The second third of the data is then used to reestimate the model parameters with a loyalty parameter. As might be expected, the in-sample log-likelihood values for our household-level Bayes estimates are approximately half of the log-likelihood values for the Guadagni and Little loyalty approach. The key question is whether the introduction of a large number of household parameters causes the predictive performance to deteriorate.

The five-observation-prior Bayes estimates outperform the loyalty-based procedures on all four performance criteria. In general, the Bayes estimates produced by the five-observation prior have the best predictive performance. Even with a strong 100-observation prior, the Bayes estimates outperform standard loyalty adjustments. The reason is that even the 100-observation prior accommodates some slope heterogeneity not allowed for in the standard procedures. For example, the price coefficient estimate from the 100-observation prior ranges from −5.0 to −7.0.

The superior predictive performance of the Bayes estimates is achieved in spite of the introduction of more than 1500 separate household slope parameters.[7] In general, there is a tradeoff in predictive performance between the increased flexibility imparted by highly pa-

[7]Counting the number of household parameters in a Bayesian approach is somewhat misleading. The use of informative priors pulls the estimates toward a common mean. With very informative priors, the effective number of parameters is undoubtedly much less than 1500. In the limiting case of an extremely tight prior, the number of parameters is the same as the number of elements in the pooled parameter vector.

Table 3
PREDICTIVE PERFORMANCE OF HOUSEHOLD ESTIMATES

Heterogeneity adjustment procedure	*Log likelihood*	*Hit rate*	*Average hit probability*	*Residual MAD*
Guadagni/Little	−2574	72.1	.580	.081
Allenby/Rossi	−2647	70.3	.582	.084
Bayes estimates				
1 observation	−2693	70.3	.624	.078
2 observation	−2640	72.0	.652	.071
5 observation	−2513	72.5	.641	.072
10 observation	−2433	71.9	.608	.078
100 observation	−2506	71.9	.593	.081

rameterized models and the sampling error introduced by a larger number of estimated parameters. However, in this case, the incorporation of slope heterogeneity via the Bayes estimates captures an important aspect of the data and is balanced by the sampling error imparted by the larger number household parameters. The predictive performance of the Bayes estimates corroborates our findings in Table 1 that a substantial amount of heterogeneity in the slope coefficients is present in the data.

CONCLUDING REMARKS

For scanner panel data, the accurate estimation of household parameters in models of consumer behavior is difficult. The number of observations for an individual household is often very small (<25) and households rarely exhibit enough choice variation to allow for the estimation of all parameters. For example, the fact that households seldom choose all brands in the choice set results in unidentified intercepts for the brands not selected.

Additional information is needed to identify the parameters that describe household behavior. We present a Bayesian method of introducing additional information into the estimation procedure through the prior distribution. A reference prior is proposed that aids in the implementation of the procedure. The effect of our procedure is to smooth fitted probabilities away from zero or one.

Our procedure has three basic advantages: (1) household estimates for all parameters, including slope parameters, are produced, (2) the methods can be applied by making minor modifications in present optimization routines, and (3) our methods can be applied to any model, not just the multinomial logit model considered here (see Allenby and Rossi 1992 for applications to other choice models and a discussion of an alternative Bayesian approach).

In contrast to parametric random effects models, the estimators do not require *a priori* specification of the distribution of heterogeneity. Neither the family of the distribution (e.g., normal, gamma, etc.) nor its relation to observed household characteristics needs to be identified. Hence, the estimator is particularly well suited for situations in which little is known about the determinants of demand and investigators are interested in approaching the data inductively.

We apply our procedures to panel data on tuna purchases and find strong evidence of both slope and intercept heterogeneity in the dataset. The degree of heterogeneity is three to 10 times the level expected from sampling error in the household estimates. By some measures, there is considerably more heterogeneity in the feature response coefficients than in the price or display response coefficients. Moreover, the slope heterogeneity dramatically changes aggregate estimates of market share response to marketing mix variables. Procedures that use only loyalty measures to account for heterogeneity will produce very biased estimates of market share response. By properly accounting for slope heterogeneity, we find that the response to feature advertising is much larger than what would be predicted from an intercept-only approach.

We also illustrate the value of household estimates by showing how they can be used to devise a targeted coupon drop. This example is meant to illustrate only a few of the benefits of household parameters. We hope to pursue several directions in future research. First, the availability of household-level estimates opens the possibility of customizing the face value of the coupon to the specific household. In fact, some retailers are experimenting with point-of-purchase couponing whereby households receive coupons based on their most recent set of purchases. Second, the problem of optimal couponing can be posed in a decision theoretic setting in which the decision rules that target individual households arise from the Bayesian solution of a profit maximization problem. This approach is a subject of our current research.

In summary, the proposed Bayesian estimators can use the wealth of information contained in scanner panel data to reveal differences in individual household demand functions that are fundamental to the theory and practice of marketing. The household-level estimates can provide the basis for better targeted and more effective marketing strategies and tactics.

REFERENCES

Allenby, Greg M. and Peter E. Rossi (1991a), "Quality Perceptions and Asymmetric Switching Between Brands," *Marketing Science*, 10 (3), 185–204.

——— and ——— (1991b), "There is No Aggregation Bias: Why Macro Logit Models Work," *Journal of Business and Economic Statistics*, 9 (1), 1–14.

——— and ——— (1993), "A Marginal-Predictive Approach to Identifying Household Parameters," *Marketing Letters* (forthcoming).

Blattberg, Robert and Scott Neslin (1990), *Sales Promotion: Concepts, Methods, and Strategies*. Englewood Cliffs, NJ: Prentice-Hall, Inc.

Chintagunta, Pradeep K., Dipak C. Jain, and Naufel J. Vilcassim (1991), "Investigating Heterogeneity in Brand Preferences in Logit Models for Panel Data," *Journal of Marketing Research*, 28 (November), 417–28.

Clarkson, David and Robert Jennrich (1991), "Computing Extended Maximum Likelihood Estimates for Linear Parameter Models," *Journal of the Royal Statistical Society*, B53 (2), 417–26.

Currim, Imran (1981), "Using Segmentation Approaches for Better Prediction and Understanding From Consumer Mode Choice Models," *Journal of Marketing Research*, 18 (August), 301–9.

Guadagni, Peter M. and John D. C. Little (1983), "A Logit Model of Brand Choice Calibrated on Scanner Data," *Marketing Science*, 2 (3), 203–38.

Haberman, Shelby (1974), *The Analysis of Frequency Data*. Chicago: University of Chicago Press.

Hauser, John R. and Birger Wernerfelt (1989), "The Competitive Implications of Relevant-Set/Response Analysis," *Journal of Marketing Research*, 26 (November), 391–405.

Kamakura, Wagner A. and Gary J. Russell (1989), "A Probabilistic Choice Model for Market Segmentation and Elasticity Structure," *Journal of Marketing Research*, 26 (November), 379–90.

McCulloch, Robert and Peter E. Rossi (1991), "A Bayesian Approach to Testing the Arbitrage Pricing Theory," *Journal of Econometrics*, 49 (1), 141–68.

Narasimhan, Chakravarthi (1984), "A Price Discrimination Theory of Coupons," *Marketing Science*, 3 (2), 128–46.

Poirier, Dale and Gary Koop (1990), "Bayesian Analysis of Logit Models," working paper, University of Toronto.

Roberts, John H. and James M. Lattin (1991), "Development and Testing of a Model of Consideration Set Composition," *Journal of Marketing Research*, 28 (November), 429–40.

Tierney, Luke and Jay Kadane (1986), "Accurate Approximations for Posterior Moments and Marginal Densities," *Journal of the American Statistical Association*, 81 (1), 82–6.

Vilcassim, Naufel J. and Dipak C. Jain (1991) "Modeling Purchase-Timing and Brand-Switching Behavior Incorporating Explanatory Variables and Unobserved Heterogeneity," *Journal of Marketing Research*, 28 (February), 29–41.

Zellner, Arnold and Peter E. Rossi (1984), "Bayesian Analysis of Dichotomous Quantal Response Models," *Journal of Econometrics*, 25 (3), 365–93.

Reprint No. JMR302103

[35]

JORDAN J. LOUVIERE and GEORGE WOODWORTH*

The authors integrate concepts in conjoint analysis and discrete choice theory in econometrics to develop a new approach to the design and analysis of controlled consumer choice or resource allocation experiments. The article is concerned with estimating the parameters of conjoint-type functions from discrete choice or allocation data. Emphasis is placed on the multinomial logit model and aggregate choice or allocation data to illustrate the concepts in a series of empirical examples ranging from simple to complex. The authors present limited external validity evidence to support the approach and make comparisons with traditional conjoint approaches.

Design and Analysis of Simulated Consumer Choice or Allocation Experiments: An Approach Based on Aggregate Data

Individual and aggregate consumer choice processes and models thereof are receiving increasing attention in marketing and related fields. In general, whether based on actual market data or simulated choice situations, the most closely examined models are basically variants of Luce's (1959, 1977) choice axiom (Batsell and Lodish 1981; Gensch and Recker 1979; Punj and Staelin 1978; Reibstein 1978).

Although the Luce or multinomial logit (MNL) model may be approximately true for aggregate choice data (Huber 1982), there is considerable evidence that it is unsatisfactory for individuals (Currim 1982; Tversky 1972). More important, whether the model is a reasonable approximation to aggregate choice data has not been tested in a controlled experimental manner. Despite considerable empirical work with nonexperimental, observational choice data (e.g., Currim 1982; Punj and Staelin 1978), we cannot be sure whether the MNL model merely correlates well with many types of choices or is actually an adequate theoretical representation for these choices.

What is needed is a way to test deductions from the MNL model under carefully controlled conditions so that departures from the model, if found, cannot be confused with any number of possible confounding influences. Such a test would permit much more powerful comparison of competing models than is currently possible with observational data (e.g., Currim 1982), and would allow generalizations to be made about the possible practical applications of the model to various types of choices. The latter consideration is important because even if the MNL model can be shown to be theoretically inadequate, it may still provide useful predictions in a variety of situations. Development of experimental procedures to permit testing under controlled conditions would enhance the ability of researchers to make the kinds of empirical comparisons and perform the statistical tests necessary to validate the model in a more rigorous manner than is currently possible.

The need to separate practical prediction from theo-

*Jordan J. Louviere is Associate Professor, Department of Marketing, and George Woodworth is Associate Professor, Department of Statistics, The University of Iowa. Both authors are associated with Policies and Strategies, Inc., Iowa City, Iowa. They acknowledge the assistance of the IMG Consultants, Pty., Ltd., Sydney, Australia, in data collection for several of the empirical examples discussed in the article. Both authors previously were associated with IMG and some parts of the article were written during that association.

The authors gratefully acknowledge the helpful and critical comments contributed by the following individuals on a draft of the article: Donald A. Anderson, Norman H. Anderson, David Curry, David Hensher, Joel Horowitz, Lester W. Johnson, R. Duncan Luce, Robert J. Meyer, Kent Norman, and Richard Staelin. Other helpful comments and encouragement came from Penny Baron and Gerry Eskin. The final version of the article has benefitted from the input of these individuals and two anonymous reviewers; faults and problems which remain, however, are entirely the responsibility of the authors. The assistance of Cathy Louviere and Dennis Rauch in computer programming and data analysis is gratefully acknowledged.

Journal of Marketing Research
Vol. XX (November 1983), 350-67

retical adequacy is exemplified by work seeking to forecast choice behavior from systems of individual judgment or evaluation equations, such as the POSSE system (Green, Carroll, and Goldberg 1981; see also Green, DeSarbo, and Kedia 1980). Although of practical value, current approaches for using the results of conjoint judgment studies to forecast corresponding consumer choices are theoretically inadequate on the basis of several considerations:

1. There is no formal theory relating judgments to choices; nor has it been demonstrated that the numerical scales obtained in conjoint studies satisfy the scale properties required in various choice models such as the MNL model.
2. Choice behavior across individuals at one point in time or within an individual over time is a probabilistic phenomenon; hence, the use of systems of deterministic conjoint equations to forecast choice is clearly inadequate.
3. Because scale values derived from conjoint studies are empirical estimates of true parameters, they have error distributions. All stochastic theories of choice require the assumption of an error distribution (Amemiya 1981); hence, any forecast based on the notion of "highest predicted utility from a conjoint equation equals first choice" has an error distribution and/or may be biased.
4. Because the basis of data collection in a conjoint analysis is a judgment or evaluation task (Anderson 1981; Johnson 1974; Keeney and Raiffa 1976; Krantz and Tversky 1971), little except crude information is available about variation in choice behavior due to variations in the presence/absence of alternatives in choice sets. These sources of variation in choice are critical to understanding variations in choice processes and to forecasting choices in dynamic, competitive situations. Thus, conjoint tasks currently supply only very limited information relevant to understanding these sources of variation in choice behavior.

Because the object in many conjoint studies is the prediction of choice or market share (Cattin and Wittink 1982), it seems logical to derive the scale values or parameters of the choice process of interest from choice data rather than from a (perhaps) parallel judgment or evaluation task. However, few methods currently are available whereby one can derive the parameters of choice models from controlled discrete choice experiments analogous to econometric choice studies or to conjoint studies. Although Batsell (1980) and Batsell and Lodish (1981) have examined the use of all possible choice sets with a resource allocation task to estimate the parameters of Luce or MNL models for individual subjects and Reibstein (1978) has used a resource allocation task over a single choice set containing all possible alternatives of interest to derive choice probabilities, neither approach addresses discrete choice behavior *per se*. Rather, the Batsell and Reibstein approaches are based on allocation behavior, which may not be the same as discrete choice behavior. These two research designs represent two extremes on the continuum of design or task possibilities for studying stochastic choice behavior. Compromise experimental designs for the study of choice behavior, which we propose, would be a useful addition to these two possibilities.

The Reibstein (1978) approach, for example, requires one to assume a known choice process, such as the MNL model, but it does not permit one to compare different choice models or to reject the assumed choice model if it is false, except by recourse to external forecasting criteria. External criteria, however, may tell us little about the "truth" of the choice process assumptions because the model may appear to do well even if wrong (see, e.g., Anderson and Shanteau 1977; Birnbaum 1973), or it may do poorly because the task was ill-conceived or misspecified, having little to do with model specification. The Batsell (1980) or Batsell and Lodish (1981) approach, in contrast, is very appropriate for studies of the choice or allocation process of individuals and aggregates, and is particularly appropriate for model (or process) comparisons. The major drawback of this approach is the magnitude of the task requirements, which quickly escalate for problems of any complexity. Despite academic and laboratory appeal, the Batsell approach would be difficult to apply in the field to problems involving more than a few alternatives. What is needed, therefore, is a method that retains many of the positive virtues of the Batsell approach while affording economies in application.

The purpose of our article is to describe, discuss, and illustrate an approach to the design and analysis of consumer choice studies that enables one to study choice under controlled conditions. This approach is based on considerations from the design of factorial experiments in statistics and affords considerable flexibility in the design of choice studies, depending on what one is willing or able to assume about the choice process and/or the role of the attributes of the alternatives in choice. The approach we propose enables a researcher to study simultaneously the choice process and the attribute tradeoff or evaluation process in choice. The researcher can infer the scale values of conjoint-like models from choice data, and can apply the models derived to the prediction of choice. Furthermore, by appropriate choice of experimental design, a researcher can test competing choice models and/or reject as false the deductions from an assumed model.

To explain and illustrate the proposed approach, we first develop some elementary concepts in choice necessary for the design of choice experiments. To do this we concentrate on the Luce or MNL model and aggregate choice data; the reasons for this focus are that (1) the MNL model has yet to be tested adequately for aggregate choice data, (2) the MNL model has been the object of considerable recent research attention in marketing (e.g., Batsell 1980; Currim 1982; Reibstein 1978), and (3) if the MNL model can be shown to be a reasonable approximation to aggregate choice data, it would be useful in managerial applications.

After discussing the application of the MNL model to the design of MNL model factorial choice experiments, we outline an approach to the estimation of MNL models from aggregate choice data based on an application of weighted least squares procedures similar to that proposed by Nakanishi and Cooper (1982). We then provide a variety of empirical application examples to illustrate the versatility of the design approach across a wide variety of types of choice problems. These illustrative applications range from simple choice experiments, designed to estimate market share or changes in market share on the basis of changes in choice set composition, to more complicated multiattribute experiments with fixed and variable choice set sizes.

We also illustrate the use of the experimental design ideas in association with choice simulation systems based on conjoint analysis studies. Finally, we provide some empirical evidence of external validity for three different choice studies.

CONCEPTUAL CONSIDERATIONS

We treat the case of single or repeated choices among sets of multiattribute alternatives. That is, we conceive of an individual being faced with a set of alternatives from which to choose, each of which consists of a different combination of levels or values of a set of multiple attributes. Let us denote the set of all relevant choice alternatives as α, containing J members. Subsets of α are denoted by capital letters, e.g., A, and single members by lowercase letters, e.g., a. Each of the members of A is described by some combination of levels of K attributes denoted by the vector $\mathbf{x}' = (x_1, x_2, \ldots, x_K)$. We assume that a value, V_a (utility or worth), is associated with each alternative a in a choice set A. These scale values denote how much each alternative is liked or valued (its utility) and are a function of the vector of attributes ($\mathbf{x}$) of the alternatives

$$V_a = \beta_{0a} + \sum_k \beta_{ka} \cdot x_k \tag{1}$$

where β_{ka} is the weight of attribute k in the valuation of alternative a. This linear-in-the-parameters and additive form is not restrictive, as nonlinearities and nonadditivities may be readily accommodated. For example, quadratic main effects and interaction terms may be estimated if the design permits, as in typical applications of general linear models in regression or analysis of variance problems. Examples of such designs and their analysis are given in the Empirical Examples section.

We use the multinomial logistic form of Luce's model

$$\mathrm{p}(a|A) = \frac{e^{V_a}}{\sum_{j \in A} e^{V_j}} \tag{2}$$

where $\mathrm{p}(a|A)$ is the probability that alternative a will be selected from choice set A. This model can be derived from random utility theory (Amemiya 1981; Hensher and Johnson 1981; Luce 1959, 1977; McFadden 1947a, b; Yellot 1977); however, the distributional assumptions are unintuitive. Hence, we advocate equation 2 as an empirical model of considerable flexibility and demonstrate its application to modeling aggregate choice behavior.

The operational interpretation of $\mathrm{p}(a|A)$ in equation 2 is the relative frequency with which alternative a would be chosen by a group of individuals offered the choice set A. Thus, equation 2 is a model for the marginal probabilities of choosing an alternative competing with other alternatives.[1]

The most significant feature of this model is the independence from irrelevant alternatives (IIA) property; i.e., the utility, V_a, of alternative a is not influenced by whatever other alternatives are or are not in the choice set. Stated another way, the odds of choosing (or ratio of choices of) alternative a in relation to alternative b must be constant regardless of whatever other alternatives are present. Some choice models avoid this problem, such as the EBA model (Tversky 1972), various generalized extreme value models, and multinomial probit (see Currim 1982). These models, however, are much more complicated than the MNL model and in some cases are intractible for more than a few alternatives (e.g., MN probit) or require considerable *a priori* information to make estimation manageable (e.g., nested logit).

The IIA property of the MNL model may be unfortunate, but it also may be a minor problem in many applications; evidence for the aggregate data case is insufficient at this time to generalize. In fitting the MNL model to aggregate data from repeated choice experiments we assume that the choices of an individual responding to several choice sets ($A_1, A_2, \ldots, A_I$) are unbiased; i.e., each choice set is evaluated without regard to previously presented choice sets.

We now consider methods for the design and analysis of repeated choice experiments which not only permit efficient estimation of the parameters of equation 1 but also allow tests to be made of the IIA property of model 2 and of competing models (see, e.g., Horowitz 1981a, b; McFadden, Tye, and Train 1976).

DESIGN AND ANALYSIS OF CHOICE EXPERIMENTS

Optimum designs for estimating the parameters of stochastic multiattribute choice models are not obvious and little work has been directed toward this problem because the optimum design requires *a priori* knowledge of the "true" choice probabilities. Additionally, most individuals working in the choice area are interested primarily in modeling issues and only secondarily in design issues. We believe discussion of design issues is important, particularly if such a discussion can lead to im-

[1]We make no assumptions about the joint probability, $\mathrm{p}(a_1, \ldots, a_I|A_1, \ldots, A_I)$, of choices a_1 from set A_1 through a_I from set A_I. Equation 2 is our model for the marginal probabilities:

$$\mathrm{p}(a_j|A_j) = \sum_{i \neq j} \sum_{a \in A_i} \mathrm{p}(a_1, \ldots, A_I).$$

provements in data collection and analysis.

We can immediately recognize three extreme design possibilities for multiattribute choice experiments:

1. Use all possible choice sets of two or more of the J alternatives ($2^J - J - 1$ choice sets[2]). Though possible, such an approach is rarely practical (but see Batsell 1980; Batsell and Lodish 1981) and would be particularly difficult in applied work.
2. Use all possible pairs of J alternatives as choice sets, or $J(J - 1)/2$ choice sets. This approach has been used frequently in the past (Bradley 1953, 1965; Luce 1977; Skvoretz, Windell, and Fararo 1974) and is popular in applied work, but is difficult to apply as J grows large.
3. Use one choice set in which all J alternatives are present (see, e.g., Reibstein 1978). Though this approach is ordinarily practical and theoretically acceptable if the MNL model is true, rejection of the MNL model is impossible in this case.

In practice, other choice designs have been employed, such as combinations of pairs, triples, quadruples, etc. However, neither the efficiency of such designs nor their statistical properties have been examined to our knowledge.

We propose a fairly straightforward compromise that has desirable statistical properties and follows directly from the properties of the MNL model. All possible choice sets that individuals can face are given by a 2^J factorial design of J factors (the alternatives) at two levels—present in or absent from the choice set. Thus, any choice set is a treatment combination drawn from the 2^J factorial design of J alternatives with two levels (present or absent). If the independence from irrelevant alternatives property implied by the MNL model is true, a sufficient condition for estimatability of the parameters of model 2 is that independence of all alternatives across choice sets be preserved.[3] That is, alternatives must be pairwise independent of each other across choice sets. We term any such design a *Luce design*. An illustration of a complete 2^J design is given in Table 1, which demonstrates the use of a 2^J factorial to generate choice sets.

Any orthogonal "main effects" experimental design plan drawn from the power set satisfies this condition and an example is given in Table 1 (see combinations indicated by an asterisk). In addition, selecting orthogonal main effects plans from the 2^J factorial generally will lead to a logical selection of a small number of choice sets that will permit estimation. An important limitation of these main effects plans, however, is that they allow no tests of the MNL model because most rejection tests require the estimation of cross-alternative interaction effects.

Our previous logic can be extended to develop a design strategy to permit rejection tests or statistical tests for lack of fit. For example, if the IIA property of the choice axiom is false, one would expect that the utility, V_a, of alternative a would be influenced by the presence or absence of other alternatives in the choice set. If this is true, a rejection test for the choice axiom is a test for significant interaction effects of alternative a with, say, alternatives b and c. This test can be performed by choosing choice sets according to a design plan that affords estimation of at least some of the two-way interactions among the J alternatives. Such 2^J fractional factorials are particularly easy to construct and design plans are readily available in published sources (Hahn and Shapiro 1966; National Bureau of Standards 1957).

A fractional factorial that enables one to estimate all two-way interactions probably would permit a fairly strong rejection test because if the MNL model is true, all of the interactions between the alternatives should be nonsignificant. Of course, the violations could occur in higher order interaction effects (e.g., the utility of one alternative may depend on the presence of more than one other alternative). We suspect that estimation of the two-way interactions should be sufficient to detect violations; however, if a more stringent test is desired one could design the study to ensure it. One can also examine all possible choice sets for an exhaustive test.

We have conducted some preliminary analyses comparing 2^J fractional factorials with other types of choice designs. In particular, we have compared the accuracy of estimates from the base 3 (2^3) and base 4 (2^4) fractions

Table 1
AN EXAMPLE OF A SIMPLE DOUBLE CONDITIONAL DESIGN

		Functional measurement/conjoint measurement treatment combinations (alternatives)			
		Alt. a	*Alt. b*	*Alt. c*	*Alt. d*
	Attribute I:	*Level a*	*Level a*	*Level b*	*Level b*
Choice set no.	*Attribute II:*	*Level p*	*Level q*	*Level p*	*Level q*
1	*	absent	absent	absent	absent
2		absent	absent	absent	present
3		absent	absent	present	absent
4	*	absent	absent	present	present
5		absent	present	absent	absent
6	*	absent	present	absent	present
7	*	absent	present	present	absent
8		absent	present	present	present
9		present	absent	absent	absent
10	*	present	absent	absent	present
11	*	present	absent	present	absent
12		present	absent	present	present
13	*	present	present	absent	absent
14		present	present	absent	present
15		present	present	present	absent
16	*	present	present	present	present

Asterisk refers to treatment combinations in a fractional factorial discussed in text.

[2] There are 2^J possible sets of choice sets if the sets containing single alternatives and the null set are included.

[3] That is, the $I \times J$ incidence matrix (choice sets × alternatives) forms a connected incomplete block design.

with that of designs involving all of the pairs of the J alternatives and with the complete choice set design of all J alternatives for up to 15 alternatives. This work, described in the Appendix, indicates that the orthogonal, main effects, fractional factorial designs we propose generally produce more accurate parameter estimates than the all-pairs design for the same number of subjects while requiring fewer responses per subject.

Thus, we suggest that for both practical and academic applications, the orthogonal, main effects, fractional factorial design plans are an efficient choice for the design of discrete choice or resource allocation studies. If rejection tests for MNL or other models are required, one could use design plans which allow as many relevant two-way interactions as possible to be tested.

FIXED CHOICE SET SIZE DESIGNS

We illustrate the use of 2^J main effects fractional designs in the Empirical Examples section. Other classes of choice problems are also of interest. Many choice problems do not involve variations in choice set size, but rather involve changes in one or more attributes of a fixed number of alternatives. Such problems have much in common with previous applications of econometric discrete choice models (see, e.g., Hensher and Johnson 1981). We term these problems *fixed choice set size Luce designs*, although by extension we can treat the variable choice set size case as well.

Fixed choice set size problems arise when the set of alternatives, say J products in a particular product class, is constant but one or more attributes of these alternatives vary across the choice sets. For example, many applications of econometric discrete choice theory have addressed transportation mode choice. The alternative modes are fixed (auto, bus, commuter train, etc.), but the attributes of each alternative differ among choice sets. Consequently, the alternative itself can change from choice set to choice set because each time the attribute combination for a mode changes a *different* mode results. Such designs enable one to study how choices are affected by changes in the attributes of a fixed brand or alternative in competition with others. For these choice problems, we suggest fractional factorial design plans in which the *attributes* of the alternatives are treated as factors. The size of the design is dictated by how many levels we choose to assign to each attribute of each alternative.

As in the case of the 2^J designs, main effects or main effects plus selected interactions design plans are used to ensure independence across all alternatives. That is, the attributes of bus are independent of those of train. Hence, the use of orthogonal fractional designs ensures that each of the separate alternatives is independent across sets.

We believe that these designs will permit fairly efficient estimation of parameters, but we have not run simulations to gather baseline data because we are uncertain about an appropriate basis for comparison. Two alternatives are (1) the optimal design, but it is not known *a priori*, and (2) randomly chosen sets of treatment combinations. The latter approach will entail considerable simulation work and is planned for a followup study.

PARAMETER ESTIMATION IN LUCE DESIGN EXPERIMENTS

We now discuss a simple method for parameter estimation in aggregate multinomial logistic models based on weighted least-squares regression proposed by Louviere, Woodworth, and Anderson (1981), Louviere and Hensher (1982), and Nakanishi and Cooper (1982). Other approaches to estimation are available (e.g., Batsell 1980; Nakanishi and Cooper 1974; Theil 1971, p. 632–6) which differ from the one we use. All of these approaches will yield the same parameter estimates if the appropriate weighted least squares computing forms are employed. In general, approaches using ordinary least squares (e.g., Batsell 1980; Batsell and Lodish 1981; Nakanishi and Cooper 1974) will be inefficient in comparison with their weighted counterparts which are known to be asymptotically efficient. An additional difference is the manner in which one chooses to linearize equation 2 to separate the numerator and denominator effects; in this case the approaches differ in relative ease of data preparation for analysis, not in theory. However, each method leads to a different vector of weights to be used in estimation. For example, the Theil (1971, p. 626–36) method eliminates the denominator effects by dividing both sides of equation 2 by the probability of choosing some arbitrary base alternative. The desired numerator effects then can be estimated by weighted least squares (see, e.g., Mahajan, Green, and Goldberg 1982). If used inferentially, the Theil approach must adjust all tests for the denominator degrees of freedom. A paper comparing the properties of the approach used in this article with these other approaches is available from the authors on request.

Consider equation 2 again.

$$p(a|A) = \frac{e^{V_a}}{\sum_{j \in A} e^{V_j}} \tag{3}$$

Note that the denominator in equation 3 is constant in each choice set in a particular study; that is, suppose a design involves I choice sets, $A_1, \ldots, A_I$, then

$$p(a|A_i) = \frac{\exp(V_a)}{k_i} \tag{4}$$

where all terms are as previously defined except k_i, which is a constant for the ith choice set ($i = 1, 2, \ldots, I$).

To estimate the parameters of this model we use a weighted multiple linear regression in which the dependent variable is

$$Y_{ai} = \ln(f_{ai}) \tag{5}$$

where f_{ai} is the number of times (frequency) alternative a was chosen from choice set A_i. For convenience we take log(0) = 0, although this definition is irrelevant because any observation with zero weight is effectively removed from the estimation. Now Y_{ai} is approximately normally distributed[4] with expected value

$$E(Y_{ai}) = \ln[n_i \cdot p(a|A_i)] = V_a + \log(n_i/k_i) \tag{6}$$

where n_i is the number of subjects asked to respond to choice set A_i. The variance of Y_{ai} is approximately[5]

$$\mathrm{Var}(Y_{ai}) = [n_i \cdot p(a|A_i)]^{-1} = \frac{1}{w_{ai}}, \tag{7}$$

say. Equation 6 can be rewritten as

$$Y_{ai} = \mu + \alpha_a + \gamma_i + e_{ai} \tag{8}$$

where e_{ai} is approximately normally distributed with zero mean and variance $1/w_{ai}$, μ is the constant term, $\alpha_a = V_a - \mu$, and $\gamma_i = \log(n_i/k_i)$. The parameters of this model can be estimated by weighted linear regression with weights[6] w_{ai}. The independent variables besides the constant are (1) $J - 1$ dummy (0/1) variables for the alternatives x_j, $j = 1, \ldots, J - 1$, $x_j = 1$ if $j = a$ and (2) $I - 1$ dummy (0/1) variables for the choice sets c_i, $i = 1, \ldots, I - 1$, $c_i = 1$ for choice set i. With this coding, $\mu = V_J$ and the regression coefficient of x_j, call it $\hat{\alpha}_j$, is an estimate of $V_j - V_J$. The V_j's themselves are not estimatable, only their contrasts; however, this is sufficient to estimate choice probabilities because equation 3 can be written as

$$p(a|A) = \frac{e^{(V_a - V_J)}}{\sum_{j \in A} e^{(V_j - V_J)}}. \tag{9}$$

The choice set dummy variables are analogous to "block" effects in analysis of variance and are needed to avoid biasing the V-estimates; however, their coefficients are of no interest.

If we wish to express V_a as a function of a vector of attributes, this is a straightforward extension:

$$V_a = \alpha_a + \sum_{l=1}^{L_a} \beta_{la} \cdot x_{la}, \tag{10}$$

where alternative a has L_a attributes and x_{la} is the level of its lth attribute. This model can be estimated by weighted multiple linear regression using as independent variables the (0/1) dummy variables mentioned before along with the attribute variables x_{li} with $x_{li} = 0$ if $i \neq a$ (i.e., use alternative-specific or nested coding of attributes).

The estimates derived by using weighted least squares in the manner suggested above are minimum modified chi square solutions, which have been demonstrated to be asymptotically efficient in large samples (Bhapkar 1966; Grizzle, Starmer, and Koch 1969). We illustrate the application of these regression procedures in the following section. This estimation approach was developed independently of the recent Nakanishi and Cooper (1982) proposal (see, e.g., Louviere, Woodworth, and Anderson 1981), but their approach is essentially the same as the one we suggest. Under the proper weighting conditions our approach should yield estimates identical to those obtained by approaches proposed by Theil (1971; see also Mahajan, Green, and Goldberg 1982) and by Batsell (1980).

EMPIRICAL EXAMPLES

We report a variety of empirical results to illustrate both design and analysis procedures and to demonstrate that the MNL model generally is a good approximation to a variety of aggregate choice results. We present the results in order of increasing experimental complexity.

Main Effects, Variable Choice Set Size Designs Based on 2^J Factorial Fractions

Example 1. Choices among major brands of soft drinks (fraction of 2^{11} based on a 2^4). Eleven major brands of soft drinks were selected for analysis (Coca-Cola, Pepsi, RC, Sprite, 7-Up, Fresca, Mountain Dew, Hires, Dr. Pepper, Mr. Pibb, and Orange Crush). Each soft drink was treated as a factor and a 16-treatment, orthogonal, main effects, fractional design plan was selected from the 2^{11} factorial to create choice sets (Hahn and Shapiro 1966).

Subjects were 89 undergraduate students enrolled in an upper division consumer behavior class. They were requested to indicate which of the 11 soft drinks they would be most likely to select on any given visit to a store to buy soft drinks, or to indicate "other." "Other" was a 12th alternative present in each choice set and serves as a base alternative. Subjects were shown 19 choice sets, the first four of which were used as practice and not analyzed.[7] *All subjects participated in all 15 choice sets; unless otherwise indicated this is true for all choice designs discussed hereafter.*

Data were aggregated into 103 choice frequencies within choice sets for analysis (each of the 11 alternatives appears eight times = 88 observations + "other" which appears 15 times = 103 observations). Equation 8 was estimated by the GLM procedure of the Statistical Analysis System (SAS Institute 1979), which has a weighting option and can generate dummy variables automatically. The estimated scale values (utilities) and their standard errors are given in Table 2.

Interestingly, the soft drinks form natural groupings (e.g., colas, lemon-lime types, etc.); thus, drinks within a group are more similar to one another than to other

[4] Make the Poisson approximation to the distribution of f_{ai} and apply Theorem 9.3.1 of Wilks (1962, p. 259).

[5] See footnote 4, same theorem.

[6] In practice we estimate the weights as $\hat{w}_{ai} = f_{ai}$, the observed frequency.

[7] There were 15 "designed" choice sets rather than 16 because the choice set containing no alternatives was not presented.

Table 2
ESTIMATED UTILITIES FOR SOFT DRINKS

Alternative (soft drink)	Estimate of $V_a - V_{other}$	Standard error[a]
Coca-Cola	.06	.02
Pepsi Cola	.20	.02
RC Cola	−.10	.02
Sprite	−.26	.02
7-Up	−.11	.02
Fresca	−.24	.02
Mountain Dew	.14	.02
Hires Root Beer	−.22	.02
Dr. Pepper	−.12	.02
Mr. Pibb	−.29	.02
Orange Crush	−.21	.02

[a]These nominal standard errors, as produced by the regression program, are based on the assumption that repeated responses from each subject are distributed as though made by different subjects. A valid, very conservative estimate of standard error is $\sqrt{15}$ times the above, 15 being the number of designed, not practice, responses per subject.

drinks not in the group. According to Tversky (1972), such similarities create problems for the choice axiom. The high correlation[8] (R = .95) between the logarithms of the 103 observed relative choice frequencies, f_{ai}/n_i, and the logarithms of the fitted choice probabilities (equation 8) indicates, however, that the MNL model provides a good account of the data from this task.

This particular example illustrates the use of a simple, main effects, fractional factorial, choice-set-generating design to scale a set of stimuli and estimate the market shares of the stimuli.

Example 2. Resource allocations among overseas holiday destination alternatives. This example features an allocation rather than a choice task. Eleven major overseas holiday destinations of interest to Australians were selected for study: (1) South Pacific Islands (Fiji, Tahiti, Tonga, etc.), (2) Hawaii, (3) East Coast of the USA, (4) West Coast of the USA, (5) Canada, (6) Japan, (7) New Zealand, (8) France, (9) the United Kingdom, (10) Germany, Austria, and Switzerland, and (11) Italy. Each of these destinations was treated as a factor in a 2^{11} factorial design (levels: present, absent) from which a base 4 (2^4) orthogonal factorial was selected to create choice sets. A total of 17 choice sets were used, with the first two sets treated as practice.

The 75 subjects were students, faculty, and staff in the School of Economic and Financial Studies at Macquarie University, Sydney, Australia, and employees of a major economics, management, and marketing consulting organization also located in Sydney. Subjects were instructed to imagine they had won five round-trip air tickets which had two conditions attached: (1) they had to be used in the next five years and (2) they could be used only to fly to the 11 indicated destinations. Subjects could elect not to use all the tickets and were told that if they used the tickets they must make all arrangements and pay for their other expenses themselves.

The subjects' task was to indicate how they were most likely to use the five free tickets by allocating them as they saw fit in each of the 15 target choice sets.[9] The allocation data were aggregated into frequencies of allocations per destination within choice set and equation 8 was estimated. Utility estimates are reported in Table 3. The model fits the data in Table 3 very well, accounting for about 90% of the variance in the logarithms of the allocation proportions.

This application example illustrates the use of a simple, main effects, fractional factorial, choice-set-generating design as in Example 1, but with a resource allocation task rather than a choice task. In all other aspects Example 2 is the same as Example 1.

Variable Attribute, Fixed Choice Set Designs

Example 3. Vacation destination choice as a function of destination and air travel costs. Five major overseas destinations of interest to Australians were selected for examination. Destination-specific air travel costs at three levels were the design factors: New Zealand ($200, $350, $400), Japan ($600, $850, $1100), U.S. West Coast ($1450, $1800, $2150), U.K. ($1600, $2000, $2400), and Italy ($1200, $1500, $1800). An orthogonal, main effects fraction of a 3^5 factorial was selected to create 18 choice sets (see Hahn and Shapiro 1966, Plan 19a, Master Plan 6). Forty subjects consisting of advertising executives, marketing executives, and consulting firm personnel who participated in a seminar in Sydney, Australia, were shown 20 choice sets consisting of the five destinations at different air travel cost combinations. The

[8]We urge caution in interpreting this multiple R as a goodness of fit measure. A small R could result from any of three sources: (1) high sampling error due to a small sample of subjects, (2) near indifference of alternatives leading to a small sum of squares for regression, or (3) failure of the IIA property of Luce's model.

[9]See footnote 7.

Table 3
ESTIMATED UTILITIES FOR DESTINATIONS

Alternative (destination)	Estimate $V_a - V_{Italy}$	Standard error[a]
South Pacific Islands	.257	.076
Hawaii	.200	.077
U.S. East Coast	.156	.078
U.S. West Coast	.349	.074
Canada	.184	.078
Japan	−.220	.086
New Zealand	−.280	.085
France	.187	.078
United Kingdom	.662	.072
Germany, Austria, Switzerland	.585	.072
Italy	—	—

[a]Nominal standard error; conservative estimates are not available for this allocation task.

first two choice sets were treated as practice and not analyzed. Subjects were instructed to choose one destination from the five for a holiday of 10 days duration or longer, or to select "other/none." The "other/none" alternative was a constant in each choice set and was a convenient way of coding a base alternative.

The choice data were aggregated into choice frequencies and the following regression equation was estimated.

$$(11)\quad \ln(f_{ai}) = \begin{cases} \mu + \alpha_a + \beta \cdot \text{Cost}_{ai} + \gamma_i \text{ Set}_i, \text{ if } a \neq \text{other} \\ \mu, \text{ if } a = \text{other} \end{cases}$$

The β cost term represents a generic cost coefficient for all alternatives—a constant effect due to cost regardless of destination (−.0009 as shown in Table 4); we relax this assumption in two additional steps reported hereafter. The estimated parameters of this model are reported in Table 4. The R-value for the model is .82.

Although the generic cost model is statistically significant and accounts for a sizable proportion of the variation (67%), this model seems unlikely to be realistic. Therefore a second analysis was performed in which alternative-specific linear cost coefficients were permitted. That is, a linear effect for cost was permitted to be different for each destination. The form of this regression equation estimated by weighted least squares is as follows.

$$(12)\quad \ln(f_{ai}) = \begin{cases} \mu + \alpha_a + \beta_a \cdot \text{Cost}_{ai} + \gamma_i \text{ Set}_i, \text{ if } a \neq \text{other} \\ \mu, \text{ if } a = \text{other} \end{cases}$$

where β_a, $a = 1, \ldots, 5$, are the alternative-specific linear cost effects. The results are reported in Table 4. The R^2 is .88 for this model, a significant improvement[10] over the hypothesis that the cost parameters are the same for all of the different destinations. For example, the respondents appear to have been more sensitive to airfare costs to New Zealand (−.003) and Japan (−.002) than to the costs to the remaining destinations. In fact, the cost slopes are related inversely to the mean airfare levels varied in the task, New Zealand having the lowest mean airfare ($316.67) and the U.K. having the highest ($2000); remaining levels were Japan ($850), U.S. ($1800), and Italy ($1500). The correlation between the mean fare and the cost coefficients is −.55. The same pattern is revealed in the next analysis, in which we relax the linearity assumption for cost.

To illustrate the power of the procedure, we introduce quadratic terms to test for nonlinearities in the specific cost effects. This model is identical to the preceding model with the exception that all cost variables are centered about their means and both linear and squared terms are estimated. The estimation results for this model are reported in Table 4.

The addition of quadratic terms significantly improves[11] the fit (R^2 = .92); only the U.S. West Coast appears to have a linear cost effect. Hence, the regression procedure has the capability of detecting departures from linearity in specific effects. For this problem, each travel cost function has the same form: decreasing at a decreasing rate, because the estimated linear terms are negative (e.g., New Zealand, −.001) whereas the quadratic terms are positive (e.g., New Zealand, .000015). This example illustrates the power of the choice design and analysis approach to handle strategic pricing problems among competing alternatives because it would be possible to predict the changes in market shares which would result from changing any of the airfares to any of the destinations.

Example 4. Choices among fast food menus at various prices. Nine attribute combinations consisting of a one-

[10] The F-value for the improvement in sum of squares greatly exceeds the tabled value of the .05 level.

[11] See footnote 10.

Table 4
MAIN EFFECTS AND COST COEFFICIENT(S) FOR FIVE VACATION TRAVEL DESTINATIONS

	Estimated utility: $V_a - V_{other}$		
		Destination-specific costs (standard errors[a])	
Destination	*Generic cost Model (R = .82)*	*Linear model (R = .94)*	*Quadratic model (R = .96)*
New Zealand	.36 − .0009 cost (.06) (.00008)	1.03 − .003 cost (.10) (.0003)	2.21 0.001 (cost-350) + 0.000015 (cost 350)² (0.00083) (0.000007)
Japan	.91 − .0009 cost (.08) (.00008)	1.60 − .002 cost (.10) (.0001)	2.71 − 0.0017 (cost-850) + 0.00000075 (cost-850)² (0.0001) (0.00000075)
U.S. West Coast	1.44 − .0009 cost (.15) (.00008)	.77 − .0005 cost (.18) (.0001)	2.57 − 0.0005 (cost-1800) + 0.0000006 (cost-1800)² (0.00008) (0.0000004)
United Kingdom	1.16 − .0009 cost (.17) (.00008)	.92 − .0005 cost (.17) (.00009)	5.53 − 0.0005 (cost-2000) + 0.000001 (cost-2000)² (0.00007) (0.0000003)
Italy	1.29 − .0009 cost (.13) (.00008)	1.33 − .0009 cost (.17) (.0001)	5.91 − 0.00087 (cost-1500) + 0.000002 (cost-2000)² (0.00009) (0.0000006)

[a] Figures in parentheses are nominal standard errors; multiply by $\sqrt{20}$ for valid but very conservative estimates.

third fraction of a 3^3 factorial design were selected to represent possible luncheon menus at fast food restaurants. The nine combinations consisted of levels of the factors sandwich (j = hamburger, fishburger, chickenburger), side order (k = french fries, onion rings, cole slaw), and drink (l = milk, milkshake, soft drink), drawn up according to an orthogonal main effects plan (see Hahn and Shapiro 1966, Plan 16a, Master Plan 3). These nine treatment combinations represent nine alternative meals. The nine alternatives were then treated as factors in a 2^9 factorial where the two levels were alternative-specific prices ($1.89, $2.69). A 12-combination orthogonal main effects plan was selected to create 12 choice sets of the nine menus at different levels of price (see Hahn and Shapiro 1966, Plan 8a, Master Plan 4). Subjects were requested to choose the one menu in each set that they would be most likely to select for lunch given the prices listed or to choose "none." Subjects were 99 students in an upper division undergraduate class in consumer behavior. They were shown 15 choice sets; the first three were treated as practice. All subjects completed all choice sets.

Data were aggregated to choice frequencies, f_{ai}, where alternative a is the attribute bundle (j, k, l) and i denotes the choice set. Weighted least squares regression was used to estimate the following equation.

$$\ln(f_{ai}) = \beta_0 + \beta_1 \text{Sand}_j + \beta_2 \text{Side}_k + \beta_3 \text{Drink}_l + \beta_4 \text{Cost}_{ai} + \gamma_i \text{Set}_i \tag{13}$$

This model implies that cost is generic. The three menu attributes were coded (−1, 0, 1) in order of increasing marginal choice frequency (see Table 5, footnote a). Both linear and quadratic models were estimated. The R for the linear model is .92 and the coefficient estimates (and standard errors) are

$$\underset{}{V_{\text{menu}} - V_{\text{none}}} = \underset{(.14)}{-3.10} + \underset{(.05)}{.29} \cdot \text{Sand}_j + \underset{(.05)}{.41} \cdot \text{Side}_k + \underset{(.05)}{.27} \cdot \text{Drink}_l - \underset{(.06)}{1.11} \cdot \text{Cost}. \tag{14}$$

Table 5

QUADRATIC UTILITY MODEL[a] FOR FAST FOOD MENUS

	Coefficients (standard errors[b])	
Attributes	*Linear*	*Quadratic*
Sandwich	0.28 (.05)	.005 (.03)
Side order	0.40 (.05)	.800 (.12)
Drink	0.25 (.05)	.014 (.03)
Cost	−1.10 (.06)	—
Constant	−3.12 (.14)	—

[a] $V_{\text{menu}} - V_{\text{none}} = \beta_0 + \sum_{r=1}^{3} (\beta_{r,\text{LIN}} \cdot x_r + \beta_{r,\text{QUAD}} \cdot (3x_r^2 - 2))$ where x_1 = sandwich (1 = hamburger, 0 = chicken, −1 = fish), x_2 = side order (1 = french fries, 0 = onion rings, −1 = cole slaw), and x_3 = drink (1 = soft drink, 0 = milk shake, −1 = milk). For quadratic values replace +1 and −1 with +1 and replace 0 with −2.

[b] Nominal. For a valid, conservative estimate, multiply by $\sqrt{12}$.

The quadratic model is displayed in Table 5. The R for the second model is .93; hence, it does not fit usefully better than the linear model. Because we deliberately precoded in order of choice, this finding indicates that the scale values of the attributes are at approximately equal intervals. As in conjoint and functional measurement studies, this model scales the attribute levels on interval scales with common origin (the base). Thus, this type of experimental design enables one simultaneously to test the choice axiom and scale the stimuli if the MNL model is approximately true. The analogy to conjoint analysis is obvious if one replaces the orthogonal polynomial values used in estimation (see Table 5) with standard (1, 0) dummy variables used in conjoint estimation. However, use of (1, 0) dummies would destroy the orthogonality of the design matrix.

This example illustrates the ability of the approach to handle pricing policy studies for conjoint profiles or concepts. In real markets attribute bundles compete on price or other grounds. This example illustrates how one can simultaneously assess the effects of the price and nonprice variables on choice. Because the study was just an example, we used only a main effects design for the luncheon alternatives. However, significant and managerially relevant interactions are clearly possible in this example. To examine these interactions or at least test for their presence, one could design the luncheon profiles to permit estimation of some interactions, or block the design into three main effects plans with a common base alternative in each, and assign the sample subjects into each block on a random basis. Because of the common base the separate samples could be grouped for estimation and all interactions tested if the MNL model is appropriate.

Thus, it is possible to scale conjoint-type designs with choice data instead of rankings or ratings data (see also Mahajan, Green, and Goldberg 1982 for a similar application not based on design concepts). To do so one must create two designs: (1) a conjoint design which generates alternative profiles (see Green 1974) and (2) a choice-set-generating design, such as that illustrated by the current example, to produce choice sets. The next two examples illustrate other choice-set-generating designs for conjoint profiles.

Example 5. Choices among reduced airfare tickets to the U.S. West Coast from Sydney, Australia. Twelve reduced-fare tickets to the U.S. West Coast were created according to the following procedure.

1. A half fraction of a 2^4 factorial design was used as a sampling frame to generate combinations of fare reduction (low or high), advance purchase requirement in days (low or high), number of stopovers permitted en route (low or high), and a cancellation penalty expressed as a percentage of the fare paid (low or high).
2. A range of values were selected to represent "low" or "high" and a value was drawn randomly from the range for each separate low or high level of each factor; this process generated eight combinations of ticket attributes or tickets.

3. Four additional tickets were generated by selecting two of the eight treatment combinations selected in step 2, and sampling again from the low and high ranges of each attribute. These additional tickets therefore are similar to the two tickets whose design codes were used as the basis for their creation. Thus, the three tickets within each of the two sets theoretically have identical expectations.

The eight tickets created in step 2 plus the four generated in step 3 comprise the 12 tickets used in the experiment.

The purpose of this experiment is to test for departures from the choice axiom based on correlated alternatives (Tversky 1972) and to illustrate another method of scaling conjoint analysis designs. The 12 alternative air tickets were placed in choice sets by treating the 12 tickets as factors and selecting a 16-treatment combination design plan from the 2^{12} factorial (see Hahn and Shapiro 1966, Plan 11a, Master Plan 5). Thirty-five subjects were recruited from the students and faculty of economics at Macquarie University (North Ryde, Australia) and from the employees of a major consulting firm in Sydney, Australia. They were requested to choose the one ticket in each of the 15 choice sets (the 16th set is the null set) that they would be most likely to use to fly to the U.S. West Coast on a holiday trip of at least 10 days duration, or to indicate that they would not travel to the U.S. at all.

Data were aggregated into choice frequencies, f_{ai}, for alternative a within choice set i. The following equation was estimated by means of weighted least squares regression.

$$\ln(f_{ai}) = \beta_0 + \beta_1 \text{Fare}_j + \beta_2 \text{Adv.Pur.}_k + \beta_3 \text{Stops}_l + \beta_4 \text{Cancel}_m + \gamma_i \text{Set}_i \tag{15}$$

where alternative a is the ticket defined by attribute bundle j, k, l, m (fare, advance purchase requirement, number of stopovers, and cancellation penalty, respectively). The estimation results are

$$V_a - V_{\text{Notrip}} = \underset{(.08)}{.37} - \underset{(.0001)}{.001} \cdot \text{Fare}_j + \underset{(.0005)}{.0007} \cdot \text{Advance}_k + \underset{(.02)}{.30} \cdot \text{Stop}_l - \underset{(.07)}{.48} \cdot \text{Cancel}_m. \tag{16}$$

The MNL model provides a reasonable fit to the data; the R is .89. All attributes have the correct signs, except advance purchase requirement, which is not significant at the .05 level (t = 1.37). We suspected that the sign reversal was likely to be due to unobserved interactions. However, introduction of the estimatable interactions permitted by this particular design did not resolve the sign on the number of stopovers (see Table 6). The effect for stopovers is not significant (t = −.49); hence, stopovers may have been irrelevant for this group of subjects. The discovery of apparently significant interactions also reinforces the caveat of Carmone and Green (1981) about misspecification in conjoint analysis because our experiment is an extension of conjoint analysis to discrete choice.

Table 6

UTILITY MODELS[a] FOR REDUCED AIRFARE TICKETS TO THE U.S. WEST COAST FROM SYDNEY, AUSTRALIA

Attributes	*Coefficients (standard errors[b])* — *Additive model (R = .89)*		*Interactive model (R = .92)*	
Main effects				
Fare reduction	−.001	(.0001)	−.001	(.00009)
Advance purchase requirement	.0007	(.0005)	−.00004	(.0006)
Number of stopovers	.3	(.02)	−.009	(.02)
Cancellation penalty	−.48	(.07)	−.68	(.10)
Interactions[c]				
Fare × Advance	—		−.00001	(.000004)
Fare × Stopovers	—		.0002	(.00008)
Advance × Stopovers	—		−.002	(.0008)
Stopovers × Cancel	—		−.25	(.12)
Constant	.37	(.08)	−.57	(.05)

[a]These are models for $V_{\text{ticket}} - V_{\text{notrip}}$.

[b]Nominal; multiply by $\sqrt{15}$ for valid, conservative standard errors.

[c]In the interaction model, variables are centered at their means to reduce collinearity: (fare − 685), (advance − 43.33), (cancel − .445833); stopovers are coded (−1) for ≤2 and (+1) for >2.

Example 6. Choice designs applied to modeling the output of an individual-level conjoint choice simulator. As part of a study supported by the U.S. National Institute on Aging, 450 Iowans between the ages of 50 and 65 participated in a study of retirement migration intentions. The 450 respondents each evaluated 30 different conjoint profiles describing aspects of hypothetical retirement locations and economic conditions. The 30 profiles constitute a 27-treatment-combination, orthogonal, main effects plan drawn from a 3^{10} factorial. Respondents were assigned randomly to one of 15 different such main effects plans. Each of the 15 plans had a common set of three treatment combinations (all attributes at level 1, all at level 2, all at level 3) which were administered first to anchor judgments made on a 0–9 category scale reflecting the intention to move upon retirement given the situation described by the profile. The 15 main effects plans (or blocks) aggregate into a fractional factorial design that permits independent estimation of all main effects and two-way interactions in the presence of three-way (but not higher order) interactions.

A desirable policy output of this study is the prediction of the probability that a randomly chosen Iowa retiree will choose to move to a location of a particular type given certain economic conditions. One approach to predicting such outcomes is to develop a choice simulator based on the individual conjoint equations derived from the judgment task (e.g., Green, Carroll, and Goldberg 1981). Such simulators typically involve a variety of choice rules, such as "highest predicted conjoint utility equals first choice." We illustrate the application of the experimental design concepts discussed heretofore to the development and implementation of a choice simulator. The objective is to use design concepts in such a way that a single, closed-form model can be used to summarize the output of the simulator. Development of a model of the simulator would enable one to forecast to many other choice situations not observed in the simulation process.

We illustrate the approach using all of the 15 blocks or main effects plans described above. The 10 variables are climate, terrain, proximity to water recreation opportunities, residential location (city, suburbs, rural), distance to nearest large metropolitan area, neighborhood age mix, distance to close friends and relatives, distance to full-service health care, local cost of living, and national inflation rate. Except for the distance variables expressed in miles, the cost of living expressed in dollars, and inflation rate expressed in percentage, all levels of variables are nominal. Because this example is illustrative and not substantive, we concentrate exclusively on methodological details and ignore substantive conclusions and potential interaction effects.

The 27 treatment combinations in each of the main effects blocks represent the choice alternatives of interest. We wish to put these into choice sets of various sizes and composition for use with a choice simulator. To do this we create a 2^J factorial design to generate the choice sets; there are 2^{27} possible choice sets in each of the 15 blocks for this problem. We select 32 of these sets in each of the 15 blocks using a 2^5 design as a base for constructing an orthogonal main effects plan. In this way, we create 15 × 32 choice sets for use with a choice simulator; each of the 27 treatment combinations of each main effects plan appears in 16 choice sets in this design. We implement the simulator by predicting the probability that each respondent would choose each alternative listed in a choice set, using a modified Luce model based on the predicted rating output from the conjoint judgment equation. We then sum the choice probabilities over all respondents for each choice set to generate the predicted choice frequencies in each of the 32 choice sets. We include the middle-level treatment combination (2, 2, 2, ..., 2) as a base alternative in *all* choice sets so that we can estimate a single MNL model.

The output of the simulator, therefore, is the predicted sample aggregate probability of choice for each of the 27 treatment combinations as they appear in each of the 32 choice sets. In each of the 15 blocks, 27 × 16 + 32 (464) total choice observations are available for analysis (or 6960 total across all blocks) because each alternative appeared in 16 of the 15 sets of 32 choice sets. These data may be analyzed exactly as are the data in Example 5. The results are reported in Table 7.

All the terms in Table 7 are in orthogonal polynomial units, which are one form of dummy coding. We provide no substantive interpretation of these results in the interest of brevity. However, the levels and corresponding coded values are listed in Table 7 and the interested reader can recover the estimated scale values by substituting the codes in the model and generating the predicted values. We merely note that these results are consistent with our expectations and the model is highly significant ($p(F)$ <

Table 7

WLS RESULTS OF THE APPLICATION OF THE MAIN-EFFECTS-ONLY MNL MODEL TO THE AGGREGATE SIMULATED CHOICE PROBABILITIES

Variable	*Levels*	*Code for linear*	*Code for quadratic*	*Parameter estimate*	*Standard error*
Climate	Southwestern	−1	1		
Linear	Southeastern	0	−2	.0018	.0038
Quadratic	Northern	1	1	−.1056	.0020
Terrain	Mountains nearby	−1	1		
Linear	High rolling hills	0	−2	.0600	.0036
Quadratic	Flat &/or low hills	1	1	.0189	.0021
Water rec.	Coastal location	−1	1		
Linear	Lakes nearby	0	−2	.1020	.0039
Quadratic	No water near	1	1	−.1337	.0020
Residential	Center of city	−1	1		
Linear	Suburbs	0	−2	−.2468	.0037
Quadratic	Rural	1	1	−.0249	.0021
Major metro	20,000–500,000	−1	1		
Linear	100–300,000	0	−2	−.2429	.0036
Quadratic	1,000,000+	1	1	.0560	.0022
Neighborhood	Most recent retirees	−1	1		
Linear	Most older retirees	0	−2	.1146	.0036
Quadratic	Young/old mix	1	1	.0235	.0021
Relative	<1/2 hour	−1	1		
Linear	1–2 hours	0	−2	−.1523	.0036
Quadratic	>6 hours	1	1	−.0023	.0021
Health care	<1/2 hour	−1	1		
Linear	1/2–1 hour	0	−2	−.1806	.0037
Quadratic	1–2 hours	1	1	−.0201	.0021
Living costs	10% less	−1	1		
Linear	Same as now	0	−2	−.3001	.0038
Quadratic	10% more	1	1	−.0326	.0021
Inflation	Low—5%	−1	1		
Linear	Moderate—10%	0	−2	−.2211	.0037
Quadratic	High—20%	1	1	−.0113	.0021
Intercept				−.3903	.0029

$F = 69.77$; $p(F) < .0001$; d.f. = (499,6460); $R^2 = .84$

.0001), accounting for about 84% of the variation in the logarithms of the 6960 choice proportions. To apply the model to the prediction of choice probabilities in other, new situations one postulates (1) any set of treatment combinations consistent with the levels used in the original set of 27 treatments and (2) choice sets of interest. One can then use the model to predict any probabilities of interest.

This example illustrates the ability of the approach to derive a single, closed-form model to summarize an aggregate choice response surface for a set of conjoint profiles or concepts. In essence, this example shows that one can fit a single model to the aggregate choice surface whereby management can infer tactical or strategic consequences for market share by manipulating the policy variables in the model. This approach affords a clear saving in estimation, data collection, file preparation, and computer analysis over the current simulation approaches which use files of individual conjoint equations.

GENERAL COMMENTS ABOUT THE EMPIRICAL EXAMPLES

Some general points about the approach are in order given the empirical examples presented. In all of the examples we tested the ability of the derived parameters to recover the original choice *proportions* rather than the logarithm of these proportions, which was the criterion variable in the regression analyses. In each case, the fit for the choice proportions as measured by R^2 was *higher* than the fit for the logarithms, and the number of parameters was *much lower* than for the regressions because the choice set dummies are not needed in prediction. Hence, all models fit *better* than the regression results suggest they do. It is important to realize that the parameter estimates are only asymptotically efficient in large samples. Amemiya (1981) suggests that a sample of 30 is a large sample for estimation with aggregate data, and all of our examples exceeded that number. However, controversy surrounds the efficiency issue, and theory and evidence are insufficient at this point to provide a firm conclusion. A recent study by Louviere and Hensher (1983) also demonstrates that these models validate well to holdout samples, strengthening the argument for them.

The parameter estimates can be improved by iteratively fitting the weighted least squares regression procedure we propose. At each iteration one substitutes the predicted frequencies from the previous iteration for the weights and refits the regression model. This process is continued until the analyst is satisfied that the parameters do not change beyond some prespecified value.

Of course, the correct way to analyze these data is by maximum likelihood procedures fit directly to the observed choice frequencies. We do not explore this alternative because algorithms to fit *aggregate* choice frequencies are not widely available and because, as McFadden, Tye, and Train (1976, p. 314) note, the weighted least squares method we propose is known to be more efficient than maximum likelihood but is more prone to bias. Because the analyst has control over both design and analysis, we suggest that the bias issue is less significant than it is for the nonexperimental data to which McFadden refers. Moreover, most marketing analysts have access to regression algorithms that permit weighting, and are interested in reasonable approximation procedures. We believe our approach is both computationally easy and efficient for the vast majority of applications likely to be encountered in practice.

It is also important to note that our *design* approach ensures orthogonality when a constant base alternative is used in every choice set. Our *estimation* approach, however, introduces correlations into the design matrix by the use of choice-set dummy variables and alternative-specific dummy variables. We believe the estimation properties are scarcely affected by this method. However, if orthogonality is desired, it can be achieved in either of the following ways.

1. Instead of the (1, 0) dummies we suggest, use a complete set of orthogonal polynomial dummy codes to represent the effects of interest.
2. Use the Batsell (1980) dummy coding to achieve orthogonal dummies, but estimate the model by using weighted least squares.

A technical report which compares our approach with the Batsell (1980) and/or Nakanishi and Cooper (1974) approach is available from the authors upon request. This technical report also details the appropriate estimation procedures.

In the next section we review some recent studies which reflect on the external validity of our proposed approach.

SELECTED EXTERNAL VALIDITY EVIDENCE

We briefly outline the results of three recent external validity tests of choice models derived from controlled-choice experiments as described in preceding sections. Other evidence of external validity is reviewed by Levin et al. (1983).

The first choice study using the methods described here was conducted on behalf of a major pet foods manufacturing firm. Because the results are proprietary, we provide only enough description to assess the outcome. Random samples of pet food users were taken from several major markets in the U.S., selected to be representative of the market. Interviewees were shown 16 different choice sets, consisting of combinations of 13 target pet food products based on a main effects plan (Hahn and Shapiro 1966, Design Index, p. 2, Plan Code 12a) drawn from the 2^{13} factorial. Interviewees were asked to allocate 11 points across the alternatives in each choice set so that the allocations reflected the proportion of each product they would be likely to purchase in a typical month. Allocation data were aggregated to develop proportions of allocations, and a choice model identical to that represented by equation 8 was estimated by weighted least squares regression.

Market share forecasts then were made by using the estimated scale values of each of the products derived from the regression analysis. U.S. national inventory withdrawal shares (SAMI) data were obtained for the validity test. The latter data reflect distribution outlet withdrawals from inventory sources, which are not the same as aggregate sales share data but should be closely related. The results of this test are depicted in Figure 1, a plot of forecast shares from the model against actual observed national shares. The relationship is obvious and the correlation is .83; a linear transformation would be necessary to apply the choice model developed in the interviews directly to the share data. This calibration is needed because the slope is not equal to unity, nor is the intercept equal to zero.

The second test involved a similar experimental design administered to a sample of 100 residents of a midwestern university town. The eight major supermarkets

Figure 1
VALIDATION RESULTS FOR U.S. NATIONAL PET FOOD SAMPLE

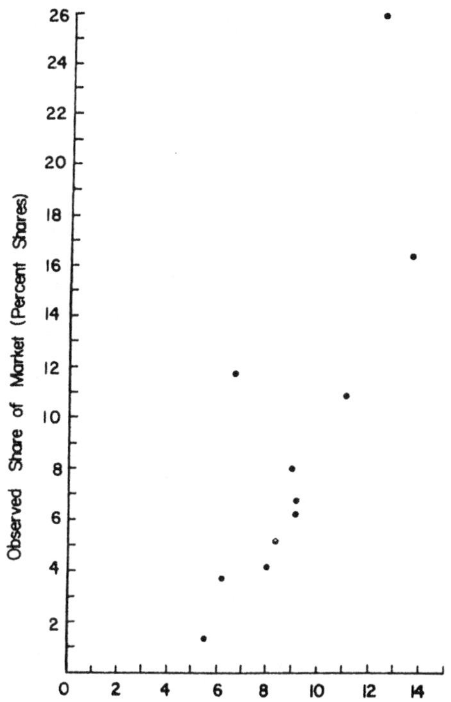

Figure 2
VALIDATION RESULTS FOR IOWA CITY SUPERMARKET STUDY

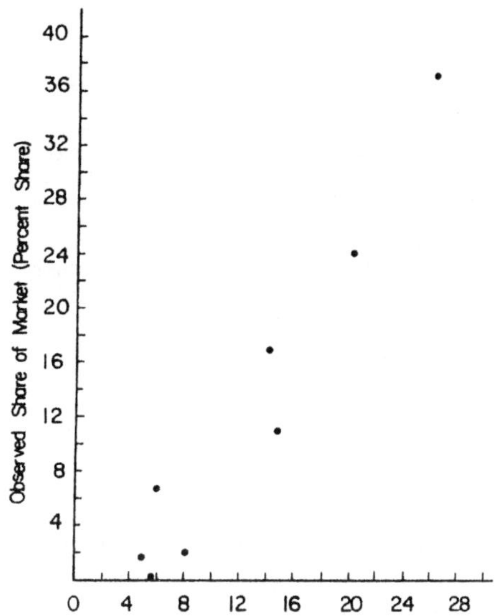

in the town were treated as factors with two levels (present, absent) and 12 choice sets were constructed by developing a main effects plan from the 2^8 factorial (Hahn and Shapiro 1966, Design Index, p. 1, Plan Code 7a) to generate choice sets. Interviewees were asked to estimate how much of their grocery shopping budget they had spent in each of the eight stores over the preceding month. They were then shown the 12 choice sets and asked to indicate which store they would be most likely to choose in each choice set.

The choice data were aggregated to relative frequencies for analysis and a model identical to equation 8 was estimated from the data. The estimated scale values for each store were used to forecast its market share, which was compared with the reported share data for the previous month's shopping obtained in the interview. The latter are plotted against the former in Figure 2. The relationship is obvious and the correlation is substantial (.96). Again, a linear transformation would be required to calibrate the laboratory model to the actual reported choice data.[12]

[12]If actual choice data are available, the model can be calibrated easily to these data to maximize external validity as indicated. If choice

The final example involves a transportation mode choice problem in Australia. For policy reasons, it was desired to assess the sensitivity of choice for travellers to and from Tasmania and mainland Australia to changes in costs and types of service by sea and air. A sample of Tasmanian and mainland Australian residents completed a choice experiment which elicited (among other things) their choices among air service at a particular price, three different sea services (overnight with berth, overnight with chair, fast daylight) at various prices, or "no travel." Respondents were shown one of three collections of 12 choice sets consisting of the four mode alternatives at different costs and the "no travel" option. The three different collections of choice sets were created to permit all possible two-way interactions among the cost components of each mode to be estimated to test the IIA property of the MNL model. Respondents were assigned randomly to each set of choice sets on an equal probability basis. The choices of respondents were aggregated for analysis by means of a multiple linear regression approximation to a choice model similar to equation 11.

The model derived from the choice data then was used to predict the current known shares by air and sea (.82 and .18, respectively). The derived model forecast the shares to be .78 and .22, respectively. This result suggests that the model requires minimum calibration and produces results consistent with actual observation. No systematic interactions were found between the cost components, as is consistent with the MNL model.

DISCUSSION AND CONCLUSIONS

We present an approach to the analysis of aggregate consumer choice behavior based on the Luce (1959) choice axiom. Through a variety of empirical examples we demonstrate that the method enables one to develop choice models which incorporate many of the advantages of conjoint analysis studies and are directly predictive of aggregate choice shares. Hence, this approach bridges the gap between the individual decomposition approach of conjoint and functional measurement (with the subsequent simulation of choice behavior) and the nonexperimental econometric approach to the development of discrete choice models. In this sense we generalize work by Reibstein (1978), Batsell (1980), and Batsell and Lodish (1981) to develop a practical approach to complex choice problems which is similar in spirit to the fractional design approach in most applications of conjoint analysis. In addition, we briefly describe preliminary evidence of the external validity of the approach for three exploratory studies. Despite the advantages mentioned and the encouraging empirical results, it is important to note that the methods of design and analysis we discuss do not replace conjoint methods. Rather, the methods are complementary because at this time conjoint techniques can handle many more attributes and permit easier individual-level analysis. Nonetheless, research should be conducted to find out whether similar results can be obtained from the two approaches and thus whether they are interchangeable in applications.

Examples of the lack of fit of Luce models are well documented for individual-level data (e.g., Slovic, Fischhoff, and Lichtenstein 1977; Tversky 1972); however, little attention has been devoted to aggregate-level data. Though we do not contend that aggregate results necessarily differ in kind from those obtained from individuals, systematic study is lacking and is needed to separate issues of theoretical significance from those of practical approximations to a variety of problems of managerial interest. To answer these questions, research extending far beyond the simplistic objectives of our article is needed.

In subsequent studies we will be concerned with generalizing the basic ideas of this article to provide rigorous tests for lack of fit of the MNL model. This work is similar to the error theory analysis available in functional measurement. The econometric theory for independent individual choice observations is now well known (Hensher and Johnson 1981; Manski and McFadden 1981); however, the case of repeated measures on single individuals is more complicated. The approach we discuss here involves repeated measures on individuals, and future work should focus on the statistical theory for this case and for the general case of repeated measures with covariates. The introduction of covariates, necessary for a rigorous analysis of market segmentation, will add complications. We plan these extensions in followup work.

The intent of our article is to illustrate the applicability of the Luce (1959) choice axiom (or the multinomial logit model) for aggregate consumer choice studies. We provide evidence that the choice axiom approximates a wide variety of choice tasks of potential interest in consumer choice studies. In addition to the empirical results reported here, we have available several other sets of choice or resource allocation data which reflect the general results presented. Further, these methods have been applied in a variety of proprietary studies in Australia and the U.S. and have produced similar results. Besides our experience, additional evidence is provided by experiments reported by Luce (1977), Batsell (1980), Batsell and Lodish (1981), and studies employing econometric discrete choice analysis (see, e.g., Arnold, Roth, and Tigert 1980; Punj and Staelin 1978).

Our research with aggregates of individuals suggests that the Luce axiom should be given renewed attention in order to show whether, like the linear model for judgments, the axiom recovers choice data well as measured by goodness of fit but can be rejected for significant lack-of-fit violations. Tests for lack of fit are rejection tests, which require an error theory. The error theory is provided by discrete choice theory in econometrics; it per-

data are not available, caution should be exercised until more is known about situations in which calibration is necessary or unnecessary. In the latter case, models should be used as relative and not absolute indicators of outcomes.

mits the analyst to test whether violations from the MNL are statistically significant. Significant violations signal a potentially important failure of the model and may lead to reformulation or comparison with other competing models. Even if shown to be theoretically inadequate, the model may provide an acceptable approximation to much aggregate choice data—a property that can be valuable in applied research. We hope the methods and results we discuss will prove useful in initiating a dialogue about the role of the choice axiom in basic and applied research in consumer behavior.

APPENDIX
EFFICIENCY OF 2^J DESIGNS

The efficiency of a design is its ability to yield precise estimates of parameters. In this Appendix we compare the efficiency of 2^J and all-pairs designs for estimating choice probabilities. Suppose J alternatives are to be included in a choice study. We refer to the design in which each subject is presented with the full set of J alternatives as the FCS (full choice set) design. Although this design does not permit a test of the choice axiom because it is a "saturated" design, it serves as a baseline against which others are compared.

The aggregate choice frequencies in the FCS design have a multinomial distribution with probabilities $p_1, p_2, \ldots, p_J$, where p_a is the probability that alternative a will be picked out of the full choice set. The maximum likelihood estimate of p_a is simply the relative frequency with which alternative a is chosen. The standard error of this estimate is given by the familiar formula,

$$SE(\hat{p}_a) = \sqrt{p_a(1 - p_a)/n}.$$

In a fractional design or an all-pairs (AP) design, alternatives are presented in a variety of incomplete choice sets. With these designs, each subject is presented with not one but several different choice sets; therefore, to make an exact computation of the standard errors of aggregate choice probability estimates for such designs, one must make some assumptions about the process by which subjects make repeated choices when presented with different subsets of the J alternatives. At one extreme, a subject's repeated choices may be completely independent—as though made by different individuals. At the other extreme, a subject's choices may be completely deterministic given his or her individual preference ordering of the J alternatives.

Faced with this ambiguity, we can provide only an upper limit on standard errors and coefficients of variation of choice probability estimates. We emphasize that the weighted least squares method suggested for estimating choice probabilities is valid regardless of the process by which individual repeated choices are made, provided the aggregate behavior is well approximated by the Luce model. It is not the estimates themselves but their standard errors which are uncertain, although we can bound them.

Table A1
STATISTICAL COMPARISON OF COEFFICIENTS OF VARIATION[a] OF ESTIMATED[b] CHOICE PROBABILITIES FOR CHOICES INVOLVING FIVE ALTERNATIVES

Alternative	*Choice probabilities (%)*	*Coefficients of variation for designs*		
		FCS	2^3	*AP*
A	8.8	.320	.328	.327
B	12.5	.264	.293	.300
C	17.8	.215	.238	.278
D	25.2	.172	.207	.256
E	35.6	.134	.171	.227

[a]The coefficient of variation (CV) is exact for the FCS design and is an upper bound on the CV's of the other two designs.
[b]Assuming n = 100 subjects.

Using the Fisher information matrix technique,[1] we computed coefficients of variation[2] of market share estimates derived from "all-pairs" designs and 2^J designs for a variety of distributions of choice probabilities over the J alternatives.

For example, with five alternatives (say A, B, C, D, and E) in the full choice set, the 2^3 design would involve the following seven incomplete choice sets.

(A,B), (C,D), (A,C,E), (A,D,E), (B,C,E), (B,D,E), (A,B,D,C)

Each subject would respond to all seven choice sets. The all-pairs design would involve the 10 possible pairs of alternatives. Suppose 100 subjects were used under each design (note that 10 responses per subject would be required with the all-pairs design but only seven with the 2^3 design) and that the choice probabilities for alternatives A, B, C, D, and E in percentages are 8.8, 12.5, 17.8, 25.2, and 35.6. The coefficients of variation for the full choice set design, the all-pairs design, and the 2^3 design with a sample of 100 subjects are reported in Table A1. The 2^3 and AP designs are upper bounds—they represent the "worst" case in which the analyst discards all but one response from each subject to ensure independence. In practice, all responses are used and these two designs have lower coefficients of variation.

[1]The Fisher information matrix is defined as the expected value of the negative of the matrix of second partial derivatives, with respect to the parameters, of the logarithm of the probability of the data.

[2]The coefficient of variation (CV) of the estimated choice probability is the standard error (SE) expressed as a fraction of the quantity estimated, i.e.,

$$CV(p_a) = \frac{SE(\hat{p}_a)}{p_a} = \frac{1 - p_a}{\sqrt{p_a}} \cdot \frac{1}{\sqrt{n}}.$$

It can be shown (Woodworth and Louviere 1982, available upon request from authors) that the CV is nearly equal to the SE of the estimated scale values of the Luce model, $\hat{V}_a = \ln(\hat{p}_a)$. Hence, we report the CV for estimates derived from various designs.

The results in Table A1 show that the 2^3 design performs very well for smaller choice probabilities. This finding is not surprising because alternatives with small choice probabilities rarely are chosen in the full choice set design as they must always compete with high-probability alternatives. In the 2^3 or all-pairs designs, however, there are choice sets in which low-probability alternatives are not pitted against high-probability alternatives.

In addition to this example, we calculated upper bounds on coefficients of variation of estimated choice probabilities for 2^3 or 2^4 designs and all-pairs (AP) designs for choices involving from 5 to 15 alternatives under a variety of choice probability distributions. The results can be summarized as follows.

- —For very small choice probabilities (0 to about 3%), the AP design is slightly more accurate than the 2^J or the FCS design.
- —In all other situations, the 2^J design is more accurate than the AP design.
- —For higher choice probabilities (25% and up), the 2^J design is much more accurate than the AP design.

Figure A1

STATISTICAL COMPARISON OF FCS, 2^3, AND ALL-PAIRS DESIGNS FOR CHOICES INVOLVING FIVE ALTERNATIVES (N = 100 SUBJECTS)

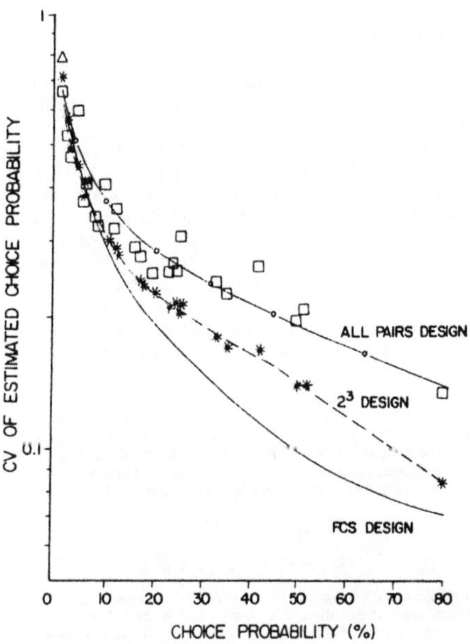

Figure A2

STATISTICAL COMPARISON OF FCS, 2^4, AND ALL-PAIRS DESIGNS FOR CHOICES INVOLVING NINE ALTERNATIVES (N = 100 SUBJECTS)

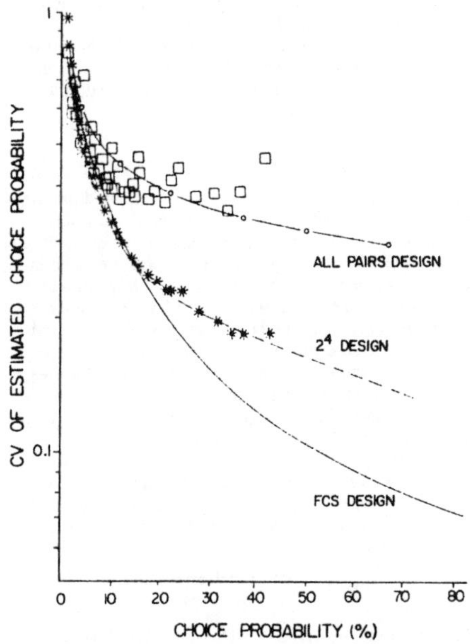

These points are illustrated in Figures A1 and A2, which are plots of upper bounds on coefficients of variation of choice probability estimates of 2^J and AP designs for five and nine alternatives. Individual points on the graph correspond to choice probabilities for individual alternatives. A variety of distributions of choice probabilities are used, ranging from uniform to geometric. These results strongly support the conclusion that 2^J designs are always almost as efficient as the FCS design and generally more efficient than AP designs. The 2^J designs, therefore, afford a good compromise for the study of choice behavior if the choice probabilities are approximated reasonably well by the Luce model.

REFERENCES

Ajzen, I. and M. Fishbein (1977), "Attitude-Behavior Relations: A Theoretical Analysis and Review of Empirical Research," *Psychological Bulletin*, 84, 888–918.

Amemiya, T. (1981), "Qualitative Response Models: A Survey," *Journal of Economic Literature*, 19, 1483–1536.

Anderson, N. H. (1981), *Foundations of Information Integra-*

tion Theory. New York: Academic Press.
——— and J. Shanteau (1977), "Weak Inference with Linear Models," *Psychological Bulletin*, 84, 1155–70.
Arnold, S. J., V. Roth, and D. G. Tigert (1980), "Conditional Logit Versus MDA in the Prediction of Store Choice," *Advances in Consumer Research*, 8, 665–70.
Batsell, R. R. (1980), "Consumer Resource Allocation Models at the Individual Level," *Journal of Consumer Research*, 7, 78–87.
——— and L. M. Lodish (1981), "A Model and Measurement Methodology for Predicting Individual Consumer Choice," *Journal of Marketing Research*, 18 (February), 1–12.
Bhapkar, V. P. (1966), "A Note on the Equivalence of Two Test Criteria for Hypotheses in Categorical Data," *Journal of the American Statistical Association*, 61, 228–35.
Birnbaum, M. H. (1973), "The Devil Rides Again: Correlation as an Index of Fit," *Psychological Bulletin*, 79, 239–42.
Bradley, R. A. (1953), "Some Statistical Methods in Taste Testing and Evaluation," *Biometrics*, 9, 22–38.
——— (1965), "Another Interpretation of a Model for Paired Comparisons," *Psychometrika*, 30, 315–18.
Carmone, F. J. and P. E. Green (1981), "Model Misspecification in Multiattribute Parameter Estimation," *Journal of Marketing Research*, 18 (February), 87–93.
Cattin, P. and D. R. Wittink (1982), "Commercial Use of Conjoint Analysis: A Survey," *Journal of Marketing*, 46, 44–53.
Currim, I. S. (1982), "Predictive Testing of Consumer Choice Models Not Subject to Independence of Irrelevant Alternatives," *Journal of Marketing Research*, 19 (May), 208–22.
Curry, D. J., J. J. Louviere, and M. J. Augustine (1980), "On the Sensitivity of Brand-Choice Simulations to Attribute Importance Weights," *Decision Sciences*, 12 (July), 502–16.
———, ———, and ——— (1983), "The Aggregate Effects of Induced Changes in Consumer Decision Structures," *Research in Marketing*, 6, Greenwich: JAI Press, Inc.
Gensch, D. H. and W. W. Recker (1979), "The Multinomial, Multiattribute Logit Choice Model," *Journal of Marketing Research*, 16 (February), 124–32.
Green, P. E. (1974), "On the Design of Choice Experiments Involving Multifactor Alternatives," *Journal of Consumer Research*, 1, 61–8.
———, J. D. Carroll, and S. M. Goldberg (1981), "A General Approach to Product Design Optimization Via Conjoint Analysis," *Journal of Marketing*, 45 (3), 17–27.
———, W. S. DeSarbo, and P. K. Kedia (1980), "On the Insensitivity of Brand-Choice Simulations to Attribute Importance Weights," *Decision Sciences*, 11, 439–50.
Grizzle, J. E., C. F. Starmer, and G. G. Koch (1969), "Analysis of Categorical Data by Linear Models," *Biometrics*, 25, 489–504.
Hahn, G. J. and S. S. Shapiro (1966), "A Catalog and Computer Program for the Design and Analysis of Symmetric and Asymmetric Fractional Factorial Experiments," *Technical Report No. 66-C-165*, General Electric Research and Development Center, Schenectady, NY.
Hensher, D. A. and L. Johnson (1981), *Applied Discrete Choice Modelling*. London: Croom-Helm.
Horowitz, J. L. (1981a), "Identification and Diagnosis of Specification Errors in the Multinomial Logit Model," *Transportation Research*, 15B, 345–60.
——— (1981b), "Testing the Multinomial Logit Model Against the Multinomial Probit Model Without Estimating the Probit Parameters," *Transportation Science*, 15, 153–63.
Huber, J. (1982), "Accounting for Attraction Bias in Choice: An Examination of Center Seeking and Reweighting Explanations," paper presented to 13th Annual Conference of Association for Consumer Research, San Francisco (October).
Johnson, R. M. (1974), "Tradeoff Analysis of Consumer Values," *Journal of Marketing Research*, 11 (May), 121–7.
Keeney, R. L. and H. Raiffa (1976), *Decisions with Multiple Objectives: Preferences and Value Tradeoffs*. New York: John Wiley & Sons, Inc.
Krantz, D. H. and A. Tversky (1971), "Conjoint-Measurement Analysis of Composition Rules in Psychology," *Psychological Review*, 78, 151–69.
Levin, I. P., J. J. Louviere, K. L. Norman, and A. Schepanski (1983), "External Validity Tests of Laboratory Studies of Information Integration," *Organizational Behavior and Human Performance*, 31, 173–93.
Louviere, J. J. (1981), "On the Identification of the Function Form of the Utility Expression and Its Relationship to Discrete Choice," Appendix B in *Applied Discrete Choice Modelling*, D. A. Hensher and L. Johnson. London: Croom-Helm, 385–416.
——— and D. A. Hensher (1982), "On the Design and Analysis of Simulated Choice or Allocation Experiments in Travel Choice Modelling," *Transportation Research Record No. 890*, 11–17.
——— and ——— (1983), "Forecasting Consumer Demand for a Unique Cultural Event: An Approach Based on an Integration of Probabilistic Discrete Choice Models and Experimental Design Data," *Journal of Consumer Research*, December, in press.
———, G. G. Woodworth, and D. A. Anderson (1981), "Predicting Consumer Choice of Destination and Ticket for International Travel from Australia," paper presented to South Pacific Meetings of Regional Science Association, Surfers' Paradise, Queensland, Australia (August).
Luce, R. D. (1959), *Individual Choice Behavior: A Theoretical Analysis*. New York: John Wiley & Sons, Inc.
——— (1977), "The Choice Axiom After Twenty Years," *Journal of Mathematical Psychology*, 3, 215–33.
Mahajan, V., P. E. Green, and S. M. Goldberg (1982), "A Conjoint Model for Measuring Self- and Cross-Price/Demand Relationships," *Journal of Marketing Research*, 19 (August), 334–42.
Manski, C. F. and D. McFadden, eds. (1981), *Structural Analysis of Discrete Data*. Cambridge, MA: MIT Press.
McFadden, D. (1974a), "Conditional Logit Analysis of Qualitative Choice Behavior," in *Frontiers in Econometrics*, P. Zarembka, ed. New York: Academic Press, 105–42.
——— (1974b), "The Measurement of Urban Travel Demand," *Journal of Public Economics*, 303–28.
——— (1979), "Quantitative Methods for Analyzing Travel Behavior of Individuals: Some Recent Developments," in *Behavioural Travel Modelling*, D. A. Hensher and P. R. Stopher, eds. London: Croom-Helm, 279–318.
———, W. Tye, and K. Train (1976), "Diagnostic Tests for the Independence from Irrelevant Alternatives Property of the Multinomial Logit Model," *Working Paper No. 7616*, Institute of Transportation Studies, University of California, Berkeley.

Nakanishi, M. and L. G. Cooper (1974), "Parameter Estimation for a Multiplicative Competitive Interaction Model—Least Squares Approach," *Journal of Marketing Research*, 11 (August), 303–11.

——— and ——— (1982), "Simplified Estimation Procedures for MCI Models," *Marketing Science*, 1 (3), 314–22.

National Bureau of Standards (1957), *Fractional Factorial Experimental Designs for Factors at Two Levels*, NBS Applied Mathematics Series, No. 48.

Punj, G. N. and R. Staelin (1978), "The Choice Process for Graduate Business Schools," *Journal of Marketing Research*, 15 (November), 588–98.

Reibstein, D. J. (1978) "The Prediction of Individual Probabilities of Brand Choice," *Journal of Consumer Research*, 5, 163–8.

SAS Institute (1979), *SAS User's Guide*. Cary, NC.

Skvoretz, J., P. Windell, and T. J. Fararo (1974), "Luce's Axiom and Occupational Prestige: Test of a Measurement Model," *Journal of Mathematical Sociology*, 3, 147–62.

Slovic, P., B. Fischhoff, and S. Lichtenstein (1977), "Behavioral Decision Theory," *Annual Review of Psychology*, 28, 1–39.

Theil, H. (1971), *Principles of Econometrics*. New York: John Wiley & Sons, Inc.

Timmermans, H. T. and K. J. Veldhuisen (1981), "Behavioural Models and Spatial Planning: Some Methodological Considerations and Empirical Tests," *Environment and Planning A*, 13, 1485–98.

Tversky, A. (1972), "Elimination by Aspects: A Theory of Choice," *Psychological Review*, 79, 281–99.

Westin, R. B. and P. L. Watson (1975), "Reported and Revealed Preferences as Determinants of Mode Choice Behavior," *Journal of Marketing Research*, 12 (August), 282–9.

Wilks, S. S. (1962), *Mathematical Statistics*. New York: John Wiley & Sons, Inc.

Yellot, J. E. (1977), "The Relationship Between Luce's Choice Axiom, Thurstone's Theory of Comparative Judgment, and the Double Exponential Distribution," *Journal of Mathematical Psychology*, 15, 109–44.

[36]

JOFFRE SWAIT and JORDAN LOUVIERE*

Multinomial logit (MNL) models are widely used in marketing research to analyze choice data, but it is not generally recognized that the unit of the utility scale in a MNL model is inversely related to the error variance. This means that, for instance, parameters of two identical utility specifications estimated from different data sources with unequal variances will necessarily differ in magnitude, even if the true model parameters that generated the utilities are identical in both sets. Despite a growing number of papers that compare MNL coefficients, no examples of appropriate tests of the joint and separate hypotheses of scale and parameter equality in MNL models exist in the marketing literature. The purpose of this paper is to address the proper procedure for MNL parameter comparisons between different data sets and to propose a simple relative scaling test that can be implemented with standard MNL estimation software. Several examples are given to illustrate the approach.

The Role of the Scale Parameter in the Estimation and Comparison of Multinomial Logit Models

INTRODUCTION

Multinomial logit (MNL) choice models are now well established in the marketing research literature (e.g., Guadagni and Little 1983; Louviere and Woodworth 1983; Kamakura and Russell 1989; Gensch 1985). Yet, despite widespread application and research interest, relatively little attention seems to have been paid to the role of the MNL scale parameter in cross-data set model comparisons. Among others, Ben-Akiva and Lerman (1985) show that the MNL model can be derived from random utility theory, assuming that the error component is IID Gumbel.

The Gumbel distribution is characterized by two parameters: a location parameter and a scale factor. The scale factor is known to be inversely related to the variance (Ben-Akiva and Lerman 1985, pp. 104–105) but cannot be identified in any particular model because of confounding with the vector of utility parameters. Hence, it is arbitrarily set to one when dealing with any given model. Consequently, the estimated parameters of two or more data sets to be compared are confounded with their respective scale factors; thus, scale factor differences (i.e., variance differences) must be isolated before comparing parameters. Such comparisons arise often in marketing research: for example, (1) tests of equality of parameters for a priori segments, (2) differences in experimental manipulations between different conditions, and (3) utilities estimated from different ranks in a ranking task using exploded logit.

In such situations MNL parameter comparisons require that the hypothesis that differences are the result of scale factor differences (i.e. variance differences) first be ruled out before testing whether observed differences are attributable to actual parameter differences. Although the scale factor cannot be identified in any particular set of empirical data, the ratio of the scale factor of one data set relative to another *can* be identified. Thus,

*Joffre Swait is Senior Associate, Decision Research, Mercer Management Consulting, Lexington, MA. Jordan Louviere is Professor of Marketing, Eccles School of Business, University of Utah, Salt Lake City. The authors gratefully acknowledge the financial assistance of the U.S. Forest Service, Urban Forestry Project, Chicago, IL, in the collection of certain data used as an illustration in this paper. They also thank the editor and three anonymous reviewers for their careful and detailed study of previous versions of this article.

Journal of Marketing Research
Vol. XXX (August 1993), 305–14

if two data sets are generated by a common choice process, but one set is "noisier" than the other, standard statistical tests (such as the well-known Chow test) may lead to the conclusion that the parameter vectors differ. It would be convenient to have a simple way to test whether the scales of two or more data sets are equal and, if not, whether parameters differ *after* accounting for differences in scale.

The purpose of this paper is to provide a simple, straightforward procedure for estimating scale factor ratios for pairs of data sets. One additional advantage of this procedure is that it makes use of commonly available maximum likelihood MNL estimation software and provides likelihood ratio tests of the hypotheses mentioned previously. In the remainder of this paper, we first demonstrate the problem by discussing the role of the scale factor in the MNL model and in cross-data set comparisons. We then present our proposed approach, illustrating its use with simulated and real data. Finally, we conclude by discussing our results and some of their implications.

THE ROLE OF THE SCALE PARAMETER

Define the utility of an alternative to be $U_{in} = V_{in} + e_{in}$, where V_{in} is the systematic (or explainable) portion of the utility function and e_{in} is an error term associated with joint random variation across both individuals and alternatives. As Ben-Akiva and Lerman (1985, pp. 104–105) note, if the e_{in} are independent and identically distributed Gumbel variates, the cumulative distribution function of an individual error term is

$$F(e_{in}) = \exp[-\exp(-\mu e_{in})],\ \mu > 0 \text{ a scalar.} \tag{1}$$

This cdf implies that $V(e_{in}) = \pi^2/6\mu^2$ (see Ben-Akiva and Lerman 1985, p. 104), and the probability that a randomly observed individual n chooses alternative i from choice set C_n is

$$P_{in} = \exp(\mu\beta X_{in}) \Big/ \sum_{j \in C_n} \exp(\mu\beta X_{jn}). \tag{2}$$

Expression (2) differs from most published versions of the MNL model in marketing by the addition of the imbedded scalar constant μ, which is the scale factor for a particular data set. Because μ cannot be identified, one must estimate the product $(\mu\beta)$ in a particular application. Ben-Akiva and Lerman (1985) show that as the variance approaches infinity, μ approaches zero, causing the MNL model to predict equal choice probabilities for all alternatives; conversely, as variance goes to zero, μ approaches infinity, causing the MNL model to predict deterministically to the alternative with the highest systematic utility.

The MNL model has the Independence of Irrelevant Alternatives (IIA) property, which is a consequence of the IID Gumbel assumption across both alternatives and individuals. Violations of IIA imply error heterogeneity resulting from omitted variable bias (see McFadden 1986, p. 281); hence, our approach assumes that the MNL model is the true model in the application of interest.

Horowitz (1980, 1981) and Jones and Landwehr (1988) suggest that the MNL model is relatively robust to scale factor differences between data sets, but more recently Morikawa (1989) suggests a far more serious problem arises when significant factors are inadvertently omitted, which is likely to occur often in practice. Recent evidence also suggests that it may be more critical to account for differences in scales than previously believed. For example, (1) Ben-Akiva and Morikawa (1990) found that accounting for scale differences between revealed and stated preference data led to superior model fits, once separate data sources were pooled and rescaled; (2) Ben-Akiva, Morikawa, and Shiroishi (1992) reported that the necessary assumptions for exploding ranking data and estimating MNL models from the exploded ranks pooled over subjects may not be satisfied in real data. And they further concluded that models estimated from different ranks could not be pooled, because both scale factors and parameters differed by rank level; (3) the latter result had been previously suggested by Hausman and Ruud (1987), who used exploded logit to show that the scale factors of ranked alternatives increased as rank increased; (4) Johnson, Louviere, and Olsen (1990) found that task effects on judgment and choice tasks could largely be accounted for by differences in scale factors, a conclusion which disagreed significantly with a more naive analysis using a nonscale-adjusted Chow test; and (5) finally, numerous examples exist of improvements in MNL choice models from appropriate a priori segmentation which accounts for variance heterogeneity and, therefore, scale differences (e.g., Currim 1982; Ben-Akiva and Lerman, 1985 pp. 194–204; Salomon and Ben-Akiva 1983; Swait, Kozel, Barros, and Ben-Akiva 1984; and Swait and Ben-Akiva 1986).

Thus, marketing practice can benefit from understanding the role of the scale parameter in MNL models and accounting for it in applications. Academic research may also benefit from such an understanding, because failure to account for scale differences may explain some previous findings in the literature (e.g., the Johnson, Louviere, and Olsen task effect result). In the next section, we present a simple method for estimating the ratio of scale parameters between pairs of data sets, together with a procedure for hypothesis testing.

EMPIRICAL ANALYSIS OF THE ROLE OF THE SCALE PARAMETER IN MNL MODELS AND A SIMPLE METHOD FOR ESTIMATING SCALE PARAMETER RATIOS

In this section we consider a situation in which two data sets contain the outcomes of an identical choice observed for two different samples. We present a simple method for estimating scale factors that also allows statistical testing of parameter and scale factor equality hypotheses, as previously qualified. We also illustrate the application of the estimation methods to examine parameter and scale factor differences with simulated and experimental data. In such a case it is of interest to know whether *observed parameter estimate differences* occur because (1) they are simply the result of sampling error, since the true underlying parameters and scale factors are the same in both populations (i.e., $\beta_1 = \beta_2$, $\mu_1 = \mu_2$); (2) the true underlying parameters are the same but the scale factors are different (i.e., $\beta_1 = \beta_2$, $\mu_1 \neq \mu_2$); (3) there are *real differences* in true parameters and scale factors (i.e., $\mu_1\beta_1 \neq \mu_2\beta_2$).

Because the scale factor and parameter vector are confounded in the MNL model, it is not possible to attribute real differences in parameters and/or scale factors (condition 3 above) to parameter vector inequality and scale equality (i.e., $\beta_1 \neq \beta_2$, $\mu_1 \neq \mu_2$) versus parameter vector inequality and scale inequality (i.e., $\beta_1 \neq \beta_2$, $\mu_1 \neq \mu_2$). However, it is possible to estimate variance differences under assumed parameter equality, and then test the assumption of parameter equality.

A Simple Method for Pairwise Point Estimation of MNL Scale Factors

Suppose we have two samples and wish to test whether they share the same population parameters, *assuming that the specification of both MNL models is identical*[1] (i.e., the independent variables are the same). We then wish to test the hypothesis

$$(3) \qquad H_1\colon \beta_1 = \beta_2 \text{ and } \mu_1 = \mu_2$$

where μ_1 and μ_2 are two scale factors, and β_1 and β_2 are corresponding parameter vectors. This hypothesis can be tested using a two-stage variant of the Chow test: (1) We test whether β_1 and β_2 are equal,

$$(4) \qquad H_{1A}\colon \beta_1 = \beta_2 = \beta,$$

while permitting the scale factors to differ between data sets. If H_{1A} is rejected, H_1 is also rejected. (2) If H_{1A} cannot be rejected, then test hypothesis

$$(5) \qquad H_{1B}\colon \mu_1 = \mu_2 = \mu.$$

Both subhypotheses can be tested using standard likelihood ratio statistics.

It is important to note that a standard Chow test comparing MNL parameter vectors across data sets ignores possible unequal variances. In this test we pool the two data sets and constrain the two parameter vectors to be equal. In effect, the hypothesis thus tested is $H_1^*\colon \beta_1 = \beta_2 = \beta$, with the *implied* constraint $\mu_1 = \mu_2 = \mu$ (since the actual joint parameter estimated is $\mu\beta$, involving the scale factor for the pooled data). This differs from the procedure we suggest, in that the two scale factors are *assumed* to be equal rather than estimated from the data. In addition, the usual comparison of models across data sets does not test hypothesis H_{1B}.

The sequential test of H_1 requires us to estimate μ_1, μ_2, and β under hypothesis H_{1A}. For the two-data set case, the FIML (Full Information Maximum Likelihood) estimates of these quantities is obtained by maximizing the following log likelihood function:

$$(6) \qquad L_\mu = \sum_n \sum_{a \in C_n} f_{an} \ln P_{an} = \sum_n \sum_{a \in C_n} f_{an} \ln \left(\frac{e^{\beta W_{an}}}{\sum_{j \in C_n} e^{\beta W_{jn}}} \right)$$

where f_{an} is the observed choice frequency for alternative a and individual n, and

$$(7) \qquad \begin{aligned} W_{an} &= \mu_1 X_{an} \quad \text{if } n \in S_1 \\ &= \mu_2 X_{an} \quad \text{if } n \in S_2 \end{aligned}$$

In the above expression, S_1 refers to individuals in sample 1, and S_2 to those in sample 2. If one defines the independent variables to directly incorporate the scale factors, the joint log likelihood function under H_{1A} is the usual MNL model but with a data matrix that is not constant; instead, the independent variables of each individual are multiplied by the scale factor of the respective sample. Thus, for a given set of scale factors, estimating β reduces to calculating the parameters of a standard MNL model. This simplification permits a relatively straightforward way to maximize L_μ.

Because both scale factors are not simultaneously identifiable in (6), it is convenient to normalize μ_1 to the value of 1. In this case, μ_2 becomes a *relative* scale parameter with respect to the normalization assumption. Then, under H_{1A}, the MNL model to be estimated has the following data matrix:

$$(8) \qquad W = \begin{bmatrix} X_1 \\ \mu_2 X_2 \end{bmatrix}$$

where X_1 and X_2 are the data matrices for samples 1 and 2, respectively. This corresponds exactly to the definition in (7) but rearranges the rows of the data matrix so that all individuals in sample 1 precede those in sample 2 in the joint data set. The parameter vector corresponding to W is β, as imposed by H_{1A}.

FIML estimation of the relative scale factor and parameter vector under H_{1A} can be accomplished with a specialized code, using optimization algorithms suited to this class of problems. The operational method we propose to maximize L_μ under H_{1A} is to literally graph the log likelihood function for the combined samples as a function of μ_2. As previously noted, given μ_2, estimating β reduces to estimating a MNL model. Because the log likelihood function for the linear-in-parameters MNL model is concave under weak regularity conditions (Ben-Akiva and Lerman 1985, p. 85), there is necessarily a

[1]Our procedure assumes that the MNL is the true model (i.e., IIA holds), and systematic sources of differences across decision-makers have been accounted for by the inclusion of the appropriate variables in the utility functions. If this assumption is false, our procedure is inappropriate because the true model will *not* be MNL. To test the appropriateness of the IIA assumption in a given data set, see McFadden (1987).

Figure 1
PROCEDURE FOR PAIRWISE SCALE FACTOR ESTIMATION AND HYPOTHESIS TESTING FOR MNL MODELS

Data Matrix	Procedure	Results
X_1 and X_2	1. Estimate separate parameter vectors by sample: β_1 and $(\mu_2\beta_2)$.	1) efficient estimates of β_1 and $(\mu_2\beta_2)$ 2) L_1 and L_2
Concatenate vertically X_1 and μ_2X_2, for a range of μ_2 values.	2. Impose H1A: $\beta_1=\beta_2=\beta$. Estimate β for each trial value of μ_2.	1) consistent estimates of β and μ_2. 2) L_μ
	3. Test H1A using λ_A.	If H1A is rejected, STOP; H1 is also rejected.
Concatenate vertically X_1 and X_2.	4. Impose H1A and H1B: $\mu_1=\mu_2=\mu$. Estimate an MNL model pooling both data sets.	1) efficient estimate of $(\mu\beta)$ 2) L_p
	5. Test H1B using λ_B.	If H1B is rejected, H1 is also rejected.

unique maximum for the log likelihood function using this manual process. Each point in the graph corresponds to the coordinate pair (trial scale value, MNL log likelihood value) for which the data matrix is created by the vertical concatenation of X_1 and μ_2X_2, as shown in (8), which enables one to utilize existing MNL estimation software to implement the procedure. The estimation procedure is as follows:

1. Define a range of values of μ_2 within which you expect the log likelihood function will be maximized. One way to define this range is to plot the parameter estimates from the separate data sets, draw a best-fitting straight line, and use its slope as the midpoint.
2. Implement a one-dimensional search (e.g., simply step through the range with a fixed increment or use a Golden Section search) to obtain an estimate of the relative scale factor of the second data set. At each trial value, define the data matrix as in (8) and estimate the corresponding MNL model using any standard MNL estimation package.
3. Because of the concavity of the log likelihood function (6), a graph of the log likelihood values versus the relative scale factor necessarily will have only one peak; the estimate of the scale factor is the value corresponding to the maximum likelihood value found in the range, and the estimate of β is the corresponding estimated parameter vector.

This procedure, summarized in Figure 1, is *not* a heuristic, despite its simplicity. It yields *consistent* estimators of μ_2 and β under H_{1A} (call these estimates $\bar{\mu}_2$ and β, respectively). To obtain efficient estimates, take one Berndt et al. (1974) step of the joint log likelihood function to obtain the FIML estimate.[2] Of course, the latter step necessitates special software, which is obviated by our procedure to make it accessible to a wider audience.

Our tedious, but straightforward way to estimate μ_2 involves a loss of statistical efficiency compared to the FIML estimator. In addition, our method does not estimate the joint covariance matrix of the scale factor and parameter vector. Consequently, the significance levels of the parameters will be overstated (since the covariance matrix does not account for sampling variation in

[2]It is well known in econometrics that an efficient estimate of a parameter can be obtained by taking one Newton-Raphson step from a consistent estimate of that parameter (e.g., Berndt et al. 1974; McFadden 1981, p. 242).

the scale factor), and a confidence interval for the scale factor is not directly available.

To test whether H_{1A} can be rejected, use the likelihood ratio test statistic

$$\lambda_A = -2[L_\mu - (L_1 + L_2)], \tag{9}$$

where L_μ is the log likelihood value corresponding to the point estimate $\overline{\mu_2}$, L_1 is the log likelihood value corresponding to a separate model for sample 1 and L_2 the corresponding value of a separate model for sample 2. This test statistic is asymptotically chi-squared distributed with $(K + 1)$ degrees of freedom. K is the number of parameters in each of β, β_1, and β_2, and the additional degree of freedom arises because we allow μ_1 to vary under the alternative hypothesis.

If H_{1A} cannot be rejected, we proceed to the second stage. Under H_{1B}, we have a MNL model in which the scale factors of the two data sets are assumed to be equal. Hence, the data matrix is simply the vertical concatenation of X_1 and X_2; again, one utilizes any MNL estimation program to obtain the FIML estimate of β. The test statistic under H_{1B} is

$$\lambda_B = -2[L_p - L_\mu]. \tag{10}$$

where L_p is the log likelihood value for the model under H_{1B}, and L_μ is as previously defined. This statistic is asymptotically chi-squared distributed, but with one degree of freedom as a result of the restriction on μ_2.

Only if both H_{1A} and H_{1B} are not rejected can hypothesis H_1 be retained at a given confidence level. And only if H_{1A} is not rejected can we interpret the estimated relative scale factor μ_2 as a measure of the hetero- or homogeneity of the error variances of the two samples (true for any estimation method). If H_{1A} is rejected, the estimated value is simply an average multiplier that optimally scales the data of sample 2 to offset the imposition of the β parameter equality assumption.

Our approach does not obtain the confidence interval of the scale factor directly, because the joint covariance matrix of the scale factor and the choice model parameters is not calculated. However, the estimation process gives one a good idea of the range over which the log likelihood function is relatively insensitive to the relative scale factor by simply inspecting the graph (see Section 3.2). Alternatively, Seber and Wild (1989, p. 196) provide an asymptotic method for calculating an approximate confidence region for the MLE $\hat{\gamma}$ of a parameter γ. Because the likelihood ratio statistic $\lambda = -2[L(\hat{\gamma}) - L(\gamma_0)]$ is asymptotically chi-squared distributed with r degrees of freedom (r-the number of restrictions imposed on the parameter vector), an approximate 100(1 − α)% confidence interval can be obtained by inverting the statistic to obtain the region given by $\{\gamma: -2[L(\hat{\gamma}) - L(\gamma)] \leq \chi^2_{r,\alpha}\}$, where $\chi^2_{r,\alpha}$ is the $(1 - \alpha)$ critical value from the chi-squared distribution with r d.f.s. Given the assumptions necessary for the asymptotic properties of MLE estimators to hold, a consistent estimator converges in distribution to the true estimate; hence, we can calculate an approximate confidence region for the consistent estimator $\overline{\mu_2}$. Seber and Wild's method identifies the end points of the confidence interval as those values of the relative scale factor at which the joint model (utility parameters equal, but scale factors differ) and the separate models (both utility parameters and scale factors vary) becomes significantly different at the desired level of α. In a graph like that shown in Figure 3, draw a horizontal line at $(L_1 + L_2) - \chi^2_{K+1,\alpha}/2$; the region between the points at which this horizontal line intersects the log likelihood curve is the approximate confidence region.

Our procedure estimates the scale factor of one data set with respect to another, for which we make the normalization assumption that its scale is one. Inverting the order of the data sets simply produces scale factor estimates that are the inverse of each other; hence, it is unimportant which data set is used as the base.

Omission of relevant variables from the utility function of a MNL model necessarily results in a heterogeneous error term. Such a misspecification may (and depending on the influence of the omitted variable, most probably will) erroneously lead to the conclusion of different parameter vectors and/or scale factors in the two data sets. Therefore, it is important that analysts specify the utility function as completely as possible, removing every identifiable source of systematic heterogeneity before applying the procedure.

If we turn our attention to expression (8), which defines the joint scaled data matrix W used for estimating the MNL model corresponding to a given scale factor value, it should be noted that the likelihood of rejecting the scaling hypothesis increases with the increasing dimensionality of W.[3] That is, the more variables to be scaled, the less likely that proportionality will hold between *all* variables across both data sets. However, this is an empirical, not a theoretical issue, which suggests that one might wish to investigate or hypothesize *which* data items will scale proportionately across data sets (see example in Section 3.4).

An Example of MNL Scale Factor Estimation Using Simulated Data

Consider a trinomial choice problem in which two variables, X and Y, define the utilities. Let the utility functions be given by

$$U_1 = \gamma_1 + \gamma_3 X_1 + \gamma_4 Y_1 + \epsilon_1 \tag{11a}$$

$$U_2 = \gamma_2 + \gamma_3 X_2 + \gamma_4 Y_2 + \epsilon_2 \tag{11b}$$

$$U_3 = \gamma_3 X_3 + \gamma_4 Y_3 + \epsilon_3 \tag{11c}$$

where γ is a parameter vector, X_i and Y_i are the values of the independent variables for alternative i, and the ϵ_i's

[3] We thank an anonymous reviewer for this insight.

are the corresponding error terms (assumed IID Gumbel).

Five data sets, each with 500 draws, were randomly generated. X's and Y's were independently drawn, from uniform distributions on [0,100] and [0,1000], respectively. The chosen alternative was the one with the highest utility value. Each data set represents a different assumption about the parameter estimates γ and the scale factors of the underlying Gumbel distributions, as noted below:

Data Set 1: $\gamma^1 = (1.0, 0.3, -0.03, 0.005)$, $\mu_1 = 1$

Data Set 2: $\gamma^2 = (1.0, 0.3, -0.03, 0.005)$, $\mu_2 = 1$

Data Set 3: $\gamma^3 = (1.0, 0.3, -0.03, 0.005)$, $\mu_3 = 2$

Data Set 4: $\gamma^4 = (2.0, 0.1, -0.04, 0.008)$, $\mu_4 = 1$

Data Set 5: $\gamma^5 = (2.0, 0.1, -0.04, 0.008)$, $\mu_5 = 2$

We considered the ability of the proposed method to detect parameter and scale factor differences by applying it in the four cases defined below; each case represents the combination of data set 1 (as the base) with another data set.

Scale Factors β Parameters	Equal	Different
Equal	**Case 1:** Data Sets 1 + 2	**Case 2:** Data Sets 1 + 3
Different	**Case 3:** Data Sets 1 + 4	**Case 4:** Data Sets 1 + 5

Table 1 contains the results of applying our proposed estimation and testing procedure to each case. In the first two cases the estimates of the scale factor of the second data set in the pair (denoted $\overline{\mu_2}$ in the table) are equal or very close to the true value. This is to be expected, because the underlying parameter vectors are the same in each pair of samples. In cases 3 and 4, however, estimates of the scale factors do not resemble the true values, which graphically illustrates that the relative scale factor estimated by this (or any other) procedure can be interpreted as a parameter of the underlying Gumbel distribution, only if hypothesis H_{1A} is not rejected. As expected, only Case 1 retains the hypothesis of parameter and scale parameter equality across both data sets at the 95% confidence level.

An Empirical Example of MNL Scale Factor Estimation Using Experimental Choice Data

Johnson, Louviere, and Olsen (1990) presented research findings about potential differences between judgment and choice tasks resulting from the effects of question order, attribute order, and practice trials. These task effects were manipulated according to a 2^4 full factorial between-subjects design, producing sixteen experimental conditions. A difficulty comparing results from different manipulations arises because judgments (ratings) and choices (discrete categorizations) are not directly comparable. Johnson, Louviere, and Olsen utilized a first-choice rule to predict the expected choices in each choice condition based on individual-level (conjoint) models estimated from the judgments (ratings), which produced a comparable metric (i.e., both results were choices; one observed, the other predicted). Johnson, Louviere, and Olsen wished to test whether statistically significant parameter differences existed between the judgment and choice tasks and used MNL regression analysis to test this hypothesis.

We use the data of Johnson, Louviere, and Olsen to illustrate how to use our procedure to test whether the underlying structural models describing choice and judgment are the same. That is, we wish to test whether the parameter vectors and scale parameter (i.e., error variances) are the same in the two tasks, given that a MNL model underlies both data sets. The choice data is used as the reference set.

First, we estimated separate 8-parameter MNL models for each data set, obtaining log likelihood values of -2079.0 ($=L_1$) for the choice data and -2235.6 ($=L_2$) for the judgment data. We then tested hypothesis H_{1A} by assuming the parameters are the same in both data sets but that scale factors differed: the value of the log likelihood of the 10-parameter joint model was -4351.6 ($=L_\mu$), corresponding to a relative scale factor estimate of 1.075. The chi-squared statistic for the H_{1A} hypothesis is $-2[-4351.6-(-2079.0 - 2235.6)] = 74.0$, with 9

Table 1

ESTIMATION AND TESTING RESULTS FOR SIMULATED DATA

Case	$\overline{\mu_2}$	L_1	L_2	L_μ	λ_A	*Reject* H_{1A}?[1]	L_p	λ_B	*Reject* H_{1B}?[2]
1	1.00	−318.25	−325.84	−644.67	1.16	No	−644.67	.00	No
2	2.05	−318.25	−178.38	−499.00	4.74	No	−522.58	47.16	Yes
3	1.75	−318.25	−210.76	−538.86	19.70	Yes	—	—	—
4	3.89	−318.25	−75.40	−431.36	75.42	Yes	—	—	—

1. Chi-squared statistic for 5 d.f. and 95% confidence level = 11.07.
2. Chi-squared statistic for 1 d.f. and 95% confidence level = 3.84.

Figure 2
TRAIL CHOICE VERSUS CONSIDERATION MNL COEFFICIENTS

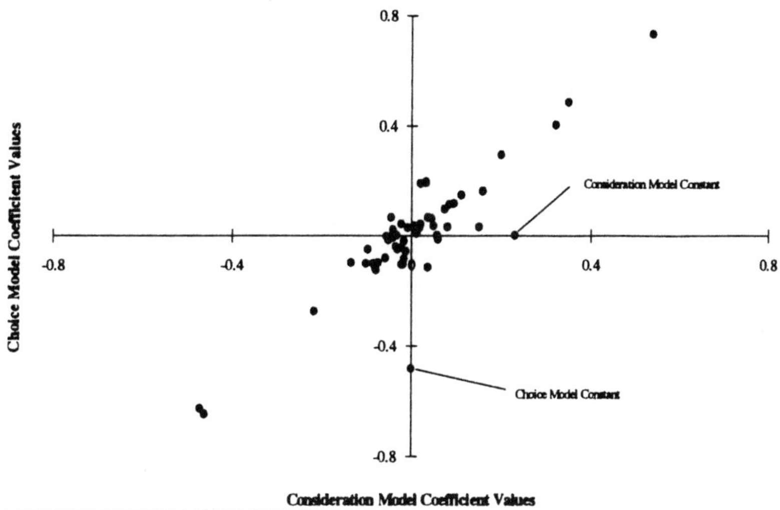

degrees of freedom, and the corresponding critical value of the chi-squared distribution at the 95% confidence level is 16.92; therefore, we roundly reject the hypothesis of parameter equality. The rejection means that our estimate for the relative scale factor (1.075) is not valid, since it was premised on the equality of the two parameter vectors. This result implies that the judgment and choice tasks have underlying models with different parameters, *assuming the MNL model is appropriate for the data*, which suggests that each task measured a different cognitive process. However, we should note that the difference may be the result of the process used to transform the judgments into a comparable choice metric.

An Example of MNL Scale Factor Estimation to Compare Choice and Consideration Tasks

Louviere, Anderson, and Louviere (1991) studied bicycle trail users' perceptions and trail choice behavior in Chicago. The study manipulated eighteen factors (e.g., trail length, surface type, presence of walkers) and observed trail choices in response to changes in these factors. Randomly selected respondents from Chicago were asked to perform the following two tasks (among others):

1. *Trail consideration*: For each of sixteen pairs of hypothetical trails (sampled from a $2^5 \times 4^9 \times 6^2 \times 8^2$ factorial design), respondents indicated whether one or both trails were considered to be an acceptable trail to use. Respondents were randomly assigned to four blocks of such trails.
2. *Trail choice*: For the same sixteen pairs, respondents were asked to indicate which one of the two trails, or streets and highways, they would choose to use, assuming that these were the only options available to them.

We now apply our procedure to test whether respondents view the consideration and choice tasks in a fundamentally different way.

As a first step, it is useful to graph the coefficients of the two MNL models against one another (Figure 2). This graph strongly suggests that both trail choice and consideration coefficients differ only by a multiplicative scalar, equal to the slope of a straight-line fit to the pairs of coefficient values. This straight line suggests that the scale parameters of the two sets may differ, but the model parameters may be equal. However, two parameters are farther from the straight line than other points: these are the intercepts or constants of the two models. Alternative-specific constants ensure that the aggregate shares of the alternatives are *exactly* replicated by MNL models. Therefore, not surprisingly, these two intercepts are not near the straight line. This suggests the following hypothesis: The trail choice and consideration tasks capture

Figure 3

TRAIL CHOICE AND CONSIDERATION MODEL JOINT LOG LIKELIHOOD AS A FUNCTION OF CONSIDERATION MODEL RELATIVE SCALE

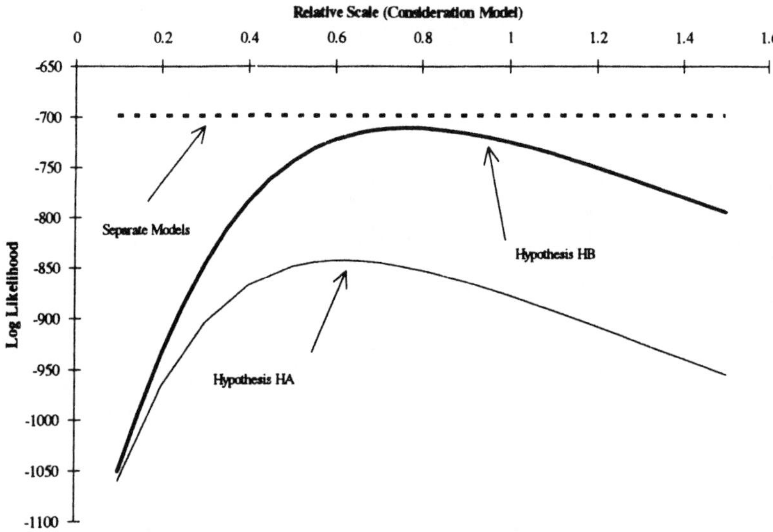

the *tradeoffs* between factors in an identical fashion, but the aggregate shares of alternatives should be allowed to differ, because the choice task permits the selection of a third alternative, streets and highways. Thus, we have two alternative scale hypotheses (H_A and H_B) that could be pursued with these data:

$$(12) \quad H_A: \begin{pmatrix} \theta_1 \\ \beta_1 \end{pmatrix} = \mu_2 \begin{pmatrix} \theta_2 \\ \beta_2 \end{pmatrix} \qquad H_B: \begin{pmatrix} \theta_1 \\ 0 \\ \beta_1 \end{pmatrix} = \mu_2 \begin{pmatrix} 0 \\ \theta_2 \\ \beta_2 \end{pmatrix}$$

θ_1 and θ_2 are constants, respectively, for the choice and consideration MNL models; β_1 and β_2 are corresponding parameter vectors; and μ_2 is the relative scale of the trail consideration model. Hypothesis H_A tests whether the scale factor applies to all parameters, whereas H_B excludes the effect of the scale factor from the constants.

Using the procedure in Figure 1, the joint log likelihood of the two data sets is graphed as a function of μ_2 in Figure 3, in which the trail choice data's scale parameter is normalized to one. The horizontal line represents the joint likelihood of the two models estimated separately (the alternate hypothesis for both H_A and H_B). Clearly, the joint model under H_B is superior to the joint model under H_A, because H_B is retained but H_A is strongly rejected, at the 95% confidence level. This suggests that both consideration and choice tasks measure the same tradeoffs between factor levels, but yield dissimilar aggregate shares (expected as a result of the different task forms). We obtain a consistent estimate of μ_2 under H_B of about 0.775; however, the theoretical interpretation of μ_2 as a parameter of an underlying error distribution may not hold under H_B.

CONCLUSIONS

Since the review process for this paper began, its ideas have been applied to a wide variety of problems involving comparisons between data sets representing different response tasks. In most cases, we found consistent evidence of cross-task validity after accounting for scale differences, which suggests that a very large proportion of differences in task effects may be the result of measurement reliability differences and not real cognitive processing differences. These comparisons have involved choice of college by U.S. high school students (Horowitz and Louviere 1990, 1993); choice of ski areas (Louviere 1992); choice of outdoor water recreation opportunities (Adamowicz, Louviere, and Williams 1992); choice of vacation destination (Louviere, Fox, and Moore

1992); and choice of toothpaste and supermarkets (Horowitz and Louviere 1992). The behavior of the scale factor and the estimation and testing procedure provided in this paper suggest ways to compare these disparate sets of data and test whether scale differences explain most of the task and outcome differences.

Our approach is practical for comparing a small number of data sets, but we need more efficient and practical procedures for comparing multiple data sets. For example, a general-purpose FIML estimation procedure would be a welcome academic and practical contribution. Finally, we might note that even if one rejects scale and parameter equality among the data sets being compared, our approach still provides a way to scale data to maximize the fit and improve parameter estimates for pooled data sets. Similarly, one of our examples (Section 3.4) illustrates the value of partial parameter vector rescaling: We allowed intercept parameters to vary apart from the proportionality restriction placed on remaining utility parameters. More work is needed to establish the statistical properties of this latter approach and to develop more efficient methods for estimating parameters subject to various scaling constraints, but the results and examples presented in this paper suggest that this is a potentially fruitful area for further research.

REFERENCES

Adamowicz, Wiktor, Jordan Louviere, and Michael Williams (1992), "Combining Revealed and Stated Preference Methods to Value Environmental Amenities," unpublished working paper, Department of Rural Economy, University of Alberta, Canada, (May).

Ben-Akiva, Moshe and Steve Lerman (1985), *Discrete Choice Analysis: Theory and Application to Travel Demand*. Cambridge, MA. MIT Press.

——— and Takayuki Morikawa (1990), "Estimation of Travel Demand Models From Multiple Data Sources," in *Transportation and Traffic Theory*, M. Koshi, ed. New York: Elsevier, pp. 461–76.

———, Takayuki Morikawa, and Fumiaki Shiroishi (1992), "Analysis of the Reliability of Preference Ranking Data," *Journal of Business Research*, 24 (2), 149–64.

Berndt, E., B. Hall, R. Hall and J. Hausman (1974), "Estimation and Inference in Nonlinear Structural Models," *Annals of Economic and Social Measurements*, 3, 653–65.

Currim, Imran (1982), "Predictive Testing of Consumer Choice Models Not Subject to the Independence of Irrelevant Alternatives," *Journal of Marketing Research*, 19 (May), 208–22.

Gensch, David (1985), "Empirically Testing a Disaggregate Choice Model for Segments," *Journal of Marketing Research*, 22 (November), 462–67.

Guadagni, Peter and John Little (1983), "A Logit Model of Brand Choice Calibrated on Scanner Data," *Marketing Science*, 2 (Summer), 203–38.

Hausman, Jerry and Paul Ruud (1987), "Specifying and Testing Econometric Models for Rank-Ordered Data," *Journal of Econometrics*, 34, 83–104.

Horowitz, Joel (1980), "Sources of Error and Uncertainty in Behavioral Travel Demand Models," in *New Horizons in Travel-Behavior Research*, P. Stopher, A. Meyburg, and W. Brog, eds. Lexington, MA: Lexington Books, pp. 543–58.

——— (1981), "Sampling, Specification and Data Errors in Probabilistic Discrete-Choice Models," in *Applied Discrete-Choice Modelling*, D. Hensher and L. Johnson, eds. New York: Wiley, pp. 417–35.

——— and Jordan Louviere (1990), "The External Validity of Choice Models Based on Laboratory Choice Experiments," in *Spatial Choices and Processes*, M. M. Fischer, P. Nijkamp, and Y. Y. Papageorgiou, eds. Amsterdam: Elsevier North Holland, pp. 247–63.

——— and Jordan Louviere (1992), "What Do Consideration Sets Really Measure?" unpublished working paper, Department of Marketing, Eccles School of Business, University of Utah, April.

——— and Jordan Louviere (1993), "Testing Predicted Choices Against Observations in Probabilistic Discrete Choice Models," *Marketing Science*, in press.

Johnson, Richard, Jordan Louviere, and Doug Olsen (1990), "Order and Practice Effects in Judgment and Choice Tasks," presented at the Annual Meeting of the Marketing Science Institute, Champagne-Urbana, IL.

Jones, J. Morgan and Jane Landwehr (1988), "Removing Heterogeneity Bias from Logit Model Estimation," *Marketing Science*, 7(1), 41–59.

Kamakura, Wagner and Gary Russell (1989), "A Probabilistic Choice Model for Market Segmentation and Elasticity Structure," *Journal of Marketing Research*, 26 (November), 379–90.

Louviere, Jordan (1992), "Cross-Validating Different Conjoint Methods: Maybe It's Just a Question of Differing Variances?" working Paper, Eccles School of Business, University of Utah.

——— and George Woodworth (1983), "Design and Analysis of Simulated Consumer Choice or Allocation Experiments: An Approach Based on Aggregate Data," *Journal of Marketing Research*, 20 (November), 350–67.

———, Don Anderson, and Cathy Louviere (1991), "Bike Trail Choice Among Chicago Area Trail Users: Final Report to the Urban Forestry Project," Department of Statistics, University of Wyoming.

———, Michael Fox, and William Moore (1992), "The Brand Constants Differ, but the Attribute Effects Are the Same: A Cross-Task Comparison of MNL Choice Models Estimated From Different Types of Stated Preference Data," unpublished working paper, Department of Marketing, Eccles School of Business, University of Utah, (April).

McFadden, Daniel (1981), "Econometric Models of Probabilistic Choice," in *Structural Analysis of Discrete Data With Econometric Applications*, C. Manski and D. McFadden, eds. Cambridge, MA: MIT Press, pp. 198–272.

——— (1986), "The Choice Theory Approach to Market Research," *Marketing Science*, 5(4), 275–97.

——— (1987), "Regression-Based Specification Tests for the Multinomial Logit Model," *Journal of Econometrics*, 34, 63–82.

Morikawa, Takayuki (1989), "Incorporating Stated Preference Data in Travel Demand Analysis," unpublished PhD dissertation, Department of Civil Engineering, MIT, Cambridge, MA.

Salomon, Ilan and Moshe Ben-Akiva (1983), "The Use of the Life-Style Concept in Travel Demand Models," *Environment and Planning A*, 15, 623–38.

Seber, George and Christopher Wild (1989), *Nonlinear Regression*. New York: Wiley.

Swait, Joffre and Moshe Ben-Akiva (1986), "Constraints on Individual Travel Behavior in a Brazilian City," *Transportation Research Record* 1085, 75–85.

———, Valerie Kozel, Raimundo Barros, and Moshe Ben-Akiva (1984), "A Model System of Individual Travel Behavior in a Brazilian City," *Transportation Policy and Decision-Making*, 2, 451–80.

[37]

ESTIMATION OF TRAVEL DEMAND MODELS FROM MULTIPLE DATA SOURCES

MOSHE BEN-AKIVA* AND TAKAYUKI MORIKAWA**
* Department of Civil Engineering, Massachusetts Institute of Technology, Cambridge, Massachusetts 02139, U.S.A.
** Department of Transportation Engineering, Kyoto University, Sakyo-ku, Kyoto, 606, Japan

ABSTRACT

The method developed in this paper combines multiple data sources in estimating travel demand models. Alternative data sources have different levels of accuracy and contain various types of biases. The aim is to exploit the relative advantages of the different data sources and obtain more reliable parameter estimates than those estimated from a single data source. The general framework of combining multiple data sources is presented, followed by its application to combining revealed preference (RP) and stated preference (SP) data to estimate discrete choice models. SP data have complementary characteristics to RP data and are widely used in marketing research. However, the use of SP data has often been rejected by transportation practitioners because of their unknown reliability. Combining RP and SP data uses information from SP data on trade-offs among attributes to help identify those parameters while correcting biases potentially contained in SP data. A case study is conducted using RP and SP data on intercity travel mode choice to demonstrate the usefulness and practicality of the method. It is shown that some model parameters are estimated successfully only by the combined estimation method. It is also confirmed that the SP data contain biases which are detected by contrasting SP and RP data.

INTRODUCTION

Estimation of travel demand models is usually based on a single data source. For example, discrete choice models are frequently estimated from disaggregate data obtained by a traveler survey. A single data source, however, may not have sufficient information to identify or accurately estimate all the model parameters. This paper presents a framework and estimation methods for using multiple data sources in estimating travel demand models. Dissimilar data sources have different types of biases and random error properties. Therefore, model estimation with multiple data sources requires explicit consideration of the different characteristics of those data sources.

The following two contexts will elucidate the idea of combining various data sources. Data from a questionnaire survey are the principal source of information on individual characteristics. But survey data have the following two major drawbacks:

i) High data collection costs and small budgets lead to small sample sizes and consequently large sampling errors; and
ii) Nonsampling errors such as nonresponse may result in biased statistics.

These drawbacks are generally not present in data obtained by passive data collection methods such as counts of passengers. These methods do not require an active participation of individual travelers and therefore only convey information on groups of individuals. Hence, this kind of data is called "aggregate data." For example, counts of passengers boarding and alighting from public transport vehicles give the numbers of passengers having a common origin or destination. The passengers are "grouped" with respect to origins or destinations. Therefore, these counts do not provide direct information on origin to destination flows and their estimation must rely on additional data sources such as an on-board survey which asks a respondent for the origin and the destination of the trip.

Published 1990 by Elsevier Science Publishing Co., Inc.
Transportation and Traffic Theory
M. Koshi, Editor

Another complementary pair of data sources consists of data on actual behavior, or revealed preferences (RP), and data of expressed preferences to hypothetical scenarios, or stated preferences (SP). Although RP data are supposed to have high face validity, they often do not convey enough information on the choice set considered and trade-offs among attributes due to multicollinearity and lack of variability. SP data could provide purer information on those issues because the experimenter can specify hypothetical choice contexts. However, the responses are highly subjective and might not be fully consistent with actual behavior. Thus, combing RP and SP could exploit the advantages of each data source if the potential inconsistencies between RP and SP data are properly corrected.

Model estimation with multiple sources of data is known as "mixed estimation" in econometrics (Judge et al. [1]). In transportation research, data from different sources have been combined in a statistical estimation of origin-destination (O-D) trip tables using least squares methods (e.g., Hendrickson and McNeil [2]) and maximum likelihood estimation (e.g., Ben-Akiva, Macke, and Hsu [3] and Ben-Akiva and Morikawa [4]). The idea of using multiple data sources has also been applied to the estimation of discrete choice models from disaggregate and aggregate data (Gonzalez [5] and Yai et al. [6]).

Ben-Akiva [7] presented a general framework for statistical estimators which combine data from multiple sources. This framework is the basis of Ben-Akiva and Morikawa's [4] data fusion method which combines two or more complementary data sources into a single data base.

The same framework also serves as the basis for this paper in which the focus is on the estimation of discrete choice models from multiple sources of data. The estimation method developed here is designed to exploit the advantages of SP data and to overcome their limitations. It combines SP data with traditional aggregate and/or disaggregate RP travel demand data.

The key features of the combined estimation methods are:

i) Bias correction: explicit response models for SP data that include both preference and bias parameters;
ii) Efficiency: joint estimation of preference parameters from all the available data; and
iii) Identification: estimation of tradeoffs among attributes that are not identifiable from RP data.

The paper first presents a general framework for the combined estimators and then develops estimators of discrete choice models using RP and SP data. Then, an empirical case study is presented to demonstrate the usefulness of the combined estimator.

COMBINED ESTIMATION FROM MULTIPLE DATA SOURCES

General Framework

Data and models are used to make inferences about characteristics of a population. In survey expansion, descriptive data analysis and forecasting, the population characteristics of interest appear as percentages of certain subgroups of a population (e.g., the percent of commuters residing in a specific zone and using public transport) or sizes of population segments (e.g., the number of trips from an origin to a destination and the number of car-owning households in a zone). These unknown population characteristics are estimated directly from the data or are predicted by a parametric model which is a function of explanatory variables and a few unknown parameters. In the former case, the unknown parameters are the characteristics of the population themselves. In estimating an O-D table with ten traffic zones, for example, a *non-modeling* approach must estimate $10 \times 10 = 100$ parameters (or cell entries), while a *modeling* approach based, for instance, on a gravity model would estimate only a small number, say 5 - 12, of model parameters. A modeling approach is usually adopted when the analysis aims to develop a model to infer the underlying behavior and apply it for forecasting. If the number of unknown parameters is prohibitively large, the use of a model in a descriptive data analysis could also be beneficial.

Principal unknown parameters For a descriptive analysis, we usually employ a non-modeling approach. In that case the principal unknown parameters are the sizes (or percentages) of population segments (or subgroups), which are denoted by T_k, where $k=1,...,K$ represents the population segments. In a modeling approach we would express these parameters as functions using an underlying model, i.e., $T_k=f(\beta, \mathbf{x}_k)$, $k=1,...,K$, where β is a vector of "deep" model parameters whose length is significantly less than K and $\mathbf{x}_k$ is a vector of known characteristics of segment k. Then, in a modeling approach T is replaced by β which is the vector of principal unknown parameters.

Primary data *Primary data* provide direct information on the principal unknown parameters. For behavioral models of individuals, a disaggregate survey is the primary data source. In combining RP and SP data to estimate discrete choice models, RP data serve as the primary data because the purpose of the model is to describe actual behavior of travelers. In a non-modeling approach, measurements from a survey sometimes provide direct observations of the principal unknown parameters, and, therefore, those data are called *direct measurements*. For instance, the percentage of commuters residing in a given area who use a specific travel mode can be directly estimated from a population-based questionnaire survey.

Secondary data *Secondary data* provide indirect information on the principal unknown parameters. In a modeling approach, aggregate and SP data provide secondary data sources. In a non-modeling approach, secondary data provide *indirect measurements* of the principal unknown parameters usually in the form of observations of population characteristics which depend on two or more of the principal unknown parameters. Typically, these measurements represent aggregations of population segments. For instance, if the primary parameters are cell entries of an O-D table, then traffic generation and attraction (i.e., row sums and column sums, respectively) are indirect measurements. Indirect measurements may be obtained from sources such as traffic counts and official census data.

Measurement bias Some measurement techniques are often subject to biases. For example, survey data are subject to various biases (such as nonresponse bias) originating from diverse systematic nonsampling errors which depend among other things on survey administration procedures. SP data may contain significant response biases if the decision making protocols employed by respondents are different from those governing their actual behavior. This issue will be discussed in more detail in the next subsection.

As discussed above, one of the key features of the combined estimation method is bias correction. The structure of biases potentially contained in each data source should be modeled using mathematical measurement models which contain unknown bias parameters. For instance, SP bias may be captured by introducing for the SP data an additional alternative specific constant in the utility function of a discrete choice model.

Random measurement errors Direct measurements from disaggregate data are usually less accurate than indirect measurements from aggregate data due to the different sample sizes. These differences in randomness will be reflected in the parameters of the probability distribution function which expresses the random nature of the data. The random nature of the data justifies the probabilistic approach to estimate unknown parameters. In other words, data are viewed as realization from an underlying probabilistic model. Discrete choice models, for instance, are expressed by "choice probabilities" of discrete alternatives and, therefore, the "likelihood" of observed choices can be specified using the underlying discrete choice model. In a non-modeling approach, the primary unknown parameters represent mean values of probabilistic data generating processes and the "likelihood" of observing direct and indirect measurements may be constructed.

In short, each data source is associated with a likelihood function which reflects the underlying random nature of the phenomena of interest and the different levels of randomness among data sources are captured by additional unknown parameters which are embedded in the likelihood function.

Estimation method The problem of combining different data sources may now be stated as the task of estimating the principal unknown parameters and bias and randomness parameters of each data source. The joint likelihood function can be constructed by simply multiplying the likelihood functions from all the available data sources if they can be assumed to be statistically independent. Maximum likelihood estimators (MLE), which have most desirable statistical properties such as consistency, asymptotic normality and asymptotic efficiency, are obtained by maximizing the logarithm of the joint likelihood function.

Combining Revealed and Stated Preference Data

Characteristics of RP and SP data SP data are respondent's expressed preferences to hypothetical situations while RP data are based on actual choices made in observable situations. For model estimation, an SP survey has the following advantages:

i) it can be used to estimate preferences for non-existing travel alternatives;
ii) multicollinearity among attributes can be avoided; and
iii) attributes that are not easily quantified, such as safety, reliability, and comfort, can be incorporated.

Despite these advantages, SP data have not been widely used in model estimation due to the uncertain reliability of the elicited information under hypothetical scenarios. The reliability of SP data has two different aspects: "validity" and "stability." Lack of validity implies a discrepancy between stated and actual behavior and it corresponds to a bias in a statistical sense. It may occur if the decision making protocol exercised in a hypothetical situation differs from that exercised in a real choice context. Decision protocols for stating preferences about hypothetical scenarios can be observed in the following contexts:

i) the respondent considers only the most important attribute of the alternatives (this is called the "prominence hypothesis");
ii) the response is influenced by an "inertia" of the current actual choice (e.g., justification of the current choice);
iii) the respondent uses the questionnaire as an opinion statement for his or her own benefit (e.g., overstating usage of a new transportation system to promote its construction);
iv) the respondent does not consider situational constraints (e.g., car availability and bad weather); and
v) the respondent misinterprets or ignores an attribute if the attribute value lacks reality.

Lack of stability relates to the magnitude of random error or noise in SP data. Namely, the stability of SP data depends on the quality of the questionnaire or the settings of the experiment. The response format such as "rating," "ranking," or "matching" in SP experiments also affects the reliability of the elicited preferences (For a more detailed discussion of these issues, see Ben-Akiva et al. [8].)

Specification of RP and SP models The main purpose of demand models is to predict future demand, especially in conjunction with major changes in service levels (or attributes) or introduction of an entirely new service. In transportation demand analysis, for example, these contexts include fare increases, schedule changes, and introduction of a new transportation service. While one can easily set up hypothetical scenarios that are similar to the future situations and ask for preference statements about them, the validity of SP data is questionable. Specifically, SP data may be biased and their accuracy may differ significantly from that of RP data. These issues are addressed by combining RP and SP data and using a combined estimator of the type described below.

Suppose that the trade-offs among certain attributes cannot be estimated accurately from the available RP data. For instance, high correlation between travel cost and travel time in RP data may yield insignificant parameter estimates for their coefficients. However, a SP surveys with a design based on low or zero correlation between these attributes may provide additional information on their trade-offs. Although the SP responses may not be valid for forecasting actual behavior due to their unknown bias and error properties, they often contains useful information on trade-offs among attributes. This premise is illustrated by the following model specification.

Assume two different data generating processes: The RP model represents actual behavior, while the SP responses are modeled by the SP model. In other words, the RP and SP models generate the primary data and the secondary data, respectively.

For the sake of this exposition, consider a choice between two alternatives. Let $\mathbf{x}$ and $\mathbf{w}$ denote vectors of explanatory variables (e.g., decision maker characteristics and alternative attributes) in terms of the differences between the two alternatives. $\mathbf{z}$ is a vector of factors that affect SP responses but not actual choice behavior (also measured in terms of differences between the two alternatives).

The purpose of the analysis is to estimate the following binary choice model:

The RP model for the primary data

- structural equation (utility function):

$$U^{RP} = \beta' \mathbf{x}^{RP} + \alpha' \mathbf{w}^{RP} + \varepsilon \tag{1}$$

- measurement equation (choice indicator):

$$d^{RP} = \begin{cases} 1\text{: if } U^{RP} \geq 0 \\ -1\text{: otherwise} \end{cases} \tag{2}$$

where U is a latent variable, α and β are vectors of principal unknown parameters, and ε is an unobserved random variable.

Suppose that the SP data are obtained from binary choice experiments whose outcome is represented by the following model:

The SP model for the secondary data

- structural equation (utility function):

$$U^{SP} = \beta' \mathbf{x}^{SP} + \gamma' \mathbf{z}^{SP} + \nu \tag{3}$$

- measurement equation (preference indicator, e.g., choice):

$$d^{SP} = \begin{cases} 1\text{: if } U^{SP} \geq 0 \\ -1\text{: otherwise} \end{cases} \tag{4}$$

where γ is a vector of unknown parameters and ν is an unobserved random variable.

In the above equations, superscripts "RP" and "SP" denote the corresponding data. Bias factors inherent to stated preferences are represented by the vector of variables **z** with its corresponding coefficient vector γ. For example, a variable representing the actual choice, if such information is available, included in **z** may capture the effect of justification bias. The sharing of β by both models implies that trade-offs among attributes included in the vector **x** are the same in both actual behavior and the SP tasks. The random components of the utility functions, ε and ν, are assumed to be independently distributed with zero means and the levels of noise in the two data sources are represented by the variances of the disturbance terms, ε and ν. If RP and SP data have different levels of randomness, this can be expressed by:

$$Var(\varepsilon) = \mu^2 Var(\nu) \tag{5}$$

where μ is an unknown parameter.

If SP data contain more random noise than RP data, μ will lie between 0 and 1. μ is also known to represent the "scale" of the model coefficients. The scale of the model is set by arbitrarily fixing the variance of the random utility term in order to identify the coefficients of a discrete choice model. For instance, assuming that ε and ν are normally distributed, the scale of the probit RP model is set to one (i.e., $Var(\varepsilon) = 1$), and the RP and SP models are:

$$P(d^{RP}=1) = \Phi\left(\beta' \mathbf{x}^{RP} + \alpha' \mathbf{w}^{RP}\right), \tag{6}$$

and,

$$P(d^{SP}=1) = \Phi\left(\mu\left(\beta' \mathbf{x}^{SP} + \gamma' \mathbf{z}^{SP}\right)\right). \tag{7}$$

where $\Phi(\ )$ denotes the standard cumulative normal distribution.

Estimation Methods

The principal motivation for combined estimation is the possible gain in the accuracy of parameter estimates by sharing some parameters (i.e., β) between the RP and SP models. It is feasible because the bias and random error specific to SP data are captured by γ and μ, respectively. All of these parameters α, β, γ and μ are estimated either by i) joint MLE, using RP and SP data simultaneously, or ii) sequential MLE, using RP and SP data one after the other.

Joint estimation method The joint estimator of α, β, γ and μ is obtained by maximizing the joint log-likelihood:

$$L(\alpha,\beta,\gamma,\mu) = \sum_{n=1}^{N^{RP}} \log\left[F\left(d_n^{RP}(\beta'\mathbf{x}_n^{RP}+\alpha'\mathbf{w}_n^{RP})\right)\right] + \sum_{n=1}^{N^{SP}} \log\left[F\left(d_n^{SP}\mu(\beta'\mathbf{x}_n^{SP}+\gamma'\mathbf{z}_n^{SP})\right)\right], \tag{8}$$

where N^{RP} and N^{SP} are the numbers of observations of RP and SP data sets, respectively, and F( ) is a cumulative distribution function of the random utility component such as

$$F(\beta'\mathbf{x}_n^{RP}+\alpha'\mathbf{w}_n^{RP}) = \Phi\left(\beta'\mathbf{x}_n^{RP}+\alpha'\mathbf{w}_n^{RP}\right), \tag{9}$$

for a binary probit model.

If one can assume statistical independence of ε and v, or equivalently:

$$\mathrm{Prob}(d^{RP},d^{SP}) = \mathrm{Prob}(d^{RP})\,\mathrm{Prob}(d^{SP}), \tag{10}$$

then joint estimation yields consistent and asymptotically efficient and normal estimators. If this assumption does not hold, the joint estimators are still consistent and asymptotically normal but not fully efficient (see Amemiya [9]). In this case, a variance-covariance matrix of the ML estimates calculated as the inverse of the information matrix will be biased downwards.

The joint estimation requires using a general MLE program and programming the joint likelihood function for the model (as opposed to model specific MLE programs, e.g., for multinomial logit).

Sequential estimation method An alternative estimation method is to estimate the RP and SP models sequentially. The advantage of this method is that one can use ordinary logit or probit estimation software. The sequential estimators are consistent but not efficient.

Step 1:

Estimate the SP model (3) from SP data to obtain $\widehat{\mu\beta}$ and $\widehat{\mu\gamma}$. Define $V^{RP}=\mu\beta'\mathbf{x}^{RP}$ and form the fitted value $\widehat{V}^{RP}=\widehat{\mu\beta}'\mathbf{x}^{RP}$.

Step 2:

Estimate the following RP model with the fitted value $\widehat{V}^{RP}$ included as a variable to obtain $\hat{\lambda}$ and $\hat{\alpha}$:

$$U^{RP} = \lambda\widehat{V} + \alpha'\mathbf{w}^{RP} + \varepsilon\,. \tag{11}$$

where $\lambda=1/\mu$.

Calculate $\hat{\mu}=1/\hat{\lambda}$, $\hat{\beta}=\widehat{\mu\beta}/\hat{\mu}$, and $\hat{\gamma}=\widehat{\mu\gamma}/\hat{\mu}$.

The accuracy of $\hat{\alpha}$, $\hat{\beta}$ and $\hat{\gamma}$ can be improved by the following additional step.

Step 3:

Multiply $\mathbf{x}^{SP}$ and $\mathbf{z}^{SP}$ by $\hat{\mu}$ to obtain a modified SP data set. Pool the RP data and the modified SP data and then estimate the two models jointly to obtain $\hat{\hat{\alpha}}$, $\hat{\hat{\beta}}$ and $\hat{\hat{\gamma}}$.

EMPIRICAL CASE STUDY

The combined estimation methods are applied to the estimation of a model of the choice of mode by intercity travelers.

Description of the Survey Data

The survey was conducted during 1987 by the Hague Consulting Group for the Netherlands Railways to assess factors which influence the choice between rail and car for intercity travel. The following description of the survey data is based on a report by Bradley et al. [10].

The City of Nijmegen, in the eastern part of the Netherlands near the border with West Germany, was selected as the data collection site. This city has rail connections with the major cities in the western metropolitan area called the Randstad which contains Amsterdam, Rotterdam and The Hague. Traveling from Nijmegen to the Randstad takes approximately two hours by both rail and car. The sample consisted of residents of Nijmegen who:

- made a trip in the previous three months to Amsterdam, Rotterdam or The Hague;
- did not use a yearly rail pass, or other type of pass which would eliminate the marginal cost of a rail trip;
- had the possibility of using a car (i.e., possessed a driver's license and had a car available in the household); and
- had the possibility of using rail (i.e., did not have very heavy baggage, were not handicapped, and did not need to visit multiple destinations).

Qualifying residents of Nijmegen were identified in a random telephone survey and requested to participate in a home interview. 235 interviews were conducted out of the 365 people who were reached by telephone and satisfied the above criteria.

The home interview survey consisted of three parts:

i) the characteristics of an intercity trip to the Randstad made within the previous three months (RP data);
ii) SP experiment of a choice between rail and car (SP1 data); and
iii) SP experiment of a choice between two different rail services (SP2 data).

The home interview survey was administered using lap-top micro-computers and the respondents replied to the questions appearing on the computer screen . The main advantage of a computer administered survey is that a desirable SP experimental design can be generated on site based on the service levels of the actual trip.

The RP data have 235 observations each including the following items:

- mode used (rail or car)
- trip purpose
- cost (for both chosen and unchosen modes)
- line-haul travel time (in-vehicle travel time and transferring time; for both chosen and unchosen modes)
- terminal travel time (access, egress and waiting time; for both chosen and unchosen modes)
- number of transfers for rail mode
- subjective ratings of latent travel characteristics (e.g., relaxation, reliability) (for both chosen and unchosen modes)
- socioeconomic characteristics of the respondents (e.g., age, sex)

The SP experiments were framed in the context of the actual trip observed in the RP data and used the full-profile pairwise comparison method. The respondent was shown two hypothetical alternatives (rail versus car in experiment 1, and two different rail services in experiment 2) at a time, each of which was described by the following four attributes: travel cost, travel time, number of transfers (only for rail), and comfort level (only for rail). Then, the respondent was asked which mode would be chosen *for the particular intercity trip reported in the RP question* in terms of a five point rating scale: 1) definitely choose alternative 1; 2) probably choose alternative 1; 3) not sure; 4) probably choose alternative 2; and 5) definitely choose alternative 2. Each respondent was presented with several pairs at each experiment. Since the main concern of the survey was the mode switching behavior from car to rail or vice-versa, the attribute levels were set so that rail became more attractive and/or car became less attractive to the car users (those who actually used a car for the intercity trip) and set in the opposite direction for the rail users. The order of alternatives presentation to the respondent was randomized so as to minimize the potential response bias. SP1 data (rail vs. car) include 1,628 comparisons (an average of 7 comparisons per respondent), while SP2 data (rail vs. rail) contain 2,965 comparisons (an average of 12-13 comparisons per respondent).

Estimation with RP Data

The home interview first asked about a recent intercity trip from Nijmegen to the Randstad. The respondents were requested to report the characteristics of that trip and those of a trip to the same destination but with the other mode. So, the attribute values of both modes were provided by the respondents rather than calculated from network data.

Binary probit models were estimated from this RP data. The dependent variable takes the value of one if rail was chosen and zero if car was chosen. Accordingly, all the explanatory variables are in terms of differences between rail and car, more specifically, the values for rail minus the values for car. The model includes the following variables:

- a constant;
- travel cost per person by rail less travel cost by car (Guilders);
- line-haul travel time by rail less line-haul travel time by car (minutes);
- terminal time by rail less terminal time by car (the time required for searching parking place) (minutes);
- number of transfers by rail; and
- non-work trip dummy = 1 if the trip is not business related, 0 otherwise.

The estimation results are shown in TABLE I. The line-haul travel time has the wrong sign although it is not significant. The rail specific constant has a large positive value, which might have been affected by the sampling strategy. Specifically, if the sample for the home interview was not drawn randomly but intentionally included more rail users, the parameter of the rail specific constant will be overestimated.

TABLE I. Estimation results of RP model

Variable	Coefficient estimate	Standard error	t-statistic
Rail constant	1.74	0.318	5.47
Cost per person	-0.0257	0.00585	-4.39
Line-haul time	0.000548	0.00347	0.16
Terminal time	-0.0263	0.00595	-4.42
Number of transfers	-0.344	0.133	-2.59
Non-work trip dummy	-0.900	0.227	-3.97
$L(0) = -162.84$ $L(\hat{\beta}) = -114.84$	$\rho^2 = 0.295$	$\bar{\rho}^2 = 0.258$	$N = 235$

Estimation with SP Data

MLE for ordered categorical dependent variable As mentioned earlier, two types of SP data were collected from each respondent: SP1 data are for choice between rail and car, while SP2 data are for choice between two rail alternatives. Since the choice indicator, or dependent variable, denoted as d is a five point preference rating, an ordinary binary discrete choice model is inappropriate. The probit model with the ordered categorical dependent variable or the *ordered probit model* may be used for this type of ordered categorical dependent variable.

Since the variable d in this case study is symmetrical with respect to category 3, it is reasonable to allow for only two threshold parameters θ_1 and θ_2 in the utility scale and construct symmetrical threshold values around zero as described below:

$$P(d=1) = P(\theta_2 \le U) = 1 - \Phi(\theta_2 - \beta'\mathbf{x}), \tag{12}$$

$$P(d=2) = P(\theta_1 \le U < \theta_2) = \Phi(\theta_2 - \beta'\mathbf{x}) - \Phi(\theta_1 - \beta'\mathbf{x}), \tag{13}$$

$$P(d=3) = P(-\theta_1 \le U < \theta_1) = \Phi(\theta_1 - \beta'\mathbf{x}) - \Phi(-\theta_1 - \beta'\mathbf{x}), \tag{14}$$

$$P(d=4) = P(-\theta_2 \le U < -\theta_1) = \Phi(-\theta_1-\beta'\mathbf{x}) - \Phi(-\theta_2-\beta'\mathbf{x}) \,, \tag{15}$$

$$P(d=5) = P(U<-\theta_2) = \Phi(-\theta_2-\beta'\mathbf{x}) \,. \tag{16}$$

where $U=\beta'\mathbf{x}+\nu$ and $\nu \sim N(0,1)$. MLE is used to jointly estimate the vector β and the θ's.

Estimation with SP1 data The SP experiment 1 was designed to collect information on mode switching behavior (from rail to car, or vice-versa) by presenting to the respondents hypothetical rail and car modes which are described by line-haul travel time and travel cost. However, since the respondent was instructed to refer to the trip reported in the RP questions, he or she may have considered additional attributes such as terminal time and the number of transfers that would have been required for the trip in evaluating the hypothetical alternatives. These additional attributes have the same values as reported in the RP questions. Thus, the model estimated from SP1 data includes these additional trip attribute variables which do not vary in the SP experiment.

There may also be a bias in the stated preferences toward the mode actually used, reflecting the inertia effect, justification of past behavior, or omitted attributes that are not captured by the included variables. This bias can be estimated by including a dummy variable which indicates the actual choice.

Accordingly, the estimated model has the following explanatory variables:

- a constant;
- travel cost by rail less travel cost per person by car (Guilders), as specified in the SP experiment;
- line-haul travel time by rail less line-haul travel time by car (minutes), as specified in the SP experiment;
- terminal time by rail less terminal time by car (minutes);
- number of transfers by rail;
- non-work trip dummy = 1 if the trip is not business related, 0 otherwise; and
- inertia dummy = 1 if rail was actually used, 0 if car was actually used.

The estimated coefficients of these variables and threshold parameters, θ_{11} and θ_{12}, are shown in TABLE II. The coefficients of all the variables are estimated with the expected signs. The rail specific constant is now negative but the coefficient of the inertia dummy is large enough to cancel it out. This implies that the intercept is negative for car users and positive for rail users, which may indicate the inertia effect of the actual choice in the SP experiment. The parameter of the non-work trip dummy is not significant, which implies that in the SP context the respondent did not consider the factors associated with the purpose of the trip. This can be interpreted as evidence of the proposition that SP methods can extract pure information on the trade-offs among presented attributes because the respondents do not take into consideration the various situational constraints that affect actual choices. The monetary value of line-haul travel time is 0.45 Guilders/min. or \$13/hour. The threshold parameters are accurately estimated.

TABLE II. Estimation results of SP1 model

Variable	Coefficient estimate	Standard error	t-statistic
Rail constant	-0.966	0.122	-7.91
Cost per person	-0.00719	0.00136	-5.29
Line-haul time	-0.00324	0.00119	-2.72
Terminal time	-0.00661	0.00206	-3.22
Number of transfers	-0.0528	0.0322	-1.64
Non-work trip dummy	-0.0250	0.0775	-0.32
Inertia dummy	1.49	0.0222	21.5
θ_{11}	0.0805	0.00959	8.40
θ_{12}	0.478	0.0222	21.5

$L(0) = -2620.16$ $L(\hat{\beta}) = -1645.91$ $\rho^2 = 0.372$ $\bar{\rho}^2 = 0.369$ $N = 1628$

TABLE III. Estimation results of SP2 model

Variable	Coefficient estimate	Standard error	t-statistic
Cost per person	-0.0807	0.00318	-25.3
Line-haul time	-0.0159	0.00136	-11.7
Number of transfers	-0.156	0.0319	-4.91
Comfort	0.500	0.0337	14.8
θ_{21}	0.0180	0.00298	6.04
θ_{22}	0.277	0.0106	26.1
L(0) = -4771.98 $L(\hat{\beta})$ = -3266.96	$\rho^2 = 0.315$	$\bar{\rho}^2 = 0.314$	$N = 2965$

Estimation with SP2 data The SP experiment 2 presented to the respondent two different rail services and asked for preferences in terms of a five point rating scale. Each rail service was described by line-haul travel time, travel cost, number of transfers, and ride comfort. Ride comfort is actually a package of different aspects such as seating room and availability, quietness, smoothness of ride, heating/ventilation, and minibar service, but it is presented at only three levels and therefore coded as 2 for better level, 1 for the current level and 0 for worse level. Additional attributes from the RP data such as terminal time are not included in this model because the alternatives are both rail trips and these attributes are equal for the two rail alternatives. For the same reason, a mode specific constant is also not included in this model. Consequently, this model only includes the four explanatory variables specified in the SP2 experiment as listed below:

- fare (Guilders);
- line-haul travel time (minutes);
- number of transfers; and
- ride comfort level.

The coefficients of these variables are jointly estimated with the threshold parameters. θ_{21} and θ_{22}, using the MLE of the ordered probit model. As shown in TABLE III, all the coefficients and the threshold parameters are estimated with very small standard errors. The calculated value of line-haul travel time is 0.2 Guilders/min. or \$6/hour, which seems reasonable.

Combined Estimation with RP and SP Data

Estimation with RP and SP1 data Following the framework presented earlier, the RP and SP models are specified as follows:

Specification of the RP model:

$$U^{RP} = \beta' \mathbf{x}^{RP} + \varepsilon \ , \tag{17}$$

Specification of the SP1 model:

$$U^{SP1} = \beta' \mathbf{x}^{SP1} + \gamma_1' \mathbf{z}^{SP1} + \nu \ , \tag{18}$$

Relationship of the random terms:

$$\mathrm{Var}(\varepsilon) = \mu_1^2 \mathrm{Var}(\nu) \ , \tag{19}$$

where $\mathbf{x}^{RP}$ is the vector of the variables included in the RP model presented earlier, $\mathbf{x}^{SP1}$ contains a subset of $\mathbf{x}^{RP}$ which is included in the SP model, $\mathbf{z}^{SP1}$ is a vector of SP specific variables, β and γ_1 are vectors of coefficients, ε and ν are normally distributed random terms, and μ_1 is a parameter that represents the relative scale of the two models. The vector $\mathbf{z}^{SP1}$ includes the following variables:

- a rail specific constant;

TABLE IV. Estimation results with RP and SP1 data

Variable	Coefficient estimate	Standard error	t-statistic
Rail constant (RP)	1.61	0.292	5.50
Rail constant (SP)	-2.96	0.860	-3.44
Cost per person	-0.0240	0.00486	-4.94
Line-haul time	-0.00463	0.00241	-1.92
Terminal time	-0.0250	0.00534	-4.68
Number of transfers	-0.245	0.0895	-2.73
Non-work trip dummy (RP)	-0.900	0.216	-4.18
Non-work trip dummy (SP)	-0.129	0.263	-0.49
Inertia dummy (SP)	4.84	1.16	4.16
θ_{11}	0.0803	0.00953	8.42
θ_{12}	0.476	0.0219	21.7
μ_1	0.294	0.0689	4.27
$L(0) = -2783.00$ $L(\hat{\beta}) = -1763.56$	$\rho^2 = 0.366$	$\bar{\rho}^2 = 0.362$	$N = 1863$

- a non-work trip dummy; and
- an inertia dummy.

Note that β's are estimated for both RP and SP1 data, while the rail specific constants and the parameter of the non-work dummy are separately estimated for each data, and the coefficient of the inertia variable is only estimated for the SP1 data. The likelihood for the RP model is expressed by an ordinary binary probit model, while that for the SP1 model is expressed by the ordered probit model with threshold parameters. The unknown parameter vectors β, γ_1, θ and the scalar μ_1 can be estimated either by joint or sequential methods as described earlier.

TABLE IV shows the results of the joint estimation. All the coefficients have the expected sign. μ_1 is estimated between 0 and 1, which indicates a greater variance of the random utilities in the SP1 data. The calculated value of line-haul time is 0.15 Guilders/min. or \$4.20/hour.

Estimation with RP and SP2 data The RP and SP models are specified as follows:

Specification of the RP model:

$$U^{RP} = \beta' \mathbf{x}^{RP} + \varepsilon \,, \tag{20}$$

Specification of the SP2 model:

$$U^{SP2} = \beta' \mathbf{x}^{SP2} + \gamma_2' \mathbf{z}^{SP2} + \zeta \,, \tag{21}$$

Relationship of the random terms:

$$\text{Var}(\varepsilon) = \mu_2^2 \text{Var}(\zeta) \,, \tag{22}$$

where $\mathbf{x}^{RP}$ is the vector of the variables included in the RP model presented earlier, $\mathbf{x}^{SP2}$ contains a subset of $\mathbf{x}^{RP}$ which is included in the SP2 model, $\mathbf{z}^{SP2}$ is a vector of SP specific variables, β and γ_2 are vectors of coefficients, ε and ζ are normally distributed random terms, and μ_2 is a parameter that represents the relative scale of the two models. β is estimated for both RP and SP2 data, while γ_2 is estimated for the SP2 data.

TABLE V shows the joint estimation results. All the estimates have the expected signs and have very small standard errors. μ_2 is estimated to be greater than 1, which indicates that SP2 data have less random noise than the RP data. The calculated value of line-haul time is 0.2 Guilder/min. or \$5.60/hour, which seems more reasonable than the one calculated from the RP and SP1 data.

TABLE V. Estimation results with RP and SP2 data

Variable	Coefficient estimate	Standard error	t-statistic
Rail constant (RP)	1.44	0.244	5.93
Cost per person	-0.0242	0.00500	-4.85
Line-haul time	-0.00474	0.00102	-4.64
Terminal time	-0.0258	0.00561	-4.60
Number of transfers	-0.0487	0.0135	-3.61
Comfort (SP)	0.150	0.0322	4.67
Non-work trip dummy (RP)	-0.867	0.213	-4.08
θ_{21}	0.0180	0.00300	6.04
θ_{22}	0.277	0.0106	26.1
μ_2	3.33	0.699	4.77
$L(0) = -4934.82$ $L(\hat{\beta}) = -3385.63$	$\rho^2 = 0.314$	$\bar{\rho}^2 = 0.312$	$N = 3200$

Estimation with RP, SP1, and SP2 data Since two independent SP data sets are used, the system is composed of a RP model and two SP models:

Specification of the RP model:

$$U^{RP} = \beta'\mathbf{x}^{RP} + \varepsilon \, , \tag{23}$$

Specification of the SP1 model:

$$U^{SP1} = \beta'\mathbf{x}^{SP1} + \gamma_1'\mathbf{z}^{SP1} + \nu \, , \tag{24}$$

Specification of the SP2 model:

$$U^{SP2} = \beta'\mathbf{x}^{SP2} + \gamma_2'\mathbf{z}^{SP2} + \zeta \, , \tag{25}$$

Relationship of the random terms:

$$\text{Var}(\varepsilon) = \mu_1^2\text{Var}(\nu) = \mu_2^2\text{Var}(\zeta) \, . \tag{26}$$

As shown in TABLE VI, all the parameters are accurately estimated with the expected signs. The value of line-haul time is calculated to be 0.2 Guilders/min. or $5.60/hour.

Model Comparisons

The estimation results are compared in TABLE VII.

The first step in evaluating the usefulness of the combined estimator is to inspect the estimated coefficients of the separate RP, SP1 and SP2 models. A comparison of equivalent coefficients among these three models reveals large differences in the scales of the estimated utilities; the scale of the SP2 model is about three times greater than the scale of the RP model and the scale of the RP model is about three times greater than the scale of the SP1 model. This observation is verified by the results of the combined estimators. The ratio of the scale parameters of the SP1 and the RP models is given by μ_1 with an estimated value of about 0.3. The ratio of the scales of the SP2 and the RP models is given by μ_2 with an estimated value of about 3.2. These results indicate that the respondents were able to sharply discriminate between alternative rail services in the SP2 experiments. On the other hand, the stated choices between rail and car alternatives in the SP1 experiment were subject to significantly greater unexplained variance. Thus, a simple SP experiment such as SP2, may yield reliable information about trade-offs among attributes. However, using this information to predict

TABLE VI. Estimation results with RP, SP1 and SP2 data

Variable	Coefficient estimate	Standard error	t-statistic
Rail constant (RP)	1.43	0.240	5.95
Rail constant (SP)	-3.18	0.835	-3.81
Cost per person	-0.0250	0.00462	-5.41
Line-haul time	-0.00497	0.000973	-5.11
Terminal time	-0.0247	0.00507	-4.86
Number of transfers	-0.0520	0.0138	-3.89
Comfort	0.156	0.0301	5.16
Non-work trip dummy (RP)	-0.864	0.211	-4.09
Non-work trip dummy (SP)	-0.0745	0.259	-0.29
Inertia dummy	4.90	1.12	4.36
θ_{11}	0.0801	0.00951	8.43
θ_{12}	0.476	0.0218	21.8
θ_{21}	0.0180	0.00300	6.04
θ_{22}	0.277	0.0106	26.1
μ_1	0.298	0.0663	4.50
μ_2	3.22	0.609	5.30
$L(0) = -7554.98$ $L(\hat{\beta}) = -5034.21$	$\rho^2 = 0.334$	$\bar{\rho}^2 = 0.332$	$N = 4828$

choices between rail and car requires additional data and an estimator that allows for scale differences among different data sources.

The most convincing demonstration of the important role that SP data can play in model estimation is provided by the estimated coefficient of the line-haul travel time variable. In the RP model this coefficient has an incorrect sign and is not significantly different from zero. (This is not an unusual occurrence in the estimation of mode choice models from RP data and is due to the limited variability of the difference between car and train line-haul time.) In the SP models the coefficients of line-haul time are negative and significantly different from zero. Thus, a combined estimator that controls for the difference in scales yields a usable negative coefficient of approximately -0.005 which can now be used to predict the effects of changes in line-haul travel times.

The preference bias in the SP1 data toward the mode actually chosen was detected by the *inertia* variable. In the RP+SP1+SP2 model, for example, the rail specific constant estimated for the SP data is -3.18 for car users and 1.72 (=-3.18+4.90) for rail users. Thus, rail users have an SP rail constant of 1.72, which is greater than the RP value of 1.43, while for car users the SP rail constant is -3.18 and this is significantly smaller than the RP value. This indicates that car users have a greater preference bias toward their current mode than rail users. In other words, car users have a greater inertia or exhibit a greater justification bias than rail users.

Although the estimation results are not shown in this paper (see Morikawa [11]), we estimated the same models by the sequential method. The parameter estimates by the joint and sequential methods turned out to be very similar (mostly within 10% difference). However, the standard errors of the estimates by the sequential method are substantially underestimated by the factor of 10 to 500%.

In order to test if SP data produce the same models as RP data, likelihood ratio tests for the combined RP and SP models were performed. The likelihood value of an unrestricted model is given by the sum of likelihoods of separately estimated models, while a combined model gives the likelihood of the corresponding restricted model. Note that this is not a test of strict equality between the RP and SP parameters. It is a test of the restrictions which are embedded in the combined model. According to the test results shown in TABLE VIII, the null hypothesis of the combined RP and SP models cannot be rejected for any of the three cases at the 2% level of significance. This indicates that the information from the stated preferences as used in the combined model convey the same choice information as the revealed preferences. In other words, the introduction of parameters that capture justification bias, inertia effects and differences in random errors permitted the pooling of SP and RP data.

TABLE VII. Comparison of parameter estimates (t-statistics in parentheses)

	RP	SP1	SP2	RP+SP1	RP+SP2	RP+SP1 +SP2
Rail constant (RP)	1.74 (5.47)			1.61 (5.50)	1.44 (5.93)	1.43 (5.95)
Rail constant (SP)		-0.966 (-7.91)		-2.96 (-3.44)		-3.18 (-3.81)
Cost per person	-0.0257 (-4.39)	-0.00719 (-5.29)	-0.0807 (-25.3)	-0.0240 (-4.94)	-0.0242 (-4.85)	-0.0250 (-5.41)
Line-haul time	0.000548 (0.16)	-0.00324 (-2.72)	-0.0159 (-11.7)	-0.00463 (-1.92)	-0.00474 (-4.64)	-0.00497 (-5.11)
Terminal time	-0.0263 (-4.42)	-0.00661 (-3.22)		-0.0250 (-4.68)	-0.0258 (-4.60)	-0.0247 (-4.86)
Number of transfers	-0.344 (-2.59)	-0.0528 (-1.64)	-0.156 (-4.91)	-0.245 (-2.73)	-0.0487 (-3.61)	-0.0520 (-3.89)
Comfort			0.500 (14.8)		0.150 (4.67)	0.156 (5.16)
Non-work trip dummy (RP)	-0.900 (-3.97)			-0.900 (-4.18)	-0.870 (-4.08)	-0.864 (-4.09)
Non-work trip dummy (SP)		-0.0250 (-0.32)		-0.129 (-0.49)		-0.0745 (-0.29)
Inertia dummy		1.49 (17.5)		4.84 (4.16)		4.90 (4.36)
θ_{11}		0.0805 (8.40)		0.0803 (8.42)		0.0801 (8.43)
θ_{12}		0.478 (21.5)		0.476 (21.7)		0.476 (21.8)
θ_{21}			0.0180 (6.04)		0.0180 (6.04)	0.0180 (6.04)
θ_{22}			0.277 (26.1)		0.277 (26.1)	0.277 (26.1)
μ_1				0.294 (4.27)		0.298 (4.50)
μ_2					3.33 (4.77)	3.22 (5.30)
$\bar{\rho}^2$	0.258	0.369	0.314	0.362	0.312	0.332

TABLE VIII. Likelihood ratio tests for equality of coefficients

Case	Test statistics	Degrees of freedom	P-value	$\chi^2_{0.01}$
1. RP vs. SP1	5.62	3	0.13163	11.35
2. RP vs. SP2	7.66	2	0.02171	9.21
3. RP vs. SP1 vs. SP2	13.00	5	0.02338	15.09

Arc elasticities of rail share with respect to 10% increase in rail fare, rail line-haul time, car cost, or car line-haul time were calculated by using the sample enumeration method in the following way. First, the initial, or before-the-change, rail share is calculated by,

$$S = \frac{1}{N}\sum_{n=1}^{N}\frac{1}{1+\exp\left(-\hat{\beta}'\mathbf{x}_n^{RP}\right)}, \tag{27}$$

where

S = initial market share of rail;
$\hat{\beta}$ = vector of parameter estimates; and
$\mathbf{x}_n^{RP}$ = vector of attributes from the RP data.

Likewise, the new, or after-the-change, rail share is,

$$\tilde{S} = \frac{1}{N}\sum_{n=1}^{N}\frac{1}{1+\exp\left(-\hat{\beta}'\tilde{\mathbf{x}}_n^{RP}\right)}, \tag{28}$$

where

$\tilde{S}$ = new market share of rail; and
$\tilde{\mathbf{x}}_n^{RP}$ = modified vector of attributes (i.e., increasing one attribute in $\mathbf{x}_n^{RP}$ by 10%).

Then, the arc elasticity for a 10% change in one attribute is calculated by,

$$\frac{10(\tilde{S} - S)}{S}. \tag{29}$$

TABLE IX shows the elasticities calculated from the three models estimated separately from each data set and the three combined models. The RP model has the wrong sign for the line-haul travel time elasticities because the parameter estimate of that variable had the wrong sign. All of the three combined models show reasonable and stable values.

CONCLUSIONS

This paper described a methodology of estimating travel demand models from multiple data sources focusing on the method of using RP and SP data simultaneously. The framework presented is so general that it is applicable to wide variety of contexts such as combining disaggregate and aggregate data to estimate discrete choice models, combining survey and census data to estimate O-D trip tables, and combing data from different areas to spatially transfer a travel demand model.

The empirical case study demonstrated the practicality of the method. The data for this analysis were obtained from a survey of intercity travelers in The Netherlands and concerned the choice between rail and car. The survey included the usual RP data and two SP experiments: rail vs. car (SP1) and rail vs. rail (SP2).

Three combined models were estimated: RP data combined with SP1 (rail vs. car) data, RP data combined with SP2 (rail vs. rail) data, and RP data combined with both SP1 and SP2 data. These combined models were compared against the three models that were separately estimated from the three data sets. The RP model could not successfully identify an important parameter (the coefficient of line-haul travel time), which is a typical problem encountered in

TABLE IX. Elasticities of rail share

Model	rail cost	rail time	car cost	car time
RP	-0.643	0.0402	0.305	-0.0397
SP1	-0.415	-0.530	0.234	0.571
SP2	-1.50	-0.939	1.18	1.12
RP+SP1	-0.605	-0.337	0.288	0.342
RP+SP2	-0.628	-0.356	0.297	0.360
RP+SP1+SP2	-0.648	-0.373	0.288	0.342

estimating models from RP data. This is usually caused by lack of variation in the data and/or misspecification of the model. However, obtaining an acceptable model specification is often very difficult because the actual behavior is influenced by related attributes while the available data are limited. Furthermore, even if the correct model specification was known, estimation of model parameters could fail because of data limitations. SP experiments present simplified hypothetical choice contexts and, therefore, may provide useful information on trade-offs among attributes.

The case study provided a clear demonstration of the usefulness of the combined estimation method. Specifically, the coefficient of the line-haul travel time variable was successfully estimated by combining RP and SP data. The SP2 experiment for rail vs. rail choice provided information on the trade-offs among attributes with the least random noise. On the other hand, SP data are often not reliable because of the oversimplified hypothetical circumstances. This problem was mitigated by using additional variables from the RP data in estimating the SP model.

A potential bias in the SP data was captured by the introduction of the *inertia* variable. This variable captured the preference bias toward the mode actually chosen. As discussed above, it was found that car users had a greater inertia or habitual effect in choosing a travel mode.

Likelihood ratio test results gave a statistical justification of combining RP and SP data. The combined models also produced the most reasonable and consistent values for intuitive measurements such as value of time and elasticities.

Three alternative estimation methods for combined models were presented: joint estimation, two step sequential estimation, and three step sequential estimation. Although yielding statistically efficient estimators, joint estimation requires an special MLE program, while sequential estimation can be performed by ordinary econometric packages. Although the estimation results are not shown in the paper, we verified that the sequential methods, especially the three step method, produced very similar estimates to those of the joint estimation, whereas standard errors of parameters reported by sequential methods were substantially underestimated. These results should encourage practitioners to employ the combined estimation method.

REFERENCES

1. G. Judge, W. Griffiths, R. Hill and T.C. Lee. The Theory and Practice of Econometrics. 2nd ed. (Wiley 1982).
2. C. Hendrickson and S. McNeil. Estimation of Origin/Destination Matrices with Constrained Regression. Transportation Research Record, 976. pp. 25-32 (1984).
3. M. Ben-Akiva, P.P. Macke and P.S. Hsu. Alternative Methods to Estimate Route Level Trip Tables and Expand On-Board Surveys. Transportation Research Record, 1037. pp. 1-11 (1985).
4. M. Ben-Akiva and T. Morikawa. Data Fusion Methods and Their Applications to Origin-Destination Trip Tables. Selected Proceedings of the 5th World Conference on Transport Research, Vol. IV. pp. 279-293 (1989).
5. S.L. Gonzalez. Combining Survey and Aggregate Data for Model Estimation. Ph.D. Dissertation. Department of Civil Engineering, MIT (1985).
6. T. Yai, S. Morichi and K. Fan. Disaggregate Modelling by Multi-Source Data. Proceedings of the 5th World Conference on Transport Research, forthcoming (1990).
7. M. Ben-Akiva. Methods to Combine Different Data Sources and Estimate Origin-Destination Matrices. in Transportation and Traffic Theory. N.H. Gartner and N.H.M. Wilson eds. pp. 459-481 (Elsevier 1987).
8. M. Ben-Akiva, T. Morikawa and F. Shiroishi. Analysis of the Reliability of Stated Preference Data in Estimating Mode Choice Models. Selected Proceedings of the 5th World Conference on Transport Research, Vol. IV. pp. 263-277 (1989).
9. T. Amemiya. 1985. Advanced Econometrics. (Harvard University Press, 1985).
10. M. Bradley, T. Grosvenor and A. Bouma. An Application of Computer-Based Stated Preference to Study Mode-Switching in the Netherlands. Unpublished Working Paper. Hague Consulting Group, The Netherlands (1988).
11. T. Morikawa. Incorporating Stated Preference Data in Travel Demand Analysis. Ph.D. Dissertation. Department of Civil Engineering, MIT (1989).

[38]

ESTIMATION OF LOGIT CHOICE MODELS USING MIXED STATED-PREFERENCE AND REVEALED-PREFERENCE INFORMATION

M. A. Bradley and A. J. Daly

ABSTRACT

The need for cost-effective research techniques in transport has led to increasing use of stated-preference data, as well as the development of mixed models, based on multiple-data sources. Different types of data, as used in such models, may have different accuracy and sources of error. Such differences exist between revealed-preference and stated-preference data. The magnitude and source of errors in different types of data will be reflected in differences in both the measured components and in the unmeasured components (variance) captured in the corresponding models. When choice models are estimated on multiple-data sources, such as various types of revealed- and stated-preference data, these differences must be taken into account explicitly in the specification of the model structure and the utility functions.

The chapter discusses the main issues involved in the estimation and application of discrete-choice models with mixed data, covering:

- the theoretical framework for combining data sources;
- the specification of the model and the likelihood function;
- the suitability and accessibility of different estimation techniques;
- a case study that compares binary probit- and logit-estimation methods;
- a case study that incorporates a new mode into a nested-logit model;
- issues involved in interpreting and applying mixed-model results.

In particular, the paper describes a new approach for estimating models on mixed-data sources using the "tree-logit" estimation technique.

INTRODUCTION

Methods for using "revealed-preference" (RP) disaggregate data to model travel demand have now become well established[1]. Usually, such data contain choices reported from traveller surveys, that are then related to the characteristics of the travel alternatives available to them: either self-reported or measured from road and public-transport network data. A number of forecasting methods have been developed to extrapolate such models to the wider population and the longer-term time horizon[2,3].

Increasingly, "stated-preference" (SP) data, based on responses to hypothetical travel situations from a survey context, have been used in cases where observed choice behaviour cannot tell us enough about the choice context of interest. SP data may be used, for example, because one is interested in travel alternatives or characteristics that do not yet exist, or one is interested in qualitative factors that are very difficult to measure in actual circumstances.

In early transport applications that used SP data, such as Kocur *et al.*[4] and Sheldon and Steer[5], the methods used remained quite close to those that had been widely adopted in the field of market research[6]. In recent years, the emphasis has shifted somewhat from "stated-preference" data to "stated-choice" data that resemble RP data as closely as possible and can be analyzed with similar techniques, such as discrete choice logit or probit estimation[7]. Concerns remain, however, that stated choices may actually be measuring different aspects of behaviour than revealed choices, with the two types of data being subject to different levels of accuracy and different types of error and bias. Such differences may be particularly important in forecasting, where the size of the explanatory-variable effects relative to the unexplained variation in behaviour becomes critical[8,9,10].

For forecasting purposes, one would ideally like a methodology that can derive the essential information from SP data (the information that cannot be obtained from RP data) and that can incorporate it into a model that is suitable for application to RP-type data and that reflects actual (or expected) choice conditions. That is, it is desirable to combine the stronger features of RP and SP data. The issue addressed by the present chapter is how this combination can be achieved.

Structure of the Paper

This chapter discusses and illustrates the main issues involved in the estimation of mixed RP-SP discrete-choice models:

The second section provides background on the theoretical framework of the integrated-estimation approach, the structure of the model, and the specification of the joint-utility function. This section includes a statistical derivation of the "tree-logit" estimator of the joint likelihood function.

The third section describes a test of the tree-logit method in the binary-choice case. This case study was performed with data used in previously-published research[11], providing a direct comparison of binary-logit and probit estimation techniques.

The fourth section presents a second case study, a more difficult but more typical case, where stated-preference data are used to supplement a model from independent revealed-preference data in order to add to the model a travel mode that does not yet exist. Here, the joint-estimation approach is tested within a nested multinomial-logit structure. The fifth section provides a brief summary and some conclusions regarding the methods and results described in the paper.

THE THEORETICAL FRAMEWORK

The theoretical framework that we have adopted for integrated analysis of RP and SP data was developed by Morikawa, Ben Akiva, and McFadden[10, 11]. The framework is that of individual utility maximization by travellers. While other behavioural paradigms can be used for analysis of this type, utility maximization has been studied in detail by many other researchers and there is a consistent and coherent body of theory based on utility maximization to which reference can be made.

Formulation of the Analytical Problem

For consistency, notation similar to that used by Morikawa *et al.*[12] is used. In this notation, the (latent) utility maximized by travellers in their revealed preferences, u^{RP}, for a given traveller, for a given alternative, is given by:

$$u^{RP} = \beta . X^{RP} + \alpha . W + \epsilon \qquad (1)$$

where:

X^{RP}, W are vectors of the measured variables influencing the RP decision;

β,α are vectors of unknown parameters (to be estimated);

ϵ represents the sum of the unmeasured utility components of utility influencing the RP decision.

Similarly, the SP decision can be represented as being decided on the basis of the utility function u^{SP}:

$$u^{SP} = \beta.X^{SP} + \gamma.Z + \nu \qquad (2)$$

where:

X^{SP}, Z are vectors of the measured variables influencing the SP decision;

β, γ are vectors of unknown parameters (to be estimated);

ν represents the sum of the unmeasured utility components of utility influencing the SP decision.

In this notation, it is possible to allow for the existence of measured variables *W* that occur only in the RP context, or *Z* that occur only in the SP context. These variables would also incorporate average biases or modal preferences, which may be different in the two contexts. Generally, the mean biases are captured by including "alternative-specific constants" in the utility functions for the alternatives. These constants represent the mean net effect of all the unmeasured components of utility. This incorporation of mean bias in the measured variables allows the assumption that the mean value of the unmeasured components ϵ and ν is zero for each alternative.

Among the variables that are present only in one of the contexts (*W* or *Z*) should be included all likely context-specific biases. Among these, it is necessary to allow for any "inertia" effect, where the biases may be systematically related to each SP respondent's actual revealed behaviour. The existence of such "inertia" and other context-specific biases make it necessary in many cases to include the alternative-specific constants within the context-dependent variables *W* and *Z*, rather than in the joint variables *X*. The interpretation and use of such effects is an important issue that we return to in the last section.

The key to the use of the joint-estimation approach lies in the variables *X* that appear in ***both*** utility functions. Their coefficients, β, can be estimated using the information from ***both*** surveys. By this formulation, therefore, the objective is achieved of exploiting data from the two contexts to make ***joint*** estimates. This can be done, of course, only when there is an overlap of two or more of the *X* variables indicated in equations (1) and (2) above. When there is only one *X* variable in common, one utility function simply can be scaled to the other, using the ratio of the independent RP and SP coefficients for that variable; no joint estimation is necessary. (The same applies when there are two or more variables in common, but they have "exactly" the same ***relative*** coefficient values in independent RP and SP models.) Joint RP/SP estimation is thus needed when there are two or more variables in common, for which the different types of data, used independently, give somewhat conflicting or inconclusive results. In joint estimation, we assume that the "true" underlying relative effects of the variables in *X* are the same in the RP and SP contexts, i.e. that their marginal contribution to utility indicated by β is identical. This assumption should be tested in estimation using the likelihood-ratio test[13].

Distributional Assumptions

The theory of utility-maximizing models (see, for example, Ben-Akiva and Lerman[14]) derives choice probabilities directly from the assumptions made about the distributions of the unobserved components ε and ν. Thus, to derive the probability models necessary to analyze the data, it is necessary to specify distributions for these variables.

Apart from the assumption that the marginal utility of each common variable is equal in each of the contexts, which is necessary to make any joint use of the data, it is also necessary to make an assumption about the distribution of the unmeasured components within the population. Because of the presence of alternative-specific constants, as explained above, it is acceptable to assume that the mean value of ε and ν is zero. However, further assumptions are required about the interdependence (both between observations and between alternatives), variance, and distributional form to be taken by these variables. As is usual in analysis based on utility maximization, ε and ν are treated as random variables.

The issue of interdependence between observations is difficult. In most practical cases, a single RP choice observation is taken from each traveller and there is little question that it is reasonable to assume independence of these observations. One of the chief advantages of SP surveys, on the other hand, is that several observations can be taken from each individual. In that case, the assumption of independence must be, at best, a poor approximation. Nevertheless, this assumption is routinely made and the success that has been achieved in previous studies suggests that the problems caused by this assumption are limited in their practical effect. Until a more satisfactory theoretical framework is established for repeated choices, the assumption will be maintained. Similarly, interdependence between RP and SP observations from the same individual cannot be treated fully at present.

The existence of interdependence between SP observations from the same individual makes it impossible to assume that the variance of the unmeasured components ϵ and ν is equal. The existence of the correlation in the SP data suggests that the variance of ν will be less than that of ϵ. However, there are many other effects at work here, such as the omission of many relevant variables from most SP contexts and the existence of substantial measurement error in many RP contexts. In general, it cannot be stated *a priori* which of the two unmeasured components will have the greater variance; however, it is clear that it is *not* possible to assume that their variances are equal.

The functional form assumed for the distributions of ϵ and ν determines the functional form of the probability model that is used to estimate the coefficients α, β, and γ. In the work of Morikawa *et al.* the assumption is made that ϵ and ν are distributed normally (with zero mean and unequal variance, as suggested above), leading to 'probit' models of probability. This assumption of normal distribution facilitates analytical study of the models, but can lead to severe difficulties in empirical work, particularly in choice contexts with more than two alternatives. Special computer software is required that can require long run times and present other difficulties in finding optimum values of the parameters.

An alternative-distributional assumption is to take the limiting-value distribution, often described as "Gumbell" or "Weibull" to describe the variation of ϵ and ν. This assumption, suggested for the present context by Daly [15], leads to the use of logit models for the probability calculations. These models are characterized by their much greater simplicity in empirical work; this feature is illustrated in the subsequent sections of the present paper.

From a theoretical viewpoint, the use of the logit model is equally as appropriate as the use of probit. Intuitively, the logit model is appropriate when an alternative is viewed as being an aggregation of a number of "sub-alternatives." The probit model, on the other hand, is appropriate when the unmeasured part of the utility function is viewed as the sum of a large number of components. Because both of these viewpoints appear to be partial descriptions of the reality being modelled, there appears little theoretical basis for the choice of one model over the other.

From an empirical point of view, the results achieved for binary-choice models with the two forms are very similar, as is illustrated in the third section. The reasons for this are explained by Daly and Zachary[16]. Briefly, the major difference between the two model forms is the greater sensitivity of the probit model to "outliers" (unusual observations) in model estimation. For less unusual observations, estimation is almost identical; in forecasting there is also almost no difference between the two model forms.

For more complicated models with more than two alternatives, the differences between logit and probit forms are more significant. Logit models extend easily to a large number of alternatives, provided that an assumption of symmetry among the alternatives is made. Some forms of asymmetry can be handled with "tree-logit" forms. Very general model forms can be included in the probit family, although the computational difficulties become very severe indeed. It may be concluded that there is scope for the use of logit models in the integration of RP and SP data. While some researchers may prefer to use probit models for specific research needs, the logit model is theoretically attractive and empirically advantageous.

The "Tree-Logit" Estimation Procedure

It is assumed, as sketched out in the previous discussion, that the non-measured components of the utility ϵ and ν are distributed independently (across both individuals and alternatives, and independently of each other) with the limiting-value distribution, but with unequal variance. If we define θ^2 to be the ratio of the variances,

$$\theta^2 = var(\epsilon) \ / \ var(\nu) \tag{3}$$

then the SP utility can be scaled by θ:

$$\theta.u^{SP} = (\theta.\beta).X^{SP} + (\theta.\gamma).Z + (\theta.\nu) \tag{4}$$

so that the random variable (θ,ν) now has a variance equal to that in the RP utility (ε). It is now possible to use both RP and SP observations in a logit-estimation procedure that requires equal variance across the observations.

While for the RP estimation, the parameters to be estimated are the simple values of α and β, for the SP estimation the coefficients are (θ.β) and (θ,γ). This scaling has no other effect on the distributional assumptions, or on the conversion of the utility functions to choice probabilities. In the case of (θ,γ), because the scale of *g* is arbitrary, the presence of θ is not necessary; but in the case of (θ.β) the scaling by θ is the essential link between the RP and SP models. The SP model, however, is no longer a linear function of the parameters — an estimation problem that can be solved by existing "tree-logit" estimation software, by setting up an artificial tree structure as follows.

The artificial tree is constructed to have as many elementary alternatives as there are in all RP and SP choice sets combined. Only the RP alternatives are set as available for the RP observations, while only the alternatives from the relevant SP experiment are available for each SP observation. The utility functions in each case are as given in equations (1) and (2) (i.e. without θ). As indicated in Figure 1, the RP alternatives are placed just below the root of the tree; while the SP alternatives are each placed in a single-alternative nest. For an RP observation, the SP alternatives are set unavailable and the choice is modelled as in a standard logit model. For an SP observation, the RP alternatives are set unavailable and choice is modelled using the tree-logit structure.

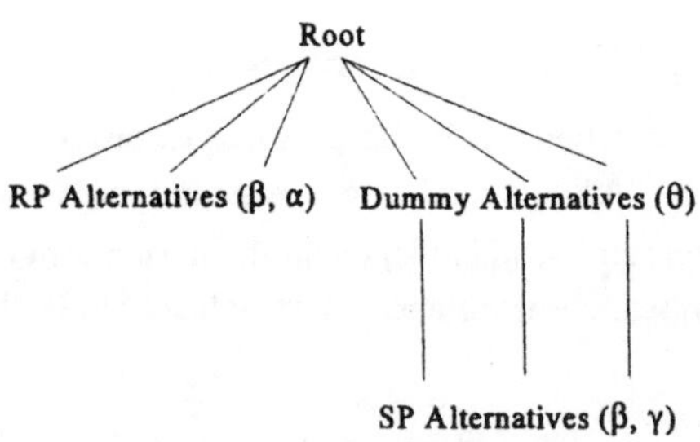

Figure 1
Artificial Tree Structure for Joint Estimation

For SP observations, the mean utility of each of the "dummy" alternatives is composed as usual in a tree-logit model (see Daly[17]):

$$V^{comp} = \theta.\ \log(\sum \exp(V^{SP})) \tag{5}$$

In equation 5, the sum is taken over all of the alternatives in the nest corresponding to the composite alternative.

$$V^{SP} = u^{SP} - \nu = \beta.x^{SP} + \gamma.z \tag{6}$$

is simply the measured part of the SP utility. Then, because each "nest" contains only one alternative in this specification:

$$V^{comp} = \theta.u^{SP} = (\theta.\beta).X^{SP} + (\theta.\gamma).Z \tag{7}$$

This is exactly the form required by equation 4, as long as the value of θ is constrained to be the same for each of the dummy alternatives. This approach can also be generalized to data from two or more different SP experiments, by using a different set of available SP alternatives and a different set of dummy alternatives with its own θ parameter for each experiment.

Because the dummy-composite alternatives are placed just below the root of the tree, as are the RP alternatives, a full-information nested-logit estimation procedure, such as Hague Consulting Group's ALOGIT program, will ensure that θ is estimated to obtain uniform variance at this level.

This method exploits software that was developed for a different purpose — the estimation of models for simultaneous nested-choice structures. It is important to note that the construction used here is artificial in that individuals are not modelled as choosing from among the RP and SP alternatives simultaneously and no assumption is required about consistency of preferences between RP and SP alternatives. Thus, the usual requirement for tree-logit models that θ should not exceed unity does not apply. The scale for SP relative to RP may be either greater than or less than unity. In fact, the decision as to whether to apply the scale factor to the RP data or the SP data is rather arbitrary, and will depend mainly on the type of data to which the model will eventually be applied for predicting behaviour.

Finally, the structure indicated above, in which the models of choice over the RP and over the SP alternatives are each simple logit in form, can be generalized. Nested-choice structures among the RP and/or SP alternatives may be introduced. An example of scaling with nested models is given in the fourth section.

CASE STUDY 1: APPLICATION TO BINARY CHOICE CONTEXTS

This section describes the application of the proposed logit estimation technique to the same data set studied by Morikawa[18]. Comparisons are made between Morikawa's probit-estimation results and results of estimation using logit models.

The Study Context

Hague Consulting Group, along with Steer Davies Gleave, was contracted by Netherlands Railways (NS) to study the potential for substitution between car and train, for intercity travel in the Netherlands as a function of rail service levels and fare. A sample of 235 individuals was selected who had recently travelled by car or rail from the Dutch city of Nijmegen, near the German border, to Amsterdam, Rotterdam, or Den Haag, all located about 125 kilometres to the West.

A computer-based home interview was designed to elicit first a detailed account of the journey that the respondent had made, including all journey costs, times, and interchanges. Respondents were then asked to give their perceptions of making the same journey by the alternative mode. These data were used as a basis for the attribute levels to be varied in stated-preference (SP) experiments, but also provided data suitable for estimating revealed-preference (RP) models, albeit with self-reported values of the car and train attributes.

The first SP experiment (SP1) was designed to measure the relative importance of four train attributes: fare, journey time, number of interchanges, and comfort level. This was thus a within-mode experiment, where all respondents compared different train options against each other. Pairwise choice questions were used, with a five-point response scale: (1) Definitely A, (2) Probably A, (3) Not Sure, (4) Probably B, and (5) Definitely B.

A second SP experiment (SP2) was a mode-choice experiment, always comparing car against train. The same four attributes for train were varied as in the first experiment. For car, although both travel cost and time were shown as attributes, only the cost was varied during the experiment. In order to create situations in which people might be induced to switch from the actual mode, the train attributes were varied to become worse than the reported levels for train users and better than the reported levels for car users. The same five-point response scale was used as in SP1. Further information on the survey and analysis results is reported in Bradley *et al.*[19]

Case Study Results

Morikawa[20] used ordered-probit estimation to analyze the interval information in the five-point scale responses in the SP1 and SP2 data, and binary-probit estimation for the RP train versus car choice. (*Ordered probit* estimates the threshold in the utility function where respondents shift from one response to the next.) For the mixed RP/SP models, Morikawa programmed the joint-likelihood function using the GAUSS microcomputer package. The results, reproduced in Table 1, contain a number of results that can be typical for the types of data used:

- the RP model does not yield a significant estimate for in-vehicle time, presumably due to insufficient variation or correlation with other variables such as cost and number of transfers (such problems are more typical when network-based attribute data are used);
- the SP1 within-mode model has the most significant estimates, but coefficients can be estimated only for the four variables that were varied in the experiment;
- the SP2 across-mode model contains fairly significant estimates for all level-of-service variables, but has values of the rail-mode constants that are different than for RP, and shows a strong inertia effect;
- the scale parameters show that the within-mode SP1 responses have significantly *less* unexplained variance than the RP data ($q>1$), and the across-mode SP2 responses have significantly ***more*** unexplained variance when compared to the RP data ($q<1$).

Table 2 contains results for models estimated on exactly the same data, with the same variable specifications as in Table 1. The models in Table 2, however, were estimated using binary-logit models and tree-logit models for the mixed RP/SP models, as explained in the second section. Estimation was done using Hague Consulting Group's ALOGIT microcomputer package.

In order to estimate binary-logit models on the five-point scale SP responses, we interpreted "Definitely A" and "Probably A" as simple choices for A, "Definitely B" and "Probably B" as simple choices for B, and "Not Sure" as half of a choice for A and half for B. (One could also omit the "Not Sure" responses to give a true discrete-choice variable.)

Table 1
Probit/Ordered Probit Parameter Estimates

Model :	RP	SP1	SP2	RP+SP1	RP+SP2	RP+SP1+SP2	RP2
N.Obs. :	235	2965	1628	3200	1863	4828	228
ρ^2 :	.295	.315	.372	.314	.366	.334	.299
(coefficients, with absolute t-values in parentheses)							
RP/SP Joint Variables							
Cost/pers	-.026	-.081	-.0072	-.024	-.024	-.025	-.027
(gld.)	(4.4)	(25.3)	(5.3)	(4.9)	(4.9)	(5.4)	(4.4)
In-V.Time	.0005	-.016	-.0032	-.0047	-.0046	-.0050	-.0050
(min.)	(0.2)	(11.7)	(2.7)	(4.6)	(1.9)	(5.1)	(1.3)
Out-V.Time	-.026		-.0066	-.026	-.025	-.025	-.026
(min.)	(4.4)		(3.2)	(4.6)	(4.7)	(4.9)	(4.7)
Transfers	-.344	-.156	-.053	-.049	-.245	-.052	-.144
(number)	(2.6)	(4.9)	(1.6)	(3.6)	(2.7)	(3.9)	(1.0)
RP-Specific Variables							
Non-work	-.900			-.870	-.900	-.864	-.691
(0/1-RP)	(4.0)			(4.1)	(4.2)	(4.1)	(2.2)
Rail ASC	1.74			1.44	1.61	1.43	0.35 *
(0/1-RP)	(5.5)			(5.9)	(5.5)	(6.0)	(1.2)
SP-Specific Variables							
Comfort		-.500		-.150		-.156	
(0/1/2-SP1)		(14.8)		(4.7)		(5.2)	
Non-work			-.025		-.129	-.075	
(0/1-SP2)			(0.3)		(0.5)	(0.3)	
Rail ASC			-.966		-2.96	-3.18	
(0/1-SP2)			(7.9)		(3.4)	(3.8)	
Inertia			1.49		4.84	4.90	
(0/1-SP2)			(17.5)		(4.2)	(4.4)	
Scale Parameters							
SP1 scaled to RP				3.33		3.22	
				(4.8)		(5.3)	
SP2 scaled to RP					.294	.298	
					(4.3)	(4.5)	

* Two additional dummy variables were included in the RP2 model, mainly affecting the value of the rail constant.

Table 2
Logit/Tree logit Parameter Estimates

Model :	RP	SP1	SP2	RP+SP1	RP+SP2	RP+SP1+SP2
N.Obs. :	235	2965	1628	3200	1863	4828
ρ^2 :	.303	.148	.338	.158	.332	.218
(coefficients, with absolute t-values in parentheses)						
RP/SP Joint Variables						
Cost/pers	-.025	-.081	-.0061	-.026	-.022	-.026
(gld.)	(4.3)	(19.8)	(3.5)	(4.7)	(4.6)	(5.0)
In-V.Time	.0040	-.016	-.0045	.0050	-.0083	-.0051
(min.)	(1.0)	(10.7)	(3.2)	(4.4)	(2.8)	(4.7)
Out-V.Time	-.024		-.0043	-.024	-.023	-.025
(min.)	(3.9)		(1.7)	(4.0)	(4.1)	(4.5)
Transfers	-.286	-.176	-.065	-.058	-.269	-.058
(number)	(2.3)	(5.4)	(1.3)	(3.6)	(2.7)	(3.8)
RP-Specific Variables						
Non-work	-.690			-.660	-.684	-.664
(0/1-RP)	(3.3)			(3.2)	(3.3)	(3.2)
Rail ASC	1.44			1.27	1.33	1.28
(0/1-RP)	(5.1)			(5.0)	(4.9)	(5.1)
SP-Specific Variables						
Comfort		-.517		-.166		-.165
(0/1/2-SP1)		(14.6)		(4.5)		(4.8)
Non-work			-.092		-.278	-.319
(0/1-SP2)			(1.1)		(1.0)	(1.0)
Rail ASC			-.880		-2.67	-3.14
(0/1-SP2)			(6.9)		(3.2)	(3.2)
Inertia			1.42		4.50	4.86
(0/1-SP2)			(15.3)		(4.2)	(3.9)
Scale Parameters						
SP1 scaled to RP				3.12		3.16
				(4.6)		(4.8)
SP2 scaled to RP					.299	.276
					(4.2)	(3.9)

There is some information lost in the transformation from the scale response to binary choice, as indicated by the lower ρ^2 measures of fit for the SP models in Table 2 as compared to Table 1. This extra explanation in the ordered-probit models is provided by two extra parameters (omitted from Table 1) that indicate the threshold utility differences that define the five symmetric scale intervals. In terms of likelihood measures, this loss of information appears more important for SP1 within-mode choices, where individuals are comparing very similar alternatives, than for the SP2 mode choices. In terms of the coefficients and their significance, however, the difference is quite small, particularly for the SP1 model.

The clearest way of comparing the probit and logit results is to compare the parameter estimates and their statistical significance in Tables 1 and 2. The logit coefficients have been divided by a factor of $\pi/\sqrt{3}$ in order to normalize the Weibull error distribution to the standard normal distribution assumed in probit[21]. None of the results are significantly different from each other in the two tables. The two coefficients which change sign between the tables — in-vehicle time for RP and the rail constant for non-workers for SP2 — are not significant in either case. The *t*-statistics are slightly lower for the logit models than for the probit models, but are very similar in the case of the RP+SP models. Perhaps most importantly, the scale factors for the RP+SP models are nearly identical in Tables 1 and 2, indicating that the tree-logit method for estimating the scale differences gives comparable results.

The estimates are most precise in the SP1 within-mode models. In particular, the inferred value of in-vehicle time from the SP1 models — about 12 gld/hr. — is very well estimated. Joint estimation on RP plus SP1 leads to a scale on the time and cost coefficients similar to RP alone but a value-of-time ratio similar to SP1 alone. If we are willing to make the reasonable assumption that this value of time is also appropriate in actual choice contexts, then the approach is successful in combining useful aspects of both data sets. Because this analysis was meant to compare the two estimation approaches, further discussion of the individual variables in the models is beyond the scope of this chapter. The inertia effect is discussed further in the fifth section.

A further interesting point is that certain results from this analysis suggest that the difference between the probit and logit results is caused by the presence of outliers, i.e. responses that are very poorly predicted by the model, often due to errors in the data. Because the error distribution assumed in probit has smaller tails than that assumed in logit, probit estimates tend to be more distorted by outliers[13]. Further evidence is provided by the RP2 model in Table 1, reported in a subsequent paper by Morikawa et al.[22] after 7 respondents had been deleted from the RP sample. These results now appear somewhat more similar to those for RP in Table 2, particularly the change of sign for in-vehicle time. The sensitivity to outliers is not a strong point for or against the use of either technique, because the best modelling practice in both cases is to identify such outliers, examine them, and eliminate them from the sample if appropriate.

CASE STUDY 2: APPLICATION TO MULTINOMIAL CHOICE CONTEXTS

The previous case study has shown that the tree-logit approach, which can be performed with currently available logit estimation software, gives results consistent with those obtained from a more complex, probit-estimation procedure. This difference is especially important for models with more than two alternatives. Existing logit-estimation packages such as ALOGIT can estimate nested, multinomial discrete-choice models, while such estimation is not currently feasible using probit analysis. The following case study shows how the scaling approach can be applied to such models. In the previous example, RP data were obtained during the SP interviews as a small supplementary data source to use in scaling the sensitivity of the SP models to that reflected in current choices. A more challenging case study is described in this study, where SP is the supplementary data source used to add additional parameters to a model that is based on ***independent*** RP data and independent network-based attribute data.

The Study Context

Hague Consulting Group, along with study team members from Macquarie University (now at the University of Sydney) and Cambridge Systematics, was contracted by CSIRO in Australia to study the market potential for a proposed high-speed rail system connecting the cities of Sydney, Canberra, and Melbourne. The objective was to identify the sensitivity of demand to key variables, such as fare and travel time, and also to predict the absolute level of demand, requiring estimation of a choice model including a mode which did not yet exist.

The first stage of the study included intercept surveys among car, air, bus, and train travellers along all routes for which the proposed Very Fast Train (VFT) would be a relevant alternative. Over 30,000 such questionnaires were completed. These data were expanded to produce origin-destination matrices of existing travel in the corridor and were also analyzed, in combination with network-based travel time and cost data, to produce RP models of mode choice among the existing alternatives.

The second stage involved over 2,500 home interviews, with roughly half of the respondents recruited out of the intercept samples, and the other half contacted at random also to include non-travellers. The SP experiment began by collecting a number of details of the most recent actual journey and of certain attributes of the alternative modes for that journey, (e.g., access/egress times from airports and train/coach stations). The VFT service was then introduced, using a realistic information/advertising brochure. The stated-preference experiment used an orthogonal design, with the travel times and costs of the existing modes and the VFT varied independently, with each respondent considering three relevant sets of hypothetical mode alternatives, supplemented with the information that they provided on access/egress times and costs. Three stated mode choices were obtained per respondent.

Although data from only the mode-choice SP experiment are discussed here, the survey also included a second, within-mode SP experiment that asked for choices among different versions of the VFT, with attributes including fare, type of seating, and entertainment facilities. Further details of the study are given in Gunn *et al.*[23]

Case Study Results

First, we should note that, because of continuing development, the models described in this section are not those that are used to forecast demand for the VFT system — the specific models shown here have been estimated for the purposes of this chapter.

Table 3 shows nested mode-choice model results, separately for business and non-business trips. For the cost variable, all models use the travel cost per person divided by the average wage per worker in the travel party, which results in a cost in units of the minutes of work time required to pay for the journey using each mode. Other variables are main line-haul in-vehicle time for each mode, access time to and egress time from each mode, mode-specific constants, and a few segmentation variables related to the choice of air travel. Note that this example uses "generic" travel-time variables across modes, but that the same approach could be extended to include different travel-time coefficients for different modes.

In the separate RP and SP models, all passenger modes — air, coach, rail, and VFT — are included in a single nest versus car, reflecting the closer substitution between those modes. The structure of the joint RP/SP nested model is shown in Figure 2. The "logsum" parameters associated with alternatives *RP Pass.* and *SP Pass.* are nested-logit structural parameters and should have a value between 0 and 1. That is the result in Table 3, with values of around .90 for the business models and .60 for the

Table 3
Nested Mode Choice Models with New Mode

	Business			Non-Business		
Data	RP	SP	RP+SP	RP	SP	RP+SP
Num. Obs.	12586	1924	14510	16317	3673	19990
ρ^2	0.368	0.261	0.343	0.129	0.203	0.141
Log-likel.	-5074	-1340	-6463	-15544	-3128	-18693
(coefficients, with absolute t-values in parenthesis)						
RP/SP Joint Variables						
Cost/Wage	-0.0016	-0.0021	-0.0016	-0.0013	-0.0009	-0.0013
(min.)	(28.2)	(6.6)	(29.3)	(40.4)	(6.9)	(40.8)
Main Time	-0.0047	-0.0057	-0.0049	-0.0022	-0.0018	-0.0021
(min.)	(32.0)	(12.8)	(34.9)	(41.2)	(9.1)	(42.5)
Access Time	0.0024	-0.0098	-0.0006	0.0012	-0.0030	0.0005
(min.)	(3.7)	(7.5)	(1.1)	(2.8)	(3.4)	(1.3)
Air-Travel	2.11	-0.216	2.10	0.069	0.300	0.075
Alone	(23.5)	(1.7)	(23.3)	(1.5)	(1.7)	(1.6)
Air-Age	-0.836	0.140	-0.831	-0.434	0.254	-0.432
<35	(11.2)	(1.1)	(11.1)	(9.7)	(1.4)	(9.7)
Air-Day	0.469	0.154	0.454	0.958	-0.094	0.930
Trip	(5.4)	(1.3)	(5.2)	(14.6)	(0.3)	(14.3)
Pass. mode-	0.823	0.943	0.821	0.566	0.683	0.579
(logsum)	(40.0)	(9.7)	(41.0)	(28.0)	(8.7)	(29.7)
RP-Specific Variables						
Air	-1.57		-1.20	-1.28		-1.12
(RP)	(11.1)		(9.1)	((12.3)		(11.6)
Coach	-2.31		-2.06	-1.69		-1.57
(RP)	(19.8)		(19.0)	(18.4)		(18.4)
Train	-2.35		-2.14	-1.73		-1.63
(RP)	(23.1)		(22.3)	(20.4)		(20.6)
SP-Specific Variables						
Air		0.377	-0.594		-1.23	-1.30
(SP)		(1.1)	(3.7)		(3.6)	(8.6)
Coach		-1.73	-2.55		-0.698	-0.931
(SP)		(2.8)	(4.1)		(3.1)	(6.3)
Train		0.615	-0.228		-0.185	-0.364
(SP)		(1.8)	(0.7)		(0.9)	(2.6)
VFT		3.00	2.22		2.00	1.80
(SP)		(9.9)	(7.8)		(7.5)	(10.9)
Inertia		2.68	2.4		2.14	2.17
(SP)		(15.1)	(11.7)		(28.8)	(23.5)
Scale Parameter			1.17			0.932
SP scaled to RP			(12.4)			(19.6)

non-business models. The SP logsum estimate is not significantly different from the RP estimate in either case. The joint RP/SP model estimate is close to the RP-only estimate in both cases.

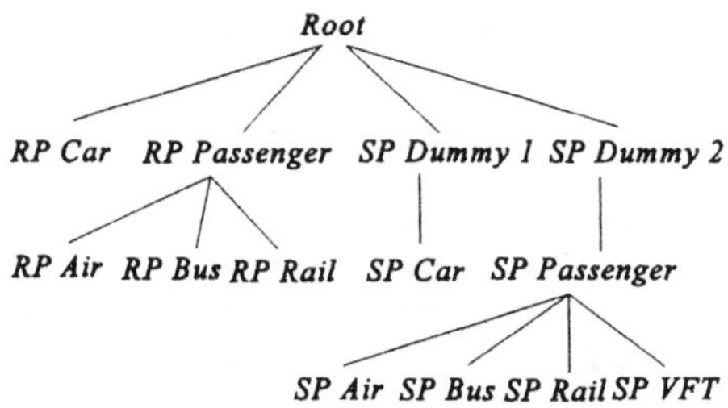

Figure 2
Tree Structure for Joint Nested Estimation

The scale parameter applied to the SP "dummy" alternatives is not a typical structural parameter, as was discussed in section 2. The resulting scale parameters in Table 3 fall on either side of unity, but quite close in both cases. This means that the proportion of unexplained variance is (coincidentally) about the same in both types of data. This is different from the results of Case Study 1.

One finding is similar to the results of the first case study: the RP models give the incorrect sign for access time, perhaps as a result of correlation with the other network-based time and cost variables. The SP models, on the other hand, give more reasonable estimates for access time at about twice as high as for main in-vehicle time. In contrast to Case Study 1, however, combining the RP and SP data did not produce a significant access-time coefficient for either purpose. The difference, in this example, is the fact that the RP sample is quite large compared to the SP sample and has a similar scale ($\theta \doteq 1$). There is no within-mode SP data with high enough measurement precision to "overrule" the RP data, as was the case in Tables 1 and 2. In practice, if one believed that the SP results were more "correct," it would be best simply to constrain the main and access-time coefficients in the RP or RP+SP model to have the same ratios as estimated in the SP-only model. This is similar to the "sequential" estimation approach, where the SP results are used to constrain the *relative* values of the coefficients of the β parameters in the RP model.

The ratio of the main in-vehicle time coefficient to the "work time-equivalent" cost coefficient is about 3.0 for the RP and SP business models, and about 2.0 for the RP and SP non-business models. For the mixed RP+SP models, the results are closest to the RP-only results due to sample size. Although not shown here, it was found that the SP and RP data did not give such similar estimates for the relative value of time and cost until *after* a nested-model structure was adopted with car versus the passenger modes. This result confirms the importance of using a correct model specification and the value of being able to apply the joint RP/SP estimation approach to nested models.

A number of further points can be made about these results. First, the extra variables for the air mode, related to day trips, travelling alone, and younger travellers, are much more significant for the RP models than the SP models. This may reflect the fact that such "background" effects have less influence on SP data, because of the highly controlled nature of the independent variables and the choice context. One might decide not to estimate these segment-specific variables for air jointly, because the two separate data sets give different results.

Second, in Table 3, two separate sets of modal constants are estimated in the joint RP/SP models. The most important constant is that related to the new VFT mode, because this is necessary for forecasting and cannot be derived from the RP data. Mode-specific constants for the existing modes are not constrained to be the same as those from the RP data, because different types of unobserved effects may influence the two types of data. The two data sources give somewhat different trends for these constants, although the SP constants are highly correlated with the "inertia" effect (see below).

Third, the SP models in Table 3 again contain an "inertia" effect, to reflect the higher probability of each respondent selecting their actual mode during the SP choice experiment. The size of the inertia effects is similar to that found in Case Study 1. Note that the inertia variable may reflect a number of unobserved effects that would otherwise be captured in the mode-specific constants. Also note that the "intertia" coefficient is similar in size to the VFT modal constant — if the inertia variable is excluded from the model (not shown here), the VFT constant becomes close to zero, while the constants for the existing modes become much larger negative. The use of the "inertia" effect and the constant for the new mode are important issues in application, and are discussed further in the final section.

Fourth, according to the likelihood-ratio test, the final likelihood of the mixed RP/SP model is significantly worse than the combined likelihoods of the separate RP and SP models for both trip purposes. This result seems to be typical for this approach[9]; the likelihood-ratio test seems to be quite a strict test for combining different data sources. One can try to improve the fit of the joint model by estimating variables separately that may be expected to have different RP and SP effects. An example in Table 3 would be to estimate RP- and SP-specific variables for the three air-related segment variables.

Finally, as noted earlier, joint estimation is not necessary (or possible) when SP experiments have only a single variable in common with RP models. An example here was a within-mode experiment, trading off a number of VFT qualitative service variables against fare level. Models, based on such data, can be applied by simply scaling all SP coefficients by the ratio of the fare coefficient in the RP model to the fare coefficient in the SP model.

Summary and Conclusions

Experience in transportation planning has confirmed the usefulness of both revealed-preference and stated-preference data. However, these two types of data each offer specific and different strengths and weaknesses. Analysis exploiting both types of data simultaneously can use the strengths of each type of data to help overcome the weaknesses of the other.

The key points in combining the two types of data are the differing systematic *biases* and random *errors* that occur in the two differing contexts. Coping with biases introduces no new methodological issues, but the fact that different levels of error are present requires special treatment in modelling.

The proposal presented in this paper is that the combination of RP and SP data can be achieved using models of the logit form. Accommodation of the differing error variances then requires the use of an artificial tree-logit construction. However, the resulting model can be estimated conveniently using existing commercial software.

The tree logit method developed has been tested on two separate case studies. In the first case study, it was shown that the results obtained from the logit approach proposed here correspond closely with those obtained from the probit approach investigated by Morikawa *et al.* Remaining differences appear to be associated with the higher sensitivity of probit models to unusual observations (outliers).

The second case study confirms the results of the first, in showing that the combined RP and SP data can improve and expand upon the results of RP data alone, while retaining the reliability of association with actual behaviour. This second example was a more rigorous test, in that it used RP and SP data from different surveys, and it used nested-logit model specifications on both types of data.

The examples demonstrate that the method can be performed using currently available software. The advantages of combining data of these two types are substantial and the results appear reliable thus far. Further examples of research and applications of this new approach will be important in making it a part of standard travel-demand modelling practice. As in using any new method, a body of experience needs to be built up in order to judge how this approach should be used best in practice — particularly in forecasting.

One important issue is the use of parameters that can be estimated only from SP data. For example, should the VFT-mode constant in the previous example be used "as is" in forecasting (after adjusting for the scale difference), or should we somehow determine its value ***relative*** to the SP-specific constants for the competing modes? The sensitivity of forecasts to this decision should be tested, because the "correct" approach is not obvious.

In this same line, the use of inertia effects needs to be considered carefully. These effects are in some ways analogous to those that can be found in longitudinal data, using information on previous behaviour. While it is clear that significant effects can be found, it is not obvious what they represent — heterogeneity in the population, actual reluctance, or "costs" of changing behaviour, or other effects that are specific to the SP experiment. In any case, such variables may be valid only for predicting switches away from the current mode in the short term. For longer-term forecasting models that are not conditional on current choices, it may be better not to include such variables in SP models, or at least to check that their inclusion does not greatly affect the SP-based estimates which ***are*** used in prediction.

In closing, we should point out that the joint-estimation method demonstrated here may have other uses than in combining RP and SP data in analysis. The scaling approach can also be applied to combine different types of RP data, or even to look for differences in data from different stages during a single SP experiment[24]. It could also be useful in combining RP information with information from other types of data from hypothetical contexts, such as "stated intentions" or "transfer prices"[25].

ACKNOWLEDGMENTS

The authors are grateful to the anonymous reviewers for their useful suggestions. The structure of the paper has been revised from that of the original Quebec version, and the second case study has been updated to take advantage of further experience using this approach since the date of the conference.

REFERENCES

1. Ben-Akiva, M., and S. Lerman, *Discrete Choice Analysis: Theory and Application to Travel Demand.* MIT Press, Cambridge, Massachussettes, 1985.

2. *Ibid.*

3. Daly, A., and J. de D. Ortúzar, "Forecasting and Data Aggregation: Theory and Practice," *Traffic Engineering and Control*, December, 1990.

4. Kocur, G., T. Adler, and W. Hyman, *Guide to Forecasting Travel Demand with Direct Utility Assessment*, U.S. Dept. of Transportation, Washington, D.C., 1982.

5. Sheldon, R., and J. Steer. "The Use of Conjoint Analysis in Transport Research," Proceedings of PTRC 10th Annual Summer Meeting, July, 1982.

6. Green, P., and V. Srinivasin, "Conjoint Analysis in Consumer Research: Issues and Outlook," *Journal of Consumer Research*, 1978, Vol. 5, pp 103-123.

7. McFadden, D., "The Choice Theory Approach to Market Research," *Marketing Science*, 1986, Vol. 5 (4).

8. Ben-Akiva, M., and B. Boccarra, "Integrated Framework for Travel Behavior Analysis," *Proceedings of the International Conference for Travel Behavior*, Aix-en-Provence, October 1987.

9. Bradley, M., and E. Kroes, "Forecasting Issues in Stated Preference Survey Research," *Selected Readings in Transport Survey Methodology*, Eucalyptus Press, Melbourne, 1992.

10. Bradley, M., and E. Kroes, "Simultaneous Analysis of Stated Preference and Revealed Preference Information," *PTRC 18th Annual Summer Meeting-Proceedings of Seminar H*, September 1990.

11. Morikawa, T., *Incorporating Stated Preference Data in Travel Demand Analysis*, Doctoral dissertation, MIT, Cambridge, Massachussettes, June 1989.

12. Morikawa, T., M. Ben-Akiva and D. McFadden, "Incorporating Psychometric Data in Econometric Demand Models," Proceedings of the Invitational Symposium on Consumer Decision Making and Choice Behavior, Banff,

May 1990.

13. Ben-Akiva, M. and S. R. Lerman, *op. cit.*

14. Ben-Akiva, M. and S. R. Lerman, *op. cit.*

15. Daly, A., "Integration of Revealed Preference and Stated Preference Data in Model Estimation," Proceedings of the Invitational Symposium on Consumer Decision Making and Choice Behaviour, Banff, May 1990.

16. Daly, A., and S. Zachary, "Commuters' Values of Time," *Local Government Operational Research Unit - Report T55*, Reading, January 1975, pp. 55-60.

17. Daly, A., "Estimation of Tree Logit Models," *Transportation Research*, 1987, Vol. 21B, pp. 251-267.

18. Morikawa, T., *op. cit.*

19. Bradley, M., T. Grosvenor, and A. Bouma, "An Application of Computer-Based Stated Preference to Study Mode Switching in the Netherlands," *PTRC 16th Annual Summer Meeting - Proceedings of Seminar D*, September 1988.

20. Morikawa, T., *op. cit.*

21. Ben-Akiva, M. and S. R. Lerman, *op. cit.*

22. Morikawa, T., *op. cit.*

23. Gunn, H., M. Bradley, and D. Hensher, "High Speed Rail Market Projection: Survey Design and Analysis," *Presented at the 3rd International Conference on Survey Methods in Transportation*, Washington, D.C., January 1990.

24. Bradley, M., and A. Daly, "Uses of the Logit Scaling Approach in Stated Preference Analysis," *Presented at the 6th World Conference on Transportation Research*, Lyon, 1992.

25. Bonsall, P., "Transfer Price Data - Its Definition, Collection and Use", *New Survey Methods in Transport*, VNU Science Press, Utrecht, 1985.

ELSEVIER

Journal of Econometrics 89 (1999) 197–221

JOURNAL OF Econometrics

Combining sources of preference data

David Hensher[a], Jordan Louviere[b], Joffre Swait[c,d,*]

[a] *Graduate School of Business, The University of Sydney, Sydney, NSW 2006, Australia*
[b] *Department of Marketing, The University of Sydney, Sydney, NSW 2006, Australia*
[c] *Advanis Inc., 12 W. University Ave., #205, Gainesville, FL 32601, USA*
[d] *College of Business Administration, University of Florida, FL, USA*

Abstract

This paper brings together several research streams and concepts that have been evolving in random utility choice theory: (1) it reviews the literature on stated preference (SP) elicitation methods and introduces the concept of testing data generation process invariance across SP and revealed preference (RP) choice data sources; (2) it describes the evolution of discrete choice models within the random utility family, where progressively more behavioural realism is being achieved by relaxing strong assumptions on the role of the variance structure (specifically, heteroscedasticity) of the unobserved effects, a topic central to the issue of combining multiple data sources; (3) particular choice model formulations incorporating heteroscedastic effects are presented, discussed and applied to data. The rich insights possible from modelling heteroscedasticity in choice processes are illustrated in the empirical application, highlighting its relevance to issues of data combination and taste heterogeneity.

JEL classification: C25

Keywords: Choice data combination; Choice models; Stated preference; Heteroscedasticity; Discrete Regression; Qualitative Choice Models

1. Introduction

Economists have traditionally focused on the actual market behaviour of economic agents for both theory inspiration and testing. Despite this traditional

* Correspondence address: Advanis Inc., 12 W. University Ave. #205, Gainesville, FL 32601, USA. E-mail: Joffre_Swait@Advanis.ca

0304-4076/99/$ – see front matter
PII: S0304-4076(98)00061-X

interest (e.g., Lancaster, 1996; McFadden, 1981) in what the literature terms *revealed preference* (RP) data, there are compelling reasons why economists also should be interested in *stated preference* (SP) data. SP data involve choices by the same economic agents, but evoked in hypothetical markets for reasons such as these:

1. Firms need to model demand for new products with new attributes or features for which there is no RP history, and/or for which one cannot safely forecast by analogy to existing products.
2. Key RP explanatory variables may exhibit little or no variability, and/or be highly collinear. Often collinearity arises from two interrelated sources: (a) *market technology*, which drives correlations among some product attributes and limits ranges over which they vary; and (b) *market forces*, which encourage competitors to offer similar attribute levels, or at least restricts ranges on certain attributes. Market forces also encourage negative correlations between attributes for a given efficient frontier, hence, some attributes may be perfectly correlated and/or linear combinations of other attributes, which can lead to identification problems.
3. As markets evolve and change, attributes previously not present may be introduced to influence choices. For example, PCs offer many new features unavailable five years ago, and these features not only may drive current choices but also may appeal to different market segments.
4. Often RP data fail to satisfy model assumptions and/or contain statistical quirks. Even with more powerful statistical tools and models, one imposes maintained assumptions to analyse data. Failure to satisfy assumptions often leads to bias, which may be ameliorated with SP data or a combined RP/SP data strategy.
5. In contrast to RP data, SP data may be less time and money intensive to collect.
6. Some products are not traded in real markets, and although RP data can be used for indirect inference in some cases, such as 'travel cost' methods used to model environmental impacts (Englin and Cameron, 1996), RP data often do not exist (see Hanemann and Kanninen, 1997).

By definition, RP data help illuminate preferences within existing or recent past market and technology structures. Although SP data may also be useful in this way, they provide insights into how preferences are likely to respond to shifts in technological frontiers. The latter use of SP data is exploited by many academic and applied researchers, and often plays a key role in informing corporate and marketing strategy. That is, understanding and predicting consumer responses to new product introductions, line extensions, etc., involve modelling likely demand and cannibalisation effects, identifying appropriate target markets, segments, etc. Such strategic decisions typically involve significant uncertainties, which motivated initial and continuing interest in SP methods and models in marketing. These observations therefore suggest that RP and SP data sources have complementary strengths and weaknesses which potentially can be exploited to enhance understanding of preference processes. Thus, not surprisingly, interest in combining RP and SP choice data (and, more generally, preference data) has been growing steadily in transportation, marketing and resource economics since 1991 (e.g. Ben-Akiva and Morikawa, 1991; Swait and Louviere, 1993; Adamowicz et al., 1994, 1996).

Therefore, the objectives of this paper are to:

1. review and discuss some key developments and advances in this stream of research;
2. present a select set of model specifications that incorporate different error structure assumptions, which lie at the heart of the data combination process, and discuss their associated parameter estimation and testing issues;
3. exemplify the types of insights that may be obtained from data combination exercises, via an empirical illustration; and
4. present and discuss conclusions and research implications arising from this stream of research.

2. Decision making and choice behaviour

2.1. *Conceptual framework*

The marketing discipline has developed a working model of consumer decision making that is loosely structured as follows. Consumers first become aware of needs and/or problems, and then search for information about products/services that could satisfy their need(s)/solve their problems. As consumers learn about products, product attributes and attribute levels, and associated uncertainties, they form beliefs about products. Eventually, they have sufficient information to form a decision strategy (or utility function) for valuing and trading off various product attributes. Once consumers have beliefs or priors about attributes possessed by product alternatives, they develop preference orderings for products; and depending upon budget and/or other constraints or considerations, decide whether to purchase/choose, and if they purchase/choose, which one or more alternatives, in what quantities, how often, etc.

Fig. 1 formalises the stages which consumers go through to form utilities or values and compare products to form overall (holistic) preferences for available sets of alternatives. The stages form a series of interrelated processes, which are consistent with economic theory and random utility operationalisation of decision processes. Importantly, the conceptual framework shows that one can 'mix and match' measures from different stages in the process to explain choice

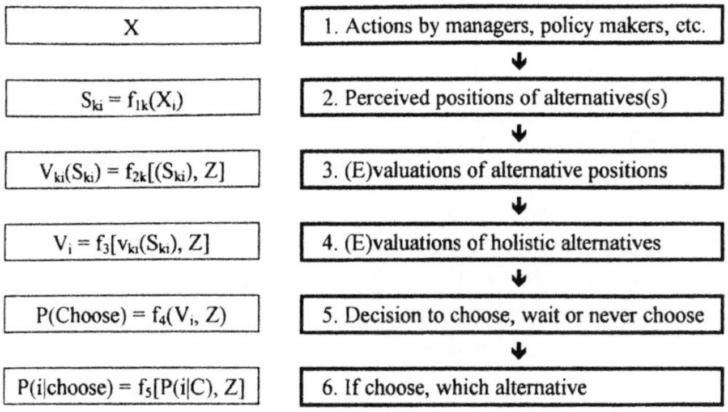

Fig. 1. Functional relationships implied by the framework.

behaviour. In this way, explanatory variables at one stage can serve as instruments or 'proxy' variables for measures at other stages, which can reduce specification errors and/or improve estimation efficiency. The framework also suggests that choices can be explained by direct observation/measurement of physical product attributes and/or managerial actions like advertising expenditures or price promotions (the vector X), but such direct estimation may obscure important intermediate processes and/or overlook the potential role of intermediate models and measures. The advantage of the latter integration is that one can explain choice behaviour in terms of

1. individual characteristics/differences (Z's),
2. physically observable and measurable (engineering) variables (X's),
3. psychophysical variables (beliefs/product positions) (S's),
4. part-worth utility measures (v's), or
5. holistic measures of each alternative's utility (V's).

SP methods primarily have been used to model processes involved in stages 2–6, although it is worth noting that there has been an enormous amount of research in psychology and neurophysiology involving stage 1 (called psychophyics, or mapping physical reality into perceptions). Econometricians are probably less familiar with SP methods and models used to study, explain and model these intermediate processes. Thus, a brief overview of SP methods and models seems apropos. Our review emphasises SP methods and models in marketing, and concentrates on recent research on combining sources of preference data to enhance our ability to explain and model the links implied in Fig. 1.

2.2. Brief overview of SP methods and models

The SP methods and models literature is large and spread over several fields, but psychology and marketing arguably contain the material likely to be of most interest to econometricians. Although there are many SP paradigms, we focus on work related to random utility theory (RUT) choice models. RUT was first proposed by Thurstone (1927) as a way to model choices of pairs of alternatives. McFadden (1974) extended RUT to the multiple choice case, although fixed (as opposed to random) utility multiple choice models were developed earlier (e.g., Luce, 1959; Restle, 1961; Rushton, 1969).

Academic marketing's interest in SP models primarily is concentrated in two research streams: (a) conjoint analysis (CA) and related work on modelling consumer tradeoffs and preferences (e.g., Green and Wind, 1971; Green and Srinivasan, 1978, 1990; Louviere, 1974, 1988a, 1994, 1995); and (b) behavioural decision theory (BDT) in marketing, psychology and economics, which seeks deeper understanding of process and more behaviourally realistic models of decision processes (e.g., Meyer et al., 1984; Kahneman and Tversky, 1979, 1984; Keller, 1993). It is fair to say that much BDT research is incompatible with RUT, and has little intellectual commonality with research on modelling preferences in econometrics and economics; consequently, we focus on the first research stream.

Conjoint analysis and related techniques are used to measure and model consumer tradeoffs, preferences and choices. The origins of these methods are axiomatic conjoint measurement, utility theory and risky decision making (e.g., Krantz and Tversky, 1971; Krantz et al., 1971; Machina, 1987), but few papers in this stream in marketing involve risky decision making (e.g., Louviere, 1988a). As well, great emphasis has been placed on practical application and prediction instead of process explanations (but see Lynch, 1985); hence, much of the published work in marketing eschews behavioural theory in favour of ad hoc statistical methods. However, conjoint analysis recently has been recast in a more behavioural framework consistent with RUT and RUT-based choice models (Louviere, 1988b, 1994, 1995). This more recent stream of research comprises the remainder of our overview, but we first briefly explain conjoint analysis as typically practiced by marketing academics and professionals.

CA is a family of preference elicitation procedures that involves the following series of design and analysis steps: (a) identification (to the extent possible) of an underlying set of product attributes that drive choice in particular applications, (b) assignment of levels to each attribute to represent ranges of likely variation expected during a period of interest, (c) use of experimental design techniques to combine attribute levels into multi-attribute descriptions or 'product profiles', (d) evaluation of the product profiles by consumers sampled from a target market of interest (usually evaluating profiles on rating scales), (e) analysis of each sampled consumer's profile rating data to estimate individual-specific models (usually via OLS regression) and (f) using the resulting equations to predict the choices expected for various scenarios of policy interest (usually predicting that alternatives with the highest predicted regression scores will be chosen). There are many variations on this general theme, including more recent methods that employ multiple choice experiments and use RUT-based discrete choice models to analyse the resulting data and make predictions using micro-simulation methods (Louviere and Woodworth, 1983; Louviere, 1994), but the preceding description is fairly close to the mark.

To date little academic research in marketing concerned with CA or BDT has evinced interest in developing formal links with theory in economics and/or real market behaviour, although lip service sometimes is paid to Lancaster (1966) product characteristics framework by CA adherents. In contrast, research into preference elicitation procedures consistent with RUT has tried to forge such conceptual and empirical links (e.g., Louviere and Hensher, 1983; Louviere and Woodworth, 1983; Hensher and Louviere, 1983; Louviere, 1988a,b; Louviere, 1994, 1995; Hensher, 1994; Swait and Louviere, 1993; Swait et al., 1993; Adamowicz et al., 1994, 1996). Indeed, since the early 1980s marketing and transportation researchers steadily have increased our understanding of the links between traditional RP models and measures and their SP counterparts. In fact, it is now fair to say that these links are reasonably well understood, and that (with some exceptions) it is possible to design research to obtain SP data that parallel RP data in most details.

By way of contrast, traditional CA and much of BDT research involves evaluation or decision tasks that bear little resemblance to choice situations faced by real consumers. For example, traditional CA typically relies on elicitation tasks that involve one-at-a-time ratings of product profiles. Such tasks may indeed elicit preferences, but they have no counterpart in consumer behaviour in real markets. Similarly, many BDT tasks involve the study of obtuse low-dimensional gambles, which often have only vague connections to real market choices. Researchers involved in the development and application of RUT-based preference elicitation methods, on the other hand, often seek to develop experiments and tasks that resemble their real market counterparts in as many essential details as possible. This has led to the development of new design theory for these types of discrete multiple choice problems (e.g., Louviere and Woodworth, 1983; Huber and Zwerina, 1996).

Thus, it is fair to say that at the present time the primary difference between more traditional RP econometric methods and models and the more recent RUT-based SP methods and models is primarily the data generation processes. Specifically, RUT-SP theory and analysis methods are identical to those that underlie the econometric analysis of cross-sectional and longitudinal discrete choices or other preference data consistent with RUT (e.g., ordered outcomes, complete rankings, joint continuous-discrete and other selection problems, etc.). Perhaps more importantly, recognition of this isomorphism between methods and models used to obtain and analyse RUT-based RP and SP data has spurred academic and applied interest in combining sources of preference data (e.g., Morikawa, 1989; Ben-Akiva and Morikawa, 1991; Swait and Louviere, 1993; Swait et al., 1993; Swait et al., 1994; Adamowicz et al., 1994, 1996; Hensher and Bradley, 1993; Louviere, 1994, 1995). This recent research interest and the resulting paradigm associated with it are the focus of our paper, and are discussed in Section 3.

The isomorphism of RUT-based RP and SP data has evolved from advances in RUT-based SP choice modelling theory and methods. Although it is well established that RUT-based discrete choice SP models can be estimated from experiments involving choices among pairs of options (e.g., Thurstone, 1927), a more general experimental basis was established only recently in marketing and transport. Specifically, Louviere and Woodworth (1983) in marketing, and Hensher and Louviere (1983) in transport pioneered a general approach to design and analyse discrete choice experiments based on McFadden's (1974) extension of RUT to the multiple choice case. More recently, there has been further progress on design theory for SP choice experiments (e.g., Hensher and Barnard, 1990; Anderson and Wiley, 1992; Bunch et al., 1996; Huber and Zwerina, 1996), but much more research is needed.

In particular, the design issues in choice experiments are (a) identification, (b) precision, (c) realism and (d) cognitive limitations. Identification refers to the possible forms of utility functions that can be identified (tested) from a given experiment under a maintained hypothesis about a choice model form (e.g., Multinomial Logit, Multinomial Probit). Precision refers to the efficiency of the estimates, given a functional form and maintained choice model hypothesis. Realism is the degree to which the experiment mirrors real marketplace choices, and cognitive limits refers to complexity and task demands. Typically, one tries to maximise identification, minimise standard errors, and maximise realism subject to management of complexity at levels that do not compromise data quality (see Swait and Adamowicz, 1997). Naturally, applied work requires compromise among these objectives.

Choice experiments are particular types of experimental designs that take identification and precision into account. A choice experiment consists of one or more sets of mutually exclusive, competing choice alternatives, which can be designed sequentially or simultaneously (Louviere, 1988a, 1994), the latter being far more common than the former:

- *Sequential design*: First, designs one or more sets of choice alternatives (often product profiles as in CA) with desirable utility function identification properties, and then assigns them to choice sets such that choice model properties and desired levels of precision are satisfied. For example, if one wishes to study how consumers choose from choice sets that consist of a fixed set of three competing options in a particular market, one could develop a sequential design as follows: (a) design three statistically equivalent sets of P total product profiles (attribute level combinations), (b) place each set of P profiles in three separate 'urns' and (c) simultaneously sample one profile randomly from each urn without replacement to create P total choice sets with three choice options. If the number of sets is sufficiently large, asymptotic properties of particular discrete choice models should be satisfied; and taken as a whole, the choice sets should have desirable statistical properties. This approach is relatively easy to implement, but cannot insure identification or precision levels without large numbers of sets.

- *Simultaneous design*: If there are N choice alternatives, and each has M attributes with exactly L levels, one can design experiments that satisfy the statistical properties of the most general member of the logistic regression family (i.e., 'Mother Logit' – McFadden et al., 1977) by treating all attributes of all alternatives as a collective factorial (i.e., L^{MN}) and selecting the smallest orthogonal main-effects design from the full factorial. This insures that the marginals (i.e., alternative-specific and/or generic parameters) are orthogonal within and between choice alternatives, which satisfies the necessary and sufficient conditions to estimate the parameters of a Mother Logit model. Mother Logit models include 'cross-effects' of attributes of one alternative in the utility function of a second alternative, thus allowing violations of the IID property of RUT choice models (Louviere and Woodworth, 1983; McFadden, 1981). Such a design allows one to estimate own-attribute and cross-attribute effects independently, which in turn allows one to relax the IID assumption in the basic MNL model derivation and permits estimation of more complex model forms.

There are other ways to design choice experiments (e.g., 2^N designs, Louviere and Woodworth, 1983), but the above encompasses much of the state of the art. Generally speaking, designs differ in (a) ability to capture utility function complexity (i.e., non-linearities and/or non-additivities), (b) number of alternatives, (c) number of attributes per alternative and (d) types of IID violations accommodated (Louviere and Woodworth, 1983; Louviere, 1988a,b; Louviere, 1994, 1995; Carson et al., 1994). It is fair to say that research on the design of RUT-based choice experiments is in its infancy, and although much has been learned, much more research is needed to fully illuminate properties of designs and develop optimally efficient designs for a wide variety of non-IID error choice processes. Specifically, there now exist a variety of ways to design choice experiments consistent with simple MNL choice processes, and progress has been made in the design of more complex experiments which relax IID error assumptions. However, little work is available to guide design selection for particular problems, because choice models are non-linear, and design optimisation requires a priori knowledge of true probabilities. That is, we know that certain types of designs are consistent with various choice process models like MNL. However, we do not yet understand how statistically efficient such designs may be for particular applications, nor how to optimise these designs for particular applications except in limited circumstances involving small numbers of alternatives and attributes (see Bunch et al., 1996; Carson et al., 1994).

3. The theory of choice data combination

3.1. The fundamental identification problem: inseparability of taste and scale

It is well known that the scale of the estimated parameters and the magnitude of the random component in all choice models based on random utility theory (RUT) are linked (see, e.g., Hensher and Johnson, 1981; Ben-Akiva and Lerman, 1985; Anderson et al., 1992). Let

$$U_{iq} = V_{iq} + \varepsilon_{iq}, \tag{1}$$

where U_{iq} is the unobserved, latent utility consumer q associates with alternative i, V_{iq} the systematic, quantifiable proportion of utility involving observables of alternatives and consumers, and ε_{iq} is the random or unobservable effects associated with the utility of alternative i and consumer q. All RUT-based choice models are derived by making assumptions about the distribution of the random effects. Imbedded in all RUT choice models are scale parameters, which are inversely related to the variance of the random component and not identifiable separately from taste parameters. The imbedded scale parameters are a consequence of the distributions assumed.

For example, the multinomial logit (MNL) choice model is derived from Eq. (1) by assuming that the ε_{iq} are IID Gumbel distributed. The Gumbel scale parameter $\lambda \geqslant 0$ is inversely proportional to the standard deviation of the random component ($\sigma_{iq} = \pi\lambda^{-1}6^{-1/2}$). The full expression of the MNL choice probability is

$$P_{iq} = \frac{\exp(\lambda V_{iq})}{\sum_{j \in C_n} \exp(\lambda V_{jq})} = \frac{\exp(\lambda \beta X_{iq})}{\sum_{j \in C_q} \exp(\lambda \beta X_{jq})}, \tag{2}$$

where P_{iq} is the choice probability of alternative i for consumer q, the systematic utility $V_{iq} = \beta X_{iq}$, and β is the vector of taste parameters. Ben-Akiva and Lerman (1985, Chapter 5) discuss the MNL model in detail and show that the parameter vector estimated from a given source of RUT-conformable preference data is actually ($\lambda\beta$), which presents one with an identification problem. A given set of data yields some value of λ, which can be normalised to a constant (e.g., unity). The analysis proceeds as if $(\lambda\beta)$ were the taste parameters.[1]

A similar identification problem exists for other generalised extreme value (GEV) choice models, such as Nested MNL, tree extreme value and ordered GEV (McFadden, 1981; Small, 1987, 1994), binary logit and probit models, and even MNP (multinomial probit) (e.g., Hausman and Wise, 1978; Daganzo, 1980; Bunch, 1991; Keane, 1995). Such identification problems arise because choice models specify a structural relationship between a categorical response and a latent variable (i.e. utility). Similar to structural equation models involving latent variables (e.g. LISREL), both origin *and* variance (i.e., 'scale') of the latent variable(s) must be specified to identify utility function parameters.

Morikawa (1989) noted that the basic scale identification problem applied to a single preference data source, but ratios of λ's in two or more sources of data were identified, which led to sequential (Swait and Louviere, 1993) and simultaneous (Morikawa, 1989; Ben-Akiva and Morikawa, 1991; Hensher and Bradley, 1993; Bhat, 1995) estimation methods for combining RP and SP data sources.

Suppose there are K preference data sources to be combined. The estimation problem above involves imposing an equality restriction on the taste parameters of the K preference data sources (i.e. $\beta_1 = \cdots = \beta_K = \beta$), and estimation of $K - 1$ additional scale parameters $(\lambda_1, \ldots, \lambda_K)$. That is, one scale parameter is fixed, say $\lambda_1 = 1$, and the $K - 1$ other parameters are inverse variance ratios relative to the reference (fixed) data source. The corresponding unrestricted model frees taste parameters and scale factors for the K data sources by estimating $(\lambda_k\beta_k)$, $k = 1, \ldots, K$. The null hypothesis is taste invariance across data sources, after permitting variance/reliability differences,[2] which can be tested using a likelihood ratio statistic, as we later discuss.

Increasing recognition of the scale parameter's role spawned several research streams, most notably (a) 'data fusion' in travel demand modelling (e.g., Morikawa, 1989; Ben-Akiva and Morikawa, 1991; Hensher and Bradley, 1993; Swait et al., 1994), and (b) combining, comparing and testing process differences in sources of preference data (e.g., Swait and Louviere, 1993; Louviere et al., 1993; Bradley and Daly, 1994; Louviere, 1994; Louviere, 1995; Swait and Adamowicz, 1997). The latter stream views scale (variance) as an integral feature of behavioural processes, whereas data fusionists seem to see scale as a nuisance

[1] Note that MNL models predict random choice as $\lambda \to 0$, and a step function as $\lambda \to \infty$ (see Ben-Akiva and Lerman, 1985). This general behaviour applies to all choice model specifications.

[2] Let each data source have L taste parameters. Under the null hypothesis, K parameter vectors can be represented in R^L as vectors of different lengths dictated by differences in reliability (i.e. more reliable measures correspond to longer vectors) superimposed upon one another. The practical importance of this is that an L component graph of two coefficient vectors that differ only in reliability (variance) should plot as a scatter of points around a straight line passing through the origin. The (positive) slope of this line is the ratio of the respective scale parameters.

parameter that must be taken into account to estimate true quantities of interest (i.e. taste parameters). The latter stream also holds a more catholic view of preference data combinations and comparisons, such as RP with RP and SP with SP, compared with the data fusionists' typical interest in joining RP and SP data sources.

The key insight that precedes both streams, however, is the role that the error structures of different preference data sources play when combining them. Real decision processes are better described if the analyst recognises the behavioural meaning of traditional statistical constructs such as variance and covariance, scale and taste weights. For example, relaxing the constant error variance assumption on the indirect utility of each alternative in a choice set allows one to avoid this key limitation of MNL models by using variance properties to satisfy a common set of statistical assumptions and combine data from different sources (Morikawa, 1989; Hensher and Bradley, 1993; Swait and Louviere, 1993). Different data collection processes may influence choice variability differentially, and if this is not recognised, may confound the real behavioural role of observed and unobserved influences on choice. The latter can be captured by appropriate specification of the error variance structure. For example, the variance of each alternative can be specified as a function of task complexity (Swait and Adamowicz, 1997) or respondent characteristics which proxy the ability to understand tasks (Bhat, 1996; Hensher, in press).

Thus, to summarise: a general view of the data combination problem recognises and accounts for error structure differences between data sources when testing for (or imposing) taste invariance across data sources. Up to this point, the literature has concentrated on modeling the differential variances (i.e. heteroscedasticity) within and between sources (see references above) when combining multiple data sets. The recognition of the role of heteroscedasticity in this research stream has made it synonymous with the concept of combining sources of preference data.

3.2. *Some alternative ways to handle heteroscedasticity in choice models*

A hierarchy of models is evolving to progressively relax some testable assumptions imposed on the error term in utility function (1). We discuss some possible ways to relax the homoscedasticity assumption with respect to ε_{iq} when combining sources of preference data, and relax certain other restrictions often imposed on choice models. Our discussion focuses on examples from the GEV family of discrete choice models (all variants of MNL) for cross-sectional choice data, but the general principles and concepts apply equally well to other choice models and data types.

3.2.1. *Random effects heteroscedastic extreme value model*

The constant variance assumption can be relaxed by specifying a more complex choice model called the heteroscedastic extreme value (HEV) model.

Allenby and Ginter (1995), Bhat (1995) and Hensher (in press) recently estimated HEV models from single-data sources, and Hensher (1998) jointly estimated one from SP and RP data. Assume the utility function is given by Eq. (1), but that errors are independently, but not identically, distributed over alternatives according to a Type I Extreme Value (or Gumbel) density function

$$f_i(t) = \exp(-t)\exp(-\exp(-\lambda_i t)), \quad -\infty < t < \infty, \tag{3}$$

where the λ_i are the respective scale parameters. The errors are, therefore, independent and heteroscedastic. If the decision rule is maximal utility, then the choice probabilities are given by

$$P_{iq} = \int_{-\infty}^{\infty} \prod_{j \neq i} F(\lambda_j)[V_{iq} - V_{jq} + \varepsilon_{iq}]\lambda_i f(\lambda_i \varepsilon_{iq})\, \mathrm{d}\varepsilon_{iq}. \tag{4}$$

The derivation of this expression is given in Bhat (1995) and Hensher (in press).

The HEV model nests the more restrictive MNL, and is sufficiently flexible to allow differential cross-elasticities among all pairs of alternatives, while avoiding the a priori identification of mutually exclusive market partitions in a nested MNL structure.[3] It is parsimonious compared to MNP, adding only $J-1$ parameters to the covariance matrix compared to an additional $[J(J-1)/2]-1$ in the more general MNP model (J is the total number of alternatives in the universal choice set). The computational burden is much less than for MNP, as only a one-dimensional integral (independent of the number of alternatives) is evaluated (MNP evaluates a $(J-1)$-dimensional integral). Importantly, and in contrast to MNP, the HEV model is easy to interpret and its behaviour intuitive (Bhat, 1995).

Hensher (in press) suggested that HEV be used to identify appropriate partitionings of MNL models into nested structures, obviating the search for structure in nested MNL partitions. Nested forms of MNL can accommodate systematic dependencies among unobserved effects that drive violations of the independence of irrelevant alternatives (IIA) property in MNL models. HEV is not closed form, but is appealing because a nested model consistent with the HEV profile of λ_i is easy to apply without the numerical integration of expression (4) (see Hensher and Bradley, 1993). HEV models can be specified for multiple data sources, jointly estimated using a FIML approach to produce a set of alternative-specific λ's across both RP and SP choice sets, by normalising on an arbitrarily selected alternative.

[3] The probabilities must be evaluated numerically because there is no closed-form solution for this single-dimensional integral. The integral can be approximated (e.g., by Gauss–Laguerre quadrature, Press et al., 1986), and computational experience suggests a 68 point approximation can accurately reproduce taste parameter estimates (Greene, 1996).

3.2.2. Parametrised heteroscedastic MNL model

Theory can be developed to explain heteroscedasticity structures in preference data of the type described in Eq. (1). For example, advertising exposures may lead to more (or less) variability in the choice behaviour of a population, depending on content. Such effects are captured partially by random effects specifications of scale parameters, but the source of variability is not explicit. It can be made explicit in parametrised heteroscedastic MNL (PHMNL) models[4] (Swait and Adamowicz, 1997; Swait and Stacey, 1996). The PHMNL model scale parameters are given by

$$\lambda_{iq} = \exp(\psi Z_{iq}), \tag{5}$$

where ψ is a parameter row-vector and Z_{iq} are covariates associated with the individual and the alternative. PHMNL choice probabilities are given by

$$P_{iq} = \frac{\exp(\lambda_{iq}\beta X_{iq})}{\sum_{j \in C_q} \exp(\lambda_{iq}\beta X_{jq})}. \tag{6}$$

The parameters to be estimated are β and ψ. PHMNL nests the MNL if $\psi = 0$. As with the HEV model described previously, PHMNL allows complex cross-substitution patterns among alternatives, the general structure of which must be specified via Z_{iq}.

Swait and Adamowicz (1997) hypothesised that SP task complexity and RP choice environment (e.g., market structure) influence levels of variability in preference data. They also proposed a way to characterise complexity and/or choice environment, which was supported in several SP and the one RP data set utilised. Their complexity measure was constant across alternatives, hence, scale parameters in their model varied across individuals and SP replications, instead of alternatives. They also found that differences in complexity between preference data sources impacted ability to combine RP and SP data.

Swait and Stacey (1996) applied PHMNL to scanner panel choice data, allowing variances (i.e. scales) to vary by person, alternative and time period as a function of brand, socio-demographic characteristics, interpurchase time, state dependence, etc. They showed that accounting for non-stationarity of the variance in terms of the explanatory variables Z_{iq} enhanced panel behaviour insights and significantly improved fits relative to models with fixed covariance matrices (e.g., MNL, nested MNL and MNP models).

[4] If scale factors are constant across alternatives the PHMNL model can be derived from a heteroscedasticity argument (Swait and Adamowicz 1997). If scale factors are alternative-specific, it can be derived as a special case of the tree extreme value model (Daly, 1987; McFadden, 1981; Hensher, 1994; Swait and Stacey, 1996). In either case, the final expression for the choice probability is given by (6).

3.3. Summary

Two models were proposed and discussed to relax the constant variance assumption of basic MNL using random effects or parametrised variance functions. Variants of these and other categorical response models can be formulated to deal with specific heteroscedastic violations. The contribution of this discussion was to illustrate general principles of controlling for heteroscedasticity in choice models, a major consideration in combining data sources.

4. Empirical example

To make the concepts of the previous sections more concrete, we focus on a data combination exercise involving two sources of data on choices of freight shipper. We use this exercise to examine the impact of error heteroscedasticity within and between data sources, and implications for data combination.

4.1. Description of the data source

Data were collected from a random sample of firms located in a single city in North America. A random sample of 500 individuals who made freight shipper choice decisions for their firms in that city were contacted by phone to solicit participation in a follow-up mail survey. The survey obtained three types of information: (1) firm characteristics, used to segment results a posteriori; (2) RP data, in the form of most recent (proportional) carrier choice (eight carriers were available in the city at the time), and an indication of which carriers were actively considered to enable specification of firm-specific choice sets and associated attributes of carriers considered; and (3) SP choice data, elicited via 16 binary choice scenarios given to each respondent. (The reader is referred to Swait et al., 1994 for further information concerning this study.)

The SP choice experiment was designed by treating the attributes of both choices as a collective set (i.e., a $8^2 \times 4^4 \times 2^{12}$), and using an orthogonal main effects design to create 80 pairs of attribute descriptions (choice sets). The 80 paired profiles were blocked into five sets of 16 choice sets each, using an extra five-level factor. Thus, each respondent supplied 16 binary choice observations.

4.2. Modelling results

Building on utility function (1), we assume that the deterministic utility of source k is given by $V_{iq}^k = \alpha_i^k + \beta^k X_{iq}^k$, where the α's are brand-specific constants and other quantities as previously defined, $k =$ RP, SP. Our objective is to combine both data sources to estimate a common taste vector, which given the above specification, requires us to test whether $\beta^{RP} = \beta^{SP} = \beta$. Note, however, that associated with the utility function are corresponding error terms; the scale (i.e. variance) of the utilities in each source may impact acceptance or rejection of the hypothesis of taste homogeneity across sources. Thus, we examine different possible assumptions about the structure of the scale differences within and between data sources, and their impact on the data combination process.

Table 1 presents several models, which we discuss in order. Model 1 is an RP Multinomial Logit (MNL) model with homoscedastic error variances (i.e., we assume that $\lambda_{iq}^{\mathrm{RP}} = 1, \forall i,q.$), arguably the standard model for such a data source. Most attribute coefficients are statistically significant and correctly signed, which is somewhat unusual because non-significance and counter-intuitive signs often occur with RP data. Note, however, that two parameters which, respectively, relate to 'better' levels of delivery speed and shipment tracing have incorrect negative signs (i.e. β_3 and β_7). We comment on this below.

Model 2 is a parametrised heteroscedastic MNL model (PHMNL) for the RP data, which relaxes the homoscedasticity restriction by allowing scale factors for three carriers (A, D and E). Lack of variability in RP attribute levels and sparse choice frequencies discourage identification of scale factors for the other carriers. Thus, the scales of alternatives B, C, F, G and H are set to unity for identification purposes. (NB: the scale of at least one alternative *must* be fixed to permit identification of the other scale factors.) Using previously introduced notation, in this second model we specify that

$$\lambda_{iq}^{\mathrm{RP}} = \exp(\psi Z_{iq}), \quad \forall q, \tag{7}$$

where Z_{iq} is basically a vector of brand constants and ψ the vector of coefficients in Table 1 (see 'scale function parameters'). The scale of carrier A relative to B, C, F, G and H is $\exp(-1.0134) \approx 0.36$, which corresponds to a variance of about 12.7 for an assumed Gumbel error variate. Carrier D has an error variance of 3.2, which is about 4 times smaller than that of A. The estimated error variances of the utility of carriers A and D not only differ from one another, but also are significantly larger than for the base group of carriers. On the other hand, carrier E has an estimated relative scale factor (variance) of about 1.26 (1.04), which is approximately equal to that of the base group.

The hypothesis that the error variances in the RP data are equal across alternatives is tested by a likelihood ratio test. Comparing Models 1 and 2 in Table 1, the calculated chi-squared statistic is 71.8 (3 degrees of freedom), which is significant at the 95% confidence level. Hence, we conclude that the RP data source exhibits strong evidence of heteroscedastic error structure.

Model 3 is the 'standard' homoscedastic MNL model for the SP data source (i.e., $\lambda_{iq}^{\mathrm{SP}} = 1, \forall\, i, q$). It should be noted that almost all parameters are statistically significant (due to the controlled design), and all have the right sign. Model 4 is a PHMNL model for the SP data, which reveals that estimated variances for all alternatives are statistically equal (i.e. the elements of ψ are essentially zero); hence, the SP data seem to satisfy variance homogeneity. In turn, this suggests

Table 1
Parametrised heteroscedastic MNL model estimation example

Parameter	Model 1 (RP) Homogenous variances (t-stats in parentheses)	Model 2 (RP) Alternative-specific variances (t-stats in parentheses)	Model 3 (SP) Homogenous variances (t-stats in parentheses)	Model 4 (SP) Alternative-specific variances (t-stats in parentheses)	Model 5 (RP + SP) Variances only between data in parentheses)	Model 6 (RP + SP) Variances between data sources and in parentheses)	Model 7 (RP + SP) Variances between data sources and alternatives (t-stats in parentheses)
Utility function							
(Taste) parameters							
Alternative-specific (Carrier) constants							
RP: Carrier A	1.7303 (5.9)	4.5262 (3.8)			0.6879 (4.8)	0.8415 (4.2)	1.0677 (4.0)
B	0.6545 (1.9)	0.6303 (1.7)			0.2632 (1.9)	0.3317 (1.6)	0.2390 (1.0)
C	0.5310 (1.5)	0.6150 (1.6)			0.5424 (4.2)	0.8030 (3.1)	0.9385 (3.1)
D	0.5176 (1.7)	0.8129 (1.8)			0.6017 (4.3)	0.7366 (2.9)	0.8713 (2.7)
E	0.8667 (2.8)	0.8546 (3.2)			0.3838 (2.8)	0.5888 (2.4)	0.6477 (2.4)
F	0.0373 (0.1)	0.3033 (0.8)			0.4042 (3.5)	0.5656 (3.0)	0.6628 (2.8)
G	0.6058 (1.7)	0.8836 (2.4)			0.3282 (2.5)	0.4136 (1.7)	0.5199 (1.4)
H	-0-	-0-			-0-	-0-	-0-
SP: Carrier A			0.8196 (4.6)	0.7512 (3.2)	1.4338 (5.0)	3.4672 (3.8)	4.1653 (3.8)
B			0.1894 (1.1)	0.1378 (0.8)	0.4799 (1.5)	0.5388 (1.7)	0.6904 (2.0)
C			0.6371 (3.8)	0.6084 (2.6)	0.2938 (0.9)	0.4063 (1.2)	0.6835 (1.9)
D			0.7245 (4.2)	0.5893 (2.5)	0.5586 (1.9)	0.7777 (1.8)	0.6811 (1.4)
E			0.4274 (2.4)	0.3764 (1.9)	0.5804 (2.0)	0.5274 (1.9)	0.9477 (3.1)
F			0.4484 (3.1)	0.4440 (2.4)	0.0242 (0.1)	0.2656 (0.7)	0.2610 (0.7)
G			0.3095 (1.8)	0.3839 (1.5)	0.4131 (1.2)	0.6058 (1.7)	0.8179 (2.2)
H			-0-	-0-	-0-	-0-	-0-
Attribute coefficients							
β_1 (Price Linear)	− 0.0509 (− 11.4)	− 0.0743 (− 10.4)	− 0.0551 (− 19.6)	− 0.0531 (− 5.4)	− 0.0434 (− 12.7)	− 0.0619 (− 10.2)	− 0.0794 (− 11.7)
β_2 (Price Quadratic)	0.0095 (3.5)	0.0124 (3.2)	0.0019 (0.6)	0.0027 (0.9)	0.0051 (2.8)	0.0075 (2.9)	0.0088 (2.9)
β_3 (RP: Delivery Speed 1)	− 0.0982 (− 0.9)	− 0.0088 (− 0.1)			0.2647 (5.3)	0.3835 (4.8)	− 0.0876 (− 0.6)

β_3 (SP: Delivery Speed 1)			0.4362 (5.7)	0.4032 (3.4)	0.2647	0.3835	0.6401 (5.3)
β_4 (Delivery Speed 2)	0.2778 4.5)	0.2818 (3.3)	0.3747 (5.1)	0.3555 (3.4)	0.2839 (6.7)	0.3261 (5.4)	0.3981 (5.4)
β_5 (Delivery Speed 3)	− 0.0439 (− 0.6)	− 0.0025 (0.0)	− 0.1066 (− 1.4)	− 0.0975 (− 1.2)	− 0.1003 (− 2.2)	− 0.0932 (− 1.5)	− 0.0421 (− 0.6)
β_6 (Pickup Time)	− 0.3023 (− 5.8)	− 0.3423 (− 5.4)	− 0.2280 (− 4.5)	− 0.2074 (− 2.5)	− 0.1906 (− 6.1)	− 0.2425 (− 5.4)	− 0.3303 (− 5.8)
β_7 (RP: Shipment Tracing)	− 0.2545 (− 3.3)	− 0.2041 (− 2.1)			0.0677 (2.2)	0.0796 (1.6)	− 0.2311 (− 2.4)
β_7 (SP: Shipment Tracing)			0.1886 (4.2)	0.1941 (3.4)	0.0677	0.0796	0.2630 (3.4)
β_8 (RP: European Coverage)	0.1437 (2.7)	0.0453 (0.7)			0.2892 (9.3)	0.3275 (7.7)	0.6543 (7.7)
β_8 (SP: European Coverage)			0.4478 (9.6)	0.4325 (4.7)	0.2892	0.3275	0.0449 (0.7)
β_9 (Refund Policy)	0.1918 (2.4)	0.0544 (0.6)	0.1995 (4.5)	0.1964 (3.8)	0.1593 (4.9)	0.1966 (4.1)	0.2277 (3.9)
β_{10} (Payment Terms)	0.0894 (1.2)	0.0298 (0.3)	0.1009 (2.1)	0.1018 (1.8)	0.0505 (1.6)	0.0826 (1.7)	0.1368 (2.2)
β_{11} (On Time Reliability)	0.2123 (4.6)	0.4208 (6.3)	0.1827 (4.0)	0.1661 (2.8)	0.1619 (5.8)	0.2583 (6.0)	0.3260 (6.5)
Scale function parameters (ψ)							
SP (1): RP (0)					0.2825 (3.3)	− 0.1182 (− 0.6)	− 0.3776 (− 2.0)
RP: Carrier A	-0-	− 1.0134 (− 5.2)			-0-	− 0.8265 (− 4.9)	− 0.9917 (− 5.5)
B	-0-	-0-			-0-	-0-	-0-
C	-0-	-0-			-0-	-0-	-0-
D	-0-	− 0.3341 (− 2.4)			-0-	− 0.2940 (− 2.1)	− 0.3941 (− 2.9)
E	-0-	0.2316 (1.8)			-0-	0.1481 (1.1)	0.0724 (0.6)
F	-0-	-0-			-0-	-0-	-0-
G	-0-	-0-			-0-	-0-	-0-
H	-0-	-0-			-0-	-0-	-0-
SP: Carrier A			-0-	0.0733 (0.3)	-0-	0.2025 (0.9)	0.1040 (0.5)
B			-0-	0.1486 (0.6)	-0-	0.0914 (0.4)	0.1165 (0.5)
C			-0-	0.0340 (0.1)	-0-	− 0.0092 (0.0)	0.0071 (0.0)
D			-0-	0.1390 (0.6)	-0-	0.1330 (0.5)	0.0927 (0.4)
E			-0-	0.0715 (0.2)	-0-	0.0012 (0.0)	0.0252 (0.1)
F			-0-	− 0.0080 (0.0)	-0-	0.0489 (0.2)	− 0.0108 (− 0.1)
G			-0-	− 0.1073 (− 0.4)	-0-	0.0529 (0.2)	− 0.1178 (− 0.5)
H			-0-	-0-	-0-	-0-	-0-
Goodness-of-fit							
Log Lik. @ conv.	− 1412.6	− 1376.7	− 810.2	− 809.3	− 2256.0	− 2230.0	− 2192.5
McFadden's ρ^2	0.22[illegible]8	0.2484	0.3556	0.3563	0.2697	0.2781	0.2903
# Parameters	18	21	18	25	26	36	39

Note: Grey cells denote structurally non-identifiable parameters within specific data source.

that unobserved characteristics do not induce different levels of variance in the SP data, in contrast to actual market choice data. As noted before, all parameter signs are correct in the SP data, but two parameters (β_3 and β_7) have opposite signs in the RP data. Of particular concern is that β_7 is statistically significant and incorrectly signed in the RP model.

We now use standard practice to combine both data sources by pooling them under the hypothesis of equal taste parameters but unequal variances between data sources (e.g. Morikawa, 1989; Ben-Akiva and Morikawa, 1991; Hensher and Bradley, 1993; Bradley and Daly, 1994), and ignoring heteroscedastcity *within* data source. As noted earlier, if this hypothesis holds, a graph of one parameter vector against the second should exhibit a positive, proportional relationship, the slope of which should equal the ratio of variances between the data sources. Fig. 2 graphs Model 1 (RP, constant variance) against Model 3 (SP, constant variance), and reveals that the expected relationship holds for all coefficients except β_3 and β_7 (these have different signs in the two data sets), in addition to β_8 (this parameter seems of greater relative importance in the SP than in the RP model).

Fig. 2 is insufficient to test the hypothesis of taste equality but data source variance inequality (see Swait and Louviere, 1993). Model 5 in Table 1 tests this standard hypothesis on the pooled RP and SP choice data. The relative scale ratio between the SP and RP data sources is about exp(0.2825), or 1.33, which differs significantly from one at the 95% significance level, and implies that under the maintained hypothesis the variance of the SP was less than that of the RP data. More precisely, the average SP variance is 75% ($\approx 1/1.33$) of the

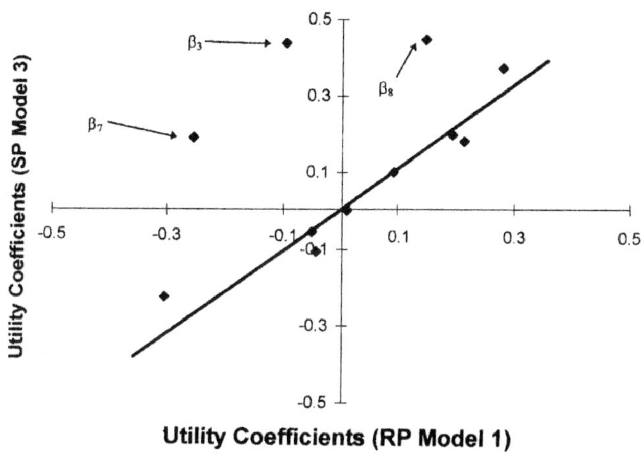

Fig. 2. Plot of MNL attribute coefficients (Models 1 and 3).

average RP variance. The chi-squared statistic for the hypothesis of taste equality and data source variance inequality contrasts Model 5 to Models 1 and 3, and equals 66.4 (= − 2[− 1412.6 − 810.2 − (− 2256.0)]) with 10 degrees of freedom; hence, the standard pooling hypothesis is rejected at the 95% confidence level.

Fig. 2 suggests that the rejection is due in part to parameter sign reversals. However, our prior analysis also suggests that variance differences between alternatives also may be responsible. The latter conjecture is supported by Model 6 (Table 1), which allows alternative-specific scale effects within data sources. Compared to Models 2 and 4, which both allow within-data source alternative-specific variance differences, the chi-squared statistic for Model 6 is 88.0 with 10 degrees of freedom. This again suggests that the two data sources cannot be combined, even if we allow within-data source heteroscedasticity.

In fact, allowing alternative-specific heteroscedasticity makes it *more* difficult to retain taste homogeneity between data sources. Swait and Adamowicz (1997) reported a similar result. They parametrised variance as a function of complexity, and found that incorporating the impact of choice context on variance made the combination of their RP and SP data less plausible. Yet, accounting for heteroscedasticity within data sources made the between-data source variance differences disappear! That is, the between-data source variance difference in Model 5 is eliminated by improved specification of the variance heteroscedasticity within-data source, particularly for the RP data.

Thus far, our results suggest that for these data sources, combination is not a statistically sound option even if we account for within-data source heteroscedasticity. Another logical possibility is to test whether it is possible to combine the data sources if we allow for differences between data sources in parameters β_3, β_7 and β_8. We previously noted that the estimate of β_7 is negative and significant in the RP data, but (correctly) positive and significant in the SP data. Parameter β_3 exhibits the same sign reversal between data sets, but is not significant in the RP data source. The last apparent difference hinted at in Fig. 2 is the greater relative importance of β_8 in the SP data compared to the RP data. Model 7 allows a separate estimate in each data source for these three parameters, which improves the log likelihood from − 2230.0 to − 2192.5 (Table 1). The removal of the equality restriction on these three parameters results in a chi-squared statistic of 13.0 with 7 degrees of freedom, compared to the critical value of 23.4 at the 95% confidence level. Our conclusion, therefore, is that the hypothesis of taste parameter equality holds across the two data sources, except for the three source-specific parameters (β_3, β_7 and β_8), as long as within-source heteroscedasticity and between-source variance differences are accounted for. Note that in this final model (1) the SP data source does not exhibit scale factors significantly different from one, indicating that the IID assumption seems warranted within that data source; (2) the RP data, however, exhibit strong heteroscedasticity via alternatives A and D, which have scale estimates of 0.37

and 0.67, respectively, in contrast to a scale of 1.0 for most of the other alternatives; and (3) that the SP data source has a scale of about 0.69, compared to a scale of 1.0 for the RP data, indicating that on average the former's variance is greater than the latter's. This last result is expected since, by construction, the SP data source has more variability in attributes than is found in the RP data.

By combining the two data sources via Model 7, we are able to utilise the well-behaved SP design matrix to correct sign and collinearity problems in the RP data. Because of the SP data, we are also able to obtain more robust parameter estimates that are valid over wider attribute ranges than found in the RP data. The availability of the RP data, on the other hand, contributes a 'real-world flavour' to the joint model by establishing alternative-specific constants that reflect population characteristics. To predict to actual market conditions, we can utilize the following subset of Model 7 parameters: RP alternative-specific constants, all jointly estimated attribute parameters, and the RP scale function parameters. In addition, a judgment call must be made by the analyst concerning the source-specific attribute parameters. In our opinion, given the counterintuitive and/or non-significant RP results for the three parameters in questions, we recommend adopting the SP estimates for (β_3, β_7 and β_8).[5]

This simple example of combining two data sources illustrates the fact that many issues must be considered in data combination, and demonstrates that such exercises should first seek to establish the best-possible specification (involving both taste and covariance parameters) within each data source. Failing to do so may result in unwitting retention of the taste homogeneity and variance difference hypothesis. Ultimately, the better the specification within each particular data set, the stronger and more generalisable will be the results obtained if data combination is actually possible. On the other hand, it must also be said that the better the specification for a data set, the less likely data combination will be due to capitalisation on chance and overfitting to source-specific nuances; sufficiently large sample sizes will then make retention of the null hypothesis of taste invariance less probable.

5. Summary and conclusion

Discrete choice models estimated from mixtures of data sources provide exciting opportunities for research into the demand for new products and services, as well as extending the attribute space of existing products and services to domains not currently available. This paper reviewed several new techniques

[5] Note that to apply the estimates shown in Table 1 for these three SP parameters, they must be divided by the corresponding scale factor from the SP data set.

being developed in marketing, resource economics and transportation to analyse, model and combine sources of preference data, and illustrated the insights possible from several generalisations of extant discrete choice models which explicitly allow for error heteroscedasticity.

Recognition that multiple data sources (e.g., RP and SP data) can be used to estimate choice models within the well-developed random utility theory framework provides opportunities for new research into ways to take both scale and taste into account, and capture complex behavioural constructs such as latent segments, random taste variation and choice dynamics, as well as extend utility spaces well beyond the domains of today's actual markets. As well, there are significant opportunities to enrich and extend choice models by paying more and closer attention to processes that lead to different scale factors, which in turn may impact many elements of choice processes and models of those processes in complex ways.

Behavioural differences in both the mean and variance of the distribution of consumer choices have both theoretical and practical implications. Theoretically, the models we discussed extend our ability to represent complex behavioural processes, and suggest future research into antecedents of variance differences, as well as more traditional research on differences in means. To our knowledge, the suggestion that the behaviour of variance components can be specified in ways consistent with random utility theory is new. In fact, this paper demonstrated that placing structure on variance components is not only possible, but practical. Moreover, our empirical illustration suggested significant gains in behavioural insights over more traditional models that focus largely on differences in means.

As discussed and demonstrated in the empirical example in this paper, variance differences have important practical implications for marketing (and other) policy. For example, differences in tastes may be less common than previously thought, but even if segments are relatively taste homogeneous, they may exhibit different variances in preferences. The latter situation has considerable practical implications for marketing policy because it suggests that resources should be devoted to understanding antecedents of variance and developing strategies to overcome and/or reduce same, rather than concentrating on serving what seem to be different taste segments. In fact, strategies based on differences in means may be wrong for populations who display variance differences, because the optimal strategy may be variance reduction.

Theory and empirical evidence provided in this paper suggests that research directed towards models that better capture differences in variances, as well as understanding sources of variance differences and their role in choice, should be interesting and fruitful. We individually and collectively are engaged in research programs consistent with these suggestions. For example, Louviere and Swait (1996) demonstrated that accounting for differences in variance often accounts for most of the differences in taste parameters in a number of new and published empirical preference and choice results. Some context effects which have produced large model differences in consumer decision-making research largely disappear if context differences in variances are taken into account. Hence, conclusions about the effects of context on means should be revisited in light of variance effects. de Palma et al. (1994) and Swait and Adamowicz (1997) studied decision task and decision environment complexity, and showed that variance has a convex relationship with decision context complexity. Brazell and Louviere (1997) reported two studies of different order and task length conditions, which showed that virtually all differences in choice model parameters were due to variance differences, and that variance (i.e. reliability) decreased up to about 40 pairs of choices, then rapidly increased until respondents saw the survey's end, at which time variance rapidly decreased again.

The above represent only a few examples of many new research avenues suggested by the theory and empirical results reviewed in this paper. Together they offer a compelling case that econometricians and marketing researchers can learn from one another to the mutual enrichment of both fields.

References

Adamowicz, W., Louviere, J., Williams, M., 1994. Combining stated and revealed preference methods for valuing environmental amenities. Journal of Environmental Economics and Management 26, 271–292.

Adamowicz, W., Swait, J., Boxall, P., Louviere, J., Williams, M., 1996. Perceptions versus objective measures of environmental quality in combined revealed and stated preference models of environmental valuation. Journal of Environmental Economics and Management 32, 65–84.

Allenby, G., Ginter, J., 1995. The effects of in-store displays and feature advertising on consideration sets. International Journal of Research in Marketing 12, 67–80.

Anderson, D.A., Wiley, J.B., 1992. Efficient choice set designs for estimating availability cross-effects models. Marketing Letters 3 (4), 357–370.

Anderson, S., de Palma, A., Thisse, J., 1992. Discrete Choice Theory of Product Differentiation. MIT Press, Cambridge.

Ben-Akiva, M., Lerman, S., 1985. Discrete Choice Analysis: Theory and Application to Predict Travel Demand. MIT Press, Cambridge.

Ben-Akiva, M., Morikawa, T., 1991. Estimation of travel demand models from multiple data sources. In: Koshi, M. (Ed.), Transportation and Traffic Theory, Proceedings of the 11th ISTTT. Elsevier, Amsterdam, pp. 461–476.

Bhat, C.R., 1995. A heteroscedastic extreme value model of intercity travel mode choice. Transportation Research 29B (6), 471–483.

Bhat, C.R., 1996. An endogenous segmentation mode choice model with an application to intercity travel. Transportation Science 31, 34–48.

Bradley, M., Daly, A., 1994. Use of the logit scaling approach to test rank-order and fatigue effects in stated preference data. Transportation 21 (2), 167–184.

Brazell, J., Louviere, J., 1997. Respondents' help, learning and fatigue. INFORMS Marketing Science Conference. University of California at Berkeley, Berkeley, CA.

Bunch, D., 1991. Estimability in the multinomial probit model. Transporation Research 25B (1), 1–12.

Bunch, D., Louviere, J., Anderson, D., 1996. A comparison of experimental design strategies for choice-based conjoint analysis with generic-attribute multinomial logit models. Unpublished working paper, UC Davis Graduate School of Management, May.

Carson, R., Louviere, J., Anderson, D., Arabie, P., Bunch, D., Hensher, D., Johnson, R., Kuhfeld, W., Steinberg, D., Swait, J., Timmermans, H., Wiley, J., 1994. Experimental analysis of choice. Marketing Letters 5 (4), 351–368.

Daganzo, C., 1980. Multinomial Probit. Academic Press, New York.

Daly, A., 1987. Estimating 'tree' logit models. Transportation Research B 21B, 251–267.

de Palma, A., Myers, G.M., Papageorgiou, Y.Y., 1994. Rational choice under an imperfect ability to choose. American Economic Review 84, 419–440.

Englin, J., Cameron, T.A., 1996. Augmenting travel cost models with contingent behavior data. Environmental and Resource Economics 7, 133–147.

Green, P., Srinivasan, V., 1978. Conjoint analysis in consumer research: Issues and outlook. Journal of Consumer Research 1, 61–68.

Green, P., Srinivasan, V., 1990. Conjoint analysis in marketing research: New developments and directions. Journal of Marketing 54 (4), 3–19.

Green, P., Wind, Y., 1971. Multiattribute Decisions in Marketing: A Measurement Approach. Dryden Press, Hinsdale, IL.

Greene, W., 1996. Heteroskedastic extreme value model for discrete choice. Working paper, New York University.

Hanemann, M., Kanninen, B., 1997. The statistical analysis of discrete-response CV data. In: Bateman, I.J., Willis, K.G. (Eds.), Valuing Environmental Preferences: Theory and Practice of the Contingent Valuation Method in the US, EC and Developing Countries. Oxford University Press, Oxford.

Hausman, J., Wise, D., 1978. AFDC participation: measured variables or unobserved characteristics, permanent or transitory. Working paper, Department of Economics, MIT, Cambridge, MA.

Hensher, D.A., Louviere, J., 1983. Identifying individual preferences for alternative international air fares: An application of functional measurement theory. Journal of Transport Economics and Policy XVII (2), 225–245.

Hensher, D., Johnson, L., 1981. Applied Discrete Choice Modelling. Croom Helm, London.

Hensher, D.A., 1994. Stated preference analysis of travel choices: The state of the practice. Transportation 21, 107–133.

Hensher, D.A., (in press). Extending valuation to controlled value functions and non-uniform scaling with generalised unobserved variances. In: Gärling, T., Laitila, T., Westin, K., (Eds.), Theoretical Foundations of Travel Choice Modeling. Pergamon, Oxford.

Hensher, D.A., (1998). Establishing a fare elasticity regime for urban passenger transport. Journal of Transport Economics and Policy 32 (2) 221–246.

Hensher, D.A., Barnard, P.O., 1990. The orthogonality issue in stated choice designs. In: Fischer, M., Nijkamp, P., Papageorgiou, Y. (Eds.), Spatial Choices and Processes. North-Holland, Amsterdam, pp. 265–278.

Hensher, D.A., Bradley, M., 1993. Using stated response data to enrich revealed preference discrete choice models. Marketing Letters 4 (2), 39–152.

Huber, J., Zwerina, K., 1996. The importance of utility balance in efficient choice set designs. Journal of Marketing Research 33, 307–317.

Kahneman, D., Tversky, A., 1979. Prospect theory: An analysis of decisions under risk. Econometrica 47, 263–291.

Kahneman, D., Tversky, A., 1984. Choices, values and frames. American Psychologist 39, 341–350.

Keane, M., 1995. Modelling heterogeneity and state dependence in consumer choice behavior. Working paper, Department of Economics, University of Minnesota.

Keller, K.L., 1993. Conceptualizing, measuring and managing customer-based brand equity. Journal of Marketing 57 (1), 1–22.

Krantz, D.H., Tversky, A., 1971. conjoint-measurement analysis of composition rules in psychology. Psychological Review 78, 151–169.

Krantz, D.H., Luce, R.D., Suppes, P., Tversky, A., 1971. Foundations of Measurement. Academic Press, New York.

Lancaster, K., 1966. A new Approach to consumer theory. Journal of political Economy 74, 132–157.

Louviere, J.J., 1995. Relating stated preference measures and models to choices in real markets: Calibration of CV responses. In: Bjornstad, D.J., Kahn, J.R. (Eds.), The Contingent Valuation of Environmental Resources. Edward Elgar, Brookfield, pp. 167–188.

Louviere, J.J., 1974. Predicting the evaluation of real stimulus objects from an abstract evaluation of their attributes: The case of trout streams. Journal of Applied Psychology 59 (5), 572–577.

Louviere, J.J., 1988a. Analyzing Decision Making: Metric Conjoint Analysis. Sage Publications, Newbury Park, CA.

Louviere, J.J., 1988b. Conjoint analysis modelling of stated preferences: A review of theory, methods, recent developments and external validity. Journal of Transport Economics and Policy 20, 93–119.

Louviere, J.J., 1994. Conjoint analysis. In: Bagozzi, R. (Ed.), Advanced Methods of Marketing Research. Blackwell Publishers, Cambridge, MA, pp. 223–259.

Louviere, J.J., Hensher, D.A., 1983. Using discrete choice models with experimental design data to forecast consumer demand for a unique cultural event. Journal of Consumer Research 10 (3), 348–361.

Louviere, J.J., Swait, J., 1996. Searching for regularities in choice processes, or the little constant that could. Working paper, Department of Marketing, Faculty of Economics, University of Sydney, August 1996.

Louviere, J.J., Woodworth, G., 1983. Design and analysis of simulated consumer choice or allocation experiments: An approach based on aggregate data. Journal of Marketing Research 20, 350–367.

Louviere, J.J., Fox, M., Moore, W., 1993. Cross-task validity comparisons of stated preference choice models. Marketing Letters 4 (3), 205–213.

Luce, R.D., 1959. Individual Choice Behavior: A Theoretical Analysis. Wiley, New York.

Lynch, J., 1985. Uniqueness issues in the decompositional modeling of multiattribute overall evaluations. Journal of Marketing Research 22, 1–19.

Machina, M.J., 1987. Choice under uncertainty: Problems solved and unsolved. Economic Perspectives 1 (1), 121–154.

McFadden, D., 1974. Conditional logit analysis of qualitative choice behaviour. In: Zarembka, P. (Ed.), Frontiers in Econometrics. Academic Press, New York, pp. 105–142.

McFadden, D., 1981. Econometric models of probabilistic choice. In: Manski, C., McFadden, D., (Eds.), Structural Analysis of Discrete Data with Econometric Applications. MIT Press, Cambridge, MA 198–272.

McFadden, D., Tye, W., Train, K., 1977. An application of diagnostic tests for independence from irrelevant alternatives property of the multinomial logit model. Transportation Research Record 637, 39–46.

Meyer, R., Levin, I., Louviere, J., 1984. Functional analysis of mode choice. Transportation Research Record 673, 1–7.

Morikawa, T., 1989. Incorporating stated preference data in travel demand analysis. Ph.D. Dissertation, Department of Civil Engineering, MIT.

Press, W.H., Flannery, B.P., Teukolsky, S.A., Vetterling, W.T., 1986. Numerical Recipes. Cambridge University Press, Cambridge.

Restle, F., 1961. Psychology of Judgment and Choice. Wiley, New York.

Rushton, G., 1969. Analysis of spatial behaviour by revealed space preference. Annals of the Association of American Geographers 59, 391–400.

Small, K., 1987. A discrete choice model for ordered alternatives. econometrica 55 (2), 409–424.

Small, K., 1994. Approximate generalized extreme value models of discrete choice. Journal of Econometrics 62, 351–382.

Swait, J., Adamowicz, W., 1997. The effect of choice environment and task demands on consumer behavior: Discriminating between contribution and confusion. Working paper, Department. of Rural Economy, University of Alberta, 39 pp.

Swait, J., Louviere J., 1993. The role of the scale parameter in the estimation and use of multinomial logit models. Journal of Marketing Research 30, 305–314.

Swait, J., Stacey, E.C., 1996. Consumer brand assessment and assessment confidence in models of longitudinal choice behavior. Presented at the 1996 INFORMS Marketing Science Conference, 7–10 March, Gainesville, FL.

Swait, J., Erdem, T., Louviere, J., Dubelaar, C., 1993. The equalization price: A measure of consumer-perceived brand equity. International Journal of Research in Marketing 10, 23–45.

Swait, J., Louviere, J., Williams, M., 1994. A sequential approach to exploiting the combined strengths of SP and RP data: Application to freight shipper choice. Transportation 21 (2), 135–152.

Thurstone, L., 1927. A law of comparative judgment. Psychological Review 34, 273–286.

[40]

JOURNAL OF APPLIED ECONOMETRICS
J. Appl. Econ. **21**: 861–878 (2006)
Published online in Wiley InterScience
(www.interscience.wiley.com) DOI: 10.1002/jae.877

HOW DO RESPONDENTS PROCESS STATED CHOICE EXPERIMENTS? ATTRIBUTE CONSIDERATION UNDER VARYING INFORMATION LOAD

DAVID A. HENSHER*
Institute of Transport and Logistics Studies, Faculty of Economics and Business, University of Sydney, Sydney, NSW 2006, Australia

SUMMARY

The popularity of stated choice (SC) experiments has produced many design strategies in which researchers use increasingly more 'complex' choice settings to study choice behaviour. When the amount of information to assess increases, we wonder how an individual handles such information in making a choice. Defining the amount of information as the number of attributes associated with each choice set, we investigate how this information is processed as we vary its 'complexity'. Four ordered heterogeneous logit models are developed, each for an SC design based on a fixed number of attributes, in which the dependent variable defines the number of attributes that are ignored. We find that the degree to which individuals ignore attributes is influenced by the dimensionality of the SC experiment, the deviation of attribute levels from an experienced reference alternative, the use of 'adding up' attributes where feasible, the number of choice sets evaluated, and the personal income of the respondent. The empirical evidence supports the view that individuals appear to adopt a range of 'coping' strategies that are consistent with how they process information in real markets, and that aligning 'choice complexity' with the amount of information to process is potentially misleading. *Relevancy* is what matters. Copyright © 2006 John Wiley & Sons, Ltd.

Received 24 March 2004; Accepted 23 March 2005

1. INTRODUCTION

How do individuals cope with the amount of information that they are asked to evaluate in a stated choice experiment? Given the number of attributes associated with each alternative, and the number of alternatives in a choice set, do individuals consider all attributes and do they combine them where feasible? Where an experienced reference alternative is used to determine the actual range and levels of attributes for a stated choice (SC) design, what role might the numerical differences in attribute levels play in influencing the information processing (IP) strategy? In particular, does this influence how many attributes are excluded from the assessment (for whatever reason—relevance or cognitive burden)? These questions are illustrative of the growing array of issues that researchers need to understand if they are to make comments on the influence of the SC experiment per se, as an appropriate instrument for revealing choice processes and outcomes.[1] This paper focuses on understanding what influences a respondent's decision to ignore (or not attend to) specific attributes in choosing amongst the offered alternatives, and the implications of not accounting for the diversity of attribute processing strategies on policy outputs such as willingness to pay.

* Correspondence to: David A. Hensher, Institute of Transport and Logistics Studies, Faculty of Economics and Business, University of Sydney, Sydney, NSW 2006, Australia. E-mail: davidh@itls.usyd.edu.au
Contract/grant sponsor: Australian Research Council Large Grants Scheme; Contract/grant number: A00103962.
[1] These types of questions are associated with the information load that is faced in making any decision, and are not specific to stated choice experiments. This is all-pervasive in real markets.

To investigate these matters we have designed a suite of SC experiments in which we systematically vary the dimensionality of the experiment, and complement it with additional questions on how the SC task is processed. This latter data is required in order to reveal the attribute processing strategy that each individual uses in choosing an alternative.

The paper is organized as follows. The next section discusses issues that may influence how an individual processes the experimental setting in terms of attribute inclusion or exclusion. We then outline the design plan required for an empirical test. Ordered heterogeneous logit models are estimated, in which the dependent variable defines the number of attributes that are ignored (or not attended to); the explanatory variables include design dimensions and processing rules. The ultimate objective of this research is to establish guidelines for how attribute processing impacts on behavioural outputs such as willingness to pay (WTP) and other related policy objectives. We derive WTP indicators for travel time savings before and after accounting for the attribute processing strategy of each individual. The substantive implications of the analysis are then presented, followed by conclusions and directions for ongoing research.

2. ISSUES FACING RESPONDENTS IN PROCESSING STATED CHOICE EXPERIMENTS

Design dimensionality is often referred to as the *complexity* of the SC experiment. It is typically implied that designs with more items to evaluate are more complex than those with less items[2] (e.g. Arentze *et al.*, 2003; Swait and Adamowicz, 2001a,b), impose cognitive burden and are consequently less reliable, in a behavioural sense, in revealing preference information. This is potentially misleading, since it suggests that complexity is an artefact of the *quantity* of information, in contrast to the *relevance* of information. For example, in the current empirical context of commuter car trip choice, for a specific choice outcome, an individual might feel more confident in making a considered choice response when the attributes offered are the components of travel time (e.g. free flow, slowed down and stop/start time) and the components of travel cost (e.g. running cost and toll cost), rather than a subset of the (relevant) attributes or even an aggregated definition (i.e. total time and total cost).

The value of providing an increasing amount of useful information can be supported by the event or attribute-splitting literature, in which 'unpacking' positive attributes of a good into multiple sub-attributes can make a good or service seem more desirable (Weber *et al.*, 1988; Starmer and Sugden, 1993). Conversely, unpacking attribute levels that are less desirable (e.g. a greater incidence of non-free flow time in total time, as revealed in the unpacking of total time) can make a good or service less desirable. Indeed, the empirical evidence supports this (Hensher, 2004)—for a given total time, an individual generally prefers a higher proportion of free flow time. Hence, such descriptions do matter; even though the 'objective total time' is the same, the outcome is different. Indeed, consistent with the editing stage of prospect theory is the option for an individual to add up attributes that share a common metric. We refer to this as attribute accumulation.

One implication is that individuals are more likely to choose particular alternatives if those containing relatively attractive consequences are subdivided into two or more components, assuming that the attribute is salient or 'relevant' to an individual. The public policy implications are profound—the risks of ignoring relevant attribute decomposition, and inclusion/exclusion, can

[2] Complexity also includes attributes that are lowly correlated, in contrast to highly correlated, the latter supporting greater ease of assessment in that one attribute represents other attributes.

DOI: 10.1002/jae

be high in settings where the differential between weights is an important element of defence for investment in a specific alterative. Thus, giving respondents more complete information (in the absence of knowing, *a priori*, individual-specific processing rules), and allowing them to impose their own rules in respect of relevancy, appears preferable to imposing a simplification rule on all respondents through limiting the dimensions of an SC design.

The behavioural paradigm herein is consistent with the view that SC designs have, in the main, assumed that all attributes are processed in what DeShazo and Fermo (2004) describe as the *passive bounded rationality* model. This model assumes that individuals attend to all information in the choice set, but increasingly make mistakes in processing that information, as the volume of information increases. Contrasting this is the *rationally adaptive* model, which assumes that individuals recognize their limited cognition has positive opportunity costs. Whether *rationally adaptive* behaviour is a product of the survey instrument and/or the nature of an individual's processing of any information is an empirical matter.

Another postulated source of attribute inclusion or exclusion is the role of the reference alternative in the choice experiment. Starmer (2000, p. 353) makes a very strong plea to support reference points:

> While some economists might be tempted to think that questions about how reference points are determined sound more like psychological than economic issues, recent research is showing that understanding the role of reference points may be an important step in explaining real economic behaviour in the field.

In particular, the reference alternative can provide the memory content necessary to make the SC profiles meaningful in a preference-revelation sense. Prospect theory (Kahneman and Tversky, 1979), as an interpretation of procedural theories that assume agents draw on decision heuristics when making choices, promotes the problem context as an important determinant of the choice-rule selection. For example, if individuals choose to ignore some attributes, then prospect theory explains this in terms of an editing routine, known as the rule of cancellation. One particular rule of interest is framing effects, of which reference dependence is a popular interpretation. It provides adaptive support in trading off the desire to make a relevant choice against the cognitive effort involved in processing the information in the SC task. For example, we might hypothesize that when the difference is greater between the reference and an SC alternative, the need to retain more (or all) attributes increases, so as to capture the differences with greater clarity.

In summary, in this study we investigate the role of five classes of influences on each respondent's inclusion or exclusion of specific attributes, describing each offered alternative that conditions their choice:

1. The dimensionality of the SC task.
2. The number of choice sets to be evaluated.
3. The deviation of the design attribute levels from the reference alternative.
4. The use of 'adding up' attributes where this is feasible.
5. The socio-economic characteristics of the respondent.

An ordered heterogeneous logit model is parameterized to identify the role of these five classes of effects. The dependent variable defines the number of attributes that are ignored (or not attended to). The zero value defines the inclusion of all attributes. The number of attributes ignored was

DOI: 10.1002/jae

identified by a series of questions in which respondents were asked to indicate which attributes they ignored in their assessment of the alternatives.

3. THE DESIGN PLAN AND APPLICATION CONTEXT

The data are drawn from a larger study, reported in Hensher (2004), in which 16 stated choice sub-designs have been embedded in one overall design, with each sub-design being used in surveying a sample of car commuter trips in Sydney in 2002. Each commuter evaluated one randomly assigned sub-design; however, across the full set of stated choice experiments, the designs differed in terms of the number, range and levels of attributes, the number of alternatives and the number of choice sets. The combination of these dimensions of each design is often seen as the source of design 'complexity' (Dellaert *et al.*, 1999), and it is within this setting that we have varied the number of attributes that each respondent is asked to evaluate.

Previous studies were used to identify candidate design dimensions (e.g. Ohler *et al.*, 2000; White *et al.*, 1998; DeShazo and Fermo, 2002; Dellaert *et al.*, 1999). The five design dimensions are shown in Table I.

Six attributes were selected for each alternative, based on previous evidence (see Hensher, in press), to characterize the options: free flow time, slowed down time, stop/start time, variability of trip time, toll cost and running costs. To explore how varying the number of attributes affects information processing, the attributes were grouped according to the following patterns, noting that aggregated attributes are combinations of existing attributes:[3]

- *Designs with three attributes:* total time (free flow + slowed down + stop/start time), trip time variability, total costs (toll + running cost).
- *Designs with four attributes:* free flow time, congestion time (slowed down + stop/start), trip time variability, total cost.
- *Designs with five attributes:* free flow time, slowed down time, stop/start time, trip time variability, total cost.
- *Designs with six attributes:* free flow time, slowed down time, stop/start time, trip time variability, toll cost, running cost.

We have selected a generic design (i.e. unlabelled alternatives) to avoid confounding the effect of the number of alternatives with the labelling (e.g. car, train). The 16 sub-design dimensions are shown in Table II, and an example of a design is given in Appendix Table AI.

Table I. Dimensionality of the design plan

Choice set size	Number of alternatives	Number of attributes	Number of attribute levels	Range of attribute levels
6	2	3	2	narrower than base
9	3	4	3	base
12	4	5	4	wider than base
15	—	6	—	—

[3] This is an important point because we did not want the analysis to be confounded by extra attribute dimensions.

Table II. The sub-designs of the overall design

Choice set of size	Number of alternatives	Number of attributes	Number of levels of attributes	Range of attribute levels
15	3	4	3	base
12	3	4	4	wider than base
15	2	5	2	wider than base
9	2	5	4	base
6	2	3	3	wider than base
15	2	3	4	narrower than base
6	3	6	2	narrower than base
9	4	3	4	wider than base
15	4	6	4	base
6	4	6	3	wider than base
6	3	5	4	narrower than base
9	4	4	2	narrower than base
12	3	6	2	base
12	2	3	3	narrower than base
9	2	4	2	base
12	4	5	3	narrower than base

Note: Column 1 refers to the number of choice sets. The 16 rows represent the set of designs (referred to as Des0, Des1, ..., Des15 in model estimation).

As a generic design, the added alternatives are exactly the same. That is, for two design alternatives, we should not expect to find the parameter for an attribute (e.g. 'free flow travel time') to be different for the set of non-reference alternatives. Therefore we do not need the attribute 'free flow time one' to be orthogonal to the attribute 'free flow time two', etc. up to 'free flow time $J - 1$'. We need to ensure that the attribute 'free flow time' representing all non-reference alternatives is perfectly[4] orthogonal to the other attributes (such as slow down time, etc.).

The designs are computer-generated. A preferred choice experiment design is one that maximizes the determinant of the covariance matrix, which is itself a function of the estimated parameters. Knowledge of the parameters, or at least some priors (such as signs) for each attribute, from past studies, provides a useful input. We found that in so doing, the search eliminates dominant alternatives. Carlsson and Martinsson (2003) have recently shown, using Monte Carlo simulation, that D-optimal designs, like orthogonal designs, produce unbiased parameter estimates but that the former have lower mean square errors. The method used finds the D-optimality plan very quickly.

The *actual* levels of the attributes shown to respondents are calculated relative to those of the experienced reference alternative—a recent car commuter trip. The levels applied to the choice task (see Appendix Table AII) differ depending on the range of attribute levels and the number of levels for each attribute. The design dimensions are translated into SC screens, illustrated in Figure 1. The number and range of attribute levels only vary *across* designs. Each sampled commuter is given a varying number of choice sets (or scenarios), but the number of attributes and alternatives remain fixed. All analysis reported herein uses the elicitation response in Figure 1 associated with a choice set that excludes the recent trip. Hensher (in press) contrasts the two elicitation responses.

[4] *Approximately* orthogonal is also acceptable given that some designs cannot guarantee complete orthogonality without loss of structure in terms of cognitive efficiency (in contrast to statistical efficiency).

DOI: 10.1002/jae

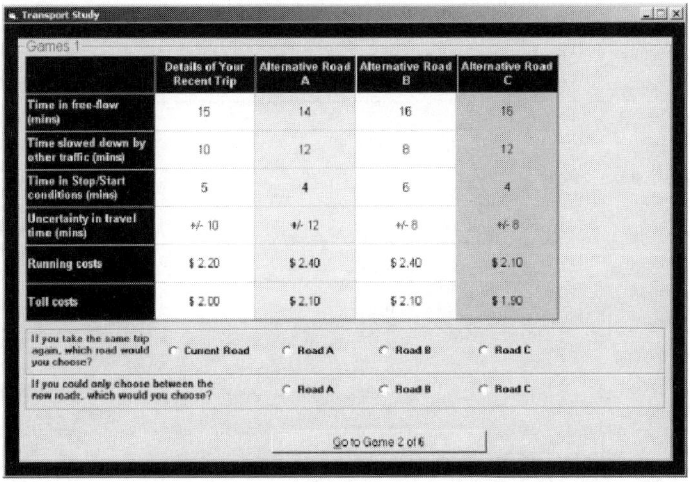

Figure 1. An example of a stated choice screen

4. THE MODELLING APPROACH

Separate ordered heterogeneous logit (OHL)[5] models are estimated for each of four design subsets (see Table I). This is necessary to enable definition of the dependent variable as the number of attributes out of the full set that were ignored in selecting an alternative. The ordered logit model allows us to include an ordinal dependent variable into the choice model in a way that explicitly recognizes the ordinality, and avoids arbitrary assumptions about scale. It does this by defining points on the *observed scale* as thresholds that recognize, in preference space, that the numerical levels of the dependent variable are not strictly linear (Winship and Mare, 1984).

Formally, let Y_i^* denote an unobserved (or latent) continuous variable $(-\infty < Y_i^* < +\infty)$, defined in utility space, and $\mu_{0,}\ \mu_1, \ldots, \mu_{J-1}, \mu_J$ denote the threshold utility points in the distribution of Y_i^*, where $\mu_0 = -\infty$ and $\mu_J = +\infty$. Define Y_i to be an ordinal (observed) variable such that $Y_i = j$ iff $\mu_{J-1} \leq Y_i^* \leq \mu_{J;}\ j = 1,\ 2,\ \ldots,\ J$ response levels. Since Y_i^* is not observed, the mean and variance are unknown. Statistical assumptions must be introduced such that Y_i^* has a mean of zero and a variance of one. To make the model operational, we need to define a relationship between Y_i^* and Y_i.

The ordered choice model is based on a latent regression model given as equation (1):

$$Y_i^* = \beta'\mathbf{x}_i + \varepsilon_i,\ \ \varepsilon_i \sim F(\varepsilon_i|\theta),\ \ \mathrm{E}(\varepsilon_i) = 0,\ \ \mathrm{Var}(\varepsilon_i) = 1 \tag{1}$$

where θ collects mean and threshold parameters. The observation mechanism results from a complete censoring of the latent dependent variable as follows:

$$Y_i. = 0 \text{ if } Y_i^* \leq \mu_0$$

[5] Ordered mixed logit (OML) models were also estimated but are not reported, given that the findings are similar. They are available on request.

DOI: 10.1002/jae

$$= 1 \text{ if } \mu_0 < Y_i^* \leq \mu_1$$

$$= 2 \text{ if } \mu_1 < Y_i^* \leq \mu_2 \quad (2)$$

$$\dots$$

$$= J \text{ if } Y_{i\ i}^* > \mu_{J-1}$$

The probabilities that enter the log-likelihood function are given by equations (3) and (4):

$$\text{Prob}(Y_i = j) = \text{Prob}(Y_i^* \text{ is in the } j\text{th range}) \quad (3)$$

$$= F(\mu_j - \beta'\mathbf{x}_i) - F(\mu_{j-1} - \beta'\mathbf{x}_i), \ \ j = 0,\ 1,\ \dots,\ J \quad (4)$$

We can generalize the unobserved variance to accommodate multiplicative heterogeneity, as we do herein, and make this variance a function of contextual variables. Behaviourally this enables us to distinguish between the influence that the SC design or process attributes have on conditioning the mean parameter estimates, and conditioning of the variance of the unobserved effects. The latter is one mechanism for revealing preference heterogeneity in the exclusion of attributes in processing the SC task.

A direct interpretation of the parameter estimates from the OHL model is not informative, given the logit transformation of the choice dependent variable. We therefore provide the marginal effects that have substantive behavioural meaning, defined as the derivatives of the choice probabilities (Hensher *et al.*, 2005a). A marginal effect is the influence a one unit change in an explanatory variable has on the probability of selecting a particular outcome, *ceteris paribus*.[6] The marginal effects need not have the same sign as the model parameters. Hence, the statistical significance of an estimated parameter does not imply the same significance for the marginal effect (see equation (5)):

$$\partial\text{Prob}(Y_i = j)/\partial\mathbf{x} = P_j(\beta_j - \overline{\beta}),\ \ \overline{\beta} = \Sigma_j P_j \beta_j \quad (5)$$

Neither the sign nor the magnitude of $\overline{\beta}$ need bear any relationship to those of β_j. β_j, equal to $\partial \log(P_j/P_0)/\partial\mathbf{x}$, is commonly defined as an interpretation of the model parameters.

5. EMPIRICAL ANALYSIS

Computer-aided personal interview (CAPI) surveys, 514 in total, were completed in the Sydney metropolitan area in 2002. A stratified random sample was applied, based on the residential location of the household. Screening questions established eligibility in respect of commuting by car. Further details are given in Hensher (in press). Final models for each of the four sub-design settings are given in Table III, with the respective marginal effects in Table IV. We report the marginal effects for the average number of attributes ignored.[7]

The evidence identifies a number of statistically significant influences on the number of attributes attended to, given the maximum number of attributes provided. Individuals clearly self-select attribute information to process in stated choice studies, just as they do in real markets, where

[6] This holds for continuous variables only. For dummy (1, 0) variables, the marginal effects are the derivatives of the probabilities given a change in the level of the dummy variable.

[7] We have retained all explanatory variables, from the various sources of influence on IP strategy, that have a t-value greater than 0.10.

DOI: 10.1002/jae

Table III. Ordered heterogeneous logit models for models with six, five, four and three attributes

Attribute	Units	OHL6	OHL5	OHL4	OHL3
Constant		4.2065 (4.78)	2.688 (5.31)	11.743 (7.0)	−0.0042 (−0.93)
Design dimensions					
No. of levels	Number	0.5299 (4.22)	0.0427 (0.98)	−0.1383 (−0.61)	0.0009 (0.82)
Narrow attribute range	1.0	1.2518 (6.03)	1.2711 (4.43)	2.2922 (2.84)	−0.00004 (−0.08)
No. of alternatives	Number	−0.8956 (−3.72)	−0.8163 (−5.23)	−2.172 (−4.62)	0.00013 (0.61)
Framing around base alt					
Free flow time for base (or total time for OHL3) minus SC alternative level	Minutes	0.0146 (1.96)	0.0319 (5.07)		−0.0000027 (−0.5)
Congested time for base (or total time for OHL3) minus SC alternative level	Minutes	0.0142 (2.42)	−0.0083 (−1.91)	0.0354 (3.43)	N/A
Attribute packaging					
Adding travel time components	1.0	−0.4922 (−3.49)	−0.9054 (−7.56)	1.2245 (4.19)	N/A
Variance decomposition					
No. of choice sets	Number	0.0345 (6.41)		0.0615 (8.23)	−0.2877 (−4.1)
Free flow time for base (or total time for OHL3) minus SC alternative level	Minutes		−0.0187 (−3.27)	−0.0049 (−1.60)	0.00074 (0.12)
Congested time for base (or total time for OHL3) minus SC alternative level	Minutes	0.0093 (4.58)		0.0072 (2.79)	
Personal income	$'000s	0.0024 (3.40)	−0.0035 (−2.0)	0.0054 (7.78)	−0.0406 (−8.4)
Threshold parameters					
Mu1		1.7896 (12.9)	2.697 (8.72)	7.435 (8.91)	0.05568 (1.47)
Mu2		3.9928 (13.6)		13.854 (8.73)	
Count of choice responses		* obs	* obs	* obs	* obs
0		6–0 1014	5–0 1415	4–0 810	3–0 1698
1		6–1 876	5–1 1080	4–1 2214	3–1 1212
2		6–2 900	5–2 66	4–2 684	3–2 48
3		6–3, 6–4 585		4–3 99	
Log-likelihood		−4518.45	−1880.52	−3847.70	−2077.95

Note: * defines maximum no. attributes minus no. ignored.

the transaction costs of seeking out, compiling and assessing large amounts of potentially useful information are often seen as burdensome and/or as producing insufficient benefit. While the evidence herein cannot establish whether an attribute reduction strategy is *strictly* linked to behavioural relevance, or to a coping strategy for handling cognitive burden, both of which are legitimate paradigms in real markets, it does provide important signposts on how many attributes provided within a specific context are processed to reflect attribute relevancy.

We now take a closer look at each OHL model, discussing the evidence under the following headings: design dimensions; framing around the base; attribute packaging; variance decomposition; other effects. The magnitude and direction of influence is given in Table IV for the marginal effects, which have to be interpreted relative to each level of the *number of attributes ignored*.[8]

[8] An earlier version of the paper presented the marginal effects for each level of the dependent variable. Two referees suggested that we report the marginal effects for the average number of attributes ignored. In the words of one referee: 'This statistic is more intuitive and provides all the information that's needed for the conclusions that the author draws'.

Table IV. Marginal effects derived from ordered heterogeneous logit models for models with six, five, four and three attributes per alternative

	OHL6 (average no. of attributes ignored)	OHL5 (average no. of attributes ignored)	OHL4 (average no. of attributes ignored)	OHL3 (average no. of attributes ignored)
Design dimensions				
No. of levels	−0.013	−0.0022*	0.0004*	−0.0076*
Narrow attribute range	−0.020	−0.0677	−0.0076	0.0003*
No. of alternatives	0.017	0.0438	0.007	−0.001*
Framing around base alt				
Free flow time for base minus SC alternative level	−0.0011	−0.0018		0.0001*
Congested time for base minus SC alternative level	−0.0002	0.0004*	−0.0001	
Attribute packaging				
Adding travel time components	−0.002	0.0483	−0.004	
Variance decomposition				
No. of choice sets	0.005		−0.421	0.00001
Free flow time for base minus SC alternative level		−0.1032	−2.155*	0.00001*
Congested time for base minus SC alternative level	−0.054		0.0252	
Personal income	−0.005	−0.0016	0.3992	0.000006

* Not statistically significant at 95% confidence level.

The interpretation is restricted to the statistically significant marginal effects (i.e. the non-starred results).

5.1. Design Dimensions

The negative marginal effect for the 'number of levels' of an attribute in OHL6 suggests that the probability of considering more attributes increases *dramatically* as the number of levels per attribute decreases, *ceteris paribus*. The number of levels is not statistically significant for OHL5, OHL4 and OHL3.

The second variable is a dummy for 'narrow attribute range'. The range has the greatest marginal effect within the five-attribute model. The probability of considering more attributes from the offered set decreases as an attribute's range narrows, *ceteris paribus*. That is, respondents ignore more attributes when the difference between attribute levels is small. This result is perhaps due to the fact that evaluation of small differences is more difficult than evaluation of large differences. An important implication is that if an analyst continues to include, in model estimation, an attribute across the entire sample that is *ignored by a respondent*, then there is a much greater likelihood of misspecified parameter estimates in circumstances where the attribute range is narrower than wider.[9]

These two results can be combined and stated in the converse as follows: respondents tend to consider more attributes (i.e. ignore fewer attributes) when the attributes have only

[9] This finding has interesting implications for the growing evidence that mean WTP for an attribute tends to be higher under a wider range for the numerator attribute (Louviere and Hensher, 2001). Simply put, the greater relevance in preserving the attribute content under a wider range will mean that such an attribute is relatively more important to the outcome than it is under a narrow range specification, and hence a higher mean WTP is inferred.

DOI: 10.1002/jae

a few levels that differ greatly, such that evaluation of each attribute is easier. Overall the respondent seems to trade-off effort spent on each attribute against the number of attributes considered.

As we increase the 'number of alternatives' to evaluate, *ceteris paribus*, the importance of considering more attributes increases, as a way of making it easier to differentiate between the alternatives. This is an important finding that runs counter to some views, for example, that individuals will tend to ignore increasing amounts of attribute information as the number of alternatives increases. Our evidence suggests that the processing strategy is dependent on the nature of the attribute information, and not strictly on the quantity.

Overall, we see a picture emerging that design dimensionality seems to have less of an influence on the attribute processing strategy when we have fewer items to process. This makes good sense but should not be taken to imply that designs with fewer items are preferred, but that preference heterogeneity in invoking an attribute processing strategy appears to decline substantially as the information content declines, for real or spurious reasons. Contrariwise, individuals appear to increasingly invoke a relevancy strategy as the amount of information to process increases. The need to capture this growing heterogeneity in IP strategies is clear and should be accounted for in behavioural choice models.

5.2. Framing Around the Base

The theoretical argument promoted in prospect theory for reference points is supported by our empirical evidence. We have framed the level of each attribute relative to that of the experienced car commute as (i) free flow time for current (or base) minus the level associated with an attribute and alternative in the SC design, and (ii) the congested travel time for the base minus the level associated with each SC alternative's attribute. Where the travel time attribute is total time, as in OHL3, we have used the single framing attribute.

The more that an SC attribute level deviates from the reference alternative's level, the more likely that an individual will process an increased number of attributes. This evidence was found for both the 'free flow time' and 'congested time' framing effects. Conversely, as the SC design attribute level moves closer to the reference alternative's level, individuals appear to use some approximation paradigm, in which closeness suggests similarity, and hence ease of eliminating specific attributes, because their role is limiting in differentiation.

Reference dependency not only has a direct (mean) influence on the number of attributes ignored (discussed above), it also plays a role via its contribution to explaining heteroscedasticity in the variance of the unobserved effects. For example, in OHL6, the effect of widening the gap between the base and SC 'congested time' reduces the heteroscedasticity of the unobserved effects across the respondents, increasing the acceptability of the constant variance condition when simpler models are specified. The same inference can be made for 'free flow time' in OHL5, but the opposite applies for OHL4.

The influence of framing via the variance of the unobserved effects reinforces the mean impact of framing for 'congested time' in OHL6 and 'free flow time' in OHL5. For OHL4, the negative influence via variance, of 'congested time', on the average number of attributes ignored outweighs the positive influence via the mean, further supporting the view that the more an SC attribute level deviates from the reference alternative's level, the more likely that an individual will process an increased number of attributes from the offered set.

DOI: 10.1002/jae

5.3. Attribute Packaging

The attribute accumulation rule in stage 1 editing under prospect theory is consistently strong for the aggregation of travel time components across the models, except the three-attribute model, where travel time is a single attribute.[10] The aggregation of cost does not have a significant influence as an attribute packaging strategy.

The strongest behavioural response is in OHL5, where running cost and toll cost are treated as a single 'total cost' attribute. The positive marginal effect for the dummy variable 'adding three travel time components' indicates that, on average, respondents who add up the time components in assessing the alternatives tend to ignore more attributes. For OHL6 and OHL4, the negative marginal effect suggests that if, on average, a respondent wants to preserve the information content of attributes, the probability of processing them through a travel time aggregation rule increases.

In contrast, the four-attribute model suggests that when the two travel time components are added up—free flow and the pre-aggregated components of congestion time—the probability of considering all but one attribute decreases. The data shows that the attribute removed by respondents was trip time variability, reducing the assessment to a comparison of total time and total cost.

There is clear evidence that a relevant simplification rule is re-packaging of the attribute set, where possible, through addition. This is not a cancellation strategy but a rational way of processing the information content of component attributes, and then weighting this information (in some unobserved way) in comparing alternatives.

5.4. Choice Set Effects and Variance Decomposition

An interesting result is the role of the 'number of choice sets' in variance decomposition.[11] As an individual considers an increasing number of attributes up to the full set, we find substantial differences in the incidence of attribute selection within each SC design, both within and between the 'number of choice sets', except for the four-attribute case. For OHL6, as the 'number of choice sets' increases from six to 15 (and for OHL4 as the number increases from nine to 15), the variance of the unobserved influences increases, as a reflection of the increasing amount of accumulated information that is being processed. The variance decreases in the case of OHL3 (with the number of choice sets varying from six to 15). This suggests some degree of interdependence between the choice sets in respect of the attribute processing response. True independence would suggest that the 'number of choice sets' has no impact on the number of attributes considered. Except for OHL4, however, the marginal effects are very small, especially for OHL3.

While the 'number of choice sets' evaluated has no direct influence on processing *each choice set per se*, there appears to be an accumulation process effect when we account for the 'number of choice sets' assessed, with its impact felt through the variance of the unobserved effects. This positioning is intuitively appealing, in the sense that capturing the overall cognitive burden of the set of SC tasks, in contrast to a single choice set task, would sit awkwardly in the set of mean influences on a *specific* SC task.

In summary, the evidence, while not the same across all four SC designs, provides accumulating evidence to support the position that the 'number of choice sets' is more a matter of cognitive

[10] This may suggest that when one gets down to so few attributes, there is a sense of simplicity being imposed on the respondent from an SC design perspective and so any gains in terms of attribute packaging are negligible. This should not be interpreted as support for simple designs; indeed, it may raise concerns about relevancy.

[11] Graphs of the distribution of respondents across the number of attributes considered for each of the evaluated number of choice sets can be provided, on request.

DOI: 10.1002/jae

recognition of other possible influences (resident in the variance term capturing the unobserved effects) on how individuals structure an attribute consideration strategy as they progress through a series of choice tasks.

5.5. Socio-economic Impacts

The socio-economic characteristics of respondents may proxy for other excluded contextual influences. A respondent's personal gross income was identified, through its influence on variance decomposition of the unobserved effects, as the only statistically significant socio-economic influence on the number of attributes considered in all OHL models. We have no priors on the likely sign of the influence on variance.

The negative marginal effect in OHL6 and OHL5 suggests that a higher personal income tends to reduce the variance of the unobserved effects, resulting in a higher probability of preserving more attributes. The inverse effect is evidence for OHL4 and OHL3, although it is very small for OHL3 and relatively strong for OHL4.

6. IMPLICATIONS FOR WILLINGNESS TO PAY

In this section we report the empirical implications of accounting for attribute exclusion and contrast it with the findings if we assumed that all design attributes are considered. We do this by estimating mixed logit models on the choice of an unlabelled alternative, as reported in a stated choice experiment illustrated in Figure 1. Mixed logit has been well documented in many sources (see McFadden and Train, 2000; Hensher and Greene, 2003; Train, 2003) and is not detailed herein. The two model specifications are defined on the assumption that (i) all attributes assessed are relevant (i.e. none are ignored for whatever reason—ML1) and (ii) an individual adopts a pre-choice response processing strategy that permits exclusion of non-relevant attributes for whatever reason (ML2).

We condition each attribute parameter on whether a respondent included or excluded the attribute in their information processing strategy. The choice probabilities are constructed in such a way that the elements of the individual-specific parameter estimates that enter the simulated maximum likelihood function are set to zero when the attribute is ignored (as are their derivatives as part of the optimization process). Further details are given in Hensher *et al.* (2005b).

The mixed logit models are estimated with a constrained triangular distribution for the random parameters. This ensures a non-negative willingness to pay for travel time savings over the entire range of the distribution. Both ML1 and ML2 specified the travel time component parameters as random, and the cost parameters as point estimates. The valuation of travel time savings is derived as the ratio of the random parameter for travel time divided by the fixed parameter estimate for travel cost.[12] The final models are presented in Table V.

The overall goodness of fit of both models is impressive. All parameters are statistically significant and of the expected sign, except for uncertainty in travel time which was removed from the final models. The values of travel time savings (VTTS) are reported in Table VI. The evidence suggests a significantly higher mean estimate of the VTTS when we do not condition parameter estimation on the attribute processing strategy, on average of the order of 18–62% depending on the specific attribute. Attribute consideration also impacts on the distribution of

[12] This ratio gives the value of travel time savings in \$/minute, which is then converted to an hourly value.

DOI: 10.1002/jae

Table V. Mixed logit choice models with alternative attribute processing conditions (3411 observations); time is in minutes, cost is in dollars (500 Halton draws)

Attribute	Alternatives	ML1	ML2
Free flow time	2–4, 6–8, 10–12, 14–16, 18–20	−0.1516 (−17.49)	−0.1521 (−17.01)
Slowed time	3, 4, 7, 8, 11, 12, 15, 16, 19, 20	−0.1166 (−11.66)	−0.1098 (−11.04)
Stop/start time	3, 4, 7, 8, 11, 12, 15, 16, 19, 20	−0.1504 (−13.90)	−0.1451 (−13.54)
Slowed/stop/start time	2, 6, 10, 14, 18	−0.1632 (−17.11)	−0.1355 (−15.03)
Cost attributes			
Running cost	4, 8, 12, 16, 20	−0.8484 (−7.74)	−1.0021 (−7.2)
Toll cost	4, 8, 12, 16, 20	−1.6939 (−24.21)	−2.3183 (−24.25)
Total cost	1–3, 5–7, 9–11, 13–15, 17–19	−0.9775 (−14.56)	−1.3358 (−15.65)
Spread of random parameter distribution			
Free flow time	2–4, 6–8, 10–12, 14–16, 18–20	0.1516 (−17.49)	0.1521 (−17.01)
Slowed time	3, 4, 7, 8, 11, 12, 15, 16, 19, 20	0.1166 (−11.66)	0.1098 (−11.04)
Stop/start time	3, 4, 7, 8, 11, 12, 15, 16, 19, 20	0.1504 (−13.90)	0.1451 (−13.54)
Slowed/stop/start time	2, 6, 10, 14, 18	0.1632 (−17.11)	0.1355 (−15.03)
Pseudo-R^2		0.590	0.593
Log-likelihood		−3783.9	−3758.9

Table VI. Values of travel time savings under the two attribute processing assumptions ($AUD per person hour); *time* = random parameter, *cost* = fixed parameter

Attribute	ML1		ML2		Ratio ML1/ML2
	Mean (std dev)	Min—Max	Mean (std dev)	Min—Max	
Free flow time	10.71 (0.69)	5.85–14.32	9.09 (0.58)	5.40–11.57	1.18
Slowed time	8.25 (0.28)	5.97–9.83	6.58 (0.26)	4.44–8.53	1.25
Stop/start time	10.61 (0.48)	5.35–13.22	8.69 (0.41)	4.49–10.88	1.22
Slowed/stop/start time	11.96 (0.68)	5.53–14.81	8.12 (0.38)	4.52–9.58	1.62

VTTS, reducing the variance as well as the minimum and maximum values. Based on this one study, we cannot conclude that the direction of behavioural impact is upwards, although it is clearly different under the two specifications (see Table V).[13]

7. CONCLUSIONS

This paper has identified the role of (i) the dimensionality of a stated choice experiment, (ii) the framing of stated choice design profiles relative to an experience profile (a reference base) and (iii) aggregating attributes, in influencing which attributes (and hence the number of attributes) are assessed in the process of selecting an alternative.[14]

[13] Recent studies by Rose *et al.* (2004) and DeShazo and Fermo (2004), in different contexts, found that the estimated marginal WTP was higher at the mean when attributes not attended to were either ignored or conditioned on this information. Rose *et al.* (2004) also report the standard deviation of the WTP which was found to be higher.

[14] This study builds on our ongoing research activity (Hensher, in press; Hensher *et al.*, 2005b; Caussade *et al.*, in press) as we search for improved ways of understanding how individuals process increasing amounts of information offered to them in stated choice experiments. There is always more to do.

DOI: 10.1002/jae

The evidence on sources of influence on how many attributes are considered, relative to the full set offered, is important in revealing candidate influences on attribute processing, and the extent to which the empirical policy outputs, such as willingness to pay, vary as a consequence of the SC design and its context. Where we might find evidence of attribute reduction (through exclusion and/or aggregation), we might reasonably speculate that the selected attribute processing strategy has elements of coping *and* relevancy. This should not necessarily be interpreted as a response to complexity, but part of the natural process of decision making.

It is unlikely that there exists a preferred SC design, given the large number of attribute (and more broadly, information) processing strategies adopted by a sampled population within a specific choice context. This is amply demonstrated herein by the range of influences on the propensity to ignore attributes. Although our findings indicate that the number of attributes ignored tends to increase as the number of levels of each attribute increases, as the range of each attribute narrows and as the number of alternatives decreases, this finding cannot be a guide as to what is the 'optimal' design from a behavioural perspective. Rather, what this study shows is that, regardless of the SC design selected, there is behavioural appeal in accounting for the process adopted by each and every sampled individual, in the way they treat each attribute in arriving at their preferred alternative. Accounting for relevancy and cognitive burden is essential if we are to accommodate individual heterogeneity in the processing of choice experiments. The fact that this has been ignored in the majority of previous stated choice experiments must be a concern. Importantly, if we want to compare the empirical findings of same-context studies (e.g. urban commuting travel) that use different SC designs, we must account for the influence of design differences.

When we compare the value of travel time savings distribution, before and after accounting for the attribute processing strategy of each individual, we find sizeable differences in the mean and the variance.

The ongoing research challenge is best stated as follows: what matters is not whether different designs require different attribute (and information) processing strategies, but whether the stated choice design per se contributes to different behavioural responses and associated attribute valuations. Importantly, the processing strategy should be viewed endogenously in future stated choice studies as illustrated in Figure 2.

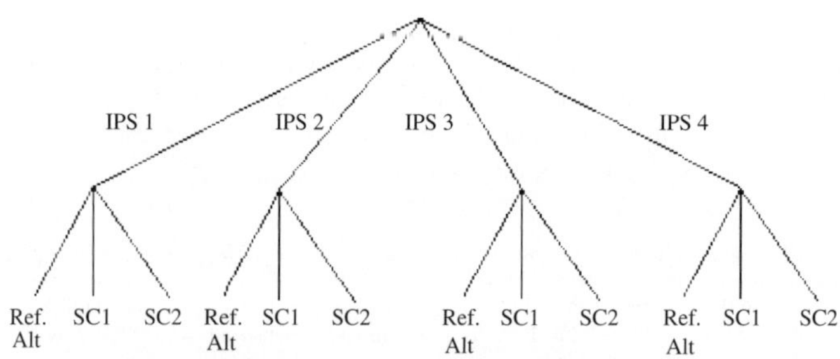

Figure 2. Endogeneity of processing strategy

DOI: 10.1002/jae

APPENDIX

Table AI. Example of a design table (one of 16 implemented designs—see Table II)

Block	Scenarios	Alternative 1			Alternative 2			Alternative 3			Alternative 4		
		Total time	Uncertainty of travel time	Total cost	Total time	Uncertainty of travel time	Total cost	Total time	Uncertainty of travel time	Total cost	Total time	Uncertainty of travel time	Total cost
1	1	2	1	2	3	2	1	0	0	3	1	3	0
1	2	0	0	1	3	2	2	1	3	0	2	1	0
1	3	2	0	0	3	3	1	0	1	2	1	2	1
1	4	2	2	0	0	1	3	3	0	1	1	3	2
1	5	2	1	1	0	0	2	3	3	0	1	2	0
1	6	1	0	2	0	2	0	2	3	3	3	1	1
1	7	0	0	1	3	2	0	2	3	0	1	1	0
1	8	3	2	3	2	0	3	1	3	1	0	1	2
1	9	0	0	3	2	2	2	1	1	1	3	3	2
2	1	2	3	1	1	0	3	3	1	0	0	2	2
2	2	3	2	3	2	1	3	0	3	3	1	0	2
2	3	2	0	1	3	3	0	0	2	0	1	1	2
2	4	0	1	3	1	2	1	2	3	0	3	0	2
2	5	1	0	3	2	3	1	3	1	2	0	2	3
2	6	0	3	1	3	0	0	2	1	3	1	2	2
2	7	1	0	3	2	2	2	3	3	0	0	1	1
2	8	1	1	3	3	0	3	0	3	2	2	2	1
2	9	0	3	0	3	2	1	2	0	2	1	1	3

DOI: 10.1002/jae

Table AII. The attribute profiles for the entire design

(units = %)	Base range			Wider range			Narrower range		
Levels:	2	3	4	2	3	4	2	3	4
Free flow time	±20	−20, 0, +20	−20, −10, +10, +20	−20, +40	−20, +10, +40	−20, 0, +20, +40	±5	−5, 0, +5	−5, −2.5, +2.5, +5
Slow down time	±40	−40, 0, +40	−40, −20, +20, +40	−30, +60	−30, +15, +60	−30, 0, +30, +60	±20	−20, 0, +20	−20, −2.5, +2.5, +20
Stop/start time	±40	−40, 0, +40	−40, −20, +20, +40	−30, +60	−30, +15, +60	−30, 0, +30, +60	±20	−20, 0, +20	−20, −2.5, +2.5, +20
Slow down–stop/start time	±40	−40, 0, +40	−40, −20, +20, +40	−30, +60	−30, +15, +60	−30, 0, +30, +60	±20	−20, 0, +20	−20, −2.5, +2.5, +20
Total travel time	±40	−40, 0, +40	−40, −20, +20, +40	−30, +60	−30, +15, +60	−30, 0, +30, +60	±20	−20, 0, +20	−20, −2.5, +2.5, +20
Uncertainty of travel time	±40	−40, 0, +40	−40, −20, +20, +40	−30, +60	−30, +15, +60	−30, 0, +30, +60	±20	−20, 0, +20	−20, −2.5, +2.5, +20
Running costs	±20	−20, 0, +20	−20, −10, +10, +20	−20, +40	−20, +10, +40	−20, 0, +20, +40	±5	−5, 0, +5	−5, −2.5, +2.5, +5
Toll costs	±20	−20, 0, +20	−20, −10, +10, +20	−20, +40	−20, +10, +40	−20, 0, +20, +40	±5	−5, 0, +5	−5, −2.5, +2.5, +5
Total costs	±20	−20, 0, +20	−20, −10, +10, +20	−20, +40	−20, +10, +40	−20, 0, +20, +40	±5	−5, 0, +5	−5, −2.5, +2.5, +5

ACKNOWLEDGEMENTS

Research funded under the Australian Research Council Large Grants Scheme, Grant A00103962. Discussions over a long period with Bill Greene, John Rose, J. R. DeShazo, Jordan Louviere, Victor Adamowitz, Ken Train, Joffre Swait and Sean Puckett have added to my understanding of this topic. Specific comments on earlier versions by John Rose, J. R. DeShazo and Sean Puckett are appreciated. The extensive comments of three referees are also appreciated, as is the advice of the co-editor Herman van Dijk. An earlier version was presented at the 2004 Australasian Conference of Economists.

REFERENCES

Arentze T, Borgers A, Timmermans H, DelMistro R. 2003. Transport stated choice responses: effects of task complexity, presentation format and literacy. *Transportation Research* **39E**: 229–244.

Carlsson F, Martinsson P. 2003. Design techniques for stated preference methods in health economics. *Health Economics* **12**: 281–294.

Caussade S, Ortúzar Juan de Dios Ortúzar J, Rizzi L, Hensher DA. 2005. Assessing the influence of design dimensions on stated choice experiment estimates. *Transportation Research B*, **39**(7): 621–640.

Dellaert BGC, Brazell JD, Louviere JJ. 1999. The effect of attribute variation on consumer choice consistency. *Marketing Letters* **10**: 139–147.

DeShazo JR, Fermo G. 2002. Designing choice sets for stated preference methods: the effects of complexity on choice consistency. *Journal of Environmental Economics and Management* **44**: 123–143.

DeShazo JR, Fermo G. 2004. Implications of rationally-adaptive pre-choice behaviour for the design and estimation of choice models. Working paper, School of Public Policy and Social Research, University of California at Los Angeles, August.

Heiner RA. 1983. The origin of predictable behaviour. *American Economic Review* **73**: 560–595.

Hensher DA. 2004. Accounting for stated choice design dimensionality in willingness to pay for travel time savings. *Journal of Transport Economics and Policy* **38**(2): 425–446.

Hensher DA. In press. Revealing differences in behavioral response due to the dimensionality of stated choice designs: an initial assessment. *Environmental and Resource Economics*, invited paper.

Hensher DA, Greene WH. 2003. The mixed logit model: the state of practice. *Transportation* **30**(2): 133–176.

Hensher DA, Rose J, Greene WH. 2005a. *Applied Choice Analysis: A Primer*. Cambridge University Press: Cambridge.

Hensher DA, Rose J, Greene W. 2005b. The implications on willingness to pay of respondents ignoring specific attributes. *Transportation* **32**(2): 203–222.

Kahneman D, Tversky A. 1979. Prospect theory: an analysis of decisions under risk. *Econometrica* **47**(2): 263–291.

Louviere JJ, Hensher DA. 2001. Combining preference data. In *The Leading Edge of Travel Behaviour Research*, Hensher DA (ed.). Pergamon Press: Oxford; 125–144.

McFadden D, Train K. 2000. Mixed MNL models for discrete response. *Journal of Applied Econometrics* **15**: 447–470.

Ohler T, Li A, Louviere J, Swait J. 2000. Attribute range effects in binary response tasks. *Marketing Letters* **11**(3): 249–260.

Rose J, Hensher DA, Greene W. 2004. Accounting for exogenous information on decision maker processing strategies in models of discrete choice: attribute exclusion strategies. Institute of Transport and Logistics Studies.

Starmer C. 2000. Developments in non-expected utility theory: the hunt for a descriptive theory of choice under risk. *Journal of Economic Literature* **XXXVIII**: 332–382.

Starmer C, Sugden R. 1993. Testing for juxtaposition and event splitting effects. *Journal of Risk and Uncertainty* **6**: 235–254.

Swait J, Adamowicz W. 2001a. The influence of task complexity on consumer choice: a latent class model of decision strategy switching. *Journal of Consumer Research* **28**: 135–148.

Swait J, Adamowicz W. 2001b. Choice environment, market complexity, and consumer behavior: a theoretical and empirical approach for incorporating decision complexity into models of consumer choice. *Organizational Behavior and Human Decision Processes* **49**: 1–27.

Train K. 2003. *Discrete Choice Methods with Simulation*. Cambridge University Press: Cambridge.

Weber M, Eisenfuhr F, Winterfeldt D. 1988. The effects of splitting attributes on weights in multi attribute utility measurement. *Management Science* **34**: 431–445.

White PJ, Johnson RD, Louviere JJ. 1998. The effect of attribute range and variance on weighted estimates. Unpublished paper, Department of Marketing, The University of Sydney.

Winship C, Mare R. 1984. Regression models with ordinal variables. *American Sociological Review* **49**: 512–525.

[41]

ECONOMETRICA

VOLUME 52 MAY, 1984 NUMBER 3

DISCRETE/CONTINUOUS MODELS OF CONSUMER DEMAND

BY W. MICHAEL HANEMANN[1]

This paper develops a unified framework for formulating econometric models of discrete/continuous consumer choices in which the discrete and continuous choices both flow from the same underlying (random) utility maximization decision. As a special case a number of models suitable for empirical application are developed where the discrete choice is among different brands of a commodity. Since these brands are essentially substitutes, the consumer prefers to buy only one brand at any time; the discrete choice is which brand to select and the continuous choice is how many units to buy.

1. INTRODUCTION

IN WORKING WITH MICRO DATA on consumer demand, one sometimes encounters situations involving qualitative, or discrete, choices in addition to the continuous choices that are the traditional focus of empirical demand analysis. For example, a consumer decides whether to rent or purchase his home, as well as how large a home to live in; a consumer decides whether to have an electric or a gas appliance, as well as how much electricity or gas to consume; a consumer decides which brand of cereal to buy, as well as how many boxes. In all of these cases, the optimal discrete choice—whether to rent or own, which type of appliance, which brand of cereal—depends partly on the outcome of the continuous choice, and vice versa. Therefore, the two choices should be modeled in a mutually consistent manner.

From a formal point of view, these mixed discrete/continuous choices can be regarded as switching regression models, and the estimation techniques developed by Amemiya [**1**], Heckman [**12**], and Lee and Trost [**17**] can be applied to them. However, it would be desirable to formulate estimating equations for the discrete and continuous choices which are derived from an underlying theoretical model of utility maximization by an individual consumer and to incorporate the restrictions resulting from this derivation into the estimation procedure. This approach is taken by King [**14**] and Dubin and McFadden [**5**], who construct specific parametric demand models for the first two consumer choices mentioned above.[2] In this paper I develop a unified framework for formulating demand models suitable for all three examples of discrete/continuous consumer choice and then employ it to construct several specific demand models for the quality-differentiated goods case.

The case of a consumer's choice among different brands of a commodity which vary in their price and quality characteristics has been studied from a theoretical point of view by Lancaster [**16**] and Novshek and Sonnenschein [**23**]. The demand models developed here provide a practical method of analyzing this

[1] I am most grateful to a co-editor and two referees for their helpful comments on earlier versions of this paper.

[2] Similar models of producer supply have been developed by Duncan [**6**] and McFadden [**19**].

type of consumer behavior with empirical data, although they have a somewhat different structure in order to ensure tractable estimating equations. These models cover a variety of functional forms, and a variety of probability distributions for the random disturbances, leading to logit, generalized logit, or probit models for the discrete choices. They, therefore, provide considerable flexibility in empirical applications.

The paper is organized as follows. Section 2 describes a general procedure for constructing discrete/continuous consumer demand models. In Section 3 this procedure is applied to the development of specific models for quality-differentiated goods. A special feature of these models is that the consumer regards the different brands essentially as substitutes and thus prefers to buy only one brand at a time. Various utility models with this property are presented in Section 3. Some extensions of these models are considered in Section 4. The conclusions are summarized in Section 5.

2. GENERAL STRUCTURE OF DISCRETE/CONTINUOUS DEMAND MODELS

Discrete / Continuous Choices

The general setup of a discrete/continuous choice model is as follows. An individual consumer has a utility function defined over the commodities $x_1, \ldots, x_N$, and z, where z is taken as the numeraire.[3] The consumer's utility may also depend on attributes of the x's, denoted by $b_1, \ldots, b_N$, which he takes as exogenous. In addition, his preferences may be influenced by his own characteristics (age, education, etc.), represented by the vector s. The utility function will be written compactly as $u(x, b, z, s)$. It is reasonable to assume that

$$x_j = 0 \rightarrow \partial u / \partial b_j = 0 \qquad (j = 1, \ldots, N), \tag{2.1}$$

which implies that the attributes of good j do not matter unless that good is actually consumed; this property is termed "weak complementarity" by Maler **[20]**.

The consumer chooses (x, z) so as to maximize u subject to a budget constraint

$$\sum p_j x_j + z = y \tag{2.2}$$

and the nonnegativity constraints

$$x_j \geq 0 \qquad (j = 1, \ldots, N), \tag{2.3}$$

$$z \geq 0. \tag{2.4}$$

Moreover, I assume that there is an element of discreteness in the consumer's choice that causes a solution to the utility maximization problem in which some

[3] The models presented below could be generalized to cases where z is a vector of goods, one of which is taken as the numeraire.

of the relations in (2.3) hold as strict equalities. Hence, the selection of the optimal x_j's simultaneously represents a discrete and a continuous choice. The discrete choice is embodied in the decision on which x_j's are to be zero; the continuous choice concerns the magnitude of the nonzero x_j's. Suppose, for example, that $N = 2$ and x_1 is the size of a house owned, while x_2 is the size of a house rented. The discrete choice here is whether to rent or to own, while the continuous choice is the amount of the housing. Alternatively, x_1 is the amount of electricity used with an electric oven, while x_2 is the amount of gas used with a gas oven; the amount of cooking is the continuous choice, and the selection of the appliance type is the discrete choice.

In this paper I will be concerned with the special case where, no matter what their prices, only one of the discrete alternatives is selected—exactly one of the relations in (2.3) holds as inequality. This is a restrictive assumption, but it is employed in almost all of the existing theoretical and empirical literature on discrete/continuous choice.[4] There are two ways in which this type of behavior can occur as a solution to the utility maximization problem. First, there may be some logical or institutional reason why the x_j's are ***mutually exclusive*** in consumption. For example, if a person has only one home, he cannot both rent and own. In effect, there is an additional constraint on the utility maximization problem of the form

$$(2.5) \qquad x_i x_j = 0, \qquad \text{all } i \neq j.$$

I will refer to the utility model (2.2)–(2.5) as the "mutual exclusivity" case.[5] Second, even if there is no logical reason why the x_j's are mutually exclusive, the consumer's tastes may be such that he naturally *prefers* to select only one of the discrete alternatives at a time. For example, there is no external reason why a person cannot have both electric and gas ovens, but this consumer may prefer to have only one type. In this case the utility maximization problem consists of (2.2)–(2.4), but the utility function must have a special structure—the indifference curves for pairs of x_j's must be linear or concave. Examples of such utility functions are presented in Sections 3 and 4. I will refer to this as the "substitute goods" case.

Thus, the essential difference between the two types of discrete/continuous choice model is the special structure of the utility function required for the latter. Apart from this, they can be analyzed in a similar manner. Before proceeding, however, it is necessary to introduce the concept of random utility.

Random Utility Models

A random utility model arises when one assumes that, although a consumer's utility function is deterministic for *him*, it contains some components which are

[4]This is the maintained hypothesis in [**5**, **6**, **14**, **16**, **19**, **23**, and **25**]. Some models where *at most* one of the x_j's is selected (i.e., there is a possibility that $x_j = 0$ all j, and $z = y$) are discussed in [**8**].

[5]The demand models in [**5** and **14**] and the supply models in [**6** and **19**] all fall into this category.

unobservable to the econometric investigator and are treated by the investigator as random variables. The unobservables could be characteristics of the consumer and/or attributes of the commodities. This concept, therefore, combines two ideas which have a long history in economics—the idea of a variation in tastes among individuals in a population and the idea of unobserved variables in econometric models. These components of the utility function will be denoted by the M-dimensional vector ϵ, and the utility function will be written $u(x,b,z,s,\epsilon)$. For the individual consumer ϵ is a set of fixed constants (or functions), but for the investigator ϵ is a random variable with some joint density function, denoted $f_\epsilon(\epsilon_1, \ldots, \epsilon_M)$, which induces a density on u. For convenience, I will still assume that (2.1) holds. Depending on whether it is a mutual exclusivity or a substitute goods-type of discrete/continuous choice model, the consumer maximizes $u(x,b,z,s,\epsilon)$ subject to the constraints (2.2)–(2.5) or (2.2)–(2.4). I assume that there are no unobservables in these constraints.

Suppose, for the moment, that the consumer has decided to consume only good j. Conditional on this decision, his utility as a function of x_j and z, the remaining choice variables, is $\bar{u}_j = u(0, \ldots, 0, x_j, 0, \ldots, 0, b_1, \ldots, b_N, z, s, \epsilon)$. By virtue of assumption (2.1), this conditional direct utility can be written as $\bar{u}_j = \bar{u}_j(x_j, b_j, z, s, \epsilon)$. The consumer maximizes $\bar{u}_j$ subject to the conditional budget constraints $p_j x_j + z = y$, and the nonnegativity conditions $x_j \geq 0$, $z \geq 0$. I assume that $\bar{u}_j$ is strictly quasiconcave in x_j and z, and none of the indifference curves intersect the z axis—i.e., x_j is essential with respect to $\bar{u}_j$. This ensures that the conditional utility maximization has a solution with $x_j > 0$. If, in addition, the indifference curves do not intersect the x_j axis, there is a solution with $z > 0$.

The resulting conditional ordinary demand functions will be denoted $\bar{x}_j(p_j, b_j, y, s, \epsilon)$ and $\bar{z}(p_j, b_j, y, s, \epsilon) = y - p_j \bar{x}_j(p_j, b_j, y, s, \epsilon)$, and the conditional indirect utility function is $\bar{v}_j(p_j, b_j, y, s, \epsilon) \equiv \bar{u}_j[\bar{x}_j(p_j, b_j, y, s, \epsilon), b_j, \bar{z}(p_j, b_j, y, s, \epsilon), s, \epsilon]$. Since $\bar{u}_j$ is a well-behaved utility function, these derived functions possess all the standard properties. In particular, $\bar{v}_j$ is quasiconvex and decreasing in p_j and increasing in y, and it satisfies Roy's Identity,

$$\bar{x}_j(p_j, b_j, y, s, \epsilon) = -\frac{\partial \bar{v}_j(p_j, b_j, y, s, \epsilon)/\partial p_j}{\partial \bar{v}_j(p_j, b_j, y, s, \epsilon)/\partial y}. \tag{2.6}$$

The quantities $\bar{x}_j$, $\bar{z}$, and $\bar{v}_j$ are known numbers to the consumer, but because his preferences are incompletely observed they are random variables from the point of view of the econometric investigator. In particular, let $f_{\bar{v}}(\bar{v}_1, \ldots, \bar{v}_N)$ be the joint density of $\bar{v}_1, \ldots, \bar{v}_N$ induced by $f_\epsilon(\cdot)$, and let $F_{\bar{v}}(\cdot)$ be the corresponding cumulative distribution.[6]

All of the foregoing is conditional on the consumer's selecting good j. The discrete choice of which good to select can be represented by a set of binary

[6] I assume that $f_{\bar{v}}$ and other derived probability distributions described below exist and are well defined. Note that if the random terms, ϵ, enter the conditional indirect utility functions in an appropriate manner, they might disappear from the ratio on the right-hand side of (2.6). In that case, the conditional quantities demanded, $\bar{x}_j$ and $\bar{z}$, would *not* be random variables for the investigator; in effect, the existence of an unobservable component of the consumer's preferences affects his discrete choice but not his continuous choice.

valued indices, $\delta_1, \ldots, \delta_N$, where $\delta_j = 1$ if $x_j > 0$, and $\delta_j = 0$ if $x_j = 0$. The choice may be expressed in terms of the conditional indirect utility functions as

$$\delta_j(p,b,y,s,\epsilon) = \begin{cases} 1 & \text{if } \bar{v}_j(p_j,b_j,y,s,\epsilon) \geq \bar{v}_i(p_i,b_i,y,s,\epsilon), \quad \text{all } i, \\ 0 & \text{otherwise.} \end{cases} \tag{2.7}$$

For the observer, the discrete choice indices are random variables with a mean $E\{\delta_j\} \equiv \pi_j$ given by

$$\begin{aligned} \pi_j(p,b,y,s,\epsilon) &= \Pr\{\bar{v}_j(p_j,b_j,y,s,\epsilon) \geq \bar{v}_i(p_i,b_i,y,s,\epsilon), \text{ all } i\} \\ &= \int_{-\infty}^{\infty} F_{\bar{v}}^j(u,\ldots,u)\,du, \end{aligned} \tag{2.8}$$

where $F_{\bar{v}}^j$ denotes the derivative of $F_{\bar{v}}(\cdot)$ with respect to its jth argument.

Now consider the original, unconditional problem of maximizing $u(x,b,z,s,\epsilon)$ subject to (2.2)–(2.5) in the mutual exclusivity case, or (2.2)–(2.4) in the substitute goods case. The unconditional ordinary demand functions associated with this problem will be denoted $x_j(p,b,y,s,\epsilon)$, $j = 1,\ldots,N$, and $z(p,b,y,s,\epsilon)$. The resulting unconditional indirect utility function is $v(p,b,y,s,\epsilon) \equiv u[x(p,b,y,s,\epsilon),b,z(p,b,y,s,\epsilon),s,\epsilon]$. The relationship between these unconditional functions and the corresponding conditional ones is given by

$$x_j(p,b,y,s,\epsilon) = \delta_j(p,b,y,s,\epsilon)\bar{x}_j(p_j,b_j,y,s,\epsilon) \qquad (j = 1,\ldots,N), \tag{2.9}$$

$$v(p,b,y,s,\epsilon) = \max\left[\bar{v}_1(p_1,b_1,y,s,\epsilon),\ldots,\bar{v}_N(p_N,b_N,y,s,\epsilon)\right]. \tag{2.10}$$

These relations can be used to analyze the probability distributions of the quantities x_j and v.

For this purpose, it is convenient to introduce the sets $A_j \equiv \{\epsilon \mid \bar{v}_j(p_j,b_j,y,s,\epsilon) \geq \bar{v}_i(p_i,b_i,y,s,\epsilon), \text{ all } i\}$, $j = 1,\ldots,N$. From f_ϵ one can construct $f_{\epsilon \mid \epsilon \in A_j}$, the conditional joint density of $\epsilon_1,\ldots,\epsilon_M$ given that $\epsilon \in A_j$, i.e., given that good j is selected. Then, the probability density of $\bar{x}_j$, $f_{x_j \mid \epsilon \in A_j}(x) = \Pr\{x_j = x \mid \epsilon \in A_j\}$, can be obtained from $f_{\epsilon \mid \epsilon \in A_j}$ by a change of variable based on (2.6). Finally, the probability density of x_j, $f_{x_j}(x) = \Pr\{x_j = x\}$, takes the form

$$f_{x_j}(x) = \begin{cases} 1 - \pi_j, & x = 0, \\ \pi_j f_{x_j \mid \epsilon \in A_j}(x), & x > 0. \end{cases} \tag{2.11}$$

In summary, the crucial building blocks for a random utility discrete/continuous choice model are the conditional indirect utility functions $\bar{v}_j(p_j,b_j,y,s,\epsilon)$, $j = 1,\ldots,N$, and the joint density f_ϵ. Once these have been specified, one can construct the densities $f_{\bar{v}}$ and $f_{\epsilon \mid \epsilon \in A_j}$ which are used to form the discrete choice probabilities and the conditional and unconditional densities of the x_j's. This procedure will be illustrated in the next section. Different random utility models can be generated by allowing the random elements ϵ to enter the conditional indirect utility functions in different ways or by making different assumptions about their joint distribution, but these models will all conform to the general structure outlined above.

The estimation of these discrete/continuous choice models will be discussed below. However, one general comment can be made. First, note that an alternative way of expressing the unconditional ordinary demand functions, besides (2.9), is the following (using the case of $N = 2$ for simplicity):

$$(2.12) \qquad x = \begin{cases} -\dfrac{\partial \bar{v}_1(p_1, b_1, y, s, \epsilon)/\partial p_1}{\partial \bar{v}_1(p_1, b_1, y, s, \epsilon)/\partial y} & \text{if } \bar{v}_1(p_1, b_1, y, s, \epsilon) \geq \bar{v}_2(p_2, b_2, y, s, \epsilon), \\ -\dfrac{\partial \bar{v}_2(p_2, b_2, y, s, \epsilon)/\partial p_2}{\partial \bar{v}_2(p_2, b_2, y, s, \epsilon)/\partial y} & \text{otherwise.} \end{cases}$$

The purpose of this formulation is to show how the theoretical random utility model generates a statistical switching regression model. The general (linear) single equation switching regression model can be written in the form[7]

$$(2.13) \qquad Y = \begin{cases} W_1\beta_1 + v_1 & \text{if } \; Z\gamma + \eta \geq 0, \\ W_2\beta_2 + v_2 & \text{otherwise,} \end{cases}$$

where Y is the dependent variable, W_1, W_2, and Z are exogenous variables, β_1, β_2, and γ are the coefficients to be estimated, and v_1, v_2, and η are random error terms. The demand model (2.12) is clearly a special case of (2.13) where, because the discrete and continuous choices both flow from the same underlying utility maximization problem, the variables W_1 and W_2 are transformations of the variables Z, the coefficients β_1 and β_2 are directly related to the coefficients γ, and the random terms v_1 and v_2 are derived from the random term η.[8] Thus, the random utility discrete/continuous demand model can be estimated by any of the statistical techniques developed for use with switching regression models while taking advantage of the additional restrictions inherent in the random utility formulation.

3. MODELS FOR SUBSTITUTE GOODS

Introduction

In this section I develop several specific discrete/continuous choice models which are suitable for empirical application. I focus on the case of substitute goods, but the procedures described below can readily be adapted to the mutual exclusivity case. Although this type of discrete/continuous choice arises in a variety of contexts, the particular paradigm I will employ here is a consumer's

[7] See, for example, Lee and Trost [**17**].

[8] Duncan's [**6**] supply model is similar to the consumption model described here in that it leads to a switching regression model of input demands and output supply with the same general form as (2.13) and with the restriction that the variables and coefficients of the continuous choice are directly related to those of the discrete choice. However, for the sake of estimation, he assumes that the random terms in the continuous choice are *independent* of those in the discrete choice. This is not fully consistent with the general notion that both choices flow from the same underlying random production model.

demand for different brands of a commodity which he regards as essentially substitutes for one another. Accordingly, x_j is interpreted as the consumption of brand $j, j = 1, \ldots, N$, and z is the consumption of all other goods. I assume that there are K different dimensions of quality. Thus, $b_j = (b_{j1}, \ldots, b_{jK})$, where b_{jk} is the amount of the kth quality characteristic associated with a unit of consumption of brand j. This generates a deterministic utility function of the form assumed above, $u = u(x,b,z,s)$.[9] To simplify the notation, I will henceforth suppress the argument s.

As noted earlier, there are many different ways to introduce a random component into the utility function, and each generates a different class of random utility models. Here I assume that $u(x,b,z,\epsilon) = u[x,\psi_1(b_1,\epsilon_1), \ldots, \psi_N(b_N,\epsilon_N), z]$. The function ψ_j may be interpreted as an index of the overall quality of the jth brand; my assumption is that it is here, in the consumer's evaluation of each brand's quality, that the random component is located.

Furthermore, depending on the requirements of the particular utility model, I assume that the random element ϵ_j enters the perceived quality index ψ_j either additively or multiplicatively. Thus, the index takes the form $\psi_j = \bar{\psi}_j(b_j) + \epsilon_j$ or $\psi_j = \bar{\psi}_j(b_j)e^{\epsilon_j}$, where $\bar{\psi}_j(b_j)$ is nonstochastic. To fix ideas I employ the specific formulas[10]

$$\psi_j(b_j,\epsilon_j) = \alpha_j + \sum_k \gamma_k b_{jk} + \epsilon_j, \tag{3.1}$$

$$\psi_j(b_j,\epsilon_j) = \exp\Big(\alpha_j + \sum_k \gamma_k b_{jk} + \epsilon_j\Big). \tag{3.2}$$

The analysis can easily be extended to other cases where $\bar{\psi}_j$ is nonlinear in the b_{jk}'s. Throughout this section, I assume that the ϵ_j's are independently and identically distributed according to the extreme value distribution, $EV(\mu,0)$, $\mu > 0$. Hence, their joint c.d.f. is

$$F_\epsilon(\epsilon_1, \ldots, \epsilon_N) = \exp\Big[-\sum e^{-\epsilon_j/\mu}\Big]. \tag{3.3}$$

The possibility of employing other probability distributions is discussed in Section 4.

This completes the stochastic specification of the random utility models. The next step is the specification of utility functions $u(x,\psi,z)$ with the property that, when maximized subject to the budget constraint (2.2), at all prices they must lead to a corner solution in which only one brand is selected. A general family of

[9] Lancaster's [15] deterministic utility model is a special case of this utility function in which $u(x,b,z) = u(\sum x_j b_{j1}, \ldots, \sum x_j b_{jK}, z)$. However, this particular formulation is too restrictive for my purposes.

[10] Another possible form, suggested by Novshek and Sonnenschein [23] and implicit in Lancaster [16], is $\psi_j = -\sum \gamma_k(\epsilon_k - b_{jk})^2$. The notion here is that, for each attribute, there is an "ideal" level of the attribute for each individual, ϵ_k; this varies among consumers and is unobservable for the econometric investigator. Each consumer seeks to minimize the weighted distance between actual and ideal attribute levels. It is difficult, however, to find a joint density, f_ϵ, which yields a sufficiently tractable form for $f_{x_j \mid \epsilon \in A_j}$.

functions with this property is

$$u = u\left[\sum x_j, \sum \psi_j x_j, \sum \psi_j \xi(x_j), z\right], \tag{3.4}$$

where $\xi_j = \xi(x_j)$ is an indicator function with $\xi_j \equiv 1$ if $x_j > 0$, and $\xi_j \equiv 0$ if $x_j = 0$. Some special cases of the general family (3.4) are considered in the remainder of this section. I should emphasize that my chief concern is to develop demand models which are practical in the sense that they yield tractable expressions for $f_{\epsilon \mid \epsilon \in A_i}$, and $f_{x_j \mid \epsilon \in A_i}$. This has guided my selection of the specific models presented below.

Perfect Substitutes Model

The best known example of (3.4) is the class of utility models with the structure

$$u(x,\psi,z) = u^*\left(\sum \psi_j x_j, z\right) \tag{3.5}$$

where u^* is a conventional bivariate utility function.[11] With this utility function, the different brands are perfect substitutes. The maximization of (3.5) subject to the budget constraint (2.2) clearly leads to a corner solution in which, except on a set of measure zero, a single brand is selected.

Given that the consumer has selected brand j, his conditional direct utility is $\bar{u}_j(x_j, \psi_j, z) = u^*(\psi_j x_j, z)$. Consider $u^*(\cdot,\cdot)$ as a function of two arguments, say, w_I and w_{II}. Clearly, if u^* is strictly quasiconcave in w_I or w_{II}, then $\bar{u}_j$ is strictly quasiconcave in x_j and z. Similarly, if w_I or w_{II} are essential with respect to u^*, then x_j or z are essential with respect to $\bar{u}_j$. Let $w_I^*(p_I, y)$ and $w_{II}^*(p_I, y)$ be the ordinary demand functions arising when $u^*(w_I, w_{II})$ is maximized subject to the constraint $p_I w_I + w_{II} = y$, and let $v^*(p_I, y) \equiv u^*[w_I^*(p_I, y), w_{II}^*(p_I, y)]$ be the corresponding indirect utility function. Then, as Muellbauer [**22**] has shown, the conditional ordinary demand functions and indirect utility function associated with $\bar{u}_j$ have the form

$$\bar{x}_j(p_j, \psi_j, y) = w_I^*(p_j/\psi_j, y)/\psi_j, \tag{3.6a}$$

$$\bar{z}(p_j, \psi_j, y) = w_{II}^*(p_j/\psi_j, y), \tag{3.6b}$$

$$\bar{v}_j(p_j, \psi_j, y) = v^*(p_j/\psi_j, y). \tag{3.6c}$$

Since v^* is decreasing in its first argument, it follows from (3.6c) that the single brand selected by the consumer is that for which (p_j/ψ_j) is lowest.

An implication is that the discrete choices depend entirely on the prices and quality characteristics of the different brands, but not on the parametric form of

[11] The application of this utility model to discrete/continuous choices is suggested in [**3**, pp. 266–269].

the bivariate utility function u^*. It is convenient here to adopt the multiplicative specification for the ψ_j's, (3.2). From (2.8), the discrete choice probabilities may be written

$$\pi_j = \Pr\{\ln p_j - \ln\psi_j \leq \ln p_i - \ln\psi_i \text{, all } i\}$$
$$= \Pr\left\{\epsilon_j + \alpha_j + \sum \gamma_k b_{jk} - \ln p_j \geq \epsilon_i + \alpha_i + \sum \gamma_k b_{ik} - \ln p_i \text{, all } i\right\}.$$

This has the general form

(3.7) $$\pi_j = \Pr\{\epsilon_j + \lambda_j \geq \epsilon_i + \lambda_i \text{, all } i\},$$

where the λ_i's contain all the nonstochastic components of the ψ_i's. Let $F_\epsilon^j(\cdot)$ denote the derivative of $F_\epsilon(\cdot)$ with respect to the jth argument. Then (3.7) becomes

(3.8) $$\pi_j = \int_{-\infty}^{\infty} F_\epsilon^j(t + \lambda_j - \lambda_1, \ldots, t + \lambda_j - \lambda_N)\, dt.$$

For the *EV* distribution (3.3),

(3.9) $$F_\epsilon^j(t + \lambda_j - \lambda_1, \ldots, t + \lambda_j - \lambda_N) = e^{-t/\mu}\exp\left[-\beta_j e^{-t/\mu}\right]/\mu$$

where

(3.10) $$\beta_j = e^{-\lambda_j/\mu} \sum_{i=1}^{N} e^{\lambda_i/\mu}.$$

Thus, from (3.7)–(3.9),

(3.11) $$\pi_j = \int_{-\infty}^{\infty} e^{-t/\mu}\exp\left[-\beta_j e^{-t/\mu}\right]\frac{1}{\mu}\, dt$$
$$= \beta_j^{-1}$$
$$= \exp\left[\bar{\alpha}_j + \sum \bar{\gamma}_k b_{jk} - \frac{1}{\mu}\ln p_j\right] \Big/ \sum \exp\left[\bar{\alpha}_i + \sum \bar{\gamma}_k b_{ik} - \frac{1}{\mu}\ln p_i\right]$$

where $\bar{\alpha}_j \equiv \alpha_j/\mu$ and $\bar{\gamma}_k \equiv \gamma_k/\mu$, which is a logit model of discrete choice.[12]

In order to develop the probability formulas for the continuous choices, let $A_j = \{\epsilon \mid \epsilon_j + \lambda_j \geq \epsilon_i + \lambda_i$, all $i\}$. Then, from (3.7), the conditional marginal density $f_{\epsilon_j \mid \epsilon \in A_j}$ takes the form:

(3.12) $$f_{\epsilon_j \mid \epsilon \in A_j}(\epsilon_j) = F_\epsilon^j(\epsilon_j + \lambda_j - \lambda_1, \ldots, \epsilon_j + \lambda_j - \lambda_N)/\pi_j.$$

[12] See [4]. Some normalization is required in order to estimate (3.11) since it is invariant to multiplication of both the numerator and denominator by e^σ for an arbitrary constant σ. An appropriate normalization would be to set $\alpha_i = 0$ for one index i.

With the *EV* distribution, one obtains from (3.10) and (3.12)

$$(3.13)\qquad f_{\epsilon_j \mid \epsilon \in A_j}(\epsilon_j) = \beta_j e^{-\epsilon_j/\mu} \exp\left[-\beta_j e^{-\epsilon_j/\mu}\right]/\mu.$$

This may be recognized as the density of a univariate *EV* random variable with scale parameter μ and location parameter $(\mu \ln \beta_j)$. For future reference, its mean and moment generating function are[13]

$$(3.14)\qquad E\{\epsilon_j \mid \epsilon \in A_j\} = \mu(\ln \beta_j + 0.57722),$$

$$(3.15)\qquad E\{e^{t\epsilon_j} \mid \epsilon \in A_j\} = \beta_j^{\mu t}\Gamma(1 - \mu t).$$

The formula for $f_{x_j \mid \epsilon \in A_j}$ is derived from $f_{\epsilon_j \mid \epsilon \in A_j}$ by a change of variable based on the formula for the conditional ordinary demand function $\bar{x}_j[p_j, \psi_j(b_j, \epsilon_j), y]$. This, in turn, can be generated from the ordinary demand function associated with u^* by applying (3.6a). As an example, consider the bivariate utility model represented by the indirect utility function

$$(3.16a)\qquad v^*(p_I, y) = \left(\frac{\theta}{\rho - 1}\right)p_I^{1-\rho} - \frac{e^{-\eta y}}{\eta}, \qquad \theta > 0, \quad \eta \neq 0.$$

The associated ordinary demand function is

$$(3.16b)\qquad w_I^*(p_I, y) = \theta p_I^{-\rho} e^{\eta y}.$$

Accordingly, the conditional ordinary demand function generated by the random utility model which consists of (3.5) and the direct utility function dual to (3.16a) is

$$\begin{aligned} \bar{x}_j(p_j, \psi_j, y) &= \theta(p_j/\psi_j)^{-\rho} e^{\eta y} \psi_j^{-1} \\ &= \theta p_j^{-\rho} \psi_j^{\rho-1} e^{\eta y}. \end{aligned}$$

Substituting (3.2) and simplifying yields

$$(3.17)\qquad \bar{x}_j(p_j, \psi_j, y) = \theta p_j^{-1} e^{\eta y} e^{(\rho-1)\lambda_j} e^{(\rho-1)\epsilon_j}$$

where, as before, $\lambda_j \equiv \alpha_j + \sum \gamma_k b_{jk} - \ln p_j$. Using (3.17) to make a change of variable in (3.13) from ϵ_j to x_j, one obtains the conditional density:

$$\begin{aligned} (3.18)\qquad f_{x_j \mid \epsilon \in A_j}(x) = {} & (\theta/p_j)^{1/\mu(\rho-1)} e^{\eta y/\mu(\rho-1)} x^{-[\mu(\rho-1)+1]/\mu(\rho-1)} \sum e^{\lambda_i/\mu} \\ & \times \exp\Big[-(\theta/p_j)^{1/\mu(\rho-1)} e^{\eta y/\mu(\rho-1)} \\ & \times x^{-1/\mu(\rho-1)} \sum e^{\lambda_i/\mu}\Big] \Big/ \mu|\rho - 1|. \end{aligned}$$

The conditional mean quantity of brand j demanded can be obtained by

[13] See, for example, [**13**, p. 278].

integrating (3.18) or, more simply, from (3.17) and (3.15):

$$
\begin{aligned}
(3.19)\qquad E\{x_j \mid \epsilon \in A_j\} &= \theta p_j^{-1} e^{\eta y} e^{(\rho-1)\lambda_j} E\{e^{(\rho-1)\epsilon_j} \mid \epsilon \in A_j\} \\
&= \theta p_j^{-1} e^{\eta y} \left(\sum e^{\lambda_i/\mu}\right)^{\mu(\rho-1)} \Gamma[1-\mu(\rho-1)].
\end{aligned}
$$

As shown below, for estimation purposes it is more convenient to work with the mean of the conditional distribution of $\ln(p_j x_j)$ which is, from (3.14),

$$
\begin{aligned}
(3.20)\qquad E\{\ln p_j x_j \mid \epsilon \in A_j\} &= \ln\theta + \eta y + (\rho-1)\lambda_j + (\rho-1)E\{\epsilon_j \mid \epsilon \in A_j\} \\
&= \ln\theta + \eta y + (\rho-1)\left[\mu \ln\left(\sum e^{\lambda_i/\mu}\right) + 0.57722\mu\right].
\end{aligned}
$$

Several comments should be made about this utility model. First, the indirect utility function (3.16a) is not quasiconvex over the entire price-income space; specifically, it is quasiconvex iff $\eta p_j \bar{x}_j \leq \rho$. In an empirical application this can be tested by comparing the estimate of ρ with the estimate of $\eta p_j E\{x_j \mid \epsilon \in A_j\}$, using the formula in (3.19). Second, it can be shown that a necessary and sufficient condition for the good w_I to be essential with respect to the utility function (3.16a) is that $\rho < 1$. This condition also suffices to ensure the existence of the term $\Gamma[1-\mu(\rho-1)]$ in (3.19). However, the good w_{II} is *not* essential with respect to this utility function—it can be seen from (3.19) that there is a nonzero probability of obtaining $z < 0$ which is meaningless economically.[14] In empirical applications it has been my experience that this probability is negligibly small, so that the problem can reasonably be ignored.[15] Finally, the socioeconomic characteristics of the consumer, s, can be introduced into the demand model by making θ and/or some of the coefficients γ_k functions of these variables.

By combining (3.5) with other indirect utility functions besides (3.16a), one can generate some alternative random utility models. Examples which are known to produce tractable demand models are

$$(3.21a)\qquad v^*(p_I, y) = \left(\frac{\theta}{\rho-1}\right)p_I^{1-\rho} + \frac{1}{1-\eta}y^{1-\eta}, \qquad \theta > 0, \quad \eta \neq 1,$$

$$(3.22a)\qquad v^*(p_I, y) = (y + \theta_1 p_I + \theta_2)p_I^{-\eta}, \qquad 0 < \eta < 1,$$

$$(3.23a)\qquad v^*(p_I, y) = (\ln y - \theta \ln p_I)p_I^{-\eta}, \qquad 0 < \theta < 1.$$

[14]To evaluate this probability, observe that the c.d.f. corresponding to (3.18) is

$$F_{x_j \mid \epsilon \in A_j}(x) = 1 - \exp\left[-x^{-1/\mu(\rho-1)}(\theta/p_j)^{1/\mu(\rho-1)} e^{\eta y/\mu(\rho-1)} \sum e^{\lambda_i/\mu}\right].$$

Thus,

$$\Pr\{z > 0 \mid \epsilon \in A_j\} = F_{x_j \mid \epsilon \in A_j}(y/p_j) = 1 - \exp\left[-y^{-1/\mu(\rho-1)} e^{\eta y/\mu(\rho-1)} \theta^{1/\mu(\rho-1)} \sum e^{\lambda_i/\mu}\right]$$

and

$$\Pr\{z > 0\} = \sum \pi_j \Pr\{z > 0 \mid \epsilon \in A_j\}.$$

[15]It should be noted that the same problem arises in other discrete/continuous choice models which have appeared in the literature including [**5**] and [**14**, p. 158].

The ordinary demand functions associated with these utility functions are

$$(3.21b)\quad w_I^*(p_I, y) = \theta p_I^{-\rho} y^{\eta},$$

$$(3.22b)\quad w_I^*(p_I, y) = -\theta_1 + \frac{\eta}{p_I}(y + \theta_1 p_I + \theta_2),$$

$$(3.23b)\quad w_I^*(p_I, y) = \frac{\theta y}{p_I} + \frac{\theta y}{p_I}(\ln y - \theta \ln p_I).$$

The utility model (3.21) is similar to (3.16) but implies a constant income elasticity of demand. The utility model (3.22) is the bivariate LES model, while (3.23) is a bivariate version of Muellbauer's **[21]** PIGLOG model. All of these models provide for w_I to be an essential good, and (3.22) and (3.23) also permit w_{II} to be essential. In each case one can develop formulas for $f_{x_j | \epsilon \in A_j}$ and $E\{x_j | \epsilon \in A_j\}$ analogous to (3.18)–(3.20); the details can be found in **[8]**.

Cross-Product Repackaging Models

Although it is convenient, the family of random utility models (3.5) suffers from the drawback that it implies a very direct type of substitution between quantity and quality in the consumer's preferences for the branded goods. Suppose the consumer chooses brand j; a doubling of the quantity, x_j, has exactly the same effect on his welfare, $\bar{u}_j$, as a doubling of the quality, ψ_j. Because of this, it is not always true that an increase in quality raises the consumer's demand for a brand. Indeed, (3.6a) implies that, if the price elasticity of demand for x_j is less than unity in absolute value, an increase in ψ_j *decreases* the quantity demanded. Such is the case with the utility models (3.16) and (3.21) but not (3.22) or (3.23).

It seems useful, therefore, to consider other families of random utility models which imply a different relation between quantity and quality, as a possible alternative to (3.5). In the literature on household equivalence scales, the transformation of the utility function u^* into u in (3.5) is known as "scaling." An alternative to scaling is the procedure of "translating," which in the present context produces the family of random utility models

$$(3.24)\quad u(x, \psi, z) = u^*\left[\sum (x_j + \psi_j), z\right]$$

where, as before, u^* is a conventional bivariate utility function.[16] However, there are two problems in using this family. First, (3.24) violates the weak complementarity assumption (2.1). More importantly, although (3.24) ensures that only one brand is selected, the selection depends entirely on price and not on the (random) quality index—the brand selected is that with the lowest price, p_j.

A more fruitful approach is to employ the transformation which Willig **[28]**

[16]Scaling and translating are discussed in [7 and **24**].

refers to as "cross-product repackaging":

$$(3.25)\quad u(x,\psi,z) = u^*\left(\sum x_j, z + \sum \psi_j x_j\right).$$

It turns out to be convenient here to use the additive specification for the ψ_j's in (3.1). These utility functions satisfy weak complementarity and ensure that a single brand is selected. Given that the consumer selects brand j, his conditional direct utility is $\bar{u}_j(x_j,\psi_j,z) = u^*(x_j, z + \psi_j x_j)$. It can be shown that, if u^* is strictly quasiconcave in w_I and w_{II}, then $\bar{u}_j$ is strictly quasiconcave in x_j and z.

The conditional ordinary demand functions and indirect utility function associated with $\bar{u}_j$ take the form

$$(3.26a)\quad \bar{x}_j(p_j,\psi_j,y) = w_I^*(p_j - \psi_j, y),$$

$$(3.26b)\quad \bar{z}(p_j,\psi_j,y) = w_{II}^*(p_j - \psi_j, y) - \psi_j w_I^*(p_j - \psi_j, y),$$

$$(3.26c)\quad \bar{v}_j(p_j,\psi, y) = v^*(p_j - \psi_j, y).$$

Hence, x_j is essential with respect to $\bar{u}_j$ if w_I is essential with respect to u^* but z is not necessarily essential, even if w_{II} is. Thus, there is a nonzero (but, perhaps, empirically small) probability that $z < 0$. It can be seen from (3.26a) that, as long as x_j is not a Giffen good, an increase in quality ψ_j raises the demand for x_j, the increase in demand being proportional to the absolute value of the own price elasticity of demand.

It follows from (3.26c) that the consumer chooses the brand with the lowest value of $(p_j - \psi_j)$. Therefore, the discrete choice probabilities have the same form as (3.7), but with λ_j defined as $\lambda_j \equiv \alpha_j + \sum \gamma_k b_{jk} - p_j$. With the EV distribution, these probabilities are given by the logit formula (3.12), except that the terms $\ln p_j$ and $\ln p_i$ in (3.11) are replaced by p_j and p_i.

The continuous choice probabilities are obtained from (3.26a) by a similar procedure to that employed in the derivation of (3.18)–(3.20). Rather than the utility model (3.16), it would be convenient to employ the related model

$$(3.27a)\quad v^*(p_I, y) = -\frac{e^{-\eta}}{\eta} + \frac{\theta}{\rho} e^{-\rho p_I}, \qquad \theta > 0, \quad \eta \neq 0,$$

$$(3.27b)\quad w_I^*(p_I, y) = \theta e^{-\rho p_I + \eta y}.$$

Closed form results can also be obtained with the Cobb Douglas utility function, and with Dubin and McFadden's **[5]** utility model which leads to a linear demand function of the form

$$(3.28)\quad w_I^*(p_I, y) = \theta - \rho p_I + \eta y.$$

The formulas corresponding to (3.18)–(3.20) for these models are presented in **[8]**.

Other Models

In addition to the utility transformation method, one can also generate discrete/continuous choice models by simply writing down an appropriate direct utility function. An example is the utility model originally developed by Blackburn [**2**] for the analysis of aggregate travel demand[17]

$$(3.29)\quad u(x,\psi,z)=\sum x_j\left(1+\ln\theta-ln\sum x_j\right)+hz+\sum\psi_j x_j,\qquad \theta>0,\quad h>0,$$

where the ψ_j's have the additive form (3.1). It can be shown that the resulting conditional direct utility function $\bar{u}_j$ is strictly quasiconcave with respect to x_j and z; also, x_j is essential but z is not. The conditional ordinary demand function and indirect utility function are

$$(3.30a)\quad \bar{x}_j(p_j,\psi_j,y)=\theta e^{\psi_j-hp_j},$$

$$(3.30b)\quad \bar{v}_j(p_j,\psi_j,y)=hy+\theta e^{\psi_j-hp_j}.$$

It follows from (3.30b) that the consumer selects the brand with the highest value of (ψ_j-hp_j). The discrete choice probabilities, therefore, have the same form as (3.7) but with λ_j defined as $\lambda_j\equiv\alpha_j+\sum\gamma_k b_{jk}-hp_j$. With the *EV* distribution, this produces a logit formula similar to (3.11).

The continuous choice probabilities are derived from (3.30a) in the manner outlined above. Observe that the consumer's demand for x_j rises with an increase in quality ψ_j but is independent of his income. Some alternative utility models which avoid this last feature, of the general form

$$(3.31)\quad u(x,\psi,z)=g\left(\sum x_j,z\right)+\sum\psi_j x_j,$$

are presented in [**8**], together with a fuller analysis of the Blackburn model.

Estimation

The discrete/continuous demand models presented above can all be estimated in a similar manner. Suppose one has a set of observations on T individuals and let j^* be the index of the brand selected by the tth individual and x_t^* his observed consumption of this brand. The likelihood function for the sample is

$$(3.32)\quad L=\prod_{t=1}^{T} f_{x_{j^*,t}}(x_t^*)$$

$$(3.33)\quad =\prod_{t=1}^{T}\left\{f_{x_{j^*,t}|\epsilon\in A_{j^*,t}}(x_t^*)\cdot\pi_{j^*t}\right\},$$

[17]Blackburn never explicitly presents this formula for the utility function, but it is implicit in his analysis.

where, for the model consisting of (3.5) and (3.16), π_{j^*t} is given by (3.11) and $f_{x_{j^*t} \mid \epsilon \in A_{j^*t}}(x_t^*)$ is given by (3.18), and similarly for the other models. In principle, all the unknown parameters can be estimated by full information maximum likelihood.[18] Following the argument of Amemiya [**1**], it can be shown that the MLE is consistent and asymptotically normal and efficient. In practice, however, the normal equations may have multiple roots and, unless one starts from an initial consistent estimator, there is no guarantee of convergence to the global maximum.

As an alternative, one can exploit the decomposition in (3.33) by employing a two-stage estimation procedure along the lines originally suggested by Heckman [**12**] and Lee and Trost [**17**] for the switching regression model with normal errors. I will describe this for the model consisting of (3.5) and (3.16); the details vary slightly for the other demand models. The first step is maximum likelihood estimation of the logit model for the discrete probabilities alone, (3.11). This yields estimates of $\bar{\alpha}$, $\bar{\gamma}$, and $(1/\mu)$ which are consistent but not efficient, since they ignore the information contained in the data on the continuous choices. With these estimates, one can form consistent estimates of $(\lambda_i/\mu)_t$. The next step is a regression analysis of the continuous choices. By virtue of (3.20), one can set up the following regression model

$$\text{(3.34)} \qquad \ln p_{j^*} x_t^* = \ln \theta_t + \eta y_t + (\rho - 1)\left\{ \mu \ln \sum e^{(\lambda_i/\mu)_t} + 0.57722\mu \right\} + v_t \qquad (t = 1, \ldots, T),$$

where the v_t's are i.i.d. $EV(\mu, -0.57722\mu)$. Hence, $E\{v_t\} = 0$ and $\operatorname{var}\{v_t\} = \pi^2\mu^2/6$.[19] The estimated values of $(\lambda_i/\mu)_t$ and μ are used to form the regressor variable in braces in (3.34) and the equation is fitted by least squares—by OLS or nonlinear least squares, depending on the form of $\ln \theta_t$. Since this is a regression with nonnormal but homoscedastic and finite-variance disturbances, the resulting estimates of μ and the coefficients in $\ln \theta_t$ are consistent.[20]

At this point, therefore, one has consistent estimates of all the unknowns in the model. The final step is to use these as initial estimates for the maximization of the likelihood function, (3.33). Since they are consistent, a single Newton–Raphson iteration will provide estimates with the same asymptotic distribution as the global MLE. Thus, these two-step maximum likelihood estimates are consistent and asymptotically normal and efficient, and their covariance matrix is consistently estimated by the information matrix.

[18] FIML is employed in [**14**]. However, the likelihood function is incorrectly specified there as the product of a discrete choice probability and an *unconditional* density, instead of a conditional density as in (3.33).

[19] From (3.15), $\operatorname{var}\{\epsilon_j \mid \epsilon \in A_j\} = \operatorname{var}\{\ln p_j x_j \mid \epsilon \in A_j\} = \pi^2\mu^2/6$.

[20] However, the usual formula for the covariance matrix of these coefficient estimates is incorrect —see Heckman [**12**].

4. SOME EXTENSIONS

Other Probability Distribution

Because they are based on the *EV* distribution (3.3), the discrete/continuous choice models presented in Section 3 are open to the objection that they exhibit the independence of irrelevant alternatives property with respect to the discrete choice probabilities, and they preclude any correlation among the random elements $\epsilon_1, \ldots, \epsilon_N$. This can be avoided by switching to some other probability distribution such as McFadden's **[18]** generalized extreme value (*GEV*) distribution or the multivariate normal (*MVN*) distribution.

With the *GEV* distribution, the joint c.d.f. of the ϵ_j's is given by

$$F_\epsilon(\epsilon_1, \ldots, \epsilon_N) = \exp\left[-G(e^{-\epsilon_1/\mu}, \ldots, e^{-\epsilon_N/\mu})\right] \tag{4.1}$$

where $\mu > 0$ and G is a nonnegative linear homogeneous function; (3.3) represents the special case of (4.1) where $G(t_1, \ldots, t_N) = \sum t_i$. Therefore,

$$\begin{aligned} &F_\epsilon^j(t + \lambda_j - \lambda_1, \ldots, t + \lambda_j - \lambda_N) \\ &\quad = e^{-t/\mu}G_j(e^{\lambda_1/\mu}, \ldots, e^{\lambda_N/\mu})\exp\left[-\beta_j e^{-t/\mu}\right]/\mu \end{aligned} \tag{4.2}$$

where G_j is the derivative of G with respect to its jth argument, and

$$\beta_j \equiv e^{-\lambda_j/\mu}G(e^{\lambda_1/\mu}, \ldots, e^{\lambda_N/\mu}). \tag{4.3}$$

Applying (3.8) to (4.2), one obtains

$$\pi_j = e^{\lambda_j/\mu}G_j(e^{\lambda_1/\mu}, \ldots, e^{\lambda_N/\mu})/G(e^{\lambda_1/\mu}, \ldots, e^{\lambda_N/\mu}), \tag{4.4}$$

where, for the model consisting of (3.2) and (3.5), $\lambda_j = \alpha_j + \sum \gamma_k b_{jk} - \ln p_j$. The marginals of the *GEV* are univariate *EV* distributions. Thus, when (3.12) is applied to (4.2), one obtains the same formula as (3.13) for the conditional marginal density $f_{\epsilon_j \mid \epsilon \in A_j}(\epsilon_j)$, except that β_j is now defined by (4.3). Similarly, (3.14) and (3.15) carry over with β_j defined by (4.3). It follows that the formulas (3.18)–(3.20) carry over except that the term $\sum e^{\lambda_i/\mu}$ is now replaced by $G(e^{\lambda_1/\mu}, \ldots, e^{\lambda_N/\mu})$.

The *MVN* has some advantages over the *GEV* distribution in that it offers a less restricted covariance structure for the ϵ_j's and permits one to adopt a random coefficient formulation of ψ_j in (3.1) or (3.2): following Hausman and Wise **[11]**, one can assume that the γ_k's are themselves *MVN* random variables. However, these advantages are obtained at the cost of much greater computational complexity.

Suppose that $\epsilon_1, \ldots, \epsilon_N$ are *MVN* with mean zero and some covariance matrix $\Sigma \equiv \{\sigma_{ij}\}$. For convenience, I will denote the T dimensional *MVN* density with mean μ and covariance matrix Σ by $\phi_T(\cdot\,; \mu, \Sigma)$, and the corresponding c.d.f. by $\Phi_T(\cdot\,;\mu,\Sigma)$. For each j, define the $(N-1)$ dimensional vector $\nu_j = (\nu_{j1}, \ldots, \nu_{j,j-1}, \nu_{j,j+1}, \ldots, \nu_{jN})$, where $\nu_{jl} = (\epsilon_l - \epsilon_j)/\omega_{jl}^{1/2}$, and $\omega_{jl} = (\sigma_j^2 + \sigma_l^2 - 2\sigma_{jl})$. Then, the density of ν_j is $\phi_{N-1}(\nu_j; 0, \Omega_j)$ where $\Omega_j \equiv (\omega_{j,lk}^*)$, $\omega_{j,ll}^* \equiv \operatorname{var}(\nu_{jl}) = 1$, and $\omega_{j,lk}^* \equiv \operatorname{cov}(\nu_{jl}, \nu_{jk}) = (\sigma_{lk} - \sigma_{jl} - \sigma_{jk} + \sigma_j^2)/\omega_{jl}^{1/2}\omega_{jk}^{1/2}$. It can be shown that the discrete choice probabilities (3.7) take the form of a probit model

$$\pi_j = \Phi_{N-1}(\Delta_j; 0, \Omega_j), \tag{4.5}$$

where $\Delta_j = (\Delta_{j1}, \ldots, \Delta_{j,j-1}, \Delta_{j,j+1}, \ldots, \Delta_{jN})$, and $\Delta_{jl} = (\lambda_j - \lambda_l)/\omega_{jl}^{1/2}$. Similarly, it can be shown that conditional marginal density $f_{\epsilon_j | \epsilon \in A_j}$ takes the form

$$\begin{aligned} (4.6) \quad & f_{\epsilon_j | \epsilon \in A_j}(\epsilon_j) \\ &= \pi_j^{-1} \cdot \int_{-\infty}^{\Delta_{j1}} \cdots \int_{-\infty}^{\Delta_{j,j-1}} \int_{-\infty}^{\Delta_{j,j+1}} \cdots \int_{-\infty}^{\Delta_{jN}} \phi_1\left(\epsilon_j; \rho_j'\Omega_j^{-1}\nu_j, \sigma_j^2 - \rho_j'\Omega_j^{-1}\rho_j\right) \\ &\quad \times \phi_{N-1}(\nu_j; 0, \Omega_j)\, d\nu_{j1}, \ldots, d\nu_{j,j-1}, d\nu_{j,j+1}, \ldots, d\nu_{jN}, \end{aligned}$$

where $\rho_j' = (\rho_{j1}, \ldots, \rho_{j,j-1}, \rho_{j,j+1}, \ldots, \rho_{jN})$, and $\rho_{jl} \equiv \operatorname{cov}(\epsilon_j, \nu_{jl}) = (\sigma_j^2 - \sigma_{jl})/\omega_{jl}^{1/2}$. Finally, using the results of Tallis **[26]**, one obtains

$$E\left\{e^{t\epsilon_j} \mid \epsilon \in A_j\right\} = e^{t^2\sigma_j^2/2}\Phi_{N-1}(\Delta_j - t\rho_j; 0, \Omega_j)/\Phi_{N-1}(\Delta_j; 0, \Omega_j), \tag{4.7}$$

$$E\left\{\epsilon_j \mid \epsilon \in A_j\right\} = -\rho_j'\kappa_j, \tag{4.8}$$

where $\kappa_j = [\partial\Phi_{N-1}(\Delta_j; 0, \Omega_j)/\partial\Delta_j]/\Phi_{N-1}(\Delta_j; 0, \Omega_j)$.

The formulas (4.5)–(4.8) can be used to generate *MVN* versions of the *EV* demand models presented in Section 3. In principle, these can be estimated by the two-step procedure described in Section 3. The details may be found in **[8]**. It should be noted, however, that (4.5)–(4.8) involve $(N-1)$ dimensional multiple integrals which become computationally unwieldy if N is at all large.

Generalized Translation Models

A feature of the discrete/continuous choice models presented in Section 3 is that, in every case, the discrete choice depends on the prices and quality characteristics of the alternative brands but not on the consumer's income. There are several ways to introduce income into the discrete choices. First, an indirect method is to make some of the coefficients γ_k in (3.1) or (3.2) functions of socioeconomic characteristics of the consumer which are correlated with his income such as age or occupation. A second method is to introduce the consumption of the numeraire good, z, directly into the quality indices so that they have the form $\psi_j(b_j, z, \epsilon_j)$. In principle, these quality indices can be combined with the utility functions (3.5), (3.24), or (3.31) to generate models in which the discrete choices depend on income as well as prices and quality characteristics. It is difficult, however, to find parametric utility functions and formulas for

$\psi_j(b_j, z, \epsilon_j)$ which yield closed-form expressions for the conditional demand function, $\bar{x}_j$, and the conditional indirect utility function, $\bar{v}_j$.

A more promising approach is based on the families of utility models

$$u(x,\psi,z) = u^*\left[\sum x_j + \sum \psi_j \xi(x_j), z\right], \tag{4.9}$$

$$u(x,\psi,z) = u^*\left[\sum x_j, z + \sum \psi_j \xi(x_j)\right], \tag{4.10}$$

where u^* is a conventional bivariate utility function, and $\xi(x_j) \equiv 1$ if $x_j > 0$ and $\xi(x_j) \equiv 0$ if $x_j = 0$.[21] I will refer to these as "generalized translation models." They appear similar to (3.24) and (3.25), but, unlike (3.24), they satisfy weak complementarity and, unlike both (3.24) and (3.25), they generate discrete choices which depend explicitly on the consumer's income. Since the utility model (4.10) has some attractive properties, I focus on it here. With this model, the conditional direct utility function is $\bar{u}_j = u^*(x_j, z + \psi_j)$. Clearly, if u^* is strictly quasiconcave in w_I and w_{II}, then $\bar{u}_j$ is strictly quasi-concave in x_j and z. The resulting conditional ordinary demand functions and indirect utility functions are

$$\bar{x}_j(p_j, \psi_j, y) = w_I^*(p_j, y + \psi_j), \tag{4.11a}$$

$$\bar{z}(p_j, \psi_j, y) = w_{II}^*(p_j, y + \psi_j) - \psi_j, \tag{4.11b}$$

$$\bar{v}_j(p_j, \psi_j, y) = v^*(p_j, y + \psi_j). \tag{4.11c}$$

Thus, x_j is essential with respect to $\bar{u}_j$ if w_I is essential with respect to u^*, but z is not necessarily essential. Furthermore, an increase in quality ψ_j raises (lowers) the demand for x_j according as x_j is a normal (inferior) good.[22]

It is clear from (4.11c) that the discrete choices are dependent on the parametric form of the utility function v^*. To illustrate this, I employ the utility model in (3.16). I assume that the ψ_i's have the additive specification (3.1). Also, for simplicity, I assume that the ϵ_i's follow the EV distribution (3.3). Substituting (3.16a) into (4.11c), one obtains

$$\bar{v}_j(p_j, \psi_j, y) = \left(\frac{\theta}{\rho - 1}\right) p_j^{1-\rho} - \frac{1}{\eta} \exp\left[-\eta\left(y + \alpha_j + \sum \gamma_k b_{jk} + \epsilon_j\right)\right]. \tag{4.12}$$

Define the new random variables τ_i, $i = 1, \ldots, N$, by $\tau_i \equiv -\exp[-\eta(y + \alpha_i + \sum \gamma_k b_{ik} + \epsilon_i)]$. Given that the ϵ_i's have the joint c.d.f. (3.3), the joint c.d.f. of

[21] Novshek and Sonnenschein [23] employ a model with the structure $u(x, \psi, z) = h[g(\sum x_j, z), \sum \psi_j \xi(x_j)]$. While the discrete choices depend on the ψ_j's in this case, the continuous choices are independent of the ψ_j's. Since the random elements enter through the ψ_j's, this implies that the continuous choices are nonstochastic. This is an example of the phenomenon mentioned in footnote 6.

[22] By constrast, with the utility model (4.9) x_j is not necessarily essential with respect to $\bar{u}_j$ even if w_I is essential with respect to u^*, and an increase in quality raises (lowers) the demand for x_j accordingly as the numeraire z is an inferior (normal) good. This utility model is discussed in [8].

the τ_i's is

$$(4.13) \quad F_\tau(\tau_1, \ldots, \tau_N) = \prod_{i=1}^{N} \exp\left[-\beta_i \tau_i^{1/\eta\mu}\right]$$

where $\beta_i \equiv \exp[(y + \alpha_i + \sum \gamma_k b_{ik})/\mu]$. From (4.12), the discrete choice of probabilities take a form similar to (3.7) and (3.8)

$$(4.14) \quad \pi_j = \Pr\{\tau_j + \lambda_j \geq \tau_i + \lambda_i, \text{ all } i\}$$
$$= \int_{-\infty}^{0} F_\tau^j(\tau + \lambda_j - \lambda_1, \ldots, \tau + \lambda_j - \lambda_N)\, d\tau$$

where now $\lambda_j \equiv \eta\theta p_j^{1-\rho}/(\rho - 1)$ and F_τ^j is the derivative of F_τ with respect to its jth argument. Although the integral in (4.14) can be evaluated numerically, it does not yield a closed-form expression such as (3.11).

Substituting (3.16b) in (4.11a), one obtains the formula for the conditional ordinary demand function

$$(4.15) \quad \bar{x}_j(p_j, \psi_j, y) = \theta p_j^{-\rho} e^{\eta(y+\psi_j)} = -\theta p_j^{-\rho} \tau_j^{-1}.$$

Since there is no closed-form expression for $f_{\tau_j | \epsilon \in A_j}$, one cannot express the conditional density $f_{x_j | \epsilon \in A_j}$ in closed form. However, there is a closed-form expression for the unconditional density (for $x > 0$):

$$(4.16) \quad f_{x_j}(x) = F_\tau^j\left[\lambda_j - \frac{\theta p_j^{-\rho}}{x} - \lambda_1, \ldots, \lambda_j - \frac{\theta p_j^{-\rho}}{x} - \lambda_N\right].$$

The mean, $E\{x_j\}$, can be obtained by numerical integration. Given this, one can numerically evaluate the conditional mean $E\{x_j | \epsilon \in A_j\} = E\{x_j\}/\pi_j$.

It follows that one cannot employ the two-step maximum likelihood estimation procedure described in Section 3. Nevertheless, one can still estimate the parameters of the model by directly maximizing the likelihood function consisting of (3.32) and (4.16) in a single step.[23] The same procedure can also be applied to several other utility models besides (3.16). Examples include the bivariate LES model, (3.22), the models (3.27) and (3.28), and the bivariate CES utility model; the specification and estimation of these models are discussed in **[8]**.

5. SUMMARY

In this paper, I have developed a unified framework for formulating econometric models of discrete/continuous consumer choices based on the random utility concept. In these models, the consumer's discrete and continuous choices both flow from a single underlying utility maximization decision. Moreover, the random elements which affect the consumer's discrete choices—representing

[23] Since one cannot initiate the iterative solution of the normal equations with a set of consistent parameter estimates, it might be desirable to try several different starting values in order to test for convergence to a global maximum.

unobservables and differences in tastes—also affect his continuous choices. This interrelationship can be exploited in the estimation of the resulting equations for the discrete and continuous choices.

Discrete/continuous consumer choices arise in a variety of contexts. These can be classified into two main groups: cases where, for logical or institutional reasons, the discrete alternatives are mutually exclusive and cases where the discreteness occurs because the alternatives are perceived by the consumer as essentially substitutes.[24] Both types of models have a similar structure and can be analyzed in a similar manner, but the latter requires additional restrictions on the form of the utility functions.

The existing literature on discrete/continuous choices has focused largely on the mutual exclusivity case. Here, however, I have devoted some attention to substitute goods models, several of which were presented in Sections 3 and 4. The paradigm is a consumer's choice among different brands of a commodity which vary in their prices and quality attributes. The random elements are located in the consumer's assessment of each brand's quality. These models permit a variety of functional forms for the continuous choice demand equations—they can accommodate normal or inferior goods and constant or variable income and price elasticities. They also permit several different types of discrete choice model —logit, generalized logit, and probit. The logit versions of the demand models are easy to estimate. The generalized logit versions, which allow some correlation among the random elements associated with the discrete alternatives, are also fairly simple to estimate. The probit versions, which permit the most general covariance structure for the random elements, are inherently more difficult to estimate and could become computationally burdensome if there were more than a few discrete alternatives.

New discrete/continuous demand models could be generated by introducing the random element into the utility function in a different manner from that adopted here. More importantly, it would be desirable to relax the assumption, used here and in almost all of the existing literature on discrete/continuous choices, that the consumer selects only one of the discrete alternatives—i.e., he always buys only one brand. In principle, one would like to allow for a more general corner solution in which the consumer may select *any* subset of the brands—not necessarily one of them, but not necessarily all of them. Such behavior has been modeled in [**10** and **27**], but these models are severely limited with respect to the parametric form of the utility function and the number of discrete alternatives which can be accommodated. More work remains to be done in order to match the variety and computational convenience of the models presented here.

University of California, Berkeley

Manuscript received May, 1982; final revision received April, 1983.

[24] A third case, where the commodities are lumpy and may be consumed only in discrete amounts, is considered in [**9**].

REFERENCES

[1] AMEMIYA, T.: "Regression Analysis When the Dependent Variable is Truncated Normal," *Econometrica*, 41(1973), 997–1016.

[2] BLACKBURN, A. J.: "An Alternative Approach to Aggregation and Estimation in the Non-Linear Model," Chapter 9 in *The Demand for Travel: Theory and Measurement*, ed. by R. E. Quandt. Lexington: D. C. Heath, 1970.

[3] DEATON, A., AND J. MUELLBAUER: *Economics and Consumer Behavior*. Cambridge: Cambridge University Press, 1980.

[4] DOMENCICH, T. A., AND D. MCFADDEN: *Urban Travel Demand: A Behavioral Analysis*. Amsterdam: North-Holland, 1975.

[5] DUBIN, J. A., AND D. MCFADDEN: "An Econometric Analysis of Residential Electric Appliance Holdings and Consumption," *Econometrica*, 52(1984), 345–362.

[6] DUNCAN, G. M.: "Formulation and Statistical Analysis of the Mixed, Continuous/Discrete Dependent Variable Model in Classical Production Theory," *Econometrica*, 48(1980), 839–852.

[7] GORMAN, W. M.: "Tricks with Utility Functions," in *Essays in Economic Analysis*, ed. by M. Artis and R. Nobay. Cambridge: Cambridge University Press, 1976.

[8] HANEMANN, W. M.: "Notes on Discrete/Continuous Demand Models," University of California —Berkeley Department of Agricultural and Resource Economics, December, 1982.

[9] ———: "Applied Welfare Analysis with Qualitative Response Models," University of California —Berkeley Department of Agricultural and Resource Economics Working Paper No. 241, October, 1982.

[10] ———: "A Methodological and Empirical Study of the Recreation Benefits from Water Quality Improvement," Harvard University Department of Economics, Ph.D. dissertation, 1978.

[11] HAUSMAN, J. A., AND D. A. WISE: "A Conditional Probit Model for Qualitative Choice: Discrete Decisions Recognizing Interdependence and Heterogeneous Preferences," *Econometrica*, 46(1978), 403–426.

[12] HECKMAN, J. J.: "Sample Selection Bias as a Specification Error," *Econometrica*, 47(1979), 153–161.

[13] JOHNSON, N. L., AND S. KOTZ: *Distributions in Statistics: Continuous Univariate Distributions—1*. Boston: Houghton Mifflin, 1970.

[14] KING, M. A.: "An Econometric Model of Tenure Choice and Demand for Housing as a Joint Decision," *Journal of Public Economics*, 14(1980), 137–159.

[15] LANCASTER, K. J.: *Consumer Demand: A New Approach*. New York: Columbia University Press, 1971.

[16] ———: *Variety, Equity, and Efficiency*. New York: Columbia University Press, 1979.

[17] LEE, L. F., AND R. P. TROST: "Estimation of Some Limited Dependent Variable Models with Application to Housing Demand," *Journal of Econometrics*, 8(1978), 357–382.

[18] MCFADDEN, D.: "Modelling the Choice of Residential Location," in *Spatial Interaction Theory and Planning Models*, ed. by A. Karlquist, L. Lundquist, F. Snickars, and J. L. Weibull. Amsterdam: North-Holland, 1978.

[19] ———: "Econometric Net Supply Systems for Firms with Continuous and Discrete Commodities." Massachusetts Institute of Technology Department of Economics Working Paper, 1979.

[20] MALER, K.: *Environmental Economics*. Baltimore: Johns Hopkins, 1974.

[21] MUELLBAUER, J.: "Community Preferences and the Representative Consumer," *Econometrica*, 44(1976), 979–999.

[22] ———: "The Cost of Living and Taste and Quality Changes," *Journal of Economic Theory*, 10(1975), 269–283.

[23] NOVSHEK, W., AND H. SONNENSCHEIN: "Marginal Consumers of Neoclassical Demand Theory," *Journal of Political Economy*, 87(1979), 1368–1376.

[24] POLLAK, R. A., AND T. J. WALES: "Demographic Variables in Demand Analysis," *Econometrica*, 49(1981), 1533–1551.

[25] SMALL, K. A., AND H. S. ROSEN: "Applied Welfare Economics with Discrete Choice Models," *Econometrica*, 49(1981), 105–130.

[26] TALLIS, G. M.: "The Moment Generating Function of the Truncated Multi-Normal Distribution," *Journal of the Royal Statistical Society*, Series B, 23(1961), 223–229.

[27] WALES, T. J., AND A. D. WOODLAND: "A Random Preference Model for the Estimation of Consumer Demand Systems with Binding Nonnegativity Constraints," University of British Columbia Department of Economics Discussion Paper No. 79-32, September, 1979.

[28] WILLIG, R. D.: "Incremental Consumer's Surplus and Hedonic Price Adjustment," *Journal of Economic Theory*, 17(1978), 227–253.

[42]

Econometrica, Vol. 52, No. 2 (March, 1984)

AN ECONOMETRIC ANALYSIS OF RESIDENTIAL ELECTRIC APPLIANCE HOLDINGS AND CONSUMPTION[1]

BY JEFFREY A. DUBIN AND DANIEL L. MCFADDEN

Recent micro-simulation studies of the demand for electricity by residences have attempted to model jointly the demand for appliance and the demand for electricity by appliance. Within this context it becomes important to test the statistical exogeneity of appliance dummy variables typically included in demand for electricity equations. If, as the theory would suggest, the demand for durables and their use are related decisions by the consumer, specifications which ignore this fact will lead to biased and inconsistent estimates of price and income elasticities.

The present paper attempts to test this bias using a subsample of the 1975 survey of 3249 households carried out by the Washington Center for Metropolitan Studies (WCMS) for the Federal Energy Administration. We discuss and derive a unified model of the demand for consumer durables and the derived demand for electricity.

To determine the magnitude of the bias resulting from estimating a unit electricity consumption (UEC) equation by ordinary least squares when unobserved factors influence both choice of appliances and intensity of use, we introduce and estimate a joint water-heat space-heat choice model, and conclude with the consistent estimation and specification of demand for electricity equations.

1. INTRODUCTION

THE ECONOMETRIC SPECIFICATION AND ESTIMATION of the demand for electricity have posed a rich set of problems for the econometrician. Early studies recognized that the demand for electricity was derived through the use of energy using durables. Somewhat later it was recognized that the long and short run responses to price changes might differ greatly as households adjusted their appliance portfolios.[2] Recently, micro-simulation studies have attempted to model jointly the demand for appliances and the demand for electricity by appliance, termed unit electricity consumption (UEC).[3] Within this latter context it becomes important to test the statistical exogeneity of appliance dummy variables typically included in demand for electricity equations. If, as the theory would suggest, the demand for durables and their use are related decisions by the consumer, specifications which ignore this fact will lead to biased and inconsis-

[1]This research has been supported by NSF Grant No. 79-20052. We are indebted to Cambridge Systematics, Inc. for provision of data and unpublished research reports. We have benefited from discussions with D. Brownstone, A. Goett, J. Hausman, R. Parks, and S. Sen. This paper revises and extends a paper presented by McFadden to an EPRI Workshop on the Choice and Utilization of Energy-Using Durables, November, 1979.

[2]Classical studies of aggregate electricity consumption given appliance stock are Houthakker [**23**], Houthakker and Taylor [**24**], and Fisher and Kaysen [**11**]. A number of other studies postulate an adaptive adjustment of consumption to long-run equilibrium, which can be attributed to long-run adjustments in holdings of appliances; see Taylor [**32**].

[3]Cross-section studies with this structure are McFadden–Kirschner–Puig [**30**], the residential forecasting model of the California Energy Conservation and Development Commission [**5**], and the micro-simulation model developed by Cambridge Systematics/West for the Electric Power Research Institute.

tent estimates of price and income elasticities. As these long-run simulations are very costly and important for future energy policy, it would appear useful to test commonly used demand equations for specification error. This problem has been noted and discussed in McFadden, Kirschner, and Puig [**30**].

The present paper attempts to test this bias using a subsample of the 1975 survey of 3249 households carried out by the Washington Center for Metropolitan Studies (WCMS) for the Federal Energy Administration. Matched with these observations were the actual rate schedules faced by each household. The use of disaggregated data in this form is desirable as we can avoid the confounding effects of either misspecification due to aggregation bias or misspecification due to approximations of rate data.

The demand systems derived below are simultaneous equations with dummy endogenous variables. Functional forms have been chosen which offer relatively easy implementation while maintaining economic consistency between discrete decisions on durable purchase and continuous decisions on usage. We use econometric methods adapted from Heckman [**20**]. Related studies are the papers by Lee and Trost [**26**] on housing demand and by Hay [**19**] on wage earnings.

In Section 2 we discuss and derive a unified model of the demand for consumer durables and the derived demand for electricity. In Section 3 we introduce and estimate a joint water-heat space-heat choice model. In Section 4 we conclude with the estimations and specification tests of demand for electricity equations under alternative assumptions. Variable definitions and constructions are discussed in an Appendix.

2. UTILITY MAXIMIZING MODELS FOR DISCRETE/CONTINUOUS CHOICE

In this section we specify a unified model of the demand for electricity consistent with discrete appliance choice. Within this model we illustrate several technical points relating to the economic theory of the demand for electricity. Particular functional forms are chosen that attempt to remain within the spirit of previous work in this area. Finally, we indicate the source of the simultaneous equation bias mentioned above.

Economic analysis of the demand for consumer durables suggests that such demand arises from the flow of services provided by durables ownership. The utility associated with a consumer durable is then best characterized as indirect. Durables may vary in capacity, efficiency, versatility, and of course will vary correspondingly in price. Although durables differ, the consumer will ultimately utilize the durable at an intensity level that provides the "necessary" service. Corresponding to this usage will be the cost of the derived demand for the fuel that the durable consumes. The optimization problem posed is thus quite complex. The consumer unit in the spirit of the theory must weigh the alternatives of each appliance against expectations of future use, future energy prices, and current financing decisions.

We first outline several econometric models consistent with utility maximization which could be used to describe appliance choice and electricity consumption. In the present analysis, block rate structure will be ignored, and electricity treated as a commodity available in any quantity at a fixed marginal (= average) price.[4] Also, appliance holding decisions will be analyzed as if they are contemporaneous with usage decisions, and do not involve intertemporal considerations —a realistic assumption only if there are perfect competitive rental markets for consumer durables.[5] The approach we use combines the method of development of discrete choice models from conditional indirect utility functions employed in McFadden [**29**] and the method developed by J. Hausman [**16**] for recovery of indirect utility functions from econometric partial demand systems.

The consumer faces a choice of m mutually exclusive, exhaustive appliance portfolios, which can be indexed $i = 1, \ldots, m$. Portfolio i has a rental price (annualized cost) r_i. Given portfolio i, the consumer has a conditional indirect utility function

$$u = V(i, y - r_i, p_1, p_2, s_i, \epsilon_i, \eta) \tag{1}$$

where p_1 is price of electricity, p_2 is price of alternative energy sources, y is income, s_i is observed attributes of portfolio i, ϵ_i is unobserved attributes of portfolio i, r_i is price of portfolio i, η is unobserved characteristics of the consumer, and all prices and income are deflated by an index of nonenergy commodity prices. Electricity and alternative energy consumption levels, given portfolio i, are (by Roy's identity)

$$x_1 = \frac{-\partial V(i, y - r_i, p_1, p_2, s_i, \epsilon_i, \eta)/\partial p_1}{\partial V(i, y - r_i, p_1, p_2, s_i, \epsilon_i, \eta)/\partial y}, \tag{2}$$

$$x_2 = \frac{-\partial V(i, y - r_i, p_1, p_2, s_i, \epsilon_i, \eta)/\partial p_2}{\partial V(i, y - r_i, p_1, p_2, s_i, \epsilon_i, \eta)/\partial y}. \tag{3}$$

The probability that portfolio i is chosen is

$$\begin{aligned} P_i = \operatorname{Prob}\{(\epsilon_1, \ldots, \epsilon_m, \eta) : {} & V(i, y - r_i, p_1, p_2, s_i, \epsilon_i, \eta) \\ & > V(j, y - r_j, p_1, p_2, s_j, \epsilon_j, \eta) \text{ for } j \neq i\}. \end{aligned} \tag{4}$$

Any function V with the necessary and sufficient properties of an indirect utility

[4]For a discussion of the treatment of rate structure in demand for electricity, see Dubin [**8**].

[5]A neoclassical consumer will base appliance purchase, replacement, and retirement decisions on the life-cycle capital and operating costs of alternative appliance portfolios. The first econometric problem in analyzing appliance choice is that the components of life-cycle appliance cost are usually not all observable. A second difficulty is that contemporary energy prices may be a poor indicator of the operating cost expectations of a household. A third, and more fundamental, difficulty in analyzing appliance choice decisions lies in the question of the interaction of supply and demand. These issues are discussed in Dubin [**7**].

function can be used to construct econometric forms for joint discrete/continuous choice.[6]

A second method of obtaining a discrete/continuous demand system is to start from a parametric specification of the UEC equation, treat Roy's identity as a partial differential equation whose solution defines a conditional indirect utility function, and then define the discrete choice probabilities from the indirect utility function. This procedure can be carried through for functions in which UEC levels exhibit some income elasticity.

First consider systems in which the UEC equation is linear in income,

$$(5)\qquad x_1 = \beta_i(y - r_i) + m^i(p_1, p_2) + \nu_{1i},$$

with m^i linear in parameters and the distribution of ν_{1i} depending in general on discrete choice i. A general solution for an indirect utility function yielding this demand equation is

$$(6)\qquad u = \psi\left(\left[M^i(p_1, p_2) + y - r_i + \nu_{1i}/\beta_i\right]e^{-\beta_i p_1}, p_2, \nu_{2i}\right),$$

where

$$(7)\qquad M^i(p_1, p_2) = \int_{p_1}^{0} m^i(t, p_2)e^{\beta_i(p_1 - t)}\,dt$$

and ψ is a function which is increasing in its first argument.[7] The demand for substitute energy satisfies

$$(8)\qquad x_2 = -M_2^i(p_1, p_2) - e^{-\beta_i p_1}\psi_2/\psi_1,$$

where $M_2^i = \partial M^i/\partial p_2$ and $\psi_2/\psi_1 = (\partial\psi/\partial p_2)/(\partial\psi/\partial p_1)$ is evaluated at the arguments in (6).

Consider a special case of (6) in which $\nu_{2i} = \nu_{21}$ is the same for all i. The discrete choice probabilities satisfy

$$(9)\qquad P_i = \text{Prob}\left\{\left[M^i(p_1, p_2) + y - r_i + \nu_{1i}/\beta_i\right]e^{-\beta_i p_1} \geq \left[M^j(p_1, p_2) + y - r_j + \nu_{1j}/\beta_j\right]e^{-\beta_j p_1} \text{ for } j \neq i\right\}.$$

A special case of this system which yields simple functional form is

$$(10)\qquad u = \ln\left\{\left[\alpha_0^i + \frac{\alpha_1^i}{\beta} + \alpha_1^i p_1 + \alpha_2^i p_2 + \beta(y - r_i) + \nu_{1i}\right]e^{-\beta p_1}\right\} - \alpha_5 \ln p_2$$

[6] A function $V(y, p_1, p_2)$ of normalized income and prices is the indirect utility function of some locally nonsatiated utility function if and only if it is lower semicontinuous, quasi-convex, increasing in y, nonincreasing in (p_1, p_2), and has $V(\lambda y, \lambda p_1, \lambda p_2)$ nondecreasing in λ.

[7] Additional restrictions on ψ and M^i will be imposed by the lower semicontinuity, monotonicity, and quasi-convexity of the indirect utility function.

with $\beta_i = \beta$ common across alternatives, and

$$(11) \qquad x_1 = \alpha_0^i + \alpha_1^i p_1 + \alpha_2^i p_2 + \beta(y - r_i) + \nu_{1i}$$

$$(12) \qquad x_2 = \frac{\alpha_2^i}{\beta}(\alpha_5 - 1) + \frac{\alpha_5}{\beta}\left(\alpha_0^i + \frac{\alpha_1^i}{\beta}\right)\frac{1}{p_2} + \frac{\alpha_5\alpha_1^i}{\beta}\frac{p_1}{p_2} + \alpha_5\frac{(y - r_i)}{p_2} + \frac{\alpha_5\nu_{1i}}{\beta p_2}.$$

Alternatively, consider the special case of (6) in which $\nu_{1i} = \eta$ and

$$(13) \qquad u = \left[M^i(p_1, p_2) + y - r_i + \eta/\beta_i\right]e^{-\beta_i p_1} + \nu_{2i}.$$

Analogously to (10) define

$$(14) \qquad u = \left(\alpha_0^i + \frac{\alpha_1^i}{\beta} + \alpha_1^i p_1 + \alpha_2^i p_2 + \beta(y - r_i) + \eta\right)e^{-\beta p_1}$$

$$- \alpha_5 \ln p_2 + \nu_{2i}.$$

The UEC equation is then

$$(15) \qquad x_1 = \alpha_0^i + \alpha_1^i p_1 + \alpha_2^i p_2 + \beta(y - r_i) + \eta$$

and the choice probabilities satisfy

$$(16) \qquad P_i = \text{Prob}(\nu_{2j} - \nu_{2i} < W_i - W_j \text{ for } j \neq i)$$

with

$$(17) \qquad W_i = V_i e^{-\beta p_1} = \left(\alpha_0^i + \frac{\alpha_1^i}{\beta} + \alpha_1^i p_1 + \alpha_2^i p_2 - \beta r_i\right)e^{-\beta p_1}.$$

Econometric studies of UEC have in most cases assumed, implicitly or explicitly, statistical independence of appliance portfolio choice and the additive error in the UEC equation and have proceeded to estimate the UEC equation by ordinary least squares. Examples are Houthakker [**23**], McFadden–Kirschner–Puig [**30**], Cambridge Systematics [**6**], California State Energy Commission [**5**], and Parti and Parti [**31**]. In practice some correlation of unobserved variables is likely. For an appliance such as an air conditioner, an unobserved effect which increases the utility of the service supplied by the appliance (e.g., poor natural ventilation in a housing unit) is likely to increase both its probability of selection and its intensity of use. For an appliance such as a water heater, unobserved factors which increase intensity of use (e.g., tastes for hot water clothes washing) are likely to decrease the probability of choosing the electric alternative which has a higher operating to capital cost ratio than the alternative fuel. In either case, ordinary least squares estimation of the UEC equation induces a classical bias due to correlation of an explanatory variable and the equation error.[8]

In our empirical work, we adopt the specifications (15)–(17) with modifications to accommodate varying climate and household characteristics and employ statistical procedures which are consistent in the presence of the suspect correlation.

3. A SPACE AND WATER HEAT CHOICE MODEL

Household demand for electricity is determined by choice of space and water heating fuel type, ownership of electrical appliances such as an air conditioner, range, dishwasher, clothes dryer, and color T.V., and the intensity of use of these devices. Table I summarizes typical saturations and UEC's.

Our analysis isolates the space and water heating choice, treating the portfolio of other appliances owned by the household as statistically exogenous. The space and water heating choice is usually associated with selection of a housing unit. This choice is often made at a different point in time than purchase or retrofit decisions on portable appliances, so that a hypothesis of behavioral independence is plausible.

We make the following assumptions on housing market behavior: First, the supply of housing units of each heating fuel type is assumed to be perfectly

TABLE I

TYPICAL APPLIANCE SATURATIONS AND UEC

Appliance	Saturation[a]	UEC[b]
Electric space heat	.23	6440[c]
Electric water heat	.23	3431[d]
Dishwasher	.49	1453[e]
Central air conditioner	.39	2856[f]
Room air conditioner	.37[g]	413
Freezer	.56	1340
Electric range	.67	780
Color TV	.81	480
Electric dryer	.56	1030

[a] From WCMS survey, 1975, subsample of 313 households.
[b] Annual consumption in KWH, from BLS survey, 1972, fitted by regression of consumption on household appliance dummies. (These estimates are subject to the potential bias discussed in the text.)
[c] The average number of heating degree days per year is 4318.
[d] Excludes hot water consumption by a dishwasher.
[e] UEC determined by hot water consumption if electric water heat.
[f] The average number of cooling degree days per year is 1229.
[g] Average number of room air conditioners/number of households.

[8] Alternatively, an ordinary least squares regression of individually metered consumption by appliance for a sample of households who have chosen portfolios containing this appliance induces a sample selection bias, with positive UEC residuals and low electricity prices more common in appliance holding households.

elastic at price differentials which accurately reflect the contemporary capital costs of these systems. Second, real capital costs of heating systems evolve sufficiently slowly so that real prices in 1975 reflect costs at date of housing unit acquisition. Third, consumer evaluation of heating system life cycle operating costs at the time of housing choice anticipates future real energy prices equal to 1975 levels.

The assumptions above permit us to model space and water heating type holdings and electricity consumption in 1975 as a contemporaneous decision, with choices of other durables treated as exogenous. In reality these assumptions are at best only approximately true, and should be tested against a more complete dynamic model of expectations, durable purchase, and intensity of use, using panel data on consumer behavior.

Our model of space and water heat choice and electricity consumption employs a version of the indirect utility function (14):

$$u = \left(\alpha_0^i + \frac{\alpha_1}{\beta} + \alpha_1 p_1 + \alpha_2 p_2 + w'\gamma + \beta(y - r_i) + \eta\right)e^{-\beta p_1} + \epsilon_i \tag{18}$$

where p_1 is electricity price, p_2 is the price of alternative energy (in KWH equivalents), i indexes the water and space heating alternatives, r_i is the annualized total life cycle cost of alternative i, and w is a vector of household characteristics, including number of persons, climate, and the portfolio of portable appliances.

Annualized total life cycle cost is assumed to have the form

$$r_i = \sum_{j=1}^{m} p_j q_{ji} + \rho r_{ki}, \tag{19}$$

where

$$\rho = \rho_0 + \rho_1 y, \tag{20}$$

$$q_{ji} = \tilde{q}_j + \tilde{q}_{ji}, \tag{21}$$

r_{ki} is the capital cost of portfolio alternative i, ρ is the discount rate, and q_{ji} is the typical total annual consumption by the household of fuel type j given portfolio i. Equation (21) writes q_{ji} as the sum of two terms, $\tilde{q}_j$, the typical annual consumption of fuel j which is independent of portfolio choice, and $\tilde{q}_{ji}$, the annual consumption of fuel j by portfolio i. In our analysis q_{ji} is calculated using typical UEC, as detailed in the Appendix, and hence is exogenous. All q_{ji} are calculated in KWH equivalents. The discount rate ρ is assumed to be a linear function of income, to reflect credit availability; ρ_0 and ρ_1 are unknown parameters.

The unobserved factors ϵ_i in (18) are assumed to have independent extreme value distributions,

$$\text{(22)} \qquad \text{Prob}(\epsilon_i \leq \epsilon) = \exp(-e^{-\epsilon\pi/\lambda\sqrt{3}-\gamma}),$$

where $\gamma = .577\ldots$ is Euler's constant. The distribution of η conditional on $(\epsilon_1, \epsilon_2, \ldots, \epsilon_m)$ is assumed to have mean $(\sqrt{2}\,\sigma/\lambda)\sum_{i=1}^m R_i\epsilon_i$ and variance $\sigma^2(1 - \sum_{i=1}^m R_i^2)$ where $\sum_{i=1}^m R_i = 0$ and $\sum_{i=1}^m R_i^2 < 1$. Then R_i is the correlation of η and ϵ_i, ϵ_i has unconditional mean zero and unconditional variance $\lambda^2/2$, and η has unconditional mean zero and unconditional variance σ^2.

The expected value of ϵ_i given that portfolio j is chosen satisfies

$$\text{(23)} \qquad E[\epsilon_i \mid \delta_j(\epsilon) = 1] = \begin{cases} -\ln P_j \cdot \lambda\sqrt{3}/\pi & \text{if } i = j, \\ \dfrac{P_i}{1 - P_i}\ln P_i \cdot \lambda\sqrt{3}/\pi & \text{if } i \neq j, \end{cases}$$

where $\delta_j(\epsilon)$ is an indicator random variable which is one if and only if j is the chosen alternative.

It then follows that

$$\text{(24)} \qquad E(\eta \mid \delta_j(\epsilon) = 1) = \frac{\sqrt{6}\,\sigma}{\pi} \cdot \left[\sum_{i=1}^m R_i \frac{P_i}{1 - P_i} \ln P_i - R_j \frac{\ln P_j}{(1 - P_j)} \right].$$

The portfolio choice probabilities have a nonlinear multinomial logit form

$$\begin{aligned} \text{(25)} \qquad P_i &= \text{Prob}[u_i > u_j \text{ for } j \neq i] \\ &= \text{Prob}\big[\epsilon_j - \epsilon_i < (\alpha_0^i - \alpha_0^j - \beta(p_1(q_{1i} - q_{1j}) + p_2(q_{2i} - q_{2j})) \\ &\qquad - \beta\rho(r_{ki} - r_{kj}))e^{-\beta p_1} \text{ for } j \neq i\big] \\ &= \frac{\exp[(\alpha_0^i - \beta(p_1 q_{1i} + p_2 q_{2i}) - \beta\rho r_{ki})(e^{-\beta p_1})/\theta]}{\sum_{j=1}^m \exp[(\alpha_0^j - \beta(p_1 q_{1j} + p_2 q_{2j}) - \beta\rho r_{kj})(e^{-\beta p_1})/\theta]} \end{aligned}$$

where $\rho = \rho_0 + \rho_1 y$ and $\theta = \sqrt{3}\,\lambda/\pi$ is a positive scale factor.

We have estimated the model (25) using a subsample of 313 households from the 1975 WCMS survey for whom water and space heat were either both electric or both gas. Mixed systems were excluded because of the difficulty of measuring their capital cost. If the logit specification for portfolio choice is correct, then no bias is introduced by restricting analysis to a subset of alternatives; see McFadden [**29**]. The subsample also eliminated households with missing data; details are given in the Appendix.

Table II gives the variables used in the choice model and their sample means. The maximum likelihood parameter estimates are given in Table III.

TABLE II

VARIABLES IN THE WATER-SPACE HEAT CHOICE MODEL

Variable	Mnemonic	Means by Alternative: Electric space and water	Means by Alternative: Gas space and water
Choice Dummy	Choice	.2332	.7668
Annual operating cost ($)	*PIOP*[a]	392.8	208.0
Capital cost ($)	*PICP*[b]	996.1	1136.0
Capital Cost · Income ($ · 10³$)	*PICPY*	17160.	20100.
Gas availability index in alternative one	*GASAV*751	.7294	0
Marginal price of electricity in alternative one	*WMPE*751	.02194	0
Electricity price ($/KWH)	p_e, p_1, *WMPE*75	.02194	.02194
Gas price ($/KWH equivalent)	p_g, p_2, *MPG*75	.006449	.006449
Annual typical electric demand (KWH)	q_{1i}	17570.	6432.
Annual typical gas demand (KWH equivalent)	q_{2i}	0.	11138.0
Income (10^3)	y	14.97	17.55

[a] $PIOP_i \equiv \sum_{j=1}^{m} p_j q_{ji}$.
[b] $PICP_i \equiv r_{ki}$.

TABLE III

ESTIMATED WATER-SPACE HEAT CHOICE MODEL

Alternative	Frequency	Proportion
Electric water and space	73	23.32
Gas water and space	240	76.68
	313	100.00

Explanatory Variable	Estimated Coefficient	Standard Error	Asymptotic t-Statistic
Capital Cost (*PICP*)	− 0.0229	0.0084	− 2.73
Capital Cost · Income (10^3) (*PICPY*)	0.621	0.244	2.55
Annual Operating Cost (*PIOP*)	− 0.0604	0.026	− 2.29
Gas availability in alternative one (*GASAV*751)	− 7.16	3.49	− 2.05
Alternative one dummy (*C*1)	− 1.32	2.32	− 0.57
Marginal price of electricity in alternative one (*WMPE*751)	496.77	228.20	2.18
Utility scale factor Exp$((-\beta)*WMPE75)$	− 39.09	14.30	− 2.73
Log Likelihood:			
at convergence	− 102.4		
with alternative dummy only	− 217.0		

Note that the coefficients of *PIOP*, *PICP*, and *PICPY* are $-\beta/\theta$, $\beta\rho_0/\theta$, and $-\beta\rho_1/\theta$, respectively. From the estimates of these parameters and their asymptotic covariances, one obtains the linear-in-income predicted discount factor

$$\hat{\rho} = \underset{(0.0780)}{0.3793} - \underset{(0.00289)}{0.01028} \cdot (\text{Annual Income}) \tag{26}$$

with annual income in thousands of 1975 dollars and standard errors in parentheses. The negative estimate of ρ_1 implies that the discount rate declines with income. This result is consistent with a similar finding of Hausman **[17]**. The formula yields a predicted discount factor of 0.205 at the sample mean income of $16,948. Classical economic consumers who are not credit constrained can be expected to have discount factors equal to the real interest rate plus depreciation rate, roughly 0.10 to 0.15. This range is attained for households with incomes over $22,300. Households below this income level appear to be credit constrained. However, it should be noted that failure of consumers to correctly anticipate energy price increases between the time of housing choice and 1975, or an imperfectly elastic housing market in which the capital cost variable *PICP* overestimates the implicit capital cost component in the price of houses with systems which have higher expected operating costs in 1975 than at the time of construction, both introduce specification errors which bias upward the estimate of ρ.

Observe from Table III that we have defined $\alpha_0^i \equiv (\gamma_0 \cdot GASAV75 + \gamma_1 p_e + \gamma_2) \cdot C1_i$. It then follows that the elasticity of demand for alternative i with respect to the price of electricity satisfies

$$\frac{\partial \ln P_i}{\partial \ln p_e} = p_e\left[\left(\frac{\gamma_1}{\theta}\right)e^{-\beta p_e}(C1_i - P_1) + (\beta)\sum_{j=1}^{2} P_j \ln\left(\frac{P_j}{P_i}\right) - \left(\frac{\beta}{\theta}\right)\left(\tilde{q}_{ei} - \sum_{j=1} P_j \tilde{q}_{ej}\right)e^{-\beta p_e}\right]. \tag{27}$$

Noting that (γ_1/θ) and $(-\beta/\theta)$ are respectively the coefficients of *WMPE751* and *PIOP* in Table III and that β is estimated in the utility scale factor term $e^{-\beta p_e}$, the elasticities calculated at the means of right-hand side variables are -0.473 for electric water and space heat and $+0.144$ for gas. For the price of gas, the elasticity is given by the analogue of (27) with $\tilde{q}_{ei}$ replaced by gas consumption (in KWH equivalents); the elasticity of P_i with respect to the price of gas is

$$\frac{\partial \ln P_i}{\partial \ln p_g} = \left(\frac{-\beta}{\theta}\right)(p_g)(e^{-\beta p_e})\left[\tilde{q}_{gi} - \sum_{j=1}^{2} P_j \tilde{q}_{gj}\right]. \tag{28}$$

For the electric and gas portfolios these are $+1.41$ and -0.43 respectively.

4. THE DEMAND FOR ELECTRICITY

Application of Roy's identity to (18), taking into account the dependence of life cycle cost r_i on the price of electricity in (19), but treating the discount rate ρ as exogenous to the household, yields annual electricity demand conditioned on space and water heating choice i,

$$x = q_{1i} + \alpha_0^i + \alpha_1 p_1 + \alpha_2 p_2 + w'\gamma + \beta(y - r_i) + \eta. \tag{29}$$

A more convenient form for estimation is

$$x - q_{1i} = \sum_{j=1}^{m} \alpha_0^j \delta_{ji} + \alpha_1 p_1 + \alpha_2 p_1 + w'\gamma + \beta\left(y - \sum_{j=1}^{m} PIOP_j \cdot \delta_{ji}\right) - \beta\rho \sum_{j=1}^{m} PICP_j \cdot \delta_{ji} + \eta \tag{30}$$

where δ_{ji} is a dummy variable which is one when $i = j$. The postulated distribution of η and ϵ_i implies $E\eta = 0$ and

$$\begin{aligned} E(\eta \mid i) &= \frac{\sigma\sqrt{6}}{\pi}\left[\sum_{j=1}^{m} \frac{R_j P_j}{1 - P_j} \ln P_j - \frac{R_i}{1 - P_i} \ln P_i\right] \\ &= \sum_{j=1}^{m} \left[\frac{\sigma\sqrt{6}\, R_j}{\pi}\right]\left[\frac{\ln P_j}{(1 - P_j)}\right] \cdot (P_j - \delta_{ji}) \\ &= \sum_{j \neq 1}^{m} \left[\frac{\sigma\sqrt{6}\, R_j}{\pi}\right]\left[\frac{P_j \ln P_j}{1 - P_j} + \ln P_i\right]. \end{aligned} \tag{31}$$

One can estimate (29) using ordinary least squares, and by three alternative methods which are consistent in the presence of correlation of the residual η and the choice dummies δ_{ji}:

(i) Instrumental Variable Method: The estimated probability, $\hat{P}_j$, from the discrete choice model is used as an instrument for δ_{ji}: the list of instruments is $p_1, p_2, w, y - \sum_{j=1}^{m} PIOP_j \cdot \hat{P}_j, \sum_{j=1}^{m} PICP_j \cdot \hat{P}_j$, and $\hat{P}_1, \ldots, \hat{P}_m$.

(ii) Reduced Form Method: Ordinary least squares is applied to the equation

$$x - q_{1i} = \sum_{j=1}^{m} \alpha_0^j \hat{P}_j + \alpha_1 p_1 + \alpha_2 p_2 + w'\gamma + \beta\left(y - \sum_{j=1}^{m} PIOP_j \cdot \hat{P}_j\right) - \beta\rho \sum_{j=1}^{m} PICP_j \cdot \hat{P}_j + \xi_1. \tag{32}$$

(iii) Conditional Expectation Correction Method: Ordinary least squares

TABLE IV
VARIABLES ENTERING THE ELECTRICITY DEMAND EQUATION

Variable	Mnemonic	Mean
Income less energy cost (chosen alternative)($)	*NETINC*	16710.
Capital cost (chosen alternative)($)	*PICPI*	1044.
Gas availability index if alternative one chosen	*GASAV751*	.1509
Marginal price of electricity if alternative one chosen	*WMPE751*	.004526
If alternative one chosen	*A1*	.2332
If homeowner	*OWN*	.9457
Gas availability index	*GASAV75*	.7294
Number of persons in household	*PERSONS*	3.78
Number of rooms	*ROOMS*	6.265
Marginal price of electricity ($/KWH)	*WMPE75*	0.02194
Marginal price of gas ($/KWH equivalent)	*MPG75*[a]	0.00645
Annual electricity consumption (KWH)		
Households choosing alternative 1	—	24240.
Households choosing alternative 2	—	8645.

[a]Conversion factor equals 4.6597×10^{-2} so that marginal price of gas in dollars per KWH equivalent is $(4.6597 \times 10^{-2}) \times$ (marginal price of gas in dollars per therm). Details are given in the Appendix.

is applied to the equation

$$(33) \qquad x - q_{1i} = \sum_{j=1}^{m} \alpha_0^j \delta_{ji} + \alpha_1 p_1 + \alpha_2 p_2 + w'\gamma + \beta\left(y - \sum_{j=1}^{m} PIOP_j \cdot \delta_{ji} \right)$$

$$- \beta\rho \sum_{j=1} PICP_j \delta_{ji} + \sum_{j \neq i}^{m} \gamma_j \left[\frac{\hat{P}_j \ln \hat{P}_j}{1 - \hat{P}_j} + \ln \hat{P}_i \right] + \xi_2$$

where the terms involving estimated probabilities permit a consistent estimate of $E(\eta \mid i)$.

Table IV lists the variables included in the estimation of (30) and gives their sample means. Table V gives the ordinary least squares estimates of (30) as well as the estimates from the three procedures outlined above. These procedures utilized a corrected covariance matrix whose form was derived using the methods of Amemiya [**2**].[9]

Note that the dependent variable in (33) is net consumption defined above as the difference between annual electricity consumption and "typical electric usage" of appliances which are not included in the modeled portfolio decision. As a consequence, explanatory dummy variables indicating ownership of an electric clothes dryer, electric range, air conditioning system, color television, etc., are excluded from the demand specification.

Using net consumption as the dependent variable follows our definition of the annualized total cost r_i. Recall that r_i is defined as the operating plus discounted capital cost for alternative i plus the charge for typical fuel usage by appliances

[9]Dubin [**9**] presents the form of the corrected covariance matrix for each consistent procedure. Details are available on request.

which are not choice specific. The inclusion of this latter cost which is constant across alternatives for each individual cannot have an effect on the coefficient estimates within the logit model. This follows as only the differences in the explanatory variables between alternatives enter the probability calculation. However, the inclusion of this term does imply a specification with net consumption as the dependent variable.

The price and income elasticities implied by the fitted equations are given in

TABLE V

ESTIMATED ELECTRICITY DEMAND MODEL

Explanatory[a] Variable	OLS Estimates COEFF. (std. error)	Method 1[b] IV Estimates COEFF. (std. error)	Method 2[c] COEFF. (std. error)[e]	Method 3[d] COEFF. (std. error)[e]
NETINC	.04020 (.03579)	.01102 (.03823)	.03254 (.04093)	.01416 (.03947)
PICPI	4.653 (.9748)	6.260 (1.149)	5.844 (1.418)	6.073 (1.2820)
GASAV751	− 4779. (3211.)	− 2477. (5674.)	− 3453. (6669.)	− 5316. (3514.5)
WMPE751	− .2262*E* + 6 (.7956*E* + 5)	− .3594*E* + 6 (.1366*E* + 6)	− .3492*E* + 6 (.1599*E* + 6)	− .2789*E* + 6 (.9387*E* + 5)
A1	.1275*E* + 5 (2886.)	.1206*E* + 5 (5468.)	.1327*E* + 5 (6449.)	.1245*E* + 5 (3284.2)
OWN	− 260.0 (1078.)	134.2 (1122.)	345.7 (1167.)	− 254.4 (1113.8)
GASAV75	− 1320.0 (1796.)	− 3465. (2314.)	− 2676. (2597.)	− 2347. (2009.6)
PERSONS	918.2 (151.4)	929.5 (156.7)	930.4 (165.9)	871.8 (160.9)
ROOMS	− 193.0 (213.3)	− 345.1 (225.0)	− 445.3 (242.4)	− 288.2 (232.8)
WMPE75	8728. (.3790*E* + 5)	.1662*E* + 5 (.4351*E* + 5)	.3012*E* + 5 (.4899*E* + 5)	− 1323. (.4087*E* + 5)
MPG75	− .1243*E* + 6 (.1319*E* + 6)	− .4898*E* + 5 (.1402*E* + 6)	− .1334*E* + 6 (.1549*E* + 6)	− .3985*E* + 5 (.1477*E* + 6)
ONE	− 3602. (2047.)	− 2934. (2434.)	− 2954. (2522.)	− 3060. (2189.4)
H1	— —	— —	— —	987.1 (603.93)[f]
Standard error of regression	4139.	4270.	4205.6[e]	4239.1[e]

[a] Estimated on a sub-sample of 313 observations from the 1975 WCMS survey. The dependent variable is electricity consumption. For variable definitions, see Table 4 and the Appendix.

[b] The instruments are the listed explanatory variables, except for *NETINC*, *PICPI*, *WMPE751*, *GASAV751*, and *A1*. Instruments for these variables are formed by replacing the dummy variable indicating actual choice of alternative one by the estimated probability from the logit model.

[c] Explanatory variables are those listed except *NETINC*, *PICPI*, *GASAV751*, *WMPE751*, and *A1*. These variables are replaced by their instruments as defined in b.

[d] Included variables are those listed and the variable $H1 = [(ESTPB1 - A1)\cdot \log(ESTPB1)/ESTPB2 - (ESTPB2 - A2)\cdot \log(ESTPB2)/ESTPB1]$. *ESTPB1* is the probability of choosing alternative one, estimated in the discrete choice model.

[e] Corrected standard errors.

[f] Standard error uncorrected is 409.11.

TABLE VI

PRICE AND INCOME ELASTICITIES

	Least Squares	Method 1 Instrumental Variable	Method 2 Reduced Form	Method 3 Conditional Expectation Correction
Elasticities of electricity demand with electric space and water heat				
with respect to income	0.028	0.008	0.023	0.010
with respect to price of electricity	− 0.197	− 0.310	− 0.289	− 0.254
with respect to price of gas	− 0.033	− 0.013	− 0.035	− 0.011
Elasticities of electricity demand with gas space and water heat				
with respect to income	0.079	0.022	0.064	0.028
with respect to price of electricity	0.021	0.042	0.076	− 0.004
with respect to price of gas	− 0.093	− 0.037	− 0.100	− 0.030
Elasticities of expected electricity demand, including portfolio shift				
with respect to income	0.06	0.02	0.05	0.02
with respect to price of electricity	− 0.22	− 0.26	− 0.23	− 0.26
with respect to price of gas	0.35	0.39	0.35	0.40

[a] Calculated at sample means.

Table VI. The formula used for the calculation of price elasticity is modified to include the effects of a change in price on the variable net income. Net income is defined simply as the difference between income and annual operating cost in the chosen alternative. The first two sets of elasticities in Table VI are calculated to correspond to short-run responses conditional on a particular choice of water-heat space-heat portfolio. In principle the conditional expectation of the error term in the usage equation is a function of the portfolio choice probabilities which in turn respond to changes in price. In making our conditional elasticity calculations we are holding this effect constant by assuming that the representative individual cannot switch his appliance portfolio in the short-run.

The last set of elasticities includes the effect of portfolio shift. We make these calculations by writing expected consumption as a probability weighted sum of the conditional expectations: $Ex = E(x \mid 1) \cdot P_1 + E(x \mid 2) \cdot P_2$ where $E(x \mid 1)$ is the expected consumption of electricity given that portfolio one is chosen and P_1 is the probability of choosing portfolio one. Then if $\epsilon[x, p]$ denotes the elasticity of x with respect to p we have:

$$(34) \qquad \epsilon[Ex, p] = \epsilon[E(x \mid 1), p]P_1 E(x \mid 1)/Ex + \epsilon[E(x \mid 2), p]P_2 E(x \mid 2)/Ex + P_1(E(x \mid 1) - E(x \mid 2))/EX \cdot \epsilon[P_1, p].$$

Each of the consistent procedures produced elasticities which are quantitatively similar. Portfolio shifts are the primary contributor to the price sensitivity of average demand calculated from (34).

Comparing the final group of elasticities, we see that the elasticity of income is both smaller than the ordinary least squares estimates and considerably smaller than previous studies have shown. Own price elasticity is larger in magnitude for methods one and three than those given by ordinary least squares. Finally, we note that the cross-elasticity of the demand for electricity with respect to the price of gas (in KWH equivalents) is larger when estimated by consistent procedures one and three compared to the least squares estimates. Again the price sensitivity comes almost entirely from portfolio shift. Based on a qualitative comparison, reasonable point estimates for average demand under the consistent methods would be $+0.02$ for income elasticity, -0.26 for own price elasticity, and $+0.39$ for cross-price-elasticity.

We have performed two tests of the independence of the choice variables and the error in (29). Method one, the instrumental variable method, was compared to the least squares estimates using the Wu–Hausman statistic.[10] The statistic $\Upsilon = (\hat{\gamma}_{IV} - \hat{\gamma}_{LS})'(\hat{V}_{IV} - \hat{V}_{LS})^{-1}(\hat{\gamma}_{IV} - \hat{\gamma}_{LS})$ computed for the estimates in Table V on the suspected endogenous variables *PICPI*, *GASAV*751, *WMPE*751, and *A*1 is 15.07. (*NETINC* is excluded because to the limits of numerical accuracy it is perfectly correlated with its instrument.) Under the null hypothesis, this statistic is asymptotically Chi-squared with four degrees of freedom and thus exceeds the 95 per cent critical level of 9.49.

The second specification test compares the results of the least squares and Heckman methods of estimation and is identical to the Wald test of the significance of the "Heckman type" correction term.[11] Recall that the variable *H*1 entered as the conditional expectation correction factor in procedure three has coefficient $(-\sigma\sqrt{6}\, R_2/\pi)$. This implies that the consistently estimated value of R_2 is -0.299 with a standard error (corrected) of 0.179. The unadjusted standard error (given in Table V, footnote f) is correct for the null hypothesis of no correlation between η and ϵ. Under the null hypothesis of no correlation, the coefficient of *H*1 would be zero. The asymptotic t statistic for the Wald test of this hypothesis is 2.41 which exceeds the 95 per cent critical level.[12]

[10] For details regarding this test see Hausman **[15]** and Hausman and Taylor **[18]**.

[11] We wish to thank an anonymous referee for directing our attention to this identity derived in Holly **[22]**. We should emphasize that the Heckman estimation method embodies specific assumptions regarding the joint distribution of η and ϵ while the instrumental variable and reduced form methods are more robust in this sense. The appropriate degrees of freedom for Wu–Hausman tests using these latter estimation methods is four which is the number of dummies and their interactions whose exogeneity is under test.

The single degree of freedom in the Wu–Hausman test utilizing the Heckman estimation method reflects the imposition of the implicit distributional assumptions.

[12] An alternative method of obtaining consistent estimates of the correlation coefficient R_2 is to run an auxilary regression of the squared fitted residuals from procedures one, two, or three against an expression for conditional expectation given portfolio choice, evaluated at the estimated choice probabilities. The point estimates of R_2 are -0.369, -0.337, and -0.332 respectively. These estimates are close to the estimate of -0.299 obtained earlier from the coefficient of *H*1. Details of the calculation are available from the authors on request.

One might thus infer that an unobserved effect which increases the attractiveness of all gas heat alternative tends to decrease simultaneously usage of electricity. This pattern could be produced, for example, by an unobserved marginal cost of electricity component.

We therefore reject the null hypothesis that the unobserved factors influencing portfolio choice are independent of the unobserved factors influencing intensity of use. If these results are confirmed in further analysis, one must conclude that estimation of UEC by least squares decomposition of total demand has the potential for severe bias, and that appropriate statistical methods, such as the instrumental variables procedure, are feasible and have satisfactory statistical properties.

California Institute of Technology
and
Massachusetts Institute of Technology

Manuscript received June, 1981; final revision received March, 1983.

APPENDIX

This section presents an account of variable construction and definition for the two-alternative all electric versus all gas water heat space heat choice model. The WCMS data survey with matched rate structure and temperature information consisted of 1502 observations. To have comparable information for both the water-heat space-heat model and the demand for electricity equation we selected a sample of 313 observations for which there were no missing observations and for which: (i) income, rate, and cost data were strictly positive (this included the marginal prices of electricity and gas in 1975 as well as space-heating capital costs as calculated by Hittman Associates for CSI/WEST); (ii) annual consumption of electricity in 1975 was positive; (iii) housing units used either gas or electric water-heat fuel and either gas or electric space-heat fuel but were selected so that the same fuel choice was made for both appliances in the portfolio; (iv) the date of housing construction was not before 1950.

WATER HEAT AND SPACE HEAT OPERATING COSTS

The definition of operating costs for water heaters and space heaters by fuel type is as follows:

Gas:

$$\begin{aligned}\$/\text{year} = {} & (\$/\text{therm-in})(\text{therm-in}/\text{Btu-in}) \\ & \cdot (\text{Btu-in}/\text{Btu-out})(\text{Btu-out}/\text{KWH-out}) \\ & \cdot (\text{KWH-out}/\text{KWH-in})(\text{KWH-in}/\text{day})(\text{days}/\text{year}),\end{aligned}$$

Electric:

$$\$/\text{year} = (\$/\text{KWH-in})(\text{KWH-in}/\text{day})(\text{days}/\text{year}),$$

where \$/therm-in is marginal price of gas in 1975, \$/KWH-in is marginal price of electricity in 1975, therm/Btu = 1/100000, Btu/KWH = 3413, Btu-in/Btu-out = 1/.72, KWH-out/KWH-in = .983, KWH-in/day is average consumption. Average consumption for electric water heating depends on the number of residents. (See p. 5-13 of EPRI report EA-682, "Patterns of Energy Use by Electrical Appliances.")

Average consumption for electric space heat per day is related to the number of rooms in the residence as well as the number of heating degree days. Heating degree days are the number of degrees the daily average temperature is below 65 degrees fahrenheit. Normally heating is not required when the outdoor temperature averages above 65 degrees. Using (BLS) data the following relationship was constructed:

$$\frac{\text{KWH-in}}{\text{day}}\left[\begin{array}{c}\text{for electric}\\ \text{space heat}\end{array}\right] = 5.9 - (.00217)(ANNUAL\ HDD) + (.000833)(ROOMS \cdot ANNUAL\ HDD).$$

Note: Sample means and definitions for all variables may be found in Table II.

The operating cost used in our econometric analysis differed in one minor respect. As discussed in the text it proved useful to add the annual operating cost for base consumption of all other electric using appliances to the space heat operating cost. As this cost is constant across alternatives its inclusion allows one to think of the household as choosing a certain space heat-water heat portfolio as well as the portfolio of all other electric utilizing durables. This latter portfolio of durables is predetermined across the choices we are modelling.

Using the MRI survey we have constructed an electric utilization base rate which depends on the presence of appliance durables measured at their average or base usage rates. Thus, we have defined:

$$\begin{aligned} QEBASE = {} & 2496 + (82.8 + .93 \cdot CDD + .51 \cdot ROOMS \cdot CDD) \\ & \cdot (\text{Central Air Conditioning}) + (-144.6 + .447 \cdot CDD) \\ & \cdot (\text{Number of Room Air Conditioners}) + 1340 \cdot FOODFRZ \\ & + 780 \cdot ELECRNGE + 480 \cdot CLRTV + 1030 \cdot ECLTHDR \end{aligned}$$

WATER HEAT AND SPACE HEAT CAPITAL COSTS

Capital costs for water heaters were not available within the WCMS data set. Estimates were obtained from the National Construction Estimator (Craftsman Book Co., Solano Beach, CA., 1978). These constructions again follow the specifications of CSI WEST (1979). They are then related to 1975 prices with a consumer price index adjustment.

Space heating capital costs for each fuel type were available within the WCMS matched data set. These numbers had been calculated using a residential thermal load model developed by Hittman Associates.

REFERENCES

[1] AMEMIYA, T.: "Regression Analysis when the Dependent Variable is Truncated Normal," *Econometrica*, 41(1973), 997–1016.

[2] ———: "The Estimation of a Simultaneous Equation Generalized Probit Model," *Econometrica*, 46(1978), 1193–1206.

[3] AMEMIYA, T., AND G. SEN: "The Consistency of the Maximum Likelihood Estimator in a Disequilibrium Model," Tech. Report 238, Institute for Math. Studies in Social Sciences, Stanford, 1977.

[4] ANDERSON, K.: "Residential Energy Use: An Econometric Analysis," RAND Corporation, 1973.

[5] CALIFORNIA STATE ENERGY CONSERVATION: "California Energy Demand 1978--2000," Working Paper, 1979.

[6] CAMBRIDGE SYSTEMATICS/WEST: "An Analysis of Household Survey Data in Household Time-of-Day and Annual Electricity Consumption," Cambridge Systematics/West, Working Paper, 1979.

[7] DUBIN, J.: "Economic Theory and Estimation of the Demand for Consumer Durable Goods and Their Utilization: Appliance Choice and the Demand for Electricity," Massachusetts Institute of Technology Energy Laboratory Discussion Paper No. 23, MIT-EL 82-035WP, 1982.

[8] ———: "Rate Structure and Price Specification in the Demand for Electricity," mimeo, Massachusetts Institute of Technology, 1980.

[9] ———: "Two-Stage Single Equation Estimation Methods: An Efficiency Comparison," mimeo, Massachusetts Institute of Technology, 1981.

[10] DUNCAN, G.: "Formulation and Statistical Analysis of the Mixed Continuous/Discrete Variable Model in Classical Production Theory," *Econometrica*, 48(1980), 839–852.
[11] FISHER, F., AND C. KAYSEN: *A Study in Econometrics: The Demand for Electricity in the U.S.* Amsterdam: North Holland, 1962.
[12] GOETT, A.: "A Structured Logit Model of Appliance Investment and Fuel Choice," Cambridge Systematics/West, Working Paper, 1979.
[13] GOLDFELD, S., AND R. QUANDT: "The Estimation of Structural Shifts by Switching Regressions," *Annals of Economic and Social Measurement*, 2(1973), 475–485.
[14] ———: "Techniques for Estimating Switching Regression" in *Studies in Non-Linear Estimation*, ed. by S. Goldfeld and R. Quandt. Cambridge: Ballinger, 1976.
[15] HAUSMAN, J.: "Specification Tests in Econometrics," *Econometrica*, 46(1978), 1251–1271.
[16] ———: "Exact Consumer's Surplus and Deadweight Loss," *American Economic Review*, 71(1979), 663–676.
[17] ———: "Individual Discount Rates and the Purchase and Utilization of Energy-Using Durables," *The Bell Journal of Economics*, 10(1979), 33–54.
[18] HAUSMAN, J., AND W. TAYLOR: "A Generalized Specification Test," *Economic Letters*, 8(1981), 239–245.
[19] HAY, J.: "An Analysis of Occupational Choice and Income," Ph.D. Dissertation, Yale University, 1979.
[20] HECKMAN, J.: "Dummy Endogenous Variables in a Simultaneous Equation System," *Econometrica*, 46(1978), 931–960.
[21] ———: "Sample Selection Bias as a Specification Error," *Econometrica*, 47(1979), 153–162.
[22] HOLLY, A.: "A Remark on Hausman's Specification Test," *Econometrica*, 50(1982), 749–759.
[23] HOUTHAKKER, H.: "Some Calculations of Electricity Consumption in Great Britain," *Journal of the Royal Statistical Society*, Series A, 114(1951), 351–371.
[24] HOUTHAKKER, H., AND L. TAYLOR: *Consumer Demand in the U.S.*, 2nd edition. Cambridge: Harvard University Press, 1970.
[25] LEE, L. F.: "Simultaneous Equations Models with Discrete and Continuous Variables," in *Structural Analysis of Discrete Data*, ed. by C. Manski and D. McFadden. Cambridge: MIT Press, 1981.
[26] LEE, L. F., AND R. TROST: "Estimation of Some Limited Dependent Variable Models with Applications to Housing Demand," *Journal of Econometrics*, 8(1978), 357–382.
[27] MADDALA, G., AND F. NELSON: "Maximum Likelihood Methods for Markets in Disequilibrium," *Econometrica*, 42(1974), 1013–1030.
[28] McFADDEN, D.: "Conditional Logit Analysis of Qualitative Choice Behavior," in *Frontiers in Econometrics*, ed. by P. Zarembka. New York: Academic Press, 1973.
[29] ———: "Econometric Models of Probabilistic Choice," in *Structural Analysis of Discrete Data*, ed. by C. Manski and D. McFadden. Cambridge: MIT Press, 1981.
[30] McFADDEN, D., D. KIRSCHNER, AND C. PUIG: "Determinants of the Long-run Demand for Electricity," in *Proceedings of the American Statistical Association*, 1978.
[31] PARTI, M., AND C. PARTI: "The Total and Appliance-Specific Conditional Demand for Electricity in the Household Sector," *Bell Journal of Economics*, 11(1980), 309–321.
[32] TAYLOR, L.: "The Demand for Electricity: A Survey," *Bell Journal of Economics*, 6(1975), 74–110.

[43]

Available online at www.sciencedirect.com

SCIENCE DIRECT®

ELSEVIER

Transportation Research Part B 39 (2005) 679–707

TRANSPORTATION RESEARCH PART B

www.elsevier.com/locate/trb

A multiple discrete–continuous extreme value model: formulation and application to discretionary time-use decisions

Chandra R. Bhat *

Department of Civil Engineering, The University of Texas at Austin, 1 University Station C1761, Austin, TX 78712-0278, USA

Received 14 April 2004; accepted 24 August 2004

Abstract

Several consumer demand choices are characterized by the choice of multiple alternatives simultaneously. An example of such a choice situation in activity-travel analysis is the type of discretionary (or leisure) activity to participate in and the duration of time investment of the participation. In this context, within a given temporal period (say a day or a week), an individual may decide to participate in multiple types of activities (for example, in-home social activities, out-of-home social activities, in-home recreational activities, out-of-home recreational activities, and out-of-home non-maintenance shopping activities).

In this paper, we derive and formulate a utility theory-based model for discrete/continuous choice that assumes diminishing marginal utility as the level of consumption of any particular alternative increases (i.e., satiation). This assumption yields a multiple discreteness model (i.e., choice of multiple alternatives can occur simultaneously). This is in contrast to the standard discrete choice model that is based on assuming the absence of any diminishing marginal utility as the level of consumption of any alternative increases (i.e., no satiation), leading to the case of strictly single discreteness. The econometric model formulated here, which we refer to as the multiple discrete–continuous extreme value (MDCEV) model, has a surprisingly simple and elegant closed form expression for the discrete–continuous probability of not consuming certain alternatives and consuming given levels of the remaining alternatives. To our knowledge, we are the first to develop such a simple and powerful closed-form model for multiple discreteness in the literature. This formulation should constitute an important milestone in the area of multiple discreteness, just as the multinomial logit (MNL) represented an important milestone in the area of single discreteness. Further, the

* Tel.: +1 512 471 4535; fax: +1 512 475 8744.
E-mail address: bhat@mail.utexas.edu

0191-2615/$ - see front matter
doi:10.1016/j.trb.2004.08.003

MDCEV model formulated here has the appealing property that it collapses to the familiar multinomial logit (MNL) choice model in the case of single discreteness. Finally, heteroscedasticity and/or correlation in unobserved characteristics affecting the demand of different alternatives can be easily incorporated within the MDCEV model framework using a mixing approach.

The MDCEV model and its mixed variant are applied to analyze time-use allocation decisions among a variety of discretionary activities on weekends using data from the 2000 San Francisco Bay Area survey.

1. Introduction

Several consumer demand choices related to travel decisions are characterized by the choice of multiple alternatives simultaneously. Examples of such choice situations include vehicle type holdings and usage, and activity type choice and duration of time investment of participation. In the former case, a household may hold a mix of different kinds of vehicle types (for example, a sedan, a minivan, and a pick-up) and use the vehicles in different ways based on the preferences of individual members, considerations of maintenance/running costs, and the need to satisfy different functional needs (such as being able to travel on weekend getaways as a family or to transport goods). In the case of activity type choice and duration, an individual may decide to participate in multiple kinds of recreational and social activities within a given time period (such as a day) to satisfy variety seeking desires. Of course, there are several other travel-related and other consumer demand situations characterized by the choice of multiple alternatives, including airline fleet mix and usage, carrier choice and transaction level, brand choice and purchase quantity for frequently purchased grocery items (such as cookies, ready-to-eat cereals, soft drinks, yoghurt, etc.), and stock selection and investment amounts.

Classical discrete and discrete–continuous models deal with situations where only one alternative is chosen from a set of mutually exclusive alternatives. Such models assume that the alternatives are perfectly substitutable for each other. On the other hand, the simultaneous demand for multiple alternatives discussed above corresponds to the situation where the alternatives are imperfect substitutes for one another. In this paper, we formulate a new econometric model for such multiple discreteness in demand that is based on utility maximization theory. Specifically, we assume a translated non-linear, but additive, form for the specification of the direct utility function, as proposed recently by Kim et al. (2002). The translated non-linear form allows for multiple discreteness as well diminishing marginal returns (i.e., satiation) as the consumption of any particular alternative increases. This is in contrast to standard discrete and discrete–continuous choice models that allow only single discreteness and assume a linear utility structure (i.e., no satiation effects). The econometric model formulated here, which we refer to as the multiple discrete–continuous extreme value (MDCEV) model, is based on introducing a multiplicative log-extreme value error term into the utility function. The result of such a specification is a surprisingly simple closed form expression for the discrete–continuous probability of not consuming certain alternatives and consuming given levels of the remaining alternatives. To our knowledge, we are the first to develop such a simple and powerful model for multiple discreteness in the literature. Further, the MDCEV model has the appealing property that it collapses to the familiar multinomial logit (MNL) choice model in the case of single discreteness, and represents an extension of the single discrete–continuous models of Dubin and McFadden (1984), Hannemann (1984), Chiang (1991), Chintagunta (1993), and Arora et al. (1998). Finally, heteroscedasticity and/or correlation in unobserved characteristics affecting the demand of different alternatives can be easily incorporated within the MDCEV model framework. Such an extension represents the multiple discrete–continuous equivalent of the mixed multinomial logit (MMNL) model (see Bhat (2003) or Train (2003) for detailed reviews of the MMNL model).

There have been several relatively recent studies in the marketing literature on the topic of multiple-discreteness. Hendel (1999) and Dube (2004) consider the purchase of multiple varieties within a particular product category as the result of a stream of expected (but unobserved to the analyst) future consumption decisions between successive shopping occasions (see also Walsh, 1995). Due to varying tastes across individual consumption occasions between the current shopping purchase and the next, consumers are observed to purchase a variety of goods at the current shopping occasion. The above studies use a linear utility function at each individual consumption occasion, with the utility parameters varying across consumption occasions. A Poisson distribution is assumed for the number of consumption occasions and a normal distribution is assumed regarding varying tastes to complete the model specification. Such a "vertical" variety-seeking model may be appropriate for frequently consumed grocery items such as carbonated soft drinks, cereals, and cookies. However, in many other choice occasions, such as time allocation to different types of discretionary activities, the true decision process may be better characterized as "horizontal" variety-seeking, where the consumer selects an assortment of alternatives due to diminishing marginal returns for each alternative. Kim et al. (2002) propose a utility structure for such "horizontal" variety-seeking with a non-linear utility function to accommodate satiation behavior. This is the overall structure maintained in the current paper. However, the econometric development and the estimation procedure are different between our paper and Kim et al.'s paper. The MDCEV model formulated here also represents a very simple and parsimonious model structure compared to the model proposed in Kim et al. (2002). To be sure, Kim et al.'s model is not practical for realistic applications, while the MDCEV model of this paper is very practical even for situations with a large number of discrete consumption alternatives. In fact, we submit that the MDCEV model structure is the MNL model-equivalent for multiple discrete–continuous choice analysis. Extensions of the MDCEV model to accommodate unobserved heteroscedasticity and error correlation among alternatives is straightforward and is similar to the movement from the MNL to the MMNL model in the standard discrete choice literature. [1]

In the current paper, we develop the multiple discrete–continuous extreme value (MDCEV) model in the context of individual time use in different types of activity pursuits using data from

[1] There have also been other formulations proposed to handle multiple-discreteness in the literature. These include the mixed multinomial-Poisson approach of Terza and Wilson (1990) and the multivariate probit (logit) approaches of Manchanda et al. (1999), Baltas (2004), Edwards and Allenby (2003), and Bhat and Srinivasan (2004). But all these formulations do not model the continuous component in a multiple discreteness setting. Further, the multiple discreteness is handled through statistical methods that generate correlation between univariate utility maximizing models of single discreteness rather than being fundamentally derived from a rigorous underlying utility maximization model for multiple discreteness. The resulting multiple discrete models also do not collapse to the standard discrete choice models when all individuals choose one and only one alternative at each choice occasion. However, these non-utility maximization models of multiple discreteness are also of value, and can be extended to include a continuous component in a flexible manner.

the 2000 San Francisco Bay area. However, the formulation is applicable to any other multiple discrete–continuous choice situation.

The next section of the paper introduces the importance of time use analysis in travel demand modeling, and briefly reviews earlier literature in the area. Section 3 advances the econometric framework for the MDCEV model of time allocation. Section 4 discusses the data source and sample used in the empirical analysis. Section 5 presents empirical results. The final section provides a summary and identifies directions for future research.

2. Overview of time-use analysis

2.1. Time-use analysis in the travel demand context

In the past several years, the activity-based approach to travel demand analysis has received much attention and seen considerable progress (see Bhat and Koppelman, 1999; Pendyala and Goulias, 2002, and Arentze and Timmermans, 2004). A fundamental difference between the commonly-used trip-based approach and the activity-based approach is the way time is conceptualized and represented in the two approaches (Pas, 1996; Ye et al., 2004). In the trip-based approach, time is reduced to being simply a "cost" of making a trip. The activity-based approach, on the other hand, treats time as an all-encompassing continuous entity within which individuals make activity/travel participation decisions. Thus, the central basis of the activity-based approach is that individuals' travel patterns are a result of their time-use decisions. Individuals have 24 h in a day (or multiples of 24 h for longer periods of time) and decide how to use that time among activities (and with whom) subject to their schedule, socio-demographic, locational, and other contextual constraints. These decisions determine the generation and scheduling of trips (see Bhat et al., forthcoming for details of an implementation of an activity-based approach to travel demand modeling).

2.2. Earlier studies relevant to current research

The study of activity time use has received attention in several fields, including psychology, anthropology, sociology, urban planning, economics, and travel behavior analysis. Qualitative paradigms and frameworks of time use have emerged from all these fields, while most of the mathematical frameworks have been developed in the microeconomics and travel demand fields. The next two sections provide a very brief overview of the mathematical studies in the microeconomics and travel demand fields that are relevant to the current research effort. Section 2.3 positions the current research effort in the context of the earlier studies.

2.2.1. Microeconomic studies

The economic approach to time use is based on the assumption that individuals (and the households of which they are a part) use their time so that the total utility derived from all the activities is maximized. Each person in the household allocates time as well as money income to various activities—receiving income from time expended in the market place and receiving utility from spending this income on the consumption of goods and services (Gramm, 1975; Gronau, 1973; Becker, 1981, 1965; Mincer, 1962, 1963). Individuals "produce" non-market activities using "inputs"—their time and market goods and services. An individual's choice of work time and time in other non-market activities depends on market wages and prices of the "inputs" used to produce non-market activities. In particular, non-market time and consumer goods used in "production" of each non-market activity is chosen so as to maximize utility subject to constraints imposed by wages, prices of consumption goods, and time (Juster, 1990). Recently, Jara-Diaz (2003) has focused on the technological relationship between time and goods consumption in more detail, and shed new light on the technological relations and constraints characterizing the utility maximization problem.

The economic studies of time use have been comprehensive in their frameworks, and have considered a variety of constraints under which individuals make their time-use decisions. However, most of these studies are rather theoretical in nature (but see Jara-Diaz and Guevara, 2003 for a study that formulates and applies a microeconomic model).

2.2.2. Travel behavior analysis

Travel behavior researchers have turned to the examination of activity time use from a need to better understand and forecast travel. Some of these studies are based on frameworks that are not rigorously derived from utility theory (for example, see Allaman et al., 1982; Damm and Lerman, 1981; Lu and Pas, 1999; Bhat, 1998), while others use frameworks with utility theory as the fundamental basis for time use (Munshi, 1993; Kitamura et al., 1996; Yamamoto and Kitamura, 1999; Bhat and Misra, 1999; Meloni et al., 2004). It is not at all clear that one type of studies is necessarily better than the other; in fact, both classes of studies have provided important insights into time use behavior. It should also be noted that utility-theoretic based models in the travel behavior research arena have generally considered time as being the only constraint in time allocation, and focused on discretionary activities.

2.2.3. The current research effort

The research in this paper is aligned with the utility-theoretic class of studies in the travel behavior area. As with earlier studies within this class, time is the only resource constraint considered and the empirical focus is on allocation among discretionary activities. The current research, however, generalizes earlier models by formulating a structure that is applicable to allocation among any number of activity categories (rather than just two categories). The underlying utility structure of the proposed structure is also very closely tied to preference and indifference curve theory, as discussed next.

3. Utility structure

Kim et al.'s (2002) proposed utility structure remains at the core of the current research effort. However, for completeness and also because our model development procedure in Section 3.1 is different from Kim et al.'s, the discussion here begins from first principles. In Section 3.2, we specify an alternative error structure specification to the one used in Kim et al. and adopt a different way of writing the likelihood function leading to a much simpler model formulation.

Let there be K different activity purposes that an individual can potentially allocate time to. Let t_j be the time spent in activity purpose j ($j = 1,2,\ldots,K$). We specify the utility accrued to an individual as the sum of the utilities obtained from investing time in each activity purpose. Specifically, we define utility over the K purposes as:

$$U = \sum_{j=1}^{K} \psi(x_j)(t_j + \gamma_j)^{\alpha_j} \tag{1}$$

where $\psi(x_j)$ is the baseline utility for time invested in activity purpose j, and γ_j and α_j are parameters (note that ψ is a function of observed characteristics, x_j, associated with purpose j).

As discussed by Kim et al. (2002), the utility form in Eq. (1) belongs to the family of translated utility functions, with γ_j determining the translation and α_j influencing the rate of diminishing marginal utility of investing time in activity purpose j. The function in Eq. (1) is a valid utility function if $\psi(x_j) > 0$ and $0 < \alpha_j \leqslant 1$ for all j. Further, the term γ_j determines if corner solutions are allowed (i.e., an individual does not participate in one or more activity purposes) or if only interior solutions are allowed (i.e., an individual is constrained by formulation to participate in all activity purposes). To see this, consider the case where an individual has a total time T available to participate in one or both of two activity purposes and spends all the time T between these two activity purposes. Thus $t_1 + t_2 = T$, which serves as the constraint when maximizing utility. Fig. 1 presents this two activity purpose case. The slope of the indifference curve at any point (t_1, t_2) in Fig. 1, is given by:

$$\text{Slope } (t_1, t_2) = \frac{(\partial U/\partial t_1)}{(\partial U/\partial t_2)} = \frac{(t_2 + \gamma_2)^{1-\alpha_2}}{(t_1 + \gamma_1)^{1-\alpha_1}} \times \frac{\psi(x_1)}{\psi(x_2)} \times \frac{\alpha_1}{\alpha_2} \tag{2}$$

The indifference curve is shown in Fig. 1a and b for the case where $\psi(x_2) = 2\psi(x_1)$ and $\alpha_1 = \alpha_2 = 0.5$. In Fig. 1a, $\gamma_1 = \gamma_2 = 0$, which leads to the case where the slope of the indifference curve approaches infinity at the y-axis (i.e., $t_1 = 0$ in Eq. (2)) and approaches zero at the x-axis (i.e., $t_2 = 0$ in Eq. (2)). Thus, the indifference curve is tangential to both axes, and only interior solutions are possible. In the figure, the linear line indicates a time budget of 5 h, and the optimal consumption point is 1 h of activity purpose 1 and 4 h of activity purpose 2. Fig. 1b shows the case when $\gamma_1 = 1.25$, but $\gamma_2 = 0$. In this situation, the indifference curve has a finite slope at the y-axis (since the slope is non-zero and finite by Eq. (2) when $t_1 = 0$ and $\gamma_1 \neq 0$). But the indifference curve remains tangential to the x-axis (since the slope is zero by Eq. (2) when $t_2 = 0$ and $\gamma_2 = 0$). In such a case, it is possible that no amount of time is invested in activity purpose 1, as is the case in Fig. 1b (note, however, that an interior solution is still possible in Fig. 1b depending on the values of the,, and parameters in an individual's utility function; the values in Fig. 1b have been set such that a corner solution results). Fig. 1c shows the reverse case when $\psi(x_2) = 0.5\psi(x_1)$, $\alpha_1 = \alpha_2 = 0.5$, $\gamma_1 = 0$, and $\gamma_2 = 1.25$. Here, the indifference curve is tangential to the y-axis, but has a finite non-zero slope at the x-axis. The values of the parameters are such that a corner solution arises with no consumption of activity purpose 2.

The discussion above indicates that the utility form of Eq. (1) is flexible enough to accommodate both internal and corner solutions. Specifically, if $\gamma_j \neq 0$, it is possible that individual q allocates no time to activity purpose j. On the other hand, if $\gamma_j = 0$, it implies that individual q allocates some non-zero amount of time to activity purpose j. In addition, the utility form is also able to accommodate a wide variety of time allocation situations based on the values of $\psi(x_j)$ and α_j ($j = 1,2,\ldots,J$). A high value of $\psi(x_j)$ for one activity purpose (relative to all other activity

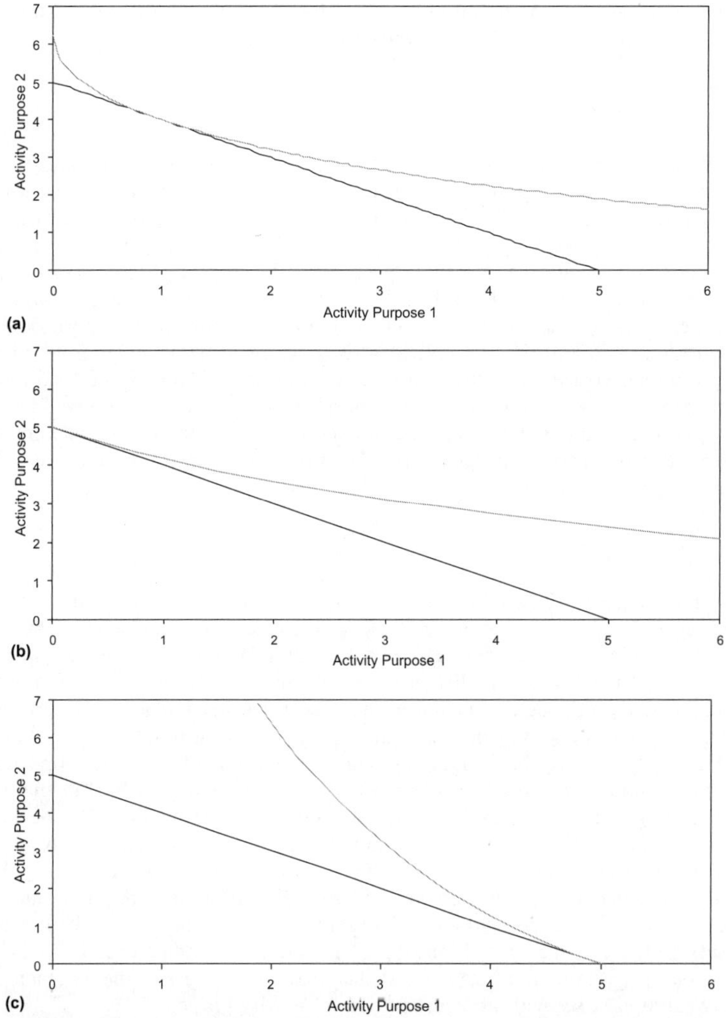

Fig. 1. Indifference curves and optimal consumption points (a) $\gamma_1 = \gamma_2 = 0$; $\alpha_1 = \alpha_2 = 0.5$; and $\psi(x_2) = 2\psi(x_1)$. (b) $\gamma_1 = 1.25$, $\gamma_2 = 0$; $\alpha_1 = \alpha_2 = 0.5$; and $\psi(x_2) = 2\psi(x_1)$. (c) $\gamma_1 = 0$, $\gamma_2 = 1.25$; $\alpha_1 = \alpha_2 = 0.5$; and $\psi(x_2) = 0.5\psi(x_1)$.

purposes), combined with a value of α_j close to 1, implies a high baseline preference and a very low rate of satiation for activity purpose j. This represents the situation when individual q allocates almost all her/his time to only activity purpose j (i.e., a "homogeneity-seeking" individual). On the other hand, about equal values of $\psi(x_j)$ and small values of α_j across the various purposes j represents the situation where the individual invests time in almost all activity purposes (i.e., a "variety-seeking" individual). More generally, the utility form allows a variety of situations characterizing an individual's underlying behavioral mechanism with respect to time allocation to activity purpose j, including (a) low baseline preference and high satiation (low ψ_j and low α_j), (b) high baseline preference and high satiation (high ψ_j and low α_j), (c) low baseline preference and low satiation (low ψ_j and high α_j), and (d) high baseline preference and low satiation (high ψ_j and high α_j).

3.1. Random utility model

We develop a statistical model from the utility structure of the previous section by adopting a random utility specification. Specifically, we introduce a multiplicative random element to the baseline utility as follows:

$$\psi(x_j, \varepsilon_j) = \psi(x_j) \cdot e^{\varepsilon_j} \tag{3}$$

where ε_j captures idiosyncratic (unobserved) characteristics that impact the baseline utility for purpose j. The exponential form for the introduction of random utility guarantees the positivity of the baseline utility as long as $\psi(x_j) > 0$. To ensure this latter condition, we further parameterize $\psi(x_j)$ as $\exp(\beta' x_j)$, which then leads to the following form for the baseline random utility:

$$\psi(x_j, \varepsilon_j) = \exp(\beta' x_j + \varepsilon_j) \tag{4}$$

The x_j vector in the above equation includes a constant term reflecting the generic preference in the population toward purpose j. The overall random utility function then takes the following form:

$$\tilde{U} = \sum_j \left[\exp(\beta' x_j + \varepsilon_j)\right] \cdot (t_j + \gamma_j)^{\alpha_j} \tag{5}$$

From the analyst's perspective, the individual is maximizing random utility ($\tilde{U}$) subject to the time budget constraint that $\sum_{j=1}^{K} t_j = T$, where T is the time available for allocation among the K activity purposes. The analyst can then solve for the optimal time allocations by forming the Lagrangian and applying the Kuhn–Tucker conditions. The Lagrangian function for the problem is:

$$\mathscr{L} = \sum_j \left[\exp(\beta' x_j + \varepsilon_j)\right](t_j + \gamma_j)^{\alpha_j} - \lambda\left[\sum_{j=1}^{K} t_j - T\right] \tag{6}$$

where λ is the Lagrangian multiplier associated with the time constraint. The Kuhn–Tucker (K–T) first-order conditions for the optimal time allocations (the t_j^* values) are given by:

$$\begin{aligned}&\left[\exp(\beta' x_j + \varepsilon_j)\right]\alpha_j(t_j^* + \gamma_j)^{\alpha_j - 1} - \lambda = 0, \quad \text{if } t_j^* > 0,\ j = 1, 2, \ldots, K\\&\left[\exp(\beta' x_j + \varepsilon_j)\right]\alpha_j(t_j^* + \gamma_j)^{\alpha_j - 1} - \lambda < 0, \quad \text{if } t_j^* = 0,\ j = 1, 2, \ldots, K\end{aligned} \tag{7}$$

The above conditions have an intuitive interpretation. For all activity purposes to which time is allocated (i.e., $t_j^* > 0$), the time investment is such that the marginal utilities are the same across purposes (and equal to) at the optimal time allocations (this is the first set of K–T conditions; note that the first term on the left side of the K–T conditions corresponds to marginal utility). Also, for an activity purpose j in which no time is invested, the marginal utility for that activity purpose at zero time investment is less than the marginal utility at the consumed times of other purposes (this is the second set of K–T conditions in Eq. (7)).

The optimal demand satisfies the conditions in Eq. (7) plus the time budget constraint $\sum_{j=1}^{K} t_j^* = T$. The time budget constraint implies that only $K - 1$ of the t_j^* values need to be estimated, since the time invested in any one purpose is automatically determined from the time invested in all the other purposes. To accommodate this constraint, designate activity purpose 1 as a purpose to which the individual allocates some non-zero amount of time (note that the individual should participate in at least one of the K purposes, given that $T > 0$). For the first activity purpose, the Kuhn–Tucker condition may then be written as:

$$\lambda = [\exp(\beta' x_1 + \varepsilon_1)]\alpha_1 (t_1^* + \gamma_1)^{\alpha_1 - 1} \tag{8}$$

Substituting for λ from above into Eq. (7) for the other activity purposes ($j = 2,\ldots,K$), and taking logarithms, we can rewrite the K–T conditions as:

$$\begin{aligned} &V_j + \varepsilon_j = V_1 + \varepsilon_1 \quad \text{if } t_j^* > 0 \ (j = 2, 3, \ldots, K) \\ &V_j + \varepsilon_j < V_1 + \varepsilon_1 \quad \text{if } t_j^* = 0 \ (j = 2, 3, \ldots, K) \text{ where} \\ &V_j = \beta' x_j + \ln \alpha_j + (\alpha_j - 1)\ln(t_j^* + \gamma_j) \ (j = 1, 2, 3, \ldots, K) \end{aligned} \tag{9}$$

The satiation parameter, α_j, needs to be bounded between 0 and 1, as discussed earlier. To enforce this condition, we parameterize α_j as $1/[1 + \exp(-\delta_j)]$. Further, to allow the satiation parameters to vary across individuals, we write $\delta_j = \theta_j' y_j$, where y_j is a vector of individual characteristics impacting satiation for the jth alternative, and θ_j is a corresponding vector of parameter. Also, note that, in Eq. (9), a constant cannot be identified in the $\beta' x_j$ term for one of the K alternatives (because only the difference in the V_j from V_1 matters). Similarly, individual-specific variables are introduced in the V_j's for $(J - 1)$ alternatives, with the remaining alternative serving as the base (these identification conditions are similar to those in the standard discrete choice model).

3.2. Econometric model

3.2.1. Basic structure

To complete the model structure, we specify a standard extreme value distribution for ε_j and assume that ε_j is independent of x_j ($j = 1,2,\ldots,K$). The ε_j's are also assumed to be independently distributed across alternatives. From Eq. (9), the probability that the individual participates in M of the K activity purposes ($M \geqslant 2$), given ε_1, is

$$P(t_2^*, t_3^*, \ldots, t_M^*, 0, 0, \ldots, 0)|\varepsilon_1 = \left\{ \left(\prod_{i=2}^{M} g(V_1 - V_i + \varepsilon_1) \right) |J| \right\} \times \left\{ \prod_{s=M+1}^{K} G(V_1 - V_s + \varepsilon_1) \right\} \tag{10}$$

where g is the standard extreme value density function, G is the standard extreme value distribution, the first M activity purposes are taken to be the ones in which the individual participates for notational convenience, and J is the Jacobian whose elements are given by:

$$J_{ih} = \frac{\partial[V_1 - V_{i+1} + \varepsilon_1]}{\partial t^*_{h+1}}, \quad i,h = 1,2,\ldots,M-1 \tag{11}$$

The term in the first parenthesis in Eq. (10) is the continuous density component corresponding to the optimal time investment for the M purposes in which the individual participates (the first purpose does not appear in this component because it is always selected for participation and because the optimal time allocation for this purpose is implicitly determined by the time allocation to other purposes). To see that the term in the first parenthesis in Eq. (10) corresponds to the continuous density component, note from the first-order conditions in Eq. (9) that the optimal time for activity purposes with non-zero time investment is governed by the nonlinear function given by $\varepsilon_i = V_1 - V_i + \varepsilon_1$ ($i = 2,3,\ldots,M$). A change-of-variable technique is used to obtain the density of $t^* = (t^*_2, t^*_3, \ldots, t^*_M)$ from ε ($= \varepsilon_2, \varepsilon_3, \ldots, \varepsilon_M$), and results in the Jacobian term J. The term in the second parenthesis in Eq. (10) is a discrete distribution component corresponding to the purposes in which the individual does not participate.

Substituting the extreme value density and distribution functions for $g(\cdot)$ and $G(\cdot)$, respectively, Eq. (10) can be equivalently written as:

$$\begin{aligned}
&P(t^*_2, t^*_3, \ldots, t^*_M, 0, 0, \ldots, 0)|\varepsilon_1 \\
&= \left\{\prod_{i=2}^{M} e^{-(V_1 - V_i + \varepsilon_1)} \cdot e^{-e^{-(V_1 - V_i + \varepsilon_1)}}\right\}\left\{\prod_{s=M+1}^{K} e^{-e^{-(V_1 - V_s + \varepsilon_1)}}\right\} \cdot |J| \\
&= \left\{\left[\prod_{i=2}^{M} e^{-(V_1 - V_i)}\right]\left[(e^{-\varepsilon_1})^{M-1}\right]\left[\prod_{i=2}^{M} e^{-e^{-(V_1 - V_i + \varepsilon_1)}}\right]\right\}\left\{\prod_{s=M+1}^{K} e^{-e^{-(V_1 - V_i + \varepsilon_1)}}\right\} \cdot |J| \\
&= \left\{\left[\prod_{i=2}^{M} e^{-(V_1 - V_i)}\right]\left[(e^{-\varepsilon_1})^{M-1}\right]\left[\prod_{j=2}^{K} e^{-e^{-(V_1 - V_j + \varepsilon_1)}}\right]\right\} \cdot |J| \\
&= \left\{\left[\prod_{i=2}^{M} e^{-(V_1 - V_i)}\right]\left[(e^{-\varepsilon_1})^{M-1}\right]\left[e^{-\sum_{j=2}^{K}\left[e^{-(V_1 - V_j + \varepsilon_1)}\right]}\right]\right\} \cdot |J|.
\end{aligned} \tag{12}$$

Next, the determinant of the Jacobian term can be derived to be as follows (see Appendix A):

$$|J| = \left(\prod_{i=1}^{M} c_i\right)\left(\sum_{i=1}^{M} \frac{1}{c_i}\right), \quad \text{where } c_i = \left(\frac{1 - \alpha_i}{t^*_i + \gamma_i}\right) \tag{13}$$

Finally, one can uncondition out ε_1 from Eq. (12) to obtain the following unconditional probability expression:

$$\begin{aligned}
&P(t^*_2, t^*_3, \ldots, t^*_M, 0, 0, \ldots, 0) \\
&= \left[\prod_{i=1}^{M} c_i\right]\left[\sum_{i=1}^{M} \frac{1}{c_i}\right]\left[\prod_{i=2}^{M} e^{-(V_1 - V_i)}\right] \int_{\varepsilon_1=-\infty}^{+\infty} \left\{(e^{-\varepsilon_1})^{M-1} \cdot e^{-\sum_{j=2}^{K}\left[e^{-(V_1 - V_j + \varepsilon_1)}\right]} \cdot e^{-\varepsilon_1} \cdot e^{-e^{-\varepsilon_1}}\right\} d\varepsilon_1 \\
&= \left[\prod_{i=1}^{M} c_i\right]\left[\sum_{i=1}^{M} \frac{1}{c_i}\right]\left[\prod_{i=2}^{M} e^{-(V_1 - V_i)}\right] \int_{\varepsilon_1=-\infty}^{+\infty} \left\{(e^{-\varepsilon_1})^{M-1} \cdot e^{-\sum_{j=1}^{K}\left[e^{-(V_1 - V_j + \varepsilon_1)}\right]} \cdot e^{-\varepsilon_1}\right\} d\varepsilon_1
\end{aligned} \tag{14}$$

The integral above can be simplified as shown in Appendix B. The final result is a remarkably elegant and compact closed form structure:

$$P(t_2^*, t_3^*, \ldots, t_M^*, 0, 0, \ldots, 0) = \left[\prod_{i=1}^{M} c_i\right]\left[\sum_{i=1}^{M} \frac{1}{c_i}\right]\left[\frac{\prod_{i=1}^{M} e^{V_i}}{\left(\sum_{j=1}^{K} e^{V_j}\right)^M}\right](M-1)! \tag{15}$$

In the case when $M = 1$ (i.e., only one alternative is chosen), the model in Eq. (15) collapses to the standard MNL model (if $M = 1$, the continuous component drops out, because the time invested in the chosen activity will be T). Also, note that the utilities are assumed to be linear in the standard MNL model (i.e., $\alpha_j = 1$ for all j). This results in the V_j's in Eq. (9) becoming linear. Thus, the model proposed in this paper is a multiple discrete–continuous extension of the standard MNL model. In addition, the model also represents a multiple discrete–continuous extension of the single discrete–continuous models of Dubin and McFadden (1984), Hannemann (1984), Chiang (1991), Chintagunta (1993), and Arora et al. (1998). Specifically, the case of a single discrete–continuous model may be viewed as a two alternative case within the multiple discrete–continuous formulation, with one alternative (say the first) always being consumed. To see this, assume that the objective was to analyze if an individual participates in recreational activities during a certain time period and the time invested in recreational activities. Then, the first activity purpose can be labeled as "non-recreational" (essentially, an "outside good") and the second as "recreational". Since all individuals would invest some amount of time in "non-recreational" activities, $\gamma_1 = 0$. One can then use the multiple discrete–continuous formulation to model participation choice and duration of time in recreational activity, with T being the total amount of time within the period under consideration (for example, 24 h if the time period is a day).

3.2.2. Accommodating heteroscedasticity and error correlations across alternative utilities

The previous section assumed that the ε_j terms are independently and identically distributed across alternatives, and are distributed standard Gumbel. However, these assumptions are needlessly restrictive. Incorporating heteroscedasticity and error correlation in the MDCEV model is straightforward, and leads to the mixed MDCEV (or MMDCEV) model (this is similar to the movement from the MNL model to the mixed MNL model). Specifically, the error term ε_j may be partitioned into three independent components ζ_j, $\eta' w_j$, and $\mu' z_j$. The first component, ζ_j, is assumed to be independently and identically standard Gumbel distributed across alternatives. The second component, $\eta' w_j$, allows the estimation of distinct scale (variance) parameters for the error terms across alternatives. w_j is a column vector of dimension K with each row representing an alternative. The row corresponding to alternative j takes a value of 1 and all other rows take a value of 0. The vector η (of dimension K) is specified to have independent, normally distributed and mean-zero elements, each element having a variance of ω_j^2. Let ω be a vector of true parameter characterizing the variance–covariance matrix of the multivariate normal distribution of η. The third component in the error term, $\mu' z_j$, constitutes the mechanism to generate correlation across unobserved utility components of the alternatives. z_j is specified to be a column vector of dimension H with each row representing a group h ($h = 1, 2, \ldots, H$) of alternatives sharing common unobserved components. The row(s) corresponding to the group(s) of which j is a member take(s) a value of one and other rows take a value of zero. The vector μ (of dimension H) may be specified to have independent normally distributed elements, each element having a variance component σ_h^2. The result of this specification is a covariance of σ_h^2 among alternatives in group h. Let σ be a parameter vector characterizing the variance–covariance matrix of μ.

For given values of the vectors η and μ, one can follow the derivation of the earlier section and obtain the usual MDCEV probability that the individual participates in M of the J activity purposes ($M \geqslant 2$):

$$P(t_2^*, t_3^*, \ldots, t_M^*, 0, 0, \ldots, 0)|(\eta, \mu) = \left[\prod_{i=1}^{M} c_i\right]\left[\sum_{i=1}^{M} \frac{1}{c_i}\right]\left[\frac{\prod_{i=1}^{M} e^{V_i+\eta' w_i+\mu' z_i}}{\left(\sum_{j=1}^{K} e^{V_j+\eta' w_j+\mu' z_j}\right)^M}\right](M-1)! \tag{16}$$

The unconditional probability can then be computed as:

$$P(t_2^*, t_3^*, \ldots, t_M^*, 0, 0, \ldots, 0) = \int_\eta \int_\mu \left[\prod_{i=1}^{M} c_i\right]\left[\sum_{i=1}^{M} \frac{1}{c_i}\right]\left[\frac{\prod_{i=1}^{M} e^{V_i+\eta' w_i+\mu' z_i}}{\left(\sum_{j=1}^{K} e^{V_j+\eta' w_j+\mu' z_j}\right)^M}\right] \times (M-1)!\, dF(\mu|\sigma)\, dF(\eta|\omega) \tag{17}$$

where F is the multivariate cumulative normal distribution. The reader will note that the dimensionality of the integration above is dependent on the number of elements in η and μ.

3.2.3. Estimation of the mixed MDCEV model

The parameters to be estimated in the MMDCEV model of Eq. (17) include the β vector, the θ_j vectors and γ_j scalars for each alternative j (these are embedded in the V_j values), and the σ and ω vectors. Let θ be a column vector that stacks all the θ_j vectors vertically, and let γ be another column vector of the γ_j elements stacked vertically.

We use the maximum likelihood inference approach to estimate the parameters of the MMDCEV model. Introducing the index q for individuals, we can write the likelihood function as:

$$\mathscr{L}(\beta, \theta, \gamma, \sigma, \omega) = \sum_{q=1}^{Q} \log\left[\int_\eta \int_\mu \left[\prod_{i=1}^{M} c_i\right]\left[\sum_{i=1}^{M} \frac{1}{c_i}\right]\left[\frac{\prod_{i=1}^{M} e^{V_i+\eta' w_i+\mu' z_i}}{\left(\sum_{j=1}^{K} e^{V_j+\eta' w_j+\mu' z_j}\right)^M}\right] \times (M-1)!\, dF(\mu|\sigma)\, dF(\eta|\omega)\right] \tag{18}$$

We apply quasi-Monte Carlo simulation techniques to approximate the integrals in the likelihood function and maximize the logarithm of the resulting simulated likelihood function across all individuals with respect to β, θ, γ, σ, and ω. Under rather weak regularity conditions, the maximum (log) simulated likelihood (MSL) estimator is consistent, asymptotically efficient, and asymptotically normal (see Hajivassiliou and Ruud, 1994; Lee, 1992; McFadden and Train, 2000).

In the current paper, we use a scrambled version of the Halton sequence to draw realizations for η and μ from their population normal distributions. Details of the Halton sequence and the procedure to generate this sequence are available in Bhat (2003).

4. Data sources and sample formation

4.1. Data sources

The data source used for this analysis is the 2000 San Francisco Bay Area Travel Survey (BATS). This survey was designed and administered by MORPACE International Inc. for the Bay Area Metropolitan Transportation Commission. The survey collected information on all activity episodes undertaken by individuals from over 15,000 households in the Bay Area for a two-day period (see MORPACE International Inc., 2002 for details on survey, sampling, and administration procedures). The information collected on activity episodes included the type of activity (based on a 17-category classification system), start and end times of activity participation, and the whether the episode was pursued in-home or out-of-home. Furthermore, data on individual and household socio-demographics, individual employment-related characteristics, household auto ownership, and internet access and usage were also obtained.

In addition to the 2000 BATS data, we also obtained zonal-level land-use and demographics data for each of the Traffic Analysis Zones (TAZ) in the San Francisco Bay area. This data included: (1) area by land-use purpose, (2) number of housing units, (3) employment levels by sector, (4) zonal population, income and age distribution of the population, and (5) area type of the zone (core CBD, other CBD, urban, suburban, or rural). This information was used to study the impact of the characteristics of the residence zone.

4.2. Sample formation

The process of generating the sample for analysis involved several steps. First, only individuals 16 years or older were considered to focus the analysis on the subgroup of the population who clearly exercise a choice in their time-use. Second, we selected only weekend day data from the original survey sample. This was done because individuals participate more frequently, and for longer durations, in discretionary activities over the weekends than during the weekdays (as indicated earlier in the paper, our empirical focus is on discretionary activities in this paper). Individuals also participate in more variety of types of discretionary activities on the weekends than weekdays (Bhat and Lockwood, 2004). Thus, time use analysis modeling for discretionary activities is particularly interesting over the weekends. Third, social activity episodes (including conversation and visiting family/friends) and recreational activity episodes, including such activities as hobbies, exercising, and watching TV, were selected from the larger file of all activity episodes. Fourth, the total time invested during the weekend day in each of the following four activity purpose categories was computed based on appropriate time aggregation across individual episodes within each category: (1) time spent in in-home social activities (IHS), (2) time spent in in-home recreational (IHR) activities, (3) time spent in out-of-home social (OHS) activities, and (4) time spent in out-of-home recreational (OHR) activities. Fifth, out-of-home shopping activity episodes were selected from the original survey file and those episodes unrelated to grocery shopping were selected. The total time invested over the weekend day across all out-of-home non-grocery shopping episodes was then computed to provide a fifth category of discretionary time-use: time spent in out-of-home non-maintenance shopping activities. For convenience, we will refer to this fifth category as "time spent in out-of-home shopping (OHSh) activities" in the rest of this paper.

Sixth, data on individual, household, and residence zone characteristics were appropriately cleaned and added. Finally, several screening and consistency checks were performed and records with missing or inconsistent data were eliminated.

The final sample for analysis includes the weekend day time-use information of 1917 individuals. The analysis of interest is the participation and time invested in five types of discretionary activities over the weekend day: in-home social (IHS), in-home recreation (IHR), out-of-home social (OHS), out-of-home recreation (OHR), and out-of-home shopping (OHSh). Of the 1917 individuals, 1169 (61%) participated in only one activity type, 605 (31.5%) participated in two activity types, 126 (6.5%) participated in three activity types, and 17 (1%) participated in four activity types (no individual participated in all activity types). These statistics clearly indicate the problem of using standard discrete choice models, since 39% of individuals participate in more than one activity type. [2]

Table 1 provides descriptive details of participation in each type of discretionary activity. The second and third columns indicate the number (percentage) of individuals participating in each activity type and the mean duration of participation among those who participate, respectively. Several observations may be made from the statistics in these two columns. First, individuals participate most in OHSh activity over the weekend from among the various discretionary activity types. However, the duration of participation in OHSh activity is short compared to other activity types. This suggests an overall high baseline preference, but also a high level of satiation, for OHSh activity in the population. Second, there is also a high likelihood of participation in IHR activities, and the participation duration in such activities is also long. This suggests a high baseline preference and a low satiation for IHR activities. Third, there appears to be a relatively low baseline preference for IHS activities; the overall baseline preferences for the OHS and OHR activities are between those of the IHS activity type and the OHSh/OHR activity types. Fourth, the extent of satiation for IHS, OHS, and OHR activities is in the same general range, and these are between the satiation levels for OHSh and IHR activities based on the mean durations of participation. The last two columns in Table 1 indicate the split between solo participations (i.e., individual participation in only one activity type or a corner solution) and multiple activity participations (i.e., individual participation in multiple activity types or interior solutions) for each activity type. Thus, the number for the IHS activity type indicates that, of the 118 individuals participating in IHS activity, 33 (or 28%) participated only in IHS activity during the day and 85 (or 72%) participated in IHS activity along with participation in other activity types during the day. The results clearly indicate that individuals tend to participate in IHS activity more often in conjunction with participation in other activity types during the day. This may be because individual observed and unobserved factors that increase participation in IHS activity also increase participation in other activity types or because of a high satiation rate for IHS activity. The model in the paper accommodates both possibilities and can disentangle the two alternative effects. The results also show that IHR activity is more often participated in isolation than other activity

[2] In the current analysis, we assume that the total time invested in discretionary activities is given for each individual, and examine the allocation of this total discretionary time to the five types of discretionary activities. A more general empirical model would be one that considers non-discretionary activities as an "outside good", and models not only the allocation to the five different types of discretionary activities, but also the time invested in discretionary activities and non-discretionary activities.

Table 1
Descriptive statistics of activity type participation and duration over the weekend day

Activity type	Total number (%) of individuals participating[a]	Mean duration of participation (min)	Number of individuals (% of total number participating) who participate ...[b]	
			Only in activity type	In the activity type and other activity types
In-home social (IHS)	118 (6.2)	197	33 (28%)	85 (72%)
In-home recreational (IHR)	738 (38.5)	275	355 (48%)	383 (52%)
Out-of-home social (OHS)	496 (25.9)	181	180 (36%)	316 (64%)
Out-of-home recreational (OHR)	632 (33.0)	188	262 (41%)	370 (59%)
Out-of-home shopping (OHSh)	841 (43.9)	81	339 (40%)	502 (60%)

[a] Percentages across rows in the column do not sum to 100% because some individuals participate in more than one activity type.
[b] Percentages sum to 100% for each row across the two columns, since the percentages are with respect to the total number of individuals participating in each activity type (the second column in the table).

types. Again, this may reinforce the notion of low satiation for the IHR activity type (as discussed earlier) or may reflect a strong preference for IHR activity by some individuals.

5. Empirical analysis

5.1. Variables considered

Several types of variables were considered in the discretionary time-use model. These included household sociodemographics (household size, presence and number of children, number of household vehicles, number of bicycles in the household, household income, family structure, and dwelling type), household location attributes (discussed below), individual demographics and employment characteristics (age, license holding to drive, student status, employment status, number of days of work, internet use, and ethnicity), and day of week/season of year.

The household location variables included a land-use mix diversity variable, fractions of detached and non-detached dwelling units, area type variables classifying zones into one of 6 categories (core central business districts, central business districts, urban business, urban, suburban, and rural), and residential density and employment density variables. The first of these variables, the land-use mix diversity variable, is computed as a fraction between 0 and 1. Zones with a value closer to one have a richer land-use mix than zones with a value closer to zero. Three categories of land-uses are considered in the computation of the mix diversity variable: acres in residential use (r), acres in commercial/industrial use (c), and acres in other land-uses (o). The actual form of the land-use mix diversity variable is:

$$\text{Land} - \text{use mix diversity} = 1 - \left\{ \frac{\left|\frac{r}{L} - \frac{1}{3}\right| + \left|\frac{c}{L} - \frac{1}{3}\right| + \left|\frac{o}{L} - \frac{1}{3}\right|}{(4/3)} \right\}, \tag{19}$$

where $L = r + c + o$. The functional form assigns the value of zero to zones in which land-use is focused in only one category, and assigns a value of 1 to zones in which land-use is equally split among the three land-use categories.

Finally, the day of week/season variables were introduced to capture the day of weekend (Saturday or Sunday) and season of year effects (fall, winter, spring, or summer).

5.2. Empirical results

5.2.1. Model specification and error-component specification

As discussed in Section 3, the utility form of Eq. (1) includes the γ_j translation parameters to allow the possibility of corner solutions for each activity type (i.e., zero consumption of each activity type). However, we found it difficult to identify the γ vector and the satiation vector α separately, because both these vectors determine the slope of the indifference curves at the corner points (see Eq. (2)). Thus, we fixed the elements of the γ vector to 1.0 (see also Kim et al., 2002).

In our analysis, we considered several error component specifications to introduce unobserved heteroscedasticity and correlation in the utilities of the five activity types. The best statistical result included the following error components: (1) five error components, one for each alternative, to capture the variance of the baseline utility terms, (2) one error component to accommodate correlation between the two in-home activities (IHS and IHR), and (3) one error component to accommodate correlation between the OHS and OHSh activity types. In the first category of error components, corresponding to pure variance elements, the variances of the out-of-home activity types were constrained to be equal for identification and stability.

5.2.2. Variable effects

The final specification results of the leisure time-use model are presented in Table 2. In the following sections, we discuss the effect of variables by variable category. In instances where some alternatives do not appear for a variable, the excluded alternatives constitute the base category.

5.2.2.1. Household sociodemographics. Among the household sociodemographic variables, the effect of the number of adults indicates that individuals in households with several adults have a higher baseline preference for IHR activity compared to individuals in households with few adult members. This may be a reflection of the increased opportunity for joint in-home recreational participation in households, such as watching a movie or television at home with other adults (see Bhat and Misra, 1999; Kitamura et al., 1996 for a similar result using a Dutch dataset).

The presence of very young children (0–4 years of age) increases the baseline preference for out-of-home activity types (OHS, OHR, and OHSh), perhaps because of a stronger need of adults in such households to have a change from the activity of caring for children inside the home. The same higher baseline propensity to participate in out-of-home activities is also observed among adults in households with young children (5–15 years of age), though the out-of-home activity types tend to be recreational or shopping rather than social. The higher propensity of adults in households with young children to participate in recreational activity is perhaps a result of the outdoor recreational pursuits with young children (such as participation in youth soccer and baseball leagues, family walks, and bicycle trips; see Mallett and McGuckin, 2000 for a similar result).

The next household attribute is the number of bicycles in the household. As the number of bicycles increases in an individual's household, the individual is more likely to pursue OHR activity. This is quite reasonable. Households who own more bicycles may be more outdoor-oriented by nature, and owning bicycles also provides an additional means to participate in outdoor recreation.

Finally, among the set of household sociodemographics, the results indicate that individuals in low income households have a higher baseline preference for in-home recreation than those in high income households. Further, individuals in the middle income range (35,000 to 95,000 dollars per annum) are more likely to participate in out-of-home recreation than those in the low or high income ranges. This non-monotonic income effect on time investment in OHR activity deserves additional attention; it appears that increasing income does increase the ability to participate in out-of-home recreation, but other constraints set in at high incomes.

5.2.2.2. Household location variables. Among the many household location variables considered in the analysis, the only ones having a marginally significant effect on time use were the area type

Table 2
Effect of exogenous variables on baseline preference to participate in each activity type

Explanatory variables	Parameter	*t*-Statistic
Household sociodemographics		
Number of adults		
In-home recreation	0.2738	2.51
Presence of very young children (0–4 years of age)		
Out-of-home social, out-of-home recreation, and out-of-home shopping	0.5141	1.77
Presence of young children (5–15 years of age)		
Out-of-home recreation	0.9801	2.93
Out-of-home shopping	0.7069	2.60
Number of bicycles		
Out-of-home recreation	0.1142	1.45
Low annual household income (<35,000 dollars)		
In-home recreation	0.9323	3.64
Medium annual household income (35,000–90,000 dollars)		
Out-of-home recreation	0.5596	2.21
Household location variables		
Central business district		
Out-of-home recreation	0.6771	1.03
Diversity in land use-mix		
Out-of-home shopping	0.4846	0.92
Individual demographics and employment characteristics		
Age		
Out-of-home recreation	−2.1541	−2.65
Age 16 or 17 years		
Out-of-home social	1.1916	1.75
Out-of-home shopping	−1.7242	−2.54
Age 18–29 years		
Out-of-home social	0.5489	1.617
Age > 65 years		
In-home recreation	0.3701	1.213
Out-of-home shopping	−0.7306	−1.913
Driver's license		
Out-of-home social, out-of-home recreation, and out-of-home shopping	1.4007	3.22
Employed		
Out-of-home shopping	0.3359	1.33
Male		
In-home recreation	0.5915	3.49
Shopping on the internet		
Out-of-home shopping	0.7958	1.81
African–American		
Out-of-home recreation	−2.3893	−1.92
Hispanic-American		
Out-of-home social	1.2894	2.40
Asian–American		
Out-of-home social	−0.7621	−2.26

Table 2 (*continued*)

Explanatory variables	Parameter	*t*-Statistic
Day of the week and seasonal effects		
Sunday		
In-home recreation and in-home social	1.0757	5.14
Winter		
Out-of-home recreation	−0.9564	−2.23
Fall		
Out-of-home recreation	−0.5128	−1.96
Baseline preference constants		
In-home recreation	1.9300	3.08
Out-of-home social	0.8161	1.07
Out-of-home recreation	2.2227	2.66
Out-of-home shopping	3.0191	3.75

variable and the land-use mix variables. The results indicate that individuals residing in CBD areas have a higher baseline preference for OHR activity compared to individuals residing in non-CBD areas. This is possibly because of the "pedestrian-oriented" urban forms associated with the high density of CBD areas. In addition, CBD areas are likely to be correlated with better accessibility to recreational activity centers. The effect of the land-use mix variable indicates a higher propensity to participate in shopping activities among individuals residing in areas with a diverse land-use mix, perhaps because of the increased ease of reaching shopping activity centers and combining shopping with other out-of-home activity participations.

5.2.2.3. Individual sociodemographics and employment characteristics. Several individual characteristics were tested in the model, but only those related to age, vehicle license holding, employment, whether or not the individual shops over the internet, gender, and ethnicity appeared in the final specification. The results indicate that older individuals are less likely to participate in OHR activity compared to younger individuals. Further, teenagers (16–17 years of age) are less likely to participate in shopping, and teenagers and young adults (18–29years of age) are more likely to participate in out-of-home social (OHS) activity. Also, the elderly (greater than 65 years of age) are more likely to participate in IHR activity and less likely to pursue shopping activity relative to younger individuals, perhaps reflecting mobility constraints.

The availability of a license to drive has a positive effect on participation in all out-of-home activity types, which can be attributed to the greater mobility to reach out-of-home activity centers. Employed individuals have a higher propensity to participate in shopping activity over the weekend than do unemployed individuals, perhaps because of the inability to access shopping activity centers and pursue shopping during the course of the work week. The effect of the male variable indicates that men pursue more IHR activity than women, a reinforcement of the notion of men being "glued to the tube". Individuals who shop over the internet also pursue more OHSh activity, suggesting a complementary effect of internet use on OHSh activity. Alternatively, it may be that the same unobserved shopping orientation factors affect both use of the internet for shopping and out-of-home shopping. The race-related variables indicate that African-Americans are less likely to pursue out-of-home recreation (OHR) activity relative to other races. This finding is similar to those of previous works in the area of recreational activity participation (see Bhat and Gossen, 2004 and Mallett and McGuckin, 2000). Also, Hispanic Americans participate more in OHS activity, while Asian Americans are less likely to pursue OHS activity, relative to other races.

5.2.2.4. Day of week and seasonal effects. The results for the day of week effects shows a higher level of preference for in-home activities (IHS and IHR) on Sundays relative to Saturdays. This is reasonable since Sundays serve as a transition day between the weekend and the work week, and many individuals use it as an in-home "rest" day.

The seasonal effects reflect a lower propensity to participate in OHR activity during the winter season and, to a lesser extent, the fall season compared to the spring and summer seasons. This is intuitive, since the spring and summer seasons provide more conducive weather conditions for outdoor recreation than the fall and winter seasons in the San Francisco Bay area.

5.2.2.5. Baseline preference constants. The baseline preference constants do not have any substantive interpretations because of the presence of two continuous exogenous variables (age and land-use mix). But since almost all of the variables are dummy variables, the constants may be viewed informally as providing the baseline preferences for the "base" individual defined by the combination of the base dummy variable categories. From this perspective, the constants reinforce our discussion in Section 4.2. Specifically, the IHS activity type (the base activity type) is least preferred of all activity types at the point when no time has yet been invested in any activity type. On the other hand, the OHSh activity type clearly has the highest baseline preference of all the activity types.

5.2.3. Satiation parameters

The satiation parameter, α_j, for each activity type j is parameterized as $1/[1 + \exp(-\delta_j)]$, where $\delta_j = \theta_j' y_j$ (see Section 3.1). This parameterization allows α_j to vary based on individual and day of week/seasonal characteristics and still be bounded between 0 and 1. In our empirical analysis, we did not find any statistically significant variation in the α_j parameters based on individual and day of week/season of year characteristics for the IHS, IHR, OHS, and OHR activity types. However, there was variation in the satiation parameter for the OHSh activity type based on the sex of the individual. After estimating the θ_j parameters, one can compute the δ_j parameters and then the α_j parameters.

Table 3 provides the estimated values of α_j and the t-statistic with respect to the null hypothesis of $\alpha_j = 1$ (note that standard discrete choice models assume $\alpha_j = 1$). Several important observations may be drawn from the table. First, all the satiation parameters are significantly different from 1, rejecting the linear utility structure employed in standard discrete choice models. Thus, there are clear satiation effects in discretionary time use decisions. Second, satiation effects are lower for the in-home activity types than for the out-of-home activity types. Between the two in-home activity types, there is lower satiation for IHR compared to IHS. Third, the highest satiation occurs in the OHSh category. This indicates that individuals are not willing to invest too much time on shopping activity. The satiation effect for shopping is higher for men relative to women (that is, women tend to shop longer than men).

Table 3
Satiation parameters

Activity type	Parameter	t-Statistic[a]
In-home social (IHS)	0.8794	3.09
In-home recreational (IHR)	0.9556	3.47
Out-of-home social (OHS)	0.7660	6.34
Out-of-home recreational (OHR)	0.7822	6.39
Out-of-home shopping (OHSh)		
Women	0.4586	7.60
Men	0.4028	7.50

[a] The t-statistic is computed for the null hypothesis that the satiation parameter is equal to 1. Equivalently, the t-statistic is for the test that there are no satiation effects or that the utility structure is linear.

5.2.4. Variance–covariance parameters

The error components introduced in the baseline preference function (see Section 5.2.1) generate heteroscedasticity and covariance in unobserved factors across activity types. From the estimated standard deviations of the error components, it is straightforward to compute the estimatedvariance–covariance matrix. This is presented in Table 4. The variance terms (i.e., the diagonal elements) indicate higher variance due to unobserved factors for the out-of-home activity types relative to the in-home activity types. Further, the matrix is dominantly diagonal, indicating that there is not much covariance in unobserved factors between the various activity types after controlling for the observed factors. However, there is significant covariance between the two in-home activity types, reflecting individual-specific unobserved components (such as inertial tendencies and preference for privacy of the home) that predispose individuals to in-home activity pursuits. The implied correlation between the baseline preferences of the in-home activity types is 0.5. There is also a marginally significant covariance in the baseline preferences of the out-of-home social and out-of-home shopping activity types due to unobserved individual-specific factors. The implied correlation is, however, very low at 0.05.

Table 4
Variance–covariance matrix

Activity type	Activity type				
	In-home social	In-home recreational	Out-of-home social	Out-of-home recreational	Out-of-home shopping
In-home social (IHS)	7.87 (2.98)	3.04 (2.50)	0	0	0
In-home recreational (IHR)		4.74 (3.85)	0	0	0
Out-of-home social (OHS)			11.88 (4.26)	0	0.64 (1.21)
Out-of-home recreational (OHR)				11.24 (4.11)	0
Out-of-home shopping (OHSh)					11.88 (4.26)

5.3. Overall likelihood-based measures of fit

The log-likelihood value at convergence of the final mixed multiple discrete–continuous extreme value (MMDCEV) model is −10,053. The corresponding value for the MMDCEV model with only the constants in the baseline preference terms, the satiation parameters, and the variance–covariance terms is −10,142. The likelihood ratio test for testing the presence of exogenous variable effects is 178, which is substantially larger than the critical chi-square value with 25 degrees of freedom at any reasonable level of significance. This clearly indicates variations in the baseline preferences for the discretionary activity types based on household demographics/location variables, individual demographics/employment attributes, and day of week/seasonal effects. Further, the log-likelihood value at convergence of the MDCEV model that does not allow unobserved heteroscedasticity and correlation across the baseline preferences of the different activity types is −10,102. The likelihood ratio test for comparing the MDCEV model with the MMDCEV model is 98, which is again substantially larger than the critical χ^2 value with five degrees of freedom (corresponding to the five parameters estimated to characterize the variance–covariance matrix). Thus, there is statistically significant unobserved variation across individuals in their baseline preferences, and statistically significant correlation between the IHS and IHR activity types and the OHS and OHSh activity types.

5.4. Prediction procedure

The final end-objective of the discretionary time model is to be able to predict the time use of individuals in the several discretionary activity types. This prediction provides information on participation, as well as the level of participation in each discretionary activity type.

The MMDCEV model can be used in a rather straight forward manner for prediction purposes. Note that consumer q allocates time to the various activities based on maximizing $\tilde{U}_q$ in Eq. (5) subject to the time budget constraint that $\sum_j t_{jq} = T_q$ and $t_{jq} \geqslant 0$ for all j (the index q for individual is introduced in the notation here). Thus, the consumer's time allocation is based on the following problem:

$$\text{Max} \quad \tilde{U}_q = \sum_j \left\{ \left[\exp(\beta' x_{qj} + \zeta_{qj} + \eta_q' w_j + \mu_q' z_j) \right] \cdot (t_{qj} + \gamma_j)^{\alpha_{qj}} \right\} \tag{20}$$

subject to

$$\sum_j t_{jq} = T_q, \quad t_{qj} \geqslant 0 \quad \text{for all } j \ (j = 1, 2, \ldots, K)$$

Of course, the error components ζ_{qj}, $\eta_q' w_j$, and $\mu_q' z_j$ are not observed to the analyst, making $\tilde{U}_q$ random. Thus, the predictions for individual q may be obtained by solving the following optimization problem:

$$\begin{aligned} \text{Max} \quad \tilde{U}_q = & \int_{\eta_q=-\infty}^{\infty} \int_{\mu_q=-\infty}^{\infty} \int_{\zeta_{q1}=-\infty}^{\infty} \int_{\zeta_{q2}=-\infty}^{\infty} \cdots \int_{\zeta_{qK}=-\infty}^{\infty} \\ & \times \sum_j \left\{ \left[\exp(\beta' x_{qj} + \zeta_{qj} + \eta_q' w_j + \mu_q' z_j) \right] \cdot (t_{qj} + \gamma_j)^{\alpha_{qj}} \right\} \\ & \times \mathrm{d}G(\zeta_{q1})\, \mathrm{d}G(\zeta_{q2}) \cdots \mathrm{d}G(\zeta_{qs})\, \mathrm{d}F(\mu_q|\sigma)\, \mathrm{d}F(\eta_q|\omega) \end{aligned} \tag{21}$$

subject to

$$\sum_j t_{jq} = T_q, \quad t_{qj} \geqslant 0 \quad \text{for all } j$$

where G is the standard cumulative Gumbel distribution and F is the multivariate normal distribution function. The objective function above can be evaluated using simulation techniques and the time allocations t_{jq} can be predicted using a constrained optimization routine. In the current paper, the optimization was achieved using the constrained optimization application of the GAUSS matrix programming language. The multidimensional integral in the objective function was evaluated using 5000 random draws (we tested the sensitivity of the t_{jq} values to the number of draws for the first several observations and found little difference in the predicted t_{jq} values beyond 5000 draws).

The prediction procedure discussed above can be used to assess the performance of the model by comparing the actual time allocations to the predicted time allocations in the estimation sample. Table 5 shows the actual and predicted time allocations for the first 5 individuals in the sample. The predicted time allocations in Table 5 are rounded to the closest minute. As can be noticed, the predictions satisfy the non-negativity constraint and the total time budget constraint because of the constrained optimization prediction process.

Summary disaggregate non-likelihood measures of fit can be computed in several ways based on a comparison of actual and predicted time allocations. Two measures of fit are presented here to reflect the discrete as well as continuous nature of the predictions from the MMDCEV model. The first measure evaluates the ability of the model to correctly predict participation in the various activity types (this is the discrete component of the model). This measure, which we label as the "hit rate" measure, indicates the percentage of correct predictions across all individuals and activity types regarding participation, and is computed to be 66%. The second measure evaluates the ability of the model to predict the duration of participation conditional on a correct prediction regarding participation (this is the continuous component of the model). This measure, computed as the mean absolute percentage error (MAPE) ratio, is 29%. Both the "hit rate" and MAPE ratio measures indicate reasonable prediction fits, but also suggest that we are perhaps missing individual-specific factors (such as, for example, the intrinsic attitude/lifestyle preference for each kind of discretionary activity) that impact participation in different kinds of discretionary activity pursuits. Such individual-specific factors can be accommodated if data on multiple weekend days are collected from the same individual.

Table 5
Predicted and actual discretionary time allocations for the first five individuals in the sample

Individual number	Predicted (actual) time use in ...				
	In-home social activity	In-home recreational activity	Out-of-home social activity	Out-of-home recreational activity	Out-of-home shopping activity
1	0 (0)	116 (120)	0 (0)	0 (0)	4 (0)
2	0 (0)	238 (240)	0 (0)	0 (0)	2 (0)
3	0 (0)	7 (0)	0 (0)	6 (0)	2 (15)
4	0 (0)	84 (0)	9 (0)	0 (0)	27 (120)
5	0 (0)	330 (240)	0 (0)	0 (90)	0 (0)

6. Conclusions

Classical discrete and discrete–continuous models deal with situations with only one alternative chosen from a set of mutually exclusive alternatives. On the other hand, many consumer demand situations are characterized by the choice of multiple alternatives simultaneously. Until recently, there has been limited research on modeling such multiple discreteness situations in the literature. This paper formulates a new model for multiple discreteness in demand that is derived from utility maximization theory. Specifically, based on Kim et al. (2002), we assume a translated non-linear, but additive, form for the specification of the utility function, which allows for multiple discreteness as well diminishing marginal returns (i.e., satiation) as the consumption of any particular alternative increases. The econometric model formulated here, which we refer to as the multiple discrete–continuous extreme value (MDCEV) model, is derived by introducing a multiplicative log-extreme value error term into the utility function. The result of such a specification is a surprisingly simple closed form expression for the discrete–continuous probability of not consuming certain alternatives and consuming given levels of the remaining alternatives. The paper proposes a mixing distribution to accommodate heteroscedasticity and covariance in unobserved characteristics affecting the demand for different alternatives, leading to the mixed MDCEV (or MMDCEV) model structure. Estimation of the MDCEV model is straightforward and easily achieved using a maximum likelihood inference procedure, while estimation of the MMDCEV model is accomplished using a simulated maximum likelihood procedure.

In the current paper, we demonstrate an application of the model to individual time use in different types of discretionary activity pursuits on weekend days using data from the 2000 San Francisco Bay area. The analysis included several different kinds of variables, including household demographics, household location variables, individual demographics and employment characteristics, and day of week and season of year. Important findings from the analysis include the following:

1. Individuals in households with several other adults and in households with low incomes have a high propensity to participate in in-home recreation over the weekend days; on the other hand, individuals in households with children, with medium household incomes, and with bicycles prefer out-of-home leisure activities relative to in-home leisure activities.
2. Household location variables do not significantly impact time use in leisure activities. However, this finding may be the result of using a coarse spatial level for computing location characteristics in the current study.
3. Older individuals, men, and African–Americans are less likely to participate in out-of-home recreation than younger individuals, women, and non-African-Americans, respectively. Young adults (16–17 years), Hispanic Americans, and individuals with a motor vehicle driving license are more likely to participate in out-of-home social pursuits than adults over the age of 17 years, non-Hispanic Americans, and individuals without a driving license, respectively. Young adults are not very likely to participate in out-of-home shopping activities over the weekend, while employed individuals and those who shop on the internet have a high likelihood of participating in out-of-home shopping activities. Men prefer in-home recreation more so than women.

4. Individuals prefer to pursue in-home leisure activities on Sundays relative to Saturdays. Individuals participate less in out-of-home recreation during the winter and fall seasons.

The model can be used to assess the impacts of changing demographics and employment patterns on time-use patterns, using the prediction process described in Section 5.4. Such an analysis is important at a time when demographics and employment characteristics are changing rapidly. The predicted changes in time use patterns can then be used within an activity-based modeling framework to examine the implied travel changes (see Bhat et al., forthcoming).

Acknowledgments

The author would like to thank Ken Vaughn and Chuck Purvis of the Metropolitan Transportation Commissions (MTC) in Oakland for providing help with data related issues. The author appreciates the efforts of Sudeshna Sen and Aruna Sivakumar on data assembly and preparation of the figure in the paper. The author is grateful to Lisa Weyant for her help in typesetting and formatting this document. The author also thanks Marcela Munizaga, Sergio Jara-Diaz, and students at the Universidad de Chile for helpful comments during an informal presentation of the model in Chile. Finally, the author appreciates the valuable comments of two anonymous reviewers on an earlier version of the paper.

Appendix A. Computation of the determinant of the Jacobian in probability expression

From Eq. (11), the elements of the Jacobian are given by:

$$J_{ih} = \frac{\partial[V_1 - V_{i+1} + \varepsilon_1]}{\partial t^*_{h+1}}, \quad i, h = 1, 2, \ldots, M-1. \tag{A.1}$$

Using Eq. (9) in the text, we can write:

$$V_i = d_i + a_i \ln(t^*_i + \gamma_i), \quad i = 1, 2, \ldots, M, \tag{A.2}$$

where $d_i = \beta' x_i + \ln \alpha_i$ and $a_i = (\alpha_i - 1)$.

Then the element ih of the Jacobian is:

$$\begin{aligned} J_{ih} &= \frac{\partial[d_1 + a_1 \ln(t^*_1 + \gamma_1) - d_{i+1} - a_{i+1} \ln(t^*_{i+1} + \gamma_{i+1}) + \varepsilon_1]}{\partial t^*_{h+1}} \\ &= \frac{\partial\left[d_1 + a_1 \ln\left(T - \sum_{r=2}^{K} t^*_r + \gamma_1\right) - d_{i+1} - a_{i+1} \ln(t^*_{i+1} + \gamma_{i+1}) + \varepsilon_1\right]}{\partial t^*_{h+1}} \\ &= -\frac{a_1}{(t^*_1 + \gamma_1)} - z_{ih} \frac{a_{i+1}}{(t^*_{i+1} + \gamma_{i+1})}, \quad i, h = 1, 2, \ldots, M-1, \end{aligned} \tag{A.3}$$

where $z_{ih} = 1$ if $i = h$ and $z_{ih} = 0$ if $i \neq h$. To compute the determinant of the Jacobian, consider a case where an individual participates in 4 activity types. Then the Jacobian matrix is:

$$J=\begin{bmatrix} \left(-\frac{a_1}{t_1^*+\gamma_1}-\frac{a_2}{t_2^*+\gamma_2}\right) & -\frac{a_1}{t_1^*+\gamma_1} & -\frac{a_1}{t_1^*+\gamma_1} \\ -\frac{a_1}{t_1^*+\gamma_1} & \left(-\frac{a_1}{t_1^*+\gamma_1}-\frac{a_3}{t_3^*+\gamma_3}\right) & -\frac{a_1}{t_1^*+\gamma_1} \\ -\frac{a_1}{t_1^*+\gamma_1} & -\frac{a_1}{t_1^*+\gamma_1} & \left(-\frac{a_1}{t_1^*+\gamma_1}-\frac{a_4}{t_4^*+\gamma_4}\right) \end{bmatrix} \quad \text{(A.4)}$$

It is straightforward to see that, because of the structure of the Jacobian, the determinant of the Jacobian is given by:

$$|J|=\left[\prod_{i=1}^{4}\left(-\frac{a_i}{t_i^*+\gamma_i}\right)\right]\left[\sum_{i=1}^{4}\left(\frac{t_i^*+\gamma_i}{a_i}\right)\right] \quad \text{(A.5)}$$

In the general case when the individual participates in M alternatives, the determinant is given by the following expression after substituting $a_i = \alpha_i - 1$:

$$|J|=\left[\prod_{i=1}^{M}\left(\frac{1-\alpha_i}{t_i^*+\gamma_i}\right)\right]\left[\sum_{i=1}^{M}\left(\frac{t_i^*+\gamma_i}{1-\alpha_i}\right)\right] \quad \text{(A.6)}$$

Appendix B. Derivation of the structure of the multiple discrete–continuous extreme value (MDCEV) model

From Eq. (14) of the text.

$$P(t_i^*>0 \text{ and } t_s^*=0; i=2,3,\ldots,M \text{ and } s=M+1,\ldots,K)$$
$$=\left[\prod_{i=1}^{M}c_i\right]\left[\sum_{i=1}^{M}\frac{1}{c_i}\right]\left[\prod_{i=2}^{M}\mathrm{e}^{-(V_1-V_i)}\right]\left[\int_{\varepsilon_1=-\infty}^{+\infty}(\mathrm{e}^{-\varepsilon_1})^{M-1}\cdot\mathrm{e}^{-\sum_{j=1}^{K}\left[\mathrm{e}^{-(V_1-V_j+\varepsilon_1)}\right]}\cdot\mathrm{e}^{-\varepsilon_1}\cdot\mathrm{d}\varepsilon_1\right] \quad \text{(B.1)}$$

Now, consider the last term with the integral in the expression above, and let $k=e^{-\varepsilon_1}$. Then $\mathrm{d}k=-\mathrm{e}^{-\varepsilon_1}\cdot\mathrm{d}\varepsilon_1$, and we can write:

$$\int_{\varepsilon_1=-\infty}^{+\infty}(\mathrm{e}^{-\varepsilon_1})^{M-1}\cdot\mathrm{e}^{-\sum_{j=1}^{K}\left[\mathrm{e}^{-(V_1-V_j+\varepsilon_1)}\right]}\cdot\mathrm{e}^{-\varepsilon_1}\cdot\mathrm{d}\varepsilon_1=-\int_{k=+\infty}^{0}k^{M-1}\cdot\mathrm{e}^{-\left[k\cdot\sum_{j=1}^{K}\mathrm{e}^{-(V_1-V_j)}\right]}\cdot\mathrm{d}k \quad \text{(B.2)}$$

Next, let $b=-ak$, where $a=\left[\sum_{j=1}^{K}\mathrm{e}^{-(V_1-V_j)}\right]$. Then, $\mathrm{d}b=-a\mathrm{d}k$, and the integral in (B.2) can be rewritten as:

$$-\int_{b=-\infty}^{b=0}\left(-\frac{b}{a}\right)^{M-1}\cdot\mathrm{e}^{b}\cdot\left(-\frac{1}{a}\right)\cdot\mathrm{d}b=-\left(-\frac{1}{a}\right)^{M}\cdot\int_{-\infty}^{0}b^{M-1}\cdot\mathrm{e}^{b}\cdot\mathrm{d}b$$
$$=(-1)^{M+1}\cdot\frac{1}{a^M}\int_{-\infty}^{0}b^{M-1}\cdot\mathrm{e}^{b}\cdot\mathrm{d}b \quad \text{(B.3)}$$

To evaluate the final integral, one can use the following recursive formula:

$$\int b^{M-1}\cdot e^{b}\cdot db = b^{M-1}\cdot e^{b} - (M-1)\int b^{M-2}\cdot e^{b}\cdot db \tag{B.4}$$

This results in the following:

$$\begin{aligned}\int_{-\infty}^{0} b^{M-1}\cdot e^{b}\cdot db &= \left[\begin{matrix} b^{M-1}e^{b} - (M-1)b^{M-2}\cdot e^{b} + (M-1)(M-2)b^{M-3}\cdot e^{b} - \\ (M-1)(M-2)(M-3)b^{M-4}\cdot e^{b} + \cdots \\ (M-1)(M-2)(M-3)\cdots 1\cdot e^{b}\end{matrix}\right]_{b=-\infty}^{b=0} \\ &= (-1)^{M-1}\cdot (M-1)!\end{aligned} \tag{B.5}$$

Putting the values of the integral back in (B.3), we get:

$$\int_{\varepsilon_1=-\infty}^{+\infty} (e^{-\varepsilon_1})^{M-1}\cdot e^{-\sum_{j=1}^{J}\left[e^{-(V_1-V_j+\varepsilon_1)}\right]}\cdot e^{-\varepsilon_1}\cdot d\varepsilon_1 = (-1)^{2M}\cdot\frac{(M-1)!}{\left[\sum_{j=1}^{K} e^{-(V_1-V_j)}\right]^{M}} = \frac{(M-1)!}{\left[\sum_{j=1}^{K} e^{-(V_1-V_j)}\right]^{M}} \tag{B.6}$$

Finally, we can re-write Eq. (B.1) as:

$$P\left(t_i^* > 0 \text{ and } t_s^* = 0;\ i = 2,3,\ldots,M \text{ and } s = M+1,\ldots,K\right)$$

$$= \left[\prod_{i=1}^{M} c_i\right]\left[\sum_{i=1}^{M}\frac{1}{c_i}\right]\left[\prod_{i=2}^{M} e^{-(V_1-V_i)}\right]\left[\frac{1}{\left[\sum_{j=1}^{K} e^{-(V_1-V_j)}\right]^{M}}\right](M-1)! \tag{B.7}$$

$$= \left[\prod_{i=1}^{M} c_i\right]\left[\sum_{i=1}^{M}\frac{1}{c_i}\right]\left[\frac{\prod_{i=1}^{M} e^{V_i}}{\left(\sum_{j=1}^{K} e^{V_j}\right)^{M}}\right](M-1)! \tag{B.8}$$

References

Allaman, P.M., Tardiff, T.J., Dunbar, F.C., 1982. New approaches to understanding travel behavior. NCHRP Report, 250, Transportation Research Board, Washington, DC.

Arentze, T.A., Timmermans, H.J.P., 2004. Albatross—a learning-based transportation oriented simulation system. Transportation Research Part B 38 (7), 613–633.

Arora, N., Allenby, G.M., Ginter, J.L., 1998. A hierarchical Bayes model of primary and secondary demand. Marketing Science 17, 29–44.

Baltas, G., 2004. A model for multiple brand choice. European Journal of Operational Research 154, 144–149.

Becker, G.S., 1965. A theory of the allocation of time. Economic Journal 75, 493–517.

Becker, G.S., 1981. A Treatise on the Family. Harvard University Press, Cambridge, Massachusetts.

Bhat, C.R., 1998. A model of post home-arrival activity participation behavior. Transportation Research Part B 32, 387–400.

Bhat, C.R., 2003. Simulation estimation of mixed discrete choice models using randomized and scrambled Halton sequences. Transportation Research Part B 37 (9), 837–855.

Bhat, C.R., Gossen, R., 2004. A mixed multinomial logit model analysis of weekend recreational episode type choice. Transportation Research Part B 38 (9), 767–787.

Bhat, C.R., Koppelman, F.S., 1999. A retrospective and prospective survey of time-use research. Transportation 26 (2), 119–139.

Bhat, C.R., Lockwood, A., 2004. On distinguishing between physically active and physically passive episodes and between travel and activity episodes: An analysis of weekend recreational participation in the San Francisco Bay area. Transportation Research Part A 38 (8), 573–592.

Bhat, C.R., Misra, R., 1999. Discretionary activity time allocation of individuals between in-home and out-of-home and between weekdays and weekends. Transportation 26, 193–209.

Bhat, C.R., Srinivasan, S., 2004. A multidimensional mixed ordered-response model for analyzing weekend activity participation. Transportation Research Part B 39 (3), 255–278.

Bhat, C.R., Guo, J.Y., Srinivasan, S., Sivakumar, A., forthcoming. A comprehensive econometric microsimulator for daily activity-travel patterns. Transportation Research Record.

Chiang, J., 1991. A simultaneous approach to whether to buy, what to buy and how much to buy. Marketing Science 4, 297–314.

Chintagunta, P.K., 1993. Investigating purchase incidence, brand choice and purchase quantity decisions of households. Marketing Science 12, 194–208.

Damm, D., Lerman, S.R., 1981. A theory of activity scheduling behavior. Environment and Planning 13A, 703–818.

Dube, J.P., 2004. Multiple discreteness and product differentiation: Demand for carbonated soft drinks. Marketing Science 23 (1), 66–81.

Dubin, J.A., McFadden, D.L., 1984. An econometric analysis of residential electric appliance holdings and consumption. Econometrica 52 (2), 345–362.

Edwards, Y.D., Allenby, G.M., 2003. Multivariate analysis of multiple response data. Journal of Marketing Research 40, 321–334.

Gramm, W.L., 1975. Household utility maximization and the working wife. American Economic Review 65 (1), 90–100.

Gronau, R., 1973. The allocation of time: The value of the housewife's time. American Economic Review 63 (4), 635–651.

Hannemann, M., 1984. The discrete/continuous model of consumer demand. Econometrica 52, 541–561.

Hajivassiliou, V.A., Ruud, P.A., 1994. Classical estimation methods for LDV models using simulations. In: Engle, R., McFadden, D. (Eds.), Handbook of Econometrics, vol. IV. Elsevier, New York, pp. 2383–2441.

Hendel, I., 1999. Estimating multiple-discrete choice models: An application to computerization returns. Review of Economic Studies 66, 423–446.

Jara-Diaz, S.R., 2003. On the goods-activities technical relations in the time allocation theory. Transportation 30 (3), 245–260.

Jara-Diaz, S.R., Guevara, C.A., 2003. Behind the subjective value of travel time savings: The perception of work, leisure, and travel from a joint mode choice activity model. Journal of Transport Economics and Policy 37 (1), 29–46.

Juster, F.T., 1990. Rethinking utility theory. The Journal of Behavioral Economics 19, 155–179.

Kim, J., Allenby, G.M., Rossi, P.E., 2002. Modeling consumer demand for variety. Marketing Science 21, 229–250.

Kitamura, R., Yamamoto, T., Fujii, S., Sampath, S., 1996. A discrete–continuous analysis of time allocation to two types of discretionary activities which accounts for unobserved heterogeneity. In: Lesort, J.-B. (Ed.), Transportation and Traffic Theory: Proceedings of the 13th International Symposium on Transportation and Traffic Theory. Pergamon, New York, pp. 431–453.

Lee, L.-F., 1992. On the efficiency of methods of simulated moments and maximum simulated likelihood estimation of discrete response models. Econometric Theory 8, 518–552.

Lu, X., Pas, E.I., 1999. Socio-demographics, activity participation and travel behavior. Transportation Research Part A 33, 1–18.

Mallett, W.J., McGuckin, N., 2000. Driving to distractions: Recreational trips in private vehicles. Transportation Research Record 1719, 267–272.

Manchanda, P., Ansari, A., Gupta, S., 1999. The shopping basket: A model for multicategory purchase incidence decisions. Marketing Science 18, 95–114.

McFadden, D., Train, K., 2000. Mixed MNL models of discrete response. Journal of Applied Econometrics 15, 447–470.

Meloni, I., Guala, L., Loddo, A., 2004. Time allocation to discretionary in-home, out-of-home activities and to trips. Transportation 31 (1), 69–96.

Mincer, J., 1962. Labor force participation of married women: A study of labor supply. In Aspects of Labor Economics, National Bureau of Economic Research, Princeton University Press, Princeton, NJ, pp. 63–97.

Mincer, J., 1963. Market prices, opportunity costs and income effects. In: Christ, C.F., Freidman, M., Goodman, L.A., Griliches, Z., Harberger, A.C., Liviatan, N., Mincer, J., Mundlak, Y., Nerlove, Patinkin, D., Tesler, L.G., Theil, H. (Eds.), Measurement in Economics. Stanford University Press, Stanford, CA, pp. 67–82.

MORPACE International, Inc., 2002. Bay Area Travel Survey Final Report. March 2002. Available from <ftp://ftp.abag.ca.gov/pub/mtc/planning/BATS/BATS2000/>.

Munshi, K., 1993. Urban passenger travel demand estimation: A household activity approach. Transportation Research Part A 27 (6), 423–432.

Pas, E.I., 1996. Time and travel demand analysis and forecasting: Theory, data collection and modeling. Presented at the Conference on Theoretical Foundations of Travel Choice Modeling, Stockholm, Sweden, August 7–11.

Pendyala, R.M., Goulias, K.G., 2002. Time use and activity perspectives in travel behavior research. Transportation 29 (1), 1–4.

Terza, J.V., Wilson, P.W., 1990. Analyzing frequencies of several types of events: A mixed multinomial-Poisson approach. The Review of Economics and Statistics 72, 108–115.

Train, K., 2003. Discrete Choice Methods with Simulation. Cambridge University Press, Cambridge, United Kingdom.

Walsh, J.W., 1995. Flexibility in consumer purchasing for uncertain future tastes. Marketing Science 14, 148–165.

Yamamoto, T., Kitamura, R., 1999. An analysis of time allocation to in-home and out-of-home discretionary activities across working days and non-working days. Transportation 26 (2), 211–230.

Ye, X., Pendyala, R.M., Gottardi, G., 2004. An exploration of the relationship between mode choice and complexity of trip chaining patterns. Presented at the 83rd Annual Meeting of the Transportation Research Board, Washington, DC, January 11–15.

[44]

DISCRETE CHOICE MODELS IN PREFERENCE SPACE AND WILLINGNESS-TO-PAY SPACE

Kenneth Train
Department of Economics, University of California, Berkeley
train@econ.berkeley.com

Melvyn Weeks
University of Cambridge, Cambridge, U.K.
mw217@econ.cam.ac.uk

Abstract In models with unobserved taste heterogeneity, distributional assumptions can be placed in two ways: (1) by specifying the distribution of coefficients in the utility function and deriving the distribution of willingness to pay (*WTP*), or (2) by specifying the distribution of *WTP* and deriving the distribution of coefficients. In general the two approaches are equivalent, in that any mutually compatible distributions for coefficients and *WTP* can be represented in either way. However, in practice, convenient distributions, such as normal or log-normal, are usually specified, and these convenient distributions have different implications when placed on *WTP*'s than on coefficients. We compare models that use normal and log-normal distributions for coefficients (called models in preference space) with models using these distributions for *WTP* (called models in *WTP* space). We find that the models in preference space fit the data better but provide less reasonable distributions of *WTP* than the models in *WTP* space. Our findings suggests that further work is needed to identify distributions that either fit better when applied in *WTP* space or imply more reasonable distributions of *WTP* when applied in preference space.

Keywords: Mixed logit, random parameters, random willingness to pay.

1. Introduction

In many applications of discrete choice models with random coefficients, the price coefficient is held constant, especially when the goal is to estimate the distribution of consumers' willingness to pay for alternative attributes (e.g., Revelt and Train, 1998; Goett *et al.*, 2000; Layton and Brown, 2000; Scarpa *et al.*, 2002; Hensher *et al.*, 2004) and/or to infer the willingess to pay of individual consumers from their observed choices and the population distribution (Train, 2003, Ch. 11; Scarpa *et al.*, 2005; Greene *et al.*, 2005.) This restriction allows the distributions of willingness to pay (*WTP*) to be calculated easily from the distributions of the non-price coefficients, since the two distributions take the same form. For example, if the coefficient of an attribute is distributed normally, then *WTP* for that attribute, which is the attribute's coefficient divided by the price coefficient, is also normally distributed. The mean and standard deviation of *WTP* are simply the mean and standard deviation of the attribute coefficient scaled by the inverse of the (fixed) price coefficient. The restriction also facilitates estimation. As Ruud (1996) points out, a model with all random coefficients, including the price coefficient, can be practically unidentified empirically, especially in datasets with only one observed choice for each decision-maker.

A fixed price coefficient,[1] however, implies that the standard deviation of unobserved utility, which is called the scale parameter, is the same for all observations. Louviere (2003) discusses the importance of recognizing that the scale parameter can, and in many situations clearly does, vary randomly over observations and that ignoring this variation in estimation can lead to erroneous interpretation and conclusions. For example, if the price coefficient is constrained to be fixed when in fact scale varies over observations, then the variation in scale will be erroneously attributed to variation in *WTP*.

In this paper we investigate alternative ways to specify random coefficients and *WTP* when the price coefficient varies. Cameron and James (1987) and Cameron (1988) introduced the concept of parameterizing a fixed-coefficient model in terms of *WTP* rather than coefficients. We extend their analysis to models with random coefficients, where distributional assumptions and restrictions can be placed on the coefficients or on the *WTP*'s. The two approaches are formally equivalent, in the sense that any distribution of coefficients translates into some derivable distribution of *WTP*'s, and vice-versa. However, the two approaches differ in terms of numerical convenience under any given distributional assumptions. For example, a model with an attribute coefficient that is normally distributed and a price coefficient that is log-normal implies that *WTP* for the attribute is distributed as the ratio of a normal to a log-normal.

[1] Or, more generally, any fixed coefficient, or uncorrelated random coefficients.

A researcher working directly in *WTP* space is unlikely to choose this inconvenient distribution for *WTP*'s. Conversely, a model with normal *WTP* and log-normal price coefficient implies that the attribute coefficient is the product of a normal and log-normal, which is a distribution that has never, to our knowledge, been applied in preference space. Restrictions are also asymmetric. For example, uncorrelated preference coefficients translate into *WTP*'s that are correlated in a particular way that would be hard to implement and test in the context of *WTP* distributions, and vice-versa.

We estimate and compare models that are parameterized in terms of coefficients, called "models in preference space," and models parameterized in terms of *WTP*, called "models in *WTP* space." For the models in preference space, a convenient distribution is specified for the coefficients, and the parameters of this distribution (such as its mean and variance) are estimated. The distribution of *WTP*'s is then derived from the estimated distribution of coefficients. This is currently the standard practice for application of choice models. For the models in *WTP* space, convenient distributions are specified for the *WTP*'s and the price coefficient. The parameters of this distribution are estimated, from which the estimated distribution of utility coefficients is derived.

We find that models using convenient distributions in preference space fit the data better, both within sample and out-of-sample, than models using convenient distributions in *WTP* space. However, the distributions of *WTP* that are derived from these models have unreasonably large variance, which translates into an untenable implication that many people are willing to pay an enormous amount of money to have or avoid an attribute. Stating the conclusions in combination: the models that fit better give less reasonable distributions for *WTP*. These results suggests that alternative distributional specifications are needed that either fit the data better when applied in *WTP* space or imply more reasonable *WTP* distributions when applied in preference space.

Our analysis and findings mirror those of Sonnier, Ainslee, and Otter (2003), with one exception. In similar comparisons as ours they find that their models in preference space fit the within-sample data better than their models in *WTP* space but provide unreasonably large variances in *WTP*. In these regards, their results match ours. However, they find that their models in *WTP* space attain better out-of-sample fit than their models in preference space, which is opposite of what we find. Sonnier *et al.* (2003) use a different method for evaluating out-of-sample fit than we do, which might account for the difference. However, differences like this one are to be expected over different datasets, since the issue under investigation is the performance of various distributional specifications and the appropriate distribution is necessarily situation-dependent.

2. Specification

In this section we describe the two types of models. Decision-makers are indexed by n, alternatives by j, and choice situations by t. To facilitate discussion, we specify utility as separable in price, p, and non-price attributes, x:

$$U_{njt} = -\alpha_n p_{njt} + \beta_n' x_{njt} + \epsilon_{njt} \tag{2.1}$$

where α_n and β_n vary randomly over decision-makers and ϵ_{njt} is i.i.d. We assume ϵ_{njt} is distributed extreme value, though the analysis is the analogous for other distributions. The variance of ϵ_{njt} can be different for different decision-makers: $Var(\epsilon_{njt}) = k_n^2(\pi^2/6)$, where k_n is the scale parameter for decision-maker n.

Though the utility specification is not yet normalized, the current formulation allows us to clarify the circumstances under which the scale parameter can be expected to vary over decision-makers. A random scale parameter is conceptually different from random values for α and β. α_n and β_n represent the tastes of person n, and these parameters vary over decision-makers because different people have different tastes. In contrast, the scale parameter does not represent a term within the utility function in any given choice situation but rather the standard deviation of utility over different choice situations. By allowing the scale parameter to be random, the researcher gives a variance to a variance. The question arises: what would cause the variance of ϵ to vary? Two prominent situations arise:

1 The unobserved term ϵ might reflect factors that are actually random or quixotic from the decision-maker's perspective, rather than, as in the usual derivation, factors that are known to the decision-maker but unknown by the researcher. In this situation, the variance of ϵ reflects the degree of randomness in the decision-maker's process, which can be expected to differ over decision-makers. This concept of randomness is particularly relevant with stated preference data, where respondents differ in their attention to the task and in their constructs of unlisted attributes. However, randomness in behavior can arise in revealed preference data as well.

2 In panel data settings, each decision-maker faces a sequence of choice situations with unobserved factors differing in each choice situation. It is reasonable to believe in this situation that the variance of these unobserved factors over choice situations for each decision-maker is different for different decision-makers, even when the unobserved factors are known to the decision-maker and unobserved only by the researcher.

These two situations also clarify the converse: When ϵ represents factors that are known to the decision-maker but unknown by the researcher, and only one choice situation is observed for each decision-maker such that each observation represents a different decision-maker, there is perhaps little need or meaning to allowing the scale parameter to vary over decision-makers. In this circumstance, the scale parameter captures variance over observations in factors that the researcher does not observe; this variance is defined on the researcher, not the decision-maker, and takes a given (i.e., fixed) value for the researcher.

Dividing utility (2.1) by the scale parameter does not affect behavior and yet results in a new error term that has the same variance for all decision-makers:

$$U_{njt} = -(\alpha_n/k_n)p_{njt} + (\beta_n/k_n)'x_{njt} + \varepsilon_{njt} \tag{2.2}$$

where ε_{njt} is i.i.d. type-one extreme value, with constant variance $\pi^2/6$. The utility coefficients are defined as $\lambda_n = (\alpha_n/k_n)$ and $c_n = (\beta_n/k_n)$, such that utility is written:

$$U_{njt} = -\lambda_n p_{njt} + c_n' x_{njt} + \varepsilon_{njt} \tag{2.3}$$

Note that if k_n varies randomly, then the utility coefficients are correlated, since k_n enters the denominator of each coefficient. Specifying the utility coefficients to be independent implicitly constrains the scale parameter to be constant. If the scale parameter varies and α_n and β_n are fixed, then the utility coefficients vary with perfect correlation. If the utility coefficients have correlation less than unity, then α_n and β_n are necessarily varying in addition to, or instead of, the scale parameter.

Equation (2.3) is called the model in preference space. Willingness to pay for an attribute is the ratio of the attribute's coefficient to the price coefficient: $w_n = c_n/\lambda_n$. Using this definition, utility can be rewritten as

$$U_{njt} = -\lambda_n p_{njt} + (\lambda_n w_n)' x_{njt} + \varepsilon_{njt}, \tag{2.4}$$

which is called utility in *WTP* space. Under this parameterization, the variation in *WTP*, which is independent of scale, is distinguished from the variation in the price coefficient, which incorporates scale.[2]

The utility expressions are equivalent of course. Any distribution of λ_n and c_n in (2.3) implies a distribution of λ_n and w_n in (2.4), and vice-versa. The general practice has been to specify distributions in preference space, estimate the parameters of those distributions, and derive the distributions of *WTP* from these estimated distributions in preference space (e.g., Train, 1998.) While fully general in theory, this practice is usually limited in implementation by the use of convenient distributions for utility coefficients. Convenient distributions for utility coefficients do not imply convenient distributions for *WTP*, and

[2] Any coefficient can be used as the base that incorporates scale, with each other coefficient expressed as the product of this coefficient and a term that is independent of scale. The only reason to use the price coefficient as the base is that the scale-free terms become *WTP*'s, which are easy to interpret.

vice-versa. As stated above, if the price coefficient is distributed log-normal and the coefficients of non-price attributes are normal, then *WTP* is the ratio of a normal term to a log-normal term. Similarly, normal distributions for *WTP* and a log-normal for the price coefficient implies that the utility coefficients are the product of a normal term and a log-normal term. The placement of restrictions is similarly asymmetric. It is fairly common for researchers to specify uncorrelated utility coefficients; however, this restriction implies that scale is constant, as stated above, and moreover that *WTP* is correlated in a particular way. It is doubtful that a researcher in specifying uncorrelated coefficients is actually thinking that *WTP* is correlated in this way. Similarly, uncorrelated *WTP*, which the researcher might want to assume or test, implies a pattern of correlation in utility coefficients that is difficult to implement in preference space.

The issue becomes: does the use of convenient distributions and restrictions in preference space or *WTP* space result in more accurate and reasonable models? The answer is necessarily situationally dependent, since the true distributions differ in different applications. However, some insight into the issue can be obtained by comparisons on a given dataset. This is the topic of the next section.

3. Data

We use the stated-preference data collected by Train and Hudson (2000) on households' choice among alternative-fueled vehicles, including gas, electric, and hybrid gas-electric vehicles. 500 respondents were presented with 15 choice situations apiece. For each choice situation, the respondent was given a card that described three vehicles and was asked to state which of the vehicles he/she would choose to buy. Each vehicle was described in terms of the following variables:

- Engine type (gas, electric, or hybrid),
- Purchase price, in dollars,
- Operating cost, in dollars per month,
- Performance (grouped into three levels, which we call "low," "medium," and "high,"[3]
- Range between recharging/refueling, in hundreds of miles,

[3]Performance was described on the card in terms of top speed and seconds required to reach 60 mph. However, these two components were not varied independently, and only three combinations of the two components were utilized.

- Body type (10 types ranging from mini car to large van).

Each of the attributes varied over choice situations and over respondents. Range varied for electric vehicles but was constant for gas and hybrid vehicles, since the purpose of this variable was to determine consumers' response to the relatively restricted range of electric vehicles. All but a few respondents completed the fifteen choice tasks, giving a total of 7,437 observations for estimation. These data have been previously used by Hess *et al.* (2003) and Train and Sonnier (2005) for other purposes. We use the data to compare specifications in preference and *WTP* space.

4. Estimation

4.1 Uncorrelated coefficients in preference space

Our first model is specified in preference space with a random coefficient for each variable and no correlation over coefficients. As discussed above, uncorrelated coefficients implies that the scale parameter is fixed. This model can therefore be seen as a version that does not allow for random scale. It is compared with models, described below, that allow random scale.

For this and other models in preference space, the attributes that are desirable, or undesirable, for everyone are given log-normally distributed coefficients. These attributes are: price, operating cost, range, a dummy for medium performance or higher, and a dummy for high performance. The coefficient for the first of the performance variables captures the extra utility associated with increasing performance from low to medium, while the coefficient for the second performance variable reflects the extra utility associated with increasing performance from medium to high. Price and operating cost are entered as negative, since the log-normal distribution implies positive coefficients. The other attributes can be either desirable or undesirable, depending on the views and tastes of the consumer. These attributes are: dummies for electric and hybrid engines, whose coefficients reflect the value of these engine types relative to gas; and dummies for each body type except mid-sized car, whose coefficients reflect the value of these body types relative to a mid-sized car (holding other attributes constant, of course.) The coefficients of these variables are given normal distributions.

The model, and all the ones which follow, was estimated by Bayesian MCMC procedures, using diffuse priors. These procedures for mixed logit models are described by Train (2003) in general and by Train and Sonnier (2005) in relation to these particular data. 10,000 iterations were used as "burn-in" after which every tenth draw was retained from 10,000 additional iterations, providing a total 1,000 draws from the posterior distribution of the parameters. Previous analysis of these data by Train and Sonnier, as well as our own analysis, indicates that the MCMC sequences converged within the burn-in period.

Table 1.1. Model in Preference Space with Uncorrelated Coefficients

Attribute	*Parameter*	*Estimate*	*St. error*
Price in $10,000's	Mean of ln(–coeff.)	–0.2233	0.0508
	Variance of ln(–coeff.)	0.5442	0.0635
Operating cost in $/month	Mean of ln(–coeff.)	-3.5540	0.0993
	Variance of ln(–coeff.)	0.7727	0.1449
Range in 100's of miles	Mean of ln(coeff.)	–0.7272	0.1298
	Variance of ln(coeff.)	0.3317	0.1209
Electric engine	Mean of coeff.	–1.9453	0.1354
	Variance of coeff.	1.6492	0.2820
Hybrid engine	Mean of coeff.	0.8331	0.1102
	Variance of coeff.	1.4089	0.1797
High performance	Mean of ln(coeff.)	–3.0639	0.3546
	Variance of ln(coeff.)	3.3681	0.8493
Medium or high performance	Mean of ln(coeff.)	–1.3030	0.2630
	Variance of ln(coeff.)	1.4041	0.5204
Mini car	Mean of coeff.	–3.0325	0.1767
	Variance of coeff.	3.5540	1.0535
Small car	Mean of coeff.	–1.3966	0.1240
	Variance of coeff.	1.3086	0.4290
Large car	Mean of coeff.	–0.4008	0.1272
	Variance of coeff.	1.3084	0.7080
Small SUV	Mean of coeff.	–0.8499	0.1072
	Variance of coeff.	0.7032	0.3655
Midsize SUV	Mean of coeff.	0.2490	0.1449
	Variance of coeff.	0.9772	0.3548
Large SUV	Mean of coeff.	–0.1295	0.1765
	Variance of coeff.	2.4334	0.9578
Compact pickup	Mean of coeff.	–1.3201	0.1507
	Variance of coeff.	1.3209	0.4484
Full-sized pickup	Mean of coeff.	–0.7908	0.1544
	Variance of coeff.	3.1370	0.8326
Minivan	Mean of coeff.	–0.5219	0.1441
	Variance of coeff.	2.6569	0.6334
Log likelihood at convergence		–6,297.81	

The Bernstein-von Mises theorem states that, under fairly benign conditions, the mean of the Bayesian posterior is a classical estimator that is asymptotically equivalent to the maximum likelihood estimator. Also, the variance of the posterior is the asymptotic variance of this estimator. See Train (2003) for an explanation with citations. Therefore, even though the model is estimated

Table 1.2. Mean and standard deviations of coefficients and *WTP*, implied by estimated parameters of model in preference space (Table 1.1)

Attribute	*Coefficient Mean*	*Coefficient Std. dev.*	*WTP Mean*	*WTP Std. dev.*
Price in $10,000's	−1.0499	0.8948		
Operating cost in $/month	−0.0421	0.0453	−0.0690	0.1130
Range in 100's of miles	0.5701	0.3576	0.9365	1.1077
Electric engine	−1.9453	1.2842	−3.1957	3.8605
Hybrid engine	0.8331	1.1870	1.3703	2.8062
High performance	0.2518	1.1829	0.4164	2.7611
Medium or high performance	0.5483	0.9581	0.9004	2.1917
Mini car	−3.0325	1.8852	−4.9773	5.8563
Small car	−1.3966	1.1439	−2.2938	3.1446
Large car	−0.4008	1.1439	−0.6598	2.5314
Small SUV	−0.8499	0.8386	−1.3952	2.1607
Midsize SUV	0.2490	0.9885	0.4060	2.1527
Large SUV	−0.1295	1.5599	−0.2120	3.3620
Compact pickup	−1.3201	1.1493	−2.1702	3.0874
Full-sized pickup	−0.7908	1.7712	−1.3032	3.9653
Minivan	−0.5219	1.6300	−0.8621	3.5859

by Bayesian procedures, the results can be interpreted from a purely classical perspective.

Table 1.1 gives estimation results for our model in preference space with uncorrelated coefficients. The estimate for each parameter is the mean of the 1,000 draws from the posterior, and the standard error of the estimate is the standard deviation of these draws. Presenting the results in this way facilitates interpretation by researchers who maintain a classical perspective: the estimates and standard errors can be interpreted the same as if they had been obtained by maximum likelihood procedures. The results can also, of course, be interpreted from a Bayesian perspective, with the mean and standard deviation of the draws providing summary information about the posterior. The log-likelihood value given at the bottom of table 1.1 is calculated in the classical way at the parameter estimates.[4]

For the log-normally distributed coefficients, the estimates in Table 1.1 are the mean and variance of the log of coefficient, which are difficult to interpret directly. Table 1.2 gives the estimated mean and standard deviation of the co-

[4] A Bayesian log-likelihood would be calculated by integrating the log-likelihood over the posterior or, as described by Sonnier *et al.* (2003), by integrating the inverse of the log-likelihood over the posterior and then taking the inverse.

efficients themselves, derived from the estimated parameters in Table 1.1. The estimates seem generally reasonable. Electric vehicles are considered worse than gas vehicles by the vast majority of the population, even if the two types of vehicles could cost the same and have the same range. The mean and standard deviation of the electric vehicle coefficient imply that 94 percent of the population place a negative value of electric vehicles relative to gas. Hybrid vehicles, on the other hand, are preferred to gas vehicles by most consumers, if they were to cost the same. The estimated mean and standard deviation imply that 75 percent have a positive coefficient for the hybrid dummy. Performance is valued at a decreasing rate, as expected. The average utility associated with moving from low to medium performance is greater than that for moving from medium to high performance (0.5483 and 0.2518 respectively.) The standard deviation of the range coefficient is much lower than of the two performance variables. This difference indicates that consumers are more similar in their desire for extra range than in their value for higher top speed and acceleration. The body type coefficients seem reasonable, with mid-sized cars and SUVs being preferred, on average, to either smaller or larger versions (holding price and operating cost constant). And pickups are valued less, on average, than comparably sized SUVs.

The estimated parameters in preference space imply distributions of *WTP*. A draw from the estimated distribution of *WTP* for an attribute is simulated by taking a draw from the estimated distribution of the attribute's coefficient and dividing by a draw from the estimated distribution of the price coefficient. Statistics for the distribution of *WTP* are obtained by taking numerous such draws and calculating the requisite statistic for these draws. The estimated mean and standard deviation of the *WTP* for each attribute is given in the final two columns of Table 1.2.

The most distinguishing aspect of the estimated distributions of *WTP* is the prevalence of large standard deviations. The standard deviation exceeds the mean for all *WTP*'s, and are more than twice the means for eight of the fifteen. These large standard deviations imply that a nontrivial share of people are willing to pay enormous amounts of money to obtain/avoid some attributes. For example, ten percent the population is estimated to have a *WTP* for range that exceeds 2. Given the units for price and range, a *WTP* over 2 means that the consumer is willing to pay more than $20,000 to have an extra 100 miles of range. Similarly, ten percent of the population is estimated to be willing to pay over $20,000 to move from low to medium performance. We return to this issue after presenting results of a model estimated in *WTP* space, where the distribution of *WTP* is estimated directly rather than derived from estimated coefficient distributions.

As stated above, a model with uncorrelated coefficients in preference space implies correlated *WTP*, with the correlation being the fairly arbitrary outcome

Table 1.3. Correlations between *WTP* for attributes, implied by estimated parameters of model in preference space (Table 1.1)

Attribute	*Op. cost*	*Range*	*Electric*	*Hybrid*	*Hi Perf*	*Med Perf*
Operating cost	1.0000	0.3687	–0.3627	0.2129	0.0679	0.1784
Range	0.3687	1.0000	–0.5029	0.2965	0.0958	0.2496
Electric	–0.3627	–0.5029	1.0000	–0.2855	–0.0929	–0.2411
Hybrid	0.2129	0.2965	–0.2855	1.0000	0.0584	0.1433
High perf	0.0679	0.0958	–0.0929	0.0584	1.0000	0.0439
Med–hi Perf	0.1784	0.2496	–0.2411	0.1433	0.0439	1.0000

(in the sense that the researcher does not specify it directly) of the estimated means and variances of the coefficients themselves. The correlation of *WTP* over attributes is given in Table 1.3. To conserve space, the correlation matrix does not contain the body types. As the table indicates, correlations among *WTP*'s are fairly large; researchers assuming uncorrelated coefficients might not be aware that they are implicitly assuming fairly large correlations among *WTP*'s.

4.2 Uncorrelated *WTP*'s in *WTP* space

We estimated a model with utility specified as in equation (2.4), where the coefficient of each non-price attribute is the product of the *WTP* for that attribute times the price coefficient. This model allows for random scale. If only scale varies, then the correlation between each pair of coefficients is one; correlations below one in coefficients imply that *WTP* varies as well as scale.

The price coefficient $-\lambda_n$ is given a log-normal distribution. The elements of ω_n (*WTP*'s) associated with operating cost, range, and the two performance variables are also specified to be log-normal, while the elements of ω_n associated with engine and body types are, instead, normal. The *WTP*'s are assumed to be uncorrelated over attributes. Note, of course, that when *WTP* for an attribute is normally distributed and the price coefficient is log-normal, the coefficient of the attribute is not normal (as in the previous model). Also, as stated above, uncorrelated *WTP* implies correlated coefficients (unlike the previous model), due to the common influence of the price coefficient on each other coefficient. The current model differs from the previous one in both of these ways.

Table 1.4 gives the estimation results. The log-likelihood is considerably lower than that for the model in Table 1.1. However, the distributions of *WTP* seem more reasonable. Comparing Table 1.5 with Table 1.2, the main dis-

Table 1.4. Model in *WTP* Space with Uncorrelated *WTP*'s

Attribute	*Parameter*	*Estimate*	*St. error*
Price in $10,000's	Mean of ln(–coeff.)	–0.0498	0.0602
	Variance of ln(–coeff.)	0.9014	0.1234
Operating cost in $/month	Mean of ln(*WTP*)	–3.4106	0.1100
	Variance of ln(*WTP*)	0.7847	0.1530
Range in 100's of miles	Mean of ln(*WTP*)	–0.4045	0.1286
	Variance of ln(*WTP*)	0.2706	0.0939
Electric engine	Mean of *WTP*	–2.5353	0.2369
	Variance of *WTP*	1.9828	0.4443
Hybrid engine	Mean of *WTP*	0.8738	0.1090
	Variance of *WTP*	2.1181	0.2745
High performance	Mean of ln(*WTP*)	–1.8854	0.2840
	Variance of ln(*WTP*)	1.7172	0.5898
Medium or high performance	Mean of ln(*WTP*)	–1.7380	0.2917
	Variance of ln(*WTP*)	2.4701	0.7310
Mini car	Mean of *WTP*	–3.4645	0.1894
	Variance of *WTP*	6.5767	1.3889
Small car	Mean of *WTP*	–1.5992	0.1451
	Variance of *WTP*	1.7010	0.5337
Large car	Mean of *WTP*	–0.6148	0.1716
	Variance of *WTP*	1.9353	0.6750
Small SUV	Mean of *WTP*	–1.0671	0.1287
	Variance of *WTP*	0.8203	0.5776
Midsize SUV	Mean of *WTP*	0.2173	0.1611
	Variance of *WTP*	1.8544	0.4389
Large SUV	Mean of *WTP*	–0.7559	0.2923
	Variance of *WTP*	8.2263	2.3072
Compact pickup	Mean of *WTP*	–1.4752	0.1398
	Variance of *WTP*	1.2675	0.5266
Full-sized pickup	Mean of *WTP*	–1.1230	0.1843
	Variance of *WTP*	5.7762	1.2558
Minivan	Mean of *WTP*	–0.7406	0.1827
	Variance of *WTP*	3.9847	0.9252
Log likelihood at convergence		–6,362.13	

tinction is that the means and especially the standard deviations of *WTP*'s are smaller for the model in *WTP* space than the model in preference space. This difference means that there is a smaller share with unreasonably large *WTP*'s. For example, the model in *WTP* space implies that 1.7 percent are estimated to be willing to pay more than $20,000 for 100 miles of extra range, while, as stated above, the model in preference space implies over 10 percent. Sim-

Table 1.5. Mean and standard of preference coefficients and *WTP*, implied by estimated parameters of model in *WTP* space (Table 1.4)

Attribute	*Coefficient Mean*	*Coefficient Std. dev.*	*WTP Mean*	*WTP Std. dev.*
Price in $10,000's	−1.4934	1.8123		
Operating cost in $/month	−0.0732	0.1616	−0.0489	0.0531
Range in 100's of miles	1.1406	1.7027	0.7636	0.4257
Electric engine	−3.7870	5.6565	−2.5353	1.4081
Hybrid engine	1.3053	3.7585	0.8738	1.4554
High performance	0.5335	1.7974	0.3584	0.7563
Medium or high performance	0.8951	4.5679	0.6047	1.9542
Mini car	−5.1712	8.6579	−3.4645	2.5645
Small car	−2.3849	4.1887	−1.5992	1.3042
Large car	−0.9180	3.4259	−0.6148	1.3912
Small SUV	−1.5914	2.8561	−1.0671	0.9057
Midsize SUV	0.3151	3.1997	0.2173	1.3618
Large SUV	−1.1336	6.8725	−0.7559	2.8682
Compact pickup	−2.2029	3.7700	−1.4752	1.1258
Full-sized pickup	−1.6858	5.9893	−1.1230	2.4034
Minivan	−1.1161	4.8729	−0.7406	1.9962

ilarly, but not as dramatically, the share who are willing to pay over $20,000 to move from low to medium performance is estimated to be 6 percent in the model in *WTP* space, which is less than the 10 percent implied by the model in preference space.

In conclusion, for both preference coefficients and *WTP* values, the indirect way of estimating the distributions results in larger means and standard deviations than when the distributions are estimated directly. As discussed above, the larger standard deviations in *WTP* imply implausible shares of the population willing to pay large amounts for an attribute. The meaning of larger means and standard deviations of coefficients is not clear.

Table 1.6 gives the correlations between coefficients that are implied by the estimated distributions of *WTP* and the price coefficient. The correlations are fairly high, due to the fact that each *WTP* is multiplied by the common price coefficient. These high correlations suggest that models with uncorrelated coefficients in preference space are incompatible empirically (as well as theoretically, of course) with independent *WTP*'s and price coefficient. Researchers, when considering independence over attributes, must be careful in distinguishing whether they want to assume that *WTP*'s are independent or

Table 1.6. Correlations between preference coefficients of attributes, implied by estimated parameters of model in *WTP* space (Table 1.4)

Attribute	*Price*	*Op. cost*	*Range*	*Electric*	*Hybrid*	*Hi Perf*	*Med Perf*
Price	1.0000	0.5526	0.8117	–0.8080	0.4157	0.3570	0.2242
Op cost	0.5526	1.0000	0.4481	-0.4456	0.2322	0.2087	0.1281
Range	0.8117	0.4481	1.0000	-0.6532	0.3375	0.2895	0.1796
Electric	–0.8080	–0.4456	–0.6532	1.0000	–0.3343	–0.2853	–0.1857
Hybrid	0.4157	0.2322	0.3375	-0.3343	1.0000	0.1439	0.0945
Hi perf	0.3570	0.2087	0.2895	-0.2853	0.1439	1.0000	0.0794
Med/Hi Perf	0.2242	0.1281	0.1796	–0.1857	0.0945	0.0794	1.0000

that utility coefficients are independent, since independence of one implies non-independence of the other.

4.3 Correlated coefficients and *WTP*

In general, neither coefficients nor *WTP*'s are independent. We estimated a model in preference space with correlated coefficients and a model in *WTP* space with correlated *WTP*'s. The model in preference space incorporates random scale, since it allows correlation between all coefficients. The two models (in preference space and *WTP* space) are therefore the same in allowing for random scale and differ only in the distributional assumptions for coefficients and *WTP*. Both models assume a log-normal price coefficient. The model in preference space assumes normal and log-normal non-price coefficients, which implies that *WTP*'s are distributed as the ratio of a normal or log-normal to a log-normal. The model in *WTP* space assumes normal and log-normal *WTP*'s, which implies coefficients that are the product of a log-normal with a normal or log-normal.

To save space, we do not present the estimates of these model; they are available to interested readers upon request. The results are consistent with those obtained above, namely: (1) the model in preference space obtains a higher log-likelihood, but (2) the estimated distribution of *WTP* is more reasonable (with smaller means and variances) for the model in *WTP* space. In addition, several conclusions can be drawn concerning correlations:

- The hypothesis that coefficients in preference space are uncorrelated can be rejected. The model in preference space attains a log-likelihood of -6,178.12 with correlated coefficients, compared to -6,297.81 for the model given in Table 1.1 with uncorrelated coefficients. The likelihood ratio test statistic is therefore 239.4 for the hypothesis that all 120 covariances are zero, which is greater than the 99-percentile value of the chi-square with 120 degrees of freedom.

- The estimated correlations among coefficients are generally small or moderate in size. 47 of the 160 correlations are below 0.1 in magnitude, and only 12 are above .4 in magnitude.
- The model in *WTP* space attains a log-likelihood of -6,228.31 when the *WTP*'s and price coefficient are all allowed to be correlated and -6,362.13 when they are constrained to be uncorrelated. The hypothesis of no correlation can be rejected.
- The estimated correlations between *WTP*'s for the model in *WTP* space are generally small or moderate, similar to the estimated correlations between coefficients for the model in preference space.
- The correlations among coefficients that are derived from the model in *WTP* space are considerably larger in magnitude than those estimated directly in the model in preference space. Similarly, the correlations among *WTP*'s that are derived from the model in preference space are considerably larger than those estimated directly in the model in *WTP* space. These findings are similar to those given above for variances, i.e., that larger variances in coefficients are obtained when they are estimated indirectly instead of directly, and larger variances in *WTP*'s are obtained when estimated indirectly than directly. It seems that the process of combining estimated distributions (dividing a normal by a log-normal for *WTP* or multiplying a normal by a log-normal for a coefficient) tends to inflate the estimated variances and covariances.

Sonnier *et al.* (2003) estimated models in preference space and *WTP* space, using the terms "linear models" and "nonlinear models" instead of our terminology to denote that the random customer-level parameters enter utility linearly in the former and nonlinearly in the later. Their results are consistent with our main conclusions, in that they obtained better within-sample fit for their model in preference space but more reasonable *WTP* distributions for their model in *WTP* space. However, their results differ from ours in one regard. They performed out-of-sample analysis and concluded that their model in *WTP* space fits better out-of-sample, even though it fits worse in-sample.

To examine this issue, we divided our sampled respondents into two equal-sized sub-samples, estimated each model on one sub-sample, and evaluated the log-likelihood of the estimated models on the other sub-sample. In each comparison (estimation on first half with evaluation on the second half, and estimation on the second half with evaluation on the first half), the model in preference space obtained a higher log-likelihood than the model in *WTP* space on the out-of-estimation sub-sample.

Our results therefore differ in this regard from those of Sonnier *et al.* (2003). The difference can perhaps be explained by the fact that we used a somewhat different method to evaluate out-of-sample fit than they did. We estimated on half the respondents using all of their choice situations and then calculated the log-likelihood for all the choice situations for the other half of the respondents, while they estimated the model on all but one choice situation for each respondent and then calculated the log-likelihood for this one "hold-out" choice situation for each respondent.

However, there is no reason to expect the same results in different settings, since the answer to the question "Which distributions fit better?" is necessarily situation-dependent. The purpose of the explorations is to focus our attention on the relation between distributions of coefficients and distributions of *WTP*, rather than to attempt to identify the appropriate distributions to use in all situations.

5. Conclusions

This paper examines consumer choice among alternative-fueled vehicles, including gas, electric, and gas/electric hybrids. The empirical results indicate that the vast majority of consumers would need to be compensated through a lower price (i.e., have a negative willingness to pay) for electric vehicles relative to gas vehicles, even if operating cost, performance, and range were the same. In contrast, most consumers are willing to pay extra for a hybrid relative to a gas vehicle with the same non-price attributes. This result is consistent with the market experience in the U.S. The few electric cars that have been introduced in the U.S. have fared poorly in the market, and models are being discontinued. In contrast, the initial offerings of hybrids have been relatively popular, and more models, such as hybrid SUVs, are being launched.

Discrete choice models were estimated with convenient distributions (normal and log-normal) in preference space and in willingness-to-pay *WTP* space. The models in preference space were found to fit the data better, both within-sample and out-of-sample, than the models in *WTP* space. However, the models in *WTP* space provided more reasonable distributions of *WTP*, with fewer consumers having untenably large *WTP*'s, than the models in preference space. This comparison implies that research is needed to identify distributions that fit the data better when applied in *WTP* space and/or provide more reasonable distributions of *WTP* when applied in preference space.

References

Cameron, T. and James, M. (1987). Efficient estimation methods for closed-ended contingent valuation survey data. Review of Economics and Statistics, 69:269–276.

Goett, A., Hudson, K., and Train, K. (2000a). Consumers' choice among retail energy suppliers: The willingness-to-pay for service attributes. The Energy Journal, 21:1–28.

Greene, W. H., Hensher, D. A., and Rose, J. M. (2005). Using classical simulation based estimators to estimate individual willingness to pay values. In Scarpa, R. and Alberini, A., editors, Applications of simulation methods in Environmental and Resource Economics. Springer-Kluwer Academic Press, Boston, MA.

Hensher, D., Shore, N., and Train, K. (2994). Households' willingness to pay for water service attributes. Working Paper, Department of Economics, University California, Berkeley.

Hess, S., Train, K. E., and Polak, J. W. (2004). On the use of a modified latin hypercube sampling (MLHS) method in the estimation of a mixed logit model for vehicle choice. Transportation Research B, forthcoming.

Layton, D. F. and Brown, G. (2000). Heterogeneous preferences regarding global climate change. The Review of Economics and Statistics, 82(4):616–624.

Louviere, J. (2003). Random utility theory-based stated preference elicitation methods: Applications in health economics with special reference to combining sources of preference data. Working Paper, Faculty of Business, University of Technology, Sydney.

Revelt, D. and Train, K. (1998). Mixed logit with repeated choices: households' choices of appliance efficiency level. Review of Economics and Statistics, 80(4):647–657.

Ruud, P. A. (1996). Simulation of the multinomial probit model: An analysis of covariance matrix estimation. Working Paper, Department of Economics, University of California.

Scarpa, R., Spalatro, F., and Canavari, M. (2002). Investigating preferences for environment friendly production practices. AgEcon Search Working Paper 03-3, http://agecon.lib.umn.edu/.

Scarpa, R., Willis, K. G., and Acutt, M. (2005). Individual-specific welfare measures for public goods: a latent class approach for residential customers of Yorkshire Water. In Koundouri, P., editor, Econometrics Informing Natural Resource Management, chapter 14. Edward Elgar Publisher, London, U.K.

Sonnier, G., Ainslie, A., and Otter, T. (2003). The influence of brand image and product style on consumer brand valuations. Working Paper, Anderson Graduate School of Management, University of California, Los Angeles.

Train, K. (1998). Recreation demand models with taste variation. Land Economics, 74:230–239.

Train, K. (2003). Discrete Choice Methods with Simulation. Cambridge University Press, Cambridge, MA, U.S.A.

Train, K. and Hudson, K. (2000). The impact of information in vehicle choice and the demand for electric vehicles in California. Project report, National Economic Research Associates.

Train, K. and Sonnier, G. (2995). Mixed logit with bounded distributions of correlated partworths. In Scarpa, R. and Alberini, A., editors, Applications of simulation methods in Environmental and Resource Economics. Chapter 7 of this volume. Springer, Boston, MA, U.S.A.